MW00659343

UNIVERSITY CASEBOOK SERIES®

CORPORATE FINANCE

PRINCIPLES AND PRACTICE

FIFTH EDITION

WILLIAM J. CARNEY
Charles Howard Candler Professor of Law Emeritus
Emory University

ROBERT P. BARTLETT, III
W. A. Franke Professor of Law and Business
Stanford Law School

GEORGE S. GEIS
William S. Potter Professor of Law
University of Virginia

860 Blue Gentian Road, Suite 350
Eagan, MN 55121
1-877-888-1330

Published in the United States of America

ISBN: 979-8-88786-285-9

To Jane, Vicky, and Laurel

PREFACE TO THE FIFTH EDITION

The lines between law and business are increasingly vanishing. Corporate leaders routinely ask their lawyers for business advice, and business executives must now be familiar with the laws that impact their strategic decisions. This is especially true for the field of corporate finance. How can a firm raise money? Where should it spend it? When should it repay investors? And why might other players in the firm's ecosystem object to any given strategy? These and other critical questions occupy the heart of this field and answering them sensibly requires knowledge that sits right at the intersection of law *and* business.

Accordingly, this book offers a blended approach that is designed to incorporate the most important insights from both fields. We start with the basics of business by reviewing key concepts from accounting and finance. Our assumption is that students will not have had previous training at a business school, and we aim to position the material in a highly accessible manner. From there, we move into a discussion of how firms decide where to raise their money. Once the strategy is set, the balance of the book digs into the exact steps needed to execute on any given financing plan: common stock, preferred stock, bonds, and so on.

In many respects, this class can be considered a continuation of the foundational course in business associations. But fundamentally, this class is about deals. A clear understanding of the law is necessary to understand how courts will interpret a given term or when investors might win a fiduciary duty lawsuit against management. Yet, as suggested, lawyers also need to understand the economics behind a deal—so they can help clients adopt features that set the desired incentives for all the relevant players. Will a new stock issuance dilute existing shareholders? If so, does this create a problem? Will a leveraged buyout impose greater risk on existing creditors? If so, should we expect to lose a lawsuit? The only way to answer these questions is to work through specific examples and problems, and this book takes a highly practical approach to corporate finance. Yes, we will analyze cases, but a great deal of our study also involves open-ended questions and problems that will put you into the shoes of a lawyer who must advise a client on critical strategic decisions.

This fifth edition of the casebook represents a significant update to the materials. The discussion and examples within each chapter have been extensively edited to present a straightforward approach that also reflects very recent developments in the field. In addition, given the growing expectation that lawyers have a working knowledge of spreadsheets and financial modeling, this edition also provides step-by-step instructions on how to use Microsoft Excel in a number of different contexts, along with sample spreadsheets. The sample spreadsheets, which are referenced by name in various sections of the casebook, can be found on the casebook website located at https://faculty.westacademic.com/Book/Detail?id=349672#teachingresources.

Lastly, we would like to note that Bill Carney has stepped back from the book as a lead editor. We are so grateful for all his work crafting and shaping the material over the years—and you will still hear his voice in many of the pages that follow. We hope you will enjoy this book as much as we have enjoyed writing it!

WILLIAM J. CARNEY
ROBERT P. BARTLETT, III
GEORGE S. GEIS

June 2024

EDITORIAL NOTE AND ACKNOWLEDGMENTS

We are grateful to our many colleagues and students at Berkeley, Virginia and Stanford for their valuable suggestions and careful help during the editing of this book. Special thanks go to Shruti Sethi, Michael Barton, and Rahul Ramesh for exceptional research assistance for this Fifth edition. Prior editions of the casebook also benefited from the outstanding research efforts of Gayatri Babel, Kathleen Kong, Tianyi Bao, John Kellam, and Trevor Lamb. Of course, the errors that remain are ours alone. We also want to thank our families for their endless support and cheerful encouragement.

As is customary in casebooks, we have taken certain liberties with judicial opinions. Citations are omitted without indication. Editing has removed sections of opinions important to the individual case but not to the pedagogical mission of this book. Formatting of headings follows a consistent approach in the book, which often will not be identical to the formatting in the original opinion.

With appreciation, this acknowledgment is made for the publishers and authors who gave permission for the reproduction of excerpts from the following materials:

American Bar Association

Committee on Corporate Laws, Section of Business Law, American Bar Association, Report of the Committee on Corporate Laws, Vol. 34. The Business Lawyer, pp. 1867–68 (1979). Copyright 1979 © by The American Bar Association. Reprinted with permission. This information or any portion thereof may not be copied or disseminated in any form or by any means or stored in an electronic database or retrieval system without the express written consent of the American Bar Association.

Model Simplified Indenture, sections 6.01, 6.02, 6.05, and 7.01, in Vol. 38, The Business Lawyer, pp. 756–759 (1983). Copyright 1983 © by The American Bar Association. Reprinted with permission. This information or any portion thereof may not be copied or disseminated in any form or by any means or stored in an electronic database or retrieval system without the express written consent of the American Bar Association.

American Bar Foundation

COMMENTARIES ON MODEL DEBENTURE INDENTURE PROVISIONS, pp. 324–26, 426–27 (1971).

Bloomberg L.P.

Matt Levine, Bed Bath Moves Into the Beyond, Money Stuff (April 24, 2023).

Elsevier Inc. B.V.

Michael Jensen and William Meckling, Theory of the Firm: Managerial Behavior, Agency Costs and Ownership Structure, Vol. 3, Journal of Financial Economics, pp. 333–34 (1976).

Clifford W. Smith, Jr. and Jerold B. Warner, On Financial Contracting: An Analysis of Bond Covenants, Vol. 7, Journal of Financial Economics, pp. 117–119, 125–132, 134–144, 146, 148–149, and 151–152 (1979).

Fordham School of Law

Robert P. Bartlett, III, Taking Finance Seriously: How Debt Financing Distorts Bidding Outcomes in Corporate Takeovers, Vol. 76, Fordham Law Review, p. 1975 (2008).

Northwestern University

Marcel Kahan and Edward Rock, Hedge Fund Activism in the Enforcement of Bondholder Rights, Vol. 103, Northwestern Law Review, pp. 283–288.

University of Notre Dame

William J. Carney and Leonard A. Silverstein, The Illusory Protections of the Poison Pill, Vol. 79, Notre Dame L. Rev., pp. 183–191 (2003).

SUMMARY OF CONTENTS

TABLE OF CONTENTS

TABLE OF CASES

The principal cases are in bold type.

UNIVERSITY CASEBOOK SERIES®

CORPORATE FINANCE

PRINCIPLES AND PRACTICE

FIFTH EDITION

CHAPTER 1

INTRODUCTION

Few law school casebooks must "defend" or "sell" their subject's importance and relevance. Corporate Finance may be different. After all, this subject is taught in business schools, isn't it? And most law students came to law school because of a facility with words and perhaps a distaste for numbers. So why not leave finance to the MBAs? One answer might be that the subject is too important to leave to the MBAs. They may not always be around when you need them. Another reason is that successful business lawyers must be able to understand their clients' (and prospective clients') businesses, so they can discuss how legal services can help them structure transactions to add value. The "rainmaker" in a law firm is generally a lawyer with a broad understanding of business as well as legal problems, who can relate to the clients' full range of concerns, and integrate that knowledge into the provision of legal services.

Additionally, central to the study of corporate finance is the question of how to value financial cash flows. This makes the study of corporate finance—and valuation methods that are central to—relevant for a wide range of lawyers. For example, if you are a personal injury lawyer and an insurance company offers your client either a lump sum settlement or a structured settlement, payable over time, how can you compare them, to ascertain that you're getting the best deal for your client? And can you explain to your client why one is better than the other, or the way in which your client should compare them? If you represent a party to a divorce, and the other party has a pension that will start paying in five years, how can you measure its value for purposes of a lump sum settlement? Suppose the other side offers a lump sum payment to be made in five years? What is it worth today, for purposes of settlement calculations?

Not surprisingly, questions about valuing cash flows are especially common in the context of business law. Suppose you represent a small business that has sought financing from a venture capitalist. The venture capitalist is prepared to invest a large sum of money in your client's business at a stated dividend rate on preferred stock. So far you know and understand the cost of obtaining this capital, right? But now suppose the venture capitalist also wants the right to convert the preferred stock into shares of common stock in your client over the next five years at a stated conversion price. Does this add to the cost? How much? And how can you begin to think about this issue with your client? If you want to represent your client effectively, you should at least know what questions to raise, and how to unpack these issues.

This is all aside from the more conventional ways of thinking about corporate finance—about advising clients in the context of raising capital in public stock markets or by issuing corporate bonds. While the lawyer's job is generally thought of as writing the documents to implement plans put together by the client and its financial advisers, the lawyer who understands the underlying financial issues will be far better equipped to participate in these activities. That is, why might a firm choose to finance itself with equity rather than debt or the many hybrid securities that sit between these two types of financial instruments? How do investors view the risks of holding these different instruments, and how do these risks shape the contracts used to execute a particular financing transaction? The answers to the questions (and more) will be addressed in this book.

Lastly, a working knowledge of corporate finance is increasingly expected of lawyers working in business law. For instance, when the Sarbanes-Oxley Act was passed in 2002, it required many directors to learn more about accounting and finance so they could effectively establish and assess internal financial controls. Similarly, hiring lawyers who understand these topics has become even more important in today's innovative capital markets where firms and investors face a dizzying array of financial choices. Lawyers need to develop a clear sense of what people value in financial transactions—and how economic value can be created and protected. Given these considerations, a lawyer's understanding of finance may often exceed that of her clients.

To commence this educational journey, we begin with an overview of the business system that informs all of business law and how corporate finance fits within it.

1. THE BUSINESS SYSTEM

How does a company work? Or, said differently, what is the overall conceptual framework for any business system. Here is one way to think about it: Imagine that you want to start a business. What is the first thing you need?

Money.

No firm can get going without seed capital, an initial investment to support its chosen activities. Practically, most ventures will have several different choices about where to get this money. You might tap into your own reserve savings or solicit your friends and family (sometimes called F&F financing) for the initial investment. Or you might walk down to the local bank to meet with a loan officer. Perhaps you could even call up your favorite investment banker to launch an initial public offering of stock or sell some corporate bonds. The set of choices that firms make about where to raise money is known as the capital structure decision. The various tradeoffs that a firm's managers face when making these decisions will be discussed in Chapter 4, and the legal and practical consequences of executing against specific capital structure decisions occupy the second half of this book. These topics comprise the core of any practice in corporate finance.

For the moment, however, imagine that you have raised some money, and there is a big pot of cash sitting on the boardroom table. What happens next? You now need to make a series of decisions about how to spend this money. You might hire some workers or build a factory or purchase some products to resell. The specific steps that managers take to make these decisions are known as capital budgeting and project analysis. This is not a primary focus of this text, but we will see some examples as we go that illustrate how managers might conduct project analysis.

Back to your new business, as you spend the money, the wheels of commerce begin to turn. The business ticks along, and you sell products or provide services to customers. Your investments in the various business inputs will (hopefully) begin to generate profits as operations ensue. These proceeds can, in turn, eventually be returned to the firm's financial backers in the form of interest payments, dividends, stock buybacks, and the like.

This entire process is known as the business system (see Figure 1-1). As long as the dollar signs from operations are larger than the dollar signs from the initial investment, then everyone should be happy. The firm is creating value and the investors make money. The cycle can begin anew. (If the dollar signs from operations are smaller than the initial investment in the firm, you will need to take a class in bankruptcy to help sort out the mess.)

Figure 1-1. The Business System

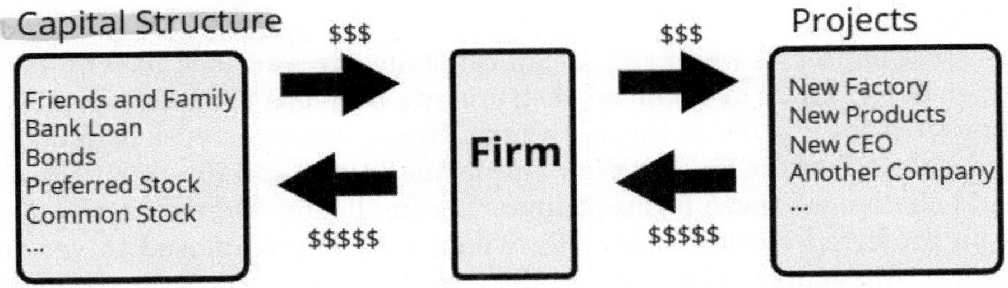

With this business system in mind, consider how several subjects relate to the overall framework. Accounting deals with the question of "how is it all going?" We need a way to measure how any given business system is performing, and this is the job of accountants. A class on corporations or business entities deals with the "who" question: who is empowered to make and execute the various decisions. Will stockholders have the final say on a given matter, or will the board of directors call the shots? Finally, corporate finance deals with the "where" question—that is, the choices firms make about where to get their money or where to spend it. This is where we will spend most of our time in this course.

2. THE PATH FORWARD

The flow of this book roughly follows the steps of the business system outlined above. Chapter 2 introduces financial statements, and it is positioned for students who have not taken a previous accounting course. It will be an abbreviated introduction, as the objective is not to produce accountants, but rather lawyers whose eyes do not glaze over when presented with financial statements. Understanding financial statements is critical, because they inform us about a company in a most basic way—what it owns, what it owes and what it earns (or loses), and how the shareholders are doing. The output of accounting is information that we need in order to be able to say something about the value of a business, the next subject of the book. In short, you can't think about value without having the numbers needed to calculate value. The focus of this chapter is on understanding the basic financial statements.

Chapter 3 covers the basics of valuation. This is perhaps the most financially oriented chapter in the book, because it lies at the heart of the subject. We use cases only to examine how these techniques operate in the courts, not for any financial wisdom they might impart. This book will employ a certain amount of algebra, which is essential in the expression of some finance concepts. Nothing more than high school algebra is required, and we will make use of spreadsheet worksheets (and share them online) to help with the most complex calculations. Thus far the book concentrates on basic theories about financial information and financial valuation that could appear in any corporate finance book, whether used in a business school or a law school. This is the prologue to the material that integrates legal doctrine with finance in the rest of the book.

In Chapter 4, we examine capital structure and look at why firms differ in the kinds of financial instruments they use to raise capital. We then turn specifically to the key alternatives—common stock (Chapter 5) and debt (Chapter 6)—with an emphasis on the specific financial and legal challenges these forms of financing implicate. After that, the focus is on preferred stock (Chapter 7), which is widely employed in venture capital financings. Convertible debt and options are also examined (Chapter 8), which requires us to explore option pricing theory and how it relates to our understanding of valuation. Finally, having covered how firms raise capital, we conclude with an examination of how firms can distribute earnings back to investors and what impact this may have on value (Chapter 9).

This book differs from many other law school corporate finance casebooks by putting first things first—an understanding of financial principles before proceeding to the legal doctrines involved. It also emphasizes drafting, documentation, and real-world examples. Along the way we also try to pass along a working knowledge of spreadsheets—a seemingly mundane but vitally important skill for any lawyer working in corporate finance. By the time you finish this course, you should have a solid understanding that a company's choice of financing vehicle raises specific risks to investors and issuers that drive the financial contracting task. For instance, we shall see how the risks posed in a debt financing are qualitatively different from the risks posed in a simple common stock financing, which are in turn different than the risks posed in a preferred stock financing. Understanding how widely used financial contracts respond to specific financing problems—in addition to learning the core legal doctrine of corporate finance—is one of the primary goals of this book. Finally, much in the style of business school texts, many of the chapters will contain questions and problems to test and expand your understanding of the material.

CHAPTER 2

FINANCIAL ACCOUNTING: MEASURING FIRM PERFORMANCE

1. INTRODUCTION

Accounting is the process of collecting, summarizing, and analyzing information about business transactions. Many new students worry that accounting is some mysterious endeavor—arcane, quirky, and difficult to understand. Our overriding goal in this chapter is to dispel this mystery. We want to provide a high-level understanding of how financial accounting works, and what information it seeks to convey, so that you will be able to read and evaluate a firm's financial statements. This is a foundational requirement for working in the field of corporate finance, and it can often be valuable for other purposes as well.

Who would ever want to review financial accounting reports? Well, suppose you are preparing to loan your best friend $1000 so she can reopen her summer lemonade stand. You might like to know how things went last year before writing the check. If she sold very little lemonade last summer, it might be wise to rethink your loan. And if you do lend the money, then you will want information about how your friend's stand is performing this summer. In other situations, in addition to current and prospective investors, many other parties might take an interest in the performance of a given company: tax collectors, regulators, financial analysts, employees, large customers, and even competitors.* Businesses need a way to express how well they function.

Accounting is the language of business. For non-accountants, financial documents can appear to be written in a code. Too often lawyers are unwilling or unable to engage in a close reading of financial statements that will give them a deeper understanding of their clients' business. In some cases, a lack of such understanding can lead to serious errors that may prove harmful to clients. Conversely, the best lawyers are usually able to understand the business motivations behind various decisions, and accounting often provides the gateway to such insights. In this chapter we hope to introduce you to a basic familiarity with financial

---

* A firm's own managers will also focus on the company's performance, of course, to set future strategies and evaluate the profitability of different divisions or products. These managers will typically use special accounting reports, however, that include confidential information about specific units, products, or customers. This is sometimes referred to as cost accounting or managerial accounting. By contrast, our focus here is on the standard financial accounting reports provided to outside parties.

statements and to provide a beginning for further learning as your career progresses.

Before examining the key financial statements, we need to cover a few general principles that underlie all of accounting:

Standards, Not Rules. Accounting is not a science. While some may think of the accounting process as a single set of rules that must be followed, it is better to think of it as a collection of standards that leave considerable discretion for management and accountants to choose the method of reporting many transactions. For example, a sports equipment firm sells a tennis racket to a customer. There are ten identical rackets in the store, but the firm paid different prices to buy each racket. Should the racket that was sold be costed at the price of the first one purchased (described as "first-in-first-out" treatment), the last one purchased ("last-in-first-out") or on some other basis? Each option will lead to a different calculation of the profits from the sale, and all are plausible approaches. (We'll return to this question shortly.)

The ultimate goal of accounting professionals should be to create financial statements that fairly present the financial picture of the firm. But you should also recognize that other factors, such as tax minimization, may impact the exercise of this discretion. More nefariously, the fact that accounting grants discretion about how to report some transactions can empower disreputable managers with enough slack to attempt fraud. You should be familiar with the parts of the accounting process that especially lend themselves to abuse to better spot questionable treatment.

More generally, you should recognize that accounting seeks to strike a balance between two objectives. On the one hand, standards should be flexible enough to allow differently situated firms to make the choices that will promote the clearest understanding of their financial performance. Firms conduct diverse activities and some variance in reporting is often necessary to develop the most meaningful reports. On the other hand, some guide rails must be established to prevent a Wild West culture where anything goes and to enable relevant comparisons between firms. How is this balance established?

Generally Accepted Accounting Principles (GAAP). In the United States, accountants have developed a collection of standards called generally accepted accounting principles (known as *GAAP*). Importantly, GAAP is not a rigid collection of rules; firms still retain significant discretion in the preparation of financial statements. But GAAP does offer a consistent framework for exercising this discretion and seeks to ensure that accountants will follow similar procedures. It also promotes explicit disclosure of the choices that accountants do make when a reporting area calls for judgement. Under GAAP, firms should report results on a consistent basis from one period to the next, and they should prefer methods that will be comparable to those of other firms in the industry.

Imagine, for example, that you work in the accounting department of a firm that sells expensive telecommunications equipment to small- and medium-sized businesses. Most of your sales are conducted on credit: you give customers the equipment, and they promise to pay you over time. To develop an accurate picture of sales revenue, you need to recognize that some customers will never pay their bills. To reflect this, you should make a deduction from your total revenues each accounting period for this bad debt expense. You may have several different options for estimating the amount of bad debt that will ultimately arise, but the specific method you do elect to use needs to be consistent with GAAP.* Further, your financial statements will disclose (usually in the footnotes) the estimation method that you are using along with other assumptions underlying your calculations.

GAAP is not stagnant; it is subject to change as accountants revise their views about optimal accounting procedures. We will briefly discuss this process, as well as the institutions that help develop GAAP, at the end of this chapter.

Methodological Consistency. Once a method is determined, accounting reports should remain as consistent as possible. For example, all reports are made on a monetary basis, which, in the U.S., means in dollars. U.S. companies with world-wide operations must convert their foreign currency transactions into dollars for purposes of financial statements. These financial reports also assume the firm is a *going concern*, a company that will continue to operate for the indefinite future. In all cases, accounting entries are made when there is an "event," which generally means a "transaction" with a third party. Transactions are reported on a conservative basis; that is, if two methods of reporting a transaction are reasonable, accountants should use the more prudent one that may understate rather than overstate profits, because understatement is likely to cause less financial harm to anyone relying on the financial statements.

For this reason, most transactions are reported on a company's books at historical cost and, with only minor exceptions, not at higher market values.† This is called the cost principle. From it you can see that accounting is historical in its approach, recording transactions at the historical price at which value is exchanged. Accounting reports should also be reliable, reasonably free from error, complete, and verifiable. But they should also be cost effective, and need only report material

---

* The exact calculations used to estimate bad debt expense are beyond the scope of this chapter. But, to illustrate conceptually, you might take historical information about the percentage of sales on credit that ultimately proved uncollectable and apply this same percentage to the current period sales. Or you might engage in an aging analysis that increases the probability that outstanding debt will not be repaid as more time passes.

† U.S. GAAP has been moving toward *fair value accounting* ("FVA") principles in recent years, but GAAP remains a hybrid system. That is, it is an evolving mixture of historical-cost, *lower-of-cost-or-market* ("LOCOM") and fair-value accounting principles.

information—that is, information of a magnitude that might influence decisions.

Reports must be made for an economic entity, which means the entire enterprise. Typically, this means that reports for a corporation and its subsidiaries are *consolidated* into a single report issued by the parent entity. Where there are transactions between parent and subsidiary, these transactions are eliminated for consolidated reporting purposes. In some historical financial scandals, controversy surrounded the use of "special purpose entities" that were allegedly separate from the main business and allowed concealment of losses.

Finally, financial reports are divided into accounting periods, which are typically yearly, and frequently quarterly or even monthly.* Many corporations report on a calendar year basis, but others select a fiscal year ending on some other date, typically one that ends immediately after a busy period. The clothing retailer Lululemon Athletica Inc. (trading under the ticker symbol "LULU"), for example, sets the end of its fiscal year at January 31—after the conclusion of the busy holiday season. Most firms also use an accrual system, as opposed to a cash system, to present a more accurate representation of the company's economic performance. This means that they try to match income and expenses to the period when they are earned or incurred, rather than when the cash actually flows in or out of the door. We explore accrual accounting in more detail in the following sections.

2. THE KEY FINANCIAL STATEMENTS

Firms use four main accounting statements to report their performance: (1) the *balance sheet* listing the company's assets and liabilities at a given point in time; (2) the *income statement* describing the firm's operating performance over a period of time; (3) the *cash flow statement* detailing the sources and uses of cash over a period in time; and (4) the *statement of changes in stockholders' equity* over a period in time. Public firms are required to file these reports periodically with the Securities and Exchange Commission ("SEC"), and you may easily access this information online.†

* The Securities and Exchange Commission (SEC) requires companies that are registered under the Securities Exchange Act of 1934 ("Exchange Act") to file publicly their audited annual financial statements on Form 10-K and their unaudited quarterly financial statements on Form 10-Q.

† More specifically, publicly traded companies are governed by the periodic reporting requirements of § 13 of the Exchange Act. The central reporting requirement under that Exchange Act is Form 10-K, the annual report that must be filed with the SEC and the essence of which must be delivered to shareholders. Item 8 of Form 10-K requires financial statements meeting the requirements of Regulation S–X, 17 C.F.R. § 210.1 et seq., the SEC's accounting regulation. Rules 3.01, 3.02, 3.04 of Regulation S–X require filings to include balance sheets for the two most recent fiscal years, audited statements of income and cash flows for the three most recent fiscal years, and a statement of changes in stockholders' equity in periods between income statements required to be presented. The SEC's website contains the financial reports of all companies filing with the SEC. These documents are located on the SEC's Electronic Data

It is important to understand, at least at a high level, how these four statements fit together (accountants call this process financial statement articulation). You should think of the balance sheet as generating a snapshot of the firm's position at a single moment in time. Two balance sheets can thus bookend an ongoing period of performance. For example, Lululemon might create a balance sheet on January 31, 2023. It will then operate over the next year in a way that is captured by the other three financial statements. Finally, Lululemon will create another balance sheet on January 31, 2024 to illustrate its assets and liabilities at the close of the fiscal year.

In reviewing a company's financial statements, always keep in mind the amount of discretion a company has in applying GAAP. Details regarding the exercise of this discretion (such as a summary of the company's accounting policies) will ordinarily be disclosed in the footnotes that accompany the financial statements. Young lawyers tasked with reviewing financial statements (e.g., as part of due diligence in an M&A transaction or corporate financing) are often tempted to focus only on the four financial statements themselves. However, without reading the footnotes, such an approach can lead to an incomplete understanding of a company's financial position. Reading the footnotes is therefore a critical part of financial statement analysis.

With these concepts in mind, let's take a closer look at each of the four key financial statements.

A. THE BALANCE SHEET

The balance sheet is our best starting point. It lists summary information about the assets owned by the firm (e.g., cash, tangible and intangible property, investment securities, etc.) and the liabilities and claims it has incurred in acquiring these assets (e.g., accounts payable owed to suppliers, debt owed to banks, equity issued to stockholders, etc.). The balance sheet uses the fundamental accounting equation:

Assets = Liabilities + Equity

This is another way of saying that all the assets of a business can be claimed by someone. If the business is dissolved, either creditors or the equity owners—such as proprietors, partners, members of a limited liability company ("LLC"), or stockholders—will receive a distribution of the remaining assets. A balance sheet simply reflects the firm's array of assets, and the claims against them, on any stated date.

Figure 2-1 presents a simplified balance sheet for Lululemon as of January 2023.* The conventional way to present a balance sheet is to list

Gathering and Retrieval ("EDGAR") system, available at http://www.sec.gov/edgar/searchedgar/webusers.htm.

* Students interested in reviewing the full financial statements of Lululemon can locate them within Lululemon's Form 10-K for 2023 which was filed with the SEC on March 28, 2023.

all the asset accounts on the left side and all the liabilities and equity accounts on the right side. The total at the bottom of each side sums to the same number, showing that the balance sheet is indeed in balance.* We can see from this figure that Lululemon had total assets of $5,607 million, total liabilities of $2,458 million, and total equity of $3,149 million (5,607 = 2,458 + 3,149).

Figure 2-1. Balance Sheet
Lululemon Athletica Inc. (LULU)
January 29, 2023
($ Millions)

Assets		Liabilities	
Cash	1,155	Accounts Payable	173
Receivables	133	Other Current Liabilities	1,319
Inventory	1,447	Total Current Liabilities	1,492
Other	424	Non-Current Liabilities	966
Current Assets	3,159	Total Liabilities	2,458
		Common Stock	1
PPE	1,270	Capital Surplus	475
Goodwill	24	Retained Earnings	2,926
Other Assets	1,154	Other Adjustments	(253)
		Total Equity	3,149
Total Assets	5,607	Total Liabilities & Equity	5,607

i. ASSETS

Common sense suggests that assets are just the things owned by a business. For Lululemon, this might include pants, shirts, store fixtures, and land. A more traditional definition of an asset is a probable future economic benefit owned or controlled by the business that is obtained in a "transaction" to which accountants can attach a price. In other words,

The Form 10-K is available for viewing through the SEC's Edgar database located at https://www.sec.gov/edgar/searchedgar/companysearch.html. We present the financial statements for Lululemon in a simplified format for ease of presentation.

* Some new accounting students are amazed to find that the column totals do indeed match every time that the entries are tallied. This is not a wonderful coincidence; it just reflects the double entry bookkeeping process whereby every asset entry also generates a corresponding entry (or entries) in another account to keep things in balance. We will see a few examples of this shortly.

the firm must have legal title or some other clear right to use the asset. And the asset must be expected to possess future benefits that can be measured. Lululemon might use $1 million to buy a new delivery of yoga pants. This should clearly be seen as an asset: the firm has legal title to the clothing, and the pants are expected to generate future economic benefits when they are sold to customers. By contrast, if Lululemon decides to spend the $1 million to host a massive end of the year party, this would not create an asset. Employees may remember the event for a long time, and they may even work harder at the firm because they enjoyed the party. But this type of economic benefit is speculative, and any future economic value cannot be ascertained.

After an asset is recorded on a company's books, generally no adjustments are made for future changes in market value (subject to a few exceptions). Thus, if a business had purchased land on Michigan Avenue immediately after the Chicago fire, and continued to hold it, the land would be shown on the books at its original cost. There are two important exceptions to this rule: inventory should be recorded at the lower of cost or market, meaning that firms sometimes need to mark down obsolete products that can no longer be valued at cost. Also, marketable securities held for sale can be reported at fair market value.

This preference for historical cost asset valuation reflects accounting's strong emphasis on reliability. There is a disadvantage to this approach, of course, because some balance sheets may significantly undervalue assets that have appreciated in value. Disney's balance sheet, for example, lists the value of the Anaheim land on which Disneyland sits at cost ($879,000), when it is undoubtedly worth much, much more (the purchase took place over 70 years ago and Southern California property values have not been too shabby in recent decades). Accordingly, a balance sheet does not necessarily present the best information about the true economic value of a firm. This is one reason why takeover offers can be made for a much higher price than accounting value—often known as "book value."* But this downside is trumped by the reliability that can be provided with historical cost valuation. Accountants fret that more flexible methods of asset valuation will lead to unreliable financial statements.

Assets are classified as either current or non-current. *Current assets* include cash or its equivalent, as well as assets that are expected to be converted into cash within one year as the result of operations. By convention, assets are also listed on the balance sheet in order of liquidity, which means cash and equivalents (marketable securities) come first, followed by accounts receivable, inventory, and other assets expected to be used within the year. *Non-current assets* are all those

* This is not to say, however, that book value is useless. Some contracts will reference book value as a quick and easy way to estimate a firm's liquidation value, and professional assessors will sometimes refer to book value to triangulate the reasonableness of other valuation methods.

assets not expected to be converted into cash within a year. They are also listed in order of liquidity: long-term investments are typically followed by equipment, buildings, and then land.

On the Lululemon balance sheet in Figure 2-1, you can see that this company holds just over 20% of its assets as cash and equivalents. This is followed by $133 million in "receivables," also known as "accounts receivable" or "A/R." What is this? Accounts receivable represents the payment obligations of buyers for products that the company has already sold. In other words, Lululemon has extended credit to some customers, and its legal entitlement to collect this money is considered an asset. Normally, receivables are due on a short cycle, perhaps thirty days or less. As alluded to earlier in this chapter, firms will also make a deduction (allowance) for doubtful accounts, representing the company's best estimate of the amount of its receivables it will be unable to collect. The number you see in Figure 2-1 is for net receivables, meaning that this allowance has already been subtracted. Details concerning the company's estimate for doubtful accounts are provided in the footnotes to the financial statements.

Four other types of asset accounts are shown in Lululemon's balance sheet: (1) inventory ready for sale; (2) PP&E (Property, Plant and Equipment), such as store fixtures, fabric manufacturing machines, office buildings, and distribution centers; (3) goodwill and intangible assets; and (4) other assets (both for current and non-current assets). Inventory includes finished goods that are intended for sale, inventories in transit, and raw materials for producing finished goods. As noted previously, inventory provides an exception to the historical cost principle, as inventory is recorded at the lower of cost or fair value. PP&E likewise has special rules regarding the application of the historical cost principle. In particular, PP&E is recorded at cost, but the value of PP&E is reduced over time through something called depreciation which, in principle, reflects how much the value of the PP&E has declined by being used. For instance, most of us are aware that if we buy a delivery truck and use it for a year, its value will be reduced by having been utilized in making deliveries. Depreciation seeks to estimate how much value is "used up", and PP&E is recorded at historical cost of a firm's property, plant and equipment, net of these accumulated depreciation charges. Note that real estate is not subject to depreciation. (We shall return to how depreciation is calculated later in this chapter.)

Goodwill is created when a company acquires another firm and can often represent a substantial amount of a company's book value of assets. Technically, goodwill is the excess of the purchase price paid for an acquired business over the fair value of the acquired firm's assets (net of liabilities) on the acquisition date. As such, it represents the excess consideration paid over and above the book value of the acquired firm. Why would a company pay more for a firm than the book value of the acquired firm's assets? We know from our earlier discussion that one reason may stem from the simple fact that, under GAAP, many of the acquired firm's assets will have been recorded at historical cost. Another relates to the possibility that the target firm has a high market value due to going-concern value, monopoly power, or other economic rents. Finally, the bidder may simply be overpaying. These considerations suggest that today's goodwill may not necessarily be tomorrow's goodwill, and under GAAP, goodwill must be tested for impairment at least annually. The accounting treatment of goodwill can create dramatic changes in a company's balance sheet. Consider, for example, Time Warner's disastrous acquisition of AOL in 2000. Before the acquisition, Time Warner's book value of assets was in the range of $25 billion. After the merger, the combined company's book value increased to the range of $85 billion because, given the nature of AOL's operations, much of the acquisition price was recorded on Time Warner's balance sheet as goodwill. But during 2000, it became increasingly obvious that Time Warner had massively overpaid for AOL, and in early 2002, the company took a massive $54 billion charge to goodwill associated with the acquisition.

Finally, we aggregate Lululemon's remaining assets into the category of "other assets," which includes several different types of assets that are beyond the scope of this chapter.

ii. LIABILITIES

Let's turn to the right side of the balance sheet. *Liabilities* are defined as obligations to provide economic benefits to a third party in the future. This includes the obvious debts, such as accounts payable, promissory notes and long-term bonds. While liabilities usually involve obligations to pay money, they may include a variety of other obligations as well. For example, in order to finance production, a manufacturer may sell inventory to a third party for current cash payments, with an agreement to repurchase the inventory in the future (an unconditional purchase obligation). Accounting treats this as essentially creation of a debt (which, incidentally, is secured by the inventory). Or, to take another example, a lawyer may accept a retainer in exchange for an agreement to perform specific legal services in the future. This is a legal obligation and creates a liability in the same way. This is sometimes called "deferred revenue" or "unearned revenue." Other liabilities might include product warranty claims, product liability claims, and environmental clean-up obligations.

Three conditions are generally required to report something as a balance sheet lability. First, a future obligation must be probable. Second, the amount of the obligation must be known or can be reasonably estimated. Third, the transaction or event that caused the obligation must have already occurred. Possible liabilities or future legal commitments that do not meet these three conditions will go unreported on the balance sheet (though they may be disclosed in footnotes). This means that fully executory contractual obligations are not treated as liabilities until execution against the contract occurs. Similarly, some legal risks may go unreported. For instance, when Lululemon compiled the balance sheet in Figure 2-1, it faced several lawsuits relating to intellectual property disputes, personal injury claims, and employment disputes. Should it disclose the possibility of loss from one of these lawsuits as a liability? The answer will depend on several factors, such as the probability that it will lose the case and the degree to which damages can be estimated. This type of situation is known as a *contingent liability*. If the contingent liability is probable, and the amount of damages can be reasonably estimated, the company must take a charge against earnings in the current period (an entry on the income statement) and include the amount as a liability (an entry on the balance sheet). You can bet that Lululemon's accountants conferred with its lawyers to determine the proper treatment of these lawsuits. If there is reasonable uncertainty about either a case outcome or the resulting damages, then a contingent liability may be disclosed only in the financial statement footnotes (which is what Lululemon did for these lawsuits).

As on the asset side, liabilities are classified as current or non-current, depending on whether they are payable within the current 12-month accounting cycle. Corporate bonds may represent both kinds of liabilities—the portion due and payable within the current accounting cycle will be listed as current, with the remainder being classified as long-term. Figure 2-1 lists just two current liability entries for Lululemon: accounts payable and other liabilities. Accounts payable are a common type of liability; they reflect amounts that a firm owes to suppliers for goods and services that have been bought on credit. Other common current liabilities include accrued liabilities for expenses that have been recorded but not yet paid (such as wages that have been earned by employees before a payday or, for company like Lululemon, unredeemed gift cards) and short-term borrowing from banks or other creditors.

Once again, each liability account is sorted by maturity. Accounts payable, usually due within 10–30 days after being incurred, are often presented first, while taxes that may be payable later in the current accounting cycle are often listed near the end of the list of current liabilities. Non-current liabilities come next. Because all liabilities are prior claims to those of stockholders in insolvency or bankruptcy, they are listed before equity.

iii. STOCKHOLDERS' EQUITY

Equity reflects the capital investments of shareholders and represents the final element in the balance sheet equation. (If this were another form of business, we might call it owners' equity or partners' equity.) Rearranging the fundamental accounting equation tells us that assets minus the liabilities will equal equity. By way of analogy, if you own a house, then your equity position equals the total value of the home (the asset value) minus your mortgage (the liability value). For this reason, equity is often referred to as the residual interest or net worth of the corporation.

If a company has issued preferred stock, then this will be listed first in the equity section of the balance sheet. (We will discuss preferred stock in more detail later in the book; for now, think of it as a highly flexible security that usually has a senior claim in a liquidation over common stock.) Typically, preferred stock is listed at its par or nominal value, a concept that we discuss in the next paragraph. Lululemon has not issued any preferred stock, so there is no corresponding equity account listed in Figure 2-1.

Common stock is presented next. Understanding the accounting treatment of common stock requires a brief discussion of the concept of par value. A company will typically designate, upon formation, a par or stated value for its common stock (and its preferred stock, if it creates any). This figure is usually arbitrary (perhaps a penny or even a fraction of a penny) and does not necessarily reflect true economic value. Some investors might be willing to pay much more than par value for a share of stock. But par value has legal implications because state laws often do not permit dividend payments that reduce the equity balance below par. Historically, a creditor might have relied on this minimum equity cushion as a way of protecting the firm's repayment obligation. Today, the concept has been relaxed, and several states now allow firms to issue stock with no par value. But some companies still use par value, and the accounting treatment of common stock investments reflects this historical treatment.

When an investor buys shares of common stock from a company, the proceeds are divided between two different accounts: the amount of the investment that corresponds to the par value will be placed in a "common stock" account, and any excess consideration will be placed in an account named "additional paid-in capital" or "capital surplus."* Lululemon, for example, designates its common stock with a par value of half a penny ($0.005), so there is a very small entry in its balance sheet for common stock. Most of the money that investors paid to purchase the shares is placed into the capital surplus account; therefore, we would need to add these two accounts to obtain a realistic sense of how much investors paid the company to acquire these shares of common stock.

You may have noticed that Lululemon's largest equity account is retained earnings. This number does not reflect the initial investment in common stock but rather tracks how much residual money has been earned by the firm over time. Because the common stockholders are the ultimate claimants after all creditors and preferred stockholders are

* If the firm has issued stock with no par value, then all the proceeds are typically allocated to the common stock account and no amount is designated as additional paid-in capital.

paid, the value of their claims will fluctuate based on the firm's fortunes. If the corporation earns a profit in a given year, it now faces a choice: pay the money out directly to shareholders as dividends or keep the money in the corporation and use it to fund future projects. (Many firms opt to do both, earmarking some profits for shareholder dividends and retaining the balance.) Common stockholders' claims will increase by the amount of retained earnings, and this account is used to track the (paper) gains. Similarly, if the corporation only has losses, the retained earnings will be diminished by the amount of the losses. This can even give rise to a negative entry, in which case the account is sometimes retitled "accumulated deficit." Lululemon has clearly not suffered from this problem, and the large retained earnings account should tip you off that the firm has enjoyed profitable performance over the years.

One other equity concept worth mentioning is treasury stock. This is simply stock that has been issued and then repurchased later by the firm through a stock buyback. Instead of cancelling the shares, accountants will track the resulting decrease in equity financing by presenting treasury stock as a negative number. If the firm decides to resell all the treasury stock to investors, then an asset account (typically cash) will increase to reflect the proceeds, and the treasury stock account will zero out.*

iv. RECORDING TRANSACTIONS ON THE BALANCE SHEET

Let's consider a short problem to illustrate how some basic transactions are recorded on the balance sheet.

Problem 2.1

On July 1, Leon Ponce decides to start a company named Perpetual Youth ("PY") to sell probiotic vitamin supplements. Ponce immediately takes several steps to launch the business:

(A) On July 1, Ponce invests $10,000 in cash to fund the business. He receives 1000 shares of PY common stock ($1 par value) in return.

(B) On July 1, PY borrows $10,000 in cash from the local bank. PY promises to repay the money in one year, along with an interest payment of $100 within five days after the end of each month.

(C) On July 1, PY locates a great store location next to the local gym and agrees to rent the site for $2000 per month. As the contract is signed, PY pays $2000 in cash to the landlord as a security deposit.

* This example assumes (unrealistically) that the amount received for reissuing the treasury stock is *exactly* the same as the amount paid by the company during the buyback. If this is not the case, then the accounting treatment is more complicated, but we do not need to get into those details here.

(D) On July 1, PY buys the hottest new "killer chia kombucha supplement pills" from a supplier for $5000. It pays half of this price in cash and promises to pay the rest of the money by the end of the month.

How should each of these transactions be recorded on the balance sheet?

To analyze balance sheet treatment of these transactions, we must first recognize that accountants will use different accounts to track changes to the various types of assets, liabilities, and equity balances. We have seen some of the most prominent accounts already: cash, accounts receivable, inventory, accounts payable, short-term debt, common stock, and retained earnings. As you grow increasingly familiar with balance sheets, you will come to recognize the most common accounts and whether they represent assets, liabilities, or equity. Some firms also use fewer common accounts—or different names for accounts that track identical business effects—but you will get the hang of this before long.

The second important concept to recognize is that accountants use double entry bookkeeping. Thought to date back to medieval times, this conceptual innovation has greatly improved the accuracy and usefulness of financial reports. Every business transaction gives rise to at least two account changes that, taken together, maintain the fundamental accounting equation: Assets = Liabilities + Equity. For instance, if a firm buys a new factory for cash, one asset will decrease (cash) while another asset (PP&E) will increase by this same amount. The liability and equity accounts will not be impacted by this transaction, yet the fundamental accounting equation will still balance.

We are now ready to analyze Problem 2.1. Accountants often use specialized concepts and terms to record the effects of a transaction (you may be familiar with T-accounts, journal entries, debits, and credits). We do not need to get into these details here, however, and can just track the changes with a spreadsheet that lists several accounts across the top of the columns along with an equal sign reminding us that the total of the asset accounts must match the total of the liability and equity accounts for every transaction. Here is what this spreadsheet might look like at the very start of Perpetual Youth's life:

Assets						Liabilities			Equity	
Cash	A/R	Inventory	PP&E	Other	=	A/P	Bank Loan	+	Common Stock	Additional Paid-in Capital
0	0	0	0	0	=	0	0	+	0	0

Now consider the changes that arise from the issue of $10,000 in stock (transaction A). Has any asset account been impacted? You will hopefully recognize that there has indeed been a change to cash: the banking coffers of PY have swelled by $10,000. Because the firm's assets have increased, we know that an offsetting entry for the transaction must increase either liabilities or equity (or decrease some other asset account). Does the stock issue lead to a liability for the firm? Recall that liabilities are defined as obligations to provide economic benefits to a third party in the future. In this case, the firm has incurred no obligation; Ponce, as shareholder, just retains the residual value of the firm. Accordingly, we should conclude that the total equity value of the firm has also risen by $10,000. Because the par value of the stock is $1 per share, the common stock account will increase by $1000 ($1 times 1000 shares) and the additional paid-in capital will increase by $9000 (the rest of the investment, or $9 times 1000 shares). For this transaction, then, there will actually be three accounts impacted. But we can see from the following worksheet, that the fundamental accounting equation still holds (10,000 = 1000 + 9000).

Assets					=	Liabilities		+	Equity	
Cash	A/R	Inventory	PP&E	Other		A/P	Bank Loan		Common Stock	Additional Paid-in Capital
10,000	0	0	0	0	=	0	0	+	1,000	9,000

Let's analyze transaction B. Again, you should recognize that cash increases because money comes into the firm via the loan. We then need to find the offsetting transaction that balances out this $10,000 increase in an asset account. (Often, it can be helpful to start with any change in cash.) Unlike the stock investment, however, PY is obligated to repay the loan in a year, so this should be considered a liability. We don't need to worry about the interest payment yet; this is an expense, the cost of borrowing money, that will accrue as time passes on the loan (and be reflected in the income statement). Our worksheet now looks like this:

Assets					=	Liabilities		+	Equity	
Cash	A/R	Inventory	PP&E	Other		A/P	Bank Loan		Common Stock	Additional Paid-in Capital
10,000	0	0	0	0	=	0	0	+	1,000	9,000
10,000	0	0	0	0	=	0	10,000	+	0	0

Consider transaction C: Perpetual Youth locates a great store location next to the local gym and agrees to rent the site for $2000 per month. As the contract is signed, PY pays $2000 in cash to the landlord as a security deposit. This one is a little trickier, but, before reading on, take a minute to think about what accounts might change from this deal.

You should recognize that cash is decreasing by $2000, so we will certainly need to decrease that asset account and find an offsetting account to adjust. Should we record the rent that we will owe later in the month as a liability? It sure seems like a future obligation—and indeed it is one as a matter of contract law. But remember the third requirement for classification as a liability: the transaction or event that caused the obligation has already occurred. Here we only have a future legal commitment, so it is not considered to give rise to an accounting liability. We will wait until we actually owe rent, due to the passage of time, before recording anything on the balance sheet.* This same principle also explains why we do not yet have to record a liability for interest payments on the loan.

What is the offsetting account for the $2000 decrease in cash? This money goes toward PY's security deposit, which is something of value that the firm expects to get back in the future (assuming PY's workers do not trash the building). We can consider it to be another type of asset. Notice that no change to the right side of the equation occurs, but the fundamental accounting equation still works. One asset has decreased, and a different asset has increased by the exact same amount (−2000 + 2000 = 0 + 0).

Assets					=	Liabilities		+	Equity	
Cash	A/R	Inventory	PP&E	Other		A/P	Bank Loan		Common Stock	Additional Paid-in Capital
10,000	0	0	0	0	=	0	0	+	1,000	9,000
10,000	0	0	0	0	=	0	10,000	+	0	0
−2,000	0	0	0	2,000	=	0	0	+	0	0

Finally, we get to transaction D: Perpetual Youth buys the hottest new "killer chia kombucha supplement pills" from a supplier for $5000. It pays half of this price in cash and promises to pay the rest of the money at the end of the month. Three accounts are impacted by this purchase; see if you can identify them before moving on.

We might start by recognizing that the supplement pills are inventory, something that PY holds now with an expectation of selling later. We will value the increase to the inventory account at cost ($5000) even though the firm may eventually wind up selling the inventory for a higher amount (that is, after all, the goal of the venture). We need to balance this increase to assets, and we can again work off of the cash: $2500 of the purchase price came from cash, so PY's cash account must decrease by this amount. The rest of the purchase price came from a

* Accounting treatment for this transaction would be different if PY paid the rent in advance. If so, cash would decrease by the payment, and another asset called "prepaid rent" would be created for the same amount. This latter account might not seem like an asset, but PY does enjoy the benefit of using the space for the next month.

promise to pay at the end of the month. We should view this commitment as an increase to a liability account (accounts payable or A/P).*

Assets					=	Liabilities		+	Equity	
Cash	A/R	Inventory	PP&E	Other		A/P	Bank Loan		Common Stock	Additional Paid-in Capital
10,000	0	0	0	0	=	0	0	+	1,000	9,000
10,000	0	0	0	0	=	0	10,000	+	0	0
−2,000	0	0	0	2,000	=	0	0	+	0	0
−2,500	0	5,000	0	0	=	2,500	0	+	0	0
15,500	0	5,000	0	2,000	=	2,500	10,000		1,000	9,000

At this point, if we wanted to prepare a balance sheet reflecting the firm's position at the end of the first day, we could sum the totals for each account and transpose the results into the conventional balance sheet format:

Balance Sheet
Perpetual Youth Inc.
July 1
($ Dollars)

Assets		Liabilities	
Cash	15,500	Accounts Payable	2,500
Receivables	0	Bank Loan	10,000
Inventory	5,000	Total Liabilities	12,500
Current Assets	20,500		
		Common Stock	1,000
PP&E	0	Additional Paid-in Capital	9,000
Other Assets	2,000	Retained Earnings	0
Total Assets	22,500	Total Liabilities & Equity	22,500

* A careful reader might ask why does the promise to pay rent at the end of the month in transaction C not give rise to a liability while the promise to pay the rest of the inventory purchase price at the end of the month does? The answer is subtle. With the inventory, PY has already received full performance by the seller (it got the pills). With the rent contract, both obligations are still executory (PY has not yet received the benefit of inhabiting the store location). More generally, this should reinforce the fact that a balance sheet does not always reflect the full economic picture of a firm.

Both sides of the balance sheet add to the same total, so things look good. This problem has also presented several of the most common patterns underlying balance sheet transactions:

- An asset increase funded with equity (transaction A)
- An asset increase funded with a liability (transaction B and part of transaction D)
- An asset increase funded by a decrease in a different asset account (transaction C and part of transaction D)

The transactions are relatively straightforward, but this is exactly the type of analysis that accountants routinely perform to track business changes and, eventually, to create a balance sheet.

Before moving on to the income statement, it is worth emphasizing the relevance of understanding these concepts not just for Leon but also for PY's lawyers. As we discuss in Chapter 9, Leon's ability in the future to conduct a cash distribution to PY's shareholders will likely require PY's lawyers to analyze PY's balance sheet to ensure compliance with state corporate law limitations on shareholder distributions, as well as fraudulent conveyance statutes. Corporate loans (such as the one obtained by PY) will also contain a variety of contract restrictions on corporate distributions based on a company's balance sheet. Likewise, if PY later raises venture capital financing, the preferred stock issued to the investor may permit the investor to redeem the shares if the company's balance sheet meets specific metrics. As the following case illustrates, effective drafting of these contract provisions requires a firm understanding of the accounting rules for balance sheets.

Albert D. Bolt v. Merrimack Pharmaceuticals, Inc.

503 F.3d 913 (9th Cir. 2007)

■ O'SCANNLAIN, CIRCUIT JUDGE.

We are called upon to interpret a corporation's articles of organization to decide whether it has an obligation to redeem certain shares of its stock.

Albert D. Bolt owns 52,488 shares of Series A Redeemable Preferred Stock ("Series A Stock") issued by Merrimack Pharmaceuticals, Inc. ("Merrimack"), a biotechnology company organized under the laws of Massachusetts. Bolt now wants to redeem those shares [for $10 each].

The relevant redemption provision of Merrimack's Restated Articles of Organization provides:

> At any time from and after December 31, 1997, if the net worth of the Corporation, determined in accordance with generally accepted accounting principles and as shown on the balance sheet of the Corporation as of the end of the fiscal quarter then most recently ended, equals or exceeds five million

dollars ($5,000,000.00), then upon the request of the holder of [the Series A] Preferred Stock, the Corporation shall redeem at the Redemption Price any and all shares of [the Series A] Preferred Stock which such holder, by such request, offers to the Corporation for redemption.

The following statement provides a snapshot of Merrimack's balance sheet as of December 31, 2001:

Assets	
Total assets	$11,331,070
Liabilities, redeemable convertible preferred stock and stockholders' deficit	
Total liabilities	$1,270,230
Redeemable convertible preferred stock:	
Series A redeemable preferred stock	$548,380
Series B convertible preferred stock	$11,915,267
Total redeemable convertible preferred stock	$12,463,647
Total stockholders' deficit	($2,402,807)
Total liabilities, redeemable convertible preferred stock, and stockholders' deficit	$11,331,070

PricewaterhouseCoopers LLP audited Merrimack's financial statements, and opined that Merrimack's balance sheet referred to above "presents fairly, in all material respects, the financial position of Merrimack Pharmaceuticals, Inc. at December 31, 2001 in conformity with accounting principles generally accepted in the United States of America."

During 2001, Merrimack had issued 3,315,201 shares of Series B Redeemable Convertible Preferred Stock ("Series B Stock") with a book value of $11,915,267. The Series B Stock is redeemable at the option of the holder upon a "deemed liquidation," defined as (1) a merger with another company, after which the Merrimack stockholders would no longer hold a majority of the voting power, or (2) the sale of Merrimack's business assets. The Series B Stock appears in the "mezzanine" of the balance sheet, between the liabilities section and the stockholders' deficit (equity) section. *See* David R. Herwitz & Matthew J. Barrett, *Accounting for Lawyers* 505 (4th ed. 2006) (explaining that the "section between liabilities and equity on the balance sheet" is commonly referred to as the "mezzanine").

On April 11, 2001, and again on March 28, 2002, Bolt sent written requests to Merrimack for the redemption of his shares of Series A Stock. In a letter dated June 13, 2002, Merrimack rejected Bolt's demands for redemption. Bolt filed suit in federal district court seeking a declaratory judgment that Merrimack's net worth exceeded $5 million as of December 31, 2001. On cross-motions for summary judgment, the district court granted summary judgment for Bolt, concluding that Merrimack's net worth exceeded $5 million as of that date.

Merrimack timely appealed.

II

We are faced with the task of interpreting Merrimack's Restated Articles of Organization to determine if it indeed has an obligation to redeem the Series A Stock held by Bolt. The dispositive issue, of course, is whether Merrimack's net worth, determined in accordance with generally accepted accounting principles ("GAAP") and as shown on the balance sheet, equaled or exceeded $5 million as of December 31, 2001. The district court held that it did. We agree.

A

We must first determine the meaning of the term "net worth," the threshold yardstick to determine whether Merrimack has an obligation to redeem the Series A Stock as Bolt requests. Merrimack's Restated Articles of Organization fail to define that term. Nor does GAAP define that term. And no item on Merrimack's balance sheet is specifically labeled "net worth."

* * *

The common and well-established meaning of the term "net worth" is the difference between a corporation's total assets and its total liabilities.[2] Merrimack's total assets and total liabilities, as shown on its December 31, 2001 balance sheet, equal $11,331,070 and $1,270,230, respectively. Accordingly, employing the well-established meaning, Merrimack's net worth equals $10,060,840, well in excess of the $5 million threshold set by the Restated Articles of Organization.

Merrimack suggests that net worth is sometimes referred to as stockholders' equity. This reference is often accurate because a balance sheet generally involves only three basic accounting elements—assets, liabilities, and equity—and equity by definition equals the residual

[2] *See, e.g.*, Herwitz & Barrett, *supra*, at 3 ("The difference between what a business owns—its *assets*—and what it owes—its *liabilities*—represents its *net worth*, which accountants sometimes refer to as *equity*."); Black's Law Dictionary (4th ed. 2004) (defining net worth as "[a] measure of one's wealth, usu. calculated as the excess of total assets over total liabilities"); *see also Am. Pac. Concrete Pipe Co., Inc. v. N.L.R.B.*, 788 F.2d 586, 590–91 (9th Cir. 1986) (calculating net worth for purposes of the Equal Access to Justice Act by "subtracting total liabilities from total assets"); *Overnite Transp. Co. v. Comm'r of Revenue*, 54 Mass. App. Ct. 180, 764 N.E.2d 363, 365 n.1 (Mass. App. Ct. 2002) (defining net worth for purposes of Massachusetts's tax revenue laws as "the book value of [the company's] total assets less its liabilities").

interest in the assets after subtracting liabilities. Yet, under this reasoning, Merrimack's net worth would still exceed $5 million.

But Merrimack goes further, arguing that the definition of net worth for purposes of its Restated Articles of Organization equals *only* Merrimack's total stockholders' deficit of $2,402,807, excluding Merrimack's total redeemable convertible preferred stock of $12,463,647. Merrimack contends that limiting the meaning of net worth to this amount is appropriate here because the Restated Articles of Organization point to net worth "as shown on the balance sheet" and call for no further calculations. While this argument has surface appeal, we ultimately are unpersuaded. The Restated Articles of Organization indeed point us to "net worth. . . *as shown* on the balance sheet." (emphasis added.) But there is no item so labeled on the balance sheet involved here. Thus, such an interpretation of net worth is "shown" on the balance sheet only to the extent that we accept an additional premise necessary to connect it to the net worth reference in the Restated Articles of Organization. Either we accept Merrimack's premise that net worth is limited to total stockholders' equity (deficit) on the balance sheet, or we accept Bolt's premise that net worth is commonly defined as the difference between total assets and liabilities. Regrettably, the Restated Articles of Organization provide no further guidance as to the proper definition of the term. Given the common and well-established meaning of the term "net worth" as the difference between total assets and total liabilities, we cannot accept that the document reflects an intentionally narrower, more nuanced definition of that term that would equal only total stockholders' equity (deficit) simply because it employed the phrase "as shown on the balance sheet." We therefore decline to adopt Merrimack's definition here.

B

Nevertheless, our analysis does not end with our construction of the term "net worth." The Restated Articles of Organization specify that the balance sheet relied upon must be determined in accordance with GAAP.[6] If the balance sheet incorrectly reports total assets or total liabilities under GAAP, our determination of net worth necessarily would be affected.

To determine whether the balance sheet is prepared in accordance with GAAP, we do not take off our judicial black robes and reach for the accountant's green eyeshade. Rather, because " 'generally accepted accounting principles' are far from being a canonical set of rules that will ensure identical accounting treatment of identical transactions[, and] tolerate a range of 'reasonable' treatments," we generally defer to the

[6] Unfortunately, GAAP is not found in a single source. *See* Herwitz & Barrett, *supra*, at 182. Instead, in the United States, GAAP consists of a hodgepodge of accounting sources, which find their respective places in the hierarchical structure established by the American Institute of Certified Public Accountants ("AICPA"). . . . [Eds. The rest of this footnote appears near the end of this chapter to illustrate the complex array of institutions that can sometimes play a part in the determination of GAAP].

professional judgment of the accountant who audited or prepared the financial statements, unless a GAAP authority *demands* a contrary accounting treatment.

Merrimack argues on appeal that the Series B Stock, which is presented in the mezzanine section of the balance sheet, is akin to a liability under GAAP authorities. Of course, if the Series B Stock were considered a liability, Merrimack's net worth would not equal or exceed $5 million. But Merrimack's balance sheet does not show the Series B Stock to be part of total liabilities. Nor do we believe that GAAP requires such accounting classification. [The court went on to discuss arguments on both sides of this classification question.]

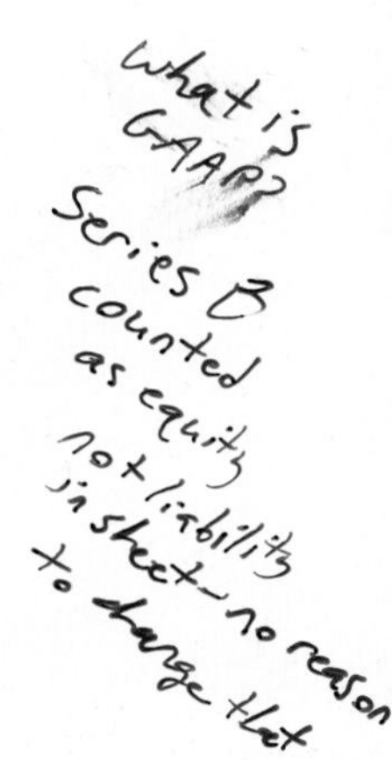

what is GAAP?
Series B counted as equity not liability in sheet - no reason to change that

* * *

In sum, finding no GAAP authority that requires classifying Merrimack's Series B Stock as part of total liabilities, we defer to PricewaterhouseCooper's conclusion that Merrimack's balance sheet "presents fairly, in all material respects, the financial position of Merrimack Pharmaceuticals, Inc. at December 31, 2001 in conformity with accounting principles generally accepted in the United States of America." We therefore agree with the district court's conclusion that Merrimack's balance sheet as of December 31, 2001 was determined according to GAAP.

Merrimack has an obligation to redeem Bolt's Series A Stock if its net worth equals or exceeds $5 million. Because we conclude that the term "net worth" for purposes of the Restated Articles of Organization should be given its well-established meaning as the difference between total assets and total liabilities, and because Merrimack's total assets and total liabilities equaled $11,331,070 and $1,270,230, respectively, as shown on the December 31, 2001 balance sheet calculated in conformity with GAAP, Merrimack's net worth exceeded $5 million. Accordingly, the district court's grant of summary judgment in favor of Bolt is AFFIRMED.

QUESTIONS

1. What exactly does Bolt want the company to do? On the basis of the balance sheet presented in the case, can you speculate about how Merrimack's business is performing? Could this explain why Bolt wants to redeem his stock?
2. Is preferred stock that (1) promises a certain annual dividend rate and (2) a right to force the company to redeem it upon the occurrence of certain events more like debt or stock? Why does it matter for resolution of this case?
3. Is this a drafting error on the part of lawyers? When Merrimack and Bolt entered into their agreement, Merrimack had a simple capital

structure, with no other classes of preferred stock. Thus, increases in "net worth," absent new financings, could only have come from earnings (retained earnings) that belonged to the common stockholders. Bolt's $548,380 investment would have represented little more than 10% of "net worth" (defined as common stockholders' equity) if the $5 million net worth had been reached.

4. What language could Merrimack's lawyers have used when the firm issued the Series A stock to Bolt to prevent this outcome?

5. Note the allusions to the complexity of authority in the determination of GAAP. This case should reinforce your understanding that the accounting profession uses standards more than rules.

B. THE INCOME STATEMENT

The second accounting report is the income statement (sometimes called the statement of earnings). This reflects a firm's financial performance over a certain period of time: how much did the company sell, and what expenses were incurred to generate this revenue. Ultimately, the income statement yields the firm's net income or profits (sometimes described as the bottom line). But the income statement also presents useful information along the way about how the firm generated that profit.

One of the most important accounting concepts to understand in relation to the income statement is the *matching principle*. For each accounting period, all expenses incurred to generate the reported sales are included under the *accrual* method of accounting—even if the actual bill is paid before or after the period. (Some small corporations and other non-corporate entities, by contrast, use the cash method of accounting, in which revenues and expenses are only recognized when cash trades hands.) Under the accrual method, accountants allocate income to the period when earned, regardless of the time of receipt, and expenses to the period when incurred, regardless of the time of payment. In other words, revenue is recognized when the activities associated with earning the revenue have been performed, such as delivery of goods or services. And any expenses supporting that revenue are also recognized during the same period.

This method becomes especially important if the firm has long-term projects that spread over multiple periods. The accrual method of accounting requires judgments to be made about when income should be recognized as earned, and when to recognize expenses as incurred. These judgments normally should be transparent; that is, the methods used for recognition should be described in accounting statements. The failure to make these judgments transparent can lead to confusion on the part of readers of financial statements, and, in some cases, to charges of fraud. For example, some telecommunication firms have gotten into trouble by engaging in "swaps" of capacity. One firm might recognize revenue from the "sale" of capacity in the current period and defer recognition of the costs of buying capacity until a later period.

While a balance sheet offers a snapshot of a business at a particular moment in time, the income statement is more like an historical novel. It begins on the first day of a fiscal period and tells the reader how the corporation's balance sheet came to look the way it does at the end of the period. Accordingly, it is the link between two balance sheets. Let's illustrate by returning to the retailer Lululemon to look at a standard example. Its income statements for 2021, 2022, and 2023 appear in Figure 2-2.

Figure 2-2. Income Statement
Lululemon Athletica Inc.
($ Millions)

	Year Ending		
	2023	2022	2021
Net Revenue	8,111	6,257	4,402
Cost of Goods Sold	3,618	2,648	1,938
Gross Profit	4,492	3,609	2,464
Selling General and Admin.	2,757	2,225	1,609
Research and Development	–	–	–
Other Expense	9	9	5
Operating Income	1,726	1,375	850
Other Income/Expense	(393)	(41)	(31)
EBIT	1,333	1,334	819
Interest Expense	–	–	–
Income Tax Expense	478	359	230
Net Income	855	975	589
Earnings Per Share (Basic)	$6.70	$7.52	$4.52
Earnings Per Share (Diluted)	$6.68	$7.49	$4.50

i. SALES (REVENUE)

The income statement begins with revenue, the dollar amount of goods and services that a company sold during each period. For

Lululemon, we see a steady increase in net revenue, from about $4.4 billion for the fiscal year ending in 2021 to more than $8.1 billion in 2023. If nothing else, this signals healthy customer demand for its clothing and other offerings. Again, this number is presented using the accrual method. Suppose Lululemon sells 10,000 shirts to a wholesaler firm on the very last week of the fiscal year—perhaps to clear out old inventory—but the buyer won't pay for the goods until after the next fiscal year begins. Should Lululemon recognize the revenue now? The answer is probably yes: under the matching principle the sales have occurred this period even if the cash has not yet arrived.*

Notice also that this revenue is reported on a net basis. This means that Lululemon calculated its net sales by subtracting product returns (and possibly making some other adjustments) from its overall gross sales. The methodology for calculating this net revenue figure, as well as other assumptions underlying the firm's revenue recognition policies, are discussed in the second footnote to the financial statements.

ii. EXPENSES: COST OF GOODS SOLD AND GROSS MARGIN

After the revenue line, an income statement will list expenses, grouped into different categories, along with several subtotals. Each category of expenses offers information about the firm's cost structure, and the subtotals facilitate comparison between different firms.

In Figure 2-2, the first category of expenses is cost of goods sold (sometimes called cost of sales). This represents the cost of merchandise shipped or services rendered. For Lululemon, it likely includes raw material purchases and other costs of making the apparel. It does not include marketing, selling costs, and other overhead expenses (these will come next). Subtracting the cost of goods sold from net revenue leads to the first subtotal: gross profit (also called gross margin). Think of this as a subtotal showing the difference between the total amount received for the apparel and the total amount needed to make the apparel. This subtotal is especially important for manufacturers and retailers because other operating expenses need to be paid from gross profits.

Gross profit, by itself, has little significance for legal purposes, but it is important when analyzing the results of operations. If, for example, the cost of goods sold is increasing as a percentage of net sales, the resulting "gross profit" will be declining. This might be explained by rising costs of raw materials, competitive pressures on selling prices, or some similar factor. We can see that Lululemon's overall gross profit has increased steadily from 2021 to 2023. Does this mean that the firm's performance is improving? Maybe, but we would also want to conduct

---

* This assumes that the sale is final and not offered under a consignment arrangement (which would raise more complicated issues of revenue recognition). Relatedly, large sales that arise very late in an accounting period are a perennial topic of concern for accountants, who worry about fraudulent "channel stuffing" practices. For instance, some companies have gotten into trouble by executing large sales at the end of the period with the understanding that the customer would return the product for a refund after the period ends.

additional analysis. For example, we could state the gross profits as a percentage of revenues by dividing the former number into the latter. If we do this for 2021 and 2023, we see that the gross profit percentage has actually decreased from 56.0% in 2021 (2,464/4,402 = 56.0%) to 55.4% in 2023 (4,492/8,111 = 55.4%). This decline could be the result of costlier manufacturing processes, price competition, a shift in product mix to less profitable clothing lines, or some other reason. All else being equal, however, it should be taken as a negative development for the company.

The treatment of inventory is one of the most important issues underlying the cost of goods sold calculation. A company will not usually specifically identify each product as it passes through the supply chain for sale. It thus needs to make assumptions about which items were actually sold, and this assumption can have an impact on the cost of goods sold when the company spends different amounts to make or buy the relevant product.

For example, imagine that Lululemon made 50,000 pairs of its latest new shorts during the 2023 year, but different raw material costs over the period meant that half of the shorts cost $10 to make, and the other half cost $15. Assume further that Lululemon sells all the shorts for the same price. If everything is sold during the same period, it becomes easy to calculate the cost of goods sold (25,000 * 10 + 25,000 * 15 = $625,000). But if only 25,000 shorts are sold in one period, the firm faces a choice: should it view the cheaper shorts as the ones sold or the more expensive ones? The first option will lead to greater reported profits for the period (costs will be lower) and a larger inventory account remaining on the balance sheet. The second option has the opposite effect: lower reported profits and a smaller inventory account. A full class in accounting would spend much more time on the impact of different costing methods (including tax effects). For now, you should just recognize that different approaches are viable and that accountants will pay significant attention to this decision.

Depreciation expense is a second important topic related to calculating cost of goods sold. This is a charge taken against the current year's revenues to reflect the diminution in value of long-term assets used to produce the sales—those with an expected life of more than one accounting cycle. These assets may diminish in value because they wear out from use, as in the case of many pieces of machinery, or because they become obsolete, as in the case of computers. A periodic charge is taken, representing some proportion of the value of these assets each year of the expected useful life of the asset.* For example, suppose a company buys an asset for $100, and management determines that the useful life of the asset is 10 years and that the asset will be worthless at the end of this time period (i.e., it has no "salvage value"). Under "straight line"

* Similarly, when intangible assets have a finite life, they are amortized over their useful lives, a process similar to depreciation. Thus, the book value of a patent that is purchased might be amortized over its remaining legal life.

depreciation, a depreciation expense would be taken every year in the amount of $10. At the same time, the value of the asset on the company's balance sheet would also be diminished by $10 such that by the end of year 10, its value would be $0. This is another manifestation of the matching principle. The exact charge may not correspond to the loss of market value of these assets, and different methods may be used to estimate depreciation expense. As with inventory costing methods, we will not get into the precise calculations, but it is important to understand conceptually that depreciation will lead to expenses on the income statement and reduce the value of long-term assets (like a factory) on the balance sheet.

Some of a firm's depreciation expenses may not be grouped into the cost of goods sold category. But if the long-term asset that is being depreciated contributes directly to the production of products, then it will probably be included in cost of goods sold. For example, Lululemon might have a weaving machine with a ten-year life that it uses to make shirts. If 10% of the machine's value is depreciated every year, then this amount should be included somewhere in the cost of goods sold line item. By contrast, some long-lived assets might not be directly used in the creation of goods, and depreciation expenses from these assets will appear further down in the income statement. The depreciation of Lululemon's corporate headquarters office building, for example, is probably not treated as a cost of goods sold expense item.

iii. EXPENSES: SG&A, R&D, AND OPERATING INCOME

We can move more quickly through the other operating expense categories. Below the gross profit subtotal, we see three expense groupings: (1) selling, general, and administrative (usually called "SG&A"); (2) research and development ("R&D"); and (3) other expenses. These are all expenses that do not relate to production of the firm's good or service but must still be incurred as the company does business. SG&A includes expenses related to advertising, marketing, sales agent salaries, general officer salaries, and many other centralized expenses. The charge that a firm takes to reflect bad debt expense (alluded to earlier in this chapter) is also placed here as a cost of selling. Think of this category as a collection of overhead expenses that must be supported from gross profits. It can be comprised of both immediate expense items (such as a one-time payment for a newspaper ad) and depreciation expenses from longer-lived assets (as mentioned above). SG&A can be a large expense component for many firms; we see in Figure 2-2, for instance, that Lululemon spends almost as much on SG&A as it does to make its products.

R&D comprises, as you would expect, expenses relating to the research and development of new products or services. The treatment of this expense category highlights another important accounting distinction: whether a given cost should be "capitalized" and placed on the balance sheet as a longer-term asset or expensed in the current year. For something like R&D, a firm might prefer the former approach, because it would allow these costs to become assets instead of immediate expense items that reduce the current period's profit calculation. But accounting standard-setters are nervous about allowing R&D expenditures to be capitalized because it is possible that much of this spending might not really pan out. The typical treatment, then, is to require firms to expense R&D in the current period.* You might recognize that this is another reason why a firm's balance sheet does not necessarily reflect the firm's full economic value: an innovative company could have expensed some R&D years ago that is still quite valuable but does not appear as an asset. Some firms will invest heavily in R&D; others, like Lululemon, may spend nothing on this category.

There may also be some other operating expenses that don't fit into another category. We see, for example, that Lululemon listed very small expenses here for each year. Another subtotal is usually presented after these expenses called operating income.

iv. EBIT AND NET INCOME

After the operating income subtotal comes a line for other income or expense items. Think of these as very unusual revenue or expense items that are not related to normal operations and not expected to repeat in future years. For example, if a business has sold some operations during the year, a comparison with the previous year's activity isn't possible without some adjustments. In these cases, it is helpful to the reader to add a line to the income statement for "Discontinued Operations," and to place it in this section. In the Lululemon exhibit, we see that it reported a huge $393 million expense in 2023, which we would certainly wish to investigate further before making a large investment in the company. (The actual financial statements and the footnotes tell us that this expense reflects a large goodwill impairment charge relating to the firm's earlier purchase of MIRROR—later rebranded as Lululemon Studio. Apparently, that deal hasn't worked out as well as the firm expected.)

The other type of transaction that often appears in this section is a non-recurring item. A company may sell a factory or division for a price well in excess of its book value. This creates a profit for the company, but when was it earned? It is recognized in the current year, but the appreciation in the value of the business may have occurred over a long

---

* By contrast, a firm that buys another company to obtain its technology is typically permitted to capitalize the purchase price as an asset. For example, a company may own a copyright in software developed by its engineers, but this intangible asset will not appear on the company's balance sheet. Rather, the cost of developing the copyright will have appeared as expenses on the company's income statement as it developed the software (e.g., as wages paid to the engineers). However, if this company is acquired, the acquiring firm will be entitled to allocate a portion of the acquisition consideration to the value of the acquired copyright, which will appear as an intangible asset on the *acquiring* firm's balance sheet. Some have argued that this treatment of intangible assets discourages in-house R&D and encourages the use of serial acquisitions to obtain similar advancements.

period of time. Conversely, a company might suffer a major uninsured loss, perhaps through an unexpected flood of a plant, where it did not carry flood insurance. While this is truly a current event, to show this as a charge against operating income would distort comparisons with previous years. Thus, when these events occur, it is appropriate to add a line to the income statement to show "Net Income from Current Operations," and then disclose these extraordinary items below that line.

Finally, a company may decide to close a plant down rather than sell it. In this case there is no transaction with which to recognize a loss, but assets have been removed from production, and most likely have lost much, if not all, of their value. In such cases companies take a one-time restructuring charge as an extraordinary item against earnings. While this has the effect of reducing current income, management might characterize this as an extraordinary item and list this charge here. As with other aspects of financial statement presentation, management has considerable discretion in whether to separate these costs in this fashion, as opposed to including them as part of operating expenses. Regardless of where these charges are presented, they are another part of the financial statements to watch very closely. Some firms have gotten into trouble by writing off "too much," thus making it easier to achieve higher earnings in later periods.

We have still another subtotal after the presentation of operating income: Earnings Before Interest and Taxes ("EBIT"). This is an especially important number for comparing other companies in the same business. EBIT is independent of financial factors like interest expense and taxes, which will vary from firm to firm, even among firms making virtually identical products. In most cases this is useful because it summarizes all of the income available to pay claimants—whether creditors or shareholders—of the business.

After EBIT, the income statement will present line items for interest expense and taxes. This leads to the firm's net income for the period. It is also usually presented on a per-share basis, called "earnings per share" or "EPS." EPS is often displayed on both a basic and diluted basis. The latter measure assumes that all outstanding convertible securities, like options or convertible debt, are exercised and recalculates the EPS on this fully diluted basis. In Figure 2-2, we see that the EPS numbers for Lululemon are essentially identical, but we will see some later examples where a diluted EPS calculation might make more of a difference. These are highly salient numbers for most firms and often the first place that analysts will look when new statements are released. It is worth emphasizing, however, that savvy analysts will consider the other parts of the financial statements (including the footnotes) and not place too much emphasis on the bottom line.

Sidebar: Contracting for a Net Profit Interest

Lawyers frequently draw contracts that depend on a determination of net profits. Formerly such contracts were used by actors and writers working on Hollywood films. Humourist Art Buchwald agreed to take a percentage of net profits for his idea for the film Coming to America, a blockbuster starring Eddie Murphy. Sadly for Mr. Buchwald, Paramount Pictures reported that there were no profits on the film, which led to litigation over whether Paramount had understated revenues associated with the film and overstated costs assigned to it. You can also imagine a client going to work to turn around a troubled subsidiary corporation and contracting for a percentage of the profits if successful. In other cases, where buyers and sellers are unable to agree on the value of a business, they resolve the matter by providing that the sellers will receive an "earn-out" if future net profits reach certain targets.

You now know that simply stipulating that a company's books be kept in accordance with GAAP isn't enough protection. In addition to assuring no changes from existing depreciation and amortization practices, you would want to protect your client's expectations by assuring that the parent corporation didn't raise expenses by assigning additional overhead from the parent to the subsidiary, or by engaging in parent-subsidiary dealings at the expense of the subsidiary's profits. Would this be enough? If you represent the seller, you might want other assurances that expenses charged to the business do not increase to wipe out all profits. What protections would you want to write into such a contract?

v. RECORDING TRANSACTIONS ON THE BALANCE SHEET AND INCOME STATEMENT

Let's return to Perpetual Youth Inc. to continue our basic illustration of the accounting process.

Problem 2.2

After completing the transactions outlined in Problem 2.1, Perpetual Youth opens its doors for business on July 2. Throughout the month, several new events occur:

(E) On July 2, PY pays $1200 to buy an advertisement on a local internet search firm.

(F) During the rest of July, PY sells 80% of the supplement pills that it bought in Problem 2.1 (D). The customers pay a total of $12,000.

(G) On July 31, Perpetual Youth makes the $2000 monthly rent payment that is due under its lease contract.

(H) On July 31, Perpetual Youth pays its supplier the remaining $2500 that it owes from transaction D.

(I) On July 31, Perpetual Youth wants to estimate the interest expense that has accumulated on its bank loan during this month (no actual payment is made however).

(J) On July 31, Perpetual Youth wants to estimate the tax expense that has accumulated on any profits earned this month. You should assume that PY has a 20% tax rate and that the interest expense will be tax deductible. (Again, no actual payment is made.)

How should each of these transactions be recorded on the spreadsheet from Problem 2.1 in a way that maintains the fundamental accounting equation? How might we construct a balance sheet and income statement for PY at the end of its first month of operations?

To take on this problem, we might start by returning to the spreadsheet created for Problem 2.1. At the end of the analysis, it looked like this:

Assets					=	Liabilities		+	Equity	
Cash	A/R	Inventory	PP&E	Other		A/P	Bank Loan		Common Stock	Additional Paid-in Capital
10,000	0	0	0	0	=	0	0	+	1,000	9,000
10,000	0	0	0	0	=	0	10,000	+	0	0
−2,000	0	0	0	2,000	=	0	0	+	0	0
−2,500	0	5,000	0	0	=	2,500	0	+	0	0

No income statement transactions occurred during Problem 2.1, but Perpetual Youth has now conducted some activities that generate revenue and expenses. Accordingly, we will want to add a second worksheet with income statement columns:

Revenues	−	Expenses	=	Net Income
0		0		0

We will use this worksheet to track transactions that appear on the income statement. Before analyzing transaction E, however, we should briefly discuss how the income statement worksheet links to the balance sheet worksheet. At the end of an accounting period, accountants will take a series of steps to "close the books," and prepare the financial statements. We will not discuss this process in detail, but one thing that occurs is that the net income balance is transferred to an equity account. This makes sense: a positive net income means that the firm has created value during the period. Shareholders, as residual claimants of the firm, are entitled to these gains if the company is liquated. With a little reflection, we can treat increases in revenues as analogous to increases in equity for the fundamental accounting equation. And increases in expenses can be treated conceptually as decreases in equity. (The changes to equity won't happen until the end of the period, but we can keep this effect in mind as we work to ensure that the fundamental accounting equation holds true.)

Let's illustrate with transaction E: On July 2, PY pays $1200 to buy an advertisement on a local internet search firm. What accounts are impacted? As before, it can be helpful to start with cash. We know that PY spent $1200, so cash must decrease by that amount. What is the offsetting entry? One tempting possibility might be to treat the advertisement as an intangible asset because it could create a future benefit for PY by increasing customer activity. But this is too speculative, and accountants do not permit this type of expenditure to be capitalized. Instead, we should treat this as an operating expense for the month by increasing expenses on the second worksheet. The fundamental equation still holds because an asset decrease (cash) is balanced by an equity decrease. (Recall that increasing an expense will effectively decrease net income and thus decrease equity at the end of the period.)

Assets					=	Liabilities			+	Equity	
Cash	A/R	Inventory	PP&E	Other		A/P	Other	Bank Loan		Common Stock	Additional Paid-in Capital
−1,200	0	0	0	0		0	0	0		0	0

Revenues	−	Expenses	=	Net Income
0		1,200		0

Transaction F: During the rest of July, PY sells 80% of the supplement pills that it bought in Problem 2.1 (D). The customers pay a total of $12,000. You might recognize that there are two different things happening here: PY is reducing the number of pills in inventory, and PY is taking in cash from customers. We need to deal with both effects. Start with the $12,000 received by PY. The customers have paid in cash (not credit), so we know that this asset will increase by that amount. The offsetting entry is for revenues—an increase in net assets that PY earned by delivering goods and services to customers. The second effect must reduce the inventory account (PY has fewer pills on hand to sell), but we need to calculate the amount of the inventory reduction. We had $5000 in total inventory and sold 80% of this, so the account reduction is for $4000. This same number will be entered as an expense (cost of goods sold) to balance the books:

Assets					=	Liabilities			+	Equity	
Cash	A/R	Inventory	PP& E	Other		A/P	Other	Bank Loan		Common Stock	Additional Paid-in Capital
−1,200	0	0	0	0		0	0	0		0	0
12,000	0	−4,000	0	0		0	0	0		0	0

Revenues	−	Expenses	=	Net Income
0		1,200		0
12,000		4,000		0

Transaction G: On July 31, Perpetual Youth makes the $2000 monthly rent payment that is due under its lease contract. This transaction is handled like the advertising payment. Cash is reduced, and expenses increase. (Formally, we define expenses as a drop in net assets used to generate revenue and support the firm's operations.) The worksheet does not specify the type of expense, but we would probably consider this SG&A (selling, general and administration).

Assets					=	Liabilities			+	Equity	
Cash	A/R	Inventory	PP& E	Other		A/P	Other	Bank Loan		Common Stock	Additional Paid-in Capital
−1,200	0	0	0	0		0	0	0		0	0
12,000	0	−4,000	0	0		0	0	0		0	0
−2,000	0	0	0	0		0	0	0		0	0

Revenues	−	Expenses	=	Net Income
0		1,200		0
12,000		4,000		0
0		2,000		0

Transaction H: On July 31, Perpetual Youth pays its supplier the remaining $2500 that it owes. Cash will again decrease. Is there another expense item to balance the books? No! PY is just paying off the accounts payable liability that was created by transaction D. Since PY follows the matching principle, it does not recognize an expense related to inventory purchase until that product is sold for revenue (as in transaction F). Accordingly, there are no changes to the income statement worksheet from this transaction; only the balance sheet accounts are impacted.

Assets					=	Liabilities			+	Equity	
Cash	A/R	Inventory	PP&E	Other		A/P	Other	Bank Loan		Common Stock	Additional Paid-in Capital
−1,200	0	0	0	0		0	0	0		0	0
12,000	0	−4,000	0	0		0	0	0		0	0
−2,000	0	0	0	0		0	0	0		0	0
−2,500	0	0	0	0		−2,500	0	0		0	0

Revenues	−	Expenses	=	Net Income
0		1,200		0
12,000		4,000		0
0		2,000		0
0		0		0

Transaction I: On July 31, Perpetual Youth wants to estimate the interest expense that has accumulated on its bank loan during this month (no actual payment is made however). If we want to get a complete picture of PY's performance over the period, we should recognize that it has accrued some interest expense on the bank loan during the month. Recall that PY borrowed $10,000 in transaction B and promised to pay $100 after the end of every month. Even though PY has not yet paid this interest by the end of July (presumably it will pay in a few days), the company should still include an expense for the loan. This is just another illustration of the matching principle: accountants will match the interest expense with each month of borrowing.

How do we account for this? We can't work off a change to cash, but we should realize that the expense account will increase by the $100. What's the offsetting entry? Accountants would set up a liability account, called interest payable, and increase that account. If you think about it, this should make sense: PY owes the interest to the bank, just like it might owe money to suppliers under an accounts payable liability. Then, when PY actually makes the interest payment to the bank the following month, both cash and the interest payable account will decrease. For now, however, our worksheet will look like this (we placed the interest payable account in an "other" liabilities column):

Assets					=	Liabilities			+	Equity	
Cash	A/R	Inventory	PP&E	Other		A/P	Other	Bank Loan		Common Stock	Additional Paid-in Capital
−1,200	0	0	0	0		0	0	0		0	0
12,000	0	−4,000	0	0		0	0	0		0	0
−2,000	0	0	0	0		0	0	0		0	0
−2,500	0	0	0	0		−2,500	0	0		0	0
0	0	0	0	0		0	100	0		0	0

Revenues	−	Expenses	=	Net Income
0		1,200		0
12,000		4,000		0
0		2,000		0
0		0		0
0		100		0

Transaction J: On July 31, Perpetual Youth wants to estimate the tax expense that has accumulated on any profits earned this month. You should assume that PY has a 20% tax rate and that the interest expense will be tax deductible. (Again, no actual payment is made.) As with the accrued interest, we should recognize that PY will need to pay taxes on any profits from this period. Like before, accounting for this will increase both expenses and a new liability account—this time called taxes payable. But first we need to calculate what this tax bill will be. We can do this by starting with the revenue balance and then subtracting all the expenses thus far: 12,000 − 1,200 − 4,000 − 2,000 − 100 = 4,700. (Note that we include the interest expense from transaction I because the problem tells us that this is also tax deductible.) We can then multiply this $4,700 by the 20% tax rate to get an accrued tax expense of $940 for PY's operations in July. Finally, we can make the relevant accounting entries (again putting the taxes payable liability in the "other" column):

Assets					=	Liabilities			+	Equity	
Cash	A/R	Inventory	PP&E	Other		A/P	Other	Bank Loan		Common Stock	Additional Paid-in Capital
−1,200	0	0	0	0		0	0	0		0	0
12,000	0	−4,000	0	0		0	0	0		0	0
−2,000	0	0	0	0		0	0	0		0	0
−2,500	0	0	0	0		−2,500	0	0		0	0
0	0	0	0	0		0	100	0		0	0
0	0	0	0	0		0	940	0		0	0

Revenues	–	Expenses	=	Net Income
0		1,200		0
12,000		4,000		0
0		2,000		0
0		0		0
0		100		0
0		940		0

We are ready to prepare an income statement for the month by following the format from earlier in the chapter and picking off the relevant line items from the worksheet. The main challenge is to properly categorize each expense: accountants would probably place the cost of the pills into cost of goods sold, the interest and tax expenses on their own lines (below EBIT) and all the other expenses into SG&A.

Income Statement

Perpetual Youth Inc.

	July
Net Revenue	$12,000
Cost of Goods Sold	4,000
Gross Profit	8,000
Selling General and Admin.	3,200
Research and Development	–
Other Expense	–
Operating Income	4,800
Other Income/Expense	0
EBIT	4,800
Interest Expense	100
Income Tax Expense	940
Net Income	3,760

Adding up all the numbers takes us to the bottom line: PY earned $3,760 in net income for the month. Not bad! Eventually, when we close the books and start a new accounting period, the $3,760 in net income will be transferred to the retained earnings equity account, and all the net income accounts will reset to zero (i.e., we increase the retained earnings account by $3,760 and decrease each of the revenue and expense accounts by the amounts needed to reset them to zero). The accounting cycle begins anew. After this occurs, the updated balance sheet for PY would look like this:

Balance Sheet
Perpetual Youth Inc.
July 31
($ Dollars)

Assets		Liabilities	
Cash	21,800	Accounts Payable	0
Receivables	0	Other Liabilities	1,040
Inventory	1,000	Bank Loan	10,000
Current Assets	22,800	Total Liabilities	11,040
		Common Stock	1,000
PP&E	0	Additional Paid-in Capital	9,000
Other Assets	2,000	Retained Earnings	3,760
Total Assets	24,800	Total Liabilities & Equity	24,800

One of the more common forms of financial statement fraud involves accelerating the recognition of revenues. This can occur because managers are eager to show period-to-period revenue and profit growth and to meet analysts' expectations. Disappointed analysts can often lead to a substantial drop in a stock's price. Keep in mind that top managers may receive a significant portion of their compensation in "restricted stock" (that cannot be resold immediately) and stock options, which are valuable only if the stock price rises above the price at the time of issuance of the options—so there are often personal incentives for senior managers to prevent a stock rout. The following two cases offer examples of revenue recognition timing concerns.

Alaiyan v. Insightful Corporation

128 Wash. App. 1002 (2005)

■ KENNEDY, J.

Wajih Alaiyan was hired by Insightful Corporation on August 13, 2001, to manage Insightful's consulting services division. He performed well, and by January 2002 he had been promoted to the position of director of professional services for North America. His new duties included oversight of domestic consulting, training, and educational services as well as oversight of department profit and loss statements and revenues and earnings from Insightful's North American operations. In this new position, Alaiyan reported directly to Shawn Javid, Insightful's Chairman, President and Chief Executive Officer (CEO). Javid abruptly fired Alaiyan on March 29, 2002. Alaiyan was an at-will employee during his entire period of employment.

Insightful is a publicly traded software company listed on the NASDAQ exchange. Alaiyan claims that while employed at Insightful, he discovered that Insightful was recognizing revenue prematurely and mismanaging expenses on five accounts that Alaiyan and his team were servicing. Alaiyan asserts that Insightful was recognizing revenue at least a quarter earlier than it should have, or, in some cases even years earlier. Specifically, Alaiyan assert[s] that dating back to 1999, Insightful recognized revenue from some projects before services were performed, or booked consulting fees for which payment was not received. [He also claims that Insightful] failed to report project expenses when they occurred, contrary to statements contained in Insightful's SEC Form 10-K dated December 31, 2002. Alaiyan contends that this illustrated a pattern of misleading accounting practices that made the corporation appear more profitable to investors and creditors in quarters when revenue was prematurely recognized, especially if expenses had been incurred in connection with those projects that were not timely posted. At the same time, Alaiyan and his team were expected to complete work on accounts on which revenue had been recognized months or years earlier; thus his department would not, he believed, be given credit on the quarterly profit and loss statements for revenues that should have been recognized as the work was done rather than earlier, before Alaiyan was hired. And sometimes the department was required to recognize expenses as the work was performed, with no offsetting revenue to balance the expenses out, on the quarterly balance sheet for the department. Alaiyan believed that this would result in lower merit bonuses for him and his team.

Alaiyan first expressed concerns about these practices just prior to his promotion, during a few meetings with the Vice President of Insightful's Professional Services Department. Alaiyan further expressed his concerns to Insightful's senior management during a meeting on January 29, 2002. He continued to communicate these concerns at weekly meetings with Insightful's management, and further discussed their effect on specific client accounts in at least three separate meetings with individual members of Insightful's management in February and March of 2002. On March 26, 2002, Javid informed Alaiyan by e-mail that he was worried about the performance of Insightful's consulting group and that he had expected the relationship between sales and consulting to improve under Alaiyan's leadership. Alaiyan contends this was the first time he had heard any complaints about his leadership in his new position, and that he had [previously] received consistent praise for his work performance. Javid and Alaiyan met on March 29, 2002, and Javid terminated Alaiyan's employment, allegedly for poor performance by the consulting group and Alaiyan's inability to work cooperatively with the sales group. Alaiyan believed that this was pretense and that he was actually discharged for objecting to what he claimed were deceptive accounting practices.

He brought a complaint in King County Superior Court against Insightful on December 13, 2002, seeking damages for wrongful termination and asserting that his wrongful termination claim implicated a clear public policy against deceptive accounting practices. Insightful raised the affirmative defense that Alaiyan was fired for poor performance and inability to work cooperatively. Alaiyan responded that this was pretense. Alaiyan admitted during deposition that he was not an expert in generally accepted accounting principles and did not know whether Insightful's accounting practices violated a specific statute or law, and further admitted that a company has a certain amount of discretion in the manner in which it recognizes revenue and expenses from quarter to quarter. However, Alaiyan asserted that he believed that Insightful's revenue and expense recognition practices were inappropriate and that it was his duty as director of professional services to report his concerns to Insightful's management.

Alaiyan moved for an order granting partial summary judgment that his wrongful termination claim implicated a clear public policy prohibiting deceptive accounting practices. Insightful also moved for summary judgment, asserting that Alaiyan had made an insufficient showing of a clear mandate of public policy applicable to the facts of this case. The court allowed Alaiyan leave to amend his complaint to further clarify the public policy that he alleged was violated by his termination. Alaiyan's amended complaint provided various bases for finding a mandate of public policy, including various Washington State and federal statutes.

Employees in Washington are generally at will and can be discharged without reason. However, a discharge of an at-will employee is wrongful if done in violation of a clearly articulated public policy. In order to establish a claim for wrongful discharge in violation of a public policy sufficient to avoid summary judgment, Alaiyan was required to establish each of three elements: (1) the existence of a clear public policy; (2) that discouraging the conduct in which he engaged complaining to his boss and management about the accounting practices relating to five specific accounts would jeopardize the public policy; and (3) that the public policy-linked conduct caused the dismissal. Insightful must not be able to show an 'overriding justification for the dismissal.' The public policy exception to the at-will doctrine has been recognized by Washington courts in four situations: (1) employee fired for refusing to commit illegal act; (2) employee fired for performing public duty or obligation such as jury duty; (3) employee fired for exercising a legal right or privilege; or (4) employee fired in retaliation for reporting employer misconduct.

Alaiyan claims that he was fired in retaliation for reporting internally that the company was improperly recognizing revenues and expenses relating to five specific accounts, and that his discharge violated the public policy articulated in various state and federal statutes against deceptive accounting practices. Insightful does not claim that Alaiyan did not complain about the accounting methods. Rather, Insightful reminds us that the public policy exception to the general terminable-at-will rule is cautiously applied by the courts and that the authorities Alaiyan cites provide insufficient support for the alleged public policy particularly as related to revenue recognition principles governing software companies. Alaiyan cites a number of Washington State and federal statutes, and one judicial decision, to illustrate what he perceives to be a clearly articulated public policy against deceptive accounting practices by publicly traded companies. Whether a particular statute contains a clear mandate of public policy is a question of law.

* * *

None of the authorities cited by Alaiyan provide a clear mandate of public policy of the type here at issue. None of the authorities address the specific accounting practices at issue here: decisions regarding the timing of recognition of revenue by a software company. None of them discuss complaints by employees regarding internal accounting practices. At the most, they articulate a general policy that accounting practices and financial reports of publicly trading companies should be truthful and not fraudulent and that purchasers of securities from these companies may have an action for fraudulent reporting. However, Alaiyan has not shown that this general policy translates into a clear mandate of a public policy protecting employees who claim that the accounting practices of their company are or might be improper.

Although we think Alaiyan was treated harshly and perhaps unfairly, at-will employment carries that risk. We cannot provide a remedy in the absence of a clear mandate of public policy that applies to the termination at issue. Accordingly, we affirm.

QUESTIONS

1. What motivated Alaiyan to report his concerns to the CEO? Does this matter?
2. Software contracts can present especially tricky revenue recognition questions because they often involve multiple elements, such as software use licenses, ongoing training and support obligations, and multi-year terms of use. GAAP requires the sale price to be allocated among each element according to the fair value of each good or service provided, but determining the correct split may require judgement. If

Insightful did recognize some revenues (but not expenses) prematurely, what would the financial impact be on net income for that initial year? What would the impact be during later years when the expenses (but not the revenues) were recognized?

3. Given your answers to question 2, why would Insightful ever bother to pursue the accounting gamesmanship alleged by Alaiyan?
4. Should the law protect at-will employees who challenge questionable accounting practices at public companies from termination?

In re IMAX Securities Litigation

587 F.Supp.2d 471 (S.D. N.Y. 2008)

■ BUCHWALD, J.

Plaintiffs brought this securities fraud class action under Sections 10(b) and 20(a) of the Securities Exchange Act, and Rule 10b–5 promulgated thereunder on behalf of all persons and entities who purchased or acquired common stock in IMAX Corporation between February 27, 2003 and July 20, 2007. This opinion addresses the IMAX defendants' motions to dismiss the complaint pursuant to Fed.R.Civ.P. 12(b)(6).

BACKGROUND

IMAX is an entertainment technology company specializing in the design and manufacture of large-format, two and three-dimensional theater systems. An IMAX theater system traditionally consists of: an advanced, high-resolution projection system, a digital sound system, a screen with proprietary coating technology, a digital theater control system, and extensive theater planning, design and installation services.

Although IMAX marketed several product and service lines during the class period, such as the production and distribution of films and film products and the operation and management of IMAX theaters, the majority of IMAX's revenue was derived from the sale and lease of theater systems to third-party owners of large-format theaters. Throughout the class period, IMAX reported relatively strong, upward-trending financial results: 16 theater system installations ("installs") and $71 million revenue for fiscal year 2002; 21 installs and $75.8 million revenue for 2003; 22 installs and $86.6 million revenue for 2004; and 39 installs and $97.7 million revenue for 2005. On March 9, 2006, IMAX filed its Form 10-K for the fiscal year ending December 31, 2005 ("2005 10-K"), which described a "record" 14 theater system installations and $35.1 million revenue in the fourth quarter. A press release issued on the same day revealed that IMAX's Board of Directors was exploring several avenues for maximizing shareholder value, including such strategic alternatives as a sale of the company or a merger with another entity.

On August 9, 2006, IMAX announced that it was in the process of responding to an informal inquiry from the SEC concerning the timing of revenue recognition, and specifically, its application of multiple element arrangement accounting to revenue derived from theater system sales and leases. Management also disclosed that discussions with potential buyers and strategic partners had faltered. By the time of the closing bell on the following day, the price of IMAX shares had fallen from $9.63 to $5.73.

Eleven months later, on July 20, 2007, IMAX filed its Form 10-K for the fiscal year ending December 31, 2006 ("2006 10-K"), which included a restatement of its financial results for fiscal years 2002 through the first three quarters of 2006. As disclosed in the 2006 Form 10-K:

> . . . the Company revised its policy to require that (i) the projector, sound system and screen system be installed and are in full working condition, the 3D glasses machine, if applicable, be delivered and projectionist training be completed, and (ii) written customer acceptance thereon received, or the public opening of the theater take place, before revenue can be recognized.

Acknowledging that "errors had occurred in its prior accounting for theatre systems," IMAX "revised its policy with regard to revenue recognition for theatre systems" and "restated its financial results in accordance with the revised policy." The restatement of IMAX's theater systems revenue had the effect of shifting revenue from the period in which it had been originally reported to subsequent periods. In total, 16 installation transactions representing $25.4 million in revenue shifted between quarters in their originally reported years, and 14 installation transactions representing $27.1 million in revenue shifted between fiscal years. The first of these consolidated actions followed shortly after IMAX released its restated financial results.

The complaint alleges that, "beginning in fiscal year 2002, and continuing throughout the Class Period, the Company improperly segregated the individual components of the [theater system] and recognized revenue on such individual components separately, thereby improperly accelerating its revenue recognition on the theater systems." The treatment of theater system revenue in this manner allegedly violated both Generally Accepted Accounting Principles ("GAAP") and IMAX's stated revenue recognition policy. We briefly review the accounting standards at play in this case . . . before turning to the merits of the defendants' motions.

The Relevant Accounting Principles

In December 1999, the SEC published Staff Accounting Bulletin No. 101 ("SAB 101"), which sets forth the general principle that revenue should not be recognized until it is "realized or realizable and earned," or, in other words, when: (i) persuasive evidence of an arrangement exists; (ii) delivery has occurred or services have been rendered; (iii) the seller's price to the buyer is fixed or determinable; and (iv) collectibility is reasonably assured. "Delivery," according to SAB 101, occurs when the seller has "substantially complete[d] or fulfill[ed] the terms specified in the arrangement."

Although SAB 101 provided specific criteria for when revenue may be recognized, it did not directly address the precedent question of what is the unit of accounting—a complicated issue in arrangements involving multiple elements. The extent of SAB 101's guidance in this regard is found in the interpretive response to one of the hypothetical questions meant to illustrate the application of revenue recognition principles:

> If an arrangement . . . requires the delivery or performance of multiple deliverables, or "elements," the delivery of an individual element is considered not to have occurred if there are undelivered elements that are essential to the functionality of the delivered element because the customer does not have the full use of the delivered element. Thus, the SEC's framework for revenue recognition required the deferral of theater system revenue until: (i) each element essential to the functionality of the theater system had been "delivered," and (ii) IMAX's obligations with respect to these elements were substantially complete. IMAX allegedly recognized revenue on individual components without awaiting delivery of certain elements that were, according to plaintiffs, "required before the system was substantially complete and functional."

In May 2003, the Emerging Issues Task Force ("EITF") of the Financial Accounting Standards Board ("FASB") attempted to resolve any uncertainty surrounding the applicable GAAP standards for determining when arrangements containing multiple revenue-generating elements must be treated as separate units of accounting. EITF 00–21, issued on that date, provided:

> In an arrangement with multiple deliverables, the delivered item(s) should be considered a separate unit of accounting if all of the following criteria are met:
>
> a. The delivered item(s) has value to the customer on a standalone basis. That item (s) has value on a standalone basis if it is sold separately by any vendor or the customer could resell the delivered item(s) on a standalone basis. In the context of a customer's ability to resell the delivered item(s), the Task Force observed that this criterion does not require the existence of an observable market for that deliverable (s).
>
> b. There is objective and reliable evidence of the fair value of the undelivered item(s).
>
> c. If the arrangement includes a general right of return relative to the delivered item, delivery or performance of the undelivered item(s) is considered probable and substantially in the control of the vendor.

Plaintiffs contend that these criteria never could have been satisfied as to IMAX's theater systems because (i) customers paid for the theater systems in installments, with the payment schedule calibrated to the progress of the delivery and installation of the entire system, and not its individual components; (ii) the theater components were either the property of IMAX or licensed by IMAX, and thus, buyers were unable to resell the components on the market; and (iii) the IMAX components were not independently saleable because they are only compatible with one another.

DISCUSSION

A. Scienter

The [law] requires plaintiffs asserting securities fraud claims to "state with particularity facts giving rise to a strong inference that the defendant acted with the required state of mind." The requisite intent may be established "either (a) by alleging facts to show that defendants had both motive and opportunity to commit fraud, or (b) by alleging facts that constitute strong circumstantial evidence of conscious misbehavior or recklessness."

[The Court first considered the plaintiff's "motive and opportunity" arguments and held that the allegations failed to plead a case at the required level of specificity.]

2. Conscious Disregard or Recklessness

A securities fraud claim predicated upon recklessness or conscious misbehavior must allege the defendants' knowledge of facts contradicting their public statements, their failure to review information that they were obligated to monitor, or their ignorance of clear and obvious signs of fraud. In each case, the burden remains on the plaintiff to set forth the specific reports, information or other indicia of fraud that rendered the defendants' conduct "highly unreasonable, representing an extreme departure from the standards of ordinary care."

Although the question is a close one, we believe that, with respect to the IMAX defendants, the complaint fairly pleads an inference of scienter based on recklessness or conscious disregard that is at least as compelling as the most compelling opposing inference—namely that IMAX violated its own accounting policy by mistake and the application of multiple element accounting to theater system revenue was a considered judgment, reflecting the advice of [its auditor] after open consultations.

The IMAX defendants undoubtedly appreciated that theater system revenue was of singular importance to the financial well-being and market perception of the Company. Theater system revenue was the single largest component of total revenue recognized during fiscal years 2002 through 2005, and, thus, represented one of the "most important metrics" of IMAX's growth. IMAX reported the number of installs and executed installation contracts ("backlogs") on a quarterly and annual basis, and repeatedly highlighted the number of installs and backlogs as a barometer of its financial health.

Plaintiffs also have alleged that IMAX executives had specific knowledge of the progress of each theater system installation. IMAX apparently had employees at each installation site who would report back to senior executives on its status. Reports containing schedules for theater installations were sent by the Finance Department to the attendees of a weekly meeting held at IMAX's Canadian headquarters, the purpose of which was to discuss theater openings and address the timeliness of the projects. The complaint further alleges that monthly sales reports detailing the number of theater systems installations were circulated via e-mail.

The complaint suggests that the IMAX defendants had a sophisticated understanding of the relevant accounting principles, yet employed aggressive (and on at least one occasion, questionable) tactics to meet their revenue targets. According to the complaint, IMAX executives appreciated the distinction between "physical installs" and "revenue recognition installs," the former being installations in the lay sense and the latter being the "installation" of a theater system element that would permit the revenue associated with the element to be recognized. As discussed supra, IMAX's disclosed policy toward the accounting treatment of theater system revenue became increasingly aggressive during the six years preceding the restatement. Moreover, the complaint alleges that, in the second quarter of 2006, an IMAX executive asked a theater owner to accept a projector, reel unit and sound system, notwithstanding the fact that construction issues were going to delay the theater's completion, "because IMAX had planned on recognizing revenue in the second quarter and still wished to do so." In the fourth quarter of 2005, according to the complaint, IMAX allegedly installed equipment in a theater without a roof but later removed the equipment so that it could be stored in a warehouse pending completion of the theater, but IMAX recorded revenue on the installation nonetheless.

Moreover, the allegation that IMAX was recognizing revenue on theater system elements in 2002 and 2004, when its stated policy was to await the installation of the entire theater system, is troublesome. Although the defendants maintain that IMAX's stated policy was simply to apply GAAP, and thus, an alleged violation of corporate accounting policy adds nothing to the analysis, the 2002 10-K and 2004 10-K expressly provide that revenue would be recognized "upon installation of the theater system." Regardless of whether certain "theater system" elements were perfunctory or whether the application of multiple element accounting to theater system revenue was proper under GAAP, IMAX's 10-Ks could be read to create an obligation to abide by a more conservative accounting policy.

If this were merely a GAAP violation case, we might have been persuaded that the complaint fails to allege scienter with respect to the

IMAX defendants because the applicable accounting rules appear to be highly complex and to involve subjective judgments and because of the complaint's allegations about the participation of [its auditors], which could provide a basis for a reliance argument by IMAX. Indeed, the violations alleged here are far more technical than those in other cases where the defendants faced civil liability for the premature recognition of revenue in contravention of GAAP. However, plaintiffs also have pleaded (i) the crucial contribution of theater system revenue to IMAX as a going concern; (ii) the IMAX defendants' understanding of the relevant accounting rules, their application to the facts before us, and the ramifications of selecting certain interpretations of the rules over others; (iii) the existence of extensive documentation indicating the progress of theater system installations and the IMAX defendants' knowledge of, or access to, those documents; (iv) the increasingly aggressive accounting of theater system revenue; (v) the failure of the IMAX defendants to conform the financial results to IMAX's own publicly disclosed accounting policy; and (vi) at least one alleged transaction that . . . appears to subvert the purpose of the applicable accounting rules. We therefore find that plaintiffs have adequately pleaded scienter with respect to the IMAX defendants.

B. Loss Causation

Under the [law] plaintiffs have "the burden of proving" that the defendant's misrepresentations "caused the loss" for which they seek recovery. The so-called "loss causation" element of a securities fraud claim is sufficiently pleaded when the complaint provides "notice of what the relevant economic loss might be" and "what the causal connection might be between that loss" and the alleged misrepresentations. The essence of loss causation is the notion that the alleged "misstatement or omission concealed something from the market that, when disclosed, negatively affected the value of the security." Accordingly, the complaint must allege that the "market reacted negatively to a corrective begin[ning] to leak out." The SEC inquiry related directly to the misrepresentations alleged in this case—the application of multiple element accounting to theater system revenue—and culminated in the restatement of IMAX's earnings and revenues for fiscal years 2002 through 2005. After the announcement, IMAX shares traded at a discount to their price on the previous day, reflecting, in part, the probability and magnitude of a restatement of previously reported revenue. Although "the truth here was revealed not in a neat and tidy single disclosure," it is sufficient that the SEC's informal inquiry and subsequent discussions with IMAX concerned the subject matter of the alleged fraud and eventually led to a restatement. And, of course, IMAX's denial of accounting irregularities was irrelevant once the SEC inquiry had alerted the market to their possibility.

As to the defendants' suggestion that the stock drop was precipitated by the contemporaneous announcement of the Board's inability to attract a suitable merger or acquisition proposal, and not the informal inquiry by the SEC, we find—regardless of the plausibility of the argument—that the issue is inappropriate for resolution at this time. To survive a motion to dismiss, a plaintiff need only provide "some indication of the loss and the causal connection [he or she] has in mind." Accordingly, the defendants will be entitled to interpose their defense of intervening facts, such as the fact of the failed merger and acquisition discussions, at trial.

CONCLUSION

For the reasons stated above, the motions to dismiss are DENIED.

QUESTIONS

1. What is a "unit of accounting" for an IMAX theater sale?
2. Did the firm or its managers have any plausible incentives to recognize revenue on an accelerated basis?
3. How were the plaintiffs harmed in this case? Was an accounting problem at IMAX the real cause of this harm? How would this question be litigated at trial?

C. THE STATEMENT OF CASH FLOWS

Accrual accounting recognizes income when earned, regardless of when it is received. It also recognizes expenses when incurred, regardless of when paid. As a result, the income statement cannot accurately reflect the cash available to a business to pay its bills and to declare dividends to shareholders. In the past, this distinction between available cash and stated earnings has sometimes become painfully apparent. When a business has substantial short-term debt, for example, and its interest expense increases dramatically during a period of rising interest rates, it might have trouble meeting obligations even with a substantial (but illiquid) reported net worth. Accordingly, GAAP requires companies to provide a statement of cash flows in published financial statements. This statement is designed to show how much more (or less) cash a business has at the end of the year than it had at the beginning. In that sense, it is the accountants' response to "show me the money."

The statement of cash flows is divided into three parts. The first section shows the cash provided by operating activities. It begins with the net income from the income statement and adds back any non-cash expenses, such as depreciation and amortization.* Additionally, it adjusts for changes in current assets that either increase or decrease cash. For example, a decrease in accounts receivable from the beginning of the year

* Depreciation expense is a non-cash expense because it allocates the cost of a large upfront purchase, like an office building or factory, to multiple periods that approximate the useful life of the asset. The entire purchase price is typically paid at the outset, however, and depreciation expense just divides some of the total cost to each period. But no cash is actually paid in subsequent periods, which is why this expense should be added back to net income in the statement of cash flows. Amortization expense, which is used for intangible assets, presents identical treatment issues.

means that more receivables have been converted into cash. The same holds true for inventories. On the liabilities side, an increase in accounts payable frees up more cash. For example, a higher accounts payable balance means the company is holding its cash rather than paying its expenses (which are reflected in net income), so this is added to operating cash flows.*

The second section deals with cash provided by investing activities. The company may, for example, sell a subsidiary or a plant, thus raising cash. Or it might invest in long-term assets, which decreases cash. In both situations these changes are measured from beginning to end of the year.

The final section focuses on financing activities during the relevant accounting period, which may be either a source or use of cash. If the company sells stock or bonds during the year, the net increase in these accounts will contribute to cash. On the other hand, the repayment of bonds as they come due, the payment of cash dividends to stockholders, and the repurchase of stock all represent drains on cash.

Let's look at the 2023 statement of cash flows for Lululemon. Recall that the firm's balance sheet in Figure 2-1 shows that the company held $1,155 million in cash at the end of fiscal 2023. If we examined the balance sheet for 2022, we would see a cash balance of $1,260 million. In other words, Lululemon spent down $105 million in cash over the year. But net income during this fiscal year was $855 million. Why is this number different than the change in cash? What happened? These questions can be answered by the Statement of Cash Flows.

Figure 2-3. Statement of Cash Flows
Lululemon Athletica Inc.
($ Millions)

	Year Ending		
	2023	2022	2021
Cash Flows From Operating Activities			
Net Income	855	975	589
Adjustments to reconcile net income to net cash provided by operating activities:			

* The directional impact of these balance sheet changes is not always obvious to students. An increase in an asset account over the period will, holding everything else equal, effectively lead to a decrease in cash from operations. For example, if a firm's inventory account rises over time, then the firm effectively spent more cash during the period to buy inventory. Conversely, an increase in a liability account will typically lead to an increase in cash from operations. If a firm's accounts payable balance increases over the period, for example, then it is effectively leaning more heavily on "trade credit" and/or paying its bills more slowly. All else being equal, this will increase the firm's cash.

Depreciation and Amortization	292	224	185
Other Adjustments	417	60	76
Changes in Operating Assets and Liabilities			
Inventory	(511)	(324)	(97)
Other Operating Activities	(217)	(80)	(174)
Liabilities	131	533	223
Net Cash Provided by Operating Activities	966	1,389	803
Cash Flows From Investing Activities			
Purchase of Property and Equipment	(639)	(395)	(229)
Other Investing Activities	69	(33)	(466)
Net Cash Used in Investing Activities	(570)	(428)	(696)
Cash Flows From Financing Activities			
Repurchase of Common Stock	(444)	(813)	(64)
Net Borrowing	–	–	–
Other Financing Activities	(23)	(32)	(17)
Net Cash Used in Financing Activities	(467)	(845)	(81)
Effect of Exchange Rate Changes on Cash	(34)	(7)	30
Increase (Decrease) in Cash	(105)	109	57
Cash: Beginning of Period	1,260	1,151	1,094
Cash: End of Period	1,155	1,260	1,151

As promised, we see from this statement that the cash changes are divided into the three main sections (plus a final line item to adjust for exchange rate effects from foreign operations). Looking at the 2023 column, we start with a net income of $855. This links directly to the bottom line of the income statement in Figure 2-2. We then move into each of the three main activities—operating activities, investing activities, and financing activities and look at the effects to cash over the year.

Operating Activities. The first adjustment involves adding back non-cash expenses. As mentioned earlier, we add back depreciation and amortization because no cash is really paid out for these items—that was done when Lululemon bought the relevant assets. After that, we need to adjust for changes in various asset accounts that were impacted by operating activities. For example, inventory balances have been increasing in recent years, and this requires additional operating cash to support (thus the negative numbers over the past three years). There are a few other adjustments from the balance sheet account changes, but the figure does not provide a more detailed explanation. The subtotal for this section shows that the company generated almost $1 billion in operating cash for 2023, which is impressive (though also down from the prior year).

Investing Activities. The purchase of investments consumes cash, and these cash outflows don't typically show up on the income statement because they are capitalized as assets (rather than treated as current period expenses). Buying new manufacturing equipment, for instance, might be necessary to replace obsolete or worn-out machines, as well as to support growth in sales or the production of new products. We see that Lululemon has consistently spent significant amounts on these types of investments, which are generally referred to as capital expenditures. Recall that the expenditures will eventually impact the income statement through depreciation charges, but the actual cash is spent upfront. This is why the investing section shows a negative number for the cash used for capital expenditures. In addition to providing information on a company's use of cash, capital expenditures also provide investors with a way to estimate how much cash a company needs to maintain and replace its capital equipment. As such, we shall see that this information also plays an important role in estimating a company's *future* free cash flows. This concept will become especially relevant when we discuss discounted cash flow analysis in Chapter 3.

In addition to capital expenditures, this section of the cash flow statement will also include information on cash expended or received from the sale or purchase of other assets, such as marketable securities. In the case of Lululemon, Other Investing Activities for 2023 included the proceeds received from the sale of an administrative office, which effectively converted a non-cash asset into cash.

Financing Activities. Lululemon's financing activity during the year was straightforward. It did not raise cash by issuing new stock or bonds; if it did, we would see an inflow of cash from these transactions in this subsection. Similarly, it does not appear to have paid cash dividends to shareholders. Rather, the only significant transaction involves the repurchase of common stock: the firm spent $444 million buying back its own stock during 2023. (We will explore why a company might wish to do this later in the book.)

Taken together, these three sections of the Cash Flow Statement explain how and why the company decreased its cash holding by $105 million during 2023. In sum, the firm generated $966 million in cash from operations, spent roughly $570 million in cash on new investments, spent $467 million on stock buybacks (and other minor financing items), and lost the balance through some unspecified foreign exchange rate effects.

Your understanding of cash flows at this point should make it clear that net income isn't the last word on how well a company is doing. In many ways, Lululemon's Statement of Cash Flows provides more enlightening information. We know from that statement that the company decreased its cash and equivalents by $105 million. But this doesn't exactly tell us how the company performed, because cash was also used by the purchase of new investments and the repurchase of stock. Net cash provided by operating activities was actually higher than net income, and this is another number that analysts would look to as a key indicator of how the firm performed during the year.

Sidebar: The Cash Flow Cycle

As our earlier discussion of the business system suggests, companies at different stages in their lives often face very different cash flow situations. For example, a company that has recently gone public might raise more cash than it intends to use immediately and invest the surplus cash in short term securities. Lululemon is perhaps a good example of this: it went public in 2007 and still retains a relatively large amount of cash and equivalents on its balance sheet.

A typical manufacturing company might gradually spend its cash to buy equipment and raw materials and hire more employees to expand production. At this point it becomes far less liquid, with much of its capital tied up in illiquid investments. The ultimate value of these investment decisions will then depend upon the market's acceptance of the firm's products. If the products sell well, the company may convert much of its inventory and payroll expense into accounts receivable. While the company will hope these more liquid assets are valuable, uncertainty may continue (especially if customer credit risk is a major concern).

The cycle may then repeat if business is good. New products, or general growth of the company, may require expansion, and all available cash may thus be reinvested—along with newly borrowed cash or the proceeds from additional stock sales.

D. THE STATEMENT OF CHANGES IN STOCKHOLDERS' EQUITY

We've now discussed three key financial statements for Lululemon: the balance sheet, the income statement, and the statement of cash flows. Many analysts would consider these to be the most important reports. But one question remains: how have the stockholders fared? At this stage, we know from the income statement that the firm generated positive overall profits. And we can determine that it paid out none of these profits as shareholder dividends by looking at the financing section of the statement of cash flows. If we compare the 2023 balance sheet in Figure 2-1 to the 2022 balance sheet for the firm (not presented in the figure), we would see that total stockholders' equity increased over the year by $409 million (from $2,740 million in 2022 to $3,149 million in 2023). In the absence of dividend payments, is this the right measure of overall stockholders' gains? Not necessarily. Recall that the company also bought stock back during the year. In other cases, a firm might issue new stock during the period, which would also increase the total equity account. So we can't just look at the net change in equity as the final word on stockholder gains for the year. This question about how stockholders fared is best answered by looking at the fourth accounting statement: the statement of changes in stockholders' equity.

If we imagine a business where all of the capital was invested at incorporation, and remained invested for years, the statement of changes in stockholders' equity would be a relatively simple document. It would simply record each year's profits, minus any losses that might occur, less dividends paid. Often, however, some additional transactions are reflected in this report, which are illustrated below. You should also recognize that equity is a cumulative account, so the starting point for this statement is the ending equity balance from last year. Let's examine Lululemon's 2023 statement (in reduced format):

Figure 2-4. Statement of Stockholder's Equity
Lululemon Athletica Inc.
($ Millions)

	Contributed Capital	Retained Earnings	Other Stockholder's Equity	Total
Balance, Jan. 30, 2022	423	2,513	(196)	2,740
Stock Issuance	–	–	–	–
Net Income		855		855
Dividends	–	–	–	–
Repurchase of Stock	(2)	(442)	–	(444)
Other Changes	54	–	(57)	(2)
Balance, Jan. 28, 2018	475	2,926	(253)	3,149

During the year, we can see that Lululemon's equity balance increased from $2,740 million over the 2023 fiscal year due to net income gains (+$855 million), stock repurchases (–$444 million), and a few other changes (-2 million).* The statement classifies these changes into three categories: (1) *contributed capital*, representing amounts initially invested; (2) *retained earnings*, representing profits that are plowed back

* For the curious, these other changes related primarily to net effects from equity and stock-based employee compensation.

into the firm; and (3) *other stockholder's equity* effects. Each relevant transaction occurring during the period is classified into the appropriate equity column. If, for example, Lululemon had issued more stock during the period, then the increase to equity would be listed in the contributed capital column. If the firm had issued dividends, then this would be subtracted from retained earnings. We see that the firm's repurchase of stock impacted both the contributed capital and the retained earnings columns. Can you figure out why?*

Just as the statement of cash flows shows why a firm's cash balance increased or decreased over the year, the statement of changes in stockholders' equity explains the reasons for changes to equity. Much of the information in this report could be gathered from the other financial statements, but this is a helpful place to look when you are trying to determine exactly what happened to equity over the period.

3. ANALYSIS OF FINANCIAL STATEMENTS

At this point, having reviewed Lululemon's financial statements, do you think 2023 was a good year for the company? It's probably tempting to answer yes. After all, the firm generated more than $850 million in net income, and it took in over $950 million in cash from operations. Moreover, Lululemon's assets vastly exceed its liabilities. With this much equity, it should be able to withstand some hard times and be able to borrow more funds if necessary. So, things seem pretty good for the apparel firm.

But this only scratches the surface; financial statements can tell you a lot more than this. The purpose of this section is to give you an introduction to some of the tools that investors, creditors, and other analysts might use to evaluate a company's performance. We will look at common-size comparative analysis, return on investment, protection for creditors, and the role of GAAP vs. Non-GAAP financial measures in evaluating financial statements.

A. COMMON-SIZE COMPARATIVE ANALYSIS

One frequent technique for evaluating a company's performance is to restate key metrics on a percentage basis. By "common-sizing" the financial results in this manner, it becomes much easier to quickly see how these key ratios have changed over time for the same firm—and also to see how they compare with competing firms of different sizes during

---

* The answer is that Lululemon had to buy back the stock on the market for more than the initial purchase price paid by investors. More specifically, $2 million of the $444 million purchase price went to offset the initial investment account, and the balance of the buyback purchase price came from retained earnings. (Clearly the stock price has gone up a lot since Lululemon's initial public offering!) If, counterfactually, the firm paid exactly the same price to buy back the stock that it initially received from investors, then all of the $444 million purchase price would be subtracted from the contributed capital column.

the same economic period. Let's consider two common-size metrics: gross profit percentage and net income percentage.

Gross Profit Percentage. This metric comes from the income statement and offers a measure of the business's profitability from selling its products, separate from operating expenses (selling, general and administrative). It is expressed as a percentage for comparative purposes, on the theory that a company with a high gross profit percentage may enjoy some competitive advantage over the competition:

$$\frac{\text{Gross Profit (Margin)}}{\text{Revenue}}$$

Said differently, we can take the gross profit number as a percentage of overall sales as an indicator of how expensive it is for the firm to make or source its products or services. For Lululemon's 2023 results, this ratio can be calculated using data from Figure 2-2 as follows:

Gross Profit:	$ 4,492
Net Revenue:	$ 8,111

Gross Profit %: $\frac{4{,}492}{8{,}111}$ = 55.4%

Is this good? It tells us that Lululemon can make or buy its clothing (and other offerings) for a little less than half of the total sales price. But to put this in context, we might want to compare the ratio with earlier years of performance for the same company and with contemporaneous results from other apparel retailers.

Start with same-firm performance. Using Figure 2-2, can you calculate the gross profit percentages for 2022 and 2021? What do these results tell us about Lululemon's performance in 2023? You should arrive at gross profit percentages of 57.7% for 2022 and 56.0% for 2021.* All else being equal, this suggests that 2023 was a down year for the company. We don't know exactly why the drop took place, but some likely explanations include pricing pressures, more expensive sourcing and supply chain costs, or a shift in the mix of products that it sold to lower margin (less profitable) lines of clothing. Managers will usually pay close attention to this ratio, as even a few percentage points can impact the stock price.

We would also want to conduct a similar analysis for competing firms. This is important because the 2023 fiscal year might have presented a significantly different business environment than earlier years. If so, results that look good from an internal historical perspective

---

* 2022: 3609/6257 = 57.7%. 2021: 2464/4402 = 56.0%.

may still disappoint investors when viewed next to the competition. Here are some comparable ratios for two competitors: Nike earned a gross profit of 43.5% and Under Armour earned a gross profit of 44.9%.* The companies may not have identical business models, but the higher gross margin percentage for Lululemon offers additional evidence that the firm had a good year.

Gross profit percentage might be helpful, but it is rarely the final word on a company's performance. Indeed, firms with different business models will often have very different gross margin percentages. For instance, compare a grocery store with a luxury car dealership. The grocery store likely has a relatively low gross margin on its products, but it sells a lot of items each day. The car dealer, by contrast, may have a much higher gross margin percentage but only sells a few cars each week. Either model might be viable, because both margin percentage and turnover volume can drive economic gains.

Profit Margin. This is sometimes called return on sales, and measures how much of each sales dollar winds up as net income. This differs from the gross profit percentage by now including other sales and overhead costs and is considered a primary measure of any company's operating performance. It is represented by:

$$\frac{\text{Net Income}}{\text{Sales (Net Revenue)}}$$

For Lululemon's 2023 results, this can be calculated from Figure 2-2 as follows:

Net Income:	$ 855	= 10.5%
Sales:	$ 8,111	

This result tells us that the company retained just over 10 percent of its sales as bottom line profits during the year. As with the gross profit percentage, we need some context to judge this number. Listed below are some comparable profit margins. After considering these additional results, do you feel more or less confident about the hypothesis that 2023 was a successful year for Lululemon?

Net Income Comparable Analysis	
Lululemon (2023):	10.5%
Lululemon (2022):	15.6%
Lululemon (2021):	13.4%

* It is important to emphasize that the numbers are not perfectly comparable because the firms have different fiscal years, meaning that the performance only includes some overlapping months. Specifically, Lululemon's fiscal year ended in January 2023, while Nike's ended in May 2023 and Under Armour's ended in March 2023.

Nike (2023):	9.9%
Under Armour (2023)*:	6.5%

B. RETURN ON INVESTMENT

Common-size results are useful, but there is a limit to how much we can learn from this type of analysis because they typically focus on relationships within one financial statement. But we might learn more from calculations that draw upon multiple statements. For instance, return on investment measures will typically divide some measure of periodic performance (usually from the income statement) by some average amount of investment for the same period (from the balance sheet).

The need to go beyond bottom line income statement results when evaluating firm performance is an important business concept to understand. Think about it this way: imagine that you have two companies that earned *exactly* the same net income last year. The first company, a mining company, required extensive investment in land, heavy machinery, and other assets to generate the profit. The second company, Uber, had almost no capital requirements; it just used a software matching program to link drivers and customers. Which firm would you rather own? Most people would prefer the asset-light Uber because very little investment money is needed to generate the profits. But an analyst who only looked at the bottom line of the income statement might erroneously judge the performance of these two firms as identical. In other words, capital investors, whether debt or equity, seek a return, and the less investment required to generate a given level of profits, the better (for residual equity holders). Let's examine two different metrics for evaluating return on investment.

Earnings Per Share ("EPS"). This represents the most common statement of how well shareholders are doing. It shows how much of a company's earnings are available to common stockholders, after paying interest on debt, taxes, and any dividends on preferred stock.

$$\frac{\text{Net Income After Preferred Dividends}}{\text{Weighted Average Outstanding Shares During the Period}}$$

Recall that Lululemon has not issued preferred stock, so to calculate its EPS for 2023, we would just need information about the average number of shares outstanding during this period.† "Weighted average," in this context, means using the average of the number of outstanding

* As stated earlier, the fiscal years do not line up directly for Nike and Under Armour; the numbers presented are the most directly comparable to Lululemon's 2023 fiscal year.

† Firms are also required by GAAP to report EPS on a "diluted" basis, which includes shares to be issued upon exercise of outstanding options and conversion rights. The concept of dilution (and the determination of a company's fully-diluted capitalization) will be discussed in Chapter 5.

shares at the beginning and end of the accounting period. During 2023, Lululemon had roughly 127.7 million shares outstanding on average. (This number should appear in the section of a company's balance sheet that summarizes stockholders' equity). The EPS calculation thus runs as follows:

Net Income ($ millions):	$855	= $6.70
Average outstanding shares (in millions):	127.7	

EPS is a salient number for investors, and a firm's share price might plummet when reported results fail to match investor expectations for a given period.

Return on Equity ("ROE"). This is another primary summary of company performance that focuses on the calculation of profits as a percentage of total stockholders' equity. It is computed as follows:

$$\frac{\text{Net Income}}{\text{Average Stockholders' Equity}}$$

The average stockholders' equity is determined by adding the beginning and ending equity balances and dividing the result by two. You can think of ROE as an overall measure of performance for the firm. Look to a firm's statement of stockholder's equity to find the average equity. Let's calculate this metric for Lululemon's 2023 fiscal year:

Average stockholders' equity is the average of ending equity for 2022 and 2023 (see Figure 2-4).

2022:	$2,740	
2023:	$3,149	
Total:	$5,889/2	= $2,945

2023 Net Income:	$ 855	= 29.0%
Average Equity:	$ 2,945	

Is an ROE of 29.0% good? We would again want context for this number and might compare it to previous years and to the performance of competitors. More generally, the topic of how much return equity holders should demand for their investment is critical for corporate finance. As we will see in later chapters, the answer is thought to depend on the level of risk—both operational risk and financial risk—that is associated with the company. A company can often use greater debt financing, or leverage, to increase overall risk and boost ROE, but this comes with additional financial risk for the equity investor. This means that an ROE of 29% might be phenomenal for a low-risk firm, but it might be horrible for a very high-risk venture. So please stay tuned. . .

C. PROTECTION FOR CREDITORS

An additional set of analytical tools relates to debt investors' common concerns about a company and its performance. Does the firm have too much debt, such that a threat of bankruptcy looms? Does recent performance suggest that the firm might have trouble making its interest payments on time? These are critical questions for creditors, and they will scrutinize the financial statements to evaluate a firm's solvency and liquidity. These ratios are especially important for corporate finance lawyers who work with debt financing transactions because many note or bond contracts explicitly use ongoing ratio requirements to impose limits on the amount of new debt that a borrower can assume, or to set other warning signs that a borrower might be on thin ice. In some cases, the inability of a corporate borrower to maintain a specific financial ratio can constitute an *event of default* (more on this term and its implications in Chapter 6). For this reason, contractual commitments like this are frequently referred to as "maintenance covenants" and will often be based on some of the ratios discussed in this section.

Debt to Total Assets Ratio ("Debt Ratio"). This describes the percentage of total assets supplied by creditors and offers an overall measure of the firm's capital structure. The higher this ratio, the greater the burden of interest and debt repayments. This, in turn, can lead to two difficulties for a firm: a higher variance in returns to shareholders, and a greater probability of default and bankruptcy. A caution: like most ratios, it uses book values of assets, rather than fair market value. While this means the ratio isn't a perfect measure, it may not be as bad as it first appears, because it can be difficult to realize full market value in a distress sale. (Recall that you can look back to the balance sheet to find a firm's total liabilities and total assets.)

$$\frac{\text{Total Liabilities}}{\text{Total Assets}}$$

For Lululemon in 2023, this is calculated as follows:

$$\begin{array}{lcl} \text{Total Liabilities:} & \$2{,}458 & = \quad 43.8\% \\ \hline \text{Total Assets:} & \$5{,}607 & \end{array}$$

In other words, about 44% of the firm's assets are funded by debt-related capital, and the other 56% are funded by equity.

Debt to Equity Ratio ("DER"). This is simply another way of presenting the information revealed by the previous ratio. Instead of dividing liabilities by total assets, analysts will divide the liabilities by total equity. Some people prefer the prior measure as more intuitive, because it shows debt as a portion of total financing, but the DER is also commonly used to describe the leverage of a firm.

$$\frac{\text{Total Liabilities}}{\text{Total Equity}}$$

For Lululemon in 2023, DER is calculated as follows:

$$\begin{array}{ll} \text{Total Liabilities:} & \dfrac{\$2{,}458}{\$3{,}149} = 0.78 \\ \text{Total Equity:} & \end{array}$$

If a company raises more than half of its capital though debt financing, this number becomes larger than one. A firm with a DER of 9.0, for example, would have $9 in debt for every dollar of equity (and would be considered a far riskier venture for equity investors and potential debt investors).

Current Ratio. Current assets are defined as those assets that can reasonably be expected to be converted into cash within the current accounting cycle: cash and equivalents (liquid short-term securities), accounts receivable, inventory, and other assets that are expected to be used within the year. Correspondingly, current liabilities are defined as those liabilities due and payable within the same cycle. The current ratio defines the relationship between current obligations and the assets available to meet them. It can be considered a rough indication of a firm's ability to service its looming obligations. Generally, the higher the current ratio, the greater the "cushion" between current obligations and a firm's ability to pay them.

$$\frac{\text{Total Current Assets}}{\text{Total Current Liabilities}}$$

For Lululemon in 2023, this is calculated as follows:

$$\begin{array}{ll} \text{Current Assets:} & \dfrac{\$3{,}149}{\$1{,}492} = 2.1 \\ \text{Current Liabilities:} & \end{array}$$

This result tells us that Lululemon has far more assets that it expects to convert to cash in the next year than liabilities payable during this time period. This fact should help convince investors that the firm is unlikely to run into a solvency or liquidity problem in the near future. If, counterfactually, the current asset and current liability numbers were reversed for the firm, then the current ratio would be 0.47 (1,492/3,149 = 0.47). This would send frantic alarm signals through any company, as managers and investors would face a real possibility that the company could not pay near term debts unless it received an emergency injection of new capital.

Times-Interest Earned (Interest Coverage) Ratio. This final measure of creditor risk looks more closely at the extent to which interest obligations can be covered from earnings before interest and taxes (EBIT). This ratio is frequently employed to protect creditors in loan agreements and bond contracts; when a debtor falls below a required coverage ratio, a default may be triggered unless the debtor can cure it within a brief time.* A high ratio may indicate that a borrower would have little difficulty meeting the interest obligations of a loan.

$$\frac{\text{Earnings Before Interest \& Taxes (EBIT)}}{\text{Annual Interest Expense}}$$

We can see from Lululemon's income statement in Figure 2-2 that the company has no interest expense in 2023. From this, we can infer that the firm has no formal loans, and that the liabilities are comprised of trade credit (accounts payable) and other types of obligations. Accordingly, an interest coverage calculation is not relevant for this company in 2023. For illustration purposes, however, imagine that Lululemon did have $2,500 million in bonds outstanding during the year at an interest rate of 5%. If so, we would calculate the interest coverage ratio as follows:

EBIT (from the income statement):	$1,333	= 10.7
Annual Interest Expense†:	$125	

An interest coverage ratio this high would probably raise no concerns. But lower interest coverage ratios might begin to worry creditors or even trigger contractual default clauses.

D. GAAP VS. NON-GAAP FINANCIAL MEASURES

As the last section should make clear, financial statement analysis commonly involves the mixing and matching of different items from a company's financial statements. The rationale for doing so is straightforward: the off-the-rack metrics required by GAAP to be disclosed in a company's financial statements simply don't convey the full story about either a company's operating performance or the particular aspect of a company that might be of interest to an investor. When these alternative financial metrics seek to adjust formal GAAP metrics (e.g., net income) by excluding or including other GAAP metrics (e.g., interest or taxes)

* In some cases, this ratio is calculated on the basis of EBIT plus depreciation.

† The annual interest expense is calculated by multiplying the $2,500 million in bonds times the interest rate of 5% = $125 million.

they are often referred to as non-GAAP financial measures.* For instance, as noted above, a company will often disclose a company's EBIT, which calculates a company's operating profit without regard to the payment of interest or taxes. While this information may be of interest to investors, it is not a financial measure required to be included in a company's income statement, making it technically a non-GAAP financial measure. We summarize here two other non-GAAP financial measures that are commonly used to evaluate a company's operating performance and that we will use extensively in Chapter 3 when we discuss firm valuation.

EBITDA. By excluding the effect of interest and taxes on a company's bottom line, EBIT effectively shows a company's operating profit and the net income that is available to pay the primary claimants on a company's profits, who generally consist of investors and the government. However, because EBIT still reflects the consequence of non-cash expenses such as depreciation and amortization, it does not necessarily reflect the amount of *actual income* (i.e., revenues less actual expenses incurred during the year) that is available to pay these claimants. For instance, we saw previously that Lululemon incurred a depreciation and amortization expense of $292 million in 2023, meaning that Lululemon's EBIT of $1,333 million reflects the effect of a large expense that was not actually incurred during the year. To estimate the amount of income produced by the company's operations that excludes this "non-cash" charge, we would turn to EBITDA, or Earnings Before Interest, Taxes, Depreciation and Amortization. To calculate EBITDA for Lululemon, we simply add the company's $292 million depreciation and amortization expense to its EBIT of $1,333 million to arrive at EBITDA of $1,625 million.

Free Cash Flow. The intuition behind EBITDA is a desire to understand the total amount of profits generated by a company's operations in light of the fact that many expenses used in calculating net income reflect an accounting concept that spreads *past* capital expenditures over *future* accounting periods. For instance, if a company paid $100 million for a factory in the past, it might have to spread part of that cost into the future through depreciation charges, but its future revenue will never actually have to be used to pay for the factory since that money has already been spent. An investor trying to understand how much "true profit" is available for distribution to all investors and the government might accordingly be drawn to EBITDA as a more useful metric than EBIT. However, most investors also understand that while depreciation reflects past expenditures, those investments nevertheless have to be maintained and replaced. Prudence therefore suggests that some amount of EBITDA must be set aside for capital expenditures and be viewed as unavailable for distribution to the company's claimants. In

* When used by a company in an SEC filing, non-GAAP measures implicate special scrutiny by the Securities and Exchange Commission under Regulation G of the Exchange Act.

practice, investors will typically estimate this amount to be set aside for reinvestment needs based on the capital expenditures as reported in the company's Statement of Cash Flows. For Lululemon, the resulting figure, typically referred to as "free cash flow," would be calculated as follows:

2023 EBITDA:	$1,625
Reported 2023 Capital Expenditures:	−$570
2023 Free Cash Flow:	$1,055

Interestingly, Lululemon's free cash flow is less than EBIT. This result is due to the fact that the company's 2023 capital expenditures exceeded its depreciation and amortization expense, reflecting a company that is growing its capital investments as it grows in size.

This section has only offered an introductory list of analytical tools; professional analysts will conduct a much more thorough review of a firm's financial statements. It is also worth emphasizing that any analytical exercise is limited by the quality of the information that the firm reports. Assets may be stated at book value instead of market value. Different firms may make different assumptions about customer default rates or the useful life of similar equipment. Or they may simply choose different approaches to a similar accounting issue—such as accounting for inventory and the cost of goods sold. In short, it is important to understand the limits, as well as the power, of these analytical techniques.

That being said, after working through this chapter, you should already have a much better sense of how to understand and evaluate a firm's performance. We will continue to build upon these tools and techniques as we get into more specific financing situations.

4. REGULATION AND OVERSIGHT OF ACCOUNTING AND AUDITING

As we have emphasized throughout this chapter, accounting is not a strict set of rules. It is a collection of standards that are described as generally acceptable accounting principles (GAAP). This approach provides flexibility to companies, so they have some discretion to select accounting methods that they feel will best reflect the firm's financial performance in an accurate and cost-effective manner.* But there must clearly be some limits on accounting methods to mitigate the risk of fraud and manipulation. Who sets these limits, and how is compliance with

* In Statement of Financial Accounting Standards No. 2, the Financial Accounting Standards Board ("FASB") stated that "the better choice is one that, subject to considerations of cost, produces from among the available alternatives information that is most useful for decision making." Where this kind of variance is allowed, it becomes critical for the financial reports to reveal the choices made.

GAAP enforced? This final section describes some of the institutions and practices that underlie the regulation and oversight of accounting.

How exactly is GAAP created? This is a rather complicated question. The short answer, however, is that GAAP continues to be generated by a series of organizations over time. While the SEC has authority to establish accounting standards for use in reports filed with the SEC, it has exercised its authority with relative restraint, leaving development of GAAP standards to the profession.*

The principal professional organization for accountants is the American Institute of Certified Public Accountants ("AICPA"). From 1939 to 1959 its Committee on Accounting Procedure issued Accounting Research Bulletins addressing specific problems. It was replaced by the Accounting Principles Board ("APB"), whose members were elected by the AICPA, which issued 31 opinions that were considered official and became part of GAAP. Because of criticism of its lack of independence from AICPA, it was replaced in 1973 by a seven-member *Financial Accounting Standards Board* ("FASB").

FASB currently maintains primary responsibility for setting GAAP in the United States. It is comprised of representatives from the accounting profession and from business, education and government. The accountants on this full-time board are required to sever their relations with their firms, and FASB is supported by a full-time research staff. It has published over 160 accounting statements that govern the development of financial reports. These, along with other bulletins, interpretive memos, options, and earlier standards, form the basis of GAAP. As you might imagine, however, there can be substantial differences of opinion about what GAAP requires in a complex or unusual matter.† Given this complexity, it is very common to have accounting

---

* Regulation S-X states requirements about the form and content of filings, and the SEC periodically provides policy statements in its Accounting Series Releases ("ASRs"), but to a large extent these reflect standards developed by the profession.

† Consider the following excerpt from a footnote in the Bolt case that we examined earlier in this chapter:

> There are five categories in the GAAP hierarchy. Officially established accounting principles, referred to as Category (a) authority, are the highest level and include the Financial Accounting Standards Board ("FASB") Statements of Financial Accounting Standards and Interpretations, Accounting Principles Board ("APB") Opinions, and AICPA Accounting Research Bulletins.... Moreover, Securities Exchange Commission ("SEC") rules and interpretative releases take an authoritative weight similar to Category (a) authority for companies registered with the SEC. Category (b) authority, the next highest level, consists of FASB Technical Bulletins and, if cleared by FASB, AICPA Industry Audit and Accounting Guides and AICPA Statements of Position.... The third level of authority, Category (c), consists of AICPA Accounting Standards Executive Committee Practice Bulletins that have been cleared by FASB and consensus positions of the FASB Emerging Issue Task Force. Category (d), the fourth level of authority, consists of AICPA accounting interpretations and implementation guides published by the FASB staff, and practices that are widely recognized and prevalent either generally or in the industry. In the absence of established accounting principles, auditors may consider accounting literature in the fifth and final level of authority, which includes FASB Statements of Financial Accounting Concepts; APB Statements; AICPA Issues Papers; International Accounting Standards of the International Accounting Standards Committee ("IASC");

professionals serve as expert witnesses about GAAP requirements when lawsuits raise questions about the appropriate treatment of an accounting issue.

In 2002, in reaction to disclosures of numerous financial and accounting frauds at major corporations—and the charges that accountants had failed to discover and reveal these frauds—Congress passed the Sarbanes-Oxley Act. For public companies, § 302 of Sarbanes-Oxley now requires Chief Executive Officers ("CEOs") and Chief Financial Officers ("CFOs") to personally certify the accuracy of corporate financial statements. They must also certify that the corporation has sufficient internal controls to assure accuracy.

Even with these managerial guarantees, however, investors and markets demand additional efforts to promote the truthfulness of accounting statements. This additional oversight is provided by auditors, and the financial statements of publicly traded companies must be audited by an independent audit firm. Some people think that auditors review every single accounting transaction and essentially replicate the efforts of a company's internal accountants, but this is not the case. Rather, auditing involves sampling techniques to test the accuracy of financial statements, designed to provide "reasonable assurance" that the statements fairly present the firm's financial condition and results of operations. Ultimately this process will result in an auditor opinion letter, but even a "clean" letter (indicating no material concerns) should not be taken as an absolute assurance of accuracy.

Figure 2-5. Regulation and Oversight

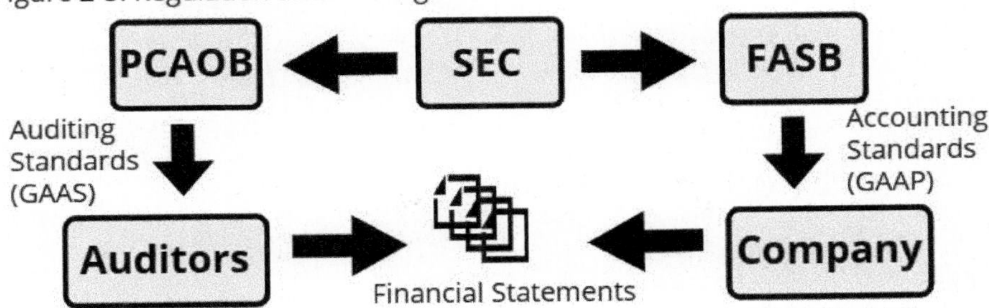

The steps that auditors take to review a firm's transactions are governed by a parallel set of standards, called *generally acceptable auditing standards* (GAAS). The elements of GAAS are beyond the scope of this book, but if you take additional classes in this area, you may learn more about the specific steps that auditors take to conduct a review. Sarbanes-Oxley also addressed a perceived concern of inadequate auditing practices by creating a new Public Company Accounting

Governmental Accounting Standards Board ("GASB") Statements, Interpretations, and Technical Bulletins; pronouncements of other professional associations or regulatory agencies; AICPA Technical Practice Aids; and accounting textbooks, handbooks, and articles.

Oversight Board ("PCAOB") to govern the auditing profession. Figure 2-5 summarizes the oversight relationship for accounting and auditing.

Finally, we should recognize that many firms operate in a global context and that different countries will use different accounting practices. International standards are heavily influenced by the *International Accounting Standards Board* ("IASB") which oversees and coordinates accounting outside the United States. More than 100 countries, including those in the European Union, require the use of *International Financial Reporting Standards* ("IFRS") that are developed by IASB. These standards are often similar to GAAP, but there can be some significant differences. In recent years, there have been efforts to harmonize GAAP and IFRS to create a unified global approach to accounting, but to date, this has not occurred. In 2012, the SEC declined to recommend IFRS adoption by the United States—despite a previous "road map" that had been developed for such an adoption.

CHAPTER 3

VALUING FIRM OUTPUT

1. INTRODUCTION

Corporate finance classes offered at business schools are often described as classes about "valuation." The reason is straightforward: As a business seeks to raise external financing, its ability to do so will depend on whether investors believe the investment opportunity is fairly priced. Imagine you start a business by yourself and eventually seek to raise $1 million from an investor in a common stock financing. If the investor insists that after the financing you each own 50% of the company, the investor is assuming you are each bringing $1 million of value to the table. Why? Because if the investor is buying half of your company for $1 million, the whole post-financing company (both the pre-financing value and the $1 million of new money) must be worth $2 million. But how can either you or the investor determine if $1 million is a fair value for the company you have created? The same challenge naturally occurs in the context of mergers and acquisitions, where would-be buyers must decide how much to offer for an entire business and a target's stockholders must decide how much to demand.

Given this challenge, it takes little imagination to see why lawyers would be expected to have some fluency in the language of valuation when representing issuers, investors, and acquirers in corporate finance transactions. As we shall see, the need for lawyers to obtain a solid understanding of valuation principles is made all the more pressing given the considerable discretion involved in assessing valuation and the unique role lawyers often play in the exercise of this discretion. Perhaps the most obvious example is in the context of litigation over the sale of a company. As we shall see, there are a variety of reasons why mergers are subsequently challenged through litigation, placing courts in the position of having to determine the value of the acquired firm. These proceedings typically entail a battle of valuation experts where seemingly minor differences in the experts' assumptions can lead to dramatic differences in valuation. A lawyer familiar with valuation principles will naturally have an advantage in selecting a competent valuation expert as well as interrogating a rival expert. Likewise, for the deal lawyer, a solid foundation in valuation is necessary to ensure that the economic bargain reached between the parties is, in fact, the economic bargain that is reflected in the underlying transaction documents. We shall return to both of these contexts in the pages that follow.

Before proceeding, we make an important preliminary observation. Having just covered financial accounting, it may be tempting to think about valuation in corporate finance as we did in financial accounting. But it is important to resist this temptation for at least two reasons.

First, as we saw in Chapter 2, book value—the most readily available estimate that we have for all of the assets owned by a firm—will commonly depart from fair value for many of a firm's assets due to historical cost reporting, as well as depreciation. Some assets, such as intangible property, may not even appear on a company's balance sheet for the reasons discussed in Chapter 2.

Moreover, even if we could obtain the fair value of all assets owned by a firm, the configuration of these assets in a business may produce value above and beyond the value of these assets when considered individually (i.e., "the whole is greater than the sum of its parts.") Imagine, for example, four singers who can individually fill a nightclub. But together as a group they might be the next Beatles or One Direction or Fifth Harmony (you get the point) and fill an entire stadium. Likewise, so long as those future ticket sales and music royalties exceed what the singers would get individually, the group should want to remain together.

This simple example underscores an important point about the valuation of business enterprises, which is that the focus is on *future cash flows* (i.e., upcoming ticket and record sales) as opposed to the value of individual assets. To be sure, there may be situations when these two values are the same, or even when the fair value of the individual assets exceeds the value of holding the assets together.* However, these are distressed firms that lack any reason to continue (or in accounting parlance, the firm lacks "going concern value") and will typically be liquidated with the firm's assets being sold at their fair values. (In keeping with our analogy, these would be situations when the band decides to break up, with the members going their separate ways.)

Our focus in this chapter will be primarily on valuing going concern businesses. Therefore, we begin our discussion of valuation with how we should think about future cash flows.

2. CALCULATING FUTURE CASH FLOWS AND PRESENT VALUE

A. THE INTUITION BEHIND VALUATION

At its core, most of finance revolves around a straightforward pair of questions: If I invest a dollar today in an investment opportunity, what

* Within economics, the notion that a firm may be valued at more than its component parts is captured by the concept of Tobin's Q, named for Nobel Laureate James Tobin, to whom the concept is credited. Tobin's Q is defined as the market value of a firm over the replacement value of its assets. Where Tobin's Q exceeds 1, Tobin theorized that a firm's managers should have incentives to invest in more of the firm's assets since the market valued them at greater than their cost; likewise, when Q was less than 1, managers should commence selling off assets in the market. In practice, Tobin's Q is often used as a rough indicator of a firm's investment opportunities and growth prospects. Replacement value of assets is unobservable (and thus incalculable); therefore, book value is often used as a substitute despite its infirmities as such a measure.

will be my expected cash flows from this investment? And given these expected cash flows, will they adequately compensate me for the risks associated with this investment? Often, the answer to these questions will be obvious. Imagine, for example, that you have $10,000 to invest and that you are offered an opportunity to loan $10,000 to a new cryptocurrency startup called CryptoX. In exchange for the loan, CryptoX agrees to repay you exactly $10,001 in one year's time. Will you make the investment? Most readers, we suspect, would decline. Your promised future cash flows are $10,001, giving you just $1 of compensation, or 0.01% of your investment. This seems pretty paltry, especially given that the risk of receiving far less than this amount is considerable. Indeed, your *expected* cash flows—that is, the cash flows you expect to receive given the probability of non-payment—are likely far lower than $10,000. You would be better off investing the $10,000 at your local bank.

This simple hypothetical illustrates the intuition behind valuation: (a) Estimate the probability-weighted expected cash flows, (b) compare them to the cost of the investment, and (c) assess whether the compensation is sufficient given the associated investment risk. Note that the focus is on the future cash flows based on the weighted-probability that they will be realized. In our hypothetical, for instance, imagine there was a 50% chance of repayment and a 50% chance of receiving $0. Our expected cash flows would therefore be $5,000.50 ($10,001 × .5 + $0 × .5). Moreover, *actual* outcomes could differ from these expected outcomes. This is no different from observing that, in flipping a fair coin ten times, actual outcomes will often depart from the expected outcome of observing 5 heads and 5 tails. In valuation, we account for the possibility that actual cash flows might be more or less than our expected cash flows by applying a discount rate that incorporates the risk associated with the investment. We will have much more to say about risk and discount rates, but for now just consider it as a discount that we will apply to the expected cash flows. Thus, the intuition behind valuation can therefore be thought of as asking whether the following equation is true:

$$\textit{Cost of the Investment Today} \leq \textit{Expected Cash Flows} \times \textit{Discount for Risk}$$

When the cost of the investment today (the left-hand side of the equation) is exactly equal to the risk-adjusted expected cash flows (the right-hand side of the equation), we say the investment is fairly priced. When the cost of the investment today is less than the risk-adjusted expected cash flows, the investment is priced at a bargain to the investor. And if the cost of the investment today is *more* than the risk-adjusted expected cash flows, the investment is over-priced and should be avoided.

Before exploring these concepts in more detail, there is an important complication that our hypothetical side-stepped in the interests of simplicity. Recall that the CryptoX investment opportunity involved just one investment (your loaning $10,000) and one future cash flow

(CryptoX's repayment of $10,001 in one year). In reality, both the investment and the future cash flows could instead be made periodically over multiple periods. For instance, instead of repaying $10,001 in one year, CryptoX could promise to pay you $1,000.10 per year over the next 10 years. Understanding how to account for periodic payments requires a more detailed discussion of compounding and rates of return.

B. COMPOUNDING AND RATES OF RETURN

Many investment opportunities will produce regular payments, such as annually, semi-annually (once every 6 months) or quarterly (once every 3 months). Take, for instance, a conventional deposit account at your local bank. When you deposit money, the bank can use these funds to extend loans to others, earning a profit on the interest it receives. As a result, the bank will compensate depositors in hopes of drawing more deposits from which it can make loans. This compensation, of course, takes the form of interest payments that the bank makes on your deposited funds. (The interest a bank pays depositors will, not surprisingly, be less than the interest that the bank receives on the loans it makes with these funds).

The amount of interest will typically be stated as an annual rate. For instance, if the bank pays interest at 10% per year and you deposit $100, the bank will pay you $10 ($100 × .1) after one full year. In theory, the bank could agree to pay you 10% per year using your original investment of $100 as the benchmark for calculating the annual interest payment. In other words, the bank would pay you $10 per year for as long as you held your money at the bank. This form of interest is referred to as *simple interest*, and there are occasionally circumstances where a borrower and a lender will agree to use it. In most situations, however, a borrower (such as our bank seeking depositors) will agree to pay *compound interest*. Why? Because the bank knows that if it paid only simple interest you would withdraw your money as soon as interest had been paid on your account, and redeposit the increased sum (perhaps with another bank). As a result, the bank is forced by competition to pay interest on the interest it has already paid into your account; this is known as compound interest.

Consider a straightforward example. Assume that you have one hundred dollars that you can invest at 10% interest for a five-year period. If interest compounds annually at the end of each year, how much will you have at the end of five years? The solution is to multiply the year-end balance by the interest rate and add this to your principal amount used to calculate interest for the following year. This is shown in the following table:

Table 3-1: Compounding

Year	Balance at Start of Year	Interest Earned During Year	Balance at End of Year
Year 1:	$100 *	.10 = $10	$110
Year 2:	$110 *	.10 = $11	$121
Year 3:	$121 *	.10 = $12.10	$133
Year 4:	$133 *	.10 = $13.30	$146
Year 5:	$146 *	.10 = $14.60	$161

As shown in the table, with compound interest, you will have $161 at the end of the five-year period. With simple interest, by contrast, you would have only $150 ($100 + (5 * $10) = $150). This may not be a huge difference, but over long time periods the increased amount from compounding can be enormous.

This can be presented more formally. The *future value* ("FV_1") of a sum (S) that is invested for one year at interest rate (r), compounded annually, is determined as follows:

$$FV_1 = S(1 + r)$$

If interest will be compounded annually and the investment is held for two years, the balance at the end of the first year (i.e., S(1 + r)) would grow by (1 + r) over the second year. Thus, the future value at the end of two years ("FV_2") of a sum (S) that is invested for two years at interest rate (r), compounded annually, is determined as follows:

$$FV_2 = S(1 + r)(1 + r)$$

This in turn can be stated as:

$$FV_2 = S(1 + r)^2$$

Similarly, the value of S at the end of year 5 is equal to $FV_5 = S(1 + r)^5$. On the day that you deposit $100, you can therefore estimate the amount of money that will be in your bank account at the end of year 5 as $\$100(1 + .1)^5$. That is, the future value ("FV") will be a function of your present value of $100 ("PV"), the annual interest rate ("r") and the number of annual periods that you wait ("t"). This logic gives rise to the standard future value formula with annually compounded returns:

$$FV = PV(1 + r)^{(t)}$$

So far, this example has assumed that a bank has agreed to compound interest annually. Can it instead agree to compound interest more frequently? For example, instead of calculating interest at the end of each year and adding it to your principal balance at the end of the year, could a bank do this at the end of every 6 months (i.e., semi-annually) or at the end of every 3 months (i.e., quarterly)? This could be beneficial in attracting deposits since the deposit account would not have to wait a full 12 months before it started earning interest on that year's interest.

Assume, for instance, that a bank pays 10% annual interest on your initial investment of $100, but the bank compounds interest quarterly. In considering the consequences of this arrangement, it is important to understand that stated interest rates are not generally all-or-nothing concepts, but instead represent compensation that is earned constantly over time. In our example, the 10% annual rate is the *cumulative* interest that the account earns over an entire year, beginning from the moment you deposit your funds. Thus, if you deposit $100 at a bank at 10% annual interest and hold your funds at the bank for 3 months, you have earned 25% of the year's interest (i.e., 3/12). If the bank compounds interest quarterly, that means that 25% of the year's interest (or 2.5% of $100) is compounded into your bank balance, and you thereafter start earning interest on not only your original $100 deposit, but also on the interest of $2.50 you've earned over that 3 month period. By the time another 3 months elapses, you will have earned 2.5% on $102.50. Because this arrangement accelerates the compounding of interest, your account will earn more the more frequent the compounding. Table 3-2 illustrates this concept by showing your account balance with quarterly compounding.

Table 3-2:
Quarterly Compounding

Beginning Balance	$100.00
Quarter 1:	
Interest: .025 × $100	2.50
Ending Balance	102.50
Quarter 2:	
Interest: .025 × $102.50	2.56
Ending Balance	105.06
Quarter 3:	
Interest: .025 × $105.06	2.63
Ending Balance	107.69
Quarter 4:	
Interest: .025 × $107.69	2.69
Ending Balance	$110.38

Recall that annual compounding would have yielded an account with only $110.00.

This example underscores how understanding the future value of an investment depends both on the interest rate *and* on the frequency of compounding. It also underscores the need to match the frequency of compounding with the rate of return for an investment. For instance, the future value formula $FV = PV(1 + r)^t$ assumes that the rate of return (r) is the rate of return over one year and that interest is compounded annually. In our earlier example of annual compounding, the formula worked because the bank compounded *annually* and the interest rate was an *annual* interest rate. When we move to compounding quarterly, Table 3-2 indicates that we need to be careful when using the future value formula to calculate the balance in your account at the end of the year. By the end of the year, you will have experienced four compound periods (one every 3 months). However, you will not have earned 10% over each of these compound periods; you will have only earned 2.5% over each period for the reasons discussed previously. Thus, we need to make a slight modification of our future value formula to account for the possibility of non-annual compounding:

$$FV = PV(1 + \frac{r}{n})^{(t \times n)}$$

In this modified formula, *r* is still the annual interest rate, and *t* is still the length of the investment in years. However, the number *n* represents the number of times interest is compounded each year. Thus, in our example, we would apply the formula as follows:

$$FV = \$100(1 + \frac{.1}{4})^{(1 \times 4)}$$

$$FV = \$100(1 + .025)^{(4)}$$

$$FV = \$110.38$$

If you held the investment for two years, the rate per compound period would remain the same (2.5%), but the number of compound periods would increase from 4 to 8:

$$FV = \$100(1 + \frac{.1}{4})^{(2 \times 4)}$$

$$FV = \$100(1 + .025)^{(8)}$$

$$FV = \$121.84$$

Could a bank offer to compound interest even more frequently than quarterly? Of course. A bank could even promise to compound interest *continuously*. Indeed, we shall see later that the concept of continuously compounded returns often plays an important role in finance. To calculate continuously compounded returns, we use the future value formula and assume that n approaches infinity (∞):

$$FV = PV(1 + \frac{r}{n \to \infty})^{(t \times n \to \infty)}$$

Fortunately, this formula has mathematical properties that allow us to calculate continuously compounded returns using the following, simplified formula:

$$FV = PVe^{rt}$$

The symbol e represents Euler's constant and is approximately 2.718. (Like Pi, Euler's constant has a decimal expansion that continues forever without repetition; in practice, one usually uses an approximation of e from a financial calculator or Microsoft Excel). Thus, the future value of an investment of $100 at a 10% annual rate, compounded continuously, would be the following after two years:*

$$FV = \$100e^{.1 \times 2}$$

$$FV = \$122.14$$

Note that, despite the continuous compounding of interest, the future value is only modestly larger than the result obtained with quarterly compounding.

Finally, what about situations where "t" (the length of the investment) is not a nice round number? After all, it seems unlikely that investors will typically make investments that last for *exactly* one year, or *exactly* one quarter. For instance, what happens if you deposit your $100 on January 1 of one year and wait one year and one month before withdrawing it? Assuming 10% interest compounded annually, we approach the problem in two steps. First, we calculate the balance owed as of the end of however many whole compound periods the loan was outstanding. In this case, interest is compounded annually; therefore, we can calculate the future value after one whole year: $\$100(1 + .1)^1 = \$110$. This leaves us with a "stub" period of one whole month. As noted previously, interest is earned continuously, so we will earn $1/12 \times 10\%$, or 0.83% on the balance in our account as of the end of the last compound

* Microsoft Excel has a built-in estimate of Euler's constant that one can use to calculate continuously compounded interest. In this example, one would enter in a cell: =100*exp(.1*2). Typing "exp(.1*2)" in an equation in Excel instructs the program to calculate $e^{(.1 \times 2)}$ using Excel's build-in estimate of Euler's constant. We discuss in the Sidebar how to use Microsoft Excel to calculate future values.

period. Because this amount was $110, the future value at the end of the final month would be: $110 × 1.0083, or $110.91.

Even this last example might seem a bit fanciful insofar that we are still assuming investors routinely hold investments for a round number of months. What about the more realistic scenario where a loan is redeemed in the middle of a week or month? Given that lawyers are commonly expected to calculate interest owed on redeemed loans (or to oversee its calculation), the question is a non-trivial one for law students. In the Sidebar, we illustrate how to use Microsoft Excel to the solve this challenge.

Sidebar: Calculating Future Values with Microsoft Excel

Based on the future value formula, calculating future value becomes a simple matter of arithmetic once we obtain the correct parameters for PV, r, n and t. While a basic calculator is more than sufficient to do these calculations, using Microsoft Excel (or a similar spreadsheet program) offers a number of advantages. For one, Excel offers a built-in function to calculate future value, which some students may find helpful. On the Casebook website, we provide an example of how to use this function in the Future Value Worksheet. (The Casebook website is located at: https://faculty.westacademic.com/Book/Detail?id=349672#teachingresources; the worksheets are in the directory entitled "Student Supplemental Worksheets.") On the tab entitled "Future Value Function," we calculate the future value of a loan of $1 (PV) invested at an annual interest rate of 10% (r) compounded annually and held for 5 years. In using the Future Value function, it is important to keep in mind that the function thinks in terms of "compound periods." This requires us to enter the interest paid *per compound period* and to provide Excel with the *total number of compound periods.* Here, the interest rate is 10% per year, compounded annually, and the investment is for five years. Thus, we will need to instruct Excel that the interest rate per compound period is 10% and that there are 5 "compound periods." Excel's Future Value function also anticipates the possibility that an additional payment is made to or from the investor at the end of each compound period. We call this possible annual payment a "Payment" below, but with this first example there is no extra payment—just the interest on the loan. In Excel, we could enter these parameters separately in Cells B1, B2, B3 and B4, as shown below. To use the Future Value formula, we type in Cell B6 "=FV(", which calls the future value function and prompts us to point the function to the relevant parameters. Specifically, typing these four keystrokes in Cell B6 will produce:

VLOOKUP × ✓ *fx* =fv(

FV(**rate**, nper, pmt, [pv], [type])

	A	B
1	Present Value (PV)	1
2	Interest Rate	0.1
3	Payment	0
4	Periods	5
5		
6	Future Value	=fv(

Note that Excel is requesting that we provide it with "rate, nper, pmt, [pv], [type]" inside the parentheses. These abbreviations stand for the interest rate per compound period (rate), the number of compound periods (nper), the amount of payment made to or from the investor at the end of each compound period (pmt), the present value of the starting investment (pv), and something referred to as "type." This last concept refers to whether interest payments to the investor are made at the end of the compound period or at the beginning. If interest is paid at the end of each compound period (as in our example), type=0; if made at the beginning of the compound period, type=1. We separate each parameter by a comma. Accordingly, we type in Cell B6 "=FV(.1,5,0,−1,0)", which produces the answer or $1.61. We enter the present value as the negative of the value in B1 because the "purchase price" is a cash outflow from the investor's perspective. The interest rate is entered as a decimal. We could also enter the formula by pointing Excel to the cells containing these parameters, or =FV(B2,B4,B3,-B1,0). We use this latter approach in the example provided on the Casebook website.

Students who find this approach unduly complicated can alternatively calculate future values by treating Excel as a dynamic calculator. We refer to Excel as a dynamic calculator because you can enter formulas as a function of other cells rather than simply real numbers. Thus, we could calculate the future value in B6 by directly entering the future value formula as "=B1*(1 + B2)^B4". The symbol ^ instructs Excel to treat the number that follows as an exponent. Changing the contents of B1, B2 or B4 will result in an automatic re-calculation of the future value in Cell B6. We provide an example of this approach in Cell B8 on the Excel worksheet.

Excel becomes particularly useful in calculating future values when trying to determine the amount due on a loan that has been outstanding for an uneven number of days. Imagine, for instance, that we seek to determine the amount owed on the example above if the loan occurred from January 1, 2018 to March 5, 2023. This period includes 5 full years, so we begin by calculating the amount owed as of the end of the last full year before the 2023 "stub" year. This is the amount we previously calculated as $1.61. We next calculate the fraction of the year represented from January 1, 2023 through March 5, 2023. On the tab entitled "Uneven Dates Example," we provide an example of how to do this using Excel. In the example, we first enter the two dates in two separate cells, formatting them as dates (in the worksheet, we enter them in cells B9 and B10). Subtracting B10 from B9 yields the number of days the loan has been outstanding, which is 63 days:

SUM × ✓ fx =B10-B9

	A	B	C
1	Present Value (PV)	1	
2	Interest Rate	0.1	
3	Payment	0	
4	Full Periods	5	
5			
6	Future Value at Year 5:	$1.61	*Value after 5 full periods*
7			
8	Stub Period:		
9	Start:	1/1/23	
10	End:	3/5/23	
11	Total Days:	=B10-B9	

We can then use this number to calculate the fraction of the year the loan earns 10% interest. Loan documents will conventionally stipulate whether to use a 365- or 360-day year, so depending on the language of the loan document, we would divide 63 by either 365 or 360. Assuming a 365-day year, the additional interest for the 2023 stub year would be (63/365) × 10% x $1.61, or approximately $0.03.

Sidebar: Average vs. Geometric Returns

The discussion of compounding was focused primarily on understanding how to calculate the future value of an investment given (a) the beginning investment amount, (b) the expected rate of return, and (c) the compounding frequency. However, this framework is also useful for evaluating *past* investment performance. Consider, for example, an investment in a single share of common stock of Yahoo! made on January 2, 2001 and held through January 4, 2018. The following chart shows the price of Yahoo! common stock on the annual anniversary of the investment, as well as the annual return:

End of Year:	Date	Value	Return
	1/2/01	$ 18.66	
1	1/2/02	$ 8.62	–54%
2	1/2/03	$ 9.10	6%
3	1/2/04	$ 23.49	158%
4	1/3/05	$ 35.21	50%
5	1/3/06	$ 34.38	–2%
6	1/3/07	$ 28.31	–18%
7	1/2/08	$ 19.18	–32%
8	1/2/09	$ 11.73	–39%
9	1/4/10	$ 15.01	28%
10	1/3/11	$ 16.12	7%
11	1/3/12	$ 15.47	–4%
12	1/2/13	$ 19.63	27%
13	1/2/14	$ 36.01	83%
14	1/2/15	$ 43.99	22%
15	1/4/16	$ 29.51	–33%
16	1/4/17	$ 44.07	49%
17	1/4/18	$ 74.76	70%

What was the average annual rate of return on this investment? Many people might make the mistake of looking at the annual returns in the last column and taking the average. That is, the simple average of the annual returns shown in the last column is approximately 19%. Not bad! However, this result seems inconsistent with the actual financial results: An investment of $18.66 and held for 17 years at 19% interest should yield a future value of:

$$\$18.66(1.19)^{17} = \$349.10$$

But we can see that our ending balance on January 4, 2018 is actually just $74.76. What went wrong with our initial analysis? The answer is that we made the mistake of calculating returns by using the simple average of annual returns, or what is known as the *arithmetic mean*. Investment returns should instead be calculated in terms of the annualized rate of return from the time the investment is made until future cash flows are realized. This is known as the *geometric mean* and can be calculated using our Future Value formula. For the investment in Yahoo!, we know the starting amount (or PV) was $18.66 and the ending amount (of FV) was $74.76. Moreover, we know the investment was held for 17 years. To calculate the implied annual rate of return with annual compounding, we solve for the missing term, r:

$$
\begin{aligned}
& \$74.76 &=& \ \$18.66(1+r)^{17} \\
\Longrightarrow\ & \$74.76/\$18.66 &=& \ (1+r)^{17} \\
\Longrightarrow\ & (4.00)^{1/17} &=& \ 1+r^{*} \\
\Longrightarrow\ & 1.085 &=& \ 1+r \\
& 8.5\% &=& \ r
\end{aligned}
$$

The geometric average rate of return is therefore 8.5%. (It is also worth noting, when evaluating total investment returns, that Yahoo paid no dividends during this period.) We provide an example of this approach on the tab entitled "Geometric Return Example" on the Future Value Worksheet on the Casebook website.

* From high school algebra, recall that $y=x^n$ is equivalent to $y^{1/n}=x$. Thus, $4.00 = (1 + r)^{17}$ is equivalent to $(4.00)^{1/17} = 1 + r$. Using Excel, we can calculate $(4.00)^{1/17}$ by entering in a cell "=4^(1/17)", which equals 1.085.

C. PRESENT VALUES

i. THE BASIC FRAMEWORK

Our examination of compounding showed how much money you would have at some future date if you invested a certain sum today. Using a little algebra, we can also use this framework to determine how much money we need *today* given (a) a specified rate of return for investing it and (b) the money *we want to have in the future*. For instance, imagine that you wanted to have $100,000 in your savings account in 10 years. How much money would you need to deposit today if your bank pays a fixed interest rate of 3% per year, compounded annually? In short, we have a future value ($100,000), a rate of return (3%), and a time period, which are three of the four variables needed in our future value equation with annual compounding:

$$FV = PV(1 + r)^t$$

As you may recall from high school algebra, we can divide both sides of an equation by the same number without changing the identity of the equation, so dividing both sides by $(1 + r)^t$ gives us:

$$\frac{FV}{(1+r)^t} = PV\frac{(1+r)^t}{(1+r)^t}$$

$$=> \frac{FV}{(1+r)^t} = PV$$

In this way, our future value equation can be transformed into a present value equation that we can use to answer the question. In this case, the equation tells us that we need approximately $75,000 today in order to have $100,000 in ten years.*

$$\frac{\$100{,}000}{(1.03)^{10}} = \$74{,}409.39$$

Before moving on, it is worth pausing to consider a couple of features of the present value equation. First, notice the effect of changing the interest rate. Imagine that instead of just depositing your money in a savings account, you buy a 10-year certificate of deposit that pays interest of 5% per year, compounded annually. Substituting 5% for 3% in the equation above yields $61,391.33; you need to save less today to have $100,000 in 10 years. Why? Because your money is receiving more interest during this time period. This may seem obvious, but the example demonstrates an important point about calculating present values: They are inversely related to the rate of return.

Second, notice the effect of extending the timeframe. What if we were willing to save for 100 years at a 3% interest rate, compounded annually? How much money would we need today to have $100,000 in our account at year 100? Substituting 100 years for 10 years in the equation above yields $5,203.28. As this example shows, delaying the receipt of a future payment can have a dramatic effect on its present value. Indeed, as Figure 3-1 illustrates, if you wait long enough, the payment loses all present value.

---

* To calculate this formula in Excel, you would enter into a cell: = "100,000/1.03^10".

Figure 3-1:
Effect of Time on Present Value of $100,000 Earning 3% Annual Interest

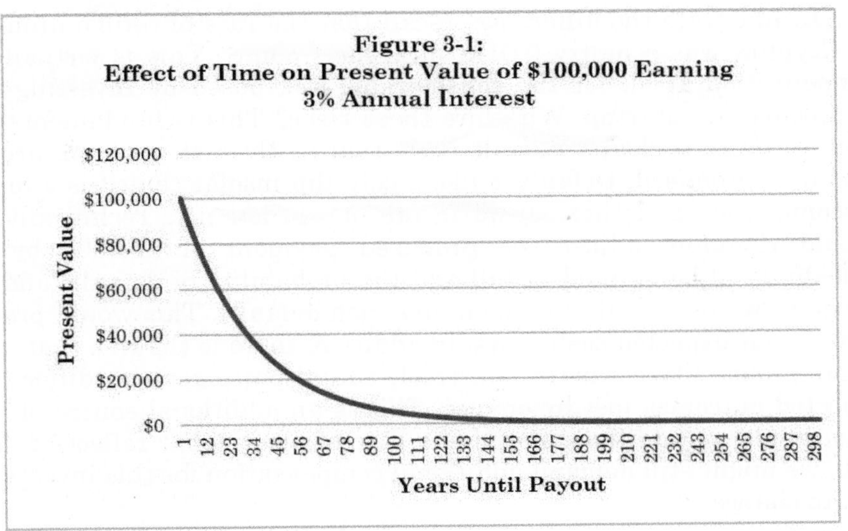

> **Quick Check Question 3.1**
>
> It is your brother's tenth birthday, and your grandparents give him a $10,000 savings bond that matures in eight years, when he is expected to begin college. The interest rate on the bond is 7% per year. Your brother writes down "$10,000" on his list of gifts received. How can you explain his error to him? Can you tell him what the present value of this gift is?

The present value formula can be incredibly useful in analyzing projects where we need to save funds today for cash needs that will arise in the future. However, most of our focus on present values in the remainder of this chapter will be in a slightly different context where we will be using the present value equation for purposes of valuation. To illustrate, recall again the hypothetical we posed earlier where you were presented with an opportunity to loan $10,000 to CryptoX. In the hypothetical, CryptoX was promising to pay you $10,001 in one year's time in exchange for your $10,000. That is, it was promising you a future value (FV) of $10,001, in exchange for your $10,000 today. Is this a fairly priced investment? Does the promise to receive $10,001 in one year have a present value of at least $10,000?

The present value equation allows us to answer these questions. The primary difference with our simple savings example is that we need to calculate the present value of a promised future payment (i.e., $10,001) but we are not given r, the rate of return. Rather, we will have to determine r based on our assessment of the risk profile of the investment. That is, in this context, the r we need to use is *not* the rate of return promised by CryptoX; it is the rate of return that you should expect from this type of investment given its risk profile.

To illustrate the difference, recall that the rate of return promised by CryptoX was a paltry 0.01%, or 1 basis point.* This is virtually no compensation at all for the considerable risk posed by investing in a cryptocurrency startup. What are these risks? This is fundamentally a loan, so there is clearly default risk—that is, the risk that you are not repaid as promised. Default is like a coin-flip insofar that it is a binary outcome: you are either repaid in full or you are not. Technically, we should therefore adjust the promised payment of $10,001 by the probability of being paid in full and the probability of default (and the payment we expect, if any, upon any such default). This would provide us with our expected cash flows. In addition, there is the risk that, even if our probability estimate is correct, actual outcomes can differ from expected outcomes just by chance. This is an additional source of risk; accordingly, in addition to setting a rate of return that reflects default risk, we might still demand additional compensation for this investment due to chance.

Below, we discuss in more detail the concept of determining the proper r to use in the present value formula when valuing an investment opportunity. But for now, it is sufficient to say that it needs to reflect a rate of return that will entice investors to acquire the investment given its risk profile. Accordingly, in the case of a $10,000 loan to CryptoX, we should be using a rate of return associated with a one-year loan to a cryptocurrency startup like CryptoX. For instance, what if we discover that all of CryptoX's competitors are paying interest rates of 20% for a one-year loan? This information would suggest that a fair rate of return for loans to risky companies like CryptoX is closer to 20%. Putting this expected rate of return into the equation above will then yield an estimate of the present value of this investment opportunity:

$$\frac{\$10{,}001}{(1+.2)^1} = \$8{,}334.17$$

In exchange for your $10,000, you would thus be receiving a contractual promise to get $10,001 in one year, which has a present value of $8,334.17. Assuming 20% is the correct rate of return for an investment with this risk profile, paying $10,000 for this contractual promise would be overpaying by $1,665.83. We now have numerical evidence for our initial conclusion that we should pass on this investment. This example also illustrates why r is often referred to in this context as a "discount rate": It is the rate we use to discount future cash flows to their present value.

As the example suggests, determining the correct discount rate can be conceptually challenging. Indeed, the question of how to select the appropriate r to use has spawned an entire asset pricing literature in finance that continues to evolve. And expert witnesses frequently debate

* A basis point is 1/100 of a percent.

which discount rate to use during lawsuits about valuation. Our objective for now is to introduce the present value equation, so we shall postpone discussing the methods used to estimate *r* until Section 3 and simply stipulate the correct discount rate to use for the time being. The immediate goal is to explore the most common applications of discounting to present value and to underscore how each application simply repeats the framework we used to evaluate the CryptoX investment opportunity.

Quick Check Question 3.2

Your law school is engaged in a capital funds campaign. You read in the school paper that a prominent alumnus has pledged $1,000,000 in her will to support the law school. Assume the alum is now 65 years old, with a life expectancy of 85. If the appropriate discount rate is 7%, what is the present value of her pledge? How should the law school report it to other alumni?

ii. APPLICATION: VALUING BONDS AND ANNUITIES

Having learned how to value a promise to receive a single payment in the future, we are now ready to value a corporate bond. A bond is a promise of a series of (annual)* interest payments, often called coupon payments, plus repayment of principal at the maturity of the bond. It can last anywhere from one year to 100 years (although 100-year bonds have been rarely seen). The easiest way to value a bond is to separate the payments. For example, suppose a $1,000 bond pays 10% interest annually at the close of each year for ten years. At the end of the tenth year, the bond also pays back the principal amount of $1,000. If 10% remains the appropriate discount rate during the bond's life, we can discount each interest payment to present value. We can also use this technique to value the repayment of principal (the "terminal payment") at the end of year 10. Moreover, we know from the prior section that doing this for each of these payments of interest and principal will turn future dollars into today's dollars. As a result, we can sum these present values together to arrive at the total present value of the bond. We illustrate this technique in Table 3-3.

Table 3-3: Valuing a Bond

Year 1:	$\$100 \div 1.10^1$	= $90.91
Year 2:	$\$100 \div 1.10^2$	= $82.64
Year 3:	$\$100 \div 1.10^3$	= $75.13
Year 4:	$\$100 \div 1.10^4$	= $68.30

* Corporate bond interest is typically paid semi-annually, but for simplicity we will assume annual payments in these examples.

Year 5:	$100 ÷ 1.10^5	= $62.09
Year 6:	$100 ÷ 1.10^6	= $56.45
Year 7:	$100 ÷ 1.10^7	= $51.32
Year 8:	$100 ÷ 1.10^8	= $46.65
9 years	$100 ÷ 1.10^9	= $42.41
10 years	$100 ÷ 1.10^{10}	= $38.55
Total PV of interest payments:		614.45
Principal PV:	$1,000 ÷ 1.10^{10}	385.55
Discounted Present Value:		$1,000.00

In this example, the $1,000 bond should trade for exactly $1,000. That's how much it is worth. Of course, that should not be very surprising because the coupon rate paid by the bond and the discount rate demanded by investors over this entire period are both 10%.

Any stream of future payments, such as that found in a bond, is called an "*annuity*," although common usage frequently limits the term to annuity policies sold by insurance companies. As you can see, the present value of an annuity is simply the sum total of the discounted present value of each payment. It's also worth mentioning that the present value of an annuity of $1 per period for n years can be calculated by a special formula:

$$PV = \frac{1}{r} - \frac{1}{r(1+r)^n}$$

If this equation strikes you as unpleasant to view, rest assured that you can safely disregard it so long as you are comfortable working with a spreadsheet program. As we show in the Sidebar, the present value of any annuity, such as a corporate bond, can be easily calculated using a spreadsheet such as Microsoft Excel (allowing you to ignore the annuity formula).

Like stocks, bonds commonly trade in the secondary market, so investors holding long-term bonds have a means to liquidate (i.e., monetize) their positions before maturity. Conventionally, bonds trade in $1,000 increments (based on the original principal, or face value, amount) to facilitate trading. As time passes, how do investors determine the price at which to buy and sell bonds? The answer is by calculating the present value of a bond's remaining future cash flows. Imagine, for example, that you were among the original investors in the $1,000 10-year bonds discussed previously. After holding the bond for exactly 9 years, you look to sell it in the open market. By this point in time, you would have received 9 interest payments of $100, meaning that the purchaser of the bond will be entitled to one payment of $1,100 of interest and principal in one year's time. Applying the PV equation, we have the following:

$$\frac{\$1{,}100}{(1+r)^1} = ?$$

Determining the appropriate r requires us to keep in mind that r is *not* the interest rate specified in the bond (i.e., the 10% coupon rate), but it is the discount rate that should capture the rate of return investors expect from this type of investment given its risk profile. After 9 years, is this issuer likely to present *exactly* the same risk profile it posed when it priced the original loan at 10%? If this is indeed the case, then you should be able to sell the bond for $1000 (do you see why?). But as with people, the credit risk of a firm usually varies over time, suggesting that the discount rate may very well be higher or lower than 10%. Moreover, as we shall see, investors demand compensation simply because they have to wait to be paid, implicating the risk of inflation. In an inflationary environment, a dollar tomorrow has less buying power than a dollar today.

These considerations explain why bond investors focus on credit risk as well as interest rate (i.e., inflation) risk. Consider what happens to the value of your bond at year 9 if investors in the bond market believe the issuer of the bond has become so risky that it could issue *new* debt only if it promised an interest rate of 20%:

$$\frac{\$1{,}100}{(1+.2)^1} = \$916.67$$

The price of the bond on trading markets will decline from $1,000 to $916.67. The same outcome would arise if the credit risk of the issuer remained stable but, because overall interest rates in the economy have increased, the company can only issue new debt at an interest rate of 20%. Conversely, if interest rates in the economy fell so that the company could issue new debt at 5%, the value of your bond would increase to $1,047.62:

$$\frac{\$1{,}100}{(1+.05)^1} = \$1{,}047.62$$

In effect, the decline in interest rates means that the issuer is paying you an above market interest rate of 10%, justifying the price premium.

Note that interest rate risk exists regardless of the credit quality of an issuer. The fact that all debt investors bear interest rate risk is a partial explanation for why investors typically insist on higher rates of return on long-term bonds than on short-term obligations. We shall return to this issue again in Section 3 when we discuss the determinants of discount rates.

Some issuers may wish to provide investors with lower inflation risk in order to get a lower interest rate on long-term debt, which they can do by using a variable interest rate. Doing so, however, places the interest rate risk on the company who must now plan for the possibility that interest rates in the economy might spike, greatly increasing the amount of interest it must pay to meet its debt obligations. (Homeowners face very similar considerations when deciding whether to take out a fixed or variable rate mortgage loan.)

Sidebar: Calculating Annuity Values with Microsoft Excel

Spreadsheet programs such as Microsoft Excel make calculating the present value of an annuity a simple process of "copying and pasting." The primary challenge is setting up the valuation model. As an example, consider the 10-year annuity presented in the main text: a 10-year bond paying $100 per year in interest (10%) with a $1,000 principal payment at the end of year 10. We will value the bond as of the issue date, so we assume 10% is also the proper discount rate.

In the Present Value Worksheet on the Casebook website, we provide a valuation model for this annuity on the tab entitled "Basic Annuity." We present below a screenshot of the model showing the contents of each cell. In the first four rows of the model, we simply record the parameters of the annuity, which we will use to calculate its value.

	A	B	C	D
1				
2		Annuity Present Value Model		
3				
4		Periodic Payment		100
5		Final Payment:		1000
6		Discount rate:		0.1
7		Payment Periods:		10
8				
9		Year	Payment	PV
10		0	0	=C10/(1+$D$6)^B10
11		1	=$D$4	=C11/(1+$D$6)^B11
12		2	=$D$4	=C12/(1+$D$6)^B12
13		3	=$D$4	=C13/(1+$D$6)^B13
14		4	=$D$4	=C14/(1+$D$6)^B14
15		5	=$D$4	=C15/(1+$D$6)^B15
16		6	=$D$4	=C16/(1+$D$6)^B16
17		7	=$D$4	=C17/(1+$D$6)^B17
18		8	=$D$4	=C18/(1+$D$6)^B18
19		9	=$D$4	=C19/(1+$D$6)^B19
20		10	=$D$4	=C20/(1+$D$6)^B20
21		10	=D5	=C21/(1+$D$6)^B21
22				
23		Total:		=SUM(D10:D22)

Rows 10–21 calculate the annuity's present value, payment by payment. We begin in Row 10 with the present value of any payments received immediately, or when Year=0. Of course, we know we receive nothing immediately from this bond, but we recommend starting with

Year=0 in any present value pricing model so that the model is flexible enough to capture situations where a payment is made immediately.

Because we receive nothing from this annuity at Year=0, we enter $0 in Cell C10. Next, for year 1, we enter $D$4 in Cell C11. Our goal is to create a valuation model based on the annuity terms set forth in the first four rows, so $D$4 instructs Excel to look to Cell D4, where we've specified that the periodic payment is $100 per year. The "$" before the D and the 4 instructs Excel to keep D4 as a fixed reference when the contents of C11 are copied and pasted elsewhere. This is important because our next step is to copy (Ctrl-C) Cell C11 and paste (Ctrl-V) its contents into cells C11–C20. Had we omitted the $ in Cell C11, Excel would assume that we want to increment "D4" by one row for every row we paste below C11 (e.g., Excel would paste D5 into Cell C12; D6 into cell C13, etc.). As shown below, using $D$4 in Cell C11 forces Excel to insert $D$4 into C12–C20 when we "copy & paste" from C12 down through C20. That leaves only the principal repayment, which we capture in Cell C21 by referencing D5. Note that year "10" is repeated in cells B20 and B21 because both an interest payment and the principal payment are made at the end of that year (be careful not to put year 11 in cell B21). We need to discount both payments by the same ten-year period.

Next in Column D, we calculate the present value of each of these payments. We do so by using the Present Value Formula for each payment; however, we enter it only once in Cell D10 as follows:

=C10/(1 + $D$6)^B10

With this format, copying the contents of D10 and pasting them downward into cells D11–D21 will ensure that these cells automatically adjust the formula for the proper payment and year. The reason is because as we paste down from D10, Excel will increment all row references by 1 for each row we move down from D10, except for references that are "locked" in place by a $ prefix. This means that the exponent reference (B10) will reference the appropriate year in Column B, and the payment (C10) will reference the appropriate payment in Column C. At the same time, the reference to the interest rate ($D$6) will remain locked at D6.

Finally, Cell D23 adds together the present values calculated in Cells D10 through D21, obtaining the present value of the annuity. As shown in the cell, the present value of the bond is $1,000.

Of course, one need not utilize this specific method to calculate the value of an annuity. For example, we also present on the same tab two alternative methods to value this annuity for the sake of comparison: Using the "PV" function in Excel and the annuity formula discussed in the text. Using the method described here, however, has the advantage of illustrating why calculating the present value of an annuity is nothing more than an application of the basic present value formula.

iii. APPLICATION: VALUING PERPETUITIES AND STOCKS

So far, we have dealt with finite payment streams on the assumption that we know (presumably from their contract terms) that they will terminate on a certain date. What about payments that continue forever, such as cash flows arising from a company's equity securities? For instance, a share of common stock may pay a regular dividend that is expected to continue for the life of a firm. Because firms have indefinite lives, how should we calculate the present value of a share of stock assuming it pays a fixed dividend forever? Similarly, the British government issued bonds in the 19th century that were not repayable at any particular time—they just paid a stated rate of interest forever. Both examples are a special form of annuity, called a "*perpetuity*."

Using the approach taken for valuing bonds, we could attempt to value a perpetuity by continuing to make annuity calculations for a very long period. As we saw from Figure 3-1, the present value of a future payment decays rapidly as we push that payment into the future. As a result, this approach to valuing perpetuities works perfectly fine despite the fact that payments continue forever. Depending on the discount rate, payments after 40 or 50 years will generally have a value that approaches zero, meaning that we effectively can treat a perpetuity as an annuity that expires when the present value of future payments nears zero. We discuss how to use Excel to value perpetuities in this fashion in the Sidebar.

In contrast to annuities, however, there is a very simple formula that can also be used to determine the present value of a perpetuity. The simplest way to derive this formula is to consider how much money you would have to invest at an interest rate of 10% to assure yourself an annual payment of $10.00 forever. The answer is obvious: $100. (Note with a perpetuity you never get your principal back, so you don't have to worry about valuing a terminal payment, as you do with a bond.) The general formula for valuing a perpetuity is simply to divide the annual payment by the discount rate. Thus:

$$Present\ Value\ of\ a\ Perpetuity = \frac{Payment\ (P)}{Discount\ Rate\ (r)}$$

The similarity between an actual perpetuity and a share of common stock that regularly pays dividends has not been lost on financial economists. The dividend discount model (DDM), in particular, is a method for valuing a company's common stock that assumes that the value of a share of stock is simply the sum of all expected future dividends, discounted to present value. For example, if a stock is expected to pay \$2.00 in dividends per year and has a discount rate of 20%, the model would conclude the present value of the stock is \$10 (i.e., \$2.00/.2).

The assumption that the dividend amount will be level throughout time is relaxed in a variant of the DDM, known as the Gordon Growth Model (GGM). In the GGM, the dividend amount is assumed to grow annually at a particular rate. Modifying the previous example slightly, we might assume that a stock that just paid a dividend of \$2.00 per share will increase dividends by 3% per year as it grows profits. A payment stream that lasts forever but grows at a specified rate is known as a growing perpetuity. As with a conventional perpetuity, payments made in the distant future have effectively zero value, so they can also be valued by simply summing the present value of all future payments until these present values converge to zero. They can also be valued using a modified version of the perpetuity formula, which accounts for the growth rate in the payment. The formula for valuing such a growing perpetuity is:

$$\textit{Present Value of a Growing Perpetuity} = \frac{\textit{Initial Payment}}{\textit{Discount Rate} - \textit{Growth Rate}}$$

Or:

$$\frac{P}{r-g}$$

where g is the growth rate, r is the discount rate, and P is the Initial Payment.

One caveat: the formula will not work if the growth rate (g) exceeds the discount rate (r). Also, when analyzing growing perpetuities, it is important to keep in mind that *P* represents the first payment to be received in the future. In our example, if a company *just* paid an annual dividend of \$2.00 and is expected to grow dividends 3% per year, the first payment to be received in the future would be \$2.06 (or \$2.00 × 1.03). We would accordingly calculate the value of such a share using the following growing perpetuity formula (again assuming a 20% discount rate):

$$PV = \frac{\$2.06}{.2 - .03} = \frac{\$2.06}{.17} = \$12.12$$

To state the obvious, these valuation models rest on several assumptions that may not be appropriate depending on the context. For instance, many stocks (such as technology stocks) do not pay dividends at all. Moreover, even when a company does pay dividends, the assumption of steady and growing dividends seems unlikely to hold for many companies. Accordingly, the valuation of common stock often involves using alternative methodologies that focus on first valuing the entire enterprise through a discounted cash flow analysis and/or a comparable company analysis, and then calculating the value of common equity. We shall discuss these approaches in more detail following our discussion of how to calculate discount rates.

Quick Check Question 3.3

What is the value of a share of preferred stock carrying an expected $8.00 annual dividend, discounted at 7%, assuming it is neither redeemable by the company ("callable") nor subject to forced redemption by the holder? What if we assume the initial $8.00 dividend grows at 2% per year?

Sidebar: Calculating Perpetuity Values with Microsoft Excel

As we did with annuities, we can calculate the value of a perpetuity using the basic present value formula and leveraging the power of a spreadsheet program such as Microsoft Excel. The primary difference is that there is no terminal payment. However, we know from Figure 3-1 that future payments received far into the future have a present value that approximates $0. As such, we simply calculate the present value of each expected periodic payment until their present value nears $0.

In the Present Value Worksheet on the Casebook website, we provide an illustration using Quick Check Question 3.3 on the tab entitled "Perpetuities." We present below a screenshot of the model showing the first ten years of payments. By year 10, the present value of the $8 payment declines to $4.07.

	A	B	C	D	E
1					
2		Simple Perpetuity Calculation: Method A			
3					
4		Annual Payment		$ 8	
5		Discount rate:		7%	
6					
7					
8					
9		Years	Payment	PV	
10		0	$ -	$ -	
11		1	$ 8.00	$ 7.48	
12		2	$ 8.00	$ 6.99	
13		3	$ 8.00	$ 6.53	
14		4	$ 8.00	$ 6.10	
15		5	$ 8.00	$ 5.70	
16		6	$ 8.00	$ 5.33	
17		7	$ 8.00	$ 4.98	
18		8	$ 8.00	$ 4.66	
19		9	$ 8.00	$ 4.35	
20		10	$ 8.00	$ 4.07	

The following screenshot illustrates how by years 311–320, the present value of $8 is effectively nothing. Summing up all 320 years of payments (after discounting to present value) yields a total present value for the stream of payments of $114.286.

321	311	$	8.00	$ 0.00000001
322	312	$	8.00	$ 0.00000001
323	313	$	8.00	$ 0.00000001
324	314	$	8.00	$ 0.00000000
325	315	$	8.00	$ 0.00000000
326	316	$	8.00	$ 0.00000000
327	317	$	8.00	$ 0.00000000
328	318	$	8.00	$ 0.00000000
329	319	$	8.00	$ 0.00000000
330	320	$	8.00	$ 0.00000000
331				
332	TOTAL			$ 114.286

For comparison, we also calculate on the tab the value of the perpetuity using the perpetuity formula and obtain the same value. As shown on the tab, we can also calculate a growing perpetuity using this same approach.

iv. APPLICATION: CAPITAL BUDGETING

Discounting to present value is also a common method of analysis when a firm is deciding how to invest its own money. This process is often referred to as capital budgeting. For example, various investment options may offer different cash flows at different periods, making comparisons difficult. However, one of the useful aspects about present value calculations is that you can compare two investments with different expected cash flows in different periods and decide which one is better. Suppose, in the following example, that each investment will require $400,000 invested at the beginning of year one. Assume that both pose the same level of risk and that a discount rate of 10% is appropriate. Here are the expected returns:

Project A:		**Project B:**	
End of Year	Return	End of Year	Return
1	$200,000	1	$100,000
2	150,000	2	100,000
3	150,000	3	325,000
Total:	$500,000	Total:	$525,000

Here are the discounted present values:

Project A:			**Project B:**		
Year:	Gross Return:	PV:	Year:	Gross Return:	PV:
1	$200,000 ÷ 1.1^1	$181,818	1	$100,000 ÷ 1.1^1	$90,909
2	150,000 ÷ 1.1^2	123,967	2	100,000 ÷ 1.1^2	82,645

3	$150{,}000 \div 1.1^3$	112,697	3	$325{,}000 \div 1.1^3$	244,177
	Total PV:	$418,482		Total PV:	$417,731

Thus Project A has the higher discounted present value, despite the higher nominal (undiscounted) value of Project B. The reason stems from the fact that Project B's cash flows are concentrated in year 3, whereas Project A has greater cash flows in years 1 and 2.

Taking this logic one step further, we can also incorporate into our analysis of projects the present value of any expected expenditures. Assume, for example, that you are a manager at a pharmaceutical company and are presently considering an expansion of your existing drug lines. A new drug will require an investment in three stages: A large investment today and two smaller investments at the end of years 1 and 2. We will additionally assume this investment is expected to yield no revenue until year 5 when you expect to sell the drug to a larger company for $3,500,000. Investors in this company expect annual returns of 20% given the risk profile of the company's pharmaceutical business, so you apply a 20% discount rate.

OUTLAYS:

Time of Payment	Amount			Present Value
Immediately	$1,000,000	÷	1.2^0	$1,000,000
End of Year 1	200,000	÷	1.2^1	166,667
End of Year 2	300,000	÷	1.2^2	208,333
			Total PV:	$1,375,000

RECEIPTS:

Time of Payment	Amount			Present Value
End of Year 5	$3,500,000	÷	1.2^5	$1,406,572

Note that this is just a variation on the valuation of bonds, which also have different payments in different periods. But the important fact is that we have made the value of cash outlays comparable to those for future cash receipts. And the present value of the future receipts exceeds the present value of the outlays. When the present value of expected returns exceeds that of investments, we say that the project has a positive *net present value.* That means we should invest in this project, assuming that we have used the correct discount rate.

How do we know if 20% is in fact the correct discount rate? In general, the answer can be found in the same logic we have been applying throughout this chapter: the discount rate should reflect the risk of the investment opportunity. We have stipulated that the investment will expand the company's existing drug lines. If investors expect 20% from the existing business, then this should be a reasonable estimate of the required return for this new product line. What about the fact that we are also applying this discount rate to our expenditures? The same logic applies: if investors in this company expect returns from this business of 20%, a manager making additional investment in the assets of the business needs to make sure that these new investments are also expected to produce returns of at least 20% to keep investors happy. For this reason, the discount rate in capital budgeting is often referred to as the *cost of capital*—it's the rate of return that investors expect for investing in the business. Consequently, it's the rate of return a manager must expect from an investment to justify deploying additional capital by the company into its business.

Quick Check Question 3.4

A factory costs $400,000. You calculate that it will produce net cash after operating expenses of $100,000 in year 1, $200,000 in year 2, and $300,000 in year 3, after which it will shut down with zero salvage value (assume the expenses occur at the end of each year). Calculate the net present value, using a 10% discount rate.

Sidebar: Alternative Capital Budgeting Approaches: Payback Period

Companies sometimes use a *payback* period to calculate whether to accept or reject a project. This simply calculates the number of years it takes for the initial investment to be repaid from project cash flows. Firms using this method pick an arbitrary period for the payback as a trigger for the investment decision (e.g., we will invest in all projects with a payback period of six years or less). This method gives equal weight to all cash flows received within the payback period, in contrast to NPV calculations. The method avoids the difficulties of determining a discount rate (as is required for NPV calculations), but at considerable cost. For instance, because this method cuts off later cash flows that occur after the payback period, it may undervalue a project that will have increasing cash flows in later years. Likewise, if the payback period is too long, it will permit acceptance of projects that may have negative NPVs. For these reasons, the payback period method is generally considered an inferior way to evaluate projects.

Sidebar: Alternative Capital Budgeting Approaches: Internal Rate of Return

In many industries, it is common to evaluate investment projects using the concept of the *internal rate of return*, or "IRR." IRR is closely related to NPV; the IRR is the discount rate at which net present value turns out to be zero. In the pharmaceutical example above, the investment under consideration had an NPV equal to $31,572 (i.e., $1,406,572 – $1,375,000). This was obtained using a specified discount rate of 20%. The IRR is the discount rate that would reduce this NPV to exactly $0. A bit of trial and error shows that using a discount rate of 20.6% would achieve this result, so the IRR for this investment is 20.6%. Microsoft Excel includes a specific IRR function, so IRR can also be calculated in Excel provided one formats the data correctly. Assuming cash outlays and cash receipts occur at one-year intervals, Excel will calculate the IRR if the user inputs annual cash flows within a single column, listed chronologically from top to bottom. The data also needs to indicate whether a cash payment is an outlay (recorded as a negative number) or a receipt (recorded as a positive number). Using a range of A1:B8, one could calculate the IRR for the investment opportunity discussed in the text by entering the following:

	A	B
1	Year	Cash Flow
2	0	-1000000
3	1	-200000
4	2	-300000
5	3	0
6	4	0
7	5	3500000
8	IRR:	=IRR(B2:B7)

Students can find this example on the tab entitled "IRR" in the Present Value Worksheet on the Casebook website. In general, IRRs can be thought of as capturing the annualized rate of return on an investment that requires sequential investments and/or sequential disbursements of cash. As a result, the metric is especially popular in venture capital finance and private equity where investments tend to be staged over time.

Despite its popularity, there are two well-known problems with IRR. First, if a project has initial positive cash flows, followed by periods of negative cash flows that require further investments, followed by more positive cash flows, the IRR can produce two different rates of return. In these settings, IRR cannot be used. The second problem is that the mathematics underlying IRR can cause a project with large, early distributions to look more favorable than it would appear if it were discounted with its "true" discount rate (i.e., the project's actual cost of capital.) Consider, for instance, the following projects, both of which have a discount rate of 10%:

Project:	**A**	**B**
Start (investment)	($400,000)	($400,000)
Cash Flows after Year 1	$400,000	$50,000
Cash Flows after Year 2	$100,000	$450,000
Cash Flows after Year 3	0	$50,000
Net cash flows	$100,000	$150,000
Net Present Value @10%	$42,070	$49,930
IRR	21%	17%

Using the net present value methodology, Project B produces a higher net present value, and should be selected. But IRR produces a dramatically different result. This is because the $400,000 cash flow in Year 1 for Project A inflates its IRR relative to Project B, which produces just $50,000 in Year 1 but $450,000 and $50,000 in Years 2 and 3, respectively.

3. DETERMINING DISCOUNT RATES

So far, we have largely stipulated the appropriate discount rate to use in the preceding examples. But how are discount rates determined in practice? It turns out that this is among the most complicated (and debated) questions in finance, so we will not pretend to provide a comprehensive answer in the pages that follow. Nevertheless, there are a core set of *principles* that are generally accepted within finance as being informative of how discount rates are determined within well-functioning markets. We will focus on developing a working knowledge of these principles to provide context for a subsequent discussion of some of the *methods* that are used to derive actual discount rates. In practice, the application of these methods will typically be left to non-lawyers; however, as we shall see, there is considerably less agreement within finance on the application of these methods, or whether they are in fact appropriate methodologies at all. Consequently, whether it is selecting a valuation expert or evaluating a fairness opinion from an investment bank, lawyers who leave calculating discount rates "to the expert" do so at their peril.

A. SOME FIRST PRINCIPLES ABOUT DISCOUNT RATES

i. IN EFFICIENT MARKETS, DISCOUNT RATES COMPENSATE INVESTORS FOR THE AMOUNT OF WORRY AND WAIT ASSOCIATED WITH AN INVESTMENT

At the most general level, basic intuition tells us that determining an appropriate discount rate has something to do with compensating investors. Recall our CryptoX hypothetical in which you had an opportunity to loan $10,000 to the company in exchange for a promised repayment in one year of $10,001. We concluded that a promised return of just $1.00 seems pretty paltry given the risk of non-payment. You might even lose sleep worrying about whether you'd even see one penny of your money again. Can't you demand a higher return as compensation for this worry? Plus, even if you were repaid in full, you would have to wait a *full year* to see it again, depriving yourself of $10,000 that you could use in the intervening time to consume or to make alternative investments. Can't you also demand compensation for having to wait a year for your return?

As it turns out, investors do in fact require compensation proportionate to these two features of investing: The amount of risk that causes them to *worry*, and the amount of time that they have to *wait*. It is also the reason why we say that discount rates in efficient markets are determined by the amount of return necessary to compensate investors for the worry and wait associated with a particular investment. To see why, first consider what we mean by an "efficient market." For present purposes, we will define an efficient market as one where there is competition among firms and no major information asymmetries between investors and firms (i.e., investors are pretty good at assessing a firm's "risk profile."). In such a market, you will have many different places to invest your $10,000, inducing firms to compete for your investment dollars.

Imagine, for instance, that CryptoX has two competitors, CryptoY and CryptoZ, with identical business models and overall risk profiles as CryptoX. Assuming all three firms require capital, competition will force Crypto X to offer you an appropriate return as compensation for the worry and wait associated with loaning it $10,000 or else you will invest elsewhere (perhaps in CryptoY or CryptoZ). CryptoY and CryptoZ face an identical incentive, forcing them to likewise offer you an appropriate rate of return given the level of worry and wait associated with the investment. From the company's perspective, the return it needs to pay you will be the cost of acquiring outside funding. This is why the company will refer to this rate of return as its *cost of capital.*

From an investor's perspective, the observed cost of capital for these firms should also be the discount rate you use to value investments in any of the firms. Imagine, for example, that the true cost of capital for these firms is 20% per year. As before, CryptoX promises to pay you $10,001 in one year for a $10,000 loan today. However, CryptoZ promises to pay you $12,000 in one year for a $10,000 loan today. As we concluded previously, the present value of CryptoX's promise is just $8,334.17—you would be wildly overpaying for the promised payment of $10,001. In contrast, the present value of CrytoZ's promise is exactly $10,000. Only the latter is fairly priced at $10,000 because CryptoZ is promising exactly the amount of return (20%) that compensates investors for the amount of worry and wait associated with this type of investment.

Of course, this all assumes the market for crypto firms is moderately efficient. We shall return to this assumption below, but first, we explore in more detail why investors demand compensation for worrying and waiting. We begin with waiting.

ii. INVESTORS DEMAND A TIME PREMIUM EVEN IN RISK-FREE INVESTMENTS

For most students, the notion that investors demand a return for waiting is intuitively obvious. Imagine you win the lottery and have two options for how to receive the payment. Option A allows you to receive $10,000,000 today. Option B allows you to receive $10,000,000 in one year. Even if you were 100% confident of receiving the money under either option, we suspect you would choose Option A. Why? Among other things, money you have today is money you can use today. You don't want to wait a year to buy that new mansion or Ferrari. For another, money you receive today generally has more purchasing power than money you receive in a year due to inflation. Money you have today also will earn interest if you save it. Finally, inflation and interest rates are not constant, but fluctuate in unpredictable ways. Waiting one year to receive your cash may therefore cause you to worry a bit about inflation and interest rate risk, and most people prefer not to worry if they can avoid it.

These are some of the primary reasons why investors demand compensation for investing, even if the future cash flows are 100% certain to occur. We can even observe this phenomenon by looking at the interest rates that the U.S. government has to pay investors when it needs to borrow funds. When the U.S. government issues bonds to investors, payments on these bonds are considered risk-free insofar that there is 100% certainty the interest and principal payments will be made. After all, the government owns the presses that print money and can always repay, in nominal currency (although it may be much depreciated through inflation of the currency). In Table 3-4 we present the daily "yield curve rates" for U.S. treasury bonds having the maturity dates listed in the first column.* U.S. bonds trade in the over-the-counter market, so it is possible to infer from the current trading price the discount rate that

* Daily yield curve rates can be found at https://www.treasury.gov/resource-center/data-chart-center/interest-rates/Pages/TextView.aspx?data=yieldYear&year=2018.

investors are placing on the government's risk-free promise to repay principal and interest having different maturity dates.*

Table 3-4:
Yields on U.S. Treasuries in December 2023

Time to Maturity	Yield (%)
1 Mo	5.57
6 Mo	5.28
1 Yr	4.82
5 Yr	3.83
10 Yr	3.84
30 Yr	3.98

If the U.S. government were to issue new securities, these are approximately the interest rates the government would have to pay investors to buy the new bonds. It is notable (and unusual) that these 2023 rates decrease for longer maturities—a phenomenon known as an inverted yield curve. In normal times, as the maturity date extends, the interest rate is usually higher. The fact that yields typically increase for longer-dated U.S. treasuries despite their risk-free character is one way to visualize the fact that investors demand compensation simply for waiting.†

Sidebar: The Term Structure of Interest Rates—Alternative Theories

Our discussion of why interest rates correlate with length of maturity (or what is often referred to as the term structure of interest rates) assumed that the market for 30-year bonds was different than the market for 1-year bonds. That is, it assumed that investors in 1-year bonds would demand compensation for being exposed to inflation and interest rate risk over a 1-year horizon, while investors in 30-year bonds would demand higher compensation for being exposed to inflation and interest rate risk over a 30-year horizon. This explanation for the term structure of interest rates is often referred to as the

---

* Recall the present value formula is PV = Future Payment/$(1 + r)^t$. Because U.S. treasury securities are traded, we can observe the PV from looking at market prices. Moreover, the future payments are known from the terms of the bond. As a result, we can calculate the discount rate (r). For instance, assume a one-year U.S. bond will pay principal of $1,000 and interest of $100 in one year and is trading at $1,075. The market-implied discount rate is approximately 2.2% ($1,075 = $1,100 / $(1 + r)^1$, or $1,100 / $1,075 = 1 + r.)

† We say that the yields "typically" increase for longer-dated maturities because—as we observe for 2023—there are instances when the yield curve can in fact decrease for longer-dated maturities. Such "inverted" yield curves are rare and are often believed to predict a weakening economy. Recall that the yield curve is derived from observed prices, so if investors believed the economy was weakening and that long-term inflation was going to be low, this could cause prices of long-dated U.S. bonds to increase and their yields to decline.

"Segmented Markets Theory." However, it is not the only theory for why investors demand a time premium.

Under the "Expectations Theory," investors in bonds focus on predicting short-term rates and assume that bonds of differing maturities are perfect substitutes. For instance, suppose one-year rates over the next five years are expected to be 5%, 6%, 7%, 8% and 9%. If bonds of different maturities are perfect substitutes, then the interest rate on a two-year bond would be: (5% + 6%)/2 = 5.5%. And interest on a five-year bond would be: (5% + 6% + 7% + 8% + 9 %)/5 = 7%. Thus, under this theory, long-term rates are all averages of expected future short-term rates. The appeal of the expectations theory is that investors *should* price a 1-year bond with some regard to expectations about future short-term rates. However, the expectations theory cannot explain why long-term yields are normally higher than short-term yields: if there is an equal chance of short-term rates going up as down, the yield curve should sometimes slope upwards and sometimes slope downwards.

A modification of the expectations theory, the "Liquidity Premium Theory", assumes investors price bonds based on expectations about future short-term rates (as in the Expectations Theory) but do not view bonds of different maturities to be perfect substitutes because most investors prefer short-term bonds to long-term bonds given concerns about inflation and interest rate risk. As such, long-term bonds must pay a premium to compensate investors for enhanced exposure to interest rate and inflation risk, similar to the Segmented Markets Theory. Note that under all three theories investors demand a time premium—the alternative theories simply provide different explanations for this empirical phenomenon.

iii. WITH RISKY DEBT INVESTMENTS, INVESTORS WILL DEMAND A DEFAULT PREMIUM TO ACCOUNT FOR DEFAULT RISK

Let's assume we live in a world where everyone is risk-neutral. In such a world, people only care about *expected* returns. To illustrate this concept, imagine you win a contest and are offered a choice of two prizes. One prize is a payment today of $10. The alternative prize is the "double-your-money-gamble." If you choose the gamble, the contest operator flips a fair coin. If it comes up heads you will be paid $20 today; if it comes up tails, you get nothing. The coin is fair, so you know the expected value of the gamble is exactly $10 (50% x $20 + 50% x $0). In a risk-neutral world, you are indifferent between the two prizes since they have the same expected values.

Now consider how you might behave as an investor in such a world. For example, imagine a company is raising capital by selling a 1-year, zero coupon bond that pays out $100,000 in one year (a zero-coupon bond pays a fixed amount at the end the term, with no interim interest payments). The risk of default is 50%, and if the company defaults, the investment will be worth $0. So the expected repayment is $50,000 (50% x $100,000 + 50% x $0). In a risk-neutral world, investors will be indifferent between this zero-coupon bond and a guaranteed payment of $50,000 in one-year since they have the same expected values. However, whether it is a guaranteed payment of $50,000 or the payment on the zero-coupon bond, the investors have to wait one year. Thus, even in this risk-neutral world, investors will demand compensation in the form of a time premium for investing in this one-year bond, but this will be their only form of compensation.

What about the 50% default risk? Investors will indeed use this to discount the promised payment of $100,000, but the discount takes the form of a default premium. It is the default premium that converts the promised payment into an expected payment. For example, if the rate of return on a one-year, risk-free bond was 3%, the present value of a risk-free expected payment of $50,000 in one year would be: $50,000/(1.03) = $48,544. In a risk-neutral world, this must also be the present value of the $100,000 zero-coupon bond issued by our hypothetical company. The promised payment of $100,000 is our future cash flow. Therefore, using our present value formula, we can calculate the discount rate as follows:

$$\frac{\$100{,}000}{(1+r)^1} = \$48{,}544$$

Solving for r, the discount rate is 106%, of which 3% is the time premium. The remaining 103% is the default premium and reflects the fact that when pricing risky debt, investors will price the debt based on its expected value. But it is important to keep in mind that a default premium is not technically compensation. After all, in the coin toss example, you were not offered any compensation for taking the gamble instead of the $10 payment. And here, issuers will not compensate investors for default risk since investors are already pricing the bond as if it is equivalent to a risk-free payment of $50,000.

Finally, note that the discount rate we use to value a bond payment does not necessarily have to include a default premium. We could, instead, approach the valuation task in two stages: First, we could calculate the expected future value of the cash flow ($100,000 × .5 + $0 × .5 = $50,000). Second, we could then discount this expected future value ($50,000) by the risk-free rate of 3% to reflect the time premium (assuming investors do not require any other compensation). As we shall see later, many valuation settings take this two-step approach and focus on discounting expected future cash flows. The conventional treatment for bond valuation, however, is to use the one-step approach and include a default premium in the rate of return. This approach is due, in part, from the fact that bonds are often publicly traded, allowing us to infer an overall expected rate of return from comparing the promised future payments to the prevailing trade price. This market-derived rate of return is known as the *yield-to-maturity*.

> **Quick Check Question 3.5**
>
> Imagine you find a bond trading in the market at a price of $900. Upon inspection, you discover that the bond pays zero interest but will ultimately pay its holder $1,000 in exactly 3 years' time. What is the rate of return that the market expects on this bond?

iv. RISK AVERSION CREATES INCENTIVES TO DIVERSIFY INVESTMENTS

In the previous example, we assumed a world where everyone was risk-neutral. This may not be too far-fetched when we have low value decisions like the double-your-money-gamble in the prior section. However, it is much less likely to reflect actual human behavior when the stakes are higher. In these settings, humans are more likely to demonstrate risk-aversion.

Consider again the 1-year, zero coupon bond being offered by the hypothetical company. Imagine that after several years of saving, you've accumulated savings of $50,000. (Perhaps you've been saving up for several years to buy a house, to further your education, or to propose to your loved one.) When presented with the opportunity to purchase the $100,000 zero-coupon bond, would you really consider it to be equivalent to a risk-free payment of $50,000? If you do and purchase it for $48,544, you will more than double your savings if the note pays out as promised. With just over $100,000 in savings, perhaps you could buy that new car you've had your eye on. On the other hand, a default wipes out virtually all of your savings that you've worked so hard to build. For most people, these "best case" / "worse case" scenarios probably don't seem equivalent in how they would impact your overall well-being (or as an economist would say, how they would impact your "utility.") While the best-case scenario would certainly be nice, the worst-case scenario would be devastating to your emotional and financial health. This is an example of the declining marginal utility of wealth: As we accumulate more wealth, we value it less than our initial accumulation of wealth because it is those initial dollars that allow us to achieve the most basic needs in life.

Because of the declining utility of wealth, individuals will generally avoid a risky investment that could result in a drop in their wealth unless they receive compensation for taking this risk. In general, the amount of compensation should reflect the degree of risk posed. How might we quantify the degree of risk? In asset pricing, we typically measure risk by assessing the expected variation of returns, relative to the expected return. For example, in our example, the expected value of the bond payout was $50,000. However, in one year the bond was *actually* going to pay either $0 or $100,000. So the variation of possible payouts relative to the expected payout is −$50,000 and +$50,000. The expected payout is $50,000, but the actual variation could overshoot this by $50,000 or undershoot it by $50,000. That's a lot of possible variation, and thus a lot of risk.

For this all-or-nothing investment, we can thus get an intuitive sense of the variation of returns just by thinking through the best-case/worst-case scenarios. However, there is a formal method for calculating the variation of returns (or an investment's *variance*), which is important to understand since investments are seldom this simple. The idea is to compare each possible outcome to the expected outcome, and then weight it by the probability that it will occur. If we then sum these numbers, we will get a sense for how much the actual outcomes overshoot or undershoot the expected outcome. However, given that some outcomes will undershoot the expected outcome, this will result in negative numbers, which will cancel out any positive numbers when we add them together. As a result, when taking the difference between a possible outcome with the expected outcome, we square this figure so that we add only positive numbers. In our example, we would calculate variance as follows:

Possible Outcome	Expected Outcome	Deviation from Expected Outcome	Deviation Squared	Probability	Probability x Deviation Squared
$0	$50,000	($50,000)	$2,500,000,000	0.5	$1,250,000,000
$100,000	$50,000	$50,000	$2,500,000,000	0.5	$1,250,000,000
				Sum:	$2,500,000,000

The variance of this investment is thus $2,500,000,000. Clearly, this is a very large number due to the squaring of deviations, making it hard to interpret intuitively. As a result, it is common to "undue" the squaring by taking the square root of variance, which produces the *standard deviation*. Here, the square root of the variance is $50,000, which is more in line with our earlier observation that actual returns were going to over-shoot or under-shoot expected payouts by $50,000. The standard deviation has some helpful statistical properties that can be used to think about risk. For instance, if there are reasons to believe the investment returns are normally distributed (i.e., they have a "bell shaped" distribution), 68% of the results of the distribution of outcomes will fall within one standard deviation of the expected return, and 95% will fall within two standard deviations. In statistics, standard deviation is referred to as "σ," or "sigma." In finance, it is also referred to as "volatility."

Calculating variance and standard deviation in this more formal manner allows us to explore the importance of diversification for a risk-averse investor. Suppose we discover another company that is also selling zero coupon bonds with the exact same default risk and that this risk is uncorrelated with that of the original firm's bond. (Perhaps this second company is in an entirely different industry). What happens if you divide your investment so that you purchase a $50,000 zero-coupon bond from each company? As before, your expected payment would be $50,000:

(.5 × $50,000 + .5 × $0) + (.5 × $50,000 + .5 × $0) = $50,000

Note, however, that the variation of your likely returns has changed considerably. Instead of receiving either $0 or $100,000 with equal probability, there are now four possible outcomes:

Scenario	Payout on Bond #1	Payout on Bond #2	Total Payout	Probability
1	$0	$0	$0	25%
2	$0	$50,000	$50,000	25%
3	$50,000	$0	$50,000	25%
4	$50,000	$50,000	$100,000	25%

If we calculate variance, we find that it has declined by 50% from $2,500,000,000 to $1,250,000,000:

Total Payout from Each Scenario	Expected Outcome	Deviation from Expected Outcome	Deviation Squared	Probability	Probability x Deviation Squared
$0	$50,000	($50,000)	$2,500,000,000	25%	$625,000,000
$50,000	$50,000	$0	$0	25%	$0
$50,000	$50,000	$0	$0	25%	$0
$100,000	$50,000	$50,000	$2,500,000,000	25%	$625,000,000
				Sum:	$1,250,000,000

In fact, as a matter of mathematics, dividing the investment into N independent securities (i.e., increasing the degree of diversification of the portfolio) will cause variance to decline by a factor of 1/N relative to putting your investment into just one of these securities. For instance, were we able to divide our $50,000 investment into 1,000 1-year, zero-coupon bonds promising $100 each, we would have an expected payout of $50,000 (1,000 × $50) but a variance and standard deviation of just $2,500,000 and $1,581, respectively. Indeed, in theory we could eliminate variance entirely as the number of investment positions in our portfolio approached infinity. This works, however, only if each position truly behaves independently of other positions within the portfolio—that is, it assumes there is no correlation in default tendencies between Bond #1 and Bond #2.

Does this principle apply for other investment securities, such as common stock? As lawyers, we know the answer must be yes. Common stock is a residual claim on a company's assets, meaning that common stock has value only to the extent that all fixed claims (such as lenders, landlords, workers, and vendors) are paid first. Accordingly, investment returns to common stock reflect the extent to which, at the time a stockholder seeks to monetize its investment, a firm has grown in value above and beyond the amount of these fixed claims. For this reason, if a company is unable to repay its bonds, the common stock presumably has very little (if any) value. Indeed, because of the seniority of debt, common stock will decline in value whenever a firm encounters financial distress and available assets are deployed to satisfy fixed claims. This means that we can expect stock returns to have even greater volatility than a company's debt returns. Yet two firms can have very different performance outcomes, particularly when they operate in different industries. Thus, as in the example with bonds, one can invest in stocks that are less correlated with each other without altering the overall expected return. Table 3-5, for instance, illustrates the reductions in risk resulting from diversifying a stock portfolio that is constructed by randomly choosing stocks listed on the New York Stock Exchange. The analysis focuses on the standard deviation of investment returns, or portfolio volatility, using a one-year horizon.

Table 3-5:
Effects of Increasing Diversification on Return Volatility

Number of Stocks in Portfolio	Average Volatility of Annual Portfolio Returns	Ratio of Portfolio Volatility to Volatility of a Single Stock
1	49.24%	1.00
2	37.36	0.76
4	29.69	0.60
6	26.64	0.54
8	24.98	0.51
10	23.93	0.49
20	21.68	0.44
30	20.87	0.42
40	20.46	0.42
50	20.20	0.41
100	19.69	0.40
200	19.42	0.39
300	19.34	0.39
400	19.29	0.39

500	19.27	0.39
1,000	19.21	0.39

Source: Meir Statman, *How Many Stocks Make a Diversified Portfolio?*, 22 JOURNAL OF FINANCIAL AND QUANTITATIVE ANALYSIS 353–64 (1987), as reported in Zvi Bodie & Robert Merton, FINANCE, 301 (2000).

Note that by investing in just ten stocks rather than one stock, the table suggests volatility of the portfolio declines by half. This highlights how one can obtain many of the risk-reducing benefits of diversification by spreading investment across a relatively small number of stock positions. Recall, however, that the stocks in Table 3-5 were chosen at random; you might not get such a large reduction in risk if you selected, say, ten technology companies. Moreover, the table also shows that there are declining marginal returns from increasing diversification: In both the 100 stock and 1,000 stock portfolios, volatility remains at roughly 19%. What might explain why this additional diversification has no effect on portfolio volatility? The answer lies in the fact that diversification can reduce volatility only when returns are uncorrelated. And as we discuss in the next section, randomly choosing stocks guarantees that some residual correlation of returns will persist among stocks.

The importance of diversification as a means to reduce risk is difficult to overstate. As we discussed earlier, risk averse investors might rationally demand compensation for taking on risky investments. However, it turns out that diversifying investments across uncorrelated assets effectively eliminates much of this risk, meaning that investors cannot demand compensation for it so long as they are competing with other investors. This brings us to our final principle, which explores when even diversified risk-averse investors can demand compensation for investing in risky assets.

v. RISK AVERSION CAUSES DISCOUNT RATES TO INCLUDE COMPENSATION FOR NON-DIVERSIFIABLE RISK

The preceding section showed that if a sufficiently large number of stocks are held in a portfolio, the risk associated with investing in the securities of individual firms can be largely eliminated. Firm risk, or *firm-specific risk* (also called *unsystematic risk* or *diversifiable risk*) stems from the fact that many of the perils that face an individual company are not faced by all other companies. Indeed, what is risk for one company may be an opportunity for another. When it rains, for example, Suntan Lotion Co., may suffer from low sales, but Umbrella Co. will prosper. Thus, in a properly diversified portfolio, individual firm risk is irrelevant.

Yet there are also risks that are general to all securities. The most obvious of these risks are ones associated with the performance of the economy generally. This risk, called *systematic risk* because it is associated with the economic system, cannot be eliminated through diversification. For instance, when the Department of Labor releases unexpected good news about the economy, even well-diversified investors will see a positive return in their portfolios that day. Likewise, even well-diversified investors suffered large losses when Lehman Brothers filed for bankruptcy on September 15, 2009 because the filing sent a signal about the dire state of our financial system. Because systematic risk affects the overall financial market, it is also referred to as *market risk*.

The fact that investors cannot eliminate market risk through diversification has an important implication for our understanding of discount rates. Recall that risk averse investors require some form of compensation for taking on risky investments—that is, they require compensation for worrying. In the prior section, however, we also saw that many of the most obvious investment risks—for example, whether a company's research and development efforts will succeed or fail, whether a company has a good or bad management team, whether a company's key customer will go bankrupt—are firm specific risks that can be avoided through diversification. An investor who tried to demand compensation for these firm-specific risks through imposing a steep discount rate would therefore lose out whenever the investor was competing with a more diversified investor. For instance, recall again our company selling a one-year, zero coupon bond that pays out $100,000 with a 50% default risk. Previously, we valued this bond at $48,544 using a discount rate of 106%, of which 103% constituted a default premium and 3% constituted a time premium. If a prospective investor added an additional premium of 10% to compensate for firm-specific risk, this would decrease the price she was willing to pay to $46,296 (i.e., $100,000/(1 + 1.16)). Other, more diversified investors would not require this additional risk premium, enabling them to outbid the investor by paying up to $48,544 for the bond.

Consider now the consequences if the performance of this zero-coupon bond is dependent to some degree on the overall economy. For instance, perhaps the company is thinly-capitalized and has very few financial resources; an economy-wide recession could push the company toward a higher risk of default. Even well-diversified investors will now demand an additional discount as compensation for this non-diversifiable market risk. As a result, we should then expect the discount rate for debt securities to consist of three component parts, assuming we are discounting future promised payments:

Cost of Debt = Time Premium + Default Premium + Non-Diversifiable Risk Premium

For a company's equity securities, in lieu of a default premium, we account for the possibility of non-payment by calculating future cash flows as the probability-weighted expected cash flows to equity. In other words, an adjustment for a default—or for something less than the most optimistic cash flow forecast—will already be incorporated in the expected cash flow estimates. By calculating future cash flows in this manner, the cost of equity will consist of just a Time Premium and a Non-Diversifiable Risk Premium:

Cost of Equity = Time Premium + Non-Diversifiable Risk Premium

We will discuss in the following section common approaches to estimating the non-diversifiable market risk premium for a security, as well as how to calculate risk premiums that appear to compensate for other non-diversifiable risks. But for now, we want to emphasize the more fundamental point that if even well-diversified investors remain subject to non-diversifiable risk, we should expect investors to price a security using a discount rate that reflects the degree to which non-diversifiable risk can affect the performance of the security.

Note, too, the subtle but important distinction between firm-specific risk and non-diversifiable risk highlighted by this example. The fact that our hypothetical company is thinly capitalized is one of the risks that is unique to this firm and thus a firm-specific risk. However, this firm-specific risk is not itself the basis for adding a risk premium to the discount rate. Rather, it is the *implications* of this firm-specific characteristic on the firm's exposure to market risk that justifies the risk premium. Thus, one should expect the size of this market risk premium to differ across firms based on characteristics that make firms either more or less sensitive to overall market forces. In short, not all securities are similarly affected by market risk. Some securities are relatively immune to the fluctuations of the business cycle, while others are severely impacted by it.

Estimating an appropriate non-diversifiable risk premium to apply therefore requires finding a method to estimate both the size of the risk premium as well as the degree to which a security is exposed to non-diversifiable risk. We turn to these estimation challenges in the following section.

B. METHODS FOR ESTIMATING DISCOUNT RATES

In the preceding section, we focused on a core set of principles that are generally accepted within finance as being informative of how discount rates are determined in well-functioning markets. Here, we move into more contested terrain by providing an overview of some of the prevailing methods for actually estimating discount rates. We begin with the cost of equity.

i. THE CAPITAL ASSET PRICING MODEL (CAPM)

a. *Overview*

First introduced through a series of research papers in the 1960s,* the Capital Asset Pricing Model (CAPM) remains one of the most common methodologies for estimating the discount rate for a company's equity securities. CAPM builds directly off of the preceding discussion and assumes that there is just one non-diversifiable risk that matters: market or systematic risk:

$$\textit{Cost of Equity} = \textit{Time Premium} + \textit{Market Risk Premium}$$

Previously, we discussed how we could estimate the compensation that investors require for waiting (i.e., the time premium) by looking at returns to risk-free securities, such as those issued by the U.S. government. So long as markets are efficient, the compensation that the U.S. government pays to investors should reflect the compensation that investors require for waiting.

Using a similar logic, we can likewise estimate the compensation that investors require for worrying about market risk by looking to the compensation investors actually receive for bearing this risk. For example, investors holding a broad portfolio of securities, such as those that comprise the S&P500 Index, have eliminated firm-specific risk through diversification. But these investors remain subject to market risk. As a result, their investment returns should reflect a Time Premium and a Market Risk Premium. We can accordingly estimate the Market Risk Premium by looking to the historical returns of the S&P500, less the risk-free rate of return. For instance, between 1950 and 2022, the S&P500 had an annualized arithmetic return (assuming reinvestment of dividends) of approximately 12.6%. (We discuss below why we might use the arithmetic return rather than the geometric return.) Assuming this is a good estimate of annual expected returns from a market portfolio, one might conclude that 12.6% is the annual return a well-diversified investor requires for investing in the overall stock market. However, because this figure also includes compensation investors demand for waiting, we would need to deduct from it the time premium (e.g., the one-year yield on U.S. treasuries) to derive the market risk premium. Using this approach, the market risk premium is typically assumed to be in the 6–8% range.

This approach gives us an estimate for the market risk premium, but what about the fact that individual firms can differ in their exposure to

* History generally accords the development of the Capital Asset Pricing Model to the works of William Sharpe, *Capital Asset Prices: A Theory of Market Equilibrium Under Conditions of Risk*, 19 JOURNAL OF FINANCE 425 (1964), John Lintner, *The Valuation of Risk Assets and the Selection of Risky Investments in Stock Portfolios and Capital Budgets*, 47 REVIEW OF ECONOMICS AND STATISTICS 13 (1965) and Fischer Black, *Capital Market Equilibrium with Restricted Borrowing*, 45 JOURNAL OF BUSINESS 444 (1972).

market risk? For instance, early-stage technology companies would seem to be particularly exposed to market fluctuations, as "down" markets might make it more difficult for them to secure financing while "up" markets make it easier. Conversely, the performance of a firm like WalMart or Target would seem less related to how the overall market is performing. To address this issue, CAPM relies on the concept of "beta" (represented as β) to calibrate the size of the Market Risk Premium for a particular security. A stock's beta captures how much a stock's returns are correlated with the returns to a market portfolio, such as the S&P500. Technically, beta represents the coefficient β on the following equation, which estimates the relationship between a stock's return and the return of the market over some time period measured in t periods (usually days or months):

$$StockReturn_t = a_t + \beta \times MarketReturn_t$$

As you might recall from eighth-grade algebra, this equation looks strikingly similar to the equation of a straight line (y = b + mx). The reason is because beta assumes a linear relationship between the return on a market portfolio and the return on an individual stock. Under this assumption, imagine a stock that has a beta of 1. If the S&P500 goes up 5%, the price of this stock will likewise be expected to increase 5%; if the S&P500 goes down 5%, the price of this stock will be expected to decline by 5%. Conversely, if the beta of a stock was 0.5 (which is approximately the beta of WalMart in 2023), the stock price would be expected to increase by half the amount of an increase in the return of the S&P500 and would be expected to decline by half the amount of a decline in the index. In other words, Walmart's performance is less sensitive to overall market fluctuations.

How does one know the beta of a security? Typically, a stock's beta is estimated by looking at the historical relationship between a stock's daily (or monthly) return and the return of a market portfolio. As an example, consider the common stock of Apple, Inc. during 2022. In Figure 3-2, we have taken the daily returns for Apple for each day of 2022 (the y-axis) and plotted them against the daily returns for the S&P500 for the same days (the x-axis). The line in the graph is the line of best fit, which we can use to estimate β and a in the equation above. Specifically, a is the point on the y-axis where the line crosses it when the x-axis has a value of zero (here, 0.0005%) and β is the slope of the line that estimates how much Apple's daily return changed as a function of the return on the S&P500. According to the line, β is 1.31, meaning that when the S&P increased by 1%, Apple's stock price is expected to have increased by approximately 1.31%. Note, however, that beta is simply an estimate of the relationship between the daily returns of the S&P500 and Apple. Clearly, there were many days where Apple's stock price moved quite a bit, despite very little movement in the S&P for that day.

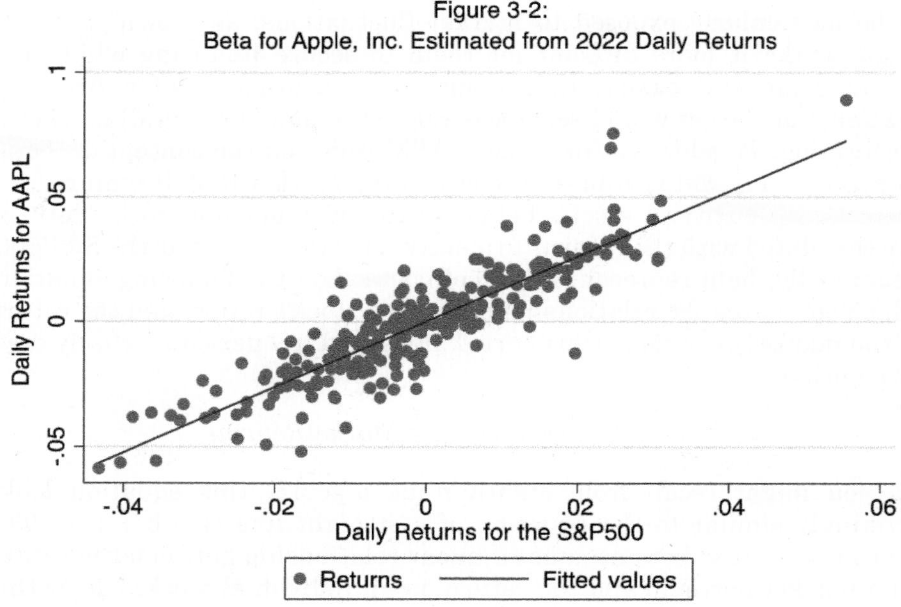

Figure 3-2:
Beta for Apple, Inc. Estimated from 2022 Daily Returns

> **Quick Check Question 3.6**
>
> To build you intuition about what beta means, consider whether each of the following firms is likely to have a relatively large beta (highly sensitive to market conditions) or a relatively small beta (insensitive to market conditions):
>
> (1) A fast food restaurant
> (2) An airline company
> (3) A funeral home company
> (4) A biotechnology company

Under CAPM, knowing a stock's beta allows an investor to determine how much of the Market Risk Premium to demand when investing in a stock. Holding a stock with a beta of 1 is equivalent to holding a market portfolio, so investors will demand the full market risk premium (which, as discussed previously, we assume is 6%–8% per year). Holding a stock with a beta of 0.5 means investors are exposed to half the market risk of a market portfolio, entitling investors to demand half of the market risk premium. We can therefore summarize the method for determining the cost of equity under CAPM as follows:

$$\textit{Cost of Equity} = \textit{Return}_{rf} + \beta \times \textit{Return}_{\textit{Market Premium}}$$

$\textit{Return}_{rf}$ is typically the risk-free rate on one-year treasury securities and $\textit{Return}_{\textit{Market Premium}}$ is the estimated market risk premium (e.g., 8%, not the total market return). Applying this formula to Apple and using a 4% risk-free rate and a 8% market risk premium, we would conclude that Apple's cost of equity is 4% + 1.31(8%), or 14.48% per year. In other words, according to CAPM, this is the annual return that investors expect from investing in Apple's common stock—at least assuming these are the correct numbers to use.

We shall return again to this assumption in a moment, but first, we must explore one remaining component of CAPM, which is why one should expect stock prices to adhere to this model. The answer has to do with several important assumptions inherent in CAPM. These include an assumption that markets are perfectly competitive, investors can borrow and lend at the risk-free rate, investors all share the same beliefs concerning the distribution of security returns, and investors seek to maximize expected returns while minimizing the variance of returns. Without getting too bogged down by the math, an important consequence of these assumptions is that investors will gravitate towards holding the market portfolio given the benefits of diversification. That is, the market portfolio will provide investors with the optimal trade-off between risk and return. But even the market portfolio has risk (i.e., volatility) that some investors might seek to avoid. Imagine, for example, a retiree who depends on portfolio income as his or her sole source of financial support. This investor probably wishes to avoid large swings in the value of her retirement account. Why would this investor be drawn to the market portfolio?

However, recall that CAPM assumes investors can easily invest at the risk-free rate, allowing them to allocate investments between a risky investment (such as in the market portfolio) and risk-free investments. For example, assume that the risk-free rate is 4% and that the market portfolio has an expected return of 10% per year and annual volatility of 15%. (We use these numbers to keep the math simple). This means that while the market portfolio is expected to increase 10% per year on average, we should expect that over the long-term, actual annual returns will range between –5% and 25%. That's a lot of risk for a retiree. On the other hand, our hypothetical investor could choose to allocate just a fraction of his or her savings into the market portfolio, investing the rest in risk-free treasuries. Consider, for instance, a set of possible portfolio allocations set forth in Table 3-6:

Table 3-6: Returns on Portfolios Containing Risk-Free Treasuries and the Market Portfolio

% Treasury Bonds	Rate of Return	% Market Portfolio	Rate of Return	Total Expected Return to "Blended" Portfolio	Volatility of "Blended" Portfolio*	Sharpe Ratio
99%	4%	1%	10%	4.06%	0.15%	0.4
75%	4%	25%	10%	5.50%	3.75%	0.4
50%	4%	50%	10%	7.00%	7.50%	0.4
25%	4%	75%	10%	8.50%	11.25%	0.4
0%	4%	100%	10%	10.00%	15.00%	0.4

Thus, our investor need not invest all of his or her savings in the market portfolio but can seek out returns in excess of the risk-free rate by investing just a fraction in the market portfolio, with the rest held in risk-free treasuries. Of course, returns will be lower than a 100% market portfolio, but so too will be the riskiness of the portfolio (in terms of volatility). Moreover, it turns out that for a given level of volatility, the returns from these "blended" portfolios will represent the best possible combination of risk and return. This is reflected in the final column where we present the *Sharpe Ratio* for each possible portfolio. The Sharpe Ratio is a way to capture the risk-reward tradeoff in a portfolio: the higher the ratio, the more return you receive for a given level of volatility.† The final row shows that the Sharpe Ratio is .4 for the portfolio where savings are placed 100% in the market portfolio. Because this portfolio maximizes the benefits of diversification, any Sharpe Ratio below this number means that investors are taking on too much risk for a given level of return. Thus, Table 3-6 shows that our hypothetical investor can perfectly calibrate his or her desired level of risk-reward by looking solely to the market portfolio and risk-free treasuries.

What about an investor who is willing to take on more risk in exchange for an expected return greater than 10%? The same conclusion

---

* The variance of a two-asset portfolio consisting of asset "a" and asset "b" is calculated as:

$$w^2_a\sigma^2_a + w^2_b\sigma^2_b + 2w_aw_bcov(a,b)$$

where w represents each asset's portfolio weight, σ^2 is each asset's variance (i.e., volatility squared), and cov(a,b) is the covariance of the two assets. The covariance of a risk-free treasury and the market portfolio is zero; therefore, the variance of the portfolios in Tables 3-6 and 3-7 is simply $w^2_a\sigma^2_a + w^2_b\sigma^2_b$. As noted previously, the volatility is the square root of the variance, or $(w^2_a\sigma^2_a + w^2_b\sigma^2_b)^{0.5}$.

† The Sharpe Ratio is calculated as: (Portfolio Return – Risk Free Rate)/(Portfolio volatility).

follows due to the assumption that investors can borrow freely at the risk-free rate. In particular, by borrowing funds, investors can "leverage" their investments in the market portfolio, and achieve returns that are even higher than those offered by it. For instance, if an investor can borrow at 4% and can obtain a 10% return if the funds are invested in the market portfolio, the 6% difference represents an increase in the total rate of return on the investor's own funds that are also invested in the market portfolio. Consider, for instance, the following five portfolios, starting with the simple "un-leveraged" portfolio where an investor invests only her own funds in the market portfolio:

Table 3-7:
Returns on Market Portfolios Using Investor's Own Funds + Borrowed Funds

% of Own Funds Invested in Market Portfolio	Rate of Return on Own Funds	% of Portfolio Invested with Borrowed Funds	Interest Rate	Interest Expense	Net Portfolio Return	Volatility of Leveraged Portfolio	Sharpe Ratio
100%	10%	0%	4%	0	10.00%	15.00%	0.4
125%	12.50%	25%	4%	1.00%	11.50%	18.75%	0.4
150%	15%	50%	4%	2.00%	13.00%	22.50%	0.4
175%	17.50%	75%	4%	3.00%	14.50%	26.25%	0.4
200%	20%	100%	4%	4.00%	16.00%	30.00%	0.4

Thus, our risk-seeking investor can achieve net returns in excess of the market portfolio by investing in the market with borrowed funds.* As with our risk-averse investor, the final column shows that all of these strategies have a Sharpe Ratio of .4; thus, this strategy will permit the investor to maximize the risk-reward tradeoff for any given level of expected returns.

* An investor must pay interest on any borrowed funds; therefore, the net return will be "Rate of Return on Own Funds" – "Interest Expense." In the final row, for instance, assume an investor invests $200 in the market portfolio, of which $100 comes from personal savings and $100 comes from borrowing at 4%. If the investor expects a 10% annual return from the market portfolio, this means the $200 portfolio is expected to grow by $20; however, the investor must pay interest of $4 at the end of one year. So the investor expects to net $16, or a 16% expected return on the original $100 of personal savings. However, expected volatility also increases by borrowing funds to make the $200 investment. Had the investor used only her $100 of personal savings, the 15% volatility of the market portfolio would mean that there was roughly a 68% chance she could see the portfolio grow from $100 to as much as $125 ($100 × (1 + (.1 + .15))) and to as low as $95 ($100 × (1 + (.1 – .15))) in one year. By investing $200 with $100 of borrowed funds, the 15% volatility of the market portfolio would mean that there was roughly a 68% chance she could see the $200 portfolio grow to as much as $250 ($200 × (1 + (.1 + .15))) and to as low as $190 ($200 × (1 + (.1 – .15))). After repaying $104 of principal and interest, the comparable range of *net* portfolio returns would therefore span from $146 (a 46% return on the $100 of savings) down to $86 (a −14% return on the $100 of savings). Thus, rather than the expected portfolio growth/loss being 15% above/below the 16% expected return for the leveraged portfolio, it would be 30% above/below the 16% expected return for this portfolio—that is, twice the volatility of the unleveraged portfolio.

The fundamental point is that under CAPM investors can have differing risk preferences and yet they will still invest solely in the market portfolio and risk-free securities. Moreover, if investors are only investing in the market portfolio, this tells us that an *individual* security will be priced exclusively by how much it contributes to the risk of the market portfolio. That is, a security whose price varies with the rest of the market portfolio adds more risk to the market portfolio, and it should compensate investors by paying more of the equity risk premium (Rm-Rf). Conversely, a security whose price does not move with the market portfolio adds less risk to the market portfolio and will pay less of the equity risk premium.*

We can now say something about how stock prices should be set according to CAPM. According to the CAPM, all investment assets should provide expected returns based on how much they contribute to the risk of the market portfolio (i.e., their betas). This concept is visually depicted in Figure 3-3 where we have drawn a line representing the expected return of an asset (the y-axis) as a function of its beta (the x-axis). We assume that the risk-free rate is 3% (which would be the expected return of an asset with a beta of zero) and that the market portfolio has an expected return of 11%, so the market premium is 11%–3%, or 8%. This visualization of the CAPM is referred to as the "Security Market Line" (SML). Now imagine a stock, such as that of Company B in Figure 3-3, with a beta of 1.0 that sits below the Security Market Line. That is, its expected return is insufficient to compensate investors for the market risk associated with Company B's stock. An investor could earn a better return for this amount of beta (market risk) by selling the stock and purchasing the market portfolio. Selling by enough investors will reduce the price of the stock until its return is equal to that of the market portfolio. If, on the other hand, one observed a stock having a beta of 1.0 that sat above the Security Market Line (e.g., shares of Company A), an investor should sell some of the market portfolio and buy the (temporarily) overperforming stock. Repeated purchases by traders should drive its price up to the point where its expected returns lie on the Security Market line.

---

* This is why beta is frequently defined as:

$$\beta = \frac{Cov(r_i,r_m)}{\sigma_m^2}$$

Where $Cov(r_i,r_m)$ is the covariance of the Returns of asset i with the returns of the market portfolio, and σ^2_m is the variance of the market portfolio. While the calculation of beta results in the same number obtained through regression, it underscores how CAPM sets individual security prices by reference to the relative marginal contribution of asset i to the risk of the market portfolio.

Figure 3-3

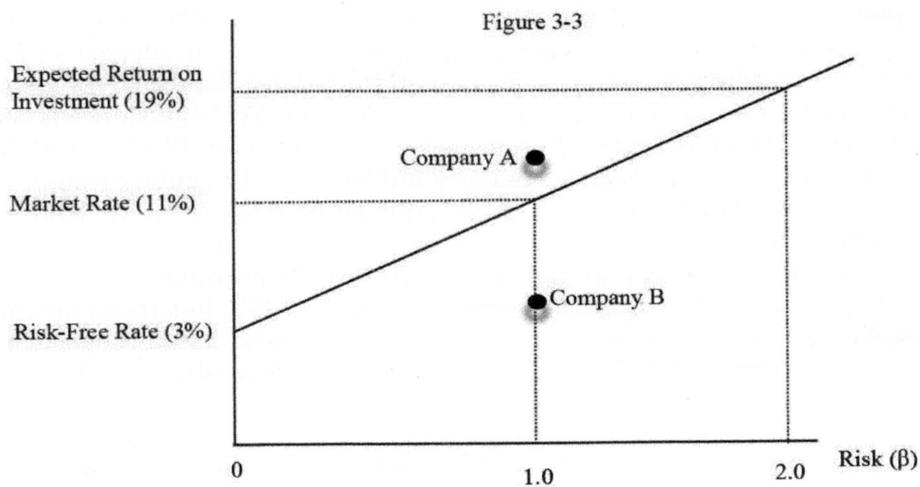

b. Limitations of CAPM

As a model, CAPM is elegant in its simplicity: The only risk that matters is a stock's exposure to market or systematic risk, as reflected in its beta. Perhaps because of its simplicity, it remains widely used in practice. As summarized in a leading treatise used by valuation experts, "[f]or more than 30 years, financial theorists generally have favored the notion that using the Capital Asset Pricing Model (CAPM) is the preferred method to estimate the cost of equity capital."*

But can a single factor (the correlation of a stock with the market portfolio) actually explain expected returns for *every* stock? Several early studies found a positive relationship between average stock returns and stocks' betas using data from 1926 through the late 1960s.† However, subsequent research in the 1980s found the relationship between beta and average returns had disappeared when using stock market data commencing with 1962.‡ Writing in 1992, famed financial economists Eugene Fama and Kenneth French found that "market beta seems to have no role in explaining the average returns on NYSE, AMEX, and NASDAQ stocks for 1963–1990. . ."§ They described this finding as "a shot straight at the heart of the [CAPM] model. . ."

Additionally, by the late 1970s, scholars had identified a number of empirical contradictions of the CAPM model. CAPM postulates that, not only is there a positive expected premium for beta, but that beta is the

* Shannon P. Pratt and Roger J. Grabowski, COST OF CAPITAL: APPLICATIONS AND EXAMPLES (3rd ed.).

† See, e.g., Fischer Black, Michael Jensen and Myron Scholes, *The Capital Asset Pricing Model: Some Empirical Tests*, STUDIES IN THE THEORY OF CAPITAL MARKETS (M. Jensen Ed., 1972).

‡ See, e.g., Marc. R. Reinganum, *A New Empirical Perspective on the CAPM*, 16 JOURNAL OF FINANCIAL AND QUANTITATIVE ANALYSIS 439 (1981).

§ Eugene F. Fama and Kenneth R. French, *The Cross-Section of Expected Stock Returns*, 47 JOURNAL OF FINANCE 427 (1992).

only factor needed to explain expected returns. Yet researchers discovered several market "anomalies" that seemed to suggest other factors might be driving stock returns. For instance, in 1981 Rolf Banz published a seminal paper documenting a "size effect."* Consider Figure 3-4, which plots the average excess returns between 1930 and 2000 (returns minus the 1-month Treasury bill rate) for 10 equally-weighted portfolios of all publicly-traded firms, grouped by size each year. That is, each year the largest 10% of firms are placed in the first portfolio and the smallest 10% of firms are placed in the tenth portfolio.† Note that portfolio returns for the largest firms sit on the SML, but those for the smaller firms sit above it. The reason stems from the fact that the returns for smaller company stocks were greater than those predicted by CAPM.

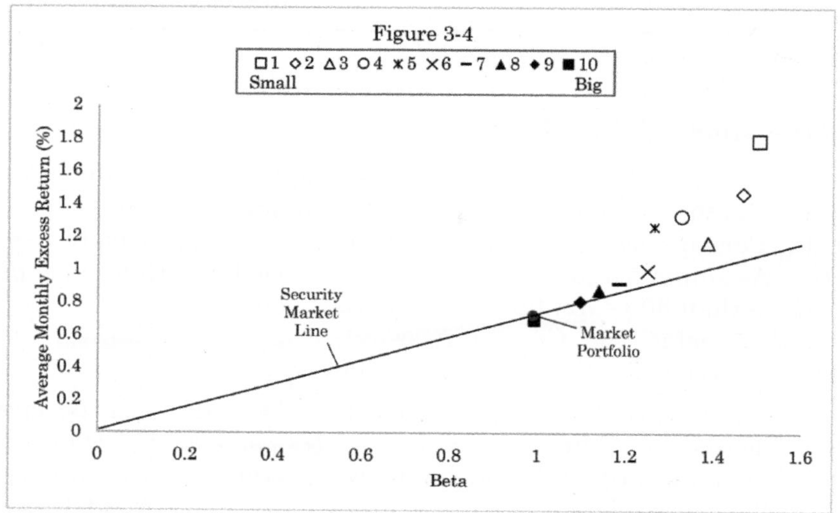

Researchers also discovered that the average returns on U.S. stocks are positively related to the ratio of a firm's book value of common equity to its market value.‡ Consider, for instance, Figure 3-5, which plots the average excess returns between 1930 and 2000 (returns minus the 1-month Treasury bill rate) for 10 equally-weighted portfolios of all publicly-traded firms, grouped each year by firms' book-to-market ratios.§ Stocks with high book-to-market ratios are often referred to as

---

* Rolf W. Banz, *The Relationship Between Return and Market Value of Common Stocks*, 9 JOURNAL OF FINANCIAL ECONOMICS 3 (1981).

† Portfolios were constructed using Ken French's dataset of Portfolios Formed on Size, available at https://mba.tuck.dartmouth.edu/pages/faculty/ken.french/data_library.html. The time period of the sample data is January 1931 through December 1999. The portfolios were constructed in June of each year.

‡ Dennis Stattman, *Book Values and Stock Returns*, 4 THE CHICAGO MBA: A JOURNAL OF SELECTED PAPERS 25 (1980); Barr Rosenberg, Kenneth Reid, and Ronald Lanstein, *Persuasive Evidence of Market Inefficiency*, 11 JOURNAL OF PORTFOLIO MANAGEMENT 9 (1985).

§ Portfolios were constructed using Ken French's dataset of Portfolios Formed on Book-to-Market, available at https://mba.tuck.dartmouth.edu/pages/faculty/ken.french/data_

"value stocks" since the market price of the firm's equity does not place a large premium over its book value. Figure 3-5 shows that "value" stocks earned excess returns relative to what CAPM would have predicted.

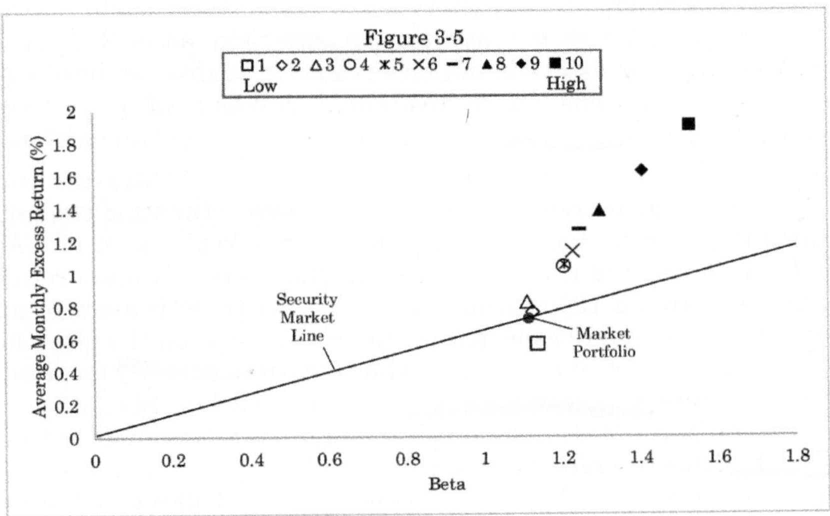

And these are not the only apparent anomalies. For example, Werner DeBondt and Richard Thaler found that stocks with low long-term past returns tend to have higher future returns, suggesting a stock's past performance was predictive of its future returns.* In a similar vein, Narasimhan Jegadeesh and Sheridan Titman found that the predictive effect of past-returns was the opposite for the *recent* past: short-term returns tend to continue in the near-term.† Specifically, stocks with higher returns in the previous twelve months tend to have higher current returns, while stocks that had low returns in the past twelve months continued to have lower current returns. Other studies have used empirical analysis to show that a firm's average stock return is related to its earnings/price (E/P) ratio,‡ its cash flow/price (C/P) ratio,§ and its past sales growth.** In combination, these anomalies point to one of two problems with CAPM: Either the market is inefficient in pricing

library.html. As in Figure 3-4, the time period of the sample data is January 1931 through December 1999. The portfolios were constructed in June of each year.

* Werner F. DeBondt and Richard Thaler, *Does the Stock Market Overreact?*, 40 JOURNAL OF FINANCE 793 (1985).

† Narasimhan Jegadeesh and Sheridan Titman, *Overreaction, Returns to Buying Winners and Selling Losers: Implications for Stock Market Efficiency*, 48 JOURNAL OF FINANCE 65 (1993).

‡ S. Basu, *Investment Performance of Common Stocks in Relation to Their Price Earnings Ratios: A Test of the Efficient Market Hypothesis*, 32 JOURNAL OF FINANCE 663 (1977).

§ Josef Lakonishok, Andrei Shleifer, and Robert Vishny, *Contrarian Investment, Extrapolation, and Risk*, 49 JOURNAL OF FINANCE 1541 (1994).

** *Id.*

securities according to beta, or CAPM does not accurately predict a security's future returns.

Even on its own terms, CAPM poses considerable estimation challenges. Consider the market risk premium. Technically, it should capture the market risk for investing in *any* risky asset, but this all-inclusive market for assets is not observable in reality. In practice, we therefore tend to focus on a diversified portfolio of public equity securities, such as the S&P500, which is a small subset of all risky assets.

Moreover, even assuming such a portfolio constitutes the correct proxy to use for the market price of risk, it raises estimation challenges. For instance, in introducing the concept of market risk in our Apple example, we presented it using the arithmetic average annual return to the S&P500 between 1950 through 2022. The arithmetic average might be a fair way to estimate expected future returns, but on the other hand, we know that if we are interested in what investors *actually* received, we need to compute geometric returns (see the earlier Sidebar in this chapter). The S&P500 is also a value-weighted index composed of the largest 500 firms, thereby adding potential bias from the excess weight given to larger stocks. Perhaps an equal-weighted index of the entire market of firms represents a better means to estimate the overall market return. Yet, at the same time, an equal-weighted portfolio gives identical weight to each company, and most companies are small- and mid-capitalization firms, implicating the small cap premium. And even if we stick with arithmetic returns for the S&P500, what time frame shall we use? For instance, extending the estimation to include the time period 1928–2022 reduces average annual returns from 12.6% to 11.5% owing to the Great Depression.

There are also alternative approaches to estimating the equity premium that avoid entirely the use of historical data. For instance, Robert Ibbotson and Peng Chen propose a "supply-side" model of the equity premium that assumes that stock market returns are generated by the performance of companies in the real economy. Thus, their estimates of the equity premium are derived from estimates of inflation, income return, growth in real earnings per share, and growth in the aggregated price/earnings (P/E) ratios.*

A similar set of challenges confront estimates of beta. In our example of calculating beta for Apple, we used the S&P500. But as with the equity premium, using this proxy for the market may introduce undesirable bias relative to other proxies. This is especially the case with Apple: As the world's largest company, it is not only included in the S&P500, but because the S&P500 is a value-weighted index, returns to Apple comprise nearly 4% of the S&P500's returns. Likewise, the beta of firms will change over time; for instance, for the calendar year 1981 (the year

* Roger G. Ibbotson and Peng Chen, *Long-Run Stock Returns: Participating in the Real Economy*, 59 FINANCIAL ANALYSTS JOURNAL 88 (2003).

following its IPO), we estimate beta for Apple to be 1.79 (37% higher than what we estimated for 2022). This shouldn't be too surprising, as firms can change their business models, but it calls into question the relevant estimation period to use when calculating a firm's beta.

We mention all of these issues merely to disabuse any readers from concluding that one can ever conclusively calculate the cost of equity with CAPM. Despite its widespread use, the empirical evidence suggests CAPM alone cannot explain equity returns. And even if one decides to use CAPM, one must confront a host of assumptions that can materially affect the estimated cost of equity.

ii. ALTERNATIVES TO CAPM: FACTOR MODELS

a. *Overview*

Given the empirical evidence against CAPM, it should hardly be surprising that alternative models for estimating a firm's cost of capital have been proposed within the asset pricing literature. Most notably, Stephen Ross and others have developed an alternative pricing model, called the Arbitrage Pricing Theory ("APT").* This theory argues that a security's expected returns depend on the security's exposure to specific macroeconomic factors that represent non-diversifiable risks. For example, these macroeconomic factors may include the spread in yields between long-term government bonds and short-term Treasury bills, the interest rate, the change in the value of the dollar compared to a market basket of other currencies, changes in forecasts of Gross National Product, and changes in forecasts of inflation.†

In many ways, APT is similar to CAPM insofar that APT assumes investors can demand a risk premium only for bearing risks that are non-diversifiable. CAPM is also similar to APT in that CAPM posits that a security's expected returns are a linear function of the security's exposure to a macroeconomic factor, represented by the returns to a market portfolio. However, APT is much more flexible in that it imposes no theoretical set of non-diversifiable factors as determining expected returns, but it is instead a multi-factor model. This can be seen in formally presenting the APT as follows:

$$E(r_i) = r_f + \beta_1 RP_1 + \beta_2 RP_2 + \cdots + \beta_n RP_n$$

As in CAPM, $E(r_i)$ is the expected return on security i and r_f is the risk-free rate of return. Each *"RP"* represents the return premium for a security's exposure to a specific risk-factor and each β represents the

* Stephen A. Ross, *The Arbitrage Theory of Capital Asset Pricing*, 13 JOURNAL OF ECONOMIC THEORY 341 (1976); Richard W. Roll and Stephen A. Ross, *The Arbitrage Pricing Theory Approach to Strategic Portfolio Planning*, 51 FINANCIAL ANALYSTS JOURNAL 122 (1995).

† These factors were not identified by Roll and Ross, but appear in E.J. Elton, M.J. Gruber and J. Mei, *Cost of Capital Using Arbitrage Pricing Theory: A Case Study of Nine New York Utilities*, 3 FINANCIAL MARKETS, INSTITUTIONS, AND INSTRUMENTS 46 (1994).

security's sensitivity to that risk-factor. Thus, if one were to believe that expected returns were entirely driven by exposure to the overall stock market, our model of expected returns would be the following:

$$E(r_i) = r_f + \beta_1(\textit{Risk Premium for Market Risk})$$

which is effectively the same model used to estimate expected returns in CAPM.

But if APT does not specify the systematic factors that affect expected returns, how do we know what they are? Under APT, we let the data tell us, which is why APT is largely an empirically-based model for expected returns. Imagine, for instance, that we postulated that all security returns are determined by the GDP Growth Rate and changes in the yield on 10-year treasuries. (It seems reasonable to believe that some securities may be more adversely affected by a slowdown in the overall economy as well as by changes in interest rates and that even diversified investors are exposed to these risks). Using various statistical techniques, we could then estimate how the returns to various diversified portfolios relate to changes in these two factors, as we did with Apple when illustrating the calculation of beta in CAPM.

An especially influential application of APT has been the multi-factor model of Eugene Fama and Kenneth French. As noted above, Fama and French found in their 1992 paper that CAPM betas seemed to have no role in explaining the average returns for stocks. In contrast, they found average returns were strongly related to two previously documented market anomalies. One was the finding that diversified stock portfolios consisting of smaller firms earned systematically higher returns than diversified portfolios consisting of large firms. The other was the finding that diversified stock portfolios consisting of firms with high book-to-market ratios (i.e., so-called "value" stocks) earned systematically higher returns than diversified portfolios consisting of firms with low book-to-market ratios (i.e., so-called "growth stocks"). (Each of these phenomena are presented visually in Figures 3-4 and 3-5, respectively). Fama and French found that these two factors—a firm's size and its book-to-market ratio—explained the cross-section of stock returns far more than a stock's beta. Moreover, they found that several other previously documented market anomalies (e.g., the documented finding that average stock returns were related to a firm's earnings/price ratio) disappeared once they accounted for the correlation of returns with a firm's size and its book-to-market ratio.*

In short, Fama and French's initial 1992 findings suggested that, while beta from CAPM was a poor predictor of average stock returns, the same could not be said of a firm's size and its book-to-market ratio. These two characteristics seemed to explain most of the variation in average

---

* Eugene Fama and Kenneth French, *The Cross-Section of Expected Stock Returns*, 47 JOURNAL OF FINANCE 427 (1992).

stock returns. The next step for Fama and French was to determine why these return premia should exist if our stock markets functioned in a rational manner. After all, a firm's size and its book-to-market ratio are both observable characteristics for firms. Why should investors demand excess returns for holding small stocks or stocks with high book-to-market ratios? Fama and French postulated that it must be because these firms posed higher risks even in diversified portfolios.* According to Fama and French, size is simply a proxy for profitability, as small firms tend to be less profitable than large firms, thus creating considerable volatility in their profitability and survival. Likewise, firms with high book-to-market ratios are firms having low market values (relative to their book values), signaling potential distress and enhanced volatility. While these explanations have not gone without objection, they nevertheless permitted Fama and French to pose a serious alternative to CAPM for estimating a firm's cost of capital.

How does one use the Fama and French model to select a discount rate? The method is closely related to how we estimated beta in the Apple example. That method entailed assessing the relationship between the daily return for bearing "market risk" (proxied by the daily return of a broadly diversified index, like the S&P500) (our x-axis) and the daily return to Apple's common stock (the y-axis). That relationship is what is captured by CAPM's beta, which we estimated to be 1.31. Based on this number, when the daily return to the S&P500 is 1%, we would expect Apple's stock to return to be a positive 1.31%.

Using similar logic, the Fama and French model seeks to estimate the extent to which a stock's daily return is a function of its exposure to the following: (a) the risk free rate to capture the time premium (as in CAPM), (b) the daily return to the overall market portfolio to capture a stock's exposure to market risk (as in CAPM), (c) the daily return to a portfolio of stocks exposed to "small company risk" (which they labeled an SMB portfolio), and (d) the daily return to a portfolio of stocks exposed to "value stock risk" (which they labeled an HML portfolio). The complete Fama-French model is then:

$$\textit{Excess Return}_{Stock} = \textit{Return}_{rf} + \beta \times \textit{Return}_{Market} + S \times \textit{Return}_{SMB} + H \times \textit{Return}_{HML}$$

Note that the first part of the model is identical to CAPM, including an estimate of beta. The fact that the Fama and French model includes three risk factors—a market risk factor (as in CAPM), an SMB factor and an

* Fama and French initially suggested that a firm's size and its book-to-market ratio could reflect risk factors in their 1992 study, *The Cross-Section of Expected Stock Returns*, 47 JOURNAL OF FINANCE 427 (1992). They formally tested this hypothesis in their subsequent paper, *Size and Book-to-Market Factors in Earnings and Returns*, 50 JOURNAL OF FINANCE 131 (1995).

HML factor—is why it is generally referred to as a the Fama-French Three Factor Model.*

Sidebar: Estimating the SMB and HML Risk Premiums

To estimate the SMB and the HML risk premiums, Fama and French constructed two diversified portfolios. The first, the Small-Minus-Big (SMB) portfolio, estimates the additional return (or the "size premium") that diversified investors have historically received by investing in stocks of companies with relatively small market capitalizations. The portfolio is reconstructed annually by investing in the smallest 30% of stocks and short selling the largest 30% of stocks, with the size of each stock (and therefore, its portfolio assignment) determined as of June in each year. (Short selling means an investor borrows a share of stock, immediately sells it, and then repurchases it in the future to return it to the lender, thus allowing an investor to profit from declining prices; we discuss this further in Chapter 8.) A positive SMB return in a month means that small cap stocks outperformed large cap stocks. The second portfolio, the High-Minus-Low (HML) portfolio, estimates the "value premium" provided to diversified investors for investing in companies with high book-to-market values. It is constructed each year in a similar fashion to SMB by investing in the top 50% of stocks ranked by book-to-market ratios as of June in each year, and short selling stocks in the bottom 50%. A positive HML return in a month means that value stocks outperformed growth stocks in that month.

Using the daily (or monthly) returns to SMB and HML, one can then use linear regression to estimate the relationships between changes in these returns and a stock's daily (or monthly) return, just as we did in calculating CAPM's beta. This method gives us slope coefficients for the SMB and HML factors, which we label *S* and *H*, respectively, in the presentation of the Fama-French model. The final step is determining what SMB premium and what HML premium to apply for purposes of estimating future returns. (Recall that in CAPM we determined Apple's cost of capital by multiplying 1.31 by the assumed market risk premium of 8%). As was the case with CAPM, there are varying approaches, but the historical averages of the SMB and HML returns are often used. For instance, data from Ken French's website indicates that the historical average from 1927 through 2022 of the annual SMB factor

---

* Given Fama and French's 1992 paper showing that beta does not explain average returns, one might wonder why they include a market risk factor at all. However, Fama and French subsequently determined that beta has strong explanatory power for the difference in returns between the average returns to stocks and the risk-free rate. See Eugene Fama and Kenneth French, *Common Risk Factors in the Returns on Stocks and Bonds*, 33 JOURNAL OF FINANCIAL ECONOMICS 3 (1993). In other words, beta is very relevant for explaining excess returns, or returns in excess of the risk-free rate. This is why in practice beta and the coefficient estimates for SMB and HML are all estimated by simultaneously regressing a firm's excess returns (e.g., its daily return less the risk-free rate) on the market return, the return to the SMB portfolio, and the return to the HML portfolio.

was approximately 2.92%. The historical average for the annual HML factor for the same time period was 4.47%.*

*(Professor French's data repository can be found at https://mba.tuck.dartmouth.edu/pages/faculty/ken.french/data_library.html.

The Fama-French model has been extraordinarily influential in how we think about what determines a firm's cost of capital, but it would be a mistake to conclude that it constitutes the final chapter on the subject. On the contrary, Fama and French themselves conceded that even their model could not explain all observed instances where particular stocks appeared to earn returns that were not captured by their three-factor model. The most notable of these was the short-term "momentum anomaly" documented in 1993 by Jegadeesh and Titman. As we mentioned above, these authors found that stocks that had positive returns within the past twelve months tended to have positive current returns. Conversely, stocks that had negative returns within the past twelve months tended to have negative current returns.

As with a stock's size or its book-to-market ratio, these findings were a puzzle. If one could determine whether a stock would be a "winner" or a "loser" simply by looking at its recent returns, shouldn't investors pile into those stocks that had strong returns over the past twelve months? And shouldn't investors sell the recent losers? In either case, this trading behavior should drive stock prices up for winners and down for losers, eliminating the phenomenon. Yet it seemed to persist. Were recent "winners" somehow riskier, as reflected in their higher near term returns? Or were these securities simply mispriced by an irrational market?

There is no widely accepted explanation for why recent winners might represent more volatile, risky investments. Nonetheless, in the mid-1990s Mark Carhart, then a doctoral student of Eugene Fama's at the University of Chicago, sought to add a fourth factor to the three-factor model to capture the excess returns to recent winning stocks.* By adding this momentum factor (which he labeled PR1YR) to the original Fama-French three factor model, this Fama-French-Carhart model estimates a stock's expected return as a function of its association with the risk-free rate, the market factor, the SMB factor, the HML factor and the "momentum factor":

* To estimate the momentum factor, Carhart used historical stock prices to construct diversified portfolios of stocks for each month that consisted of stocks having the highest 30 percent returns over the past twelve months, while shorting stocks having the lowest 30% returns over the same time period. Like the SMB and HML portfolios, the returns for this new portfolio, which he called PR1YR (for prior year's returns), estimate the "momentum premium" provided to diversified investors for investing in stocks having high stock returns over the past year.

$$Excess\ Return_{Stock} = Return_{rf} + \beta \times Return_{Market} + S \times Return_{SMB} + H \times Return_{HML} + M \times Return_{PR1YR}$$

Since Carhart published his findings in 1997, the Fama-French three factor and the Fama-French-Carhart four factor models have been the primary multi-factor models used in the academic literature to analyze stock prices. However, even with the addition of a momentum factor, pricing anomalies persist, suggesting that stock returns (and thus, a firm's cost of capital) remain dependent on other factors. This has led to an assortment of competing factor models as researchers search for better and better explanations for why stocks act the way they do. Indeed, recent years have witnessed a proliferation of competing factor models; one paper counts 59 new factors in various models between 2010 and 2012 alone![*]

b. *Limitations of Factor Models*

As the preceding section indicates, the emergence of factor models has revolutionized the field of asset pricing. It has also spawned an array of "factor based" investment funds that are focused on exploiting the return premia identified by these factor-based models.[†] Notwithstanding their significant influence, however, factor-based models suffer from several limitations when they are used to estimate a firm's cost of capital.

First, as empirically driven models, factor-based models are only as reliable as the empirical findings that support them. What are we to make of a factor-based model if it loses explanatory power? Indeed, one might even expect these models to lose explanatory power over time.

Consider, for instance, the size premium. As noted previously, this anomaly was initially identified in a 1981 research paper by Rolf Banz. If, as Banz documented, investing in small cap stocks provides diversified investors with a means to achieve additional return without significantly adding more risk, shouldn't investors start buying more small cap stocks after 1981? And if so, wouldn't this drive up the price of small cap stocks, thereby reducing their expected returns and consequently, the historical small cap premium? It turns out that the empirical evidence suggests this may very well have occurred. For example, one study suggests that the small-firm anomaly disappeared shortly after the initial publication

---

* Campbell R. Harvey, Yan Leu, and Heqing Zhu, . . .*and the Cross-Section of Expected Returns*, 29 REVIEW OF FINANCIAL STUDIES 5 (2016).

† One of the most notable proponents of factor-based investing is AQR Capital (short for "Applied Quantitative Research") which has been led, since it was founded in 1998, by Cliff Asness, a former PhD student of Eugene Fama. Factor based investment funds (or "Smart Beta" funds, as they are also known) are today offered by virtually all major asset management firms. Vanguard, for instance, provides an assortment of mutual funds and ETFs having varying exposures to "value" and "momentum", as well as other factors that have been identified in the academic literature. See https://investor.vanguard.com/etf/factor-funds.

of the papers that discovered it, coinciding with an explosion of small cap-based funds and indices.*

Our ability to rely on empirical evidence supporting a factor model is also complicated by the possibilities of model misspecification and data mining. Model misspecification refers to a situation where the results of an empirical model are unreliable because the model itself suffers from some defect, such as the omission of an important variable. For instance, by including a momentum factor, one can view the Fama-French-Carhart four factor model as "fixing" the model misspecification of the Fama-French three factor model. By analogy, the problem with discarding a small cap premium based on its apparent disappearance is that perhaps there *is* a small cap premium, but existing factors models have inaccurately captured it.†

Efforts to find a better calibrated empirical factor model also have a potential dark side: the risk of atheoretical data mining. In 2018, Fama and French summarized this risk in discussing a new 5-factor model that they had introduced in 2015. Their new 5-factor model omitted any reference to the momentum factor, and Fama and French observed that many practitioners were reluctant to give up using the momentum factor. Accordingly, Fama and French added a momentum factor to their 5-factor model making it a 6-factor model. They noted:

> We include momentum factors (somewhat reluctantly) now to satisfy insistent popular demand. We worry, however, that opening the game to factors that seem empirically robust but lack theoretical motivation has a destructive downside: the end of discipline that produces parsimonious models and the beginning of a dark age of data dredging that produces a long list of factors with little hope of sifting through them in a statistically reliable way.‡

In short, factor models are supposed to explain how assets are priced based on their exposure to specific risk factors. Adding more variables like momentum might help empirically explain asset prices, but is there a theoretical reason to believe it represents a *risk* factor? Absent theory, Fama and French rightfully note the enhanced risk that a new factor model is simply the result of data mining.

In addition to uncertainty over *which* factors matter, there is also uncertainty about the correct return premium to use when using a factor

---

* William G. Schwert, *Anomalies and Market Efficiency*, THE HANDBOOK OF THE ECONOMICS OF FINANCE 937–972 (G. Constantinides, et al. eds. 2003).

† This is precisely the punchline of a 2018 paper by Cliff Asness and others. They find that "no reliable size premium is evident" over the period 1957–2012 if one simply controls for a stock's exposure to HML and momentum. Cliff Asness et al., *Size Matters, If You Control Your Junk*, 129 JOURNAL OF FINANCIAL ECONOMICS 479 (2018). However, they find that among "high quality" stocks, there is a large and persistent size premium. This finding leads Asness to advocate for including a "quality" factor to the Fama-French three factor model.

‡ Eugene Fama and Kenneth French, *Choosing Factors*, 128 JOURNAL OF FINANCIAL ECONOMICS 234 (2018).

model to estimate a firm's cost of capital. Recall that this was also an issue with CAPM insofar that scholars and valuation experts differ on what risk premium to use. While we may assume a market risk premium of 6–8% based on historical returns to equity, the truth is that we can't actually observe the risk premium diversified investors demand for being exposed to market risk; we have to rely on noisy proxies. The same problem applies to estimating the premium diversified investors demand for being exposed to a risk factor such as HML or SMB. Indeed, while Fama and French initially speculated in 1993 that their new three factor model could "be used to estimate the expected return on a firm's securities, for purposes of judging its cost of capital,"* their subsequent research called this possibility into question. In seeking to estimate the average cost of capital across industries, they found that uncertainty about the true risk premium led to extremely noisy estimates when they tried to use their model (as well as CAPM) to estimate an industry's cost of capital. Or in their words, "[e]stimates of the cost of equity are distressingly imprecise."†

Finally, an especially important limitation of all factor models is their fundamental assumption about market efficiency—an assumption that is commonly referred to as the Efficient Capital Markets Hypothesis (ECMH). Indeed, this assumption also goes to the heart of CAPM. Why is the ECMH so central to asset pricing models? Recall that all of the models we have discussed share a common belief that investors price securities based on their exposure to non-diversifiable risk. It is this belief that allows scholars to say things like "*Wow! The historical returns on high book-to-market stocks are higher than the returns on low book-to-market stocks. This must mean high book-to-market stocks are riskier*!" But is this the only conclusion one could draw from observing this empirical relationship? Not at all. So-called "value" stocks could be just that—under-valued and cheap, thus leading to their high returns as the market corrects itself. And the poor returns to growth stocks could likewise represent the market over-pricing these securities, which would likewise result in these stocks having lower future returns. Indeed, many might say this was exactly what happened during the Internet bubble of 1999–2000. Every factor model necessarily assumes that the market doesn't tend to make systematic mistakes in pricing securities and is capable of evaluating the risk profile of each security as well as estimating future cash flows.

How realistic is this assumption? A large literature in finance suggests that, on the whole, it generally holds up in deep, highly liquid capital markets such as those represented by U.S. stock exchanges. This is especially true for large capitalization firms. Stocks in these companies

* Eugene Fama and Kenneth French, *Common Risk Factors in the Returns on Stocks and Bonds*, 33 JOURNAL OF FINANCIAL ECONOMICS 3, 54 (1993).

† Eugene Fama and Kenneth French, *Industry Costs of Equity*, 43 JOURNAL OF FINANCIAL ECONOMICS 153 (1997).

are subject to mandatory periodic disclosure obligations imposed by the SEC and are typically followed closely by research analysts, investors, and financial journalists. Moreover, a host of empirical studies document that when these firms release market-moving news—such as an earnings announcement, an M&A transaction, or a stock dividend—the stock price adjusts virtually instantaneously, consistent with "the market" pricing all publicly disclosed information.

The same, however, cannot be said of certain other markets. For instance, over-the-counter stocks and bonds may be issued by firms that are exempt from the mandatory disclosure obligations imposed by U.S. securities regulations. Likewise, few (if any) research analysts may study these securities. Not surprisingly, the empirical evidence gives us less reason to believe that markets are continuously pricing these securities to account for their risk profile and accurately estimating their future cash flows. Moreover, even markets that are typically efficient at processing information—such as the market for securities listed on U.S. stock exchanges—can experience episodes of apparent mispricing. Examples include the May 6, 2010 "Flash Crash," the mispricing of risk within financial firms prior to the Financial Crisis, and many other phenomena. For instance, the small cap premium appears largely in the month of January and then disappears for the remainder of the year. Does this fact reflect small cap firms being exposed to higher risk in this particular month? Or does it relate to some other behavioral characteristic of investors? The difficulty of refuting either possibility is why such phenomenon are simply referred to as "anomalies" by those who study asset prices.

We shall return again to the important role played by ECMH in valuation in Section 4(C). For now, we simply note that factor models assume efficient markets, but markets probably vary in the degree to which they efficiently incorporate public information into stock prices. This simple fact has two important implications for those who seek to use a factor model or CAPM to estimate a firm's cost of capital.

First, empirical evidence showing that a particular model fails to explain returns does not necessarily mean the model is inaccurate. Consider, for instance, the original Fama-French three factor model's inability to explain the momentum anomaly (i.e., returns from last year's "winners" were associated with next year's winners.) If one assumes the market is efficient, the fact that last year's winners tend to have expected returns that exceed those predicted by the 3-factor model forces one to conclude that the model is flawed and needs to be "fixed" by adding a risk factor for momentum. On the other hand, if one relaxes the assumption that markets are efficient, this leads to an alternative interpretation: the model is correct but the market is not very efficient. For instance, if stock prices only react partially to good news, then the announcement of good news will induce strong stock performance initially as well as in the ensuing several months. If this is the case, accounting for momentum in a firm's cost of equity would be inappropriate since it would reflect market inefficiencies and not compensation that investors demand for bearing non-diversifiable risk. To this day, a debate continues about whether momentum returns are due to investor under-reaction or market compensation for bearing some form of systematic risk.*

Second, the possibility that markets can be inefficient also has implications for whether it is appropriate to adopt any particular factor model just because it can explain historical returns. This is simply an extension of the previous point. For instance, use of the Fama-French three factor model is generally justified on the basis that it accounts for the compensation investors demand for holding value stocks and small stocks, based on the historical evidence. But as noted previously, what if this historical evidence is simply picking up a behavioral anomaly unrelated to a stock's systematic risk? We noted previously that the size effect is concentrated almost entirely in the month of January. This empirical finding remains a puzzle, but one possible explanation involves tax incentives for retail investors. One study, for instance, has argued that small cap investors tend to sell losing stocks in December to capture tax losses and then reinvest the proceeds after the New Year, augmented by cash infusions from year-end bonuses.† The theory remains contested, but it highlights the assumption made when using a multi-factor model: The markets are efficient, so the return premium observed on a particular factor must therefore reflect compensation investors demand for bearing risk. Ultimately, however, it is exceptionally difficult to know whether a model that fails to predict returns suffers from some missing factor (i.e., *market are efficient but we just forgot something*) or whether the results have been distorted by an irrational moment in the trading markets.

For practical purposes, the takeaway message from this should be clear: Whenever you use a factor model, you are assuming that the return premium for a factor reflects compensation for bearing non-diversifiable risk and not some other feature of market inefficiency.

iii. ALTERNATIVES TO CAPM AND FACTOR MODELS: INDUSTRY MODELS

We round out this discussion of equity discount rates by summarizing a final cluster of alternative approaches. In practice, survey evidence indicates that the CAPM remains the dominant method used by investment banking professionals to estimate a firm's cost of capital in corporate finance transactions as well as by chief financial officers (CFOs) in making capital budgeting decisions.‡ Yet alternative "industry"

---

* For a summary of the contending explanations, see Narasimhan Jegadeesh and Sheridan Titman, *Momentum*, 3 ANNUAL REVIEW OF FINANCIAL ECONOMICS 493 (2011).

† Jay Ritter, *The Buying and Selling Behavior of Individual Investors at the Turn of the Year*, 43 JOURNAL OF FINANCE 701 (1988).

‡ Robert F. Bruner et al., *Best Practices in Estimating the Cost of Capital: Survey and Synthesis* 8 FINANCIAL PRACTICE AND EDUCATION 13, 17 (1998) (reporting that 80% of advisers

approaches have also emerged, particularly among valuation experts working with smaller, private firms (e.g., a private family-run firm may need to be valued as part of the family's estate planning process). Surprisingly, these latter approaches are often at odds with the vast finance literature that we have just surveyed, making us hesitant to describe them as "alternatives" at all. However, because lawyers are commonly tasked with identifying a valuation expert in certain settings, it is important to consider these other approaches as well. If nothing else, this discussion will underscore how much these industry models often contradict basic principles of finance.

One especially popular industry approach, known as the "build-up method,"* estimates the cost of equity as the sum of the following components:

$$Return_{equity} = R_f + RP_m + RP_s + RP_u$$

R_f is the risk-free rate, and RP_m represents the "general equity risk premium." Similar to CAPM, this equity premium represents the compensation investors demand for investing in equities rather than risk-free assets. However, contrary to CAPM, it is a fixed rate of return (e.g., 5%) imposed on every equity security and is based on the historical rate of return paid on equity securities over U.S. treasury obligations. The third variable RP_s is a size premium that is also added to the risk-free rate and is based on the size of the company under investigation. Note that while this concept is similar in spirit to the small cap premium estimated by the Fama-French three factor model, the build-up model determines the size of RP_s solely from the size of the company. More specifically, using the historical return premia that firms of similar sizes have returned over the predicted return estimates from CAPM, a valuation expert would simply use this excess return as the RP_s for *every* firm of that size. A Fama-French model, in contrast, would estimate the premium by first running a regression to estimate the association of a particular stock with SMB, and then use this estimate to determine the percentage of the small cap premium to attribute to the stock. In short, two small firms of the same size could have different small cap premiums under the Fama-French model.

Finally, and most problematically, the build-up model includes RP_u, which represents, according to one leading treatise, the "[r]isk premium attributable to the specific company or to the industry."† If this concept sounds similar to firm-specific or non-systematic risk, it's because it is—

surveyed use CAPM to calculate the cost of equity); John R. Graham & Campbell R. Harvey, *The Theory and Practice of Corporate Finance: Evidence from the Field*, 60 JOURNAL OF FINANCIAL ECONOMICS 187, 201 (2001) (73.5% of respondents in a survey of CFOs always or almost always use the CAPM).

* See Shannon P. Pratt & Roger J. Grabowski, COST OF CAPITAL: APPLICATIONS AND EXAMPLES Ch. 7 (3rd ed. 2008).

† *Id.*

as the same authors note "the *u* stands for unsystematic risk."* The company-specific premium is left to the discretion of the analyst, based on her subjective perception of the company's general riskiness according to a multitude of factors. The justification given for using the build-up approach, instead of the CAPM, is that the assumptions underlying the CAPM do not hold for small owner-managed companies whose owners are undiversified and exposed to company-specific risks. Despite the intuitive appeal of this argument, the build-up model provides no theory as to how undiversified an owner must be before a premium might be warranted, nor does it provide empirical evidence for the size of this premium. On the contrary, empirical finance research provides evidence against the existence of company-specific risk premia in the real world, even for undiversified investors. For instance, even for small private companies where lack of diversification is a valid concern, the available evidence suggests that returns to the owners of small private companies are no larger than returns generated by their public-company counterparts.†

To be sure, these industry valuation guides also provide instruction for utilizing CAPM. Yet even here, they continue to depart from conventional practice, adopting what one practitioner calls a "modified CAPM."‡ Like the build-up method, this modified CAPM includes a blunt size premium for smaller companies based purely on their size, such that every firm in a particular size category receives the same premium. It also provides for a discretionary, company specific risk factor, thus contradicting a foundational principle undergirding the CAPM itself.

Despite their inconsistency with academic research, these industry models are nevertheless used in some valuation proceedings. And they are not just limited to valuations of private, family-run firms for intra-family estate planning. One study, for instance, documents their use in Chapter 11 bankruptcy proceedings and finds judges approving company-specific risk premia as large as 10%.§ Likewise, the following case demonstrates their use by experts in an appraisal lawsuit arising in the context of a merger of two firms. As the case illustrates, however, relying on an expert who uses an "industry" model to estimate a firm's cost of capital can raise serious reliability and admissibility issues.

---

* *Id.*

† See Tobias J. Moskowitz & Annette Vissing-Jorgensen, *The Returns to Entrepreneurial Investment: A Private Equity Premium Puzzle?*, 92 AMERICAN ECONOMIC REVIEW 745 (2002).

‡ See Shannon Pratt and Alina Niculita, VALUING A BUSINESS: THE ANALYSIS AND APPRAISAL OF CLOSELY HELD COMPANIES 193 (5th ed. 2008).

§ Kenneth Ayotte and Edward Morrison, *Valuation Disputes in Corporate Bankruptcy*, 166 UNIVERSITY OF PENNSYLVANIA LAW REVIEW 1819 (2018).

In re Appraisal of the Orchard Enterprises, Inc.

2012 WL 2923305 (Del. Ch. 2012)

■ STRINE, CHANCELLOR.

I. *Introduction*

This is the post-trial decision in an appraisal arising out of a merger in which the common stockholders of The Orchard Enterprises, Inc. were cashed out at a price of $2.05 per share by Orchard's controlling stockholder, Dimensional Associates, LLC (the "Going Private Merger" or the "Merger"). [Eds. In an appraisal action, a court must determine the fair value of the shares of a firm that was acquired in an all cash transaction, exclusive of any value arising from the acquisition; we discuss appraisal proceedings in Section 5 of this Chapter.] Relying upon a discounted cash flow ("DCF") analysis, the petitioners, who together owned 604,122 shares of Orchard's common stock, claim that each Orchard common share was worth $5.42 as of the date of the Going Private Merger. By contrast, the respondent Orchard contends that the Merger price was generous and that Orchard common shares were worth only $1.53 a piece as of the date of the Merger.

* * *

The largest disagreement between the parties over DCF value is over the discount rate to use. Each side's expert used three different methods to come to a discount rate. Two of these methods are versions of the so-called "build-up" model. The build-up model is a method larded with subjectivity, and it incorporates elements that are not accepted by the mainstream of corporate finance scholars. By contrast, the third method each of the experts used is based on the capital asset pricing model ("CAPM") that remains the accepted model for valuating [sic] corporations. The experts used a modified CAPM method that takes into account academic acceptance that the size of a corporation affects the expected rate of return and should be factored into the calculation of a corporation's discount rate.

II. *Factual Background*

A. *Orchard's Business And Capital Structure Before The Merger With Dimensional*

Orchard primarily makes money from the retail sale (through digital stores such as Amazon and iTunes) and other forms of exploitation of its controlled, licensed music catalogue, which includes artists ranging from the rapper Pitbull to jazz musician Wynton Marsalis. As of 2010, this core business made up 90% of Orchard's total revenue, with the other revenue coming from the distribution of other digital content. Until Dimensional, a private equity investor, cashed out Orchard's common stockholders in the Going Private Merger, Orchard was traded on the NASDAQ.

[Eds. As is customary in appraisal proceedings, the court had to assess the value of Orchard's shares based on conflicting valuation reports submitted by two expert witnesses. Timothy Meinhart served as expert for the plaintiff shareholders; Robert Fesnak served as expert for Orchard. After resolving a conflict between these experts over which cash flows to use in the valuation analysis, the court then turned to a dispute over the proper discount rate to apply to these cash flows.]

b. *Discount Rate*

Both experts calculated a cost of equity for Orchard using three different methods: CAPM, the build-up rate model, and the Duff & Phelps Risk Premium Report model. The latter two methods are related, with the Duff & Phelps model being a variation of the build-up rate model.

I am uncomfortable using the latter two methods for a few reasons. I begin with the important one that the build-up model is not, in my view, well accepted by mainstream corporate finance theory as a proper way to come up with a discount rate. Indeed, its components involve a great deal of subjectivity and expressly incorporate company-specific risk as a component of the discount rate. This is at odds with the CAPM, which excludes company-specific risk from inclusion in the discount rate, on the grounds that only market risk should be taken into account because investors can diversify away company-specific risk. Relatedly, corporate finance theory suggests that concern about the achievability of the company's business plan and thus its generation of cash flows should be taken into account by adjustments to the cash flow projections, and not by adjusting the discount rate. The build-up model, however, allows for a variety of risks to be poured into the discount rate, including so-called projection risk and other factors.

Because of these factors, this court has been at best ambivalent about indulging the use of the build-up method, and has preferred the more academically and empirically-driven CAPM model when that can be applied responsibly. In contrast to the build-up model, which has not gained acceptance among distinguished academicians in the area of corporate finance, the CAPM method is generally accepted, involves less (but still more than comfortable) amounts of subjectivity, and should be used where it can be deployed responsibly. In deploying that method, this court has taken into account, as it will here, evolving views of the academy and market players regarding its appropriate application. For example, both parties here accept the evolving view that the returns to the firm are influenced by size and that a size premium is therefore appropriate to take into account in calculating the discount rate. This court has done so on prior occasions too, and will do so here.

There is another reason I choose not to deploy the two versions of the build-up method. Ultimately, I am coming up with one cost of capital. Formulas can be useful, but when they are used simply to make a discretionary human judgment about a debatable subject [they] seem to have a false precision, [and] they are obscurantist, obfuscating, and less of an aid to clear thinking than a way of dissembling about what the real reason for the outcome is. For example, in this case, Meinhart came up with a 15.3% discount rate using the CAPM method, a 16.5% discount rate using the Duff & Phelps method, and a 16.1% discount rate using the build-up method, and then chose a discount rate of 16% for use in his DCF analysis. Meanwhile, Fesnak came up with a 17.8% discount rate using the CAPM method, a 19.5% discount rate using the Duff & Phelps method, and a 21.1% discount rate using the build-up method, and then chose a discount rate of 20% for use in his DCF analysis. In each case, why did the experts choose their ultimate discount rates? I still don't really know and I have read the reports and listened to the testimony.

As a law-trained judge who has to come up with a valuation deploying the learning of the field of corporate finance, I choose to deploy one accepted method as well as I am able, given the record before me and my own abilities. Even if one were to conclude that there are multiple ways to come up with a discount rate, that does not mean that one should use them all at one time and then blend them together. Marc Vetri, Mario Batali, and Lidia Bastianich all make a mean marinara sauce. Is the best way to serve a good meal to your guest to cook up each chef's recipe and then pour them into a single huge pot? Or is it to make the hard choice among the recipes and follow the chosen one as faithfully as a home cook can? This home cook will follow the one recipe approach and use the recipe endorsed by Brealey, Myers and Allen and the mainstream of corporate finance theory taught in our leading academic institutions, *i.e.*, the CAPM method.

Under CAPM, the cost of equity is calculated as follows: Cost of Equity = $r_f + ß * (r_m - r_f)$, where r_f is the risk-free rate of return, ß is the beta of the company, which measures the risk and volatility of the company's securities relative to the overall market portfolio, and r_m-r_f is the equity risk premium, or risk differential between investment in a particular company and investment in a diversified stock portfolio. A size premium is a generally acceptable addition to the CAPM formula in the valuation of smaller companies to account for the higher rate of return that investors demand as compensation for the greater risk associated with small company equity. As noted, both parties agree that a size factor should be considered in applying the CAPM method to Orchard, based on empirical evidence regarding the performance of stocks of different market capitalizations.

Because the experts largely agree on the components of their CAPM estimates of the discount rate,[116] I focus only on the areas of disagreement, which are: (i) whether a historical or supply-side equity risk premium should be used; (ii) whether a 1% company-specific risk premium should be added to the CAPM; and (iii) whether the 6.3% size premium added to the CAPM by both experts should be adjusted if the

---

116 The experts agree that the appropriate risk-free rate of return at the time of the Merger was 3.9%. They also agree on an industry beta of 1.0.

supply-side equity risk premium is used instead of the historical equity risk premium.

I address these issues in turn.

i. Equity Risk Premium

Fesnak calculated a discount rate under a modified CAPM using the historical equity risk premium of 6.7% published in the 2010 Ibbotson SBBI Valuation Yearbook (the "Ibbotson Yearbook"). Meinhart relied on the Ibbotson Yearbook's supply-side equity risk premium of 5.2%. Ibbotson's historical equity risk premium is generated using historical market returns from 1926 to the relevant valuation date. Ibbotson's supply-side equity risk premium uses the same historical data, but separates the components of the equity risk premium into those attributable to a stock's price-to-earnings ratio and those attributable to a stock's expected earnings growth, excluding the former and including the latter. This is because the supply-side premium assumes that actual equity returns will track real earnings growth, not the growth reflected in the price-to-earnings ratio.

Meinhart's use of a 5.2% equity risk premium has substantial support in professional and academic valuation literature. I recently reviewed this literature and addressed the choice between the historical equity risk premium and the supply-side equity risk premium in *Global GT LP v. Golden Telecom, Inc.*[123] In *Golden Telecom,* although recognizing that the historical equity risk premium is the more traditional estimate, I concluded that the academic community has shifted toward greater support for equity risk premium estimates that are closer to the supply-side rate published by Ibbotson. I therefore determined that using an equity risk premium based on Ibbotson's supply-side rate in my DCF valuation of the subject company was appropriate. I noted that when academics and experts have "mined additional data and pondered the reliability of past practice and come, by a healthy weight of reasoned opinion, to believe that a different practice should become the norm, this court's duty is to recognize that practice if, in the court's lay estimate, the practice is the most reliable available for use in an appraisal." . . . . Orchard has not provided me with a persuasive reason to revisit the supply-side versus historical equity risk premium debate. I therefore find that the Ibbotson Yearbook's supply-side equity risk premium of 5.2% is an appropriate metric to be applied in valuing Orchard under the CAPM.

ii. Company-Specific Risk Premium

Fesnak included a 1% company-specific risk premium in his calculation of the discount rate under the CAPM "to account for the specific risks facing Orchard that were not otherwise captured within the other components of the cost of capital." Although Meinhart indicated in his report that a company-specific risk premium, if appropriate, is part

[123] 993 A.2d 497 (Del. Ch.2010), aff'd, 11 A.3d 214 (Del.2010).

of a modified CAPM, he concluded that addition of this factor is inappropriate here. I do not believe that a company-specific risk premium should be used in a CAPM calculation of a discount rate, especially in a case like this.

A company-specific risk premium is not an addition to the CAPM that is accepted by corporate finance scholars, but is sometimes added to the discount rate by practitioners valuing a company to reflect that the company has risk factors that they believe have not already been captured by the equity risk premium as modified by beta and (if applicable) the small company size premium. "Pure proponents of the CAPM argue that only systemic risk as measured by beta is relevant to the cost of capital and that company-specific risks should be addressed by appropriate revisions in cash-flow estimates."

More generally, for a corporation that operates primarily in the United States and where there are sound projections, the calculation of a CAPM discount rate should not include company-specific risk for the obvious reason that it is inconsistent with the very theory on which the model is based. If there are concerns about projection risk because the projections were generated by an inexperienced management team, the company's track record is such that estimating future performance is difficult even for an experienced management team, or projections seem[] to be infected with a bias, it would be better for the expert to directly express his skepticism by adjusting the available projections directly in some way, to make plain his reasoning. Admittedly, this would involve as much subjectivity as heaping on to the discount rate, but it would also force more rigor and clarity about the expert's concern. Here, where management under the control of Dimensional came up with various scenarios and Orchard's expert gave overwhelming weight to management's base case scenario, no extra discounting is warranted and the CAPM method should be applied on its own terms, and not be infected by an ingredient from the build-up method.

Moreover, this is not an appraisal action in which the respondent's expert is given management-prepared projections that he believes are inaccurate. Fesnak, whose firm was hired by the special committee as its financial advisor in the Going Private Merger, had his hands deep in the dough of the projections used in the fairness opinion and then in his valuation report, and I accept his 90–10 weighting of the base case and aggressive case scenarios. Fesnak gave the following reasons for his addition of a company-specific risk premium: (i) Orchard's "ability to achieve revenue levels and profitability as forecasted;" (ii) Orchard's "ability to capitalize on its business strategy;" and (iii) "the impact on [Orchard] of the general economic recession." These are risk factors that Orchard management presumably considered at the time of the Merger, with Fesnak's participation, and thus Fesnak's argument that the cash flow projections must be further adjusted by an addition to the discount rate is even weaker than it might be had he had no access to management at the time the projections were made.

In terms of projection risk, I suppose I can see the rough utility of "stress testing" projections when they are from an unreliable source. No doubt private equity and venture capital firms use hurdle rates to see how far off the projections of unproven managers can be for an investment to still make sense. Having no way to directly adjust the cash flows in the manner that some standard valuation treatises suggest is proper (but do not explain how to do), some market participants no doubt use the discount rate as a crude way of applying a doubt factor to the projections. In this way, they are "discounting", but not coming up with a discount rate in a way consistent with CAPM. Rather, they are conflating what is being discounted with the discount rate.

Although I have some sympathy with this short-cut (*i.e.*, a "heuristic" to academics), there is no justification for it here. Orchard had experienced management who were under the control of Dimensional. There is no reason to think the projections used by Fesnak [were] biased, except in a way that favors his client. Fesnak chose to give almost no weight to the aggressive case, and 90% weight to the base case. Fesnak therefore dealt with projection risk already through weighting the projections. As the petitioners' expert Meinhart pointed out at trial, the addition of a 1% company-specific risk premium to Fesnak's CAPM analysis double counts Orchard's risks of failing to achieve projections that are already included in Fesnak's probability weighting of the different scenarios, and the appropriate way to deal with company-specific risk would be to weight the cash flows differently. Fesnak's larding onto the discount rate was simply a form of additional discounting that he did not justify as warranted.

Furthermore, Fesnak explained in his expert report that his addition of the company-specific risk premium was in part attributable to the "company-specific" risk factor for the state of the general economy. How this general risk has a worse effect on Orchard than on all other market participants is not clear to me and provides no basis in my view for an addition to the discount rate. More fundamentally, this is again a risk that should be reflected in the estimated cash flows, not heaped into a CAPM discount rate. It has no place there.

For these reasons, Orchard has failed to convince me of the appropriateness of the company-specific risk premium used by Fesnak in his valuation of the company. I therefore reject Fesnak's addition of 1% to the discount rate under the CAPM.

iii. Size Premium

Meinhart and Fesnak relied upon the same size premium of 6.3% in their respective CAPM calculations of Orchard's cost of capital, which is the size premium for the broader 10th decile published in the 2010 Ibbotson Yearbook. A size premium is an accepted part of CAPM because there is evidence in empirical returns that investors demand a premium for the extra risk of smaller companies. The petitioners describe the 6.3% premium as, if anything, too high, and Orchard argues it is conservative and is not justified if other inputs to the CAPM are modified, such as the equity risk premium.

The Ibbotson Yearbook divides the stock returns of public companies into deciles by size, measured by the aggregate market value of the companies' common equity. The smaller the company, the greater the excess return over the basic realized returns. The 10th decile encompasses companies with a market capitalization of approximately $1 million to $214 million, and is further broken down into sub deciles. The parties agree that Orchard technically falls into sub decile 10z, which includes companies with a market capitalization of $1 to $76.1 million. The Ibbotson Yearbook size premium for sub decile 10z is 12.06%, which is nearly twice the size premium chosen by the parties' experts. But, a rote application of the 12.06% premium to Orchard is improper because the 10z sub decile includes troubled companies to which Orchard, which is debt free, is not truly comparable. The Ibbotson Yearbook does not exclude speculative or distressed companies whose market capitalization is small because they are speculative or distressed. Before one uses the size premium data for 10z, one needs to determine if the mix of companies that comprise that sub decile are in fact comparable to the subject company. Both Meinhart and Fesnak concluded that a size premium as high as 12.06% was inappropriate for Orchard. Meinhart explained at trial that he was cautious to use the 10z sub decile because doing so would "run the risk of including companies in there that may be going through financial distress or other situations that may, in fact, skew [the] size premium numbers."

Rather than making the argument that Orchard's cost of capital should include an adjustment to the size premium for the broader 10th decile to account for Orchard's being among the smallest companies in that decile, Orchard merely asserts that the size premium of 6.3%, albeit adopted by Fesnak, should be increased in the event that the court does not adopt the rest of Fesnak's inputs to the CAPM. Specifically, Orchard uses Fesnak's application of a conservative size premium as a back-door way to argue in favor of using a historical, rather than supply-side, equity risk premium. Orchard claims that using the supply-side equity risk premium with the Ibbotson Yearbook's size premium understates the cost of capital, and a supply-side equity risk premium must therefore "be offset by [ ] a higher size premium." In support of this argument, Orchard cites to an article by James Hitchner which suggests that use of the Ibbotson Yearbook's supply-side equity risk premium mandates an upward adjustment to the size premium employed in valuation. Specifically, Hitchner writes:

> [The Ibbotson Yearbook's] size premiums . . . take the actual return of that decile over a period . . ., and then they subtract the expected

return calculated using the [CAPM]. . . . However, . . . [Ibbotson's] size premium data is not calculated using the supply side equity risk premium. It's calculated using the [historical] equity risk premium, so you have a little bit of 'apples and oranges.' It would be nice if [Ibbotson] could start publishing supply side size premiums, but currently, they don't. If the expected return using supply side is less, which it would be when using a smaller equity risk premium, mathematics would dictate that the size premium itself would go up because the 'in excess' of CAPM would be higher. As such, much of the decrease in the return due to using the [supply side equity risk premium] would be offset by a higher size premium.[153]

Orchard's citation to this article fails to convince me that the size premium must be adjusted if a supply-side, rather than historical equity risk premium is used, for reasons explained in a source cited by the petitioners. Shannon Pratt and Roger Grabowski explain in their valuation treatise *Cost of Capital: Applications and Examples* that the Ibbotson size premium data should not be adjusted if the supply-side equity risk premium is used because "[i]f one believes that economic factors not expected to recur caused the returns on the broad market to be higher than one would have expected, then the returns of stocks comprising all deciles were probably influenced by the same factors."[154] The use of a size premium with the CAPM model is already a nod in Orchards direction, and Orchard has not persuaded me that simply because I use the supply-side equity risk premium, I should add more to the size premium.[155] By adding a hefty 6.3% into the CAPM formula for size, Orchard is treated fairly in my view, even though I acknowledge that academic and practitioner thinking this area seems to be in a period of active evolution.

IV. *Conclusion*

For the reasons I have explained, I accept the financial projections used in Fesnak's fairness opinion and disclosed in Orchard's Schedule 13E, without the changes to the tax rate proposed by Fesnak in his valuation report. . . . After modifying these inputs to Fesnak's model, I applied a discount rate of 15.3% and arrived at a value of $4.67 per share for Orchard as of the date of the Going Private Merger. . . .

IT IS SO ORDERED.

---

153 James R. Hitchner, *Cost of Capital Insights,* FINANCIAL VALUATION AND LITIGATION EXPERT, Issue 12, Apr./May 2008).

154 Shannon P. Pratt & Roger J. Grabowski, COST OF CAPITAL: APPLICATIONS AND EXAMPLES 239 (4th ed.2010).

155 It is conceivable that I might have added 1% to the size premium because of where Orchard falls in the broader 10th decile. An addition of 1% to the size premium for the broader 10th decile might have been a justifiable way to account for Orchard's small size without equating the company with the distressed and speculative companies in the 10z category. But, Fesnak did not argue that this factor justified his addition for company-specific risk in his report, which is where it should have been.

NOTES

1. *Modified CAPM.* The Chancery Court's rejection of the build-up model in favor of the plaintiff's modified CAPM model appears rooted in a desire to stay true to the academic asset pricing literature. In the words of the Court, "[i]n contrast to the build-up model, which has not gained acceptance among distinguished academicians in the area of corporate finance, the CAPM method is generally accepted, involves less (but still more than comfortable) amounts of subjectivity, and should be used where it can be deployed responsibly." The expert report submitted by the plaintiff's expert Timothy J. Meinhart reveals that his "modified CAPM" took the following form:

$$K_e = R_f + [\beta * E_{RP}] + S_{RP} + \alpha$$

In the equation, R_f is the risk-free rate, E_{RP} is the equity risk premium, S_{RP} is a small company premium and α is an "Unsystematic equity risk premium" to compensate for company-specific risks. Meinhart declined to use a company-specific risk factor since expected cash flows were based on the "probability-weighted projected net cash flows that were prepared by Company management." Using an industry publication that summarized average and median betas for different industries, he used a beta of 1.0 based on "(1) the median unlevered beta of the guideline publicly traded companies and (2) industry beta data for companies in [the industry classified by] SIC 7379." Based on this information, how faithful is the modified CAPM to the academic literature?

2. *Accounting for a Size Premium.* Both experts agreed to apply a small size premium of 6.3% to the discount rate used for Orchard Enterprises. This discount rate was obtained from the widely used *Ibbotson Valuation Yearbook*, which estimates a size premium to apply to firms that fall within different size deciles according to their market capitalizations. As noted in the opinion, 6.3% is the size premium for the 10th size decile of firms. Consider whether this, too, is faithful to the empirical findings of a small size premium incorporated in the Fama-French three factor model. As discussed previously, the Fama-French model assumes firms can vary in their exposure to the small company risk factor proxied by *SMB*. In Figure 3-6, for instance, we estimate the regression coefficient for SMB for the stocks of the approximately 600 publicly-traded firms falling within the 10th size decile in March 2010—the month in which the Orchard Enterprises transaction was announced.* Is this distribution consistent with the idea that all firms of a similar size should have a uniform size premium applied to their cost of equity?

* We estimated SMB using monthly returns between March 2008 and March 2010. For presentation purposes, we exclude in Figure 3-6 any firms where the estimate of SMB was greater than 5 or less than −5.

Figure 3-6
Coefficient on SMB for All Firms in Size Decile 10 As of March 30, 2010

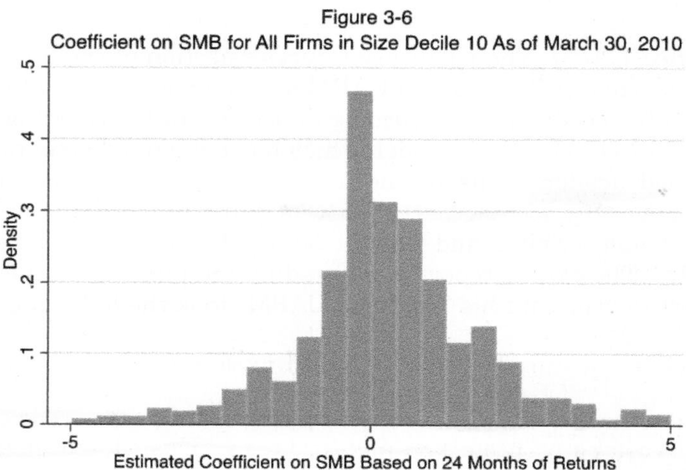

iv. ESTIMATING THE COST OF DEBT

We previously defined the cost of debt as follows:

Cost of Debt = Time Premium + Default Premium + Non-Diversifiable Risk Premium

As a formal matter, one could estimate the cost of debt as we did with the cost of equity by taking the sum of the three component parts listed above. You may recall that we took this approach when we calculated the cost of debt for a hypothetical one-year, zero-coupon bond promising $100,000 in one-year's time. The note had a 50% default rate and a time premium of 3%. Based on these two parameters, we calculated the cost of debt at 106%.

In the example, we assumed that risk was fully diversifiable, in part because we had yet to cover how to estimate the risk premium for non-diversifiable risk. Having now covered these methods, we could seek to estimate the third component of the cost of debt—the risk premium for bearing non-diversifiable risk. To the extent the debt is publicly traded, for instance, we might seek to estimate its beta using CAPM. Alternatively, if we had an estimate for the time premium and the default premium, we could infer the risk premium by looking at the trading price.

Example: Inferring Risk Premiums

Assume that a zero-coupon bond has the following payoff scenarios: the probability of receiving full payment of $210 in one year is 95%, the probability of receiving $100 is 4%, and the probability of receiving absolutely no payment is 1%. Time-equivalent Treasuries offer a rate of return of 5%. The bond is trading today at $187.50. What is the time premium, the default premium, and the risk premium?

Answer. The expected payoff is \$203.50 (= 210 * 95% + 100 * 4% + 0 * 1%). The promised payoff is \$210, and the stated price is \$187.50. Thus, while the quoted rate of return is 12% (\$210/\$187.50 – 1), the expected rate of return (net of default risk) is \$203.50/\$187.50 – 1 = 8.53%. Given that the time premium (the Treasury rate) is 5%, the risk premium is 3.53% (= 8.53% – 5%). The remaining 3.47% (= 12% – 8.53%) is the default premium.

In practice, a firm's cost of debt is estimated directly rather than "assembled" piece by piece as we do with the cost of equity from a model like CAPM. For publicly-traded bonds, this technique is made possible by the fact that the market price of bonds provides an estimate of the present value of the bond's cash flows, which are specified in the bond contract. Imagine, for instance, that we observe a bond that trades today at \$877 and promises to pay \$100 in interest over the following two years, along with a principal payment of \$1000 at the end of year 2. Assuming the markets are efficient, we can estimate the cost of debt (r) for this bond by using the present value formula:

$$\$877 = \frac{\$100}{(1+r)^1} + \frac{\$1{,}100}{(1+r)^2}$$

Solving for r yields 17.84%. This is known as the yield-to-maturity, or the overall cost of debt reflected by the market price.* In short, 17.84% is overall cost of debt (i.e., the left-hand side of the equation at the beginning of this section), but we don't necessarily know how much of this reflects the time premium vs. the default premium vs. the non-diversifiable risk premium.

When a company does not have traded debt, an alternative approach is to estimate the cost of debt based on the yield-to-maturities of other firms having a similar default risk. This is made possible by the fact that major credit rating agencies such as Standard & Poor's and Moody's periodically publish the average yield-to-maturity on firms having different credit ratings. So if you know, for example, that CryptoX has an "A" credit rating, then you might look to published estimates for yield-to-maturities at other A-rated firms to obtain an estimate of CryptoX's cost of debt.

Finally, if a firm has issued secured bank debt and has a low risk of default, the cost of debt is often assumed to be the existing interest rate

---

* In Excel, we can estimate r using the IRR formula by entering in a range of cells (here, we use A1:A4):

–877
100
1100
=IRR(A1:A4)

This calculation will solve for r in the equation above, giving us an answer of 17.84%.

that is payable on the debt. Note that taking this approach assumes the interest rate negotiated at the commencement of the loan agreement fully reflects the cost of debt over the life of the loan. For fixed rate debt, such an assumption may be highly questionable, particularly if the company's credit profile has changed since the loan was issued.

Theoretically, calculating the cost of debt as the observed rate of return demanded by debt investors—e.g., using the yield-to-maturity or the stated interest rate on floating rate loans—overstates the forward-looking cost of debt because of default risk. In an ideal world, we would calculate the cost of debt by estimating the discount rate applied by the market to expected returns, net of default risk. The problem raised by risky debt is that only the promised yield is observable, leaving us with an estimated cost of debt that conflates the default premium with the compensation investors demand for investing in an issuer's debt securities. Naturally, this issue becomes material only where a firm has a non-trivial risk of default.

v. WEIGHTED AVERAGE COST OF CAPITAL

We conclude this discussion of calculating discount rates with a discussion of the Weighted Average Cost of Capital. In general, the Weighted Average Cost of Capital (or WACC) is the discount rate a company uses when estimating the present value of a new investment or when estimating the value of the company itself. Often, it is simply referred to as a company's overall cost of capital. As we shall see, the WACC requires the ability to estimate a company's cost of equity and its cost of debt and constitutes one of the most important concepts in valuation. Think of it as a balanced r for the entire firm.

To understand the relevance of a company's WACC, recall our discussion in Section 2(C)(iv) where we introduced the concept of capital budgeting. In the example used there, a pharmaceutical company sought to determine whether to invest in a new drug line that would require three investments: $1 million today, $200,000 in one year, and $300,000 in two years. We further expected the project to generate $3,500,000 after five years when the company sold the product line. The manager's task was to determine the net present value of the project and thus whether it would be an acceptable investment. If the NPV were positive, then the firm should take the project; a negative number, however, would suggest that the firm should pass on the idea. Recall that we used a 20% discount rate. In so doing, we assumed that 20% was the company's cost of capital and, therefore, its WACC.

More specifically, we noted that we were using this 20% rate because this was the rate of return that the company's investors expected from the business. As a result, any new investments in existing business activities would need to produce this return (or more) to keep these investors happy. This is a critical concept to understand, so it's worth exploring it in a bit more detail. However, to keep things simple, let's assume our manager is now choosing to invest just \$100 in one of two alternative projects. Each project has the same risk profile as the company's existing business, but the projects have different expected payoffs which will occur in exactly 1 year:

Project	Investment Cost Today	Total Expected Payout in 1 Year	Rate of Return
A	\$100	\$117	\$117/100 – 1 = 17%
B	\$100	\$121	\$121/100 – 1 = 21%

Which one of these projects will keep the firm's investors happy? If the investors are expecting at least a 20% rate of return from the company's pharmaceutical business, Project B will do the trick. By using 20% as a discount rate, the manager assures herself that when taking on a positive net present value investment in the company's business, she will be accepting projects that will keep her investors happy. To illustrate, consider the implications of calculating the net present value of the two projects with the correct discount rate (20%, as shown in the first column) and two incorrect discount rates (15% and 30%, the second and third columns, respectively):

Project	NPV using 20% Discount Rate	NPV using 15% Discount Rate	NPV using 30% Discount Rate
A	(\$117/1.2) – \$100 = –\$2.5	(\$117/1.15) – \$100 = \$1.74	\$117/1.3 – \$100 = –\$10
B	(\$121/1.2) – \$100 = \$0.83	(\$121/1.15) – \$100 = \$5.21	\$121/1.3 – \$100 = –\$6.92

As shown in the second column, using an incorrect discount rate of 15% produces a net present value for Project A that is too high, making the project look more valuable than it is given its risk profile. At the same time, the third column shows that using a discount rate that is too high poses the risk of making Project B look undesirable as reflected in the NPV of –\$6.92. Yet Project B would actually create value and be perfectly acceptable to the company's investors given that it is expected to produce a 21% return. Using the right discount rate leads to a straightforward decision rule: accept projects with a positive NPV and reject those with a negative NPV.

How does one determine a company's cost of capital in the real world? The short answer is that we look to the rate of return that investors expect to receive for investing in the company's overall business. The simplest case is where a company has financed itself entirely by issuing common stock, as illustrated in Figure 3-7:

Figure 3-7. All Equity Firm

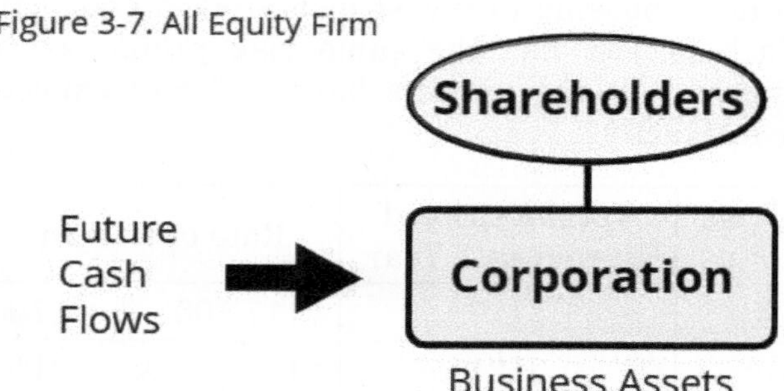

In such a setting, shareholders have the only legal claim to the cash flows arising from the company's business. Investing in a share of this company is therefore equivalent to investing directly in a pro-rata share of the company's business projects and its future cash flows. Indeed, but for the legal construct of the corporation, investors effectively own the underlying business assets. If markets are efficient, the rate of return that shareholders expect from each share will therefore reflect the rate of return shareholders expect from holding a pro rata share in the company's underlying business. The logic is as follows:

Value of business	=	Aggregate value of stock
Risk of business	=	Risk of stock
Rate of return on business	=	Rate of return on stock
Investors' required return from business	=	Investors' required return from stock

We now have another application for estimating a company's return on equity (e.g., by using CAPM): it allows us to estimate the rate of return investors expect for investing in the underlying business of an all equity firm. This same r is also the expected rate of return that investors will require on new investments that do not change the overall risk of the company's cash flows.

Self Check: Estimating the Cost of Capital for an All Equity Firm

The Newell Soup Company manufactures and sells a variety of soups in retail grocery outlets around the world. Its beta is 1.2, and it has no outstanding debt. Newell is considering an expansion of its operations by investing in a new soup factory. If the risk-free rate is 3% and the market risk premium is 6%, what discount rate should the company use to evaluate the NPV of this proposed investment?

In contrast to Figure 3-7, most companies issue debt as well as equity, as illustrated in Figure 3-8. Note that adding the bank as a claimant on the company's assets has no effect on the company's underlying business or its future cash flows. We shall explore this reasoning in more detail in the following chapter. But for now, you should view the addition of a lender as simply requiring the company's future cash flows to be shared among the company's shareholders and its debt investor (i.e., the bank).

Figure 3-8. Debt and Equity Financing

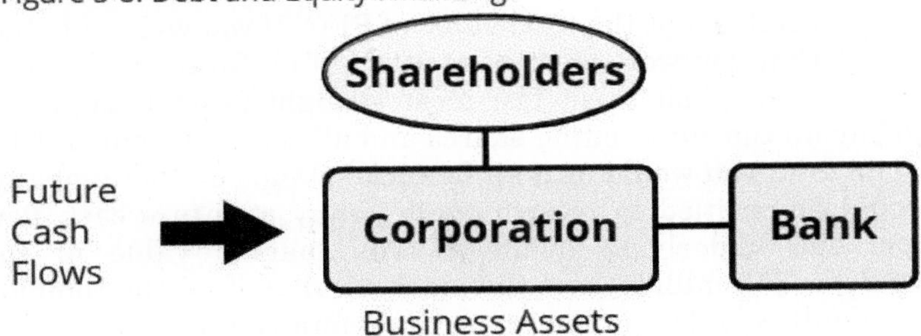

As we know, lenders also demand a return on investment based on the investment risk posed by the business. Of course, their ability to be paid first in the event of distress makes debt investments less risky, resulting in a lower expected return relative to a company's equity investors. Nevertheless, the expected returns on debt and the expected returns on equity both reflect the compensation or payments that investors require for investing in the company's business.* So as in the case of an all-equity company, it should be possible to infer the company's cost of capital by combining these returns. This is the concept of a company's WACC: It is a way of estimating a company's current cost of capital in light of the fact that different types of investors will demand different rates of return from the company. From a manager's perspective, one can view the WACC as answering the question "*What rate of return must the underlying business produce each year to keep all of a company's investors content?*"

For a company that has both debt and equity investors, calculating the WACC requires just a small amount of arithmetic, assuming we can estimate the cost of equity and the cost of debt. We'll illustrate with a simple example and, to avoid complications, let's ignore for now the fact that corporations have to pay income tax. (We'll add the effect of taxes later).

> *Example*: Imagine you are a manager at Performance Electronics Corporation (PEC), a manufacturer of consumer home products. PEC generates all cash flows from the sale of consumer products manufactured at a factory located in

* Technically speaking, the cost of debt includes a default premium, which is not compensation to investors. Nonetheless, a company must pay the default premium along with the other components of the cost of debt to keep its investors content, thus making it part of the gross expected returns expected by debtholders.

Columbus, Ohio. To finance itself, PEC has issued long-term bonds with a market value of $50 million, and they currently yield 9%. It also has 4 million shares of common stock outstanding, which trade for $10 each. At this price, the shares offer an expected return of 18%. What is PEC's WACC?

To derive the WACC we need to take an average of the cost of debt and the cost of equity, weighted by the fractions of the company that consist of debt and equity, respectively. How do we determine these fractions? First, think about the total value of PEC. If you wanted to buy the company so that you were entitled to 100% of all future cash flows, how could you accomplish this? The most straight-forward approach would be to buy all the outstanding shares and all the outstanding debt. If you could do that, you would own all financial claims on the company, and you would be entitled to receive every penny of future cash flow arising from the underlying business. The market value of the outstanding debt ($50 million) and the market value of all the common stock ($10 × 4 million = $40 million) must therefore be the total value of the firm. This gives us our denominator for calculating the fraction of the firm that consists of debt and equity.

Security	Market Value	Fraction of the Firm:
Debt	$50 million	50/90 = 55.6%
Equity	$40 million	40/90 = 44.4%
Total:	$90 million	100%

Recall that the cost of debt is 9% and the cost of equity is 18% per year. Using these figures, we can now calculate the average, weighted by the share of the company comprised of debt and equity, respectively:

$$(55.6\% \times 9\%) + (44.4\% \times 18\%) = 13\%$$

The WACC of PEC is therefore 13%. It is the rate of return that PEC must generate on business activities to satisfy both equity and debt investors. We can even check our math. Recall that the company's equity has a current market value of $40 million, and equity investors expect a return of 18% per year. This means these investors are expecting the equity component of the company to return annually $7.2 million ($40 million × 18%). Meanwhile, the company's debt has a market value of $50 million, and the debt yields 9% per year, which is the amount the company must return to its debtholders each year. With $50 million of outstanding debt, that translates to $4.5 million per year ($50 million × 9%). In total, the company's business therefore needs to return a total of $11.7 million. As noted above, the company's aggregate value is $90 million; therefore, if the company's business returns $11.7 million, that would be a return of exactly 13% ($11.7 million / $90 million).

Sidebar: Using Market vs. Book Values for WACC

You undoubtedly noticed that in calculating the WACC for PEC we used the market values of the company's equity and debt, rather than book values (which the problem did not specify). We did this because the cost of capital for a company must be based on what investors are actually willing to pay for the company's outstanding securities. This calculation requires an assessment of market values. Recall that market value usually differs from the book value of equity and debt that is recorded on a firm's balance sheet. This is because the book value of equity has a historical perspective; it reflects funds raised in the past from shareholders or reinvested by the firm on their behalf. If a company has positive future growth prospects, the market value of equity should be much higher than book value. Discount rates are used to evaluate *future* cash flows, which are reflected in market values—not book values. In calculating WACC, it is important to always use the market values of outstanding securities.

Having illustrated how to calculate a company's WACC in a world without taxes, let's return to the real world where corporate cash flows are subject to taxes. Taxes are relevant in calculating WACC because interest payments can usually be deducted from income before corporate taxes are calculated. Consequently, the cost to the company of an interest payment is reduced by the amount of this tax saving.

For example, let's assume the corporate tax rate for PEC is 35%. Each year, the company must make a 9% interest payment to the company's debt holders, but this payment also reduces PEC's profits, which reduces PEC's tax liability. So the actual amount of money the company needs to generate from its business to keep its investors content is less than if it had to pay taxes on 100% of its income. Imagine, for instance, that PEC has $10 million in earnings before interest and taxes (EBIT). In Table 3-8, we present two scenarios. In the first scenario, PEC must pay debt holders 9% interest on a $50 million loan (or $4.5 million per year). In the second scenario, PEC has no debt outstanding, so its stockholders are entitled to 100% of the company's cash flow after taxes. Which one results in the company having a larger amount of cash flow to pay to *all* of its investors?

**Table 3-8:
Cash Flows to PEC's Investors**

	PEC (with debt)	PEC (with no debt)
EBIT	$10.0	$10.0
Interest Expense	$4.5	0.0
Taxable Income	$5.5	$10.0

Taxes Owed (@35% tax rate)	$1.925	$3.5
Net income to equity investors	$3.575	$6.5
Total income to ALL Investors (debt and equity)	$8.075	$6.5

As shown in the table, the scenario in which PEC relies on debt financing results in more cash flow to its investors. Why? By shielding some of the company's EBIT from taxes, the company has more of its EBIT left over to distribute to its investors. In particular, the $4.5 million of interest payments means that $4.5 million of EBIT will be exempt from the 35% tax rate, putting an additional $1.575 million in the pockets of the company's investors. This is why interest payments are often referred to in finance as "tax shields." (Note that this example assumes that the entire interest tax shield can be used in the current year; we'll revisit this concept, along with some legal limits on interest deductibility, in the next chapter when we explore how a firm determines the optimal mix of equity and debt financing.) This also means that the company doesn't have to generate as much EBIT each year to meet the return expectations of its investors, thus lowering the company's WACC. We account for the effect of interest payments in lowering WACC in this way by using the after-tax cost of debt in the WACC formula:

After-tax cost of debt = pretax cost of debt x (1 – tax rate)
= 9% x (1 – .35)
= 5.85%

We now have everything we need to calculate a company's WACC, which is given in the following formula:

$$WACC = \left[\frac{D}{V} \times (1 - T_c) \times r_{debt}\right] + \left[\frac{E}{V} \times r_{equity}\right]$$

D/V and E/V represent the fraction of the firm comprised of equity and debt, respectively, using market values as shown previously. T_c is the corporate tax rate. And r_{debt} and r_{equity} are the costs of debt and equity, respectively. Applying this formula to PEC and assuming a 35% tax rate, the WACC for PEC would be:

$$11.25\% = \left[\frac{50}{90} \times (1 - .35) \times 9\%\right] + \left[\frac{40}{90} \times 18\%\right]$$

Sidebar: What if There Are More than Two Sources of Financing?

In our example, PEC had only two sources of financing: equity and debt. But what if a company has additional sources of financing, such as preferred stock? In such cases, the calculation of WACC proceeds along the same lines that we have discussed: you simply calculate the weighted-average after-tax return of each security that is outstanding. For example, suppose PEC also has some preferred stock. As we shall see, preferred stock often shares many characteristics of fixed-income securities like bonds insofar that it may pay out a stream of annual dividends that are fixed at a specific annual rate (e.g., \$0.08/share). Like any investment, investors will price preferred stock by discounting future cash flows at the required rate of return. What would be the WACC for PEC if it had outstanding preferred stock that had an aggregate market value of \$10 million and preferred stock investors demanded an annual return of 12%? (Assume that the market value of common stock and the market value of debt remain \$40 million and \$50 million, respectively.) We simply expand our WACC formula to account for the fact that there are now three types of investors that can claim the future cash flows from PEC's business:

$$11.33\% = \left[\frac{50}{100} \times (1 - .35) \times 9\%\right] + \left[\frac{40}{100} \times 18\%\right] + \left[\frac{10}{100} \times 12\%\right]$$

Now that we understand how to calculate the WACC for PEC, we close this section by pulling everything together with an extended problem. Assume that PEC is offered an opportunity to expand its production capacities by opening another factory in nearby Cincinnati. The company's managers expect the new factory to cost \$30 million (immediately), and it will generate revenue of \$10 million per year with operating expenses of \$4 million per year. Assume these cash flows occur at the end of each year (commencing exactly one year after the \$30 million expenditure) and will last forever. Is this a good use of corporate funds?

The central task is to determine whether the expected cash flows from this investment have a present value of at least \$30 million. We first estimate expected future after-tax cash flows:

Revenue	\$10.0
Less Operating Expenses	(\$4.0)
Pretax operating cash flow	\$6.0
Less Taxes (@35% tax rate)	(\$2.1)
After-tax cash flow	\$3.9

Again, these cash flows are expected to occur in perpetuity. Note that they are calculated on an after-tax basis as if the company had no debt payments to make. Why did we do that if we know the company has outstanding debt? The answer is that capital budgeting analysis forecasts revenues, costs, and taxes as if projects are financed entirely with equity; any interest tax shields are accounted for by using the after-tax cost of debt in the WACC.

Having calculated the after-tax perpetual cash flows from the project, we know that we can estimate their present value by using the formula for valuing a perpetuity:

$$\text{Present Value of a Perpetuity} = \frac{\text{Annual Payment}}{\text{Discount Rate}}$$

If \$3.9 million is the annual payment, what discount rate should we use? Note that this is a project that would expand the company's *existing* assets. As such, we can use the company's existing after-tax WACC of 11.25% as the relevant discount rate since it reflects investors' expected returns to PEC's overall business.

$$\$34.67 \text{ million} = \frac{\$3.9 \text{ million}}{.1125}$$

Since \$34.67 million – \$30 million = \$4.67 million, we can conclude that the Cincinnati expansion has a positive NPV and is therefore a smart business decision.

As this example shows, always keep in mind that the WACC represents the company's cost of capital for its *existing* business based on its *existing* capital structure. This feature of WACC is important when managers use the WACC to evaluate potential investment projects. Had the company proposed investing in a business with a different risk profile (e.g., imagine PEC was considering an acquisition of a software company), it would need to use a discount rate that reflected the cost of capital for a business with that risk profile. Using the same 11.25% WACC might lead to an incorrect decision. Likewise, had the company proposed financing the new factory with a different mix of equity and debt, it would be necessary to make an adjustment to the size of the tax shields and recalculate a WACC for this specific project with the new financing proportions.

Self Check: Estimating the Cost of Capital for an All Equity Firm

Return again to the hypothetical involving The Newell Soup Company. Assume that instead of a new soup factory, the company wanted to diversify its business and was considering the construction of a new semi-conductor manufacturing plant. Upon investigation, you discover that the average cost of equity capital for several industries are as follows:

Large retail grocery stores: 12%

Airlines: 15%

Semi-conductor manufacturers: 22%

Given these facts, would you still use the existing cost of capital for The Newell Soup Company to calculate the NPV of this project? If not, which industry cost of capital would be the appropriate cost of capital to use? Should you use a blended average of two industry rates for the expansion decision?

4. VALUING ENTIRE FIRMS

Having covered the fundamental concepts behind valuing a firm's securities and its possible investment projects, we're now ready to focus on common methods for valuing entire firms. As we shall see, disputes concerning the valuation of entire firms are a common source of litigation, requiring practicing lawyers to have some degree of familiarity with the most common valuation methods. Here, we explore three common techniques: Comparables, Discounted Cash Flow Analysis, and Market Analysis.

A. COMPARABLES

When a firm lacks an existing market value (e.g., it is privately held), comparables analysis is perhaps the most straight-forward approach to obtaining a value for the company. This is true, in part, because it resembles how we value many items in our personal lives. Imagine, for instance, that a distant relative bequeaths to you a 1968 Chevy Bel-Aire. If you wanted to estimate its value, you would probably look to the market for used cars and try to find an automobile with similar characteristics, such as Make, Model, Mileage, Condition, etc.

Now imagine you are trying to value a family-owned company or a company that otherwise has no publicly-traded securities. As with the 1968 Chevy Bel-Aire, a comparables analysis would require that you look for the most similar company you can find with an observable market price. For instance, perhaps you can find a similar company that is publicly-traded on Nasdaq or a similar company that has recently been acquired for a purchase price announced in the public domain.

When searching for comparables, the goal is to find other firms that display "value characteristics" similar to those of the company under investigation. Like Make, Model, and Mileage in the used car market, these value characteristics can include company features such as industry, growth rate, and size. They can also include more idiosyncratic characteristics for a specific context (e.g., daily active users for a social media company) that can help better isolate a set of truly similar firms.

Once a set of comparable firms has been identified, it then becomes necessary to infer the value of the company by comparing specific performance metrics across the subject company and the comparable companies. Suppose, for instance, that we are seeking to estimate the value of Rockland, Inc., a private company that operates several rock quarries. While Rockland is privately held, its two most significant competitors—Pebbles, Inc. and Stones, Inc.—are publicly traded on the New York Stock Exchange. The aggregate value of the common stock of Pebbles, Inc. is currently $1 billion, and the aggregate market value of equity for Stones, Inc. is $850 million. Neither company has any debt outstanding, so assuming efficient markets, these numbers reflect the total value of these comparable firms.

Here are some select performance metrics for the most recent fiscal year for Rockland, Pebbles, and Stones:

From the Companies' Balance Sheets			
Item:	Rockland, Inc.	Pebbles, Inc.	Stones, Inc.
Total Assets (millions)	$160	$750	$550
Stockholders Equity (millions)	$80	$284	$144

From the Companies' Income Statements			
Item:	Rockland, Inc.	Pebbles, Inc.	Stones, Inc.
Revenues (millions)	$350	$769	$699
EBITDA (millions)	$45	$131	$107
Net Income (millions)	$30	$48	$62

A key assumption in any comparables analysis is that the equity markets are rationally pricing firms based on specific performance metrics, such as the ones presented in these tables. The next step is therefore to examine how the publicly available market values of Pebbles, Inc. and Stones, Inc. relate to these metrics. (You can think of this as a way to "common size" the key variables, just like how you might use automobile mileage in a car comparable valuation.) In the following table, we do this by dividing the firms' market values by the performance variables that we think are most relevant. For simplicity, we'll focus on revenues, EBITDA, and net income:

Comparable Market Data:	Pebbles, Inc.	Stones, Inc.	Average
Market Value/Revenues	1.30	1.22	1.26
Market Value/EBITDA	7.63	7.94	7.79
Market Value/Net Income	20.83	13.71	17.27

Having determined the multiples by which the market appears to be valuing these firms, we can now apply them to Rockland's performance metrics. Again, the assumption is that, were Rockland publicly traded, the market would value it based on the same multiples by which it values comparable firms. While comparables analysis sometimes does this firm-by-firm (i.e., calculating Rockland's value using Pebble's multiples and Rockland's value using Stones' multiples), we will simply use the average of the two companies:

Metric:	Value of Metric for Rockland:	Average Multiple from Above:	Firm Value Estimate (in millions)
Revenues (millions)	$350	1.26	$441
EBITDA (millions)	$45	7.79	$351
Net Income (millions)	$30	17.27	$518

In this simple example, our comparables analysis suggests that the market value of Rockland is in the range of $351 to $518 million.

While a comparables analysis is simple to implement, there are a number of limitations to this type of valuation methodology. These include the difficulty of finding truly comparable companies with observable valuations, as well as the assumption that markets are efficiently valuing these firms based on the identified performance metrics. Moreover, it should be obvious from this example that comparables analysis gives enormous discretion to the analyst; therefore, its reliability hinges critically on the exercise of sound judgment. The need for sound judgement is especially important in the selection of performance metrics. Some analysts or managers may advocate for metrics that are not great estimates of the firm's value. In the Rockland example, for instance, we might think that the EBITDA or Net Income calculations yield better estimates because revenues are a long way from the bottom-line profitability of a firm. Should we really ignore the entire cost structure when estimating Rockland's value?

In general, common performance metrics used in these analyses include the market value divided by net income (or share price / earnings per share, which yields the P/E ratio), the market value of equity divided by total revenue, and the market value of equity divided by total shareholders' equity. Yet even these ratios can be misleading. For example, the price-to-earnings ratio can be influenced by a firm's capital structure and its use of debt-financing. Using EBITDA avoids this problem, but at the cost of ignoring the value of the tax shields provided by a company's decision to use debt-financing.

Finally, an especially vexing problem with comparables analysis is the question of whether an illiquidity discount should be applied to the firm under-investigation and, if so, how much to apply. In our example, for instance, one could reasonably argue that, as a private company, the equity of Rockland is far less marketable than the common stock of Pebbles and Stones (which trades freely on the NYSE). Implying a value of $351 to $518 million may therefore overstate the value of Rockland as a private firm if investors require compensation for owning illiquid stock. In practice, valuation professionals may use illiquidity discounts for private firms in the range of 25–30%.*

Somewhat surprisingly, illiquidity discounts can also arise in a comparables valuation for a public firm. For instance, comparables analysis is often among the methods used to evaluate whether an acquisition of a public firm provides fair value to the company's investors, either in negotiating an agreement or in an ex post legal challenge of the transaction. In several notable cases, courts have imposed an illiquidity discount in this context. But rather than apply a discount to reduce the imputed value of the firm, these courts have used it to *inflate* the estimated value. In a survey of the cases, Professors Wachter and Hammermesh note that the valuations derived from a comparables analysis can be inflated by as much as 30% due to the so-called "implicit minority discount."† If applied to our example with Rockland, Inc., the valuation range would increase to $456 million to $673 million. However, as emphasized by Professors Wachter and Hammermesh, "not a single piece of financial or empirical scholarship affirms the core premise of the [implicit market discount]—that public company shares systematically trade at a substantial discount to the net present value of the corporation." Rather, as they show, the concept developed in the case law primarily through a combination of happenstance and the path-dependency of *stare decisis*, creating the doctrinal equivalent of a financial urban legend.‡

B. DISCOUNTED CASH FLOW ANALYSIS

An alternative method for valuing firms is a discounted cash flow (DCF) analysis. Fundamentally, a DCF analysis is just an extension of the discounting method we have been using throughout this chapter. However, rather than calculating the present value of a stream of interest payments or dividends, we calculate the present value of the cash flows arising from a company's entire business. For instance, recall Figure 3-8 from Section 3:

* Shannon Pratt & Alina Niculita, VALUING A BUSINESS: THE ANALYSIS AND APPRAISAL OF CLOSELY HELD COMPANIES, Ch.17. (5th ed. 2008).

† See Lawrence Hammermesh and Michael Wachter, *The Short and Puzzling Life of the "Implicit Minority Discount" in Delaware Appraisal Law*, 157 U. PENN. L. REV 1 (2007).

‡ More recent Delaware cases have also begun to cast doubt on this theory, though none have gone so far as to reject it outright as a categorical rule. See, e.g., HBK Master Fund L.P. v. Pivotal Software, Inc. 2023 WL 5199634, (Del. Ch. Aug. 14, 2023) (declining to add a control premium to account for the implicit minority discount in a comparables analysis).

Figure 3-8. Debt and Equity Financing

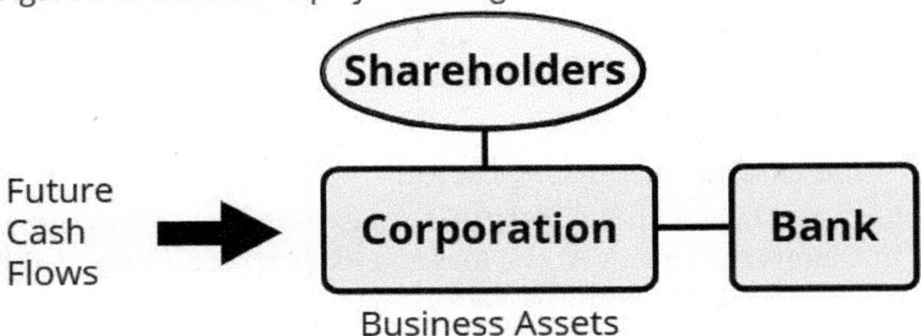

The goal of a DCF analysis is to determine the present value of the future cash flows that can be claimed by the corporation given its ownership of the underlying business.

To illustrate just how much the DCF analysis relies on the present value framework presented in Section 2(C), imagine the business depicted in Figure 3-8 is expected to produce $100 million per year in cash flows forever (as is possible given a corporation's perpetual existence). If we stipulated that the discount rate for these cash flows was 10%, we could calculate their present value using the perpetuity formula:

$$\frac{\$100\ Million}{.1} = \$1\ Billion$$

This simple DCF analysis indicates the value of the firm is $1 billion.

In practice, of course, few firms can be valued with such a simple set of assumptions. For one, what exactly are the "cash flows" that we should be discounting to present value? What about the possibility that they change over time? And where exactly do we find the discount rate for an entire business? We answer each of these questions in turn.

First, with regard to defining "cash flows," a DCF analysis assumes that the relevant cash flows to value are those that are free to distribute to all investors in a firm. That is, if you bought up all the securities of a firm—equity, debt, preferred stock, etc.—how much cash could the firm distribute to you after paying all of its expenses, including taxes? Like interest payments on a bond, these would be the cash flows that you would expect to receive from your investment in the firm's business; therefore, these are the cash flows that are relevant for purposes of valuing the firm. Conventionally, these "free cash flows" are calculated as follows:

$$CF_t = EBIT_t \times (1 - T) + DEPR_t - CAPX_t - \Delta NWC_t$$

where for a given year t:

CF = free cash flow

$EBIT$ = earnings before interest and taxes

T = corporate tax rate

$DEPR$ = depreciation and amortization

$CAPX$ = capital expenditures

ΔNWC = increase in net working capital

Note that this formula calculates "free cash flows," which is a concept we introduced in Chapter 2. However, the formula looks a bit different in the DCF context. Let's walk through the logic.

Recall that the goal in a DCF analysis is to estimate for all years in the future how much "free cash flow" is available to *all investors* in the firm after the company has paid its expenses (including taxes). We know from Chapter 2 that net income comes close to capturing this concept, but it isn't quite right. The problem is that net income includes as an expense any interest payments made that year on debt; however, interest payments are payments to investors, so they should be included in free cash flows. Moreover, net income includes taxes that were paid, but these taxes have been calculated based on the company's existing level of debt. As discussed previously, interest payments are tax deductible, so the company's existing level of indebtedness will influence the amount of taxes that must be paid. If the company had no debt, the amount of taxes it owed would be higher.

To address these problems with net income, the definition of "free cash flows" starts by using EBIT. EBIT should reflect the profits on the underlying business after paying all expenses but before paying any interest (BI = "before interest") and before paying taxes (BT = "before taxes"). Accordingly, if the company had no debt outstanding and you held all of the company's outstanding equity, EBIT would represent the accounting profits produced by the firm in a year before paying taxes. Of course, the company would still need to pay taxes on this amount, which is why the formula above then multiplies EBIT by (1-T). The result is EBIT, after taxes. Note that this number equals the amount of net income of the company if it was an all-equity firm. In other words, calculating a company's free cash flows assumes an all-equity capital structure.

The next two items in the formula address a problem with using after-tax EBIT as our estimate of free cash flows. We discussed this problem in Chapter 2 when we introduced you to EBITDA. Depreciation and amortization represent non-cash expenses that reduce EBIT. They are accrued operating expenses, but the firm doesn't really pay cash for these charges. This means that the actual cash flows produced by a firm (and which are actually available to be distributed to investors) will be higher than those reflected by after-tax EBIT. Yet depreciation and amortization are also meant to capture the idea that when a company invests in a capital asset, it is "used up" over time and will eventually need to be replaced. If we distributed to investors all the cash represented by these accounting entries, and made no other adjustment, the company would therefore lack funds to replenish old capital assets. As a result, we deduct the amount actually spent on capital expenditures to reflect the fact that some cash is spent each year to replenish aging capital equipment. Another way to put this is that we abandon the matching principal of accounting for long lived-assets and use the actual cash that is spent in each given year.

Finally, in calculating free cash flows, we typically need to account for growth over time. We'll see in a moment that this entails determining an appropriate growth rate to use for future years. However, if we are going to assume that the company grows its revenue, we should also hold back some of this year's profits to fund next year's revenue growth. For example, imagine we operate a manufacturing firm, and we expect to double our sales next year. This means we'll need to ramp up short term payments as we pay for advertising, hire additional workers, and purchase inventories to support this growth. In short, the more we grow the company's revenues, the more cash we'll need around to fund our day-to-day operations. *Working capital* refers to the cash a company needs to fund these day-to-day operations, and we calculate it by taking current assets and subtracting current liabilities.* Were we to calculate free cash flow without holding back a bit of cash to add to working capital, we would be assuming that this year's working capital is sufficient to fund next year's growth, and we would quickly run out of cash as the company grows. We therefore deduct ΔNWC, which is the increase in net working capital from one year to the next. For instance, if we anticipated growing our cash flow by 5% per year, we might choose to increase our working capital by 5% per year as well.

Once free cash flows are determined for the most recent fiscal year, future cash flows can be estimated, typically by assuming a short-term growth rate and a long-term perpetual growth rate. For example, an analyst might assume a firm will aggressively grow free cash flows over the next five years before settling into a slower, long-term growth rate that applies in perpetuity. This convention reflects the fact that a firm will generally seek to exploit short-term profit opportunities, producing strong short-term growth rates. However, competition among firms should eventually erode any above-market operating margins, suggesting a lower long-term growth rate might apply after the short-term growth period.† At bottom, however, we should recognize that these

---

* This concept is closely related to the calculations used for the accounting statement of cash flows in Chapter 2. Recall that net increases in current assets, like accounts receivable, requires the use of more cash (the firm is essentially extending a loan to customers). And conversely, net increases in current liabilities, like accounts payable, increases the operating cash available. With a DCF model, we need to project this same logic into the future to reflect how working capital will need to change to support future business activity and growth.

† The long-term growth rate is also confined by the growth rate of the overall economy. The reason is a simple matter of mathematics: if a firm's cash flows could grow forever at a rate that exceeded the economy's growth rate, the firm would become the economy. For firms being

growth numbers are just estimates; the accuracy of the DCF model will therefore reflect the quality of the model's assumptions.

Because long-term cash flows are assumed to grow forever at the long-term growth rate, these long-term cash flows are generally calculated by determining the present value of a growing perpetuity to be received at the end of the short-term growth period. Conceptually, it is as if the analysis assumes the company is sold for this value at the end of the short-term growth period, which is why this value is often referred to as the "terminal value." For instance, assume that in the most recent fiscal year a company had free cash flows of $100 million, and these cash flows are assumed to grow at 5% per year over the next five years and 2% per year thereafter. Future cash flows would be modeled as:

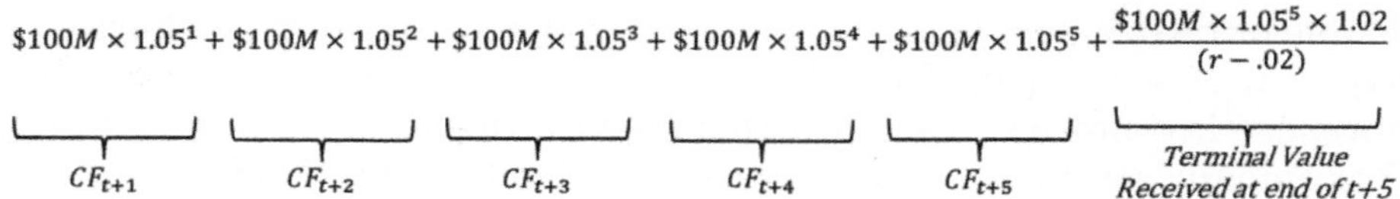

Note that for the first five years, cash flows simply grow at 5% per year.

Calculating the terminal value is conceptually more complicated because of the way that the perpetuity formula works. Recall that we need to put in the numerator of the formula the first payment to be received from the perpetuity, which will be the estimated cash flows in year 6. Year 6 is assumed to be the first year where cash flows grow at an annual rate of 2%, so this will be 2% higher than year 5 cash flows (as noted above, year 5 cash flows will be $100M × 1.05^5$, so year 6 cash flows will be 2% higher than this amount). The present value of a growing perpetuity is determined by dividing this number by (r-.02), which is the discount rate (r) less the long-term growth rate.

What discount rate (r) should we use for all of these future cash flows? Based on the prior section, it must be the company's weighted average cost of capital, or WACC. As noted previously, the WACC reflects the compensation investors demand for investing in the underlying business of a firm; therefore, it is also the discount rate we use when applying a DCF analysis to value a firm. For example, using the same numbers from above for future cash flows, if we assume a WACC of 15%, the full DCF analysis would be:

$$\text{PV for: } \underbrace{\frac{\$105M}{1.15^1}}_{CF_{t+1}} + \underbrace{\frac{\$110.25M}{1.15^2}}_{CF_{t+2}} + \underbrace{\frac{\$115.76M}{1.15^3}}_{CF_{t+3}} + \underbrace{\frac{\$121.55M}{1.15^4}}_{CF_{t+4}} + \underbrace{\frac{\$127.63M}{1.15^5}}_{CF_{t+5}} + \underbrace{\frac{\$1,001M}{1.15^5}}_{\text{Terminal Value}}$$

valued in U.S. dollars, this puts an upper limit on the perpetual growth rate of approximately 3–4% per year.

Or about \$882 million. Note how much value of the company is captured by the terminal value, underscoring its importance in a DCF analysis. (Note also that in calculating its present value, we discount the terminal value by 1.15^5 since the perpetuity formula prices its value at the end of year 5. Don't be tempted to discount this amount back by six years.)

Estimating firm values by a DCF analysis is widely regarded as technically sound; however, the large number of assumptions and estimates make it unrealistic to arrive at a single point-estimate for the value of a firm. As a result, cash flows are typically estimated under a "best case," "most likely case," and "worst case" scenario, and different estimates for WACC and terminal growth rates are often adopted to give a range of firm values under the different scenario assumptions. Probabilities can then be assigned to these scenarios such that a specific weighted average can be calculated, but keep in mind that the result will, at best, remain a rough estimate of firm value. In short, one must always be mindful of the risk of false precision when using a DCF analysis.

C. MARKET PRICES

We have saved for last what is at once the most straight-forward as well as the most contested method for valuing firms whose securities trade on public trading venues: simply look at the trading price of the firm's securities. Where a firm's securities are publicly traded, the total value of its outstanding securities—stock, bonds, preferred stock, etc.—should reflect the present value of the underlying business. We discussed the rationale previously: If you wanted to own 100% of the cash flows arising from this business, you would have to pay for all of the securities that are entitled to receive these future cash flows. Thus, the total purchase price of these securities should reflect the total value of the firm.

The reliability of this approach, however, rests critically on the accuracy of the prices that we observe in the trading markets. Previously, we discussed how estimating a firm's cost of capital based on its stock price rests on a critical assumption about market efficiency reflected in the Efficient Capital Market Hypothesis (ECMH). Similarly, the merits of using observable market prices to estimate firm value are likewise inexorably tied to the ECMH.

i. OVERVIEW OF ECMH

In general, the ECMH posits that asset prices fully reflect all available information affecting an asset. The intuition behind the ECMH is that it is information that determines the value of financial assets; therefore, traders are highly motivated to seek out and trade on any value-relevant information. As such, any "good" or "bad" information about a security will cause the price to increase or decrease, respectively, as traders discover the information and trade on it. But what exactly does it mean to say that asset prices fully reflect "all available information"?

Different answers to this question can give rise to different conceptions of an "efficient market." Following the emergence of the ECMH as a formal theory during the 1960s, financial economists have focused on three different answers, giving rise to three different theories of the ECMH: the "weak" form, the "semi-strong" form, and the "strong" form.

Weak Form of the ECMH. Under the weak form of the ECMH, the current market price of a security reflects all past information concerning that security. If the weak form of ECMH holds, an investor who observes in 2023 a stock trading on the NYSE for $150 per share should feel confident that $150 reflects the value of all past information regarding that stock. For instance, if the company had strong revenue growth in 2021, this information would already be incorporated into the $150 price per share in 2023, and the stock price will not increase further on account of revenue growth that occurred in 2021. Likewise, if the stock price had increased 5% per year over the past five years, the $150 stock price would also reflect this information as well, so there should be no possibility of another automatic 5% increase next year. In short, the weak form of the ECMH assumes that technical analysis—for example, trading on price trends—cannot be profitable. For the same reason, the weak form of the ECMH suggests that short term stock prices should move in a "random walk." After all, if today's market price already reflects all past information, tomorrow's price will be a function of purely new information. And since the future is uncertain, so too will be the news and, consequently, its implications for the stock price.

Semi-Strong Form of the ECMH. The semi-strong form of the ECMH builds on the weak form of the ECMH; however, it incorporates the fact that information regarding a security can be publicly available (e.g., past stock prices, disclosures made in SEC filings, newspaper stories about the firm's CEO) as well as non-publicly available (e.g., confidential laboratory results for a new pharmaceutical compound). According to the semi-strong form of the ECMH, security prices reflect only information that is publicly-available. Moreover, in keeping with the notion that traders are constantly seeking out value-relevant information, the semi-strong form also posits that security prices will react quickly to the public dissemination of information. For instance, if the hypothetical company above were to disclose that its R&D team had just discovered a cure for Alzheimer's, the stock price would immediately increase as traders adjusted their assessment of the company's future cash flows and valuation.

Strong Form of the ECMH. The strong form of the ECMH posits that the current price of a security incorporates all current information regardless of whether the information has been publicly-disclosed. That is, under the strong form of the ECMH, an efficient market is omniscient, and stock prices will reflect even proprietary, non-public information. For instance, if the strong form of the ECMH applied to the stock market, public announcement by our hypothetical company of its discovery of a cure for Alzheimer's would not have affected the stock price. Why?

Because the market price would reflect this positive news in real time as the company pursued its R&D endeavors.

ii. DO CAPITAL MARKETS ADHERE TO THE ECMH?

Numerous empirical tests have been conducted to evaluate whether any of these forms of the ECMH describe our capital markets. The vast majority of these tests have focused on stocks trading on U.S. stock exchanges. Within this market, the evidence has largely confirmed that stock returns tend to move according to a random walk, consistent with the weak form of the ECMH. That is, yesterday's stock price return is a poor predictor of tomorrow's stock price return. Moreover, abundant evidence also suggests that the U.S. stock market adheres to the semi-strong form of the ECMH. Indeed, this evidence appears in the fact that stock prices routinely jump (or fall) almost instantaneously whenever a company releases its quarterly earnings results or announces a seemingly major corporate development.

In contrast, there is very little evidence in support of the strong form of the ECMH. Corporate insiders who trade in their company's equity securities can earn systematically high returns, which is one of the reasons why the practice is banned by U.S. insider trading laws. If the stock market adhered to the strong form of the ECMH, insiders could not profit from insider trading since the market price would already reflect the value of all corporate information.

Evidence that the U.S. stock market generally adheres to the semi-strong (but not the strong) form of the ECMH has a number of important implications for investors.* Perhaps most notably, if today's stock price reflects all past information, it means there is no point to the type of technical analysis offered by investment advisors. On the contrary, if stock prices move randomly, these investment professionals can offer no reliable means to earn investment returns. Worse, their large fees will reduce whatever returns the advisor manages to obtain. Accordingly, a better investment would be to diversify across a large number of stocks and simply earn compensation for bearing systematic risk, as postulated by the CAPM. This conclusion is, in many ways, behind the tremendous growth in index funds over the past several decades. In general, an index fund is type of mutual fund with a portfolio constructed to match or track the components of a financial market index, such as the Standard & Poor's 500 Index. The fund is passive insofar that its managers simply follow the index and exercise no discretion in choosing investments. As such, management fees are a fraction of the cost of an actively managed mutual fund. Indexed assets under management have grown from almost

---

* Additionally, this evidence has important implication for lawyers when litigating corporate valuation disputes, as we shall see in Section 5. Outside of this context, this evidence also has been influential in U.S. securities regulation, both with respect to the design of the U.S. mandatory disclosure regime as well as how class action litigation is permitted to proceed under U.S. securities laws. These latter topics are typically covered in a basic securities regulation class.

zero in the 1980s to about 46% of registered fund assets globally at the end of 2022.*

It would be a mistake, however, to conclude that either the semi-strong or weak form of the ECMH constitutes an absolute law of the capital markets. For one, when we move beyond publicly-traded U.S. stocks, there is far less evidence that asset prices reflect current or past information. Consider, for instance, the common stock of a closely-held company. These shares can trade infrequently, if at all. As such, any given market transaction—and therefore, the market price—may reflect stale, outdated information as well as the idiosyncratic preferences or liquidity considerations of the transacting parties. The same is true for corporate debt securities, which typically trade rarely. Indeed, the fact that these markets are generally inefficient in pricing securities has given rise to the venture capital and private equity industries. Because there is no reliable market price for a private company, investors rely on the expertise of a venture capitalist or a private equity fund manager to identify underpriced investment opportunities.

Additionally, even among stocks that trade on U.S. stock exchanges, there are countless examples where the market does not adhere strictly to either the weak or semi-strong forms of the ECMH. In Section 3(B), for example, we discussed the "momentum" anomaly. As we summarized there, stocks that have positive returns within the past twelve months tend to have positive current returns, while stocks that have negative returns within the past twelve months tend to have negative current returns. This phenomenon should not be possible if the U.S. stock market truly adhered to the weak form of the ECMH.

Nor do stock prices always respond timely to what would appear to be important information. For instance, in their single-firm event study of the pharmaceutical company EntreMed, Gur Huberman and Romer Regev found that EntreMed's stock price soared following the release of positive news concerning its cancer-curing drugs in the *New York Times*, even though the information had been published previously in *Nature* five months earlier. In contrast with the *Times* story, however, EntreMed's stock price hardly responded to this earlier news release.† The opposite situation—over-reaction—can also occur. For instance, in 2017 the Long Island Iced Tea Corp., a struggling iced tea company listed on Nasdaq, announced its intent to change its name to the Long Blockchain Corp. Its stock priced jumped nearly 300% on the news before returning to its original price three months later.‡ Examples such as these underscore the fact that market efficiency is not a binary concept

---

* See Investment Company Institute, Investment Company Fact Book 2023, available at https://www.ici.org/system/files/2023-05/2023-factbook.pdf.

† See Gur Huberman and Tomer Regev, *Contagious Speculation and a Cure for Cancer: A Nonevent that Made Stock Prices Soar*, 56 JOURNAL OF FINANCE 387, 387–88 (2001).

‡ *Long Island Iced Tea Soars After Changing Its Name to Long Blockchain*, BLOOMBERG (Dec. 21, 2017), available at https://www.bloomberg.com/news/articles/2017-12-21/crypto-craze-sees-long-island-iced-tea-rename-as-long-blockchain.

in which a market is either efficient or not efficient; rather, it is a matter of degree. That is, even within markets that generally adhere to the semi-strong form of the ECMH, there can be instances when security prices do not appear to respond accurately to public information.

Any valuation that seeks to rest entirely on market prices must therefore assess whether it is appropriate to assume that a market is sufficiently efficient to justify relying on these prices. In this regard, it is useful to set forth some of the central assumptions of the ECMH.

Zero Transaction Costs in Securities. In positing that traders will immediately trade on discovering price-relevant information, the ECMH assumes it is costless to trade on this information. Obviously, transaction costs can never reach zero in markets; it takes time and money to locate trading partners and to complete a transaction. Nonetheless, there are ways that they can be significantly reduced in certain markets. Stock exchanges, for instance, are a key means to bring together investors looking to buy and sell stocks. Likewise, the abolition of fixed commissions and the development of discount brokers has dramatically reduced trading costs for U.S. public equities. These features of the U.S. stock market help explain its significant liquidity: When an investor seeks to buy or sell securities of a NYSE listed firm, she can generally do so immediately and without affecting the stock's price. However, the same cannot be said of many other markets where transaction costs remain high. It is far more difficult, for instance, to find counter-parties in the market for shares of private companies or even shares of publicly-traded firms that trade in the over-the-counter market. These latter markets should therefore be expected to be less efficient than the market for exchange-listed stocks.

All Available Information is Costlessly Available to Market Participants. In its strongest form, the ECMH assumes all price-relevant information is costless to acquire. The failure of this assumption accounts for the fact that the strong form of the ECMH does not apply to our capital markets. Inside information is not costlessly available to market participants, other than to the insiders themselves. This helps explain why it is profitable (but illegal) for insiders to trade on it. In contrast, macroeconomic information—about the economy generally, for example—is generally known to market participants. But what about publicly disclosed information about a specific firm? This news might seem more costly to acquire insofar that investors will have to be focused on following the firm in question. Yet certain markets may have institutions that make even this information relatively easy and cheap to acquire.

For example, a widely cited description of how firm-specific information is made available to market participants is offered by

Professors Ronald Gilson and Reinier Kraakman.* These authors argue that publicly-disclosed, firm-specific information is disseminated broadly when a significant subset of market participants—e.g., informed traders and research analysts—are aware of the information. These market participants are the most active traders, and they have strong incentives to study firm-specific disclosures and trade on it (or, in the case of analysts, to encourage others to trade on it). As a result, these market participants disseminate the essence of any news through their trading activities and research reports. Thus, the security prices should reflect firm specific information more in a market where these participants operate than in a market where they do not. For example, according to the ECMH, one should expect the transaction prices in the shares of a large-cap stock such as Apple (which is followed by dozens of analysts) to be more reflective of firm-specific information than the transaction prices in the shares of a thinly-traded firm on the over-the-counter market or in the shares of a private company.

Agreement on the Implication of Current Information for Stock Prices. The ECMH also assumes that traders will agree on information for a specific security. In some situations, this assumption may indeed be true, such as when the Federal Reserve announces a change in interest rates. In other cases, however, there may be more uncertainty. For instance, Gilson and Kraakman point out that some information, such as a technological innovation or a new form of security, may create more difficulties in deciphering its meaning. In these cases, markets may discount the value of the innovation until some traders can verify its value independently of the issuer's claims. Deciphering the full significance of the results of clinical tests of new drugs, for example, may require expert knowledge of the molecular structure of the subject drug, compared to other drugs.

Sufficient Capital to Engage in Risky Arbitrage. While not incorporated in the early articulation of the ECMH, this last assumption has emerged in response to a critique of the ECMH made by behavioral economists. In general, behavioral economists have criticized ECMH on the grounds that it fails to incorporate the way in which traders can act in seemingly irrational ways, thereby making markets inefficient. Consider, for instance, the case of the Long Island Iced Tea Corp. discussed previously. One might imagine that the 300% price increase triggered by the company's decision to add "blockchain" to the firm's name was the result of unsophisticated "noise" traders seeking to ride the Bitcoin bubble that existed in December 2017. Even if that were the case, however, the stock for the Long Island Iced Tea Corp. could still be relatively efficient if sophisticated investors can counter-act the effect of

* Ronald J. Gilson and Reinier H. Kraakman, *The Mechanisms of Market Efficiency*, 70 VA. L. REV. 549 (1984).

these noise traders by short-selling the company's over-priced shares.* That is, defenders of the ECMH would posit that these noise traders simply create a short-term arbitrage opportunity that should be traded away quickly.

But how easy is it for traders to exploit the arbitrage opportunities created by noise traders? It is here that behavioral economists have mounted one of their central challenges to the ECMH theory. According to behavioral economists, real-world arbitrage is risky and, as a result, may not be capable of correcting the mispricings that arise when investors depart from classic assumptions of rationality. Among other things, for instance, the ability to engage in arbitrage requires the availability of close substitutes for securities that are mispriced. Consider a classic example provided by Andrei Shleifer, a leading behavioral economist.† Shleifer points to a hypothetical investor in 1998 who might have believed that large American corporations were over-valued given the extremely high prices that they were trading at relative to their profitability. However, the S&P500 Index lacks a good substitute, so any attempt to short-sell the index would have posed considerable risk for the investor. To illustrate, Shleifer notes that if the investor had sold short the S&P500 at the beginning of 1998 and bought the Russell 2000 Index of smaller companies as a hedge (on the theory that smaller companies were not as mispriced), this investor would have lost 30.8 percent by the end of 1998. In short, the absence of close substitutes for many financial assets means that investors face the risk that prices can move further out of line, making arbitrage extremely risky. As Shleifer concludes, "The bottom line of this work is that theory by itself does not inevitably lead a researcher to a presumption of market efficiency."

The Warren Buffett Phenomenon (or Anomaly)

We conclude this discussion of the ECMH with a look at Warren Buffett. As noted previously, the weak form of the ECMH posits that there should be no value in professional investment advice, making Buffett's extraordinary investment returns one of the lasting puzzles faced by proponents of the ECMH. Warren Buffett is one of a handful of investment managers to achieve long-run success in beating the market. Among others are John Maynard Keynes, who managed the endowment for King's College Cambridge through the great Depression and achieved positive returns during a period when the market overall had declined, Phil Fisher, Charlie Munger (who managed an investment partnership before becoming Buffett's colleague at Berkshire-Hathaway), Lou Simpson, who managed GEICO's investments, William Ruane who

* Short selling means an investor borrows a share of stock, immediately sells it, and then repurchases it in the future to return it to the lender, thus allowing an investor to profit from declining prices; we discuss short-selling in Section 3(A) of Chapter 8.

† See Andrei Shleifer, INEFFICIENT MARKETS: AN INTRODUCTION TO BEHAVIORAL FINANCE 10–16 (2000).

managed the Sequoia Fund and William Miller, who managed the Legg Mason Value Trust. Buffett himself described many of these legendary investors as members of "Graham and Doddsville," after legendary finance teacher Benjamin Graham and his successor and co-author David Dodd, at Columbia University.* From them Buffett and the others learned their basic approach to investing.

In theory, Buffett's ability to beat the market portfolio for so many years is entirely consistent with market efficiency. In particular, as a matter of statistics, if you have a billion people engaged in a coin-flipping contest, only one will be the ultimate winner, boasting an extraordinarily large number of heads (or tails). Might Buffett just be lucky? We suspect this explanation is less than satisfying for most readers.

Buffett has generally described his approach as one of intensive examination of a company in which he is considering investing, which he calls "focus investing." Rather than hold the widely diversified portfolio of many financial managers, which generally underperform market averages and index funds because of transaction costs and the taxable nature of gains on frequent sales of stock, Buffett and his peers prefer a close examination to find companies (not stocks) they really like, and limiting their portfolios to a handful of such stocks. In each instance, these investors value each company independent of market valuations. They do this by looking for businesses that are simple and understandable (Buffett avoided the dot.com crash of the early 2000s by adhering to this principle). They look for a consistent operating history and good long-term prospects. Second, they look for capable and rational managers who are candid with shareholders about mistakes, and who avoid the pressure of mutual fund managers to produce short-term quarterly results. They look for companies with high profit margins, which often means these firms dominate their respective markets.

What does Buffett make of the ECMH? The following is from Buffet's report to Berkshire-Hathaway shareholders in 1988:

To the Shareholders of Berkshire Hathaway Inc.:

Our gain in net worth during 1988 was $569 million, or 20.0%. Over the last 24 years (that is, since present management took over), our per-share book value has grown from $19.46 to $2,974.52, or at a rate of 23.0% compounded annually. We've emphasized in past reports that what counts, however, is intrinsic business value—the figure, necessarily an estimate, indicating what all of our constituent businesses are worth. By our calculations, Berkshire's intrinsic business value significantly exceeds its book value. Over the 24 years, business value has grown somewhat faster than book value; in 1988, however, book value grew the faster, by a bit.

* See Warren Buffett, *The Superinvestors of Graham-and-Doddsville*, HERMES, THE COLUMBIA BUSINESS SCHOOL MAGAZINE (Apr. 1984).

* * *

Efficient Market Theory The preceding discussion about arbitrage makes a small discussion of "efficient market theory" (EMT) also seem relevant. This doctrine became highly fashionable—indeed, almost holy scripture in academic circles during the 1970s. Essentially, it said that analyzing stocks was useless because all public information about them was appropriately reflected in their prices. In other words, the market always knew everything. As a corollary, the professors who taught EMT said that someone throwing darts at the stock tables could select a stock portfolio having prospects just as good as one selected by the brightest, most hard-working security analyst. Amazingly, EMT was embraced not only by academics, but by many investment professionals and corporate managers as well. Observing correctly that the market was *frequently* efficient, they went on to conclude incorrectly that it was *always* efficient. The difference between these propositions is night and day.

In my opinion, the continuous 63-year arbitrage experience of Graham-Newman Corp. Buffett Partnership, and Berkshire illustrates just how foolish EMT is. (There's plenty of other evidence, also.) While at Graham-Newman, I made a study of its earnings from arbitrage during the entire 1926–1956 lifespan of the company. Unleveraged returns averaged 20% per year. Starting in 1956, I applied Ben Graham's arbitrage principles, first at Buffett Partnership and then Berkshire. Though I've not made an exact calculation, I have done enough work to know that the 1956–1988 returns averaged well over 20%. (Of course, I operated in an environment far more favorable than Ben's; he had 1929–1932 to contend with.)

All of the conditions are present that are required for a fair test of portfolio performance: (1) the three organizations traded hundreds of different securities while building this 63- year record; (2) the results are not skewed by a few fortunate experiences; (3) we did not have to dig for obscure facts or develop keen insights about products or managements—we simply acted on highly-publicized events; and (4) our arbitrage positions were a clearly identified universe—they have not been selected by hindsight.

Over the 63 years, the general market delivered just under a 10% annual return, including dividends. That means $1,000 would have grown to $405,000 if all income had been reinvested. A 20% rate of return, however, would have produced $97 million. That strikes us as a statistically-significant differential that might, conceivably, arouse one's curiosity.

Yet proponents of the theory have never seemed interested in discordant evidence of this type. True, they don't talk quite as much about their theory today as they used to. But no one, to my knowledge, has ever said he was wrong, no matter how many thousands of students he has sent forth misinstructed. EMT, moreover, continues to be an integral part of the investment curriculum at major business schools. Apparently, a reluctance to recant, and thereby to demystify the priesthood, is not limited to theologians.

Naturally the disservice done students and gullible investment professionals who have swallowed EMT has been an extraordinary service to us and other followers of Graham. In any sort of a contest—financial, mental, or physical—it's an enormous advantage to have opponents who have been taught that it's useless to even try. From a selfish point of view, Grahamites should probably endow chairs to ensure the perpetual teaching of EMT.

All this said, a warning is appropriate. Arbitrage has looked easy recently. But this is not a form of investing that guarantees profits of 20% a year or, for that matter, profits of any kind. As noted, the market is reasonably efficient much of the time: For every arbitrage opportunity we seized in that 63- year period, many more were foregone because they seemed properly-priced.

An investor cannot obtain superior profits from stocks by simply committing to a specific investment category or style. He can earn them only by carefully evaluating facts and continuously exercising discipline. Investing in arbitrage situations, per se, is no better a strategy than selecting a portfolio by throwing darts.

5. VALUATION AND THE COURTS

Courts are routinely required to assess firm values. In corporate bankruptcy, for instance, valuation disputes lie at center of the Chapter 11 reorganization process. If a firm is worth more as a going-concern than if liquidated, a bankruptcy court may agree to avoid a liquidation and instead distribute new securities in the reorganized company to the company's old investors. In the corporate law context, courts are likewise commonly called upon to decide what a company is worth. The settings can range from mundane corporate transactions to the most significant of corporate events. For example, under Section 155 of the Delaware General Corporation Law ("DGCL"), a company that conducts a simple reverse stock split may have to "pay in cash the fair value of fractions of a share" resulting from the split. Thus, a company that conducts a 1-for-100 reverse stock split will have to pay in cash the fair value of any pre-split shares held by a stockholder who holds fewer than 100 pre-split shares.*

More importantly, high stakes litigation over firm value frequently occurs when a company chooses to engage in an important strategic transaction, such as an acquisition, a sale, or a reorganization. For instance, when a transaction is undertaken with a related party (e.g., a management buyout of the company led by a company's CEO), the board of the selling firm may find its approval of the transaction subject to enhanced judicial scrutiny. Under enhanced scrutiny, the board of directors has the burden of demonstrating why the transaction was the product of a "fair process" and resulted in a "fair price." Perhaps even more important is the right of shareholders to obtain a judicial appraisal of their shares in the sale of a company. For instance, Section 262(h) of the DGCL provides that, upon a qualified petition for appraisal by stockholders, the Court of Chancery:

> "shall determine the fair value of the shares exclusive of any element of value arising from the accomplishment or expectation of the merger or consolidation, together with interest, if any, to be paid upon the amount determined to be the fair value. In determining such fair value, the Court shall take into account all relevant factors. . ."

In contrast to an entire fairness challenge where a court must determine if the price was "fair," appraisal requires an actual determination of fair value, thus placing the court squarely in the position of setting a specific price per share. In recent years courts have increasingly found themselves in the position of having to make these fair value determinations. For instance, Charles Korsmo and Minor Myers document a tenfold increase in appraisal litigation from 2004 to 2013.† Likewise, Matt Cain, Jill Fisch, Steven Davidoff-Solomon, and Randall Thomas found that in 2015, thirty-three deals were targeted with fifty-one appraisal petitions, while in 2016, forty-eight deals were challenged by seventy-seven appraisal petitions.‡ Following the *Dell* case below, the rate of appraisal petitions has declined, but a sizeable number continue to be filed each year. During 2022, for instance, twenty-two petitions were filed in the Delaware Chancery Court.§

For a court tasked with valuing a firm, the preceding sections necessarily raise a host of difficult questions. For example, what

---

* See Samuels v. CCUR Holdings, Inc., 2022 WL 1744438 (Del. Ch. May 31, 2022) (holding that Delaware law permits direct claims against a corporation for violating the requirement to pay fair value under DGCL Section 155).

† See Charles R. Korsmo & Minor Myers, *Appraisal Arbitrage and the Future of Public Company M&A*, 92 WASH U. L. REV. 1551, 1553 (2015).

‡ See Matthew Cain et al., *The Shifting Tides of Merger Litigation*, 71 VAND. L. REV. 603, 604 (2018).

§ See Cornerstone Research, Appraisal Litigation in Delaware: Trends in Petitions and Opinions 2006–2022, available at https://www.cornerstone.com/wp-content/uploads/2023/04/Appraisal-Litigation-in-Delaware-2006-2022.pdf.

valuation method should be utilized? To the extent one uses a comparables analysis, how can one reliably determine firm value given the considerable discretion required? To the extent one uses a DCF analysis, how much confidence should courts have in the result given the uncertainty of predicting future cash flows and the outsized influence of terminal values? Similarly, how much confidence can courts place in a DCF methodology when the academic literature on determining discount rates remains in flux? And even if a court seeks to avoid these issues by utilizing market prices, how much confidence should it have in market prices when both the behavioral finance literature and experiences such as the 2008 Financial Crisis highlight how market prices might also depart from intrinsic value? These are difficult questions that go to the heart of legal valuation efforts.

With this in mind, it should hardly be surprising that courts have struggled with valuation disputes. Notably, within Delaware, it was not until Weinberger v. UOP, Inc., 457 A.2d 701 (Del. 1983) that the courts even embraced modern valuation techniques such as DCF analysis. Rather, from 1950 until 1983, the judicially-crafted "Delaware block method" was the exclusive method for resolving valuation disputes. According to this method, courts assessed the value of a firm using three distinct techniques, generally by evaluating evidence offered by expert testimony. First, a court assessed a market-based value estimated using any reliable market data. Second, it assessed value based on a separate analysis of the company's assets. Finally, it assessed value based on the company's earnings by applying an appropriate multiple (similar to a comparables analysis). The court then assigned a percentage weight to each of the three valuations based on factors purportedly relating to the relevance of each valuation. A weighted-average value of the firm was then calculated. Given Delaware's prominence as a source of corporate law, most states also mandated the use of the Delaware block method. Recently, however, many states have gradually followed *Weinberger's* embrace of any valuation method that is generally accepted by the financial community. See, e.g., Athlon Sports Communications, Inc. v. Duggan, 549 S.W.3d 108 (Tenn. 2018) (abandoning mandatory use of Delaware block method and adopting "the *Weinberger* approach of giving trial courts the flexibility to choose the valuation method that best fits the circumstances").

By opening the door for alternative valuation techniques, however, courts also expanded the terrain over which valuation experts could duel. For example, even if valuation experts stick to a standardized DCF analysis using the framework described earlier in this chapter, there is ample opportunity for experts to present vastly different valuations. Consider, for instance, the simple DCF described in Section 4(B). There, we calculated that a firm with free cash flows of $100 million growing at 5% per year over the next five years and 2% thereafter has a value of approximately $882 million. This value was derived from a DCF analysis using a WACC of 15%. As shown in Table 3-9, however, modifying the WACC by only +/– 2% and the long-term growth rate by +/– 1% gives a range of values from $733 million to over $1.1 billion.

Table 3-9:
Sensitivity Analysis of Hypothetical DCF

		Terminal Growth Rate:		
		0.01	0.02	0.03
	0.13	$986	$1,046	$1,117
WACC:	0.15	$842	$882*	$928
	0.17	$733	$761	$794

*original estimate

Even the most diligent valuation expert cannot be absolutely certain about a firm's long-term growth rate. And as discussed in Section 3(B), reasonable minds can differ on any number of parameters that might affect a firm's true discount rate—such as the calculation of beta, the size of the risk premium, or the use of factor adjustments to estimate risk premiums. The challenge of resolving the "dueling experts" problem becomes all the greater when we introduce the very real possibility that experts might adopt industry models with additional variables. By allowing experts to determine discount rates by reference to concepts such as a company-specific risk factor these methods gives experts seemingly boundless discretion.

In light of these challenges, market-based estimates of firm value represent an attractive alternative. Yet courts must remain cautious about the challenges of relying entirely on market prices. Referring to the 1929 market crash, a 1934 Delaware appraisal action summarized these concerns as follows:

> The experience of recent years is enough to convince the most causal [sic] observer that the market in its appraisal of values must have been woefully wrong in its estimates at one time or another within the interval of a space of time so brief that fundamental conditions could not possibly have become so altered as to affect true worth.

Chicago Corp. v. Munds, Del.Ch., 172 A. 452, 455 (1934). Likewise, writing in 1992, the Delaware Supreme Court noted that "*Munds'* succinct evaluation of the market has lost none of its lustre." Rapid-American Corp. v. Harris, Del.Supr., 603 A.2d 796, 806 (1992).

These considerations have loomed large as courts sought to wade through the surge in appraisal actions in recent years and the resulting challenge of selecting a price in the midst of "dueling experts." These tensions came to a head in the following case relating to an appraisal action stemming from the 2013 buyout of Dell, Inc.

Dell, Inc. v. Magnetar Global Event Driven Master Fund Ltd.

177 A.3d 1 (Del. 2017)

[Eds. On October 30, 2013, Dell, Inc. was acquired in a management buyout led by Dell's founder and Chief Executive Officer, Michael Dell, and affiliates of a private equity firm, Silver Lake Partners. The transaction valued Dell at approximately $25 billion and represented the largest technology buyout in history. The controversial transaction also induced a number of Dell shareholders to oppose the transaction and exercise their appraisal rights under DGCL Section 262. Arguing before Vice Chancellor Travis Laster, the company defended the $13.75 per share transaction price (excluding a special dividend) as representing fair value for the company's stock prior to the transaction on the basis that the Company's board of directors had thoroughly searched for alternative bidders. It also presented the expert testimony of Glenn Hubbard, Dean of the Columbia University Graduate School of Business, who used a DCF analysis to opine that the Company had a fair value of $12.68 per share on the closing date. The petitioning shareholders, on the other hand, presented the expert testimony of Bradford Cornell, a financial economist and well-known valuation expert, whose DCF analysis showed that the Company had a fair value of $28.61 per share. As summarized by Vice Chancellor Laster, "[t]wo highly distinguished scholars of valuation science, applying similar valuation principles, thus generated opinions that differed by 126%, or approximately $28 billion."

In his Chancery Court ruling, Vice Chancellor Laster rejected the Company's argument that the merger price represented the most reliable value of the Company due to several deficiencies in the negotiation of the merger price. The Vice Chancellor was especially concerned about the fact that in negotiating the transaction, all parties focused on the premium of the deal price to the current trading price of Dell's stock; however, a "valuation gap" appeared to exist between "the market's perception and the Company's operative reality." In particular, the Vice Chancellor appeared to agree with the petitioners that the gap was driven by "(i) analysts' focus on short-term, quarter-by-quarter results and (ii) the Company's nearly $14 billion investment in its transformation, which had not yet begun to generate the anticipated results." Vice Chancellor Laster was also concerned that, because the transaction only attracted the interest of financial sponsors (as opposed to a strategic buyer, such as Hewlett Packard) the price reflected financial sponsors' need to generate a sufficient IRR on the transaction. At the same time, Vice Chancellor Laster found that the evidence did not support the valuation advanced by Bradford Cornell, the petitioner's expert. Rather, by modifying some of the assumptions of the DCF utilized by the Company's expert, the Vice Chancellor arrived at a fair value calculation of $17.62 per share. The revised price was 28% higher than the deal price, thus implying the deal undervalued Dell by nearly $7 billion. On appeal, the Delaware Supreme Court issued the following decision.]

■ VALIHURA, JUSTICE:

The petitioners left standing in this long-running appraisal saga are former stockholders of Dell Inc. ("Dell" or the "Company") who validly exercised their appraisal rights instead of voting for a buyout led by the Company's founder and CEO, Michael Dell, and affiliates of a private equity firm, Silver Lake Partners ("Silver Lake"). In perfecting their appraisal rights, petitioners acted on their belief that Dell's shares were worth more than the deal price of $13.75 per share—which was already a 37% premium to the Company's ninety-day-average unaffected stock price.

Our appraisal statute, 8 Del. C. § 262, allows stockholders who perfect their appraisal rights to receive "fair value" for their shares as of the merger date instead of the merger consideration. The appraisal statute requires the Court of Chancery to assess the "fair value" of such shares and, in doing so, "take into account all relevant factors." The trial court complied: it took into account all the relevant factors presented by the parties in advocating for their view of fair value—including Dell's stock price and deal price—and then arrived at its own determination of fair value.

The problem with the trial court's opinion is not, as the Company argues, that it failed to take into account the stock price and deal price. The trial court did consider this market data. It simply decided to give it no weight. But the court nonetheless erred because its reasons for giving that data no weight—and for relying instead exclusively on its own discounted cash flow ("DCF") analysis to reach a fair value calculation of $17.62—do not follow from the court's key factual findings and from relevant, accepted financial principles.

Here, the trial court gave no weight to Dell's stock price because it found its market to be inefficient. But the evidence suggests that the market for Dell's shares was actually efficient and, therefore, likely a possible proxy for fair value.

I.

A. Dell

In June 2012, when the idea of an MBO first arose, Dell was a mature company on the brink of crisis: its stock price had dropped from $18 per share to around $12 per share in just the first half of the year. The advent of new technologies such as tablet computers crippled the traditional PC-maker's outlook. The Company's recent transformation struggled to generate investor optimism about its long-term prospects. And the global economy was still hungover from the financial crisis of 2008.

Other than a brief hiatus from 2004 to his return in 2007, Michael Dell had led Dell as CEO, from the Company's founding in his first-year dorm room at the University of Texas at Austin when he was just nineteen years old, to a Fortune 500 behemoth with global revenues hitting $56.9 billion in the fiscal year ending February 1, 2013. Dell was indisputably one of the world's largest IT companies.

i. Michael Dell's Return and the Company's Challenges

Upon his return to the Company in 2007, Mr. Dell perceived three key challenges facing Dell. First, low-margin PC-makers such as Lenovo were muscling into Dell's market share as the performance gap between its higher-end computers and the cheaper alternatives narrowed. Second, starting with the launch of Apple's iPhone in 2007, the impending onslaught of smartphones and tablet computers appeared likely to erode traditional PC sales. Third, cloud-based storage from the likes of Amazon.com threatened the Company's traditional server storage business.

In light of these threats, Mr. Dell believed that, to survive and thrive, the Company should focus on enterprise software and services, which could be accomplished through acquisitions in these spaces. From 2010 through 2012, the Company acquired eleven companies for approximately $14 billion. And Mr. Dell tried to sell the market on this transformation. He regularly shared with equity analysts his view that the Company's enterprise solutions and services divisions would achieve annual sales growth in the double-digits and account for more than half of Dell's profits by 2016.

Yet despite Dell's M & A spurt and Mr. Dell's attempts to persuade Wall Street to buy into the Company's future, the market still "didn't get" Dell, as Mr. Dell lamented. It still viewed the Company as a PC business, and its stock hovered in the mid-teens.

ii. The Market for Dell's Stock

Dell's stock traded on the NASDAQ under the ticker symbol DELL. The Company's market capitalization of more than $20 billion ranked it in the top third of the S & P 500. Dell had a deep public float and was actively traded as more than 5% of Dell's shares were traded each week. The stock had a bid-ask spread of approximately 0.08%. It was also widely covered by equity analysts, and its share price quickly reflected the market's view on breaking developments. Based on these metrics, the record suggests the market for Dell stock was semi-strong efficient, meaning that the market's digestion and assessment of all publicly available information concerning Dell was quickly impounded into the Company's stock price. For example, on January 14, 2013, Dell's stock jumped 9.8% within a minute of Bloomberg breaking the news of the Company's take-private talks, and the stock closed up 13% from the day prior—on a day the S & P 500 as a whole fell 0.1%.

B. The Sale Process

The first inkling of a Dell MBO can be traced to June 2012, when private equity executive Staley Cates of Southeastern Asset Management suggested to Mr. Dell that he might consider taking the Company private. Mr. Dell was intrigued as he believed it would be easier to execute the Company's transformation plan unencumbered by stockholder pressure.

Dell's earnings for the second quarter of Fiscal 2013 . . . underscored the Company's challenges: revenue was down 8% from the prior year, and earnings per share dropped 13%. The Company's revenue fell short of expectations, and its management further revised its EPS forecast down 20% for Fiscal 2013. Dell management said that the Company was amid a "long-term strategy" expected to "take time" to reap benefits. But one analyst called the Company a "sinking ship" and emphasized that "Dell's turnaround strategy is fundamentally flawed [and] the fundamentals are bad. Dell may have responded too late to save itself." Many analysts also revised their price targets downward.

[T]he Company's third-quarter earnings, released on November 15, 2012, brought more bad news for Dell: revenue dropped 11% from the prior year, and EPS was down 28%. During this period when Dell was trying to sell its long-term vision without success, it kept failing the quarterly tests on which so many market analysts focus. By way of example, this was the sixth of the past seven quarters that revenue fell below consensus estimates. As research analysts lowered their price targets out of concern for the future of the PC industry and growing skepticism about Dell's turnaround strategy, even CFO Brian Gladden acknowledged that "[m]anagement projections appear optimistic given valuation & sell-side estimates of Dell['s] future value." The Committee enlisted Boston Consulting Group ("BCG") to formulate independent projections for the Company.

[Eds. The court then summarized the negotiation of the merger agreement by the Company, Michael Dell, and affiliates of Silver Lake Partners, along with the pre-signing and post-signing canvassing of the market for alternative bidders.]

D. The Appraisal Trial

The four-day appraisal trial in October 2015 featured 1,200 exhibits, seventeen depositions, live testimony from seven fact witnesses and five expert witnesses, a 542-paragraph-long pre-trial order, and 369 pages of pre- and post-trial briefing. Petitioners argued that, as demonstrated through their expert's DCF analysis, the fair value of the Company's common stock at the effective time of the Merger was actually $28.61 per share—more than double the deal price of $13.75. If this valuation were correct, the Buyout Group obtained Dell at a $26 billion discount to its actual value. In contrast, Dell maintained that its DCF analysis yielding a $12.68 per share valuation was a more appropriate approximation of fair value, but that, in light of the uncertainties facing the PC industry, fair value could be as high as the deal price (but not greater).

E. The Court of Chancery's Determination of Fair Value

The Court of Chancery acknowledged that "[t]he consideration that the buyer agrees to provide in the deal and that the seller agrees to accept is one form of market price data, which Delaware courts have long considered in appraisal proceedings." However, the court believed that flaws in Dell's sale process meant that the deal price of $13.75 should not be afforded any weight here since it was "not the best evidence of [the Company's] fair value." Accordingly, the trial court disregarded both Dell's pre-transactional stock price and the deal price entirely.

The Court of Chancery identified three crucial problems with the pre-signing phase of the sale process that contributed to its decision to disregard the market-based indicators of value.

First, the primary bidders were all financial sponsors who used an LBO pricing model to determine their bid prices—meaning that the per-share deal price needed to be low enough to facilitate an IRR of approximately 20%. As the court saw it, the prospective PE buyers, the Buyout Group, Mr. Dell, and the Committee never focused on determining the intrinsic value of the Company as a going concern.

Second, the trial court believed that Dell's investors were overwhelmingly focused on short-term profit, and that this "investor myopia" created a valuation gap that purportedly distorted the original merger consideration of $13.65. Thus, under the Court of Chancery's logic, the efficient market hypothesis—which teaches that the price of a company's stock reflects all publicly available information as a consensus, per-share valuation—failed when it came to Dell, diminishing the probative value of the stock price. This phenomenon also allegedly depressed the deal price by anchoring deal negotiations at an improperly low starting point.

Third, the trial court concluded that there was no meaningful price competition during the pre-signing phase as, at any given time during the pre-signing phase, there were at most two private equity sponsors competing for the deal, creating little incentive to bid up the deal price.

II. Analysis

We agree with petitioners that the trial court did consider all relevant factors presented, including Dell's stock price and deal price. But we reverse because the reasoning behind the trial court's decision to give no weight to any market-based measure of fair value runs counter to its own factual findings. After reviewing our appraisal statute and accompanying jurisprudence, we explore why the facts fail to support the Court of Chancery's reasoning for disregarding, in particular, the deal price.

A. The Relevant Legal Framework

The General Assembly created the appraisal remedy in 1899 after amending the corporate code to allow a corporation to be sold upon the consent of a majority of stockholders instead of unanimous approval as was previously required. Given that a single shareholder could no longer hold up the sale of a company, the General Assembly devised appraisal in service of the notion that "the stockholder is entitled to be paid for that which has been taken from him."[79] Stockholders who viewed the sale price as inadequate could seek "an independent judicial determination of the fair value of their shares" instead of accepting the per-share merger consideration.[80] There is one issue in an appraisal trial: "the value of the dissenting stockholder's stock."[81]

i. "What" the Court is Valuing

We have explained that the court's ultimate goal in an appraisal proceeding is to determine the "fair or intrinsic value" of each share on the closing date of the merger. To reach this per-share valuation, the court should first envisage the entire pre-merger company as a "going concern," as a standalone entity, and assess its value as such. "[T]he corporation must be viewed as an on-going enterprise, occupying a particular market position in the light of future prospects." The valuation should reflect the " 'operative reality' of the company as of the time of the merger."

Because the court strives "to value the corporation itself, as distinguished from a specific fraction of its shares as they may exist in the hands of a particular shareholder," the court should not apply a minority discount when there is a controlling stockholder. Further, the court should exclude "any synergies or other value expected from the merger giving rise to the appraisal proceeding itself." [93]

---

79 Tri-Continental Corp. v. Battye, 74 A.2d 71, 72 (Del. 1950). In [DFC Global Corp. v. Muirfield Value Partners], we stated that the purpose of appraisal is to "make sure that [stockholders] receive fair compensation for their shares in the sense that it reflects what they deserve to receive based on what would fairly be given to them in an arm's-length transaction." 172 A.3d at 370–71, 2017 WL 3261190, at *18.

80 Alabama By-Prod. Corp. v. Cede & Co., 657 A.2d 254, 258 (Del. 1995); Cede & Co. v. Technicolor, Inc., 542 A.2d 1182, 1186 (Del. 1988) ("An appraisal proceeding is a limited legislative remedy intended to provide shareholders dissenting from a merger on grounds of inadequacy of the offering price with a judicial determination of the intrinsic worth (fair value) of their shareholdings.").

81 Technicolor, 542 A.2d at 1186 (quoting Kaye v. Pantone, Inc., 395 A.2d 369, 374–75 (Del. Ch. 1978)).

93 Global GT LP v. Golden Telecom, Inc., 993 A.2d 497, 507 (Del. Ch. 2010), aff'd, 11 A.3d 214 (Del. 2010); DFC, 172 A.3d at 368, 2017 WL 3261190, at *16 (The Court should exclude "any value that the selling company's shareholders would receive because a buyer intends to operate the subject company, not as a stand-alone going concern, but as a part of a larger enterprise, from which synergistic gains can be extracted." (quoting Union Ill. 1995 Inv. LP v. Union Fin. Grp., Ltd, 847 A.2d 340, 356 (Del. Ch. 2004))). As noted in DFC, there are policy reasons for excising the synergistic value: "the specific buyer [should] not end up losing its upside for [the] purchase by having to pay out the expected gains from its own business plans for the company it bought to the petitioners." 172 A.3d at 368, 2017 WL 3261190, at *16. Further, "the broader excision of synergy gains could have also been thought of as a balance to the Court's decision to afford pro rata value to minority stockholders." Id.

Then, once this total standalone value is determined, the court awards each petitioning stockholder his pro rata portion of this total—"his proportionate interest in [the] going concern" plus interest.

ii. "How" the Court Should Approach Valuation

This Court has relied on the statutory requirement that the Court of Chancery consider "all relevant factors" to reject requests for the adoption of a presumption that the deal price reflects fair value if certain preconditions are met, such as when the merger is the product of arm's-length negotiation and a robust, non-conflicted market check, and where bidders had full information and few, if any, barriers to bid for the deal.[98] In *Golden Telecom*, we explained that Section 262(h) is "unambiguous[ ]" in its command that the Court of Chancery undertake an "independent" assessment of fair value, and that the statute "vests the Chancellor and Vice Chancellors with significant discretion to consider 'all relevant factors' and determine the going concern value of the underlying company."[99] In *DFC*, we again rejected an invitation to create a presumption in favor of the deal price.[100] Even aside from the statutory command to consider all relevant factors, we doubted our ability to craft the precise preconditions for invoking such a presumption.[101]

As such, "the trial of an appraisal case under the Delaware General Corporation Law presents unique challenges to the judicial factfinder."[102] And this task is complicated by "the clash of contrary, and often antagonistic, expert opinions of value," prompting the trial court to wade through "widely divergent views reflecting partisan positions" in arriving at its determination of a single number for fair value.[103]

In the end, after this analysis of the relevant factors, "[i]n some cases, it may be that a single valuation metric is the most reliable evidence of fair value and that giving weight to another factor will do nothing but distort that best estimate. In other cases, it may be necessary to consider two or more factors."[104] Or, in still others, the court might apportion weight among a variety of methodologies. But, whatever route it chooses, the trial court must justify its methodology (or methodologies)

---

98 See DFC, 172 A.3d at 348, 2017 WL 3261190, at *1 ("We decline to engage in that act of creation, which in our view has no basis in the statutory text, which gives the Court of Chancery in the first instance the discretion to 'determine the fair value of the shares' by taking into account 'all relevant factors.' " (quoting 8 Del. C. § 262(h)).

99 11 A.3d at 217–18.

100 DFC, 172 A.3d at 366–67, 2017 WL 3261190, at *15.

101 Id.

102 PetSmart, 2017 WL 2303599, at *1 (citing Ancestry.com, 2015 WL 399726, at *2).

103 Shell Oil, 607 A.2d at 1222.

104 DFC, 172 A.3d at 387–88, 2017 WL 3261190, at *31; see also M.G. Bancorp., 737 A.2d at 525–26 ("[T]he Court of Chancery has the discretion to select one of the parties' valuation models as its general framework or to fashion its own."); Id. at 526 ("[A]lthough not required to do so, it is entirely proper for the Court of Chancery to adopt any one expert's model, methodology, and mathematical calculations, in toto, if that valuation is supported by credible evidence and withstands a critical judicial analysis on the record.").

according to the facts of the case and relevant, accepted financial principles.[105]

Given the human element in the appraisal inquiry—where the factfinder is asked to choose between two competing, seemingly plausible valuation perspectives, forge its own, or apportion weight among a variety of methodologies—it is possible that a factfinder, even the same factfinder, could reach different valuation conclusions on the same set of facts if presented differently at trial. There may be no perfect methodology for arriving at fair value for a given set of facts, and the Court of Chancery's conclusions will be upheld if they follow logically from those facts and are grounded in relevant, accepted financial principles. "To be sure, "fair value" does not equal "best value."[108]

B. The Court of Chancery's Reasons for Disregarding Deal Price Do Not Follow from the Record

i. The Trial Court Lacked a Valid Basis for Finding a "Valuation Gap" Between Dell's Market and Fundamental Values

The Court of Chancery presumed "investor myopia" and hangover from the Company's "nearly $14 billion investment in its transformation, which had not yet begun to generate the anticipated results" produced a "valuation gap" between Dell's fundamental and market prices. That presumption contributed to the trial court's decision to assign no weight to Dell's stock price or deal price. The trial court believed that short-sighted analysts and traders impounded an inadequate—and lowball—assessment of all publicly available information into Dell's stock price, diminishing its worth as a valuation tool. But the record shows just the opposite: analysts scrutinized Dell's long-range outlook when evaluating the Company and setting price targets, and the market was capable of accounting for Dell's recent mergers and acquisitions and their prospects in its valuation of the Company.

Further, the Court of Chancery's analysis ignored the efficient market hypothesis long endorsed by this Court. It teaches that the price produced by an efficient market is generally a more reliable assessment of fair value than the view of a single analyst, especially an expert witness who caters her valuation to the litigation imperatives of a well-heeled client.

A market is more likely efficient, or semi-strong efficient, if it has many stockholders; no controlling stockholder; "highly active trading"; and if information about the company is widely available and easily

---

105 The statute does not instruct the Court of Chancery to create an investment bank-like football field and use it to come to a formulaic determination of value. In many situations, certain valuation methods (e.g., comparables-based analysis) may be of no reliable utility. Our cases stress that the statute assigns the Court of Chancery the duty to consider the relevant methods of valuation argued by the parties and then determine which method (and inputs), or combination of methods, yields the most reliable determination of value.

108 See DFC, 2017 WL 3261190, at 369–71, at *18.

disseminated to the market. In such circumstances, a company's stock price "reflects the judgments of many stockholders about the company's future prospects, based on public filings, industry information, and research conducted by equity analysts." In these circumstances, a mass of investors quickly digests all publicly available information about a company, and in trading the company's stock, recalibrates its price to reflect the market's adjusted, consensus valuation of the company.[116]

The record before us provides no rational, factual basis for such a "valuation gap." Indeed, the trial court did not indicate that Dell lacked a vast and diffuse base of public stockholders, that information about the Company was sparse or restricted, that there was not an active trading market for Dell's shares, or that Dell had a controlling stockholder—or that the market for its stock lacked any of the hallmarks of an efficient market. In fact, the record shows that Dell had a deep public float, was covered by over thirty equity analysts in 2012, boasted 145 market makers, was actively traded with over 5% of shares changing hands each week, and lacked a controlling stockholder. As noted in the expert reports, Dell's stock price had a track record of reacting to developments concerning the Company. For example, the stock climbed 13% on the day the Bloomberg first reported on Dell's talks of going private.

Further, the trial court expressly found no evidence that information failed to flow freely or that management purposefully tempered investors' expectations for the Company so that it could eventually take over the Company at a fire-sale price, as in situations where long-term investments actually led to such valuation gaps. In fact, Mr. Dell tried to persuade investors to envision an enterprise solutions and services business enjoying double-digit sales growth and which would more than compensate for any decline in end-user computing. And he pitched this plan for a "prolonged" period, approaching nearly three years.

There is also no evidence in the record that investors were "myopic" or shortsighted. Rather, the record shows analysts understood Dell's long-term plans. But they just weren't buying Mr. Dell's story. . .

The Court of Chancery's myopia theory also overlooks that, at an earlier stage in its history, Dell was a growth stock trading at large multiples to its then-current cash flow. That is, for much of its history, analysts bought Mr. Dell's long-term vision. But, by the early years of the second decade of the 21st century, they were no longer doing so.

Further, the prospective bidders who later reviewed Dell's confidential information all dropped out due to their considerable discomfort with the future of the PC market. The record simply does not

[116] Id. at 370, at *18 ("[C]orporate finance theory reflects a belief that if an asset—such as the value of a company as reflected in the trading value of its stock—can be subject to close examination and bidding by many humans with an incentive to estimate its future cash flows value, the resulting collective judgment as to value is likely to be highly informative and that, all estimators having equal access to information, the likelihood of outguessing the market over time and building a portfolio of stocks beating it is slight.").

support the Court of Chancery's favoring of management's optimism over the public analysts' and investors' skepticism—especially in the face of management's track record of missing its own projections. (Even Mr. Dell doubted his management team's forecasting abilities and conceded at trial, "We're not very good at forecasting.") And the Court of Chancery does not justify why it chose to do so. In short, the record does not adequately support the Court of Chancery's conclusion that the market for Dell's stock was inefficient and that a valuation gap in the Company's market trading price existed in advance of the lengthy market check, an error that contributed to the trial court's decision to disregard the deal price.

ii. The Lack of Strategic Bidders Is Not a Credible Reason for Disregarding the Deal Price

The trial court's complete discounting of the deal price due to financial sponsors' focus on obtaining a desirable IRR and not "fair value" was also error.

Here, it is clear that Dell's sale process bore many of the same objective indicia of reliability that we found persuasive enough to diminish the resonance of any private equity carve out or similar such theory in *DFC*. . . The Committee, composed of independent, experienced directors and armed with the power to say "no," persuaded Silver Lake to raise its bid six times. Nothing in the record suggests that increased competition would have produced a better result. JPMorgan also reasoned that any other financial sponsor would have bid in the same ballpark as Silver Lake.

The bankers canvassed the interest of sixty-seven parties, including twenty possible strategic acquirers during the go-shop.

The Court of Chancery stressed its view that the lack of competition from a strategic buyer lowered the relevance of the deal price. But its assessment that more bidders—both strategic and financial—should have been involved assumes there was some party interested in proceeding. Nothing in the record indicates that was the case. Fair value entails at minimum a price some buyer is willing to pay—not a price at which no class of buyers in the market would pay. The Court of Chancery ignored an important reality: if a company is one that no strategic buyer is interested in buying, it does not suggest a higher value, but a lower one.

Other than the Buyout Group, as mentioned, all prospective buyers who reviewed the Company's confidential information retreated for the same reasons that the public markets were purportedly undervaluing Dell—trepidation about the future of the PC industry and the prospects of Dell's long-term turnaround strategy. This consistency confirms that management did not intentionally depress the Company's stock price in order to take advantage of a "trough" that public investors failed to recognize. In fact, the trial court expressly found that, "unlike other situations that this court has confronted, there is no evidence that Mr. Dell or his management team sought to create the valuation disconnect so that they could take advantage of it," and "[t]o the contrary, they tried to convince the market that the Company was worth more." Prospective buyers just did not believe the potential for a turnaround outweighed the risk of further erosion of PC sales and, accordingly, the Company's balance sheet. This coherence in views also makes it hard to take seriously the notion that Dell investors were incapable of accounting for Dell's long-term strategy. And it reinforces the integrity of both Dell's stock price and deal price.

Overall, the weight of evidence shows that Dell's deal price has heavy, if not overriding, probative value. The transaction process exemplifies many of the qualities that Delaware courts have found favor affording substantial, if not exclusive, weight to deal price in the fair value analysis. Even the Court of Chancery's own summary remarks suggest the deal price deserves weight as the court characterized the sale process as one that "easily would sail through if reviewed under enhanced scrutiny" and observed that "[t]he Committee and its advisors did many praiseworthy things," too numerous to catalog in its opinion, as the trial court noted. Given the objective indicia of the deal price's reliability and our rejection of the notion of a private equity carve out, to the extent that the Court of Chancery chose to disregard Dell's deal price based on the presence of only private equity bidders, its reasoning is not grounded in accepted financial principles, and this assessment weighs in favor of finding an overall abuse of discretion. As explained below, there are other reasons that lead us to this conclusion.

C. Market Data Conclusion

Taken as a whole, the market-based indicators of value—both Dell's stock price and deal price—have substantial probative value. But here, after examining the sale process, the Court of Chancery summarized that, "[t]aken as a whole, the Company did not establish that the outcome of the sale process offers the most reliable evidence of the Company's value as a going concern." These two statements are not incongruous, and the Court of Chancery's statement is not a rational reason for assigning no weight to market data. There is no requirement that a company prove that the sale process is the most reliable evidence of its going concern value in order for the resulting deal price to be granted any weight. If, as here, the reasoning behind the decision to assign no weight to market data is flawed, then the ultimate conclusion necessarily crumbles as well—especially in light of the less-than-surefire DCF analyses—as demonstrated below.

In so holding, we are not saying that the market is always the best indicator of value, or that it should always be granted some weight. We only note that, when the evidence of market efficiency, fair play, low barriers to entry, outreach to all logical buyers, and the chance for any topping bidder to have the support of Mr. Dell's own votes is so compelling, then failure to give the resulting price heavy weight because the trial judge believes there was mispricing missed by all the Dell stockholders, analysts, and potential buyers abuses even the wide discretion afforded the Court of Chancery in these difficult cases. And, of course, to give no weight to the prices resulting from the actions of Dell's stockholders and potential buyers presupposes that there is a more plausible basis for determining Dell's value in the form of expert testimony, such as from the petitioners' expert, who argued that his DCF analysis showed the fair value of Dell's stock is $28.61 per share—almost three times higher than the unaffected stock price of $9.97 per share and more than two times higher than the deal price of $13.75 per share.

D. The Discounted Cash Flow Analyses

We pause to note that this appraisal case does not present the classic scenario in which there is reason to suspect that market forces cannot be relied upon to ensure fair treatment of the minority. Under those circumstances, a DCF analysis can provide the court with a helpful data point about the price a sale process would have produced had there been a robust sale process involving willing buyers with thorough information and the time to make a bid. When, by contrast, an appraisal is brought in cases like this where a robust sale process of that kind in fact occurred, the Court of Chancery should be chary about imposing the hazards that always come when a law-trained judge is forced to make a point estimate of fair value based on widely divergent partisan expert testimony.

As is common in appraisal proceedings, each party—petitioners and the Company—enlisted highly paid, well-credentialed experts to produce DCF valuations. But their valuations landed galaxies apart—diverging by approximately $28 billion, or 126%. Petitioners' expert arrived at a per-share valuation of $28.61 as of the merger date, and the Company's expert produced a valuation of $12.68 per share. The Court of Chancery recognized that "[t]his is a recurring problem," and even believed the "market data is sufficient to exclude the possibility, advocated by the petitioners' expert, that the Merger undervalued the Company by $23 billion." Thus, the trial court found petitioners' valuation lacks credibility on its face. We agree. Yet, the trial court believed it could reconcile these enormous valuation chasms caused by the over 1,100 variable inputs in the competing DCFs and construct a DCF that more appropriately reflected the fair value of Dell's stock than the market data. And, reconciling the various agreements and divergences among the experts, the trial court determined fair value to be $17.62.

To underscore our concern with the Court of Chancery's decision to give no weight to Dell's stock market price or the deal price and, instead, arrive at a value nearly $7 billion above the transaction price, we consider the trial court's concluding explanation for its reasoning:

> The fair value generated by the DCF methodology comports with the evidence regarding the outcome of the sale process. The sale process functioned imperfectly as a price discovery tool,

> both during the pre-signing and post-signing phases. Its structure and result are sufficiently credible to exclude an outlier valuation for the Company like the one the petitioners advanced, but sufficient pricing anomalies and disincentives to bid existed to create the possibility that the sale process permitted an undervaluation of several dollars per share. Financial sponsors using an LBO model could not have bid close to $18 per share because of their IRR requirements and the Company's inability to support the necessary levels of leverage. Assuming the $17.62 figure is right, then a strategic acquirer that perceived the Company's value could have gotten the Company for what was approximately a 25% discount. [But g]iven the massive integration risk inherent in such a deal, it is not entirely surprising that HP did not engage and that no one else came forward. Had the valuation gap approached what the petitioners' expert believed, then the incentives to intervene would have been vastly greater.
>
> Because it is impossible to quantify the exact degree of the sale process mispricing, this decision does not give weight to the Final Merger Consideration. It uses the DCF methodology exclusively to derive a fair value of the Company.[186]

What this statement means is that the Court of Chancery's DCF value was the antithesis of any economist's definition of fair market value. The Court of Chancery conceded that its DCF value did not reflect a value deemed attractive to the buyers of Dell's 1,765,369,276 publicly traded shares. Further, it did not reflect the value that private equity buyers (including the biggest players such as KKR, TPG, and Blackstone) put on it, as it was too high for any of them to pay. The trial court also picked a price higher than any strategic would pay because, in economic terms, no strategic believed it could exploit a purported $6.8 billion value gap because the risks and costs of acquiring Dell and integrating it into its company dwarfed any potential for profit and synergy gains if Dell were purchased at the Court of Chancery's determination of fair value. And, of course, as to all buyers, strategic and financial, the Court of Chancery found that a topping bid put them at hazard of overpaying and succumbing to a winner's curse.

When an asset has few, or no, buyers at the price selected, that is not a sign that the asset is stronger than believed—it is a sign that it is weaker. This fact should give pause to law-trained judges who might attempt to outguess all of these interested economic players with an actual stake in a company's future. This is especially so here, where the Company worked hard to tell its story over a long time and was the opposite of a standoffish, defensively entrenched target as it approached the sale process free of many deal-protection devices that may prevent

---

186 Dell Trial Fair Value, 2016 WL 3186538, at *51.

selling companies from attracting the highest bid. Dell was a willing seller, ready to pay for credible buyers to do due diligence, and had a CEO and founder who offered his voting power freely to any topping bidder.

Given that we have concluded that the trial court's key reasons for disregarding the market data were erroneous, and given the obvious lack of credibility of the petitioners' DCF model—as well as legitimate questions about the reliability of the projections upon which all of the various DCF analyses are based—these factors suggest strong reliance upon the deal price and far less weight, if any, on the DCF analyses.

In addition to the relatively sound economic reasons, there are also important policy reasons supporting this result. If the reward for adopting many mechanisms designed to minimize conflict and ensure stockholders obtain the highest possible value is to risk the court adding a premium to the deal price based on a DCF analysis, then the incentives to adopt best practices will be greatly reduced. Although widely considered the best tool for valuing companies when there is no credible market information and no market check, DCF valuations involve many inputs—all subject to disagreement by well-compensated and highly credentialed experts—and even slight differences in these inputs can produce large valuation gaps. Here, management's projections alone involved more than 1,100 inputs, and the experts' fair value determinations . . . landed on different planets. Rather than gambling on an appraisal's battle of the experts, transactional planners might instead propose alternative routes (such as squeeze-outs) to CEOs and founders that will be less attractive for diversified investors in public companies and will likely result in going-private transactions occurring at a lower, not higher, value.

III. Fair Value Conclusion

Despite the sound economic and policy reasons supporting the use of the deal price as the fair value award on remand, we will not give in to the temptation to dictate that result. That said, we give the Vice Chancellor the discretion on remand to enter judgment at the deal price if he so chooses, with no further proceedings. If he decides to follow another route, the outcome should adhere to our rulings in this opinion, including our findings with regard to the DCF valuation. If he chooses to weigh a variety of factors in arriving at fair value, he must explain that weighting based on reasoning that is consistent with the record and with relevant, accepted financial principles.

NOTES

1. *Valuation in Appraisal Proceedings.* The *Dell* opinion reflects the customary approach to appraisal proceedings in Delaware insofar that appraisal actions should award dissenting stockholders their proportional share of the value of the 'going concern' exclusive any value arising from the transaction, such as value created by operating synergies or the benefits of consolidated control. Nor do these benefits include the elimination of any

agency costs arising by virtue of the transaction. Why should courts exclude these other factors?

2. *The Primacy of Market Prices?* When the *Dell* decision was handed down, Vice Chancellor Laster was in the midst of deciding another appraisal proceeding involving Hewlett-Packard's acquisition of a company called Aruba Networks Inc. The Vice Chancellor ultimately awarded the Aruba petitioners $17.13 per share—the stock's trading price prior to the merger's announcement and $7.54 *below* the deal price. The Vice Chancellor arrived at this conclusion for two reasons. First, he felt the *Dell* decision compelled him to look to market-based indicators of value. Second, he believed the other market metric—the deal price—included a premium for "reduced agency costs" that were inappropriate to award to the petitioning shareholders, as discussed in the previous Note. In reversing the Chancery Court, the Delaware Supreme Court rejected the notion that the deal price included a reduction in agency costs that was separate from the estimate of deal synergies offered by Aruba; therefore, it awarded the petitioners $19.10 per share, or the merger price minus the estimated value of these synergies. In justifying its willingness to depart from the market price, the Supreme Court noted that there were reasons to believe Hewlett-Packard possessed nonpublic information concerning Aruba in negotiating the merger price. See Verition Partners Master Fund Ltd. v. Aruba Networks, Inc., 210 A.3d 128 (Del. 2019). Following *Aruba,* there was understandably some confusion about the role of market-based indicators of value in Delaware appraisal proceedings. Should courts prioritize deal price or market prices? And what role should traditional approaches such as a DCF or comparables play?

Two additional Delaware Supreme Court cases decided in 2020 appeared to suggest a rough pecking order. First, in Structures Fund Ltd. v. Stillwater Mining Co., 240 A.3d 3 (Del. 2020) the Court held that the Chancery Court did not abuse its discretion when it held that deal price (less synerges) was a reliable indicator of fair value if the court concluded that the sales process had "objective indicia" of reliability. Second, in Fir Tree Value Master Fund, LP v. Jarden Corporation, 236 A.3d 313 (2020), it held that the Chancery Court was within its discretion to use the unaffected, pre-merger trading price to support its determination of fair value after concluding that the deal price resulted from a flawed sales process. In light of *Dell* and *Aruba,* these cases appeared to suggest that appraisal proceedings should first give priority to deal price (less synergies) so long as the court could conclude that the sales process had "objective indicia" that the deal price fully valued the company. Absent such a conclusion, a court could then look to pre-transaction market prices so long as the court had no reason to believe that the stock price was distorted (e.g., because there was nonpublic material information that was not reflected in the stock price or because the stock did not trade in an informationally efficient market). If neither of these market-based measures could be used, a court could then rely on a DCF or comparables analysis. While this pecking order was not explicitly stated by the Delaware Supreme Court, the Chancery Court had largely adopted it by 2023. See, e.g., HBK Master Fund L.P. v. Pivotal Software, Inc. 2023 WL 5199634, (Del. Ch. Aug. 14, 2023) (noting "recent decisions of Delaware courts suggested a pecking order of methodologies for determining fair value. . .") How might the prioritization of market values by courts explain the drop off in appraisal petitions since 2017?

3. *Market Values in the Federal Courts.* As in *Dell*, federal courts have in some cases rejected expert testimony in favor of market evidence. For instance, VFB LLC v. Campbell Soup Co., 482 F.3d 624 (3d Cir. 2007) affirmed a lower court holding that rejected expert testimony in favor of market values in a case involving a fraudulent transfer in an unsuccessful corporate spin-off. Similarly, the Bankruptcy Court followed this approach in In re Iridium Operating LLC, 373 B.R. 283 (Bankr. S.D.N.Y. 2007), stating that "the public markets constitute a better guide to fair value than the opinions of hired litigation experts whose valuation work is performed after the fact and from an advocate's point of view." *Id.* at 291.

4. *Minority and Illiquidity Discounts.* As noted in *Dell*, the appraisal action contemplates determining the aggregate value of a firm and then awarding each shareholder his or her pro rata interest in it, without regard to a minority discount or illiquidity discount. For instance, where a company's stock is dominated by a controlling shareholder, the shares held by minority stockholders could, in theory, be valued at a discount given their inability to control the firm. Likewise, where a company's stock trades infrequently, the shares may trade at a discount given the difficulty of selling the stock. The rejection of any such discounts was articulated by the Delaware Supreme Court in Cavalier Oil Corp. v. Hartnett, 564 A.2d 1137 (Del. 1989), in which the Supreme Court approved of the chancery court's interpretation of Section 262's objective as valuing "the corporation itself, as distinguished from a specific fraction of its shares as they may exist in the hands of a particular shareholder."* The Revised Model Business Corporation presently takes a similar approach. Revisions to Model Business Corporation Act ("Model Act") § 13.01 now define "fair value" for appraisal purposes as follows:

> " 'Fair value' means the value of the corporation's shares determined:
>
> (i) immediately before the effectiveness of the corporate action to which the shareholder objects;
>
> (ii) using customary and current valuation concepts and techniques generally employed for similar businesses in the context of the transaction requiring appraisal; and

---

* As the Court noted in *Cavalier*, this approach to valuation does not necessarily rule out the possibility that a court might account for the presence of a controller in its valuation analysis. For instance, if the presence of a controller depresses the stock price of a company (e.g., because of controller agency costs), a court might provide an upward adjustment of the market value *of the firm* to account for the discount the market places on the firm's value. After making this adjustment, the court would then assess each shareholder's proportionate interest without any further discounts. As the Court noted, there is a "distinction between applying the discount at the company level [to determine firm value] . . . . and its use to further devalue a shareholder's proportionate interest." In Delaware, the former is permitted, while the latter is not.

(iii) without discounting for lack of marketability or minority status except, if appropriate, for amendments to the articles of incorporation pursuant to section 13.02(a)(5)."

The cases in other jurisdictions are mixed on the application of a minority discount. See, e.g., English v. Atromick International, Inc., 2000 Ohio App. LEXIS 3580 (2000) (applying both a minority discount and marketability discount).

CHAPTER 4

CAPITAL STRUCTURE

1. INTRODUCTION

We are ready to explore how a company decides where to get its funds. Should it sell stock, issue bonds, borrow from a bank, or tap into some other source of money to support operations? As mentioned earlier, a firm's collective choices in this area are known as its capital structure. Even a cursory glance at two companies can show that managers often take very different approaches to this issue. The company Alphabet, Inc. (the holding company for Google), for instance, has historically taken on almost no long-term debt, while Apple secures roughly half its funding in this manner. Why would two close competitors make such different choices?

A good place to start is by asking whether funding decisions can create incremental value for a company. On the operating side (as opposed to the fundraising side of the business) there are many plausible ways to generate value. A firm might be first to invent a revolutionary new product. Or it might gain economies of scale that allow it to produce something for less than everyone else. Or it might identify another strategy for generating positive net present value investments. Indeed, this is at the heart of what businesses do.

By contrast, creating value through corporate fundraising decisions is usually considered much more difficult. There are two main ways to create value via fundraising. First, the firm could "fool" investors by issuing a security and selling it for an excessively high price. Second, it might seek to reduce some other type of cost through fundraising activities.

The first possibility, fooling investors, takes us back to our previous discussion of efficient capital markets. From an investor standpoint, securities of different firms are usually viewed as economic substitutes for each other.* The exact price of one company's stock will differ from that of another company, of course, in a way that reflects the firm's future

* As you may have studied in an economics class, rival or competing goods are often described as substitutes. In the consumer context, a price increase (decrease) for one product will typically increase (decrease) demand for its substitute. For imperfect substitutes, the effect may only be partial. If a city's underground metro raises ticket prices, for example, some people will start riding the bus, but other die-hard riders will stick with the metro. For perfect substitutes, however, a price increase will theoretically cause consumers to move all business to the substitute. A food buyer might view identical crops on neighboring farms in this manner. This concept of economic substitutes is relevant to corporate financing decisions. For instance, we saw this implicitly in Chapter 3 when we determined the cost of equity capital by examining how you could construct a portfolio using risk-free government securities, risky common stock, and risky borrowings. Having determined the rates of return for various combinations, we could then calculate the rates that investors would demand for stock portfolios with various levels of risk. This enabled us to derive the capital market line, along which all returns must lie.

expected cash flows and risk. But once prices are in equilibrium, an investor is unlikely to pay a premium for, say, Nike stock simply because she likes that firm more. If Nike did try to levy a "popularity premium," then investors would shift their money to a different stock that offered a superior risk-return tradeoff.

For this reason, many firms seeking to raise capital focus more on cost minimization. Will one type of funding be less expensive to obtain? Will it drive down any other costs for the firm? Some fundraising expenses arise through transaction costs, of course, such as the need to pay lawyers or bankers to help execute a financing plan. But, as we will see, there may be other types of costs that a firm seeks to minimize—such as taxes or a risk of bankruptcy. Moreover, different firm circumstances can lead to different choices about what the best capital structure looks like. A brand-new biotech venture may not make the same funding decisions as an established steel conglomerate, but both firms might be financed optimally for their specific situations. This chapter explores both the variety of instruments used to raise capital and the different reasons why firms might choose one pattern of financing over others.

2. THE RANGE OF FINANCIAL CHOICES

Problem 4.1

Your new client, E-Toaster Inc., makes web-enabled toasters for smart homes. ("Dial up your crispness, punch start through the Wi-Fi, and hit that snooze button on your alarm.") Recent business has been good, and E-Toaster has $200 million in assets (comprised of cash, receivables, inventory, and some manufacturing assets). It is capitalized as follows:

(A) $25 million from a short-term bank line of credit

(B) $25 million from long-term bonds (due in 20 years)

(C) $150 million from common stock (stockholders' equity)

E-Toaster forecasts free cash flow of $50 million per year for the near future. It has never paid out dividends to its shareholders. But recently, an activist shareholder has convinced the company's CEO to start paying $25 million in dividends each year, and the company has agreed to commence paying dividends next year. E-Toaster now wants to expand into Wi-Fi waffle makers, and it needs to raise $50 million during the next year to purchase new manufacturing equipment and support expanded working capital needs.

E-Toaster's CEO and CFO have just stopped by your office to ask for advice about how the firm should obtain this new capital. They mention that they are considering several options: (1) funding the project from retained earnings; (2) issuing more common stock; (3) issuing a new series of preferred stock; (4) trying to increase the bank line of credit;

or (5) issuing additional bonds. They are also open to any other ideas that you might have. What should you tell them?

When faced with new capital needs, many firms might begin by asking whether they can (and should) finance the incremental funding with cash retained from operations (option 1 in Problem 4.1). New projects are often supported by profits from prior activities that can be plowed back into the firm, thereby avoiding the need to tap external sources of capital. This is sometimes called bootstrapping. Of course, this financing option is not free; the opportunity cost of doing something else with the money, including returning it to shareholders, must be considered. Will retained earnings work as a financing option for E-Toaster in Problem 4.1? The short answer is no, not unless the company is willing to break its promise to begin paying a common stock dividend. While it does expect to generate $50 million in free cash flow over the next year, half of this will be used in the $25 million dividend. Accordingly, internal funding may go part of the way, but E-Toaster will also need to find another option.

Each of the other possibilities mentioned in this problem offers an array of tradeoffs for the firm and investors. E-toaster could issue more common stock (option 2) to avoid incurring a fixed repayment obligation (which arises with debt), but current shareholder rights—including voting control—will be diluted. The firm might also need to arrange a larger total dividend payout unless it wants to pay less to each share. Issuing preferred stock (option 3) could enable the firm to avoid common stock dilution (depending on the exact terms), but it would probably grant the new investors liquidation priority and perhaps some other preferences.

The two suggested debt options, short-term bank borrowing (option 4) and longer-term bonds (option 5), offer still different tradeoffs. Each would lock in a fixed payment obligation, take seniority over most other investor claims, and (probably) generate a tax break for the firm through the deductibility of interest payments. Short-term borrowing might allow for cheaper interest rates than long-term borrowing, but it could expose the firm to additional risks if E-Toaster needs to "roll over" this financing when payment on the bank credit line is due. These and many other factors—such as the firm's existing debt level, relevant contractual obligations, and expectations about future financing conditions—must be considered.

Moreover, to provide comprehensive advice to E-Toaster, you would want to be familiar with an even broader menu of fundraising alternatives. Your clients have suggested some good possibilities, but the complete range of financing instruments is as broad as the imaginations of investment bankers and attorneys. We will offer a much closer look at many of these alternatives in the chapters that follow. But, for now, let's turn to an overview of the primary types of fundraising vehicles.

A. EQUITY-RELATED FINANCING

Before examining different types of equity-related financing, it may be helpful to discuss the overall purpose of equity financing. Like debt, the sale of equity—partial ownership in a firm—is a fundraising tool used by entities to obtain capital that can be used to fund the expenses of running or growing the business. However, unlike debt, the sale of equity does not typically carry an obligation to repay the principal amount invested or interest on that amount at a later date. Instead, equity owners are entitled to a residual claim on the value of the business and to any distributions of profit that the business chooses to make as it operates, such as dividends or share repurchases. Equity investors also enjoy the possibility of gain on their investment in the form of appreciation in value of the shares purchased as the business grows.

Options and Warrants. If we were to start with the riskiest forms of investments in corporations, most would expect to start with common stock. Common stock, after all, represents the residual claim on the earnings and assets of the firm, after all other claimants have been paid off. But there are instruments that are even riskier than common stock, represented by options to purchase stock. In general, stock options represent a contract right to purchase stock at a specified price per share. You may be familiar with the concept of a stock option from the employment context: Employees (especially at technology companies) often receive stock options as part of their compensation package. But stock options can also be acquired by individuals who are not employees. In this latter context, stock options are called "warrants" when they are issued by the company, and "call options" when written by others, as we will explore in Chapter 8. Options and warrants are considered riskier than stock because they might expire as worthless even when the firm is solvent and the stock itself has value.

As noted above, options and warrants convey a right—but not an obligation—to purchase a share of common stock at a specified price over a specified period of time. For example, I might pay e-Toaster $5 to buy a warrant that allows me to purchase a share of common stock for $50 (known as the exercise price or strike price) any time over the next year. If the underlying stock price never exceeds the exercise price during the life of the warrant, the warrant expires and is worth nothing. There is no reason to pay $50 for a share of e-Toaster stock under the warrant if I can buy it on the market for less. If, on the other hand, the price of the stock rises above the strike price, then a warrant holder will exercise the warrant by paying $50 and will receive one share of common stock. From a corporate governance standpoint, option and warrant holders have no right to vote or receive earnings from the corporation until they exercise their option to buy stock; rights under a warrant are strictly contractual. This short discussion of options also highlights why companies issue stock options to employees: Because options only have value if the underlying stock price exceeds the exercise price, the employee will have strong incentives to increase the value of the company and its stock price. However, it is important to keep in mind that options can also appear in some other funding situations, as we shall see.

Common Stock. Common stock is considered the prototypical form of investment in a corporation. Shareholders are generally regarded as the "residual" claimants on the firm, entitled to all income and assets after the rights of senior claimants (listed below) are satisfied. Because of their residual status, shareholders also receive voting rights, with the right to vote for election (and removal) of directors and to vote for fundamental changes in the corporate contract like charter amendments, mergers, sales of all assets, liquidations, and dissolution. Common shareholders are also owed fiduciary duties by a firm's directors, who generally must look out for the rights of the shareholders (as opposed to those of other claimants). Common shares may also be issued in classes with different rights, such as non-voting common and voting common, or common with super-voting rights compared to other common shares. Some technology firms, for example, have concentrated control in an influential founder through a super-voting class of common stock.

Common shareholders are not automatically entitled to regular payments on their investment, but they may receive recurring dividend payments from the firm. A board retains discretion, however, to reduce or discontinue dividend payments at any point in time. That being said, firms recognize that a dividend cut is usually taken as a signal of upcoming financial trouble, and they may endeavor to maintain (or even slowly increase) current dividend plans. Some corporations may prefer stock buybacks to dividends as a way to distribute cash to common stock investors in a tax-advantaged manner. We will discuss dividend policy, including the legal limits on a firm's ability to pay dividends, in a later chapter.

Preferred Stock. You should think of preferred stock as a highly flexible investment that sits between common stock and debt on a firm's balance sheet. Formally it is considered an equity investment, but the only way to understand the legal rights held by a holder of preferred stock is to look closely at the issuing company's charter. Preferred stock must be specifically authorized in a company's charter which must set forth all of the rights, preferences, and privileges that attach to the preferred stock. Moreover, a company will often authorize a class of preferred stock and further subdivide it into separate "series" of preferred stock, each having its own rights and preferences, as specified in the charter.

Preferred stock is largely a creature of contract, with few if any rights created by law. In this case, the contract is the corporate charter. There is not a standard array of features that all issues of preferred stock will adopt. Given this flexibility, preferred stock is often favored in certain specialized contexts. For example, start-up companies seeking outside equity financing ("seed capital" at the earliest stage and "venture capital" later on) will often issue preferred stock to the outside investors, while the founders retain common stock. As we shall see, the reason stems from the flexibility of preferred stock, which has permitted venture capitalists to craft a unique form of financing that treats the investor as a common stockholder for highly successful startups (thus sharing in the large residual claim) while also granting the investor debt-like protections when a startup fails.

As noted above, shares of preferred stock must be authorized in the company's charter, which means that authorizing any shares of preferred stock requires amending the company's charter. However, most state laws authorize the charter to create a class of "blank check preferred" stock, which the board of directors can later subdivide into one or more series, and specify the rights and preferences as new series are authorized.* In these cases, whenever the board creates a new series of preferred stock and specifies its rights, it files a "certificate of designation" with the relevant state regulatory agency, which amends the charter to include the new terms. Importantly, designating a series of blank check preferred stock does not generally require shareholder approval. This flexibility has made blank check preferred useful for creating hostile takeover defenses, as well as for raising capital.

In general, the rights and preferences of preferred stock can be classified as involving "economic" preferences and "control" preferences. For example, with regard to economic preferences, a company's charter might grant preferred stock special dividend rights. Preferred stock dividends are usually specified either as a dollar amount or as a percentage of the original price of the preferred stock. As in the case of common stock, receipt of dividends is not a property right of the preferred shareholder; the board of directors retains flexibility to decide whether to pay the dividend in any given period. The only assurance that preferred shareholders have is that no dividends can be paid on the common stock unless and until a dividend is first paid on the preferred. "Straight" preferred stock only prohibits paying a dividend on the common in any year that no dividend is paid on the preferred. That is, the holders of straight preferred stock must be paid if the holders of common are to be paid. Because this permits the board to skip preferred stock dividends for many years, then pay a single year's earmarked dividend on the preferred and a larger dividend of accumulated earnings to the common stockholders, wise investors might wish to avoid this form of preferred.† It is more typical, therefore, for the preferred stock to "cumulate" unpaid dividends—so that if the firm does not pay a stated preferred dividend in any given year, the amount will carry over to the following year (and thereafter). Eventually, the firm must pay the total

* See, e.g., DGCL § 151(a); Model Act § 6.02.

† If the preferred stock is convertible into shares of common stock, it is possible for the terms of the preferred stock to grant the holder of preferred stock the right to participate in any common stock dividends as if the preferred stock had been converted into shares of common stock. This type of preferred stock dividend is common in venture capital finance.

amount of the accumulated dividends to preferred shareholders before anything can be paid out to the common shareholders.

Another common economic entitlement of preferred stock is a liquidation preference. In general, a liquidation preference entitles the holder of preferred stock to receive from the company a designated amount per share of preferred (often its original purchase price) before any distributions can be made to common stockholders. While the term might suggest this preferential payment is limited to the dissolution of a company, the terms of the preferred stock can also make it apply to other settings, such as an acquisition of the company.

"Control" preferences generally focus on the voting rights of preferred stock, which can vary greatly. Publicly issued preferred stock frequently will have no voting rights in the ordinary course of business, but will obtain, by statute or contract, voting rights on any amendment of the preferred stock's terms and, in some cases, on the issue of new classes or series of preferred with rights and preferences that would be senior to those of the current, outstanding preferred. Publicly issued preferred stock can also be granted the right to elect some or all directors if dividends are skipped on the preferred for some specified number of periods.* By contrast, preferred stock issued in the startup context will often have full voting rights, equal to (or even better than) those of the common stock.

As we will see in Chapter 7, preferred stock sometimes includes other, more complex features. For example, in addition to having a liquidation preference and preferential dividend rights, preferred stock might also be convertible into a specified number of shares of common stock and/or redeemable by the firm or investor (or both) according to a set formula. Convertible preferred stock might also have a "participation" feature that gives holders the right to be treated as a common stockholder even after receiving any preferential payments owed to the preferred stock. For instance, venture capital investors might acquire participating preferred stock that, upon the acquisition of a startup company, entitles the venture capitalist to receive its liquidation preference before the common stockholders receive any payments and to thereafter receive distributions on its preferred stock as if it had converted its preferred stock into common stock. Again, the hallmark of preferred stock is flexibility, and the security is used for many different purposes.†

* New York Stock Exchange Listed Company Manual Section 313.00(c) provides: "Preferred stock, voting as a class, should have the right to elect a minimum of two directors upon default of the equivalent of six quarterly dividends. The right to elect directors should accrue regardless of whether defaulted dividends occurred in consecutive periods."

† For example, the flexibility of preferred stock makes it a popular vehicle for delivering the anti-takeover defense known as the poison pill. Or, to take another example, floating rate preferred (sometimes called "floaters") is a preferred stock with a dividend rate that varies with short-term interest rates. This is sometimes issued by banks and sold to corporations with excess cash available for short-term investment. Floating rate preferred can be an attractive alternative to short-term debt instruments for tax reasons (the dividends received deduction available to corporations).

B. DEBT-RELATED FINANCING

As noted earlier, debt-related financing is the primary alternative to equity-related financing for companies seeking to obtain external capital. While preferred stock is "contractual" in the sense that the terms of preferred must be specified in a company's charter, debt financing is truly a creature of contract. As a result, the number of permutations that debt can take is enormous, and we cannot discuss all of them here. What follows is merely an overview of some of the more common varieties; we will provide a more elaborate discussion of debt financing in Chapter 6.

Before we begin, we note that a distinguishing feature of virtually all forms of debt financing is that the debtor company is contractually obligated to repay a fixed sum of money.* In some cases, the obligation arises because the company has borrowed money, but in others, the obligation arises because the company received some other form of value (e.g., inventory or other assets). As we saw in Chapter 2, debt obligations are typically recorded on a company's balance sheet as a liability and classified as either short-term debt or long-term debt. Short-term debt is generally thought of as debt that will be due within one year from the time it is incurred. This kind of debt financing is typically used to support current operations, often involving seasonal cash requirements, such as the need of retail merchants to build up extra inventory in advance of holiday sales. On the balance sheet this is classified as current debt (see Chapter 2), and long-term debt is often described as "funded debt."

1. *Bank Loans.* For many readers, the concept of debt financing might bring to mind a loan officer at your local bank who spends her day making commercial loans to businesses. Consistent with this intuition, banks represent a core source of debt financing for many companies; however, other institutions, such as commercial finance companies and factors, may also duplicate much of the financing available through banks. We describe here some of the more common forms of bank financing, acknowledging that in practice, a bank need not be the party to whom a company is obligated. Additionally, in all of the examples that follow, note that the lender will typically demand compensation for the loan through an interest rate that may be fixed or that may float with a reference rate, such as SOFR (Secured Overnight Financing Rate), which is the interest rate major U.S. financial institutions pay each other for

---

* Note that the concept of debt financing is typically confined to situations where the firm itself is contractually obligated to repay borrowed funds. Thus, it would exclude situations where borrowed funds are indirectly used to fund a corporation's operations. For instance, the promoters of many new corporations will borrow funds personally to invest in their business, generally by making equity investments. While the promoters expect to repay these loans from the profits earned in the business, as far as contractual obligations are concerned, these remain the personal obligation of the promoter, and are generally not thought of as part of corporate finance.

overnight loans.* Yields on various U.S. Treasury securities and other benchmarks are also used as reference points for interest obligations.

For companies looking to finance long-term operations, banks can offer *term loans*, often secured by tangible assets of a business, like equipment or real estate. These loans generally span several years, with terms often ranging between 5 to 10 years. Interest rates typically float on these loans. Banks are limited by federal regulation to lend not more than 10% of their capital to any one borrower. When a borrower's needs are larger than a bank's capacity, it frequently brings in additional banks to participate in the loan (a syndication). Similar loans are made by other financial institutions, including pension funds and insurance companies. More recently, large private credit funds, run by private equity asset managers like Blackstone and Apollo, have also increasingly moved into the direct lending business.

For shorter term borrowing requirements, companies might turn to some of the following options:

Accounts receivable financing is most often used by businesses facing short-term cash flow needs. Many lenders will lend firms as much as 75% of their recent accounts receivable balance. But as accounts grow older, lenders will reduce the percentage of face value they will lend or, in some cases, may refuse to lend in this manner at all as bad debt risk grows. This form of financing is a type of secured loan in which accounts receivable are pledged as collateral in exchange for cash. The loan is repaid within a specified short-term period as the receivables are collected. In other cases, finance companies may purchase the receivables outright (known as "factoring"), which does not create a liability on the debtor's books.

Inventory financing is similar to accounts receivable financing, except the business' current inventory is used as collateral for the secured loan. For current retail inventory that retailers expect to sell soon, the firm may be able to borrow 60–80% of a conservative valuation of the inventory. By contrast, manufacturers' inventories, consisting of component parts and unfinished materials, may fetch as little as 30%. The key factor is the merchantability of the inventory—how quickly and for how much money the inventory can be sold. Imagine, for instance, that you are a lender who extends inventory financing. If a clothing retailer approaches you about a loan based on leftover outfits from last year, you might grow nervous about placing a high value on this possibly stale inventory. Like accounts receivable financing, this is current financing, and it is often used to purchase new inventory.

Businesses can also finance current transactions with a *line of credit* that establishes a maximum amount of funds available from a bank that can be drawn down as needed for ongoing working capital or other uses.

* Beginning in January 2022, SOFR replaced the London Interbank Offered Rate (LIBOR) as a benchmark interest rate for new loans in the U.S.

These credit lines are offered for renewable periods, which may range up to several years. Typically, banks want the line to reach zero at some point during each year to ensure that the line of credit is not being used to finance long-term projects. Interest rates float at the current rate, and most lines of credit are secured by receivables or inventory. (Established businesses with good cash flows and credit histories might be able to borrow on an unsecured basis.) These commitments are sometimes called "revolving credit facilities" or "revolvers." A commitment fee may be assessed by the bank for making a line of credit available to the borrower, even if the full amount is never used. Interest accrues only on the amount actually borrowed, however, so a firm with seasonal cash needs may find this an especially attractive option.

More generally, businesses can also turn to *short-term commercial loans* for current financing needs. Although these loans are sometimes used to finance the same type of operating costs as a working capital line of credit, they are different because a commercial loan is usually taken out for a specific expenditure (e.g., to purchase a specific piece of equipment or repay a particular debt). Unlike accounts receivable or inventory financing, short-term commercial loans are also not typically contingent on the value of specific current assets like receivables or inventory. A fixed amount of money is borrowed for a set time with interest paid on the lump sum. These loans are typically secured and can be either short-term or for periods of three to five years.

Companies may also work with banks to obtain less obvious forms of short-term debt financing. For instance, a company might ask a bank to issue *a letter of credit* on the company's behalf. The letter guarantees payment by the bank to the recipient of the letter upon proof that contract terms between the company and the letter recipient have been completed. These letters are often used for international credit purchases or to guarantee a company's obligations under a contract (e.g., a company's lease obligations). For example, a buyer of goods might obtain a letter of credit, under which the bank promises to pay the foreign seller a stipulated purchase price upon satisfactory delivery of the goods. The seller might take comfort from the letter, knowing that it doesn't need to rely solely on the buyer's creditworthiness; indeed, it might not be willing to do business without such a letter. The issuing bank will typically deliver the funds to the seller's bank upon receipt of satisfactory documentation proving the goods were delivered. The bank would then seek reimbursement from the buyer.

2. *Other Forms of Debt-Financing*. Over the past few decades, corporate borrowers have also been able to turn directly to the capital markets for debt financing. Instead of going to a bank for a loan, the firm might issue bonds or another type of financing instrument to raise debt-related funds from a broader base of investors. Again, the range of strategies for obtaining credit in the capital markets is diverse. Let's consider a few options.

Commercial paper involves short-term, unsecured promissory notes, typically with maturities of no more than nine months (to take advantage of securities law exemptions). Proceeds are normally used for current transactions, such as payroll or accounts payable. Many different types of companies issue commercial paper, but it has been especially important for financial services firms. Issuers can market paper directly to buyers (other companies that invest on a short-term basis) or sell through a dealer, like an investment bank or a subsidiary of a commercial bank, that resells in the commercial paper market. Commercial paper is usually issued in denominations of $100,000 or more. The Federal Reserve Board publishes commercial paper rates for specific maturities. Commercial paper is also rated by credit rating agencies, such as Moody's Investors Services and Standard and Poor's, Inc.

The short maturity of commercial paper comes with an obvious downside: issuers of commercial paper will need to repay it in just a matter of months (or even days). Most issuers manage this repayment risk by issuing a new batch of commercial paper as pre-existing obligations mature, the proceeds of which are used to satisfy the company's repayment obligation. This process of "rolling over" commercial paper works so long as investors stand ready to purchase an issuer's commercial paper. During the Financial Crisis of 2007–2008, however, many investors abandoned the commercial paper market, contributing to the liquidity crisis faced by large financial firms.

Debentures. Unsecured corporate debt sold in public markets is generally called a debenture, although short-term debt may be called "notes." There is no legal or economic distinction between the two. In some cases, debentures may be expressly subordinated to other debt, such as debts owed to general creditors or term loans. If so, the risk attached to subordinated debt begins to approach the risks borne by stockholders, and higher interest rates will be needed to attract investors. When the risk is sufficiently high, the debt will not be rated as investment grade by the rating services and will be called "high yield" debt or, in the vernacular, "junk bonds." Because of the requirements of the Trust Indenture Act of 1939,* debentures sold in amounts in excess of $50 million must typically be issued pursuant to a trust indenture, which names a trustee to act as agent on behalf of the holders to enforce the terms of the contract. Indentures (the formal debt contracts) are also written in standardized terms, as we shall see in Chapter 6. Some debentures are convertible into common stock, a subject examined in Chapter 8. Like other loans, interest rates may be fixed or variable on debentures.

Bonds. Bonds are also promissory notes, with terms very much like those of debentures, except the term "bond" is typically used to describe obligations that are secured by collateral. This gives them a priority in

* 15 U.S.C. §§ 77aaa et seq. The specific requirements of the Trust Indenture Act are discussed in Chapter 6.

bankruptcy, to the extent of the collateral, over unsecured claims. (In some cases, however, a security interest in fixed assets that are specific to a business may be worth little if the salvage value of the assets is low.) Like debentures, they are issued under a trust indenture. Sometimes the term "bond" is loosely used to describe unsecured debt, so the distinction becomes less important.

Structured Financing is another technique that might be used by borrowers to obtain a lower interest rate than they could obtain on the basis of their overall credit rating. The strategy involves taking high-quality assets (such as accounts receivable) and separating them from the risks of the borrower's overall business. The firm accomplishes this separation by selling these assets to a special-purpose vehicle ("SPV") (sometimes called a "special purpose entity," or "SPE"), which in turn sells securities against the pool of assets that the SPV has acquired. If the sale of assets to the SPV is a true sale for value and does not leave the borrower with unreasonably small capital, concerns about the potential bankruptcy of the operating business do not attach to the SPV. Accordingly, the transaction is not viewed as a fraudulent conveyance or a voidable preference in bankruptcy. Even so, how do you think a pre-existing creditor, such as a bank, would feel after a company completes this type of transaction? They may not be enamored with the change and might even try to prevent such moves in the initial lending contract.

Finally, we should mention *capital leases* as yet another form of financing. It may sound strange to think about a lease contract as financing, but businesses frequently use long-term leases as an alternative to borrowing cash and purchasing assets. Typically, these leases are for a significant portion of the expected economic life of the asset. Lease payments are calculated to return to the lender (either a commercial finance company or a subsidiary of a bank) the asset's entire purchase price plus interest. At the termination of the lease, the lessee may then have the right to purchase the asset at a nominal price. This arrangement is thus quite similar, economically speaking, to borrowing money from the lessor and purchasing the asset.

Equipment leasing is an important form of corporate finance in some industries. Airlines frequently lease airplanes, and shippers frequently lease rail cars. Other companies may lease vehicles. In some cases, companies may also sell currently owned assets and lease them back to execute a capital structure change. Leasing fungible assets, such as railroad cars or trucks, eliminates much of the lessor's need to engage in a credit investigation of the lessee; the lease terminates if the lessee defaults, and the equipment can quickly be leased (or sold) to others. One of the other reasons for the popularity of this arrangement is that leasing can have some tax advantages over outright ownership.*

* Normally the lessor obtains the depreciation deduction on the asset, and where the lessor's tax rate is higher than the lessee's, this has the net effect of reducing taxes. In some cases, businesses may not be able to take full advantage of aggressive depreciation deductions

3. MODIGLIANI AND MILLER'S IRRELEVANCE HYPOTHESIS

By now, you should realize that firms have many different options for raising capital. Different firms will also make different choices about the right proportion of debt, preferred stock and common stock. Even the same firm will sometimes change its mind about the optimal financing strategy. In 2013, for example, Apple had a debt to equity ratio of roughly 0.1. By 2023, that same ratio approached 2.0. This diversity in firm financing has persisted over long periods of time and through different market conditions and tax regimes. All of this suggests that capital structure must be useful in maximizing value for investors in firms. Otherwise, why would we observe such variety? This intuition is sound: capital structure does matter.

Nevertheless, we are going to disregard this intuition at the outset and begin a discussion of capital structure strategy with the hypothesis that capital structure is irrelevant to firm value. This is widely known as Modigliani and Miller ("M&M") Proposition I, named after a seminal study in the 1950s that ultimately led to a Nobel Prize.* To paraphrase, this proposition asserts that a firm is only worth the discounted present value of its future cash flows from operations—regardless of capital structure. Or, as commonly stated in more colloquial terms, you cannot increase the total size of the pie simply by slicing it up into different-sized pieces.

A quick warning: most people do not believe that the M&M Proposition I reflects empirical reality. As we stated a moment ago, firms can often benefit from different financing choices, and capital structure decisions command senior management attention. But we can derive some helpful insights about how that value is created by starting with M&M's work and then considering where the assumptions in their theory may differ from observations in the real world.

Let's back up a little to build our understanding of this proposition. Imagine that you've found the perfect company to buy: a trendy local

---

available to others. Under the Internal Revenue Code, it is possible to deduct more depreciation expense in the early years of the life of an asset than the company would like to report as an expense to investors. Thus, the company may choose to report financial results using "straight line" depreciation, in which it deducts an equal amount of depreciation expense in each year of the asset's useful life. At the same time, it may choose to use accelerated depreciation for tax purposes, which allows it to deduct more in the early years of the life of the asset. But if the company has "too many" such deductions, which are treated as "tax shelters," it may become subject to the alternative minimum tax, which is at a higher rate than taxes computed the regular way. But lease payments are not treated as a tax shelter, so the company can deduct the entire lease payment, and the lessor is not subject to the alternative minimum tax, thus reducing the total tax burden. You might wonder why lessees would care about the ability of lessors to take generous tax deductions, but there is an easy answer. In a world of competition lenders will be forced to give some of these tax breaks back to the lessees in the form of lower lease payments.

* Franco Modigliani and Merton Miller, *The Cost of Capital, Corporation Finance and the Theory of Investment*, 48 AMERICAN ECONOMIC REVIEW 261 (1958). Modigliani was awarded the Nobel Prize in Economics, for this and other work, in 1985.

coffee shop named "Jumpstarter" that is known for its strong brews. The seller is asking $1 million, and you think this is a pretty good deal (but are not sure). You could pay cash for the entire company, but your favorite lender also proposes two alternative financing strategies:

- Option 1: You put down $900,000 of your own money as equity and borrow $100,000 from the bank (at a 10% interest rate) to complete the purchase.
- Option 2: You put down $100,000 of your own money as equity and borrow $900,000 from the bank (also at a 10% interest rate) to complete the purchase.

In both cases, the loan will be secured by the assets of the coffee shop, and you will not need to guarantee the debt personally. (Let's also ignore taxes for the moment.) Should you buy the coffee shop? If so, which financing strategy should you use?

To decide whether this is a good opportunity, you might start with two key questions: How much cash flow will the coffee shop generate in the future, and what is the present value of these cash flows? There is clearly uncertainty about what Jumpstarter's performance will look like in the coming years, as this depends on countless questions that cannot be answered today. Can the shop attract new customers? Will a nearby competitor come along with better coffee? What will the price of coffee beans be next year? And so on. You might, however, still devise several future scenarios and project how Jumpstarter is expected to perform under each one. You could then assign probabilities to each scenario to obtain a point estimate of future cash flows. Finally, as described in the last chapter, these cash flows can be discounted back to present value in a way that reflects the firm's risk.

Suppose, for example, that you construct three scenarios for Jumpstarter's future performance:

- Base Case: $120,000 operating cash flow per year
- Bad Case: $20,000 operating cash flow per year
- Good Case: $220,000 operating cash flow per year

If you assume that each scenario is equally likely to occur and that the cash flows will continue in perpetuity (both big assumptions), then you can derive a point estimate of $120,000 per year in expected cash flow: (1/3 * $120) + (1/3 * $20) + (1/3 * $220) = $120. Suppose you have also determined that the appropriate discount rate for Jumpstarter's business is 12%. Jumpstarter doesn't have any outstanding debt obligations, so if you owned all the shares of Jumpstarter, you would own 100% of Jumpstarter's business. We can therefore use the perpetuity formula to estimate the total value of the company with all-equity financing:

$$\text{Value} = \frac{\$120{,}000}{.12} = \$1 \text{ million}$$

According to these estimates, then, the coffee shop is priced fairly. It is not an amazing deal, but you are also not overpaying.

Turn now to the key question asked by Modigliani and Miller: can you increase the value of a firm like Jumpstarter by tinkering with its capital structure? Or does this just divide a same-sized pie into different pieces? Let's consider the impact of debt. As mentioned above, you have the option to take on some debt financing at a 10% interest rate. Moreover, if the bank loans the company money at 10% interest, the cost of debt for the company would be less than the cost of equity. Why? Recall that for an all-equity firm, the expected return on equity is equal to the expected return on the underlying business, which we have determined to be 12% per year. In short, the bank would expect a 10% rate of return while equity investors would expect a 12% rate of return (recall that lenders bear less risk and may be satisfied with a lower return). For a long time, the conventional wisdom on capital structure planning stated that if the cost of debt is lower than the rate of return demanded by investors in a firm's stock, then the firm should borrow to finance any activity that is expected to return a rate equal to (or greater than) the discount rate for equity.

Return to the Jumpstarter financing decision. If you pay cash for the company, then all future cash flows will effectively belong to you as the sole equity investor. You will (or should) demand a 12% return, and, as calculated above, the company is worth $1 million when you discount all the forecasted future cash flows back to present value using a 12% discount rate. With debt financing, however, the future cash flows must be shared: the required interest payment is first paid to the lender, and you will receive anything that is left over. How does this impact Jumpstarter's total value?

To answer this question, we need to calculate what is left over for you after deducting the interest payments to the lender. We can consider both of the bank's proposed financing options:

	Option 1	Option 2
Expected operating cash	$120,000	$120,000
Less: interest	−$10,000	−$90,000*
Net Income	$110,000	$30,000

We should then use the perpetuity formula, as before, to value Jumpstarter's equity. Before M&M's work, analysts would typically look only at operating risk (i.e., the risk arising from the company's business)

* The interest payments are calculated as follows. Option 1: $100,000 in debt * 10% interest rate = $10,000. Option 2: $900,000 in debt * 10% interest rate = $90,000.

to determine the right discount rate. Under this assumption, the expected earnings should still be discounted at 12%.

$$\text{Option 1: } \frac{\$110{,}000}{.12} = \$916{,}667$$

$$\text{Option 2: } \frac{\$30{,}000}{.12} = \$250{,}000$$

This gives us the total equity value for each option. But to calculate Jumpstarter's total value, we also need to add the value of the debt.* Start with option 1: If the company has $916,667 worth of equity plus $100,000 in debt,† then it must be worth a total of $1,016,667. We've seemingly boosted the value of a company by over $16,000 just by tinkering with the capital structure. And if a little debt helps, then why not take on even more of a good thing? Under option 2, the company should be worth $250,000 in equity plus $900,000 in debt for a total of $1,150,000. Bring on financing option 2!

Such was the conventional wisdom when Modigliani and Miller first considered this question of capital structure. But the discussion so far glosses over an important point: the expected earnings associated with the two debt financing options are more volatile than in an all-equity capital structure. This is true because creditors maintain a fixed right to their interest payments regardless of whether the firm has a good year or not. This fact amplifies the range of possible returns to equity investors under a concept known as financial leverage. We can illustrate this by calculating the returns to Jumpstarter under all three operating scenarios:

All Equity Purchase (000's)	Bad Case	Base Case	Good Case
Gross earnings	$20	$120	$220
Interest	$0	$0	$0
Earnings to shareholders	$20	$120	$220

Lender's Option 1 (000's)	Bad Case	Base Case	Good Case
Gross earnings	$20	$120	$220

* This step is not always immediately obvious to new students, as many assume that debt will detract from the value of a company. But remember that debt investors and equity investors are simply two different groups who each have claims on the firm. We therefore want to add the value of both claims to determine the total value of the company.

† There is another implicit assumption in this calculation: the current market rate of interest for the debt remains at 10%. If markets shift after the debt was issued, then the fair value of this debt may be higher or lower.

Interest	$(10)	$(10)	$(10)
Earnings to shareholders	$10	$110	$210

Lender's Option 2 (000's)	Bad Case	Base Case	Good Case
Gross earnings	$20	$120	$220
Interest	$(90)	$(90)	$(90)
Earnings to shareholders	($70)	$30	$130

Let's also calculate the rate of return for the equity investment under each scenario:

All Equity Purchase:	Earnings to Shareholders	Rate of Return (on equity)
Bad	$20	2.0%*
Base	$120	12.0%
Good	$220	22.0%

Lender's Option 1:	Earnings to Shareholders	Rate of Return (on equity)
Bad	$10	1.1%
Base	$110	12.2%
Good	$210	23.3%

Lender's Option 2:	Earnings to Shareholders	Rate of Return (on equity)
Bad	$(70)	-70%
Base	$30	30%
Good	$130	130%

Under option 1, with a little leverage, the returns range from 1.1% to 23.2%. These represent a slightly wider span (or variance) than the range that occurs if Jumpstarter is financed entirely by equity (2% to 22%). But the variance of returns really kicks in with financing option 2 when the range goes from −70% to 130%. As equity owner, you more than double your investment in the good case scenario but lose almost everything after one year if the bad case scenario emerges. This seems

* Calculated as $20,000 / $1,000,000. Other numbers in this column are calculated in a similar manner: return to equity / initial equity investment.

almost as risky as taking your money to a Las Vegas roulette wheel. In short, greater financial leverage causes greater variance, and thus increases risk for equity investors.

We have already seen that equity investors will demand higher compensation for expected returns that have greater variance (i.e., for returns that pose more risk). Under this reasoning, why should you still be satisfied earning only 12% as an equity investor under the leveraged financing scenarios, when you are bearing this additional risk? In 1958, a conceptual revision began as Modigliani & Miller took up this exact question.

As the prior example demonstrates, leverage might conceivably increase the value of a company, but only if investors don't recognize that they are bearing increased levels of risk. Or, alternatively, equity investors could be willing to pay a premium for the ability to make an investment in a leveraged entity. But M&M asked why this should be the case—especially when equity investors can create their own leverage by borrowing money personally and investing the extra proceeds in larger equity positions. In other words, why pay more for a leveraged firm when you can do it yourself? This is the great insight of Modigliani and Miller's irrelevance hypothesis.* However, because Modigliani and Miller's thesis is primarily a heuristic, designed to enable us to see certain essential features, it abstracts from real-world conditions.† For example, it assumes a world with the following features:

- No taxes;
- No bankruptcy costs;
- No difference in borrowing costs between corporations and shareholders;
- Symmetry of market information, meaning companies and investors have the same information; and
- Low transaction costs, so investors can readily shift between investments.

To illustrate M&M Proposition I, imagine that you have decided to skip buying a coffee shop in order to invest directly in the stock of large coffee bean companies. You still have $1 million in cash to invest, and you can personally borrow up to another $1 million at 10%. You are considering investing in one of two firms: Starbucks and Moonbucks. Both companies are identical, except that Starbucks has a 100% equity capital structure, while Moonbucks is financed with 50% equity and 50% debt. You've estimated that equity investors should demand a 12% return

---

* Franco Modigliani and Merton H. Miller, *The Cost of Capital, Corporation Finance and the Theory of Investment*, 48 AMERICAN ECONOMIC REVIEW 261 (1958). This is also called M&M Proposition One.

† It's not clear M&M intended it to be this way. Assuming away taxes may have been an error. The title of their subsequent article adjusting for taxes suggests this: "*Corporate Income Taxes and the Cost of Capital: A Correction*", 53 AMERICAN ECONOMIC REVIEW 422 (1963).

for investing in shares of coffee bean companies. (Having never studied the M&M Irrelevance Hypothesis, you assume equity investors should expect a 12% return regardless of a company's capital structure.) At the moment you are considering two possible investment choices:

Choice A: An investment in Starbucks using "home-made" leverage. You put $500,000 of your own money into Starbucks stock and borrow an additional $500,000 at a 10% interest rate. You also invest this latter amount in Starbucks stock. Your total investment in the company is expected to earn a 12% annual rate of return ($120,000 on your $1 million investment).

Choice B: An unleveraged investment in Moonbucks. You put $1 million of your money own into Moonbucks stock for an expected 12% annual rate of return ($120,000 on your $1 million investment).

Which investment do you prefer?

With Choice B, given your assumption that all coffee bean companies have a cost of equity of 12%, you expect to earn 12% from this equity investment in Moonbucks. With Choice A, however, you can expect to earn 14% on your equity investment:

$120,000	total income
– 50,000	Interest
$70,000	net income

$$\text{Equity return} = \frac{\$70{,}000}{\$500{,}000} = 14\%$$

As noted in the example, this can be called "home-made leverage." Instead of relying on Moonbucks to obtain a leveraged position, you have created your own leverage by borrowing money in an individual capacity to buy a larger amount of equity. You can enjoy a leveraged return if you want to amplify possible outcomes by personally bearing more risk.

For this reason, an investor should never pay extra for a leveraged firm because she can "home-make" the same set of results. Why would you ever be satisfied with the 12% return offered by Moonbucks when you can get a 14% return with Starbucks for bearing the exact same level of financial and operating risk. You wouldn't. Something must be wrong with the assumption that equity investors will be satisfied with the same return for leveraged and unleveraged capital structures. They should demand more to take equity in a leveraged company. This also highlights why it was an error to assume that the expected return on equity for

Starbucks and Moonbucks would be the same at 12%. Just as you would expect a higher return of 14% in Choice A because of your "home-made leverage," investors in Moonbucks would expect more than 12% due to the company's leveraged capital structure. This is just another way of saying that investors will not place any extra value on the fact that Moonbucks has chosen to finance itself with debt because this decision does not create any value that the investors can't create themselves. This is the essence of M&M Proposition I.

Armed with this insight, M&M turned to a second proposition: the expected discount rate on the common stock of a levered firm will increase in proportion to the debt-equity ratio of the firm. This should make sense. The required return on equity should rise with any increase in debt because leverage increases the variance of expected returns. Thus, the higher the leverage, the greater the probability that the firm will be unable to generate enough revenue to pay its debts as they come due.

Accordingly, we need to reconsider the discount rate that is used to value equity investments in leveraged firms. Let's return to the Jumpstarter coffee shop example and financing options 1 and 2. M&M Proposition II suggests that the correct discount rate for both options will rise in a way that keeps the total value of the company steady at $1 million. With financing option 1, then, we would need to revise the valuation with an equity discount rate of about 12.222%:

$$\text{Revised Option 1:} = \frac{\$110{,}000}{.12222} = \$900{,}000$$

We are back to a firm that is worth $1 million (comprised of equity worth $900,000 and debt worth $100,000). Any expected return below 12.222% doesn't fully compensate investors for the riskiness of their shares in this leveraged firm. The same holds true for financing option 2, except that the discount rate that equity investors require is even higher to compensate for the much greater spread in returns. According to M&M proposition II, this rate should jump to 30%

$$\text{Revised Option 2:} = \frac{\$30{,}000}{.30} = \$100{,}000$$

Again, the total value of Jumpstarter is $1 million (comprised of equity worth $100,000 and debt worth $900,000).*

* There should also be some intuitive appeal in M&M Proposition II. Note that in Option 2, the variance of returns was plus/minus 100% (i.e., relative to the base case expected return of 30%, the best case/worst case outcome would produce returns that were 130% and −70%, respectively). This was 10 times the variance of returns of an all equity financing (i.e., relative to the base case expected return of 12%, the best case/worse case outcome in an all equity Jumpstarter would produce returns that were 22% and 2%, respectively). Equity investors in Option 2 would therefore be subject to 10 times the risk relative to investors in an all-equity Jumpstarter. Moreover, if the company's cost of debt is 10% and the expected return on its core

Before this work by Modigliani and Miller, financial planners would have asked if there was some optimal ratio of debt and equity that could maximize the value of a firm. But M&M's hypotheses suggested that any capital structure decision is just as good (or bad) as another. If you take on more debt, then the discount rate on equity will rise. If you take on less debt, then the discount rate will fall. Either way, a firm's value will be the result of future operating prospects—and not the specific decisions that managers make about how to finance these operations. According to M&M, a firm cannot change the total value of its securities just by splitting the cash flows into different streams through different securities.

This work has been extremely influential, and no one challenges the basic logic of the M&M thesis. But no matter what you do, do not walk into your first corporate finance planning meeting as a new lawyer, climb up on the boardroom table and shout to your clients, "It just doesn't matter! Look at the M&M propositions! Raise the money any darn way you want!" Because here's the kicker: Most people believe that M&M's irrelevance hypothesis does not reflect reality because of its assumptions noted previously. Let us turn, then, to the real world, and consider how relaxing some of the M&M assumptions might shed light on how firms actually make capital structure choices.

Sidebar: M&M Proposition II and WACC

M&M Proposition II can also be derived from a company's weighted-average cost of capital (WACC). Recall from Chapter 3 that in a world without taxes a company's WACC is calculated as:

$$WACC = \left[\frac{D}{V} \times r_{debt}\right] + \left[\frac{E}{V} \times r_{equity}\right]$$

where D is the market value of a company's debt, V is the aggregate value of the company's securities, E is the market value of equity, r_{debt} is the expected return on debt, and r_{equity} is the expected return on equity. In general, a company's WACC estimates the expected return on a company's underlying business, and in the case of Jumpstarter, we stated that the expected return on its core business was 12%. We also stipulated that the expected rate of return on debt was 10%. Given M&M Proposition I, the total value of Jumpstarter is $1 million regardless of its financing structure, so we could calculate the expected return on equity in Option 2 as follows:

business is 12%, this indicates that the equity risk premium of an unlevered firm is 2% (i.e., 12% – 10%). Because equity investors in Option 2 are subject to 10 times the risk of an unlevered firm, they should be expected to impose a risk premium that is 10 times larger, or 20% (i.e., 10 * 2%). Using a 20% risk premium over the cost of debt also produces a total cost of equity of 30% (i.e., 10% + 20%).

$$.12 = \left[\frac{\$900{,}000}{\$1{,}000{,}000} \times .1\right] + \left[\frac{\$100{,}000}{\$1{,}000{,}000} \times r_{equity}\right]$$

Solving for r_{equity}, we obtain 30%.

Rather than using the WACC formula, M&M Proposition II is also commonly expressed in the following (mathematically equivalent) form:

$$r_{equity} = r_{assets} + \frac{D}{E}(r_{assets} - r_{debt})$$

where r_{assets} is the return on the company's core business assets and D/E is the company's debt-to-equity ratio. Thus, in the case of Option 2:

$$r_{equity} = .12 + \frac{\$900{,}000}{\$100{,}000}(.12 - .1)$$

which also produces an expected return on equity of 30%. This latter formulation makes clear that a company's cost of equity increases as a function of its debt-to-equity ratio.

4. THE REAL WORLD

Even Modigliani and Miller acknowledge that we observe the use of debt and preferred stock in capital structures, and that these capital structures vary across firms. Explaining why this happens—and what firms really do—requires us to relax the simplifying assumptions of the M&M thesis. In the real world, corporate finance managers pay constant attention to a firm's capital structure. How do they decide where to raise funds? In the balance of this chapter, we mostly consider one of the "big picture" questions: what mix of debt and equity should a firm prefer? In later chapters we will consider some of the more specialized situations that often call for a different investment vehicle like preferred stock or convertible debt.

A. DEBT AND TAXES

Let's relax the "no taxes" assumption of M&M and consider the impact of tax planning on real-world capital structures. Individuals and corporations both pay taxes, of course, but a firm that raises money via debt might offset part of the total tax bill by deducting interest payments. Dividend payouts, by contrast, are not deductible and therefore result in double taxation. Accordingly, tax savings is another important feature of debt financing—beyond the risk amplification effects for stockholders described in the last section—and this can play a meaningful role in capital structure decisions. (We also recognized this tax benefit from debt in Chapter 3 during our discussion of WACC calculations.)

We can illustrate this concept by returning to the Jumpstarter coffee shop problem and examining the effect of taxes on investor cash flows. Let's assume that corporations are subject to a top marginal tax rate of 20%.* Now let's consider how much money would be available after taxes to Jumpstarter's investors each year under the three financing scenarios mentioned earlier: (1) all equity financing, (2) modest borrowing, (3) and highly leveraged borrowing.

All Equity Financing. You invest $1 million and expect pretax earnings of $120,000. After corporate income taxes, $96,000 is left to be paid as a dividend to shareholders.

	Corporate Level	Investor Payments
Net corporate income	$120,000	
Less corporate taxes @20%:	(24,000)	
Corporate income after taxes	$96,000	
Dividend to shareholders	($96,000)	$96,000

Modest Borrowing. You invest $900,000 equity and borrow $100,000. Expected pretax and pre-interest earnings remains $120,000, but after the interest payment of $10,000, the company has only $110,000 of taxable income. Following the payment of corporate taxes, this leaves $88,000 to be distributed to shareholders. However, when added to the $10,000 of interest paid, the total payments to investors is $98,000.

	Corporate Level	Investor Payments
Operating income	$120,000	
Less interest	(10,000)	$10,000
Net income	$110,000	
Less corporate taxes @ 20%	(22,000)	
Corporate income after taxes	$88,000	
Dividend to shareholders	($88,000)	$88,000
Totals:		$98,000

* As of publication, the top corporate rate is 21%. We have also ignored the choice between individual debt and corporate debt in these examples. If individual taxpayers can obtain more tax benefits from interest deductions than corporations, then individual borrowing may be preferable. But if some shareholders pay no current taxes on corporate income (as in the case of non-profit organizations and pension plans where all taxes are paid by plan beneficiaries on a deferred basis), then corporate borrowing is clearly preferable. Thus, in our examples, if you can borrow the same $100,000 or $900,000 at 10%, the individual interest expense deduction at 40% will exceed the corporate deduction at 20%. For investors in lower brackets, corporate borrowing will be more attractive.

Highly Leveraged Borrowing. You invest just $100,000 equity and borrow $900,000. Expected pretax and pre-interest earnings remains $120,000, but after the interest payment of $90,000, the company has only $30,000 of taxable income. Following the payment of corporate taxes, this leaves $24,000 to be distributed to shareholders. However, when added to the $90,000 of interest paid, the total payments to investors is $114,000.

	Corporate Level	**Investor Payments**
Operating income	$120,000	
Less interest	(90,000)	$90,000
Net income	$30,000	
Less corporate taxes @ 20%	(6,000)	
Corporate income after taxes	$24,000	
Dividend to shareholders	($24,000)	$24,000
Totals:		$114,000

This analysis shows how debt financing can generate more cash flows for investors. With all-equity financing, the company's investors (consisting of just equity investors) should expect $96,000 in investor payments from the company. With modest borrowing, that number rises to $98,000, consisting of $10,000 of interest payments and $88,000 of dividends. And with highly leveraged borrowing, it increases still further to $114,000. Why? Every dollar paid out as interest reduces corporate taxes by the amount paid times 20%. Thus, in the highly leveraged borrowing option, the interest tax shield is 0.2 times the interest payments, or 0.2 * $90,000 = $18,000. These are funds that are available to the company's investors each year but are not available in an all-equity firm. Naturally, investors will take this additional after-tax income into account when valuing the firm. The "tax shield" for debt thus raises the value of the leveraged firm. Indeed, Modigliani and Miller would subsequently amend their Proposition I to account for this fact. Specifically, their revised Proposition I states that the value of a levered firm (V_L) that pays corporate taxes is equal to the value of an unlevered firm (V_U) plus the present value of the tax shields from debt.

How should one calculate the present value of these tax shields? A common convention is to assume that the company will maintain its existing debt level in perpetuity, thus making these tax shields an annual payment to the investors in the firm. From Chapter 3, we know that we can determine the present value of a perpetuity by discounting the annual payments by a discount rate that reflects their risk. What discount rate should investors use in this context? As we saw in the last chapter, investors often use a firm's beta to determine a company's cost of equity. But we all know that nothing is more certain than death and taxes. So as long as the firm expects to earn at least enough to cover its interest payments, the tax deduction becomes quite certain, and should thus be discounted at a relatively low rate. The most common assumption used in valuing these deductions is that they are as certain as the interest payments on the debt, so that the interest rate creditors charge is the appropriate discount rate. Thus, in our previous example, if debt carries a 10% interest rate, we would calculate the present value of the tax shields in the highly leveraged scenario as follows:

$$\frac{(.1)(900{,}000)(.2)}{.1} = \$180{,}000$$

Notice that the interest rate of 10% appears in both the numerator and the denominator. From high school algebra, you might recall that this means that we can divide .1 by .1, thus eliminating it from the equation. We can therefore value the tax shields from debt by simply multiplying the outstanding indebtedness ($900,000) by the company's tax rate (20%). As such, we can summarize the M&M Proposition I in a world with taxes as follows:

$$V_L = V_U + T_C D$$

where V_L is the value of a levered firm, V_U is the value of the firm with an all equity capital structure, and T_cD is the present value of the tax shields from debt.

From a policy perspective, the wisdom of providing a tax deduction for interest payments has long been the subject of debate. Critics argue that it puts a thumb on the capital structure scale for debt in a way that is unjustified and may lead to other distortions (discussed later in this chapter). Proponents argue that the deduction is helpful for promoting corporate investment and that a major change to such settled treatment would be disruptive. In 2018, however, Congress decided to limit the corporate interest deduction as part of a broader tax reform package. Following this change, many firms are no longer able to deduct interest expenses that exceed roughly 30% of their adjusted taxable income.* They are permitted to carry forward any unused deduction, however, for a later tax year when interest payments do fall below the cap.

The impact of this change is complicated. But the reform will reduce the total benefit of interest tax shields for some firms. In the Jumpstarter example, the cap in interest deductions would have no effect because the

* During a phase in period from 2018 to 2021, adjusted income was defined as EBITDA. After 2021, the definition was changed to EBIT, thereby lowering the deductibility cap even further for many firms. The legal revisions contain other rules as well. For example, any additional interest income earned by a firm is also fully deductible. And small corporations and some other industry-specific ventures may be exempted from the deduction limits.

corporation is small enough to be exempted from the limit. But if we were to increase every number in the example by three zeros, the deduction attempted in the highly leveraged financing plan might not pass muster. Assuming we are looking at 2022 or later, the firm's EBIT will be used as adjusted taxable income for this cap. 30% of a $120 million EBIT (remember we have added three zeros to every number) is $40 million, which is far less than the $90 million in interest that we would otherwise like to deduct. The tax changes can thus impact some highly leveraged firms.

Despite this limit, a tax shield persists for some debt financing. This tax shield explains part of the attraction of leveraged buyouts ("LBOs"), which we will examine in more detail at the end of the chapter. Firms that carry too little debt might be foregoing potential tax savings associated with more debt. In some cases, this can attract takeover offers. Bidders might be able to make an offer based on the projected value of the cash flows of a leveraged firm—including the discounted present value of the tax shield—to offer more for the firm than the current market value.

Sidebar: M&M Proposition II and Corporate Taxes

Accounting for the existence of corporate taxes also affects M&M Proposition II. Because every dollar of interest reduces a company's tax bill, the after-tax cost of debt is the nominal interest rate multiplied by one minus the corporate tax rate. For example, in the Jumpstarter example involving the highly leveraged scenario, the pre-tax interest rate was 10%, resulting in annual interest payments of $90,000. Given the company's 20% tax rate, this means the company saves $18,000 in taxes when it deducts these interest expenses. Thus, Jumpstarter will only pay $72,000 on its debt (i.e., $90,000 – $18,000), which equates to an 8% after-tax interest rate, or 10% * (1 – .2).

As a result, we need to modify M&M Proposition II to account for the presence of corporate taxes. The result is the following formula:

$$r_{equity} = r_{assets} + \frac{D}{E}(1-T)(r_{assets} - r_{debt})$$

where *T* is the corporate tax rate and all other terms are the same as in the previous Sidebar. Applying this formula to the highly leveraged scenario, we would get the following:

$$r_{equity} = .12 + \frac{\$900{,}000}{\$100{,}000}(1-.2)(.12-.1)$$

Or 26.4%. This is slightly lower than the 30% return on equity we calculated previously, illustrating how the presence of corporate taxes moderates the effect of leverage on the cost of equity.

Sidebar: Combining CAPM with M&M Proposition II—The Hamada Equation

The fact that M&M Proposition II provides a formula for calculating the return on equity has a natural parallel with CAPM, which can also be used to calculate the expected return on equity. The difference, however, is that CAPM accomplishes this by way of a stock's "beta", which reflects the correlation between a stock's return and the market portfolio's return. How should we think about CAPM in light of M&M Proposition II? Recall from Chapter 3 that we estimate a stock's beta by examining empirically how a stock's returns (e.g., its daily returns) relate to the returns to a portfolio of stocks (e.g., the daily returns to the S&P 500). This approach largely ignores a company's debt-to-equity ratio; however, we now know from M&M Proposition II that the expected return on equity will be a function of this ratio. This means that whatever equity returns we calculate using a stock's estimated beta must be a function of the company's debt-to-equity ratio. Imagine, for instance, that we estimate a stock's beta as 1.0 using its daily returns, and we learn that the company has no debt on its balance sheet. The return on equity we calculate using CAPM would thus reflect the return on equity of a company with a debt-to-equity ratio of 0. We could therefore refer to the company's beta as "unlevered" because the company has no financial leverage (i.e., debt). Conversely, imagine instead that after estimating a stock's beta as 1.0, we learn that the company's debt-to-equity ratio is 2.0. In this case, the return on equity we estimate with CAPM would reflect a return on equity in a company where D/E in M&M Proposition II is 2.0. We would therefore refer to the company's beta as a "levered beta." Indeed, because a stock's beta determines its expected return in CAPM, we can express a stock's beta as a function of the company's debt-to-equity ratio using the following equation:

$$\beta_L = \beta_A(1 + \frac{D}{E}(1 - T))$$

This equation is analogous to M&M Proposition II, except that instead of calculating the return on equity as a function of the company's debt-to-equity ratio, it calculates a stock's beta as a function of the company's debt-to-equity ratio. (The equation is often referred to as Hamada's equation after Robert Hamada, a professor of finance at the University of Chicago).* In the equation, β_A is the beta of the company were it to have no leverage (referred to as "asset beta"), T is the company's tax rate, and β_L is the beta of the company if it has debt valued at D and equity valued at E. Why is this useful? Because it allows us to "unlever" and/or "relever" a company's beta to determine the expected return on equity under different capital structures.

As an example, imagine you run a private equity fund and are considering the acquisition of NewCo, a private company. From Chapter 3, you know that to value NewCo requires an estimate of its weighted average cost of capital. You therefore look to a publicly-traded company, LeverageCo, which has an identical business, to form this estimate. Your favorite financial website tells you that LeverageCo's stock currently has an observed beta of 2.0. If the risk-free rate is 3% and the equity premium is 8%, we could use CAPM to estimate the cost of equity of LeverageCo as 18% (i.e., 2% + 2.0(8%)). However, LeverageCo has a debt-to-equity ratio of 2:1, and NewCo has no debt at all. If we re-write Hamada's equation to solve for LeverageCo's "asset beta", we can use that asset beta as the asset beta for NewCo given that they have identical businesses. And because NewCo has no debt, its equity beta must equal its asset beta. If both companies have a tax rate of 20%, the procedure yields:

$$\beta_A = \frac{\beta_L}{(1 + \frac{D}{E}(1 - T))}$$

$$\beta_A = \frac{2.0}{(1 + \frac{2}{1}(1 - .2))}$$

The asset beta for companies like LeverageCo and NewCo is therefore ~ 0.769, and NewCo's cost of equity (using CAPM) would be roughly 8% (i.e., 2% + .769(8%)). We now have a discount rate to use when valuing NewCo's cash flows.

---

* Hamada's equation can be derived algebraically from combining CAPM and M&M Proposition II. Recall that CAPM is $R_* = R_f + \beta_* (R_M - R_f)$. ($R_*$ and β_* reflect the return and beta for the financial asset in question). Next, substitute the CAPM expressions for R_{assets} and R_{equity} in the M&M formula. If we assume that debt has no risk premium (i.e., its beta is zero), we have:

$$R_f + \beta_L(RM - Rf) = Rf + \beta_A(R_M - R_f) + \frac{D}{E}(1 - T)(R_f + \beta_A(R_M - R_f) - R_f + 0(R_M - R_f))$$

And after canceling out R_f and $(R_M - R_f)$, we have

$$\beta_L = \beta_A + \frac{D}{E}(1 - T)(\beta_A)$$

which is the same as

$$\beta_L = \beta_A(1 + \frac{D}{E}(1 - T))$$

B. THE COST OF FINANCIAL DISTRESS

Extensive debt financing might generate tax savings, but there is an obvious downside to consider: a greater risk of bankruptcy and other forms of financial distress. As a firm takes on more debt, it runs a greater chance that operations won't be as strong as expected and that it will default on repayment obligations. The cost of financial distress should therefore mitigate any temptation to take on too much leverage. Modigliani and Miller emphasized this point as well, arguing that a tax subsidy did not counsel an all-debt capital structure because of the introduction of bankruptcy costs.* (Recall that the absence of bankruptcy costs was one of the assumptions for the M&M Irrelevance Propositions to hold.)

Most people think of bankruptcy as a sad ending to a firm's life. But it is worth emphasizing that bankruptcy is really just part of a legal system where shareholders use their limited liability to walk away from debts that a firm cannot pay. This is valuable, from the ex-ante shareholder perspective, and not something that equity investors would wish to abdicate. Said differently, the "sad event" is not bankruptcy itself, but rather the fact that the firm's asset values and operations have bottomed out in a way that do not allow it to satisfy current obligations.

Yet bankruptcy is not a zero-sum game. The litigation and transaction costs of bankruptcy can be substantial, and creditors will almost inevitably receive less than the value of the company pre-bankruptcy. It is this expense of working through a bankruptcy proceeding that decreases the total size of the pie for investors. As a corporation takes on more and more debt, the risk of incurring deadweight losses associated with financial distress grows, and the market value of the firm might decrease accordingly. Future creditors could also recognize this risk and demand higher interest payments to compensate them for the possibility of default; this also reduces the residual value of the firm to shareholders.

Just how expensive are the legal fees and other costs of bankruptcy? For high profile bankruptcies, the amounts can be significant. Enron, which filed for bankruptcy in 2001, is said to have spent over $1 billion in legal and other professional fees. The Lehman Brothers bankruptcy in 2008 seems to have come close to that number; it paid attorneys and advisors over $850 million. Some judges balk at legal fee requests in bankruptcy proceedings, but the ultimate costs can still seem staggering. That being said, several studies have argued that the cost of financial distress is not always large—especially when it is considered in relation to the total size of a firm's assets.†

In addition to the direct administrative and professional costs of bankruptcy, a firm might also incur less obvious costs as it enters or approaches insolvency. Governance flexibility may decrease when business decisions require court approval, and good opportunities may be

* Franco Modigliani and Merton H. Miller, *Corporate Income Taxes and the Cost of Capital: A Correction*, 53 AMERICAN ECONOMIC REVIEW 422, 442 (1963).

† Jerold B. Warner, *Bankruptcy Costs: Some Evidence*, 26 JOURNAL OF FINANCE 337 (1977); Lawrence A. Weiss, *Bankruptcy Resolution: Direct Costs and Violation of Priority of Claims*, 27 JOURNAL OF FINANCIAL ECONOMICS 285 (1990). One study found that bankruptcy costs consumed about three percent of the debtor's estate. Stephen J. Carroll et al., *RAND Inst. for Civil Justice*, ASBESTOS LITIGATION COSTS AND COMPENSATION 72 (2002).

missed. Lenders may place additional restrictions or conditions on firm activities before agreeing to refinance existing debt or extend additional credit. It is often difficult to estimate the cost of these indirect effects, but we will study some of the problems more extensively in later chapters.

This short discussion of the costs of financial distress thus highlights how the tax benefits of debt-financing must be considered against these costs, especially for highly leveraged firms. In fact, the notion that a firm's managers explicitly trade-off the tax benefits of debt against the costs of financial distress constitutes one of the main theories for why firms differ in their choice of capital structure. Under this "trade-off theory," companies with safe, tangible assets and plenty of taxable income should have relatively high debt-to-equity ratios. Why? The fact that these firms have high taxable income means that they stand to gain from the tax shields of debt. At the same time, the presence of tangible assets should diminish the costs of financial distress since these assets can be more easily valued and sold in a bankruptcy than, say, intangible assets. For the same reasons, the trade-off theory suggests that unprofitable companies with risky intangible assets should instead rely on equity financing when they need to raise external capital.

Consistent with the trade-off theory, we do indeed observe many industry differences in capital structure. For example, utility companies, which generally have both large amounts of taxable income as well as sizeable amounts of tangible property (as well as real estate) generally rely on debt financing far more than high-tech growth companies. However, the trade-off theory is less successful in explaining other empirical observations. Consider, for instance, the ExxonMobil Corporation. The company has reported tens of billions of dollars of taxable income during recent years. Moreover, the company reports over $200 billion of property, plant, and equipment and its existing debt is rated AAA by Moody's, thus suggesting it could borrow considerable sums without incurring large financial distress costs. Despite these characteristics, however, the company has utilized very little long-term debt.* The existence of companies like ExxonMobil suggests that the trade-off theory cannot be the only theory for explaining capital structure decisions.

C. A PECKING ORDER THEORY

Recall that the M&M Irrelevance Proposition also assumed that there was symmetry of market information, meaning that companies and investors had the same information concerning a company and its prospects. But in the real world, of course, investors face an information asymmetry when investing in firms because investors usually know less

* In fiscal year 2022, for instance, ExxonMobil recorded long-term debt of $40.5 billion while its market capitalization of equity was over $400 billion. Notably, the company maintained even lower levels of long-term debt in the years prior to the 2018 tax reform, when the tax benefits of debt were even greater.

about a firm than its managers. Accounting for this information asymmetry has led to an alternative theory that might explain why profitable companies borrow less than predicted under the trade-off theory. Under this "pecking order" theory, a company's managers are assumed to act in the best interests of its current shareholders and seek to minimize the negative wealth effects to a firm associated with raising external capital. These negative wealth effects arise from these information asymmetries. In particular, prospective equity investors will recognize that even well-meaning managers have an incentive to sell equity securities to the public when managers believe the market overvalues their firm. Consequently, outside investors will interpret a new equity issuance as a signal that management believes its shares are overvalued, and investors will therefore discount the market prices of firms that issue equity securities—a prediction that has been confirmed in numerous studies.

In general, because debt investors can minimize these information asymmetries through elaborate debt contracts, these negative wealth effects should be greater for equity issuances than for debt issuances and can be avoided entirely if a company can use internal funds to finance its new investments. Moreover, this theory also points towards the value of "financial slack." Having financial slack means having cash, marketable securities and ready access to debt markets (or to bank financing) so that financing is quickly available for new investments. Accordingly, the theory suggests that managers will first look to internal funds before turning to external financing, and to the extent external financing is needed, managers will issue debt rather than equity. Because financial slack is most valuable to firms with positive-NPV growth opportunities, the theory should be particularly applicable to growth firms.

Overall, this "pecking order" is consistent with the general pattern in which U.S. corporations have historically chosen to finance their operations. Specifically, most of the aggregate gross investment by U.S. corporations has been financed from internal cash flows, with external financing accounting for less than twenty percent of corporate financing needs, the vast majority of which has consisted of debt. The theory also predicts that profitable firms with retained earnings should borrow less than non-profitable firms, notwithstanding the fact that profitable firms have the most to gain from the tax shield of debt. Thus, in contrast to the trade-off theory, it has the capacity to explain the low borrowing levels of a firm such as ExxonMobil.

D. CAPITAL STRUCTURE AND AGENCY COSTS

Finally, let's consider one other variable that might impact a firm's preference for equity or debt in the real world. Note that the trade-off theory and the pecking order theory both assume that managers determine a company's capital structure based on what maximizes the value of the company. However, at least since Adam Smith, economists have observed that corporate managers don't always behave as investors might like.* Managers may not work as hard as possible, or they may waste corporate funds on private benefits like high salaries, fancy offices, corporate jets, and so on. They may take incredible risks with investor's money in the hope that a lucky bet will boost the value of their stock options. Or they may reinvest profits in negative net present value projects, perhaps seeking to build a larger empire. The range of concerns, known collectively as the agency cost problem, is vast, and is often viewed as an inevitable byproduct of the corporation. Empowering someone else to make decisions about your money has costs as well as benefits.

When it comes to capital structure decisions, the existence of managerial agency costs can cut in a number of different directions. Perhaps most obviously, managers may prefer financial slack not because it is in the best interests of the firm and its investors but because it makes life easier for a firm's managers. As the saying goes "equity is soft; debt is hard." The manager of a firm with large levels of corporate debt must use corporate cash flow to make interest and principal payments, regardless of how the firm performs. In contrast, an all-equity firm with financial slack permits managers to take it easy, expand their perks or empire-build with cash that should be paid back to shareholders. In other words, there is a dark side to financial slack once we introduce the possibility of managerial agency costs.

At the same time, equity investors are not naïve and will anticipate this behavior, potentially imposing a steep discount on the value of a company's shares. This dynamic suggests a counter-vailing influence of managerial agency costs: Equity investors' preoccupation with agency costs could induce some entrepreneurs to avoid using the diffuse public equity markets where concerns about these agency problems loom large. Instead, the incentive might be for these entrepreneurs to "bootstrap" their firms using personal resources, and when necessary, turn to debt markets for additional financing. Yet even in these situations, managerial agency costs persist given that the interests of the owner-manager and debt investors will often diverge, creating the prospect that the owner-manager will use her discretionary authority to maximize her personal interests over those of her outside investors. If debt investors harbor large concerns about this aspect of the agency problem, we could very well see agency problems pushing firms back toward using outside equity.

---

* "The directors of such companies, however, being the managers of other people's money than of their own, it cannot well be expected that they should watch over it with the same anxious vigilance with which the partners in a private copartnery frequently watch over their own. Like the stewards of a rich man, they are apt to consider attention to small matters as not for their master's honor, and very easily give themselves a dispensation from having it. Negligence and profusion, therefore, must always prevail, more or less, in the management of the affairs of such a company." Adam Smith, THE WEALTH OF NATIONS (1776, Cannan edition, 1937), p. 700.

Two influential academics, Michael Jensen and William Meckling, modeled the agency cost problem in the 1970s. They argued that a manager's decisions diverged from those of an owner-manager, because the manager did not bear the full costs of any decisions nor obtain the full benefit of them. They then described some of the devices designed to reduce these divergences, such as monitoring (by outside accountants and directors, for example) and bonding (often in the form of incentive compensation). Even where these devices are successful, they are also costly, leading the authors to the conclusion that there were irreducible costs associated with the agency relationship, and that they were the sum of the costs of divergence from the owners' goals plus the monitoring and bonding costs incurred.

Might a firm's capital structure be adjusted in a way that eliminates, or at least mitigates, the agency cost problem? Consider the following excerpt from Jensen and Meckling's seminal article:

Theory of the Firm: Managerial Behavior, Agency Costs and Ownership Structure

by Michael Jensen and William Meckling
3 Journal of Financial Economics 305, 333–34 (1976)

"In general if the agency costs engendered by the existence of outside owners are positive it will pay the absentee owner (i.e., shareholders) to sell out to an owner-manager who can avoid these costs. This could be accomplished in principle by having the manager become the sole equity holder by repurchasing all of the outside equity claims with funds obtained through the issuance of limited liability debt claims and the use of his own personal wealth. This single-owner corporation would not suffer the agency costs associated with outside equity. Therefore there must be some compelling reasons why we find the diffuse-owner corporate firm financed by equity claims so prevalent as an organizational form.

"An ingenious entrepreneur eager to expand, has open to him the opportunity to design a whole hierarchy of fixed claims on assets and earnings, with premiums paid for different levels of risk. Why don't we observe large corporations individually owned with a tiny fraction of the capital supplied by the entrepreneur in return for 100 percent of the equity and the rest simply borrowed? We believe there are a number of reasons: (1) the incentive effects associated with highly leveraged firms, (2) the monitoring costs these incentive effects engender, and (3) bankruptcy costs.

* * *

"We don't find many large firms financed almost entirely with debt type claims (i.e., non-residual claims) because of the effect such a financial structure would have on the owner-manager's behavior. Potential creditors will not loan $100,000,000 to a firm in which the entrepreneur has an investment of $10,000. With that financial structure the owner-manager will have a strong incentive to engage in activities (investments) which promise very high payoffs if successful even if they have a very low probability of success. If they turn out well, he captures most of the gains, if they turn out badly, the creditors bear most of the costs."

Agency cost theory has been extraordinarily influential in explaining not only why firms might choose a particular capital structure, but also why different financing choices entail different forms of financial contracts. Once a firm has growth opportunities and needs more financing than an owner-manager can personally supply, it faces a dilemma. If investors (and markets) are rational, they will anticipate the increased shirking of the owner-manager and will value the company on a reduced basis. For the owner-manager, selling off part ownership of the company under these conditions means that he will receive a disappointing amount for the sale of shares in the business. Alternatively, as we see in the venture capital context, outside equity investors can also demand any number of "bonding" and "monitoring" covenants that could ultimately cause the manager to lose control of her firm. One solution, of course, is for the manager to finance expansion with her own funds. This may be impractical for several reasons. The obvious one is that the manager may not have enough money to finance a large (and potentially profitable) expansion. Although a manager could personally borrow additional funds, pledging her interest in the business as well as her personal assets, she may be reluctant to incur that much risk, by placing all her eggs in one basket.

One major solution to this valuation problem is to use outside debt financing by the corporation. Because of limited liability, the manager will not bear the increased risks of this financing. But debt, as we shall see, is a powerful disciplinary tool. Creditors, whether banks or public investors, are not naive. If the manager is left unconstrained, creditors will wish to compensate themselves ex ante for the high risk of default on firm loans with a high interest rate (which may itself increase the risk of default). In a default, the creditors will capture all firm assets, leaving the original owner-manager with worthless stock. The manager can contractually agree to certain terms to assure outside investors that she will not increase agency costs as much as anticipated, and thus attempt to reduce interest costs. These include limits on salaries and dividends, covenants against increasing the riskiness of the firm's activities, and performance measures that must be met to avoid default. Performance measures, of course, require outside monitoring, usually in the form of audited financial statements (see Chapter 2). Some of these are costs that would also be incurred with the use of outside equity. In both cases, outside investors, whether stockholders or creditors, would probably prefer some outsiders on the board of directors to serve as monitors (and, in today's world, as an audit committee of the board).

All of this leads us to a few general observations:

1. Agency costs rise with the use of outside equity.
2. Outside debt financing often reduces agency costs because of the discipline imposed, and because the owner/manager still bears the agency costs imposed on residual claimants.
3. Agency costs of debt rise with increasing use of debt (e.g., owner/managers are tempted to take higher risks because shareholders capture all the gains while bondholders suffer a large share of the losses).
4. Agency costs can be reduced (but not eliminated) through various monitoring and bonding mechanisms to protect outside investors, whether shareholders or creditors.

It is worth saying a little more about the problem suggested by observation number 3. Although highly leveraged debt financing may help to mitigate agency costs that arise between managers and shareholders (for the reasons mentioned in observations 1 and 2), this same reliance on debt might present other concerns. Investors might grow worried about managerial behavior that benefits shareholders at the expense of debt investors (referred to above as the agency costs of debt). There are many potential concerns, but one especially salient manifestation of the problem is known as "betting on resurrection." Consider the following illustration, where a management team may have bet on resurrection by taking on new risks during a period of insolvency.

Quadrant Structured Products Company, Inc. v. Vertin

115 A.3d 535 (Del. Ch. 2015)

■ LASTER, VICE CHANCELLOR.

Plaintiff Quadrant Structured Products Company, Ltd. ("Quadrant") owns debt securities issued by defendant Athilon Capital Corp. ("Athilon" or the "Company"), a Delaware corporation. Quadrant contends that Athilon is insolvent and has asserted derivative claims for breach of fiduciary duty against the individual defendants, who are members of Athilon's board of directors (the "Board"). Quadrant . . . asserts that . . . the Board breached its fiduciary duties by transferring value preferentially to Athilon's controller, defendant EBF & Associates ("EBF"), and to [another EBF affiliate].

I. FACTUAL BACKGROUND

Athilon was formed before the financial crisis of 2008 to sell credit protection to large financial institutions. The Company's wholly owned subsidiary, Athilon Asset Acceptance Corp. ("Asset Acceptance"), wrote credit default swaps on senior tranches of collateralized debt obligations. Athilon guaranteed the credit swaps that Asset Acceptance wrote.

[Eds.—A credit default swap is a financial contract where the buyer of the swap makes payments (premiums) to the seller of the swap. In return, the seller promises to compensate the buyer if a specified debt obligation goes into default or experiences another adverse credit event (as defined in the swap contract). For example, a firm like Asset Acceptance might sell you a credit default swap where you agree to pay premiums of $100 each month, and it agrees to pay you $100,000 if The Coca-Cola Company defaults on its 3.15% bonds due 15 November 2030. You might wish to buy this swap to hedge your risk on the Coca-Cola bonds (if you also have a direct position in these bonds) or because you think that Coca-Cola is likely to default on its bonds. The credit default swap market grew significantly in the early 2000's. Firms like Asset Acceptance found themselves in enormous trouble, however, as a result of the 2008 financial crisis. Numerous companies defaulted on their bonds, and large payout obligations were triggered for sellers of credit default swaps.

It is also worth noting that the plaintiff's position in this case is unusual because a debt investor does not ordinarily have standing to initiate derivative litigation on behalf of a corporation; these claims are typically brought by a shareholder. However, when a corporation is insolvent, debt investors become the beneficiaries of directors' fiduciary duties, allowing them to have standing to bring a derivative claim.]

To fund its operations, Athilon secured approximately $100 million in equity capital and $600 million in long-term debt. The debt was issued in multiple tranches comprising $350 million in Senior Subordinated Notes, $200 million in Subordinated Notes, and $50 million in Junior Subordinated Notes.

On the strength of its $700 million in committed capital, Athilon guaranteed more than $50 billion in credit default swaps written by Asset Acceptance. In the heady days before the financial crisis, the rating agencies gave Athilon and Asset Acceptance "AAA/Aaa" debt ratings and investment grade counterparty credit ratings.

Athilon suffered significant losses as a result of the financial crisis. It paid $48 million to unwind one credit default swap in 2008 and an additional $320 million to unwind another credit default swap in 2010. Athilon's GAAP financial statements showed a net worth of negative $513 million in 2010. As a result, Athilon and its subsidiary lost their AAA/Aaa ratings. Standard & Poor's gave the Company's Junior Subordinated Notes a credit rating of CC, indicating that default on the notes was a "virtual certainty." Athilon's securities traded at deep discounts, reflecting the widely held view that the Company was insolvent.

In 2010, EBF acquired significant portions of Athilon's debt. EBF's purchases included:

- Senior Subordinated Notes with a par value of $149.7 million, purchased for $37 million.
- Subordinated Notes with a par value of $71.4 million, purchased for $7.6 million.
- Junior Subordinated Notes with a par value of $50 million, purchased for $11.3 million, comprising the entire outstanding issuance.

EBF decided initially not to purchase Athilon's equity. Vincent Vertin, the EBF partner responsible for the investment, perceived that Athilon was insolvent and did not see any value in its stock. He wrote in June 2010, "What would I pay for this equity? Probably zero."

Later in 2010, EBF revisited this decision and decided to acquire all of Athilon's equity. The reason? Control. As an internal EBF document explained, "[e]quity ownership along with significant related party debt ownership affords the opportunity to control exit strategies, including the timing and size of any debt repayments, asset management fees and future dividends."

Using the control conferred by its status as Athilon's sole stockholder, EBF reconstituted the Board. At the time [of the lawsuit], the Board members were Vertin, Michael Sullivan, Patrick B. Gonzalez, Brandon Jundt, and J. Eric Wagoner. Vertin was a partner at EBF, and Sullivan was an in-house attorney for EBF. Gonzalez was the CEO of Athilon. Jundt was a former employee of EBF. He and Wagoner appear at this stage to be independent directors

Quadrant filed this derivative action on October 28, 2011. In its original complaint, Quadrant alleged that Athilon was insolvent, that its business model of writing credit default swaps had failed, and that the constitutive documents governing Athilon prohibited [it] from engaging in other lines of business. At the time of suit, Athilon's business consisted of a legacy portfolio of guarantees on credit default swap contracts written by Asset Acceptance that would continue to earn premiums until the last contracts expired in 2014 or shortly thereafter. Quadrant contended that given this situation, a well-motivated board of directors would maximize the Company's economic value for the benefit of its stakeholders by minimizing expenses during runoff, then liquidating the Company and returning its capital to its investors.

Quadrant alleged that instead, the Board transferred value to EBF by continuing to make interest payments on the Junior Subordinated Notes, which the Board had the authority to defer without penalty. Quadrant alleged that the Board did not exercise its authority to defer the payments because EBF owned the Junior Subordinated Notes. The Complaint also alleged that the Board transferred value from Athilon to

EBF by causing the Company to pay excessive fees to [another entity] which EBF indirectly owns and controls.

Finally, Quadrant alleged that the Board changed the Company's business model to make speculative investments for the benefit of EBF. As an example of the shift in investment strategy, Athilon increased its holdings of auction rate securities in the first quarter of 2011. Athilon's assets previously consisted of mainly of cash, cash equivalents, blue-chip corporate equities, and a limited amount of illiquid auction rate securities. Athilon sold liquid securities with a par value of $25 million and purchased additional illiquid auction rate securities.

The Complaint alleged that by adopting an investment strategy that involved greater risk, albeit with the potential for greater return, the Board acted for the benefit of EBF and contrary to the interests of the Company's more senior creditors. The strategy benefited EBF because EBF owned the Company's equity and Junior Subordinated Notes, which were underwater and would not bear any incremental losses if the investment strategy failed. If the riskier investment strategy succeeded, then these securities would rise in value and EBF would capture a substantial portion of the benefit.

. . .

In February 2015, the defendants moved for summary judgment on the theory that Athilon had returned to solvency. Citing an unaudited balance sheet, they argued that as of December 31, 2014, on a GAAP basis, Athilon's total assets were valued at $593,909,343 and its total liabilities at $441,699,117, resulting in positive stockholder equity of $152,210,225. After the completion of briefing, the defendants supplied an audited balance sheet reflecting marginally more positive figures.

II. LEGAL ANALYSIS

The defendants contend that summary judgment should be granted in their favor because Quadrant lacks standing to sue derivatively. "[T]he creditors of an insolvent corporation have standing to maintain derivative claims against directors on behalf of the corporation for breaches of fiduciary duties." N. Am. Catholic Educ. Programming Found., Inc. v. Gheewalla, 930 A.2d 92, 101 (Del. 2007). The defendants say that although Athilon once might have been insolvent (a point they contest), it is insolvent no longer. Because Quadrant is no longer a creditor "of an insolvent corporation," the defendants contend that Quadrant's claims should be dismissed for lack of standing. By making this argument, the defendants advocate the imposition of a continuous insolvency requirement, under which a creditor only can maintain a derivative claim during the time that a corporation actually is insolvent. Whether Delaware law imposes a continuous insolvency requirement presents a question of first impression.

The defendants also contend that summary judgment should be granted in their favor because to have standing to sue derivatively,

Quadrant must establish not only that Athilon's liabilities exceed its assets but also that Athilon has no reasonable prospect of returning to solvency. The latter test—irretrievable insolvency—is one that Delaware courts use when determining whether to appoint a receiver. The defendants say it should govern whether a creditor has standing to pursue derivative claims.

How one views these arguments depends in part on the nature of a creditor's claim for breach of fiduciary duty. If that claim is (i) an easily invoked theory that a creditor can assert directly as the firm approaches insolvency, (ii) a powerful cause of action that defendant directors will struggle to defeat because of an inherent conflict between their duties to creditors and their duties to stockholders, and (iii) a vehicle for obtaining a judicial remedy that would involve a forced liquidation of a firm that otherwise might continue to operate and return to solvency, then strong arguments can be made in favor of counterbalancing hurdles like a continuous insolvency requirement and a need to plead irretrievable insolvency.

But if a creditor's claim for breach of fiduciary duty is less potent and more closely aligned with the interests of the firm as a whole, then the need for additional hurdles recedes. If the claim is (i) something creditors only can file derivatively once the corporation actually has become insolvent, (ii) subject by default to the business judgment rule and not facilitated by any inherent conflict between duties to creditors and duties to stockholders, and (iii) only a vehicle for restoring to the firm self-dealing payments and other disloyal wealth transfers, then strong arguments can be made against the additional requirements as unnecessary and counterproductive impediments to the effective use of the derivative action as a meaningful tool for oversight.

Which is it? In my view, Gheewalla and a series of decisions by Chief Justice Strine, writing while a member of this court answered the matter definitively in favor of the latter characterization. In doing so, they significantly altered the landscape for evaluating a creditor's breach-of-fiduciary-duty claim.

[The court went on to evaluate the case in more detail.]

III. CONCLUSION

To establish standing to assert derivative claims as a creditor on behalf of Athilon, Quadrant must first plead and later prove that Athilon was insolvent at the time of suit. Quadrant need only show that Athilon was insolvent under the traditional balance sheet test. For purposes of the current motion for summary judgment, Quadrant has come forward with evidence sufficient to create a genuine issue of fact as to Athilon's solvency. The defendants' motion for summary judgment is denied.

QUESTIONS

1. How was Athilon able to obtain the highest credit rating on its debt obligations yet face such financial difficulty just a few years later?
2. Why is the plaintiff upset? Is this a situation where EBF is using Quadrant's money to "bet on resurrection?" How? Who would benefit from this decision?
3. Do you agree with the court's decision about when creditors should be able to assert a derivative action for a possible breach of fiduciary duty? We will return to the question of when creditors might maintain a fiduciary duty claim in Chapter 6, when we consider the important Gheewalla case referenced above.

To quickly sum up, agency cost considerations can push both ways for debt financing. More debt financing might theoretically reduce agency cost distortions between managers and shareholders by imposing external limits on managerial misbehavior. Even the need to make a regular interest payment, for example, might restrain an otherwise selfish manager's impulses by giving them "less slack" on the firm's spending. But greater debt in the capital structure can also introduce new distortions between the interests of shareholders and those of debt investors, as suggested by the previous case. Some of these latter concerns might be addressed ex ante by contract, and we will consider numerous methods for doing so in Chapter 6. But some problems are still likely to persist because debt investors cannot contract for every contingency. This means that the net effect of these various agency cost concerns on capital structure decisions will likely depend on industry- or even firm-specific characteristics related to regulation, governance, transparency, and other factors.

5. ADJUSTING CAPITAL STRUCTURE

As the discussion thus far might suggest, many companies seem to embrace a trade-off theory of financing. A wise fundraiser might seek to optimize a firm's use of debt by borrowing robustly to secure tax benefits, while also maintaining enough equity financing to avoid tilting the firm towards an excessive risk of financial distress. In addition, the firm might weigh various agency cost concerns (and possibly some other factors) when making this decision. All of this suggests that there should be some optimal amount of debt that a firm prefers to use in its capital structure. But this "ideal ratio" should also be expected to differ across firms and industries according to these different considerations. And some firms may hold off on debt financing entirely, perhaps to preserve flexibility for major strategic moves like borrowing heavily in the future to acquire another company. This diversity of approaches is, of course, exactly what we observe in the real world.

Moreover, capital structure decisions are not stagnant. A firm that set a highly leveraged capital structure ten years ago may wish to revisit this balance in light of new tax laws or riskier business endeavors. Or a firm that has historically eschewed borrowing may wish to wade into debt financing to reap new tax advantages. In this final section of the chapter, we examine how a company can take specific actions to adjust its capital structure. In addition to looking at the methods for each change, we will also ask why a firm might wish to take such action and examine some of the legal problems that might accompany the change.

A. RECAPITALIZATIONS

Often, capital structure adjustments involve internal financing changes which are also called recapitalizations. These can take many different forms, but usually a firm will execute a recapitalization for one of two primary reasons: to significantly increase the debt to equity ratio, or to significantly decrease this ratio. Let's begin with the decision to take on more debt.

i. ISSUING DEBT TO BUY BACK STOCK

Between 2010 and 2023 Coca-Cola boosted its debt to equity ratio from about 0.2 to 1.6. For such a large firm, this involved billions of dollars in borrowing. One way to accomplish such a change, of course, is simply to hold equity levels steady while borrowing large volumes of money over time to fund new expansion. But what about a firm that wishes to recapitalize without changing its total size? For such a firm, another option might be to issue new debt and then use the proceeds to buy back some outstanding stock. This allows a company to rapidly increase its debt to equity ratio by simultaneously changing both the numerator and the denominator.

For example, imagine that you are the CFO of The Coca-Cola Company in 2010. Your corporation has issued about $5 billion in long term debt and about $25 billion in equity—for a debt-to-equity ratio of 0.2. You now want to recapitalize the firm to take on more leverage and thereby shield a greater portion of your operating income from taxes. Your investment bankers tell you that it should be relatively easy to issue $10 billion in new Coca-Cola bonds at a very competitive interest rate. How should you proceed?

Assuming that you do decide to issue the bonds, the use of these proceeds will be tightly connected to the firm's strategic plan. If, for example, Coca-Cola is pursuing a strategy of acquiring regional bottling companies to distribute more of its products directly, then it may make sense to use the entire $10 billion bond issue to accelerate these plans. (Indeed, such a strategic move will often drive the financing decision, not the other way around.) This action would still increase Coca Cola's debt to equity ratio as follows:

	Before	After
Total Assets	$30 billion	$40 billion
Equity	$25 billion	$25 billion
Debt	$5 billion	$15 billion
Debt to Equity Ratio	0.2	0.6

But if Coca-Cola wants to execute a more dramatic recapitalization, then you might consider an alternative plan: Issue the $10 billion in bonds and use these proceeds to buy back some of the firm's stock. To implement this plan, you would need to purchase Coca-Cola stock at market prices (or possibly at a slight premium to market). For simplicity, assume that Coca-Cola instructs its investment bank to buy shares of Coca-Cola on the New York Stock Exchange, where the company's common stock is traded. As we saw in Chapter 2, this may not be the same price as the book value of the equity, which is currently reflected in the total amount of equity on the balance sheet. But to simplify, let's assume that book value and market value are equal at this moment in time. In this case, the entire $10 billion debt issuance would be used to decrease equity by an equivalent amount*:

	Before	After
Total Assets	$30 billion	$30 billion†
Equity	$25 billion	$15 billion
Debt	$5 billion	$15 billion
Debt to Equity Ratio	0.2	1.0

Shifting $10 billion in this manner from equity to debt would alter Coca Cola's capital structure more dramatically than the expansion plan. This could allow the firm to reduce taxes significantly because, as described above, the resulting interest payments may generate a tax shield. It is worth noting, however, that the Inflation Reduction Act of 2022 will now cause share buybacks by most public firms to incur an additional excise tax, currently set at 1%. (We will explore the economics of share buybacks more thoroughly in Chapter 9.) Of course, this recapitalization will also increase the risk that Coca-Cola might suffer

* The actual accounting treatment of share buybacks is more complex. Accountants will typically decrease the cash account and increase a treasury stock account that is known as a "contra-equity" account. This has the effect of decreasing the equity balance, but it also continues to track the pool of treasury stock in case the firm decides to resell these shares to investors in the future.

† Total assets remain at $30 billion because the $10 billion in cash that is received in the bond issuance is immediately paid out to equity investors in the stock buyback for a net change of zero.

losses related to financial distress if business prospects diminish. The most obvious cost of excessive debt is bankruptcy, as we have noted above. But excessive debt, or at least an unusually large proportion of debt in a capital structure, can also lead to other legal consequences—which we will consider closely in Chapter 6.

Sometimes a corporation might execute this type of recapitalization to discourage a hostile takeover attempt. Suppose you have heard rumors that your archrival PepsiCo is considering a hostile buyout of Coca-Cola with high levels of debt financing (a leveraged buyout). Could a recapitalization help you fight off PepsiCo? Consider the following excerpt from a seminal case in the area:

Revlon, Inc. v. McAndrews & Forbes Holdings Inc.

506 A.2d 173 (Del. 1986)

■ MOORE, JUSTICE:

. . .

The prelude to this controversy began in June 1985, when Ronald O. Perelman, chairman of the board and chief executive officer of Pantry Pride, met with his counterpart at Revlon, Michel C. Bergerac, to discuss a friendly acquisition of Revlon by Pantry Pride. Perelman suggested a price in the range of $40–50 per share, but the meeting ended with Bergerac dismissing those figures as considerably below Revlon's intrinsic value. All subsequent Pantry Pride overtures were rebuffed, perhaps in part based on Mr. Bergerac's strong personal antipathy to Mr. Perelman.

Thus, on August 14, Pantry Pride's board authorized Perelman to acquire Revlon, either through negotiation in the $42–$43 per share range, or by making a hostile tender offer at $45. Perelman then met with Bergerac and outlined Pantry Pride's alternate approaches. Bergerac remained adamantly opposed to such schemes and conditioned any further discussions of the matter on Pantry Pride executing a standstill agreement prohibiting it from acquiring Revlon without the latter's prior approval.

On August 19, the Revlon board met specially to consider the impending threat of a hostile bid by Pantry Pride. At the meeting, Lazard Freres, Revlon's investment banker, advised the directors that $45 per share was a grossly inadequate price for the company. Felix Rohatyn and William Loomis of Lazard Freres explained to the board that Pantry Pride's financial strategy for acquiring Revlon would be through "junk bond" financing followed by a break-up of Revlon and the disposition of its assets. With proper timing, according to the experts, such transactions could produce a return to Pantry Pride of $60 to $70 per share, while a sale of the company as a whole would be in the "mid 50" dollar range. Martin Lipton, special counsel for Revlon, recommended two defensive measures: first, that the company repurchase up to 5 million of its nearly 30 million outstanding shares; and second, that it adopt a Note Purchase Rights Plan. [Eds. This latter defense, the details of which are excluded here, is commonly described as a "poison pill."] . . .

Pantry Pride made its first hostile move on August 23 with a cash tender offer for any and all shares of Revlon at $47.50 per common share and $26.67 per preferred share, subject to (1) Pantry Pride's obtaining financing for the purchase, and (2) the [Note Purchase] Rights being redeemed, rescinded or voided.

The Revlon board met again on August 26. The directors advised the stockholders to reject the offer. Further defensive measures also were planned. On August 29, Revlon commenced its own offer for up to 10 million shares, exchanging for each share of common stock tendered one Senior Subordinated Note (the Notes) of $47.50 principal at 11.75% interest, due 1995, and one-tenth of a share of $9.00 Cumulative Convertible Exchangeable Preferred Stock valued at $100 per share. Lazard Freres opined that the notes would trade at their face value on a fully distributed basis. Revlon stockholders tendered 87 percent of the outstanding shares (approximately 33 million), and the company accepted the full 10 million shares on a pro rata basis. The new Notes contained covenants which limited Revlon's ability to incur additional debt, sell assets, or pay dividends unless otherwise approved by the "independent" (non-management) members of the board. . . .

[The court went on to hold that these defenses (but not some other defenses that were adopted later by the board) were legally permissible.]

QUESTIONS

1. Ignore the poison pill defense, as we have omitted the court's discussion of this strategy's details. How would the other defenses change Revlon's capital structure?
2. Why would Revlon's managers and professional advisors believe that these recapitalizations might discourage Pantry Pride from pursuing a hostile takeover?
3. Can you think of any effective response by Perelman to the recapitalization defenses?

---

ii. ISSUING DEBT TO PAY LARGE DIVIDENDS

A closely related recapitalization strategy involves borrowing money and using the proceeds to pay a large dividend to shareholders. This should also have the effect of increasing a firm's debt to equity ratio, and the economic effect of such behavior is comparable to share buyback recapitalizations. The additional debt will obviously increase the firm's borrowings. And a large dividend payout will decrease the firm's equity balance. If the entire amount of the debt proceeds is paid out as a special dividend, then there may be little net effect on the firm's cash balance.

Some activist shareholders have lobbied in recent years for incumbent managers to pursue this type of recapitalization. Why do you suppose they might want this to happen? Consider the following letter* from one such investor during the run-up to the Dell appraisal lawsuit discussed in Chapter 3:

Icahn Enterprises L.P.

March 5, 2013

Board of Directors

Dell Inc.

One Dell Way

Round Rock, Texas 78682

Attn.: Laurence P. Tu, Senior Vice President, General Counsel and Secretary

Re: Agreement and Plan of Merger, dated as of February 5, 2013 (the "Going Private Transaction").

Dear Board Members:

We are substantial holders of Dell Inc. shares. Having reviewed the Going Private Transaction, we believe that it is not in the best interests of Dell shareholders and substantially undervalues the company.

Rather than engage in the Going Private Transaction, we propose that Dell announce that in the event that the Going Private Transaction is voted down by shareholders, Dell will immediately declare and pay a special dividend of $9 per share comprised of proceeds from the following sources: (1) $4.26 per share, or $7.4 Billion, from available cash as proposed in the Going Private Transaction, (2) $1.73 per share, or $3 Billion, from factoring existing commercial and consumer receivables as proposed in the Going Private Transaction, and (3) $4.26, or $5.25 Billion in new debt.

We believe that such a transaction is superior to the Going Private Transaction because we value the pro forma "stub" at $13.81 per share using a discounted cash flow valuation methodology based on a consensus of analyst forecasts. The "stub" value of $13.81 combined with our proposed $9.00 special dividend gives Dell shareholders a total value of

---

* The full text of this letter, along with Dell's immediate response, is available at: https://www.sec.gov/Archives/edgar/data/826083/000119312513094825/0001193125-13-094825-index.htm.

$22.81 per share, representing a 67% premium to the $13.65 per share price proposed in the Going Private Transaction. We have spent a great deal of time and effort in determining the $22.81 per share value and would be pleased to meet with you to share our analysis and to understand why you disagree, if you do.

We hope that this Board will agree to adopt our proposal by publicly announcing that the Board is committed to implement our proposal if the Going Private Transaction is voted down by Dell shareholders. This would avoid a proxy fight.

However, if this Board will not promise to implement our proposal in the event that the Dell shareholders vote down the Going Private Transaction, then we request that the Board announce that it will combine the vote on the Going Private Transaction with an annual meeting to elect a new board of directors. We then intend to run a slate of directors that, if elected, will implement our proposal for a leveraged recapitalization and $9 per share dividend at Dell, as set forth above. In that way shareholders will have a real choice between the Going Private Transaction and our proposal. To assure shareholders of the availability of sufficient funds for the prompt payment of the dividend, if our slate of directors is elected, Icahn Enterprises would provide a $2 billion bridge loan and I would personally provide a $3.25 billion bridge loan to Dell, each on commercially reasonable terms, if that bridge financing is necessary.

Like the "go shop" period provided in the Going Private Transaction, your fiduciary duties as directors require you to call the annual meeting as contemplated above in order to provide shareholders with a true alternative to the Going Private Transaction. As you know, last year's annual meeting was held on July 13, 2012 (and indeed for the past 20 years Dell's annual meetings have been held in this time frame) and so it would be appropriate to hold the 2013 annual meeting together with the meeting for the Going Private Transaction, which you have disclosed will be held in June or early July.

If you fail to agree promptly to combine the vote on the Going Private Transaction with the vote on the annual meeting, we anticipate years of litigation will follow challenging the transaction and the actions of those directors that participated in it. The Going Private Transaction is a related party transaction with the largest shareholder of the company and advantaging existing management as well, and as such it will be subject to intense judicial review and potential challenges by shareholders and strike suitors. But you have the opportunity to avoid this situation by following the fair and reasonable path set forth in this letter.

Our proposal provides Dell shareholders with substantial cash of $9 per share and the ability to continue as owners of Dell, a stock that we expect to be worth approximately $13.81 per share following the dividend. We believe, as apparently does Michael Dell and his partner

Silver Lake, that the future of Dell is bright. We see no reason that the future value of Dell should not accrue to ALL the existing Dell shareholders—not just Michael Dell.

As mentioned in today's phone call, we look forward to hearing from you tomorrow to discuss this matter without the need for us to bring this to the public arena.

Very truly yours,
Icahn Enterprises L.P.

By:
Carl C. Icahn
Chairman of the Board

---

iii. ISSUING EQUITY TO REPAY (OR BUY BACK) DEBT

A third type of recapitalization involves the issuance of new equity combined with the repurchase of some of the corporation's debt. The effect on the firm's capital structure of this plan is exactly the opposite of the previous two recapitalizations: the debt-to-equity ratio will decrease. Why might a company decide to follow this strategy—which is sometimes called a deleveraging recapitalization? The most obvious reason is to reduce an impending risk of bankruptcy or financial distress. Deleveraging is usually a primary component of a distressed firm's workout plan: new equity may come into the company (often as preferred stock) in exchange for a reduction in the firm's debt. And the debt repurchase might not occur at 100 cents on the dollar if everyone agrees to share some pain in order to secure the new equity cushion. We will see several examples of debt workouts later in the book. For now, consider the following case:

S. Muoio & Co. LLC. v. Hallmark Entertainment Investments

2011 WL 863007 (Del. Ch. 2011)

■ CHANDLER, CHANCELLOR:

This action challenges the fairness of the June 29, 2010 recapitalization (the "Recapitalization") of Crown Media Holdings, Inc. ("Crown" or the "Company") orchestrated by Crown's controlling stockholder and primary debt holder, Hallmark Cards, Inc. and its affiliates (collectively "Hallmark"). For years, Crown was unable to make its debt payments, and was forced to obtain extensions on the debt from Hallmark. In the Recapitalization, Hallmark exchanged its Crown debt for an increased percentage of Crown's Class A common stock, new preferred stock and a new and far smaller amount of debt with longer maturities, thereby permitting Crown to avoid a debt default and bankruptcy.

Hallmark initially proposed a recapitalization on May 28, 2009. Crown's board immediately created a Special Committee to consider the proposed recapitalization. Before the Special Committee could even consider the proposed recapitalization, S. Muoio & Co. LLC (a Crown stockholder) filed this action on July 13, 2009, seeking to enjoin the proposed transaction. The parties agreed to a stay of the litigation while the Special Committee considered Hallmark's proposal. . . .

Almost seven months later, on February 9, 2010, Crown announced that Hallmark and Crown had approved and executed a non-binding term sheet in connection with the Recapitalization. On March 1, 2010, Crown announced it had entered into a Master Recapitalization Agreement memorializing the terms of the Recapitalization. After receiving that notice, however, Muoio [sought] rescission of the transaction. The Recapitalization closed on June 29, 2010.

Plaintiff contends that the Recapitalization was consummated at an unfair price and drastically undervalued Crown. In so doing, plaintiff asserts that Crown should be valued based on a discounted cash flow ("DCF") analysis, and that a properly conducted DCF analysis establishes that Crown's stock is worth far more than the Recapitalization, which is valued at $2.59 per share. Plaintiff also contends that Hallmark imposed the Recapitalization on the Company through an unfair process, that the Hallmark-dictated terms of the new debt and preferred stock are unfair, and that the Recapitalization unfairly transferred significant value and voting power from the Crown minority stockholders to Hallmark. . . .

The parties concede that the appropriate standard of review is entire fairness. . . . Ultimately, my decision turns on the following factual findings: the Crown board's process was not flawed; the Special Committee was independent and negotiated at arm's length; and the record clearly demonstrates that Crown was underwater at the time of the Recapitalization—that is, it could not pay its debts as they became due and absent the Recapitalization, default or bankruptcy seemed inevitable. In addition (as is now quite common in cases of this nature), the valuation question, in part, resulted in a battle of the experts—and in this case, plaintiff's expert lost. His proffered opinion was far less credible and persuasive than defendants' experts. For the reasons more fully explained below, I find in favor of defendants and conclude that the Recapitalization was entirely fair.

I. BACKGROUND

A. The Parties

Plaintiff Muoio is a New York securities advisory firm and a holder of Crown's Class A common stock.

Defendant Hallmark, a Missouri corporation headquartered in Kansas City, Missouri, is engaged in the manufacture and distribution of personal expression products. Immediately before the Recapitalization proposal, Hallmark controlled approximately 80.1% of Crown's outstanding shares; following the proposal it now controls approximately 90.3%.

Nominal Defendant Crown is a Delaware corporation with its principal place of business in Studio City, California. Crown's revenues are largely tied to advertising revenue, which in turn is driven by the ratings and demographics of its cable television channels. Crown competes for both ratings and key demographics with large media companies that are able to spread their costs across multiple cable channels. . . .

B. Crown's Formation and its Debt Crisis

In 1991, Hallmark created the family entertainment platform that became Crown following a review of its business units, which also include Crayola and other family oriented subsidiaries. In the early 1990s, Hallmark acquired an extensive production library of programming that was designed to appeal to all ages. . . . The network was later renamed as "Hallmark Channel." Crown Media Holdings was created in 2000 to effectuate an initial public offering of Crown, providing the Company with additional capital to fund its development.

In January 2001, Crown acquired a library of over 700 original television movies, representing over 3,000 hours of programming, from a Hallmark subsidiary (the "Library Transaction"). This programming was used, among other things, to populate the Hallmark Channel and the Hallmark Movie Channel. With the Library Transaction, Crown assumed $220 million of debt and ultimately issued 33.3 million shares of stock to Hallmark. Over the years, Hallmark supplied Crown with needed capital injections, and agreed to extend maturities on the debts owed to it by Crown. By spring 2009, however, Crown owed Hallmark over $1.1 billion in debt. Crown also held a credit revolver with J.P. Morgan (the "JPM Revolver") guaranteed by Hallmark, and it owed $25 million [on this credit line].

C. Crown's Attempts to Find a Buyer

In August 2005, the Crown board formed a special committee . . . (the "2005 Special Committee") to seek a buyer for the Company and also consider other alternatives. The 2005 Special Committee retained independent legal and financial advisors, Wachtell, Lipton, Rosen & Katz and Citigroup, to engage in an extensive sales process involving key players in the cable industry as well as private equity firms. The object was to help identify a buyer for Crown. Not a single offer resulted from the 2005 Special Committee process. Thereafter, Hallmark itself engaged in discussions with several potential acquirers or other sources of financing for Crown, but was similarly unsuccessful.

In August 2006, Tim Griffith became Hallmark's interim CFO and assumed responsibility for the management of Hallmark's investment in Crown. At this point, Hallmark held $1 billion of Crown's outstanding debt. Crown's financial situation was precarious because Crown had never made a profit and (as stated above) efforts to sell the Company had failed up to this point. To allow Crown to continue operating as a going concern, Hallmark had previously granted Crown a waiver and standstill on its debt payments. The waiver and standstill agreement was revisited every quarter, with extensions being effective for one year from the date Hallmark extended. Without the waivers and extensions, Crown's auditors would have issued a going concern qualification on Crown's financial statements for one simple reason: Crown could not pay interest on its debt (much less pay the principal of the notes due upon expiration of the standstill).

In 2006, Crown hired a new CEO, Henry Schleiff, who was specifically recruited to find a buyer for Crown. Schleiff had successfully sold another cable channel before joining Crown. Schleiff contacted numerous parties but ultimately failed to locate a buyer for Crown during his three year tenure as CEO. In 2007, Schleiff's efforts produced three prospective buyers: Liberty Media, Time Warner, and Hearst. Each potential buyer did due diligence and spoke with management. Liberty Media expressed interest in Hallmark's stake in Crown, valuing Crown at around $800 million. Liberty Media continued to show its interest, raising its enterprise value to $1 billion by 2008. In other words, Liberty Media viewed Crown's enterprise value to be below the value of Crown's debt. Similarly, Time Warner did not make an offer, but put an enterprise value on Crown of $1 billion (again, below the value of its debt). Hearst never formally made an offer. In 2008 and 2009, Schleiff also turned up other potential buyers, including CBS, Hasbro, and Fox. None made an offer above Crown's debt to Hallmark. Fox did make a proposal, in which it put the total enterprise value of Crown at $500 million and which would have required Hallmark to write off 85% of the Hallmark debt and give Fox control of the Company. Hallmark was unwilling to accept those terms. Concurrently, Hallmark extended Crown's waiver and standstill to May 2010.

In sum, despite continuous efforts to shop Crown since 2005, no potential buyer had placed a value on Crown that exceeded the Hallmark debt, and the most recent offer for Crown was $500 million—less than half of its debt to Hallmark. At least in Hallmark's view, given that refinancing Hallmark's debt with a third party was impossible, a recapitalization was the best path forward either to a future refinancing or a future sale. Although plaintiff disputes this, it appears that Hallmark's view was that if there was no recapitalization, bankruptcy or foreclosure were the likely alternatives.

D. The Recapitalization Proposal

On May 28, 2009, Hallmark sent the Crown board a proposal for recapitalizing the Hallmark debt (the "Hallmark Proposal"). Under the Hallmark Proposal, Hallmark's equity ownership would increase from 67% to at least 90.1 % (possibly even up to 95%), while its voting power would increase from 80.1% to 90.3%. The Hallmark Proposal included restructuring $500 million of principal amount of the Hallmark debt into a $300 million cash-pay term loan bearing an annual interest rate of 12% and a $200 million pay-in-kind term loan with an annual interest rate of 15%, both maturing on September 30, 2011. The remaining Hallmark debt, which is about $600 million, would be exchanged for convertible preferred stock with a liquidation preference of approximately $640 million and a conversion price of $1.00 per share. Along with this proposal, Hallmark also advised Crown that it would not continue to extend the waiver and standstill. Hallmark was neither willing, nor legally obligated, to invest further in Crown.

E. Creation of the Special Committee

After receiving the Hallmark Proposal, the Crown board on June 2, 2009, formed the Special Committee, composed of [three] independent directors. . . . According to the resolutions creating the Special Committee, the Special Committee was empowered to "consider such matters as it deems advisable with respect to the Recapitalization Proposal," and authorized to "take such further action, at the Company's expense, as the Special Committee deems appropriate in order to carry out the intent and purposes" of the authorizing resolutions. The resolutions prohibited the Crown board from approving or authorizing an agreement with respect to the Hallmark Proposal "without a prior favorable recommendation of the Recapitalization Proposal or the relevant part thereof by the Special Committee."

F. Process of the Special Committee

The Special Committee's first task was to select its independent legal and financial advisor. The Special Committee retained Richards, Layton & Finger, P.A. ("RLF") as its independent legal counsel. After receiving presentations from various firms, the Special Committee retained Morgan Stanley as its financial advisor. Once Morgan Stanley was engaged, the Special Committee promptly authorized a press release announcing the engagement, stating expressly that the Committee was "considering Hallmark Cards' proposal as well as the Company's other alternatives."

After being retained by the Special Committee, Morgan Stanley engaged in extensive due diligence of Crown, including meetings with Crown's senior management to discuss the Company's business plans and financial viability. Morgan Stanley reviewed Crown's current financial condition and provided the Special Committee with information regarding comparable companies. Based on its analysis, on September

11, 2009, Morgan Stanley advised the Special Committee that it had determined a preliminary value of Crown of between $500 million and approximately $1 billion, with a mid-point at approximately $700 to $750 million—less than the amount Crown owed to Hallmark. . . .

The Special Committee knew it had few options. Those options included: (1) refinancing the Hallmark debt; (2) pursuing a third-party sale; (3) accepting Hallmark's Proposal; or (4) negotiating the Hallmark Proposal. The Special Committee, with advice from Morgan Stanley, acknowledged that none of those options were optimal, but the status quo (i.e., doing nothing) was not feasible because Crown simply could not service its debt burden and would be unable to satisfy its debts on the maturity dates. Morgan Stanley took the position (and so advised the Special Committee) that Crown could not refinance the Hallmark debt with a third party in light of Crown's capital structure and debt market conditions in 2009. Moreover, given past failed sales efforts, the Special Committee determined that a third-party sale was unlikely. The Special Committee reached this decision based on its own members' extensive industry experience as well as Morgan Stanley's advice.

Ultimately, the Special Committee determined that, absent a recapitalization of its debt, Crown faced a potential bankruptcy. Morgan Stanley advised that Crown's non-Hallmark stockholders likely would not receive any value in a bankruptcy proceeding. On the other hand, there were potential downsides to Hallmark in a bankruptcy, and Morgan Stanley considered it unlikely that Hallmark wanted to place Crown into bankruptcy. As stated above, Hallmark, with its original proposal, had no intention of continuing to extend the waiver and standstill, and it simply did not want to invest further in Crown. Likewise, the Special Committee and Morgan Stanley believed that further extending the debt waivers and putting off Crown's significant capital structure issues were not in the best interests of Crown or its minority stockholders, because the debt owed to Hallmark would continue to grow. Therefore, the Special Committee decided not to pursue or to ask for further debt extensions. Given the potential risks and costs of a bankruptcy, Morgan Stanley believed Hallmark would be inclined to renegotiate a solution to the debt issues for Crown; Morgan Stanley also considered the Hallmark Proposal to have numerous deficiencies. It was against this background that Morgan Stanley advised the Special Committee that a go-private transaction was the best alternative for the non-Hallmark stockholders. In the event Hallmark would not consider taking Crown private at a fair price, Morgan Stanley believed the Special Committee should try to negotiate for better terms in a recapitalization.

[The court described extensive negotiation efforts between the Special Committee and Hallmark. Eventually the parties reached a recapitalization agreement.]

II. ANALYSIS

. . .

A transaction between a majority stockholder and the company in which it owns a majority stake is generally reviewed under the entire fairness standard and the controlling stockholder (or the party standing on both sides of the transaction) bears the burden of proof. Given Hallmark's role in the Recapitalization, the applicable standard of review for this case under Delaware law is therefore entire fairness. As its name implies, entire fairness has two components: fair dealing and fair price. These prongs are not independent and the Court does not focus on each of them individually. Rather, the Court "determines entire fairness based on all aspects of the entire transaction." . . .

If defendant can show that the challenged transaction was negotiated and approved by "an independent committee of directors" or an informed majority of the minority, however, the burden of proof shifts to "the challenging shareholder-plaintiff." To determine whether the burden shifts in this case, I must consider "whether the special committee was truly independent, fully informed, and had the freedom to negotiate at arm's length." . . .

I find that all three members of the Special Committee were independent, and approved the transaction after an arm's length negotiation. Thus, plaintiff bears the burden of showing that the Recapitalization was unfair given the undisputed evidence that the transaction was approved by an independent and disinterested special committee of directors. . . .

Along with the board's composition and independence, "fair dealing addresses the timing and structure of negotiations as well as the method of approval of the transaction." Considering these factors, for the reasons set forth below, I find that the process followed here was entirely fair.

1. Hallmark's Timing of the Recapitalization

Plaintiff argues that Hallmark opportunistically timed its original Recapitalization proposal to burden Crown with debt as the initial step in a devised plan in which it could exercise leverage over Crown to maneuver a "perfect storm" and force recapitalization at a critical moment in Crown's life cycle. Given the fact that Hallmark had all along sought a meaningful solution to Crown's crumbling capital structure, I do not accept plaintiff's contention that Hallmark had devised an elaborate scheme to unfairly time the Recapitalization. . . .

Unfortunately that is not all of the bad news for the plaintiff. There are other reasons why plaintiff's unfair timing theory fails as well. Plaintiff's unfair timing theory is premised almost entirely on the approximately $3 billion valuation of Crown by plaintiff's expert witness, Daniel R. Schechter.

I am not able to accept this theory, however, when Schechter's valuation cannot explain why no potential buyer or valuation expert (other than Schechter himself) ever perceived Crown's value to exceed its debt.

. . .

The Special Committee met formally twenty-nine times over a period of nine months. The Special Committee's legal advisors were present at each one of them. After Morgan Stanley was retained, representatives of Morgan Stanley (usually including Robert Kindler, the Global Head of Mergers and Acquisitions at Morgan Stanley) attended every one of the Special Committee's meetings. The members of the Special Committee relied on the professional advice provided by their legal and financial advisors. Notably, each member of the Special Committee assumed an active role in the process (outside its internal meetings) including speaking with a third party regarding potential interest in Crown, meeting with Muoio to discuss his concerns, actively facilitating negotiations, and negotiating face-to-face with Hallmark.

. . .

In the end, the Special Committee got a great result for Crown's minority stockholders. Its advisors believed and advised the Special Committee that the Recapitalization was a more attractive and viable option for Crown's minority stockholders than any other alternatives available to the Company. Accordingly, I find that the negotiated Recapitalization terms were the product of a thorough, effective, and independent Special Committee.

[The court went on to consider an expert witness battle over the valuation of the company. The plaintiff's expert used a discounted cash flow method that "valued Crown nearly three times higher than all the other valuations at $2.946 billion."]

In sum, because Crown's outstanding debt exceeded the value of its equity before the Recapitalization, and because defendants' proffered expert testimony persuasively and thoroughly supported their valuation conclusions (and plaintiff's experts failed to convince me otherwise), I conclude that the Recapitalization was entirely fair.

QUESTIONS

1. What were Hallmark's options at the time of the proposed recapitalization? Why did it ultimately decide to advocate for Crown's recapitalization?
2. If the economic effect of the recapitalization was to reduce the financial pressure on Crown, then why would the plaintiff shareholder be upset? Shouldn't Muiou prefer this outcome to bankruptcy?
3. Why did Crown need to go through the extensive process of establishing a special committee? Couldn't the board just make the recapitalization decision for the corporation?

The exchange transaction conducted by Hallmark represents a fairly typical way for distressed debtors to reduce their debt-to-equity ratio. The basic model for these exchange transactions is for the debtor company to negotiate directly with its lenders to find a bundle of securities (typically involving a combination of the company's equity and/or new debt with more lenient repayment terms) that the lenders will accept in exchange for the company's existing debt. In the case of Crown Media Holdings, Inc., this was facilitated by the fact that Hallmark was both Crown's primary lender as well as its Crown's controlling stockholder. Of course, that fact is also why the recapitalization was subjected to entire fairness review. In other contexts, the debtor and lenders may lack any such relationship. In these settings, any debt exchange is unlikely to be subject to entire fairness review, but the debtor will face a potentially larger problem: How can it persuade a lender to surrender its debt for a security that is more junior or that has less favorable claims? Indeed, where the debt is held across many lenders, the debtor may have to persuade a large number of lenders to complete a recapitalization. In Chapter 6, we shall explore various "hard ball" strategies that debtors have used to compel lenders to make such a trade.

iv. RECAPITALIZING DISTRESSED FIRMS: DISCLOSURE CHALLENGES, TOXIC DEATH SPIRALS, AND MEME STOCK FINANCE

In addition to a debt-for-equity swap, a debtor could also reduce its debt-to-equity ratio by simply selling equity to stockholders. This act alone will reduce the ratio, and of course, the company can also use the proceeds to repay its debt, which will reduce it even more. However, when a firm is in financial distress due to its debt burden, a natural question arises: Why would anyone buy its stock? If the firm were to go bankrupt, the equity would almost certainly become worthless. This risk is especially acute where the financial distress is severe. Conventionally, distressed firms have turned to one of two solutions to find a path forward for new equity sales.

The first approach is to give investors a reason to believe the financial distress is not severe and will be short-lived. However, such a reason may not exist or may be highly uncertain. Where a distressed company seeks to issue equity, it should hardly be surprising that the SEC will be especially attentive to what the company has disclosed to investors to ensure investors are making an informed investment decision and are not mislead into having false hope.

The second approach is to compensate investors for making such a risky investment. In a transaction following this approach, one or more investors will typically purchase from the company newly issued convertible notes or convertible preferred stock. We cover convertible securities in Chapter 8, but for now, it is sufficient to know that these securities allow the holder to exchange the face value of the instrument for shares of the company's common stock. The exact number of shares will be determined by a formula set forth in the convertible security, and this formula can be drafted to provide compensation to investors. For instance, imagine you are among a group of investors that each purchase from a company a convertible note for $10,000 at a time when the company's stock trades at $5 per share. Each note provides that upon conversion, the holder will receive the number of shares that is equal to $10,000 divided by $2.50 (the conversion price), or one-half the current trading price of the stock. Upon conversion, you would therefore be entitled to 4,000 shares that you can then sell at $5 per share on the stock market for a total of $20,000. Congratulations! You just doubled your money by investing in a distressed firm.

Of course, this simple example ignores several facts that will complicate the ultimate outcome. Perhaps most importantly, there is no guarantee that the stock price will remain at $5 per share. On the contrary, the price should be expected to fall in value as investors convert and sell stock on the open market. Due to this risk, investors might require the conversion formula to be written so that the conversion price is equal to 50% of the stock price at the moment of conversion. However, this is likely to create a toxic "death-spiral": As the stock price declines, each $10,000 note is converted into more shares, which are then sold, further depressing the company's stock price, resulting in more shares being issued and sold upon conversion of the other notes, further depressing the stock price, and on and on. You better convert fast before the stock zeros out!

Equally important, the obvious and adverse impact of this transaction on the company's common stock raises a number of issues under U.S. securities regulation. While these issues are beyond the scope of this book, one way to comply with these rules would be to file a registration statement covering the convertible notes and underlying shares of common stock, which will effectively disclose to the public these adverse consequence on the company's common stock. In an efficient market, this disclosure itself should prompt a sharp drop in the price of the company's stock.* This only adds to the challenge of successfully securing investors for this type of equity offering.†

---

* Of course, the company could choose to sell the convertible securities in an unregistered private placement, assuming it could satisfy the requirements for an unregistered offering. (We discuss these requirements in Part 6 of Chapter 5.) However, note that for convertibles sold in unregistered private placements, U.S. securities laws will generally require the investor to wait at least six months before converting and selling shares on a stock exchange.

† It should perhaps come as no surprise that equity offerings of this nature tend to occur mostly on the Over-the-Counter (OTC) Market, often by way of unregistered offerings. As a result, the stock price of OTC securities may be less sensitive to the issuance of a toxic convertible as the OTC Market is not regarded as informationally efficient. Yet even here, efforts to profit from an investment in a toxic convertible before the company's price plummets has led investors to violate U.S. securities laws. See Securities and Exchange Commission v. Joshua Sason, et al., No. 19-cv-1459 (S.D.N.Y. filed February 15, 2019). Not surprisingly, the SEC takes a very dim view of these offerings.

In short, the conventional recipes for a successful equity offering by a distressed firm are not especially compelling ones. The fundamental problem is one of valuation. If the value of the underlying business is less than the value of the company's debt, M&M tells us that there can be no value for equity. Selling shares of common stock to pay down debt is simply a wealth transfer from the buyers of shares to the company's creditors. This is wonderful for creditors (who previously stood to be paid only from the company's existing business assets) but nonsensical for the shareholder investors.

But what if shareholders viewed investing in distressed firms as fun? Sure, your position as a shareholder is likely to be zeroed out if a company goes bankrupt, but how can one really tell if a company is valued at less than its debt? Maybe things will turn around! Or perhaps there are symbolic reasons you might want to invest in a company that Wall Street financiers have abandoned. For whatever reason, the past several years witnessed the entry of a large number of retail traders who appear to hold these perspectives. Evidence of this new breed of retail trader was perhaps most vividly revealed in the dramatic surge in the stock prices of video game retailer GameStop and movie chain AMC during 2021, despite the growing risk that both firms might shutter in the wake of declining sales (in part due to the COVID-19 pandemic). In general, this form of trading is believed to be heavily influenced by social media, memes, and the hype generated in online communities, especially on platforms like Reddit's WallStreetBets. These stocks often become popular not because of the underlying company's financial performance, but due to viral sharing of memes and posts that encourage a large number of retail investors to buy shares. As such, stocks that are subject to such trading waves have become known as "meme" stocks.

The fact that a large swath of investors may find utility in purchasing shares of distressed firms changes the conventional calculus for new equity financing. First, the need to clearly and forcibly alert investors to the company's financial distress and risk of bankruptcy will not deter meme stock investors from buying a company's stock. Second, the adverse impact of a toxic convertible offering should be diminished.

As an example of the first point, consider the bankruptcy of the car rental company Hertz Global Holdings, Inc. The COVID-19 pandemic resulted in a virtual shutdown of the entire car rental market, forcing Hertz to file for bankruptcy in 2020. Yet Hertz's stock, which traded under $1 per share prior to the bankruptcy filing, soared above $5 per share after the filing—a puzzling scenario given the company's financial distress. Seeking to capitalize on this momentum, Hertz announced an at-the-market offering, in which it would sell $500 million of new equity to raise capital.* Notably, the offering prospectus made abundantly clear

* An at-the-market offering allows a company to sell shares directly to the retail market through a designated broker-dealer at current market prices over a given period of time. As such, an investor who buys shares over an exchange during an at-the-market offering could be

the risk investors faced by purchasing shares.* However, the move quickly drew scrutiny from the SEC, which questioned the prudence of allowing investors to purchase equity that might soon be rendered worthless under bankruptcy proceedings. Hertz would eventually pull the offering due to the SEC's saber-rattling.

Roughly three years later, a convertible offering by the retailer Bed Bath and Beyond (BBBY) provided an example of the second point. In the spring of 2023, BBBY stood on the doorstep of bankruptcy after making a number of operational missteps that caused its revenue to plummet. BBBY had failed to secure a buyer and was widely rumored to be planning a bankruptcy filing. Nonetheless, it had become a meme stock, and its highly volatile shares were still worth about $300 to $400 million in total market capitalization. In February 2023, it announced a $1 billion registered offering of convertible preferred stock (reportedly anchored by the hedge fund Hudson Bay Capital). In the registration statement, the company disclosed the large discount that investors would receive on converting their preferred shares into BBBY common stock. Moreover, because both the preferred shares and the underlying common shares were being registered with the SEC, investors could convert and immediately resell the common shares to retail investors. In effect, BBBY was using the offering as a conduit to tap into the retail interest in BBBY as a meme stock. Moreover, it would be doing so in fashion that would risk creating a toxic death spiral. BBBY would also eventually conduct an at-the-market offering to raise additional capital, much as Hertz had originally planned. In the end, BBBY would indeed file for bankruptcy, but this did not happen until several months after the new equity financing transactions had occurred. In the meantime, BBBY's status as a meme stock would enable millions of dollars to flow to the company's creditors from presumably retail traders. The columnist Matt Levine provided the following post-mortem.

Bed Bath Moves Into the Beyond

Money Stuff, April 24, 2023
by Matt Levine.

On Jan. 20, Bed Bath & Beyond Inc. had about 117.3 million shares of common stock outstanding; the stock closed that day at $3.35 per share. On March 27, it had about 428.1 million shares outstanding, at $0.7881 each. On April 10, it had 558.7 million shares outstanding, at $0.2961 each. Yesterday, April 23, when it filed for bankruptcy, it had 739,056,836 shares outstanding. The stock closed at $0.2935 on Friday.

---

purchasing newly issued (primary) shares from the company or previously outstanding (secondary) shares from another selling investor.

* For instance, the cover page of the prospectus noted in bold: "We are in the process of a reorganization under chapter 11 of title 11, or Chapter 11, of the United States Code, or Bankruptcy Code, which has caused and may continue to cause our common stock to decrease in value, or may render our common stock worthless."

So in the last two weeks, Bed Bath & Beyond has sold about 180 million shares to retail investors, more shares than it had outstanding in January. The stock averaged about $0.31 per share over those two weeks, meaning that the company raised maybe $55 million, in those two weeks, as it has been sliding into bankruptcy. Since January, Bed Bath & Beyond has sold about 622 million shares, or almost 50 million shares a week, raising a few hundred million dollars.

Here is Bed Bath's first-day declaration in the bankruptcy case, which describes what the company has been up to over the last few months. The points that I would highlight are:

- In December 2022, "Bed Bath & Beyond triggered multiple events of defaults under its financing facilities" and began its slow move into bankruptcy.
- Also in December 2022, its financial advisers at Lazard "commenced a process to solicit interest in a going-concern sale transaction that could be effectuated in chapter 11," that is, to find someone who was interested in buying the company out of bankruptcy and continuing to operate its business.
- They failed: By mid-January, "Lazard had engaged with approximately 60 potential investors to solicit interest in serving as a plan sponsor, acquiring some or all of the Debtors' assets or businesses, or providing postpetition financing," but "to date, the Company has been yet to identify an executable transaction."
- So, as of mid-January, it seems that the company's plan was to file for bankruptcy, close all its stores, liquidate its inventory and hand whatever cash was left to its creditors.
- But Bed Bath did have one thing going for it. It was "part of the 'meme-stock' movement started and fueled on Reddit boards and social media websites," because it "checked the two boxes needed to become a meme-stock: (i) a troubled financial situation and (ii) nostalgia value."
- So someone had the bright idea of delaying things for a bit by selling tons and tons of stock to Bed Bath's retail shareholders at whatever prices they'd pay. "Certain third-party investors expressed interest in providing the Debtors with substantial equity financing in light of the Company's depressed share price and continued trading volatility. More specifically, the Debtors were approached by Hudson Bay Capital Management, LP" about a weird stock deal that we discussed in January; this ended up raising about $360 million. After the Hudson Bay deal ran its course—basically, after Hudson Bay and Bed Bath drove the stock price from above $3 to below $1 by pounding out about 311

> million shares to retail investors—Bed Bath and its brokers at B. Riley Securities Inc. sold another 311 million shares to retail investors, but at ever-declining prices, so they raised a lot less money. Still something, though.

It was not enough, though, and ultimately this weekend Bed Bath & Beyond filed for exactly the sort of bankruptcy it was contemplating in January: Close all the stores, liquidate the inventory, hand whatever cash is left to the creditors. "The Debtors are committed to achieving the highest or otherwise best bid for some or all of the Debtors' assets by marketing their assets pursuant to the Bidding Procedures, and, if necessary, conducting an auction for any of their assets," the company says, but it has had like four months to find someone interested in buying the business, and if no one has shown up yet no one is going to. And: "The Debtors estimate that the aggregate net sales proceeds from all Sales will be approximately $718 million," against about $1.8 billion of debt to pay off. Nonetheless:

> While the commencement of a full chain wind-down is necessitated by economic realities, Bed Bath & Beyond has and will continue to market their businesses as a going-concern, including the buybuy Baby business. Bed Bath & Beyond has pulled off long shot transactions several times in the last six months, so nobody should think Bed Bath & Beyond will not be able to do so again. To the contrary, Bed Bath & Beyond and its professionals will make every effort to salvage all or a portion of operations for the benefit of all stakeholders.

I said above that the few hundred million dollars that Bed Bath raised by selling 622 million shares of stock since it started preparing for bankruptcy "was not enough" to solve its problems, but it's actually a bit worse than that. Bed Bath's bankruptcy filing tells a story in which the company got into a bad place due to a combination of pandemic/supply-chain issues and its own management mistakes; in particular, its former chief executive officer pushed private-label brands instead of the well-known brands that its customers wanted. Bed Bath realized its mistakes and began correcting them—that CEO "was excused on June 29, 2022"—but that takes money; "the Company needed real runway to turn around its inventory and liquidity position."

But the story is not that it then went out and raised several hundred million dollars to build up its inventory and make its business more attractive. No, the story is that it went out and raised several hundred million dollars to hand directly to its creditors:

> Unfortunately, under the terms of the Second Amended Credit Agreement, the Debtors were required to use the net proceeds from the initial closing of the [Hudson Bay] Offering, along with the FILO Upsize, to repay outstanding revolving loans under the Debtors' Prepetition ABL Facility, including repayment of the nearly $200 million overadvance. At this point the

> Company's sales had dropped 60% on a comparable store basis, resulting in substantial ongoing losses from operation; therefore, the remaining Offering proceeds went to cover operational losses rather than to restoring inventory levels. . . .
>
> The net proceeds from the B. Riley ATM Program were used to prepay outstanding revolving loans under the Debtors' Prepetition ABL Facility and cash collateralize outstanding letters of credit, resulting in new credit under the Debtors' Prepetition ABL Facility. . . .
>
> The Debtors' cash burn continued while sales further declined due to lack of incoming merchandise, thus, preventing the Debtors from implementing their anticipated long-term operational restructuring while satisfying their restrictive debt obligations.

That is, Bed Bath had an asset-based lending facility (its most senior debt) and a first-in-last-out term loan (effectively its second-most-senior debt); as of November 2022, it had borrowed $550 million on the ABL (plus $186.2 million of letters of credit) and $375 million on the FILO. As of Sunday there was $80.3 million outstanding on the ABL (plus $102.6 million of letters of credit) and $547.1 million outstanding on the FILO. Since this all began, Bed Bath has raised a bit more than $400 million from shareholders and handed about $300 million of it directly to its lenders, while the business collapsed and it had no money to fix things. Now it will hand the rest of its money over to the lenders.

I don't know what to say? All of this was quite well disclosed. Back when Bed Bath did the Hudson Bay deal in January, it said in the prospectus that it intended to use all the money it raised to repay debt, and that if it didn't raise a billion dollars in that deal (it did not) then it "would not have the financial resources to satisfy its payment obligations," it "will likely file for bankruptcy protection," "its assets will likely be liquidated" and "our equity holders would likely not receive any recovery at all in a bankruptcy scenario." All of the legal documents were pretty clear that Bed Bath was raising money by selling stock to retail investors, that it was handing that money directly to its creditors, that the money probably wouldn't be enough, that Bed Bath was probably going bankrupt, and that when it did the stock that it had just sold to those retail investors would be worthless. And things have worked out exactly as promised. No one can be surprised!

And yet it is one of the most astonishing corporate finance transactions I've ever seen?[4] The basic rules of bankruptcy are:

---

4 Its closest competition is when Hertz Global Holdings Inc. sold stock to meme-stock investors *in bankruptcy*, which was incredible, but (1) the US Securities and Exchange Commission shut that deal down almost as soon as it launched, so it never raised much money and (2) Hertz was trying to reorganize in bankruptcy, not liquidate; it succeeded and the equity actually recovered, so buying (and, thus, selling) the stock was not *that* crazy. To be clear, that is still a possibility here—"Bed Bath & Beyond has pulled off long shot transactions several

1. When a company is bankrupt, the shareholders get zero dollars back, and the creditors get whatever's left.
2. The shareholders don't get less than zero. They don't put more money in.[5]

Here, I mean, Bed Bath was kind of like "hey everyone, we went bust, sorry, but our lenders are such nice people and they could really use a break, we're gonna pass the hat and it would be great if you could throw in a few hundred million dollars to make them feel better." And the retail shareholders did! With more or less complete disclosure, they bought 622 million shares of a stock that (1) was pretty clearly going to be worthless and (2) now is worthless, so that Bed Bath could have more money to give to its lenders when it inevitably liquidated.

I have over the past few years been impressed by AMC Entertainment Holdings Inc.'s commitment to the meme-stock bit. In particular, AMC's management was early and aggressive in realizing that being a meme stock could be a tool of corporate finance, that when people on Reddit are bidding up your stock for no clear reason, the correct reaction is not to chuckle in disbelief but to sell them stock. But AMC at least has a story; AMC is using its meme investors' money to pay down debt, sure, but also to keep its theaters open and buy a gold mine.

No, this is the peak of meme stocks. Bed Bath & Beyond sold 50 million shares a week for three months with, as far as I can tell, no story, no plan, nothing but "a troubled financial situation and nostalgia value." Bed Bath saw that its retail shareholders wanted to throw their money away, and that its sophisticated lenders wanted to get their money back, and realized that there was a trade to be done that would make everyone, temporarily, happy. So it did the trade. It's amazing. The lawsuits are gonna be great.

Do you agree with Levine's assessment? Or might there have been a financial case for retail investors to buy shares of BBBY in the spring and summer of 2023?

B. LEVERAGED BUYOUTS (LBOS)

In corporate finance, many actions that can be accomplished with internal changes can also be accomplished through a merger. Recapitalizing the balance sheet is a good example of this. A corporation with modest amounts of debt might be transformed into a highly indebted one through a leveraged buyout (or "LBO"). This is just a merger where

times in the last six months, so nobody should think Bed Bath & Beyond will not be able to do so again"—and I will feel dumb and amazed if the people who bought Bed Bath stock on Friday at $0.29 end up making a fortune on the trade.

[5] This is a little loose, and there are scenarios where some equity owner might put in more money in a bankruptcy-type situation in order to *keep control of the company*. "An equity owner throws in more money and comes out with zero stake in the company" is . . . less common.

the buying company uses significant amounts of debt that is secured by the target company assets to pay for the buyout. (The consumer analogy is a home purchase using a large mortgage.) When the smoke clears on this transaction, the selling firm's former shareholders may be cashed out, and a new group of shareholders might own the firm. And because new debt has been issued to pay for the LBO, the surviving company will have a more leveraged capital structure. In other words, this can transform a firm's capital structure in a manner akin to the first two types of recapitalizations in the prior section.

The Jensen and Meckling article from earlier in this chapter laid the theoretical foundation that explained many of the LBOs of the 1980s. Agency costs of outside equity had apparently increased during 1960s and 1970s with the creation of conglomerates. All too often, managers were reinvesting free cash flows in new projects that were negative net present value projects rather than paying funds to shareholders. Debt provided discipline for managers: By obligating managers to pay interest and repay principal, debt forces a company's managers to be more efficient in their use of capital, lest they default and lose control of the firm. A new set of entrepreneurs arose to provide 100% ownership of the equity of these firms. Generally, they formed relatively small investment partnerships to raise the equity capital for a leveraged buyout, which they combined with large sums of debt-financing to buy entire firms. Moreover, in order to reduce agency costs and better align incentives, they often required managers of the acquired firm to invest heavily—all of their available wealth—in the equity of the acquired firm. Figure 4-1, for example, illustrates the typical structure for an LBO transaction.

Figure 4-1. Typical LBO Structure

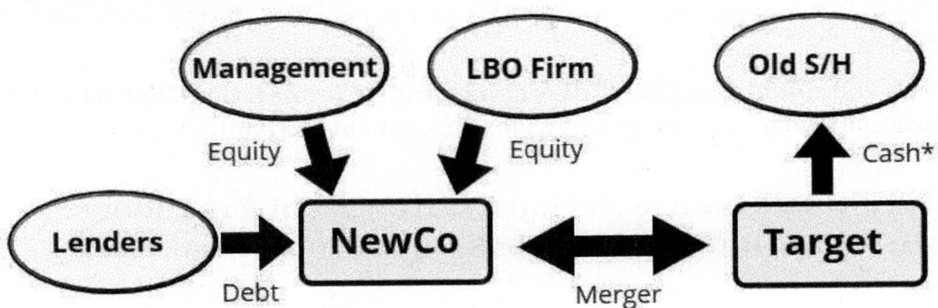

* Cash to Target shareholders represents the merger consideration, sourced from NewCo's equity and debt financings

Not all firms were appropriate subjects for this kind of highly-leveraged transaction. The best candidates possessed stable cash flows that reduced some of the risk of high leverage. Ideally, they also had fungible assets, that provided collateral that can be resold at a high percentage of value by creditors in the event of a default. Many were mature businesses, with few opportunities for reinvesting capital in positive net present value projects.

A later leveraged buyout boom in the early years of the 21st century was driven to some extent by a different factor—extraordinarily low interest rates that probably did not fully reflect the risks borne by lenders, due to an expansionary Federal Reserve policy. This second LBO wave also witnessed the application of the LBO model to high-technology firms. These latter deals differed significantly from the classic conglomerate LBO insofar that earnings were both more volatile and assets consisted of more intangibles. It remains an open question whether the extension of the LBO model to technology firms was simply an artifact of undisciplined lending prior to the financial crisis or whether it represented the ability of LBO sponsors to minimize the financial distress costs associated with highly-levered technology firms.

The leveraged buyout movements of the 1980s and the early years of the 21st century represented the most extreme examples of the widespread use of leverage in capital structures. Both LBO buyers of firms and their lenders recognized the bankruptcy risks, and often attempted to provide incentives for these lenders to abstain from putting troubled debtors into Chapter 11 reorganization. One way to do this was to provide the LBO lenders with a large portion of the equity in the acquired or refinanced firm. Under ordinary circumstances this would not prevent bankruptcy initiatives from creditors, because the LBO lenders could sell either the stock they received or the debt instruments they had acquired. The solution in some cases was to "staple" the debt and equity together (called "strip financing"),* so there would be few possible gains for a creditor to push a debtor into bankruptcy. On the other hand, making creditors into shareholders would reduce shareholder incentives to undertake risky projects at the expense of creditors.

As you might imagine, LBOs can be controversial. Consider whether adoption of such a strategy might lead to suboptimal outcomes:

Taking Finance Seriously: How Debt Financing Distorts Bidding Outcomes in Corporate Takeovers

by Robert P. Bartlett, III
76 Fordham Law Review 1975 (2008)

As the foregoing analysis indicates, debt-financing provides a potentially powerful way for managers to increase the value of a firm.

* Michael C. Jensen, *Agency Costs of Free Cash Flow, Corporate Finance, and Takeovers*, 76, No. 2 AM. ECON. REV. 323, 325–26 (186). Strip financing was involved in most of the LBOs of the early 1980s, but declined thereafter, replaced by public debt. The loss of the monitoring of financial institutions caused by this shift is one of the explanations for the higher default rate on these later deals. Steven N. Kaplan & Jeremy C. Stein, *The Evolution of Buyout Pricing and Financial Structure (Or, What Went Wrong) in the 1980s*, THE NEW CORPORATE FINANCE: WHERE THEORY MEETS PRACTICE, 600, 609 (2000) (Donald C. Chew, Ed.).

For similar reasons, a bidder that finances an acquisition with debt rather than equity can significantly increase its ultimate valuation of a target. In effect, the bidder will have chosen to recapitalize target with debt, thereby lowering target's cost of capital due to the deductibility of interest payments. . . Yet for the same reason, the fact that firms have different preferences for debt-financing allows this form of financing to affect bidding outcomes. In particular, in a bidding contest for a target, the fact that one bidder chooses to be more aggressive in using debt-financing may very well give it a competitive edge over other bidders, regardless of whether it is the bidder that could best put target's assets to productive use. . . .

Consider again the case of BigCo except now assume that BigCo's management has decided to put the company up for sale. [Eds. The article previously describes BigCo as a publicly-traded company with 100,000 outstanding shares of Common Stock, an annual pre-tax income of $125,000, an effective tax rate of 35%, a market value of $650,000, and a cost of equity of 12.5%.] As in the original example, BigCo has no debt outstanding and has the same economic attributes discussed previously. For simplicity, let us further assume there are only two potential buyers interested in BigCo, ManagementCo and StrategyCo. ManagementCo represents a group of BigCo's senior executives who are proposing a management buyout. The group anticipates no post-acquisition synergies or cost-savings, believing instead that BigCo will simply maintain its current level of annual pre-tax operating income of $125,000 for the foreseeable future. StrategyCo, in contrast, represents BigCo's primary competitor who hopes to achieve considerable operating synergies through a merger. In particular, it believes it can increase BigCo's operating income by 3% per year forever. Thus, from the perspective of allocational efficiency, StrategyCo is clearly the bidder that can put BigCo's assets to the most productive use.

Who will actually put forth the best price? It depends on how each finances its bid. If ManagementCo is a typical management buyout, we can expect it to use a high degree of debt-financing in its acquisition, effectively recapitalizing BigCo with more debt. As a result, ManagementCo will be able to utilize the implicit government subsidy provided by the resulting tax deductions when it forms its valuation of BigCo. StrategyCo, in contrast, may be at a competitive disadvantage in bidding if it is unable or unwilling to finance its offer with debt. For instance, if StrategyCo is a software company that uses no debt in its operations, StrategyCo would finance its bid with all equity, resulting in an ultimate valuation of $880,921.[62] Even though this value represents

[62] This valuation was obtained using the Gordon Growth Model, which is one of the oldest methods for valuing firms. . . . For purposes of valuing BigCo, the perpetual stream of cash flows to be expected would equal BigCo's last full year of net operating income after taxes [$81,250], and assuming nothing has changed the underlying risk of BigCo's business, BigCo's cost of equity would still equal 12.5%. Accordingly, the Gordon growth model would calculate the discounted present value of BigCo as follows: (81,250 × 1.03) / (.125 – .03) = $880,921. Because

a premium of 36% to BigCo's existing market value, ManagementCo would be able to beat it by obtaining a loan commitment of $660,000 and financing the rest of the acquisition consideration through equity contributions.[63] Assuming ManagementCo were to keep this debt outstanding after the acquisition, the present value of the resulting tax shields would be $231,000,[64] allowing ManagementCo to put forth a maximum bid of $881,000.[65] Consequently, even without any change to BigCo's pre-existing cash-flows, ManagementCo could win the bidding contest.

To be sure, StrategyCo could avoid this problem if it anticipated larger operating synergies from the acquisition. Moreover, there is only so much debt ManagementCo could seek to use, thereby placing an upper limit on the value of the tax shields. For instance, even assuming ManagementCo could utilize every dollar of operating income ($125,000) to service its debt burden, the maximum amount of debt it could use would be $1,000,000 (i.e., $125,000/.125), creating a maximum tax shield of $350,000. As Figure 5 shows, ManagementCo's willingness to utilize significant debt-financing would therefore allow ManagementCo to match any bid by StrategyCo assuming StrategyCo used a permanent annual growth rate of 4% or less, but not if StrategyCo modeled its valuation of BigCo using a permanent annual growth rate of more than 4%.

$880,921 represents the value of all anticipated future cash flows from BigCo discounted to present value, it should be the maximum price StrategyCo should pay for BigCo.

[63] Although such a loan would be large in magnitude, it would be well-within the range of debt multiples used in LBOs during 2006.

[64] The present value of the tax shields can be calculated by discounting to present value the anticipated annual tax savings resulting from target's interest payments. Given the assumption that this debt would remain outstanding forever and given a 35% tax rate, target could expect to save each year $660,000 × (rate of interest) × 35%. Moreover, because tax shields are largely assumed to have the same risk as that of the interest payments generating them, the most common assumption is to discount the tax shields at the rate of interest. As a result, the actual interest rate becomes irrelevant for purposes of calculating the present value of the tax shields, and the method for calculating the present value of tax shields is simplified as (tax rate) × (debt outstanding). In the case of ManagementCo's bid for BigCo, this can be demonstrated by using the following perpetuity formula: (660,000 × (r) × .35)/(r) = $660,000 × .35 = $231,000.

[65] This value was obtained using the Adjusted Present Value (APV) methodology . . . In our example, the APV method would [ ] add the present value of the anticipated tax shields arising from ManagementCo's financing structure ($231,000) to the value of BigCo assuming ManagementCo financed it with all equity. Because ManagementCo expects no change in BigCo's cash flows after the acquisition, this latter figure would equal $650,000—the same valuation of the all-equity BigCo prior to the acquisition. . . .

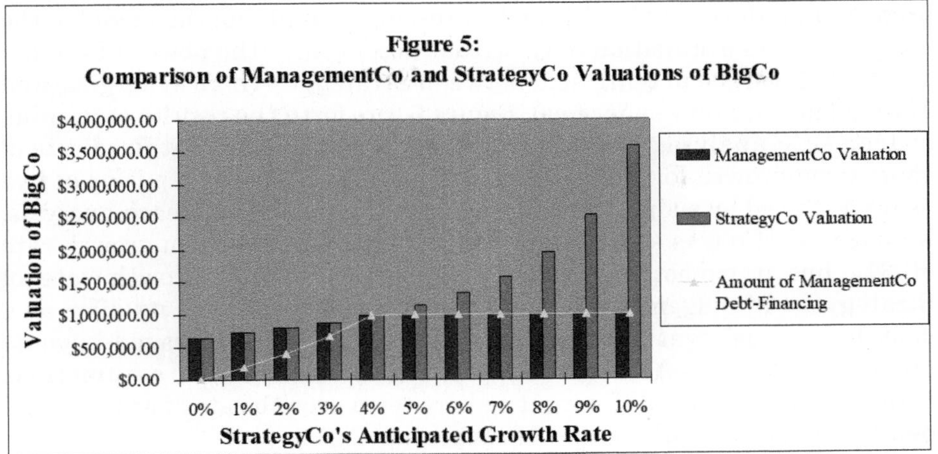

Figure 5:
Comparison of ManagementCo and StrategyCo Valuations of BigCo

Yet even assuming StrategyCo could significantly increase BigCo's operating income, the foregoing discussion oversimplifies how ManagementCo and StrategyCo would likely model their valuations in at least two important respects. First, while StrategyCo might reasonably assume a significant increase in BigCo's rate of growth in the near term, it is less tenable to maintain this assumption for long periods of time. Assuming BigCo operates in a competitive industry, competition among firms must eventually erode above-market operating margins. Moreover, any valuation model using a constant growth rate must use a growth rate that is less than or equal to the economy's overall growth rate. The reason is a simple matter of mathematics: if a firm's cash flows could grow forever at a rate that exceeded the economy's growth rate, the firm would become the economy. For firms being valued in U.S. dollars, this puts an upper limit on the perpetual growth rate of approximately 5–6% per year.

Second, it is extremely unlikely that ManagementCo would anticipate level operating income in the foreseeable future. At a minimum, ManagementCo could expect some cost savings from taking BigCo private. . . . Additionally, ManagementCo might also expect some enhanced operating efficiencies. As noted above, highly-leveraged firms can create significant incentives among managers to generate cash flow. For ManagementCo, this incentive should be particularly enhanced given the increased ownership stake of BigCo's managers in the post-acquisition firm. If BigCo's managers fail to execute their business plan, it will be their own money they have lost.

As a result of these two considerations, a more realistic understanding of how ManagementCo and StrategyCo form their valuations of BigCo would be to assume that both bidders expect significant short-term operating efficiencies, followed by a lower constant growth rate. In fact, this discounted-cash flow (DCF) methodology is routinely recommended by both academics and practitioners as the preferred method to value firms. Interestingly, applying the model to the case of BigCo's acquisition only further accentuates the power of the tax shields to level the playing field between StrategyCo (high synergies) and ManagementCo (low synergies). Figure 6 sets forth the results of running sixteen DCF analyses assuming StrategyCo used a different fixed rate of short-term growth for BigCo ranging from 0% to 15% for a period of five years, followed by a long-term annual growth rate of 3%. In each analysis, ManagementCo was also assumed to anticipate a long term growth rate of 3%, but it expected only one-half the short-term growth rate of StrategyCo. ManagementCo was also assumed to finance its offer at a debt level consistent with the average of all U.S. leveraged-buyouts occurring in 2006. As Figure 6 illustrates, under these assumptions StrategyCo would need to expect a short-term growth rate of at least 13% per year before it could outbid ManagementCo.

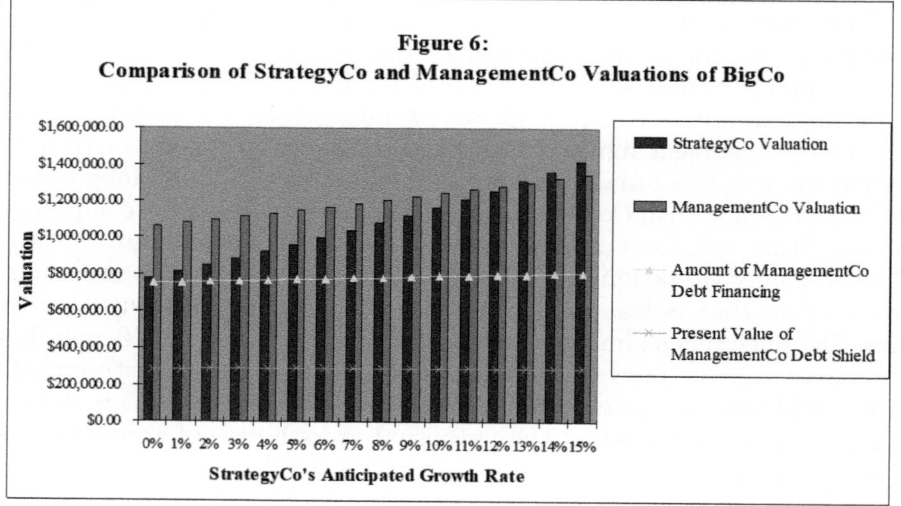

Admittedly, real-life bidders analyze expected synergies and cost-savings with considerable more refinement than used in this example. But the central insight offered here must apply for even these more complex valuation models: the use of debt-financing effectively subsidizes a bidder's ultimate valuation of a target. Indeed, it is for this reason that the present value of the tax shields arising from debt-financing appear as a fundamental element in every significant form of discounted cash flow analysis. At the same time, the long-standing debate over capital structure tells us that not every bidder will use this subsidy to the same extent given bidders' divergent financing policies. The result of these two factors is a *de facto* subsidy that benefits some bidders but not others.

When an LBO succeeds, the sponsors of the deal can generate enormous profits. Returning to the consumer mortgage analogy, if you invest a very small amount of equity in a new home purchase—borrowing the rest from a bank—then your equity gains and losses will be magnified. If your home value appreciates at a rate higher than your mortgage interest rate, you will enjoy leveraged returns on your equity investment. The reverse is also true. In the LBO context, new owners will usually try to secure operational improvements to the business, and small gains can have an outsized effect on their own personal returns. Corporate tax savings from the debt interest deductions can be the icing on this cake. During some legendary LBOs, for instance, equity investors have netted personal gains in the tens or even hundreds of millions of dollars on a single buyout.

But when an LBO fails, you know where we are headed: better sign up for that class on Bankruptcy Law. In the next and final case of this chapter, we examine a situation where one LBO didn't turn out as planned. Don't worry, we'll stop before we get to the thorny bankruptcy problems, but the case offers a useful look at the structure of an LBO deal and at the complex array of players who can sometimes get involved when things go badly.

In re Tribune Media Co.

799 F.3d 272 (3d Cir. 2015)

■ AMBRO, CIRCUIT JUDGE:

In December 2007, the Tribune Company (which published the Chicago Tribune and the Los Angeles Times and held many other properties) was facing a challenging business climate. Sensing an opportunity, Sam Zell, a wealthy real estate investor, orchestrated a leveraged buy-out ("LBO"), a transaction by which a purchaser (in this case, an entity controlled by Zell and, for convenience, referred to by that name in this opinion) acquires an entity using debt secured by assets of the acquired entity. Before the LBO, Tribune had a market capitalization of approximately $8 billion and about $5 billion in debt.

The LBO was taken in two steps: Zell made a tender offer to obtain more than half of Tribune's shares at Step One, followed by a purchase of all remaining shares at Step Two. In this LBO, as is typical, Zell obtained financing (called here the "LBO debt") to purchase Tribune secured by Tribune's assets, meaning that Zell had nothing at risk. The transaction took Tribune private and saddled the company with an additional $8 billion of debt. Moreover, as a part of the sale, Tribune's subsidiaries guaranteed the LBO debt. The holders of the debt that Tribune carried before Zell took it over (the "pre-LBO debt") had recourse only against Tribune, not against the subsidiaries. Thus the LBO debt, guaranteed by solvent subsidiaries, had "structural seniority" over the pre-LBO debt.

Unsurprisingly, Tribune, in a declining industry with a precarious balance sheet, eventually sought bankruptcy protection. It filed under

Chapter 11 in December 2008, and at some later point Aurelius, a hedge fund specializing in distressed debt, bought $2 billion of the pre-LBO debt and became an active participant in the bankruptcy process. (We do not know how much Aurelius paid for this debt.)

Ten days after the filing, the U.S. Trustee appointed the Official Committee of Unsecured Creditors (the "Committee"), which obtained permission to pursue various causes of action (e.g., breach of fiduciary duty and fraudulent conveyance) on behalf of the estate against the LBO lenders, directors and officers of old Tribune, Zell, and others (collectively called the "LBO-Related Causes of Action," see In re Tribune Co., 464 B.R. 126, 136 n. 7 (Bankr.D.Del.2011)). As the Bankruptcy Court put it, "[f]rom the outset ... the major constituents understood that the investigation and resolution of the LBO-Related Causes of Action would be a central issue in the formulation of a plan of reorganization."

Various groups of stakeholders proposed plans of reorganization; the important ones for the purposes of this appeal are Aurelius's (the "Noteholder Plan") and one sponsored by the Debtor, the Committee, and certain senior lenders, called the "DCL Plan" (for Debtor/Committee/ Lender) or simply the "Plan." The primary difference between the Noteholder and the DCL Plans was that the proponents of the former (the "Noteholders") wanted to litigate the LBO-Related Causes of Action while the DCL Plan proposed to settle them.

Kenneth Klee, one of the principal drafters of the Bankruptcy Code of 1978, was appointed the examiner in this case, and he valued the various causes of action to help the parties settle them. Professor Klee concluded that whether Step One left Tribune insolvent (and was thus constructively fraudulent) was a "very close call" if Step Two debt was included for the purposes of this calculation. He further concluded that a court was "somewhat likely" to find intentional fraud and "highly likely" to find constructive fraud at Step Two. He also valued the recoveries to Aurelius's and the Trustees' classes of debt under the various litigation scenarios and concluded that the DCL Plan settlement offered more money ($432 million) than all six possible litigation outcomes except full avoidance of the LBO transactions, which would have afforded the pre-LBO lenders $1.3 billion. Given these findings for both steps of the LBO, full recovery was a possibility.

The DCL Plan restructured Tribune's debt, settled many of the LBO-Related Causes of Action for $369 million, and assigned other claims to a litigation trust that would continue to pursue them and pay out any proceeds according to a waterfall structure whereby the pre-LBO lenders stand to receive the first $90 million and 65% of the Trust's recoveries over $110 million (this aspect of the Plan we refer to as the "Settlement"). Aurelius objected because it believes the LBO-Related Causes of Action are worth far more than the examiner or Bankruptcy Court thought and that it can get a great deal more money in litigation than it got under the Settlement. The Bankruptcy Court's opinion on confirmation, thoroughly done by Judge Kevin Carey, discussed the parties' disagreement at length and ultimately concluded that it was "uncertain" that litigation would result in full avoidance of the LBO. And full avoidance was the only result the Bankruptcy Court's opinion suggests could plausibly result in greater recovery than the Settlement. Thus the Court held that the Settlement was reasonable, and, on July 23, 2012, the DCL Plan was confirmed over Aurelius's objection.

[The DCL Plan was substantially consummated, and the subsequent objections of Aurelius were dismissed.]

QUESTIONS

1. How much of an impact did Zell's LBO have on Tribune's capital structure? Why did Zell seek to execute such a risky buyout?
2. Imagine that you held debt in Tribune immediately before the Zell LBO. How do you feel after the LBO is announced? Why? Can you think of any way to protect against this possibility in your initial bond contract with Tribune? We will revisit this question, along with some of the potential legal claims mentioned in this case, in Chapter 6.
3. Why did Aurelius want to buy the pre-existing debt of Tribune *after* the LBO had failed? How would you describe the business strategy of a hedge fund investor like Aurelius?

CHAPTER 5

COMMON STOCK

Having covered some of the factors that explain a firm's choice of capital structure, we turn now to an analysis of the primary issues that often arise when executing different financing choices. As we shall see, each external financing strategy raises specific risks that need to be addressed in the relevant transaction documents. Because the initial source of financing for firms tends to be in the form of common equity, we begin with a discussion of the issues that frequently arise in a common stock financing.

1. THE BASICS OF STOCK

Recall Perpetual Youth, Inc. ("PY"), our hypothetical start-up company from Chapter 2. Upon forming PY, its founder, Leon Ponce, invested $10,000 in exchange for 1,000 shares of PY Common Stock. It was hardly an accident that we made this financing the first transaction for the company. Upon forming an entity—whether it's a corporation, a partnership or an LLC—a simple equity financing tends to be the first step in a company's lifecycle. Not only does it provide a firm with vital seed financing to commence operations, it also allows founders to establish the control and cash flow arrangements that will govern the firm. The reason stems from the fact that common stockholders are the "residual claimants" on a firm's assets and cash flows.

Most students taking this class have already had some exposure to the notion that common stock is a "residual claim" through earlier coursework. The concept reflects the legal requirement that, under state corporate statutes, upon the winding-up or sale of a firm, common stockholders stand last in line in terms of receiving any distributions on their investment claims. In other words, it is only after the contractual claims of fixed claimants (e.g., workers, lenders, landlords, vendors and others holding a contractual right to payment) are satisfied that common stockholders are entitled to receive any distributions from the firm's remaining assets. Notably, however, to the extent common stockholders receive anything, they are entitled to *all* of whatever is left after satisfying these fixed claimants.

For this reason, if Leon Ponce believes that the long-term value of PY will exceed what it owes to its fixed claimants, he will naturally want to hold the company's common stock as that is what entitles him to all of the upside from the business he is building. Relatedly, because common stock is a residual claim, state corporate statutes give common stockholders important governance rights. Indeed, vesting common stockholders with governance rights over the firm might seem sensible because common stockholders should have powerful incentives to run the firm in a fashion that ensures there is value in the residual claim. As such, state corporate statutes provide common stockholders with default voting rights of one vote per share. See, e.g., DGCL § 212(a) ("Unless otherwise provided in the certificate of incorporation and subject to § 213 of this title, each stockholder shall be entitled to 1 vote for each share of capital stock held by such stockholder.") This means that, as a default matter, common stockholders have the right to elect the company's board of directors. And it is the board of directors that state corporate statutes vest with the discretionary authority to manage a corporation's business and affairs, including the ability to delegate this authority to executive officers. As the founder of the firm, Leon therefore has an additional reason to hold the Company's common stock: it will allow him to control the composition of the board of directors. (Indeed, Leon's lawyer will undoubtedly have drafted a set of incorporation documents that name Leon as the initial director of PY, as well as a board consent naming Leon as the company's Chief Executive Officer.)

This description of Leon Ponce's common stock financing highlights several key features that tend to drive the structure of common stock financing transactions (which we will discuss in detail in the pages that follow). First, by choosing to invest in common stock, common stockholders generally care about cash flow rights and control rights that flow to them as a matter of default corporate law. Notably, these rights are not fixed in an amount for individual shareholders but are instead allocated to shareholders based on the *percentage* of common stock owned by them. For instance, so long as Leon Ponce is the sole stockholder of PY, he will be entitled to 100% of the residual claim as well as 100% of the voting power in any election of directors. But if PY issues new shares to additional stockholders, then Leon's percentage claim on the residual value of PY, and his percentage claim on the common stock voting power, will be diminished accordingly. As we shall see, this feature of common stock creates the risk of dilution, and as a result, most common stock financings will focus a great deal on methods to address this risk.

Second, the fact that state corporate statutes define the default rights of common stock means that locating the exact bundle of rights that flow to a given stockholder requires an analysis of both the relevant state corporate statute and the specific company's formation documents. Most notably, state corporate laws typically provide a set of default economic and cash flow rights for common stock that can only be modified by a contrary provision in the company's Certificate of Incorporation ("COI," which is also called the charter or the articles of incorporation by some states). Indeed, it is probably impossible to overstate the importance of a company's COI in defining the rights of common stockholders. The COI is where a firm will authorize the creation of the company's capital stock and establish the number of classes into which it is divided. The COI also specifies any special rights, preferences or privileges that apply to the stock. Some of these adjustments can be transformative.

For example, Figure 5-1 illustrates the initial paragraphs of the COI for Meta Platforms, Inc. ("Meta") after the company changed its name from Facebook, Inc. in 2021. In Article IV, Meta's COI specifically authorizes 9,241,000,000 shares of capital, which are divided into the following three classes: (a) 5,000,000,000 shares of Class A Common Stock, (b) 4,141,000,000 shares of Class B Common Stock, and (c) 100,000,000 shares of Preferred Stock. Were we to keep reading its COI, we would discover that the Class A Common Stock is entitled to 1 vote per share while the Class B Common Stock is entitled to 10 votes per share. The Class B Common Stock is held largely by Mark Zuckerberg, Meta's founder and CEO, ensuring that he maintains control of the firm. Note that Meta is incorporated in Delaware, and this is not the default voting power conferred on the common stock by the DGCL (which is 1 vote per share). Rather, this is an example of how the default rights of common stock can be altered by a contrary provision in the COI. For similar reasons, any special rights of preferred stock also have to be set forth in the COI—a topic we shall revisit when discussing preferred stock in Chapter 7.*

Figure 5-1: Select Provisions of Meta Platforms Certificate of Incorporation

META PLATFORMS, INC.

AMENDED & RESTATED CERTIFICATE OF INCORPORATION

ARTICLE I: NAME

The name of the corporation is Meta Platforms, Inc.

ARTICLE II: AGENT FOR SERVICE OF PROCESS

The address of the corporation's registered office in the State of Delaware is 251 Little Falls Drive, Wilmington, New Castle County, 19808. The name of the registered agent of the corporation at that address is Corporation Service Company.

ARTICLE III: PURPOSE

The purpose of the corporation is to engage in any lawful act or activity for which corporations may be organized under the General Corporation Law of the State of Delaware ("***General Corporation Law***").

ARTICLE IV: AUTHORIZED STOCK

1. **Total Authorized.**

The total number of shares of all classes of capital stock that the corporation has authority to issue is 9,241,000,000 shares, consisting of: 5,000,000,000 shares of Class A Common Stock, $0.000006 par value per share ("***Class A Common Stock***"), 4,141,000,000 shares of Class B Common Stock, $0.000006 par value per share ("***Class B Common Stock***" and together with the Class A Common Stock, the "***Common Stock***") and 100,000,000 shares of Preferred Stock, $0.000006 par value per share. The number of authorized shares of Class A Common Stock or Class B Common Stock may be increased or decreased (but not below the number of shares thereof then outstanding) by the affirmative vote of the holders of capital stock representing a majority of the voting power of all the then-outstanding shares of capital stock of the corporation entitled to vote thereon, irrespective of the provisions of Section 242(b)(2) of the General Corporation Law.

---

* Note that the COI must also set forth the par value of any authorized stock. We discussed the concept of par value in Chapter 2.

Notwithstanding the centrality of the COI to common stockholders, there is nothing prohibiting a company's stockholders from voluntarily agreeing to act (or to refrain from acting) in particular ways. As a result, it is also common to see stockholders enter into different types of stockholder agreements that can also materially affect a stockholder's economic or voting entitlements. One example involves the use of voting agreements among stockholders of a closely held firm; in these agreements, stockholders agree to vote for specific individuals (or nominees of individuals) at any election of the board of directors. The possibility for such stockholder agreements complicates the task of determining the bundle of rights and obligations that applies to a particular stockholder. We shall discuss below some of the standard stockholder agreements that arise in a common stock financing.

Finally, when working with common stock, it is vital to keep in mind that the relationship between a stockholder and the company is also shaped by the fiduciary duties that a company's board of directors owes to the common stockholders. Within corporate legal scholarship, it is often said that these fiduciary duties provide "gap-filling" rules that help define the investment contract that exists between common stockholders and the company. Among other things, for instance, these duties obligate directors to use their discretionary authority to advance "the best interests of the corporation for the benefit of its shareholder owners." N. Am. Catholic Educ. Programming Found., Inc. v. Gheewalla, 930 A.2d 92, 101 (Del. 2007). As we shall see, these fiduciary duties can provide important substantive rights to common stockholders when they believe that a board has acted adversely to their financial interests.

Sidebar: Authorized vs. Outstanding Stock

A company can lawfully sell shares of common stock only if those shares exist. The process for creating shares of common stock is regulated by state corporate statutes, which typically provide that any equity securities (including shares of common stock and preferred stock) are created when they are "authorized" in a company's charter document. See, e.g., DCGL § 151(a) ("Every corporation may issue 1 or more classes of stock or 1 or more series of stock within any class thereof . . . and which classes or series may have such voting powers, full or limited, or no voting powers, and such designations, preferences and relative, participating, optional or other special rights, and qualifications, limitations or restrictions thereof, as shall be stated and expressed in the certificate of incorporation or of any amendment thereto. . ."). Thus, Meta's 5,000,000,000 shares of Class A Common Stock, 4,141,000,000 shares of Class B Common Stock, and 100,000,000 shares of Preferred Stock were created when the company filed its certificate of incorporation authorizing them.

Once shares are authorized, the process of actually selling them to investors or awarding them to employees or service providers occurs when the company's board of directors approves their "issuance" in exchange for some form of consideration. In Delaware corporations, for instance, the board of directors may "authorize capital stock to be issued for consideration consisting of cash, any tangible or intangible property or any benefit to the corporation, or any combination thereof." DCGL § 152. Where stock has par value, however, the board of directors is prohibited from issuing any share of stock for consideration having a value less than par value. See DCGL § 153. (We discuss this topic in more detail in Section 5 below). Once shares have been validly issued, they are referred to as "outstanding" shares. Only shares that are outstanding can be voted or be entitled to a distribution or other form of payment. Thus, in determining who can vote at a shareholders' meeting or who "owns" the residual claim, it is only outstanding shares that count.

2. PRICING A COMMON STOCK FINANCING

An initial challenge in any common stock financing relates to pricing: How much must an investor pay for each share that is acquired? Not surprisingly, the answer to this question is closely related to our discussion of valuation in Chapter 3 and will depend on the value of the company. However, from a deal lawyer's perspective, pricing common stock requires two additional pieces of information: (a) the capitalization of the company and (b) the amount of money to be invested in a given financing.

To understand the importance of these three pieces of information for deal pricing, let's consider a hypothetical startup transaction:

Problem 5.1

NewCo, Inc. is a Delaware firm recently formed by Francis Founder, a talented data scientist. NewCo's COI has authorized 100 shares of Common Stock. Of these authorized shares, 40 were issued to Francis upon formation, which represent all of the shares that are currently outstanding. Francis is now seeking a common stock investment of $600 from Janet, an angel investor. Francis and Janet agree that, based on Francis' hard work, NewCo has a pre-financing value of $400. How many shares should Janet receive for the $600 investment?

Under these facts, we can determine the price per share that Janet should pay in the financing as $10/share. Why? First, Francis and Janet have agreed that the pre-financing value of the company is $400. Since there is no debt outstanding, this must also be the aggregate value of the company's equity, which consists of 40 shares of common stock. (Note that while the company has 100 *authorized* shares, only 40 shares have been *issued* by NewCo prior to Janet's investment). Because each share of stock is entitled to an equal pro-rata claim on the company's residual claim, each share can be valued as follows:

$$\frac{Pre - Financing\ Valuation}{Pre - Financing\ Capitalization} = \frac{\$400}{40\ Shares} = \$10/Share$$

Janet is investing \$600, so at \$10/share, Janet will receive 60 shares (i.e., \$600/\$60). While this is obviously a simplified scenario, this approach to deal pricing is standard in any common stock equity financing, from a startup-financing to a company's public offering of common stock.

Before moving on, it is important to note that Janet will probably require one additional task from her lawyer before signing off on this deal: constructing a post-financing, "pro-forma" capitalization table. These tables summarize what the company's ownership structure will look like assuming the deal is closed at the proposed pricing. In Problem 5.1, the pro-forma capitalization table would appear as follows:

Table 5-1:
Pro-Forma Cap Table of NewCo
Following Janet's Investment

Stockholder	Common Stock	% of Fully Diluted Stock
Francis	40	40%
Janet	60	60%
Total	**100**	**100%**

Why would Janet care to see this table? In general, the table provides a way to check that \$10/share is the correct price per share based on the fundamental economics of the transaction. From Janet's perspective, the price per share is simply a way to ensure that she receives the correct percentage claim of the common equity based on her investment. Recall that she is contributing \$600 of value to this firm. Before this contribution, she and Francis agreed that the value of the firm was \$400, so in total, this means that the post-financing value of the firm must be \$600 + \$400, or \$1,000. Her economic contribution to the firm will therefore be 60%; if she receives anything less than 60% in the pro-forma cap table, that will tip her off that something went wrong in pricing the transaction.

Finally, note that the final column refers to "% of Fully Diluted Stock," which means the capitalization table should capture the currently outstanding shares of common stock plus any shares of common stock that *might* become outstanding because of existing options or other contract rights to acquire shares of common stock. Investors care about these contract rights because if they are exercised, they can reduce the investor's ownership claim. In Problem 5.1, we are aware of no such contract rights, so the number of outstanding shares is the same as the number of fully-diluted shares. We shall investigate below what happens when this is not the case.

3. THE PROBLEM OF DILUTION

A. VOTING DILUTION VS. ECONOMIC DILUTION

Dilution represents an especially worrisome problem for investors in a company's residual claim. This obviously includes holders of a company's common stock, but as we shall see in subsequent chapters, it also includes investors who have options to acquire common stock (such as holders of a company's convertible preferred stock, convertible notes, common stock options, and common stock warrants). In general, dilution comes in two primary forms: voting dilution and economic dilution. For most students, voting dilution is more intuitive to understand, so we begin with it.

As an example, let's return to our start-up company, NewCo, a company incorporated in Delaware. Assume Janet invests $600 in NewCo on the terms discussed previously, thereby acquiring 60 shares. As shown above, these 60 shares represent 60% of the company's outstanding common stock after the financing. Further assume that NewCo's Bylaws provide that the board shall consist of 3 directors, who are elected by the holders of a majority of the outstanding shares. Additionally, according to the DGCL, NewCo's COI can be amended if approved by (1) a majority of the company's board of directors; and (2) a majority vote of the outstanding shares of common stock.

Under these facts, Janet will clearly hold a lot of influence over NewCo. As a 60% stockholder, she will have the ability to determine the company's board of directors, and she has the power to block any amendment to the company's COI. However, what would happen to this influence if the company issues 100 new shares of common stock to a new investor, Arigo Ventures? In Table 5-2, we present a pro-forma cap table assuming this new issuance of common stock. As shown in the table, such a scenario would reduce Janet's voting power from 60% to 30%, representing a dramatic change in her ability to elect the company's directors or block any changes to the company's COI. This simple example illustrates how a new issuance of stock can result in voting dilution for pre-existing shareholders.

**Table 5-2:
Pro-Forma Cap Table of NewCo Following
Arigo Venture's Investment**

Stockholder	Common Stock	% of Fully Diluted Stock
Francis	40	20%
Janet	60	30%
Arigo Ventures	100	50%
Total	**200**	**100%**

But how much does Janet need to worry about this scenario? Under these facts, very little. Recall that NewCo's COI states that there are only 100 authorized shares of Common Stock. Before issuing any new common stock, the company would need to amend its COI to increase the number of authorized shares. However, amending a company's COI requires the amended document to be approved by a majority of the company's board of directors and a majority vote of its stockholders. As a 60% stockholder, Janet could veto any amendment that she opposes. These facts illustrate how a stockholder such as Janet can protect herself against voting dilution by obtaining control rights over the ability of a company to issue additional shares of equity.* That said, however, there may be circumstances when issuing additional shares of equity is necessary, requiring an alternative approach to protecting against voting dilution in the form of contractual preemptive rights. We will see how this works in a moment.

How does voting dilution differ from economic dilution? Let's return to NewCo's situation following Janet's $600 investment. Assume that the number of authorized shares of common stock is now 200. Let's further assume that the company's board approves a sale of 100 shares of common stock to Arigo Ventures at $10/share immediately after Janet's investment. Now consider the economic consequences to Janet:

Before the issuance to Arigo Ventures:

Voting % represented by Janet's 60 shares = 60%

Economic value represented by Janet's 60 shares = $600

After the issuance to Arigo Ventures:

Voting % represented by Janet's 60 shares = 30%

Economic value represented by Janet's 60 shares = $600

Let's walk through the logic. Before the sale of stock to Arigo Ventures, Janet's 60 shares represented 60% of the total shares, resulting in her

* Additionally, a company's COI can also include an express provision that requires a majority (or a supermajority) of outstanding shares to be voted in favor of issuing any new shares, providing even stronger protection over subsequent stock issuances.

60% voting position. Recall that we also determined that when Janet invested, the value of the company was $1,000 due to the combination of the $400 of value that existed before her investment and Janet's $600 cash infusion. She paid $10, which was the fair value for her 60 shares, or $600 in total. From Table 5-1, we also see that she has a 60% economic claim in a company that is worth $1,000, so that also points to a $600 value for her shares.

After the sale of stock to Arigo Ventures, Janet suffers voting dilution from the issuance of the 100 shares, as in the prior example. But what's the economic value of her 60 shares? Note that Arigo Ventures is paying $10 per share for their 100 shares. Assuming this is an arms-length transaction, that suggests the common stock is valued at $10/share, indicating that Janet's 60 shares continue to be worth $600. Alternatively, we could say that the post-financing value of the company is now $2,000 (i.e., the $1,000 cash infusion is added to the $1,000 value of the company that existed after Janet's investment). Janet now holds a 30% claim on a company worth $2000; her economic position remains $600.

In short, this is an example of Janet suffering voting dilution but not economic dilution because the economic value of her claim stays the same.

Now, suppose that Arigo Ventures acquires their 100 shares for free. What are the economic consequences to Janet?

Before the issuance to Arigo Ventures:

Voting % represented by Janet's 60 shares = 60%

Economic value represented by Janet's 60 shares = $600

After the issuance to Arigo Ventures:

Voting % represented by Janet's 60 shares = 30%

Economic value represented by Janet's 60 shares = $300

As in the previous example, the issuance of 100 shares results in Janet losing half of her voting power. However, now she also loses half of the economic value of her investment. Why? In this example, Arigo Ventures is adding no value to the company; they receive their stock for free. Since the stock issuance happens right after Janet's investment, this suggests that the company has the same overall value of $1,000. But now Janet holds just a 30% economic claim to this company, or a claim worth $300. This particular stock issuance thus causes Janet to suffer from both voting dilution *and* economic dilution.

The reason Janet suffered economic dilution in this example stems from the fact that the company gave away shares to Arigo Ventures. Because Arigo Ventures received a right to the company's residual value without providing equivalent value, the 50% claim issued to Arigo Ventures was effectively paid for by the pre-existing stockholders. This results in economic dilution. In contrast, the prior example assumed that

Arigo Ventures paid \$10/share, which was exactly equal to the fair value of the stock. If Arigo Ventures pays fully for its percentage claim (50%), then the pre-existing stockholders do not need to subsidize the percentage claim obtained by this new investor. It turns out that any time a company sells stock for less than its fair market value, the pre-existing stockholders are effectively paying for a portion of the new stockholder's investment, resulting in economic dilution to these earlier investors.

Is this also true if the company sells stock at a price that is simply below the price paid by prior investors? Imagine, for example, that immediately after Janet's \$600 investment, NewCo sells Arigo Ventures 100 shares at \$8/share (\$2 less than what Janet paid). *Even if \$8/share is fair value*, Janet may still feel that she is experiencing economic dilution. To see why, let's once again look at her voting position and economic position before and after the transaction:

Before the issuance to Arigo Ventures:

Voting % represented by Janet's 60 shares = 60%

Economic value represented by Janet's 60 shares = \$600

After the issuance to Arigo Ventures:

Voting % represented by Janet's 60 shares = 30%

Economic value represented by Janet's 60 shares = \$480

By now, it should be clear why Janet suffers voting dilution; voting dilution happens simply by virtue of the company issuing 100 additional shares. But why did she experience a decline in the economic value of her shares? The reason is that Janet appears to have overpaid! Recall that we have assumed in this example that the fair value of the common stock is \$8/share, indicating that the total value of the company's 200 shares of common stock is \$1,600 (i.e., \$8/share × 200 shares). After the transaction with Arigo Ventures, Janet holds 30% of these shares, which is \$480 in value (30% x \$1,600). As a result, even if the company is selling stock at fair value, a company's pre-existing investors may nonetheless feel like they've experienced economic dilution. Indeed, for her \$600 investment, Janet now holds stock worth just \$480.

In the real world, of course, a second investor like Arigo Ventures might not be able to buy shares at a lower price immediately after another stock sale. But as time passes, it is indeed possible that a firm may only be able to sell more shares by dropping the price for new investors. A moment's reflection suggests that this scenario is probably the most worrisome for an investor who is concerned about economic dilution—especially for investments in private firms that lack a public trading market. After all, for any observed sale of stock, it may be quite challenging to know whether it was made at, above, or below fair value. In contrast, it is quite easy to determine whether a future stock sale is made at, above, or below the price paid by a prior investor. Moreover, for private firms, these early investors may have good reason to worry about whether they over-paid for their stock; it is tough to value nascent ventures. Consequently, an investor like Janet will naturally worry about *any* issuance of stock at a price below $10/share, prompting her to request several protections against such dilutive issuances. Before turning to those protections, however, we first return to the concept of preemptive rights.

B. ADDRESSING THE RISK OF DILUTION

We noted previously that, in theory, a stockholder could avoid the risk of voting dilution and economic dilution simply by obtaining a veto right over the future issuance of a company's equity securities. Because both forms of dilution can occur when a company issues new shares, a stockholder who has the ability to veto new sales could technically prevent any dilution arising from a new issuance of shares. And consistent with this logic, one does observe equity investors, such as venture capital firms, demanding the right to veto any new issuance of shares as a condition to their investment.* This approach to the risk of dilution, however, is problematic for at least two reasons. First, not all investors will have enough negotiating leverage to obtain such veto rights. Indeed, a company is likely to resist any such request given the possibility that it could imperil the firm's ability to raise capital when it desperately needs more money. This consideration also points toward the second concern about an absolute veto: it may be in the best interests of the company to issue additional equity. So instead of using a blanket veto right, stockholders will often use a different strategy to protect themselves against the risk of dilution. Let's consider three other possibilities.

i. PREEMPTIVE RIGHTS

One approach that allows a company to sell equity securities while also minimizing the risk of dilution for existing stockholders involves preemptive rights. In their simplest form, preemptive rights guarantee that if a company proposes to issue any new shares of common stock, it must first offer these shares to its pre-existing stockholders in proportion to their ownership percentages. Recall, for example, the hypothetical above where NewCo proposed selling 100 shares of Common Stock to Arigo Ventures for $8 per share. Just before the issuance, Janet held 60% of the company's outstanding Common Stock and Francis held 40%. If both stockholders had preemptive rights, then the company would be obligated to first offer these shares to Janet and Francis in these proportions. Thus, the company could still sell 100 shares at $8/share, but it would first have to offer 60 shares to Janet and 40 shares to

* Typically, these veto rights appear in the Company's COI as a special voting right that applies to the class of preferred stock received by the venture capital investor. We shall discuss preferred stock in Chapter 7.

Francis. If Janet and Francis both exercise their right to participate, their ownership percentages will remain the same, thus avoiding any dilution to their claims on the firm.

But why would a company's pre-existing stockholders have these rights? Initially, preemptive rights emerged as an inherent common law right of shareholders in the United States. In particular, the doctrine can be traced back to Gray v. Portland Bank, 3 Mass. 364 (1807), which held that since the power to authorize new shares resided in the shareholders, they had an equitable interest in any new shares that were subsequently created. The *Gray* majority reasoned that, like partners, only the shareholders had the right to admit new owners, and that the value of shares in the hands of later shareholders benefitted from the investments of the earlier owners. Based on this reasoning, courts typically ruled that a corporation "held" its authorized but unissued shares in trust for its shareholders, subject to their paying for them in the future.

This early approach to preemptive rights is illustrated in the following case.

Stokes v. Continental Trust Company

78 N.E. 1090 (N.Y. 1906)

■ JUDGES: VANN, J. HAIGHT, J. (dissenting). CULLEN, CH. J., WERNE and HISCOCK, JJ., concur with VANN, J.; WILLARD BARTLETT, J., concurs with HAIGHT, J.; O'BRIEN, J., absent.

■ VANN, J.

[Eds. Plaintiff, W.E.D. Stokes, sued to compel a corporation to issue at par the number of shares to which he allegedly was entitled by virtue of his preemptive rights to a new stock issue, and in case such shares could not be delivered, for damages. The trial court found in favor of the plaintiff, but the Appellate Division reversed.]*

* * * [T]he question presented for decision is whether according to the facts found the plaintiff had the legal right to subscribe for and take the same number of shares of the new stock that he held of the old?

The subject is not regulated by statute and the question presented has never been directly passed upon by this court, and only to a limited extent has it been considered by courts in this state.

* * *

The leading authority is Gray v. Portland Bank, decided in 1807 and reported in 3 Mass. 364.

* * *

---

* Eds. W.E.D. Stokes was a prominent figure in New York business and social circles at the turn of the 20th century. He was an heir to the Phelps Dodge company fortune, and a prominent real estate developer. See Fred S. McChesney, *The Story of Stokes v. Continental Trust Co.: What'd I Say?*, CORPORATE LAW STORIES, 7 (J. Mark Ramseyer, ed., 2009).

The court held that stockholders who held old stock had a right to subscribe for and take new stock in proportion to their respective shares. As the corporation refused this right to the plaintiff he was permitted to recover the excess of the market value above the par value, with interest. In the course of its argument the court said: "A share in the stock or trust when only the least sum has been paid in is a share in the power of increasing it when the trustee determines or rather when the cestuis que trustent agree upon employing a greater sum.

* * *

A vote to increase the capital stock, if it was not the creation of a new and disjointed capital, was in its nature an agreement among the stockholders to enlarge their shares in the amount or in the number to the extent required to effect that increase.

* * *

If from the progress of the institution and the expense incurred in it any advance upon the additional shares might be obtained in the market, this advance upon the shares relinquished belonged to the whole, and was not to be disposed of at the will of a majority of the stockholders to the partial benefit of some and exclusion of others."

This decision has stood unquestioned for nearly a hundred years and has been followed generally by courts of the highest standing. It is the foundation of the rule upon the subject that prevails, almost without exception, throughout the entire country.

* * *

In the case before us, the new stock came into existence through the exercise of a right belonging wholly to the stockholders. As the right to increase the stock belonged to them, the stock when increased belonged to them also, as it was issued for money and not for property or for some purpose other than the sale thereof for money. By the increase of stock, the voting power of the plaintiff was reduced one-half, and while he consented to the increase he did not consent to the disposition of the new stock by a sale thereof to Blair & Company at less than its market value, nor by sale to any person in any way except by an allotment to the stockholders. The increase and sale involved the transfer of rights belonging to the stockholders as part of their investment. The issue of new stock and the sale thereof to Blair & Company was not only a transfer to them of one-half the voting power of the old stockholders, but also of an equitable right to one-half the surplus which belonged to them. In other words, it was a partial division of the property of the old stockholders. The right to increase stock is not an asset of the corporation any more than the original stock when it was issued pursuant to subscription. The ownership of stock is in the nature of an inherent but indirect power to control the corporation. The stock when issued ready for delivery does not belong to the corporation in the way that it holds its real and personal property, with power to sell the same, but is held by it with no power of alienation in trust for the stockholders, who are the beneficial owners and become the legal owners upon paying therefor. The corporation has no rights hostile to those of the stockholders, but is the trustee for all including the minority. The new stock issued by the defendant under the permission of the statute did not belong to it, but was held by it the same as the original stock when first issued was held in trust for the stockholders. It has the same voting power as the old, share for share. The stockholders decided to enlarge their holdings, not by increasing the amount of each share, but by increasing the number of shares. The new stock belonged to the stockholders as an inherent right by virtue of their being stockholders, to be shared in proportion upon paying its par value or the value per share fixed by vote of a majority of the stockholders, or ascertained by a sale at public auction. While the corporation could not compel the plaintiff to take new shares at any price, since they were issued for money and not for property, it could not lawfully dispose of those shares without giving him a chance to get his proportion at the same price that outsiders got theirs. He had an inchoate right to one share of the new stock for each share owned by him of the old stock, provided he was ready to pay the price fixed by the stockholders. If so situated that he could not take it himself, he was entitled to sell the right to one who could, as is frequently done. Even this gives an advantage to capital, but capital necessarily has some advantage. Of course, there is a distinction when the new stock is issued in payment for property, but that is not this case. The stock in question was issued to be sold for money and was sold for money only. A majority of the stockholders, as part of their power to increase the stock, may attach reasonable conditions to the disposition thereof, such as the requirement that every old stockholder electing to take new stock shall pay a fixed price therefor, not less than par, however, owing to the limitation of the statute. They may also provide for a sale in parcels or bulk at public auction, when every stockholder can bid the same as strangers. They cannot, however, dispose of it to strangers against the protest of any stockholder who insists that he has a right to his proportion. Otherwise the majority could deprive the minority of their proportionate power in the election of directors and of their proportionate right to share in the surplus, each of which is an inherent, preemptive and vested right of property. It is inviolable and can neither be taken away nor lessened without consent, or a waiver implying consent. The plaintiff had power, before the increase of stock, to vote on 221 shares of stock, out of a total of 5,000, at any meeting held by the stockholders for any purpose. By the action of the majority, taken against his will and protest, he now has only one-half the voting power that he had before, because the number of shares has been doubled while he still owns but 221. This touches him as a stockholder in such a way as to deprive him of a right of property. Blair & Company acquired virtual control, while he and the other stockholders lost it. We are not discussing equities, but legal rights, for this is an action at law, and the plaintiff was deprived of a strictly legal right. If the result gives him an advantage over other stockholders, it is because he stood upon his legal rights, while they did not. The question is what were his legal rights, not what his profit may be under the sale to Blair & Company, but what it might have been if the new stock had been issued to him in proportion to his holding of the old. The other stockholders could give their property to Blair & Company, but they could not give his.

A share of stock is a share in the power to increase the stock, and belongs to the stockholders the same as the stock itself. When that power is exercised, the new stock belongs to the old stockholders in proportion to their holding of old stock, subject to compliance with the lawful terms upon which it is issued. When the new stock is issued in payment for property purchased by the corporation, the stockholders' right is merged in the purchase, and they have an advantage in the increase of the property of the corporation in proportion to the increase of stock. When the new stock is issued for money, while the stockholders may provide that it be sold at auction or fix the price at which it is to be sold, each stockholder is entitled to his proportion of the proceeds of the sale at auction, after he has had a right to bid at the sale, or to his proportion of the new stock at the price fixed by the stockholders.

We are thus led to lay down the rule that a stockholder has an inherent right to a proportionate share of new stock issued for money only and not to purchase property for the purposes of the corporation or to effect a consolidation, and while he can waive that right, he cannot be deprived of it without his consent except when the stock is issued at a fixed price not less than par and he is given the right to take at that price in proportion to his holding, or in some other equitable way that will enable him to protect his interest by acting on his own judgment and using his own resources. This rule is just to all and tends to prevent the tyranny of majorities which needs restraint, as well as virtual attempts to blackmail by small minorities which should be prevented.

* * *

■ HAIGHT, J. (dissenting). I agree that the rule that we should adopt is that a stockholder in a corporation has an inherent right to purchase a proportionate share of new stock issued for money only, and not to purchase property necessary for the purposes of the corporation or to effect a consolidation. While he can waive that right he cannot be deprived of it without his consent, except by sale at a fixed price at or above par, in which he may buy at that price in proportion to his holding or in some other equitable way that will enable him to protect his interest by acting on his own judgment and using his own resources. I, however, differ with Judge Vann as to his conclusions as to the rights of the plaintiff herein. Under the findings of the trial court the plaintiff demanded that his share of the new stock should be issued to him at par, or $100 per share, instead of $450 per share, the price offered by Blair & Company and the price fixed at the stockholders' meeting at which the new stock was authorized to be sold. This demand was made after the passage of the resolution authorizing the increase of the capital stock of the defendant company and before the passage of the resolution authorizing a sale of the new stock to Blair & Company at the price specified. After the passage of the second resolution he objected to the sale of his proportionate share of the new stock to Blair & Company and again demanded that it be issued to him, and the following day he made a legal tender for the amount of his portion of the new stock at $100 per share. There is no finding of fact or evidence in the record showing that he was ever ready or willing to pay $450 per share for the stock. He knew that Blair & Company represented Marshall Field and others at Chicago, great dry goods merchants, and that they had made a written offer to purchase the new stock of the company provided the stockholders would authorize an increase of its capital stock from five hundred thousand to a million dollars. He knew that the trustees of the company had called a special meeting of the stockholders for the purpose of considering the offer so made by Blair & Company. He knew that the increased capitalization proposed was for the purpose of enlarging the business of the company and bringing into its management the gentlemen referred to. There is no pretense that any of the stockholders would have voted for an increase of the capital stock otherwise than for the purpose of accepting the offer of Blair & Company. All were evidently desirous of interesting the gentlemen referred to in the company, and by securing their business and deposits increase the earnings of the company. This the trustees carefully considered, and in their notice calling the special meeting of the stockholders distinctly recommended the acceptance of the offer. What, then, was the legal effect of the plaintiff's demand and tender? To my mind it was simply an attempt to make something out of his associates, to get for $100 per share the stock which Blair & Company had offered to purchase for $450 per share; and that it was the equivalent of a refusal to pay $450 per share, and its effect is to waive his right to procure the stock by paying that amount. An acceptance of his offer would have been most unjust to the remaining stockholders. It would not only have deprived them of the additional sum of $350 per share, which had been offered for the stock, but it would have defeated the object and purpose for which the meeting was called, for it was well understood that Blair & Company would not accept less than the whole issue of the new stock. But this is not all. It appears that prior to the offer of Blair & Company the stock of the company had never been sold above $450 per share; that thereafter the stock rapidly advanced until the day of the completion of the sale on the 30th of January, when its market value was $550 per share; but this, under the stipulation of facts, was caused by the rumor and subsequent announcement and consummation of the proposition for the increase of the stock and the sale of such increase to Blair & Company and their associates. It is now proposed to give the plaintiff as damages such increase in the market value of the stock, even though such value was based upon the understanding that Blair &

Company were to become stockholders in the corporation, which the acceptance of plaintiff's offer would have prevented. This, to my mind, should not be done. I, therefore, favor an affirmance.

QUESTIONS

1. What business reasons motivated the increase in authorized stock and the sale to Blair & Co.?
2. Do you have any reason to believe that $450 per share was an unfairly low price for the sale of new shares in Continental Trust Company? The stock was trading between $350 and $400 on market rumors of a deal with Blair & Co.
3. Would it have been fair to other shareholders to allow Stokes to purchase newly issued shares at their par value of $100?
4. Why would the other shareholders vote to dilute their own share of ownership by selling new shares to Blair at $450?
5. What effect would honoring Stokes' preemptive rights have on Blair's interest in acquiring one-half of the total shares of Continental?
6. Does the majority opinion suggest any limits on the preemptive rights doctrine that might provide a way for Blair and the other shareholders to avoid Stokes' claims? If so, how would you suggest restructuring the transaction if you represented Blair or the majority of the shareholders?

Stokes was rooted in a common law interpretation of New York law, but state statutes during this time period often took a similar approach to the issue of preemptive rights. Indeed, through much of the twentieth century, many state statutes granted preemptive rights unless the corporation opted out of them in its articles of incorporation. As in *Stokes*, the typical statutory provisions provided that preemptive rights gave shareholders the right to buy any newly issued shares at the same price offered to others. But a default rule granting preemptive rights posed a variety of challenges in practice. For instance, should these rights apply when a company issues a different class of common stock (e.g., one without voting rights or dividend rights)? What about the issuance of preferred stock? Or options to acquire common stock? And how exactly should a corporation, perhaps unaware that preemptive rights even exist, cure a violation when it issues shares to new investors?

Due in part to these tricky questions, the notion that preemptive rights should be a default right of shareholders eventually lost ground—to be replaced by an approach that required investors to demand these rights expressly through the power of contract. For example, the modern approach is exemplified by Model Act § 6.30(a) which states specifically that no preemptive rights exist unless provided in the articles of incorporation. Note that a simple statement in the articles that "the corporation elects to have preemptive rights" gets shareholders a standard form set of preemptive rights, unless the articles of incorporation vary them. Model Act § 6.30(b). A similar approach is taken in Delaware under DGCL § 102(b)(3).

In practice, stockholders often obtain preemptive rights through a separate contract formed by the company and the investors at the time of the initial financing. For instance, Section 4.1 of the Model Investor Rights Agreement published by the National Venture Capital Association (NVCA) is entitled "Rights to Future Stock Issuances" and provides a contractual right for a company's venture capital (VC) investors to purchase their pro-rata share of future stock offerings. As we shall see, VC investors typically purchase shares of a company's convertible preferred stock, which the investor can convert into shares of common stock initially at a ratio of 1:1. For present purposes, this distinction is only relevant for how the contract defines an investor's pro-rata share. Here is the language from one company that adopted the NVCA language:*

> 4. Rights to Future Stock Issuances.
>
> 4.1 Right of First Offer. Subject to the terms and conditions of this Section 4.1 and applicable securities laws, if the Company proposes to offer or sell any New Securities, the Company shall first offer such New Securities to each Major Investor. . . .
>
> (a) The Company shall give notice (the "Offer Notice") to each Major Investor, stating (i) its bona fide intention to offer such New Securities, (ii) the number of such New Securities to be offered, and (iii) the price and terms, if any, upon which it proposes to offer such New Securities.†
>
> (b) By notification to the Company within twenty (20) days after the Offer Notice is given, each Major Investor may elect to purchase or otherwise acquire, at the price and on the terms specified in the Offer Notice, up to that portion of such New Securities which equals the proportion that the Common Stock then held by such Major Investor (including all shares of Common Stock then issuable (directly or indirectly) upon conversion and/or exercise, as applicable, of the Preferred Stock and any other Derivative Securities then held by such Major Investor) bears to the total number of shares of Common Stock of the Company then

* This provision is taken from the Amended and Restated Investors' Rights Agreement dated August 24, 2018, of Fulcrum Therapeutics, Inc., available at https://www.sec.gov/Archives/edgar/data/1680581/000104746919003793/a2239080zex-10_1.htm.

† "New Securities" is defined elsewhere in the agreement to mean "collectively, equity securities of the Company, whether or not currently authorized, as well as rights, options, or warrants to purchase such equity securities, or securities of any type whatsoever that are, or may become, convertible or exchangeable into or exercisable for such equity securities."

> outstanding (assuming full conversion and/or exercise, as applicable, of all shares of Preferred Stock and other Derivative Securities).* At the expiration of such twenty (20) day period, the Company shall promptly notify each Major Investor that elects to purchase or acquire all the shares available to it (each, a "Fully Exercising Investor") of any other Major Investor's failure to do likewise. During the ten (10) day period commencing after the Company has given such notice, each Fully Exercising Investor may, by giving notice to the Company, elect to purchase or acquire, in addition to the number of shares specified above, up to that portion of the New Securities for which Major Investors were entitled to subscribe but that were not subscribed for by the Major Investors, which portion is equal to the proportion that the Common Stock issued and held, or issuable upon conversion and/or exercise, as applicable, of Preferred Stock and any other Derivative Securities then held, by such Fully Exercising Investor bears to the number of shares of Common Stock issued and held, or issuable (directly or indirectly) upon conversion and/or exercise, as applicable, of the Preferred Stock and any other Derivative Securities then held, by all Fully Exercising Investors who wish to purchase such unsubscribed shares. The closing of any sale pursuant to this Section 4.1(b) shall occur within the later of one hundred twenty (120) days after the date that the Offer Notice is given and the date of initial sale of New Securities pursuant to Section 4.1(c).
>
> (c) If all New Securities referred to in the Offer Notice are not elected to be purchased or acquired as provided in Section 4.1(b), the Company may, during the ninety (90) day period following the expiration of the periods provided in Section 4.1(b), offer and sell the remaining unsubscribed portion of such New Securities to any Person or Persons at a price not less than, and upon terms no more favorable to the offeree than, those specified in the Offer Notice. . . .

Compared to the conventional concept of preemptive rights in *Stokes*, note several points about how the NVCA provision is implemented. First, the contract limits the right to a "Major Investor" which is a term defined elsewhere in the contract to include investors holding a specified number of shares of preferred stock. This illustrates how, even in a venture capital financing, only the largest investors are granted these rights. Additionally, as noted in the contract, an investor's

---

* "Derivative Securities" is defined elsewhere in the agreement to mean "any securities or rights convertible into, or exercisable or exchangeable for (in each case, directly or indirectly), Common Stock, including options and warrants."

pro rata share is defined by reference to the number of shares of common stock actually held by a Major Investor or common stock "issuable" upon conversion of any preferred stock or other derivative securities held by a Major Investor. The total number of shares of common stock outstanding is also based on the number of shares of common stock outstanding, as well as common shares that are issuable upon conversion of the preferred stock or other derivative securities. In our NewCo example, for instance, if Janet had initially acquired 60 shares of convertible preferred stock, her pro-rata percentage would be calculated as follows:

Table 5-3:
Pro-Forma Cap Table of NewCo Following Arigo Venture's Investment

Stockholder	Common Stock	Preferred Stock (as converted)	Pro-Rata %
Francis	40	0	40%
Janet	0	60	60%
Total	**40**	**60**	**100%**

Thus, assuming Janet is a Major Investor, the contract language would give her the right to acquire 60% of any new stock sale, allowing her to maintain her existing ownership percentage (even if she has not converted the preferred to common). An "alternative" approach provided in the NVCA model, however, would calculate a Major Investor's pro-rata share based on the number of shares held by the Major Investor relative to all shares "then held by all the Major Investors." Were this language used and if Janet was the only Major Investor, her pro rata percentage would be 100% (i.e., 60 shares/60 shares), allowing her to buy all the shares being offered and thereby *increase* her ownership position. Finally, note the effect of the second half of Section 4.1(b). Where there are multiple Major Investors and one of them chooses *not* to participate, the other Major Investors can purchase the shares offered to the non-participating Major Investors. This provision might also allow investors to increase their ownership in the company.

Finally, the existence of preemptive rights can pose a dilemma for a company that wants not only to raise financing but wants the financing to come from a *particular* new investor. For example, a large corporation might seek to make a strategic investment in a pharmaceutical company whose product it will be distributing. Or a large financial investor might seek a controlling position as part of a strategic growth equity investment. The existence of preemptive rights can potentially disrupt these arrangements unless the firm can obtain a waiver of any preemptive rights or structure the deal in some other way that accommodates the rights. We elaborate on this latter point in the Sidebar.

Sidebar: Pricing an Equity Financing with Preemptive Rights

Despite its 1906 publication date, the *Stokes* case represents a setting that could quite easily arise today. Just as a private equity fund might seek a controlling position when making a growth equity investment, Blair & Co. had negotiated with Continental Trust to obtain a 50% stake in the company for its investment of $2,250,000. Stokes' assertion of preemptive rights, however, complicated this arrangement insofar that the company would have to sell 4.42% of the offering to Stokes rather than to Blair & Co., cutting Blair & Co. back to a $2,150,550 investment. Assuming Blair & Co insists on investing $2,250,000 for a 50% equity position, Stokes' assertion of preemptive rights risked impeding the transaction.

We illustrate here a common technique designed to allow the company to honor the original financial terms with Blair & Co. while also honoring Stokes' preemptive rights. The technique leverages the pricing equation cited earlier that is used for a common stock financing:

$$\frac{Pre - Financing\ Valuation}{Pre - Financing\ Capitalization} = Price\ Per\ Share\ (PPS)$$

The facts of the case state that Stokes held 221 shares out of 5,000 shares prior to the financing and that Blair & Co was to pay $450/share for 5,000 shares. In combination, these facts indicate a pre-financing valuation of $2,250,000 ($450 × 5,000 pre-financing capitalization). To ensure that Blair & Co. receives 50% of the company's equity for an investment of $2,250,000, we need to ensure that the denominator includes any shares that would reduce Blair's equity claim. This obviously includes any outstanding shares, but it should also include any shares that might be contingent, such as stock options. Under this same reasoning, it should also include any shares existing stockholders have a right to acquire pursuant to preemptive rights. Here, Stokes has the right to purchase 4.42% (221/5000) of any new shares, so the pricing equation would appear to be:

$$\frac{Pre - Financing\ Valuation}{Pre - Financing\ Capitalization + Stokes'\ Shares}$$

$$= \frac{\$2{,}250{,}000}{5{,}000 + (4.42\%\ x\ 5{,}000)} = \$430.95$$

Recall that the original price per share was $450/share, so this lower price per share will ensure that Blair obtains more shares for its $2,250,000 investment. This should make sense since the company must issue more shares to get Blair & Co. a 50% ownership stake, assuming Stokes is also acquiring more shares to maintain his 4.42% ownership stake. For instance, at $430.95/share, Blair & Co. would receive approximately 5,221 shares ($2,250,000/$430.95). And if Stokes also purchases 221 shares (4.42% × 5,000), this would give Blair & Co. a 50% equity position since the total number of shares outstanding after the financing would be 10,442 (i.e., 5,000 (pre-financing shares) + 221 (new shares to Stokes) + 5,221 (new shares to Blaire & Co)).

While this comes close to solving the problem, we have one wrinkle: Stokes is entitled to purchase 4.42% of any shares offered by the company. The calculation above assumed that Stokes would be buying 221 shares, which is 4.42% of the original 5,000 shares offered to Blair & Co. However, by lowering the price per share to $430.95, the company will be issuing 5,221 shares to Blair & Co.—not 5,000. Honoring Stokes' preemptive rights would entitle him to buy 4.42% of these additional 221 shares. Indeed, we seem to have something of an iterative loop: We once again need to reduce the price per share to account for Stokes' right to acquire 4.42% of the additional 221 shares, which increases the number of shares sold to Blair. Yet Stokes' has the right to purchase 4.42% of these additional shares, forcing us to lower the price per share *again* in hopes of getting Blair & Co. to a 50% ownership position.

The note at the end of this Sidebar shows how to solve this challenge using basic algebra; however, in practice, deal lawyers solve this "iterative loop" problem using Microsoft Excel. This is made possible by Excel's ability to "iterate" through equations that have circular references. And this is precisely the problem that we have encountered. We can see the circular reference if we re-write the equation above as follows:

$$\frac{\$2{,}250{,}000}{5{,}000 + 4.42\% \times \mathit{Total\ Shares\ Sold}} = \mathit{Price\ Per\ Share\ (PPS)}$$

The problem is that *Total Shares Sold* depends on the Price Per Share, which is what we are trying to figure out. At the same time, we can break *Total Shares Sold* into two components: Shares sold to Blair & Co. (which will be $2,250,000/PPS) and shares issued to Stokes (which will be 4.42% of *Total Shares Sold*). Using Excel, we simply ask the program to calculate *PPS* and then ask it to calculate *Total Shares Sold* as the sum of (a) shares sold to Blair & Co. (calculated as above) and (b) shares issued to Stokes (calculated as above):

	A	B
1		
2	Price Per Share:	=2250000/(5000+B5)
3		
4	Shares to Blair & Co.:	=2250000/B2
5	Shares to Stokes:	=0.0442*B6
6	Total Shares Sold:	=SUM(B4:B5)

Notice how B2 depends on B5 (Shares to Stokes), which in turn depends on B6 (Total Shares Sold). Yet B6 is the sum of B5 and B4 (which, in turn, depends on B2)! These formulas are thus "circular" and entering them in Excel will prompt a warning that there are circular references. However, if we instruct Excel to use "iterative" calculation, the program will seek to find answers for B2, B4 and B5 (which would end the iterative loop) through an algorithm that resembles trial & error. In Excel for Mac, we enable this functionality by going to Preferences→Calculation and checking the box next to "Enable Iterative Calculation." In Excel for Windows, we enable it by going to Options→Formulas→Calculation Options and check the box for "Enable Iterative Calculation." We provide an example of this solution on the tab entitled "Fixing Stokes" on the "Common Stock Worksheet" on the casebook website. As the worksheet reveals, issuing a total of 5,485 shares at $429.19/share will permit the company to sell 50% of the company's equity to Blair & Co., while honoring Stokes' right to purchase 4.42% of the overall offering.*

It is important to note, however, that one of the implications of taking this approach is to increase the dilution experienced by all other stockholders. The reason stems from the fact that $429.19 price per share implies a pre-financing valuation of $2,145,951 (i.e., $429.19 × 5,000 pre-financing fully-diluted shares). And, obviously, we have only taken account of one shareholder, Stokes, who wishes to exercise preemptive rights; if additional pre-existing shareholders have the same preemptive rights and want to do the same thing, then we would need to adjust our calculations.

* We can solve this problem algebraically if consider two facts. First, shares acquired by Blair & Co. will be determined by dividing $2,250,000 by PPS, or $2,250,000/PPS. Second, the total shares issued to Blair & Co will be equal to 95.58% of the *Total Shares Sold*, once we account for the 4.42% acquired by Stokes. Thus, in the PPS equation noted above, we can substitute for *Total Shares Sold* the following: ($2,250,000/PPS) x (1/.9558). Solving for PPS yields $429.19.

ii. ANTI-DILUTION PROTECTION

Preemptive rights represent an important method for pre-existing stockholders to avoid dilution if they are willing to invest in a subsequent sale of a company's securities. But what about situations where an investor is unwilling or unable to purchase additional shares? Whether such an investor would find a future issuance of stock worrisome depends in large measure on the price at which the company sells its securities. Consider, for instance, the case of Janet in the previous example. Recall that she paid $10/share for 60 shares causing her to own 60% of the company's fully-diluted capitalization. If the company subsequently sells to a new investor 100 shares of Common Stock at $20/share, Janet's ownership position will be reduced to 30%; however, the economic value of her claim will have *increased* from $600 to $1,200 (i.e., 60 × $20/share). While Janet's non-participation affects her voting control, she experiences no economic dilution. Depending on the circumstances, this may be perfectly acceptable to Janet.*

More troubling to Janet is a future stock issuance below the price that she paid for the stock (a so-called "cheap stock issuance"). As discussed previously, this will produce both voting dilution and economic dilution. Consequently, Janet may demand, as part of her initial investment, some protections against a cheap stock issuance. In addition to the right to veto the sale of stock, these protections may take the form of price-based antidilution provisions in her investment agreements.

In general, price-based antidilution protection is designed to protect against the *economic dilution* that occurs when a company sells stock at a price below the price paid by a prior investor. Consider again the scenario where Janet buys her stock and the company then issues 100 common shares to Arigo Ventures at $8/share. This transaction suggests that the 60 shares held by Janet now hold an aggregate value of $480, indicating a $120 decline in her investment (recall that she paid $600). Had Janet negotiated for antidilution protection, however, these provisions would have ensured that the decline was less than this amount. Indeed, a generous antidilution provision might even ensure that she suffers *no* economic dilution in her $600 investment.

How is this possible? In the case of a common stockholder such as Janet, a typical antidilution provision works by simply issuing the stockholder additional shares of stock at no new cost. For instance, imagine that when Janet made her initial stock purchase, the investment agreement included the following language:

> *If the Company issues or sells any Common Stock at a purchase price (the New Issuance Price) per share less than $10/share, then the Company shall issue to Janet a number of shares of Common Stock equal to the following:*

$$New\ Shares = \frac{\$10}{New\ Issuance\ Price} \times 60 - 60$$

Now consider the implications of this contract provision on Janet following the sale of 100 shares to Arigo Ventures at $8/share. The first question to ask is whether the anti-dilution provision is triggered at all.

---

* This example illustrates a more general point about early-stage investing, which is that some degree of voting dilution is always expected by early investors in a company. As a company grows, it will need additional investments of both labor and capital, and a company may choose to pay for these investments by issuing common stock (or, in the case of employee labor, common stock options). These additional issuances of common stock will reduce the ownership claim of prior investors, but if they are building value in the company, the investors will ideally find themselves in a situation such as in this example where their voting percentages decline but their economic stakes grow in value. That said, even in the most successful start-up companies, early investors will typically participate at some level in the next several equity financings of the company to minimize their voting dilution—as well as to signal their support for the company to new investors. (Failure to participate might be interpreted by prospective new investors as a lack of confidence in the firm's future prospects.)

The language says it applies if the company sells stock at a price below \$10/share, so the answer is yes: it is clearly triggered when the company sells 100 shares to Arigo Ventures for \$8/share. The next step is to plug numbers into the equation to see how many shares must be given to Janet. The New Issuance Price is \$8/share, so the equation is:

$$New\ Shares = \frac{\$10}{\$8} \times 60 - 60$$

If we run the numbers, we can see that Janet will receive 15 additional shares. Now let's examine the capitalization table for NewCo when all the dust settles:

Table 5-4: Cap Table of NewCo Following Arigo Venture's Investment with Janet's Antidilution Provision		
Stockholder	Common Stock	% of Fully Diluted Stock
Francis	40	18.60%
Janet	75	34.88%
Arigo Ventures	100	46.52%
Total	**215**	**100%**

Recall that in this example, we stipulated that \$8/share was the fair value of the shares prior to the financing, indicating a pre-financing value of the firm of \$800 (i.e., 100 shares x \$8/share). Arigo Ventures is investing \$800, so the post-financing value of the company would therefore be \$1,600. Note that following the receipt of 15 shares, Janet has a 34.88% claim on the firm's value of \$1,600, which is equal to approximately \$558. This is a substantial improvement to her economic condition relative to a scenario where she has no antidilution protection (recall that, with no antidilution protection, she wound up with an economic stake worth just \$480).

However, before concluding, there is one additional consideration we need to discuss. Notice that Arigo Ventures no longer holds a 50% position despite the fact that its investment comprises exactly one-half of the company's \$1,600 post-financing valuation. Indeed, were it to see the capitalization table in Table 5-4 it would no doubt be puzzled and upset about why it doesn't hold 50% of the company's fully-diluted capitalization given the pre-financing valuation of \$800 and its investment amount of \$800. The explanation, of course, is that Arigo Ventures was diluted by the issuance of the 15 shares to Janet. As a result, Arigo Ventures and its lawyers need to treat Janet's antidilution protection like any other contingent right to acquire stock and include these shares as part of the company's pre-financing capitalization. We can accomplish this by using our pricing equation with the following adjustment to the pre-financing capitalization in the denominator:

$$\frac{\$800}{100 + \frac{\$10}{New\ Issuance\ Price} \times 60 - 60} = New\ Issuance\ Price$$

It might seem odd that the New Issuance Price is itself determined by the New Issuance Price. However, as we show in the Sidebar below, this is easily solvable using Microsoft Excel. As we illustrate there, the result is a price per share of $5/share, entitling Arigo Ventures to 160 shares of Common Stock for its $800 investment. Likewise, using $5/share for the New Issuance Price in Janet's antidilution formula results in her receiving 60 additional shares of Common. The final capitalization table is therefore:

Table 5-5: Cap Table of NewCo Following Arigo Venture's Investment with Janet's Antidilution Provision

Stockholder	Common Stock	% of Fully Diluted Stock
Francis	40	12.50%
Janet	120	37.50%
Arigo Ventures	160	50.00%
Total	**320**	**100.00%**

Note that, given the $1,600 valuation of the company, Janet's 37.5% ownership position now translates into exactly $600 (i.e., 37.5% x $1,600). Thus, the consequence of Janet's antidilution protection is to protect her against *any* economic dilution from the sale of stock at a price below $10/share. In practice, this form of price protection is referred to as a "full ratchet" provision or a "full price protection" provision.

Given the role of equity finance for venture capital, it turns out that antidilution protection is an especially important topic in venture capital finance. There are a number of different provisions to reflect various negotiation compromises. In general, these provisions typically rely on conversion rights within the venture capital preferred stock, so we shall reserve discussion of these other varieties of antidilution protection until Chapter 7 when we discuss convertible securities, including convertible preferred stock.

Sidebar: Pricing an Equity Financing That Triggers Antidilution Protection

If an equity financing will trigger pre-existing stockholders' antidilution protection, a new investor (and its lawyers) must take care to account for the antidilution provision when pricing the transaction.

Otherwise, it will dilute the new investor and cause the investor to hold less of an ownership claim than it expects from the economics of the financing. As was done in the case of preemptive rights, we can accomplish this pricing modification by including any "antidilution" shares as part of the pre-financing fully-diluted capitalization. As noted previously, in the example involving Janet and Arigo Ventures, the share pricing equation would be:

$$\frac{\$800}{100 + \frac{\$10}{New\ Issuance\ Price} \times 60 - 60} = New\ Issuance\ Price$$

As with the example of preemptive rights, this equation includes a circular reference in that New Issuance Price (the right-side of the equation) depends on New Issuance Price (which also appears in the left-side of the equation). Using Excel's iterative calculation, however, we can solve this problem by breaking apart the equation into two cells. In one, we calculate the *New Issuance Price* (i.e., $800 pre-money valuation/(100 pre-money fully-diluted shares + new shares issuable to Janet)), and in the other, we calculate the new shares issuable to Janet (i.e., $10/New Issuance Price × 60 – 60), taking care that the calculation of *New Issuance Price* is linked to the cell calculating the number of shares issuable to Janet and vice versa:

	A	B
1	New Issuance Price	=800/(100+B2)
2	New Shares to Janet	=10/B1*60-60

By turning on the "iterative" calculation functionality (see prior Sidebar), the program will produce a price per share of $5/share. We provide an example of this solution on the tab entitled "Arigo Ventures" on the "Common Stock Worksheet" on the casebook website.

Sidebar: Cash Payments as Antidilution Protection

Most antidilution provisions involve modifying an investor's equity position in a company to minimize the economic dilution arising from an issuance of stock at a price lower than that paid by the pre-existing stockholder. However, a company can also protect a stockholder against economic dilution through more direct methods, such as a simple cash payment upon a dilutive issuance. For instance, this approach was taken by the private equity firm TPG Capital in its April 2008 investment in Washington Mutual, Inc. (WaMu), a bank that was struggling with its large exposure to subprime mortgages. In the $7 billion financing, WaMu sold 176 million shares of common stock to TPG and other investors at price of $8.75 per share. Section 4.11 of the

Investment Agreement* between WaMu, TPG, and the other investors provided as follows:

4.11 Reset.

(a) If, from the date hereof until the date that is eighteen months after the Closing Date:

(1) the Company issues or sells, or agrees to issue or sell, more than $500 million of Common Stock . . . at a purchase . . . price (the [Reset Price]) per share less than the Reference Purchase Price [Eds. This term was elsewhere defined to be $8.75.] (a Reset Issuance) . . .

then . . . the Company shall make a payment to each Investor (the Reset Payment), equal to the product of (i) an amount equal to the (z) Reference Purchase Price minus the Reset Price, divided by (y) the Reference Purchase Price multiplied by (ii) the aggregate amount paid by such Investor pursuant to Article I . . .

To see how this provision protects TPG, imagine that WaMu's financial condition continued to deteriorate inducing WaMu to sell another $1 billion shares of Common Stock six months after the financing at price of $5/share (assume this is the current fair market value). Since TPG purchased $2 billion in the original financing, the provision would work as follows:

Reference Purchase Price:	$8.75
Reset Price:	$5.00
TPG Original Investment:	$2 billion
Payment to TPG:	($8.75 – $5.00)/$8.75 × $2 billion => $857,142,857

Note that since TPG invested $2 billion in WaMu, it would have received approximately 228,571,428 shares of common stock (i.e., $2 billion / $8.75). Assuming these shares now have a value of $5/share, they would be worth $1,142,857,143, or just 57.14% of their original value. However, when we add the value of the cash payment now owed to TPG, its overall economic position remains $2 billion ($1,142,857,143 + $857,142,857 = $2 billion). This is another version of full ratchet antidilution protection.

If you represented the new investor, how would you feel upon discovering that TPG is owed this amount? Does this suggest a potential limitation to the effectiveness of this antidilution provision?

* The Investment Agreement can be found at https://www.sec.gov/Archives/edgar/data/933136/000127727708000181/exhibit101.htm.

iii. FIDUCIARY DUTIES

The final method of protecting against dilution is for a stockholder to challenge the board's approval of a dilutive stock issuance. While the approval of a stock sale is ordinarily subject to the business judgment rule, a court may be willing to evaluate the transaction under the exacting enhanced scrutiny standard where directors personally benefit from the transaction. In Chapter 7, we shall see that this issue has become increasingly relevant for venture capital investors, who often make multiple investments in their portfolio companies while having a representative sit on the board of directors. In the first case that follows, we consider how the situation can arise in the more straight-forward setting of a company financed solely with common stock. The second case then explores a practical constraint on the ability of stockholders to protect against dilution by means of a fiduciary duty claim following the acquisition of a company—a setting that is highly likely to create incentives for diluted stockholders to bring such claims.

Katzowitz v. Sidler et al.

249 N.E.2d 359 (N.Y. 1969)

■ JUDGES BURKE, SCILEPPI, BERGAN, BREITEL and JASEN concur with JUDGE KEATING; CHIEF JUDGE FULD dissents and votes to affirm on the opinion at the Appellate Division.

■ KEATING, J.

Isador Katzowitz is a director and stockholder of a close corporation. Two other persons, Jacob Sidler and Max Lasker, own the remaining securities and, with Katzowitz, comprise Sulburn Holding Corp.'s board of directors. Sulburn was organized in 1955 to supply propane gas to three other corporations controlled by these men. Sulburn's certificate of incorporation authorized it to issue 1,000 shares of no par value stock for which the incorporators established a $100 selling price. Katzowitz, Sidler and Lasker each invested $500 and received five shares of the corporation's stock.

The three men had been jointly engaged in several corporate ventures for more than 25 years. In this period they had always been equal partners and received identical compensation from the corporations they controlled. Though all the corporations controlled by these three men prospered, disenchantment with their inter-personal relationship flared into the open in 1956.

* * *

In December of 1961 Sulburn was indebted to each stockholder to the extent of $2,500 for fees and commissions earned up until September, 1961. Instead of paying this debt, Sidler and Lasker wanted Sulburn to loan the money to another corporation which all three men controlled. Sidler and Lasker called a meeting of the board of directors to propose that additional securities be offered at $100 per share to substitute for the money owed to the directors. The notice of meeting for October 30, 1961 had on its agenda "a proposition that the corporation issue common stock of its unissued common capital stock, the total par value which shall equal the total sum of the fees and commissions now owing by the corporation to its * * * directors". (Emphasis added.) Katzowitz made it quite clear at the meeting that he would not invest any additional funds in Sulburn in order for it to make a loan to this other corporation. The only resolution passed at the meeting was that the corporation would pay the sum of $2,500 to each director.

With full knowledge that Katzowitz expected to be paid his fees and commissions and that he did not want to participate in any new stock issuance, the other two directors called a special meeting of the board on December 1, 1961. The only item on the agenda for this special meeting was the issuance of 75 shares of the corporation's common stock at $100 per share. The offer was to be made to stockholders in "accordance with their respective preemptive rights for the purpose of acquiring additional working capital". The amount to be raised was the exact amount owed by the corporation to its shareholders. The offering price for the securities was 1/18 the book value of the stock. Only Sidler and Lasker attended the special board meeting. They approved the issuance of the 75 shares.

Notice was mailed to each stockholder that they had the right to purchase 25 shares of the corporation's stock at $100 a share. The offer was to expire on December 27, 1961. Failure to act by that date was stated to constitute a waiver. At about the same time Katzowitz received the notice, he received a check for $2,500 from the corporation for his fees and commissions. Katzowitz did not exercise his option to buy the additional shares. Sidler and Lasker purchased their full complement, 25 shares each. This purchase by Sidler and Lasker caused an immediate dilution of the book value of the outstanding securities.

On August 25, 1962 the principal asset of Sulburn, a tractor trailer truck, was destroyed. On August 31, 1962 the directors unanimously voted to dissolve the corporation. Upon dissolution, Sidler and Lasker each received $18,885.52 but Katzowitz only received $3,147.59

The plaintiff instituted a declaratory judgment action to establish his right to the proportional interest in the assets of Sulburn in liquidation less the $5,000 which Sidler and Lasker used to purchase their shares in December, 1961.

Special Term (Westchester County) found the book value of the corporation's securities on the day the stock was offered at $100 to be worth $1,800. The court also found that "the individual defendants * * * decided that in lieu of taking that sum in cash [the commissions and fees due the stockholders], they preferred to add to their investment by having the corporate defendant make available and offer each stockholder an additional twenty-five shares of unissued stock." The court reasoned that Katzowitz waived his right to purchase the stock or object to its sale to Lasker and Sidler by failing to exercise his preemptive right and found his protest at the time of dissolution untimely.

The Appellate Division (Second Department), two Justices dissenting, modified the order of Special Term. The modification was procedural. The decretal paragraph in Special Term's order was corrected by reinstating the complaint and substituting a statement of the parties' rights. On the substantive legal issues and findings of fact, the Appellate Division was in agreement with Special Term. The majority agreed that the book value of the corporation's stock at the time of the stock offering was $1,800. The Appellate Division reasoned, however, that showing a disparity between book value and offering price was insufficient without also showing fraud or overreaching. Disparity in price by itself was not enough to prove fraud. The Appellate Division also found that the plaintiff had waived his right to object to his recovery in dissolution by failing to either exercise his pre-emptive rights or take steps to prevent the sale of the stock.

The concept of pre-emptive rights was fashioned by the judiciary to safeguard two distinct interests of stockholders—the right to protection against dilution of their equity in the corporation and protection against dilution of their proportionate voting control. After early decisions, legislation fixed the right enunciated with respect to proportionate voting but left to the judiciary the role of protecting existing shareholders from the dilution of their equity.

It is clear that directors of a corporation have no discretion in the choice of those to whom the earnings and assets of the corporation should be distributed. Directors, being fiduciaries of the corporation, must, in issuing new stock, treat existing shareholders fairly. Though there is very little statutory control over the price which a corporation must receive for new shares the power to determine price must be exercised for the benefit of the corporation and in the interest of all the stockholders.

Issuing stock for less than fair value can injure existing shareholders by diluting their interest in the corporation's surplus, in current and future earnings and in the assets upon liquidation. Normally, a stockholder is protected from the loss of his equity from dilution, even though the stock is being offered at less than fair value, because the shareholder receives rights which he may either exercise or sell. If he exercises, he has protected his interest and, if not, he can sell the rights, thereby compensating himself for the dilution of his remaining shares in the equity of the corporation.

When new shares are issued, however, at prices far below fair value in a close corporation or a corporation with only a limited market for its shares, existing stockholders, who do not want to invest or do not have the capacity to invest additional funds, can have their equity interest in the corporation diluted to the vanishing point.

The protection afforded by stock rights is illusory in close corporations. Even if a buyer could be found for the rights, they would have to be sold at an inadequate price because of the nature of a close corporation. Outsiders are normally discouraged from acquiring minority interests after a close corporation has been organized. Certainly, a stockholder in a close corporation is at a total loss to safeguard his equity from dilution if no rights are offered and he does not want to invest additional funds.

Though it is difficult to determine fair value for a corporation's securities and courts are therefore reluctant to get into the thicket, when the issuing price is shown to be markedly below book value in a close corporation and when the remaining share-holder-directors benefit from the issuance, a case for judicial relief has been established. In that instance, the corporation's directors must show that the issuing price falls within some range which can be justified on the basis of valid business reasons. If no such showing is made by the directors, there is no reason for the judiciary to abdicate its function to a majority of the board of stockholders who have not seen fit to come forward and justify the propriety of diverting property from the corporation and allow the issuance of securities to become an oppressive device, permitting the dilution of the equity of dissident stockholders.

The defendant directors here make no claim that the price set was a fair one. No business justification is offered to sustain it. Admittedly, the stock was sold at less than book value. The defendants simply contend that, as long as all stockholders were given an equal opportunity to purchase additional shares, no stockholder can complain simply because the offering dilutes his interest in the corporation.

The defendants' argument is fallacious.

The corollary of a stockholder's right to maintain his proportionate equity in a corporation by purchasing additional shares is the right not to purchase additional shares without being confronted with dilution of his existing equity if no valid business justification exists for the dilution.

A stockholder's right not to purchase is seriously undermined if the stock offered is worth substantially more than the offering price. Any purchase at this price dilutes his interest and impairs the value of his original holding. "A corporation is not permitted to sell its stock for a legally inadequate price at least where there is objection. Plaintiff has a right to insist upon compliance with the law whether or not he cares to exercise his option. He cannot block a sale for a fair price merely because he disagrees with the wisdom of the plan but he can insist that the sale price be fixed in accordance with legal requirements." Judicial review in this area is limited to whether under all the circumstances, including the disparity between issuing price of the stock and its true value, the nature of the corporation, the business necessity for establishing an offering price at a certain amount to facilitate raising new capital, and the ability of stockholders to sell rights, the additional offering of securities should be condemned because the directors in establishing the sale price did not fix it with reference to financial considerations with respect to the ready disposition of securities.

Here the obvious disparity in selling price and book value was calculated to force the dissident stockholder into investing additional sums. No valid business justification was advanced for the disparity in price, and the only beneficiaries of the disparity were the two director-stockholders who were eager to have additional capital in the business.

It is no answer to Katzowitz' action that he was also given a chance to purchase additional shares at this bargain rate. The price was not so much a bargain as it was a tactic, conscious or unconscious on the part of the directors, to place Katzowitz in a compromising situation. The price was so fixed to make the failure to invest costly. However, Katzowitz at the time might not have been aware of the dilution because no notice of the effect of the issuance of the new shares on the already outstanding shares was disclosed. In addition, since the stipulation entitled Katzowitz to the same compensation as Sidler and Lasker, the disparity in equity interest caused by their purchase of additional securities in 1961 did not affect stockholder income from Sulburn and, therefore, Katzowitz possibly was not aware of the effect of the stock issuance on his interest in the corporation until dissolution.

No reason exists at this time to permit Sidler and Lasker to benefit from their course of conduct. Katzowitz' delay in commencing the action did not prejudice the defendants. By permitting the defendants to recover their additional investment in Sulburn before the remaining assets of Sulburn are distributed to the stockholders upon dissolution, all the stockholders will be treated equitably. Katzowitz, therefore, should receive his aliquot share of the assets of Sulburn less the amount invested by Sidler and Lasker for their purchase of stock on December 27, 1961.

Accordingly, the order of the Appellate Division should be reversed, with costs, and judgment granted in favor of the plaintiff against the individual defendants.

QUESTIONS

1. What does it mean that the book value of Sulburn's shares was $1,800 at the time the stock was offered to the three shareholders?
2. Is book value the ultimate test of the price at which shares should be offered in a corporation? Why or why not?
3. If you represented Katzowitz at the time new shares were offered at $100 each, how would you advise him assuming he did not have a pressing need for the $2,500 he had just received from Sulburn? Why?
4. The court states that preemptive rights were created by the courts to protect two distinct rights of shareholders—their equity in the corporation and their proportionate voting control. Which is more important here?

5. If shares had been offered to each shareholder at $1,800 per share, would Katzowitz have any complaint?
6. Is this an offer that normally a shareholder like Katzowitz can't refuse? If so, can you think of any justification for allowing directors to make such an offer?
7. If the right to purchase shares for $100 that are worth $1,800 is offered, and Katzowitz chooses not to exercise these rights, is there any other way he can obtain value from the right? If so, why didn't he do so?
8. If you represent a minority investor about to buy shares in a newly organized company, can you think of ways to give someone in Katzowitz's position a veto power over the price of new issues?

Note that, while the dilutive issuance occurred in December 1961, Katzowitz did not bring suit until Sulburn was dissolved and its assets distributed with 46.15% going to Lasker, 46.15% going to Sidler and just 7.7% going to Katzowitz. These proportions reflected each stockholder's ownership position following the December issuance to Lasker and Sidler, but it was the skewed distributions in late 1962 that no doubt prompted Katzowitz to initiate the lawsuit. More generally, it should hardly be surprising that a primary context in which dilution claims arise is the winding-up of a corporation when its residual value is distributed among stockholders according to their ownership positions, as occurs in a liquidation or acquisition. This setting is when the consequence of a dilutive issuance (which may have occurred well in the past) are acutely felt by diluted stockholders.

For Delaware-incorporated companies, this simple fact can raise a practical problem for stockholders seeking to bring dilution claims following the Delaware Supreme Court's 2021 decision in Brookfield Asset Mgmt., Inc. v. Rosson.* Prior to *Brookfield*, a stockholder's standing to bring a claim alleging breach of fiduciary duty relating to a dilutive issuance was governed by the Delaware Supreme Court's 2006 decision in Gentile v. Rossette, 906 A.2d 91 (Del. 2006). *Gentile* held that when a controlling stockholder caused a corporation to issue stock to the stockholders for insufficient consideration (or in the words of the Court, to "overpay" for the consideration with its stock), two types of injuries occur. First, the corporation is harmed by overpaying for an asset, thus giving rise to a potential stockholder derivative claim. In addition, the overpayment transaction also directly harms other stockholders because "the end result of this type of transaction is an improper transfer—or expropriation—of economic value and voting power from the public shareholders to the majority or controlling stockholder." Thus, under *Gentile*, such claims could be brought by a stockholder either as a derivative or a direct action. (For a summary of the difference, see the accompanying sidebar). Moreover, while *Gentile* involved a corporation

* Brookfield Asset Mgmt., Inc. v. Rosson, 261 A.3d 1251 (Del. 2021).

issuing stock to a controlling stockholder, the Delaware chancery court interpreted *Gentile* to permit stockholders to pursue direct challenges to any self-interested, dilutive stock issuances when the facts alleged support a viable claim for breach of the board's duty of loyalty. See Carsanaro v. Bloodhound Tech, Inc., 65 A.3d 618 (Del. Ch. 2013).

Sidebar: Direct vs. Derivative Actions

Formally, fiduciary duties are owed by the directors of a corporation not to shareholders *per se,* but rather to "the corporation." Therefore, a breach of any fiduciary duty gives rise to a potential legal claim against the offending fiduciary that belongs to the corporation. This creates a legal conundrum of sorts, particularly when the offending party or parties sit at the very hub of authority in the firm, including authority over whether to pursue legal claims against negligent or disloyal fiduciaries. It would hardly be surprising if corporate boards proved reluctant to authorize litigation against themselves or a subset of board members, officers, or significant block shareholders.

The principal mechanism to contend with this incentive problem is the shareholder derivative lawsuit—a procedural device that allows a self-appointed shareholder to act as a champion on behalf of the corporation's interest and effectively force the corporation to sue its own fiduciary(ies). Should the shareholder champion prevail, any remedy (non-monetary or monetary) generally goes to the corporation, and thus the shareholder profits only "derivatively" through the change of value in her shares. Courts place significant procedural limits on derivative litigation, requiring heightened pleading standards, continuity of ownership for the filing shareholder, and convincing evidence that the company's board was itself untrustworthy in deciding whether the company should itself pursue litigation.

In certain types of cases, shareholders may have an option to avoid the derivative litigation process altogether and instead sue a fiduciary directly, alleging the breach of a legal duty owed directly to them (rather than derivatively through the corporation). Shareholders may benefit from specific entitlements granted to them through a shareholder agreement or other legal writing that gives them a right to proceed individually (or as a class action) against the offending fiduciary without the need to characterize it derivatively. For Delaware corporations, the dividing line between derivative and direct actions is typically policed by the Delaware Supreme Court's test in Tooley v. Donaldson, Lufkin & Jennette, Inc., 845 A.2d 1031 (Del. 2004). Under the *Tooley* test, determining whether a stockholder's claim is direct or derivative turns on the following two questions: "(1) who suffered the alleged harm (the corporation or the stockholders, individually); and (2) who would receive the benefit of any recovery or other remedy (the corporation or the stockholders, individually)?"

In *Brookfield,* the Delaware Supreme Court overruled *Gentile,* agreeing with the lower court that "dilution claims are classically derivative, i.e., 'the quintessence of a claim belonging to an entity: that fiduciaries, acting in a way that breaches their duties, have caused the entity to exchange assets at a loss.' " As a result, a stockholder seeking to bring a fiduciary duty claim alleging wrongful dilution must now proceed solely by way of a derivative claim. The problem for such a stockholder, however, is that derivative claims require something not required for direct claims: Satisfaction of the continuous ownership rule. Specifically, to have standing to bring a derivative action, a plaintiff must establish that her share ownership was continuous and uninterrupted from the time of the alleged wrongs through the pendency of the action.

Now recall that diluted shareholders are apt to delay bringing a claim for wrongful dilution until a liquidity event when shareholders experience the consequence of the dilutive issuance. Critically, because of the continuous ownership rule, all diluted shareholders will lack standing to bring a derivative claim alleging wrongful dilution if the liquidity event happens to be a merger of the issuing company, which formally swaps a stockholder's share entitlement for the merger consideration. To be sure, the merger does nothing to remedy the corporate injury that occurred from the cheap stock issuance, and the right to pursue an action against the fiduciaries who caused it to occur remains an entitlement of the issuing corporation. But like all assets and rights of the issuing corporation, the right to bring such an action is henceforth "owned" by the acquiring firm.

Does all of this mean that, following a merger, the former shareholders of the merged company have no ability to pursue wrongful dilution claims? In *Brookfield,* the Delaware Supreme Court said "no" and provided a potential path forward using a framework it had previously articulated in In re Primedia, Inc. Shareholders Litigation, 67 A.3d 455 (Del. Ch. 2013). In particular, while such shareholders have no right to bring a derivative action, *Primedia* focused on the fact that such shareholders nevertheless retain the right to bring a direct claim with regard to the *merger*. For instance, shareholders have long been entitled to bring a direct action alleging that a board breached its *Revlon* duties to seek the highest value reasonably available for shareholders in the context of a corporate sale or change of control. By analogy, *Primedia* suggested that if a merged corporation's shareholders held derivative claims that will pass to the buyer, these shareholders would have the right to challenge the merger for insufficiently valuing the underlying claims. For instance, just as a former shareholder would have a direct claim that the merger delivered insufficient consideration for a tangible piece of property conveyed in the merger, a shareholder would have a direct claim that insufficient consideration was paid by the buyer for intangible assets that are similarly conveyed, such as the right to bring a lawsuit.

In the case that follows, the venture capital firm New Enterprise Associates (NEA) took up the challenge of bringing such an action alleging wrongful dilution. At about the time *Brookfield* was decided, one of NEA's portfolio companies had conducted an equity financing that severely reduced NEA's ownership position shortly before the company was acquired via a merger. Because of *Brookfield*, NEA lacked standing to challenge the dilutive issuance after the merger, so it sought to attack the transaction instead by challenging the merger itself. (While the equity financing involved the issuance of preferred stock rather than common stock, note that the question of standing at the center of the case would be the same regardless of whether the company had issued common stock or preferred stock in the transaction.) As you read the case, consider the extent to which this type of *Primedia* claim is an adequate substitute for a direct action relating to a dilutive stock issuance.

New Enterprise Associates v. George S. Rich

292 A.3d 112 (Del. Ch. 2023)

■ LASTER, J. TRAVIS, VICE CHANCELLOR.

1. FACTUAL BACKGROUND

A. The Company

Founded in 2012, [Fugue, Inc. or the Company] provides tools to build, deploy, and maintain a cloud infrastructure security platform. Josh Stella was a co-founder of the Company and serves as its Chief Executive Officer.

In 2013, plaintiff Core Capital Partners III, L.P. ("Core Capital") led the Company's seed round. . . .

In 2014, plaintiffs New Enterprise Associates 14, L.P., NEA Ventures 2014, L.P., and NEA: Seed II, LLC, invested in the Company. Each is an investment vehicle or fund sponsored by New Enterprise Associates, a name-brand venture capital firm. The distinctions among the entities are not important for this decision, which for simplicity refers to them as "NEA."

Across multiple rounds of financings, NEA invested a total of $36.1 million in the Company, and Core Capital invested a total of $1.7 million. In return for their investments, NEA and Core Capital received shares of preferred stock.* The rights conferred by their preferred stock included an aggregate liquidation preference equal to their invested capital, and NEA and Core Capital each received the right to appoint one member to the Board. During this period, the Board had five members.

* Preferred stocks are a class of stock which have a preferred right to receive an earmarked dividend payment and the right to payment before common stock if the issuer liquidates. We cover preferred stock in Chapter 7.

B. The Failed Sale Process And The Recapitalization

In the second half of 2020, the Company began exploring strategic alternatives. The principal goal was to find a potential acquirer. The process continued throughout 2020 and into the first quarter of 2021. During that time, the Company engaged with more than fifteen possible buyers.

Toward the end of the first quarter of 2021, Stella told the Board that the Company's efforts to find a buyer had failed. Stella also represented that that Company was running out of money and needed additional capital to continue operating. He indicated that the Company would use the new money to grow its business and position itself better as an acquisition target. According to Stella, that process would take two to three years.

To provide the growth capital that the Company needed, Stella recommended that the Company engage in a recapitalization that would involve the issuance of Series A-1 Preferred Stock to a group of investors led by [George] Rich (the "Recapitalization"). [Eds: Rich was another investor in the company.] Stella represented to the Board and the Company's existing investors that the Recapitalization was the only option available and that a market check for other financing sources had not generated any alternatives.

Based on Stella's representations, the Board authorized management to proceed with the Recapitalization.

C. The Terms Of The Recapitalization

The Company raised roughly $8 million in the Recapitalization. In return for this capital, it issued 13,129,810 shares of Series A-1 Preferred Stock (the "Preferred Stock"), reflecting a purchase price of $0.61 per share. The Recapitalization valued the Company's pre-transaction equity at $10 million.

Rich invested in the Recapitalization through two vehicles: GRI Ventures, LLC, and JMI Fugue, LLC (together, the "Rich Entities"). Both of the Rich Entities were special purpose vehicles that Rich formed for the investment. Rich controlled those vehicles through Rich Family Ventures, LLC. GRI Ventures was designated as the "Lead Investor" for the round. It invested $4,189,999.51 in return for 6,876,743 shares of Preferred Stock. JMI Fugue invested $999,999.62 in return for 1,641,227 shares of Preferred Stock. Together, the Rich Entities held 8,511,970 of the shares of Preferred Stock, representing 65% of the issuance.

Twenty-three other investors participated in the Recapitalization. Eleven already owned common stock in the Company. Another five were Company employees. Only seven appear to be new investors.

NEA and Core Capital were invited to participate. They declined.

For the Company's existing investors, the terms of the Recapitalization were onerous. In the Recapitalization, all of the existing preferred stock was converted into common stock. Before the Recapitalization, the preferred stock held by the Company's investors carried an aggregate liquidation preference of $74.6 million, with $37.7 million associated with shares of preferred stock held by NEA and Core Capital. The conversion into common stock wiped out the liquidation preference.

After the Recapitalization, only the new Preferred Stock carried a liquidation preference. Not only that, but it was a supercharged liquidation preference equal to two times invested capital. The Preferred Stock was also participating preferred, meaning that if there was a liquidity event, the holders of Preferred Stock would (i) receive a payment equal to two times their invested capital before any amounts reached the common stockholders and (ii) have the right to participate pro rata with the common stockholders in any further distributions.

The effect of the Recapitalization on the existing investors was dramatic. NEA's economic ownership in the Company declined from 32% of the equity value before the Recapitalization to 14% afterward. Core Capital's economic ownership in the Company declined from just under 3% before the Recapitalization to less than 1% afterward.

From a governance standpoint, the effect of the Recapitalization was even more significant. The Company's post-transaction capital structure consisted of 8,921,712 shares of common stock and 13,129,810 shares of Preferred Stock. The Preferred Stock voted on an as-converted basis, giving it 60% of the Company's voting power. The Preferred Stock also carried class voting rights, and the approval of the Preferred Stock voting as a separate class was required for significant corporate actions, including engaging in a merger, a sale of assets, or any issuance of shares; increasing the number of directors; amending the certificate of incorporation or the bylaws; and dissolving the Company. Because the Rich Entities acquired 65% of the issuance, they controlled the voting rights that the Preferred Stock carried. On a fully diluted basis, the Rich Entities owned shares carrying 39% of the Company's voting power.

As part of the Recapitalization, the Company and certain of its stockholders entered into a Fourth Amended and Restated Voting Agreement dated as of April 30, 2021 (the "Voting Agreement"). All of the purchasers of Preferred Stock executed the Voting Agreement, as did twenty-nine holders of common stock, including NEA and Core Capital (the "Signatory Stockholders").

Under the Voting Agreement, the Signatory Stockholders agreed to vote for (i) one director designated by GRI Ventures, who initially was Rich, (ii) a second director designated by the holders of a majority of the Preferred Stock, who initially was [David] Rutchik, (iii) a third director elected by a majority of the Preferred Stock held by investors other than GRI Ventures, who initially was John Morris, (iv) a fourth director who would be the CEO, and (v) a fifth director designated by all the outstanding stock voting together as a single class, who initially was

Wayne Jackson. Because the Rich Entities held approximately 65% of the Preferred Stock, they had the contractual authority to designate the first two of the five directors. Because the Rich Entities controlled 39% of the Company's fully diluted voting power, they had an outsized voice in the selection of the fifth director.

Morris and Jackson had been directors of the Company before the Recapitalization. Rutchik was one of the twenty-three individuals and entities who participated in the Recapitalization. Through the Rutchik Descendants' Trust (the "Rutchik Trust"), Rutchik paid $324,999.41 to acquire 533,398 shares of Preferred Stock. Rutchik also was affiliated with Nodozac LLC, which paid $99,999.54 to acquire 164,122 shares of Preferred Stock. Through his affiliates, Rutchik acquired a total of 697,520 shares, representing 5% of the issuance. . . .

The Recapitalization became effective on April 30, 2021. Shortly before the effective time, Stella and Rich proposed to increase the size of the Recapitalization from $8 million to $10 million. The Board, which still included representatives of NEA and Core Capital, rejected that proposal. It is reasonable to infer that the existing investors did not want to suffer the additional dilution from a larger investment and believed that the slightly smaller investment would fund the Company to a liquidity event. At a minimum, having $8 million on its books would put the Company in a stronger position to negotiate if it sought additional capital.

D. An Expression Of Interest

In late June 2021, something unexpected happened. Guy Podjarny, the founder and CEO of Snyk Limited, contacted Stella about a potential strategic transaction. Snyk is an England-registered corporation with its headquarters in Boston, Massachusetts. Snyk provides a developer security platform. . . . The Board did not disclose Snyk's expression of interest to any of the stockholders. . . .

E. The Second Offering

On July 14, 2021, Morris and Jackson resigned from the Board, leaving Rich, Rutchik, and Stella as the only three directors. One week later, on July 21, the Board authorized the Company to issue a total of 3,938,941 additional shares of Preferred Stock, which increased the outstanding shares of Preferred Stock by 18% (the "Second Offering").

Rather than treating the Second Offering as a new transaction, the Board decided to amend the terms of the stock purchase agreement governing the Recapitalization to encompass the Second Offering. By doing so, the Board permitted the shares to be issued at the same price and with the same generous terms that Rich and his co-investors had extracted in April 2021 when the Company was low on cash, had no other sources of financing, and had no prospect of a near-term sale. Three months later, the Company had $8 million on its books and had received an inbound expression of interest. . . . .

The buyers in the Second Offering were the Rich Entities, the Rutchik Trust, and six other entities and individuals. . .

The Rich Entities acquired another 2,790,086 shares of Preferred Stock, representing 70% of the Second Offering. That purchase brought their total ownership to 11,302,056 shares of Preferred Stock, or 66% of the class. George Rich, Jr. acquired 164,122 shares of Preferred Stock, representing 5% of the Second Offering and another 1% of the class. After the Second Offering, Rich and his son controlled 44% of the Company's outstanding voting power.

Rutchik acquired another 328,245 shares, representing 8% of the Second Offering. Through the Rutchik Trust, he already owned 533,398 shares of Preferred Stock, and through Nodozac, he owned another 164,122 shares, giving him a total of 1,025,765 shares, or 6% of the class. After the Second Offering, the shares Rutchik controlled carried 3.9% of the Company's outstanding voting power. If Rich and Rutchik acted together, they controlled 48% of the Company's outstanding voting power.

The Second Offering raised another $2,402,754.01 for the Company. When added to the $8 million raised in the Recapitalization, the Company had raised a total of $10.4 million, before transaction costs. . . .

F. The Option Grants

On July 29, 2021, the Board granted stock options to acquire 6,029,555 shares of common stock at an exercise price of $0.10 per share (the "Option Grants"). Of that total, 2,945,352 options were issued to thirty-one different employees and two advisors (the "Disinterested Grants"). The remaining 3,084,203 options, representing 51% of the total, went to the members of the Board (the "Interested Grants").

Stella received the vast majority of the Interested Grants, presumably because he was the CEO. His grant of 2,050,227 options represented two thirds of the Interested Grants and one third of the Option Grants as a whole. . . . Rutchik received 886,265 options, representing 29% of the Interested Grants and 15% of the Option Grants as a whole. He received the largest grant of options after Stella. . . . Rich received options on 147,711 shares, the same as the sixth-highest employee after Stella. . . .

G. The Merger Negotiations And Term Sheet

While these events were transpiring, discussions with Snyk moved forward. . . . On December 18, 2021, the Board informed the Company's stockholders that Snyk had agreed to a term sheet to acquire the Company for $120 million in cash. That was the first time that the plaintiffs heard about the discussions with Snyk. Before then, the plaintiffs believed that the Company had abandoned its efforts to find an acquirer in April and that management was focusing on growing the business. . . .

* * *

I. The Merger

On February 17, 2022, the Company announced that it had entered a merger agreement with Snyk and closed the transaction (the "Snyk Merger"). . . .

The waterfall showed that the Rich Entities received $14,570,213.04 in proceeds for the 3,282,453 shares of the Preferred Stock they had purchased in the Second Offering for $2,002,296.33, reflecting an increase in value of 728%. The Rutchik Trust received $1,457,019.97 in proceeds for the 328,245 shares of the Preferred Stock it purchased in the Second Offering for $200,229.45, thereby achieving the same percentage gain. On a per share basis, the Rich Entities and the Rutchik Trust bought shares of Preferred Stock at $0.61 per share. Through the Snyk Merger, they sold at $4.44 per share of Preferred Stock.

Stella, Rich, and Ruchik's options vested as a result of the Snyk Merger. In the transaction, the common stock was valued at $3.22 per share. Net of the exercise price of $0.10 per share, the option holders received $3.10 per share. The Interested Grants generated total net proceeds of $9,623,389.20: Stella received net proceeds of $6,397,158.18; Rutchik received net proceeds of $2,765,340.43; and Rich received net proceeds of $460,890.59.

In total, through the Second Offering and the Interested Grants, Rich, Rutchik, and Stella received $25,650,622.21 in net proceeds from the Snyk Merger.

Part of the defendants' gains came at the expense of the Company's other stockholders. Without the Second Offering and Interested Grants, the merger consideration that Rich, Rutchik, and Stella received for those shares would have been available for distribution pro rata to all of the stockholders. Yes, the Rich Entities and the Rutchik Trust would have received their proportionate share based on the Preferred Stock they acquired in the Recapitalization, but their pro rata share would have been a fraction of the amounts they extracted through the Second Offering and the Interested Grants. Through those transactions, the Rich Entities and the Rutchik Trust increased their net take at the expense of the Company's other stockholders. Through the Interested Grants, Stella gained all of the equity interests that provided him with a share of the merger consideration. . . .

H. This Litigation

On May 9, 2022, NEA and Core Capital filed this lawsuit. The operative complaint contains eight counts. . .

Counts VI, VII, and VIII challenge the Snyk Merger. Count VI contends that Rich, Rutchik, and Stella breached their fiduciary duties as directors by approving the Snyk Merger. Count VII advances a similar theory against the Rich Entities for breaching their fiduciary duties as controlling stockholders. Count VIII alleges that the Rutchik Trust aided and abetted the fiduciaries' breaches of duty. . . .

II. LEGAL ANALYSIS

The defendants have moved to dismiss the complaint under Rule 12(b)(6) on the grounds that it fails to state a claim on which relief can be granted. . . .

I have previously attempted to explain why a claim involving the issuance of equity to an insider inflicts both an injury at the entity level and an injury at the investor level, with the injury primarily felt at the investor level and the corporate-level injury deriving only from the legal construct that a corporation's shares (representing proportionate ownership interests in the firm) are assets of the firm itself.[26] But that doctrinal battle has been lost, with the Delaware Supreme Court holding definitively that claims for equity dilution are only and always derivative. *Brookfield*, 261 A.3d at 1263.

* * *

E. Count VI: The Claim That The Director Defendants Breached Their Fiduciary Duties By Approving The Snyk Merger

In Count VI of the complaint, NEA and Core Capital challenge the Snyk Merger on the theory that (i) it was an interested transaction that conferred unique benefits on the defendants by extinguishing the plaintiffs' standing to maintain derivative claims and (ii) the merger consideration did not take into account the value of the derivative claims. In advancing this theory, the plaintiffs allege that the Second Offering and Option Grants were interested transactions in their own right and that the defendants would not have been able to show that those transactions were entirely fair (the "Interested Transaction Claims"). . . .

Evaluating whether the plaintiffs have stated a claim against the Snyk Merger involves a two-step process. First, the plaintiffs must show that they have standing to challenge the Snyk Merger. Second, the plaintiffs must have stated a claim against the defendants on which relief can be granted.

---

26 See *In re El Paso Pipeline P'rs, L.P. Deriv. Litig.*, 132 A.3d 67, 95–118 (Del. Ch. 2015) (holding that purchase of asset from controller in return for stock inflicted an injury that was primarily direct but, at a minimum, both derivative and direct, such that plaintiffs retained standing to pursue a claim after a subsequent controller squeeze-out), rev'd sub nom. *El Paso Pipeline GP Co., L.L.C. v. Brinckerhoff*, 152 A.3d 1248 (Del. 2016) (holding that purchase of asset from controller in return for stock was solely derivative such that standing to pursue a claim was extinguished by a subsequent controller squeeze-out merger leaving plaintiff with alternative of challenging the fairness of the merger); *Carsanaro v. Bloodhound Techs., Inc.*, 65 A.3d 618, 654–61 (Del. Ch. 2013) (holding that interested recapitalization involving dilutive issuance inflicted an injury that was primarily direct but, at a minimum, both derivative and direct), abrogated in part by El Paso, 152 A.3d at 1264 (rejecting analysis of dilution claim as having both direct and derivative components).

1. The Plaintiffs' Standing To Challenge The Snyk Merger

The Delaware Supreme Court has endorsed a pleading-stage framework that this court used in the *Primedia* decision to evaluate whether a plaintiff had standing to challenge a merger based on the extinguishment of derivative standing. . . . The *Primedia* decision described the framework as follows:

> A plaintiff claiming standing to challenge a merger directly under *Parnes* because of a board's alleged failure to obtain value for an underlying derivative claim must meet a three part test. First, the plaintiff must plead an underlying derivative claim that has survived a motion to dismiss or otherwise could state a claim on which relief could be granted. Second, the value of the derivative claim must be material in the context of the merger. Third, the complaint challenging the merger must support a pleadings-stage inference that the acquirer would not assert the underlying derivative claim and did not provide value for it.

In re Primedia, Inc. S'holders Litig., 67 A.3d 455, 477 (Del. Ch. 2013). In this case, the plaintiffs can meet all of the *Primedia* requirements.

a. Viable Derivative Claims

The first *Primedia* element is met because the plaintiffs have pled derivative claims that would survive a Rule 12(b)(6) motion to dismiss. . . .

The Second Offering was an interested transaction to which the entire fairness test would apply. At the time of the Second Offering, the Board comprised Rich, Rutchik, and Stella. None qualify as disinterested and independent.

For a director to be disinterested, the director "can neither appear on both sides of a transaction nor expect to derive any personal financial benefit from it in the sense of self-dealing, as opposed to a benefit which devolves upon the corporation or all stockholders generally." *Aronson,* 473 A.2d at 812. The benefit that the director receives must be sufficiently material to rebut the presumption of loyalty. *Technicolor*, 634 A.2d at 363. "Directorial interest also exists where a corporate decision will have a materially detrimental impact on a director, but not on the corporation and the stockholders." *Rales*, 634 A.2d at 936.

Rich and Rutchik both approved the Second Offering and participated in it. They stood on both sides of the transaction and benefitted from it. . . .

Stella was the CEO. He reported to the Board majority consisting of Rich and Rutchik, and Rich controlled the Company through the Rich Entities. Under the great weight of Delaware precedent, senior corporate officers generally lack independence for purposes of evaluating matters that implicate the interests of either a controller or a conflicted board majority. Stella did not participate in the Second Offering and therefore was not interested in that transaction, but he was not independent of Rich and Rutchik for purposes of the decision to approve it.

Because there were no disinterested and independent directors to approve the Second Offering, the entire fairness standard applies. The plaintiffs have pled facts supporting an inference of unfairness. When approving the Second Offering, Rich, Rutchik, and Stella allowed the participating stockholders, including Rich and Rutchik and their affiliates, to acquire Preferred Stock at the same price and on the same terms that Rich had extracted three months before, in April 2021, when the Company was running out of money and had spent six months exploring a potential sale in an effort that failed to generate any interest. When Rich negotiated that transaction, he was the only game in town, and he held all the cards. He was able to secure a deal that valued the Company's existing equity at only $10 million, he forced all of the existing preferred stockholders to convert their shares into common stock and give up all of their special rights, and he extracted Preferred Stock with powerful terms, including a 2× liquidation preference. After the Recapitalization injected $8 million into the Company, the situation was different. The Company had enough cash to operate for a significant period. Moreover, the Company had received the inbound expression of interest from Snyk. Although preliminary, that expression of interest changed the environment from one in which no one had shown any interest that would validate the Company's worth to one in which a third party had expressed interest in an acquisition. It is reasonable to infer that using the distressed-entity pricing from April for a non-distressed transaction in July was not entirely fair. . .

It is reasonable to infer that the Second Offering would be subject to the entire fairness test and that the transaction was not entirely fair. It is therefore reasonable to infer that a derivative claim challenging the Second Offering would survive a motion to dismiss. . . .

[With respect to the Interested Grants, they] covered 3,084,203 shares and represented 51% of the total Option Grants. Rich, Rutchik, and Stella thus granted themselves more options than they awarded to thirty-one different employees and two advisors. . . .

When directors make sizable grants of in-the-money options to themselves, the directors must establish the fairness of their actions. Using the $1.12 per share figure as a plug number, the directors granted themselves options that were in the money to the tune of $2,091,231, setting aside any increase in value above $1.12 from the Company's improved position relative to April 2021, and setting aside any additional contingent value calculated by another method. . . .

A derivative challenge to the Interested Grants would survive a motion to dismiss under Rule 12(b)(6).

b. A Material Amount In The Context Of The Snyk Merger

The second *Primedia* element is met because it is reasonably conceivable that the value of the Interested Transaction Claims was material in the context of the Snyk Merger. There is no bright-line figure for materiality. *Goldstein*, 2022 WL 1797224, at *11. One place to look for pleading-stage guidance is the 5% rule of thumb that laypeople use as a rough guide. *Id.*

Based on the complaint and the documents it incorporates by reference, it is possible to make some rough, pleading-stage estimates of the value of the Interested Transaction Claims. Working backwards from the complaint's allegations that each share of Preferred Stock received $4.44 in the deal and each share of common stock received $3.22, it is possible to estimate total deal consideration at $123,324,378.68 (without the proceeds from option exercise).[38]

Using the waterfall of a liquidation preference for the Preferred Shares equal to two times the purchase price of $0.61 per share, followed by a distribution of the remaining proceeds pro rata to all holders of common and Preferred Stock, it is possible to estimate that the Second Offering alone resulted in Rich, Rutchik, and Stella receiving $5 million more than they would have received if the Second Offering had not taken place. That amount represents 4% of the transaction proceeds, which is inferably a material percentage of the transaction consideration. . . .

Based on the court's estimates, the Interested Grants alone resulted in Rich, Rutchik, and Stella receiving $5.4 million more than they would have received if the Interested Grants had not taken place. That amount represents 4.4% of the transaction proceeds, which is again a material percentage of the transaction consideration. . .

Based on the court's estimates, the combination of the Second Offering and the Interested Grants resulted in Rich, Rutchik, and Stella receiving $11.9 million more than they would have received if the Interested Grants had not taken place. That amount represents 9.7% of the transaction proceeds, which is again a material percentage of the transaction consideration. . . .

Those are headline numbers. Any litigation involves risk, so the risk-adjusted value of the Interested Transaction Claims would be lower. It also seems likely that the defendants would be able to prove that Stella was entitled to an option grant of some magnitude. His grant is quite large, and perhaps the plaintiffs are correct that a portion of it represented a reward for supporting the Recapitalization and going along

---

[38] 8,921,712 shares of common stock plus 6,029,555 additional shares from option exercise = 14,951,267 shares of common.

14,951,267 shares of common * $3.22 per share = $48,143,079.74.

17,068,751 shares of Preferred Stock * $4.44 = $75,785,254.44.

Total distributions include $602,955.50 from option exercise at $0.10 per share.

$48,143,079.74 + $75,785,254.44 – $602,955.50 = $123,325,378.68.

with the Second Offering. *See* Compl. ¶ 60. But some of it (maybe most or all of it) represented legitimate incentive compensation for his role as CEO. All of those issues can be hashed out later in the case. At the pleading stage, it is reasonably conceivable that the value of the Interested Transaction Claims was material.

c. Whether Snyk Would Assert The Derivative Claims

The third *Primedia* element asks whether the complaint challenging the merger supports a pleading-stage inference that the acquirer would not assert the underlying derivative claims and did not provide value for them. The facts of the complaint strongly support an inference that Snyk will not assert the Interested Transaction Claims or the Disclosure Claim.

When evaluating whether an acquirer is likely to assert a derivative claim and therefore to have included value for that claim in the deal consideration, it is helpful to divide the litigation assets that an acquirer might purchase and assert into two categories: (i) external claims against third parties, such as contract claims, tort claims, and similar causes of action ("External Claims") and (ii) internal claims against sell-side fiduciaries ("Internal Claims").[44] There is no reason to think either that an acquirer would not determine disinterestedly whether to assert an External Claim or that the merger price would not incorporate an assessment of the value of that claim.[45] By contrast, there is ample reason to think that an acquirer would never assert, and therefore would not pay for, Internal Claims.[46]

It is reasonable to infer that Snyk will not cause the Company to challenge the Second Offering or the Interested Grants by asserting the Interested Transaction Claims or the Disclosure Claim. The third and final element of the *Primedia* test is met.

2. Whether The Challenge To The Snyk Merger States A Viable Claim

Meeting the *Primedia* test establishes that the plaintiff has standing to challenge a merger based on its failure to provide value for derivative claims. The existence of standing to sue does not mean that a complaint necessarily states a claim on which relief can be granted. . . . The court must separately analyze whether there are grounds to second-guess the merger.

"Any board negotiating the sale of a corporation should attempt to value and get full consideration for all of the corporation's material

---

[44] *See Primedia,* 67 A.3d at 483–84; Note, *Survival of Rights of Action After Corporate Merger*, 78 Mich. L. Rev. 250, 263–70 (1979) [hereinafter Survival of Rights].

[45] *See Primedia,* 67 A.3d at 483–84; Survival of Rights, *supra*, at 263–66.

[46] *Golaine v. Edwards*, 1999 WL 1271882, at *5 (Del. Ch. Dec. 21, 1999) (noting that such claims "usually die as a matter of fact"); *Penn Mart Realty Co. v. Perelman*, 1987 WL 10018, at *2 (Del. Ch. Apr. 15, 1987) ("I agree that it is highly unlikely that Pantry Pride, which now controls Revlon, will seek to redress the allegedly excessive severance payments or allegedly excessive fees and therefore these abuses (if they are abuses) are not likely to be addressed.").

assets," including litigation assets. *Massey Energy*, 2011 WL 2176479, at *3; *accord Merritt v. Colonial Foods, Inc.*, 505 A.2d 757, 764 (Del. Ch. 1986) (Allen, C.). "The degree to which a court will examine a board's success at this task depends on the standard of review." *Primedia*, 67 A.3d at 486. If the business judgment rule applies to the decision to approve the merger, then the court will not second guess the board's effort. If the entire fairness standard applies, then a plaintiff who has already gained standing to sue by pleading facts supporting an inference that the merger consideration did not include value for the derivative claims will have stated a claim on which relief can be granted.

The analysis in this case is straightforward. Rich, Rutchik, and Stella were the directors who approved the Second Offering and the Interested Grants. Their actions gave rise to the Interested Transaction Claims and the Disclosure Claim, which were assets of the Company. *Orbit/FR*, 2023 WL 128530, at *4 (explaining that a controller's pre-transaction looting of the company gave rise to "a chose-in-action as an asset belonging to Orbit[ ] for breach of fiduciary duty"). Rich, Rutchik, and Stella then approved a sale of the Company to Snyk that inferably did not afford any value to those assets, and the merger simultaneously conferred a benefit on the directors by extinguishing the sell-side stockholders' standing to assert the Interested Transaction Claims and the Disclosure Claim. All three members of the Board were therefore interested in the Snyk Merger, and the entire fairness test applies. *Cf. id.* at *4 (applying entire fairness test where the interested defendant was a controller).

For the reasons already discussed, it is reasonably conceivable that the consideration received by the stockholders who were not affiliated with the directors was not entirely fair because the directors approved a merger that diverted consideration to themselves through the shares of Preferred Stock issued in the Second Offering and the options granted in the Interested Grants. That is another way of saying that the consideration did not afford value for the Interested Transaction Claims and the Disclosure Claim. It is therefore reasonably conceivable that the Snyk Merger was not entirely fair. The plaintiffs have stated a claim on which relief can be granted.

[Eds. The court used the same two-part framework to assess whether NEA had standing to bring Count VII (the claim that the Rich Entities breached their fiduciary duty to NEA as a controlling stockholder by approving the Synk merer) and Count VIII (the claim that Rutchik Trust aided and abetted the directors in breaching their fiduciary duties by approving the Synk merger). In both instances, the court first found that, prior to the merger, NEA would have had a material derivative claim against Rich as a controlling stockholder in participating in the dilutive transactions as well as a material aiding and abetting claim against the Rutchik Trust for its knowing participation in the fiduciary breaches relating to the dilutive transactions. Having established NEA's standing to bring each claim, the court then concluded each claim represented a viable cause of action since one could reasonably infer that the Snyk merger did not afford any value to these claims. Thus, the court refused to dismiss any of the claims.]

QUESTIONS

1. The third *Primedia* factor asks whether the buyer is likely to pursue the alleged derivative claim. Why did the court infer that Synk would be unlikely to pursue a claim against Rich, Stella or Rutchik? If it is indeed a viable claim, why wouldn't Synk want to collect whatever it could against these individuals for breaching their fiduciary duty to Fugue prior to the merger?
2. To the extent NEA prevails in its claim that the merger provided insufficient value for Fugue's derivative claims, what damages will it be entitled to receive?
3. Recall the damages awarded in the *Katzowitz* case. In effect, Katzowitz was placed in the same economic position that he would have enjoyed if the dilutive transaction never occurred. By this logic, what damages should NEA receive to be made whole for the wrongful dilution that occurred from the Second Offering and the Interested Grants? Would this amount be more or less than the amount you calculated when answering the prior question? What do you think is the proper measure of damages for a stockholder who receives a de minimis payout in a merger due to a board's wrongful dilutive issuances in the past?

C. DILUTION BY DESIGN

As suggested by the *Katzowitz* case, stockholder concerns about the risk of dilution might also make it a potentially useful tool to encourage stockholders to continue to provide financing to a company. Most notably, an early-stage firm may need multiple rounds of investment as it develops its business plan. In these situations, an initial group of investors may each agree to invest a certain sum in the enterprise. But when all of the funds are not needed immediately—as can be the case when a project is built, developed or acquired in stages—then the stockholders could agree to contribute some initial sum along with a commitment to supply additional funds later as needs arise. For example, they might agree to make specified payments over time or agree that the firm can simply issue a call on them for additional funds as necessary—perhaps when specified business milestones have been met. But what happens if an investor fails to pay his or her agreed share at that later point in time? This may occur because the investment no longer looks so rosy, or because the investor now has found a higher-yielding project for the remaining funds. In some cases, it may be that if the investor fails to contribute, the remaining investors will feel compelled to make-up the difference by contributing more than they originally planned. If things have gone badly, and more money is needed to salvage some part of the investment, the non-contributing investor may benefit from the investments of the others, at no cost to him—a free rider problem. In such a setting, a company and its investors may agree to use "penalty dilution" to mitigate the likelihood of this problem.

To see how penalty dilution works, let's return to the NewCo problem immediately after Janet's original purchase of 60 shares of Common Stock for $10/share. As before, assume that the capitalization of the company is set forth in Table 5-1 with Janet holding 60 shares of Common Stock and Francis Founder holding 40 shares of Common Stock. Now imagine that NewCo has gotten off to a bad start: it has encountered some unexpected difficulties developing a key product, and the valuation of NewCo has declined to $500. It is in desperate need of $1,000.

Let's consider the incentives of Janet to purchase her pro-rata share of a new offering of Common Stock using a pre-money valuation of NewCo equal to its fair market value of $500. The company's fully-diluted capitalization prior to the financing is 100 shares, so the company might offer 200 shares at $5/share (i.e., $500 pre-money valuation/100 pre-money fully-diluted shares suggests a current price of $5 per share). If successful in raising the funds, this would mean the post-financing value of the company would be $1,500 ($500 pre-financing value + $1,000 of new cash). The company hopes Janet can purchase her pro-rata share, or 120 shares for $600 (i.e., 60% × 200 shares). Consider the economic consequences to Janet of participating (and assuming others purchase the remaining 40% of the offering):

Janet's Economic Position if She Participates at Pro-Rata:

Post-Financing Economic Position: (60 + 120)/300 × $1,500	=	$900
Total Investment: −$600 (original $) + −$600 (new $)	=	−$1,200
Loss:	=	−$300

Now let's look at her position if she sits on the sidelines, and the company is forced to raise the capital from new investors:*

Janet's Economic Position if She Does NOT Participate at Pro-Rata:

Post-Financing Economic Position: 60/300 × $1,500	=	$300
Total Investment: −$600 (original $)	=	−$600
Loss:	=	−$300

In either scenario, she expects a $300 loss. But if she participates, Janet will have placed an additional $600 at risk. Given the company's difficulties, this may strike Janet as an unappealing risk to take.

* This assumes that, as in the original scenario, Janet does not have any antidilution protection.

Now consider Janet's incentives if the company raises the $1,000 by selling 500 shares of Common Stock at $2/share—a price well below the fair market value of $5/share. If she participates at her pro-rata share, she would purchase 300 shares (i.e., 500 × 60%) for $600.

Janet's Economic Position if She Participates at Pro-Rata:

Post-Financing Economic Position: (60 + 300)/600 × $1,500	=	$900
Total Investment: −$600 (original $) + −$600 (new $)	=	−$1,200
Loss:	=	−$300

Not much appears to have changed relative to the company offering stock at $5/share. However, when we look at the cost to Janet of not participating, we see the downside to Janet is much greater when the stock offering is set at $2/share:

Janet's Economic Position if She Does NOT Participate at Pro-Rata:

Post-Financing Economic Position: 60/600 × $1,500	=	$150
Total Investment: −$600 (original $)	=	−$600
Loss:	=	−$450

Thus, by offering stock at a price below its fair market value, a company can put considerable pressure on existing stockholders to participate in a stock financing. Of course, just because the economics of dilution produce this result does not necessarily mean it is a viable or wise strategy for a company to pursue. Among other things, the transaction would have to be approved by the company's board of directors and, potentially, by the company's stockholders as well (depending on whether the company has sufficient authorized shares and on whether stockholders have special voting rights over new issuances of stock). Likewise, we saw in the *Katzowitz* case that if any directors (or affiliates of directors) participate in the stock financing, a court could subsequently review the transaction under the entire fairness standard of review. Nonetheless, when a board legitimately believes it is necessary to induce stockholders to participate in a stock financing, there may be valid reasons to price the issuance at a sufficiently cheap price to punish any non-participating stockholders.

D. DILUTION AS A TAKEOVER DEFENSE—THE POISON PILL

Another strategic use of dilution appears in a poison pill takeover defense. The standard poison pill defense (formally known as a shareholder rights plan) involves a company's promise to issue new shares of common stock to all shareholders if an uninvited bidder for control acquires a specified percentage of the company's shares. The pill is painful to the uninvited bidder for two reasons. First, the right to acquire new shares is discriminatory: it goes to all shareholders *except* the uninvited bidder. Second, the new shares can be purchased at a price that is far below fair market value. The goal is not to trigger the pill, but rather to force the uninvited bidder to negotiate with the board instead of pursuing a hostile tender offer. Accordingly, the board is also given the power to redeem the pill for a nominal amount. This means that if the uninvited bidder can convince the board that the transaction makes sense, then the board can remove the pill and the deal can proceed without any dilution.

It is undeniable that the basic design of a poison pill makes it painful to an uninvited bidder, if triggered. But is dilution alone sufficient to deter a determined hostile bidder? Consider the following analysis.

The Illusory Protections of the Poison Pill

by William J. Carney and Leonard A. Silverstein
79 Notre Dame Law Review 179 (2003)

I. THE OPERATION OF A RIGHTS PLAN

Rights are issued as pro rata distributions to all common stockholders.[11] The right is typically the right to purchase one unit of a new series of preferred stock.[12] The preferred stock unit has rights that are essentially equivalent to those of the common, with minor distinctions.[13] These rights are exercisable at the projected "long term value" of the common stock—the price the stock is predicted to reach at the end of the ten year life of the rights—a price typically three to five times higher than the current market price of the common stock.[14] To reach these valuations, financial advisers to the adopting company's board are required to make heroic assumptions about growth rates for company profits—typically in excess of 17% per year compounded for the ten year life of the rights plan.[15]

These rights are initially "stapled" to the common stock, in the sense that they can only be transferred with the common stock, and are not

---

[11] The date of the declaration of the dividend of rights is generally called the "Record Date" or the "Rights Dividend Declaration Date."

[12] While there are no legal barriers to using whole shares of preferred, many companies lack sufficient authorized but unissued shares to accomplish this, and thus use fractions of a share.

[13] Each unit has the same dividend and liquidation rights as the common, with the theoretical difference that the preferred shareholder's rights to payment are "prior" to those of the common, to satisfy what are thought to be legal requirements of a priority of some kind.

[14] See, e.g., Wachtell, Lipton, Rosen & Katz, *The Share Purchase Rights Plan* (1996), *reprinted in* Ronald J. Gilson & Bernard S. Black, THE LAW AND FINANCE OF CORPORATE ACQUISITIONS: 1999 SUPPLEMENT 10, 15 and Martin Lipton & Erica H Steinberger, 1 TAKEOVERS & FREEZEOUTS § 6.03[4][b][i], at 6–61 (Release 27, 1999). A recent study of 341 rights plans adopted in 1998 showed median exercise prices were 5.1 times the price of the common stock at the time of the announcement, but only 3.5 times the high stock price for the 12 months preceding adoption of the rights plan, suggesting that declining stock prices may be a primary motivating factor in the adoption of rights plans. Houlihan Lokey Howard & Zukin, *Stockholder Rights Plan Study* 4 (1999).

[15] The implied annual growth rate for earnings required to achieve these valuations was 17.7%. *Id.*

immediately exercisable on issue.[16] The rights separate from the common stock certificates and rights certificates are issued and become transferable apart from the common stock on a "Distribution Date." This occurs when a bidder appears, either by making a tender offer for a significant block of target shares, typically 30%,[17] or by becoming an "Acquiring Person" by acquiring a somewhat smaller block, typically 15% on the "Acquisition Date".[18] This makes it more difficult for a bidder to make a tender offer for a package that includes both the common stock and the rights because those who hold rights certificates are no longer necessarily identical with the shareholders. Prior to the Acquisition Date, the rights are redeemable for a nominal amount.[19]

The board's power to redeem the rights for a nominal amount generally terminates on the Acquisition Date.[20] This prevents a bidder that has taken a substantial position from waging a proxy fight to replace the board with new members, who will redeem the rights using the bidder's newly acquired shares to win the contest.[21]

More importantly, at the Acquisition Date, the rights are no longer exercisable to acquire a preferred stock unit at an unrealistic price—it was never contemplated that the preferred stock rights would be exercised on their original terms.[22] In the event the bidder acquires a specified substantial block and becomes an "Acquiring Person," the rights "flip in" and become exercisable for the target's common stock (the "flip-in") at a discount, typically 50% of current market value.[23] The exercise

---

16 By the terms of the rights agreement, the rights are initially represented by the common stock certificates, which will contain a notation to this effect.

17 In some plans the rights separate ten days after the date of first announcement that the bidder either acquires the triggering amount of shares or announces a tender offer that would result in such ownership. Wachtell, Lipton, Rosen & Katz, *supra* note 14 at 15.

18 A survey of rights plans adopted in 1998 found thresholds ranging from 10% to 35%, with a median of 15% and a mean of 16%. Houlihan Lokey Howard & Zukin, *supra* note 14 at 2. In 1999, the triggers may have been somewhat lower. More than 75% of the firms adopting or amending rights plans in 1999 set the trigger at or below 15%, with two-thirds of all adopting firms selecting the 15% level. Pat McGurn, *Guest Features—Poison Pills: The Storm of 1999 Trickles into 2000*, INVESTOR RELATIONS BUSINESS, Mar. 20, 2000, in LEXIS/NEWS/ALLNWS. The ISS Study shows that approximately 95 out of 115 plans used a 15% threshold, while approximately ten set the threshold at 10%. ISS Study, *supra* note 1.

19 McGurn, *supra* note 18, at 16.

20 *Id.*

21 It does not prevent a bidder who has not yet reached the triggering amount from waging such a proxy fight, however, as AT&T did in its fight for control of NCR, and as Farley Industries did in its successful attempt to take over West Point-Pepperell, a fabric manufacturer. This threat was the inspiration for the "dead hand" pill, that attempted to protect the tenure of incumbent directors who were not otherwise protected by provisions for a staggered board, removal only for cause, and prohibitions against board-packing.

22 The Internal Revenue Service has concluded that the probability of exercise of these rights is so remote that the distribution of the rights as a dividend does not constitute the distribution of stock or property to shareholders, and thus has no tax consequences—shareholders do not realize any taxable income on the receipt of rights. Rev. Rul. 90–11, 1990–1 C.B. 10.

23 Thus, the holder of a right would obtain the right to purchase $200 worth of target common stock at an exercise of price of $100. See Wachtell, Lipton, Rosen & Katz, *supra* note 14 at 15 and 1 Lipton & Steinberger, *supra* note 14 at § 6.03[4][b][i], at 6–62.

price for the preferred becomes the exercise price for multiple shares of common stock. Thus, if the exercise price was $100 per unit of preferred, the holder of a right now has the right to purchase common stock with a market value (pre-Acquisition Date) of $200 for $100.[24] The key to the operation of this plan is discrimination against the bidder—rights are void in the bidder's hands.

These rights have an important anti-destruction provision—a merger of the target into the bidder does not destroy the rights—they "flip over" to become exercisable in the bidder's common stock, on the same bargain basis as the flip-in rights—a 50% discount, using the same exercise price. Thus the dilution of the bidder's shareholders is identical, whether the flip-in or flip-over rights are triggered.[25]

II. THE IMPACT OF A RIGHTS PLAN

A. *Introductory Problems*

We now examine how a rights plan would operate if triggered. We begin with a simple observation: a rights plan can only dilute the investment that a bidder has already made when it crosses the threshold that triggers the rights. If the threshold is 15%, that is the most that can be taken from a bidder through dilution, hardly enough, by itself, to deter a determined bidder prepared to pay a premium for a target it perceives to be undervalued. Because most rights plans only provide a 50% discount from market price, they will not appropriate all of the bidder's initial investment.

One of the difficulties in examining the operation of rights plans is that none have operated. In the 1980s Sir James Goldsmith acquired a sufficient amount of the stock of Crown Zellerbach Corporation to make its flip-over rights non-redeemable, but did not engage in a self-dealing event, such as a takeout merger, that allowed exercise of the flip-over

---

[24] Because companies may lack sufficient authorized but unissued shares of common stock to honor the rights, some plans now provide for a flip-in to be exercisable in "common stock equivalents," which are generally preferred share units with terms comparable to common stock. The number of preferred units is increased, so the exercise obtains for the rights holder a number of units equal to the number of shares of common stock that two times the exercise price could acquire. Because "blank check" preferred shares can be divided by the board into as many units as the board determines, and because these preferred units are the economic equivalent of the common stock, there is no limit to the number of shares that can be issued on exercise of the rights. See Wachtell, Lipton, Rosen & Katz, *supra* note 14 at 37 (Section 11(a) of the Rights Plan). Another solution provided by many rights plans is to allow the board to exchange the rights for one share of common stock. This avoids forcing shareholders to pay cash to exercise the rights. The difficulty, as we will show, is that the smaller number of dilutive shares issued reduces the dilution of the bidder's investment. See Table 5, *infra*. Finally, many rights plans provide that in the event the issuer lacks sufficient shares to honor all the rights, it will be obligated to pay rights holders "damages"—the difference between the value of what they receive on exercise and the value of what they were entitled to. To avoid insolvency issues, these obligations are generally conditioned on availability of sufficient cash, and create a continuing obligation to pay cash as it becomes legally available for payment.

[25] See text *infra* at Part II.B.7. Both the flip-in and flip-over rights have antidilution protection for rights holders of the type commonly found in convertible securities and options.

rights.[26] No flip-in plan has ever been deliberately triggered,[27] although the authors experienced a close call in one case, and there have been a few other apparently inadvertent triggering events.[28] Several uncertainties present themselves in assessing the impact of a rights plan. If the rights plan flips in, will rights holders exercise immediately or will they wait until immediately before expiration, as rational holders of conventional options will do? While shares should be valued on a fully diluted basis in efficient markets, uncertainty about the target's receipt of cash and its investment or disposition by the target could influence the market value of its stock after the flip-in, and thus the cost of acquisition. We discuss this issue in sections II.B.2 and II.B.6, *infra*.

Because of the lack of operational experience, several other questions cannot be answered definitively. What will a target do with proceeds received from the exercise of the rights? If rights are exercised, the target would receive cash representing a multiple of the aggregate market value of its current equity, and would be unlikely to have any massive positive net present value projects in which to invest. In essence, it will probably hold cash or equivalents. If the proceeds are simply held by the target, the bidder can recapture them upon obtaining 100% control. If they are distributed to other shareholders in a discriminatory manner, the bidder's dilution losses are increased. We explore this in Part II.B.6, *infra*. Similarly, what if rights are not exercised immediately, but are only exercised after the bidder has increased its ownership beyond the minimum amount required to trigger the rights? The obvious answer is that this means the bidder has a larger investment subject to dilution, and thus larger losses. This is also explored in Part II.B.6.

B. *Calculating Bidder Dilution*

We begin our discussion of bidder dilution with a caution: it is only half the picture. Too often analysis stops with an observation that a

---

26 See Carney *supra* note 4 at 264. The earliest rights plans lacked a flip-in feature; they only operated if the bidder engaged in a merger or other business combination with the target.

27 1 Arthur Fleischer, Jr. and Alexander R. Sussman, TAKEOVER DEFENSE, § 5.02[A], 5–18 to –19 (6th ed. 2002).

28 In our case, the investor that crossed the triggering threshold also failed to file a timely Schedule 13D, so there was no public announcement of the acquisition of the amount that would have constituted it an "Acquiring Person," which allowed a settlement. Among the issuers that experienced inadvertent triggering events are Pediatrix Medical Group, Michel Chandler, *Shareholder Nearly Triggers a Poison Pill at Ailing Pediatrix*, MIAMI HERALD, Sept. 21, 1999, C3; Newcor, Inc., News Digest, RUBBER & PLASTICS NEWS, July 24, 2000, p. 4; *Worldtex, Inc., Business Briefs*, THE CHARLOTTE OBSERVER, Mar.29, 2000, LEXIS: News: Allnews; Illini Bank, Craig Woker, *Illinois Bank Sweeps Legal Doubleheader*, THE AMERICAN BANKER, Mar. 3, 2000, 5; Rawlings Sporting Goods Co. Inc., Al Stamborski, *Rawlings and 2 Investors Avoid Triggering Poison Pill*, ST. LOUIS POST DISPATCH, May 7, 1999, C11; BJ Services, David Ivanovich, *BJ Services Swallows Poison Pill; Takeover Defense Set Off by Mistake*, THE HOUSTON CHRONICLE, Jan. 7, 1994, Business Section, 1. Harold Simmons did trigger separation of a flip-in, flip-over plan of NL Industries in the 1980s, by acquiring 20% of its shares, but the flip-in rights did not become exercisable until occurrence of a business combination or the bidder's increase in its holdings by more than 1%. Amalgamated Sugar Co. v. NL Industries, 644 F. Supp. 1229 (S.D.N.Y. 1986). Newell Cos. announced that it would swallow a poison pill of Wm. E. Wright Co., but there is no indication whether it was a flip-in pill. *Newell to Swallow "Poison Pill,"* CHICAGO TRIBUNE, Oct. 21, 1985, Business Section, 3.

hostile bidder's initial investment will be massively diluted by crossing the threshold that permits exercise of the flip-in rights. While this is true, it gives an incomplete picture of the costs imposed by a rights plan on a determined bidder; it is a static rather than a dynamic analysis. As we noted earlier, the typical rights plan's flip-in rights are triggered by a 15% acquisition. If a bidder's initial investment is totally destroyed by the exercise of the rights, the rights plan has added only 15% to the bidder's costs of a total acquisition. Dilution is never 100% because the bidder remains the owner of some diminished percentage of the outstanding shares, so the bidder's actual losses (added costs) will be somewhat less.[29]

We begin our analysis by examining the operation of a typical preferred stock rights plan, with flip-in rights triggered at the 15% level, with the rights exercisable at a 50% discount from market price. We assume that rights have been issued at an exercise price four times the current (pre-bid) market price of the common stock. We further assume immediate exercise of the rights, and receipt of the proceeds by the target. We will then show that triggering flip-in rights at the minimum ownership level is a dominant strategy, because triggering with the bidder owning larger amounts always puts more of the bidder's investment at risk—at least until unrealistically high levels of ownership are attained. Table 1 below sets out the assumptions in our examples:

TABLE 1. ASSUMPTIONS FOR A TYPICAL PREFERRED STOCK RIGHTS PLAN

1.	Target shares outstanding:	1,000,000
2.	Pre-bid market price per share	$ 10.00
3.	Bidder's per share cost for the first 15%:	$ 15.00[30]
4.	Expected takeover bid price per share:	$ 15.00
5.	Exercise price for preferred stock rights:	$ 40.00
6.	Assumed market value per share of target shares for calculating common stock acquisition price:	$ 15.00
7.	Flip-in trigger:	15%
8.	Flip-in discount:	50%
9.	Shares issuable per right if the market price is $15:	5.3333333

1. The Operation of a Flip-In Rights Plan

We now assume that a bidder acquires the minimum amount of shares necessary to trigger the rights, so that shares now trade on a fully diluted basis. Because the bidder receives no rights and suffers dilution,

---

[29] It is impossible for a rights plan to destroy the bidder's entire investment, because whatever the percentage, the bidder retains some shares in the target.

[30] This is a simplifying assumption; it is likely that the bidder's average cost per share for the first 15% will be less than $15 per share. The differences in results are modest, however. See Part II.B.4, *infra*.

its percentage ownership is severely diluted, from 15% to 2.7%. [Eds. Note that, as shown in Table 2, total shares following exercise of the rights will increase from 1,000,000 to 5,333,333; thus, the bidder's 150,000 share position as a percent of outstanding shares declines from 15% to 2.7%]. But, unlike prior examples, we assume that the bidder is determined, and then proceeds to acquire the remaining public shares at the takeover premium of 50% over the pre-bid value of the target.

Table 2 shows the bidder's costs of a complete acquisition using these assumptions:

TABLE 2. BIDDER'S COST OF ACQUISITION USING A MINIMUM PURCHASE WITH A PREFERRED STOCK RIGHTS PLAN

Bidder's initial acquisition of 150,000 shares @ $15.00:		$ 2,250,000
Rights flip in for 5.3333333333 shares for 850,000 rights—		
Shares Outstanding:		
New shares	4,533,333.333	
Original shares	1,000,000	
Total shares	5,533,333.333	
Proceeds of exercise: (*850,000 × $40*):	$34,000,000	
Market's estimate of value of target:	$49,000,000	
Value per fully diluted share (*$49,000,000/5,533,333*):	$ 8.855421	
Value of bidder's 150,000 shares:	$ 1,328,313	
Bidder's dilution losses:	$ 921,688	
Bidder's cost for remaining shares (*5,383,333 × $8.855422*) =		47,671,688
Total Cost to Bidder:		$49,921,688
Less: Dividend of cash proceeds of rights exercise		(34,000,000)
Net Cost to Bidder:		$15,921,688

If we assume that the proceeds of exercise of the rights have been retained intact by the target, once the bidder has gained control it can capture the $34,000,000 proceeds, leaving a net cost of $15,921,688. The dilution loss, $921,688, represents 41% of the bidder's initial investment.[31] Put another and more dynamic way, it represents 9.2% of the target's pre-bid value, or 6.1% of the bidder's original estimate of the

[31] If the target immediately conducted a dividend of the proceeds, before the bidder completed the acquisition, the bidder would receive a small portion (2.71%) of the $34,000,000 dividend. This would amount to $921,400, virtually eliminating the dilution of its investment (but not its ownership percentage) previously suffered. This is explored *infra* in Part II.B.6.

cost of an acquisition, absent the rights plan. Premiums of this general magnitude are supported by studies of the premiums added to the cost of acquisitions by the presence of rights plans.[32]

The expected cost of a rights plan to a bidder is the bidder's cost per share times the number of shares held by the bidder, minus the post-issue (fully diluted) market value of the target's shares held by the bidder, which is a function of the market value of the entire company divided by the post-issue number of target shares. This can be expressed as equation (1):

$$L = ca - \frac{(mx + p)}{x + d} \quad (1)$$

where L = bidder's loss through dilution; c = bidder's average pre-trigger cost per share; m = pre-trigger market price; a = bidder's share ownership at the time flip-in rights are triggered; x = shares outstanding before dilutive issuance; d = number of shares issued in dilutive distribution; p = proceeds from exercise of rights $(x\text{-}a)e$; and e = exercise price of rights.

Equation (1) expresses the obvious truth that the bidder's loss can be no more than the bidder's investment in the target (ma) at the time the rights become exercisable, ameliorated by the new value received upon exercise of the rights (p), and limited by the fact that the bidder will retain some percentage ownership in the firm absent issuance of an infinite number of new shares at a zero exercise price.

At this point you may be wondering whether (and when) a board of directors should be legally authorized to issue a security that discriminates against large shareholders and deters the interest of

[32] The presence of a rights plan increased premiums by almost 8% of firm value, as reported in Georgeson & Company Inc.'s study of premiums obtained by companies with and without pills for the period 1992–1996. Georgeson & Co., *Mergers & Acquisitions: Poison Pills and Shareholder Value, 1992–1996*, https://www.westlaw.com/Document/Ia2277ad1e69a11dbbc53a2a4c439050e/View/FullText.html?transitionType=Default&contextData=(sc.Default)&VR=3.0&RS=cblt1.0. (visited 6/11/03). An earlier study found bid improvements of 14% for targets with pills that were subsequently taken over. Office of the Chief Economist, Securities and Exchange Commission, *The Effects of Poison Pills on the Wealth of Target Shareholders*, 41 (1986). This study examines early versions of rights plans in a small sample, given the date of the study. A Morgan Stanley study of deals between 1988 and 1995 reports gains to firms with pills of approximately 16%. Mark S. Porter, *Poison Pills Add Premium to Deal Pricing*, 10 No. 31 INVESTMENT DEALERS' DIGEST 2 (Aug. 4, 1997); John C. Coates IV, *Empirical Evidence on Structural Takeover Defenses: Where Do We Stand?*, 54 U. MIAMI L. REV. 783, 794, text at n. 44 (2000). Coates notes an update that produced similar results. *Id.* At n. 45, citing Kenneth A. Bertsch, *Poison Pills*, Investor Responsibility Research Center, Corporate Governance Series 1998 Background Report E at 21 (Jun. 25, 1998). Comment & Schwert, *supra* note 1, at 30–31, also find premium increases in this range. These percentage gains are higher than the dilution inflicted by our model. This may be a result of the issuance of more shares than our model suggests. A magazine reported a Morgan Stanley study of acquisitions since 1997 showed a median premium for firms with pills of 35.9% vs. 31.9% for firms without pills. *Daily Briefing: The Bids Sure Are Getting Hostile*, BUSINESS WEEK ONLINE, Jan. 4, 2002, LEXIS. Table 3 demonstrates how increasing the number of shares issued can increase bidder dilution.

would-be acquirers. Delaware took up these important topics in the following seminal case.

Moran v. Household International, Inc.

500 A.2d 1346 (Del.1985)

■ MCNEILLY, JUSTICE.

This case presents to the Court for review the most recent defensive mechanism in the arsenal of corporate takeover weaponry—the Preferred Share Purchase Rights Plan ("Rights Plan" or "Plan"). The validity of this mechanism has attracted national attention. Amici curiae briefs have been filed in support of appellants by the Security and Exchange Commission ("SEC")[1] and the Investment Company Institute. An amicus curiae brief has been filed in support of appellees ("Household") by the United Food and Commercial Workers International Union.

In a detailed opinion, the Court of Chancery upheld the Rights Plan as a legitimate exercise of business judgment by Household. Moran v. Household International, Inc., Del. Ch., 490 A.2d 1059 (1985). We agree, and therefore, affirm the judgment below.

I

The facts giving rise to this case have been carefully delineated in the Court of Chancery's opinion. A review of the basic facts is necessary for a complete understanding of the issues.

On August 14, 1984, the Board of Directors of Household International, Inc. adopted the Rights Plan by a fourteen to two vote.[2] The intricacies of the Rights Plan are contained in a 48-page document entitled "Rights Agreement." Basically, the Plan provides that Household common stockholders are entitled to the issuance of one Right per common share under certain triggering conditions. There are two triggering events that can activate the Rights. The first is the announcement of a tender offer for 30 percent of Household's shares ("30% trigger") and the second is the acquisition of 20 percent of the Household's shares by any single entity or group ("20% trigger").

If an announcement of a tender offer for 30 percent of Household's shares is made, the Rights are issued and are immediately exercisable to purchase 1/100 share of new preferred stock for $100 and are redeemable by the Board for $.50 per Right. If 20 percent of Household's shares are acquired by anyone, the Rights are issued and become non-redeemable

---

1 The SEC split 3–2 on whether to intervene in this case. The two dissenting Commissioners have publicly disagreed with the other three as to the merits of the Rights Plan. 17 Securities Regulation & Law Report 400; The Wall Street Journal, March 20, 1985, at 6.

2 Household's Board has ten outside directors and six who are members of management. Messrs. Moran (appellant) and Whitehead voted against the Plan. The record reflects that Whitehead voted against the Plan not on its substance but because he thought it was novel and would bring unwanted publicity to Household.

and are exercisable to purchase 1/100 of a share of preferred. If a Right is not exercised for preferred, and thereafter, a merger or consolidation occurs, the Rights holder can exercise each Right to purchase $200 of the common stock of the tender offeror for $100. This "flip-over" provision of the Rights Plan is at the heart of this controversy.

Household is a diversified holding company with its principal subsidiaries engaged in financial services, transportation and merchandising. HFC, National Car Rental and Vons Grocery are three of its wholly-owned entities.

Household did not adopt its Rights Plan during a battle with a corporate raider, but as a preventive mechanism to ward off future advances. The Vice-Chancellor found that as early as February 1984, Household's management became concerned about the company's vulnerability as a takeover target and began considering amending its charter to render a takeover more difficult. After considering the matter, Household decided not to pursue a fair price amendment.[3]

In the meantime, appellant Moran, one of Household's own Directors and also Chairman of the Dyson-Kissner-Moran Corporation, ('D-K-M'), which is the largest single stockholder of Household, began discussions concerning a possible leveraged buy-out of Household by D-K-M. D-K-M's financial studies showed that Household's stock was significantly undervalued in relation to the company's break-up value. It is uncontradicted that Moran's suggestion of a leveraged buy-out never progressed beyond the discussion stage.

Concerned about Household's vulnerability to a raider in light of the current takeover climate, Household secured the services of Wachtell, Lipton, Rosen and Katz ("Wachtell, Lipton") and Goldman, Sachs & Co. ("Goldman, Sachs") to formulate a takeover policy for recommendation to the Household Board at its August 14 meeting. After a July 31 meeting with a Household Board member and a pre-meeting distribution of material on the potential takeover problem and the proposed Rights Plan, the Board met on August 14, 1984.

Representatives of Wachtell, Lipton and Goldman, Sachs attended the August 14 meeting. The minutes reflect that Mr. Lipton explained to the Board that his recommendation of the Plan was based on his understanding that the Board was concerned about the increasing frequency of "bust-up"[4] takeovers, the increasing takeover activity in the financial service industry, such as Leucadia's attempt to take over Arco, and the possible adverse effect this type of activity could have on employees and others concerned with and vital to the continuing successful operation of Household even in the absence of any actual bust-

[3] A fair price amendment to a corporate charter generally requires supermajority approval for certain business combinations and sets minimum price criteria for mergers.

[4] "Bust-up" takeover generally refers to a situation in which one seeks to finance an acquisition by selling off pieces of the acquired company.

up takeover attempt. Against this factual background, the Plan was approved.

Thereafter, Moran and the company of which he is Chairman, D-K-M, filed this suit. On the eve of trial, Gretl Golter, the holder of 500 shares of Household, was permitted to intervene as an additional plaintiff. The trial was held, and the Court of Chancery ruled in favor of Household. Appellants now appeal from that ruling to this Court.

II

The primary issue here is the applicability of the business judgment rule as the standard by which the adoption of the Rights Plan should be reviewed. Much of this issue has been decided by our recent decision in Unocal Corp. v. Mesa Petroleum Co., Del. Supr., 493 A.2d 946 (1985). In Unocal, we applied the business judgment rule to analyze Unocal's discriminatory self-tender. We explained:

> When a board addresses a pending takeover bid it has an obligation to determine whether the offer is in the best interests of the corporation and its shareholders. In that respect a board's duty is no different from any other responsibility it shoulders, and its decisions should be no less entitled to the respect they otherwise would be accorded in the realm of business judgment.

Other jurisdictions have also applied the business judgment rule to actions by which target companies have sought to forestall takeover activity they considered undesirable.

* * *

This case is distinguishable from the ones cited, since here we have a defensive mechanism adopted to ward off possible future advances and not a mechanism adopted in reaction to a specific threat. This distinguishing factor does not result in the Directors losing the protection of the business judgment rule. To the contrary, pre-planning for the contingency of a hostile takeover might reduce the risk that, under the pressure of a takeover bid, management will fail to exercise reasonable judgment. Therefore, in reviewing a pre-planned defensive mechanism it seems even more appropriate to apply the business judgment rule. See Warner Communications v. Murdoch, D. Del., 581 F. Supp. 1482, 1491 (1984).

Of course, the business judgment rule can only sustain corporate decision making or transactions that are within the power or authority of the Board. Therefore, before the business judgment rule can be applied it must be determined whether the Directors were authorized to adopt the Rights Plan.

III

Appellants vehemently contend that the Board of Directors was unauthorized to adopt the Rights Plan. First, appellants contend that no provision of the Delaware General Corporation Law authorizes the issuance of such Rights. Secondly, appellant, along with the SEC, contend that the Board is unauthorized to usurp stockholders' rights to receive hostile tender offers. Third, appellants and the SEC also contend that the Board is unauthorized to fundamentally restrict stockholders' rights to conduct a proxy contest. We address each of these contentions in turn.

A.

While appellants contend that no provision of the Delaware General Corporation Law authorizes the Rights Plan, Household contends that the Rights Plan was issued pursuant to 8 Del. C. §§ 151 (g) and 157. It explains that the Rights are authorized by § 157[7] and the issue of preferred stock underlying the Rights is authorized by § 151.[8] Appellants respond by making several attacks upon the authority to issue the Rights pursuant to § 157.

Appellants begin by contending that § 157 cannot authorize the Rights Plan since § 157 has never served the purpose of authorizing a takeover defense. Appellants contend that § 157 is a corporate financing statute, and that nothing in its legislative history suggests a purpose that has anything to do with corporate control or a takeover defense. Appellants are unable to demonstrate that the legislature, in its adoption of § 157, meant to limit the applicability of § 157 to only the issuance of Rights for the purposes of corporate financing. Without such affirmative evidence, we decline to impose such a limitation upon the section that the legislature has not. Compare Providence & Worcester Co. v. Baker, Del. Supr., 378 A.2d 121, 124 (1977) (refusal to read a bar to protective voting provisions into 8 Del. C. § 212(a)).

As we noted in Unocal:

> [O]ur corporate law is not static. It must grow and develop in response to, indeed in anticipation of, evolving concepts and

---

[7] The power to issue rights to purchase shares is conferred by 8 Del. C. § 157 which provides in relevant part:

> Subject to any provisions in the certificate of incorporation, every corporation may create and issue, whether or not in connection with the issue and sale of any shares of stock or other securities of the corporation, rights or options entitling the holders thereof to purchase from the corporation any shares of its capital stock of any class or classes, such rights or options to be evidenced by or in such instrument or instruments as shall be approved by the board of directors.

[8] 8 Del. C. § 151(g) provides in relevant part:

> When any corporation desires to issue any shares of stock of any class or of any series of any class of which the voting powers, designations, preferences and relative, participating, optional or other rights, if any, or the qualifications, limitations or restrictions thereof, if any, shall not have been set forth in the certificate of incorporation or in any amendment thereto but shall be provided for in a resolution or resolutions adopted by the board of directors pursuant to authority expressly vested in it by the provisions of the certificate of incorporation or any amendment thereto, a certificate setting forth a copy of such resolution or resolutions and the number of shares of stock of such class or series shall be executed, acknowledged, filed, recorded, and shall become effective, in accordance with § 103 of this title.

needs. Merely because the General Corporation Law is silent as to a specific matter does not mean that it is prohibited.

Secondly, appellants contend that § 157 does not authorize the issuance of sham rights such as the Rights Plan. They contend that the Rights were designed never to be exercised, and that the Plan has no economic value. In addition, they contend the preferred stock made subject to the Rights is also illusory, citing Telvest, Inc. v. Olson, Del. Ch., C.A. No. 5798, Brown, V.C. (March 8, 1979).

Appellants' sham contention fails in both regards. As to the Rights, they can and will be exercised upon the happening of a triggering mechanism, as we have observed during the current struggle of Sir James Goldsmith to take control of Crown Zellerbach. See Wall Street Journal, July 26, 1985, at 3, 12.* As to the preferred shares, we agree with the Court of Chancery that they are distinguishable from sham securities invalidated in Telvest, *supra*. The Household preferred, issuable upon the happening of a triggering event, have superior dividend and liquidation rights.†

Third, appellants contend that § 157 authorizes the issuance of Rights "entitling holders thereof to purchase from the corporation any shares of its capital stock of any class . . ." (emphasis added). Therefore, their contention continues, the plain language of the statute does not authorize Household to issue rights to purchase another's capital stock upon a merger or consolidation.

Household contends, *inter alia*, that the Rights Plan is analogous to "anti-dilution" provisions which are customary features of a wide variety of corporate securities. While appellants seem to concede that "anti-destruction" provisions are valid under Delaware corporate law, they seek to distinguish the Rights Plan as not being incidental, as are most "anti-destruction" provisions, to a corporation's statutory power to finance itself. We find no merit to such a distinction. We have already rejected appellants' similar contention that § 157 could only be used for financing purposes. We also reject that distinction here.

"Anti-destruction" clauses generally ensure holders of certain securities of the protection of their right of conversion in the event of a merger by giving them the right to convert their securities into whatever securities are to replace the stock of their company. See Broad v. Rockwell International Corp., 5th Cir., 642 F.2d 929, 946, cert. denied, 454 U.S. 965 (1981); Wood v. Coastal States Gas Corp., Del. Supr., 401 A.2d 932, 937–39 (1979); B.S.F. Co. v. Philadelphia National Bank, Del.

* Eds. At the time of adoption of the rights plan, the Household common stock was trading in the range of $30–33. Because each 1/100 had the same dividend and liquidation rights as the common, it was highly unlikely that any shareholder would ever exercise rights to purchase the preferred stock. Rights in Crown Zellerbach preferred were not exercised after Sir James Goldsmith's acquisition of its common stock.

† Eds. Each 1/100 of a share of preferred stock had the same dividend and liquidation rights as the common stock, except (to the extent this is possible), they were prior and superior to the rights of the common stock.

Supr., 204 A.2d 746, 750–51 (1964). The fact that the rights here have as their purpose the prevention of coercive two-tier tender offers* does not invalidate them.

* * *

Having concluded that sufficient authority for the Rights Plan exists in 8 Del. C. § 157, we note the inherent powers of the Board conferred by 8 Del. C. § 141(a), concerning the management of the corporation's "business and affairs" (emphasis added), also provides the Board additional authority upon which to enact the Rights Plan. Unocal, 493 A.2d at 953.[11]

B.

Appellants contend that the Board is unauthorized to usurp stockholders' rights to receive tender offers by changing Household's fundamental structure. We conclude that the Rights Plan does not prevent stockholders from receiving tender offers, and that the change of Household's structure was less than that which results from the implementation of other defensive mechanisms upheld by various courts.

Appellants' contention that stockholders will lose their right to receive and accept tender offers seems to be premised upon an understanding of the Rights Plan which is illustrated by the SEC amicus brief which states:

> "The Chancery Court's decision seriously understates the impact of this plan. In fact, as we discuss below, the Rights Plan will deter not only two-tier offers, but virtually all hostile tender offers."

The fallacy of that contention is apparent when we look at the recent takeover of Crown Zellerbach, which has a similar Rights Plan, by Sir James Goldsmith. Wall Street Journal, July 26, 1985, at 3, 12. The evidence at trial also evidenced many methods around the Plan ranging from tendering with a condition that the Board redeem the Rights, tendering with a high minimum condition of shares and Rights, tendering and soliciting consents to remove the Board and redeem the Rights, to acquiring 50% of the shares and causing Household to self-tender for the Rights. One could also form a group of up to 19.9% and solicit proxies for consents to remove the Board and redeem the Rights.

* Eds. When a bidder makes a tender offer (an invitation to shareholders to tender their shares) at an attractive price above the current market price, and assures those who do not tender that the bidder will engage in a "freeze-out" merger at a lower price, public shareholders may well feel that they are coerced into accepting the offer.

[11] 8 Del. C. § 141(a) provides:

> (a) The business and affairs of every corporation organized under this chapter shall be managed by or under the direction of a board of directors, except as may be otherwise provided in this chapter or in its certificate of incorporation. If any such provision is made in the certificate of incorporation, the powers and duties conferred or imposed upon the board of directors by this chapter shall be exercised or performed to such extent and by such person or persons as shall be provided in the certificate of incorporation.

These are but a few of the methods by which Household can still be acquired by a hostile tender offer.

In addition, the Rights Plan is not absolute. When the Household Board of Directors is faced with a tender offer and a request to redeem the Rights, they will not be able to arbitrarily reject the offer. They will be held to the same fiduciary standards any other board of directors would be held to in originally approving the Rights Plan.

In addition, appellants contend that the deterrence of tender offers will be accomplished by what they label "a fundamental transfer of power from the stockholders to the directors." They contend that this transfer of power, in itself, is unauthorized.

The Rights Plan will result in no more of a structural change than any other defensive mechanism adopted by a board of directors. The Rights Plan does not destroy the assets of the corporation. The implementation of the Plan neither results in any outflow of money from the corporation nor impairs its financial flexibility. It does not dilute earnings per share and does not have any adverse tax consequences for the corporation or its stockholders. The Plan has not adversely affected the market price of Household's stock.

Comparing the Right Plan with other defensive mechanisms, it does less harm to the value structure of the corporation than do the other mechanisms. Other mechanisms result in increased debt of the corporation. See Whittaker Corp. v. Edgar, *supra*, (sale of "prize asset"), Cheff v. Mathes, *supra*, (paying greenmail to eliminate a threat), Unocal Corp. v. Mesa Petroleum Co., *supra*, (discriminatory self-tender).

There is little change in the governance structure as a result of the adoption of the Rights Plan. The Board does not now have unfettered discretion in refusing to redeem the Rights. The Board has no more discretion in refusing to redeem the Rights than it does in enacting any defensive mechanism.

The contention that the Rights Plan alters the structure more than do other defensive mechanisms because it is so effective as to make the corporation completely safe from hostile tender offers is likewise without merit. As explained above, there are numerous methods to successfully launch a hostile tender offer.

C.

Appellants' third contention is that the Board was unauthorized to fundamentally restrict stockholders' rights to conduct a proxy contest. Appellants contend that the "20% trigger" effectively prevents any stockholder from first acquiring 20% or more shares before conducting a proxy contest and further, it prevents stockholders from banding together into a group to solicit proxies if, collectively, they own 20% or more of the stock.[12] In addition, at trial, appellants contended that read literally, the Rights Agreement triggers the Rights upon the mere acquisition of the right to vote 20% or more of the shares through a proxy solicitation, and thereby precludes any proxy contest from being waged.[13]

Appellants seem to have conceded this last contention in light of Household's response that the receipt of a proxy does not make the recipient the "beneficial owner" of the shares involved which would trigger the Rights. In essence, the Rights Agreement provides that the Rights are triggered when someone becomes the "beneficial owner" of 20% or more of Household stock. Although a literal reading of the Rights Agreement definition of "beneficial owner" would seem to include those shares which one has the right to vote, it has long been recognized that the relationship between grantor and recipient of a proxy is one of agency, and the agency is revocable by the grantor at any time. Henn, Corporations § 196, at 518. Therefore, the holder of a proxy is not the "beneficial owner" of the stock. As a result, the mere acquisition of the right to vote 20% of the shares does not trigger the Rights.

The issue, then, is whether the restriction upon individuals or groups from first acquiring 20% of shares before waging a proxy contest fundamentally restricts stockholders' right to conduct a proxy contest. Regarding this issue the Court of Chancery found:

> Thus, while the Rights Plan does deter the formation of proxy efforts of a certain magnitude, it does not limit the voting power of individual shares. On the evidence presented it is highly conjectural to assume that a particular effort to assert shareholder views in the election of directors or revisions of corporate policy will be frustrated by the proxy feature of the Plan. Household's witnesses, Troubh and Higgins described recent corporate takeover battles in which insurgents holding less than 10% stock ownership were able to secure corporate control through a proxy contest or the threat of one.

We conclude that there was sufficient evidence at trial to support the Vice-Chancellor's finding that the effect upon proxy contests will be minimal. Evidence at trial established that many proxy contests are won with an insurgent ownership of less than 20%, and that very large holdings are no guarantee of success. There was also testimony that the key variable in proxy contest success is the merit of an insurgent's issues, not the size of his holdings.

---

[12] Appellants explain that the acquisition of 20% of the shares trigger the Rights, making them non-redeemable, and thereby would prevent even a future friendly offer for the ten-year life of the Rights.

[13] The SEC still contends that the mere acquisition of the right to vote 20% of the shares through a proxy solicitation triggers the rights. We do not interpret the Rights Agreement in that manner.

IV

Having concluded that the adoption of the Rights Plan was within the authority of the Directors, we now look to whether the Directors have met their burden under the business judgment rule.

The business judgment rule is a "presumption that in making a business decision the directors of a corporation acted on an informed basis, in good faith and in the honest belief that the action taken was in the best interests of the company." Aronson v. Lewis, Del. Supr., 473 A.2d 805, 812 (1984) (citations omitted). Notwithstanding, in Unocal we held that when the business judgment rule applies to adoption of a defensive mechanism, the initial burden will lie with the directors. The "directors must show that they had reasonable grounds for believing that a danger to corporate policy and effectiveness existed. . . [T]hey satisfy that burden 'by showing good faith and reasonable investigation. . .' " In addition, the directors must show that the defensive mechanism was "reasonable in relation to the threat posed." Unocal, 493 A.2d at 955. Moreover, that proof is materially enhanced, as we noted in Unocal, where, as here, a majority of the board favoring the proposal consisted of outside independent directors who have acted in accordance with the foregoing standards. Then, the burden shifts back to the plaintiffs who have the ultimate burden of persuasion to show a breach of the directors' fiduciary duties.

There are no allegations here of any bad faith on the part of the Directors' action in the adoption of the Rights Plan. There is no allegation that the Directors' action was taken for entrenchment purposes. Household has adequately demonstrated, as explained above, that the adoption of the Rights Plan was in reaction to what it perceived to be the threat in the market place of coercive two-tier tender offers. Appellants do contend, however, that the Board did not exercise informed business judgment in its adoption of the Plan.

Appellants contend that the Household Board was uninformed since they were *inter alia*, told the Plan would not inhibit a proxy contest, were not told the plan would preclude all hostile acquisitions of Household, and were told that Delaware counsel opined that the plan was within the business judgment of the Board.

As to the first two contentions, as we explained above, the Rights Plan will not have a severe impact upon proxy contests and it will not preclude all hostile acquisitions of Household. Therefore, the Directors were not misinformed or uninformed on these facts.

Appellants contend that Delaware counsel did not express an opinion on the flip-over provision of the Rights, rather only that the Rights would constitute validly issued and outstanding rights to subscribe to the preferred stock of the company.

To determine whether a business judgment reached by a board of directors was an informed one, we determine whether the directors were grossly negligent. Smith v. Van Gorkom, Del. Supr., 488 A.2d 858, 873 (1985). Upon a review of this record, we conclude the Directors were not grossly negligent. The information supplied to the Board on August 14 provided the essentials of the Plan. The Directors were given beforehand a notebook which included a three-page summary of the Plan along with the articles on the current takeover environment. The extended discussion between the Board and representatives of Wachtell, Lipton and Goldman, Sachs before approval of the Plan reflected a full and candid evaluation of the Plan. Moran's expression of his views at the meeting served to place before the Board a knowledgeable critique of the Plan. The factual happenings here are clearly distinguishable from the actions of the directors of Trans Union Corporation who displayed gross negligence in approving a cash-out merger.

In addition, to meet their burden, the Directors must show that the defensive mechanism was "reasonable in relation to the threat posed". The record reflects a concern on the part of the Directors over the increasing frequency in the financial services industry of "boot-strap" and "bust-up" takeovers. The Directors were also concerned that such takeovers may take the form of two-tier offers.[14] In addition, on August 14, the Household Board was aware of Moran's overture on behalf of D-K-M. In sum, the Directors reasonably believed Household was vulnerable to coercive acquisition techniques and adopted a reasonable defensive mechanism to protect itself.

V

In conclusion, the Household Directors receive the benefit of the business judgment rule in their adoption of the Rights Plan.

The Directors adopted the Plan pursuant to statutory authority in 8 Del. C. §§ 141, 151, 157. We reject appellants' contentions that the Rights Plan strips stockholders of their rights to receive tender offers and that the Rights Plan fundamentally restricts proxy contests.

The Directors adopted the Plan in the good faith belief that it was necessary to protect Household from coercive acquisition techniques. The Board was informed as to the details of the Plan. In addition, Household has demonstrated that the Plan is reasonable in relation to the threat posed. Appellants, on the other hand, have failed to convince us that the Directors breached any fiduciary duty in their adoption of the Rights Plan.

While we conclude for present purposes that the Household Directors are protected by the business judgment rule, that does not end the matter. The ultimate response to an actual takeover bid must be judged by the Directors' actions at that time, and nothing we say here relieves them of their basic fundamental duties to the corporation and its

---

[14] We have discussed the coercive nature of two-tier tender offers in Unocal, 493 A.2d at 956, n.12. We explained in Unocal that a discriminatory self-tender was reasonably related to the threat of two-tier tender offers and possible greenmail.

stockholders. Their use of the Plan will be evaluated when and if the issue arises.

Affirmed.

NOTE ON RIGHTS PLANS

Flip-over rights, of the kind employed by Household, were approved in Horwitz v. Southwest Forest Industries, Inc., 604 F.Supp. 1130 (D.Nev. 1985). Flip-in plans were approved in APL Corp. v. Johnson Controls, Inc., 85 Civ. 990 (E.D.N.Y. 1985) (applying Wisconsin law); Gelco Corp. v. Coniston Partners, 652 F.Supp. 829 (D. Minn.1986); affirmed in part and vacated in part, 811 F.2d 414 (8th Cir.1987) and Harvard Industries, Inc. v. Tyson, [1986–87 Decisions] Fed. Sec. L. Rep. (CCH) ¶ 93,064 (E.D. Mich.1986).

A flip-in plan, of the kind described in Carney & Silverstein, *supra*, was first approved in Delaware in Stahl v. Apple Bancorp, Inc., [1990 Decisions] Fed. Sec. L. Rep. (CCH) ¶ 95,412 (1990). Unlike the plan in *Moran*, this plan expressly excluded from the definition of beneficial ownership possession of revocable proxies obtained through a public proxy solicitation. The Chancery Court concluded that the poison pill was not an invalid infringement on shareholders' voting rights, because it left the holder of a number of shares less than the triggering percentage free to solicit proxies to remove the board and replace them with directors with the power to redeem the rights. It held that the minor restrictions imposed on a bidder, such as entering into agreements with other shareholders to serve on the board or to share expenses were immaterial. Still, the court cautioned that "It is troubling in either context if the side in control of the levers of power employs them with respect to an election to coerce its opposition to restrict its legitimate electioneering activities." 1990 WL 114222 at *5.

On the other hand, flip-in rights plans have been questioned more closely by the courts, since they can dilute the investment of the bidder in the target, and thus deter takeover bids altogether. Several courts have applied the "heightened scrutiny" of Unocal Corp. v. Mesa Petroleum Co., 493 A.2d 946 (Del. 1985), to closely examine whether the terms of the flip-in represented an overreaction to possible threats. Dynamics Corp. of America v. CTS Corp., 637 F.Supp. 406 (N.D. Ill.), aff'd, 794 F.2d 250 (7th Cir.1986), reversed on other grounds, 481 U.S. 69, 107 S. Ct. 1637 (1987); and R. D. Smith & Co., Inc. v. Preway, Inc., 644 F.Supp. 868 (W.D.Wis.1986).

Other courts have examined whether rights plans that exclude bidders represent unlawful discrimination. See The Amalgamated Sugar Company v. NL Industries, 644 F.Supp. 1229 (S.D.N.Y. 1986) (applying New Jersey law), which followed Minstar Acquiring Corp. v. AMF Inc., 621 F.Supp. 1252 (S.D.N.Y.1985) and Asarco Inc. v. Court, 611 F.Supp. 468 (D.N.J.1985). It was followed in West Point-Pepperell, Inc. v. Farley, Inc., 711 F.Supp. 1088 (N.D.Ga.1988).

Legislatures have responded to the questions raised by poison pills in a variety of ways. In nearly every case where a pill was invalidated by a court as in excess of statutory authority, the statute was later amended to authorize such discriminatory features. Even states that did not experience such rulings took steps to amend their statutes. It is worth noting, however, that some poison pills have been written in a way that only permit the same directors who adopted the pill to rescind it (or that delays redemption by a subsequent board for some period of time). The goal, of course, is to prevent a motivated hostile acquirer from launching a proxy contest to first vote in new directors and then rescind the pill. These so called "dead-hand" or "slow-hand" pills have been viewed with disfavor in Delaware. See, for example, Quickturn Design Systems Inc. v. Shapiro, 721 A.2d 1281 (Del. 1998).

---

4. SHAREHOLDER AGREEMENTS

Poison pills represent responses to the threat that a bidder might gain majority control of a target corporation's shares, and through its control of both the board and future shareholder votes, dictate the terms of a cash-out merger to minority shareholders. This represents just one way in which shareholders' interests may conflict. In the context of the publicly traded corporation, it represents by far the most notable example. Other conflicts that might arise among individual shareholders in these corporations are resolved in different ways. For instance, investors can select the type of corporation they wish to invest in based on their preferences for risk, dividend policies, or other investment goals. That is, investors in publicly-traded firms can minimize investor conflicts simply by virtue of the fact that public equity markets provide a menu of investment options, ranging from mature companies that adhere to generous dividend polices to more risky "growth" companies that pay no dividends at all and use whatever cash flows they generate to finance future growth. Similarly, some investors will avoid investments they regard as socially damaging, and others will pursue them. In theory, investors in publicly traded corporations can readily change their investments at relatively low cost if a company changes its strategies, whether on dividends, risky projects, or otherwise, in a manner the individual investor does not prefer.

The situation for the shareholder in a closely-held corporation is quite different, because there is no ready market into which one can sell shares in a closely-held enterprise. These shareholders are "locked in" and have, in effect, provided permanent capital for the enterprise unless the majority chooses to liquidate and sell the entire business, or to buy out the minority shareholder. Mr. Katzowitz represents a typical example of such a minority shareholder.

The solution for many of these conflicts must be found in advance planning that recognizes that shareholder conflicts may arise, even among investors with long relationships, as in the case of Katzowitz,

Sidler and Lasker. The general response to these conflicts is for shareholders to use the power of contract to address potential pitfalls in advance, at least to the extent they can be foreseen and anticipated. Note, however, that the concept of a "shareholder contract" can be quite expansive insofar that shareholders may agree to contract terms that appear in both a corporation's governing documents (e.g., the corporation's COI and its By-Laws) as well as more conventional shareholder agreements. Venture capitalists, for instance, regularly demand a set of contract terms that are negotiated in contracts entered into directly among shareholders (e.g., a Voting Agreement, an Investor Rights Agreement, a Right of First-Refusal and Co-Sale Agreement) as well as terms that are added directly to the Company's COI.

To the extent shareholders choose to bind the company to an agreement outside its COI, however, drafters must be mindful of statutory provisions such as DGCL § 141(a), which provides that "the business and affairs of every corporation . . . shall be managed by or under the direction of a board of directors, except as may be otherwise provided in this chapter or in its certificate of incorporation." Accordingly, such private agreements cannot override the board's obligation to use its discretion to manage the business and affairs of the corporation, except as may be set forth in its COI. See, e.g., In West Palm Beach Firefighters' Pension Fund v. Moelis & Co., 2024 WL 747180 (Del. Ch. Feb. 23, 2024) (holding that provisions in stockholder agreement between a company and its majority stockholder were facially invalid because they unduly constrained the board's discretion in violation of DGCL § 141(a)); Abercrombie v. Davies, 123 A.2d 893 (Del. Ch. 1956) (holding that governance restrictions in private agreements violate DGCL § 141(a) when they "have the effect of removing from directors in a very substantial way their duty to use their own best judgment on management matters").

We will examine some of the basic conflicts below, and the range of devices available to deal with them in advance. Keep in mind that many shareholder agreements require shareholders to give up default rights and powers generally available under corporate law, subject, in egregious cases, to equitable intervention from the courts. Obviously, such ex post solutions are expensive for all concerned, when compared to advance planning and agreement.

A. DISTRIBUTIONS

Where individuals form a business in which they expect to work full time, they obviously expect a steady income to replace that foregone in previous employment. Since all employees are employed at will absent some agreement, it is clear that employment agreements are critical at this juncture. These may be for a set term, or "for life" during one's active working years, but in order to be enforceable in many jurisdictions, such a contract should allow termination "for cause," which can be narrowly defined if necessary. In some cases employment might last as long as one remains a shareholder in the firm, but in this case provision should be made to avoid a forced sale by the individual—as in a cash-out merger, where the other shareholders own all the stock in the new entity.

One difficulty with employment agreements is that they are static; they may provide for an initial level of compensation, but not for upward (or downward) adjustments over time. If this is left to the discretion of the board, a shareholder who finds herself at odds with the others may find her compensation lagging. Another difficulty may be that one's responsibilities will change over time, while a rigid salary agreement will not provide for appropriate adjustments. Where all participants are equals, requiring equal compensation may be a solution, but it does not provide for all contingencies.

By law all shares of the same class or series must generally be treated alike, so if dividends are to be paid, they will be paid equally on all shares, eliminating the risk of unequal treatment. But dividends are paid only at the discretion of the board, and where disagreements arise, some shareholders may be disappointed.

One solution in a closely held firm is to assure that all shareholders are also directors, each with an equal say in these decisions. This requires a shareholders' agreement in which each shareholder agrees to vote for all the others in the election of directors. Another solution is the use of separate classes of voting common stock for each shareholder, with a charter provision assuring each class board representation.

But none of these solutions address the retirement problem. When a shareholder retires from employment, the shareholder's salary disappears, and absent other investments, the shareholder is dependent on corporate distributions for income. Guaranteeing a dividend level for common stock is generally not feasible, but converting common stock to preferred, with a cumulative dividend, and an obligation to pay it if earned (see Chapter 7) could provide a reasonable assurance of continued income. Other solutions, to be discussed below, include a potential buyout of retiring shareholders, or contributions to tax-sheltered retirement plans during one's working years.

B. RISKY INVESTMENT CHOICES

Shareholders face the problem of changing preferences for risk (and reinvestment of profits) over time. The make-up of the shareholder group may change, bringing in younger investors with a longer time horizon and different attitudes toward risk. In other cases, the investor group may begin with age differentials, which become most important when one or more shareholders reaches normal retirement age. (Creditors worry about the same problem, as discussed in Chapter 6.) One solution is to specify the business to be conducted by the firm in the articles of incorporation, rather than use the broader purpose of "any lawful business" that is permitted by most states. Any change would therefore require a board and shareholder vote to amend the articles of incorporation, which would at least give some voice to the shareholders. The minority's voice can be increased by requiring supermajority voting to amend this provision, if desirable. Generally state laws also require shareholder votes for mergers and the sale of substantially all assets, which could also be made subject to supermajority votes. Increasing the governance approvals needed to make these types of decisions, however, might also expose the firm to situations where it is unable to gather sufficient consensus to pursue a seemingly attractive opportunity.

C. LIQUIDITY: EXIT

A shareholder's departure from a firm can create difficult problems for close corporations. Small firms often lack the liquidity for an immediate buy-back from a withdrawing shareholder. And valuing shares where there is no market is especially tricky, as we have seen in Chapter 3. For a retired shareholder, holding non-dividend paying shares for which there is no market is the worst possible situation.

A common approach is for shareholders to enter into a buy-sell agreement with the corporation. At a minimum, this agreement might obligate the corporation to repurchase shares upon retirement at a normal retirement age or at an earlier death or disability. The corporation can fund these obligations by purchasing "key person" insurance on each shareholder, which will develop cash values to fund the buyout (or a death benefit). If funding is difficult, the buyout might be over a period of years. It is difficult to overstate the importance of a buy-sell agreement in the close corporation context, and transaction planners will often give serious thought to the various mechanisms and terms of these agreements.

A related problem is valuation. Book value is obviously a very inaccurate measure of fair market value in most cases, but it has the benefit of avoiding other calculation expenses and disputes. Appraisal by an independent expert might also be used. In some cases shareholders have agreed periodically on a value at which any of them might be bought out, which may work if all shareholders are operating behind a true veil of ignorance: that is, all of them are about the same age and health, so which one retires first is truly unknown. As soon as this changes, the one most likely to retire faces the moral hazard that the others may undervalue the shares.

D. TRANSFER RESTRICTIONS AND TAG-ALONG, DRAG-ALONG RIGHTS

Unlike partnerships, shareholder approval is not required for the transfer of shares under corporate law. Shares are private property and are regarded as freely transferable absent some restrictions by agreement. Accordingly, there is a risk that a majority of the shares may be transferred to new owners with different goals than the original shareholders. This could give rise to the "Tony Soprano" problem: you might be perfectly happy being a small shareholder at a firm where your friend owns most of the shares. But if she sells out to Tony Soprano (a fictional mafia leader), you're going to get nervous. Not surprisingly, share transfer restrictions are common in closely held corporations. To be enforceable against third parties, these restrictions must generally be noted conspicuously (such as by means of a legend placed on the stock certificates). See, e.g., Model Act § 6.27.

One type of transfer restriction mimics the partnership by requiring the consent of other shareholders. But unlike most partnership interests, shares are private property and presumptively freely transferable. So unreasonable restraints on alienation are disfavored by the courts and may not be enforced. As a result, simple majority consent requirements are more likely to be upheld than a unanimous consent requirement, which gives every other shareholder a veto right over any stock transfer. Consent restraints are often qualified by a condition that consent will not be unreasonably withheld. Obviously, this is an "open" term that will be left to the judgment of a court in the event of a dispute.

A less controversial restraint involves granting the company or other shareholders a right of first refusal to purchase the seller's shares at the price offered by a third party. Unless all the shares are purchased, such a right of first refusal risks leaving the seller with an unmarketable remainder, and worse off than the original terms offered by a third party. So if the remaining shareholders are to be allowed to purchase pro rata, it is wise to provide that if not all shares are taken, any shareholder can offer to buy the remainder. Further, to protect the seller, there should be a provision that unless all are taken, the seller may proceed with the original sale.

Finally, suppose a shareholder wishes to sell out to a third party, perhaps one not previously known to the other shareholders. In some cases, the remaining shareholders may not wish to buy out the departing shareholder (e.g., by exercising a right of first refusal) but would instead prefer to sell their own shares to the third party on the same terms as those offered to the departing shareholder. To ensure their ability to do this, investors often obtain "tag-along" or "co-sale" rights upon making an investment in a company's equity. These rights grant shareholders the right to sell their shares on the same terms as a departing shareholder. In other cases, an investor may identify a potential buyer of its shares who wants to buy all the company's shares, or none at all. For this reason, an investor may require that pre-existing shareholders in a company provide the investor with "drag-along" rights—the right to force the shareholders to sell their shares to a bidder if required by the investor. This latter term is sufficiently harsh that it can usually only be obtained when the shareholders really want an investment enough to make this concession.

5. CREDITOR PROTECTION: LEGAL CAPITAL

You might recall from Chapter 2 that common stock investments are typically divided between two separate accounting classifications: part of the investment, corresponding to par value, is placed in a "common stock" account, and any excess consideration is placed in an account named "additional paid-in capital" or "capital surplus." Why do we do this? The short answer is that, once upon a time, founders of a business enterprise needed to obtain permission from state legislatures to create a corporation. Sometimes this permission was only granted if the founders could commit a minimum amount of capital—embodied in the stock's par value. Eventually the need to petition state legislatures to create a corporation was dropped, but the concept of guaranteeing some minimum amount of legal capital continued as a way to convince creditors that the firm has a sufficient equity cushion. These days, legal capital may not really provide much benefit to creditors. It can, however, serve as a trap for unwary directors who inadvertently declare a dividend that depletes the firm of this required equity cushion (a topic we discuss in Chapter 9). And it is still necessary to delve into some of the history here because lawyers are often asked to render an opinion that a firm's stock has been "duly authorized and validly issued."

Legal capital—that is, the assignment of a nominal ("par") value to shares—had its origin in the era of special chartering, when a charter was a contract between the sovereign and a corporation's promoters. In exchange for a monopoly franchise, the sovereign extracted a commitment from the promoters to provide enough capital to accomplish the enterprise. The charters provided that shares must have a nominal value, and that the nominal value of all authorized shares was equal to the amount of capital stock authorized by the sovereign. This nominal value was called "par value." Before the franchise was valid, all shares had to be subscribed for, and a minimum amount paid in for these shares. Shareholders were liable for the balance of the subscription. Hence the state was assured that in exchange for a monopoly franchise, the promoters would actually raise the capital to conduct the business, which was, in the eighteenth and early nineteenth century, typically a quasi-public enterprise with natural monopoly characteristics, such as building and operating bridges, toll roads, canals, mills, and finally railroads.

Americans grew accustomed to obtaining charters from the state for incorporation, which carried privileges of monopoly and limited liability. More conventional business corporations, such as the New England woolen and cotton mills, lacked the natural monopoly elements, and thus were not given exclusive franchises. But the use of requirements of minimum subscribed capital continued. Whether this was simply legislative inertia or a more conscious use of legal capital requirements for creditor protection is less obvious.

In the nineteenth century states began to pass General Corporation Laws, under which anyone could create a corporation without the need to obtain individualized legislative approval. Competition from low-cost states drove special chartering out of business. In the process, this eliminated the notion of a bargain with the state over the amount of capital committed to a business—and the original purpose of minimum capital commitments disappeared. At the same time, however, the idea that par value could be used to protect those dealing with the corporation began to take root. In particular, the requirement that shareholders pay the full par value of shares came to be seen as a mode of protecting creditors and a means to disclose to creditors how much shareholders had invested in the business. The general idea behind these legal capital requirements was to assure a creditor of a business that the aggregate par value of a corporation's shares had actually been invested by its shareholders and, further, that this capital would remain locked in the corporation to minimize the risk of insolvency.

A moment's reflection, however, should reveal several limitations with this approach to creditor protection. First, even if a company sells shares at par value, it only tells creditors how much shareholders originally invested (or committed to invest), not what their investment is currently worth. Moreover, in most cases, the par value of stock will not even reflect the total amount invested in a company's shares. For instance, recall that the par value of Meta's Class A and Class B common stock is a mere $0.0000006/share. Is this the amount that Meta's common stockholders paid for each share? Hardly. Rather, the par value of stock is fixed in a company's charter upon authorizing a class of capital stock. This means that the par value of stock is ultimately determined by a corporation's board and shareholders who, as reflected in Meta's charter, may have incentives to keep it as low as possible to permit more generous shareholder distributions in the future. The price at which a company actually sells its stock is instead determined by a company's board of directors at the moment the corporation issues it. See DGCL § 152 and Model Act § 6.21(c).*

Second, the usefulness of par value depends on what shareholders give up in exchange for shares. If they give cash in the amount of par value, it is at least an accurate history of the value contributed for shares' par value, which is all accounting purports to accomplish. If they give assets valued at inflated prices, it is not necessarily even accurate history.

Over time, several judicial doctrines developed to deal with this second problem. Where investors contributed over-valued assets, the

* As noted above, when a company sells stock for more than its par value, the excess is recorded on its balance sheet as "additional paid-in capital."

shares were considered "watered" to the extent of the overstatement of the value of the assets.* Where investors received shares for no consideration, these were called "bonus" shares. In each case, shareholders were liable, either to the company or to creditors, for the difference between the value given and par value. Various theories were used to rationalize holding shareholders liable in this fashion.

1. *The "Trust Fund" Theory*. This theory held that the corporation held its capital in trust for the benefit of creditors of the corporation. Shareholders who failed to pay in the full par value of shares were also trustees to the extent of their underpayments. This doctrine was properly rejected as pure fiction in Hospes v. Northwestern Mfg. & Car Co., 48 Minn. 174, 50 N.W. 1117 (1892). The court recognized that corporations hold their capital for the benefit of shareholders, not for the benefit of creditors.
2. *The "Misrepresentation" Theory*. This theory held that only those creditors who were deceived by the overstatement of capital and who relied on it in extending credit were entitled to make a claim. The difficulty with this theory is that after a few years of operations, which could involve profits, losses, or changes in asset values not reflected in accounting statements, no one should be deceived or rely on original contributions, and few creditors really look to this as any indication of a company's well-being. Issues of deceit are now more commonly and easily dealt with under securities laws (as we discuss in the next subsection).
3. *The "Statutory Obligation" Theory*. This theory held that purchasing shares for less than par value creates a statutory obligation to pay the difference to creditors when the firm is insolvent. Consistent with this theory, many corporate statutes also restricted the form of consideration that could be used to purchase stock. For instance, prior to 1980, Model Act § 19 stated that promissory notes and promises of future services could not be used to purchase shares of stock. The same rule also applied in Delaware until 2004, in DGCL § 152 (prior to 2004, this section provided that shares shall be deemed fully paid and nonassessable if "(1) the entire amount of such consideration has been received by the corporation in the form of cash, *services rendered*, personal property. . .") (emphasis added).

For lawyers, the upshot of all of this greatly complicated two common issues in the life of a corporation: issuing capital stock and paying

* The origins of the phrase lie in cattle markets, where sharp sellers would cause their cattle to drink heavily before weighing.

shareholder distributions. We shall postpone discussion of the latter until Chapter 9 and focus here on the challenge of issuing capital stock.

When a corporation issued and sold capital stock, these legal capital considerations historically made it critical to assess whether the corporation was receiving both (a) the proper *amount* of consideration for the shares as set forth by a board resolution and (b) the proper *form* of consideration, especially with regard to the payment of par value. In particular, where shares were issued in exchange for promissory notes or future services, a lawyer would not be able to render an opinion that the shares were duly authorized and validly issued. Today, however, the need to focus on the proper form of consideration is greatly diminished by amendments to corporate statutes. For instance, in 1978, the Model Act eliminated all vestiges of par value and legal capital. The Official Comments to § 6.21 give the reason for this change:

> "Practitioners and legal scholars have long recognized that the statutory structure embodying "par value" and "legal capital" concepts is not only complex and confusing but also fails to serve the original purpose of protecting creditors and senior security holders from payments to junior security holders. Indeed, to the extent security holders are led to believe that it provides this protection, these provisions may be affirmatively misleading."

As a result, under the Model Act, par value has been abolished, and the obligation to pay for shares is generally purely contractual, and not statutory. See Model Act § 6.22:

> § 6.22. Liability of Shareholders
>
> (a) A purchaser from a corporation of its own shares is not liable to the corporation or its creditors with respect to the shares except to pay the consideration for which the shares were authorized to be issued (Section 6.21) or specified in the subscription agreement (Section 6.20).
>
> (b) Unless otherwise provided in the articles of incorporation, a shareholder of a corporation is not personally liable for the acts or debt of the corporation except that he may become personally liable by reason of his own acts or conduct.

In contrast to the Model Act, Delaware continues to retain the concept of par value, and under DGCL § 153, shares with a par value still cannot be issued for consideration less than the stated par value in the company's COI. However, in 2004, Delaware amended DGCL § 152 to permit capital stock to be issued "for consideration consisting of cash, any tangible or intangible property or any benefit to the corporation, or any combination thereof." Thus, even in Delaware, a company can sell its stock for any form of consideration, so long as a company sells it for at least par value.

We close this subsection with a discussion of a related, practical challenge that often arises in the context of a corporation issuing shares for other than cash or tangible property. In particular, many new firms often have some investors that are willing to put up cash while others (often the founders) commit to invest their labor, or "sweat equity." Even aside from the legal capital challenges these arrangements historically posed, it can be challenging to establish the parties' desired governance and profit-sharing arrangement in a corporation, especially if they want to be "50-50" partners. In a partnership, if they want a 50-50 arrangement for splitting profits and losses, they get this 50-50 arrangement by default, regardless of any disparity in capital contributions. Uniform Partnership Act ("UPA"), § 18(a). Partners also get equal voting rights regardless of capital, unless they agree otherwise. UPA § 18(e). In contrast, in a corporation having just common stock, both dividends and votes are proportional to shares issued, which can pose a problem if only one set of investors is furnishing the capital.

Imagine, for instance, that Arigo Ventures and Francis form NewCo as 50-50 partners, in which Arigo will invest capital and Francis will invest labor. How can Arigo Ventures and Francis agree to take equal shares for their contributions? In a Delaware corporation, DGCL § 152 (discussed previously) now permits Francis to pay for shares with future services. For example, if Arigo Ventures and Francis agree to form a company as 50-50 partners with Arigo contributing $10,000 of cash and Francis contributing services, the company could issue stock at $1 per share with Arigo receiving 10,000 shares for Arigo's $10,000 contribution and Francis receiving 10,000 shares for Francis' future services. The downside of this arrangement is if the firm suddenly liquidates. For example, if the corporation were to be quickly dissolved (perhaps because of a deadlock), Francis would get one-half of the remaining capital—a windfall.

As a result, Arigo Ventures and Francis are likely to utilize an alternative structure, such as one of the following:

1. Have Arigo Ventures & Francis each buy voting common shares for a low par value (recall that in states such as Delaware, par represents the minimum price that can be paid for each share), and have Arigo Ventures lend the balance of the capital to the firm. This protects Arigo Ventures in dissolution by giving it more of the profits and assets on dissolution than Francis would get. However, to the extent that the vast majority of Arigo Ventures' and Francis' total contributions are represented by Arigo's claim as a creditor, this may create the danger of creditor liability for Arigo Ventures. (See Chapter 6).
2. Have Arigo Ventures & Francis each buy voting common shares for a low par value, and have Arigo buy nonvoting preferred shares with the balance of its capital. As we shall see in Chapter 7, the preferred can be designed to have a dividend and liquidation preference that gives Arigo

Ventures more than Francis on a liquidation, just as in a loan. The dividend rate can be made quite small (or non-existent). The liquidation preference needs to be at least the amount invested to protect Arigo's investment in dissolution.

3. Have Arigo Ventures and Francis buy separate classes of stock, as above, but have Arigo's shares be convertible into the class of stock held by Francis. For instance, Francis can buy 10,000 shares of common stock at a low price per share (e.g., $.01/share), while Arigo Ventures purchases the same number of shares of convertible preferred stock at a higher price per share (e.g., $1.00/share). The terms of the preferred stock will have a liquidation preference equal to the original purchase price, which will entitle Arigo to a return of its capital contribution in the event of an early liquidation before Francis receives any liquidation proceeds. Additionally, the conversion feature of the preferred will allow Arigo to convert each share of preferred stock into one share of common stock if the venture succeeds. This ensures Arigo Ventures and Francis split the residual claim 50-50 in good states of the world. Finally, the preferred stock will vote on an "as-converted to common stock basis" on all matters on which common stockholders are entitled to vote. This latter provision will ensure Arigo Ventures and Francis each hold 50% of the company's voting power. As we shall see in Chapter 7, this third solution is commonly used in conventional venture capital financings.

Thus, even though the legal capital regime plays only a minor role today in issuing stock, a number of practical challenges can arise when some participants will be investing labor while others will be investing capital. In such cases, the ability to issue multiple classes of stock may prove useful in achieving the investors' governance and economic objectives.

6. PUBLIC SECURITIES MARKETS AND REGULATION

While this chapter has focused on the financial issues that arise when a company issues common stock, it is worth noting that any sale of securities (including common stock) by a company also implicates the need to assess whether the issuance complies with state and federal securities laws. Although a full discussion of these issues is beyond the scope of this book, we provide here an overview of how U.S. securities laws regulate the issuance and trading of common stock.

A. THE FEDERAL SECURITIES LAWS IN A NUTSHELL

After the great stock market crash of 1929, Congress began to hold hearings about the causes of the crash. While many economists today believe that the crash was caused to a large extent by the monetary policies of the Federal Reserve Bank, which shrank the money supply by one-third, that was not the common view in 1929 and thereafter. The view was that Wall Street was the source of the crash, and that practices on Wall Street needed to be changed. These hearings focused on several perceived problems: (1) excessive speculation by ill-informed investors; (2) manipulation of prices on established markets by market insiders; and (3) excessive use of credit in buying stocks.

Congress responded with a series of laws during the 1930s. We will address only two of these laws—the Securities Act of 1933, 15 U.S.C. §§ 77a et seq. (the "Securities Act") and the Securities Exchange Act of 1934, 15 U.S.C. §§ 78a et seq. (the "Exchange Act"). These two laws continue to establish the foundation for modern securities regulation and were important parts of Franklin D. Roosevelt's "New Deal" legislation of the 1930s.

i. THE SECURITIES ACT: REGULATING "PUBLIC" OFFERINGS

The Securities Act was adopted within the first 100 days of the New Deal, and thus illustrates the importance that Congress and the President attached to reforming the securities markets. A principal justification for the Securities Act was to fill in the gap left by state regulation that could not effectively reach transactions that occurred across state lines. Congress used the state laws (as well as certain provisions of the English Companies Act) as models for the Securities Act. But Congress had to decide which model of state regulation to use when a firm or investor offered and sold securities: (1) merely prohibiting fraud in offering and selling securities; (2) requiring registration of the securities to be offered in the form of requiring a mandatory disclosure document distributed to investors, or (3) providing that the government would judge the merits of offerings to determine which could be sold to the public. Congress chose a combination of (1) and (2). The philosophy was one of full disclosure. For companies offering or selling securities, the Securities Act requires the preparation of an elaborate disclosure document called a registration statement.

In general, the Securities Act has delegated to the Securities and Exchange Commission the authority to declare what information must be included in a registration statement, which it has done through the creation of various registration statements that differ by the type of securities offering. The default registration statement is Form S-1, which requires (among other things) a description of the issuer's business, a description of the securities, a description of the offering and, perhaps most importantly, a set of audited financial statements covering the past several accounting periods. The vast majority of these required disclosures are contained in Part I of the registration statement, which is referred to as a "prospectus" and is the portion of the registration statement that must be distributed to any offerees.

The heart of the Securities Act is section 5, 15 U.S.C. § 77e, which requires that securities be registered before they may be offered or sold. Section 5 also requires that the prospectus that is part of the registration statement must be delivered to all prospective buyers. The Act applies both to the issuer of the securities, as well as to all those who assist an issuer in distributing its securities to the public, defined as "underwriters." Section 5 is enforced by provisions in section 12, 15 U.S.C. § 77*l*, that make those who offer and sell securities without registration liable to buyers, for the full amount of the sale price. It is also enforced by provisions in section 11, 15 U.S.C. § 77k, that make both the offering company, its directors, significant officers, as well as underwriters, liable for any materially false or misleading statements in the registration statement. In short, this system of offering regulation is rooted in a theory of mandatory disclosure of information, combined with a regime for ensuring that this information is not materially misleading. Note that the Securities Act is *not* a "merit" statute that regulates the substantive "quality" of a security or issuer (e.g., as we do in the context of regulating new pharmaceuticals). As such, it permits anyone to offer any kind of security to the public, so long as they make full and accurate disclosure about its merits and risks.

Congress recognized that the registration process would be time-consuming and expensive, and so it provided a series of exemptions from the registration requirements. These exemptions are particularly important for small, emerging growth firms that need to raise capital by selling securities and would find the registration process both time consuming and expensive—both in terms of the monetary cost of compliance as well as the non-monetary costs incurred in the form of disclosing in a public document information regarding the company's business or finances before it is ready to do so. These exemptions took two forms—exemptions for classes of securities, largely in section 3, 15 U.S.C. § 77c, and exemptions for particular transactions in securities, also found in section 3, but most importantly in section 4, 15 U.S.C. § 77d. The exemptions for classes of securities were generally available where some other set of laws was likely to provide investors with equivalent protection—such as bank deposits, insurance policies, and securities issued with specific regulatory and/or court approval. The transaction exemptions contained some recognition that other laws might provide protections—as in the case of an offering made entirely within a single state, where state securities laws would apply and could be enforced effectively. In addition, these exemptions recognized that in some cases investors either did not need the protection of the securities laws, because they were capable of protecting themselves, or in some cases, the cost of protection was just too high, given the amounts being offered. Finally, the SEC has formalized exemptions for offerings to non-U.S. persons that take place entirely outside the United States, provided precautions are taken to assure that these securities do not flow back into the United States immediately, and the non-U.S. investors bear the risks of investment before resales can occur in the U.S.*

Despite the formal existence of these exemptions from the registration requirement, the statutory provisions that contain them can often be vague and confusing. Section 4(a)(2) of the Securities Act, for example, provides an exemption from registration for "transactions by an issuer not involving any public offering." Nowhere in the Securities Act, however, is the term "public offering" defined. Moreover, in its first decision interpreting this language, the U.S. Supreme Court held that the exemption only applied where all offerees were able to "fend for themselves," in terms of being able to obtain the same information that registration would have provided, and being able to evaluate the merits and risks of the investment. This vague standard created conflicting interpretations in the lower courts, and, with the SEC staff taking a most restrictive approach, to the gradual narrowing of this exemption.

Beginning in the 1970s the SEC recognized that it had closed off access to capital for some smaller offerings, and began a program of introducing "safe harbors" by rule-making to provide greater clarity for when an exemption from registration applied to a particular offering of securities. The most notable attempt to do so is Regulation D, 17 C.F.R. §§ 230.501 et seq., which has two exemptive rules. First, for offerings under a certain dollar figure occurring within a 12-month period ($10 million as of this edition of the casebook), a flat exemption is provided, so long as the issuer avoids a "general solicitation" when offering the securities. (To avoid a general solicitation, an issuer should restrict the offering to persons with whom it has a pre-existing relationship). For larger offerings of any amount, an alternative exemption is available if the issuer avoids a general solicitation *and* sales are restricted to 35 persons, provided that (a) they are sufficiently experienced in business and financial matters that they can judge the merits and risks of the investment and (b) they receive largely the same sort of information that would have been provided by a registration statement. In addition, the latter offering may include *an unlimited* number of "accredited investors," a group which includes certain financial institutions and wealthy individuals who are entitled to no specific information at all (though, of course, they may privately demand information from the

* Formally, the Section 5 registration requirement applies to *anyone* who makes a public offering of securities, which can include individual investors reselling to other investors on a stock exchange. A separate exemption under Section 4 exempts the vast majority of these non-issuer transactions so long as the transaction does not involve the issuer of the securities, an underwriter or a dealer. For reasons that are beyond the scope of this subsection, this exemption means that Section 5 applies to individual investors only if the investor is someone who controls the issuer, such as a corporate insider.

issuer as a condition to their investment). Because of the additional requirements that apply to including non-accredited investors in these larger exempt offerings, many issuers attempting such an exempt offering will limit their sales to "accredited investors."

ii. THE EXCHANGE ACT: PERIODIC REPORTING FOR "PUBLIC" COMPANIES

While the Securities Act focuses on the initial issue and distribution of securities, the Exchange Act focuses on the provision of information about companies whose shares are either (a) traded on a registered stock exchange or (b) otherwise held by either more than 500 non-accredited investors or 2,000 security holders (in either case, excluding security holders who acquired their shares through employee compensation arrangements). The Exchange Act requires a company meeting either clause (a) or (b) to register with the SEC by providing comprehensive information about the company and its securities under section 12, 15 U.S.C. § 78*l*.* (This information is comparable to that required in a Securities Act registration statement, except, of course, there is no description of an offering.) The SEC is empowered by section 13, 15 U.S.C. § 78m, to adopt regulations concerning periodic reports, which have resulted in three core periodic reporting requirements. First, registered companies are required to file an annual report on Form 10-K that contains similar information to that contained in a registration statement, updated annually. Second, registered companies are required to file quarterly financial reports on Form 10-Q, containing the company's unaudited financial statements and an accompanying management's discussion and analysis of financial condition. Finally, SEC Form 8-K requires filings within four days after a list of specific corporate events occurs. The list of events represents the SEC's determination of transactions and corporate activities that require immediate disclosure to the company's shareholders, as opposed to a delayed disclosure in a company's annual report or in a Form 10-Q. Among other things, this list of events includes: the creation or termination of a material definitive agreement, the declaration of bankruptcy, a substantial acquisition or disposition of assets, replacement of certain executive officers or directors, and a change in auditors. A full list of events is set forth in Form 8-K, which is available at https://www.sec.gov/files/form8-k.pdf.

In addition to the foregoing mandatory disclosure forms, the SEC was also given authority to regulate disclosures made by any registered corporation seeking proxies from its shareholders to be voted at a shareholders' meeting, and to set the terms of those disclosures, by section 14 of the Exchange Act, 15 U.S.C. § 78n. These regulations specify the information required to be distributed to shareholders, including an

---

* In the case of (b), the company will be subject to mandatory disclosure requirements only if it also has assets in excess of $10 million.

annual report that includes most of the information in the annual report filed with the SEC on Form 10-K, and require companies to include certain shareholder proposals in the company's proxy materials.

As with the Securities Act, the Exchange Act also includes a number of provisions designed to ensure that any information disclosed by a company—whether voluntarily provided or whether required by an SEC report—is not materially misleading. The antifraud provisions of the Exchange Act cover a wide range of actions. Section 9, 15 U.S.C. § 78i, covers some of the manipulations that had been observed in the 1920s, and prohibits them. Section 10(b), 15 U.S.C. § 78j(b), the general antifraud provision, was originally part of section 9 of the bill, and was described as a catch-all antifraud measure, to cover manipulations and frauds not expressly prohibited. It gave the SEC authority to adopt rules to prevent fraud and manipulation, which the SEC used to adopt Rule 10b–5, 17 C.F.R. § 240.10b–5, in 1942. While the rule is silent on whether a private right of action exists, courts early on implied that one existed, thus giving investors the ability to pursue a federal fraud action involving the purchase or sale of a security. From those beginnings has grown an enormous body of law, and class action lawsuits alleging accounting fraud or other deceptive conduct are frequently brought today as 10b–5 private actions.

Since the mid-1990s, all of these filings (including registration statements required by the Securities Act) can be viewed on the SEC's Electronic Data Gathering, Analysis, and Retrieval (EDGAR) database located at https://www.sec.gov/edgar/searchedgar/companysearch.

B. THE NEW ISSUES MARKET

Corporations can issue stock or debt in a variety of transactions. Small businesses typically issue securities in negotiated transactions to persons known to the promoters of the business. In many cases these investors expect to participate actively in the operation of the business. Their negotiations are face to face, and may include, in addition to the price and terms of the securities, agreements over the role these investors will play in the management of the business. This may involve a position on the board of directors of the corporation, or full-time employment with the corporation.

As a corporation grows larger and needs capital beyond the means of those actively involved in the business, it may seek what is called a "private placement" of additional securities, which is typically structured as an offering to satisfy Regulation D (discussed above). In some cases, the corporation may deal with a venture capital firm, which seeks investments in promising young businesses likely to offer securities to the public at a later date or to be acquired by a larger firm. Venture capital firms often raise their capital from financial institutions, pension plans, university endowments, as well as from wealthy investors willing to take the high risks associated with new ventures. Venture capitalists negotiate directly with start-up firms, and typically put start-ups under pressure to succeed within a few years, by taking preferred stock. If the business does not succeed, preferred stock gives the venture capitalist a priority over the original founders and investors (who typically hold common stock) in the sale or liquidation of the firm. If the business succeeds, these securities typically have conversion rights—to convert the preferred stock into common stock of the corporation, to allow the venture capitalist to share in the growth in value of the firm. Typically, the issuing corporation hopes to offer its securities to the public within a few years (though some firms have grown comfortable with longer stints as a private company) or to be acquired by a larger firm. Venture capital transactions are discussed more fully in Chapters 7 and 8.

Today, it is increasingly common for early-stage companies to raise "seed" or "pre-seed" capital prior to soliciting venture capital investors. These transactions are typically structured as a private placement with an organization focused on developing very early-stage companies (Y-Combinator and Techstars are two well-known examples) and/or wealthy investors. These latter investors are sometimes described as "angel" investors, and invest at an early stage, before venture capital financing. Historically, these investors would often buy common stock in the corporation. Over the past decade, it is more common for these investors to acquire promissory notes (or similar instruments) that convert into the shares of preferred stock issued in the company's first venture capital financing. These convertible securities allow these early investors to postpone a formal negotiation over the valuation of the firm and instead convert at a discount to the valuation ultimately negotiated by the venture capitalist and the entrepreneur.

More recently, smaller enterprises with specific projects that would appeal to individuals as worthy learned to use the internet for "crowd-funding" to seek capital in relatively modest amounts. They avoided the application of the securities laws by asking for contributions, rather than investments. In some cases, those who put up funds would receive a token reward, such as a t-shirt, a recording if and when produced, or the like. Web sites developed to facilitate these transactions. After the stock market collapse of 2007–2008 and public pressure to permit firms to use crowdfunding to raise capital by selling securities such as common stock, Congress enacted a "crowdfunding" exemption to the Securities Act contained in the 2012 Jumpstart our Business Startups ("JOBS") Act. There are several different features of this law, but the crowdfunding exemption, in § 4(a)(6) of the Securities Act, is designed to exempt an offering of securities through crowdfunding if a firm sells no more than $1 million of securities in any 12 month period (adjusted for inflation) and follows a variety of additional requirements. These additional requirements include obligations to make certain disclosures both before and after an offering and to market the offering only through approved intermediary web sites.

Another exemption added by the JOBS Act covered expanded offerings under the "small offering" exemption of Section 3(b) of the Securities Act, which previously exempted offerings of up to $5 million from the full disclosure requirements and expenses of registration. Dubbed by some as "Regulation A+", this exemption applies to offerings of up to $75 million of securities, provided an issuer complies with a number of requirements under Regulation A+ (including the preparation of a lengthy disclosure document that resembles an abbreviated registration statement).

Rather than raise equity capital through an exempt offering, a company can also raise equity capital through a registered public offering. A registered offering allows an issuer to solicit anyone and everyone, thus greatly expanding the range of potential investors. Moreover, a registered offering also positions a company to list its equity securities on a stock exchange, thereby providing a source of liquidity to its stockholders.

Investment bankers usually play a central role in a registered offering. In the typical registered public offering, officials of a corporation approach an investment banker and explain their business and its need for funds. Investment banks are especially important for a company conducting its initial public offering (an "IPO"), where the bank can help market the securities of a newly public firm. (In this regard, hiring an investment bank to underwrite the IPO is analogous to hiring a real estate agent to help sell a house.) In these transactions, the terms of the offering are typically negotiated with the investment banker. After an initial evaluation of the corporation and its prospects, if the investment banker determines that the corporation represents a promising investment opportunity, it will enter into a tentative agreement to underwrite the corporation's securities. This tentative agreement is called a "letter of intent." It is an agreement that is binding only in limited respects. The investment banker does not make a binding commitment to underwrite the securities, but only to use its best efforts to secure financing. The only binding part of the letter of intent is the allocation of expenses of the offering, whether or not it proceeds.

The underwriter can then agree to underwrite the offering in two primary ways. The first and most common is called a "firm commitment underwriting," and involves a commitment to take the securities and pay for them, regardless of the underwriter's ability to resell them at the public offering price. Underwriters will only commit to this form of offering where they feel confident that the offering will be well received by investors. The underwriters do not commit in advance to pay a specific price for the shares. Instead, they and the issuer's representatives conduct "road shows" before interested institutional investors, seeking to determine investor interest and at what price the shares can be marketed. Once a price is determined, the underwriters then purchase shares from the company at this price (less a commission) before selling them to investors at the same price. In other cases, where the underwriters are less confident in the offering, underwriters will only commit to a "best efforts" offering, in which they only commit to use their best efforts to sell the securities as agents on behalf of the issuer. In these cases investment bankers function in an agency capacity, and do not commit their own capital to the offering.

Once a letter of intent is signed, the issuer and the underwriter begin the preparation of a "registration statement," as required by the Securities Act and discussed previously. This registration statement will be filed with the Securities Exchange Commission ("SEC"), where it will be reviewed by the SEC staff for completeness and fairness of presentation. The period during which the SEC staff reviews the registration statement is one in which the issuer and underwriter are legally prohibited from selling the securities by Section 5 of the Securities Action, but they are permitted to offer them. It is called the "waiting period." Typically, the staff is not fully satisfied with the manner of disclosure and writes the issuer a "letter of comments" detailing its concerns. The issuer is expected to make appropriate revisions in the registration statement to satisfy the SEC staff's concerns. When an amendment is filed with the SEC staff, it is typically reviewed quickly, and if the staff is satisfied, the issuer is notified.

At this time the managing underwriter is in possession of information about the probable success of the offering, from the indications of investor interest obtained by the underwriting syndicate and from the selling dealers. Only now does the underwriter make a commitment to a firm underwriting by signing a binding underwriting agreement. At this point the underwriter not only knows the extent of investor interest, but can also see how the securities market has performed since it made its initial commitment in a letter of intent. It can price the common stock to reflect the prices and quantities investors have indicated they will buy. Indeed, the underwriter has an incentive to set the offering price on the low side, to make it easier to sell the offering, and to reduce the underwriter's risk of failure. If the public offering price is perceived by investors to represent a bargain, the offering will be oversubscribed, and will become a "hot issue." This means the issuer has not obtained the highest price it might have obtained and has "left money on the table."* Once it has set the price, the registration statement is

---

* The problem of underpricing has induced some firms to seek alternative structures when "going public." For instance, in 2004 Google conducted its IPO by means of a "Dutch Auction." In a typical Dutch Auction, an issuer asks interested investors to offer the highest price they are willing to pay for its stock. Once enough investors have made bids to buy all of the offered shares, all successful (high) bidders will be sold shares at the lowest price of any successful bid. Likewise, in 2018–2019, firms such as Spotify and Slack opted to transition from privately-held firms to publicly-traded firms by directly listing their common shares on stock exchanges, avoiding an IPO altogether. This latter approach is made possible by, among other things, the fact that these firms did not need to raise capital at the time they decided to become publicly-listed firms. In theory, direct listings can also be used to raise capital for a firm without the risk of IPO underpricing. Since 2019, a handful of other firms have followed Spotify's use of a direct listing to enable its stockholders to resell their securities into the public trading market;

amended to reflect this price, and the SEC staff permits the registration statement to become "effective." Effectiveness means that the securities can then be sold, bringing this process to a close.

An alternative system of underwriting has developed in the past thirty-five years in the U.S. in response to competitive pressures from European capital markets. The registration process for new offerings in the U.S. is both time-consuming and costly. It is not unusual for the SEC staff to take 30 days or more to review and comment upon a registration statement. In the meantime, the issuer and underwriter may offer, but they cannot sell, the securities. In times of volatile interest rates this can mean that issuers attempting to raise capital through debt offerings will find that interest rates have risen before they can complete their sales. In response to this many larger American companies whose names were recognized in Europe sought to raise capital in European capital markets, where less regulation meant quicker access to funds when interest rates were favorable.

In response, the SEC developed an alternative method of registration for companies that were already subject to the Exchange Act reporting regime. Under this technique, a U.S. company may file a registration statement for a large amount of securities which it does not commit to offer currently. The registration statement is approved by the SEC staff of an offering "for the shelf," which means for future use. For particularly large issuers that already have securities registered under the Exchange Act (in general, Exchange Act companies having more than $700 million of equity held by non-affiliates), the registration statement becomes automatically effective upon filing it with the SEC. Then, when market conditions appear favorable, the issuer need only amend the registration statement to name the underwriter for an offering and specify the price and amount of the registered securities to be sold. This amendment process can take place in a few days rather than in weeks or months, and the issuer can take advantage of the current interest rates or stock prices. This has been enhanced by SEC rules that allow issuers with some history of SEC filings to incorporate much of the information previously filed with the SEC in their registration statements, often reducing the document to a series of incorporations by reference from these filings plus a description of the offering, underwriters and use of proceeds.

One other type of shelf offering is the "at the market" (or "ATM") offering, where an issuer uses the shelf registration statement to "dribble out" relatively small amounts of stock at the current market price. The issuer may do this directly or through an underwriter functioning in an agency capacity. This allows an issuer to wait until it believes its stock is favorably priced before selling, and to stop whenever the price is

---

however, as of this writing, no firm has yet attempted to use a direct listing for capital-raising purposes.

unacceptable. Generally, the amounts that can be sold in this manner are smaller than in conventional offerings.*

One consideration in making a public offering of securities is the ongoing cost of filing periodic reports with the SEC. These costs have risen for smaller companies over the past fifteen years, in part because of increased auditing costs imposed by the Sarbanes-Oxley Act in 2002. Today, most companies seeking to list on a national stock exchange are considerably larger than was the case in the late 1990s, resulting in a dramatic reduction in the number of firms listed on U.S. stock exchanges.

* As discussed in Chapter 4, during the COVID-19 pandemic-fueled stock market rally, ATMs become attractive vehicles for some "meme-stock" companies to raise capital at favorable prices. For instance, AMC Holdings Inc. would raise $325 million via an ATM offering in September 2023. In Chapter 4, we discuss additional ATM offerings during this time by Hertz (while it was in bankruptcy!) and Bed Bath and Beyond.

CHAPTER 6

CORPORATE DEBT

1. INTRODUCTION

Suppose you're advising a corporation that wants to raise money through debt financing. Perhaps the shareholders do not wish to give up more residual control of the firm, or perhaps the company believes that debt financing will bring tax advantages. As you explore the various borrowing options (which we previewed in Chapter 4) with the firm's leaders, the conversation will probably turn to whether your client should use publicly issued debt, in the form of bonds and debentures, or whether it should turn to a private arrangement. If the firm wants to issue, say, bonds in the public markets, then the process will mirror that of a stock offering—but most transactions will also be subject to an additional legal regime known as the Trust Indenture Act of 1939 (more on this shortly). If your client decides instead to engage in private borrowing, perhaps by approaching a bank or private credit fund like Blackstone or Apollo, then you will need to negotiate a private loan agreement on their behalf.

Much of what we will discuss in this chapter involves public debt. But it is important to note that most of the problems we deal with here, and the contractual approaches we will observe, also are employed in privately negotiated loan agreements. Indeed, in some cases the restraints on debtors may be tighter in private agreements because both parties recognize the opportunity for renegotiation should it seem appropriate under changed circumstances. Creditors that are repeat players in loan markets have incentives to maintain a reputation for commercial reasonableness and might display a willingness to accommodate debtors when their circumstances change. Renegotiation is far more difficult in public debt markets, as we shall observe.

Why might a corporation borrow both from banks and other financial institutions as well as borrow through public markets? Banks and financial institutions, after all, are intermediaries—they pay interest on the money they possess and then re-lend to corporate borrowers. Larger corporations use banks mostly for short-term financing, seasonal working capital, or bridge loans before more permanent financing is obtained. Frequently corporations that expect to have short-term needs will obtain a line of credit on which they can draw as needed. To assure the bank that this is not long-term financing, banks may require that this line be paid down to zero at least once a year. In some cases, these loans will be secured—perhaps by the firm's accounts receivables or inventory.

In many countries, such as Germany and Japan, most corporate borrowing has traditionally occurred through large banks and public debt markets have played a relatively smaller role in debt financing. The United States is different as many corporations offer debt in public securities markets by registering the offering with the SEC. Until the 1980s, smaller American corporations were largely excluded from the public debt market and relied more on bank financing, which made growth more difficult. The advent of junk bonds in the early 1980s improved the access of smaller companies to public debt markets and decreased their reliance on banks. American corporations also offer debt to institutions in what the securities laws often characterize as a private offering, but it can be semi-public, in the sense that debt may be sold to large numbers of institutional investors. And even if this debt is not registered under the securities laws, it may still trade in separate markets maintained for institutional buyers.

For most public companies, the cost of issuing underwritten public debt has dropped dramatically over the past few decades. Underwriting commissions have fallen precipitously, as competition among underwriters has increased and private options have multiplied. Years of Federal Reserve policies keeping interest rates low also contributed to the attractiveness of corporate borrowing, though rates have ticked up in recent years.

Where debt issues exceed $50 million (originally $10 million but increased in 2015) and are offered to the public, the offered bonds or debentures must be issued subject to an indenture of trust. This is used to solve collective action problems and to comply with the Trust Indenture Act ("TIA"). Unlike private lending agreements, which are typically executed via a direct contract between a borrower and lender, deals subject to the TIA are structured in a less intuitive way. A bank trust department is typically named as the primary counterparty to the borrowing firm; it then serves as a trustee for the bondholders to enforce the terms of the indenture and monitor the debtor's compliance with its covenants. The indenture contains the terms of the obligations, and the actual public investors are legally viewed as beneficiaries of this trust. This obviously increases the complexity of a public bond offering. But it also provides a dedicated monitor for the lending relationship and is thought to offer additional coordination benefits. (If a debtor defaults, having thousands of bondholders race to the courthouse to get paid first doesn't make any more sense here than in bankruptcy.) As we will see later in this chapter, trust indentures are highly regulated documents, and the TIA mandates some key terms.

While the choice between a public offering or a private loan is perhaps the biggest consideration in any debt transaction, there are many other crucial decisions for issuers. Corporate debt comes in many different variants, and it can be used to accomplish diverse fundraising goals. Here are a few additional questions that might arise:

1. *Should You Borrow on a Short-Term Basis or on a Long-Term Basis?* Some loan agreements, such as commercial paper, may

contemplate a term of 30 days or less. Other bonds may last for 20 years or more (a few deals even provide for perpetual debt). A corporation will often be able to borrow at a lower interest rate with shorter-term debt, although it might also take on other risks if it plans to "roll over" the debt into a new loan upon expiration.

2. *Should You Borrow Using a Fixed Rate of Interest or a Variable Rate of Interest?* As with a home mortgage, a corporation might pay a flat rate of interest on the debt, or it may select a reference benchmark and have the interest payment vary according to that benchmark.

3. *Should You Borrow on a Secured or Unsecured Basis?* Offering security might be a way to attract funds at a lower rate, but the lender can, of course, seize the collateral upon default. Pre-existing lenders might also have viewpoints (or even legal restrictions) related to new security interests.

4. *What Credit Rating Will the Debt Receive?* Most corporate debt that is publicly held is rated for its credit quality by a bond rating agency. Moody's Investors' Services, Standard & Poors, and Fitch's, are among the major rating services. (Appendix 6-A describes the rating categories employed by each agency.) As a practical matter, a firm's rating score is likely to have a significant impact on the effective interest rate that is paid on the debt. AAA rated debt will offer a lower rate, while junk bonds will need to pay more to investors—either by offering a higher interest rate or by trading at a price discount to face value.

5. *Should You Allow Debt Investors to Convert Their Position into an Equity Security?* Issuing convertible debt might be another way to lower the interest rate and could present some other theoretical benefits. Of course, adding a bundled option to convert is not costless for the firm to grant investors. Convertible securities present a range of special financing and legal issues, and we will take up this topic in Chapter 8.

6. *What Other Promises Should You Make to the Lender?* This question occupies much of this chapter. Lenders take an obvious risk by giving their money over to the borrowing corporation and they will usually want to take some steps to increase the probability of repayment. Indeed, the concerns here are related to a topic that we discussed in Chapter 4: the stockholder-bondholder conflict. Creditors make decisions about whether to lend, how much to lend and what interest rate to demand for a loan based on the debtor's prospects of repayment. These decisions are made at the time that credit is extended. The problem is that loans are not a one-day occurrence; they may remain outstanding for years. And much can change during this time. A wise lender will try to anticipate some of the problems that might arise and negotiate for provisions in the loan agreement that protect their interests. Some of these terms will not be costless to the issuing firm, however, and sorting out the exact zone of agreement is one of the main tasks for professional advisors who work in this area.

Fundamentally, many of the worst problems arise because debtors have incentives to increase the riskiness of a business after they've borrowed at a fixed rate. Why? Because this becomes a "heads I win, tails you lose" type of game once the borrowing has occurred, and the creditor is locked into a fixed interest rate for a fixed term.

Consider a simple example. Assume a firm has raised $10,000 through the sale of common stock and $100,000 through the sale of bonds that bear an 8% interest rate (for a total interest expense of $8,000 per year). The firm is now considering two business strategies: a low-risk strategy and a high-risk strategy with the following expected payouts:

Strategy I - Low Risk

Firm Earnings	Prob.	Weighted Value	To Bondholders	Prob.	Weighted Value to Bondholders	To Stockholders	Prob.	Weighted Value to Stockholders
$6,000	0.1	$600	$6,000	0.1	$600	$0	0.1	$0
$10,000	0.8	$8,000	$8,000	0.8	$6,400	$2,000	0.8	$1,600
$14,000	0.1	$1,400	$8,000	0.1	$800	$6,000	0.1	$600
Expected Value	1	$10,000		1	$7,800		1	$2,200

Strategy II - High Risk

Firm Earnings	Prob.	Weighted Value	To Bondholders	Prob.	Weighted Value to Bondholders	To Stockholders	Prob.	Weighted Value to Stockholders
$2,000	0.4	$800	$2,000	0.4	$800	$0	0.4	$0
$10,000	0.2	$2,000	$8,000	0.2	$1,600	$2,000	0.2	$400
$18,000	0.4	$7,200	$8,000	0.4	$3,200	$10,000	0.4	$4,000
Expected Value	1	$10,000		1	$5,600		1	$4,400

Notice how choosing the risky project doubles the expected value of returns for stockholders, while reducing the expected value of returns for bondholders by $2,200. In both cases, however, the expected value of the total results for the firm remains the same, at $10,000. The high-risk strategy drops expected returns to bondholders from 7.8% to 5.6%, notwithstanding the 8% coupon rate. (For this example, we assume that any default on the bonds isn't recoverable in bankruptcy.) But the high-risk strategy raises stockholders' expected returns from 22% to 44%. Once the interest rate and the creditor's claims are fixed, shareholders might gamble, at least in part, with creditors' money, because creditors will suffer losses in the worst-case scenario. Of course, if bondholders recognize these risks in advance, then they should demand a higher interest rate to compensate for this risk.

How does this gambling occur? One possibility arises if corporate leaders can initiate risky projects, such as taking all the firm's wealth and placing it on one bet at a casino. This a not an entirely irrational choice if leverage is sufficiently high. But there are also other, more subtle ways that risky investments can arise. Adding additional debt to the firm's capital structure has a similar effect, since it reduces the probability of full repayment to the first creditor. Even worse, the second creditor might obtain a security interest in firm assets, and thus gain a priority in bankruptcy over the first creditor. Shareholders can achieve the same effect by withdrawing their own capital, which will also make the firm more highly leveraged, and allow the shareholders to gamble with creditors' money. And related to this is the problem of underinvestment: in order to fund distributions to shareholders, the firm may decide not to maintain its plant and equipment or make other investments necessary to support the current business. In short, there are a myriad of potential problems, and it should not be surprising to learn that corporate lawyers have developed a host of contractual strategies that attempt to navigate the stockholder-bondholder conflict.

The rest of this chapter is organized as follows. Section 2 discusses the basics of bond agreements and how these contracts will be interpreted by courts (hint: many terms are given content as a matter of law instead of looking to the parties' subjective intent). Section 3, the heart of the chapter, examines the most important contracting problems that arise in debt financing. It looks at some famous historical disputes and explores the contractual terms that have developed in connection with these cases. Section 4 reviews the special transactional structure and legal considerations that arise for larger public transactions conducted under the TIA. Section 5 considers when the fiduciary duties of firm managers might switch over from shareholders to creditors. And Sections 6 and 7 conclude with a few additional topics related to debt financing—including discussions about disputes between creditors (sometimes referred to as "creditor-on-creditor violence"), unexpected liability for lenders and some more advanced types of lending arrangements.

2. CONTRACT INTERPRETATION

Because the stockholder-bondholder conflict is well known, the terms of bond indentures have been the subject of elaborate drafting to control the problem. The primary authority in this area was created in 1965, by a committee of bond lawyers representing issuing corporations and purchasing financial institutions. American Bar Foundation, COMMENTARIES ON THE MODEL DEBENTURE INDENTURE PROVISIONS 1965, MODEL DEBENTURE INDENTURE PROVISIONS—ALL REGISTERED ISSUES AND CERTAIN NEGOTIABLE PROVISIONS WHICH MAY BE INCLUDED IN A PARTICULAR INCORPORATING INDENTURE (1971) (hereinafter "Commentaries"). A later edition was published in 1977. In 1983, the ABA published the Model Simplified Indenture, 38 Bus. Law. 741 (1983), and in 2000 published the Revised Model Simplified Indenture, 55 Bus. Law. 1115 (2000). The simplified indentures lack the elaborate covenants found in the original document. Subsequently the ABA Committee on Trust Indentures and Indenture Trustees published Model Negotiated Covenants and Negotiated Provisions, in 61 Bus. Law. 1439 (2006) for riskier debt.

To understand the general framework of an indenture, you might wish to examine the Table of Contents from the Revised Model Simplified Indenture, which is set out in Appendix 6-B. We will also turn to some specific provisions in the next Section, drawn largely from the Commentaries, to illustrate contractual resolutions of various parts of the stockholder-bondholder conflict.

Before exploring specific terms, however, we need to discuss the general approach that courts will take when interpreting debt contracts. The following case involves one of the leading deal-makers in the telecommunications field over the past three decades.

Bank of New York Mellon Trust Company v. Liberty Media Corporation

29 A.3d 225 (Del. 2011)

■ HOLLAND, JUSTICE.

The plaintiffs-appellees, Liberty Media Corporation ("LMC") and its wholly owned subsidiary Liberty Media LLC ("Liberty Sub," together with LMC, "Liberty") brought this action for declaratory and injunctive relief against the defendant-appellant, the Bank of New York Mellon Trust Company, N.A., in its capacity as trustee (the "Trustee"). Liberty proposes to split off, into a new publicly traded company ("SplitCo") the businesses, assets, and liabilities attributed to Liberty's Capital Group and Starz Group (the "Capital Splitoff").* After Liberty announced the proposed splitoff of the businesses and assets attributable to its Capital and Starz tracking stock groups, Liberty received a letter from counsel for an anonymous bondholder.

In that letter, counsel for the bondholder stated that Liberty has pursued a "disaggregation strategy" designed to remove substantially all of Liberty's assets from the corporate structure against which the bondholders have claims, and shift those assets into the hands of Liberty's stockholders. Therefore, the bondholder contended that the transaction might violate the Successor Obligor Provision in the Indenture and threatened to declare an event of default. In response to that threat, Liberty commenced this action against the Trustee under the Indenture, seeking injunctive relief and a declaratory judgment that the proposed Capital Splitoff will not constitute a disposition of "substantially all" of Liberty's assets in violation of the Indenture.

The Capital Splitoff will be Liberty's fourth major distribution of assets since March 2004. The Trustee argues that when aggregated with the previous three transactions, the Capital Splitoff would violate a

* [Eds. A splitoff transaction involves placing a division's assets in a new subsidiary corporation of the parent company, and then allowing shareholders of the parent to exchange their parent shares for shares in the subsidiary. This is distinguished from a spinoff, which is a dividend transaction, in which the parent declares a dividend of the subsidiary's shares to the parent's stockholders.]

successor obligor provision in an indenture dated July 7, 1999 (as amended and supplemented, the "Indenture") pursuant to which Liberty agreed not to transfer substantially all of its assets unless the successor entity assumed Liberty's obligations under the Indenture ("Successor Obligor Provision"). It is undisputed that, if considered in isolation, and without reference to any prior asset distribution, the Capital Splitoff would not constitute a transfer of substantially all of Liberty's assets or violate the Successor Obligor Provision.

The Court of Chancery concluded, after a trial, that the four transactions should not be aggregated, and entered judgment for Liberty. The Court of Chancery concluded that the proposed splitoff is not "sufficiently connected" to the prior transactions to warrant aggregation for purposes of the Successor Obligor Provision. The Court of Chancery found that "[e]ach of the transactions resulted from a distinct and independent business decision based on the facts and circumstances that Liberty faced at the time," and that each transaction "was a distinct corporate event separated from the others by a matter of years," and that these transactions "were not part of a master plan to strip Liberty's assets out of the corporate vehicle subject to bondholder claims." Having held that aggregation would be inappropriate on the facts of this case, the Court of Chancery did not reach Liberty's alternative argument that, even if the identified transactions were aggregated for purposes of the Successor Obligor Provision, they collectively would still not constitute a transfer of "substantially all" of Liberty's assets.

* * *

We conclude that the judgment of the Court of Chancery must be affirmed.

FACTUAL BACKGROUND

What follows are the facts as found by the Court of Chancery in its post-trial opinion.

Liberty's Emergence and Early Evolution

For two decades, Liberty has enjoyed a dynamic and protean existence under the leadership of its founder and chairman, Dr. John Malone. Liberty emerged in 1991 from Tele-Communications, Inc. ("TCI"), then the largest cable television operator in the United States, when a threat of federal regulation led TCI to separate its programming assets from its cable systems. TCI formed Liberty and offered its stockholders the opportunity to exchange their TCI shares for Liberty shares. At the time, Dr. Malone was Chairman, CEO, and a large stockholder of TCI. After the exchange offer, Dr. Malone was also Chairman, CEO, and a large stockholder of Liberty.

* * *

In 1998, Dr. Malone convinced AT&T to acquire TCI by merger at a significant premium. In the transaction, both TCI and Liberty became wholly-owned subsidiaries of AT&T. The agreement with AT&T allowed Liberty to operate autonomously, and Liberty's assets and businesses were attributed to a separate tracking stock issued by AT&T. Dr. Malone served as Liberty's Chairman.

The Indenture

While it was a subsidiary of AT&T, Liberty entered into the Indenture with the Trustee. From July 7, 1999 through September 17, 2003, Liberty issued multiple series of publicly traded debt under the Indenture, the proceeds of which totaled approximately $13.7 billion. Liberty has since retired or repurchased much of that debt. As of September 30, 2010, debt securities with a total balance of approximately $4.213 billion remained outstanding. * * *

The Terms of the Indenture

The Indenture includes a successor obligor provision. This provision prohibits Liberty from selling, transferring, or otherwise disposing of "substantially all" of its assets unless the entity to which the assets are transferred assumes Liberty's obligations under the Indenture (thereby releasing Liberty from its obligations). Section 801 of the Indenture provides, in pertinent part:

> [Liberty Sub] shall not consolidate with or merge into, or sell, assign, transfer, lease, convey or other[wise] dispose of all or substantially all of its assets and the properties and the assets and properties of its Subsidiaries (taken as a whole) to, any entity or entities (including limited liability companies) unless:
>
> (1) the successor entity or entities . . . shall expressly assume, by an indenture (or indentures, if at such time there is more than one Trustee) supplemental hereto executed by the successor Person and delivered to the Trustee, the due and punctual payment of the principal of, any premium and interest on and any Additional Amounts with respect to all the Securities and the performance of every obligation in this Indenture and the Outstanding Securities on the part of [Liberty Sub] to be performed or observed . . .;
>
> (2) immediately after giving effect to such transaction or series of transactions, no Event of Default or event which, after notice or lapse of time, or both, would become an Event of Default, shall have occurred and be continuing; and
>
> (3) either [Liberty Sub] or the successor Person shall have delivered to the Trustee an Officers' Certificate and an Opinion of Counsel [containing certain statements required by Section 801].

A failure to comply with the obligations imposed by Article Eight constitutes an "Event of Default." *Id.* § 501.

The Indenture does not define the phrase "substantially all." Nor does the Indenture contain any covenants requiring Liberty to maintain a particular credit rating, a minimum debt coverage ratio, or a minimum asset-to-liability ratio.[2] The Indenture does not contain any provision directly addressing dividends and stock repurchases, which are the corporate vehicles to effectuate a spinoff (stock dividend) and a splitoff (stock redemption).

Liberty's Continued Evolution Since the Splitoff From AT&T

In August 2001, AT&T split off Liberty to the holders of its publicly traded Liberty tracking stock. When Liberty re-emerged as a public company, it held a "fruit salad" of assets, consisting mainly of minority equity positions in public and private entities. For example, Liberty owned single-digit-percentage stakes in large public companies such as Sprint, Viacom, and Motorola. Liberty also owned large minority positions in private companies such as Discovery Communications. Most of Liberty's assets, except for a few controlled operating businesses, did not generate any cash flow. The value of Liberty's holdings, which had been quite significant during the heady days of the internet bubble (recall that the Indenture was executed in 1999), fell significantly in 2000 and 2001 (the period leading up to the splitoff).

After the splitoff, Dr. Malone and the rest of Liberty's management team set out to build value at Liberty by rationalizing its investment portfolio. Put simply, Liberty wanted to use its minority investments to acquire controlling stakes in mutually supporting operating businesses that would generate cash flow. According to Dr. Malone,

> [I]t was always obvious that the direction that the company needed to go—which was to—out of the cosmic dust, as it were, form some gravitational units that could then pull in these investment assets, monetize them and grow. It's always been a process of how do you convert from a portfolio of investments into a series of operating businesses.

Beginning in 2001, Liberty sought to own stakes in businesses that Liberty either controlled or saw a clear path to control. If Liberty did not control an asset and could not identify a path to control, then Liberty management evaluated all possible alternative uses for the asset. Over the ensuing decade, Liberty engaged in numerous transactions in pursuit of that overall strategy, frequently structuring its deals as swaps or exchanges to avoid triggering taxable events.

---

2 *Compare, e.g.*, Committee on Trust Indentures and Indenture Trustees, ABA Section of Business Law, *Model Negotiated Covenants and Related Definitions*, 61 Bus. Law. 1439 (2006) (providing model covenants addressing these topics); Thomas O. McGimpsey & Darren R. Hensley, *Successor Obligor Clauses: Transferring "All or Substantially All" Corporate Assets in Spin-Off Transactions,* Colorado Lawyer 45 (Feb. 2001) (describing different forms of covenants).

International Cable

After separating from AT&T, Liberty looked first to build a cash-generating business in the area its management team knew best: cable television. Having sold the nation's largest cable provider to AT&T in 1999, Dr. Malone did not think it was feasible to make a comeback in the U.S. Instead, Liberty sought to expand, and consolidate, its international cable holdings.

[Beginning in 2001 Liberty acquired various international assets, including the largest cable business in Germany, owned by Deutsch Telekom. When that deal fell apart, Liberty determined that alternative means to build an international business would require huge amounts of capital, largely funded by debt. Liberty then decided to put its international cable assets into a separate entity.]

* * *

Thus, in 2004, Liberty spun off Liberty Media International, Inc. ("LMI"), which held Liberty's controlling interest . . . and stakes in other international cable companies.

The LMI spinoff was a significant transaction for Liberty. It removed $11.79 billion in assets (at book value) from Liberty's balance sheet, representing 19% of Liberty's total book value as of March 31, 2004—the date the Trustee contends should be used for purposes of determining what constituted "substantially all" of Liberty's assets. * * *

The Trustee views the LMI spinoff as the start of Liberty's disaggregation strategy. Commenting on the LMI spinoff in early 2005, Dr. Malone described it as "the first shoe to drop" and a "model we want to follow":

(Dr. Malone, testifying that Liberty's strategy was to "[c]onsolidate on the operating businesses, and figure out how to disaggregate the businesses where we couldn't find an efficient way to own, consolidate, and grow assets, that we hadn't been able to figure out how to do that").

QVC

[Consistent with that strategy, Liberty, which already owned a minority position in QVC [Shopping Network], Inc., increased that investment to obtain majority control.] * * *

Discovery

Also during 2003 and 2004, Liberty management explored alternatives for Discovery, a cable channel that Liberty owned in partnership with Cox Communications and Advance/Newhouse. Although Discovery was performing well, Liberty owned less than 50% of the equity, lacked control, did not have a clear path to control, and was restricted by a stockholders agreement from selling or otherwise monetizing its position.

* * *

With their preferred alternatives blocked, Dr. Malone and the Liberty management team decided to dividend Liberty's Discovery shares to its stockholders, thereby giving them a direct ownership interest in Discovery. * * *

The Discovery spinoff removed from Liberty's balance sheet assets with a book value of $5.825 billion, representing 10% of Liberty's total book value as of March 31, 2004.

* * *

The Trustee points to the Discovery spinoff as a continuation of Liberty's "disaggregation strategy." In its 2004 shareholder letter, Liberty management stated that:

> [s]ince Liberty's inception 14 years ago, our overriding objective has been clear and consistent: to maximize the value of our shares. Over the years, we have accomplished this by executing three core strategies: owning businesses with significant built-in growth potential; making timely acquisitions that enable us to build on that growth potential and create new business lines; and actively managing our capital structure. In 2004, we introduced a fourth strategy of disaggregating businesses by distributing them to our shareholders. While this technique actually reduces the value of our shares, it also increases the wealth of our shareholders by giving them holdings in two companies instead of one.

* * *

The Interactive and Capital Tracking Stocks

On November 9, 2005, Liberty announced the creation of two tracking stocks, one for Liberty's Interactive Group and the second for Liberty's Capital Group. Liberty created the tracking stocks to "help the investment and analyst communities to focus their attention on the underlying value of [Liberty's] assets." At the same time, Liberty management recognized that the trackers could serve as a first step toward future splitoffs. * * *

Meanwhile, Liberty continued to pursue transactions on other fronts involving both exchanges of minority positions for wholly owned assets and outright acquisitions. In April 2007, Liberty agreed to exchange its minority stake in CBS Corporation for ownership of a CBS local television station and $170 million in cash. In May 2007, Liberty exchanged a portion of its minority investment in Time Warner Inc. for ownership of the Atlanta Braves baseball organization, Leisure Arts, Inc., and $984 million in cash. During 2006 and 2007, Liberty acquired IDT Entertainment (later renamed Starz Media), Provide Commerce, Inc., FUN Technologies, Inc., BuySeasons, Inc., and Backcountry.com, Inc. In 2008, Liberty attributed Starz Media and other entertainment-related assets to a new tracking stock group called the Entertainment

Group. This resulted in Liberty's assets being divided between three tracking stock groups: the Interactive Group, the Entertainment Group, and the Capital Group.

Liberty Entertainment

The News Corp. swap [of Liberty's 16% ownership of Rupert Murdoch's company] gave Liberty an influential position in DirecTV. Consistent with its overall strategy, Liberty sought a path to control. In April 2008, Liberty purchased another 78.3 million shares of DirecTV for consideration of $1.98 billion in cash. Restrictions in the DirecTV certificate of incorporation, however, prohibited Liberty from acquiring more than 50% of DirecTV's equity unless Liberty offered to purchase 100% of the outstanding stock. To avoid triggering that provision, Liberty and DirecTV agreed that Liberty's equity ownership could exceed the 50% threshold, but Liberty's voting power would be capped at 48.5%. As a result of DirecTV's stock repurchase program, Liberty's equity ownership eventually climbed to 57%, although Liberty's voting power never exceeded 48.5%.

As 2008 wore on and the financial markets deteriorated, Liberty's management realized that financing to acquire the balance of DirecTV was not available. With the DirecTV charter provision otherwise blocking Liberty's path to control, Liberty management examined other potential alternatives. Ultimately, Liberty announced that it would split off its interest in DirecTV, along with certain other business, into a new entity called Liberty Entertainment, Inc. ("LEI"). Liberty and DirecTV then negotiated a transaction in which LEI would merge with DirecTV immediately after the splitoff. The splitoff and merger closed on November 19, 2009.

Liberty initially planned to split off all the assets attributed to the Entertainment Group, including the DirecTV stake, Starz, FUN Technologies, Inc., Liberty Sports Holdings, LLC, GSN, LLC and WildBlue Communications. Because Liberty management believed that DirecTV was undervaluing Starz and WildBlue in the merger negotiations, Liberty decided to retain those assets. Liberty management also considered the potential effect of the splitoff on bondholders. At that time, Dr. Malone stated that "[w]e had to retain [the] cash and economic value of Starz in order to reassure the bondholders in Liberty that their interests were being protected." The Trustee cites this statement as evidence that Liberty knew its disaggregation strategy was approaching the "substantially all" limit. Dr. Malone and Liberty CEO Gregory Maffei testified at trial that they did not believe Liberty was legally required to hold back Starz and cash from the splitoff, but Liberty did so to protect itself during the height of the financial crisis and reassure bondholders and lenders.

The LEI splitoff removed from Liberty's balance sheet assets with a book value of $14.2 billion, representing 23% of Liberty's asset base as of March 31, 2004. The splitoff also removed roughly $2.2 billion in short-term debt that was attributable to LEI. DirecTV is now the world's leading provider of digital television entertainment services. In 2009, DirecTV reported assets with a book value of $18.26 billion, revenues of $21.57 billion, and operating profit of $2.67 billion. Dr. Malone served as Chairman of DirecTV until April 6, 2010.

* * *

The Proposed Splitoff

In June 2010, Liberty announced the Capital Splitoff, in which Liberty proposes to split off the businesses allocated to its Capital and Starz Groups into SplitCo, a new public entity. SplitCo will own Starz Entertainment, Starz Media, Liberty Sports Interactive, Inc., the Atlanta Braves, True Position, Inc., and Liberty's interest in Sirius XM. The assets to be split off have a book value of $9.1 billion, representing 15% of Liberty's total assets as of March 2004. Dr. Malone is expected to serve as Chairman of the new entity's board, and Mr. Maffei is expected to serve as CEO.

After the Capital Splitoff, Liberty will hold the businesses attributed to Liberty's Interactive Group, consisting primarily of QVC, several e-commerce businesses (including Evite, Gifts.com, BuySeasons, and Bodybuilding.com), and minority equity stakes in Expedia, the Home Shopping Network ("HSN"), and Tree.com (which operates Lending Tree). All outstanding debt securities issued by Liberty will remain obligations of Liberty following the Capital Splitoff. Liberty's board analyzed Liberty's ability to service its outstanding debt after the splitoff, including debt at the QVC level and concluded that Liberty will have no difficulty servicing its debt.

ISSUE ON APPEAL

The parties dispute whether Liberty will breach the Successor Obligor Provision by disposing of substantially all its assets in a series of transactions. It is undisputed, however, that the Capital Splitoff, standing alone, does not constitute "substantially all" of Liberty's assets. The threshold question is, therefore, whether the Capital Splitoff should be aggregated with the prior spinoffs of LMI and Discovery and the splitoff of LEI.

The answer to that threshold question involves the construction of a boilerplate successor obligor provision in an indenture governed by New York law. That provision restricts Liberty's ability to dispose of "all or substantially all" of its assets unless the transferee assumes the Indenture debt. The question presented has not been addressed by the New York Court of Appeals, nor, to our knowledge, by any lower New York state court.

* * *

The Aggregation Principle

The Court of Chancery acknowledged that, as a theoretical matter, a series of transactions can be aggregated for purposes of a "substantially all" analysis.[7] Indeed, the Successor Obligor Provision at issue recognizes that aggregation may occur. That Provision states that Liberty can comply with the Successor Obligor Provision only if "immediately after giving effect to such transaction *or series of transactions*, no Event of Default or event which, after notice or lapse of time, or both, would become an Event of Default, shall have occurred and be continuing." Courts applying New York law have determined that, under appropriate circumstances, multiple transactions can be considered together, *i.e.*, aggregated, when deciding whether a transaction constitutes a sale of all or substantially all of a corporation's assets.[9]

Sharon Steel *Precedent*

The Court of Chancery began its analysis with the Second Circuit's 1982 decision in *Sharon Steel Corp. v. Chase Manhattan Bank, N.A.*, which the court characterized as "the leading decision on aggregating transactions for purposes of a 'substantially all' analysis" in the context of a successor obligor provision. In *Sharon Steel*, the Second Circuit addressed a transaction in which a corporation, subject to a successor obligor provision in a bond indenture, had transferred corporate assets to multiple purchasers pursuant to a plan of liquidation. The court held that "boilerplate successor obligor clauses do not permit assignment of the public debt to another party in the course of a liquidation unless 'all or substantially all' of the assets of the company at the time the plan of liquidation is determined upon are transferred to a single purchaser."

In *Sharon Steel*, after consummating a series of asset sales in furtherance of its liquidation plan, UV Industries, Inc. ("UV") sold its remaining assets to Sharon Steel in November of 1979. Sharon Steel sought to assume UV's indenture obligations under the successor obligor provision, arguing that it was permitted to do so without bondholder consent because the most recent transfer to Sharon Steel constituted a sale of "all or substantially all" of UV's assets as measured immediately

---

7 *See* Ad Hoc Committee for Revision of the 1983 Model Simplified Indenture, Revised Model Simplified Indenture, 55 Bus. Law. 1115, 1134–35, 1186–87 (2000) ("In the context of asset disposition by transfer or lease, serious consideration must be given to the possibility of accomplishing piecemeal, in a series of transactions, what is specifically precluded if attempted as a single transaction.").

9 *See* Sharon Steel Corp. v. Chase Manhattan Bank, N.A., 691 F.2d 1039, 1051–52 (2d Cir. 1982) (comparing assets acquired by successor corporation to assets held by debtor corporation one and a half years earlier, prior to two third-party asset sales, when determining whether successor corporation acquired "substantially all" of the debtor's assets); In re Associated Gas & Elec. Co., 61 F. Supp. 11, 28–31 (S.D.N.Y. 1944) (treating transfers of subsidiaries by one controlled company to a second over a course of three years as a sale of substantially all assets where the transactions were "parts of a single scheme"), *aff'd*, 149 F.2d 996 (2d Cir. 1945); U.S. Bank Nat'l Ass'n v. Angeion Corp., 615 N.W.2d 425, 432–34 (U. Minn. Ct. App. 2000) (reversing grant of summary judgment to debtor and finding that issues of fact existed as to whether two transactions viewed together constituted a sale of substantially all of the issuer's assets).

prior to the transaction. Under the indenture governing UV's debt securities, as under the Indenture in this case, a successor corporation could assume UV's obligations only if UV sold "all or substantially all" of its assets in the transaction. Certain debenture holders claimed that the assets sold to Sharon Steel did not constitute "substantially all" of UV's assets. Therefore, UV accordingly had defaulted under the indenture and as a consequence, the outstanding debt was immediately due and payable.

In *Sharon Steel*, the Second Circuit focused on the fact that all of the sales were pursued to accomplish the predetermined goal of liquidating UV under a formal plan of liquidation, even though only one asset sale had been identified at the time the liquidation plan was adopted. Characterizing the sales as a "piecemeal" liquidation, the Second Circuit explained that it would be inappropriate to regard the UV/Sharon Steel sale in isolation, given the substance and purpose of the "overall scheme to liquidate." As a result, for purposes of determining whether "substantially all" of UV's assets had been transferred to Sharon Steel, thereby permitting Sharon Steel to assume the indenture obligations, the Second Circuit held that the assets transferred to Sharon Steel had to be measured against the totality of assets UV owned at the inception of the plan of liquidation. Taking into account all the assets UV had transferred to various buyers since the adoption of the liquidation plan, the Second Circuit concluded that UV had not transferred to Sharon Steel "substantially all" of its assets. Therefore, UV had violated the successor obligor provision.

The *Sharon Steel* court was careful to distinguish the "piecemeal liquidation" at issue in that case from situations where a company disposes of assets over time and not as part of a preconceived plan of liquidation. Specifically, the Second Circuit rejected UV's "literalist approach" under which Sharon Steel necessarily acquired "all of" UV's assets because it purchased whatever assets were left at the time of the sale. In doing so, the Second Circuit distinguished sales of assets "in the regular course of UV's business" from *seriatim* sales as part of "an overall scheme to liquidate":

> To the extent that a decision to sell off some properties is not part of an overall scheme to liquidate and is made in the regular course of business it is considerably different from a plan of piecemeal liquidation, whether or not followed by independent and subsequent decisions to sell off the rest. A sale in the absence of a plan to liquidate is undertaken because the directors expect the sale to strengthen the corporation as a going concern. . . The fact that piecemeal sales in the regular course of business are permitted thus does not demonstrate that successor obligor clauses apply to piecemeal liquidations, allowing the buyer last in time to assume the entire public debt.

In *Sharon Steel*, the Second Circuit found that aggregation was appropriate because the individual sale transactions at issue were part of a "plan of piecemeal liquidation" and an "overall scheme to liquidate." Conversely, where asset transactions are not piecemeal components of an otherwise integrated, pre-established plan to liquidate or dispose of nearly all assets, and where each such transaction stands on its own merits without reference to another, courts have declined to aggregate for purposes of a "substantially all" analysis.

Sharon Steel *Applied*

* * *

The Court of Chancery's legal conclusion rests on its factual finding that aggregating the four transactions is not warranted because each transaction was the result of a discrete, context-based decision and not as part of an overall plan to deplete Liberty's asset base over time. The court stated:

> Having reviewed the documentary record and listened to the witnesses testify at trial, I find that the Capital Splitoff is not sufficiently connected to the LMI and Discovery spinoffs or the LEI splitoff to warrant aggregating the four transactions. Each of the transactions resulted from a distinct and independent business decision based on the facts and circumstances that Liberty faced at the time. Although the transactions share the same theme of distributing assets to Liberty's stockholders, they were not part of a master plan to strip Liberty's assets out of the corporate vehicle subject to bondholder claims. Rather, each transaction reflected a context-driven application of the overarching business strategy that Liberty has followed since separating from AT&T: consolidate ownership of businesses where Liberty can exercise control or has a clear path to control, while exploring all possible alternatives for assets that do not fit this profile. . . [Liberty] has not followed a strategy of disposing of substantially all of its assets.

* * *

Boilerplate Provisions Require Uniform Interpretation

Successor obligor provisions in bond indentures consist of market-facilitating boilerplate language. Courts endeavor to apply the plain terms of such provisions in a uniform manner to promote market stability. The Court of Chancery has previously noted that "boilerplate provisions" in indentures are "not the consequence of the relationship of particular borrowers and lenders and do not depend upon particularized intentions of the parties to an indenture." Therefore, in interpreting boilerplate indenture provisions, "courts will not look to the intent of the parties, but rather the accepted common purpose of such provisions." In this case, the Court of Chancery properly recognized the boilerplate character of the Indenture's Successor Obligor Provision and correctly emphasized the importance of uniform interpretation.

The Trustee responds that although the Successor Obligor Provision at issue here is "boilerplate" (*i.e.*, was not the subject of specific negotiation between the parties), it is not the standard successor obligor provision boilerplate found in any of the various iterations of the model indenture. The Trustee and Liberty both acknowledge, however, that the "series of transactions" language in the Indenture is the result of a specific recommendation contained in the comments to the *Model Simplified Indenture*, which counseled draftsmen to give "serious consideration" to the risks posed by the "piecemeal" disposition of assets through "a series of transactions." The inclusion of the phrase "series of transactions" in the Indenture, the Trustee argues, broadened the meaning and scope of the Successor Obligor Provision. That argument is not persuasive.

The "series of transactions" language first appeared in a comment to the *Model Simplified Indenture*, published five months after the *Sharon Steel* decision. That comment cautions that "serious consideration must be given to the possibility of accomplishing *piecemeal, in a series of transactions*, what is specifically precluded if attempted as a single transaction." Liberty argues that the comment was designed to address the same concerns at issue in *Sharon Steel*. In support of that argument, it points to the fact that the *Revised Model Simplified Indenture*, promulgated in May 2000, contains the same commentary, but adds a citation to *Sharon Steel*. Accordingly, Liberty submits, the only fair conclusion to be drawn from the presence of "series of transactions" language in a post-*Sharon Steel* successor obligor provision (such as the one at issue here) is that the additional language is meant to underscore that a disposition of "substantially all" assets may occur by way of either a single transaction or an integrated series of transactions, as occurred in *Sharon Steel*. We agree.

Liberty's Indenture was executed many years after the Second Circuit's decision in *Sharon Steel*. There is no evidence in the record that the "series" language was included for any reason other than to clarify that the Successor Obligor Provision should be interpreted in the same manner as the one at issue in *Sharon Steel*. The trial testimony established—and the Trustee admits—that the Successor Obligor Provision was never a subject of negotiations between the parties in the case. Had the parties to the Indenture intended to create an asset disposition covenant with a broader scope than the standard, boilerplate successor obligor covenant, it was incumbent upon them to include it in a separate, negotiated covenant. As two commentators have noted:

> *Sharon Steel* illustrates the narrow construction of indenture provisions and the underlying concerns that inform the interpretation of indenture provisions by the courts. It is therefore important that negotiated provisions in an indenture

> be not only explicit *but also distinct from boilerplate provisions*. Modifications to common indenture provisions *will unlikely yield additional rights* as courts will not look to the intent of the parties, but rather the accepted common purpose of such provisions.

In *Airgas, Inc. v. Air Products and Chemicals*, this Court recently noted that practice and understanding in the real world are relevant and persuasive, when interpreting similar language in a contractual provision. It is important to the efficiency of capital markets that language routinely used in indentures be accorded a consistent and uniform construction.

Liberty points out that at the time the Indenture was established, there were more rigorous model provisions available that explicitly required consideration of prior asset dispositions in determining the legal effect of a later disposition of any substantial part of an issuer's assets. For example, Sample Covenant 1 of Section 10–13 in the *Commentaries* states:

> Subject to the provisions of Article Eight, the Company will not convey, transfer or lease, any substantial part of its assets unless, in the opinion of the Board of Directors, such conveyance, transfer or lease, considered together with all prior conveyances, transfers and leases of assets of the Company, would not materially and adversely affect the interest of the Holders of the Debentures or the ability of the Company to meet its obligations as they become due.

The Liberty Indenture contains no such provision. As the Court of Chancery also noted, there is also no covenant "requiring Liberty to maintain a particular credit rating, a minimum debt coverage ratio, or a minimum asset-to-liability ratio," and "the Indenture does not contain any provision directly addressing dividends and stock repurchases, which are the corporate vehicles to effectuate a spinoff (stock dividend) and a splitoff (stock redemption)." This Court has consistently held that the rights of bondholders and other creditors are fixed by contract. As the Court of Chancery properly recognized, it would be inconsistent with the concept of private ordering to expand the scope of the Successor Obligor Provision by rewriting the Indenture contract to include by implication additional protections for which the parties could have—but did not—provide by way of a covenant separate and apart from the boilerplate successor obligor provision.

* * *

The Court of Chancery carefully considered and applied *Sharon Steel* to the facts before it, and concluded that the Capital Splitoff "is not sufficiently connected to the LMI and Discovery spinoffs or the [Entertainment] splitoff to warrant aggregating the four transactions."* * *

The Trustee concedes that the Capital Splitoff, viewed in isolation, does not constitute a disposition of substantially all of Liberty's assets. On the facts of this case, the Court of Chancery properly held that aggregation is not appropriate. Accordingly, Liberty was entitled to a declaration that the Capital Splitoff does not violate the Successor Obligor Provision in the Indenture.

Conclusion

The judgment of the Court of Chancery is affirmed.

QUESTIONS

1. What was the goal of the Successor Obligor Clause? How did the problem in Sharon Steel differ from the one presented by this case?
2. Sharon Steel teaches that boilerplate is to be interpreted as a matter of law. This is indeed the general approach taken today. Why? Given this approach, what relevance do comments to the *Commentaries on the Model Debenture Indenture Provisions* have in interpretation?
3. How does Liberty argue that the absence of other protective provisions, such as Sample Covenant 1 of Section 10–13 of the *Commentaries*, should affect the interpretation of the language governing sales of substantially all assets? Is such an argument consistent with the standardized interpretation of "substantially all" in boilerplate provisions? Or does it suggest that inclusion of language such as Sample Covenant 1 means that the document has been negotiated, and thus its interpretation is a question of fact rather than of law?

3. CONTRACT TERMS

A. INTRODUCTION AND SUMMARY

We are now ready to begin the integration of the theory and practice of contracting about corporate debt.* We have briefly introduced the stockholder-bondholder conflict above and it is time to expand on the nature of the problem. What types of contract terms are used to protect bondholders? As you review these materials, recall some of the financial ratios described in Chapter 2.

In essence, the stockholder-bondholder conflict stems from the different payouts that shareholders and creditors receive from a firm. Creditors obtain promises of payments at specific times with specified interest rates. They have no opportunity to participate in extraordinary profits that a firm might earn. But like stockholders, they may be disappointed if a debtor corporation runs into hard times and defaults on

---

* Much of this discussion is drawn from Clifford W. Smith and Jerold B. Warner, *Financial Contracting: An Analysis of Bond Covenants*, 7 JOURNAL OF FINANCIAL ECONOMICS 117 (1979).

its obligations. Stockholders, on the other hand, are the residual claimants. In all cases, they only get payouts after the creditors are paid. The difference, of course, is that stockholders enjoy all the gains that exceed the amounts needed to pay off creditors. Stockholders clearly bear more risk than creditors, and thus expect to earn higher rates of return as we saw in Chapter 3.

Another part of the problem stems from the fact that creditors do not have a general right to control the firm and thus have no plenary power over the management and financing of the debtor. Their main protection comes from the covenants they obtain at the original extension of credit, whether in a bond issue or a loan agreement. Shareholders, on the other hand, elect the directors who manage the business and affairs of the corporation. Because the directors are accountable to the shareholders, we should expect the board to focus primarily on shareholder wishes. This is also bolstered by the fact that directors are typically understood to owe fiduciary duties to shareholders (as well as to the corporation itself). If risky choices benefit the shareholders at the expense of the creditors, we can generally expect the board to choose the risky option.

The creditors' challenge, then, is to contract ex ante to address all future states of the world in which directors and shareholders might choose risky options that increase the risk of default to creditors. Described in that manner, the problem appears insuperable: the bounded rationality of human beings (and limited time for contracting) makes it impossible to imagine and specify all such circumstances. Fortunately, this conflict has been around for a while and creditors have observed the standard circumstances that place them at risk. As a result, contract terms to deal with most of them, embodied in the American Bar Association's COMMENTARIES ON MODEL DEBENTURE INDENTURE PROVISIONS (1971) and the later *Revised Model Simplified Indenture*, 55 BUS. LAW. 1115 (2000), guide drafters of both bond indentures and loan agreements. This is not to say that a creative board will never find a new way to take advantage of debt investors. But a wise bondholder will be expected to at least block off the easiest, and well-known, forms of opportunism. Let's consider a quick overview of the issues to be treated in the following pages.

New Debt and Claim Dilution. Recall that in Chapter 5 we examined how existing stockholders are diluted when new shares are issued. For control purposes, all new issues dilute the voting power of existing stockholders. Additionally, shareholders will experience economic dilution when new shares are issued at prices lower than the value of existing shares. Creditors, likewise, are concerned about both kinds of dilution from new debt issuances. Even where fair value is given for new credit, to the extent that such loans or bonds increase the percentage of the firm financed by creditors rather than stockholders, they reduce the "equity cushion" that protects the corporation and the creditors from default. The other concern involves issuance of new debt on more favorable terms to new creditors—typically by giving them a priority over existing creditors (such as a security interest or mortgage on the debtor's property). In the event of default, this may leave the unsecured creditors with fewer assets to satisfy their claims.

Risky Investments. If a firm sells bonds and the investors expect the proceeds to be employed in the same type of business in which the debtor is presently engaged, the interest rate demanded will be based on that expected level of risk. But if the proceeds are used to enter an entirely new and riskier type of business, the investors would have, with the benefit of hindsight, demanded a higher interest rate. Typically, in public bond offerings the use of proceeds will be disclosed to comply with federal and state securities laws. This will not generally be the case with commercial loans from banks, insurance companies and other lenders. Further, the disclosures will only cover the immediate use of the proceeds. Nothing in the securities laws prevents a subsequent application of the debtor's funds to riskier uses (the "going to Las Vegas" phenomenon). Think about the steady changes in the business of Liberty Media Corporation in the preceding case. One can imagine a company engaged in the manufacture and sale of consumer cosmetics or generic drugs such as aspirin suddenly deciding that entry into biotechnology to cure cancer would be potentially more profitable and exciting. The firm's employees and shareholders might be energized, but pre-existing bondholders will probably not be thrilled.

Dividends and Other Distributions. Creditors lend with the expectation that the proceeds will be used in the business, as discussed above. But they also expect that the existing assets of the business, most notably liquid assets, will not be withdrawn. How would you feel if you loaned a company $1000 and it immediately paid out that cash as a dividend to shareholders? Such withdrawals have the same effect on the equity cushion as additional borrowings, making equity a smaller proportion of the capital invested in the business. Distributions can come in a variety of forms. Dividends are the most common. Dividends may be in cash or in assets. The asset distribution may take the form of a spin-off in which an operating unit is placed in a new subsidiary and the shares are dividended up to the existing shareholders. Alternatively, the corporation could spend cash to repurchase shares from its shareholders. Finally, the corporation could engage in a split-off, where the shares of the subsidiary are exchanged for the corporation's own shares.

Underinvestment. The value of a debtor's assets can be reduced over time. Depreciating assets may not be replaced as a debtor allows a business to wind down while distributing cash to shareholders. Other forms of underinvestment, such as passing on new investment opportunities, forming new entities to take advantage of them, or failing to engage in adequate maintenance of existing equipment, may be more difficult to control by contract.

Recall that in Chapter 5 we discussed legal capital as a creditor protection device and learned that older forms of legal capital don't usually offer much of a benefit; they have been largely superseded by insolvency restrictions on distributions (a subject for Chapter 9). Also keep in mind that creditors lacking an elaborate loan agreement might still get protection from provisions allowing courts to set aside fraudulent conveyances. And if a corporation is subject to loan or indenture covenants that protect one group of creditors, then the other creditors such as employees, suppliers and even tort claimants can often free ride on the indenture's restrictions.

B. A DESCRIPTION AND ANALYSIS OF BOND COVENANTS

We are now ready to look at some covenants that expressly address the essence of the stockholder-bondholder conflict. Along the way, we'll also see some backup arguments that might serve as substitutes for addressing these problems.

i. AVOIDING CLAIM DILUTION: RESTRICTING NEW DEBT

The Liberty Media case offers a good example of how a company can adjust both its business and capital structure over time, as it confronts either new opportunities or obstacles. As the company reordered its business, John Malone and management were obviously aware of the possibility of creating risks for bondholders. But at least where a company is solvent, as Liberty was, the duties of management run to the shareholders, not the bondholders (except to observe the terms of the indenture). Firms may issue new securities, both debt and equity, to finance their activities over time. New debt offerings can dilute the existing bondholders' claims against the assets and cash flows of the business. The *Commentaries* offer two means of protecting bondholders: (1) a blanket prohibition on new debt; or (2) restrictions that only permit new debt if certain conditions are met.

Another way that companies can harm bondholders is by creating new debt with superior rights to the existing debt—principally by giving the new debt a senior claim on assets of the firm, often through mortgages or security interests. The *Commentaries* again suggest two means of dealing with this issue: (1) prohibit such mortgages and liens; or (2) require that the existing bondholders share in the priority.

Debtors frequently resist absolute prohibitions because they reduce flexibility and may transfer wealth from shareholders to bondholders. For example, if a firm's business is growing and producing positive net present values from new projects, a prohibition on new debt would require all new financing to come in as equity, thereby increasing the proportion of equity in the firm and reducing risk for bondholders without any commensurate reduction in interest rates. As a result, the *Commentaries* offer a range of compromises: (1) specific dollar limits on the amount of new debt; (2) limiting total debt to a specified percentage of net tangible assets (goodwill is typically excluded); (3) limiting new debt so that debt service (both interest and debt amortization) do not exceed a stated percentage of earnings; or (4) providing that the ratio of current debt not exceed some percentage of current assets (working capital tests).

When imposing these types of limits, defining debt becomes important. You might recall that in Chapter 4 we suggested that capital leases are essentially substitutes for purchase money financing. With a capital lease, the asset will appear on the balance sheet, and the corresponding lease obligation will appear as a liability. Indentures will similarly treat these leases as debt. Likewise, a sale of debtor assets coupled with a lease back to the debtor, should also be treated as debt. Even more conventional leases, such as real estate leases, can be included in the debt total by capitalizing the value of the payment obligation under the lease. Indentures will also include in the debt calculation assumptions or guarantees of debt of other parties, amounts payable in installments under purchase money agreements, and the indebtedness of subsidiaries of the borrower.

a. Sample Covenants

The covenants in this area are generally described as "negative covenants," because of the limitations they impose on debtors. Here are several versions of covenants based on Commentaries, Section 10–11, which restricts "funded debt." "Funded Debt" is defined as follows:

> " 'Funded Debt' means any obligation payable more than one year from the date of determination thereof, which under GAAP is shown on the balance sheet as a liability, including obligations under capital leases, but excluding items customarily reflected below current liabilities, such as deferred federal taxes on income and other reserves."

§ 10–11 Limitations on Additional Funded Debt.

The Company shall not, and shall not permit any Subsidiary to, create, incur, assume or issue, directly or indirectly, or guarantee or in any manner become, directly or indirectly, liable for or with respect to the payment of any Indebtedness, except for:

(1) Indebtedness under the Debentures and this Indenture;

(2) Indebtedness of the Company and any Subsidiary not otherwise referred to in this Section ___ outstanding on the Date of Issue (specifically including the full amount available to the Company or its Subsidiary pursuant to the loan agreements referred to in clauses (i) and (ii) of the definition of "Senior Indebtedness" contained in Section ___ hereof);

(3) Indebtedness (plus interest, premium, fees and other obligations associated therewith), that, immediately after giving effect to the incurrence thereof, does not cause the ratio of Funded Debt to Consolidated Tangible Net Worth plus Shareholder Subordinated Debt to exceed 7:1; or

(4) any deferrals, renewals, extensions, replacements, refinancings or refundings of, or amendments, modifications or supplements to, Indebtedness incurred under clauses (2) or (3) above, whether involving the same or any other lender or creditor or group of lenders or creditors, provided that any such deferrals, renewals, extensions, replacements, refinancings, refundings, amendments, modifications or supplements (i) shall not provide for any mandatory redemption, amortization or sinking fund requirement in an amount greater than or at a time prior to the amounts and times specified in the Indebtedness being deferred, renewed, extended, replaced, refinanced, refunded, amended, modified or supplemented, (ii) shall not exceed the principal amount (plus accrued interest and prepayment premium, if any) of the Indebtedness being renewed, extended, replaced, refinanced or refunded and (iii) shall be subordinated to the Debentures at least to the extent and in the manner, if at all, that the Indebtedness being renewed, extended, replaced, refinanced or refunded is subordinated to the Debentures.

A Variation on ABF Model Covenants, § 10–11, Sample Covenant 1: Limitations on Incurrence of Debt.

(a) The Company will not, and will not permit any Subsidiary to, incur any Debt, other than Intercompany Debt, that is subordinate in right of payment to the Notes, if, immediately after giving effect to the incurrence of such Debt and the application of the proceeds thereof, the aggregate principal amount of all outstanding Debt of the Company and its Subsidiaries on a consolidated basis determined in accordance with GAAP is greater than 60% of the sum of (i) the Company's Adjusted Total Assets as of the end of the most recent fiscal quarter prior to the incurrence of such additional Debt and (ii) the increase in Adjusted Total Assets since the end of such quarter (including any increase resulting from the incurrence of additional Debt).

(b) The Company will not, and will not permit any Subsidiary to, incur any Debt if the ratio of Consolidated Income Available for Debt Service to the Annual Service Charge on the date on which such additional Debt is to be incurred, on a pro forma basis, after giving effect to the incurrence of such Debt and to the application of the proceeds thereof would have been less than 1.5 to 1.

(c) The Company will not, and will not permit any Subsidiary to, incur any Debt secured by any mortgage, lien, charge, pledge, encumbrance or security interest of any kind upon any of the properties of the Company or any Subsidiary ("Secured Debt"), whether owned at the date hereof or hereafter acquired, if, immediately after giving effect to the incurrence of such Secured Debt and the application of the proceeds thereof, the aggregate principal amount of all outstanding Secured Debt of the Company and its Subsidiaries on a consolidated basis is greater than 40% of the sum of (i) the Company's Adjusted Total Assets as of the end of the most recent fiscal quarter prior to the incurrence of such additional Debt and (ii) the increase in Adjusted Total Assets since the end of such quarter (including any increase resulting from the incurrence of additional Debt).

(d) The Company will at all times maintain an Unencumbered Total Asset Value in an amount not less than 150% of the aggregate principal amount of all outstanding unsecured Debt of the Company and its Subsidiaries on a consolidated basis.

For purposes of the foregoing provisions regarding the limitation on the incurrence of Debt, Debt shall be deemed to be "incurred" by the Company or a Subsidiary whenever the Company or such Subsidiary shall create, assume, guarantee or otherwise become liable in respect thereof.

There are other negative covenants designed to protect against senior debt, that is, debt that is secured by the assets of the firm.

Variation on Model Covenants, § 10–10: Negative Pledge.

Neither the Company nor any Subsidiary will create, assume or suffer to exist any Lien on any asset now owned or hereafter acquired by it, except:

(a) Liens in favor of the Banks securing the Loans hereunder;

(b) Liens for taxes or assessments or other government charges or levies if not yet due and payable or if due and payable if they are being contested in good faith by appropriate proceedings and for which appropriate reserves are maintained;

(c) Liens imposed by law, such as mechanic's, materialmen's, landlord's, warehousemen's and carrier's Liens, and other similar Liens, securing obligations incurred in the ordinary course of business which are not past due for more than 30 days, or which are being contested in good faith by appropriate proceedings and for which appropriate reserves have been established;

(d) Liens under workmen's compensation, unemployment insurance, social security or similar legislation;

(e) Liens, deposits or pledges to secure the performance of bids, tenders, contracts (other than contracts for the payment of money), leases (permitted under the terms of this Agreement), public or statutory obligations, surety, stay, appeal, indemnity, performance or other similar bonds, or other similar obligations arising in the ordinary course of business;

(f) judgment and other similar Liens arising in connection with court proceedings; provided that the execution or other enforcement of such Liens is effectively stayed and the claims secured thereby are being actively contested in good faith and by appropriate proceedings;

(g) easements, rights-of-way, restrictions and other similar encumbrances which, in the aggregate, do not materially interfere with the occupation, use and enjoyment by the Company or any such Subsidiary of the property assets encumbered thereby in the normal course of its business or materially impair the value of the property subject thereto;

(h) Liens securing obligations of such a Subsidiary to the Company or another such Subsidiary;

(i) Liens set forth in Schedule III; and

(j) Liens not otherwise permitted by the foregoing clauses of this Section securing indebtedness in an aggregate principal amount at any one time outstanding not to exceed 30% of Consolidated Tangible Net Worth.

Tangible Net Worth is a defined term. Here is a sample:

> " 'TANGIBLE NET WORTH' means, as of any date, the difference of (i) Net Worth, minus (ii) to the extent included in determining the amount under the foregoing clause (i), the net book value of goodwill, cost in excess of fair value of net assets acquired, patents, trademarks, tradenames and copyrights, treasury stock and all other assets which are deemed intangible assets under Agreement Accounting Principles."

Metropolitan Life Insurance Company v. RJR Nabisco, Inc.

716 F.Supp. 1504 (S.D.N.Y. 1989)

■ WALKER, J.

I. INTRODUCTION

The corporate parties to this action are among the country's most sophisticated financial institutions, as familiar with the Wall Street investment community and the securities market as American consumers are with the Oreo cookies and Winston cigarettes made by defendant RJR Nabisco, Inc. (sometimes "the company" or "RJR Nabisco"). The present action traces its origins to October 20, 1988, when F. Ross Johnson, then the Chief Executive Officer of RJR Nabisco, proposed a $17 billion leveraged buy-out ("LBO") of the company's shareholders, at $75 per share.[1] Within a few days, a bidding war developed among the investment group led by Johnson and the investment firm of Kohlberg Kravis Roberts & Co. ("KKR"), and others. On December 1, 1988, a special committee of RJR Nabisco directors, established by the company specifically to consider the competing proposals, recommended that the company accept the KKR proposal, a $24 billion LBO that called for the purchase of the company's outstanding stock at roughly $109 per share.

The flurry of activity late last year that accompanied the bidding war for RJR Nabisco spawned at least eight lawsuits, filed before this Court, charging the company and its former CEO with a variety of securities and common law violations. The Court agreed to hear the present action—filed even before the company accepted the KKR proposal—on an expedited basis, with an eye toward March 1, 1989, when RJR Nabisco was expected to merge with the KKR holding entities created to facilitate the LBO. On that date, RJR Nabisco was also scheduled to assume roughly $19 billion of new debt. After a delay unrelated to the present action, the merger was ultimately completed during the week of April 24, 1989.

Plaintiffs now allege, in short, that RJR Nabisco's actions have drastically impaired the value of bonds previously issued to plaintiffs by, in effect, misappropriating the value of those bonds to help finance the LBO and to distribute an enormous windfall to the company's shareholders. As a result, plaintiffs argue, they have unfairly suffered a multimillion dollar loss in the value of their bonds.[4]

* * *

Although the numbers involved in this case are large, and the financing necessary to complete the LBO unprecedented, the legal principles nonetheless remain discrete and familiar. Yet while the

---

1 A leveraged buy-out occurs when a group of investors, usually including members of a company's management team, buy the company under financial arrangements that include little equity and significant new debt. The necessary debt financing typically includes mortgages or high risk/high yield bonds, popularly known as "junk bonds." Additionally, a portion of this debt is generally secured by the company's assets. Some of the acquired company's assets are usually sold after the transaction is completed in order to reduce the debt incurred in the acquisition.

4 Agencies like Standard & Poor's and Moody's generally rate bonds in two broad categories: investment grade and speculative grade. Standard & Poor's rates investment grade bonds from "AAA" to "BBB." Moody's rates those bonds from "AAA" to "Baa3." Speculative grade bonds are rated either "BB" and lower, or "Ba1" and lower, by Standard & Poor's and Moody's, respectively. *See, e.g., Standard and Poor's Debt Rating Criteria* at 10–11. No one disputes that, subsequent to the announcement of the LBO, the RJR Nabisco bonds lost their "A" ratings. [Eds. See Appendix 6-A at the end of this chapter.]

instant motions thus primarily require the Court to evaluate and apply traditional rules of equity and contract interpretation, plaintiffs do raise issues of first impression in the context of an LBO. At the heart of the present motions lies plaintiffs' claim that RJR Nabisco violated a restrictive covenant—not an explicit covenant found within the four corners of the relevant bond indentures, but rather an *implied* covenant of good faith and fair dealing—not to incur the debt necessary to facilitate the LBO and thereby betray what plaintiffs claim was the fundamental basis of their bargain with the company. The company, plaintiffs assert, consistently reassured its bondholders that it had a "mandate" from its Board of Directors to maintain RJR Nabisco's preferred credit rating. Plaintiffs ask this Court first to imply a covenant of good faith and fair dealing that would prevent the recent transaction, then to hold that this covenant has been breached, and finally to require RJR Nabisco to redeem their bonds.

RJR Nabisco defends the LBO by pointing to express provisions in the bond indentures that, *inter alia,* permit mergers and the assumption of additional debt. These provisions, as well as others that could have been included but were not, were known to the market and to plaintiffs, sophisticated investors who freely bought the bonds and were equally free to sell them at any time. Any attempt by this Court to create contractual terms *post hoc*, defendants contend, not only finds no basis in the controlling law and undisputed facts of this case, but also would constitute an impermissible invasion into the free and open operation of the marketplace.

For the reasons set forth below, this Court agrees with defendants. There being no express covenant between the parties that would restrict the incurrence of new debt, and no perceived direction to that end from covenants that are express, this Court will not imply a covenant to prevent the recent LBO and thereby create an indenture term that, while bargained for in other contexts, was not bargained for here and was not even within the mutual contemplation of the parties.

II. BACKGROUND

* * *

A. The Parties:

Metropolitan Life Insurance Co. ("MetLife"), incorporated in New York, is a life insurance company that provides pension benefits for 42 million individuals. According to its most recent annual report, MetLife's assets exceed $88 billion and its debt securities holdings exceed $49 billion. MetLife is a mutual company and therefore has no stockholders and is instead operated for the benefit of its policyholders. MetLife alleges that it owns $340,542,000 in principal amount of six separate RJR Nabisco debt issues, bonds allegedly purchased between July 1975 and July 1988. Some bonds become due as early as this year; others will not become due until 2017. The bonds bear interest rates of anywhere from

8 to 10.25 percent. MetLife also owned 186,000 shares of RJR Nabisco common stock at the time this suit was filed.

* * *

RJR Nabisco, a Delaware corporation, is a consumer products holding company that owns some of the country's best known product lines, including LifeSavers candy, Oreo cookies, and Winston cigarettes. The company was formed in 1985, when R. J. Reynolds Industries, Inc. ("R. J. Reynolds") merged with Nabisco Brands, Inc. ("Nabisco Brands"). In 1979, and thus before the R. J. Reynolds-Nabisco Brands merger, R. J. Reynolds acquired the Del Monte Corporation ("Del Monte"), which distributes canned fruits and vegetables. From January 1987 until February 1989, co-defendant Johnson served as the company's CEO. KKR, a private investment firm, organizes funds through which investors provide pools of equity to finance LBOs.

B. The Indentures:

The bonds implicated by this suit are governed by long, detailed indentures, which in turn are governed by New York contract law. No one disputes that the holders of public bond issues, like plaintiffs here, often enter the market after the indentures have been negotiated and memorialized. Thus, those indentures are often not the product of face-to-face negotiations between the ultimate holders and the issuing company. What remains equally true, however, is that underwriters ordinarily negotiate the terms of the indentures with the issuers. Since the underwriters must then sell or place the bonds, they necessarily negotiate in part with the interests of the buyers in mind. Moreover, these indentures were not secret agreements foisted upon unwitting participants in the bond market. No successive holder is required to accept or to continue to hold the bonds, governed by their accompanying indentures; indeed, plaintiffs readily admit that they could have sold their bonds right up until the announcement of the LBO. Instead, sophisticated investors like plaintiffs are well aware of the indenture terms and, presumably, review them carefully before lending hundreds of millions of dollars to any company.

Indeed, the prospectuses for the indentures contain a statement relevant to this action:

> The Indenture contains no restrictions on the creation of unsecured short-term debt by [RJR Nabisco] or its subsidiaries, no restriction on the creation of unsecured Funded Debt by [RJR Nabisco] or its subsidiaries which are not Restricted Subsidiaries, and no restriction on the payment of dividends by [RJR Nabisco].

Further, as plaintiffs themselves note, the contracts at issue "[do] not impose debt limits, since debt is assumed to be used for productive purposes."

1. The relevant Articles:

A typical RJR Nabisco indenture contains thirteen Articles. At least four of them are relevant to the present motions and thus merit a brief review.

* * *

Article Ten addresses a potential "Consolidation, Merger, Sale or Conveyance," and explicitly sets forth the conditions under which the company can consolidate or merge into or with any other corporation. It provides explicitly that RJR Nabisco "may consolidate with, or sell or convey, all or substantially all of its assets to, or merge into or with any other corporation," so long as the new entity is a United States corporation, and so long as it assumes RJR Nabisco's debt. The Article also requires that any such transaction not result in the company's default under any indenture provision.

2. The elimination of restrictive covenants:

In its Amended Complaint, MetLife lists the six debt issues on which it bases its claims. Indentures for two of those issues—the 10.25 percent Notes due in 1990, of which MetLife continues to hold $10 million, and the 8.9 percent Debentures due in 1996, of which MetLife continues to hold $50 million—once contained express covenants that, among other things, restricted the company's ability to incur precisely the sort of debt involved in the recent LBO. In order to eliminate those restrictions, the parties to this action renegotiated the terms of those indentures, first in 1983 and then again in 1985.

MetLife acquired $50 million principal amount of 10.25 percent Notes from Del Monte in July of 1975. To cover the $50 million, MetLife and Del Monte entered into a loan agreement. That agreement restricted Del Monte's ability, among other things, to incur the sort of indebtedness involved in the RJR Nabisco LBO. In 1979, R. J. Reynolds—the corporate predecessor to RJR Nabisco—purchased Del Monte and assumed its indebtedness. Then, in December of 1983, R. J. Reynolds requested MetLife to agree to deletions of those restrictive covenants in exchange for various guarantees from R. J. Reynolds. A few months later, MetLife and R. J. Reynolds entered into a guarantee and amendment agreement reflecting those terms. Pursuant to that agreement, and in the words of Robert E. Chappell, Jr., MetLife's Executive Vice President, MetLife thus "gave up the restrictive covenants applicable to the Del Monte debt . . . in return for [the parent company's] guarantee and public covenants."

MetLife acquired the 8.9 percent Debentures from R. J. Reynolds in October of 1976 in a private placement. A promissory note evidenced MetLife's $100 million loan. That note, like the Del Monte agreement, contained covenants that restricted R. J. Reynolds' ability to incur new debt. In June of 1985, R. J. Reynolds announced its plans to acquire Nabisco Brands in a $3.6 billion transaction that involved the incurrence of a significant amount of new debt. R. J. Reynolds requested MetLife to waive compliance with these restrictive covenants in light of the Nabisco acquisition.

In exchange for certain benefits, MetLife agreed to exchange its 8.9 percent debentures—which *did* contain explicit debt limitations—for debentures issued under a public indenture—which contain no explicit limits on new debt. An internal MetLife memorandum explained the parties' understanding:

> [MetLife's $100 million financing of the Nabisco Brands purchase] had its origins in discussions with RJR regarding potential covenant violations in the 8.90% Notes. More specifically, *in its acquisition of Nabisco Brands, RJR was slated to incur significant new long-term debt, which would have caused a violation in the funded indebtedness incurrence tests in the 8.90% Notes.* In the discussions regarding [MetLife's] willingness to consent to the additional indebtedness, *it was determined that a mutually beneficial approach to the problem* was to 1) agree on a new financing having a rate and a maturity desirable for [MetLife] and 2) modify the 8.90% Notes. The former was accomplished with agreement on the proposed financing, while the latter was accomplished by [MetLife] agreeing to substitute RJR's public indenture covenants for the covenants in the 8.90% Notes. In addition to the covenant substitution, RJR has agreed to "debenturize" the 8.90% Notes upon [MetLife's] request. This will permit [MetLife] to sell the 8.90% Notes to the public.

3. The recognition and effect of the LBO trend:

Other internal MetLife documents help frame the background to this action, for they accurately describe the changing securities markets and the responses those changes engendered from sophisticated market participants, such as MetLife and Jefferson-Pilot. At least as early as 1982, MetLife recognized an LBO's effect on bond values.[14] In the spring of that year, MetLife participated in the financing of an LBO of a company called Reeves Brothers ("Reeves"). At the time of that LBO, MetLife also held bonds in that company. Subsequent to the LBO, as a MetLife memorandum explained, the "Debentures of Reeves were downgraded by Standard & Poor's from BBB to B and by Moody's from Baal to Ba3, thereby lowering the value of the Notes and Debentures held by [MetLife]."

MetLife further recognized its "inability to force any type of payout of the [Reeves'] Notes or the Debentures as a result of the buy-out [which]

14 MetLife itself began investing in LBOs as early as 1980. *See* MetLife Special Projects Memorandum, dated June 17, 1989, attached as Bradley Aff. Exh. V, at 1 ("[MetLife's] history of investing in leveraged buyout transactions dates back to 1980; and through 1984, [MetLife] reviewed a large number of LBO investment opportunities presented to us by various investment banking firms and LBO specialists. Over this five-year period, [MetLife] invested, on a direct basis, approximately $430 million to purchase debt and equity securities in 10 such transactions . . .").

was somewhat disturbing at the time we considered a participation in the new financing. However," the memorandum continued,

> our concern was tempered since, as a stockholder in [the holding company used to facilitate the transaction], we would benefit from the increased net income attributable to the continued presence of the low coupon indebtedness. The recent downgrading of the Reeves Debentures and the consequent "loss" in value has again raised questions regarding our ability to have forced a payout. *Questions have also been raised about our ability to force payouts in similar future situations, particularly when we would not be participating in the buy-out financing.*

Id. (emphasis added). In the memorandum, MetLife sought to answer those very "questions" about how it might force payouts in "similar future situations."

> *A method of closing this apparent "loophole," thereby forcing a payout of [MetLife's] holdings, would be through a covenant dealing with a change in ownership.* Such a covenant is fairly standard in financings with privately-held companies . . . It provides the lender with an option to end a particular borrowing relationship via some type of special redemption . . . *Id.*, at 2 (emphasis added).

A more comprehensive memorandum, prepared in late 1985, evaluated and explained several aspects of the corporate world's increasing use of mergers, takeovers and other debt-financed transactions. That memorandum first reviewed the available protection for lenders such as MetLife:

> Covenants are incorporated into loan documents to ensure that after a lender makes a loan, the creditworthiness of the borrower and the lender's ability to reach the borrower's assets do not deteriorate substantially. *Restrictions on the incurrence of debt,* sale of assets, mergers, dividends, restricted payments and loans and advances to affiliates *are some of the traditional negative covenants that can help protect lenders in the event their obligors become involved in undesirable merger/takeover situations.*

The memorandum then surveyed market realities:

> Because almost any industrial company is apt to engineer a takeover or be taken over itself, *Business Week* says that investors are beginning to view debt securities of high grade industrial corporations as Wall Street's riskiest investments. In addition, *because public bondholders do not enjoy the protection of any restrictive covenants,* owners of high grade corporates face substantial losses from takeover situations, if not immediately, then when the bond market finally adjusts. . . There have been

> 10–15 merger/takeover/LBO situations where, *due to the lack of covenant protection, [MetLife] has had no choice but to remain a lender to a less creditworthy obligor*. . . The fact that the quality of our investment portfolio is greater than the other large insurance companies . . . may indicate that we have negotiated better covenant protection than other institutions, thus generally being able to require prepayment when situations become too risky . . . [However,] a problem exists. And *because the current merger craze is not likely to decelerate* and because there exist vehicles to circumvent traditional covenants, the problem will probably continue. Therefore, *perhaps it is time to institute appropriate language designed to protect Metropolitan from the negative implications of mergers and takeovers.* (emphasis added).[15]

Indeed, MetLife does not dispute that, as a member of a bondholders' association, it received and discussed a proposed model indenture, which included a "comprehensive covenant" entitled "Limitations on Shareholders' Payments." As becomes clear from reading the proposed—but never adopted—provision, it was "intend[ed] to provide protection against all of the types of situations in which shareholders profit at the expense of bondholders." *Id.* The provision dictated that the "corporation will not, and will not permit any subsidiary to, directly or indirectly, make any shareholder payment unless . . . (1) the aggregate amount of all shareholder payment during the period [at issue] . . . shall not exceed [figure left blank]." The term "shareholder payments" is defined to include "restructuring distributions, stock repurchases, debt incurred or guaranteed to finance merger payments to shareholders, etc."

Apparently, that provision—or provisions with similar intentions—never went beyond the discussion stage at MetLife. That fact is easily understood; indeed, MetLife's own documents articulate several reasonable, undisputed explanations:

> While it would be possible to broaden the change in ownership covenant to cover any acquisition-oriented transaction, *we might well encounter significant resistance in implementation with larger public companies* . . . With respect to implementation, we would be faced with the task of imposing a non-standard limitation on potential borrowers, *which could be a difficult task in today's highly competitive marketplace. Competitive pressures notwithstanding, it would seem that*

---

15 During discovery, MetLife produced from its files an article that appeared in *The New York Times* on January 7, 1986. The article, like the memoranda discussed above, reviewed the position of bondholders like MetLife and Jefferson-Pilot:

"Debt-financed acquisitions, as well as those defensive actions to thwart takeovers, have generally resulted in lower bond ratings. . . . Of course, a major problem for debtholders is that, compared with shareholders, they have relatively little power over management decisions. *Their rights are essentially confined to the covenants restricting, say, the level of debt a company can accrue.*"

> *management of larger public companies would be particularly opposed to such a covenant since its effect would be to increase the cost of an acquisition* (due to an assumed debt repayment), a factor that could well lower the price of any tender offer (thereby impacting shareholders).

The November 1985 memorandum explained that

> obviously, our ability to implement methods of takeover protection will vary between the public and private market. In that public securities do not contain any meaningful covenants, it would be very difficult for [MetLife] to demand takeover protection in public bonds. Such a requirement would effectively take us out of the public industrial market. A recent *Business Week* article does suggest, however, that there is increasing talk among lending institutions about requiring blue chip companies to compensate them for the growing risk of downgradings. *This talk, regarding such protection as restrictions on future debt financings, is met with skepticism by the investment banking community which feels that CFO's are not about to give up the option of adding debt and do not really care if their companies' credit ratings drop a notch or two.*

The Court quotes these documents at such length not because they represent an "admission" or "waiver" from MetLife, or an "assumption of risk" in any tort sense, or its "consent" to any particular course of conduct—all terms discussed at even greater length in the parties' submissions. Rather, the documents set forth the background to the present action, and highlight the risks inherent in the market itself, for any investor. Investors as sophisticated as MetLife and Jefferson-Pilot would be hard-pressed to plead ignorance of these market risks. Indeed, MetLife has not disputed the facts asserted in its own internal documents. Nor has Jefferson-Pilot—presumably an institution no less sophisticated than MetLife—offered any reason to believe that its understanding of the securities market differed in any material respect from the description and analysis set forth in the MetLife documents. Those documents, after all, were not born in a vacuum. They are descriptions of, and responses to, the market in which investors like MetLife and Jefferson-Pilot knowingly participated.

These documents must be read in conjunction with plaintiffs' Amended Complaint. That document asserts that the LBO "undermines the foundation of the investment grade debt market . . . ," that, although "the indentures do not purport to limit dividends or debt . . . such covenants were believed unnecessary with blue chip companies . . .", that "the transaction contradicts the premise of the investment grade market . . ."; and, finally, that "this buy-out was not contemplated at the time the debt was issued, contradicts the premise of the investment grade ratings that RJR Nabisco actively solicited and received, and is inconsistent with the understandings of the market . . . which plaintiffs relied upon."

Solely for the purposes of these motions, the Court accepts various factual assertions advanced by plaintiffs: first, that RJR Nabisco actively solicited "investment grade" ratings for its debt; second, that it relied on descriptions of its strong capital structure and earnings record which included prominent display of its ability to pay the interest obligations on its long-term debt several times over; and third, that the company made express or implied representations not contained in the relevant indentures concerning its future creditworthiness. In support of those allegations, plaintiffs have marshaled a number of speeches made by co-defendant Johnson and other executives of RJR Nabisco.[18] In addition, plaintiffs rely on an affidavit sworn to by John Dowdle, the former Treasurer and then Senior Vice President of RJR Nabisco from 1970 until 1987. In his opinion, the LBO "clearly undermines the fundamental premise of the company's bargain with the bondholders, and the commitment that I believe the company made to the bondholders . . . I firmly believe that the company made commitments . . . that require it to redeem [these bonds and notes] before paying out the value to the shareholders."

III. DISCUSSION

At the outset, the Court notes that nothing in its evaluation is substantively altered by the speeches given or remarks made by RJR Nabisco executives, or the opinions of various individuals—what, for instance, former RJR Nabisco Treasurer Dowdle personally did or did not "firmly believe" the indentures meant. The parol evidence rule bars plaintiffs from arguing that the speeches made by company executives prove defendants agreed or acquiesced to a term that does not appear in the indentures. In interpreting these contracts, this Court must be concerned with what the parties intended, but only to the extent that what they intended is evidenced by what is written in the indentures.

The indentures at issue clearly address the eventuality of a merger. They impose certain related restrictions not at issue in this suit, but no restriction that would prevent the recent RJR Nabisco merger transaction. The indentures also explicitly set forth provisions for the adoption of new covenants, if such a course is deemed appropriate. While it may be true that no explicit provision either permits or prohibits an LBO, such contractual silence itself cannot create ambiguity to avoid the dictates of the parole evidence rule, particularly where the indentures impose no debt limitations.

---

18 *See, e.g.,* Address by F. Ross Johnson, November 12, 1987, P. Exh. 8, at 5 ("Our strong balance sheet is a cornerstone of our strategies. It gives us the resources to modernize facilities, develop new technologies, bring on new products, and support our leading brands around the world."); Remarks of Edward J. Robinson, Executive Vice President and Chief Financial Officer, February 15, 1988, P. Exh. 6, at 1 ("RJR Nabisco's financial strategy is . . . to enhance the strength of the balance sheet by reducing the level of debt as well as lowering the cost of existing debt."); Remarks by Dr. Robert J. Carbonell, Vice Chairman of RJR Nabisco, June 3, 1987, P. Exh. 10, at 5 ("We will not sacrifice our longer-term health for the sake of short term heroics.").

Under certain circumstances, however, courts will, as plaintiffs note, consider extrinsic evidence to evaluate the scope of an implied covenant of good faith. However, the Second Circuit has established a different rule for customary, or boiler plate, provisions of detailed indentures used and relied upon throughout the securities market, such as those at issue. Thus, in *Sharon Steel Corporation v. Chase Manhattan Bank, N.A.*, 691 F.2d 1039 (2d Cir. 1982), Judge Winter concluded that

> boiler plate provisions are ... not the consequences of the relationship of particular borrowers and lenders and do not depend upon particularized intentions of the parties to an indenture. There are no adjudicative facts relating to the parties to the litigation for a jury to find and the meaning of boiler plate provisions is, therefore, a matter of law rather than fact. Moreover, uniformity in interpretation is important to the efficiency of capital markets ... Whereas participants in the capital market can adjust their affairs according to a uniform interpretation, whether it be correct or not as an initial proposition, the creation of enduring uncertainties as to the meaning of boiler plate provisions would decrease the value of all debenture issues and greatly impair the efficient working of capital markets ... Just such uncertainties would be created if interpretation of boiler plate provisions were submitted to juries sitting in every judicial district in the nation.

Id. at 1048. *See also* Morgan Stanley & Co. v. Archer Daniels Midland Co., 570 F. Supp. 1529, 1535–36 (S. D. N. Y. 1983) (Sand, J.) ("[Plaintiff] concedes that the legality of [the transaction at issue] would depend on a factual inquiry ... This case-by-case approach is problematic ... [Plaintiff's theory] appears keyed to the subjective expectations of the bondholders ... and reads a subjective element into what presumably should be an objective determination based on the language appearing in the bond agreement."); *Purcell v. Flying Tiger Line, Inc.*, No. 82–3505, at 5, 8 (S. D. N. Y. Jan. 12, 1984) (CES) ("The Indenture does not contain any such limitation [as the one proposed by plaintiff]. . . In light of our holding that the Indenture unambiguously permits the transaction at issue in this case, we are precluded from considering any of the extrinsic evidence that plaintiff offers on this motion ... It would be improper to consider evidence as to the subjective intent, collateral representations, and either the statements or the conduct of the parties in performing the contract.") (citations omitted). Ignoring these principles, plaintiffs would have this Court vary what they themselves have admitted is "indenture boiler plate," to comport with collateral representations and their subjective understandings.

A. *Plaintiffs' Case Against the RJR Nabisco LBO:*

1. Count One: The implied covenant:

In their first count, plaintiffs assert that defendant RJR Nabisco owes a continuing duty of good faith and fair dealing in connection with the contract [i.e., the indentures] through which it borrowed money from MetLife, Jefferson-Pilot and other holders of its debt, including a duty not to frustrate the purpose of the contracts to the debtholders or to deprive the debtholders of the intended object of the contracts—purchase of investment-grade securities.

> In the "buy-out," the company breaches the duty [or implied covenant] of good faith and fair dealing by, *inter alia*, destroying the investment grade quality of the debt and transferring that value to the "buy-out" proponents and to the shareholders.

In effect, plaintiffs contend that express covenants were not necessary because an *implied* covenant would prevent what defendants have now done.

A plaintiff always can allege a violation of an express covenant. If there has been such a violation, of course, the court need not reach the question of whether or not an *implied* covenant has been violated. That inquiry surfaces where, while the express terms may not have been technically breached, one party has nonetheless effectively deprived the other of those express, explicitly bargained-for benefits. In such a case, a court will read an implied covenant of good faith and fair dealing into a contract to ensure that neither party deprives the other of "the fruits of the agreement." Such a covenant is implied only where the implied term "is consistent with other mutually agreed upon terms in the contract." In other words, the implied covenant will only aid and further the explicit terms of the agreement and will never impose an obligation " 'which would be inconsistent with other terms of the contractual relationship.' " *Id.* (citation omitted). Viewed another way, the implied covenant of good faith is breached only when one party seeks to prevent the contract's performance or to withhold its benefits. As a result, it thus ensures that parties to a contract perform the substantive, bargained-for terms of their agreement.

In contracts like bond indentures, "an implied covenant . . . derives its substance directly from the language of the Indenture, and 'cannot give the holders of Debentures any rights inconsistent with those set out in the Indenture.' *[Where] plaintiffs' contractual rights [have not been] violated, there can have been no breach of an implied covenant.*"

* * *

The appropriate analysis, then, is first to examine the indentures to determine "the fruits of the agreement" between the parties, and then to decide whether those "fruits" have been spoiled-which is to say, whether plaintiffs' contractual rights have been violated by defendants.

The American Bar Foundation's *Commentaries on Indentures* ("the *Commentaries*"), relied upon and respected by both plaintiffs and defendants, describes the rights and risks generally found in bond indentures like those at issue:

> The most obvious and important characteristic of long-term debt financing is that the holder ordinarily has not bargained for and does not expect any substantial gain in the value of the security to compensate for the risk of loss . . . The significant fact, *which accounts in part for the detailed protective provisions of the typical long-term debt financing instrument*, is that *the lender (the purchaser of the debt security) can expect only interest at the prescribed rate plus the eventual return of the principal.* Except for possible increases in the market value of the debt security because of changes in interest rates, the debt security will seldom be worth more than the lender paid for it . . . It may, of course, become worth much less. Accordingly, the typical investor in a long-term debt security is primarily interested in every reasonable assurance that the principal and interest will be paid when due. . . . Short of bankruptcy, the debt security holder can do nothing to protect himself against actions of the borrower which jeopardize its ability to pay the debt unless he . . . establishes his rights through contractual provisions set forth in the debt agreement or indenture.

Id. at 1–2 (1971) (emphasis added).

A review of the parties' submissions and the indentures themselves satisfies the Court that the substantive "fruits" guaranteed by those contracts and relevant to the present motions include the periodic and regular payment of interest and the eventual repayment of principal. ("The Issuer covenants . . . that it will duly and punctually pay . . . the principal of, and interest on, each of the Securities . . . at the respective times and in the manner provided in such Securities . . ."). According to a typical indenture, a default shall occur if the company either (1) fails to pay principal when due; (2) fails to make a timely sinking fund payment; (3) fails to pay within 30 days of the due date thereof any interest on the date; or (4) fails duly to observe or perform any of the express covenants or agreements set forth in the agreement. Plaintiffs' Amended Complaint nowhere alleges that RJR Nabisco has breached these contractual obligations; interest payments continue and there is no reason to believe that the principal will not be paid when due.

It is not necessary to decide that indentures like those at issue could never support a finding of additional benefits, under different circumstances with different parties. Rather, for present purposes, it is sufficient to conclude what obligation is *not* covered, either explicitly or implicitly, by these contracts held by these plaintiffs. Accordingly, this Court holds that the "fruits" of these indentures do not include an implied restrictive covenant that would prevent the incurrence of new debt to facilitate the recent LBO. To hold otherwise would permit these plaintiffs to straightjacket the company in order to guarantee their investment. These plaintiffs do not invoke an implied covenant of good faith to protect a legitimate, mutually contemplated benefit of the indentures; rather, they seek to have this Court create an additional benefit for which they did not bargain.

Although the indentures generally permit mergers and the incurrence of new debt, there admittedly is not an explicit indenture provision to the contrary of what plaintiffs now claim the implied covenant requires. That absence, however, does *not* mean that the Court should imply into those very same indentures a covenant of good faith so broad that it imposes a new, substantive term of enormous scope. This is so particularly where, as here, that very term—a limitation on the incurrence of additional debt—has in other past contexts been expressly bargained for; particularly where the indentures grant the company broad discretion in the management of its affairs, as plaintiffs admit; particularly where the indentures explicitly set forth specific provisions for the adoption of new covenants and restrictions; and *especially* where there has been no breach of the parties' bargained-for contractual rights on which the implied covenant necessarily is based. While the Court stands ready to employ an implied covenant of good faith to ensure that such bargained-for rights are performed and upheld, it will not, however, permit an implied covenant to shoehorn into an indenture additional terms plaintiffs now wish had been included.

Plaintiffs argue in the most general terms that the fundamental basis of all these indentures was that an LBO along the lines of the recent RJR Nabisco transaction would never be undertaken, that indeed *no* action would be taken, intentionally or not, that would significantly deplete the company's assets. Accepting plaintiffs' theory, their fundamental bargain with defendants dictated that nothing would be done to jeopardize the extremely high probability that the company would remain able to make interest payments and repay principal over the 20 to 30 year indenture term—and perhaps by logical extension even included the right to ask a court "to make sure that plaintiffs had made a good investment." Gardner, 589 F. Supp. at 674. But as Judge Knapp aptly concluded in *Gardner*, "Defendants . . . were under a duty to carry out the terms of the contract, but not to make sure that plaintiffs had made a good investment. The former they have done; the latter we have no jurisdiction over." *Id.* Plaintiffs' submissions and MetLife's previous undisputed internal memoranda remind the Court that a "fundamental basis" or a "fruit of an agreement" is often in the eye of the beholder, whose vision may well change along with the market, and who may, with hindsight, imagine a different bargain than the one he actually and initially accepted with open eyes.

The sort of unbounded and one-sided elasticity urged by plaintiffs would interfere with and destabilize the market. And this Court, like the parties to these contracts, cannot ignore or disavow the marketplace in which the contract is performed. Nor can it ignore the expectations of that market—expectations, for instance, that the terms of an indenture will be upheld, and that a court will not, *sua sponte*, add new substantive terms to that indenture as it sees fit. The Court has no reason to believe that the market, in evaluating bonds such as those at issue here, did not discount for the possibility that any company, even one the size of RJR Nabisco, might engage in an LBO heavily financed by debt. That the bonds did not lose any of their value until the October 20, 1988 announcement of a possible RJR Nabisco LBO only suggests that the market had theretofore evaluated the risks of such a transaction as slight.

The Court recognizes that the market is not a static entity, but instead involves what plaintiffs call "evolving understanding[s]." Just as the growing prevalence of LBO's has helped change certain ground rules and expectations in the field of mergers and acquisitions, so too it has obviously affected the bond market, a fact no one disputes. To support their argument that defendants have violated an implied covenant, plaintiffs contend that, since the October 20, 1988 announcement, the bond market has "stopped functioning." They argue that if they had "sold and abandoned the market [before October 20, 1988], the market, if everyone had the same attitude, would have disappeared." What plaintiffs term "stopped functioning" or "disappeared," however, are properly seen as natural responses and adjustments to market realities. Plaintiffs of course do not contend that no new issues are being sold, or that existing issues are no longer being traded or have become worthless.

To respond to changed market forces, new indenture provisions can be negotiated, such as provisions that were in fact once included in the 8.9 percent and 10.25 percent debentures implicated by this action. New provisions could include special debt restrictions or change-of-control covenants. There is no guarantee, of course, that companies like RJR Nabisco would accept such new covenants; parties retain the freedom to enter into contracts as they choose. But presumably, multi-billion dollar investors like plaintiffs have some say in the terms of the investments they make and continue to hold. And, presumably, companies like RJR Nabisco need the infusions of capital such investors are capable of providing.

Whatever else may be true about this case, it certainly does not present an example of the classic sort of form contract or contract of adhesion often frowned upon by courts. In those cases, what motivates a court is the strikingly inequitable nature of the parties' respective bargaining positions. Plaintiffs here entered this "liquid trading market," with their eyes open and were free to leave at any time. Instead they remained there notwithstanding its well understood risks.

Ultimately, plaintiffs cannot escape the inherent illogic of their argument. On the one hand, it is undisputed that investors like plaintiffs recognized that companies like RJR Nabisco strenuously opposed additional restrictive covenants that might limit the incurrence of new debt or the company's ability to engage in a merger. Furthermore, plaintiffs argue that they had no choice other than to accept the indentures as written, without additional restrictive covenants, or to "abandon" the market.

Yet on the other hand, plaintiffs ask this Court to imply a covenant that would have just that restrictive effect because, they contend, it reflects precisely the fundamental assumption of the market and the fundamental basis of their bargain with defendants. If that truly were the case here, it is difficult to imagine why an insistence on that term would have forced the plaintiffs to abandon the market. The Second Circuit has offered a better explanation: "[a] promise by the defendant should be implied only if the court may rightfully assume that the parties would have included it in their written agreement had their attention been called to it . . . *Any such assumption in this case would be completely unwarranted.*" *Neuman v. Pike*, 591 F.2d 191, 195 (2d Cir. 1979) (emphasis added, citations omitted).

In the final analysis, plaintiffs offer no objective or reasonable standard for a court to use in its effort to define the sort of actions their "implied covenant" would permit a corporation to take, and those it would not.[28] Plaintiffs say only that investors like themselves rely upon the "skill" and "good faith" of a company's board and management, and that their covenant would prevent the company from "destroy[ing] . . . the legitimate expectations of its long-term bondholders." As is clear from the preceding discussion, however, plaintiffs have failed to convince the Court that by upholding the explicit, bargained-for terms of the indenture, RJR Nabisco has either exhibited bad faith or destroyed plaintiffs' *legitimate*, protected expectations.

* * *

2. Count Five: In Equity:

Count Five substantially restates and realleges the contract claims advanced in Count I. Along with these repetitions, plaintiffs blend in allegations that the transaction "frustrates the commercial purpose" of the parties, under "circumstances [that] are outrageous, and . . . it would [therefore] be unconscionable to allow the 'buy-out' to proceed . . ." Those very issues—frustration of purpose and unconscionability—are equally matters of contract law, of course, and plaintiffs could just as easily have advanced them in Count I. Indeed, to some extent plaintiffs did advance these claims in that Count. ("RJR Nabisco owes a continuing duty . . . not to frustrate the purpose of the contracts . . ."). For present purposes, it makes no difference how plaintiffs characterize their arguments. Their equity claims cannot survive defendants' motion for summary judgment.

In their papers, plaintiffs variously attempt to justify Count V as being based on unjust enrichment, frustration of purpose, an alleged

28 Under plaintiffs' theory, bondholders might ask a court to prohibit a company like RJR Nabisco not only from engaging in an LBO, but also from entering a new line of business-with the attendant costs of building new physical plants and hiring new workers—or from acquiring new businesses such as RJR Nabisco did when it acquired Del Monte.

breach of something approaching a fiduciary duty, or a general claim of unconscionability. Each claim fails. First, as even plaintiffs recognize, an unjust enrichment claim requires a court first to find that "the circumstances [are] such that in equity and good conscience the defendant should make restitution." Plaintiffs have not alleged a violation of a single explicit term of the indentures at issue, and on the facts alleged this Court has determined that an implicit covenant of good faith and fair dealing has not been violated. Under these circumstances, this Court concludes that defendants need not, "in equity and good conscience," make restitution.

Second, in support of their motions plaintiffs claim frustration of purpose. Yet even resolving all ambiguities and drawing all reasonable inferences in plaintiffs' favor, their claim cannot stand. A claim of frustration of purpose has three elements:

> First, the purpose that is frustrated must have been a principal purpose of that party in making the contract. . . The object must be so completely the basis of the contract that, as both parties understand, without it the transaction would make little sense. Second, the frustration must be substantial. It is not enough that the transaction has become less profitable for the affected party or even that he will sustain a loss. The frustration must be so severe that it is not fairly to be regarded as within the risks that he assumed under the contract. Third, the non-occurrence of the frustrating event must have been a basic assumption on which the contract was made.

Restatement (Second) of Contracts, 265 comment a (1981). * * * Similarly, there is no indication here that an alleged refusal to incur debt to facilitate an LBO was the "essence" or "principal purpose" of the indentures, and no mention of such an alleged restriction is made in the agreements. Further, while plaintiffs' bonds may have lost some of their value, "discharge under this doctrine has been limited to instances where a virtually cataclysmic, wholly unforeseeable event *renders the contract valueless to one party.*" That is not the case here. Moreover, "the frustration of purpose defense is not available where, as here, the event which allegedly frustrated the purpose of the contract . . . was clearly foreseeable." Faced with MetLife's internal memoranda, plaintiffs cannot but admit that "MetLife has been concerned about 'buy-outs' for several years." Nor do plaintiffs provide any reasonable basis for believing that a party as sophisticated as Jefferson-Pilot was any less cognizant of the market around it.

Third, plaintiffs advance a claim that remains based, their assertions to the contrary notwithstanding, on an alleged breach of a fiduciary duty. Defendants go to great lengths to prove that the law of Delaware, and not New York, governs this question. Defendants' attempt to rely on Delaware law is readily explained by even a cursory reading of Simons v. Cogan, 549 A.2d 300, 303 (Del. 1988), the recent Delaware

Supreme Court ruling which held, *inter alia,* that a corporate bond "represents a contractual entitlement to the repayment of a debt and does not represent an equitable interest in the issuing corporation necessary for the imposition of a trust relationship with concomitant fiduciary duties." Before such a fiduciary duty arises, "an existing property right or equitable interest supporting such a duty must exist." *Id.* at 304. A bondholder, that court concluded, "acquires no equitable interest, and remains a creditor of the corporation whose interests are protected by the contractual terms of the indenture." *Id.* Defendants argue that New York law is not to the contrary, but the single Supreme Court case they cite—a case decided over fifty years ago that was not squarely presented with the issue addressed by the *Simons* court-provides something less than dispositive support. *See* Marx v. Merchants' National Properties, Inc., 148 Misc. 6, 7, 265 N. Y. S. 163, 165 (1933). For their part, plaintiffs more convincingly demonstrate that New York law applies than that New York law recognizes their claim.[34]

Regardless, this Court finds *Simons* persuasive, and believes that a New York court would agree with that conclusion. In the venerable case of Meinhard v. Salmon, 249 N.Y. 458, 164 N. E. 545 (1928), then Chief Judge Cardozo explained the obligations imposed on a fiduciary, and why those obligations are so special and rare:

> Many forms of conduct permissible in a workaday world for those acting at arm's length, are forbidden to those bound by fiduciary ties. A trustee is held to something stricter than the morals of the market place. Not honesty alone, but the punctilio of an honor the most sensitive, is then the standard of behavior. As to this there has developed a tradition that is unbending and inveterate. Uncompromising rigidity has been the attitude of courts of equity when petitioned to undermine the rule of undivided loyalty . . . Only thus has the level of conduct for fiduciaries been kept at a level higher than that trodden by the crowd.

Id. at 464 (citation omitted). Before a court recognizes the duty of a "punctilio of an honor the most sensitive," it must be certain that the complainant is entitled to more than the "morals of the market place," and the protections offered by actions based on fraud, state statutes or the panoply of available federal securities laws. This Court has concluded

[34] The indenture provision designating New York law as controlling, *see supra* n.10, would, one might assume, resolve at least the issue of the applicable law. In quoting the relevant indenture provision, however, plaintiffs omit the proviso "except as may otherwise be required by mandatory provisions of law." Defendants, however, fail to argue that the internal affairs doctrine, which they assert dictates that Delaware law controls this question, is such a "mandatory provision of law." Nor do defendants respond to plaintiffs' reliance on First National City Bank v. Banco Para El Comercio, 462 U.S. 611, 621, 77 L. Ed. 2d 46, 103 S. Ct. 2591 (1983) ("Different conflicts principles apply, however, where the rights of third parties *external* to the corporation are at issue.") (emphasis in original, citation omitted). Ultimately, the point is academic; as explained below, the Court would grant defendants summary judgment on this Count under either New York or Delaware law.

that the plaintiffs presently before it—sophisticated investors who are unsecured creditors—are not entitled to such additional protections.

Equally important, plaintiffs' position on this issue—that "A Company May Not Deliberately Deplete its Assets to the Injury of its Debtholders,"—provides no reasonable or workable limits, and is thus reminiscent of their implied covenant of good faith. Indeed, many indisputably legitimate corporate transactions would not survive plaintiffs' theory. With no workable limits, plaintiffs' envisioned duty would extend equally to trade creditors, employees, and every other person to whom the defendants are liable in any way. Of all such parties, these informed plaintiffs least require a Court's equitable protection; not only are they willing participants in a largely impersonal market, but they also possess the financial sophistication and size to secure their own protection.

Finally, plaintiffs cannot seriously allege unconscionability, given their sophistication and, at least judging from this action, the sophistication of their legal counsel as well. Under the undisputed facts of this case, this Court finds no actionable unconscionability.

QUESTIONS

1. In the materials directly preceding this case, we saw several types of covenants that might have protected the plaintiff from this outcome. Why weren't any of these included in the indentures?
2. Why does the court suggest that uniform interpretation of boiler plate language in indentures is important?
3. Is parole evidence admissible on the intent of the parties to a debenture indenture? Should it matter whether the covenants are in publicly issued debt or in a negotiated bank loan agreement? Is it likely that interpretation of the intent of the parties in loan agreements would provide precedent for interpretation of public debt?
4. What is an implied covenant of good faith? Is there an implied covenant of good faith that issuing corporations won't harm the value of the bonds?
5. How does an implied covenant of good faith differ from a fiduciary duty?
6. What elements are required for a claim of frustration of purpose? Why aren't they present here?

NOTE

RJR Nabisco bonds dropped about 20% in value on the announcement by RJR Nabisco officials that they were considering a leveraged buyout, amounting to a $1 billion loss. Kenneth Lehn & Annette Poulsen,

Contractual Resolution of Bondholder-Stockholder Conflicts in Leveraged Buyouts, 34 J.L. & Econ. 645, 646 (1991). One contemporaneous study found that restructurings such as LBOs resulted in average bondholder losses of 2.5%. Paul Asquith & Thierry A. Wizman, Event Risk, Wealth Redistribution and the Return to Existing Bondholders in Corporate Buyouts, 27 J. Fin. Econ. 195 (1991).

After the buyout RJR had outstanding indebtedness of $29 billion, and a debt-equity ratio of 23:1. In January of 1991 RJR settled its litigation with MetLife and Jefferson Pilot by exchanging their debt for new equity and some new debt. In March and April of 1991, KKR's principals realized that RJR would default on its debt unless the debt was restructured. In March RJR made offerings of common stock and new debt, raising $1.5 billion. Several high-interest junk bond issues were repurchased in the market, reducing outstanding junk bonds from $4.8 billion to $1.7 billion over the next eight months. Another debt issue was repurchased through an exchange offer for a combination of new preferred stock and cash. The cash for these transactions was raised from the sale of Del Monte for $5.7 billion. A new loan allowed RJR to redeem an issue of increasing rate notes held by institutions. In October 1991, RJR made an exchange offer of its common stock for the preferred that it had issued a few months earlier in its debt retirement program. By December 1991, RJR's debt was reduced below $15 billion, and it lost its junk bond rating, which further reduced its interest costs.

Sidebar: More Restrictive Claim Dilution Covenants

The rise of LBO deals during this time period eventually brought some changes to indenture provisions. Here is a sample indenture term from APOGENT Technologies, Inc. dated Oct. 10, 2001 (note: "CODES" is an acronym for Senior Convertible Contingent Debt Securities).

SECTION 11.1. REPURCHASE RIGHTS.

(b) Change of Control Put.

In the event that a Change in Control shall occur, each Holder shall have the right (each, a "CHANGE OF CONTROL REPURCHASE RIGHT" and, together with the Optional Repurchase Right, each a "REPURCHASE RIGHT"), at the Holder's option, but subject to the provisions of Section 11.2 hereof, to require the Company to repurchase, and upon the exercise of such right the Company shall repurchase, all of such Holder's CODES not theretofore called for redemption, or any portion of the principal amount thereof that is equal to $1,000 or an integral multiple thereof as directed by such Holder pursuant to Section 11.3 (provided that no single CODES may be repurchased in part unless the portion of the principal amount of such CODES to be Outstanding after such repurchase is equal to $1,000 or an integral multiple thereof), on the date (the "CHANGE OF CONTROL REPURCHASE DATE" and, together with the Optional Repurchase Date, each a "REPURCHASE DATE") that is a Business Day no earlier than 30 days nor later than 60 *days after the date of the Company Notice at a purchase price in cash equal to 100% of the principal amount of the CODES to be repurchased (the "CHANGE OF CONTROL REPURCHASE PRICE" and, together with the Optional Repurchase Price, each a "REPURCHASE PRICE"), plus accrued and unpaid Interest (including Contingent Interest) to, but excluding, the Change of Control Repurchase Date; provided, however, that installments of Interest (including Contingent Interest) on CODES whose Stated Maturity is prior to or on the Change of Control Repurchase Date shall be payable to the Holders of such CODES, or one or more Predecessor Securities, registered as such on the relevant Regular Record Date according to terms and the provisions of Section 2.1 hereof.*

What is the effect of this provision? How does it protect against the claim dilution that a pre-existing creditor might experience from an LBO? Should a borrower be nervous about agreeing to such a provision?

ii. RISKY INVESTMENTS

We alluded to this issue earlier as the "going to Las Vegas" problem. Suppose you loan money to SuperSafeCo, only to have the firm bet your cash on the roulette wheel. If it lands on red, the shareholders get rich and you get repaid. But if it lands on black, then the only thing you receive is an apologetic email: "We're really sorry, but we lost all our money." That's not a great lending situation.

More realistically, think about investors who purchase bonds of a very stable business—perhaps a retail chain like Costco or a water utility company like American Water. While these firms' fortunes will vary a bit with the economy, their core cash flows seem as stable as one could ever expect. Should bondholders be concerned if these companies add riskier business lines, either through purchase or merger? Or suppose a corporation simply sells its major business (imagine Costco selling its stores to Walmart, and using the proceeds in some other high-risk business). The volatility of earnings might increase, along with the risk of default on corporate debt.

Specifying all the assets a debtor *shouldn't* own would require lenders to draft a very long list of prohibited activities—an impossible and ever-changing task. One partial solution might be an absolute ban on investments in financial instruments—such as the shares of another company—and a prohibition of mergers. But this would impose a severe loss of flexibility for the debtor. Typically, less onerous restrictions are used: some covenants simply require that net tangible assets must meet some proportion of the debtor's balance sheet or limit intangible assets to some percentage of the firm's capitalization (shareholders' equity plus long-term debt).

Another facet of the problem involves "asset substitution," where the debtor sells one type of business asset and replaces it with another. We have already seen prohibitions on the transfer of substantially all assets not in the ordinary course of business in the Liberty Media case. The Sharon Steel case, discussed in Liberty Media, makes the point that it is substantially all operating assets that count, not financial assets. Other restrictions may permit sales so long as they are not substantially all the assets of a particular division or subsidiary. Finally, these covenants may limit sales and dispositions to some specified dollar amount. In some cases, these limits may be relaxed if the proceeds are used to purchase other tangible fixed assets or to retire debt.

Similarly, mergers of the debtor with another corporation can radically change the character of the combined firm. The asset mix may be different, and perhaps much riskier, than the debtor's own assets. The capital structure of the surviving firm may contain considerably more debt, and may place liens on firm assets. The surviving firm's working capital ratio may be weaker. In private loan agreements the solution may be to prohibit mergers, with the understanding that the prohibition can be waived by the lender if the merger does not impose significantly increased risk (or if the borrower agrees to new terms, such as a higher interest rate). Indeed, institutional lenders have incentives to develop a reputation for reasonable treatment of debtors' requests for waivers. But public debt covenants, involving the consent of bondholders, are not so easily waived due to collective action problems, so intermediate solutions are required. These typically permit mergers if certain financial ratios are maintained by the surviving company—working capital ratios, debt/equity ratios, and requiring that earnings cover total debt service of the combined company by some multiple of earnings.

Covenants can add some flexibility. In the Sharon Steel case, if a sale of substantially all the assets occurred, the buyer could assume the repayment of the bonds without an event of default occurring that would cause the bonds to become immediately due and payable. In the case of mergers, the bonds may permit a transaction only if the net tangible assets of the surviving firm meet a certain dollar minimum or are a certain percentage of long-term debt. Another possible merger requirement could insist that the bonds not be in default after completion of the transaction.

An especially rigid covenant to protect against asset substitution involves giving a mortgage on firm property to secure repayment that lasts until full repayment has been completed. In public debt such a covenant is effectively permanent and can prevent value-creating sales where funds are used to purchase assets that are more valuable to the firm. Getting bondholder waivers in public issues is virtually impossible. Where such mortgages are used in loan agreements with banks and other financial institutions, it is often possible, as stated earlier, to waive such restrictions when the creditors are convinced that such a waiver will not harm them.

Along these lines, consider some model provisions that seek to manage the problems imposed by risky investments and mergers. (Note that these are taken mostly from the original 1965 Commentaries and that some agreements now use, or adapt, alternative model provisions from the 2006 Negotiated Covenants.)

Variation on Model Covenants, § 8–1. Company May Consolidate or Merge Only on Certain Terms.

The Company shall not consolidate with or merge into any other corporation or convey, transfer or lease its properties and assets substantially as an entirety to any Person, and the Company shall not permit any Person to consolidate with or merge into the Company, unless:

(a) in case the Company shall consolidate with or merge into another corporation or convey, transfer or lease its properties and assets substantially as an entirety to any Person, the corporation formed by such consolidation or into which the Company is merged or the Person which acquires by conveyance or transfer, or which leases, the properties and assets of the Company substantially as an entirety shall be a corporation organized and existing under the laws of the United States of America, any State thereof or the District of Columbia and shall expressly assume, by an indenture supplemental hereto, executed and delivered to the Trustee, in form reasonably satisfactory to the Trustee, the due and punctual payment of the principal of (and premium, if any) and interest, if any, on all the Outstanding Securities of all series and the performance of every covenant of this Indenture on the part of the Company to be performed or observed;

(b) immediately after giving effect to such transaction, no Event of Default, and no event which, after notice or lapse of time or both, would become an Event of Default, shall have happened and be continuing; and

(c) if a supplemental indenture is required in connection with such transaction, the Company shall have delivered to the Trustee an Officers' Certificate and an Opinion of Counsel, each stating that such consolidation, merger, conveyance, transfer or lease and such supplemental indenture comply with this Article and that all conditions precedent herein provided or relating to such transaction have been complied with.

Variation on Model Covenants, § 8–2. Successor Corporation Substituted.

Upon any consolidation by the Company with or merger by the Company into any other corporation or any conveyance, transfer or lease of the properties and assets of the Company substantially as an entirety in accordance with Section ___ the successor corporation formed by such consolidation or into which the Company is merged or to which such conveyance, transfer or lease is made shall succeed to, and be substituted for, and may exercise every right and power of, the Company under this Indenture with the same effect as if such successor corporation had been named as the Company herein, and thereafter, the predecessor corporation shall be relieved of the performance and observance of all obligations and covenants under this Indenture and the Securities (and any Coupons appertaining thereto), including but not limited to the obligation to make payment of the principal of (and premium, if any) and interest, if any, on all the Outstanding Securities of all series (and any Coupons appertaining thereto), and, in the event of such conveyance, transfer or lease, may be liquidated and dissolved.

Model Covenants, § 10–13: Restrictions on Dispositions of Assets.

Subject to the provisions of Section ___, the Company will not convey, transfer or lease, any substantial part of its assets unless, in the opinion of the Board of Directors of the Company, such conveyance, transfer or lease, considered together with all prior conveyances, transfers and leases of assets of the Company, would not materially and adversely affect the interest of the Holders of the Notes or the ability of the Company to meet its obligations as they become due.

Variation on Model Covenants, § 10–16: Investments.

The Company will not make, or permit any of its Subsidiaries to make, any loan or advance to any Person or purchase or otherwise acquire, or permit any such Subsidiary to purchase or otherwise acquire, any capital stock, assets, obligations or other securities of, make any capital contribution to, or otherwise invest in, or acquire any interest in, any Person (all such transactions being herein called "Investments"), except:

(a) Investments in Liquid Assets;

(b) Investments in the Company or any or its Consolidated Subsidiaries;

(c) Investments in accounts, contract rights and general intangibles (as defined in the Uniform Commercial Code) or notes or other instruments receivable, arising from the sale, lease or other furnishings of goods or services by the Company or any Subsidiary in the ordinary course of its business;

(d) Investments in equity interests (including stocks and convertible debt securities) of corporations which do not become Consolidated Subsidiaries made with the proceeds of the issuance of stock by the Company;

(e) Acquisitions permitted by Section ___;

(f) Investments (including stocks, equity interests and convertible debt securities) of corporations that do not become Consolidated Subsidiaries made with the proceeds of the sale or other disposition of any capitalized Investment permitted by clause (d), providing the

Company gives the Banks notice of such Investment under this clause; and

(g) additional Investments not exceeding in the aggregate at any one time outstanding $20,000,000.

---

iii. DISTRIBUTIONS

When corporations raise funds in public markets, the federal and state securities laws require that they disclose the intended use of their proceeds. A use of funds for other purposes subjects the debtor, and usually some officers and directors, to civil liability for fraud and perhaps to criminal prosecution as well. Not all loan transactions privately negotiated with lenders are covered by the securities laws, but these lenders are, not surprisingly, just as interested in the use of proceeds. This concern is both short term (immediate diversion) and long term (diversion of cash from the business to the stockholders). Conversely, a requirement that funds must be kept within the corporation forces the debtor to employ the funds on new business opportunities or the maintenance and replacement of assets. This, in turn, addresses (albeit indirectly) the underinvestment problem, to be discussed in a moment.

The focus of the restriction on distributions is on corporate payment of cash, debt securities or other assets to shareholders. (See Model Act § 1.40(6) for a similar definition, which is applied to prohibit extreme distributions that result in insolvency in § 6.40.) With closely held corporations, these restrictions may also extend to salaries and bonuses paid to officers and directors (to prevent *de facto* dividends to the owners). Absolute prohibitions are generally not the rule; rather, specific conditions are generally set. This occurs by establishing minimum capital requirements, such as the ratio of debt to equity, or a minimum amount of retained earnings. These provisions thus allow dividends to be paid to the extent that retained earnings exceed some minimum, or to the extent that equity capital provides enough of a cushion to maintain the required ratio. If new equity capital is raised, this permits additional dividends under the debt/equity formula. A lender may also seek minimum working capital requirements. In effect, this means that dividends must be financed out of new earnings or new equity capital.

As you review these covenants, recall our discussion of financial ratios in Chapter 2. It is also important to recognize that firms in different markets will usually have different financial benchmarks; an astute representative of a corporate borrower should know what ratios are reasonable for a lender or an underwriter to demand for firms in that industry.

Sample Covenant: Current Ratio.

The Company shall maintain at all times a ratio of Consolidated Current Assets to Consolidated Current Liabilities of not less than 1.75 to 1.

Sample Covenant: Leverage Ratio.

The Company shall maintain at all times a ratio of Total Liabilities to Consolidated Tangible Net Worth of not greater than 1 to 1.

Sample Covenant: Minimum Consolidated Tangible Net Worth.

The Company will at no time permit Consolidated Tangible Net Worth to be less than the sum of (i) $288,981,000 plus (ii) 50% of consolidated net income of the Company and its Consolidated Subsidiaries for the period from January 31, 1993 through the end of the Company's then most recent fiscal quarter (treated for this purpose as a single accounting period) plus (iii) 50% of the net proceeds received by the Company from the issuance and sale subsequent to January 30, 1993 of shares of any class of the capital stock of the Company; provided, however, that in the event the Company incurs a net loss in one or more of its fiscal quarters ending after January 30, 1993, the results of such quarter or quarters shall be excluded in calculating consolidated net income of the Company and its Consolidated Subsidiaries pursuant to clause (ii) above.

Variation on ABF Model Covenants, § 10–12: Restrictions on Dividends, Redemptions, etc.

(a) The Company will not:

(1) declare or pay any dividend or make any other distribution on any Equity Securities of the Company, except dividends or distributions payable in Equity Securities of the Company, or

(2) purchase, redeem or otherwise acquire or retire for value any Equity Securities of the Company, except (and provided all other covenants of this Indenture are complied with) Equity Securities acquired upon conversion thereof into other Equity Securities of the Company or pursuant to an insurance funded buy-sell agreement covering the death or disability of a shareholder of the Company, or pursuant to a buy-sell agreement during the life time of a shareholder of the Company if purchased under a debt obligation which is Subordinated Indebtedness of the Company with a minimum term of five years with equal annual payments (a "Buy-Sell Debt Obligation"), or

(3) permit a Subsidiary to purchase, redeem or otherwise acquire or retire for value any Equity Securities of the Company, if, upon giving effect to such dividend, purchase, redemption or the acquisition, the aggregate amount expended for all such purposes subsequent to December 31, 1995 would exceed the sum of

(1) 50% of the Consolidated Net Income accumulated subsequent to December 31, 1995;

(2) the aggregate of the net proceeds received by the Company or a Wholly-Owned Subsidiary from the sale or issuance after December 31, 1995 (other than to a Subsidiary or upon the Conversion of Equity Securities or Indebtedness or the Company or a Wholly-Owned Subsidiary) of Equity Securities of the Company, said net proceeds being deemed for the purposes of this Section to equal the aggregate of (a) the cash, if any, received by the Company or a Wholly-Owned Subsidiary from such sale or issue, plus (b) the value of any consideration, other than cash, received by the Company or a Wholly-Owned Subsidiary from such sale or issue, as determined by resolution of the Board of Directors; and

(3) the net proceeds (as above defined) received by the Company or a Wholly-Owned Subsidiary from the issuance or sale (other than to the Company or a Subsidiary) of any convertible Indebtedness of the Company which Indebtedness has been converted into Equity Securities of the Company after December 31, 1995.

(b) The Company will not (1) declare or pay any dividend or make any other distribution, other than a Regular Dividend, on any Equity Securities of the Company, except dividends or distributions payable in Equity Securities of the Company, or (2) purchase, redeem or otherwise acquire or retire for value any Equity Securities of the Company, except Equity Securities acquired upon conversion thereof into other Equity Securities of the Company or pursuant to an insurance funded buy-sell agreement covering the death or disability of a shareholder of the Company, or pursuant to a Buy-Sell Debt Obligation, (3) or, except as permitted by Section ___ herein, permit a Subsidiary to purchase, redeem or otherwise acquire or retire for value any Equity Securities of the Company, if, upon giving effect to such dividend, distribution, purchase, redemption or other acquisition, the Consolidated Tangible Net Worth of the Company would be reduced to less than an amount equal to 150% of the aggregate principal amount of Debentures and all Parity Indebtedness then outstanding.

(c) The provisions of this Section ___ shall not prevent (1) the payment of annual year-end bonuses to key employees, executive officers and shareholder employees of the Company pursuant to the bonus plan described in and consistent with the restrictions in Section ___ hereof, (2) the payment of any dividend within 60 days after the date of declaration thereof, if at such date such declaration complied with the foregoing provisions, although the dividends so paid shall be considered in determining subsequent restrictions under this Section or (3) the acquisition or retirement of any Equity Securities of the Company by exchange for, or upon conversion of, or out of the proceeds of the substantially concurrent sale (other than to a Subsidiary) of, other Equity Securities of the Company, and no effect shall be given to any such acquisition or retirement or the proceeds of any sale, conversion or exchange in any computation made under this Section. A certificate of a firm of independent certified public accountants shall be conclusive evidence of the amount of accumulated Consolidated Net Income and the amount of Consolidated Tangible Net Worth.

iv. UNDERINVESTMENT—ASSET MAINTENANCE

The underinvestment problem is one of the most difficult situations to deal with contractually. How do you handle the risk that a board might pass up decent opportunities to the lender's chagrin? While a loan contract could conceivably provide that "the debtor shall accept all positive net present value projects," one can imagine the plethora of problems this would create. What is a "project?" Is it every corporate opportunity that comes before an officer or employee, or a director? Projects outside the core competencies of the business might be positive for other firms but not for this one. And what cost of capital should be used to evaluate the opportunity? Does this change if additional financing is required to accept the project? Moreover, even if determining the expected value of a given project might be feasible, should we also worry that accepting its riskiness might alter the overall cost of capital for the firm?

Another dimension to underinvestment involves a risk that the firm won't properly maintain existing plant and equipment or replace long-lived assets as necessary to support production and sales. While a covenant requiring a borrower to keep all plant and equipment in good condition, repair and working order is aspirational, will a lender really be able to monitor and enforce this term? Many lenders may lack the expertise to make this determination. In some cases, there may be maintenance schedules that could be made enforceable. A business owning vehicles, such as a trucking company or a taxicab company, might be held to the manufacturer's maintenance schedules for the vehicles. Services provided by third parties such as dealers could be documented and submitted to the lenders. Similar requirements for drydocking vessels or servicing passenger aircraft can also be imagined.

But many businesses have assets that are not subject to such rigid maintenance schedules. One substitute, albeit a rough one, is to require the firm to maintain working capital (current assets minus current liabilities) at specified levels. Declines in working capital may provide a signal to lenders that the debtor's cash flows are declining, and are likely to lead to deferred maintenance on plant and equipment.

In some cases, lenders might use insurance requirements as a proxy for monitoring, because insurers might be better at inspecting plants and warehouses to ensure adequate maintenance. See Smith and Warner § 2.5.4. Thus, a requirement that a company carry boiler insurance will elicit an annual inspection by a boiler expert. Appropriate fire insurance requirements may force the debtor to install sprinkler systems, while workers' compensation insurance may cause insurers to engage in safety inspections that lead to improvements in the workplace. Avoidance of potential disasters will reduce the variance in the debtor's cash flows, to the benefit of lenders.

ABF Model Covenants, § 10–5: Maintenance of Properties.

The Company will cause all its properties used or useful in the conduct of its business to be maintained and kept in good condition, repair and working order and supplied with all necessary equipment and will cause to be made all necessary repairs, renewals, replacements, betterments and improvements thereof, all as in the judgment of the Company may be necessary so that the business carried on in connection therewith may be properly and advantageously conducted at all times; provided, however, that nothing in this Section shall prevent the Company from discontinuing the operation and maintenance of any of its properties if such discontinuance is, in the judgment of the Company, desirable in the conduct of its business and not disadvantageous in any material respect to the Debentureholders.

ABF Model Covenants, § 10–6: Statement as to Compliance.

The Company will deliver to the Trustee, within 90 days after the end of each fiscal year, a written statement signed by the President or a Vice President of the Company, stating, as to each signer thereof, that:

(1) a review of the activities of the Company during such year and of performance under this Indenture has been made under his supervision; and

(2) to the best of his knowledge, based on such review, the Company has fulfilled all its obligations under this Indenture throughout such year, or, if there has been a default in the fulfillment of any such obligation, specifying each such default known to him and the nature and status thereof.*

ABF Model Covenants, § 10–7: Corporate Existence.

Subject to Article 8, the Company will do or cause to be done all things necessary to preserve and keep in full force and effect its corporate existence, rights (charter and statutory) and franchises; provided, however, that the Company shall not be required to preserve any right or franchise or any minor business activity if the Board of Directors shall determine that the preservation thereof is no longer desirable in the

---

* This is contemplated by § 314(a)(2) of the Trust Indenture Act, but no rules adopted by the SEC implement it.

"Sec. 314(a) Each person who, as set forth in the registration statement or application, is or is to be an obligor upon the indenture securities covered thereby shall—

"(2) to file [sic] with the indenture trustee and the Commission, in accordance with rules and regulations prescribed by the Commission, such additional information, documents, and reports with respect to compliance by such obligor with the conditions and covenants provided for in the indenture, as may be required by such rules and regulations, . . ."

conduct of the business of the Company and that the loss thereof is not disadvantageous in any material respect to the Debentureholders.

Variation on ABF Model Covenants, § 10–9: Insurance.

The Company will at all times cause all buildings, plants, equipment and other insurable properties owned or operated by it or any Subsidiary to be properly insured and kept insured with responsible insurance carriers, against loss or damage by fire and other hazards, to the extent that such properties are usually insured by corporations owning or operation plants and properties or a similar character in the same localities; provided, however, that nothing in this Section shall prevent the Company or any Subsidiary from maintaining any self-insurance program covering minor risks if adequate reserves are maintained in connection with such program.

C. SUBSTITUTES FOR COVENANTS

As suggested by the discussion thus far, one of the most important goals of any lender involves protecting the promise to get repaid. Covenants that restrict dividends, limit additional debt, avoid risky bets outside the current line of business, and maintain the firm's equipment are all ways to protect this repayment obligation. Another more direct strategy, however, might be to just require the borrower to make ongoing payments or to set funds aside in something called a *sinking fund*—so that the lender can gain confidence that enough money will be there when repayment is due. Of course, these strategies are not mutually exclusive, and some bonds with sinking funds might also demand detailed covenants that protect the borrower's promise to repay.

Lenders might also reduce risk by requiring periodic repayment of borrowed funds. This is quite familiar to consumers in auto and home lending, where monthly payments are the norm. Periodic payments, at least of interest due on bonds, is one way for bondholders to monitor the borrower's solvency. In some cases, where the entire principal amount is due and payable at the end of a term, this increases the risk of nonpayment. As noted above, a sinking fund is a means of reducing this risk, by requiring periodic payments by the borrower. These payments are made into the sinking fund for the purpose of repurchasing the bonds. Depending on the indenture, the debtor may reinvest the funds to finance later repurchases, or repurchase bonds in one of two ways. First, the bonds may be called by lot for repurchase at par value, perhaps with a prepayment penalty in the early years. Second, the debtor may go into the market and repurchase bonds at their current market value. Obviously, if the bonds are trading below the call price, the debtor will repurchase in the market. This will usually occur only when interest rates have risen since the original issue. But there is another possibility: that the debtor's finances have deteriorated, and the bonds have declined in market value to reflect the increased risk of default. If that's the case, then a sinking fund may be only a weak form of protection.

Another possible substitute for detailed covenants can be found with convertible debt. Chapter 8 will examine options and convertible securities more thoroughly, but it's also worth a quick note here about the role conversion features play in providing some form of protection for bondholders. Typically, where convertible features are included, there are relatively few negative covenants. Often the convertible feature signals relatively risky debt, for which the issuer will pay a lower current interest rate, in exchange for the conversion feature. (As we shall see in Chapter 8, conversion features are frequently an important part of a preferred stock investments, as well.)

One specialized type of debt involves venture lending—loans made to development-stage or emerging companies that have yet to earn significant revenues, and are likely to require additional equity capital from early stage venture capitalists. There is evidence that lenders are most likely to make loans in this highly risky arena where they see prominent venture capitalists who are expected to invest in later rounds of equity financing (thus providing financing to repay the lenders). In addition to relatively high interest rates on the loans and relatively short terms (often less than four year), these lenders will typically demand warrants to purchase common stock at the current valuation of the borrower's stock for a period of seven to ten years.

It is also worth noting that with conversion rights or warrants, risky projects that succeed (like the Las Vegas roulette wheel "investment") might cause debt investors to convert in order to share in the gains. In theory, this could reduce some of the ex-ante agency distortions between creditors and equity investors, a topic we will revisit in Chapter 8.

D. CALL PROTECTION

One of the worst outcomes for preexisting creditors arises when a firm cannot repay its debt and is forced to file for bankruptcy. But there's another important type creditor risk that can occur even when a borrower is very successful: the early repayment (or call) of the bonds. In an era of declining interest rates, a borrower might find that the rate on its long-term bonds, issued years earlier, is well above current market rates. It makes perfect sense, from the debtor's perspective, to reduce interest costs by refinancing—issuing new debt at the lower market rates and calling the old bonds. (You'd do the same thing with your home mortgage.) The bondholders, on the other hand, face the loss of the higher interest rate for which they had contracted and the inability to replace the bonds with investments of comparable value. As we'll see in this section, some indentures will protect against (or price) this type of refinancing risk.

Corporate bonds, like home mortgages, may be written for relatively long periods (generally as much as 25–30 years). If bonds carry a fixed rate, they become a bet on interest rates between borrower and lender. If interest rates rise, the borrower wins the bet—because it remains able to employ the borrowed funds at the lower interest rate originally negotiated. On the other hand, if interest rates fall, the lender wins, since it obtains a rate higher than current market rates. (This is one reason why borrowers must generally pay a higher interest rate for long-term debt.)

But if a borrower is allowed to prepay the debt when interest rates fall, the bet becomes more one-sided; presumably the lender would have asked for a higher initial interest rate to compensate for the lost opportunity of holding above market-rate bonds. Corporate bonds have various ways of dealing with this problem. One solution is simply to use a variable interest rate that is reset according to some outside measure of current interest rates (such as the prime rate in the United States). But many bonds carry a fixed rate, perhaps because, like homeowners, borrowers want to be able to have more planning certainty around future interest costs. Where the bonds can be prepaid (called) by the issuer, limits are usually placed on the ability to call the bonds in order to preserve the benefits of the investors' bargain, at least for some future period. The exact limits are often the subject of negotiation. In some instances, the bonds may not be called for the first few years; in others, a "call premium" (a prepayment penalty) may be imposed—though this premium will often decline over time. The most extreme form of protection involves something called a "make-whole premium" which is discussed in a sidebar below.

In the case that follows, Archer Daniels Midland Co. borrowed by selling 30-year debentures in 1981. This was during one of the worst bouts of inflation in our nation's recent history, and ADM was forced to pay a whopping 16% rate of interest! And because most participants in credit markets probably believed that interest rates were bound to come down, ADM also needed to offer a substantial prepayment penalty. Set out below is the call premium schedule (based on the par value, or principal amount, of the bonds):

Year	Percentage	Year	Percentage
1981	115.500%	1991	107.750%
1982	114.725	1992	106.975
1983	113.950	1993	106.200
1984	113.175	1994	105.425
1985	112.400	1995	104.650
1986	111.625	1996	103.875
1987	110.850	1997	103.100

1988	110.075	1998	102.325
1989	109.300	1999	101.550
1990	108.525	2000	100.775
			and thereafter at 100%

Morgan Stanley & Co., Inc. v. Archer Daniels Midland Company

570 F.Supp. 1529 (S.D.N.Y. 1983)

■ SAND, D.J.

This action . . . arises out of the planned redemption of $125 million in 16% Sinking Fund Debentures ("the Debentures") by the defendant ADM Midland Company ("ADM") scheduled to take place on Monday, August 1st, 1983. Morgan Stanley & Company, Inc. ("Morgan Stanley") brings this suit under § 10(b) of the Securities Exchange Act of 1934 and 316(b) of the Trust Indenture Act of 1939, and other state and federal laws, alleging that the proposed redemption plan is barred by the terms of the Indenture, the language of the Debentures, and the Debenture Prospectus. Plaintiff contends, in addition, that the failure on the part of ADM to reveal its intention to redeem the Debentures, as well as its belief that such redemption would be lawful under the terms of the Indenture Agreement, amounts to an intentional, manipulative scheme to defraud in violation of federal and state securities and business laws. Morgan Stanley seeks a preliminary injunction enjoining ADM from consummating the redemption as planned, and, after full consideration on the merits, permanent injunctive relief barring the proposed transaction and damages. Both parties have pursued an expedited discovery schedule and now cross-move for summary judgment.

FACTS

In May, 1981, Archer Daniels issued $125,000,000 of 16% Sinking Fund Debentures due May 15, 2011. The managing underwriters of the Debenture offering were Goldman Sachs & Co., Kidder Peabody & Co. and Merrill Lynch, Pierce, Fenner & Smith, Inc. The Debentures ". . . provided, however, that prior to May 15, 1991, the Company may not redeem any of the Debentures pursuant to such [prepayment] option from the proceeds, or in anticipation, of the issuance of any indebtedness for money borrowed by or for the account of the Company or any Subsidiary (as defined in the Indenture) or from the proceeds, or in anticipation of a sale and leaseback transaction (as defined in Section 1008 of the Indenture), if, in either case, the interest cost or interest factor applicable thereto (calculated in accordance with generally accepted financial practice) shall be less than 16.08% per annum.

* * *

The proceeds of the Debenture offering were applied to the purchase of long-term government securities bearing rates of interest below 16.089%.

ADM raised money through public borrowing at interest rates less than 16.08% on at least two occasions subsequent to the issuance of the Debentures. On May 7, 1982, over a year before the announcement of the planned redemption, ADM borrowed $50,555,500 by the issuance of $400,000,000 face amount zero coupon debentures due 2002 and $100,000,000 face amount zero coupon notes due 1992 (the "Zeroes"). The Zeroes bore an effective interest rate of less than 16.08%. On March 10, 1983, ADM raised an additional $86,400,000 by the issuance of $263,232,500 face amount Secured Trust Accrual Receipts, known as "Stars," through a wholly-owned subsidiary, Midland Stars Inc. The Stars carry an effective interest rate of less than 16.08%. The Stars were in the form of notes with varying maturities secured by government securities deposited by ADM with a trustee established for that purpose. There is significant dispute between the parties as to whether the Stars transaction should be treated as an issuance of debt or as a sale of government securities. We assume, for purposes of this motion, that the transaction resulted in the incurring of debt.

In the period since the issuance of the Debentures, ADM also raised money through two common stock offerings. Six million shares of common stock were issued by prospectus dated January 28, 1983, resulting in proceeds of $131,370,000. And by a prospectus supplement dated June 1, 1983, ADM raised an additional $15,450,000 by issuing 600,000 shares of common stock.

Morgan Stanley, the plaintiff in this action, bought $15,518,000 principal amount of the Debentures at $1,252.50 per $1,000 face amount on May 5, 1983, and $500,000 principal amount at $1,200 per $1,000 face amount on May 31, 1983. The next day, June 1, ADM announced that it was calling for the redemption of the 16% Sinking Fund Debentures, effective August 1, 1983. The direct source of funds was to be the two ADM common stock offerings of January and June, 1983. The proceeds of these offerings were delivered to the Indenture Trustee, Morgan Guaranty Trust Company, and deposited in a special account to be applied to the redemption. The amount deposited with the Indenture Trustee is sufficient to fully redeem the Debentures.

* * *

Plaintiff's allegations can be reduced to two general claims: First, plaintiff contends that the proposed redemption is barred by the express terms of the call provisions of the Debenture and the Indenture Agreement, and that consummation of the plan would violate the Trust Indenture Act of 1939, and common law principles of contract law. The plaintiff's claim is founded on the language contained in the Debenture and Trust Indenture that states that the company may not redeem the

Debentures "from the proceeds, or in anticipation, of the issuance of any indebtedness . . . if . . . the interest cost or interest factor . . . [is] less than 16.08% per annum." Plaintiff points to the $86,400,000 raised by the Stars transaction within 90 days of the June 1 redemption announcement, and the $50,555,500 raised by the Zeroes transaction in May, 1982—both at interest rates below 16.08%—as proof that the redemption is being funded, at least indirectly, from the proceeds of borrowing in violation of the Debentures and Indenture agreement. The fact that ADM raised sufficient funds to redeem the Debentures entirely through the issuance of common stock is, according to the plaintiffs, an irrelevant "juggling of funds" used to circumvent the protections afforded investors by the redemption provisions of the Debenture. Plaintiff would have the Court interpret the provision as barring redemption during any period when the issuer has borrowing at a rate lower than that prescribed by the Debentures, regardless of whether the direct source of the funds is the issuance of equity, the sale of assets, or merely cash on hand.

The defendant would have the Court construe the language more narrowly as barring redemption only where the direct or indirect source of the funds is a debt instrument issued at a rate lower than that it is paying on the outstanding Debentures. Where, as here, the defendant can point directly to a non-debt source of funds (the issuance of common stock), the defendant is of the view that the general redemption schedule applies.

* * *

According to Morgan Stanley, the fact that the Debentures were trading at levels above the call price prior to the redemption announcement bolsters the argument that the investing public thought it was protected against early redemption. The plaintiff asserts that it would not have bought the Debentures without what it perceived to be protection against premature redemption.

ADM contends that plaintiff's allegations of securities fraud stem in the first instance from its strained and erroneous interpretation of the redemption language. Defendant argues that the redemption language itself—a boilerplate provision found in numerous Indenture Agreements—was sufficient disclosure. Moreover, defendant asserts that it had no plan or scheme at the time the Debentures were issued to exercise its call rights in conjunction with speculation in government securities or otherwise and that the provision existed solely to offer the issuer "financial flexibility." More important, defendant contends that its view of the Debenture language was the one commonly accepted by both bondholders and the investing public. In support of this contention, defendant points to the only case directly to address the issue, Franklin Life Insurance Co. v. Commonwealth Edison Co., 451 F. Supp. 602 (S.D. Ill. 1978). Franklin held, with respect to language almost identical to that contained in the ADM Debentures, that a redemption directly funded through equity financing was not prohibited despite contemporaneous borrowing by the issuer.

Defendant contends that it first seriously contemplated redemption in the Spring of 1983 upon the suggestion of Merrill Lynch, one of its investment bankers. Merrill Lynch had received legal advice that a redemption transaction of the sort contemplated was proper under the language of the Debenture and the analysis of the Court in Franklin. Moreover, the defendant asserts that Morgan Stanley itself was fully aware of this interpretation of the redemption language, although it may have disagreed with it. ADM explains the high price at which the Debentures were trading prior to the redemption announcement not as a reflection of investors' belief that the Debentures were not currently redeemable, but rather as a reflection of the belief that ADM itself, or some other interested buyer, might seek to purchase the Debentures through a tender offer or other financial transaction.

DISCUSSION

* * *

With respect to the likelihood of success on the merits, defendant's interpretation of the redemption provision seems at least as likely to be in accord with the language of the Debentures, the Indenture, and the available authorities than is the view proffered by the plaintiff. We first note that the one court to directly address this issue chose to construe the language in the manner set forth in this action by the defendant. Franklin Life Insurance Co. v. Commonwealth Edison Co., 451 F. Supp. 602 (S. D. Ill. 1978). While plaintiff is correct in noting that this Circuit is not bound by this decision, and while this case can no doubt be distinguished factually on a number of grounds, none of which we deem to be of major significance, Franklin is nevertheless persuasive authority in support of defendant's position.

Defendant's view of the redemption language is also arguably supported by The American Bar Foundation's Commentaries on Model Debenture Indenture Provisions (1977), from which the boilerplate language in question was apparently taken verbatim. In discussing the various types of available redemption provisions, the Commentaries state:

> Instead of an absolute restriction [on redemption], the parties may agree that the borrower may not redeem with funds borrowed at an interest rate lower than the interest rate in the debentures. Such an arrangement recognizes that funds for redemption may become available from other than borrowing, but correspondingly recognizes that the debenture holder is entitled to be protected for a while against redemption if interest rates fall and the borrower can borrow funds at a lower rate to pay off the debentures.

Id. at 477 (emphasis added). We read this comment as pointing to the source of funds as the dispositive factor in determining the availability of redemption to the issuer—the position advanced by defendant ADM.

Finally, we view the redemption language itself as supporting defendant's position. The redemption provision in the Indenture and the Debentures begins with the broad statement that the Debentures are "subject to redemption . . . at any time, in whole or in part, at the election of the company, at the following optional Redemption Price. . ." Following this language is a table of decreasing redemption percentages keyed to the year in which the redemption occurs. This broad language is then followed by the narrowing provision "provided, however . . . the Company may not redeem any of the Debentures pursuant to such option from the proceeds, or in anticipation, of the issuance of any indebtedness" borrowed at rates less than that paid on the Debentures.

While the "plain meaning" of this language is not entirely clear with respect to the question presented in this case, we think the restrictive phrasing of the redemption provision, together with its placement after broad language allowing redemption in all other cases at the election of the company, supports defendant's more restrictive reading.

Morgan Stanley asserts that defendant's view would afford bondholders no protection against redemption through lower-cost borrowing and would result in great uncertainty among holders of bonds containing similar provisions. In its view, the "plain meaning" of the redemption bondholders of these bonds and the investment community generally, is that the issuer may not redeem when it is contemporaneously engaging in lower-cost borrowing, regardless of the source of the funds for redemption. At the same time, however, the plaintiff does not contend that redemption through equity funding is prohibited for the life of the redemption restriction once the issuer borrows funds at a lower interest rate subsequent to the Debenture's issuance. On the contrary, plaintiff concedes that the legality of the redemption transaction would depend on a factual inquiry into the magnitude of the borrowing relative to the size of the contemplated equity-funded redemption and its proximity in time relative to the date the redemption was to take place. Thus, a \$100 million redemption two years after a \$1 million short-term debt issue might be allowable, while the same redemption six months after a \$20 million long-term debt issue might not be allowable.

This case-by-case approach is problematic in a number of respects. First, it appears keyed to the subjective expectations of the bondholders; if it appears that the redemption is funded through lower-cost borrowing, based on the Company's recent or prospective borrowing history, the redemption is deemed unlawful. The approach thus reads a subjective element into what presumably should be an objective determination based on the language appearing in the bond agreement. Second, and most important, this approach would likely cause greater uncertainty among bondholders than a strict "source" rule such as that adopted in Franklin, *supra*.

Plaintiff's fear that bondholders would be left "unprotected" by adoption of the "source" rule also appears rather overstated. The rule proposed by defendant does not, as plaintiff suggests, entail a virtual emasculation of the refunding restrictions. An issuer contemplating redemption would still be required to fund such redemption from a source other than lower-cost borrowing, such as reserves, the sale of assets, or the proceeds of a common stock issue. Bondholders would thus be protected against the type of continuous short-term refunding of debt in times of plummeting interest rates that the language was apparently intended to prohibit. Moreover, this is not an instance where protections against premature redemption are wholly absent from the Debenture. On the contrary, the Debentures and the Indenture explicitly provide for early redemption expressed in declining percentages of the principal amount, depending on the year the redemption is effected.

At this early stage of the proceedings, on the record before us, and for all the reasons outlined above, we find that plaintiff has failed to show a sufficient likelihood of its success on the merits of its contract claims as to entitle it to preliminary injunctive relief.

QUESTIONS

1. Why were the ADM debentures trading at $1,252.50 when Morgan Stanley bought them on May 5, 1983? Can you calculate the current yield on the bonds at this price?
2. What was the call price on these bonds in 1983?
3. Why do you suppose Morgan Stanley bought these bonds at such a premium? How much money did it lose?
4. What's the purpose of prohibiting redemption from the proceeds of a lower-interest bond issue? How much protection does this term really offer?
5. This debenture indenture allowed redemption on 60 days' notice beginning in 1981, with call premiums starting at 115% of par, and declining to nearly par in 2000. How can this be consistent with the prohibition at issue in this case?
6. How can you tell if a redemption comes from the proceeds of a particular financing?
7. How could a creditor protect against the type of loss sustained by Morgan Stanley? How would borrowers react? (See the next Sidebar for more discussion on this topic.)

NOTE

In theory, a firm attempting to maximize shareholder value should call bonds as soon as the market price of the bonds exceeds the call price, because this signals that the company could refinance its debt at lower current interest rates. But even in the absence of call protection in indenture covenants, companies do not always do this immediately. Two explanations have been offered. First, because a company incurs additional transaction costs when issuing new debt, it makes sense to wait until the market price of outstanding bonds is at least equal to the sum of these transaction costs and the redemption price. Second, when interest rates and bond prices are volatile, an issuer has no assurance that bond prices will remain above this sum during the time necessary to complete the redemption process. Typical bond issues give bondholders about thirty days to surrender the bond and receive the call price in cash. During this period bond prices may drop below the call price; if so, the firm will pay too much to redeem bonds that it could have repurchased more cheaply in the market. Accordingly, issuers do not typically call bonds until the market price exceeds the call price by some amount sufficient to cover not only the transaction costs of the call but also to reduce the probability of a price drop below the market price during the execution period.

Sidebar: The Make-Whole Premium

The ADM case illustrates how a ban on redemptions from lower cost debt might be sidestepped by a borrowing company that also issues stock or that generates large amounts of cash flow from current operations. Money is fungible. How, then, can creditors who really want to eliminate prepayment risk do so in a lending contract? One possibility might be to simply ban redemptions outright during the term of the loan. Another idea might be to charge an astronomical premium for redemption, perhaps 200% or 300% of par value. But even assuming that a court would uphold these terms, most issuers would be very reluctant to agree to such a strict limitation. There can be many reasons why a firm might want or need to redeem a bond issuance even when interest rates are perfectly stable. Perhaps it wants to sell the firm at an attractive price, and the bonds will need to be eliminated early to support the deal.

Instead, a lender who wants to eliminate all pre-payment risk might negotiate for something known as a *make-whole premium* or a *make-whole call*. The intuition here is that an issuer will be able to redeem the given bond issuance but that the premium it must pay to do so will be calculated to give some or all of the economic gains from a lower market rate of interest to the creditors. Sometimes the firm might even need to pay more to the current creditors than they would save from refinancing at a lower rate (suggesting that the borrowing firm is only likely to redeem the debt if it really needs to meet some other strategic goal). Consider some representative language (taken from the prospectus used in the issue of notes by Edison International):

Optional Redemption

We will be entitled to redeem the notes at our option as described below. You will not be permitted to require us to redeem or repurchase the notes at your option.

Prior to September 15, 2029 (the "Par Call Date"), we may redeem the notes at our option, in whole or in part, at any time and from time to time, at a "make-whole" redemption price (expressed as a percentage of principal amount and rounded to three decimal places) equal to the greater of:

(1) (a) the sum of the present values of the remaining scheduled payments of principal and interest thereon discounted to the redemption date (assuming the notes matured on the Par Call Date) on a semi-annual basis (assuming a 360-day year consisting of twelve 30-day months) at the Treasury Rate plus 45 basis points less (b) interest accrued to the date of redemption, and

(2) 100% of the principal amount of the notes to be redeemed,

plus, in either case, accrued and unpaid interest thereon to but excluding the redemption date.

What is the effect of this provision? It might be easiest to illustrate with an example. Suppose $10 million worth of Notes was issued in 2020 with a 10-year term (i.e., they are due in 2030). At the time of issuance, the Notes pay a 10% fixed rate of interest (assume all principal is paid at the end of the 10 years), and the relevant Treasury Rate is 8%. In 2025, with exactly five years to go, corporate interest rates have dropped to 8% (for firms with similar credit ratings) and the relevant Treasury Rate is also down 200 basis points to 6%. The firm decides to redeem, for whatever reason, and the make-whole premium is triggered. How much must the firm pay?

To answer this, we need to compare premium option (1) with premium option (2) and pick the larger number. Premium option (2) requires a redemption price of just the $10 million in principal; in effect, there is no premium to pay under this option. Premium option (1) is more complicated. We need to calculate the net present value of future interest and principal payments over the next five years. We will then discount each of these cash flows using a 6.45% discount rate (the 6% reference Treasury rate plus 45 basis points). We provide an example of this solution on the tab entitled "Make-Whole Premium" on the "Debt Worksheet" on the casebook website. As the worksheet reveals, premium option (2) yields a total redemption price of about $11.47 million, or a premium of a little more than $1.47 million, so this is the amount that the firm would need to pay for the right to call the Notes early.

Notice that that price paid to refinance early under this provision is more than the firm will save by issuing new debt at the lower 8% interest rate. We can see how much more by increasing the discount rate in the Excel Worksheet to 8%. The make-whole premium under this scenario is about $0.8 million, which is the amount the firm would save if it was planning to keep the notes until maturity. The difference between $1.47 million and $0.8 million ($0.67 million) is therefore an extra prepayment premium that the firm must pay to call the debt. The issuing firm may not like such a steep price, of course, and it could try to negotiate this down by increasing the basis point addition from 45 to a higher amount. If, for example, the firm uses a 200 basis point adjustment, then all of the refinancing savings—but not more—will go to the creditor in this example. And if it uses 300 basis points, then both creditor and debtor will split the gains from this lower interest rate refinancing. Do you see why?

It is also important to understand how this exact split can change over time if the firm's borrowing spread increases or decreases relative to Treasuries. In this example, this spread remains constant at 200 basis points during both 2020 and 2030; you might try recalculating the effect of the make-whole premium if there is a decrease in the basis point spread by 2025 to 100 bps (i.e., the borrowing rate for the corporation is 8% and the Treasury rate is 7%).

Make-whole premiums in lending contracts are usually understood to be enforceable outside of bankruptcy, but there is always a risk that an especially onerous provision might be struck down as an unenforceable liquidated damages provision under contract law. It is a closer call, however, whether this term will be enforced if a firm has entered (or is about to enter) bankruptcy; the provision may be the subject of additional litigation.

E. MONITORING COMPLIANCE

How can a creditor, or its designated agent, ensure that things are going well with a debt arrangement? Monitoring costs can be shifted to the debtor, at least in part, by requiring it to furnish audited annual financial statements to the indenture trustee. In addition, many debtors will be required to file quarterly financial reports with the SEC. These quarterly filings are not required to be audited, so the indenture will generally insist that an officer certify the accuracy of these reports. And these obligations will continue so long as any part of the debt remains outstanding. Moreover, a debtor that is subject to SEC reporting requirements will also be required to file with the SEC periodic updates on Form 8-K that can also provide bondholders with information regarding the debt. For instance, among other things, Form 8-K requires companies to disclose changes to the company's senior management or to its outside accountants, dispositions of assets, and the entry of material contracts.

Typically indentures will also require corporate officers to furnish certificates to the indenture trustee that the corporation is in compliance with the indenture covenants. The following illustrations are taken from the Revised Model Simplified Indenture, 55 Bus. Law. 1115 (2000).

***Section 4.02.* SEC Reports.**

The Company shall file with the Trustee within 15 days after it files them with the SEC copies of the annual reports and of the information, documents and other reports which the Company is required to file with the SEC pursuant to Section 13 or 15(d) of the Exchange Act. The Company will cause any quarterly and annual reports which it makes available to its stockholders to be mailed to the Holders. The Company will also comply with the other provisions of TIA Section 314(a). Delivery of such reports, information and documents to the Trustee is for informational purposes only and the Trustee's receipt of such shall not constitute notice or constructive notice of any information contained therein or determinable from information contained therein, including the Company's compliance with any of its covenants hereunder (as to which the Trustee is entitled to rely exclusively on Officers' Certificates).

***Section 4.03.* Compliance Certificate.**

The Company shall deliver to the Trustee, within [105] days after the end of each fiscal year of the Company, a brief certificate signed by the principal executive officer, principal financial officer or principal accounting officer of the Company, as to the signer's knowledge of the Company's compliance with all conditions and covenants contained in this Indenture (determined without regard to any period of grace or requirement of notice provided herein).

***Section 4.04.* Notice of Certain Events.**

The Company shall give prompt written notice to the Trustee and any Paying Agent of (i) any Proceeding, (ii) any Default or Event of Default, (iii) any cure or waiver of any Default or Event of Default, (iv) any Senior Debt Payment Default or Senior Debt Default Notice, and (v) if and when the Securities are listed on any stock exchange.

F. BREACH, AMENDMENTS, AND EXCHANGE OFFERS

We haven't really talked yet about what happens if the borrowing firm fails to keep up with its contractual obligations. Maybe a debtor promises to meet a minimum interest coverage ratio each quarter, but business has been lousy this time around, and the firm just didn't make it. What happens now?

Indentures usually treat any breach of a covenant as an event of default. This allows creditors, through the indenture trustee, to declare a default and take the remedies provided in the indenture, which will usually include acceleration of the entire indebtedness and, if there is security, foreclosure on the collateral. These events of insolvency would then allow the trustee to file an involuntary petition in bankruptcy against the debtor. Typically, a debtor will seek to convert the proceeding into a Chapter 11 reorganization, with a stay of any remedies for creditors. There will be extended delays while a plan of reorganization is proposed and sent to creditors and claimants for approval. In short, the remedies for any breach are draconian, and may involve more expense and delay than bondholders would wish. If so, the discussion may soon turn toward negotiations between the parties outside of bankruptcy to secure arrangements that would allow the bondholders to waive the covenant breach, as provided in the indenture.

What if multiple parties hold the debt, and they cannot agree on whether to adjust the contract after an event of default? For bonds subject to the TIA, Section 316 of the TIA (discussed further in Section 4 of this chapter) sets forth rules for whether and how bonds can be amended without the approval of all bondholders. In particular, changes in the specific covenants cannot usually be made without the consent of the holders of a majority in principal amount of the outstanding debt (the firm itself is not allowed to vote any debt it holds). To prevent abuse of majority rule where insiders control a large percentage of the bonds, interest payments may not be deferred without approval of holders of 75% of the bonds and then not for more than three years. Moreover, the consent of 100% of the debtholders is typically required in order to change the maturity date or principal amount of the bonds. In private placements with just a few lenders, renegotiation is typically easier.

For a distressed firm seeking to renegotiate the repayment of outstanding bonds, the requirement that 100% of its bondholders consent to an extension of the bond's maturity date or a reduction in its principal amount raises a clear collective action problem: Even if the vast majority of bondholders are willing to conduct a debt restructuring, just a handful of dissenting bondholders can derail the transaction. The following case highlights a common workaround for firms in this situation.

Katz v. Oak Industries, Inc.

508 A.2d 873 (Del. Ch. 1986)

■ ALLEN, CHANCELLOR.

A commonly used word—seemingly specific and concrete when used in everyday speech—may mask troubling ambiguities that upon close examination are seen to derive not simply from casual use but from more fundamental epistemological problems. Few words more perfectly illustrate the deceptive dependability of language than the term "coercion" which is at the heart of the theory advanced by plaintiff as entitling him to a preliminary injunction in this case.

Plaintiff is the owner of long-term debt securities issued by Oak Industries, Inc. ("Oak"), a Delaware corporation; in this class action he seeks to enjoin the consummation of an exchange offer and consent solicitation made by Oak to holders of various classes of its long-term debt. As detailed below that offer is an integral part of a series of transactions that together would effect a major reorganization and recapitalization of Oak. The claim asserted is in essence, that the exchange offer is a coercive device and, in the circumstances, constitutes a breach of contract. This is the Court's opinion on plaintiff's pending application for a preliminary injunction.

I.

The background facts are involved even when set forth in the abbreviated form the decision within the time period currently available requires.

Through its domestic and foreign subsidiaries and affiliated entities, Oak manufactures and markets component equipments used in consumer, industrial and military products (the "Components Segment"); produces communications equipment for use in cable television systems and satellite television systems (the "Communications Segment") and manufactures and markets laminates and other materials used in printed circuit board applications (the "Materials Segment"). During 1985, the Company has terminated certain other unrelated businesses. As detailed below, it has now entered into an agreement with Allied-Signal, Inc. for the sale of the Materials Segment of its business and is currently seeking a buyer for its Communications Segment.

Even a casual review of Oak's financial results over the last several years shows it unmistakably to be a company in deep trouble. During the period from January 1, 1982 through September 30, 1985, the Company has experienced unremitting losses from operations; on net sales of approximately $1.26 billion during that period it has lost over $335 million. As a result its total stockholders' equity has first shriveled (from $260 million on 12/31/81 to $85 million on 12/31/83) and then disappeared completely (as of 9/30/85 there was a $62 million deficit in its stockholders' equity accounts). Financial markets, of course, reflected this gloomy history.[2]

Unless Oak can be made profitable within some reasonably short time it will not continue as an operating company. Oak's board of directors, comprised almost entirely of outside directors, has authorized steps to buy the company time. In February, 1985, in order to reduce a burdensome annual cash interest obligation on its $230 million of then outstanding debentures, the Company offered to exchange such debentures for a combination of notes, common stock and warrants. As a result, approximately $180 million principal amount of the then outstanding debentures were exchanged. Since interest on certain of the notes issued in that exchange offer is payable in common stock, the effect

[2] The price of the company's common stock has fallen from over $30 per share on December 31, 1981 to approximately $2 per share recently. The debt securities that are the subject of the exchange offer here involved (see note 3 for identification) have traded at substantial discounts.

of the 1985 exchange offer was to reduce to some extent the cash drain on the Company caused by its significant debt.

About the same time that the 1985 exchange offer was made, the Company announced its intention to discontinue certain of its operations and sell certain of its properties. Taking these steps, while effective to stave off a default and to reduce to some extent the immediate cash drain, did not address Oak's longer-range problems. Therefore, also during 1985 representatives of the Company held informal discussions with several interested parties exploring the possibility of an investment from, combination with or acquisition by another company. As a result of these discussions, the Company and Allied-Signal, Inc. entered into two agreements. The first, the Acquisition Agreement, contemplates the sale to Allied-Signal of the Materials Segment for $160 million in cash. The second agreement, the Stock Purchase Agreement, provides for the purchase by Allied-Signal for $15 million cash of 10 million shares of the Company's common stock together with warrants to purchase additional common stock.

The Stock Purchase Agreement provides as a condition to Allied-Signal's obligation that [holders of] at least 85% of the aggregate principal amount of all of the Company's debt securities shall have tendered and accepted the exchange offers that are the subject of this lawsuit. Oak has six classes of such long term debt.[3] If less than 85% of the aggregate principal amount of such debt accepts the offer, Allied-Signal has an option, but no obligation, to purchase the common stock and warrants contemplated by the Stock Purchase Agreement. An additional condition for the closing of the Stock Purchase Agreement is that the sale of the Company's Materials Segment contemplated by the Acquisition Agreement shall have been concluded.

Thus, as part of the restructuring and recapitalization contemplated by the Acquisition Agreement and the Stock Purchase Agreement, the Company has extended an exchange offer to each of the holders of the six classes of its long-term debt securities. These pending exchange offers include a Common Stock Exchange Offer (available only to holders of the 9-5/8% convertible notes) and the Payment Certificate Exchange Offers (available to holders of all six classes of Oak's long-term debt securities). The Common Stock Exchange Offer currently provides for the payment to each tendering noteholder of 407 shares of the Company's common stock in exchange for each $1,000 9-5/8% note accepted. The offer is limited to $38.6 million principal amount of notes (out of approximately $83.9 million outstanding).

---

3 The three classes of debentures are: 13.65% debentures due April 1, 2001, 10 1/2% convertible subordinated debentures due February 1, 2002, and 11-7/8% subordinated debentures due May 15, 1998. In addition, as a result of the 1985 exchange offer the company has three classes of notes which were issued in exchange for debentures that were tendered in that offer. Those are: 13.5% senior notes due May 15, 1990, 9-5/8% convertible notes due September 15, 1991 and 11-5/8% notes due September 15, 1990.

The Payment Certificate Exchange Offer is an any and all offer. Under its terms, a payment certificate, payable in cash five days after the closing of the sale of the Materials Segment to Allied-Signal, is offered in exchange for debt securities. The cash value of the Payment Certificate will vary depending upon the particular security tendered. In each instance, however, that payment will be less than the face amount of the obligation. The cash payments range in amount, per $1,000 of principal, from $918 to $655. These cash values however appear to represent a premium over the market prices for the Company's debentures as of the time the terms of the transaction were set.

The Payment Certificate Exchange Offer is subject to certain important conditions before Oak has an obligation to accept tenders under it. First, it is necessary that a minimum amount ($38.6 million principal amount out of $83.9 total outstanding principal amount) of the 9-5/8% notes be tendered pursuant to the Common Stock Exchange Offer. Secondly, it is necessary that certain minimum amounts of each class of debt securities be tendered, together with consents to amendments to the underlying indentures.[4] Indeed, under the offer one may not tender securities unless at the same time one consents to the proposed amendments to the relevant indentures.

The condition of the offer that tendering security holders must consent to amendments in the indentures governing the securities gives rise to plaintiff's claim of breach of contract in this case. Those amendments would, if implemented, have the effect of removing significant negotiated protections to holders of the Company's long-term debt including the deletion of all financial covenants. Such modification may have adverse consequences to debt holders who elect not to tender pursuant to either exchange offer.

Allied-Signal apparently was unwilling to commit to the $15 million cash infusion contemplated by the Stock Purchase Agreement, unless Oak's long-term debt is reduced by 85% (at least that is a condition of their obligation to close on that contract). Mathematically, such a reduction may not occur without the Company reducing the principal amount of outstanding debentures (that is the three classes of outstanding notes constitute less than 85% of all long-term debt). But existing indenture covenants (See Offering Circular, pp. 38–39) prohibit the Company, so long as any of its long-term notes are outstanding, from issuing any obligation (including the Payment Certificates) in exchange for any of the debentures. Thus, in this respect, amendment to the indentures is required in order to close the Stock Purchase Agreement as presently structured.

---

4 The holders of more than 50% of the principal amount of each of the 13.5% notes, the 9-5/8% notes and the 11-5/8% notes and at least 66-2/3% of the principal amount of the 13.65% debentures, 10 1/2% debentures, and 11-7/8% debentures, must validly tender such securities and consent to certain proposed amendments to the indentures governing those securities.

Restrictive covenants in the indentures would appear to interfere with effectuation of the recapitalization in another way. Section 4.07 of the 13.50% Indenture provides that the Company may not "acquire" for value any of the 9-5/8% Notes or 11-5/8% Notes unless it concurrently "redeems" a proportionate amount of the 13.50% Notes. This covenant, if unamended, would prohibit the disproportionate acquisition of the 9-5/8% Notes that may well occur as a result of the Exchange Offers; in addition, it would appear to require the payment of the "redemption" price for the 13.50% Notes rather than the lower, market price offered in the exchange offer.

In sum, the failure to obtain the requisite consents to the proposed amendments would permit Allied-Signal to decline to consummate both the Acquisition Agreement and the Stock Purchase Agreement.

* * *

II.

* * *

As amplified in briefing on the pending motion, plaintiff's claim is that no free choice is provided to bondholders by the exchange offer and consent solicitation. Under its terms, a rational bondholder is "forced" to tender and consent. Failure to do so would face a bondholder with the risk of owning a security stripped of all financial covenant protections and for which it is likely that there would be no ready market. A reasonable bondholder, it is suggested, cannot possibly accept those risks and thus such a bondholder is coerced to tender and thus to consent to the proposed indenture amendments.

It is urged this linking of the offer and the consent solicitation constitutes a breach of a contractual obligation that Oak owes to its bondholders to act in good faith. Specifically, plaintiff points to three contractual provisions from which it can be seen that the structuring of the current offer constitutes a breach of good faith. Those provisions (1) establish a requirement that no modification in the term of the various indentures may be effectuated without the consent of a stated percentage of bondholders; (2) restrict Oak from exercising the power to grant such consent with respect to any securities it may hold in its treasury; and (3) establish the price at which and manner in which Oak may force bondholders to submit their securities for redemption.

III.

* * *

I turn first to an evaluation of the probability of plaintiff's ultimate success on the merits of his claim. I begin that analysis with two preliminary points. The first concerns what is not involved in this case. To focus briefly on this clears away much of the corporation law case law of this jurisdiction upon which plaintiff in part relies. This case does not involve the measurement of corporate or directorial conduct against that high standard of fidelity required of fiduciaries when they act with respect to the interests of the beneficiaries of their trust. Under our law—and the law generally—the relationship between a corporation and the holders of its debt securities, even convertible debt securities, is contractual in nature. Arrangements among a corporation, the underwriters of its debt, trustees under its indentures and sometimes ultimate investors are typically thoroughly negotiated and massively documented. The rights and obligations of the various parties are or should be spelled out in that documentation. The terms of the contractual relationship agreed to and not broad concepts such as fairness define the corporation's obligation to its bondholders.[7]

Thus, the first aspect of the pending Exchange Offers about which plaintiff complains—that "the purpose and effect of the Exchange Offers is to benefit Oak's common stockholders at the expense of the Holders of its debt"—does not itself appear to allege a cognizable legal wrong. It is the obligation of directors to attempt, within the law, to maximize the long-run interests of the corporation's stockholders; that they may sometimes do so "at the expense" of others (even assuming that a transaction which one may refuse to enter into can meaningfully be said to be at his expense) does not for that reason constitute a breach of duty. It seems likely that corporate restructurings designed to maximize shareholder values may in some instances have the effect of requiring bondholders to bear greater risk of loss and thus in effect transfer economic value from bondholders to stockholders. But if courts are to provide protection against such enhanced risk, they will require either legislative direction to do so or the negotiation of indenture provisions designed to afford such protection.

The second preliminary point concerns the limited analytical utility, at least in this context, of the word "coercive" which is central to plaintiff's own articulation of his theory of recovery. If, pro arguendo, we are to extend the meaning of the word coercion beyond its core meaning—dealing with the utilization of physical force to overcome the will of another—to reach instances in which the claimed coercion arises from an act designed to affect the will of another party by offering inducements to the act sought to be encouraged or by arranging unpleasant consequences for an alternative sought to be discouraged, then—in order to make the term legally meaningful at all—we must acknowledge that some further refinement is essential. Clearly some "coercion" of this kind is legally unproblematic. Parents may "coerce" a child to study with the threat of withholding an allowance; employers may "coerce" regular attendance at work by either docking wages for time absent or by rewarding with a bonus such regular attendance. Other "coercion" so

---

7 To say that the broad duty of loyalty that a director owes to his corporation and ultimately its shareholders is not implicated in this case is not to say, as the discussion below reflects, that as a matter of contract law a corporation owes no duty to bondholders of good faith and fair dealing. Such a duty, however, is quite different from the congeries of duties that are assumed by a fiduciary.

defined clearly would be legally relevant (to encourage regular attendance by corporal punishment, for example). Thus, for purposes of legal analysis, the term "coercion" itself—covering a multitude of situations—is not very meaningful. For the word to have much meaning for purposes of legal analysis, it is necessary in each case that a normative judgment be attached to the concept ("inappropriately coercive" or "wrongfully coercive", etc.). But, it is then readily seen that what is legally relevant is not the conclusory term "coercion" itself but rather the norm that leads to the adjectives modifying it.

In this instance, assuming that the Exchange Offers and Consent Solicitation can meaningfully be regarded as "coercive" (in the sense that Oak has structured it in a way designed—and I assume effectively so—to "force" rational bondholders to tender), the relevant legal norm that will support the judgment whether such "coercion" is wrongful or not will, for the reasons mentioned above, be derived from the law of contracts. I turn then to that subject to determine the appropriate legal test or rule.

Modern contract law has generally recognized an implied covenant to the effect that each party to a contract will act with good faith towards the other with respect to the subject matter of the contract. The contractual theory for this implied obligation is well stated in a leading treatise:

> If the purpose of contract law is to enforce the reasonable expectations of parties induced by promises, then at some point it becomes necessary for courts to look to the substance rather than to the form of the agreement, and to hold that substance controls over form. What courts are doing here, whether calling the process "implication" of promises, or interpreting the requirements of "good faith", as the current fashion may be, is but a recognition that the parties occasionally have understandings or expectations that were so fundamental that they did not need to negotiate about those expectations. When the court "implies a promise" or holds that "good faith" requires a party not to violate those expectations, it is recognizing that sometimes silence says more than words, and it is understanding its duty to the spirit of the bargain is higher than its duty to the technicalities of the language. Corbin on Contracts (Kaufman Supp. 1984), § 570.

It is this obligation to act in good faith and to deal fairly that plaintiff claims is breached by the structure of Oak's coercive exchange offer. Because it is an implied contractual obligation that is asserted as the basis for the relief sought, the appropriate legal test is not difficult to deduce. It is this: is it clear from what was expressly agreed upon that the parties who negotiated the express terms of the contract would have agreed to proscribe the act later complained of as a breach of the implied covenant of good faith—had they thought to negotiate with respect to that matter. If the answer to this question is yes, then, in my opinion, a court is justified in concluding that such act constitutes a breach of the implied covenant of good faith.

With this test in mind, I turn now to a review of the specific provisions of the various indentures from which one may be best able to infer whether it is apparent that the contracting parties—had they negotiated with the exchange offer and consent solicitation in mind—would have expressly agreed to prohibit contractually the linking of the giving of consent with the purchase and sale of the security.

IV.

Applying the foregoing standard to the exchange offer and consent solicitation, I find first that there is nothing in the indenture provisions granting bondholders power to veto proposed modifications in the relevant indenture that implies that Oak may not offer an inducement to bondholders to consent to such amendments. Such an implication, at least where, as here, the inducement is offered on the same terms to each holder of an affected security, would be wholly inconsistent with the strictly commercial nature of the relationship.

Nor does the second pertinent contractual provision supply a ground to conclude that defendant's conduct violates the reasonable expectations of those who negotiated the indentures on behalf of the bondholders. Under that provision Oak may not vote debt securities held in its treasury. Plaintiff urges that Oak's conditioning of its offer to purchase debt on the giving of consents has the effect of subverting the purpose of that provision; it permits Oak to "dictate" the vote on securities which it could not itself vote.

The evident purpose of the restriction on the voting of treasury securities is to afford protection against the issuer voting as a bondholder in favor of modifications that would benefit it as issuer, even though such changes would be detrimental to bondholders. But the linking of the exchange offer and the consent solicitation does not involve the risk that bondholder interests will be affected by a vote involving anyone with a financial interest in the subject of the vote other than a bondholder's interest. That the consent is to be given concurrently with the transfer of the bond to the issuer does not in any sense create the kind of conflict of interest that the indenture's prohibition on voting treasury securities contemplates. Not only will the proposed consents be granted or withheld only by those with a financial interest to maximize the return on their investment in Oak's bonds, but the incentive to consent is equally available to all members of each class of bondholders. Thus the "vote" implied by the consent solicitation is not affected in any sense by those with a financial conflict of interest.

In these circumstances, while it is clear that Oak has fashioned the exchange offer and consent solicitation in a way designed to encourage consents, I cannot conclude that the offer violates the intendment of any of the express contractual provisions considered or, applying the test set out above, that its structure and timing breaches an implied obligation of good faith and fair dealing.

One further set of contractual provisions should be touched upon: Those granting to Oak a power to redeem the securities here treated at a price set by the relevant indentures. Plaintiff asserts that the attempt to force all bondholders to tender their securities at less than the redemption price constitutes, if not a breach of the redemption provision itself, at least a breach of an implied covenant of good faith and fair dealing associated with it. The flaw, or at least one fatal flaw, in this argument is that the present offer is not the functional equivalent of a redemption which is, of course, an act that the issuer may take unilaterally. In this instance it may happen that Oak will get tenders of a large percentage of its outstanding long-term debt securities. If it does, that fact will, in my judgment, be in major part a function of the merits of the offer (i.e., the price offered in light of the Company's financial position and the market value of its debt). To answer plaintiff's contention that the structure of the offer "forces" debt holders to tender, one only has to imagine what response this offer would receive if the price offered did not reflect a premium over market but rather was, for example, ten percent of market value. The exchange offer's success ultimately depends upon the ability and willingness of the issuer to extend an offer that will be a financially attractive alternative to holders. This process is hardly the functional equivalent of the unilateral election of redemption and thus cannot be said in any sense to constitute a subversion by Oak of the negotiated provisions dealing with redemption of its debt.

Accordingly, I conclude that plaintiff has failed to demonstrate a probability of ultimate success on the theory of liability asserted.

QUESTIONS

1. In analyzing whether Oak's tender offer violates the covenant that Oak may not vote its own debentures, the court concludes that the votes will only be by "those with a financial interest to maximize return on their investment. . ." Is that the same as saying that Oak isn't effectively voting the bonds?

2. Why does the court hold that the tender offers don't violate the implied covenant of good faith and fair dealing with respect to provisions requiring redemption at stated prices? Are the noteholders coerced into consenting and tendering by the threat of losing all the covenants?

3. How would you vote in the exchange offer if you were a Noteholder? Why?

4. If Noteholders are told the company will fail if it doesn't get the $15 million from the stock sale, what would they do? Does the amendment request then become coercive because it eliminates financial covenants?

Or does it just eliminate hold-outs who want to free ride and let other Noteholders solve Oak's solvency problem?

5. If the Trust Indenture Act (and the Oak indentures) permitted indenture amendments to relieve Oak of part of its payment obligations on the Notes on some supermajority vote (perhaps 75%), would this restructuring have been conducted differently?

6. If Oak had simply offered payments to the bondholders to consent to amendments to the indentures to eliminate the financial covenants and the requirements of pro rata repurchase, would the result have been the same?

NOTE

The device used by Oak Industries has found favor in debt defaults where few resources such as bankruptcy reorganization are available to restructure debt. In particular, where sovereign nations default on their debts to international bondholders, the consent exchange offer has been used successfully to resolve debtor defaults. See Jill E. Fisch and Caroline M. Gentile, Vultures or Vanguards? The Role of Litigation in Sovereign Debt Restructuring, 53 Emory L.J. 1043, 1091–92 (2004).

G. ENFORCEMENT OF COVENANT BREACHES

Hedge Fund Activism in the Enforcement of Bondholder Rights

Marcel Kahan and Edward Rock
103 Northwestern Law Review 281 (2009)

In the past, many violations of bondholder rights have remained undetected and unsanctioned. This historic underenforcement problem was rooted in the collective action problems facing bondholders, in the lack of substantial incentives for the indenture trustee—the supposed bondholder representative—to represent bondholder interests vigorously, in contractual provisions in the bond indenture—the document that governs most bondholder rights—that provide little help in detecting violations and impose barriers on the ability of bondholders to enforce their rights, and in the relatively accommodating attitude of insurance companies and mutual funds—the traditional holders of corporate bonds.

With the rise of hedge funds, however, this historic underenforcement problem has given way to a new enforcement paradigm. Unlike traditional investors, activist hedge funds look for bonds where companies have violated, have arguably violated, or are about to violate some contractual provisions; buy up a large quantity of the issue; and then aggressively enforce their rights. Hedge funds have been able to greatly ameliorate the historic underenforcement problem because they have the sophistication to detect potential violations, the financial resources to acquire substantial amounts of a single bond issue, and the willingness to take on issuers; perhaps most importantly, they have decided to pursue, and become experienced in pursuing, this strategy.

Yet not all is peachy-keen, and not just for the companies that find themselves the unexpected targets of activism. Hedge funds are obviously motivated by the desire to make money, and how much money they make from this strategy depends on the remedy afforded to bondholders for violations of their rights. But as we show, this remedy scheme entails its own imperfections. In particular, the standard remedy for covenant violations—acceleration—can, depending on extraneous circumstances, result in payoffs that are significantly larger or significantly smaller than the harm related to the violations.

In those circumstances where the payoff exceeds the harm, and thus produces a windfall, activist bondholders have incentives to enforce their rights aggressively, leading to overenforcement. * * *

In the short run, it is likely that selective enforcement has resulted in a disequilibrium between indenture covenants—which were drafted with the expectation that they would be underenforced—and the actual, much higher level of selective enforcement. In the long run, we would expect the market to adjust to reach a new equilibrium that is likely to be more efficient than the old underenforcement equilibrium. This new equilibrium may entail less stringent and more carefully drafted covenants.

* * *

In this Part, we provide some examples to illustrate the nature and scope of recent bondholder activism. * * *

2. Spectrum Brands.—In January 2007, Sandell, Sandelman, and Xerion—three hedge funds—sent a notice of default to Spectrum Brands alleging that the company's borrowing under its Revolving Credit Facility violated the indenture for Spectrum's 8-1/2% Senior Subordinated Notes. Spectrum took the unusual step of filing with the SEC its own lengthy analysis of the indenture provision, explaining why no such violation had occurred. Apparently, however, Spectrum was not sure it would prevail. Two months later, on March 12, it announced that it had entered into an Exchange and Forbearance Agreement with Sandell and Sandelman. According to that agreement, the company agreed to offer to exchange the 8-1/2% Senior Subordinated Notes for new Toggle PIK Exchange Notes due 2013,[17] with an initial interest rate of 11%—which was to increase semi-annually to 15.25% unless redeemed—in exchange for a waiver of any defaults under the 8-1/2% notes.

[17] For $1,000 in old notes, holders were to receive $950 in new notes and a $50 cash consent payment.

* * *

2. KCS Energy.—7-1/8% Senior Notes by KCS Energy, Inc. contained a change of control repurchase right that was triggered when a majority of the directors of the "Company" were neither "nominated for election or elected" with the "approval" of a majority of KCS's premerger directors. On July 12, 2006, KCS merged into Petrohawk Energy Corp., with Petrohawk surviving the merger. Prior to the merger, the board of KCS adopted a resolution "confirming and approving" the nomination and election of all the postmerger directors.[23] But only four of nine members of the postmerger board of Petrohawk (the "Company" for purposes of the indenture) were actual premerger directors of KCS. A group of note holders, reportedly organized by W.R. Huff Asset Management (a firm specializing in high yield bonds), replaced the indenture trustee and instructed the new trustee to file a suit arguing that the merger constituted a change of control. The court ruled in favor of Petrohawk, reasoning that the note holders were "attempting to exploit imprecise contract drafting" and to "use a technicality" to obtain a benefit. [Law Debenture Trust Company of New York v. Petrohawk Energy Corp., 2007 Del. Ch. LEXIS 113.]

The authors also describe numerous cases where issuers violated indenture terms through delinquent SEC filings. In UnitedHealth Group Inc. v. Wilmington Trust Co., 548 3d Cir. 1124 (8th Cir. 2008), United failed to file timely quarterly financial reports with the SEC on Form 10-Q because it was conducting an investigation of allegedly backdated stock options, which could cause it to restate its financial statements. United did communicate with investors about the reasons for its delay, and provided its best estimate of what its earnings were, without any adjustment that might result from any required restatement. (It turned out that there was only a 1% difference.) Hedge funds that held the bonds filed a notice of default with United, alleging a violation of an indenture covenant. United subsequently filed suit against the indenture trustee seeking a declaratory judgment that it was not in violation of the covenant, which read as follows:

> So long as any of the Securities remain Outstanding, *the Company shall cause copies of all current, quarterly and annual financial reports* on Forms 8-K, 10-Q and 10-K, respectively, and all proxy statements, *which the Company is then required to file with the [Securities and Exchange] Commission pursuant to Section 13 or 15(d) of the Exchange Act to be filed with the Trustee* and mailed to the Holders of such series of Securities at their addresses appearing in the Security Register maintained by the Security Registrar, in each case, within 15 days of filing

---

[23] Law Debenture Trust Co. of N.Y. v. PetroHawk Energy Corp., No. Civ. A. 2422–VCS, 2007 WL 2248150, at 10 (Del. Ch. Aug. 1, 2007).

with the Commission. The Company shall also comply with the provisions of TIA [Trust Indenture Act] ss. 314(a).

The hedge funds urged that this meant that United was required to make timely filings, in accordance with the SEC regulations, and to mail copies of these filings within fifteen days of the scheduled date of the filings. The court rejected this argument, concluding that the indenture did not require SEC filings at any particular time, but only required mailing to the noteholders within fifteen days of the actual date of filing.

In another notable case, U.S. Bank v. Windstream Services, a hedge fund named Aurelius purchased a large position in certain notes of Windstream Services, a telecommunications firm. The hedge fund then argued that a complicated set of transactions by Windstream—involving the transfer of some wire and copper fiber assets to another entity—breached a covenant in the governing bond indenture restricting "sale and leaseback" transactions. It sought acceleration of the debt. The U.S. District Court agreed with Aurelius in a decision that caused Windstream to file for bankruptcy.

Should hedge fund investors like Aurelius be able to successfully pursue these types of claims? Are they just enforcing contractual rights that give debt investors the benefit of their bargain? Does your answer change if the hedge fund also owns a large position in credit default swaps—an economic investment that is designed to pay off if a firm files for bankruptcy (as was rumored to be the case—though this was not confirmed by Aurelius)? If this is a problem, should we blame active enforcement of debt covenants or the existence of credit default swap markets?

4. THE INDENTURE TRUSTEE AND THE TRUST INDENTURE ACT

A. THE NATURE OF THE TRUSTEE AND ITS DUTIES

The trust device is unique to common law countries. While it is frequently thought of as a device for family estate planning where management of trust assets is expected to continue well after the death of the donor, it has served commercial purposes as well. In Western states such as California and Colorado, loans secured by real estate were not secured by a mortgage, but by a deed of trust. The trustee (a public trustee in Colorado) took no possessory interest in the property, but held title until repayment of the debt. Similarly, 19th century financings of railroads, with their huge investment in land and track, were financed with bonds secured by a deed of trust to secure repayment. The trust indenture was the document employed to set out the duties and powers of the trustee and continued in use as a deed to secure repayment of debt even where no mortgage was involved. In these cases, the indenture trustee held nothing but was simply instructed to protect the interests of the bondholders and to assure prompt repayment of the debt. The result has been a mixed message about the role of the trustee: Is the trustee a classic fiduciary, with standardized duties of care and loyalty, or something else, such as a contractual stakeholder with limited agency powers and duties? For an argument that this type of trust is simply a contractual arrangement rather than the fiduciary obligation that originated with a grant of property, see John H. Langbein The Contractarian Basis of the Law of Trusts, 105 Yale L.J. 625 (1995).

The utility of the trust indenture in enforcing the terms of a bond issue sold to large numbers of the investing public is that it centralizes the monitoring and enforcement role, eliminating the collective action problems facing bondholders. In that sense, the process is analogous to a bankruptcy administration, with the exception that there is only a single class of claimant.

During the Great Depression, when there were many defaults in corporate bonds, the role of the indenture trustee came under attack. It is the debtor corporation that selects the trustee, compensates the trustee, and sets the terms of the trust. Because this is a commercial relationship, the trustee sought relief from the high fiduciary standards imposed on more conventional trustees, and the debtor was often willing to provide exculpatory language in the trust indenture. Further, the debtor was likely to select a financial institution with which it had existing banking relations to serve as trustee. This could raise questions of trustee loyalty in times of debtor distress since aggressive enforcement of the indentures' covenants might cause the debtor to shift its banking relationships to another institution. Where the trustee was also a creditor of the debtor, this conflict of interest could cause the trustee to favor its own interests over those of the bondholders. To some, this seemed like a rigged game.

While temptations might exist for trustee disloyalty, there were countervailing market pressures. Financial institutions serving as indenture trustees needed to maintain reputations for honesty and loyalty to the trust beneficiaries. It was also in the self-interest of the debtor to select a trustee with a good reputation, or the debtor might need to offer a higher interest rate to compensate for the increased risk of slack enforcement.

Nevertheless, by the 1930s, suspicion of financial institutions prevailed. Congress adopted legislation regulating the trust indenture in 1939.

The Trust Indenture Act of 1939

The Trust Indenture Act applies to the public issuance of debt securities where the aggregate outstanding value of the securities is more than $50 million (by exempting those issued pursuant to an indenture for $50 million or less).* Trust Indenture Act, § 304(a)(9), 15 USC § 77ddd(a)(9). When it applies, the Act mandates the use of an indenture for the issuance of debt, as well as the appointment of a trustee. The Act additionally imposes a number of requirements for the trustee and for the indenture.

With respect to the Trustee, the Act requires the trustee to meet certain minimum qualification standards. For instance, trustees must have capital and surplus of at least $150,000 (a number that has not changed since 1939). Section 310(a)(2), 15 USC § 77jjj(a). Further, trustees may not have specified conflicting interests once the debtor is in default.† These conflicts include being a trustee under another indenture for the same debtor (Section 310(b)(1), 15 USC § 77jjj(b)(1)); being an underwriter for a debt issue of the issuer (Section 310(b)(2), 15 USC § 77jjj(b)(2)); controlling the debtor, by owning 10% or more of the debtor's voting securities, (Section 310(b)(5), 15 USC § 77jjj(b)(5)); or holding other debt of the debtor that is in default (10% of such issue) (Section 310(b)(8), 15 USC § 77jjj(b)(8)).

With respect to the indenture, the Act also imposes several mandatory terms that must be contained in the indenture. For instance, the indenture must require that the trustee report to the bondholders annually concerning any change in its eligibility to serve as trustee and the amount, if any, owed to it by the debtor. Section 313(a), 15 USC § 77mmm(a). There are limits on the exculpation that may be given the trustee. Section 315(d), 15 USC § 77oooo(d). And in the event of default, the trustee must notify the bondholders, Section 315(b), 15 USC § 77oooo(b), and take such actions as a prudent person would take in the conduct of his own affairs. Section 315(c), 15 USC § 77oooo(c).

The Act also regulates some terms of the indenture related to amendment: As noted previously, the indenture can't be amended to change rights to payment of interest, unless holders of 75% of debt consent, and interest can't be delayed for more than 3 years. Section 316(a)(2), 15 USC § 77ppp(a)(2) Any other limits on payment obligations to a debt holder require the consent of the debt holder (unanimous consent). Section 316(b), 15 USC § 77ppp(b).

An annotated version of the act, complete with discussion of legislative history and major cases, has also been published. Committee on Trust Indentures and Indenture Trustees, ABA Section of Business Law, Annotated Trust Indenture Act, 67 Bus. Law. 977 (2012).

---

* This threshold, formerly $10 million, was changed to $50 million through a final SEC rule in 2015. Because the Act applies only to debt securities, it does not apply to loans (such as conventional bank loans) that are not securities under U.S. federal securities laws.

† Until 1990 the Act prohibited such conflicts of interest at any time. One assumes Congress concluded that potential conflicts of interest were of little concern before default, when the Trustee's duties were routine and ministerial.

Elliott Associates v. J. Henry Schroder Bank & Trust Co.

838 F.2d 66 (2d Cir. 1988)

■ ALTIMARI, CIRCUIT JUDGE.

This appeal involves an examination of the obligations and duties of a trustee during the performance of its pre-default duties under a trust indenture, qualified under the Trust Indenture Act of 1939 (the "Act"). The instant action was brought by a debenture holder who sought to represent a class of all debenture holders under the trust indenture. The debenture holder alleged in its complaint that the trustee waived a 50-day notice period prior to the redemption of the debentures and did not consider the impact of the waiver on the financial interests of the debenture holders. The debenture holder alleged further that, had the trustee not waived the full 50-day notice period, the debenture holders would have been entitled to receive an additional $1.2 million in interest from the issuer of the debentures. The debenture holder therefore concludes that the trustee's waiver was improper and constituted a breach of the trustee's duties owed to the debenture holders under the indenture, the Act and state law.

The district court dismissed the debenture holder's action after conducting a bench trial and entered judgment in favor of the defendants. The district court held that the trustee's waiver did not constitute a breach of any duty owed to the debenture holders—under the indenture or otherwise—because, as the court found, a trustee's pre-default duties are limited to those duties expressly provided in the indenture. We agree with the district court that no breach of duty was stated here. Accordingly, we affirm the district court's decision dismissing the action.

FACTS AND BACKGROUND

Appellant Elliott Associates ("Elliott") was the holder of $525,000 principal amount of 10% Convertible Subordinated Debentures due June 1, 1990 (the "debentures") which were issued by Centronics Data Computer Corporation ("Centronics") pursuant to an indenture between Centronics and J. Henry Schroder Bank and Trust Company ("Schroder"), as trustee. Elliott's debentures were part of an aggregate debenture offering by Centronics of $40,000,000 under the indenture which was qualified by the Securities Exchange Commission ("SEC") pursuant to the Act.

The indenture and debentures provided, inter alia, that Centronics had the right to redeem the debentures "at any time" at a specified price, plus accrued interest, but the indenture also provided that, during the first two years following the issuance of the debentures, Centronics' right to redeem was subject to certain conditions involving the market price of Centronics' common stock. To facilitate its right to redeem the debentures, Centronics was required to provide written notice of a proposed redemption to the trustee and to the debenture holders. Section

3.01 of the indenture required that Centronics give the trustee 50-day notice of its intention to call its debentures for redemption, "unless a shorter notice shall be satisfactory to the trustee." Section 3.03 of the indenture required Centronics to provide the debenture holders with "at least 15 days but not more than 60 days" notice of a proposed redemption.

At the option of the debenture holders, the debentures were convertible into shares of Centronics' common stock. In the event Centronics called the debentures for redemption, debenture holders could convert their debentures "at any time before the close of business on the last Business Day prior to the redemption date." Subject to certain adjustments, the conversion price was $3.25 per share. The number of shares issuable upon conversion could be determined by dividing the principal amount converted by the conversion price. Upon conversion, however, the debentures provided that "no adjustment for interest or dividends [would] be made."

Debenture holders were to receive interest payments from Centronics semi-annually on June 1 and December 1 of each year. Describing the method of interest payment, each debenture provided that the Company will pay interest on the Debentures (except defaulted interest) to the persons who are registered Holders of Debentures at the close of business on the November 15 or May 15 next preceding the interest payment date. Holders must surrender Debentures to a Paying Agent to collect principal payments. To insure the primacy of the debenture holders' right to receive interest, the indenture provided that "notwithstanding any other provision of this Indenture, the right of the Holder of a Security to receive payment of . . . interest on the Security . . . shall not be impaired."

In early 1986, Centronics was considering whether to call its outstanding debentures for redemption. On March 12, 1986, Centronics' Treasury Services Manager, Neil R. Gordon, telephoned Schroder's Senior Vice President in charge of the Corporate Trust Department, George R. Sievers, and informed him of Centronics' interest in redeeming the debentures. Gordon told Sievers that Centronics "was contemplating redemption" of all of its outstanding debentures, subject to SEC approval and fluctuations in the market for Centronics' common stock. Specifically addressing the 50-day notice to the trustee requirement in section 3.01 of the indenture, Gordon asked Sievers how much time "Schroder would need once the SEC had Centronics' registration materials and an actual redemption date could therefore be set." Sievers responded that "Schroder would only need [one] week" notice of the redemption. Sievers explained that this shorter notice would satisfy section 3.01 because Centronics was proposing a complete rather than a partial redemption, and because there were relatively few debenture holders. Sievers explained that the shorter notice therefore would provide it with sufficient time to perform its various administrative tasks in connection with the proposed redemption.

Shortly thereafter, on March 20, 1986, Centronics' Board of Directors met and approved a complete redemption of all of its outstanding debentures and designated May 16, 1986 as the redemption date. On April 4, 1986—42 days prior to the redemption—Centronics' President, Robert Stein, wrote Schroder and informed the trustee that "pursuant to the terms of the Indenture, notice is hereby given that the Company will redeem all of its outstanding 10% Convertible Subordinated Debentures due June 1, 1990, on May 16, 1986." Centronics then proceeded to file registration materials with the SEC in order to receive clearance for the redemption. Schroder was furnished with copies of all the materials Centronics had filed with the SEC.

On May 1, 1986, the SEC cleared the proposed redemption. On that same day, pursuant to section 3.03 of the indenture, Centronics gave formal notice of the May 16, 1986 redemption to the debenture holders. In a letter accompanying the Notice of Redemption, Centronics' President explained that, as long as the price of Centronics' common stock exceeded $3.75 per share, debenture holders would receive more value in conversion than in redemption. In the Notice of Redemption, debenture holders were advised, inter alia, that the conversion price of $3.25 per share, when divided into each $1,000 principal amount being converted, would yield 307.69 shares of Centronics common stock. Based upon the April 30, 1986 New York Stock Exchange closing price of $5 3/8 per share of Centronics' common stock, each $1,000 principal amount of debenture was convertible into Centronics common stock having an approximate value of $1,653.83. Debenture holders were advised further that failure to elect conversion by May 15, 1986 would result in each $1,000 principal amount debenture being redeemed on May 16 for $1,146.11, which consisted of $1,000 in principal, $100 for the 10% redemption premium, and $46.11 in interest accrued from December 1, 1985 (the last interest payment date) to May 16, 1986 (the redemption date). Finally, the notice of redemption explained that accrued interest was not payable upon conversion:

> *No adjustments for Interest or Dividends upon Conversion.* No payment or adjustment will be made by or on behalf of the Company (i) on account of any interest accrued on any Debentures surrendered for conversion or (ii) on account of dividends, if any, on shares of Common Stock issued upon such conversion. Holders converting Debentures will not be entitled to receive the interest thereon from December 1, 1985 to May 16, 1986, the date of redemption. (emphasis in original).

On May 15, 1986, the last day available for conversion prior to the May 16, 1986 redemption, Centronics' common stock traded at $6 5/8 per share. At that price, each $1,000 principal amount of debentures was convertible into Centronics' common stock worth approximately $2,038. Thus, it was clear that conversion at $2,038 was economically more profitable than redemption at $1,146.11. Debenture holders apparently recognized this fact because all the debenture holders converted their debentures into Centronics' common stock prior to the May 16, 1986 redemption.

Elliott filed the instant action on May 12, 1986 and sought an order from the district court enjoining the May 16, 1986 redemption. Elliott alleged in its complaint that Schroder and Centronics conspired to time the redemption in such a manner so as to avoid Centronics' obligation to pay interest on the next interest payment date, i.e., June 1, 1986. This conspiracy allegedly was accomplished by forcing debenture holders to convert prior to the close of business on May 15, 1986. Elliott contended that, as part of this conspiracy, Schroder improperly waived the 50-day notice in section 3.01 of the indenture and thus allowed Centronics to proceed with the redemption as planned. Elliott claimed that Schroder waived the 50-day notice without considering the impact of that waiver on the financial interests of the debenture holders and that the trustee's action in this regard constituted, inter alia, a breach of the trustee's fiduciary duties. Finally, Elliott alleged that, had it not been for the trustee's improper waiver, debenture holders would have been entitled to an additional payment of $1.2 million in interest from Centronics.

* * *

The district court decided this matter on the basis of the papers filed. The parties stipulated to the facts, as summarized above, and submitted affidavits of experts in the field who provided opinions on the custom and practice in the financial community relevant to the issues in the case. The district court filed its decision on March 17, 1987 in which it denied Elliott's motion for class certification and granted Schroder and Centronics' motions to dismiss. The district court also denied Schroder's and Centronics' motions for costs and attorneys' fees.

DISCUSSION

The central issue on this appeal is whether the district court properly held that the trustee was not obligated to weigh the financial interests of the debenture holders when it decided on March 12, 1986 to waive Centronics' compliance with section 3.01's 50-day notice requirement. We agree with the district court's conclusion that the trustee was under no such duty.

At the outset, it is important to sort out those matters not at issue here. First, Elliott does not dispute that Centronics complied in all respects with the indenture's requirement to provide notice of redemption to the debenture holders. Elliott's claim only challenges the sufficiency of the notice to the trustee and the manner in which the trustee decided to waive that notice. Moreover, Elliott does not dispute that Schroder's actions were expressly authorized by section 3.01, which specifically allows the trustee discretion to accept shorter notice of redemption from Centronics if that notice was deemed satisfactory. * * * Rather, Elliott's claim essentially is that the trustee was under a duty—

implied from the indenture, the Act or state law—to secure greater benefits for debenture holders over and above the duties and obligations it undertook in the indenture.

No such implied duty can be found from the provisions of the Act or from its legislative history. Indeed, section 315(a)(1) of the Act allows a provision to be included in indentures (which was incorporated into the indenture at issue here) providing that

> the indenture trustee shall not be liable except for the performance of such duties [prior to an event of default] as are specifically set out in [the] indenture.

Moreover, when the Act was originally introduced in the Senate by Senator Barkley, it provided for the mandatory inclusion of a provision requiring the trustee to perform its pre-default duties and obligations in a manner consistent with that which a "prudent man would assume and perform." However, the version of the Act introduced in the House of Representatives by Representative Cole excluded the imposition of a pre-default "prudent man" duty on the trustee. After extensive hearings on the House and Senate versions of the Act, during which representatives of several financial institutions expressed concern over the imposition of pre-default duties in excess of those duties set forth expressly in the indenture, Congress enacted the present version of section 315 of the Act. Thus, it is clear from the express terms of the Act and its legislative history that no implicit duties, such as those suggested by Elliott, are imposed on the trustee to limit its pre-default conduct.

It is equally well-established under state common law that the duties of an indenture trustee are strictly defined and limited to the terms of the indenture, although the trustee must nevertheless refrain from engaging in conflicts of interest.

In view of the foregoing, it is no surprise that we have consistently rejected the imposition of additional duties on the trustee in light of the special relationship that the trustee already has with both the issuer and the debenture holders under the indenture. As we recognized in Meckel [v. Continental Resources Co., 758 F.2d 811 (2d Cir. 1985)],

> an indenture trustee is not subject to the ordinary trustee's duty of undivided loyalty. Unlike the ordinary trustee, who has historic common-law duties imposed beyond those in the trust agreement, an indenture trustee is more like a stakeholder whose duties and obligations are exclusively defined by the terms of the indenture agreement.

758 F.2d at 816. We therefore conclude that, so long as the trustee fulfills its obligations under the express terms of the indenture, it owes the debenture holders no additional, implicit pre-default duties or obligations except to avoid conflicts of interest.

Our analysis here is therefore limited to determining whether the trustee fulfilled its duties under the indenture. As set forth above, section

3.01 requires that, when the company intends to call its debentures for redemption, it must provide the trustee with 50-day notice of the redemption, "unless a shorter notice shall be satisfactory to the trustee." Section 3.02 of the indenture sets forth the manner in which the trustee selects which debentures are to be redeemed when the company calls for a partial redemption. The American Bar Foundation's Commentaries on Model Debenture Indenture Provisions (1971) (the "Commentaries") explains that "notice of the Company's election to redeem all the debentures need not be given to the Trustee since such a redemption may be effected by the Company without any action on the part of the Trustee. . ." Id. at § 11–3, p. 493. Thus, it appears that section 3.01's notice requirement is intended for the trustee's benefit to allow it sufficient time to perform the various administrative tasks in preparation for redemption. While compliance with a full notice period may be necessary in the event of partial redemption, the full notice may not be required in the event of a complete redemption. We find that, although the trustee may reasonably insist on the full 50-day notice in the event of a complete redemption, it nevertheless has the discretion to accept shorter notice when it deems such shorter notice satisfactory.

* * *

CONCLUSION

In view of the foregoing, we affirm the judgment of the district court which dismissed Elliott's action. * * *

QUESTIONS

1. What was the debenture holder's complaint? Do they really have grounds to be upset?
2. What was the redemption price for a $1,000 debenture? What was the conversion value on May 15?
3. The court quotes the *Commentaries* to the effect that when all debentures are called, notice need not be given to the Trustee. How does this relate to the Company's obligation to give advance notice? Don't debenture holders have independent rights to advance notice?

NOTE

The *Elliott Associates* opinion contains at least two characterizations of the Trustee's position: (1) a mere stakeholder, with duties limited to those specified in the indenture, and (2) a trustee, with duties of loyalty to the bondholders, citing Dabney v. Chase National Bank, 196 F.2d 668 (2d Cir. 1952). But other courts have used at least two other characterizations: (3) a full trustee, with full duties to act as a "prudent man" and (4) an agent for the bondholders, with some fiduciary duties. See Smith, Case & Morrison,

The Trust Indenture Act of 1939 Needs No Conflict of Interest Resolution, 35 Bus. Law. 161, n. 30 (1979). The authors observe that originally the trustee was employed simply to serve as mortgagee for secured debt, and that the role has grown from that simple beginning. The trust was an obvious device to borrow to describe the trustee's role, since it held liens on property for the benefit of bondholders. But from the beginning the indenture severely limited the duties and liabilities of the indenture trustee. One might ask whether bailee would be a more accurate description of the trustee's role, but for the troublesome problem that in a bailment legal title to property does not pass, as it does in a mortgage (except in lien theory states).

B. THE TRUSTEE'S DUTIES IN DEFAULT

Until a default, the indenture trustee's duties are minimal in most indentures. Set out below is the definition of default from the American Bar Association's Model Simplified Indenture:

Section 6.01. Events of Default.

An "Event of Default" occurs if:

(1) the Company fails to pay interest on any Security when the same becomes due and payable and such failure continues for a period of [30] days;

(2) the Company fails to pay the Principal of any Security when the same becomes due and payable at maturity, upon redemption or otherwise;

(3) the Company fails to comply with any of its other agreements in the Securities or this Indenture and such failure continues for the period and after the notice specified below;

(4) the Company pursuant to or within the meaning of any Bankruptcy Law:

(A) commences a voluntary case,

(B) consents to the entry of an order for relief against it in an involuntary case,

(C) consents to the appointment of a Custodian of it or for all or substantially all of its property, or

(D) makes a general assignment for the benefit of its creditors; or

(5) a court of competent jurisdiction enters an order or decree under any Bankruptcy Law that:

(A) is for relief against the Company in an involuntary case,

(B) appoints a Custodian of the Company or for all or substantially all of its property, or

(C) orders the liquidation of the Company, and the order or decree remains unstayed and in effect for 60 days.

* * *

A Default under clause (3) is not an Event of Default until the Trustee or the Holders of at least [25]% in Principal amount of the Securities notify the Company and the Trustee of the Default and the Company does not cure the Default, or it is not waived, within [60] days after receipt of the notice. The notice must specify the Default, demand that it be remedied to the extent consistent with law, and state that the notice is a "Notice of Default."

What happens if there is an Event of Default? As in most installment payment agreements, the indenture gives the Trustee the power to accelerate upon default:

Section 6.02. Acceleration.

If an Event of Default occurs and is continuing, the Trustee by notice to the Company, or the Holders of at least 25% in Principal amount of the Securities by notice to the Company and the Trustee, may declare the Principal of and accrued and unpaid interest on all the Securities to be due and payable. Upon such declaration the Principal and interest shall be due and payable immediately.

These provisions are required by section 317(a) of the Trust Indenture Act.*

Recognizing that trustees may have weak incentives to enforce the indenture in the event of default, the Trust Indenture Act, section 316(a), provides that an indenture shall be deemed to provide a right for bondholders to enforce.† The Model Indenture contains complying provisions:

Section 6.05. Control by Majority.

The Holders of a majority in Principal amount of the Securities may direct the time, method and place of conducting any proceeding for any remedy available to the Trustee or exercising any trust or power conferred on the Trustee. However, the Trustee may refuse to

---

* (a) The indenture trustee shall be authorized—

(1) in the case of a default in payment of the principal of any indenture security, when and as the same shall become due and payable, or in the case of a default in payment of the interest on any such security, when and as the same shall become due and payable and the continuance of such default for such period as may be prescribed in such indenture, to recover judgment, in its own name and as trustee of an express trust, against the obligor upon the indenture securities for the whole amount of such principal and interest remaining unpaid; . . .

† § 316(a)(1) contains the following:

"The indenture to be qualified—

(1) shall automatically be deemed (unless it is expressly provided therein that any such provision is excluded) to contain provisions *authorizing the holders of not less than a majority in principal amount* of the indenture securities or if expressly specified in such indenture, of any series of securities at the time outstanding (A) *to direct the time, method and place of conducting any proceeding for any remedy* available to such trustee, under such indenture, or (B) on behalf of the holders of all such indenture securities, to consent to the waiver of any past default and its consequences; . . ." [Emphasis supplied.]

follow any direction that conflicts with law or this Indenture, is unduly prejudicial to the rights of other Securityholders, or would involve the Trustee in personal liability or expense for which the Trustee has not received a satisfactory indemnity.

Section 6.06. Limitation on Suits.

A Securityholder may pursue a remedy with respect to this Indenture or the Securities only if:

(1) the Holder gives to the Trustee notice of a continuing Event of Default;

(2) the Holders of at least 25% in Principal amount of the Securities make a request to the Trustee to pursue the remedy;

(3) the Trustee either (i) gives to such Holders notice it will not comply with the request, or (ii) does not comply with the request within [15 or 30] days after receipt of the request; and

(4) the Holders of a majority in Principal amount of the Securities do not give the Trustee a direction inconsistent with the request prior to the earlier of the date, if ever, on which the Trustee delivers a notice under Section 6.06(3)(i) or the expiration of the period described in Section 6.06(3)(ii).

A Securityholder may not use this Indenture to prejudice the rights of another Securityholder or to obtain a preference or priority over another Securityholder.

Section 315(a)(1) of the Act allows a provision in the indenture that the trustee shall not be liable except for breach of duties specifically set out in the indenture. In the event of default, the trustee must notify the bondholders, and take such actions as a prudent person would take in the conduct of his own affairs. Section 315(b) and (c) 15 USC § 77oooo(b) & (c). The Model Simplified Indenture provides the following language:

Section 7.01. Duties of Trustee.

(a) If an Event of Default has occurred and is continuing, the Trustee shall exercise such of the rights and powers vested in it by this Indenture, and use the same degree of care and skill in their exercise, as a prudent person would exercise or use under the circumstances in the conduct of its own affairs.

(b) Except during the continuance of an Event of Default:

(1) The Trustee need perform only those duties that are specifically set forth in this Indenture and no others. * * *

In the event a Trustee fails to discharge its duties under Section 315(b) and (c), most courts have held that debt holders have an implied private right of action against the Trustee. Consequently, a Trustee that fails to notify the bondholders of a default or, following a default, to take such actions as a "prudent person would take in the conduct of his own affairs" can be directly liable to bondholders for damages arising from breaching its obligations under Section 315(b) and (c). See, e.g., BlackRock Core Bond Portfolio v. U.S. Bank National Association (S.D.N.Y. February 26, 2016). This right is in addition to any state law rights that debtholders may have against a trustee whose actions following a default may cause debtholders to suffer an economic loss. For instance, consider the following case resting on both breach of contract and breach of fiduciary duty concepts.

Gresser v. Wells Fargo Bank, N.A.

2012 WL 5250553 (D.Md. 2012)

■ CATHERINE C. BLAKE, UNITED STATES DISTRICT JUDGE.

Plaintiff Anne Gresser brings this action on behalf of a putative class of bondholders alleging that, under an indenture with failed sub-prime mortgage lender KH Funding ("KH"), defendant Wells Fargo breached its duties as indenture trustee. Wells Fargo has filed a motion for judgment on the pleadings seeking to dismiss Gresser's claims. For the reasons set forth below, Wells Fargo's motion will be denied.

BACKGROUND

KH was a Maryland sub-prime mortgage lender and bond issuer. On August 4, 2004, KH entered into an indenture with defendant Wells Fargo under which it issued "Series 3 Senior Secured Investment Debt Securities" ("Series 3 Notes") and "Series 4 Subordinated Unsecured Investment Debt Securities ("Series 4 Notes"). Plaintiff Anne Gresser is a holder of Series 3 Notes that had, at one time, over $1 million in face value.

The indenture was made pursuant to the Trust Indenture Act of 1939 ("TIA"), which it incorporates by reference. Under the indenture . . . Wells Fargo undertook a variety of duties and obligations as indenture trustee. These duties include an obligation, in the event of a default, to protect the value of the Notes on behalf of their holders by "exercis[ing] such of the rights and powers vested in it by this [i]ndenture, and us[ing] the same degree of care in their exercise, as a prudent man would exercise or use under the circumstances in the conduct of his own affairs." This obligation is triggered only by an "Event of Default," a term formally defined in the indenture that includes any failure by KH "to pay interest and/or principal due on the Notes for a period of 30 days." Wells Fargo also had a duty to notify Series 3 noteholders of the existence of any default or Event of Default. The indenture further provides that Wells Fargo "may not be relieved from liabilities for its own negligent action, its own negligent failure to act, or its own willful misconduct, except that . . . [it] shall not be liable for any error of judgment made in good faith by a Responsible Officer, unless it is proved that [it] was negligent in ascertaining the pertinent facts."

On May 18, 2005, Wells Fargo, as indenture trustee, "filed an original financing statement . . . with the Maryland Department of Assessment and Taxation" on behalf of Series 3 noteholders. By filing the statement, "Wells Fargo perfected liens on and security interests in" a variety of collateral held by KH for the benefit of Series 3 noteholders. Under Maryland law a financing statement is only effective for five years from the date of filing. Wells Fargo did not file a continuation statement within five years and allowed the Series 3 noteholders' lien and security in the collateral held by KH to lapse. Wells Fargo eventually filed a second financing statement on September 7, 2010, less than 90 days before KH filed for bankruptcy.

KH suffered a series of mounting losses beginning in 2007 and coinciding with the financial crisis. KH reported these losses to the SEC. Beginning with the 2008 10-K it filed on April 15, 2009, KH also reported continuing Events of Default to the SEC. For example, on May 20, 2009, KH reported to the SEC "it was subject to approximately $1.5 million in redemption requests for Series 3 Notes that were past the 30-day grace period." On December 23, 2009, KH reported "it received notice from Wells Fargo that Wells Fargo had declared an event of default under the Indenture and that Wells Fargo intended to mail notice of such event of default to holders of the Notes." Wells Fargo had taken no action with respect to any default up until this date. On January 7, 2010, Wells Fargo notified holders that an Event of Default was occurring, and on February 5, 2010, citing its powers under the indenture, Wells Fargo gave notice it was accelerating the notes because KH "has defaulted in the payment of principal and interest on the [Notes] . . . for a period of at least 30 days, and, therefore, Events of Default have occurred and are continuing."

On December 3, 2010, KH filed for bankruptcy. Because Wells Fargo failed to continue the first financing statement, and because it had filed the second financing statement less than 90 days before KH filed for bankruptcy, KH sought in a Complaint to Avoid Preferential Transfer, under a provision of the U.S. Bankruptcy Code, to avoid application of the lien against its assets created by the second financing statement. In its answer to KH's complaint, Wells Fargo admitted it did not file the second financing statement within five years of filing the first statement. Wells Fargo and KH filed a stipulation and consent order, which was entered on May 17, 2011, under which Series 3 noteholders lost secured creditor status with respect to any of KH's assets except for two deposit accounts with a combined value of less than $55,000.

Subsequently, Gresser commenced this action on behalf of herself and all other Series 3 noteholders as of February 5, 2010. Gresser alleges that Wells Fargo breached its contractual duties to Series 3 noteholders, as third-party beneficiaries of the indenture, "by its recurrent failure to exercise its rights and powers under the Indenture despite its knowledge of repeated and continuing events of default . . ." Gresser also alleges that Wells Fargo breached its contract, or alternatively breached its duty of care as a fiduciary, by failing to file a continuation of the first financing statement leading to "a lesser recovery from [KH's] bankruptcy estate" for Series 3 noteholders.

ANALYSIS

* * *

II. Breach of Contract Claim

Gresser adequately states a claim for breach of contract as a third party beneficiary of Wells Fargo's agreement with KH. Under the indenture, "except during the continuance of an Event of Default[,]" Wells Fargo's obligations are limited to "those duties . . . specifically set forth in [the indenture] and no others, and no implied covenants or obligations" are to be read into the indenture. During an Event of Default, however, this provision does not apply, and Wells Fargo's obligations are not limited to express provisions of the indenture. Instead, Wells Fargo is to be held to a "prudent man" duty of care in determining its liabilities for actions taken or not taken to protect the interests of noteholders. Thus, in order to state a claim for breach of the indenture as a noteholder, Gresser must plead that (1) an Event of Default occurred and was continuing as defined by the agreement; (2) Wells Fargo was aware of the continuance of an Event of Default; and (3) Wells Fargo then breached its duty of care by its actions or failure to act.

Gresser's complaint easily satisfies the first requirement: she cites five KH SEC filings, beginning in April 2009, that report various amounts of at least $1.75 million of interest and principal payments that were more than 30 days late. Section 6.1 of the indenture defines an "Event of Default" as, among other possibilities, "defaults in the payment of interest" or "defaults in the payment of the principal of any Security when the same becomes due and payable at maturity . . . and the Default continues for a period of 30 days . . ." Wells Fargo's heightened duties under the indenture are only triggered by "the continuance of an Event of Default." Taking the SEC filings as accurate, there were at least five instances where an Event of Default was continuing—the dates on which KH reported to the SEC that it was past the 30 day grace period in principal and loan payments.

* * *

Wells Fargo argues that Gresser's only allegation that the trustee was aware of the continuing Events of Default is that KH indicated it was in default in its SEC filings. Wells Fargo points to § 4.3 of the indenture and a New York Court of Appeals case to show that it was under no duty to review KH's SEC filings. See Racepoint Partners, LLC v. JP Morgan Chase Bank, N.A., 928 N.E.2d 396, 398–99, (N.Y. 2010). This may be true, but it does not necessarily follow that because Wells Fargo did not need to review the filings the fact that it received the filings has no bearing on the plausibility of Gresser's claim. Because Wells Fargo received them, it is plausible that they made the trustee aware of KH's defaults.

Furthermore, the complaint not only alleges that Wells Fargo was notified of the defaults because it received the SEC filings; the complaint also alleges that KH directly informed Wells Fargo of its defaults. The complaint alleges repeatedly that "KH funding stated [in its SEC filings] that it informed Wells Fargo of [the nonpayment of principal and interest]." Taken as true, these statements indicate that Wells Fargo was notified of Events of Default for months prior to giving notice to Series 3 holders or accelerating the notes.

As to wrongdoing, Gresser's complaint describes three failures to act on the part of Wells Fargo that plausibly state a claim for breach of its duties under the indenture. First, the complaint alleges that Wells Fargo did not accelerate the notes until February 5, 2010, almost a year after Gresser alleges Wells Fargo first became aware of continuing Events of Default. * * *

Second, Wells Fargo allegedly failed to give notice of Events of Default to Series 3 holders as required by § 10.13(b) of the indenture. Wells Fargo contends that Gresser did not adequately plead this claim because the complaint only alleges that the trustee failed "to exercise its rights and powers under the [i]ndenture" and that giving notice "is a duty, not a right or power." But, in an Event of Default, § 7.1 is not limited to enumerated powers, and "implied covenants or obligations" may be read into the indenture. Thus, this section fairly encompasses the express duty to notify Series 3 holders contained in § 10.13(b) of the indenture, and this is an additional ground upon which Gresser plausibly states a claim for breach. See In re Bankers Trust Co., 450 F.3d 121, 129 (2d Cir. 2006) (finding indenture trustee breached duty to give noteholders notice of default).

Third, the complaint plausibly alleges that Wells Fargo's failure to file a continuance of the first financing statement was a breach of § 7.1 of the indenture. The indenture contains no provision that requires Wells Fargo to file such a statement. On this basis, Wells Fargo argues that § 7.1(a), which requires the trustee to "exercise such rights and powers vested in it by [the indenture,]" "expressly" limits Wells Fargo's duties to specific provisions of the indenture and that Gresser is wrongly attempting to "transform the duty into one with undefined and unlimited scope." But, a broad duty of care is precisely what § 7.1(a) appears to place on Wells Fargo during an Event of Default. Section 7.1(b) states: "Except during the continuance of an Event of Default . . . [t]he duties of [Wells Fargo] shall be determined solely by express provisions of the [i]ndenture and . . . no implied covenants or obligations shall be read into this [i]ndenture . . ." (emphasis added). It follows that, during an Event of Default, implied covenants or obligations can be read into the indenture. Though Maryland law is relatively silent as to the obligations of indenture trustees, a broad, fiduciary-like duty to protect noteholder interests seems to be what the TIA intended to vest in indenture trustees during defaults.[4] Thus, Wells Fargo's attempt to limit the term "rights and powers vested in it by [the indenture]" to only an express set of powers conflicts with § 7.1 as a whole.

Furthermore, Wells Fargo seems to have believed that filing a financing statement was not beyond its powers under the indenture, because it undertook to file the first statement in 2005 as a means of securing noteholder interests. At that time, a default was not occurring and Wells Fargo was under no obligation to do so. Once an Event of Default was occurring, however, Wells Fargo's duty to protect noteholder interests vested, and it is plausible that it breached this duty by failing to file a continuance of the financing statement. In fact, Wells Fargo did eventually file a second financing statement shortly before KH filed for bankruptcy, suggesting Wells Fargo believed it was prudent under the indenture to do so. Wells Fargo's alleged failure to file a timely continuance of the financing statement, according to the complaint, hindered its efforts to recover for the Series 3 noteholders in KH's bankruptcy proceedings. This is a third plausible ground for Gresser's claim.

* * *

IV. "Good Faith"

Finally, Gresser's complaint will not be dismissed for failing to plead specific facts that show Wells Fargo did not act in good faith. Section 7.1(c)(2) of the indenture provides that Wells Fargo "shall not be liable for any error of judgment made in good faith." The TIA itself provides that all indentures "shall automatically be deemed . . . to contain provisions protecting the indenture trustee from liability for any error of judgment made in good faith by a responsible officer . . ." 15 U.S.C. § 77ooo(d)(2). Wells Fargo contends that these provisions place a burden on the party seeking indenture trustee liability to plead facts that show a lack of good faith and that Gresser's complaint is, at most, conclusory in this regard. In this context, however, good faith more likely constitutes an affirmative defense. See CFIP Master Fund, Ltd. v. Citibank, N.A., 738 F. Supp. 2d 450, 473 n.26 (S.D.N.Y. 2010) (construing a nearly identical provision in a trust agreement as an affirmative defense).

Eventually, Gresser may be unable to prevail if Wells Fargo shows it consciously decided not to give bondholders notice of defaults, not to accelerate the notes prior to February 2010, and not to file a continuance of the financing statement. If these omissions were "judgment[s]" made by an officer or officers of Wells Fargo, then it may be entitled to a

[4] See Steven L. Schwarcz & Gregory M. Sergi, Bond Defaults and the Dilemma of the Indenture Trustee, 59 Ala. L. Rev. 1037, 1044–45 (2008) (stating that during the development of the TIA, the SEC suggested that indenture trustees "be transformed into active trustees with the obligation to exercise the degree of care and diligence which the law attaches to such high fiduciary position[s]." (citation omitted)). Wells Fargo attached this law review article to its Reply Memorandum.

presumption that they were made in good faith, regardless of their wisdom. See Speers Sand & Clay Works, Inc. v. American Trust Co., 20 F.2d 333, 335 (4th Cir. 1927).

But, Gresser does not merely allege that Wells Fargo made unwise or imprudent decisions in carrying out its duties under the indenture; rather, she alleges that Wells Fargo failed to address KH's defaults at all. While it is possible that Wells Fargo's omissions were choices entitled to protection under the "good faith" language of the indenture and TIA, it is equally plausible that they were not "error[s] in judgment" and that Wells Fargo simply ignored KH's defaults. Dismissing Gresser's claims on good faith grounds would require the court to find, as fact, that an officer or officers of Wells Fargo assessed KH's defaults and consciously decided to forgo action. Cf. CFIP Master Fund, Ltd., 738 F. Supp. 2d at 473–74 (granting summary judgment that defendant trustee acted in good faith after finding that "[t]he undisputed record shows that . . . [the defendant] made the decision" to take the allegedly negligent action after "conferring with outside counsel" and "asking . . . for further explanation"). At this stage, such a factual finding would be inappropriate.

CONCLUSION

For the forgoing reasons, Wells Fargo's motion for judgment on the pleadings will be denied.

5. CREDITOR FIDUCIARY DUTY CLAIMS

Earlier in this chapter, during the RJR Nabisco case, we saw how a firm's managers do not normally owe fiduciary duties to creditors: "a corporate bond 'represents a contractual entitlement to the repayment of a debt and does not represent an equitable interest in the issuing corporation necessary for the imposition of a trust relationship with concomitant fiduciary duties.' " This can change, however, if a corporation begins to experience financial difficulty.

It is clear, for instance, that directors owe duties to creditors when the corporation is in bankruptcy. And they may also owe duties at some time before bankruptcy. Several courts have held that once a corporation becomes insolvent, directors owe fiduciary duties to creditors.*

The following case reflects problems that arose with the overbuilding of broadband transmission capacity. The troubled corporation, Clearwire, was not alone. Worldcom filed for Chapter 11 protection in 2002 (though it was helped along this path by a massive accounting scandal). And Global Crossing, a firm with a core network that covered four continents and 200 major cities, also filed for Chapter 11 reorganization and sold its assets in 2002.

* Clarkson Co. Ltd. v. Shaheen, 660 F.2d 506 (2d Cir. 1981), cert. denied 445 U.S. 990 (1982); Bank Leumi-Le-Israel, B.M. v. Sunbelt Industries, Inc., 485 F.Supp. 556 (S. D. Ga. 1980).

North American Catholic Educational Programming Foundation, Inc. v. Rob Gheewalla, Gerry Cardinale and Jack Daly

930 A.2d 92 (Del. Supr. 2007)

■ HOLLAND, JUSTICE.

This is the appeal of the plaintiff-appellant, North American Catholic Educational Programming Foundation, Inc. ("NACEPF") from a final judgment of the Court of Chancery that dismissed NACEPF's Complaint for failure to state a claim. NACEPF holds certain radio wave spectrum licenses regulated by the Federal Communications Commission ("FCC"). In March 2001, NACEPF, together with other similar spectrum license-holders, entered into the Master Use and Royalty Agreement (the "Master Agreement") with Clearwire Holdings, Inc. ("Clearwire"), a Delaware corporation. Under the Master Agreement, Clearwire could obtain rights to those licenses as then-existing leases expired and the then-current lessees failed to exercise rights of first refusal.

The defendant-appellees are Rob Gheewalla, Gerry Cardinale, and Jack Daly (collectively, the "Defendants"), who served as directors of Clearwire at the behest of Goldman Sachs & Co. ("Goldman Sachs"). NACEPF's Complaint alleges that the Defendants, even though they comprised less than a majority of the board, were able to control Clearwire because its only source of funding was Goldman Sachs. According to NACEPF, they used that power to favor Goldman Sachs' agenda in derogation of their fiduciary duties as directors of Clearwire. In addition to bringing fiduciary duty claims, NACEPF's Complaint also asserts that the Defendants fraudulently induced it to enter into the Master Agreement with Clearwire and that the Defendants tortiously interfered with NACEPF's business opportunities.

NACEPF is not a shareholder of Clearwire. Instead, NACEPF filed its Complaint in the Court of Chancery as a putative *creditor* of Clearwire. The Complaint alleges *direct*, not derivative, fiduciary duty claims against the Defendants, who served as directors of Clearwire while it was either insolvent or in the "zone of insolvency."

Personal jurisdiction over the Defendants was premised exclusively upon 10 *Del.C.* § 3114, which subjects directors of Delaware corporations to personal jurisdiction in the Court of Chancery over claims "for violation of a duty in [their] capacity [as directors of the corporation]." * * *

For the reasons set forth in its Opinion, the Court of Chancery concluded: (1) that creditors of a Delaware corporation in the "zone of insolvency" may not assert direct claims for breach of fiduciary duty against the corporation's directors; (2) that the Complaint failed to state a claim for the narrow, if extant, cause of action for direct claims involving breach of fiduciary duty brought by creditors against directors of insolvent Delaware corporations; and (3) that, with dismissal of its fiduciary duty claims, NACEPF had not provided any basis for exercising personal jurisdiction over the Defendants with respect to NACEPF's other claims. Therefore, the Defendants' Motion to Dismiss the Complaint was granted.

In this opinion, we hold that the creditors of a Delaware corporation that is either insolvent or in the zone of insolvency have no right, as a matter of law, to assert direct claims for breach of fiduciary duty against the corporation's directors. Accordingly, we have concluded that the judgments of the Court of Chancery must be affirmed.

Facts

NACEPF is an independent lay organization incorporated under the laws of Rhode Island. In 2000, NACEPF joined with Hispanic Information and Telecommunications Network, Inc. ("HITN"), Instructional Telecommunications Foundation, Inc. ("ITF"), and various affiliates of ITF to form the ITFS Spectrum Development Alliance, Inc. (the "Alliance"). Collectively, the Alliance owned a significant percentage of FCC-approved licenses for microwave signal transmissions ("spectrum") used for educational programs that were known as "Instruction Television Fixed Service" spectrum ("ITFS") licenses.

The Defendants were directors of Clearwire. The Defendants were also all employed by Goldman Sachs and served on the Clearwire Board of Directors at the behest of Goldman Sachs. NACEPF alleges that the Defendants effectively controlled Clearwire through the financial and other influence that Goldman Sachs had over Clearwire.

According to the Complaint, the Defendants represented to NACEPF and the other Alliance members that Clearwire's stated business purpose was to create a national system of wireless connections to the internet. Between 2000 and March 2001, Clearwire negotiated a Master Agreement with the Alliance, which Clearwire and the Alliance members entered into in March 2001. * * *

Under the terms of the Master Agreement, Clearwire was to acquire the Alliance members' ITFS spectrum licenses when those licenses became available. To do so, Clearwire was obligated to pay NACEPF and other Alliance members more than $24.3 million. * * *

In June 2002, the market for wireless spectrum collapsed when WorldCom announced its accounting problems. It appeared that there was or soon would be a surplus of spectrum available from WorldCom. Thereafter, Clearwire began negotiations with the members of the Alliance to end Clearwire's obligations to the members. Eventually, Clearwire paid over $2 million to HITN and ITF to settle their claims and; according to NACEPF, was only able to limit its payments to that amount by otherwise threatening to file for bankruptcy protection. These settlements left the NACEPF as the sole remaining member of the

Alliance. The Complaint alleges that, by October 2003, Clearwire "had been unable to obtain any further financing and effectively went out of business."

NACEPF's Complaint

* * * In Count II [of the Complaint, NACEPF alleges that because, at all relevant times, Clearwire was either insolvent or in the "zone of insolvency," the Defendants owed fiduciary duties to NACEPF "as a substantial creditor of Clearwire," and that the Defendants breached those duties by:

> (1) not preserving the assets of Clearwire for its benefit and that of its creditors when it became apparent that Clearwire would not be able to continue as a going concern and would need to be liquidated and (2) holding on to NACEPF's ITFS license rights when Clearwire would not use them, solely to keep Goldman Sachs's investment "in play."

* * *

Motions to Dismiss

The Defendants moved to dismiss the Complaint on two grounds: first, for lack of personal jurisdiction under Court of Chancery Rule 12(b)(2); and, second, for NACEPF's failure to state a claim upon which relief can be granted under Court of Chancery Rule 12(b)(6). With respect to their first basis for dismissal, the Defendants noted that NACEPF's sole ground for asserting personal jurisdiction over them is 10 *Del.C.* § 3114 [which grants personal jurisdiction over nonresident directors for breaches of their duties as directors]. The Defendants argued that personal jurisdiction under § 3114 requires, at least, sufficient allegations of a breach of fiduciary duty owed by director-defendants. With respect to their second basis for dismissal, the Defendants contended that, even assuming that personal jurisdiction was sufficiently alleged, NACEPF's Complaint failed to set forth allegations which adequately supported any of its claims for relief, as a matter of law.

* * *

Therefore, to resolve the issue of personal jurisdiction, the Court of Chancery was required to decide whether, as a matter of law, Count II of the NACEPF Complaint properly stated a breach of fiduciary duty claim upon which relief could be granted.

Court of Chancery Rule 12(b)(6)

* * *

In the Court of Chancery and in this appeal, NACEPF waived any basis it may have had for pursuit of its claim derivatively. Instead, NACEPF seeks to assert only a *direct claim* for breach of fiduciary duties. It contends that such direct claims by creditors should be recognized in the context of both insolvency and the zone of insolvency. Accordingly, in ruling on the 12(b)(6) motion to dismiss Count II of the Complaint, the Court of Chancery was confronted with two legal questions: whether, as a matter of law, a corporation's *creditors* may assert *direct* claims against directors for breach of fiduciary duties when the corporation is either: first, insolvent or second, in the zone of insolvency.

Allegations of Insolvency and Zone of Insolvency

In support of its claim that Clearwire was either insolvent or in the zone of insolvency during the relevant periods, NACEPF alleged that Clearwire needed "substantially more financial support than it had obtained in March 2001." The Complaint alleges Goldman Sachs had invested $47 million in Clearwire, which "represent[ed] 84% of the total sums invested in Clearwire in March 2001, when Clearwire was otherwise virtually out of funds."

> *After March 2001,* Clearwire had financial obligations related to its agreement with NACEPF and others that *potentially* exceeded $134 million, did not have the ability to raise sufficient cash from operations to pay its debts as they became due and was dependent on Goldman Sachs to make additional investments to fund Clearwire's operations for the foreseeable future.

The Complaint also alleges:

> For example, upon the closing of the Master Agreement, Clearwire had approximately $29.2 million in cash and of that $24.3 million would be needed for future payments for spectrum to the Alliance members. Clearwire's "burn" rate was $2.1 million per month and it had then no significant revenues. The process of acquiring spectrum upon expiration of existing licenses was both time consuming and expensive, particularly if existing licenseholders contested the validity of any Clearwire offer that those license holders were required to match under their rights of first refusal.

Additionally, in the Complaint, NACEPF alleges that, "[b]y October 2003, Clearwire had been unable to obtain any further financing and effectively went out of business. Except for money advanced to it as a stopgap measure by Goldman Sachs in late 2001, Clearwire was never able to raise any significant money."

The Court of Chancery opined that insolvency may be demonstrated by either showing (1) "a deficiency of assets below liabilities with no reasonable prospect that the business can be successfully continued in the face thereof," or (2) "an inability to meet maturing obligations as they fall due in the ordinary course of business." Applying the standards applicable to review under Rule 12(b)(6), the Court of Chancery concluded that NACEPF had satisfactorily alleged facts which permitted a reasonable inference that Clearwire operated in the zone of insolvency during at least a substantial portion of the relevant periods for purposes of this motion to dismiss. The Court of Chancery also concluded that insolvency had been adequately alleged in the Complaint, for Rule 12(b)(6) purposes, for at least a portion of the relevant periods following execution of the Master Agreement.

Corporations in the Zone of Insolvency Direct Claims for Breach of Fiduciary Duty May Not Be Asserted by Creditors

In order to withstand the Defendant's Rule 12(b)(6) motion to dismiss, the Plaintiff was required to demonstrate that the breach of fiduciary duty claims set forth in Count II are cognizable under Delaware law. This procedural requirement requires us to address a substantive question of first impression that is raised by the present appeal: as a matter of Delaware law, can the *creditor* of a corporation that is operating within the *zone of insolvency* bring a *direct action* against its directors for an alleged *breach of fiduciary* duty?

It is well established that the directors owe their fiduciary obligations to the corporation and its shareholders. While shareholders rely on directors acting as fiduciaries to protect their interests, creditors are afforded protection through contractual agreements, fraud and fraudulent conveyance law, implied covenants of good faith and fair dealing, bankruptcy law, general commercial law and other sources of creditor rights. Delaware courts have traditionally been reluctant to expand existing fiduciary duties.

Accordingly, "the general rule is that directors do not owe creditors duties beyond the relevant contractual terms."

In this case, NACEPF argues that when a corporation is in the zone of insolvency, this Court should recognize a new direct right for creditors to challenge directors' exercise of business judgments as breaches of the fiduciary duties owed to them. This Court has never directly addressed the zone of insolvency issue involving directors' purported fiduciary duties to creditors that is presented by NACEPF in this appeal. That subject has been discussed, however, in several judicial opinions[27] and many scholarly articles.

In *Production Resources*, the Court of Chancery remarked that recognition of fiduciary duties to creditors in the "zone of insolvency" context may involve:

> "using the law of fiduciary duty to fill gaps that do not exist. Creditors are often protected by strong covenants, liens on assets, and other negotiated contractual protections. The implied covenant of good faith and fair dealing also protects creditors. So does the law of fraudulent conveyance. With these

[27] *Credit Lyonnais Bank Nederland N.V. v. Pathe Commc'ns Corp.*, 1991 Del. Ch. LEXIS 215, 1991 WL 277613 (Del. Ch. 1991); *Production Resources Group, L.L.C. v. NCT Group, Inc.*, 863 A.2d 772 (Del. Ch. 2004); *Trenwick America Litig. Trust v. Ernst & Young, L.L.P.*, 906 A.2d 168 (Del. Ch. 2006); *Big Lots Stores, Inc. v. Bain Capital Fund VII, LLC*, 922 A.2d 1169, 2006 Del. Ch. LEXIS 59, 2006 WL 846121 (Del. Ch. 2006).

> protections, when creditors are unable to prove that a corporation or its directors breached any of the specific legal duties owed to them, one would think that the conceptual room for concluding that the creditors were somehow, nevertheless, injured by inequitable conduct would be extremely small, *if extant*. Having complied with all legal obligations owed to the firm's creditors, the board would, in that scenario, ordinarily be free to take economic risk for the benefit of the firm's equity owners, so long as the directors comply with their fiduciary duties to the firm by selecting and pursuing with fidelity and prudence a plausible strategy to maximize the firm's value."

In this case, the Court of Chancery noted that creditors' existing protections—among which are the protections afforded by their negotiated agreements, their security instruments, the implied covenant of good faith and fair dealing, fraudulent conveyance law, and bankruptcy law—render the imposition of an additional, unique layer of protection through direct claims for breach of fiduciary duty unnecessary. It also noted that "any benefit to be derived by the recognition of such additional direct claims appears minimal, at best, and significantly outweighed by the costs to economic efficiency." The Court of Chancery reasoned that "an otherwise solvent corporation operating in the zone of insolvency is one in most need of effective and proactive leadership—as well as the ability to negotiate in good faith with its creditors—goals which would likely be significantly undermined by the prospect of individual liability arising from the pursuit of direct claims by creditors." We agree.

Delaware corporate law provides for a separation of control and ownership. The directors of Delaware corporations have "the legal responsibility to manage the business of a corporation for the benefit of its shareholders owners."[34] Accordingly, fiduciary duties are imposed upon the directors to regulate their conduct when they perform *that* function. Although the fiduciary duties of the directors of a Delaware corporation are unremitting:

> the exact course of conduct that must be charted to properly discharge that responsibility will change in the specific context of the action the director is taking with regard to either the corporation or its shareholders. This Court has endeavored to provide the directors with clear signal beacons and brightly lined channel markers as they navigate with due care, good faith, a loyalty on behalf of a Delaware corporation and its shareholders. This Court has also endeavored to mark the safe harbors clearly.

In this case, the need for providing directors with definitive guidance compels us to hold that no direct claim for breach of fiduciary duties may

[34] *Malone v. Brincat*, 722 A.2d 5, 9 (1998).

be asserted by the creditors of a solvent corporation that is operating in the zone of insolvency. When a solvent corporation is navigating in the zone of insolvency, the focus for Delaware directors does not change: directors must continue to discharge their fiduciary duties to the corporation and its shareholders by exercising their business judgment in the best interests of the corporation for the benefit of its shareholder owners. Therefore, we hold the Court of Chancery properly concluded that Count II of the NACEPF Complaint fails to state a claim, as a matter of Delaware law, to the extent that it attempts to assert a direct claim for breach of fiduciary duty to a creditor while Clearwire was operating in the zone of insolvency.

Insolvent Corporations Direct Claims For Breach of Fiduciary Duty May Not Be Asserted by Creditors

It is well settled that directors owe fiduciary duties to the corporation. When a corporation is *solvent*, those duties may be enforced by its shareholders, who have standing to bring *derivative* actions on behalf of the corporation because they are the ultimate beneficiaries of the corporation's growth and increased value. When a corporation is *insolvent*, however, its creditors take the place of the shareholders as the residual beneficiaries of any increase in value.

Consequently, the creditors of an *insolvent* corporation have standing to maintain derivative claims against directors on behalf of the corporation for breaches of fiduciary duties. The corporation's insolvency "makes the creditors the principal constituency injured by any fiduciary breaches that diminish the firm's value." Therefore, equitable considerations give creditors standing to pursue derivative claims against the directors of an insolvent corporation. Individual creditors of an insolvent corporation have the same incentive to pursue valid derivative claims on its behalf that shareholders have when the corporation is solvent.

In *Production Resources*, the Court of Chancery recognized that—in most, if not all instances—creditors of insolvent corporations could bring derivative claims against directors of an insolvent corporation for breach of fiduciary duty. In that case, in response to the creditor plaintiff's contention that derivative claims for breach of fiduciary duty were transformed into *direct* claims upon insolvency, the Court of Chancery stated:

> The fact that the corporation has become insolvent does not turn [derivative] claims into direct creditor claims, it simply provides creditors with standing to assert those claims. At all times, claims of this kind belong to the corporation itself because even if the improper acts occur when the firm is insolvent, they operate to injure the firm in the first instance by reducing its value, injuring creditors only indirectly by diminishing the

value of the firm and therefore the assets from which the creditors may satisfy their claims.[40]

Nevertheless, in *Production Resources*, the Court of Chancery stated that it was "not prepared to rule out" the *possibility* that the creditor plaintiff had alleged conduct that "might support" a *limited* direct claim. Since the complaint in *Production Resources* sufficiently alleged a derivative claim, however, it was unnecessary to decide if creditors had a legal right to bring direct fiduciary claims against directors in the insolvency context.

In this case, NACEPF did not attempt to allege a derivative claim in Count II of its Complaint. It only asserted a *direct* claim against the director Defendants for alleged breaches of fiduciary duty when Clearwire was insolvent. The Court of Chancery did not decide that issue. Instead, the Court of Chancery *assumed arguendo* that a direct claim for a breach of fiduciary duty to a creditor is legally cognizable in the context of actual insolvency. It then held that Count II of NACEPF's Complaint failed to state such a direct creditor claim because it did not satisfy the [necessary pleading requirements.]

To date, the Court of Chancery has never recognized that a creditor has the right to assert a *direct* claim for breach of fiduciary duty against the directors of an *insolvent* corporation. However, prior to this opinion, that possibility remained an open question because of the "arguendo assumption" in this case and the *dicta* in *Production Resources* and *Big Lots Stores*. In this opinion, we recognize "the pragmatic conduct-regulating legal realms . . . calls for more precise conceptual line drawing."

Recognizing that directors of an insolvent corporation owe direct fiduciary duties to creditors, would create uncertainty for directors who have a fiduciary duty to exercise their business judgment in the best interest of the insolvent corporation. To recognize a new right for creditors to bring direct fiduciary claims against those directors would create a conflict between those directors' duty to maximize the value of the insolvent corporation for the benefit of all those having an interest in it, and the newly recognized direct fiduciary duty to individual creditors. Directors of insolvent corporations must retain the freedom to engage in vigorous, good faith negotiations with individual creditors for the benefit of the corporation.

Accordingly, we hold that individual *creditors* of an *insolvent* corporation have *no right to assert direct* claims for breach of fiduciary duty against corporate directors. Creditors may nonetheless protect their interest by bringing derivative claims on behalf of the insolvent

---

[40] *Production Resources Group, L.L.C. v. NCT Group, Inc.*, 863 A.2d at 776; *see also Trenwick Am. Litig. Trust v. Ernst & Young, L.L.P.*, 906 A.2d 168, 2006 WL 2333201, at *22 n.75 (Del. Ch.).

corporation or any *other* direct nonfiduciary claim, as discussed earlier in this opinion, that may be available for individual creditors.

Conclusion

The creditors of a Delaware corporation that is either insolvent or in the zone of insolvency have no right, as a matter of law, to assert direct claims for breach of fiduciary duty against its directors. Therefore, Count II of NACEPF's Complaint failed to state a claim upon which relief could be granted. Consequently, the final judgment of the Court of Chancery is affirmed.

QUESTIONS

1. Why does it matter whether a creditor's claim for a fiduciary duty breach is direct or derivative? Does this make much of a practical difference?
2. In a typical Chapter 11 bankruptcy reorganization the shareholders participate not as creditors or "claimants" but as parties with an "interest" that stands behind that of the creditors, with only a minuscule chance of preserving any part of their investment. If they continue to have such an interest, how can the court suggest that creditors take the place of shareholders as residual claimants when the corporation is insolvent?
3. The California Court of Appeals discussed the extent of directors' duties in Berg & Berg Enterprises, LLC v. Boyle, 178 Cal. App. 4th 1020, 1038, 100 Cal. Rptr. 3d 875, 891 (Cal. App.6th Dist. 2009):

   > "Subsequent federal and out-of-state decisions discussing *Credit Lyonnais* and grappling with the question and scope of a duty owed to creditors upon insolvency have underscored that when managing a corporation that is insolvent, directors must consider the best interests of the whole "corporate enterprise, encompassing all its constituent groups, without preference to any. That duty, therefore, requires directors to take creditor interests into account, but not necessarily to give those interests priority. In particular, it is not a duty to liquidate and pay creditors when the corporation is near insolvency, provided that in the directors' informed, good faith judgment there is an alternative. Rather, the scope of that duty to the corporate enterprise is 'to exercise judgment in an informed, good faith effort to maximize the corporation's long-term wealth creating capacity.' " (citing *In re Ben Franklin Retail Stores, Inc.* (Bankr. N.D.Ill. 1998) 225 B.R. 646, 655; *Geyer v. Ingersoll Publications Co.,* (Del.Ch. 1992) 621 A.2d 784, 789–791; *In re Hechinger Inv. Co. of Delaware* (Bankr. D.Del. 2002) 274 B.R. 71, 89; *In re RSL Com Primecall, Inc.* (Bankr. S.D.N.Y., Dec. 11, 2003, Nos. 01–11457, 01–11469) 2003 Bankr. Lexis 1635, pp. *24–*25; *Production Resources v.*

NCT Group (Del.Ch. 2004) 863 A.2d 772, 787–803, overruled in part in *NACEPF v. Gheewalla* (Del. 2007) 930 A.2d 92, 103.)

Can you suggest how a lawyer should advise a corporation's directors about what this means in terms of taking risks?

6. OTHER LEGAL PITFALLS FOR LENDERS AND AFFILIATES

A. INTERCREDITOR DISPUTES

In recent years, some firms have seen the rise of intercreditor disputes, where different groups of lenders jockey for preferential treatment, typically in the shadow of a looming financial distress. Sometimes called "creditor-on-creditor violence" or "lender-on-lendor violence" these situations usually relate to opportunistic behavior by one or more of a borrower's existing creditors to gain seniority in the borrowing company's capital structure—particularly if that borrower is facing a risk of bankruptcy. But by gaining more seniority, the creditor may be *decreasing* the likelihood that another creditor will recover their investment.

For example, creditors who initially lent money with few protections, fearing that they may not recover, may seek to lend again, this time with provisions that enhance their likelihood of recovery (sometimes new creditors enter the mix as well). One strategy here is to engage in an "uptier transaction" that typically provides a company with a new liquidity infusion from a subset of lenders and/or equity investors. The new lenders might try to modify their credit agreement to allow the borrower to issue "super priority" debt with existing collateral to a subset of lenders (participating lenders) followed by an exchange of existing debt for this new super priority debt. Lenders who do not participate in this transaction may be left with a less attractive debt instrument that is now junior to the newly issued and/or exchanged debt. Should this be OK? Consider the following case:

In re Serta Simmons Bedding, LLC

No. 23-90020, 2023 WL 3855820 (Bankr. S.D. Tex. June 6, 2023)

■ JONES, UNITED STATES BANKRUPTCY JUDGE.

The Debtors are one of the largest bedding manufacturers and distributors in North America. For the ten years prior to 2020, the Debtors held the largest percentage of industry market share. The Debtors' main operating entity was formed in 2010 following the combination of the Serta® and Simmons® brands. Today, the Debtors employ approximately 3,600 employees and operate 21 bedding manufacturing facilities across the United States and Canada. Included within the Debtors' product umbrella are iconic brands such as Serta®, icomfort®, Beautyrest®, Simmons®, and Tuft & Needle®. The Debtors distribute their products through national, regional, and independent retail channels, as well as through direct-to-consumer channels. The Debtors also license their intellectual property to third-party manufacturers of bedding products.

* * *

The Post-2008 Credit Market and the 2016 Credit Agreement

The syndicated commercial loan market is a 1.4 trillion-dollar business. Following the 2008 financial crisis, commercial borrowers were able to negotiate more flexibility in their loan documents. This flexibility or "looseness," provides less protection for lenders and more opportunity for borrowers to manage their capital structure. A typical example of "looseness" evaluated by lenders is the degree to which the borrower can subsequently take on additional debt on a priority basis.

In November 2016, certain of the Debtors entered into three credit facilities which provided for (i) $1.95 billion in first lien term loans (the "2016 Credit Agreement"); (ii) $450 million in second lien term loans; and (iii) a $225 million asset-based revolving loan. The 2016 Credit Agreement is a "loose" document. The 2016 Credit Agreement contains multiple provisions providing the Debtors, as borrowers, a great deal of flexibility to engage in liability management transactions.

Section 9.05(g) of the 2016 Credit Agreement addresses the assignment of loans to "Affiliated Lenders" and the Debtors (defined in the 2016 Credit Agreement as the "Top Borrower"). Section 9.05(g) states, in relevant part, that:

> Notwithstanding anything to the contrary contained herein, any Lender may, at any time, assign all or a portion of its rights and obligations under this Agreement in respect of its Term Loans to any Affiliated Lender on a non-pro rata basis (A) **through Dutch Auctions open to all Lenders holding the relevant Term Loans on a pro rata basis or (B) through open market purchases,** in each case with respect to clauses (A) and (B), without the consent of the Administrative Agent;

(emphasis added). Thus, the 2016 Credit Agreement expressly permitted the Debtors to repurchase their debt from their Lenders on a non-pro rata basis through either a Dutch auction open to all Lenders or through open market purchases involving fewer than all Lenders.

Section 2.18 of the 2016 Credit Agreement provides that the agreement's pro rata sharing rights are "[s]ubject in all respects to the provisions of each applicable Intercreditor Agreement." The section also provides that the pro rata sharing does not apply to "any payment obtained by any Lender as consideration for the assignment of or sale of a participation in any of its Loans to any permitted assignee or participant, including any payment made or deemed made in connection with Sections 2.22, 2.23, 9.02(c) and/or Section 9.05." These exceptions were generally known to all lenders.

The 2016 Credit Agreement also provides great flexibility for future amendments. Section 9.02(b) provides that "neither this Agreement nor any other Loan Document or any provision hereof or thereof may be waived, amended or modified, except (i) in the case of this Agreement, pursuant to an agreement or agreements in writing entered into by the Top Borrower and the Required Lenders* . . . ." (footnote added). Amendments could therefore be freely made with the consent of only a simple majority of the Lenders unless the amendment involved a so-called "sacred right." Sacred rights, however, were subject to an express exception for purchases under § 9.05(g):

> [T]he consent of each Lender directly and adversely affected thereby (but not the consent of the Required Lenders) shall be required for any waiver, amendment or modification that: . . . waives, amends or modifies the provisions of Sections 2.18(b) or (c) of this Agreement in a manner that would by its terms alter the pro rata sharing of payments required thereby **(except in connection with any transaction permitted under Sections 2.22, 2.23, 9.02(c) and/or 9.05(g) or as otherwise provided in this Section 9.02)**.

(emphasis added).

The Debtor Faces Financial Challenges in 2019–2020

The Debtors began to experience financial challenges even prior to the onset of the COVID-19 public health emergency in March 2020. Direct-to-consumer sales competition and wholesale customer demands for more favorable payment terms placed increased pressure on the Debtors' liquidity. Mandated closures of over half of the Debtors' manufacturing facilities caused by governmental responses to the COVID-19 pandemic caused additional strain on the Debtors' liquidity. Further, the Debtors faced an upcoming maturity date on its ABL credit facility in 2021. The Debtors forecasted a sales to budget shortfall of $50 million for the month of March 2020 alone. The Debtors' March 31, 2020, forecast reflected a total lack of liquidity by early July.

Faced with those uncertainties, the Debtors engaged [an investment bank] in late 2019 "to evaluate both liquidity enhancement alternatives and liability management alternatives designed to capture, discount, or otherwise manage their liabilities." . . . At the time, the Debtors had outstanding approximately $1.9 billion of first lien debt, $420 million of second lien debt, $225 million of ABL facility debt and $80 million in capital lease obligations. The Debtors' "objective was to raise new liquidity in order to make sure that the company could survive, as well

* 'Required Lenders' means, at any time, Lenders having Loans or unused Commitments representing more than 50% of the sum of the total Loans and such unused commitments at such time." [Debtor Ex. 6 at § 9.02(b), Docket No. 853-6].

as potentially right-size the balance sheet through achieving discount." The failure to obtain relief by June 2020 meant that the company "might have been forced to file for bankruptcy or, worse, liquidate."

[The investment bank] immediately contacted eleven different lending groups regarding financing opportunities with seven expressing an interest. . .

The 2020 Transaction

The Debtors' increased leverage, unmet expectations and profitability shortfalls as well as the bankruptcy of a major customer and the ongoing uncertainty caused by the COVID-19 public health emergency motivated a group of the Debtors' lenders to form an ad hoc group (the "PTL Lenders") and contact the Debtors on April 7, 2020, to discuss ongoing liquidity needs and potential options. When they received no response, the PTL Lenders sent a second communication on April 24, 2020, along with the outline of a priority financing proposal that allowed for participation by all the Debtors' first and second lien lenders. The Debtors again failed to respond.

Approximately a week later, the PTL Lenders learned for the first time that at least one other group of first lien lenders (the "Objecting Lenders") had presented the Debtors with a proposed financing alternative using a "drop-down" structure in early March 2020. This group consisted of Angelo Gordon Management LLC ("Angelo Gordon"), Gamut Capital Management LP ("Gamut") and Apollo Management Holdings, L.P. ("Apollo"). The Objecting Lenders recognized that the "looseness" of the 2016 Credit Agreement allowed for (i) a liability management solution; and (ii) the stripping of first lien lender protections. Angelo Gordon had been working on crafting a proposed structure for the Debtors since January 2020. Under a drop-down structure, a borrower moves its most valuable assets to a new unrestricted subsidiary. The participating lenders then advance new money secured by the assets and provide a discount on existing debt that is then repurchased. The effect of a drop-down is to remove a borrower's most valuable assets from the non-participating lenders' collateral base. In their proposal, the Objecting Lenders utilized the open market provision under § 9.05(g) for the Debtors to repurchase their loans. In anticipation of implementing this structure, the Objecting Lenders acquired approximately $575 million of the Debtors' first lien debt at substantial discounts.

One original member of the PTL Lender group, Barings, LLC ("Barings"), withdrew from the group to propose its own transaction with the Debtors. At the time, Barings knew that the process would be competitive and that the credit agreement had "significant flexibility with respect to a liability management transaction." Barings submitted its initial proposal to the Debtors on or about May 8, 2020. The proposal utilized a drop-down of all the Debtors' intellectual property rights, involved new financing of $390–450 million and the repurchase of

Barings' existing debt at a discount. The ensuing negotiations between the parties were characterized "as being fairly typical for any competitive process, auction or competitive financing." Barings submitted its last proposal on June 4, 2020.

The Debtors invited the PTL Lender group to submit a competing proposal using a set of general guidelines. After unsuccessfully attempting to get the Objecting Lenders to work together to submit a joint proposal, the PTL Lenders submitted their own proposal to the Debtors on May 26, 2020. Multiple negotiations occurred with the primary focus on the amount of discount to be applied to the existing first and second lien debt. On June 5, 2020, the Debtors accepted the PTL Lenders' final proposal (the "2020 Transaction"). The 2020 Transaction involved the creation of a priority tranche of debt consisting of $200 million of new money plus $875 million of exchanged loans with the first lien loans exchanged at 74% and the second lien loans exchanged at 39%.* When Barings learned that the Debtors had accepted the PTL Lenders' proposal, Barings analyzed the 2020 Transaction and agreed to participate. In agreeing to participate, Barings noted that the economic effects of the 2020 Transaction were similar to the drop-down structure that it had proposed but was "a cleaner more efficient transaction." Barings noted that its analysis determined that the 2016 Credit Agreement allowed for the 2020 Transaction and that it participated in the 2020 Transaction in good faith.

Immediately after learning that the Debtors had accepted the PTL Lenders' proposal, the Objecting Lenders circulated the following internal email:

1. [The debtor's equity sponsor] has played our two groups off of each other and continues to do so

a. We concede that the [PTL Lenders' professional group] has outmaneuvered our group

b. However, we don't want to let [the debtor's equity sponsor] be the winners

c. We are concerned about two outcomes:

---

* The parties refer to the 2020 Transaction as an "uptier transaction." Generally, an uptier transaction involves the issuance of new debt by a borrower that is secured by a priming lien on the borrower's assets with the existing debt of the participating lenders purchased at a discount with a portion of the proceeds. As with a drop-down, the effect of an uptier transaction is to effectively remove a borrower's most valuable assets from the non-participating lenders' collateral base until the participating lenders are paid in full. As discussed on the record by the Court, the names ascribed to these transactions have no legal significance. They are just words. [Docket No. 968, Tr. at pg. 47:24–48:3, J. Jones]. The Court is more concerned with the effects of these transactions and whether the undertaken actions were permitted under the 2016 Credit Agreement. The fact that one person says they know drop-downs but not uptiers is to suggest that financial transactions fit nicely into static "buckets." In the modern world of commercial finance, they simply do not. The Court has referred to these transactions in the aggregate as "Position Enhancement Transactions" ("PETs") between lenders.

i. [Race to the bottom—while we would rather not, we are being encouraged/are being forced to underbid you]

ii. Litigation—risk that any transaction will result in significant litigation for all parties involved

The email then outlines a proposed offer to the PTL Lenders:

2. Outline of offer

a. We will sign a lock-up that ties us all together that [the PTL Lenders' lawyers] can draft

i. The group will only pursue transactions that treat all parties the same and are supported by the group

ii. We wait to properly restructure this business

b. Payment to [PTL Lenders' professional group]. Option:

i. Ad Hoc Group purchase of $200mm of face value at 65 cents, or

ii. $30 million fee paid directly to ad hoc group members

Angelo Gordon also contacted other lenders to garner support to stop the PTL Lenders' transaction. When those efforts proved unsuccessful, the Objecting Lenders and LCM—first lien loan holders—filed lawsuits in New York state court to enjoin the transaction. The New York state court denied the Objecting Lenders' request for a preliminary injunction based on their failure to establish a likelihood of success on the merits. After abandoning the lawsuit, the Objecting Lenders filed a second almost identical lawsuit two years later.

The Court finds the foregoing to be reflective of the true motives of the Objecting Lenders in these proceedings, including an objective lack of good faith.

[Eds. The Court proceeds to outline the procedural history of the case. It then discusses its approach to evaluating the proposed plan of reorganization and addresses objections advanced by various parties.]

The Adversary Proceeding

New York law implies a covenant of good faith and fair dealing in the performance of every contract. "[T]he implied duty must arise from the contract and the promisee's reasonable expectations," at the time of the transaction. "[T]o plead a valid cause of action for breach of the covenant of good faith, a plaintiff must allege facts sufficient to demonstrate that the plaintiff reasonably understood the contract or contractual provision at issue to state a duty to take or refrain from taking a particular action." Id. (internal quotations omitted). One party's assertion that the counter-party's actions "drastically undermined a fundamental objective of the parties' contract" is insufficient.

The Court's inquiry is an objective one focused on the plaintiff's reasonable expectations at the time of entry into the agreement. Courts should provide a level of deference in reviewing agreements negotiated and executed by sophisticated parties. The Court may not insert contractual terms where none exist.

The Court's inquiry is further constrained by the entirety of the terms in the agreement. Conduct that is expressly permitted under an agreement does not violate the implied covenant. Finally, actions taken for a "legitimate business purpose," even if self-interested, do not violate the covenant of good faith and fair dealing. Signing a contract does not "oblige [one] to become an altruist towards the other party."

The evidence adduced at trial is undeniable. The parties were keenly aware that the 2016 Credit Agreement was a "loose document" and understood the implications of that looseness. The Objecting Lenders acquired the majority of their loan holdings long after the original issuance and in anticipation of negotiating and executing a PET to the exclusion of the PTL Lenders—exactly what they complain was done to them using the same provisions of the 2016 Credit Agreement. No evidence of an improper motive on behalf of either the Debtors or the PTL Lenders was presented. The Debtors always remained transparent in their goals. Likewise, the PTL Lenders acted defensively and in good faith. On the scale of equity, it is the conduct of the Objecting Lenders that raises an eyebrow. There is no evidence of a breach of the implied duty of good faith and fair dealing by either the Debtors, the PTL Lenders or any of the other counter-defendants. There is no evidence of a breach of the 2016 Credit Agreement. The parties could have easily avoided this entire situation with the addition of a sentence or two to the 2016 Credit Agreement. They did not. And this litigation ends with each party receiving the bargain they struck—not the one they hoped to get.

PETs may or may not be a good thing. Lender exposure to these types of transactions can be easily minimized with careful drafting of lending documents. While the result may seem harsh, there is no equity to achieve in this case. Sophisticated financial titans engaged in a winner-take-all battle. There was a winner and a loser. Such an outcome was not only foreseeable, it is the only correct result. The risk of loss is a check on unrestrained behavior. As set forth above in connection with confirmation of the Plan, the Court finds that based on the overwhelming evidence adduced at trial, the 2020 Transaction was the result of good-faith, arm's length negotiations by economic actors acting in accordance with the duties owed to their respective creditors, investors and owners. The Court further finds that the 2020 Transaction was not prohibited by the 2016 Credit Agreement. The Court further finds that the 2020 Transaction is binding and enforceable in all respects. All claims for breach of the implied duty of good faith and fair dealing are denied. All claims for breach of the 2016 Credit Agreement are denied. All other requested relief is denied.

QUESTIONS

1. What exactly was the impact of the PTL June 2020 "uptier" transaction on the economic rights of each party? Why was this permitted under the 2016 credit agreement?
2. Should legal adjudication of these transactions be governed by the covenant of good faith? Is there a different approach that might be preferable to sort out claims of lender-on-lender "violence?"
3. How should creditors who are concerned about the possibility of lender-on lender "violence" protect against similar transactions in their ex-ante contracts?

B. CREDITOR LIABILITY

Most of the discussion in this chapter has explored topics related to a lender's direct investment in a borrower. How does the lender protect this investment? And what legal obligations does a borrower or trustee owe the lender once the investment is made? Said differently, we have mostly examined lawsuits where the lending party is a *plaintiff*—along with some transactional strategies that lenders might use to protect themselves in the event of a potential problem or lawsuit.

But it is also important to recognize that a creditor might face a risk of being roped into a lawsuit as a *defendant* when something has not gone well at the firm in which they've invested and another party is upset. Similarly, other affiliates, including professional advisors who help structure a troubled lending transaction, might find themselves facing a lawsuit. When will these types of problems arise?

Krivo Industrial Supply Company v. National Distillers and Chemical Corporation

483 F.2d 1098 (5th Cir. 1973)

■ RONEY, CIRCUIT JUDGE.

Plaintiffs, ten creditors of a now reorganized corporation, individually sued National Distillers and Chemical Corp., the major creditor of that corporation, on their debts. Finding that the cases all involved common questions of law and fact, the District Court consolidated them for trial on the single issue of liability. The issue of damages was severed and was reserved for subsequent proceedings. The alleged liability of National Distillers was predicated upon the rule that, when one corporation controls and dominates another corporation to the extent that the second corporation becomes the "mere instrumentality" of the first, the dominant corporation becomes liable for those debts of the subservient corporation attributable to an abuse of that control. After hearing plaintiffs' evidence, the District Court granted a directed verdict in favor of National Distillers. We affirm, finding that the evidence was insufficient to establish a jury question as to the presence of the requisite degree of control.

I. The Law

* * *

The "Instrumentality" Doctrine

We note at the outset that the case before us involves only the question of National Distillers' liability under the "instrumentality" theory. It involves no question of fraud, deceit, or misrepresentation. Nor does it involve charges that National Distillers received large amounts of security for small debt and made excessive, overreaching profits through foreclosure. Hence, we must examine the evidence exclusively within the framework of the narrow rule of corporation law known as the "instrumentality" doctrine.

Basic to the theory of corporation law is the concept that a corporation is a separate entity, a legal being having an existence separate and distinct from that of its owners. This attribute of the separate corporate personality enables the corporation's stockholders to limit their personal liability to the extent of their investment. But the corporate device cannot in all cases insulate the owners from personal liability. Hence, courts do not hesitate to ignore the corporate form in those cases where the corporate device has been misused by its owners. The corporate form, however, is not lightly disregarded, since limited liability is one of the principal purposes for which the law has created the corporation.

One of the most difficult applications of the rule permitting the corporate form to be disregarded arises when one corporation is sought to be held liable for the debts of another corporation. * * * The rationale for holding the dominant corporation liable for the subservient corporation's debts is that, since the dominant corporation has misused the subservient corporation's corporate form by using it for the dominant corporation's own purposes, the debts of the subservient corporation are in reality the obligations of the dominant corporation. In these cases, "the courts will look through the forms to the realities of the relation between the companies as if the corporate agency did not exist and will deal with them as the justice of the case may require." Here, then, the corporate form of the subservient corporation is disregarded so as to affix liability where it justly belongs. Plaintiffs' claim in this case is based on this second theory of liability.

* * *

. . . [T]wo elements are essential for liability under the "instrumentality" doctrine. First, the dominant corporation must have controlled the subservient corporation, and second, the dominant corporation must have proximately caused plaintiff harm through misuse of this control.

In considering the first element, that of control, the courts have struggled to delineate the kind of control necessary to establish liability under the "instrumentality" rule. Two problem areas have persistently troubled the process of ascertaining the extent of control. First, to what extent is stock ownership critical, and second, how much weight should be given to the existence of a creditor-debtor relationship in those cases where the debtor corporation is alleged to be the "instrumentality" of its creditor?

* * *

As with stock ownership, a creditor-debtor relationship also does not per se constitute control under the "instrumentality" theory. The general rule is that the mere loan of money by one corporation to another does not automatically make the lender liable for the acts and omissions of the borrower. The logic of this rule is apparent, for otherwise no lender would be willing to extend credit. The risks and liabilities would simply be too great. Nevertheless, lenders are not automatically exempt from liability under the "instrumentality" rule. If a lender becomes so involved with its debtor that it is in fact actively managing the debtor's affairs, then the quantum of control necessary to support liability under the "Instrumentality" theory may be achieved.

An examination of "instrumentality" cases involving creditor-debtor relationships demonstrates that courts require a strong showing that the creditor assumed actual, participatory, total control of the debtor. Merely taking an active part in the management of the debtor corporation does not automatically constitute control, as used in the "instrumentality" doctrine, by the creditor corporation.

The broad scope permitted creditors to institute various restrictions on the activities of their debtors is exemplified by Chicago Mill & Lumber Co. v. Boatmen's Bank, 234 F. 41 (8th Cir. 1916). In Chicago Mill & Lumber Co., a bank lent large sums of money to a mill and land company. To protect its investment, the bank had its assistant cashier elected president of the debtor company. The manager of the company testified that he took his directions from either the president of the bank or the assistant cashier who headed the company. After the company went into bankruptcy, a creditor sued the bank on the theory that the bankrupt company had been merely a department of the bank and that the bank's arrangements for monitoring the activities of its debtor entitled the plaintiff to a jury determination of whether or not the company was in fact controlled by the bank.

Affirming the District Court's directed verdict in favor of the bank on the issue, the Eighth Circuit accorded great importance to the fact that "the bank was a large creditor, and as such largely interested in the prosperity of the company, and most naturally should desire to keep an oversight over its doings." 234 F. at 46. Referring to various statements attributed to bank personnel indicating that the bank owned the company or was conducting the company's business in the bank's behalf, the Court stated:

> Comprehensively speaking, they are all easily and naturally referable to a legitimate and customary practice of keeping an oversight by a creditor over the business, management, and operations of a debtor of doubtful solvency. All the facts of this case and all the reasonable inferences deducible from them would not, in our opinion, have warranted a jury in finding . . . that the [bank] was carrying on the business of the [company] as a part of its own. . .

* * *

In summary, then the control required for liability under the "instrumentality" rule amounts to total domination of the subservient corporation, to the extent that the subservient corporation manifests no separate corporate interests of its own and functions solely to achieve the purposes of the dominant corporation. As Professor Fletcher states:

> The control necessary to invoke what is sometimes called the "instrumentality rule" is not mere majority or complete stock control but such domination of finances, policies and practices that the controlled corporation has, so to speak, no separate mind, will or existence of its own and is but a business conduit for its principal.

1 W. Fletcher, supra, § 43 at 204–205. No lesser standard is applied in "instrumentality" cases involving a creditor-debtor relationship. As the Court said in In re Kentucky Wagon Mfg. Co., 3 F. Supp. 958, 963 (W.D. Ky. 1932), aff'd, 71 F.2d 802 (6th Cir.), cert. denied, Laurent v. Stites, 293 U.S. 612, 55 S. Ct. 142, 79 L. Ed. 701 (1934), "it is to be noted that it is not 'controlling influence' that is essential. It is actual control of the action of the subordinate corporation."

In addition to actual and total control of the subservient corporation, the "instrumentality" rule also requires that fraud or injustice proximately result from a misuse of this control by the dominant corporation. Berger v. Columbia Broadcasting System, Inc., supra; see National Bond Finance Co. v. General Motors Corp., supra. Alabama emphatically rejects actual fraud as a necessary predicate for disregarding the corporate form, holding instead that courts may decline to recognize corporate existence whenever recognition of the corporate form would extend the principle of incorporation "beyond its legitimate purposes and [would] produce injustices or inequitable consequences."

This is the better rule, for the theory of liability under the "instrumentality" doctrine does not rest upon intent to defraud. It is an equitable doctrine that places the burden of the loss upon the party who should be responsible. The basic theory of the "instrumentality" doctrine is that the debts of the subservient corporation are in reality the obligations of the dominant corporation.

II. The Factual Background

* * *

Brad's Machine Products, Inc., was a California corporation that began its existence as a machine shop in Stanton, California. Employing approximately 25 persons, Brad's was owned by John C. Bradford and his wife Nola. In addition to the machine business, Bradford's investments included a championship quarter horse, racing boats, airplanes, an Arizona bar, an Alabama motel, Florida orange groves, and oil wells. In addition, Bradford, a country and western singer, formed a motion picture company, Brad's Productions, Inc., through which he produced a film that featured him as a singer. All of these investment activities were funded by his income from the machine shop.

The record shows that Bradford was an able and inventive machinist and that the California operation had been profitable. In 1966, Bradford saw potential profit in the munitions industry, so he employed Arnold Seitman to guide his entry into the Government contracting system. Seitman had previously supervised government contracting for a company in Gadsden, Alabama, and he soon obtained for Brad's a 2.7 million dollar contract for the production of M-125 fuses, the principal component of which was brass.

* * *

For a brief time, Brad's appeared to prosper. Bradford's wide-ranging investments, however, soon became a severe financial drain on the Brad's operation. One subsidiary, a Gadsden box plant that made wooden boxes for shells, alone lost over one million dollars. By the end of 1968, Brad's was headed for financial distress.

The M-125 booster fuse assembly was the major product manufactured by Brad's, accounted for ninety percent of its gross sales, and required substantial quantities of brass rods. In the beginning Brad's had purchased its brass requirements from three sources: Revere Brass Company, Mueller Brass Company, and Bridgeport Brass Company. Brad's principal source of supply was Bridgeport, and Brad's was one of Bridgeport's larger customers. Bridgeport is a division of the defendant, National Distillers and Chemical Corporation.

In early 1969, Bridgeport was shipping approximately $400,000–$500,000 worth of brass rod to Brad's every month. In March, 1969, Brad's owed Bridgeport approximately $1,000,000 and Bridgeport, at the request of Brad's, agreed to convert this arrearage to a promissory note. On March 28, 1969, Bridgeport accepted Brad's note, secured by (1) the personal guaranties of John C. Bradford, Chairman of the Board and sole stockholder of Brad's, and his wife and (2) a mortgage on real property owned by J-N Industries, Inc., a subsidiary of Brad's located in Tucson, Arizona. The note was payable at the rate of $40,000 per month, plus interest on the unpaid balance, and it contained a "balloon agreement" under which the final payment in March of 1970 would equal the unpaid balance. * * *

In connection with the agreement for deferred payment, Brad's and Bridgeport entered into a "financing and loan agreement." Under this agreement, Bridgeport agreed to continue to supply Brad's with brass rod, so long as Brad's paid for current brass shipments within fifteen or sixteen days (with a ten day grace period). Despite this condition, by the end of July, 1969, Bridgeport permitted Brad's to build up an additional $630,000 in brass rod accounts payable.

On August 1, 1969, Bradford, Brad's President E. J. Huntsman, and Brad's Comptroller Roy Compton, went to New York to confer with representatives of National Distillers, including Assistant General Counsel and Secretary John F. Salisbury. The representatives of Brad's stated that its current financial situation precluded continued operation unless it received additional assistance, including working capital. They blamed the unsuccessful attempts to diversify Brad's as the reason for the company's financial straits. Moreover, they needed immediate assistance because the Government had threatened to cancel the current fuse contract if the financial condition of Brad's continued to worsen. Bradford offered to put up all the assets he and the company had in exchange for the additional funds and for National Distillers' intervention with the Government on behalf of Brad's.

At the close of the August 1, 1969, meeting, National Distillers and Brad's reached an oral agreement in line with Bradford's requests. National Distillers was to (1) provide internal financial management assistance to help Brad's eliminate costly waste, (2) lend Brad's another $600,000 in cash, (3) defer payment on the $630,000 accounts receivable, (4) help Brad's and Bradford liquidate unprofitable holdings to provide more capital for Brad's, and (5) intervene with the Government to prevent cancellation of the current fuse body contract. Brad's and Bradford personally were to assign to National Distillers as collateral the various interests accumulated during the attempted diversification.

Salisbury immediately telephoned a Government official in Birmingham, Alabama, whose job included monitoring for the Defense Contract Administration Service the financial ability of Brad's to perform its Government contracts, and assured him of National Distillers' intent to aid Brad's. * * * To help the financial management at Brad's, Leon Rudd, one of National Distillers' "Internal Auditors" was sent to Gadsden to oversee its finances and to establish control procedures for managing cash and investments. Finally, Salisbury assigned one of his assistants to help him and Brad's dispose of the assets assigned to National Distillers and other assets not so assigned. Under the terms of several agreements, both formal and informal, National Distillers agreed that any income or proceeds from these unassigned assets would be used for certain designated purposes in aid of Brad's other creditors and then either would revert to Brad's or to Bradford or would belong to National Distillers outright.

Rudd remained with Brad's for fifteen months, during which National Distillers loaned Brad's an additional $169,000 in cash and deferred another $667,131.28 in accounts payable by Brad's to Bridgeport. Despite these transfusions, Brad's ceased its operations in December, 1970. These suits resulted from debts left unpaid by Brad's.

III. The Decision

After a comprehensive review of the testimony and exhibits presented by the plaintiffs in the District Court, and viewing the evidence in the light most favorable to the plaintiffs, we conclude that the evidence was not "of such quality and weight that reasonable and fair-minded men in the exercise of impartial judgment might reach different conclusions," on the issue of control. Keeping in mind that the kind of control prerequisite to liability under the "instrumentality" rule is actual, operative, total control of the subservient corporation, the evidence here was wholly insufficient to support a jury decision that Brad's had "no separate mind, will or existence of its own and [was] but a business conduit" for National Distillers. The evidence is overwhelming that Brad's maintained a separate, independent corporate existence at all times. Hence, the motion for a directed verdict in favor of defendants was properly granted.

In cases involving the "instrumentality" rule, we must take a broad approach to the question of control, examining all of the plaintiffs' evidence to ascertain if the allegedly subservient corporation in fact had no separate corporate purposes or existence. In the case before us, plaintiffs presented evidence of (1) National Distillers' ownership of majority control of Brad's, (2) National Distillers' view of its relationship to Brad's, (3) the scope of National Distillers' control over Brad's, and (4) the alleged exploitation of Brad's supposedly wrought through abuses of that control.

* * *

2. According to plaintiffs, the evidence shows that National Distillers believed that it had the power to control Bradford and his corporation and acted accordingly. A careful examination of this evidence, however, makes clear that National Distillers considered control of Brad's to be, at most, only partly shared between National Distillers and Brad's.

First, a letter from National Distillers' Salisbury to the general manager of the movie company, Brad's Productions, Inc., stated: "As I am sure you are aware, National Distillers and Chemical Corporation has taken an active role in the management and control of Brad's Machine Products, Inc., and various other undertakings of John C. Bradford." This letter, however, is not inconsistent with National Distillers' argument, which we conclude is correct, that the evidence shows that Brad's voluntarily shared control with National Distillers. The letter does not say that National Distillers had taken control of Brad's; rather, it states only that National Distillers had "taken an active role in the management and control of Brad's."

* * *

Third, plaintiffs quote Seitman's testimony that states that Salisbury at one time threatened to "fire" both Seitman and Bradford and run the Brad's operation itself. A complete reading of Seitman's testimony indicates that he believed that National Distillers' so-called power or authority to "fire" lay in its "control of the purse strings." Seitman testified that National Distillers could not "have told Brad's who its officers were to be," and he then stated that he understood Salisbury to mean that National Distillers would cease extending credit to Brad's if certain contracts were not fulfilled. Thus, it is plain that National Distillers could have "fired" Brad's personnel only by cutting off credit or loans, thereby putting Brad's out of business. The record contains no evidence showing that National Distillers conceived that it could have directed or implemented the replacement and selection of management personnel, absent credit control.

3. As to the scope of National Distillers' alleged control, the evidence shows only that National Distillers' activities were narrowly restricted to safeguarding its interests as a major creditor of Brad's, that National Distillers participated in the corporate decision-making at Brad's only to a limited degree, and that at no time did National Distillers assume actual, participatory, total control of Brad's.

The thrust of plaintiffs' contention here is that Leon Rudd, who was sent to the Gadsden plant by National Distillers in August, 1969, and who remained until late November, 1970, actively dominated the Brad's decision-making apparatus during his stay.

A reading of the testimony, especially that of the Brad's comptroller Compton, compels a conclusion that Rudd's activities were much more circumscribed than appellants argue. Rudd, an internal auditor employed by National Distillers, was transferred to Brad's in response to John Bradford's request for assistance in establishing a system of internal controls. Rudd was not thrust upon Brad's unwanted or unneeded.

Because many of the financial problems at Brad's had been precipitated by improvident investments and uncontrolled spending, Rudd immediately moved to put himself in the position of monitoring Brad's cash outlays. According to Compton's testimony, Rudd suggested, and they all "readily agreed," that no purchase orders be sent out without his prior approval. Also, Rudd's signature was made mandatory on all checks from the Brad's accounts. From these "controls," plaintiffs would extrapolate the theory that National Distillers, through Rudd, was in charge of Brad's. Such a conclusion is untenable.

First, the evidence showed that, in fact, Rudd's prior approval of purchase requisitions was not always necessary for purchases. At the trial, several of plaintiffs' purchase orders, put in evidence for other purposes, were shown to have been made up and sent out without Rudd's approval.

Second, assuming that Rudd in fact enjoyed such an all-powerful veto over purchases, this power was never exercised where Brad's proper business purposes were involved. Rather, Rudd voiced his displeasure only when expenditures were contemplated that were unrelated to the Brad's machine shop operation.

Third, Rudd's powers were essentially negative in character. The testimony showed that his function was to monitor the finances and to help Compton fend off aggressive, unhappy creditors. Although plaintiffs contend that Rudd "participated in the management" of Brad's, the evidence shows that he did so only in a limited sense. Only those decisions having an immediate effect on Brad's financial position were subject to Rudd's primary attention. He attended management meetings solely in that capacity. The record contains no evidence that he was ever substantially involved in personnel or production decisions. Rudd left the delicate task of renegotiating Government contracts to Compton. (After a Government contract had been completed, Government officials often reviewed the profits of the contracting firm, seeking the return of "excess profits").

Fourth, Rudd's position as a required signatory on all checks drawn against the Brad's general account provides little support for plaintiffs' theory. Besides Rudd's signature, the checks also required one other signer from Brad's. Hence, Rudd again had but a veto power.

Plaintiffs argue that Rudd, using his power as a required signatory, expanded his powers into management (1) by negotiating and consummating settlements of disputed claims and (2) by designating the order in which creditors were to be paid. Once again, Compton's uncontradicted testimony illuminates the extent of Rudd's "control." Because Brad's had always been short of working capital, the practice had developed of writing checks to creditors as soon as a particular bill came due and then retaining the checks until there was money in the Brad's account to pay the checks. As could be expected, irate creditors often called upon Compton to pay up. When Rudd arrived, he and Compton worked together handling creditors. Compton testified that theirs was a cooperative effort but that, since Rudd was more skilled in dealing with creditors, he had the final decision as to which creditors were paid. The factors they considered included (1) the amount of money in the account, (2) the importance of the creditor to the continued operation of the plant, (3) the age of the bill, and (4) the urgency or fervor of a particular creditor's demand. In addition, Rudd often spoke with these creditors, attempting to forestall or to settle their demands.

Rudd's activities while at Brad's simply do not amount to active domination of the corporation. His job was to provide internal financial management assistance and all that he did was in keeping with this mission. Although he kept a fairly tight rein on disbursements, the evidence shows that his role was that of providing a centralized control over purchases and disbursements. His job was two-fold: (1) to eliminate costly duplication, e.g., multiple orders of the same supply, and (2) to eliminate all disbursements not directly and immediately related to the machine shop business. These controls were strong, and Rudd was not afraid to exercise his power, but we cannot conclude from the evidence before us that his activities could justify a jury verdict that found control. Rudd limited the scope of his position to overseeing the finances of Brad's. Neither he nor anyone else from National Distillers or from Bridgeport Brass had much, if any, influence, let alone control, over other key areas of managerial decision-making at Brad's.

In addition to Rudd's activities, plaintiffs argue that other National Distillers personnel exercised control over Brad's outside investments and production.

First, they contend that Salisbury and an assistant made the final decisions as to which assets of the "mini-conglomerate" to retain and which to liquidate. Compton testified that these efforts stemmed from Bradford's earlier request for management assistance from National Distillers and that all the proceeds were returned to Brad's to provide working capital. Although National Distillers' personnel apparently did make the final decision on the disposition of these assets, in many cases this power may be traced to the transaction in which they were assigned to National Distillers for precisely such a disposition.

Second, Compton also testified that a vice president of Bridgeport, Al Jones, visited Brad's on a weekly basis for five or six months, offering his advice and assistance wherever the production personnel at Brad's might need it. Nowhere in the record is it indicated that Jones ever exercised any control over the production process. To the contrary, his function was that of a consultant, checking data and offering his analysis. Compton specifically testified that neither Rudd nor Jones was concerned with production quantity.

These activities of both Rudd and the other are not sufficient to establish the degree of control requisite to "instrumentality" rule liability. The evidence shows that, at most, National Distillers shared managerial responsibility for some but not all aspects of the Brad's operation. That is not enough.

4. Finally, plaintiffs contend that control was shown indirectly by proving abuses of the Brad's corporation by National Distillers that could have been accomplished only with the requisite control.

First, plaintiffs complain that Rudd did not exercise his supposed veto enough. They point to Rudd-approved disbursements for a new house for Bradford, for a Mercedes automobile for the Bradford family, and for racing boats. Plaintiffs argue that these examples represent the abuse of power and control by National Distillers. In view of Rudd's limited functions at Brad's, the only fair inference that can be drawn from this configuration of "abuses of control" is that, in fact, Rudd had very little control over John Bradford.

* * *

After considering the plaintiffs' evidence in the most favorable light, it is plain that Brad's never became an "instrumentality" of National Distillers. Although National Distillers' position as a major creditor undoubtedly vested it with the capacity to exert great pressure and influence, we agree with the District Court that such a power is inherent in any creditor-debtor relationship and that the existence and exercise of such a power, alone, does not constitute control for the purposes of the "instrumentality" rule. Plaintiffs had to show the exercise of that control in the actual operation of the debtor corporation. Accordingly, because plaintiffs failed to produce substantial evidence of such actual operative total control, we affirm the directed verdict granted by the District Court.

Because we hold that plaintiffs failed to establish the requisite degree of control, we do not reach the question of whether the case should have been tried before a judge or before a jury.

Costs will be taxed to appellants.

AFFIRMED.

QUESTIONS

1. Why do you think Bridgeport Brass kept shipping brass to Brad's on open account?
2. While the court does not reach the question of whether dominating a corporation so it becomes a mere "instrumentality" proximately caused injury to plaintiffs, what kinds of injury can you imagine would persuade a court that dominance caused injury?
3. As part of the August 1, 1969 deal, Brad's pledged its plant and equipment to National Distillers, thus giving National a priority over general creditors. Why wouldn't a court focus on this as inequitable conduct that constituted an abuse of National's dominance of Brad's?
4. If you represented National Distillers in the August 1, 1969 negotiations, exactly what would your goals be in committing to "provide internal financial management assistance to help Brad's eliminate costly waste"? In order to avoid potential charges of domination of the debtor sufficient to make it a mere instrumentality, what would you like the agreement to provide in this area?

5. What does the court think that National's credit manager, Zimmerman, meant when he said that National "had the power, authority to fire Bradford and run him off"?
6. The court notes that Rudd's powers "were essentially negative in character." Why would this matter if he had a veto power over all purchase orders and all checks? Isn't this veto power the substantial equivalent of the power to make affirmative decisions?
7. Rudd, who had to approve all purchase orders and had the power to veto checks by refusing to co-sign, apparently allowed Brad's to purchase a home, a Mercedes and racing boat for Bradford. Why does the court reject the argument that this is an abuse of Brad's corporation in which National Distillers was complicit?

NOTE

Another important theory that is sometimes used to find lender liability involves the creation of an agency relationship. If a lender exerts significant control over a borrower, perhaps through detailed affirmative covenants, and if the borrower is deemed to act "on behalf of" the lender, then there is a chance that a court will find that the parties have formed an agency relationship. Accordingly, as principal, the lender may be responsible for tort or contract claims by third parties that are attributable to the borrower. A good example of this risk arises in A. Gay Jensen Farms Co. v. Cargill, Inc., 309 N.W. 2d 285 (Minn. 1981). In the case, Cargill extended credit to a grain broker named Warren, and the two firms developed a highly intertwined relationship over the years. Eventually Warren was unable to pay debts to both Cargill and a group of farmers who had sold grain to Warren on credit. The farmers were ultimately allowed to recover from Cargill for Warren's obligations under an agency theory. Standard lending relationships are unlikely to pose a serious risk of lender liability, but lenders who insist on very high levels of control over borrowers may open themselves up to some exposure if things go wrong.

C. LIABILITY OF AFFILIATED PARTIES UNDER THE "DEEPENING INSOLVENCY" DOCTRINE

Those who assist a debtor in obtaining borrowings beyond its ability to repay may at first think of themselves as simply prolonging the life of the debtor, and thus giving it a chance to recover from any disasters that have placed it in a precarious financial position. But a number of courts have recognized the tort of "deepening insolvency" to hold participants liable to a bankrupt debtor's estate for the damages thus caused by increased indebtedness. The following discussion involves claims brought against attorneys and investment bankers who arranged the public marketing of additional debt by an insolvent debtor. Other cases have involved accounting firms, and in some cases commercial banks who served as depositories for funds.

Official Committee of Unsecured Creditors v. R. F. Lafferty & Co.

267 F.3d 340 (3d Cir. 2001)

■ FUENTES, CIRCUIT JUDGE.

[This case involved charges of a Ponzi scheme*, in which the family controlling the debtor corporations caused them to issue huge amounts of debt securities, which were then taken at least in part as salaries and other compensation by some of the defendants. Walnut Equipment Leasing Company experienced financial difficulties, and created a Special Purpose Entity, Equipment Leasing Corporation of America ("ELCOA") to raise capital through debt sales to acquire equipment leases from Walnut. Fraud in the offer and sale of these securities was alleged, in the form of fraudulent financial statements by both companies. Among the alleged participants in the fraud were a law firm controlled by the majority shareholder of Walnut, William Shapiro, their accountant, Cogen Sklar, LLP, and their underwriters, R. F. Lafferty & Co. and Liss Financial Services, Inc. The Court of Appeals held that Pennsylvania courts would recognize a claim for "deepening insolvency." Part of the discussion involved whether this was a claim to be brought by the bankrupt estate or by the creditors.]

We agree with the District Court's evaluation. With the exception of a single federal securities law claim, the Committee brought only state common law claims on behalf of the Debtors. According to the Amended Complaint, the defendants (including Lafferty), through their alleged

---

* Eds. Carlo "Charles" Ponzi was an Italian immigrant who lived in Boston and was considering publishing a magazine. He had written about the publication to a person in Spain, who replied and included an international postal reply coupon, which Ponzi could take to his local post office to exchange for stamps to be used to mail the magazine to Spain. Ponzi discovered that the coupon had cost the equivalent of one cent, but was exchangeable in the U.S. for six one-cent stamps. Eureka! Ponzi thought he had found the ultimate arbitrage opportunity. In order to finance this activity, he sought funds from local investors, promising a 50% return on borrowed funds within 90 days. Not unreasonable, since he could earn a 600% return with every dollar invested in postal reply coupons overseas. But the transaction costs of arbitrage were higher than he anticipated—there were long delays in transferring currency abroad, and unexpected red tape in dealing with various postal organizations. But Ponzi bragged about his scheme, and investors lined up at the door to invest with him. While he promised to repay funds with 50% interest in 90 days, in fact he repaid it in 45 days. Unfortunately, he did this with funds received from later investors. Word of these returns spread, and he was soon taking in a million dollars a week. His newly hired staff was kept so busy they were storing investors' cash in closets, desk drawers and wastebaskets. Within six months, Ponzi was living the life of a millionaire. While authorities were suspicious, no investor filed a complaint, because all had been repaid. A newspaper story questioning the legitimacy of his business led Ponzi to offer to have his books audited. Within hours of the story a run on his business occurred, but he was able to repay all of the investors who appeared, which restored confidence in the business. This continued until the auditors declared that his business was bankrupt, and it collapsed. Over 40,000 people had invested with him. He was prosecuted for fraud and sentenced to five years in federal prison, of which he served three and one-half, and was then sentenced to an additional seven to nine years in Massachusetts. While out on bond pending an appeal, Ponzi finally did what most good swindlers do much earlier—he ran and disappeared, turning up under another name in Florida to conduct a land swindle. After another conviction, he was transferred to Massachusetts to serve his sentence. Upon deportation to Italy in 1934, he still had many fans who gave him an enthusiastic send-off.

fraud and participation in the scheme, injured the Debtors by "wrongfully expand[ing] the [D]ebtors' debt out of all proportion of their ability to repay and ultimately forc[ing] the [D]ebtors to seek bankruptcy protection." In other words, the Committee alleges an injury to the Debtors' corporate property from the fraudulent expansion of corporate debt and prolongation of corporate life. This type of injury has been referred to as "deepening insolvency." As far as the state law claims are concerned, it is clear that, to the extent Pennsylvania law recognizes a cause of action for the Debtors against Lafferty, the Committee can demonstrate the injury required for standing to sue in federal court. Given Lafferty's arguments, the standing analysis then consists of three inquiries: (1) whether the Committee is merely asserting claims belonging to the creditors, (2) whether "deepening insolvency" is a valid theory giving rise to a cognizable injury under Pennsylvania state law, and (3) whether, as Lafferty contends, the injury is merely illusory.

* * *

B. Whether "deepening insolvency" is a valid theory that gives rise to a cognizable injury under state law

Having established that the Committee brought claims on behalf of the Debtors, rather than the creditors, we must now determine whether the alleged theory of injury—"deepening insolvency"—is cognizable under Pennsylvania law. Neither the Pennsylvania Supreme Court nor any intermediate Pennsylvania court has directly addressed this issue. In the absence of an opinion from the state's highest tribunal, we must don the soothsayer's garb and predict how that court would rule if it were presented with the question. Indeed, because no state or federal courts have interpreted Pennsylvania law on this subject, we will rely predominantly on decisions interpreting the law of other jurisdictions and on the policy underlying Pennsylvania tort law to make this prediction.

Drawing guidance from these authorities, we conclude that, if faced with the issue, the Pennsylvania Supreme Court would determine that "deepening insolvency" may give rise to a cognizable injury. First and foremost, the theory is essentially sound. Under federal bankruptcy law, insolvency is a financial condition in which a corporation's debts exceed the fair market value of its assets. Even when a corporation is insolvent, its corporate property may have value. The fraudulent and concealed incurrence of debt can damage that value in several ways. For example, to the extent that bankruptcy is not already a certainty, the incurrence of debt can force an insolvent corporation into bankruptcy, thus inflicting legal and administrative costs on the corporation. See Richard A. Brealey & Stewart C. Myers, Principles of Corporate Finance 487 (5th ed. 1996) ("[B]y issuing risky debt, [a corporation] give[s] lawyers and the court system a claim on the firm if it defaults."). When brought on by unwieldy debt, bankruptcy also creates operational limitations which hurt a corporation's ability to run its business in a profitable manner. Aside from causing actual bankruptcy, deepening insolvency can undermine a corporation's relationships with its customers, suppliers, and employees. The very threat of bankruptcy, brought about through fraudulent debt, can shake the confidence of parties dealing with the corporation, calling into question its ability to perform, thereby damaging the corporation's assets, the value of which often depends on the performance of other parties. In addition, prolonging an insolvent corporation's life through bad debt may simply cause the dissipation of corporate assets.

These harms can be averted, and the value within an insolvent corporation salvaged, if the corporation is dissolved in a timely manner, rather than kept afloat with spurious debt. As the Seventh Circuit explained in Schacht v. Brown:

> [C]ases [that oppose "deepening insolvency"] rest[ ] upon a seriously flawed assumption, i.e., that the fraudulent prolongation of a corporation's life beyond insolvency is automatically to be considered a benefit to the corporation's interests. This premise collides with common sense, for the corporate body is ineluctably damaged by the deepening of its insolvency, through increased exposure to creditor liability. Indeed, in most cases, it would be crucial that the insolvency of the corporation be disclosed, so that shareholders may exercise their right to dissolve the corporation in order to cut their losses. Thus, acceptance of a rule which would bar a corporation from recovering damages due to the hiding of information concerning its insolvency would create perverse incentives for wrong-doing officers and directors to conceal the true financial condition of the corporation from the corporate body as long as possible.

711 F.2d 1343, 1350 (7th Cir.1983) (citations omitted) (emphasis added).

Growing acceptance of the deepening insolvency theory confirms its soundness. In recent years, a number of federal courts have held that "deepening insolvency" may give rise to a cognizable injury to corporate debtors. See, e.g., id. (applying Illinois law and holding that, where a debtor corporation was fraudulently continued in business past the point of insolvency, the liquidator had standing to maintain a civil action under racketeering law); Hannover Corp. of America v. Beckner, 211 B. R. 849, 854–55 (M. D. La.1997) (applying Louisiana law and stating that "a corporation can suffer injury from fraudulently extended life, dissipation of assets, or increased insolvency"); Allard v. Arthur Andersen & Co., 924 F. Supp. 488, 494 (S.D.N.Y.1996) (applying New York law and stating that, as to suit brought by bankruptcy trustee, "[b]ecause courts have permitted recovery under the 'deepening insolvency' theory, [defendant] is not entitled to summary judgment as to whatever portion of the claim for relief represents damages flowing from indebtedness to trade creditors"); In re Gouiran Holdings, Inc., 165 B. R. 104, 107 (E.D.N.Y.1994) (applying New York law, and refusing to dismiss claims brought by a creditors' committee because it was possible that, "under some set of facts two years of negligently prepared financial statements could have been a substantial cause of [the debtor] incurring unmanageable debt and filing for bankruptcy protection"); Feltman v. Prudential Bache Securities, 122 B. R. 466, 473 (S. D. Fla.1990) (stating that an " 'artificial and fraudulently prolonged life . . . and . . . consequent dissipation of assets' constitutes a recognized injury for which a corporation can sue under certain conditions", but concluding that there was no injury on the facts). Some state courts have also recognized the deepening insolvency theory. See, e.g., Herbert H. Post & Co. v. Sidney Bitterman, Inc., 219 A.D.2d 214, 639 N.Y.S.2d 329 (N. Y. App. Div. 1st Dep't 1996) (applying New York law and allowing a malpractice claim for failing to detect embezzlement that weakened a company, which already was operating at a loss, thereby causing default on loans and forcing liquidation); Corcoran v. Frank B. Hall & Co., 149 A.D.2d 165, 175, 545 N.Y.S.2d 278 (N. Y. App. Div. 1st Dep't 1989) (applying New York law and allowing claims for causing a company to "assume additional risks and thereby increase the extent of its exposure to creditors").

Significantly, one of the most venerable principles in Pennsylvania jurisprudence, and in most common law jurisdictions for that matter, is that, where there is an injury, the law provides a remedy. * * * Thus, where "deepening insolvency" causes damage to corporate property, we believe that the Pennsylvania Supreme Court would provide a remedy by recognizing a cause of action for that injury.

* * *

We pause here to consider the 19th century case of Patterson v. Franklin, 176 Pa. 612, 35 A. 205 (1896), an arguably applicable decision of the Pennsylvania Supreme Court. In Patterson, an assignee standing in the shoes of an insolvent corporation brought suit against the incorporators, claiming that they had allegedly made false representations in the statement of incorporation. Id. at 206. Apparently, the false representations had allowed the corporation to contract more debts. Id. On these allegations, the Pennsylvania Supreme Court affirmed the dismissal of the assignee's claims, reasoning that, because the assignee had alleged that the corporation had benefitted from the representations, there was no viable cause of action. Id. In our view, Patterson is not controlling here. The Patterson court never expressly considered the "deepening insolvency" theory, as the opinion does not indicate that the assignee presented any version of that argument to the court. In fact, it seems that the assignee in Patterson had not even alleged an injury to the corporation at all:

> The fraud was perpetrated for its benefit. It was a gainer, not a loser because of it. It was given a considerable credit by the statement to which, as it is alleged, it had no claim whatever.

Id. (emphasis added). Thus, given the allegations in the case, it was perfectly reasonable for the court in Patterson to affirm the dismissal.

See also Kinter v. Connolly, 233 Pa. 5, 81 A. 905, 905 (1911) (rejecting receiver's claim on behalf of the corporation against the directors for fraudulent statements that induced parties to do business with the corporation because "there [was] no averment that any act or omission of those of the defendants who demur caused loss or injury to the [corporation].").

Our reading of Patterson is informed in part by its age. In the hundred-plus years between that decision and the present, the business practices of corporations in the United States have changed quite dramatically. Likewise, society's understanding of corporate theory has grown. Therefore, we decline to draw any broad principle from Patterson, a decision which did not directly address "deepening insolvency."

In sum, we believe that the soundness of the theory, its growing acceptance among courts, and the remedial theme in Pennsylvania law would persuade the Pennsylvania Supreme Court to recognize "deepening insolvency" as giving rise to a cognizable injury in the proper circumstances.

QUESTIONS

1. What does the court mean by "fraudulent debt"?
2. What is wrong with prolonging a corporation's life? How could issuing more debt, which may "deepen" insolvency, prolong a corporation's life?
3. If you are a shareholder in a potentially or actually insolvent corporation that lacks funds to pay employee salaries, would you want to persuade them to take notes in lieu of salary? If so, why?
4. Is postponing a bankruptcy filing in the interests of the corporation? Do you have to decide who is the "corporation" before you can answer this question?

NOTE

The Third Circuit declined to expand its Lafferty holding in In re CitX Corporation, Inc. v. Detweiler, 448 F.3d 672 (3d Cir. 2006). In CitX the debtor was alleged to have falsified its financial statements to deceive its accounting firm and obtain "clean" financial statements that allowed it to raise new capital through fraudulent stock sales. The court affirmed the district court's dismissal of a negligent misrepresentation claim against the accounting firm on the basis that the claim of fraudulent stock sales did not allege harm to the creditors or CitX, stating that:

> [a]ssuming for the sake of argument that Detweiler's financial statements allowed CitX to raise over one million dollars, that did nothing to 'deepen' CitX's insolvency. Rather, it lessened CitX's insolvency. Before the equity infusion, CitX was $2,000,000 in the

> red (using round numbers for ease of discussion). With the added $1,000,000 investment, it was thereby insolvent only $1,000,000. This hardly deepened insolvency."

448 F.3d at 677. Note that the fraudulent stock offering increased CitX's contingent liabilities by $1,000,000, although this would not have been recorded on the books (and even then only in a footnote) until a claim was brought on behalf of the defrauded stockholders. Once this happened, CitX would have remained $2,000,000 in the red. How does this differ from Lafferty? The Fifth Circuit rejected the doctrine in SI Restructuring, Inc. v. Faulkner (In re SI Restructuring, Inc.), 532 F.3d 355 (5th Cir. 2008).

Other federal courts have extended Lafferty's reasoning to other states. See Smith v. Arthur Andersen LLP, 421 F.3d 989 (9th Cir. 2005). OHC Liquidation Trust v. Credit Suisse First Boston, 340 B. R. 510 (Bankr. D. Del. 2006) held, on a motion to dismiss, that the Supreme Courts of Delaware, New York and North Carolina would recognize a claim of deepening insolvency. The opinion contains an extensive discussion of the origins and dubious development of the doctrine. Delaware rejected this suggestion later that same year, as we will now see.

Trenwick America Litigation Trust v. Ernst & Young, L.L.P.

906 A.2d 168 (Del. Ch. 2006)
aff'd sub nom. Trenwick America Litig. Trust v. Billett, 2007 DEL. LEXIS 357

■ STRINE, VICE CHANCELLOR.

[On motion to dismiss the complaint.]

This case is unusual. The primary defendants in this case were directors of a publicly listed insurance holding company. All but one of the eleven directors was an independent director. The other director was the chief executive officer of the holding company.

In 1998, the holding company embarked on a strategy of growth by acquisition. Within a span of two years, the holding company acquired three other unaffiliated insurance companies in arms-length transactions. The two transactions at issue in this case involved the acquisition of publicly-traded entities and were approved by a vote of the holding company's stockholders. The holding company's stockholder base was diverse and the company had nothing close to a controlling stockholder.

In connection with the last acquisition, the holding company redomiciled to Bermuda, for the disclosed reason that tax advantages would flow from that move. Consistent with the objective of reducing its tax burden, the holding company reorganized its subsidiaries by national line, creating lines of United States, United Kingdom, and Bermudan subsidiaries. As a result of that reorganization, the holding company's top U.S. subsidiary came to be the intermediate parent of all of the holding company's U.S. operations. The top U.S. subsidiary also continued and deepened its role as a guarantor of the holding company's overall debt, including becoming a primary guarantor of $260 million of a $490 million line of credit, a secondary guarantor of the remainder of that debt, and assuming the holding company's responsibility for approximately $190 million worth of various debt securities. Nonetheless, after that reorganization, the financial statements of just the top U.S. subsidiary indicated that it had a positive asset value of over $200 million.

In 2003, the holding company had to place its insurance operations in run-off globally. The holding company and its top U.S. subsidiary filed for bankruptcy. The cause of the failure was that the claims made by the insureds against the holding company's operating subsidiaries (including the insureds of the companies it had acquired) exceeded estimates and outstripped the holding company's capacity to service the claims and its debt.

The reorganization plan for the top U.S. subsidiary resulted in the creation of a Litigation Trust. That Trust was assigned all the causes of action that the U.S. subsidiary owned.

The Litigation Trust then brought this case. The essential premise of its claims is that the majority independent board of the holding company engaged in an imprudent business strategy by acquiring other insurers who had underestimated their potential claims exposure. As a result of that imprudent strategy, the holding company and its top U.S. subsidiary were eventually rendered insolvent, to the detriment of their creditors. Not only that, because the top U.S. subsidiary took on obligations to support its parent's debt and actually assumed some of that debt, the top U.S. subsidiary and its creditors suffered even greater injury than the holding company and its creditors.

* * *

[The court examined and rejected claims that the board had breached duties to creditors because Trenwick America was insolvent at the time of the reorganization and the Trenwick directors enriched themselves through the reorganization.]

D. Delaware Law Does Not Recognize A Cause Of Action For So-Called "Deepening Insolvency"

In Count II of the complaint, the Litigation Trust seeks to state a claim against the former Trenwick America directors for "deepening insolvency." The Count consists of the following cursory allegations:

> From 2000 until 2003, these [Trenwick America] Defendants fraudulently concealed the true nature and extent of [Trenwick America's] financial problems by expanding the amount of debt undertaken by [Trenwick America].
>
> The [Trenwick America] Defendants knew that [Trenwick America] would not be able to repay this increased debt, but

> fraudulently represented to creditors and other outsiders that the debt would be repaid.
>
> By these actions, [Trenwick America's] officers and directors prolonged the corporate life of [Trenwick America] and increased its insolvency, until [Trenwick America] was forced to file for bankruptcy on August 20, 2003.
>
> As a result of [those] actions, [Trenwick America] suffered damages to be proven at trail [sic], which [the Litigation Trust] is entitled to recover.

The concept of deepening insolvency has been discussed at length in federal jurisprudence, perhaps because the term has the kind of stentorious academic ring that tends to dull the mind to the concept's ultimate emptiness.

Delaware law imposes no absolute obligation on the board of a company that is unable to pay its bills to cease operations and to liquidate. Even when the company is insolvent, the board may pursue, in good faith, strategies to maximize the value of the firm. As a thoughtful federal decision recognizes, Chapter 11 of the Bankruptcy Code expresses a societal recognition that an insolvent corporation's creditors (and society as a whole) may benefit if the corporation continues to conduct operations in the hope of turning things around.[103]

If the board of an insolvent corporation, acting with due diligence and good faith, pursues a business strategy that it believes will increase the corporation's value, but that also involves the incurrence of additional debt, it does not become a guarantor of that strategy's success. That the strategy results in continued insolvency and an even more insolvent entity does not in itself give rise to a cause of action. Rather, in such a scenario the directors are protected by the business judgment rule. To conclude otherwise would fundamentally transform Delaware law.

---

[103] *See, e.g., Kittay v. Atlantic Bank of N.Y. (In re Global Servs.)*, 316 B.R. 451, 460 (Bankr. S.D.N.Y. 2004) ("The fiduciaries of an insolvent business might well conclude that the company should continue to operate in order to maximize its "long-term wealth creating capacity," or more generally, its enterprise value. In fact, chapter 11 is based on the accepted notion that a business is worth more to everyone alive than dead."). *See also NLRB v. Bildisco & Bildisco*, 465 U.S. 513, 528, 104 S. Ct. 1188, 79 L. Ed. 2d 482 (1984) ("The fundamental purpose of reorganization is to prevent a debtor from going into liquidation, with an attendant loss of jobs and possible misuse of economic resources."); *In re RSL Com Primecall, Inc.*, 2003 Bankr. LEXIS 1635, 2003 WL 22989669, at * 8 (Bankr. S.D.N.Y. Dec. 11, 2003) ("It has never been the law in the United States that directors are not afforded significant discretion as to whether an insolvent company can 'work out' its problems or should file a bankruptcy petition."); *Steinberg v. Kendig (In re Ben Franklin Retail Stores, Inc.)*, 225 B.R. 646, 655 (Bankr. N.D. Ill. 1998) (noting there is no duty "to liquidate and pay creditors when the corporation is near insolvency, provided that in the directors' informed, good faith judgment there is an alternative"), *aff'd in part & rev'd in other part*, 2000 U.S. Dist. LEXIS 276, 2000 WL 28266 (N.D. Ill. 2000); H.R. REP. No. 95–595, at 220 (1977), *as reprinted in* 1978 U.S.C.C.A.N. 1978, 5963, 6179 ("The premise of a business reorganization is that assets that are used for production in the industry for which they are designed are more valuable than those same assets sold for scrap . . . It is more economically efficient to reorganize than to liquidate, because it preserves jobs and assets.").

The rejection of an independent cause of action for deepening insolvency does not absolve directors of insolvent corporations of responsibility. Rather, it remits plaintiffs to the contents of their traditional toolkit, which contains, among other things, causes of action for breach of fiduciary duty and for fraud. The contours of these causes of action have been carefully shaped by generations of experience, in order to balance the societal interests in protecting investors and creditors against exploitation by directors and in providing directors with sufficient insulation so that they can seek to create wealth through the good faith pursuit of business strategies that involve a risk of failure. If a plaintiff cannot state a claim that the directors of an insolvent corporation acted disloyally or without due care in implementing a business strategy, it may not cure that deficiency simply by alleging that the corporation became more insolvent as a result of the failed strategy.

Moreover, the fact of insolvency does not render the concept of "deepening insolvency" a more logical one than the concept of "shallowing profitability." That is, the mere fact that a business in the red gets redder when a business decision goes wrong and a business in the black gets paler does not explain why the law should recognize an independent cause of action based on the decline in enterprise value in the crimson setting and not in the darker one. If in either setting the directors remain responsible to exercise their business judgment considering the company's business context, then the appropriate tool to examine the conduct of the directors is the traditional fiduciary duty ruler. No doubt the fact of insolvency might weigh heavily in a court's analysis of, for example, whether the board acted with fidelity and care in deciding to undertake more debt to continue the company's operations, but that is the proper role of insolvency, to act as an important contextual fact in the fiduciary duty metric. In that context, our law already requires the directors of an insolvent corporation to consider, as fiduciaries, the interests of the corporation's creditors who, by definition, are owed more than the corporation has the wallet to repay.[104]

---

[104] *See, e.g.*, Prod. Res. Group, 863 A.2d at 791 (Del. Ch. 2004) ("When a firm has reached the point of insolvency, it is settled that under Delaware law, the firm's directors are said to owe fiduciary duties to the company's creditors. This is an uncontroversial proposition and does not completely turn on its head the equitable obligations of the directors to the firm itself. The directors continue to have the task of attempting to maximize the economic value of the firm. That much of their job does not change. But the fact of insolvency does necessarily affect the constituency on whose behalf the directors are pursuing that end. By definition, the fact of insolvency places the creditors in the shoes normally occupied by the shareholders-that of residual risk-bearers. Where the assets of the company are insufficient to pay its debts, and the remaining equity is underwater, whatever remains of the company's assets will be used to pay creditors, usually either by seniority of debt or on a pro rata basis among debtors of equal priority.") (internal citations omitted); Angelo, Gordon & Co. v. Allied Riser Comm. Corp., 805 A.2d 221, 229 (Del. Ch. 2002) ("Even where the law recognizes that the duties of directors encompass the interests of creditors, there is room for application of the business judgment rule."); Geyer v. Ingersoll Publ'ns Co., 621 A.2d 784, 787 (Del. Ch. 1992) ("[W]hen the insolvency exception [arises], it creates fiduciary duties for directors for the benefit of creditors."); *see generally* Laura Lin, Shift of Fiduciary Duty Upon Corporate Insolvency: Proper Scope of Directors' Duty to Creditors, 46 VAND. L. REV. 1485 (1993).

In this case, the Litigation Trust has not stated a viable claim for breach of fiduciary duty. It may not escape that failure by seeking to have this court recognize a loose phrase as a cause of action under our law, when that recognition would be inconsistent with the principles shaping our state's corporate law. In so ruling, I reach a result consistent with a growing body of federal jurisprudence, which has recognized that those federal courts that became infatuated with the concept, did not look closely enough at the object of their ardor.[105] Among the earlier federal decisions embracing the notion—by way of a hopeful prediction of state law—that deepening insolvency should be recognized as a cause of action admittedly were three decisions from within the federal Circuit of which Delaware is a part.[106] None of those decisions explains the rationale for concluding that deepening insolvency should be recognized as a cause of action or how such recognition would be consistent with traditional concepts of fiduciary responsibility. In a more recent decision, the Third Circuit has taken a more skeptical view of the deepening insolvency concept,[107] a view consistent with the outcome reached in this decision. In fact, many of the decisions that seem to embrace the concept of deepening insolvency do not clarify whether the concept is a stand-alone

---

105 Good examples of this jurisprudence include: Bondi v. Bank of America Corp. (In re Parmalat), 383 F. Supp.2d 587 (S. D. N. Y. 2005) (explaining that "[i]f officers and directors can be shown to have breached their fiduciary duties by deepening a corporation's insolvency, and the resulting injury to the corporation is cognizable . . . that injury is compensable on a claim for breach of fiduciary duty" and declining to recognize a separate tort for deepening insolvency under North Carolina law); Alberts v. Tuft (In re Greater Southeast, Community Hosp. Corp.), 333 B. R. 506, 517 (Bankr. D.C. 2005) ("Recognizing that a condition is harmful and calling it a tort are two different things. The District of Columbia courts have not yet recognized a cause of action for deepening insolvency, and this court sees no reason why they should. . . There is no point in recognizing and adjudicating "new" causes of action when established ones cover the same ground. The Trust's duplicative claims will be dismissed."); In re Vartec Telecom, Inc., 335 B. R. 631, 641, 644 (Bankr. N. D. Tex. 2005) (describing recent cases and the trend to decline recognizing deepening insolvency as a separate tort because the injury caused is substantially duplicated by torts already in existence); In re Global Servs., 316 B. R. at 459 ("The distinction between "deepening insolvency" as a tort or damage theory may be one unnecessary to make. Prolonging an insolvent corporation's life, without more, will not result in liability under either approach. Instead, one seeking to recover for 'deepening insolvency' must show that the defendant prolonged the company's life in breach of a separate duty, or committed an actionable tort that contributed to the continued operation of a corporation and its increased debt.") (citations omitted); Sabin Willet, The Shallows of Deepening Insolvency, 60 Bus. LAW. 549 (2005) (providing detailed reasons not to recognize deepening insolvency as a cause of action). *See also* In re CitX Corp., Inc., 448 F.3d 672, 679 n.11 (3d Cir. 2006) (rejecting, as without basis in reason, a request to hold that a claim of negligence will sustain a cause of action for deepening insolvency under Pennsylvania law).

106 *See* Official Comm. of Unsec. Creditors v. R.F. Lafferty, 267 F.3d 340 (3d Cir. 2001) (recognizing deepening insolvency as a valid cause of action under Pennsylvania law where defendants used fraudulent financial statements to raise capital in the debtor's name, thereby deepening debtor's insolvency and causing bankruptcy); OHC Liquidation Trust v. Credit Suisse First Boston (In re Oakwood Homes Corp.), 340 B.R. 510, 2006 WL 864843, at *16–17 (Bankr. D. Del. Mar. 31, 2006) (holding that Delaware, New York, and North Carolina would recognize the cause of action); In re Exide Technologies, Inc., 299 B.R. 732 (Bankr. D. Del. 2003) ("based on the Third Circuit's decision in *Lafferty* and the Delaware courts' policy of providing a remedy for an injury, I conclude that Delaware Supreme Court would recognize a claim for deepening insolvency when there has been damage to corporate property").

107 *See* In re CitX Corp., 448 F.3d at 680 n.11.

cause of action or a measurement of damages (the extent of deepening) for other causes of action.[108]

7. ALTERNATIVE STRUCTURES FOR THE LENDING RELATIONSHIP

We finish this chapter by exploring some alternative approaches for structuring a lending relationship. This Section certainly does not exhaust all other possibilities; we only want to leave you with a sense that more advanced strategies and transactional structures continue to arise in this area.

A. LEASING

Leasing transactions are alternatives to buying assets. In the short-term setting, the reasons for leasing are obvious: the transaction costs of a short-term rental will be lower than the cost of buying the asset and reselling it later. (It's the same logic you use when renting a car for your vacation.) These leases are called "operating" leases or "true" leases, as opposed to the "finance" leases (formerly known as "capital" leases) discussed below. The lessor is better able to locate others interested in such assets than a buyer attempting to resell the asset would be in most cases. Further, if the lessor specializes in a certain type of equipment, its volume purchases can give it more bargaining power than individual buyers would have. In these situations, the lessor is typically responsible for maintenance of the equipment, so the operating lessee does not have to acquire the skills to maintain it. The operating lessee also does not need to tie up a large amount of capital; it simply makes the rental payments for the rental period. For example, many trucks are rented on a short-term basis by users who have seasonal needs. Or heavy construction equipment might be rented for the duration of a building project.

Large operating lessors will often keep a robust inventory of the equipment available. In some leases the term may be extended, and the lessee may also have a cancellation option. In effect, this type of lease gives the lessee some protection against rental increases during the lease term and can become an option to lease over the full term. Short-term rentals will usually command a price premium, in part because the lessor has to take into account expected periods when the equipment may not be leased. You see examples of this kind of equipment leasing on a regular basis; U-Haul and Ryder trucks, as well as auto rental and leasing companies are prime examples.

---

[108] *E.g., Lafferty*, 267 F.3d at 351, *clarified by, CitX*, 448 F.3d 672 at 677 (explaining that in *Lafferty* "we did describe deepening insolvency as a 'type of injury,' and a 'theory of injury' " but that "we never held it was a valid theory of damages for an independent cause of action.") (citations omitted).

The analysis of long-term leases is quite different. Here, buying rather than leasing is a real option. In this case, the most direct comparison is between a lease and borrowing the money to buy the asset. These leases are called "finance" leases. Typically, finance leases extend over much of the economic life of the asset. They are generally completed on a "net" basis, which means that the lessee bears all the costs of maintaining the asset. Not surprisingly, this turns a lease into a purely financial transaction from the lessor's perspective, and may introduce large financial services companies into the leasing business. In many cases, a lessee will select the desired equipment from the dealer or manufacturer and then negotiate lease terms with the leasing company—who then enters into the purchase contract for the equipment. Major airlines often obtain their airplanes through this type of arrangement.

Recall from Chapter 4 that the Modigliani-Miller Proposition I tells us that the value of an asset does not change depending on the means used to finance it. Why, then, might leasing rather than borrowing on a secured basis make sense? In some cases, taxes provide an explanation—especially if a lessor can make better use of a tax deduction than the lessee. For example, accelerated tax depreciation deductions may be of less value to a lessee than to a lessor. With a purchase, the buyer can only deduct the allowed depreciation each year plus interest on any borrowings to finance the purchase; with a lease, the lessee might be able to deduct the entire amount of the lease payment. In effect, this turns principal amortization into a current expense item. Second, the lease allows the lessee to finance the entire amount of the purchase rather than the smaller fraction it might be able to finance through secured lending.

In the past, a company might also have decided to lease, rather than borrow and purchase, in order to obtain preferable accounting treatment. In an operating lease the lessee is not thought of as the "owner" of the equipment and is not viewed as incurring a "debt" for the lease payments. As a result, the lease payments showed up in income statements, but lease obligations did not appear as liabilities of the company. Similarly, the leased equipment did not show up as an asset of the business. However, under more recent lease accounting standards, ASU 2016-02 (Topic 842), lessees are now required to recognize most leases on the balance sheet, increasing the transparency of lease obligations.

B. ASSET BACKED FINANCING

We saw previously that firms often seek to obtain loans that are secured by income-generating assets, such as accounts receivable. Imagine, for instance, that you run a successful legal practice and are hoping to obtain a loan to expand your office. If you have a large amount of accounts receivable, a lender might be willing to extend you credit using these receivables as collateral. However, if you fail to repay the loan, the lender would foreclose and your clients would thereafter pay off their outstanding legal bills by paying the lender.

Securitization rests on similar logic in that it allows a firm to convert income-generating assets into a source of financing. Rather than obtaining a loan, however, a firm holding income-generating assets will sell these assets to an entity established for the sole purpose of buying a portfolio of income-generating assets having specific characteristics (e.g., credit card receivables, student loans, mortgages, airline leases, etc.). For instance, in a securitization of home mortgages, a financial services firm will establish a special purchase vehicle (SPV) (which is often a business trust or other entity that is disregarded for tax purposes) that will sell investment securities that represent interests in the stream of principal and interest payments that will be made on the purchased mortgages. Having raised capital in this fashion, the SPV will then acquire mortgages from an originating bank.

Who typically buys a SPV's securities? In general, these securities are structured as bonds that pay principal and interest, so like any bond, they may appeal to investors seeking fixed income investments. Moreover, most SPVs can offer securities with different expected yields, further broadening the class of investors who might be interested in buying them. The SPV accomplishes this result by issuing multiple "tranches" of securities having different rights and priorities with regard to the SPV's income. For instance, an SPV might issue three classes of securities—Class A, Class B, and Class C—that have different priorities of payment. In such a setting, on any date that interest is owed on the SPV's securities, the SPV would first pay interest on the Class A securities before making any payment on the Class B or C securities. Likewise, to the extent income remains after paying the Class A interest, the SPV would pay interest on the Class B securities. Finally, to the extent income remains after that, the SPV would make payment on the Class C securities. As this simple example illustrates, the Class C securities would come with a higher risk of default while the Class A securities would come with a lower risk of default. As such, the SPV could offer yields that corresponded to these different levels of risk, appealing to a broad array of investor risk preferences. When the securities are sold in public markets, they are generally rated by one of the bond rating agencies and the top tranche will receive a very high investment grade rating. This rating further expands the market for the securities, since many regulated buyers such as insurance companies are required to hold "investment grade" securities and the more senior tranches of securization vehicles (because of tranching) will often have very high credit ratings.

Likewise, for a firm holding income-generating assets (an Originator), financing through securitization provides a number of benefits. Most obviously, it converts a quasi-liquid asset (receivables, etc.) into a slightly more liquid asset (cash). Since both are current assets, this is by itself not a major benefit for the Originator's balance sheet or its creditworthiness. But if the Originator had borrowed on a secured basis against these financial assets, it would have incurred debt, which would appear on the balance sheet, worsening its debt-equity ratio and raising its fixed charges. A sale to the SPV, however, keeps this debt off the Originator's balance sheet, which is a clear benefit. (All of this analysis changes, of course, if the sale is not a "true" sale, as discussed below.) Consider the following example, of a company that either borrows against or sells $100 million in accounts receivable:

Original Balance Sheet

Balance Sheet

LeverCo.

($millions)

Assets		Liabilities	
Cash	$100	Current Liabilities	$100
Receivables	$100	Long-Term Liabilities	$100
Plant & Equipment	$200	Total Liabilities	$200
		Shareholders' Equity	$200
Total Assets	$400	Total Liabilities + Equity	$400

Current Ratio: *2:1*

Debt-Equity Ratio: *1:1*

Now assume that Leverco borrows against its receivables on a secured basis, and is able to borrow 100% of their value:

Balance Sheet with Borrowing
LeverCo.
($millions)

Assets		Liabilities	
Cash	$200	Current Liabilities	$200
Receivables	$100	Long-Term Liabilities	$100
Plant & Equipment	$200	Total Liabilities	$300
		Shareholders' Equity	$200
Total Assets	$500	Total Liabilities + Equity	$500

Current Ratio: *3:2*

Debt-Equity Ratio: *3:2*

Now assume that LeverCo sells its receivables to an SPV:

Balance Sheet with Sale
LeverCo.
($millions)

Assets		Liabilities	
Cash	$200	Current Liabilities	$100
Receivables	0	Long-Term Liabilities	$100
Plant & Equipment	$200	Total Liabilities	$200
		Shareholders' Equity	$200
Total Assets	$400	Total Liabilities + Equity	$400

Current Ratio: *2:1*

Debt-Equity Ratio: *1:1*

There are several benefits from this difference between borrowing and selling. First, for companies with existing debt, borrowing may cause them to be in violation of debt covenants (note that borrowing increases LeverCo's debt-equity ratio, but selling receivables leaves ratios as they were before), while selling receivables for cash should not cause any difficulties. (Covenants may prohibit asset sales, of course.) Second, in terms of ratio analysis, prospective creditors down the road might be more willing to extend new credit to LeverCo if it sells receivables rather than borrows against them on a secured basis. Third, where lenders to the Originator must worry about the Originator's credit risk and engage in a thorough credit investigation, that task falls away when the financial assets are separated from the Originator. As firms become more highly leveraged and edge closer to a real risk of insolvency, there is reason to believe that the Originator may not be completely candid about its problems.* Now, when the receivables are sold to an SPV with no other assets or liabilities, investors only need to know the quality of the receivables. In some cases, especially where there are doubts about the quality of the assets being purchased, Originators may seek credit enhancement in the form of overcollateralization or a letter of credit from a bank.

As this discussion suggests, critical to the success of securitization is the ability to separate the SPV and its assets from the Originator and its creditors. Should the Originator find itself in bankruptcy reorganization, its creditors may make two types of arguments to reach the assets of the SPV. First, they may argue that the Originator's transfer of the financial assets was a fraudulent conveyance. In most cases, this is a relatively easy argument to defeat because the SPV will have paid the issuer all the proceeds from its own issue of securities, which is powerful evidence of the fair market value of the financial assets.

The second challenge to the transaction may come under the doctrine of substantive consolidation. Where there is unified operation of a parent and subsidiary corporations, courts may ignore the separate legal entities and treat all related corporations as part of a single debtor. Consolidated Rock Products Co. v. DuBois, 312 U.S. 510 (1941). One key to avoiding this problem is to make certain that the SPV is "bankruptcy remote" from the Originator. If the SPV is controlled by the Originator, it may be tempted to cause the SPV to enter Chapter 11 at the same time as the Originator, in order to bring more assets into the debtor's estate through consolidation. One solution is that the charter or other organizing document of the SPV provide against voluntary filings, by requiring approval of independent directors of the SPV. For an example of a director's causing an SPV to enter Chapter 11 along with the Originator, see the description of the Days Inn of America case in Steven L. Schwarcz, STRUCTURED FINANCE: A GUIDE TO THE PRINCIPLES OF ASSET SECURITIZATION, § 2:2.1 (3d ed. 2002).

The other key to avoiding consolidation is to assure that the financial assets are truly separated from the Originator, by a "true sale."† Part of the difficulty arises because the Originator may "over-collateralize" the SPV, by giving it more financial assets than may be needed to pay off the SPV's obligations in order to enhance the SPV's creditworthiness and reduce the interest rate that is paid by the SPV to its investors. Of course, if there are assets remaining after the SPV has repaid all its obligations,

* This is a "last period" problem for desperate managers. For a discussion of this problem in the context of securities fraud, see Jennifer Arlen and William J. Carney, *Vicarious Liability for Fraud on Securities Markets: Theory and Evidence,* 1992 U. ILL. L. REV. 691.

† The Originator also wants this transaction treated as a sale rather than a secured loan to improve its own balance sheet, as shown in the examples given above.

the Originator will want them returned. But this creates difficult questions of whether the transaction was a "true sale" or merely a secured loan by the Originator, so the assets remain part of the Originator's bankrupt estate. See, for example, In re Evergreen Valley Resort, Inc., 23 B.R. 659, 661–62 (Bankr. D. Me. 1982); In re Hurricane Elkhorn Coal Corp. 19 B.R. 609, 617 (Bank. W.D. Ky. 1982), rev'd on other grounds, 763 F.2d 188 (6th Cir. 1985). In this case, the SPV simply becomes a creditor of the bankrupt estate to share in the assets as a secured creditor. Because of the automatic stay of all collection proceedings, at the very least this imposes a delay on collection of the financial assets by the SPV. Likewise, it would not be surprising for the Originator to warrant to the SPV the quality of the financial assets, but if the Originator takes the next step to guarantee payment of the receivables, the Originator has retained the risks of an owner, and the transaction may be treated as a secured loan. See, for example, Major's Furniture Mart, Inc. v. Castle Credit Corp., 449 F.Supp. 538 (E.D. Pa. 1978), *aff'd* 602 F.2d 538 (3d Cir. 1979).

A full treatment of this subject can be found in Steven L. Schwarcz, *supra*, from which much of this discussion is drawn. Having listed other factors that influence whether a true sale has occurred, Schwarcz writes: "It is rare in modern commercial transactions for all the factors favoring a true bankruptcy sale to be met. There is inevitably a question of balance." *Id.* at 4:6.

Securitization of mortgages also played an important role in the Financial Crisis. In general, in the early years of this century, banks and mortgage origination firms issued large amounts of home mortgages to borrowers having considerable credit risk. These mortgages were generally regarded as "sub-prime" because the borrowers were unable to qualify for more conventional "prime" mortgages. As with conventional mortgages, these subprime mortgages were securitized by SPVs who issued securities in tranches, as described above. The rating agencies turned out to be terribly mistaken about the quality of many of these securities and rated them based on the agencies' past experience with other asset categories, apparently not recognizing that the subprime mortgages placed in these pools were generally of much lower quality than the other asset categories with which they were familiar. As subprime mortgage default and delinquency rates skyrocketed, the subprime mortgage market collapsed, further enhancing default rates as subprime borrowers lost the ability to refinance.

Appendix 6-A

Rating Classifications

The major ratings services provide more detailed information on their analytic methods on their web sites. We provide only the ratings categories here. These categories are for long-term corporate bonds. Separate ratings exist for short-term debt and government bonds.

Moody's Investor Services:

Moody's long-term ratings are opinions of the relative credit risk of financial obligations with an original maturity of one year or more. They address the possibility that a financial obligation will not be honored as promised. Such ratings use Moody's Global Scale and reflect both the likelihood of default and any financial loss suffered in the event of default.

Aaa Obligations rated Aaa are judged to be of the highest quality, subject to the lowest level of credit risk.

Aa Obligations rated Aa are judged to be of high quality and are subject to very low credit risk.

A Obligations rated A are considered upper-medium grade and are subject to low credit risk.

Baa Obligations rated Baa are judged to be medium-grade and subject to moderate credit risk and as such may possess certain speculative characteristics.

Ba Obligations rated Ba are judged to be speculative and are subject to substantial credit risk.

B Obligations rated B are considered speculative and are subject to high credit risk.

Caa Obligations rated Caa are judged to be speculative of poor standing and are subject to very high credit risk.

Ca Obligations rated Ca are highly speculative and are likely in, or very near, default, with some prospect of recovery of principal and interest.

C Obligations rated C are the lowest rated class and are typically in default, with little prospect for recovery of principal or interest.

Moody's will often append a further numerical modifier, from 1 to 3, to these primary ratings. A modifier of 1 indicates a higher rank in the overall rating category, a modifier of 2 indicates a mid-tier position, and a modifier of 3 indicates a lower rank. Thus debt rated Baa3 would be viewed as risker than debt rated Baa1.

Standard & Poors:

AAA An obligation rated 'AAA' has the highest rating assigned by Standard & Poor's. The obligor's capacity to meet its financial commitment on the obligation is extremely strong.

AA An obligation rated 'AA' differs from the highest-rated obligations only to a small degree. The obligor's capacity to meet its financial commitment on the obligation is very strong.

A An obligation rated 'A' is somewhat more susceptible to the adverse effects of changes in circumstances and economic conditions than obligations in higher-rated categories. However, the obligor's capacity to meet its financial commitment on the obligation is still strong.

BBB An obligation rated 'BBB' exhibits adequate protection parameters. However, adverse economic conditions or changing circumstances are more likely to lead to a weakened capacity of the obligor to meet its financial commitment on the obligation.

Obligations rated 'BB', 'B', 'CCC', 'CC', and 'C' are regarded as having significant speculative characteristics. 'BB' indicates the least degree of speculation and 'C' the highest. While such obligations will likely have some quality and protective characteristics, these may be outweighed by large uncertainties or major exposures to adverse conditions.

BB An obligation rated 'BB' is less vulnerable to nonpayment than other speculative issues. However, it faces major ongoing uncertainties or exposure to adverse business, financial, or economic conditions which could lead to the obligor's inadequate capacity to meet its financial commitment on the obligation.

B An obligation rated 'B' is more vulnerable to nonpayment than obligations rated 'BB', but the obligor currently has the capacity to meet its financial commitment on the obligation. Adverse business, financial, or economic conditions will likely impair the obligor's capacity or willingness to meet its financial commitment on the obligation.

CCC An obligation rated 'CCC' is currently vulnerable to nonpayment, and is dependent upon favorable business, financial, and economic conditions for the obligor to meet its financial commitment on the obligation. In the event of adverse business, financial, or economic conditions, the obligor is not likely to have the capacity to meet its financial commitment on the obligation.

CC An obligation rated 'CC' is currently highly vulnerable to nonpayment. The 'CC' rating is used when a default has not yet occurred, but Standard & Poor's expects default to be a virtual certainty, regardless of the anticipated time to default.

C An obligation rated 'C' is currently highly vulnerable to nonpayment, and the obligation is expected to have lower relative seniority or lower ultimate recovery compared to obligations that are rated higher.

D An obligation rated 'D' is in default or in breach of an imputed promise. For non-hybrid capital instruments, the 'D' rating category is used when payments on an obligation are not made on the date due, unless Standard & Poor's believes that such payments will be made within five business days in the absence of a stated grace period or within the earlier of the stated grace period or 30 calendar days. The 'D' rating also will be used upon the filing of a bankruptcy petition or the taking of similar action and where default on an obligation is a virtual certainty, for example due to automatic stay provisions. An obligation's rating is lowered to 'D' if it is subject to a distressed exchange offer.

NR This indicates that no rating has been requested, or that there is insufficient information on which to base a rating, or that Standard & Poor's does not rate a particular obligation as a matter of policy. *The ratings from 'AA' to 'CCC' may be modified by the addition of a plus (+) or minus (-) sign to show relative standing within the major rating categories.

Fitch Ratings

AAA: Highest credit quality.

'AAA' ratings denote the lowest expectation of credit risk. They are assigned only in cases of exceptionally strong capacity for payment of financial commitments. This capacity is highly unlikely to be adversely affected by foreseeable events.

AA: Very high credit quality.

'AA' ratings denote expectations of very low credit risk. They indicate very strong capacity for payment of financial commitments. This capacity is not significantly vulnerable to foreseeable events.

A: High credit quality.

'A' ratings denote expectations of low credit risk. The capacity for payment of financial commitments is considered strong. This capacity may, nevertheless, be more vulnerable to adverse business or economic conditions than is the case for higher ratings.

BBB: Good credit quality.

'BBB' ratings indicate that expectations of credit risk are currently low. The capacity for payment of financial commitments is considered adequate but adverse business or economic conditions are more likely to impair this capacity.

BB: Speculative.

'BB' ratings indicate an elevated vulnerability to credit risk, particularly in the event of adverse changes in business or economic conditions over time; however, business or financial alternatives may be available to allow financial commitments to be met.

B: Highly speculative.

'B' ratings indicate that material credit risk is present.

CCC: Substantial credit risk. 'CCC' ratings indicate that substantial credit risk is present.

CC: Very high levels of credit risk.

'CC' ratings indicate very high levels of credit risk.

C: Exceptionally high levels of credit risk.

'C' indicates exceptionally high levels of credit risk.

Defaulted obligations typically are not assigned 'RD' or 'D' ratings, but are instead rated in the 'B' to 'C' rating categories, depending upon their recovery prospects and other relevant characteristics. This approach better aligns obligations that have comparable overall expected loss but varying vulnerability to default and loss.

Both Standard and Poor's and Fitch may also add the modifiers "+" or "-" at the end of a rating to denote relative status within major rating categories. Thus debt rated BBB+ is viewed as less risky than debt rated BBB-.

Appendix 6-B

Revised Model Simplified Indenture

Table of Contents

CHAPTER 7

PREFERRED STOCK

1. INTRODUCTION

A. CREATING AND ISSUING PREFERRED STOCK

As you might expect, preferred stock is generally thought of as a class of stock having some preference over common stock. But what extra benefits do you actually get when you invest in preferred stock? The precise nature of these preferences can vary greatly from firm to firm. Customary preferences include the right to receive an earmarked dividend payment and the right to payment before common stock if the issuer liquidates. But not every share of preferred stock will include even these provisions, and the only way to understand what a given issue of preferred stock does is to examine its specific terms. We discuss below the specific features that are typical of preferred stock, but for now, it is important to understand that these preferences must be expressly set forth in a company's charter. The DGCL, quoted below in part, is typical of statutes authorizing preferred stock:

> § 151. Classes and series of stock; redemption; rights, etc.
>
> (a) Every corporation may issue 1 or more classes of stock or 1 or more series of stock within any class thereof, any or all of which classes may be of stock with par value or stock without par value and which classes or series may have such voting powers, full or limited, or no voting powers, and such designations, preferences and relative, participating, optional or other special rights, and qualifications, limitations or restrictions thereof, as shall be stated and expressed in the certificate of incorporation or of any amendment thereto, or in the resolution or resolutions providing for the issue of such stock adopted by the board of directors pursuant to authority expressly vested in it by the provisions of its certificate of incorporation.
>
> See also Model Act § 6.01(a).

As envisioned by these statutes, a company that wishes to issue preferred stock must first authorize shares of preferred stock in its charter (similar to common stock authorization, as discussed in Chapter 5), and this authorizing language must also specify any preferential terms. Set forth below, for instance, is an excerpt from the Certificate of Incorporation ("COI") of the ride-sharing company Lyft, Inc. just prior to its initial public offering ("IPO") of common stock in March 2019:

Article IV.

A. Classes of Stock. As of the date on which this Amended and Restated Certificate of Incorporation is accepted for filing by the Secretary of State of the State of Delaware (the "**Filing Date**"), the authorized capital stock of the Corporation shall be as follows:

This Corporation is authorized to issue two classes of stock to be designated, respectively, "**Common Stock**" and "**Preferred Stock**." This Corporation is authorized to issue 340,000,000 shares of Common Stock, par value of $0.00001 per share. This Corporation is authorized to issue 227,328,900 shares of Preferred Stock, par value of $0.00001 per share, 6,063,921 of which shall be designated "**Series Seed Preferred Stock**," 8,129,364 of which shall be designated "**Series A Preferred Stock**," 7,067,771 of which shall be designated "**Series B Preferred Stock**," 14,479,445 of which shall be designated "**Series C Preferred Stock**," 24,674,534 of which shall be designated "**Series D Preferred Stock**," 47,099,094 of which shall be designated "**Series E Preferred Stock**," 37,263,568 of which shall be designated "**Series F Preferred Stock**," 18,662,127 of which shall be designated "**Series G Preferred Stock**," 42,771,492 of which shall be designated "**Series H Preferred Stock**" and 21,117,584 of which shall be designated "**Series I Preferred Stock**."

Immediately prior to Lyft's IPO, the company had thus authorized two classes of stock: 340,000,000 shares of Common Stock and 227,328,900 shares of Preferred Stock. Further, it had sub-divided its Preferred Stock into 10 "series" of preferred stock, as permitted by § 151 of the DGCL (Lyft is a Delaware company). That seems like an awful lot of work. Why did it do this? As we shall see, a company might raise capital by conducting sequential preferred stock financings. In the case of Lyft, it raised capital through multiple "rounds" of preferred stock financing conducted between 2008 and 2018. In its first preferred stock financing, it sold Series Seed Preferred Stock at a price per share of approximately $0.23. In its most recent preferred stock financing in 2018, the company sold Series I Preferred Stock at a price per share of $47.3539. Not surprisingly, these different stock prices reflect the fact that the company had grown considerably over this ten-year period. To the extent investors at each round of financing demand different terms and pay different prices, a company can authorize and issue a separate series of preferred stock to reflect these different terms and prices. (Note that Lyft is an especially comprehensive example: most firms don't go through *that* many rounds of venture funding. Moreover, all of Lyft's preferred stock was converted into common stock at its IPO; we shall return later to why this occurs when a venture-backed start-up conducts an IPO.)

In authorizing its preferred stock, Lyft chose to "amend and restate" its COI at each financing, which allowed it to authorize a new series to reflect the terms of the particular financing. Because Lyft is a Delaware company, it had to comply with the requirements of Section 242 of the DGCL to amend its charter, meaning that it had to secure approvals from both the company's board of directors and its stockholders. However, this is not the only way a company can amend its charter to authorize the terms of preferred stock. One of the innovations of corporate law in the late 1960s was the development of so-called "blank check preferred," sometimes called simply "blank preferred." Both the DGCL and the Model Act were amended to permit companies to authorize preferred stock "in blank," leaving it to the board of directors to fill in the terms at some later date by a board resolution and the filing of a "certificate of designation" (under the DGCL) or "articles of amendment" (under the Model Act) to the articles of incorporation. See DGCL § 151 and Model Act § 6.02. In effect, blank check preferred is a way for a company's stockholders to empower the board of directors with the ability to conduct a preferred stock financing in the future without having to seek stockholder approval of the terms offered in the financing. As such, it can be a useful tool for publicly held firms where soliciting stockholders may pose a number of practical and financial challenges.

In addition to authorizing preferred stock, a company's charter (or a certificate of designation in the case of blank check preferred) must also expressly define the terms of the preferred stock. By default, all capital stock is created equal. In terms of voting rights, for instance, the default rule in both Delaware and Model Act jurisdictions is that each share has one vote, unless otherwise provided in the certificate or articles of incorporation. DGCL § 212(a); Model Act § 7.21(a). Likewise, with respect to distributions on a liquidation, failure to specify any special preference on preferred stock means that capital and surplus will be distributed ratably among common and preferred stockholders in proportion to the number of shares held by each. See Lloyd v. Pennsylvania Electric Vehicle Co., 72 A. 16 (New Jersey 1909). As we shall see, the fact that preferred stock has no default "preferences" means that a company's charter must define—and must *clearly* define—those circumstances when the preferred stock should be treated differently than common stock.

B. AN OVERVIEW OF REPRESENTATIVE TERMS

Corporate statutes provide no specific guidance as to the nature or form of the rights and obligations of preferred stock. But in practice, it is useful to think of preferred stock terms as relating to either "economic" preferences or "control" preferences. In the Appendix to this book, we include the full Amended and Restated Certificate of Incorporation of Lyft, Inc. immediately prior to its IPO, which provides a nice illustration of some of the more common economic and control preferences that are used by companies when issuing preferred stock (especially when the preferred stock is being issued to venture capital (VC) investors). Notice that the bulk of the document is contained in Article IV, which consists of Section A (the short section authorizing the preferred stock quoted previously) and Section B (a much longer section defining the "Rights, Preferences and Restrictions of Preferred Stock"). We summarize here the terms of the preferred stock set forth in Section B to provide a general overview of how these commonly used terms operate. After that, we will dive deeper into some of the legal and conceptual issues that can arise with preferred stock.

i. ECONOMIC PREFERENCES

a. Dividends

Subsection 1(a) of Article IV(B) states that if Lyft wants to pay a dividend on shares of Common Stock in a given year, it must first pay a specified dividend on each series of preferred stock. These dividend amounts per share are as follows:

Series	Annual Dividend
Seed	$0.01801333
A	$0.06101333
B	$0.1682
C	$0.339792
D	$0.810552
E	$1.5556
F	$2.143112
G	$2.572
H	$3.179688
I	$3.788312

How did the company determine these amounts? The short answer is that these amounts are exactly 8% of the price that was paid for each share of each series. This reflects the convention of defining a preferential dividend as a rate of return on the investor's original investment. For instance, if the company paid a common stock dividend every year, this provision would ensure that each preferred stock investor received at least an 8% annual return on their investment. Moreover, we shall see that Lyft's preferred stock is convertible into shares of common stock, and Subsection 1(b) of Article IV(B) states that all preferred stockholders are also entitled to any dividends that the stockholders would have received had they converted their preferred stock into shares of common stock.

But what if Lyft chooses not to pay a common stock dividend (as was the case between Lyft's incorporation and its IPO)? Based on the language of subsection 1 of Article IV(B), Lyft's preferred stockholders would have no basis for complaining; the obligation to pay an 8% dividend arises only if the company's board chooses to declare a dividend on common stock. This type of preferential dividend is generally referred to as a "straight" preferential dividend and obviously leaves an investor vulnerable to the board's decision of whether to pay (or not pay) any common stock dividends. Indeed, a preferred stockholder might worry about a board strategy to save up large piles of cash, pay out the 8% preferred dividend just one time, and then distribute the rest of the firm's money to common shareholders that same year. Of course, in the case of Lyft's preferred stockholders, this risk is eliminated by the fact that Lyft's preferred stockholders are entitled to any dividends that they would have received had they converted their preferred stock into shares of common stock. But if the preferred stock lacks this provision, the risk is very real.

An alternative form of preferential dividend avoids some of this vulnerability. "Cumulative" dividends provide that regardless of whether a company declares a dividend, preferred dividends will accumulate at a specified rate, to be paid out at a future date before the common may receive anything. For example, if Lyft's Series Seed Preferred Stock had 8% cumulative dividends, the company would incur a growing dividend obligation for each year it failed to pay the 8% dividend on the Series Seed Preferred Stock. Between the issue date of the stock in August 2008 through August 2018, this accumulated dividend would have grown to \$0.180133 (10 × \$0.0180133). Exactly when would the company have to pay out this dividend? Typically, corporate charters provide that it must be paid out (1) before any common stock dividends can be declared; (2) when the preferred stock is redeemed (if redeemable); or (3) when the company is liquidated or sold.

b. Liquidation Preference

Subsection 2(a) of Article IV(B) of Lyft's charter states that if Lyft engages in a "Liquidation Event", the holders of the preferred stock must receive a specified amount per share before any payments can be made to the holders of common stock. These amounts are:

Series	Liquidation Preference
Seed	$0.225166667
A	$0.762666667
B	$2.1025
C	$4.2474
D	$10.1319
E	$19.4456
F	$26.7889
G	$32.1500
H	$39.7461
I	$47.3539

For each series, the charter refers to these amounts as the series "original issue price", indicating that these dollar figures are the original purchase prices paid for each series of preferred stock. Following these preferential payments, all of the remaining assets and proceeds are then to be distributed to the holders of Lyft's common stock. Note as well that Subsection 2(d) of Article IV(B) defines a "Liquidation Event" to include the acquisition of Lyft. Thus, the intention of this section is to ensure that all proceeds from the liquidation of the company (including its acquisition) go to the preferred stockholders until they receive their original investment amount. After that, any remaining proceeds go to the holders of common stock.

To the extent a preferred stock investor is concerned about losing his or her investment, there is clearly a certain logic in obtaining a liquidation preference. By requiring the company to return preferred stockholders' investment capital before the holders of common stock see a penny, the provision allocates more investment risk to common stockholders than to preferred stockholders. It is also a way for preferred investors to protect against a board decision to liquidate the firm, right after the preferred investment is made, and distribute some of their investment capital to common stockholders. By ensuring that they will get repaid first, preferred stockholders avoid any risk of this trick.

At the same time, however, for preferred stock investors looking for a healthy return on investment, this arrangement seems nonsensical. Consider the Series Seed Preferred Stock. Investors in this security were Lyft's earliest investors, investing approximately $1.4 million in what was then a fledging new firm. Were Lyft to be acquired at a $20 billion valuation (just under its valuation at its IPO), these investors would receive only $1.4 million on their shares of Series Seed Preferred Stock. And they don't even have cumulative dividends to grow this payout by 8% per year. Why would any investor agree to this bargain?

The primary answer relates to another term of Lyft's preferred stock to be discussed below—namely, holders of preferred stock have the right to convert their preferred shares into shares of common stock. Thus, in our hypothetical acquisition of Lyft at $20 billion (or, as was actually the case, in its IPO), preferred stockholders would convert their preferred shares into shares of common stock, thereby participating in the large gains on the residual claim.

Even for non-convertible preferred stock, however, a liquidation preference can make sense with some types of preferred stock dividend provisions. For example, consider a company that issues non-convertible preferred stock at $10/share with (a) a $10 liquidation preference (which is payable on a liquidation or a sale of the firm) and (b) an 8% cumulative preferential dividend. If you bought this preferred stock, you can expect 8% per year in dividends, with your original investment to be returned on a liquidation event. Of course, the company could choose not to pay dividends in any given year, but the dividends would nevertheless accumulate and be payable on a liquidation. This seems close to a debt investment with flexible interest payments: just as a lender seeks a return on investment through the payment of interest (and the eventual repayment of principal), a preferred stock investor might seek a return on investment through the receipt of preferential dividends (and the eventual return on invested capital through a liquidation preference). To be sure, these payments are riskier than with a loan. But the enhanced risk also means that preferred stock investors should be able to demand dividend rates that are much higher than the company's cost of debt.

Sidebar: Other Types of Liquidation Preferences

The liquidation preference of Lyft's preferred stock represents a common form of liquidation preference, especially in the context of venture capital finance. In practice, this type of preference is often referred to as a "1× preference" that is payable "pari pasu." That is, each investor is entitled to receive its original investment amount (i.e., 1 × its original investment), and payment is made "pari pasu" across all series. This latter provision means that, in the event the company is liquidated for less than the aggregate amount of the preferred stock liquidation preferences, each share of preferred stock would receive a pro-rata portion of the available proceeds according to the amount otherwise due on such share (e.g., each series would receive the same percentage payment on its stated liquidation preference).

However, a variety of other types of liquidation preferences are occasionally used. Indeed, because preferred stock preferences must be drafted in a company's charter, the enabling feature of corporate law can give rise to any number of permutations of the basic liquidation preference described previously. Three permutations used from time to time involve: (a) requiring payment of a liquidation preference to be senior to the preference owing on any previously issued shares of preferred stock, (b) adjusting the amount of the fixed payout on each preferred share, and/or (c) allowing the investor to participate in any common stock distributions even after taking the fixed liquidation preference. For instance, when investing in a distressed company, a VC investor might insist on receiving a multiple of its original investment (e.g., 1.5×, 2×, etc.) which must be paid before any distributions are made to other preferred stock investors in the event of a liquidation or acquisition, thereby ensuring that the VC investor receives both its capital and a fixed return on investment before any proceeds can be paid to the company's other stockholders. Alternatively, a VC investor might insist that after receiving its fixed liquidation payment (e.g., 1× or 2×, as the case may be), it also participates in any distributions to common stockholders as if the investor had converted into common stock just prior to the liquidation event. An investor receiving such "participating" preferred stock thus avoids the need to choose between receiving a fixed liquidation preference and converting into common stock. A variation of this last approach might also be to limit or "cap" the amount of money a stockholder can receive as a holder of preferred stock (e.g., a preferred stockholder may be entitled to a 1× liquidation preference and will also be entitled to participate in distributions to common stockholders until the preferred stockholder receives total proceeds of 3× its original investment cost).

c. *Redemption Rights*

Subsection 3 of Article IV(B) of Lyft's Certificate of Incorporation states that "[n]either this Corporation nor the holders of Preferred Stock shall have the unilateral right to call or redeem . . . any shares of the Preferred Stock." While Lyft and its investors chose to make the preferred stock non-redeemable, many other companies will issue preferred stock that can be redeemed (or repurchased) by the company—either because the investors have the right to force a redemption or because the company has the right to call for its redemption. In either case, the redemption amount is commonly the same amount as the liquidation preference, including any accumulated dividends. As we saw in *Bolt v. Merrimack Pharmaceuticals, Inc.* in Chapter 2, preferred stock that is redeemable at the option of the preferred stockholders can pose considerable financial risk for the company. Upon a redemption demand, the company will need to somehow find cash to fund the redemption.

This risk can be mitigated, however, by some other related factors. First, the shareholder's right of redemption may be written to kick in only after several years (or possibly longer), giving the issuer time to gain a solid operating foothold. Second, the redemption provisions are often drafted such that a specified percentage of the holders must request redemption before the company is obligated to redeem the shares (as was the case in *Bolt v. Merrimack*). Finally, as we shall see below, distributions to stockholders (whether by way of dividends or stock repurchases) can only be done when the distribution does not "impair" a firm's capital under a state's corporate statute or otherwise create a risk of insolvency. For a firm with several years of net losses, these legal constraints might prevent the firm from paying more than a small fraction of the redemption amount or even block all distributions.

d. Conversion Rights

Subsection 4 of Article IV(B) of Lyft's Certificate of Incorporation gives the holder of preferred stock the right to convert each share of preferred stock into shares of common stock at the conversion rate in effect at the time of conversion. (The initial conversion rate is 1:1, but we shall see in Chapter 8 that this might be adjusted over time). We shall save a thorough exploration of this conversion right for Chapter 8, when we discuss options and convertible securities. For now, we note that when preferred stock is convertible (as in the case of Lyft), an exercise of the conversion right means that the investor forfeits all preferred stock rights for the shares that are converted into common stock. As a result, an investor will rationally convert into common stock only when the residual claim of a company has grown so large that the investor is better off abandoning its preferred stock economic preferences and taking a pro rata share of this residual claim.

ii. CONTROL PREFERENCES

a. Basic Voting Rights

As noted, by default each share of preferred stock shall have one vote, unless otherwise provided in a company's charter. Section 5 of Article IV(B) of Lyft's charter provides an example of how these default rights can be altered in practice. Section 5(a) begins by reiterating the default rule and making clear that each holder of preferred stock is entitled to vote with common stockholders on all matters presented to the Company's common stockholders. Notably, it also specifies that each share of preferred stock will be entitled to one vote for each share of common stock into which the share of preferred stock could be converted, thus tying the number of votes to the preferred stock's conversion right. Because the conversion ratio is initially 1:1, this means that each share of preferred stock gets one vote per share.

b. Preferential Voting Rights

In addition to these basic voting rights, Lyft's charter also gives its preferred stockholders two special voting rights. First, Section 5(b) of Article IV(B) gives select series of preferred stock the right to elect a specified number of directors. Specifically, the holders of the Series B, Series C, Series F, and Series H Preferred Stock are each entitled to elect one director (four directors in total), and the holders of the Series E Preferred Stock are entitled to elect two directors. This subsection also states that the holders of common stock are entitled to elect four directors, with any remaining directors to be elected by a combined vote of the common stock and preferred stock. As of its IPO, Lyft had 10 directors, consisting of the six directors elected by the preferred stockholders and the four directors elected by just the common stockholders. (There were no jointly elected directors). Note that not all preferred stockholders have the right to elect a director, nor is this right allocated equally across the different series of preferred stock (e.g., the Series E Preferred Stock has the right to elect two directors). This board configuration reflects the fact that when preferred stockholders have the right to elect directors it generally reflects idiosyncratic negotiations between the company, the new investors, and pre-existing investors at the time of a new investment. It is also important to emphasize that preferred stock investors commonly seek these rights in the context of venture capital finance, but they are less common in other situations.

The second preferential voting right of Lyft's preferred stockholders is contained in Section 6 of Article IV(B). Entitled "Protective Provisions," this section restricts the company from engaging in a lengthy list of activities without first obtaining the approval of the preferred stockholders. Notably, the section is divided into activities that require a simple majority of all outstanding shares of preferred stock voting as a single class (subsection a), as well as activities that require the approval of each series of preferred stock voting separately as disparate classes (subsections b through k). As with the provisions regarding director elections, these voting provisions reflect idiosyncratic negotiations between the company, the new investors, and pre-existing investors at the time of a new investment. As such, preferred stock protective provisions will vary greatly by company and, in some companies, may not exist at all.

C. THE USES OF PREFERRED STOCK

Companies issue preferred stock for different reasons, and the context of any given deal will inevitably shape the stock's terms. Here, we summarize three common reasons why a company might issue preferred stock (though it is worth emphasizing that the flexibility of preferred stock also causes it to be used in some rarer, specialized situations).*

* As discussed in Chapter 5, for instance, a company may also use blank check preferred stock as a way to implement a poison pill; however, in this context, there is no intention that preferred shares will actually be issued. For instance, in a typical "flip-in" poison pill, a company will distribute to all common stockholders a right to purchase one unit of a new series of preferred stock, the terms of which are governed by a shareholder rights plan that implements the poison pill. Technically, the plan permits any recipient of the right to acquire a share of the newly authorized preferred stock, but the exercise price is set at a price that would make such an exercise economically undesirable. Rather, the purpose of the shareholder rights plan is to provide that upon a triggering event (e.g., a bidder acquiring a significant block of shares), the rights "flip in" and become exercisable for the target's common stock at a discount to market value.

i. REGULATORY CAPITAL

Financial institutions commonly issue preferred stock to satisfy regulatory capital requirements. For a financial institution, such as a simple bank, the vast majority of its liabilities consist of demand deposits, which the bank might utilize to make longer-term investments (e.g., a bank will use customer deposits as a source of funding for commercial loans and mortgages). Financial institutions are thus highly leveraged, and a small decline in the value of the institution's assets (e.g., an unexpected increase in the default probability of the loans on its balance sheet) could drive the institution towards insolvency.

To address this risk, banking regulations require financial institutions to have a minimum amount of regulatory capital to absorb unexpected declines in the value of the firm's assets. While a bank could issue common stock to satisfy these requirements, financial institutions often turn to preferred stock to minimize common stock dilution. In general, banking regulations stipulate that only non-cumulative preferred stock can count towards a financial institution's "tier 1" capital; therefore, the terms of preferred stock used for this purpose generally include non-cumulative dividends with a stipulated dividend (payable quarterly) that must be paid prior to any dividend on common shares. These shares of preferred stock also tend to have no voting rights unless the firm proposes to issue a new series of preferred stock having senior or pari passu (on "equal footing") dividend rights, in which case the firm must first secure the approval of the preferred stockholders. In addition, this type of preferred stock often allows the preferred stockholders to elect one or more directors if the firm misses a specified number of dividend payments. The institution selling these preferred shares typically has no obligation to repay the original investment unless (a) the firm is liquidated (in which case, preferred stockholders receive their original investment prior to any payments to common stockholders) or (b) the institution chooses to redeem the shares at their liquidation values. Finally, in some cases, the preferred stock may also be convertible into shares of the issuer's common stock at the option of the holder. Because this conversion right allows investors to participate in the unlimited upside growth of the residual claim, it represents a valuable right that should enable the issuer to negotiate for a lower dividend rate. Preferred shares issued by financial institutions are often publicly traded on either the NYSE or Nasdaq and constitute the largest segment of publicly-traded preferred stock.*

---

* For instance, preferred stock issued by financial firms constitute over 80% of the S&P Preferred Stock Index—an index designed to track the market for publicly-traded U.S. preferred stock. See https://www.spglobal.com/spdji/en/indices/fixed-income/sp-us-preferred-stock-index/#data.

ii. BALANCE SHEET MANAGEMENT

Firms may also turn to preferred stock financing to achieve a desired level of leverage on common stock without having to issue debt. Consider, for instance, a firm that would prefer to raise outside capital by selling bonds but is constrained by debt covenants that limit the firm's debt-to-equity ratio. Or alternatively, even in the absence of these covenants, the firm might be concerned that taking on more debt might make it challenging to make all required interest payments. In either case, preferred stock represents a means for the firm to raise capital on "debt-like" terms without having to issue actual debt. Instead of selling bonds with a contractual right to periodic interest and a specified maturity date, these firms might sell shares of preferred stock with a preferential dividend rate and an obligation to repay the original investment only if the firm liquidates or chooses to redeem the preferred stock. As with preferred stock issued by financial institutions, the preferred stock issued in this context is generally non-voting, unless the firm misses a series of dividends (in which case the preferred stockholders may be entitled to elect one or more directors) or the firm proposes issuing a senior or pari passu series of preferred stock (which requires the affirmative approval of the preferred stockholders). Here, too, an issuer may choose to add a conversion right to the preferred stock to negotiate for a lower preferred dividend rate. Not surprisingly, firms issuing preferred stock in this context tend to be firms that are already highly leveraged.*

iii. VENTURE CAPITAL AND PRIVATE EQUITY

Preferred stock is also used routinely by both venture capital and private equity firms when making investments in private companies. Indeed, we saw an example of this practice when we examined the preferred stock issued by Lyft, Inc. As with the preferred stock used in the previous two contexts, the preferred stock used in venture capital and private equity transactions will contain a liquidation preference that helps provide downside protection to investors in a liquidation (which generally includes an acquisition of the firm). However, in contrast to investors purchasing the preferred stock issued by more mature companies, venture capital and private equity investors do not expect their return to come from preferential dividends; rather, they anticipate investment returns from the ability to convert their preferred stock into common stock as the firm prospers. Consequently, the preferred stock used in this setting will usually convert into common stock, at the option of the preferred stockholder, and rarely uses cumulative dividends.†

---

* For instance, aside from financial services firms, firms operating in the real estate, communication services, and utility sectors represent the most important constituents of the S&P Preferred Stock Index. See https://www.spglobal.com/spdji/en/indices/fixed-income/sp-us-preferred-stock-index/#data.

† For instance, in its quarterly survey of venture capital financing terms, the law firm Fenwick & West reports that only 2% of preferred stock financings included cumulative

Additionally, whereas preferred stock issued by mature companies often has limited voting rights, the preferred stock issued in venture capital and private equity transactions generally has preferential voting rights, as we saw in the case of Lyft. This reflects the fact that venture capital and private equity investors intend to be actively involved in overseeing a firm's growth. As we shall see, these investments can also create tricky conflicts of interest between common stockholders and the preferred stockholders (and even among preferred stockholders). One strategy for responding to these conflicts is to demand the types of protective provisions that we examined in Lyft's charter. In most cases, the terms of the preferred stock will also provide that the holders of the preferred stock are entitled to appoint one or more directors to the firm's board of directors.

Sidebar: SAFEs and Other "Pre-Seed" and "Seed" Financing Instruments

Preferred stock remains the security of choice among U.S. venture capitalists, but a very early-stage startup today is likely to issue a different type of "preferred" security before it conducts its first preferred stock financing. Consider, for instance, a recently formed startup that receives $100,000 from an angel investor or an incubator such as Y-Combinator. (This type of financing is colloquially referred to as "pre-seed" or "seed" financing, but we shall call it "seed stage" financing for simplicity). In theory, these seed-stage investors could demand that the company issue them shares of convertible preferred stock, but doing so raises a difficult valuation challenge. Specifically, as with common stock investors, investors in convertible preferred stock will demand that they receive preferred shares that, on an as-converted-to-common-stock basis, will reflect the value of their investment relative to the post-financing value of the company. As we saw in Chapter 5, this requires determining the pre-financing value of the company, which is likely to be especially hard for a company that may have nothing more than an untested business idea. Indeed, investors may be likely to assign such nascent firms very little value at all, which could leave the founder with an extremely small equity position after the financing. (As an example, a $100,000 investment in a company that has a pre-financing value of just $25,000 would result in the investor owning 80% of the post-financing fully-diluted equity, or $100,000/($25,000 + $100,000)). This could, in turn, undermine a founder's incentive to pursue the business at all.

A popular solution to this valuation challenge is to postpone assigning any valuation to the startup until it (hopefully) raises a much larger round of financing in a preferred stock financing. But what, then,

dividends in the third quarter of 2023. See Silicon Valley Venture Capital Survey—Third Quarter 2023, available at https://assets.fenwick.com/banner-images/Silicon-Valley-Venture-Capital-Survey-Third-Quarter-2023-Updated.pdf.

should the company issue to these seed-stage investors? Initially, the answer was to use a convertible promisory note with accruing interest. The face amount of the note would equal the investment amount, and the conversion feature would provide that all principal and accrued interest would automatically convert into the preferred stock issued in the company's first preferred stock financing (whenever that might occur). In other words, the seed stage investor would automatically be treated in the future as if it were purchasing the preferred shares in an amount equal to the note's principal and accrued interest. In this fashion, the founder and the investors kick the valuation can down the road until the company is more mature and ready for a larger preferred stock financing.

While this approach solves the initial valuation problem, it nevertheless raises other issues. First, the note will require some type of maturity date, raising the possibility that a company could default on the note prior to securing a preferred stock financing. Not surprisingly, a founder might view this risk as less than ideal. Second, seed-stage investors understandably demanded some form of compensation for taking seed-stage financing risk. That is, in this convertible note model, seed-stage investors receive for their extremely risky investment the same price and terms on their ultimate preferred shares as the venture capital investors leading the preferred stock financing in a more mature startup.

Over time, several innovative financing instruments were therefore introduced to improve on the convertible note financing model. The most prominent of these is Y-Combinator's Simple Agreement for Future Equity or "SAFE." As with a convertible note financing, the company issues a SAFE to an investor with a face value equal to the investment amount, and (as with a convertible note), the SAFE will automatically convert into preferred stock in the company's first preferred stock financing. However, in contrast to a convertible note, there is no interest or maturity date; it is purely a financing "placeholder" for the investment until the preferred stock financing occurs. Additionally, to accommodate the need to compensate seed-stage investors, SAFEs will typically entitle the SAFE to convert at a per share price that is slightly discounted for the SAFE holder. For instance, if the preferred stock financing closes at $1.00 per share, a $100,000 SAFE might convert at a price of $0.80 per share (reflecting a 20% discount), such that the holder receives 125,000 shares of preferred stock. This, in turn, might require the company to create various series of "shadow" preferred stock to accommodate the fact that investors in the preferred stock financing will have paid a different per share price.

While it is common to see preferred stock used in these three contexts, we again emphasize that the use of preferred stock is by no means restricted to these three domains. On the contrary, the fact that preferred stock can be drafted to resemble either debt or common equity makes it very much a "hybrid" instrument that can be adapted to suit any number of corporate needs and investor tastes. At the same time, it would be a mistake to conclude that the drafter of preferred stock operates in a true freedom of contract regime. As the following sections show, disputes concerning preferred stock terms have given rise to a variety of legal doctrines that can restrict what may be accomplished in the preferred stock contract. This, in turn, has led to some interpretive principles that can often catch both issuers and investors by surprise.

D. THE LEGAL TREATMENT OF THE PREFERRED STOCK BARGAIN

The balance of this chapter turns to the legal treatment of preferred stock. In interpreting the provisions of preferred stock, courts often invoke the principle that a company's charter "is interpreted using standard rules of contract interpretation which require a court to determine from the language of the contract the intent of the parties." Smith v. Nu-West Industries, Inc. 2000 WL 1641248 (excerpted below). Despite this interpretive principle, however, understanding the preferred stock bargain is complicated by the fact that holders of preferred stock are, to state the obvious, *stockholders*. As a result, the relationship between preferred stock investors and the company necessarily implicates a variety of legal considerations that govern the relationship between a corporation and its stockholders. In the remaining sections of this chapter, we examine four areas that have proven especially important in understanding the preferred stockholders' bargain:

1. Contracting for dividends when the discretion to declare dividends is vested in a company's board of directors;
2. Contracting for dividends and redemptions given limitations on the ability to distribute corporate assets to stockholders;
3. Modifying preferred stock terms in light of statutory rules regulating charter amendments; and
4. Implementing the preferred stock bargain against the backdrop of a board's fiduciary duties.

As you read the cases below, think about whether courts are being faithful to the principle that the preferred stock terms are "interpreted using standard rules of contract interpretation."

2. THE BOARD'S DISCRETION TO PAY (OR NOT PAY) DIVIDENDS

As noted, companies often turn to preferred stock as a substitute for issuing corporate bonds, using a preferred stock dividend as the functional equivalent of interest. Likewise, many investors acquire shares of preferred stock with the expectation that, like a debt obligation, the preferred stock will pay periodic (e.g., annual) dividends at a specified rate. But to what extent can a company commit contractually to pay a dividend? The fundamental challenge is that corporate statutes vest a company's board of directors with the discretion to manage the business and affairs of the corporation, including the declaration of dividends. For instance, DGCL § 170 states that "[t]he directors of every corporation, subject to any restrictions contained in its certificate of incorporation, may declare and pay dividends upon the shares of its capital stock." The following two cases underscore the challenge of contracting for preferred dividends.

Arizona Western Insurance Company v. L. L. Constantin & Co.

247 F.2d 388 (3d Cir. 1957)

■ BIGGS, C. J.

Arizona Western Insurance Company (Arizona) instituted this suit against L. L. Constantin & Co. (Constantin) to recover dividends on 10,000 shares of preferred stock in Constantin held by Arizona and authorized by the December 2, 1952 amendment to Constantin's certificate of incorporation. This provided in pertinent part that 'The holders of the preferred stock shall be entitled to receive, and the Company shall be bound to pay thereon, but only out of the net profits of the Company, a fixed yearly dividend of Fifty Cents (50 cents) per share, payable semi-annually.' An identical provision appeared in the preferred stock certificate. Arizona was the record holder of the stock from on or about October 1, 1954 to on or about February 1, 1956.

Constantin's Board of Directors on December 28, 1954 adopted a resolution which read: 'Resolved, that a dividend be declared on preferred stock at the interest rate of 5% to all * * * stockholders of record on December 30, 1954, payable January 15, 1955.' At the declared rate Arizona as the holder of 10,000 shares of preferred stock was entitled to dividends of $5,000. Constantin paid dividends on certain shares of its preferred stock but nothing was paid on the shares held by Arizona.

In 1955 no dividend was paid to any holder of preferred stock.

After a demand for dividends Arizona instituted suit on the basis of diversity. * * * The third count alleged that under the terms of Constantin's amended certificate of incorporation and the preferred stock certificate, Constantin was bound to pay to Arizona out of net profits a fixed yearly dividend of 50 cents per share, payable semi-annually, and that net profits were available for the payment of such a dividend. Arizona alleged that it demanded payments of the dividends, that payment was refused and that it is entitled to a judgment in the amount of $5,000 plus interest for the dividend declared in 1954 and not paid to Arizona and to a judgment in the amount of $5,000 plus interest for the unpaid dividend which, it is alleged, Constantin was bound to pay in 1955, there being net profits available.

Constantin answered in substance that . . . while admitting the declaration of a dividend on December 28, 1954, Constantin denied that any dividend had been declared in 1955, and denied also that any dividends were due in 1955 as a matter of right.

* * *

Constantin's motion for summary judgment, or judgment on the pleadings in the alternative, with respect to the third count of the amended complaint, was granted, and Arizona's cross-motion for summary judgment addressed to the third count was denied. The court below handed down no opinion explaining the reasons which caused it to take the action it did on the motions directed to the third count but on the occasion of oral argument on the motions the court expressed the view that 'notwithstanding the provision in the certificate of incorporation, a dividend should be payable only when declared in the discretion and judgment of the Board of Directors.'

* * *

Constantin contends that if this court compels the payment of a dividend, absent fraud or bad faith on the part of the Board of Directors, it will be interfering in the management and internal affairs of the corporation; that the compelling of a payment of a dividend would change the status of Arizona from a shareholder to a creditor; and that a suit to compel a declaration of a dividend is a class action and Arizona does not allege that it sues on behalf of other stockholders similarly situated.

* * *

The language employed by the Court of Chancery in Stevens v. United States Steel Corp., 68 N. J. Eq. 373, 377–378, 59 A. 905, 907 is pertinent. The Vice-Chancellor said: 'Subject, of course, to provisions in the charter, and also to the by-laws of the Company, it is for the directors to say whether profits shall be distributed to the stockholders, or retained for the purpose of the corporate business.' In Wilson v. American Ice Co., D.C.1913, 206 F. 736, 738, the United States District Court for the District of New Jersey stated, 'It is well settled, that in the absence of statutory provisions, the granting of dividends from the profits of a trading corporation is in the discretion of the directors, subject to the intervention of a court of equity for improper refusal.'

* * *

We appreciate the reluctance of courts to construe provisions relative to the declaration of dividends in such a way as to hold that the directors are bound in certain circumstances to declare dividends. But the shareholder has the right to have his contract enforced, and, if the contract as expressed in the certificate of incorporation and the stock certificate, require the construction that dividends are mandatory under specified circumstances the courts can adopt no other construction of the contract between the corporation and the stockholder.

The amended certificate of incorporation in the case at bar provides in pertinent part that, 'The holders of the preferred stock shall be entitled to receive, and the Company shall be bound to pay thereon, but only out of the net profits of the Company, a fixed yearly dividend of fifty cents (50 cents) per share, payable semi-annually.' Identical language is found in the preferred stock certificate. Words could not more clearly or plainly manifest that Constantin agreed to be bound to pay dividends where net profits were available for the purpose. We will not hold that the words were employed as a bait to prospective purchasers of preferred stock.

L. L. Constantin & Co. v. R. P. Holding Corp.

56 N.J. Super. 411, 153 A.2d 378 (1959)

■ COLIE, J. S. C.

L. L. Constantin & Co., a New Jersey corporation, filed a complaint against R. P. Holding Corp., Charles Denby, Continental Bank & Trust Co. as receiver of Inland Empire Insurance Co., and Royal American Insurance Co., seeking a declaratory judgment stating the rights and obligations of the parties hereto in connection with preferred stock issued by the plaintiff corporation. Royal American Insurance Co. has not answered and a default has been taken against it.

The controversy between the plaintiff and defendants arises from the legal effect of an amendment on December 23, 1952 of the certificate of incorporation which read, so far as pertinent:

> "By authorizing the issuance of fifty thousand (50,000) shares of preferred stock having a par value of Ten dollars ($10.00) each. The holders of the preferred stock shall be entitled to receive, and the Company shall be bound to pay thereon, but only out of the net profits of the Company, a fixed yearly dividend of fifty cents (50 cents) per share, payable semi-annually. The said dividend shall be cumulative. Preferred stockholders shall have no voting rights. The stock shall be redeemable on and after January 2nd, 1955, at Ten dollars and fifty cents ($10.50) per share."

An identical legend appears upon the face of each preferred stock certificate.

[The court recited the holding in the previous litigation, and determined that there was no collateral estoppel in this action, because R. P. Holding Corp. and its co-defendants were not parties to the previous litigation. Further, *res judicata* was not applicable here.]

* * *

[In 1956 Constantin's board passed the following resolution:]

> "The holders of the preferred stock shall be entitled to receive (cumulative) dividends, as and when declared by the Board of Directors, out of its surplus or net profits, as determined pursuant and subject to the provisions of the General Corporation Law of the State of New Jersey, at the rate of 50 cents per annum * * *."

New preferred stock certificates were printed bearing, *inter alia*, the above language.

> [The defendants all purchased their stock after these actions were taken.]
>
> At the pretrial conference, the complaint was amended to allege that "the corporate by-laws in article 7, provide that dividends are to be declared by the Board of Directors when expedient, and that unless the directors declare a dividend, the same does not become due and payable."

* * *

Standing alone, the 1952 amendment providing that "the holders of the preferred stock shall be entitled to receive, and the company shall be bound to pay * * *" presents no problem for construction. There is no ambiguity which would entitle this court to construe the above quoted direction. As the Court of Appeals said: "Words could not more clearly or plainly manifest that Constantin agreed to be bound to pay dividends where net profits were available for the purpose." However, the contract between Constantin and its preferred shareholders is to be found not alone in the language of the 1952 amendment but in the entire certificate of incorporation, as amended, and the applicable provisions of the statute in force at the time of incorporation, *i.e.*, 1947. The General Corporation Act provides that "the business of every corporation shall be managed by its board of directors * * *," and "unless otherwise provided in the certificate of incorporation, or in a by-law adopted by a vote of at least a majority of the stockholders." *R.S.* 14:8–20, from which the last quote is borrowed, reads:

> "14:8–20. Working capital; directors may vary; dividends
>
> Unless otherwise provided in the certificate of incorporation, or in a by-law adopted by a vote of at least a majority of the stockholders, the directors of every corporation organized under this title may, in their discretion, from time to time, fix and vary the amount of the working capital of the corporation and

determine what, if any, dividends shall be declared and paid to stockholders out of its surplus or net profits. Dividends may be declared and paid in capital stock with or without par value."

The legislative history behind the enactment of *R.S.* 14:8–20 demonstrates that the declaration of dividends has had the attention of the Legislature, and its attempts to limit control over dividends were deemed unsatisfactory and ended, for the time being, in the enactment last quoted. The prior legislative attempts have been commented upon by our courts in no flattering terms. " * * * [T]he legislative experiment, in controlling the discretion of the managers of corporations in respect of the distribution of profits was somewhat dangerous, and brought about a situation which was liable to be productive of mischief, and exposed corporations to malicious and injurious attacks." Stevens v. United States Steel, 68 N.J. Eq. 373 (Ch. 1905). "Naturally, the amount needed for the legitimate purposes of the company's business must be determined by the directors, who are intrusted with the management of the company." Murray v. Beattie Mfg. Co., 79 N.J. Eq. 604 (E. & A. 1911).

Public policy with respect to corporate management has been established by the mandate of the Legislature to be that "the business of every corporation shall be managed by its board of directors" and that "the directors of every corporation * * * may * * * determine what, if any, dividends shall be declared and paid to stockholders out of its surplus or net profits." Recognizing that the situation might arise in which this public policy might not be in the best interests of the corporation and its shareholders, the Legislature provided a means to permit the corporation to act contrary to such public policy. The device employed was to qualify the imposed discretion in the directors by providing that it could be avoided, but only where "otherwise provided in the certificate of incorporation, or in a by-law adopted by a vote of at least a majority of the stockholders * * *."

Article 7 of Constantin's by-laws reads:

> "The Board of Directors shall by vote declare dividends from the surplus profits of the Corporation whenever, in their opinion, the condition of the Corporation's affairs will render it expedient for such dividend to be declared."

It is, in part, the inconsistency between the discretion imposed on the directors as to dividends and the mandatory declaration allegedly provided for in the 1952 amendment that requires judicial construction as between the charter, the by-laws and the statute. It may be conceded at the outset that where inconsistency exists between by-laws and certificate of incorporation, the latter ordinarily governs and it would seem more so where, as here, the conflict arose some years after the enactment of the by-law. However, the provision in the quoted by-law is consistent with *R.S.* 14:8–20 which vested discretion in the directors as to dividend declarations, and the fact that Article 7 of the by-laws was not amended when the 1952 amendment was adopted is some evidence that the 1952 amendment was not intended to divest the directors of discretion.

Can it be said that the statement that "the holders of the preferred stock shall be entitled to receive, and the Company shall be bound to pay * * * " meets the requirements of "unless otherwise provided in the certificate of incorporation, or in a by-law * * * " of Constantin? This court must answer that question in the negative. The statute is clear that the corporate business is to be managed by its directors and that, unless otherwise provided in the charter or by-law the directors may, in their discretion determine what if any dividends shall be declared and paid. In such an important area of corporate policy as is the discretion of the board of directors as to declaration of dividends little should be left to implication. It is only by implication that the language "entitled to receive * * * and bound to pay" can be said to override the statutory discretion embodied in *R.S.* 14:8–20.

* * *

In light of the statutory provisions, the language of Article 7 of the by-laws and the well-settled attitude of the courts against implied repealers and the absence of a "clear and peremptory" denial of the directors' statutory right to discretionary control of dividends, the court holds that the amendment of 1952 does not make the payment of a dividend mandatory, if net profits are available therefor.

QUESTIONS

1. How would a court be likely to decide the dispute over Constantin's dividend obligations under the Model Act §§ 6.40 and 8.01(b)?
2. How would the Delaware courts be likely to decide this question under DGCL §§ 141 and 170?
3. Why would a company want to issue preferred stock with a dividend that was mandatory in any year where there were net profits? Why not issue corporate bonds instead?
4. Assuming that there is an ambiguity in the Constantin language governing dividends on the preferred stock, would the following provision resolve that ambiguity?

> "Dividends upon the Series B Preferred Stock shall be paid out of funds legally available therefore, annually beginning on August 1, 2001, at the rate per annum of $.27 per share (annually the "Mandatory Dividend" and collectively the "Mandatory Dividends"). In addition, commencing on August 1, 2001, the holders of Series B Preferred Stock shall be entitled to receive, out of funds legally available therefore, additional annual dividends at the rate per annum of $.27 per share (the "Elective Dividend" and collectively the "Elective

> Dividends"), when, as and if declared by the Board of Directors. Elective and Mandatory Dividends (the "Series B Accruing Dividends") shall accrue from day to day, whether or not earned or declared, and shall be cumulative, from August 1, 2001."

Articles of Incorporation of The Catalog.Com Inc.

5. Aside from attempting to make the payment of a preferred stock dividend mandatory, what other provisions could provide greater confidence to investors that specified dividends will actually be paid? Consider, for instance, the following provision from Citigroup's Certificate of Designation for its 8.125% Non-Cumulative Preferred Stock, Series AA:

> **Voting Right**. If and whenever dividends on the Series AA Preferred Stock . . . have not been paid in an aggregate amount equal . . . to at least six quarterly Dividend Periods (whether consecutive or not) (a "Nonpayment"), the number of directors constituting the Board of Directors shall be increased by two, and the Holders [of Series AA Preferred Stock], shall have the right, voting separately as a single class without regard to class or series (and with voting rights allocated pro rata based on the liquidation preference of each such class or series), to the exclusion of the holders of Common Stock, to elect two directors of the Company to fill such newly created directorships (and to fill any vacancies in the terms of such directorships). . .

The discretion of the board to declare (or not declare) dividends naturally gives rise to the possibility that the board will exercise this discretion inappropriately. In general, the board's decision regarding dividend policy will be reviewed under the deferential business judgment rule, absent a conflict of interest among directors. For instance, where the board of directors is dominated by representatives of preferred stockholders, a board's decision to pay a preferred stock dividend may be evaluated under the more exacting intrinsic fairness test. See Burton v. Exxon Corporation, 583 F.Supp. 405 (1984) (applying intrinsic fairness test to examine propriety of preferential dividend paid to preferred stockholder who employed all of the company's directors). Near the end of this Chapter we shall examine some other circumstances that can cause a preferred stockholder's director-nominees to trigger intrinsic fairness review of director conduct.

However, even in the absence of a conflicted board, might equitable principles act to constrain the board's discretion to pay dividends? This question is especially relevant for a holder of straight preferred stock. Imagine, for instance, a company that issues non-convertible preferred stock with a $1.00 per share non-cumulative preferred dividend; however, the company withholds paying any dividends for decades, allowing retained earnings to accumulate over time. If the board of directors eventually decides to distribute these retained earnings to common stockholders, compliance with the preferred stock dividend provision merely requires that the company pay preferred stockholders $1.00 per share before declaring a massive common stock dividend. As a matter of contract law, courts often turn to the duty of good faith and fair dealing to constrain the possibility that contracting parties might seek to improperly exploit contractual incompleteness. Might such a concept help protect preferred stockholders in this context?

Guttmann v. Illinois Central R. Co.

189 F.2d 927 (2d Cir.),
cert. denied 342 U.S. 867 (1951)

■ FRANK, CIRCUIT JUDGE.

The trial court's findings of facts—which are amply supported by the evidence and unquestionably are not 'clearly erroneous'—establish that the directors acted well within their discretion in withholding declarations of dividends on the non-cumulative preferred stock up to the year 1948. In so holding, we assume, *arguendo*, that, as plaintiff insists, the standard of discretion in weighing the propriety of the non-declaration of dividends on such preferred stock is far stricter than in the case of non-declaration of dividends on common stock. For, on the facts as found and on the evidence, we think the directors, in not declaring dividends on the preferred in the years 1937–1947, adopted a reasonable attitude of reluctant but contingent pessimism about the future, an attitude proper, in the circumstances, for persons charged, on behalf of all interests, with the management of this enterprise.[2]

The issue, then, is whether the directors could validly declare a dividend on the common stock in 1950 without directing that there should be paid (in addition to preferred dividends on the preferred for that year) alleged arrears of preferred dividends, the amount of which had been earned in 1942–1947 but remained undeclared and unpaid. To put it differently, we must decide whether (a) the directors had the power to declare such alleged arrears of dividends on the preferred and (b) whether they 'abused' their discretion in declaring any dividend on the common without ordering the payment of those alleged arrears.*

---

2 That the directors were not acting in the interest of the common stockholders in disregard of the interest of the preferred appears from the following: The Union Pacific Railroad holds about 25% of the outstanding common stock (i.e., 348,700 shares out of a total of 1,357,994) and was therefore pretty obviously in control of the Board of Directors. Yet, that same Railroad holds about 52% of the outstanding preferred shares (i.e., 98,270 out of a total of 186,457). Union Pacific would plainly be better off if the plaintiff were successful in this suit.

* Eds. The Certificate of Incorporation provided: "The preferred stock shall be preferred both as to dividends and assets and shall be entitled to receive out of the surplus or net profits of the Company, in each fiscal year, dividends at such rate or rates, not exceeding seven per cent, per annum, as shall be determined by the Board of Directors in connection with the issue of the respective series of said stock and expressed in the stock certificates therefor, before any dividends shall be paid upon the common stock, but such dividends shall be non-cumulative. No

Our lode-star is Wabash Railway Co. v. Barclay, 280 U.S. 197, which dealt with the non-cumulative preferred stock of an Indiana railroad corporation. There were no controlling Indiana decisions or statutes on that subject. The United States Supreme Court was therefore obliged to interpret the contract according to its own notions of what the contract meant. We have a similar problem here, since there are no Illinois decisions or statutory provisions which control or guide us. Absent such decisions and statutes, we must take the Wabash opinion as expressing the correct interpretation of the rights of non-cumulative preferred stockholders of this Illinois company. For the difference between the language of the preferred stock here and that in Wabash seems to us to be of no moment.

In the Wabash case, plaintiffs, holders of non-cumulative preferred stock, sought an injunction preventing the defendant railroad company from paying dividends on the common stock unless it first paid dividends on the non-cumulative preferred to the extent that the company, in previous years, had had net earnings available for that payment and that such dividends remained unpaid. The Court decided against the plaintiffs. It spoke of the fact that, in earlier years, 'net earnings that could have been used for the payment were expended upon improvements and additions to the property and equipment of the road'; it held that the contract with the preferred meant that 'if those profits are justifiably applied by the directors to capital improvements and no dividend is declared within the year, the claim for that year is gone and cannot be asserted at a later date.' We take that as a ruling that the directors were left with no discretion ever to pay any such dividend. For if they had had that discretion, it would surely have been an 'abuse' to pay dividends on the common while disregarding the asserted claim of the non-cumulative preferred to back dividends. Indeed, the plaintiff in the instant case contends that a payment of common dividends, whenever there is such a discretion, constitutes an unlawful 'diversion'; and such a 'diversion' would be an 'abuse' of discretion.[6]

Plaintiff, however, seeks to limit the effect of the Wabash ruling to instances where the net earnings, for a given year, which could have been paid to the non-cumulative preferred, have once been expended justifiably for 'capital improvements' or 'additions to the property or equipment.' He would have us treat the words 'non-cumulative' as if they read 'cumulative if earned except only when the earnings are paid out for

---

dividends shall be paid, declared, or set apart for payment on the common stock of the Company, in any fiscal year, unless the full dividend on the preferred stock for such year shall have been paid or provided for. Whenever in any year the dividend paid on such preferred stock is less in amount that the full dividend payable on all such stock outstanding, the dividends paid shall be divided between the series of such stock outstanding in the same proportion to the aggregate sums which would be distributable to the preferred stock of each of such series if full dividends were paid thereon."

[6] This becomes the more evident when it is noted that the plaintiff asserts that 'non-cumulative' means in effect, 'cumulative if earned.' For directors have no discretion to pay common dividends without paying arrears of cumulative preferred dividends.

capital additions.' He argues that the Wabash ruling has no application when net earnings for a given year are legitimately retained for any one of a variety of other corporate purposes, and when in a subsequent year it develops that such retention was not necessary. We think the attempted distinction untenable. It ascribes to the Supreme Court a naive over-estimation of the importance of tangibles (because they can be touched and seen) as contrasted with intangibles. Suppose the directors of a corporation justifiably invested the retained earnings for the year 1945 in land which, at the time, seemed essential or highly desirable for the company's future welfare. Suppose that, in 1948, it turned out that the land so purchased was not necessary or useful, and that the directors thereupon caused it to be sold. Plaintiff's position compels the implied concession that the proceeds of such a sale would never be available for payment of so-called arrears of unpaid non-cumulative preferred dividends, and that the directors would forever lack all discretion to pay them.[7] We fail to see any intelligible difference between (1) such a situation[8] and (2) one where annual earnings are properly retained for any appropriate corporate purpose, and where in a later year the retention proves wholly unnecessary.[9] There is no sensible ground for singling out legitimate capital outlays, once made, as the sole cause of the irrevocable destruction of the claims of the preferred. We do not believe that the Supreme Court gave the contract with the preferred such an irrational interpretation. It simply happened that in the Wabash case the earnings had been used for capital additions, and that, accordingly, the court happened to mention that particular purpose. Consequently, we think that the Court, in referring to that fact, did not intend it to have any significance. We disregard the decisions of the New Jersey courts, and the decision of the Ninth Circuit, since we think they are at odds with the rationale of the Wabash decision.

Here we are interpreting a contract into which uncoerced men entered. Nothing in the wording of that contract would suggest to an ordinary wayfaring person the existence of a contingent or inchoate right to arrears of dividends.[13] The notion that such a right was promised is,

---

7 Were plaintiff to contend that the proceeds of such a sale are available for preferred dividends he would logically be required to contend that reserves for depreciation of capital assets are similarly available. For such reserves constitute, in effect, a repayment of investment in capital.

8 Or one where, in our supposititious case, the corporation, no longer needing the land, could easily sell it at a handsome figure.

9 The attempted distinction would also come to this: (a) The noncumulative preferred irrevocably loses all rights to a dividend as of a given year, if the earnings for that year are invested in fixed capital, but (b) has an inchoate right in the form of a sort of contingent credit if those earnings are reasonably retained for future investments which are never made and which thereafter show up as wholly unnecessary. This is to say that the preferred take the risk of loss of a dividend as of a year in which it is earned when there is a reasonable need for a present capital investment, but no such risk if there is a present reasonable likelihood of a need for such an investment in the future, which later appears undesirable. We see no rational basis for such a distinction.

13 Berle, a most brilliant legal commentator on corporate finance, who may be credited with the authorship of plaintiff's basic contention, admitted that 'popular interpretation,'

rather, the invention of lawyers or other experts, a notion stemming from considerations of fairness, from a policy of protecting investors in those securities. But the preferred stockholders are not—like sailors or idiots or infants—wards of the judiciary. As courts on occasions have quoted or paraphrased ancient poets, it may not be inappropriate to paraphrase a modern poet, and to say that 'a contract is a contract is a contract.' To be sure, it is an overstatement that the courts never do more than carry out the intentions of the parties: In the interest of fairness and justice, many a judge-made legal rule does impose, on one of the parties to a contract, obligations which neither party actually contemplated and as to which the language of the contract is silent. But there are limits to the extent to which a court may go in so interpolating rights and obligations which were never in the parties' contemplation. In this case we consider those limits clear.

In sum, we hold that, since the directors did not 'abuse' their discretion in withholding dividends on the non-cumulative preferred for any past years, (a) no right survived to have those dividends declared, and (b) the directors had no discretion whatever to declare those dividends subsequently.

From the point of view of the preferred stockholders, the bargain they made may well be of a most undesirable kind. Perhaps the making of such bargains should be prevented. But, if so, the way to prevent them is by legislation, or by prophylactic administrative action authorized by legislation, as in the case of the S. E. C. in respect of securities, including preferred stocks, whether cumulative or non-cumulative, issued by public utility holding companies or their subsidiaries. The courts are not empowered to practice such preventive legal medicine, and must not try to revise, extensively, contracts already outstanding and freely made by adults who are not incompetents.

Affirmed.

QUESTIONS

1. Why doesn't the court exercise its equitable powers to provide some rights to passed dividends, when past profits are available? Does this mean the board has complete discretion about paying preferred non-cumulative dividends, as long as it acts in good faith?
2. Does the statement of the board's discretion to omit dividends on preferred stock differ in any significant way from the rule for common stock?
3. Recall the rules of interpretation for corporate bonds set forth in Chapter 6. Does this opinion suggest rules governing interpretation of

---

including that of 'investors and businessmen,' holds 'non-cumulative' to mean 'that dividends on non-cumulative preferred stock, once passed or omitted, are 'dead': can never be made up.' See Berle, Non-Cumulative Preferred Stock, 23 Columbia Law Review (1923) 358, 364–365.

preferred stock contracts are closer to those of corporate bonds or ordinary contracts? Does any rationale suggest itself for such an approach?

NOTE ON SANDERS V. CUBA RAILROAD CO.

Judge Frank's opinion in the *Guttmann* case refers to some New Jersey decisions disregarded by the court. In 1956, the New Jersey Supreme Court rejected an opportunity to conform its rule to that of the *Guttmann* and *Wabash Railway* decisions. In Sanders v. Cuba Railroad Co., 120 A.2d 849 (N.J. 1956), the corporation had paid no preferred stock dividends from 1933 through 1955, although it had been profitable for the years 1941–48 and 1951–52, and had substantial accumulated earned surplus (retained earnings). After expressing some confusion over the plaintiffs' claim for relief, the court stated:

> "The rights of the holders of the non-cumulative preferred stock rest generally (apart from statutory restrictions) upon the terms of the defendant's certificate of incorporation. See *Ballantine, Corporations,* 516, 517 (1946). Those terms conferred priority rights over common stockholders when there were annual net profits from which dividends could properly be declared. *Agnew v. American Ice Co.,* 2 *N.J.* 291, 298 (1949). If there were no such profits in a given year, then no dividends could be paid to the preferred stockholders with respect to that year, then or thereafter. If, however, there were such profits the board of directors still had broad discretionary power to withhold any declaration of dividends and retain the profits as part of the corporation's working capital. If during a later year the corporation earned net profits and its board of directors wished to declare dividends to both the non-cumulative preferred stockholders and the common stockholders, the question would then be presented as to whether the preferred stockholders were entitled to receive the earlier dividends (which were passed though they could have been paid from the annual net profits) before the common stockholders received any dividends. This question finds neither a clear nor a specific answer in the defendant's certificate of incorporation, and its determination, in an appropriate case, will involve full consideration of the precise language of the certificate and the present scope and effect of New Jersey's so-called "Cast Iron Pipe Doctrine" or dividend credit rule. See Bassett v. United States Cast Iron Pipe & Foundary Co., 74 *N.J. Eq.* 668 (Ch. 1908), affirmed 75 N.J. Eq. 539 (E. & A. 1909); *Agnew v. American Ice Co., supra.*
>
> "It may be acknowledged that New Jersey's dividend credit rule has not generally been accepted by the other states or in the federal courts. In the recent case of *Guttmann v. Illinois Central R. Co.,* Judge Frank expressed the view that nothing in the terms of the ordinary non-cumulative preferred stock contract points to "a

contingent or inchoate right to arrears of dividends" and that the contrary notion is an invention "stemming from considerations of fairness, from a policy of protecting investors in these securities." There seems to be little doubt that equitable factors did play a significant part in the development of New Jersey's doctrine. In the *Wabash Railway* case, *supra*, Justice Holmes stated that there was a common understanding that dividends which were passed (though there were profits from which they could have been declared) were forever gone insofar as non-cumulative preferred stock was concerned; but he referred to no supporting materials and there are those who have suggested a diametrically opposite understanding. See *Lattin, Non-Cumulative Preferred Stock*, 25 *Ill. L. Rev.* 148, 157 (1930). This much is quite apparent—if the common stockholders, who generally control the corporation and will benefit most by the passing of the dividends on the preferred stock, may freely achieve that result without any dividend credit consequences, then the preferred stockholders will be substantially at the mercy of others who will be under temptation to act in their own self-interest. While such conclusion may sometimes be compelled by the clear contractual arrangements between the parties there is no just reason why our courts should not avoid it whenever the contract is silent or is so general as to leave adequate room for its construction. In any event, New Jersey's doctrine has received wide approval in legal writings and there does not seem to be any present disposition in this court to reject it or limit its sweep in favor of the Supreme Court's approach in the *Wabash Railway* case. See *Frey, The Distribution of Corporate Dividends*, 89 *U. Pa. L. Rev.* 735, 750 (1941); *Berle, Non-Cumulative Preferred Stock*, 23 *Col. L. Rev.* 358 (1923); *Lattin, supra*."

QUESTIONS

1. The New Jersey Supreme Court justifies the dividend credit rule because any other rule leaves preferred shareholders at the mercy of the directors elected by the common. What situation concerns the court?
2. How can prospective investors in preferred shares protect themselves from adverse actions by directors who are aggressively representing the common shareholders?
3. Recall that the preferred stock purchased by Lyft's venture capital investors included straight, non-cumulative dividends. Assume that from 2010–2018 Lyft was profitable but never paid a dividend. Based on Lyft's charter, how are these preferred stock investors protected against the possibility that just prior to its IPO in 2019 the board pays the annual preferred dividends and then declares a much larger dividend to the common stockholders?

3. LEGAL RESTRICTIONS ON PREFERRED STOCK DISTRIBUTIONS

As discussed in greater detail in Chapter 9, there have long been general prohibitions against conveyances by debtors that were either designed to or had the effect of removing debtor assets from the reach of creditors. In the corporate context, these concerns are made manifest in statutory rules and legal doctrines that limit shareholder distributions, such as through the payment of dividends or stock repurchases. For instance, DGCL § 170 states:

> "(a) The directors of every corporation . . . may declare and pay dividends upon the shares of its capital stock . . . either (1) out of its surplus, as defined in and computed in accordance with §§ 154 and 244 of this title, or (2) in case there shall be no surplus, out of its net profits for the fiscal year in which the dividend is declared and/or the preceding fiscal year. * * * "

DGCL § 154, in turn, defines "surplus" to mean the excess of a company's net assets over the par value of the corporation's issued stock. This section further provides that "net assets" are calculated by subtracting total liabilities from total assets, which is the same as total stockholders' equity. As you might recall from Chapter 2, stockholders' equity consists of three components: (1) stated capital (par value x number of shares issued), (2) additional paid-in capital (the excess of the issue price paid for all shares sold by the company over their aggregate par value), and (3) retained earnings (equity kept in the corporation from profitable business activities). Thus, "surplus" is the sum of (2) and (3). As discussed in Chapter 5, the historical justification for provisions such as DGCL § 170 was to ensure that some level of "permanent capital" would always be available for creditors.

These statutes applied the same approach to share repurchases, which also return money to shareholders. For instance, DGCL § 160(a) provides:

> "(a) Every corporation may purchase, redeem, receive, take or otherwise acquire, own and hold, sell, lend, exchange, transfer or otherwise dispose of, pledge, use and otherwise deal in and with its own shares; provided, however, that no corporation shall—
>
> > "1. Purchase or redeem its own shares of capital stock for cash or other property when the capital of the corporation is impaired or when such purchase or redemption would cause any impairment of the capital of the corporation. . ."

To be sure, these provisions provide paltry protection for creditors. If a firm can set par value using subpenny prices (a common occurrence), then the company's stated capital might be quite modest. Moreover, note the exception in DGCL § 170(a)(2) for dividends payable out of the net profits in the current or prior fiscal year (a so-called "nimble dividend"). That is, even if a corporation had negative earned surplus (e.g., from having many years of net losses), it could still pay a dividend if it had a profitable year.

Yet even if these legal restrictions offer only weak protections for creditors, they nevertheless reflect a clear association between a company's profitability and the payment of dividends or other shareholder distributions. Moreover, while U.S. corporate statues might allow dividends to be paid from additional paid-in capital, it was far from clear whether this result should apply to *cumulative* dividends. Imagine, for instance, a company that issues preferred stock with cumulative dividends, and suppose the company never earns a profit. If the company is subsequently liquidated, should the preferred stockholders receive their accumulated dividends? After all, there were no profits from which to pay dividends. Said differently, should cumulative dividends be limited to years when the company had net profits? These questions proved vexing for courts interpreting the terms of preferred stock, as reflected in the following case.

Hay v. Hay

38 Wash.2d 513, 230 P.2d 791 (1951)

■ DONWORTH, J.

The liquidating trustees of The Big Bend Land Company, a Washington corporation, instituted this action to secure a declaratory judgment construing Article VI of its amended articles of incorporation. The question presented is whether the holders of cumulative preferred stock upon liquidation of the corporation are entitled to be paid accrued dividends from the corporate assets before the common stockholders become entitled to participate in the distribution thereof, the corporation having no earned surplus or net profits.

The trial court entered a judgment declaring that the amended articles of incorporation required that the holders of the cumulative preferred stock receive from the assets of the corporation, so far as they might reach, an amount equal to six per cent per annum computed on the par value of each share from the date of issuance thereof to date of liquidation (January 18, 1947), and that the holders of the common stock were not entitled to receive any distribution of assets until payment of the six per cent per annum accrued dividend to the preferred stockholders had been fully made. The defendant Edward T. Hay, individually and as administrator of the estate of Fayette H. Imhoff, deceased, has appealed.

* * *

Prior to December 27, 1921, the capital stock of The Big Bend Land Company consisted entirely of common stock. On that date Article VI of the articles of incorporation was amended to read as follows:

"Amended Article VI

"The amount of the capital stock of this Corporation is One Million Five Hundred Thousand ($1,500,000) Dollars, divided into fifteen thousand (15,000) shares of the par value of One Hundred ($100) Dollars each.

"The stock of this Corporation is divided into two classes, namely: common stock in the amount of eighty-five hundred (8500) shares of the par value of One Hundred ($100) Dollars each, and preferred stock in the amount of sixty-five hundred (6500) shares of the par value of One Hundred ($100) Dollars each.

"The terms on which these two classes of stock are created and the particular character of the preference of the preferred stock and the conditions and limitations applying thereto and to the common stock are as follows:

"(a) The holders of the preferred stock shall be entitled to receive, when and as declared by the Board of Trustees of this Corporation, cumulative dividends thereon from the date of issuance of said preferred stock at the rate of six (6%) per cent per annum and no more, payable out of the surplus profits of this Corporation annually on the 31st day of December of each year before any dividend shall be paid or set apart for the common stock. Dividends on the preferred stock shall be cumulative, so that if in any year dividends amounting to six (6%) per cent shall not have been paid on such stock the deficiency shall be paid before any dividend shall be declared or paid upon or set apart for the common stock. . .

"(b) This Corporation may at any time, or from time to time as shall be permitted under the laws of the State of Washington, redeem the whole or any part of its preferred stock on any annual dividend date by paying therefor in cash One Hundred and one and 50/100 ($101.50) Dollars per share, and all accrued unpaid dividends thereon at the date fixed for such redemption. . .

"(c) Out of any surplus profits of the Corporation remaining after the payment of full dividends on the preferred stock for all previous dividend periods and after full dividends thereon for the then current annual dividend period shall have been declared and paid in full or provided for, then, and not otherwise, dividends may be declared upon the common stock.

"(d) In the event of any liquidation, dissolution or winding up of the Corporation the holders of the preferred stock shall be

> entitled to be paid in full the par value thereof, *and all accrued unpaid dividends thereon* before any sum shall be paid to or any assets distributed among the holders of the common stock, but after payment to the holders of the preferred stock of the amounts payable to them as hereinbefore provided, the remaining assets and funds of the Corporation shall be paid to and distributed among the holders of the common stock."

We have italicized the words which constitute the crux of this controversy.

There are no corporate creditors involved. The holders of the preferred stock have received from the liquidating trustees the par value thereof. No dividends on the cumulative preferred stock have ever been declared or paid. No surplus profits are available with which to pay the accumulated dividends. There is a substantial amount of assets on hand, but they would all be absorbed if they should be applied in payment of accrued dividends on the preferred stock.

Appellant takes the position that the phrase "all accrued unpaid dividends" means that before there can be a dividend there must be surplus profits, and that, since none ever existed, the right to such dividends never accrued and therefore none are payable. * * *

On the other hand, it is the contention of respondents that subdivisions (a), (b), and (c) of Amended Article VI of the articles of incorporation relate to the payment of dividends to preferred stockholders out of surplus profits *while the corporation is a going concern,* but that subdivision (d) authorizes the payment of accumulated and unpaid dividends out of assets *upon liquidation of the corporation,* even though there be no surplus profits available. They argue that, the corporation being in the process of liquidation, there can be no impairment of its capital and, therefore, there is no longer any purpose in restricting the payment of dividends to surplus profits.

It seems clear, even without reference to the decisions of other courts of last resort hereinafter cited, that the two classes of stockholders contracted between themselves with respect to the division of the assets in case of liquidation. Their agreement was that the preferred stockholders should receive the par value of their stock plus an amount equal to "all accrued unpaid dividends thereon" before any assets should be distributed to the common stockholders.

It should be noted that the articles contain no condition to the effect that the surplus profits must be equal to, or greater than, the total of all accrued unpaid dividends before such distribution could be made. The parties were contracting with reference to a possible future liquidation, a situation where the statutory prohibition (Rem. Rev. Stat., § 3823) against declaration of dividends out of capital had no application.

Appellant's construction of the subparagraph (d) of Amended Article VI as being subject to an implied condition (applicable only to a going concern) that such cumulative dividends are payable only out of surplus profits, is contrary to the fundamental concept of the law of corporations. Appellant's construction of subparagraph (d) is based upon a failure to recognize the vital distinction between a corporation which is a going concern and one which is in liquidation. The reference to "all accrued and unpaid dividends" in subparagraph (d) is the only practical yardstick by which the total share of the assets (which the preferred stockholders were to receive upon liquidation) could be measured. At the time the amended article was drafted and adopted, the quoted phrase was the most definite way that the preferential rights of the preferred stockholders could have been described. It stated the method by which the amount distributable to the preferred stockholders could be computed in the event of a liquidation in the future.

The decisions bearing on this subject were formerly in direct conflict, but the great weight of authority presently supports the interpretation of subparagraph (d) adopted by the trial court in this case. 12 Fletcher, Cyclopedia, Corporations (Rev. & Perm. ed.) 198, § 5449.

* * *

Reference has previously been made to Rem. Rev. Stat., § 3823, which was in effect when the articles of incorporation here involved were amended. This statute provides:

> "It shall not be lawful for the trustees to make any dividend except from the net profits arising from the business of the corporation, nor divide, withdraw, or in any way pay to the stockholders, or any of them, any part of the capital stock of the company, nor to reduce the capital stock of the company unless in the manner prescribed in this chapter, or the articles of incorporation or by-laws; and in case of any violation of the provisions of this section, the trustees, under whose administration the same may have happened, except those who may have caused their dissent therefrom to be entered at large on the minutes of the board of trustees at the time, or were not present when the same did happen, shall, in their individual or private capacities, be jointly or severally liable to the corporation and the creditors thereof in the event of its dissolution, to the full amount so divided, or reduced, or paid out: *Provided, that this section shall not be construed to prevent a division and distribution of the capital stock of the company which shall remain after the payment of all its debts upon the dissolution of the corporation* or the expiration of its charter. . ." (Italics ours.)

This statutory enactment forbidding the declaration of dividends except from net profits specifically provides that it shall not be construed to prevent a distribution of assets upon a dissolution after the payment of corporate debts. Appellant construes this statute as applying to the very situation to which the statute says it shall have no application. This is directly contrary to its express provision. There is nothing unusual in § 3823—practically all states have statutes forbidding the declaration of dividends out of capital assets while the corporation is a going concern. Section 3823 has no bearing upon the problem involved here.

Being of the opinion that Rem. Rev. Stat., § 3823, expressly provides that it has no application to this case and also that, according to the great weight of authority, respondents are entitled under the provisions of subparagraph (d) to receive a sum equal to all accrued unpaid dividends as well as the par value of their cumulative preferred stock in the liquidation of this corporation before appellants shall be entitled to participate therein, we affirm the judgment of the trial court.

■ GRADY, J. (dissenting).

* * *

The problem presented has caused the courts much difficulty, arising out of determining what are "accrued dividends," "cumulative dividends," "accumulated dividends," or "unpaid dividends," as those words are used in articles of incorporation. The courts do not seem to have had much trouble when questions arose in the ordinary course of business of a corporation, but differences of opinion arose when on liquidation preferred stockholders sought to have a preference in the distribution of assets to reimburse them, because in certain years the corporation had earned no net profits out of which dividends could be declared or paid.

One school of thought is of the view that a dividend can come into being and exist only by affirmative declaration of the trustees of a corporation, and then only if the corporation has on hand surplus net profits earned in the transaction of its business. If net profits, or a surplus, never existed, the right to a dividend never accrued, and that which never accrued cannot be demanded out of the capital account on liquidation. This was the view of the chancellor of Delaware in Penington v. Commonwealth Hotel Const. Corp., 17 Del. Ch. 188, 151 Atl. 228.

Another school of thought is that dividends, if not regularly paid out of available earnings, may be amassed or stored up, whether earned or not earned, at regular dividend dates, and, in the absence of a controlling statute, may be paid out of assets when the corporation is liquidated if the articles of incorporation so provide. This idea found expression in Penington v. Commonwealth Hotel Const. Corp., 17 Del. Ch. 394, 155 Atl. 514, 75 A. L. R. 1136. Three judges of the court disagreed with the chancellor. Two believed his views were correct and consistent with the better and more logical reasoning. The cases cited in the majority opinion follow the reasoning of the three judges.

* * *

It seems to me apparent that whoever prepared subdivisions (a), (b), (c), and (d) of the amended articles of incorporation was familiar with the rules of law relating to the rights of holders of common and preferred stock and desired to follow Rem. Rev. Stat., § 3823 . . .

The statute contains two inhibitions: (1) against making any dividend, except from net profits arising from the business; (2) against any division, withdrawal, or payment to the stockholders of any part of the capital stock of the corporation. By the proviso, the capital stock remaining after debts are paid may be divided among the stockholders when the corporation is dissolved or its charter expires. The subjects of the two inhibitions are wholly unrelated. The first relates to dividends and forbids the making of any, except from net profits. No dividend can be made out of assets, and any article of incorporation construed as so providing would be contrary to the statute and void. The second relates to the assets of the corporation and forbids any division thereof, except on dissolution or expiration of the charter.

Making dividends and dividing assets are two different things. A dividend can never be made unless there are in existence net or surplus profits derived out of the current business done by the corporation. The capital stock or assets of The Big Bend Land Company belong to the common stockholders. The preferred stockholders had either loaned money to the corporation and received in payment shares of preferred stock or had become purchasers of such stock. The common stockholders could have received dividends as and when they were made by the trustees out of net profits and secondary to preferred stockholders. The latter could have received dividends from the same source, but on an annual percentage basis.

If at the end of any year net profits had not been earned out of which the dividends could have been made in whole or in part, then the preferred stockholder had a preference whereby he would be entitled to such dividends as soon as there were net profits available. In the case of the common stockholder, he would not necessarily be paid a dividend, even though there might be available net profits therefor, but the preferred stockholder became entitled to dividends annually *if* there were net profits out of which they could be made. If such dividends were made, but were not paid to the stockholder, or if he chose to leave them with the corporation, he would have a preference right over common stockholders later to have them paid to him. Such dividends would be property of the corporation, and when ultimately paid would not be as dividends, but as corporate funds. Such payment would not be a violation of Rem. Rev. Stat., § 3823. Dividends as such are not made when a corporation is liquidated and dissolved. They are only made while it is doing business.

It seems to me that the purpose of subdivision (d), when considered along with all of the other subdivisions of Amended Article VI and Rem. Rev. Stat., § 3823, was to provide that, when the corporation was liquidated and dissolved, the preferred stockholders were entitled to have a redemption made of their stock and to receive any dividends which had at any time been made by the trustees out of net profits but had not been paid to them, before any should be paid to or any assets distributed among the holders of the common stock. I can find nothing in subdivision (d) that authorizes the making of dividends out of assets upon liquidation and dissolution.

* * *

I think a reading of the whole of Amended Article VI in connection with Rem. Rev. Stat., § 3823, must convince one that the dividends referred to in subdivision (d) can mean only those that may have been once lawfully made by the board of trustees out of surplus profits, but which had not been paid to the preferred stockholders. If we do otherwise, we must accuse the corporation of adopting a tricky device to favor preferred stockholders and deprive the common stockholders of their property. Granting that if in any year or years no net profits are earned, dividends have nevertheless "accrued" and during successive years have "accumulated" and may be paid at some future time, they can only be paid out of surplus profits and not out of capital. If the corporation is liquidated and does not have on hand any net or surplus profits, then there is nothing out of which the "dividends" can be paid. This was the view of the court in *Michael v. Cayey-Caguas Tobacco Co.*, 190 App. Div. 618, 180 N. Y. Supp. 532, especially when fortified by a statute the same as Rem. Rev. Stat., § 3823. The court said:

> "Since no profits have been made, and so no dividends were or could have been declared, it is difficult to understand how eight per centum annual dividends could have accumulated during these intervening years to be now paid out of 'surplus assets and funds' or 'surplus profits,' to wit, the amount remaining after payment of debts and repayment of capital. No such sum exists. The amount now on hand is not profits, but is capital. . . There being no accumulated profits, when the preferred stockholders received the full par value of their stock they had received all that they were entitled to, in view of the fact that the amount remaining in the hands of the company was not sufficient to pay the par value of the common stock."

QUESTIONS

1. The dissenting judge stated that "the capital stock or assets of The Big Bend Land Company belong to the common stockholders." What does he mean by this?
2. The dissenting judge interpreted the language of the relevant charters as requiring payment on dissolution of only declared but unpaid dividends. If declared dividends are a liability of the company, how meaningful is such a provision?

3. Modern statutes, such as the Model Act, contain no legal capital requirements: shares need not have par value, no part of the price paid for shares must be segregated as "capital," and prohibitions on dividends under § 6.40(c) are couched solely in terms of insolvency, rather than impairment of "capital." What effect would incorporation under such a statute have on the reasoning of the two sides in this case?
4. If you wished to draft language for a corporate charter that would convince a court that unpaid cumulative dividends were intended to be paid on liquidation, how would you write it?

The debate about undeclared dividend arrearages on liquidation continued in Wouk v. Merin, 283 App. Div. 522, 128 N.Y.S.2d 727 (1954), where the majority held that where the governing language provided that the preferred shareholders were to receive on a company's liquidation the par value of their shares, together with "any arrearage of dividends to which the holders of such preferred stock may be entitled," they were not entitled to arrearages where the board had not declared dividends. This interpretation missed a critical legal point—had the dividends been declared, they would have become debts of the corporation, and the preferred shareholders would have claimed as creditors, not as shareholders.* Thus the court's interpretation leaves the language devoid of meaning. In Matter of Dissolution of Chandler & Co., 230 N.Y.S.2d 1012 (Sup. 1962), the charter provided that preferred shareholders were entitled to "One Hundred Dollars ($100), and also accrued dividends, before any amount shall be paid on account of the Second Preferred Stock and Common Stock." The court held that cumulative dividends "accrued" regardless of declaration. In distinguishing Wouk v. Merin, the court noted that the dissolution language in Wouk provided for payment of "any arrearage of dividends to which the holders of such preferred may be entitled."

> "Apparently, as the dissenting opinion notes . . . had the dissolution clause contained the phrase "together with any accumulated dividends due thereon" in lieu of the language actually employed as above quoted, it was conceded that the preferred stockholders would have been entitled to accumulated dividends which accrued, by mere lapse of time."

230 N.Y.S.2d at 1017.

The conflicting judicial decisions in this area demonstrate the need for clear drafting. Some examples of preferred stock liquidation provisions are set forth in the Sidebar. Do they clearly resolve any potential ambiguity about the right of preferred shareholders to receive undeclared dividends, whether from profits or not, on liquidation?

---

* See William Meade Fletcher, *12 Fletcher Cyclopedia on the law of Private Corporations § 5322* (1995 REV.).

Sidebar: When Must a Company Pay Accumulated Dividends on a Liquidation?

We present here four different efforts to describe whether preferred shareholders are entitled to dividend arrearages on a liquidation. Are they successful in making clear that any such arrearages must be paid, regardless of whether the firm earned any profits?

Here is the approach of Deere & Co.:

"2.2 DEFINITIONS

"2.21 The term "arrearages," whenever used in connection with dividends on any share of preferred stock, shall refer to the condition that exists as to dividends, to the extent that they are cumulative (either unconditionally, or conditionally to the extent that the conditions have been fulfilled), on such share which shall not have been paid or declared and set apart for payment to the date or for the period indicated; but the term shall not refer to the condition that exists as to dividends, to the extent that they are non-cumulative, on such share which shall not have been paid or declared and set apart for payment.

2.4 LIQUIDATION RIGHTS

"2.41 In the event of any liquidation, dissolution or winding up of the corporation, whether voluntary or involuntary, the holders of preferred stock of each series shall be entitled to receive the full preferential amount fixed by the certificate of incorporation or any amendment thereto, or by the resolutions of the board of directors providing for the issue of such series, including any arrearages in dividends thereon to the date fixed for the payment in liquidation, before any distribution shall be made to the holders of any stock junior to the preferred stock. After such payment in full to the holders of the preferred stock, the remaining assets of the corporation shall then be distributable exclusively among the holders of any stock junior to the preferred stock outstanding, according to their respective interests."

Here is the provision of ADOLOR CORPORATION:

"4. Preference on Liquidation. In the event of the voluntary or involuntary liquidation, dissolution or winding up of the Corporation, holders of each series of Preferred Stock will be entitled to receive the amount fixed for such series plus, in the case of any series on which dividends will have been determined by the board of directors to be cumulative, an amount equal to all dividends accumulated and unpaid thereon to the date of final distribution whether or not earned

> or declared before any distribution shall be paid, or set aside for payment, to holders of Common Stock."
>
> Here is the provision for Krispy Kreme:
>
> "SECTION 6. LIQUIDATION, DISSOLUTION OR WINDING UP. Upon any liquidation, dissolution or winding up of the Corporation, no distribution shall be made (1) to the holders of shares of stock ranking junior (either as to dividends or upon liquidation, dissolution or winding up) to the Series A Preferred Stock unless, prior thereto, the holders of shares of Series A Preferred Stock shall have received $1.00 per share, plus an amount equal to accrued and unpaid dividends and distributions thereon, whether or not declared, to the date of such payment; . . ."
>
> And here is the provision for EOG RESOURCES, INC.:
>
> "6. Liquidation Preference.
>
> "(a) Upon the dissolution, liquidation or winding up of the Corporation, voluntary or involuntary, the holders of the then outstanding shares of Series B Senior Preferred Stock shall be entitled to receive and be paid out of the assets of the Corporation available for distribution to its stockholders, before any payment or distribution of assets shall be made on the Common Stock, the Junior Preferred Stock or any other class of stock of the Corporation ranking junior to the Series B Senior Preferred Stock upon liquidation, the amount of $1,000.00 per share, plus an amount equal to the sum of all accrued and unpaid dividends (whether or not earned or declared) on such shares to the date of final distribution."

Cases such as *Hay v. Hay* highlight the importance of clear drafting if preferred stockholders intend for cumulative dividends to accumulate in unprofitable companies. A closely related issue pertains to how cumulative dividends should accrue in partial years. For instance, if a company's charter provides for an annual preferred dividend, does this mean that the specified dividend accrues annually? Or should it accrue daily, in a way that allows for a partial calculation (as is common in the case of interest on indebtedness)? This question constitutes the main issue in the following case.

Smith v. Nu-West Industries, Inc.

2000 WL 1641248,
aff'd 781 A.2d 695 (Del. Supr. 2001)

■ CHANDLER, CHANCELLOR.

Plaintiff Roger B. Smith, and the class of Nu-West Class A preferred shareholders he represents, seeks a summary judgment determination on Count I of the complaint, alleging that Nu-West Industries ("defendant" or "Nu-West") failed to pay the proper redemption price for all outstanding shares of Nu-West's Class A preferred shares. Nu-West and the other named defendants also moved for summary judgment on Count I. Plaintiff alleges that defendants miscalculated the amount of allegedly accrued but unpaid dividends owed on the Class A preferred stock. Defendants claim that Nu-West's certificate of incorporation plainly states that dividends were not payable for the period in question and, hence, were also not accruing during this period and should be excluded from the redemption price. For the reasons I set forth below, I grant plaintiff's motion for summary judgment.

I.

* * *

On December 13, 1996, Nu-West redeemed its Class A preferred stock at a price of $100 per share plus accrued and unpaid dividends of $71.50 per share, for a total of $171.50 per share. It is undisputed that dividends on Nu-West Class A preferred accumulated at the annual rate of $11 per share. To calculate the redemption price, Nu-West included $66 per share for dividends accrued during each of the six fiscal years ending June 30, 1990, through June 30, 1995, together with $5.50 per share for dividends accrued during the last six months of calendar year 1995. The redemption price did not include any payment for the dividend allegedly accruing during the period from January 1, 1996, through December 13, 1996.

On the redemption date, former plaintiff Shapiro was the record and beneficial owner of 1,126 shares of Class A preferred stock. When he received notice of Nu-West's intent to redeem the Class A preferred shares at $171.50, Shapiro questioned Nu-West's failure to include in the redemption price dividends accrued from January 1, 1996, through December 13, 1996. Nu-West responded that dividends do not accrue daily, but rather, accrue in full only at the end of each full fiscal year according to its interpretation of its certificate of incorporation. Shapiro believed that the redemption price should have included an additional $10.43 per share to account for the dividends accruing from January 1, 1996, through the date of redemption, December 13, 1996. * * * Ultimately, as noted above, Smith, the beneficial owner of 18,500 Class A preferred shares as of the redemption date, was substituted for Shapiro as the named plaintiff and the class of Class A preferred shareholders was certified.

II.

* * *

The issue the parties present for decision is the question of whether the provisions of NuWest's certificate of incorporation provide for daily accrual of preferred dividends or annual accrual of preferred dividends. I find that there are no disputes of material fact and that the class of plaintiffs are, as a matter of law, entitled to an additional $10.43 per share. Thus, plaintiffs motion for summary judgment on the Count I of the complaint is granted. As discussed more fully below, Nu-West's certificate of incorporation clearly, and unambiguously, mandates a finding that dividends accrue daily and are payable at the time of redemption.

A. The Certificate of Incorporation

As to the dividends associated with the Class A preferred shares, the relevant certificate sections provide:

> (B) Dividends and Distributions
>
> (a) From the issuance date of the Class A Preferred Stock (the "Class A Preferred Issuance Date") until the end of the first full fiscal year of the Corporation, dividends shall begin to accrue and shall be payable only to the extent of Excess Cash Flow (as hereinafter defined) for such period, and unpaid dividends for such period shall not be cumulative.
>
> (b) For the second full fiscal year of the Corporation after the Class A Preferred Issuance Date, cash dividends shall be payable only to the extent of Excess Cash Flow for such period and shall be cumulative only to the extent of the Adjusted Net Income (as hereinafter defined) for such period.
>
> (c) For the third and each subsequent full fiscal year of the Corporation after the Class A Preferred Issuance Date, cash dividends shall be payable only to the extent of Excess Cash Flow for each such period and unpaid dividends for each such period shall be cumulative.

In the event of redemption, the certificate expressly provides that "dividends shall cease to accrue from and after the Class A Redemption Date designated in the notice of redemption."

Several other certificate provisions also address the treatment of Class A preferred shares. Article IV, § 2(1)(E)(1) notes that the Class A preferred is subject to being exchanged, at the option of Nu-West, for Nu-West's 11% Subordinated Debentures due June 1, 2002. In that event, the notice of exchange was required to state, among other things, "that dividends on the shares of Class A preferred Stock to be exchanged *will cease* to accrue *on such Exchange date*." Moreover, the certificate provides that from, and after, the Exchange Date *"the right to receive dividends* [on Class A preferred] *shall cease to accrue*." Similarly, on the dissolution, liquidation, and winding up of Nu-West, holders of Class A preferred are entitled to receive $100 per share "plus a sum equal to all cumulative dividends on such shares accrued and unpaid thereon to the date of final distribution."

B. Summary of the Arguments

Plaintiff, in supporting his motion, argues that the certificate of incorporation, when read as a whole, clearly indicates that dividends for the preferred stock accrue on a daily basis. Moreover, in advancing this argument in both his brief and at the presentation of his motion, the plaintiff emphasized the distinction between the concepts of when dividends "accrue" and when they are "payable."

Defendants oppose plaintiff's motion and seek summary judgment in their favor. The gist of their argument is that the certificate of incorporation provides that dividends for preferred shares accrue to, and are payable to, shareholders at the end of the fiscal year only. In other words, defendants argue that when the certificate says "payable" it means both payable and accrued.

C. Application of the Law to the Undisputed Facts

The parties' motions ask the Court to interpret the provisions of Nu-West's Certificate of Incorporation related to preferred stock dividends.

The Certificate is interpreted using standard rules of contract interpretation which require a court to determine from the language of the contract the intent of the parties. In discerning the intent of the parties, the Certificate should be read as a whole and, if possible, interpreted to reconcile all of the provisions of the document.

If no ambiguity is present, the court must give effect to the clear language of the Certificate. A contract is not rendered ambiguous simply because the parties do not agree upon its proper construction. Rather, a contract is ambiguous only when the provisions in controversy are reasonably or fairly susceptible of different interpretations or may have two or more different meanings. . . The true test is not what the parties to the contract intended it to mean, but what a reasonable person in the position of the parties would have thought it meant.[11]

At the very root of this controversy is the distinction between when, and how, dividends accrue and when they are *payable*. The defendants argue that the concepts are one and the same. I do not agree. Three concepts are important when discussing dividends for preferred stock.[12] First, there is the concept of when these dividends are *payable*. Generally, preferred shareholders benefit from a stated and fixed dividend rate, annual or otherwise, which is payable (i.e., the shareholder actually receives the dividend) only when the corporation has a stated level of earnings to pay the dividend. Often, a corporation's articles of incorporation will provide that where there are insufficient earnings or other funds to actually pay a preferred dividend, that dividend will *cumulate*. In the simplest of terms, this means the fixed dividend from

---

[11] Kaiser Aluminum Corp. v. Matheson, Del. Supr., 681 A.2d 392, 395 (1996) (internal citations and quotations omitted).

[12] See Penington v. Commonwealth Hotel Const. Corp., Del. Supr., 17 Del. Ch. 394, 155 A. 514 (1931) and Garrett v. Edge Moor Iron Co., Del. Ch., 22 Del. Ch. 142, 194 A. 15 (1937).

the prior period is added to that of the current period. This cumulating will continue until there are funds to pay the dividends. Finally, there is the separate question of when does the shareholder's rights to a dividend accrue? A shareholder's rights to receive a dividend will vest at a particular time. At the time the rights vest, the corporation may, or may not, have the funds to pay the dividend. These are distinct concepts in the area of preferred stock dividends and care should be taken not to confuse them. This case thus reduces to a single question: When did Nu-West's shareholders' rights to a preferred dividend vest or accrue?

To answer this question, I must look to the terms of the certificate. First, I know when the preferred dividends are *payable*. Article IV, § 2(1)(B)(1)(a–c) provides that dividends are only payable to the extent of excess cash flow during the fiscal year. To the extent the excess cash flow at the end of the fiscal year is insufficient, the $11.00 dividend is not paid in that period and cumulates, or rolls forward, into the next year. This section establishes an annual system where at the end of each fiscal year either the dividend is paid or it cumulates.

The difficulty arises where there is an extraordinary event that disrupts the annual cycle. Here we are faced with the redemption of an entire class of preferred stock before the completion of a full annual cycle. The question now becomes whether, and to what extent, the shareholders' rights to that fixed $11.00 dividend have vested or accrued. If the rights do not accrue until the end of the fiscal year, as urged by the defendants, then the shareholders are not entitled to any part of the dividend. If the rights accrue daily from the first day of the fiscal year, as argued by the plaintiffs, then the shareholder will be entitled to a portion of the dividend.

While Nu-West's certificate is clear on when these preferred dividends are payable and that they cumulate if unpaid, the certificate is silent on whether the shareholders' rights to the dividends accrue daily up to the date of redemption. Mindful of this Court's duty to seek the intent of the parties from reading the contract as a whole, I find that other provisions of the certificate would lead a "reasonable person in the position of the parties" to conclude that the parties' intended the preferred dividends to accrue daily.

First, Article IV, § 2(1)(D)(5) clearly states that "dividends shall cease to accrue from and after the Class A Redemption Date designated in the notice of redemption." Logically, dividends can only cease to accrue "from and after the Class A Redemption Date" if they have been accruing continuously up to that date.

Second, Article IV, § 2(1)(E)(2)(iii) states that dividends will "cease to accrue" on the Exchange Date when preferred shares are exchanged for debt. This Exchange Date is an "extraordinary" event and not altogether different conceptually from a redemption. Likewise, Article IV, § 2(1)(G)(1) provides that upon dissolution, liquidation, and winding up, Class A preferred shareholders are entitled to receive "all cumulative dividends . . . accrued and unpaid thereon to the date of final distribution." The date of final distribution may or may not occur at the end of a fiscal year.

III.

Reading the certificate of incorporation as a whole, I conclude that a reasonable person in the position of the parties would conclude that the preferred dividend accrues daily until the occurrence of an extraordinary event stops the accrual—here the redemption of the shares. I do not find that the certificate is ambiguous, nor do I find the terms in conflict. Rather, the provisions are quite clear on their face and act in concert to compel this result. It is only in applying those provisions to this specific fact situation—redemption—that a problem in interpretation arises. While the drafters were, quite simply, less clear than they could have been, the certificate as a whole fills in any minor gaps.

The facts in this case are undisputed and clear. The parties do not contest any fact, so they are entitled to a ruling, as a matter of law, as to whether dividends accrue daily or annually. Nu-West's certificate of incorporation clearly, and unambiguously, mandates a finding that dividends accrue daily and are payable at the time of redemption.

I grant plaintiff's motion for summary judgment and deny defendants' motion for summary judgment. The defendants are directed to pay an additional $10.43 per share for each Class A preferred share redeemed.

QUESTIONS

1. Assuming cumulative preferred dividends are earned but not declared, what rights do preferred shareholders have to dividends absent a redemption or liquidation?
2. Absent a declaration of cumulative preferred dividends, what does it mean to say these dividends accrue?
3. On similar facts, what would the results be under the language governing preferred stock of Deere & Co., Adolor Corporation, Krispy Kreme and EOG Resources, Inc. set forth in the Sidebar above?

In addition to dividends, preferred stockholders can also receive distributions by means of a stock repurchase or a stock redemption. As was the case in *Nu-West Industries*, redeemable preferred stock generally entitles the holder on a redemption to both the redemption price (which is typically the original purchase price) plus any accrued dividends. By removing shareholder capital from the corporation, however, preferred stock redemptions necessarily implicate statutory limitations on shareholder distributions such as those set forth in DGCL § 160(a) (limiting shareholder distributions to distributions from "surplus capital"). By themselves, these statutory restrictions can constrain the ability of preferred stockholders to demand a redemption otherwise permitted by a company's charter.

Imagine, for instance, a venture capital fund that purchases 1,000,000 shares of a company's redeemable Series A Preferred Stock (par value $0.001 per share) at a purchase price of $1 per share. In addition, the company has issued 100,000 shares of Common Stock (par value $0.001 per share). Stated capital would therefore be $1,100 (i.e., 1,000,000 × $0.001 + 100,000 × $0.001). Further assume that the Series A Preferred Stock has the right to demand redemption at $1 per share. If the Series A Preferred Stock demands redemption at a time when the total assets of the firm are $1,000,000 and the total liabilities (consisting of accounts payable) are $900,000, the net assets would be $100,000 and surplus would be $98,900 ($100,000 – $1,100). As a result, this would be the maximum amount that the company could redeem at that time.

Yet one may naturally ask whether it should even be permissible for the company to redeem $98,900 of Series A Preferred Stock. If it did, the payment would greatly enhance the probability that the company might fail as a going concern. Indeed, following the partial redemption, the company's assets would have to lose just $1,100 in value before the company was balance-sheet insolvent. This hypothetical raises the question of whether statutory restrictions such as DGCL § 160(a) represent the only mandatory constraint on the redemption rights of preferred stockholders. The following case examines this question.

SV Investment Partners v. Thoughtworks, Inc.

7 A.3d 973 (De. Ch. 2010)

■ LASTER, VICE CHANCELLOR.

The plaintiffs are a group of affiliated investment funds and their advisor, SV Investment Partners, LLC (collectively, "SVIP"). In 2000, they purchased over 94% of the Series A Preferred Stock (the "Preferred Stock") issued by the defendant ThoughtWorks, Inc. ("ThoughtWorks" or the "Company"). The amended and restated certificate of incorporation of ThoughtWorks dated April 5, 2000 (the "Charter") granted the holders of the Preferred Stock the right to have their stock redeemed "for cash out of any funds legally available therefor" beginning five years after issuance. SVIP first exercised its redemption right in 2005.

ThoughtWorks does not have and cannot obtain the cash to redeem the Preferred Stock in full. Instead, each quarter, its board of directors (the "Board") carefully evaluates the Company's finances to determine (i) whether ThoughtWorks has surplus from which a redemption could be made, (ii) whether ThoughtWorks has or could readily obtain cash for a redemption, and (iii) whether a redemption would endanger the Company's ability to continue as a going concern. Over sixteen quarters, the Board has redeemed Preferred Stock on eight separate occasions. A total of 222,802 shares have been redeemed with a total value of $4.1 million.

SVIP objects to the Board's periodic approach. According to SVIP, the term "funds legally available" simply means "surplus." SVIP presented an expert at trial who opined that ThoughtWorks has surplus of $68–$137 million. SVIP argues that while ThoughtWorks may not have cash or the ability to get it, it nevertheless has "funds legally available" and must redeem the Preferred Stock. Because ThoughtWorks has failed to do so, SVIP believes itself entitled to a judgment for the aggregate redemption price. As of April 5, 2010, that amount was $66,906,539.

SVIP's theory breaks down because the phrase "funds legally available" is not equivalent to "surplus." A corporation can have "funds" and lack "surplus," or have "surplus" and lack "funds." The binding constraint on ThoughtWorks' ability to redeem the Preferred Stock is a lack of funds and the concomitant risk that a significant redemption will render the Company insolvent. An unbroken line of decisional authority dating back to the late nineteenth century prohibits a corporation from redeeming shares when the payment would render the corporation insolvent. Even assuming that SVIP were correct and ThoughtWorks could be deemed to have "surplus," SVIP has not shown that ThoughtWorks has "funds legally available." Judgment is therefore entered in favor of ThoughtWorks and against SVIP.

I. FACTUAL BACKGROUND

On April 5, 2000, SVIP invested $26.6 million in ThoughtWorks in exchange for 2,970,917 shares of the Preferred Stock. Another 167,037 shares were purchased by eighteen individuals who are not parties to this action.

C. The Pertinent Terms Of The Preferred Stock

The holders of the Preferred Stock are entitled to receive cumulative cash dividends at a rate of 9% per annum, compounded semi-annually and accruing semi-annually in arrears. In any liquidation, dissolution, or winding up of the Company, the Preferred Stock is entitled to a liquidation preference equal to the initial purchase price of $8.95 per share (adjusted for any stock dividends, splits, recapitalizations, or consolidations) plus all accrued and unpaid dividends, plus an amount equal to what the Preferred Stock would receive in liquidation assuming it were converted into common stock and shared ratably with the common.

Critically for the current case, Article IV(B), Section 4(a) of the Charter sets out the Preferred Stock's redemption right. It states:

> On the date that is the fifth anniversary of the Closing Date . . ., if, prior to such date, the Company has not issued shares of Common Stock to the public in a Qualified Public Offering . . . each holder of Preferred Stock shall be entitled to require the

Corporation to redeem for cash out of any funds legally available therefor and which have not been designated by the Board of Directors as necessary to fund the working capital requirements of the Corporation for the fiscal year of the Redemption Date, not less than 100% of the Preferred Stock held by each holder on that date. Redemptions of each share of Preferred Stock made pursuant to this Section 4 shall be made at the greater of (i) the Liquidation Price and (ii) the Fair Market Value (as determined pursuant to Section 4(e) below) of the Preferred Stock.

Charter art. IV(B), § 4(a) (the "Redemption Provision"). The Redemption Provision contains two limitations on the Company's obligation "to redeem for cash." First, the redemption can only be "out of any funds legally available therefor." Second, the provision excludes funds "designated by the Board of Directors as necessary to fund the working capital requirements of the Corporation for the fiscal year of the Redemption Date."

Article IV also addresses what happens if "funds of the Corporation legally and otherwise available for redemption pursuant to Section 4(a)" are "insufficient to redeem all the Preferred Stock required to be redeemed." In that event, funds to the extent so available shall be used for such purpose and the Corporation shall effect such redemption pro rata according to the number of shares held by each holder of Preferred Stock. The redemption requirements provided hereby shall be continuous, so that if at any time after the Redemption Date such requirements shall not be fully discharged, without further action by any holder of Preferred Stock, funds available pursuant to Section 4(a) shall be applied therefor until such requirements are fully discharged.

Charter art. IV(B), § 4(d). The same provision states that "[f]or the purpose of determining whether funds are legally available for redemption . . . , the Corporation shall value its assets at the highest amount permissible under applicable law" (the "Valuation Provision"). *Id.*

G. No Legally Available Funds

[Eds. Because ThoughtWorks had not conducted an IPO by the fifth year following SVIP's investment, SVIP demanded redemption of its Preferred Stock in 2005. Litigation followed concerning the interpretation of the working capital set-aside, resulting in a court order in 2006 that "the working capital set-aside applied only in fiscal year 2005, and, thus, ThoughtWorks must now redeem SVIP's preferred stock to the extent funds are legally available therefor." Shortly after the chancery court issued this order, SVIP again demanded that ThoughtWorks redeem its Preferred Stock for $45 million, representing the aggregate redemption price at the time.]

In response, at a meeting on August 24, 2006, the Board analyzed the extent to which the Company had "funds legally available" to make a redemption payment. The Board obtained legal advice from Freeborn & Peters LLP and financial advice from AlixPartners LLC. A Freeborn memorandum set out the process for the Board to follow:

> In declaring the amount of legally available funds for redemption, the Board must (a) not declare an amount that exceeds the corporation's surplus as determined by the Board at the time of the redemption, (b) reassess its initial determination of surplus if the Board determines that a redemption based on that determination of surplus would impair the Company's ability to continue as a going concern, thereby eroding the value of any assets (such as work in process and accounts receivable) that have materially lower values in liquidation than as part of a going concern, such that the value assumptions underlying the initial computation of surplus are no longer sustainable and the long term health of the Company is jeopardized, (c) exercise its affirmative duty to avoid decisions that trigger insolvency, (d) redeem for cash, (e) apply the amount declared pro rata to the Redeemed Stock, and (f) recognize the right of the Preferred Shareholders to a continuous remedy if the amount declared is not sufficient to satisfy in full the redemption obligation under the Charter.

At the August 24 meeting, the Board determined that ThoughtWorks had $500,000 of funds legally available and redeemed Preferred Stock in that amount.

In each of the subsequent sixteen quarters, the Board has followed the same process to determine the extent to which funds are legally available for redemptions. In each case, the Board has considered current financial information about the Company and consulted with its advisors. For example, in March 2010, AlixPartners advised the Board that ThoughtWorks' "net asset value" was in the range of $6.2 to $22.3 million, and its "cash availability"—net of the previously declared but still unpaid redemptions—ranged from approximately $1 million (in the worse of two downside cases) to approximately $3 million (in the base case). After deliberating, the Board determined that the Company had no funds legally available and "declare[d] a redemption of Series A Preferred Stock in the amount of $0.00." The Board departed from AlixPartners' more bullish view after learning that a significant customer was falling behind in its payments and that the Company's "days sales outstanding" had increased during the prior quarter.

To date, through this quarterly process, ThoughtWorks has redeemed a total of $4.1 million of Preferred Stock. That equates to 222,802 shares, of which 214,484 are held by SVIP. SVIP has declined to submit its stock certificates for payment.

H. SVIP Pursues The Current Litigation.

On February 8, 2007, SVIP filed this action. SVIP seeks a declaratory judgment as to the meaning of the phrase "funds legally available" and a monetary judgment for the lesser of (i) the full amount of ThoughtWorks' redemption obligation and (ii) the full amount of ThoughtWorks' "funds legally available."

II. LEGAL ANALYSIS

Section 160 of the Delaware General Corporation Law (the "DGCL") authorizes Delaware corporation to redeem its shares, subject to statutory restrictions. It provides, in pertinent part:

> (a) Every corporation may purchase, redeem, receive, take or otherwise acquire . . . its own shares; provided, however, that no corporation shall:
>
> > (1) Purchase or redeem its own shares of capital stock for cash or other property when the capital of the corporation is impaired or when such purchase or redemption would cause any impairment of the capital of the corporation, except that a corporation . . . may purchase or redeem out of capital any of its own shares which are entitled upon any distribution of its assets, whether by dividend or in liquidation, to a preference over another class or series of its stock . . . if such shares will be retired upon their acquisition and the capital of the corporation reduced in accordance with §§ 243 and 244 of this title.

8 *Del. C.* § 160(a)(1). "A repurchase impairs capital if the funds used in the repurchase exceed the amount of the corporation's 'surplus,' defined by 8 *Del. C.* § 154 to mean the excess of net assets over the par value of the corporation's issued stock." *Klang v. Smith's Food & Drug Ctrs., Inc.*, 702 A.2d 150, 153 (Del. 1997). "Net assets means the amount by which total assets exceed total liabilities." 8 *Del. C.* § 154. Under Section 160(a)(1), therefore, unless a corporation redeems shares and will retire them and reduce its capital, "a corporation may use only its surplus for the purchase of shares of its own capital stock." *In re Int'l Radiator Co.*, 92 A. 255, 256 (Del. Ch. 1914).

Section 160's restrictions on redemptions are intended to protect creditors. . . . The statute seeks to accomplish this goal by prohibiting transactions that would redistribute to stockholders assets that were part of what nineteenth and early twentieth century common law jurists deemed a permanent base of financing upon which creditors were presumed to rely when extending credit. . . . As a practical matter, the test operates roughly to prohibit distributions to stockholders that would render the company balance-sheet insolvent, but instead of using insolvency as the cut-off, the line is drawn at the amount of the corporation's capital.

SVIP contends that under the circumstances, it is entitled to a judgment against ThoughtWorks for the full amount of the redemption price. SVIP argues that: It is common practice to include in . . . mandatory redemption provisions a phrase such as funds legally available, which simply means funds that carry no legal prohibition on their use. Under Delaware law, a corporation's surplus is legally available for the redemption of its stock. Surplus is the amount by which a corporation's net assets exceed its stated capital. . . . And here, ThoughtWorks promised in its Charter that for the purpose of calculating funds legally available for redemption it would value its assets at the highest legally permissible level. . . . At trial, SVIP's expert valued ThoughtWorks' assets to determine the amount of the company's surplus [using the three standard business valuation methodologies]. . . . The discounted cash flow ("DCF") method produced the lowest figure, but even this figure resulted in surplus in excess of the amount necessary to redeem all of the preferred stock. . . . On this basis, SVIP seeks a judgment in the amount of the redemption obligation, $64,126,770.

A. The Plain Meaning Of "Funds Legally Available"

Because the existence of surplus under Section 160 most commonly constrains a corporation's ability to pay dividends or redeem stock, "funds legally available" is colloquially treated as if synonymous with "surplus." The two concepts, however, are not equivalent.

The phrase "funds legally available" . . . contemplates initially that there are "funds," in the sense of a readily available source of cash. The funds must both be "available" in the general sense of accessible, obtainable, and present or ready for immediate use, and "legally" so, in the additional sense of accessible in conformity with and as permitted by law. The Redemption Provision renders this usage of "funds" all the more clear by speaking in terms of redemption "for cash out of funds legally available therefor." The Redemption Provision thus directly links "funds" to the concept of "cash."

A corporation easily could have "funds" and yet find that they were not "legally available." . . . Outside the DGCL, a wide range of statutes and legal doctrines could restrict a corporation's ability to use funds, rendering them not "legally available." The Bank Holding Company Act of 1956, 12 U.S.C. § 1841, *et seq.*, requires bank holding companies to maintain certain capital requirements, and a subject company would need to take those restrictions into account. Federal employment taxes collected from employees are held in trust for the federal government, as are sales and use taxes collected by corporations for eventual payment to state governments. Funds subject to these and other types of restrictions would not be "legally available," whether or not the company had "surplus" under the DGCL. *See, e.g., Hurley v. Boston R. Hldg. Co.*, 54 N.E.2d 183, 198 (Mass. 1944) (noting that corporation did not have funds legally available to redeem preferred stock because its only property was stock of a railroad which, by statute under Massachusetts law at the time, could not be sold without express legislative consent).

Most significantly for the current case, the common law has long restricted a corporation from redeeming its shares when the corporation is insolvent or would be rendered insolvent by the redemption. [citations omitted] Black-letter law recognizes that "the shareholder's right to compel a redemption is subordinate to the rights of creditors." 11 *Fletcher's Cyclopedia of the Law of Private Corporations* § 5310 (perm. ed.).

As against creditors of the corporation, preferred shareholders have no greater rights than common shareholders. They have no preference over them, either in respect to dividends or capital, and have no lien upon the property of the corporation to their prejudice, except where the statute provides otherwise. On the contrary, their rights, both in respect to dividends and capital are subordinate to the rights of such creditors, and consequently they are not entitled to any part of the corporate assets until the corporate debts are fully paid. Nor can the corporation give them any preference, either in respect to the payment of principal or dividends, which will be superior to the rights of creditors, unless by virtue of express statutory authority.

Learned commentators similarly explain that the redemption right of a preferred stockholder cannot impair the rights of creditors and therefore cannot be exercised when the corporation is insolvent or would be rendered insolvent by the payment. [citations omitted]

Delaware follows these principles. Since at least 1914, this Court has recognized that, *in addition* to the strictures of Section 160, "[t]he undoubted weight of authority" teaches that a "corporation cannot purchase its own shares of stock when the purchase diminishes the ability of the company to pay its debts, or lessens the security of its creditors." *Int'l Radiator*, 92 A. at 255. In *Farland v. Wills*, 1975 WL 1960 (Del. Ch. Nov. 12, 1975), this Court enjoined payments by a corporation to its sole stockholder, including a repurchase of stock. The Court held that it was not necessary "to conclude preliminarily that there was an actual impairment of capital" under Section 160 of the DGCL. *Id.* at *6. Rather, the Court enjoined the repurchase on the legal principle that "[a] corporation should not be able to become a purchaser of its own stock when it results in a fraud upon the rights of or injury to the creditors." *Id.*

A corporation may be insolvent under Delaware law either when its liabilities exceed its assets, or when it is unable to pay its debts as they come due. *See, e.g., N. Am. Catholic Educ. Programming Found., Inc. v. Gheewalla*, 2006 WL 2588971, at *10 (Del. Ch. Sept. 1, 2006), *aff'd*, 930 A.2d 92 (Del. 2007); *Prod. Res. Gp., L.L.C. v. NCT Gp., Inc.*, 863 A.2d 772, 782 (Del. Ch. 2004). Although a corporation cannot be balance-sheet insolvent and meet the requirements of Section 160, a corporation can nominally have surplus from which redemptions theoretically could be made and yet be unable to pay its debts as they come due. The common law prohibition on redemptions when a corporation is or would be rendered insolvent restricts a corporation's ability to redeem shares under those circumstances, giving rise to yet another situation in which "funds legally available" differs from "surplus." *See In re Color Tile, Inc.*, 2000 WL 152129, at *5 (D. Del. Feb. 9, 2000) (holding that complaint alleging a Delaware corporation had incurred "debts beyond its ability to pay" validly pled that the corporation "lacked legally available funds at the time of the dividend declaration").

SVIP's claim depends on "funds legally available" being equivalent to "surplus." Because the two concepts differ, SVIP's claim fails as a matter of law. SVIP's claim also fails because it supposes that the existence of "surplus" is sufficient to establish conclusively a corporation's obligation to redeem shares, regardless of whether the corporation actually has funds from which the redemption can be made. "Funds legally available" means something different. It contemplates "funds" (in the sense of cash) that are "available" (in the sense of on hand or readily accessible through sales or borrowing) and can be deployed "legally" for redemptions without violating Section 160 or other statutory or common law restrictions, including the requirement that the corporation be able to continue as a going concern and not be rendered insolvent by the distribution.

B. The Amount Of Funds Legally Available

Under Delaware law, when directors have engaged deliberatively in the judgment-laden exercise of determining whether funds are legally available, a dispute over that issue does not devolve into a mini-appraisal. Rather, the plaintiff must prove that in determining the amount of funds legally available, the board acted in bad faith, relied on methods and data that were unreliable, or made a determination so far off the mark as to constitute actual or constructive fraud. *Klang*, 702 A.2d at 156; *accord Morris*, 63 A.2d at 584–85.

SVIP failed to prove at trial that the Board ever (i) acted in bad faith in determining whether ThoughtWorks had legally available funds, (ii) relied on methods and data that were unreliable, or (iii) made determinations so far off the mark as to constitute actual or constructive fraud. . . .

The factual record demonstrates that the Board has acted in the utmost good faith and relied on detailed analyses developed by well-qualified experts. For sixteen straight quarters, the Board has undertaken a thorough investigation of the amount of funds legally available for redemption, and it has redeemed Preferred Stock accordingly. On each occasion, the Board has consulted with financial and legal advisors, received current information about the state of the Company's business, and deliberated over the extent to which funds could be used to redeem the Preferred Stock without threatening the Company's ability to continue as a going concern. The Board's process has been impeccable, and the Board has acted responsibly to fulfill its contractual commitment to the holders of the Preferred Stock despite other compelling business uses for the Company's cash. This is not a case where the Board has had ample cash available for redemptions and simply chose to pursue a contrary course. *Cf. Mueller v. Kraeuter & Co.*, 25 A.2d 874, 877 (N.J. Ch. 1942) (compelling corporation to take steps to redeem preferred stock where directors in prior years deployed funds exceeding amount of redemption obligation for purposes of expansion).

III. CONCLUSION

Judgment is entered in favor of ThoughtWorks and against SVIP. ThoughtWorks will present a final order upon notice.

QUESTIONS

1. SVIP invested $26.6 million in Thoughtworks in 2000. As of April 5, 2010, SVIP's aggregate redemption price was almost $67 million. Where did the additional $40.4 million owed come from?
2. The court reads "any funds legally available" broadly by invoking the need to protect creditors. Is there any evidence that Thoughtworks had creditors?
3. Suppose that the terms of SVIP's redemption right read "surplus" instead of "any funds legally available therefor." Do you think the result would have been any different?

NOTE

In SV Investment Partners, LLC v. Thoughtworks, Inc. 37 A.3d 205 (Del. 2011), the Delaware Supreme Court affirmed the outcome of the Chancery Court's opinion, although it refrained from evaluating SVIP's argument that "funds legally available" was limited to "surplus." Rather, it affirmed the lower court opinion on the basis that, even if SVIP's legal definition was correct, SVIP's expert witness failed to produce evidence to rebut the board's determination that it had insufficient "legally available" funds for redemption.

Left undisturbed, the Chancery Court's distinction between restrictions imposed by Section 160 of the DGCL and restrictions imposed by Delaware common law has continued to influence the Chancery Court's assessment of redemption requests by preferred stockholders. Most notably, in TCV VI, L.P. et al v. Tradingscreen Inc. et al. (C.A. No. 10164-VCN, Delaware Court of Chancery, March 27, 2015), the court examined another attempt by preferred stockholders to exercise a redemption right similar to the one at issue in *ThoughtWorks*. However, in contrast to the redemption right in *ThoughtWorks*, the redemption right for Tradingscreen did not contain the limiting language that any redemption could only be made from "legally available funds." Nonetheless, the company refused to redeem the preferred stock, arguing that Delaware law imposes limitations "which require that any redemption of shares be made only out of legally available funds." The court agreed and held that the absence of the limiting language was not dispositive, concluding that as a matter of Delaware common law, redemptions can only be made from funds legally available. Citing *ThoughtWorks*, the court further noted that Tradingscreen "may only 'legally' deploy funds for stock redemptions if doing so does not 'violat[e] Section 160 or other statutory or common law restriction, including the requirement that the corporation be able to continue as a going concern and not be rendered insolvent by the distribution.' " (citations omitted)

In response to *ThoughtWorks* and *Tradingscreen*, the National Venture Capital Association modified the redemption section of its model Certificate of Incorporation for Series A Preferred Stock financings to include the following provision:

> 6.4 Interest. If any shares of Preferred Stock are not redeemed for any reason on any Redemption Date, all such unredeemed shares shall remain outstanding and entitled to all the rights and preferences provided herein, and the Corporation shall pay interest on the Redemption Price applicable to such unredeemed shares at an aggregate per annum rate equal to [twelve] percent ([12]% (increased by one percent (1%) each month following the Redemption Date until the Redemption Price, and any interest thereon, is paid in full), with such interest to accrue daily in arrears and be compounded [annually]; provided, however, that in no event shall such interest exceed the maximum permitted rate of interest under applicable law (the "Maximum Permitted Rate"), provided, however, that the Corporation shall take all such actions as may be necessary, including without limitation, making any applicable governmental filings, to cause the Maximum Permitted Rate to be the highest possible rate. In the event any provision hereof would result in the rate of interest payable hereunder being in excess of the Maximum Permitted Rate, the amount of interest required to be paid hereunder shall automatically be reduced to eliminate such excess; provided, however, that any subsequent increase in the Maximum Permitted Rate shall be retroactively effective to the applicable Redemption Date to the extent permitted by law.

Why do you think the NVCA would add this language given the decision in *ThoughtWorks*? Do you think it would have changed the outcome in the case had it been included in the ThoughtWorks charter? Can you think of any other strategies that might protect preferred stock investors from the outcome in *ThoughtWorks*?

4. ALTERING THE PREFERRED STOCK CONTRACT

A. GENERAL VOTING RULES AND VOTING RIGHTS

After a company issues preferred stock, it might find it necessary to modify the terms of the preferred stock contract. Often, the need to modify a contract arises from the need to sell additional shares of preferred stock. As discussed previously, when a firm sells preferred stock, the dividend rate, the liquidation preference, and other economic terms reflect the price at which the preferred stock is sold. Consequently, a company will typically need to authorize a separate series for each additional round of preferred stock financing. Where a company has blank check preferred stock, this authorization can be accomplished by a board resolution adopting a certificate of designation for the new series of preferred stock. In other cases, the company may choose to "amend and restate" its charter, as was done by Lyft, Inc.

Additionally, a company may seek to amend the preferred stock contract to modify the terms of existing preferred stock. Consider, for instance, a company that has raised \$100 million of venture capital financing through selling preferred stock with an aggregate liquidation preference of \$100 million. If the company struggles to build its business and needs to raise additional capital, it may find that new investors will insist on a reduced liquidation preference for the pre-existing stock. Why? As with any preferred stock financing, the new investment will increase the amount of the total preferred stock liquidation preference. However, if the new investor believes that a realistic "exit scenario" for the company is a sale of the company for less than, say, \$75 million, all of the acquisition proceeds will be absorbed by the preferred stock liquidation preference, leaving nothing for common stockholders. Yet the common stock is generally held by the company's managers and other key employees, who will inevitably realize that the common stock no longer has a realistic chance of having any value. To keep the company's employees motivated, the new investor will therefore demand reducing the pre-existing liquidation preference. (In practice, investors often refer to this as a problem of "liquidation overhang.") As a formal matter, accomplishing this task will require amending the charter to change the terms of the pre-existing preferred stock liquidation preference, as well as to authorize the new shares of preferred to be sold in the financing.

Because the preferred stock contract is in the company's charter, modifying the contract for either of these reasons requires complying with the technical rules for charter amendments. In general, these rules will be set forth in (a) the corporate statute for the company's state of incorporation and (b) the company's charter. As an example, imagine that instead of conducting an IPO, Lyft chose instead to raise additional capital by selling newly issued Series J Preferred Stock. Let's consider what approvals would be required.

Since Lyft is incorporated in Delaware, we would turn first to Section 242 of the DGCL which governs how to amend the certificate of incorporation of a Delaware firm. Section 242(b)(1) states that an amendment shall be effective if:

> [the company's] board of directors shall adopt a resolution setting forth the amendment proposed, declaring its advisability, and either calling a special meeting of the stockholders entitled to vote in respect thereof for the consideration of such amendment or directing that the amendment proposed be considered at the next annual meeting of the stockholders. . .

It further adds that if:

> a majority of the outstanding stock entitled to vote thereon, and a majority of the outstanding stock of each class entitled to vote thereon as a class has been voted in favor of the amendment, a certificate setting forth the amendment and certifying that such amendment has been duly adopted in accordance with this section shall be executed, acknowledged and filed and shall become effective. . .

In short, a certificate of amendment (or an amended and restated certificate of incorporation) authorizing the new Series J Preferred Stock would require the approval of Lyft's board of directors, along with the affirmative vote of a majority of its outstanding voting stock. Recall that Lyft's charter states that the preferred stock has the right to vote on an as-converted-to-common-stock basis on all matters brought before the company's stockholders. As such, a majority of all preferred stock and all common stock (voting as a single class and on an as-converted basis) would need to approve the amendment.

Before moving to any additional approvals that might be required by Lyft's specific charter, it is important to note one wrinkle in the statutory framework we just reviewed. Notice that the above-cited provision regarding stockholder approval requires a simple majority vote of stockholders, along with the approval by "a majority of the outstanding stock of each class entitled to vote thereon as a class." Lyft's charter authorizes two classes of stock: Common and Preferred. In what circumstances would either class be entitled to a separate class vote on a proposed amendment? The answer to this question is found in Section 242(b)(2), which provides:

> The holders of the outstanding shares of a class shall be entitled to vote as a class upon a proposed amendment, whether or not entitled to vote thereon by the certificate of incorporation, if the amendment would increase or decrease the aggregate number of authorized shares of such class, increase or decrease the par value of the shares of such class, or alter or change the powers,

> preferences, or special rights of the shares of such class so as to affect them adversely.

Here we see a legislative attempt to provide each class of stockholder with default rights against amendments that might adversely affect the class. These amendments include: (1) changes in the number of authorized shares of the class, (2) changes in the par value of the class, and (3) any amendment that adversely affects the contractual rights of the class.* Moreover, where a class is sub-divided into multiple series and the amendment would adversely affect just one or more series, Section 242(b)(2) states that a separate vote is required by the adversely affected series:

> If any proposed amendment would alter or change the powers, preferences, or special rights of 1 or more series of any class so as to affect them adversely, but shall not so affect the entire class, then only the shares of the series so affected by the amendment shall be considered a separate class for the purposes of this paragraph.

In our example, Lyft is proposing to authorize a new series of preferred stock which will entail increasing the total number of shares of preferred stock. As such, a majority of the preferred stock voting as a separate class would need to approve the amendment. So long as the amendment does not make any adverse changes to one or more series of preferred stock, no separate vote by a series would be required under Section 242(b)(2).

Finally, we would need to examine Lyft's charter for any additional stockholder approvals that are required to adopt the amendment authorizing the Series J Preferred Stock. As summarized earlier in this chapter, Section 6(a) of Article 4(B) ("Protective Provisions") requires the company to obtain the approval of the holders of a majority of the outstanding Preferred Stock to amend the company's charter. Thus, even without Section 242(b)(2), the company would require a separate class vote on the amendment by the holders of the outstanding Preferred Stock. Additionally, subsections 6(b) through 6(k) might require a separate *series* vote depending on the terms of the new Series J Preferred Stock. For example, if the Series J Preferred Stock were to provide that its liquidation preference must be paid in full before any other series of preferred stock (i.e., a senior liquidation preference), then the holders of a majority of *each* of the following series would need to approve the amendment: Series I, Series H, Series G, Series F, Series E, and Series D Preferred Stock.

While this analysis has focused on Lyft, Inc. as a venture-backed startup company, it is worth noting that the same type of analysis applies

* With respect to an amendment that changes the authorized number of shares of a class, Section 242(b)(2) permits the amendment to be approved by a simple majority vote of all stock if such a vote is permitted in the original certificate of incorporation, in any amendment authorizing the class, or in an amendment approved by a majority of the class.

to preferred stock issued in other contexts. Indeed, the listing rules of the New York Stock Exchange (NYSE) require that in order to list preferred stock on the NYSE, the preferred stock must have specific class voting rights in the issuer's organizational documents. These rights include both the right to elect directors upon a failure to pay dividends, as well as the right to vote separately on some types of corporate transactions. The full set of minimum voting rights is set forth in Section 313.00(C) of the New York Stock Exchange, LISTED COMPANY MANUAL:

> (C) Preferred Stock, Minimum Voting Rights Required
>
> Preferred stock, voting as a class, should have the right to elect a minimum of two directors upon default of the equivalent of six quarterly dividends. The right to elect directors should accrue regardless of whether defaulted dividends occurred in consecutive periods.
>
> The right to elect directors should remain in effect until cumulative dividends have been paid in full or until non-cumulative dividends have been paid regularly for at least a year. The preferred stock quorum should be low enough to ensure that the right to elect directors can be exercised as soon as it accrues. In no event should the quorum exceed the percentage required for a quorum of the common stock required for the election of directors. The Exchange prefers that no quorum requirement be fixed in respect of the right of a preferred stock, voting as a class, to elect directors when dividends are in default.
>
> The Exchange recommends that preferred stock should have minimum voting rights even if the preferred stock is not listed.
>
> Increase in Authorized Amount or Creation of a Pari Passu Issue—
>
> - An increase in the authorized amount of a class of preferred stock or the creation of a pari passu issue should be approved by a majority of the holders of the outstanding shares of the class or classes to be affected. The Board of Directors may increase the authorized amount of a series or create an additional series ranking pari passu without a vote by the existing series if shareholders authorized such action by the Board of Directors at the time the class of preferred stock was created.
>
> Creation of a Senior Issue—
>
> - Creation of a senior equity security should require approval of at least two-thirds of the outstanding preferred shares. The Board of Directors may create a senior series without a vote by the existing series if shareholders authorized such action by the Board of Directors at the time of the existing series of preferred stock was created.

- A vote by an existing class of preferred stock is not required for the creation of a senior issue if the existing class has previously received adequate notice of redemption to occur within 90 days. However, the vote of the existing class should not be denied if all or part of the existing issue is being retired with proceeds from the sale of the new stock.

Alteration of Existing Provisions—

- Approval by the holders of at least two-thirds of the outstanding shares of a preferred stock should be required for adoption of any charter or by-law amendment that would materially affect existing terms of the preferred stock.
- If all series of a class of preferred stock are not equally affected by the proposed changes, there should be a two-thirds approval of the class and a two-thirds approval of the series that will have a diminished status.
- The charter should not hinder the shareholders' right to alter the terms of a preferred stock by limiting modification to specific items, e.g., interest rate, redemption price.

B. MANAGING CLASS AND SERIES VETO RIGHTS

As the foregoing discussion highlights, amending the preferred stock contract may require soliciting the votes of the holders of the outstanding preferred stock voting as a separate class, as well as the holders of individual series of preferred stock. These class and series veto rights protect stockholders against amendments that might adversely affect their economic and voting rights, but these multiple veto rights also make it more difficult for the company to amend the company's charter. Indeed, they may create the risk that just a small number of stockholders can hold-up a proposed preferred stock financing or any other transaction that triggers a separate class or series vote. Moreover, this risk is heightened if the class and series veto rights require supra-majority approvals. For instance, if Lyft's certificate of incorporation required the holders of two-thirds of the outstanding preferred stock to approve an amendment to the company's charter, holders of just one-third of the outstanding shares of preferred stock would have the power to derail a proposed amendment.

Not surprisingly, companies have on occasion resorted to a variety of tactics to navigate the challenges posed by class and series veto rights.

i. MERGERS

Recall that in our discussion of amending Lyft's charter we focused on the approval framework contained in Section 242(b) of the DGCL. We did so because this section, entitled "Amendment of certificate of incorporation after receipt of payment for stock," is obviously intended to set forth the statutory rules for amending a company's certificate of incorporation. However, this is not the only statutory provision that provides a method for amending a company's charter. Might a merger do the trick? Consider Section 251, entitled "Merger or consolidation of domestic corporations." This section permits two or more corporations to merge into a single corporation and sets forth the procedural requirements:

> (b) The board of directors of each corporation which desires to merge or consolidate shall adopt a resolution approving an agreement of merger or consolidation. The agreement shall state: (1) The terms and conditions of the merger or consolidation; (2) The mode of carrying the same into effect; (3) *In the case of a merger, such amendments or changes in the certificate of incorporation of the surviving corporation as are desired to be effected by the merger*, or, if no such amendments or changes are desired, a statement that the certificate of incorporation of the surviving corporation shall be its certificate of incorporation. . . .
>
> (e) In the case of a merger, *the certificate of incorporation of the surviving corporation shall automatically be amended to the extent, if any, that changes in the certificate of incorporation are set forth in the agreement of merger.* (emphasis added)

Section 251 thus empowers the board of directors of a corporation to adopt an agreement of merger, which can be used to amend the certificate of incorporation of the surviving entity.

As with Section 242(b)(2), however, Section 251(c) also requires a stockholder vote:

> The agreement required by subsection (b) shall be submitted to the shareholders of each constituent corporation at an annual or special meeting thereof for the purpose of acting on the agreement. . . . If a majority of the outstanding stock of the corporation entitled to vote thereon shall be voted for the adoption of the agreement, that fact shall be certified on the agreement by the secretary or assistant secretary of the corporation. . . If the agreement shall be so adopted and certified by each constituent corporation, it shall then be filed and shall become effective. . . .

Now we get to the interesting part: Unlike Section 242(b)(2), Section 251 contains no requirement of a class or series vote. The affirmative vote of the holders of a simple majority of the outstanding voting stock is sufficient. Accordingly, Section 251 would appear to offer a way around class or series veto rights when proposing an amendment that adversely affects the preferred stock (or a series of preferred stock). For instance, if a company's board of directors and the holders of a majority of its voting stock support a charter amendment that diminishes a preferred stock right, might Section 251 be used to approve the amendment? This question gained heightened relevance as a result of the Great Depression of the 1930's when numerous companies had passed on cumulative preferred dividends. This caused enormous arrearages to build up and these would seemingly need to be paid off before any dividends could be declared for the common stock. As a result, common stock offerings were extremely difficult to complete because these companies could offer no promise of dividends for a very long period. Companies in need of financing thus sought for ways to reduce the amount of accumulated preferred stock dividends.

In Keller v. Wilson, 21 Del. Ch. 391, 190 A. 115 (1936), the Delaware Supreme Court considered a plan of recapitalization that was designed to address this problem. In the recapitalization, the company's existing preferred shares, which at the time had accumulated dividend arrearages of approximately $6 million, would be converted into a new class of preferred stock, thus cancelling the $6 million of arrearages. A similar arrangement was made for a second class of preferred stock, called Class A, which at the time had accumulated dividend arrearages of approximately $6.6 million. In the recapitalization, each Class A share was to be converted into five shares of common stock, which would likewise eliminate the accumulated arrearages. The conversion of the preferred stock and Class A stock was to occur by way of an amendment of the company's certificate of incorporation. The vote in favor of the recapitalization and amendment was approved by the overwhelming vote of each class. Moreover, the Delaware statute had recently been amended to permit a charter amendment that affected the rights of an outstanding class of stock if the amendment was approved by the holders of a majority of the shares of each affected class.

Nonetheless, an objecting holder of Class A stock brought suit to enjoin the recapitalization. The court noted the conventional rule that dividends do not become a liability of the corporation until declared (and no dividends had been declared) and noted the need for corporate flexibility. Yet, while conceding that these dividends were not formally vested property rights because they had not been declared, there were elements of an estoppel theory in the court's opinion insofar that it viewed the cumulative feature of the dividends as an inducement that caused investors to purchase the class. As a result, while the accumulated dividends could not legally become vested property rights until a fund of retained profits existed from which they could be paid, the court concluded that ". . . it is difficult to perceive the justice of permitting the corporation to destroy the opportunity to create the fund by action under a subsequent amendment to the law which, when the corporation was formed and the stock issued, did not permit of such destruction." 190 A. at 124. In short, because the corporate statute at the time the corporation was formed did not permit destruction of accumulated dividends, the court held that the right to accumulated arrearages "be regarded as a vested right of property secured against the destruction by the Federal and State Constitutions." 190 A. at 124–25. The court therefore enjoined the recapitalization.*

In light of the *Keller* decision, an alternative strategy for pruning preferred stock cumulative dividends was taken by the Federal United Corporation. Facing a similar problem of large dividend arrearages, it decided to execute a merger with a wholly owned subsidiary. As a result of this transaction, the old preferred stock and its arrearages were canceled and replaced by new preferred in the merged entity, together with common stock. The preferred shareholders were induced to vote for the merger, in part, by the corporation's promise that dividend payments on the new preferred would begin immediately. In upholding the transaction, the Delaware Supreme Court noted that the preferred shareholders were protected by their appraisal rights, and that the preferred shareholders bought their shares subject to the provisions of Delaware law permitting mergers upon satisfaction of certain conditions. Because of this, there was no vested property right that could permit any preferred shareholders to object to a merger when their financial interests were protected by appraisal. See Federal United Corp. v. Havender, 11 A.2d 331 (Del. 1940).

The doctrine underlying this decision was articulated more clearly by Judge Leahy in Langfelder v. Universal Laboratories, Inc., 68 F. Supp. 209 (D. Del. 1946) (applying Delaware law), involving another merger that eliminated arrearages on cumulative dividends. The opinion stated,

> Under Delaware law, accrued dividends after the passage of time mature into a debt and cannot be eliminated by an amendment to the corporate charter under Sec. 26 of the Delaware Corporation Law. But the right to be paid in full for such dividends, notwithstanding provisions in the charter contract, may be eliminated by means of a merger which meets the standard of fairness. The rationale is that a merger is an act of independent legal significance, and when it meets the requirements of fairness and all other statutory requirements, the merger is valid and not subordinate or dependent upon any other section of the Delaware Corporation Law.

Thus was born Delaware's doctrine of "independent legal significance."

Note that in cases like *Federal United*, the vast majority of preferred stockholders supported altering the preferred stock arrearages. But the company had to turn to a merger because the Delaware statute at the time did not specifically permit amendments that reduced accumulated dividends, as it currently does. See DGCL 242(a)(4). But what about proposed amendments that adversely affect a class of preferred stock and that are *opposed* by a majority of that class? Does the doctrine of

* The 1967 amendments to the DGCL added new section 242(a)(4), which specifically authorizes an amendment "[t]o cancel or otherwise affect the right of the holders of the shares of any class to receive dividends which have accrued but have not been declared."

independent legal significance still apply? If so, how can preferred stockholders protect themselves against adverse changes to their preferred stock rights that might arise through a merger? Consider the following two cases.

Elliott Associates, L.P. v. Avatex Corporation

715 A.2d 843 (Del. 1998)

■ VEASEY, CHIEF JUSTICE.

In this case of first impression, we hold that certain preferred stockholders have the right to a class vote in a merger where: (1) the certificate of incorporation expressly provides such a right in the event of any "amendment, alteration or repeal, whether by merger, consolidation or otherwise" of any of the provisions of the certificate of incorporation; (2) the certificate of incorporation that provides protections for the preferred stock is nullified and thereby repealed by the merger; and (3) the result of the transaction would materially and adversely affect the rights, preferences, privileges or voting power of those preferred stockholders. In so holding, we distinguish prior Delaware precedent narrowly because of the inclusion by the drafters of the phrase, "whether by merger, consolidation or otherwise."

Facts

Defendant Avatex Corporation ("Avatex") is a Delaware corporation that has outstanding both common and preferred stock. The latter includes two distinct series of outstanding preferred stock: "First Series Preferred" and "Series A Preferred." Plaintiffs in these consolidated cases are all preferred stockholders of defendant Avatex. The individual defendants are all members of the Avatex board of directors.

Avatex created and incorporated Xetava Corporation ("Xetava") as its wholly-owned subsidiary on April 13, 1998, and the following day announced its intention to merge with and into Xetava. Under the terms of the proposed merger, Xetava is to be the surviving corporation. Once the transaction is consummated, Xetava will immediately change its name to Avatex Corporation. The proposed merger would cause a conversion of the preferred stock of Avatex into common stock of Xetava. The merger will effectively eliminate Avatex' certificate of incorporation, which includes the certificate of designations creating the Avatex preferred stock and setting forth its rights and preferences. The terms of the merger do not call for a class vote of these preferred stockholders. Herein lies the heart of the legal issue presented in this case.

Plaintiffs filed suit in the Court of Chancery to enjoin the proposed merger, arguing, among other things, that the transaction required the consent of two-thirds of the holders of the First Series Preferred stock. Defendants responded with a motion for judgment on the pleadings, which the Court of Chancery granted, finding that the provisions governing the rights of the First Series Preferred stockholders do not require such consent.

The plaintiffs allege that, because of Avatex' anemic financial state, "all the value of Avatex is [currently] in the preferred stock." By forcing the conversion of the preferred shares into common stock of the surviving corporation, however, the merger would place current preferred stockholders of Avatex on an even footing with its common stockholders. In fact, the Avatex preferred stockholders will receive in exchange for their preferred stock approximately 73% of Xetava common stock, and the common stockholders of Avatex will receive approximately 27% of the common stock of Xetava.

Under the terms of the Avatex certificate of incorporation, First Series stockholders have no right to vote except on:

> (a) any "amendment, alteration or repeal" of the certificate of incorporation "whether by merger, consolidation or otherwise," that
>
> (b) "materially and adversely" affects the rights of the First Series stockholders.

The text of the terms governing the voting rights of the First Series Preferred Stock is set forth in the certificate of designations as follows:

> Except as expressly provided hereinafter in this Section (6) or as otherwise . . . required by law, the First Series Preferred Stock shall have no voting rights. . .
>
> So long as any shares of First Series Preferred Stock remain outstanding, the consent of the holders of at least two-thirds of the shares of the First Series Preferred Stock outstanding at the time (voting separately as a class . . .) . . . shall be necessary to permit, effect or validate any one or more of the following: . . .
>
> (b) The amendment, alteration or repeal, whether by merger, consolidation or otherwise, of any of the provisions of the Restated Certificate of Incorporation or of [the certificate of designations] which would materially and adversely affect any right, preference, privilege or voting power of the First Series Preferred Stock or of the holders thereof. . .[6]

---

6 In addition, Section 4 of the Avatex certificate of incorporation provides, in relevant part:

> So long as any of the preferred stock remains outstanding, the consent of the holders of at least a majority of all outstanding shares of preferred stock . . . shall be necessary for effecting or validating any amendment, alteration or repeal of any of the provisions of this Article [including certain board resolutions] which increase or decrease the par value of the preferred stock or would adversely affect the rights or preferences of the preferred stock, or of the holders thereof. . .

See also 8 Del. C. § 242(b)(2) (providing by statute a class vote in certain circumstances). When an amendment to a certificate of incorporation is sought to be effected under that section:

> The holders of the outstanding shares of a class shall be entitled to vote as a class upon a proposed amendment, whether or not entitled to vote thereon by the certificate of incorporation, if the amendment would increase or decrease the aggregate number of

* * *

This appeal, then, reduces to a narrow legal question: whether the "amendment, alteration or repeal" of the certificate of incorporation is caused "by merger, consolidation or otherwise" thereby requiring a two-thirds class vote of the First Series Preferred stockholders, it being assumed for purposes of this appeal that their rights would be "materially and adversely" affected. The Court of Chancery answered this question in the negative. Although we respect that Court's craftsmanlike analysis, we are constrained to disagree with its conclusion.

Relying primarily on *Warner Communications Inc. v. Chris-Craft Industries Inc.,*[16] the Court of Chancery held that it was only the *conversion* of the stock as a result of the merger, and not the *amendment, alteration or repeal* of the certificate, that would adversely affect the preferred stockholders. It is important to keep in mind, however, that the terms of the preferred stock in *Warner* were significantly different from those present here, because in *Warner* the phrase "whether by merger, consolidation or otherwise" was not included. The issue here, therefore, is whether the presence of this additional phrase in the Avatex certificate is an outcome-determinative distinction from *Warner*.

In *Warner,* the question was whether the Series B preferred stock of Warner Communications, Inc. had the right to a class vote on a proposed merger of Warner with Time, Inc. (renamed Time Warner Inc.) and TW Sub, its wholly-owned subsidiary. As the first step in a two-step transaction, Time had acquired approximately 50% of Warner's common stock in a tender offer. The second step was the "back-end" merger in which TW Sub was merged into Warner, which survived as a wholly-owned subsidiary of Time. The Warner common stock not held by Time was converted into cash, securities and other property. In the merger, the Warner Series B preferred would be converted into Time Series BB preferred stock. The parties stipulated that the Warner Series B stockholders would thereby be adversely affected.

The Chancellor held that the drafters of the Warner Series B certificate of designations did not intend for two-thirds of the Series B stockholders to have a veto over every merger in which their interest

---

authorized shares of such class, increase or decrease the par value of the shares of such class, or alter or change the powers, preferences, or special rights of the shares of such class so as to affect them adversely.

Id. Because the merger here implicates a different statute (8 Del. C. § 251, which does not itself require a class vote), the provisions of Section 242 are not implicated, the two statutes being of independent legal significance. See Warner Communications Inc. v. Chris-Craft Indus., Inc., Del. Ch., 583 A.2d 962, 970, aff'd, Del. Supr., 567 A.2d 419 (1989). Likewise, Section 4 of the Avatex certificate is not applicable. Similarly, the Avatex Series A Preferred stock, which is not implicated in this appeal, has the right to a two-thirds class vote if the corporation seeks to "amend, alter, repeal or waive" any provision of the certificate of incorporation. But the additional language of the First Series Preferred, "whether by merger, consolidation or otherwise," significantly is missing from the rights granted to the Series A Preferred.

16 583 A.2d 962.

would be adversely affected because the right to vote was conferred expressly (as it must under Delaware law), and "only in narrowly defined circumstances . . . not present here." The two provisions in the certificate of designations involved in *Warner* were as follows. Section 3.3 provided:

> So long as any shares of Series B Stock shall be outstanding and unless the consent or approval of a greater number of shares shall then be required by law, . . . the affirmative vote or written consent of the holders of at least two-thirds of the total number of the then outstanding shares of Series B Stock . . . voting as a class, shall be necessary to alter or change any rights, preferences or limitations of the Preferred Stock so as to affect the holders of all such shares adversely. . .

Section 3.4 provided:

> So long as any shares of Series B Stock shall be outstanding and unless the consent or approval of a greater number of shares shall then be required by law, without first obtaining the consent or approval of the holders of at least two-thirds of the number of shares of the Series B Stock . . . the Corporation shall not (i) amend, alter or repeal any of the provisions of the Certificate of Incorporation or By-laws of the Corporation so as to affect adversely any of the preferences, rights, powers or privileges of the Series B Stock or the holders thereof. . .

We note again that nowhere in the Series B certificate of designations was found the phrase "by merger, consolidation or otherwise," which is the key phrase in the present case. Nevertheless, the heart of the Warner rationale, which we must address here, is that it was not the amendment, alteration or repeal of the Warner certificate that adversely affected the Warner Series B stock. The Chancellor held that it was only the conversion of the Warner Series B Preferred to Time Series BB Preferred that caused the adverse effect, and, moreover, that the conversion was permissible under 8 Del. C. § 251, which (unlike 8 Del. C. § 242) does not require a class vote on a merger. Further, the Chancellor held that no contractual protection of the Warner Series B stock provided for a class vote on a merger. The Chancellor summarized his rationale in Warner as follows:

> 1. Section 3.4(i) does not create a right to a class vote on the proposed merger despite the fact that Warner's certificate of incorporation is being amended in the merger because, in the circumstances, the amendment itself will not "adversely affect" the Series B Preferred.
>
> 2. The same reasoning that supports the conclusion that the proposed merger does not trigger a class vote under Section 3.4(i) requires an identical conclusion with respect to 3.3(i).
>
> 3. If the amendment of Warner's certificate does not trigger the class vote provisions of either 3.4(i) or 3.3(i), the dispositive

question becomes whether the merger itself may trigger that result under the language of Section 3.3(i). Stated differently, the core issue here may be said to be whether the predicate words of Section 3.3(i), "alter or change," are to be read to include "convert pursuant to a merger." I conclude that Section 3.3(i) does not create a right to a class vote on a merger that will convert the Series B Preferred stock into other securities, other property or cash.

In more detail, he continued:

Section 3.4(i) provides a right to a series vote . . . in the event of a charter amendment that amends, alters or repeals any provision of the certificate of incorporation so as to adversely affect the Series B Preferred or its holders.

Warner will be the surviving corporation in the proposed merger. Its charter will be amended in the merger. . . Nevertheless, Section 3.4(i) does not, in my opinion, grant a right to a series vote in these circumstances because the adverse effect upon defendants is not caused by an amendment, alteration or repeal of any provision of Warner's certificate of incorporation. Rather it is the conversion of the Warner Series B Preferred into Time Series BB Preferred that creates the adverse effect. * * *

This conclusion is further supported by a review of other provisions of the certificate of designation. . . The drafters did expressly address the possibility of a merger in connection with the very question of a class vote by the preferred and adopted the limited protection afforded by Section 3.4(iii):

> Without . . . consent . . . of the Series B Stock . . . the Corporation shall not . . . (iii) be a party to any transaction involving a merger, consolidation or sale . . . in which the shares of Series B Stock . . . are converted into the right to receive equity securities of the surviving, resulting or acquiring corporation . . . unless such corporation shall have, after such merger, consolidation or sale, no equity securities either authorized or outstanding . . . ranking prior, as to dividends or in liquidation, to the Series B Stock or to the stock of the surviving, resulting or acquiring corporation issued in exchange therefor.

Plaintiffs here argue that *Warner* is distinguishable for three reasons: (1) the fact that the words "whether by merger, consolidation or otherwise" were not present in the Warner Series B certificate; (2) in *Warner,* unlike here, the preferred stockholders did not remain as stockholders of the surviving corporation, whose certificate arguably was amended and on which the preferred stockholders in *Warner* were relying for a right to a class vote; and (3) in *Warner,* unlike here, the merger was not an attempt simply to change the rights of the preferred stock, but rather there was economic and business substance to that transaction beyond an effort to do indirectly what could not be done directly.

In our view, only the first reason is valid in this appeal. * * *

The relevant statutory provisions are found in Sections 251(b) and 251(e) of the Delaware General Corporation Law ("DGCL"), which provide, in pertinent part:

> § 251. Merger or consolidation of domestic corporations.
>
> * * *
>
> (b) The board of directors of each corporation which desires to merge or consolidate shall adopt a resolution approving an agreement of merger or consolidation. The agreement shall state: (1) The terms and conditions of the merger or consolidation; (2) the mode of carrying the same into effect; (3) in the case of a merger, such amendments or changes in the certificate of incorporation of the surviving corporation as are desired to be effected by the merger, or, if no such amendments or changes are desired, a statement that the certificate of incorporation of the surviving corporation shall be its certificate of incorporation; (4) in the case of a consolidation, that the certificate of incorporation of the resulting corporation shall be as is set forth in an attachment to the agreement; (5) the manner of converting the shares of each of the constituent corporations into shares or other securities of the corporation surviving or resulting from the merger or consolidation and, if any shares of any of the constituent corporations are not to be converted solely into shares or other securities of the surviving or resulting corporation, the cash, property, rights or securities of any other corporation or entity which the holders of such shares are to receive in exchange . . .; and (6) such other details or provisions as are deemed desirable. . .
>
> * * *
>
> (e) In the case of a merger, the certificate of incorporation of the surviving corporation shall automatically be amended to the extent, if any, that changes in the certificate of incorporation are set forth in the agreement of merger.

In short, Section 251 of the DGCL describes three ways that a merger or consolidation can affect the certificate of a constituent corporation:

(1) Section 251(b)(3) Amendments. First, the merger agreement may call for amendments to the pre-existing certificate of the surviving corporation.

(2) Displacement and Substitution by Merger. Second, the merger can designate the certificate of one of the constituent corporations as the

certificate of the surviving entity, and thereby render the certificate of every other constituent corporation a legal nullity.

(3) Displacement and Substitution via Consolidation. Finally, in the case of a consolidation, the certificate of the resulting corporation displaces and renders a legal nullity the certificate of every disappearing constituent corporation.

In speaking of the "amendment, alteration or repeal" of the Avatex certificate by "merger, consolidation or otherwise," the drafters must have been referring to some or all of the events permitted by Section 251. Therefore, Section 251 provides the relevant backdrop for the interpretation of the First Series Preferred voting rights.

Avatex argued below, and the Court of Chancery appears to have agreed, that *only* a Section 251(b)(3) Amendment to the surviving corporation's charter amounts to an "amendment, alteration or repeal" within the meaning of the provisions defining the voting rights of the preferred stockholders. Accordingly, the argument runs, these provisions would apply *only* in the circumstance (not present here) where Avatex survives the merger and its certificate is amended thereby. Since the proposed merger with Xetava does not contemplate any such amendments to the disappearing Avatex certificate, the argument goes, the transaction can go forward without a First Series class vote.

The difficulty with this reading is that it fails to account for the word *consolidation,* which appears in the phrase "by merger, consolidation or otherwise." A consolidation cannot entail a Section 251(b)(3) Amendment because in a consolidation there is no "surviving corporation" whose pre-existing certificate is subject to amendment. The resulting corporation in a consolidation is a completely new entity with a new certificate of incorporation. All the certificates of the constituent corporations simply become legal nullities in a consolidation. In short, Avatex' proposed reading of the relevant provisions would render the word *consolidation* mere surplusage, and is problematic for that reason.[37]

Although the transaction before us is not a consolidation, the drafters' use of the word *consolidation* is significant. They must have intended the First Series Preferred stockholders to have the right to vote on at least some mergers or other transactions whereby the Avatex certificate—and indeed, Avatex itself—would simply disappear. Consolidation, by definition, implicates the disappearance of all constituent corporations. Here, Avatex disappears, just as it would in a consolidation. Under the terms of the proposed merger, Xetava will be the surviving entity and, since Avatex will cease its independent existence, its certificate becomes a legal nullity, as defendants concede. In our view, this constitutes a repeal, if not an amendment or alteration.

---

[37] *See Sonitrol Holding Co. v. Marceau Investissements,* Del. Supr., 607 A.2d 1177, 1184 (1992) (under "cardinal rule of contract construction," court should give effect to all contract provisions).

Thus, the proposed merger is potentially within the class of events that trigger First Series Preferred voting rights.

The first question is: What will happen as a result of the merger to the "rights, preferences, privileges or voting power" of the Avatex First Series Preferred stock as set forth in the existing Avatex certificate? They disappear when the preferred stockholders of Avatex become common stockholders of Xetava under its certificate that does not contain those protections. We assume, as did the trial court, that their elimination would affect the First Series Preferred stockholders adversely.

The second question is: What act or event will cause this adverse effect if the merger is consummated? The trial court held that, "as in Warner," the adverse effect on the plaintiffs "will not flow from any 'amendment, alteration or repeal' of the First Series Certificate (however accomplished) but from the conversion into common stock of the First Series Preferred in the Proposed Merger." The Court so held notwithstanding that it had noted the distinguishing language of the certificate here—not present in *Warner*—"whether by merger, consolidation or otherwise." But the Court dismissed this distinction by concluding that this "language only modifies the phrase 'amendment, alteration and repeal' and does not independently create a right to a class vote in the case of *every merger.*" But that is not the issue here where there is no contention that the First Series Preferred have a right to a class vote on *every merger*.

* * *

In our view, the Court of Chancery misapplied *Warner's* holding that "the amendment contemplated [as a "housekeeping" measure post-merger] is necessitated by the merger [and the] amendment, like the conversion, flows from the merger and is not a necessary condition of it." This was the case in *Warner,* but is not here. The error of the trial court here was in its conclusion that the observation in *Warner* quoted above "is at least equally apposite here, where *Avatex* is to be merged with and into Xetava and will simply cease to maintain a separate corporate existence as a matter of law, without the necessity of any amendment, alteration or repeal" of the certificate.

In our view, the merger does cause the adverse effect because the merger is the corporate act that renders the Avatex certificate that protects the preferred stockholders a "legal nullity," in defendants' words. That elimination certainly fits within the ambit of one or more of the three terms in the certificate: *amendment* or *alteration* or *repeal.* The word *repeal* is especially fitting in this context because it contemplates a nullification, which is what defendants concede happens to the Avatex certificate.

* * *

In our view, the rights of the First Series Preferred are expressly and clearly stated in the Avatex certificate. The drafters of this instrument could not reasonably have intended any consequence other than granting to the First Series Preferred stock the right to consent by a two-thirds class vote to any merger that would result in the elimination of the protections in the Avatex certificate if the rights of the holders of that stock would thereby be adversely affected. The First Series Preferred stock rights granted by the corporate drafters here are the functional equivalent of a provision that would expressly require such consent if a merger were to eliminate any provision of the Avatex certificate resulting in materially adverse consequences to the holders of that security.

The drafters were navigating around several alternatives. First, all parties agree that pure amendment protection available to the First Series Preferred stockholders as granted by Section 242(b)(2) of the DGCL and Section 4 of the certificate does not—absent the very phrase at issue here—apply to this merger. Although *Warner* was decided after the Avatex certificate of designations became effective, *Warner* clearly supports this view and it continues to be valid precedent for that proposition. Second, all parties agree that if Avatex would have been the survivor, and its certificate were amended in the merger as contemplated by 8 *Del. C.* § 251(c)(3), the First Series Preferred would have the right to consent by two-thirds class vote. * * *

If Section 6 of the certificate does not guarantee a class vote to the First Series Preferred in this merger, what could it conceivably be interpreted to mean? Defendants argue that the certificate can be construed to apply *only* in the second instance noted above—namely, in the case where Avatex is the survivor and *its* certificate is amended, altered or repealed, as contemplated by Section 251(b)(3). But, as plaintiffs point out, this cannot be the *only* outcome the drafters intended because the certificate grants the First Series Preferred this protection in a consolidation where Section 251(b)(3) does not apply. Because the word *consolidation* is included, it cannot reasonably be argued that the protections of Section 6 of the certificate applicable to the First Series Preferred are confined to a Section 251(b)(3) amendment. Therefore, the term *consolidation* cannot be ignored or wished away as surplusage, as defendants argue. It is well established that a court interpreting any contractual provision, including preferred stock provisions, must give effect to all terms of the instrument, must read the instrument as a whole, and, if possible, reconcile all the provisions of the instrument.

Conclusion

The Court of Chancery held, and defendants contend on appeal that *Warner* compels a different result from that which we reach because *Warner* held that there it was only the stock conversion, not the amendment that adversely affected the preferred. But the short answer here is that the language of the First Series Preferred stock is materially different from the language in *Warner* because here we have the phrase, "whether by merger, consolidation or otherwise." This provision entirely changes the analysis and compels the result we hold today. Here, the repeal of the certificate and the stock conversion cause the adverse effect.

It is important to place what we decide today in proper perspective. The outcome here continues a coherent and rational approach to corporate finance.[51] The contrary result, in our view, would create an anomaly and could risk the erosion of uniformity in the corporation law. The Court of Chancery was mindful of this concern in referring to our general observations in *Kaiser* that the courts should avoid creating enduring uncertainties as to the meaning of boilerplate provisions in financial instruments. To be sure, there are some boilerplate aspects to the preferred stock provisions in the Avatex certificate and those found in other cases. But one is struck by the disuniformity of some crucial provisions, such as the differences that exist when one compares the provisions in *Warner* and *Sullivan* with those presented here. That lack of uniformity is no doubt a function of (a) the adaptations by different drafters of some standard provisions; (b) negotiations by preferred stock investors seeking certain protections; (c) poor drafting; or (d) some combination of the above. The difference between the provisions in the Warner certificate and the Avatex provisions are outcome-determinative because we find there is no reasonable interpretation of the Avatex certificate that would deny the First Series Preferred a class vote on an "amendment, alteration or repeal . . . by merger, consolidation or otherwise" of the protective provisions of the Avatex certificate.

The path for future drafters to follow in articulating class vote provisions is clear. When a certificate (like the Warner certificate or the Series A provisions here) grants only the right to vote on an amendment, alteration or repeal, the preferred have no class vote in a merger. When a certificate (like the First Series Preferred certificate here) adds the terms "whether by merger, consolidation or otherwise" and a merger results in an amendment, alteration or repeal that causes an adverse effect on the preferred, there would be a class vote. When a certificate grants the preferred a class vote in any merger or in any merger where the preferred stockholders receive a junior security, such provisions are broader than those involved in the First Series Preferred certificate. We agree with plaintiffs' argument that these results are uniform,

---

[51] *See* [Richard M. Buxbaum, *Preferred Stock-Law and Draftsmanship*, 42 CAL. L. REV 242, 243 (1954)]:

> PREFERRED STOCK is an anomalous security. It is a debt security when it claims certain absolute rights. . . It is an equity security when it tries to control the enterprise through a practical voting procedure or to share in excess distributions of corporation profits. Of course, a share of preferred stock is actually a composite of many rights.
>
> * * *
>
> The primary source of a share's legal rights is the share contract. There is no ideal preferred stock but only a collection of attributes which the share contract says makes up a share of preferred stock. The share contract, in turn, is found in the articles of incorporation and the applicable state statutes.

(footnotes omitted).

predictable and consistent with existing law relating to the unique attributes of preferred stock.

The judgment of the Court of Chancery is reversed and the matter is remanded for further proceedings consistent with this Opinion.

QUESTIONS

1. The court concludes that "[t]he path for future drafters to follow in articulating class veto provisions is clear." What does it mean by this?
2. The court rejected Avatex's argument that § 251(b)(3) provides that only a merger in which Avatex is the surviving corporation would amend or alter the certificate of incorporation and require a preferred shareholder vote. The court rejects this argument because it ignores the language in the charter that states "by merger, *consolidation* or otherwise." (Emphasis added) Why does the inclusion of the word "consolidation" in this phrase have so much importance for the court?
3. What is a "consolidation"? It is not a defined term in the DGCL. It nearly always appears as part of the phrase "merger or consolidation." The only statutory hint appears in § 252(c)(5). How does the court describe a consolidation?
4. If the holders of First Preferred wanted to avoid adverse changes to the terms of the First Preferred, why not simply draft the veto right to cover "any corporate action that would materially and adversely affect any right, preference, privilege or voting power of the First Series Preferred Stock or of the holders thereof"? Do you think the court would find that this language covers the transaction at issue in *Avatex*?

Benchmark Capital Partners IV, L.P. v. Vague

2002 WL 1732423 (Del. Ch.)

■ NOBLE, VICE CHANCELLOR.

I. Introduction

This is another one of those cases in which sophisticated investors have negotiated protective provisions in a corporate charter to define the balance of power or certain economic rights as between the holders of junior preferred stock and senior preferred stock. These provisions tend to come in to play when additional financing becomes necessary. One side cannot or will not put up more money; the other side is willing to put up more money, but will not do so without obtaining additional control or other diminution of the rights of the other side. In short, these cases focus on the tension between minority rights established through the corporate charter and the corporation's need for additional capital.

In this case, Plaintiff Benchmark Capital Partners IV, L.P. ("Benchmark") invested in the first two series of the Defendant Juniper

Financial Corp.'s ("Juniper") preferred stock. When additional capital was required, Defendant Canadian Imperial Bank of Commerce ("CIBC") was an able and somewhat willing investor. As a result of that investment, Benchmark's holdings were relegated to the status of junior preferred stock and CIBC acquired a controlling interest in Juniper by virtue of ownership of senior preferred stock. The lot of a holder of junior preferred stock is not always a happy one. Juniper's Fifth Amendment and Restated Certificate of Incorporation (the "Certificate") contains several provisions to protect the holders of junior preferred stock from abuse by the holder of senior preferred stock. Two of those provisions are of particular importance here. The Certificate grants the junior preferred stockholders a series vote on corporate actions that would "[m]aterially adversely change the rights, preferences and privileges of the [series of junior preferred stock]." In addition, the junior preferred stockholders are entitled to a class vote before Juniper may "[a]uthorize or issue, or obligate itself to issue, any other equity security . . . senior to or on a parity with the [junior preferred stock]."

The Certificate provides that those provisions protecting the rights of the junior preferred stockholders may be waived by CIBC. CIBC may not, however, exercise this power "if such amendment, waiver or modification would . . . diminish or alter the liquidation preference or other financial or economic rights" of the junior preferred stockholders or would shelter breaches of fiduciary duties.

Juniper now must seek more capital in order to satisfy regulators and business requirements, and CIBC, and apparently only CIBC, is willing to provide the necessary funds. Juniper initially considered amending its charter to allow for the issuance of another series of senior preferred stock. When it recognized that the protective provisions of the Certificate could be invoked to thwart that strategy, it elected to structure a more complicated transaction that now consists principally of a merger and a sale of Series D Preferred Stock to CIBC. The merger is scheduled to occur on July 16, 2002 with a subsidiary merging with and into Juniper that will leave Juniper as the surviving corporation, but with a restated certificate of incorporation that will authorize the issuance of a new series of senior preferred stock and new junior preferred stock with a reduced liquidation preference and will cause a number of other adverse consequences or limitations to be suffered by the holders of the junior preferred. As part of this overall financing transaction, Juniper, after the merger, intends to issue a new series of preferred, the Series D Preferred Stock, to CIBC in exchange for a $50 million capital contribution. As the result of this sequence of events, the equity holdings of the junior preferred stockholders will be reduced from approximately 29% to 7%. Juniper will not obtain approval for these actions from the holders of the junior preferred stock. It contends that the protective provisions do not give the junior preferred stockholders a vote on these plans . . .

Benchmark, on the other hand, asserts that the protective provisions preclude Juniper's and CIBC's heavy-handed conduct and brings this action to prevent the violation of the junior preferred stockholder's fundamental right to vote on these corporate actions as provided in the Certificate and to obtain interim protection from the planned evisceration of its equity interest in Juniper.

III. Factual Background

A. Benchmark and CIBC Invest in Juniper

Benchmark became the initial investor in Juniper when in June 2000, it invested $20 million and, in exchange, was issued Series A Preferred Shares. Juniper raised an additional $95.5 million in August 2000 by issuing its Series B Preferred Shares. Benchmark contributed $5 million in this effort. It soon became necessary for Juniper to obtain even more capital. Efforts to raise additional funds from existing investors and efforts to find new potential investors were unavailing until June 2001 when CIBC and Juniper agreed that CIBC would invest $27 million in Juniper through a mandatory convertible note while CIBC evaluated Juniper to assess whether it was interested in acquiring the company. CIBC also agreed to provide additional capital through a Series C financing in the event that it chose not to acquire Juniper and if Juniper's efforts to find other sources for the needed funding were unsuccessful.

In July 2001, CIBC advised Juniper that it would not seek to acquire Juniper. After reviewing its options for other financing, Juniper called upon CIBC to invest the additional capital. The terms of the Series C financing were negotiated during the latter half of the summer of 2001. A representative of Benchmark, J. William Gurley, and its attorney were active participants in these negotiations. Through the Series C Transaction, which closed on September 18, 2001, CIBC invested $145 million (including the $27 million already delivered to Juniper). With its resulting Series C Preferred holdings, CIBC obtained a majority of the voting power in Juniper on an as-converted basis and a majority of the voting power of Juniper's preferred stock. CIBC also acquired the right to select six of the eleven members of Juniper's board. As required by Juniper's then existing certificate of incorporation, the approval of the holders of Series A Preferred and Series B Preferred Stock, including Benchmark, was obtained in order to close the Series C Transaction.

B. The Certificate's Protective Provisions

Juniper's Certificate protects the holders of Series A Preferred and Series B Preferred from risks associated with the issuance of any additional equity security that would be senior to those shares by requiring their prior approval through a separate class vote as prescribed in Section C.6.a(i):

> So long as any shares of Series A Preferred Stock or Series B Preferred Stock remain outstanding, the Corporation shall not, without the vote or written consent by the holders of at least a

> majority of the then outstanding shares of the Series A Preferred Stock and Series B Preferred Stock, voting together as a single class; provided, however, that the foregoing may be amended, waived or modified pursuant to Section C.4.c: (i) Authorize or issue, or obligate itself to issue, any other equity security (including any security convertible into or exercisable for any equity security) senior to or on a parity with the Series A Preferred Stock or Series B Preferred Stock as to dividend rights or redemption rights, voting rights or liquidation preferences (other than the Series C Preferred Stock and Series C Prime Preferred Stock sold pursuant to, or issued upon the conversion of the shares sold pursuant to, the Series C Preferred Stock Purchase Agreement . . .)

Under Section C.6.a(ii), Juniper also must provide the holders of the junior preferred stock with a class vote before it may proceed to dispose of all or substantially all of its assets or to "consolidate or merge into any other Corporation (other than a wholly-owned subsidiary Corporation)."

Because CIBC was investing a substantial sum in Juniper, it insisted upon greater control than it would have obtained if these voting provisions (and other comparable provisions) could be exercised without limitation by the holders of Series A Preferred and Series B Preferred shares as a class. Thus, it sought and obtained a concession from the Series A Preferred and Series B Preferred holders that it could amend, waive, or modify, inter alia, the protective provisions of Section C.6. [Eds. This right was contained in Section C.4.c of the Certificate, referenced in Section C.6.a above.] The right of CIBC to waive the voting rights of the Series A Preferred and Series B Preferred holders was limited by excluding from the scope of the waiver authority any action that "would (a) diminish or alter the liquidation preference or other financial or economic rights, modify the registration rights, or increase the obligations, indemnities or liabilities, of the holders of Series A Preferred Stock, Series A Prime Preferred Stock or Series B Preferred Stock or (b) authorize, approve or waive any action so as to violate any fiduciary duties owed by such holders under Delaware law."

Another protection afforded the holders of both the Series A Preferred and Series B Preferred Stock was set forth in Sections C.6.c(ii) & C.6.d(ii) of the Certificate. Those provisions require a vote of the holders of each series, provided that the requirement for a series vote was not amended or waived by CIBC in accordance with Section C.4.c, if that corporate action would "[m]aterially adversely change the rights, preferences and privileges of the Series A Preferred [and Series B] Preferred Stock."

C. Additional Financing Becomes Necessary

By early 2002, Juniper was advising its investors that even more capital would be necessary to sustain the venture. Because Juniper is in the banking business, the consequences of a capital shortage are not merely those of the typical business. Capital shortfall for a banking entity may carry the potential for significant and adverse regulatory action. Regulated not only by the Federal Reserve Board and the Federal Deposit Insurance Corporation but also by the Delaware Banking Commissioner, Juniper is required to maintain a "well-capitalized" status. Failure to maintain that standard (or to effect a prompt cure) may result in, among other things, regulatory action, conversion of the preferred stock into a "senior common stock" which could [then] be subjected to the imposition of additional security through the regulatory authorities, and the loss of the right to issue Visa cards and to have its customers serviced through the Visa card processing system.

Juniper, with the assistance of an investment banking firm, sought additional investors. The holders of the Series A Preferred and Series B Preferred Stock, including Benchmark, were also solicited. Those efforts failed, thus leaving CIBC as the only identified and viable participant available for the next round of financing, now known as the Series D Transaction.

D. The Series D Preferred Transaction

Thus, Juniper turned to consideration of CIBC's proposal, first submitted through a term sheet on March 15, 2002, to finance $50 million through the issuance of Series D Preferred Stock that would grant CIBC an additional 23% of Juniper on a fully-diluted basis and reduce the equity interests of the Series A Preferred and Series B Preferred holders from approximately 29% to 7%.

The board, in early April 2002, appointed a special committee to consider the CIBC proposal.[14] As the result of the negotiations among Juniper, the special committee, and CIBC, the special committee was able to recommend the Series D Transaction with CIBC.

In general terms, the Series D Transaction consists of the following three steps:

1. Juniper will carry out a 100-1 reverse stock split of its common stock.

2. Juniper Merger Corp., a subsidiary of Juniper established for these purposes, will be merged with and into Juniper which will be the surviving corporation. The certificate of incorporation will be revised as part of the merger.

[14] The special committee consisted of Mr. Tolleson, who Benchmark challenges as a friend and colleague of Mr. Vague, and two directors who were appointed to the board by the Series A Preferred and the Series B Preferred stockholders in accordance with the Prior Investors' Rights Agreement. Benchmark has not challenged the independence of these two directors. Benchmark, however, does challenge the authority and the performance of the special committee, but Benchmark has not advanced those arguments in support of its pending application for a preliminary injunction. [Eds. Richard Vague was a co-founder and CEO of the company.]

3. Series D Preferred Stock will be issued to CIBC (and, at least in theory, those other holders of Series A, B and C Preferred who may exercise preemptive rights) for $50 million.

Each share of existing Series A Preferred and each share of existing Series B Preferred will be converted into one share of new Series A Preferred or Series B Preferred, respectively, and the holders of the existing junior preferred will also receive, for each share, a warrant to purchase a small fraction of a share of common stock in Juniper and a smaller fraction of a share of common stock in Juniper. A small amount of cash will also be paid. Juniper will receive no capital infusion as a direct result of the merger. Although the existing Series A Preferred and Series B Preferred shares will cease to exist and the differences between the new and distinct Series A Preferred and Series B Preferred shares will be significant,[20] the resulting modification of Juniper's certificate of incorporation will not alter the class and series votes required by Section C.6. The changes to Juniper's charter as the result of the merger include, inter alia, authorization of the issuance of Series D Preferred Shares, which will be senior to the newly created Series A Preferred and Series B Preferred Stock with respect to, for example, liquidation preferences, dividends, and as applicable, redemption rights. Also the Series D Stock will be convertible into common stock at a higher ratio than the existing or newly created Series A Preferred and Series B Preferred Stock, thereby providing for a currently greater voting power. In general terms, the equity of the existing Series A Preferred and Series B Preferred holders will be reduced from approximately 29% before the merger to approximately 7% after the Series D financing, and CIBC will hold more than 90% of Juniper's voting power.

IV. Contentions of the Parties

Benchmark begins its effort to earn a preliminary injunction by arguing that the junior preferred stockholders are entitled to a vote on the merger on a series basis under Sections C.6.c(ii) & C.6.d(ii) because the merger adversely affects, inter alia, their liquidation preference and dividend rights and on a class basis under Section C.6.a(i) because the merger, through changes to Juniper's capital structure as set forth in its revised certificate of incorporation, will authorize the issuance of a senior preferred security.[23] Benchmark also invokes its right to a class vote to

---

[20] For example, the holders of the newly created Series A Preferred and Series B Preferred Stock will have an aggregate liquidation preference of $15 million as compared to the liquidation preference of the existing Series A Preferred and Series B Preferred holders of approximately $115 million. Moreover, "[t]he dividend payable . . . to the holders of the New Series A Stock will be reduced from $0.1068 per share to $0.020766 per share and the dividend payable . . . to the holders of the New Series B Preferred Stock will be reduced from $0.23 per share to $0.030268 per share." The redemption rights and other preferences of the existing Series A Preferred and Series B Preferred holders will similarly be compromised by the conversion to the New Series A Preferred and New Series B Preferred Stock as a result of the merger. Finally, the New Series A Preferred and New Series B Preferred Stock will be subordinate to another series of preferred stock, the Series D Preferred Stock.

[23] While the Verified Complaint asserts general fiduciary duty and disclosure claims relating to the alleged scheme to dilute wrongfully the interests of the junior preferred

challenge the Series D Purchase Agreement under Section C.6.a(i) because that agreement obligates Juniper to issue a senior preferred security. . .

In response, Juniper and CIBC argue that the junior preferred stockholders are not entitled to a class or series vote on any aspect of the Series D financing, particularly the merger. The adverse effects of the transaction arise from the merger and not from any separate amendment of the certificate of incorporation, which would have required the exercise of the junior preferred stockholders' voting rights. Juniper and CIBC emphasize that none of the junior preferred stock protective provisions expressly applies to mergers.

V. Analysis

* * *

B. Reasonable Probability of Success on the Merits

1. General Principles of Construction

[A court's function in ascertaining the rights of preferred stockholders] is essentially one of contract interpretation against the background of Delaware precedent. These precedential parameters are simply stated: Any rights, preferences and limitations of preferred stock that distinguish that stock from common stock must be expressly and clearly stated, as provided by statute. Therefore, these rights, preferences and liquidations will not be presumed or implied.[29]

These principles also apply in construing the relative rights of holders of different series of preferred stock.

2. Challenges to the Merger

Benchmark presents two distinct challenges to the merger. First, it argues that Section C.6.c(ii), which protects the rights of the holders of Series A Preferred, and Section C.6.d(ii), which protects the rights of the holders of Series B Preferred, preclude the merger without a series vote because the merger "[m]aterially adversely changes the rights, preferences and privileges" of those classes of preferred stock. Second, Benchmark asserts that the merger cannot go forward, without a class vote by the holders of the Series A Preferred and Series B Preferred Stock combined, because of Section C.6.a(i), which precludes the authorization of a senior preferred stock without such a vote. The Series D Preferred Stock, when issued, will have rights superior to the Series A Preferred and Series B Preferred Stock, either in existing form or in the post-merger form. Because the merger agreement provides the mechanism for the authorization of the Series D Preferred Stock through the

stockholders, Benchmark has not relied upon these claims in pursuing its application for a preliminary injunction.

29 Elliot Assocs., L.P. v. Avatex Corp., 715 A.2d 843, 852–53 (Del. 1998) (footnotes omitted). See 8 Del. C. § 151. The Supreme Court in Avatex further noted that "strict construction" as an analytical methodology is "problematic" in interpreting such provisions in corporate charters. See id. at 853 n. 46.

accompanying restatement of Juniper's certificate of incorporation, it falls within the reach of Section C.6.a(i), or so Benchmark argues.

a. Merger as Changing the Rights, Preferences and Privileges

Benchmark looks at the Series D Preferred financing and the merger that is integral to that transaction and concludes that the authorization of the Series D Preferred Stock and the other revisions to the Juniper certificate of incorporation accomplished as part of the merger will materially adversely affect the rights, preferences, and privileges of the junior preferred shares. Among the adverse affects to be suffered by Benchmark are a significant reduction in its right to a liquidation preference, the authorization of a new series of senior preferred stock that will further subordinate its interests in Juniper, and a reduction in other rights such as dividend priority. These adverse consequences will all be the product of the merger. Benchmark's existing Series A Preferred and Series B Preferred shares will cease to exist as of the merger and will be replaced with new Series A Preferred Stock, new Series B Preferred Stock, warrants, common stock, and a small amount of cash. One of the terms governing the new junior preferred stock will specify that those new junior preferred shares are not merely subordinate to Series C Preferred Stock, but they also will be subordinate to the new Series D Preferred Stock. Thus, the harm to Benchmark is directly attributable to the differences between the new junior preferred stock, authorized through the merger, and the old junior preferred stock as evidenced by the planned post-merger capital structure of Juniper.

Benchmark's challenge is confronted by a long line of Delaware cases[32] which, in general terms, hold that protective provisions drafted to provide a class of preferred stock with a class vote before those shares' rights, preferences and privileges may be altered or modified do not fulfill their apparent purpose of assuring a class vote if adverse consequences flow from a merger and the protective provisions do not expressly afford protection against a merger. This result traces back to the language of 8 Del. C. § 242(b)(2), which deals with the rights of various classes of stock to vote on amendments to the certificate of incorporation that would "alter or change the powers, preferences, or special rights of the shares of such class so as to affect them adversely." That language is substantially the same as the language ("rights, preferences and privileges") of Sections C.6.c(ii) & C.6.d(ii). Where the drafters have tracked the statutory language relating to charter amendments in 8 Del. C. § 242(b), courts have been reluctant to expand those restrictions to encompass the separate process of merger as set forth in 8 Del. C. § 251,

[32] See Avatex, 715 A.2d 842; Warner Communications, Inc. v. Chris-Craft Indus., Inc., 583 A.2d 962 (Del. Ch. 1989), aff'd, 567 A.2d 419 (Del. 1989); Sullivan Money Mgmt., Inc. v. FLS Holdings, Inc., Del Ch, C.A. No. 12731, mem. op., Jacobs, V.C. (Nov. 20, 1992), aff'd, 628 A.2d 84 (Del.1993); Starkman v. United Parcel Service of America, Inc., Del. Ch., C.A. No. 17747, Lamb, V.C. (Oct. 18, 1999) (transcript of oral ruling).

unless the drafters have made clear the intention to grant a class vote in the context of a merger.

> The draftsmen of this language . . . must be deemed to have understood, and no doubt did understand, that under Delaware law (and generally) the securities whose characteristics were being defined in the certificate of designation could be converted by merger into "shares or other securities of the corporation surviving or resulting from [a] merger or consolidation" or into "cash, property, rights or securities of any other corporation." 8 Del. C. § 251(b); Federal United Corporation v. Havender, Del. Supr., 11 A.2d 331 (1940). . . .

The range of Sections C.6.c(ii) and C.6.d(ii) is not expressly limited to changes in the Certificate. However, given the well established case law construing the provisions of certificates of incorporations and the voting rights of classes of preferred stockholders, I am satisfied that the language chosen by the drafters (i.e., the "rights, preferences, and privileges") must be understood as those rights, preferences and privileges which are subject to change through a certificate of incorporation amendment under the standards of 8 Del. C. § 242(b) and not the standards of 8 Del. C. § 251.

Finally, the corporate charter of Juniper was adopted after our Supreme Court's decision in Avatex and the drafters of the Certificate are charged with knowledge of its holding and the following:

> The path for future drafters to follow in articulating class vote provisions is clear. Where a certificate (like the Warner certificate or the Series A provisions here) grants only the right to vote on an amendment, alteration or repeal, the preferred have no class vote in a merger. When a certificate (like the First Series Preferred certificate here) adds the terms "whether by merger, consolidation or otherwise" and a merger results in an amendment, alteration or repeal that causes an adverse effect on the preferred, there would be a class vote.[38]

In short, to the extent that the merger adversely affects the rights, preferences and privileges of either the Series A Preferred or Series B Preferred Stock, those consequences are the product of a merger, a corporate event which the drafters of the protective provision could have addressed, but did not. Accordingly, I am satisfied that Benchmark has not demonstrated a reasonable probability of success on the merits of its claim that Sections C.6.c(ii) and C.6.d(ii) require a series vote on the merger contemplated as part of the Series D Transaction.

---

38 Avatex, 715 A.2d at 855; see also Sullivan Money Mgmt., mem. op. at 9 ("Unarguably had the Certificate's drafters intended to expressly entitle the Series A Preferred Stockholders to a class vote on a merger, they knew fully well how to do so.").

b. Authorization of Series D Preferred Shares Through the Merger Process

Benchmark's straightforward argument that it is entitled to a class vote on the authorization of the Series D Preferred Stock through the merger can easily be set forth. By Section C.6.a(i) of the Certificate, the holders of the Series A Preferred and Series B Preferred Stock have the right, unless that right is properly waived by CIBC, to a class vote on the authorization of a senior preferred security. The Series D Preferred Stock will be on parity with the Series C Preferred Stock and, thus, will be senior to be [sic] the existing junior preferred and the newly created junior preferred that will be created as part of the merger. The protective provisions of the Certificate do not distinguish between authorization through amendment of the Certificate under 8 Del. C. § 242(b) and those changes in the Certificate resulting from a recapitalization accompanying a merger pursuant to 8 Del. C. § 251. Thus, according to Benchmark, it matters not how the result is achieved. Moreover, Section C.6.a(i) does not track or even resemble the "privileges, preferences and special rights" language of 8 Del. C. § 242(b)(2) that was important to the analysis in the Warner line of cases. Benchmark thus argues that the clear and unambiguous words of Section C.6.a(i) guarantee (at least in the absence of an effective waiver by CIBC) it and the other holders of Series A Preferred and Series B Preferred shares a class vote before the Series D Preferred Stock may be authorized. While Benchmark has advanced an appealing and rational analysis, I conclude, for the reasons set forth below, that it has failed to demonstrate a reasonable probability of success on the merits of this argument.

In ascertaining whether a class of junior preferred stockholders has the opportunity to vote as a class on a proposed corporate action, the words chosen by the drafters must be read "against the background of Delaware precedent." For example, Sullivan Money Management, Inc. v. FLS Holdings, Inc. involved the question of whether a class vote was required in order to change critical rights of preferred shareholders " 'by amendment to the Certificate of Incorporation of [FLS Holdings, Inc.] or otherwise.' " In interpreting the charter of FLS Holdings, Inc., the Court was urged to treat the phrase "or otherwise" as including mergers. The Court, in rejecting this contention, set forth the following:

> The word "merger" is nowhere found in the provision governing the Series A Preferred Stock. The drafters' failure to express with clarity an intent to confer class voting rights in the event of a merger suggests that they had no intention of doing so, and weighs against adopting the plaintiffs' broad construction of the words "or otherwise."

Here, the authorization of the Series D Preferred Stock results from the merger and the restatement of Juniper's certificate of incorporation as part of that process. Warner and the cases following it, and Starkman in particular, demonstrate that certain rights of the holders of preferred stock that are secured by the corporate charter are at risk when a merger leads to changes in the corporation's capital structure. To protect against the potential negative effects of a merger, those who draft protective provisions have been instructed to make clear that those protective provisions specifically and directly limit the mischief that can otherwise be accomplished through a merger under 8 Del. C. § 251.[44]

In sum, Benchmark complains of the harm which will occur because of alterations to Juniper's capital structure resulting from modifications of the certificate of incorporation emerging from the merger. General language alone granting preferred stockholders a class vote on certain changes to the corporate charter (such as authorization of a senior series of stock) will not be read to require a class vote on a merger and its integral and accompanying modifications to the corporate charter and the corporation's capital structure.[45] To reach the result sought by Benchmark, the protective rights " 'must . . . be clearly expressed and will not be presumed.' "[46] Unfortunately for Benchmark, the requirements of a class vote for authorization of a new senior preferred stock through a merger was not "clearly expressed" in the Certificate. Against this background, I am reluctant both to presume that protection from a merger was intended and, perhaps more importantly, to create uncertainty in a complex area where Avatex has set down a framework for consistency.

QUESTIONS

1. As noted in the opinion, the charter for Juniper required the consent of the holders of the Series A and Series B Preferred Stock to "consolidate or merge into any other Corporation (other than a wholly-owned subsidiary Corporation)." Doesn't this language suggest the Series A and Series B Preferred Stockholders intended to have a class vote on a merger? Given *Avatex*, why do you think the veto right excluded a merger with a wholly-owned subsidiary? Is this the result of shoddy

---

44 See Avatex, 715 A.2d at 855; Starkman, tr. at 18–22. As a general matter, drafting guidance, such as that provided in Avatex, may be read as creating a "safe harbor" or as a prudential suggestion and is not typically to be read as the exclusive means of achieving the desired goal. Given what some may view as the peculiar nature of preferred stock, however, finding any safe haven may be difficult without substantial adherence to the guidance set forth in Avatex.

45 Benchmark correctly points out that the "preferences, privileges and special rights" language of Section 242(b)(2) which has been significant in the Warner line of cases cannot be found in any recognizable form in Section C.6.a(i). See Avatex, 715 A.2d at 854–55 (commenting on the significance of the uniformity of crucial provisions and the interplay of "boilerplate" provisions in the drafting process). However, as observed by this Court in Sullivan Money Mgmt, Inc., mem. op. at 6, certificate language comparable to that found in 8 Del. C. § 242(b)(2) is but one consideration in concluding that the merger has separate and independent significance or function.

46 Avatex, 715 A.2d at 853 n. 46 (quoting Rothschild Int'l Corp. v. Liggett Group, 474 A.2d 133, 136 (Del. 1984)).

lawyering, or might there be some other goal at play? Why didn't the court inquire more about the intended purpose of the carve-out?

2. Historically, the doctrine of independent legal significance has generally been relevant for charter amendments that adversely affect the terms of a company's preferred stock. Benchmark argues that it should therefore not apply to the "authorization" of the Series D Preferred Stock, which would appear to be captured by its class veto right. Why does Vice Chancellor Noble reject this argument?

3. Vice Chancellor Noble notes that the task of interpreting preferred stock terms "is essentially one of contract interpretation against the background of Delaware precedent," which includes the principle that "any rights, preferences and limitations of preferred stock that distinguish that stock from common stock must be expressly and clearly stated." Yet note 29 also distinguishes this interpretive principle from "strict construction." Is there a meaningful difference between a "clear and express" statement rule and "strict construction"?

NOTE: THE DOCTRINE OF INDEPENDENT LEGAL SIGNIFICANCE UNDER THE MODEL ACT

While Section 251 of the DGCL creates no preferred class voting rights in mergers, in contrast to charter amendments, The Model Act provides an integrated approach to charter amendments and mergers. For instance, Section 10.04 of the Model Act (the analog to DGCL § 242) requires a separate vote of a class or series if a charter amendment would "change the rights, preferences, or limitations of all or part of the shares of the class." Section 11.04 (the analog of DGCL § 251) requires board and stockholder approval of a merger, noting that shareholders are "entitled to vote as a separate group on a provision in the plan [of merger] that constitutes a proposed amendment to the articles of incorporation of a surviving corporation that requires action by separate voting groups under section 10.04." See Section 11.04(f).

Is there a good justification for the differing Delaware approach, or is this just a trap for the unwary?

---

ii. VOTE BUYING

The *Avatex* and *Benchmark* cases emerged from transactions where the companies were unable to convince the objecting stockholders to vote in favor of the transactions. However, as shown in *Avatex*, this cramdown strategy may not work where the preferred stock protective provisions encompass any adverse change to the preferred stock "whether by merger, consolidation or otherwise." Consistent with the Coase Theorem, preferred stockholders will have considerable leverage to bargain with the company in these situations.* Given that the preferred stockholders

* Recall that the Coase Theorem posits that where transaction costs are sufficiently low, parties will bargain to an efficient outcome regardless of the allocation of property rights. The

will effectively be selling their votes through these negotiations, these bargains can often raise the question of whether such "vote buying" is permissible.

Schreiber v. Carney

447 A.2d 17 (Del. Ch.1982)

■ HARTNETT, VICE CHANCELLOR.

In this stockholder's derivative action, Leonard I. Schreiber, the plaintiff, brought suit on behalf of defendant-Texas International Airlines, Inc. ("Texas International"), a Delaware corporation, challenging the propriety of a loan from Texas International to defendant Jet Capital Corporation ("Jet Capital"), the holder of 35% of the shares of stock of Texas International. Also joined as individual defendants were Texas International's board of directors—several of whom also served on Jet Capital's board of directors. The matter is presently before the Court on cross-motions for summary judgment. Defendants' motion is based on their contention that there has been no showing of waste and that plaintiff lacks standing to bring this suit. Plaintiff's motion is based on his contention that the transaction was tainted by vote-buying and is therefore void. For the reasons set forth below, both motions must be denied.

I

The essential facts are undisputed. The lawsuit arises out of the corporate restructuring of Texas International which occurred on June 11, 1980. The restructuring was accomplished by way of a share for share merger between Texas International and Texas Air Corporation ("Texas Air"), a holding company formed for the purpose of effectuating the proposed reorganization. Texas Air is also a Delaware corporation. At the annual meeting held on June 11, 1980 the shareholders voted overwhelmingly in favor of the proposal. As a result the shareholders of Texas International were eliminated as such and received in trade for their stock an equal number of shares in Texas Air. Texas International in turn became a wholly-owned subsidiary of Texas Air.

Prior to the merger Texas International was engaged in the airline business servicing the cities of Houston and Dallas, Texas. All concede that the purpose of the merger was to enable Texas International—under a new corporate structure—to diversify, to strengthen itself financially and in general to be transformed into a more viable and aggressive enterprise. According to the proxy statement issued in connection with the merger, management indicated that although there were no commitments at that time, it was actively considering the possibility of

---

holding of *Avatex* effectively means that a properly drafted protective provision gives preferred stockholders a property right against adverse changes to the terms of the preferred stock. The Coase Theorem suggests these stockholders might be willing to waive this entitlement with some inducement.

acquiring other companies engaged in both related as well as unrelated fields.

During the formulation of the reorganization plan, management was confronted with an obstacle, the resolution of which forms the basis for this lawsuit, because Jet Capital, the owner of the largest block of Texas International's stock, threatened to block the merger. Jet Capital's veto power resulted from a provision in Texas International's Certificate of Incorporation which required that each of its four classes of stock participate in the approval of a merger. At that time, Texas International's four classes of outstanding stock consisted of 4,669,182 shares of common stock and three series of convertible preferred stock; 32,318 shares of Series A stock, 66,075 shares of Series B stock and 2,040,000 shares of Series C stock. According to the Certificate of Incorporation a majority vote was required of both the common stockholders and the Series A preferred stockholders voting as separate classes. Similarly, a majority vote was required of the Series B and Series C preferred stockholders, but voting together as a single class. Because Jet Capital owned all of the Series C preferred stock—the larger class—it was in a position to block the merger proposal. Jet Capital indicated that although the proposal was indeed beneficial to Texas International and the other shareholders, it was nevertheless compelled to vote against it because the merger, if approved, would impose an intolerable income tax burden on it. This was so because the merger had an adverse impact on Jet Capital's position as the holder of certain warrants to purchase Texas International's common stock which would expire in 1982. There were warrants outstanding for the purchase of 1,029,531 shares of Texas International common stock at $4.18 per share and, of these, Jet Capital owned sufficient warrants to acquire 799,880 shares of Texas International's common shares. As the holder of these warrants, Jet Capital was faced with three alternatives.

The first alternative for Jet Capital was for it to participate in the merger and exchange its Texas International warrants for Texas Air warrants. However, according to an Internal Revenue Service ruling obtained by management, each holder of an unexercised Texas International warrant would be deemed to have realized taxable income from the merger as if the warrant had been exercised. Thus, it was estimated that Jet Capital would incur an $800,000 federal income tax liability. Because Jet Capital was a publicly held company, its management could not justify the assumption of such a tax liability and, therefore, did not consider this a viable alternative.

The second alternative was for Jet Capital to exercise the warrants prematurely. The merger would then be tax free to it as it would be to the other shareholders. This, however, was also not deemed to be feasible because Jet Capital lacked the approximately three million dollars necessary to exercise the warrants. Jet Capital's assets—other than its Texas International stock—were worth only $200,000. In addition, borrowing money at the prevailing interest rates in order to finance an early exercise of the warrants was deemed prohibitively expensive by the management of Jet Capital.* In any event, this alternative was considered to be imprudent because the early exercise of the warrants posed an unnecessary market risk because the market value of Texas International's stock on the date of the early exercise might prove to be higher than that on the expiration date. As a result, this alternative was also not considered viable.

The third and final alternative was for Jet Capital to vote against the merger and thus preclude it. Given these alternatives, Jet Capital obviously chose to oppose the restructuring.

In order to overcome this impasse, it was proposed that Texas International and Jet Capital explore the possibility of a loan by Texas International to Jet Capital in order to fund an early exercise of the warrants. Because Texas International and Jet Capital had several common directors, the defendants recognized the conflict of interest and endeavored to find a way to remove any taint or appearance of impropriety. It was, therefore, decided that a special independent committee would be formed to consider and resolve the matter. The three Texas International directors who had no interest in or connection with Jet Capital were chosen to head up the committee. After its formation, the committee's first act was to hire independent counsel. Next, the committee examined the proposed merger and, based upon advice rendered by an independent investment banker, the merger was again found to be both a prudent and feasible business decision. The committee then confronted the "Jet Capital obstacle" by considering viable options for both Texas International and Jet Capital and, as a result, the committee determined that a loan was the best solution.

After negotiating at arm's length, both Texas International and Jet Capital agreed that Texas International would loan to Jet Capital $3,335,000 at 5% interest per annum for the period up to the scheduled 1982 expiration date for the warrants. After this period, the interest rate would equal the then prevailing prime interest rate. The 5% interest rate was recommended by an independent investment banker as the rate necessary to reimburse Texas International for any dividends paid out during this period. Given this provision for anticipated dividends and the fact that the advanced money would be immediately paid back to Texas International upon the exercise of the warrants, the loan transaction had virtually no impact on Texas International's cash position.

As security Jet Capital was required to pledge all of its Series C preferred stock having a market value of approximately 150% of the amount of the loan. In addition, Jet Capital was expected to apply to the prepayment of the loan any after tax proceeds received from the sale of

* Eds. By April 1980 the prime rate charged by banks to their best customers was 20%. https://fred.stlouisfed.org/series/PRIME.

any stock acquired by Jet Capital as a result of the exercise of the 1982 warrants.

The directors of Texas International unanimously approved the proposal as recommended by the committee and submitted it to the stockholders for approval—requiring as a condition of approval that a majority of all outstanding shares and a majority of the shares voted by the stockholders other than Jet Capital or its officers or directors be voted in favor of the proposal. After receiving a detailed proxy statement, the shareholders voted overwhelmingly in favor of the proposal. There is no allegation that the proxy statement did not fully disclose all the germane facts with complete candor.

The complaint attacks the loan transaction on two theories. First, it is alleged that the loan transaction constituted vote-buying and was therefore void. Secondly, the complaint asserts that the loan was corporate waste. In essence, plaintiff argues that even if the loan was permissible and even if it was the best available option, it would have been wiser for Texas International to have loaned Jet Capital only $800,000—the amount of the increased tax liability—because this would have minimized Texas International's capital commitment and also would have prevented Jet Capital from increasing its control in Texas International on allegedly discriminatory and wasteful terms. Plaintiff also points out that the 5% interest rate on the loan was only equal to the amount of dividends Texas International would have been expected to pay during the period between the time of the early exercise and the date the warrants expired. Jet Capital, therefore in effect it is urged, received an interest free loan for the nearly two-year period preceding the 1982 warrant expiration date.

* * *

IV

* * *

It is clear that the loan constituted vote-buying as that term has been defined by the courts. Vote-buying, despite its negative connotation, is simply a voting agreement supported by consideration personal to the stockholder, whereby the stockholder divorces his discretionary voting power and votes as directed by the offeror. The record clearly indicates that Texas International purchased or "removed" the obstacle of Jet Capital's opposition. Indeed, this is tacitly conceded by the defendants. However, defendants contend that the analysis of the transaction should not end here because the legality of vote-buying depends on whether its object or purpose is to defraud or in some manner disenfranchise the other stockholders. Defendants contend that because the loan did not defraud or disenfranchise any group of shareholders, but rather enfranchised the other shareholders by giving them a determinative vote in the proposed merger, it is not illegal per se. Defendants, in effect, contend that vote-buying is not void per se because the end justified the means. Whether this is valid depends upon the status of the law.

The Delaware decisions dealing with vote-buying leave the question unanswered. In each of these decisions, the Court summarily voided the challenged votes as being purchased and thus contrary to public policy and in fraud of the other stockholders. However, the facts in each case indicated that fraud or disenfranchisement was the obvious purpose of the vote-buying.

* * *

The present case presents a peculiar factual setting in that the proposed vote-buying consideration was conditional upon the approval of a majority of the disinterested stockholders after a full disclosure to them of all pertinent facts and was purportedly for the best interests of all Texas International stockholders. It is therefore necessary to do more than merely consider the fact that Jet Capital saw fit to vote for the transaction after a loan was made to it by Texas International. As stated in Oceanic Exploration Co. v. Grynberg, Del. Supr., 428 A.2d 1 (1981), a case involving an analogous situation, to do otherwise would be tantamount to "[d]eciding the case on . . . an abstraction divorced from the facts of the case and the intent of the law."

A review of the present controversy, therefore, must go beyond a reading of Macht v. Merchants Mortgage & Credit Co., [Del. Ch. 194 A. 19 (1937)] *supra*, and consider the cases cited therein. There are essentially two principles which appear in these cases. The first is that vote-buying is illegal per se if its object or purpose is to defraud or disenfranchise the other stockholders. A fraudulent purpose is as defined at common law, as a deceit which operates prejudicially upon the property rights of another.

The second principle which appears in these old cases is that vote-buying is illegal per se as a matter of public policy, the reason being that each stockholder should be entitled to rely upon the independent judgment of his fellow stockholders. Thus, the underlying basis for this latter principle is again fraud but as viewed from a sense of duty owed by all stockholders to one another. The apparent rationale is that by requiring each stockholder to exercise his individual judgment as to all matters presented, "[t]he security of the small stockholders is found in the natural disposition of each stockholder to promote the best interests of all, in order to promote his individual interests." In essence, while self interest motivates a stockholder's vote, theoretically, it is also advancing the interests of the other stockholders. Thus, any agreement entered into for personal gain, whereby a stockholder separates his voting right from his property right was considered a fraud upon this community of interests.

The often cited case of Brady v. Bean, 221 Ill. App. 279 (1921), is particularly enlightening. In that case, the plaintiff—an apparently influential stockholder—voiced his opposition to the corporation's proposed sale of assets. The plaintiff feared that his investment would be wiped out because the consideration for the sale appeared only sufficient enough to satisfy the corporation's creditors. As a result and without the knowledge of the other stockholders, the defendant, also a stockholder as well as a director and substantial creditor of the company, offered to the plaintiff in exchange for the withdrawal of his opposition, a sharing in defendant's claims against the corporation. In an action to enforce this contract against the defendant's estate, the Court refused relief stating:

> "Appellant being a stockholder in the company, any contract entered into by him whereby he was to receive a personal consideration in return for either his action or his inaction in a matter such as a sale of all the company's assets, involving, as it did, the interests of all the stockholders, was contrary to public policy and void, it being admitted that such contract was not known by or assented to by the other stockholders. *The purpose and effect of the contract was apparently to influence appellant, in his decision of a question affecting the rights and interests of his associate stockholders, by a consideration which was foreign to those rights and interests and would likely to induce him to disregard the consideration he owed them and the contract must, therefore, be regarded as a fraud upon them.* Such an agreement will not be enforced, as being against public policy." (emphasis added) 221 Ill. App. at 283.

In addition to the deceit obviously practiced upon the other stockholders, the Court was clearly concerned with the rights and interests of the other stockholders. Thus, the potential injury or prejudicial impact which might flow to other stockholders as a result of such an agreement forms the heart of the rationale underlying the breach of public policy doctrine.

An automatic application of this rationale to the facts in the present case, however, would be to ignore an essential element of the transaction. The agreement in question was entered into primarily to further the interests of Texas International's other shareholders. Indeed, the shareholders, after reviewing a detailed proxy statement, voted overwhelmingly in favor of the loan agreement. Thus, the underlying rationale for the argument that vote-buying is illegal per se, as a matter of public policy, ceases to exist when measured against the undisputed reason for the transaction.

Moreover, the rationale that vote-buying is, as a matter of public policy, illegal per se is founded upon considerations of policy which are now outmoded as a necessary result of an evolving corporate environment. According to 5 Fletcher Cyclopedia Corporation (Perm. Ed.) § 2066:

> "The theory that each stockholder is entitled to the personal judgment of each other stockholder expressed in his vote, and that any agreement among stockholders frustrating it was invalid, is obsolete because it is both impracticable and impossible of application to modern corporations with many widely scattered stockholders, and the courts have gradually abandoned it."

In addition, Delaware law has for quite some time permitted stockholders wide latitude in decisions affecting the restriction or transfer of voting rights. In Ringling Bros., Etc., Shows, Inc. v. Ringling, Del. Supr., 53 A.2d 441 (1947), the Delaware Supreme Court adopted a liberal approach to voting agreements which, prior to that time, were viewed with disfavor and were often considered void as a matter of public policy. In upholding a voting agreement the Court stated:

> "Generally speaking, a shareholder may exercise wide liberality of judgment in the matter of voting, and it is not objectionable that his motives may be for personal profit, or determined by whims or caprice, so long as he violates no duty owed his fellow stockholders." (citation omitted)

The Court's rationale was later codified in DGCL § 218(c), which permits voting agreements.

Recently, in Oceanic Exploration Co. v. Grynberg, Del. Supr., 428 A.2d 1 (1981), the Delaware Supreme Court applied this approach to voting trusts. The Court also indicated, with approval, the liberal approach to all contractual arrangements limiting the incidents of stock ownership. Significantly, Oceanic involved the giving up of voting rights in exchange for personal gain. There, the stockholder, by way of a voting trust, gave up his right to vote on all corporate matters over a period of years in return for "valuable benefits including indemnity for large liabilities." 428 A.2d at 5.

Given the holdings in Ringling and Oceanic it is clear that Delaware has discarded the presumptions against voting agreements. Thus, under our present law, an agreement involving the transfer of stock voting rights without the transfer of ownership is not necessarily illegal and each arrangement must be examined in light of its object or purpose. To hold otherwise would be to exalt form over substance. As indicated in Oceanic more than the mere form of an agreement relating to voting must be considered and voting agreements in whatever form, therefore, should not be considered to be illegal per se unless the object or purpose is to defraud or in some way disenfranchise the other stockholders. This is not to say, however, that vote-buying accomplished for some laudable purpose is automatically free from challenge. Because vote-buying is so easily susceptible of abuse it must be viewed as a voidable transaction subject to a test for intrinsic fairness.

V

Apparently anticipating this finding, plaintiff also attempts to cast the loan agreement as one seeking to accomplish a fraudulent purpose. As indicative of fraud, plaintiff points to the fact that no other warrant holder was given a similar loan to enable an early exercise of the warrants. However, despite this contention, I am satisfied that, based on the record, there is no evidence from which an inference of a fraudulent object or purpose can be drawn.

As to the other warrant holders who did not get a loan, they were merely the holders of an expectant and contingent interest and, as such, were owed no duty by Texas International except as set forth in the warrant certificates. FOLK, The Delaware General Corporation Law, Little, Brown (1972) § 155, p. 126. In any event, the record fails to show any evidence that Texas International's ultimate decision to fund Jet Capital's early exercise of the warrants was motivated and accomplished except with the best interests of all Texas International stockholders in mind.

VI

I therefore hold that the agreement, whereby Jet Capital withdrew its opposition to the proposed merger in exchange for a loan to fund the early exercise of its warrants was not void per se because the object and purpose of the agreement was not to defraud or disenfranchise the other stockholders but rather was for the purpose of furthering the interest of all Texas International stockholders. The agreement, however, was a voidable act. Because the loan agreement was voidable it was susceptible to cure by shareholder approval. Michelson v. Duncan, Del. Supr., 407 A.2d 211 (1979). Consequently, the subsequent ratification of the transaction by a majority of the independent stockholders, after a full disclosure of all germane facts with complete candor precludes any further judicial inquiry of it.

* * *

VIII

In summary plaintiff's motion for summary judgment on the grounds that the transaction before the Court was permeated by vote-buying and was therefore void or voidable is denied. Defendants' motion for summary judgment on the grounds that plaintiff lacks standing to bring this suit or on the grounds that there is no factual basis for a claim of waste is denied.

It is so ordered.

QUESTIONS

1. What's so bad about vote buying? Who is harmed? Can you imagine a situation where it might lead to bad policy outcomes?
2. In Section IV of its opinion, the Schreiber court discussed the holding in Brady v. Bean, 221 Ill. App. 279 (1921), where a shareholder who was also a creditor of the corporation sought to cause the corporation to sell its assets and dissolve. To facilitate the dissolution, the creditor offered to share his gains as a creditor with another shareholder if he would drop his opposition and vote in favor of the dissolution. The court characterizes this as causing a potential injury to other shareholders, because the motivating force was a creditor's claim, "a consideration which was foreign to those rights and interests [of the other stockholders]." How does this differ from the interests of Jet Capital? Do you think the Schreiber court would have decided Brady v. Bean the same way?
3. As noted in the opinion, the court concludes that vote buying was not void "because the object and purpose of the agreement was not to defraud or disenfranchise the other stockholders but rather was for the purpose of furthering the interest of all Texas International stockholders." However, the court then notes that "it must be viewed as a voidable transaction subject to a test for intrinsic fairness." In light of the court's conclusion that the vote buying was beneficial to Texas International stockholders, what exactly would a test for intrinsic fairness entail? Why did the court skip this test?

NOTE

While *Schreiber* involved a situation where the preferred stockholders were selling their votes, it should hardly be surprising that vote buying also occurs when the consent of common stockholders is required. For instance, in Goldman v. Postal Telegraph, Inc., 52 F. Supp. 763 (D. Del. 1943), the court sustained what was in effect a payment to holders of common stock to secure their consent to a liquidating asset sale. The suit was brought by a holder of preferred stock, who complained that the proceeds of the sale were less than the original liquidation preference of the preferred stock. Specifically, in the vote submitted to the shareholders to approve the sale, it was proposed to amend the company's charter to provide that the preferred stockholders would receive stock of the buyer at a formula that left approximately 16% of the sale proceeds for the common stockholders. If the company had been liquidated, the plaintiff complained, the common stockholders would have received nothing. Accordingly, he argued that this amendment was simply a payment to the common stockholders to secure their votes, which were necessary to approve the sale. The court dismissed the complaint, stating:

> "The reality of the situation confronting Postal's management called for some inducement to be offered the common stockholders

to secure their favorable vote for the plan. * * * The fact is something had to induce the common stockholders to come along. This court and the Delaware courts have recognized the strategic position of common stock to hamper the desires of the real owners of the equity of a corporation, and the tribute which common stock exacts for its vote under reclassification and reorganization."

Today, formal voting agreements are routinely used in preferred stock financings to implement governance agreements required by preferred stock investors. For instance, venture capital financing transactions will entail the execution of a voting agreement that commits preferred stockholders and the largest common stockholders to vote in favor of directors nominated by select investors, directors nominated by common stockholders (who will typically be the company's founders), and "industry directors" acceptable to both the investors and the founders. This agreement thus supplements charter provisions (such as seen in Lyft's charter) granting preferred stockholders and common stockholders the right to nominate a specified number of directors. See NVCA Model Voting Agreement, available at https://nvca.org/resources/model-legal-documents/. The voting agreement may also require common stockholders to vote in favor of any acquisition of the company approved by the board of directors and a specified percentage of preferred stockholders. This latter provision, referred to as a "drag-along" provision, helps ensure that common stockholders will not veto an acquisition where most of the acquisition consideration will be absorbed by the preferred stock liquidation preferences. The Trados case, *infra*, involves a case arising from such an acquisition.

The final case in this sub-section explores how innovations in the derivatives market can disrupt traditional understandings of how class veto rights function. In theory, a protective provision that grants preferred stockholders a veto right over adverse modifications to the preferred does so because the drafters assume that holders of the preferred stock voting rights will have similar economic interests. But what if the economic rights of the preferred can be separated from their voting rights?

Corre Opportunities Fund, LP v. Emmis Communications Corporation

892 F.Supp.2d 1076 (S.D. Ind. 2012)

■ SARAH EVANS BARKER.

This cause is before the Court on Plaintiffs' Motion for Preliminary Injunction. . . Plaintiffs, Corre Opportunities Fund, LP . . . seek a preliminary injunction barring Defendants, Emmis Communications Corporation ("Emmis") . . . from, inter alia, holding a Special Meeting to vote on the Proposed Amendments set forth in Emmis's March 13, 2012

Preliminary Proxy Statement and from voting, directing others to vote, or taking any action on votes cast for the Proposed Amendments.

A hearing was held on July 31 and August 1, 2012, at which the parties presented evidence and oral argument. Having considered the parties' briefing, the documentary and testimonial evidence, and oral arguments, the Court hereby DENIES Plaintiffs' motion for injunctive relief.

Factual Background

Relevant Rights and Protections of Preferred Stock

In 1999, Emmis issued 2,875,000 shares of 6.25% Series A Cumulative Convertible Preferred Stock ("Preferred Stock") for $50 per share, raising approximately $144 million. Plaintiffs are all shareholders who own, or manage funds that own, more than 800,000 shares of Emmis's Preferred Stock.

Emmis's Articles of Incorporation sets out the rights and protections associated with the Preferred Stock, which include, inter alia: (1) a right to cumulative annual cash dividends at a rate per annum equal to 6.25% of the stock's $50 liquidation preference; (2) a bar on Emmis's ability to pay dividends to its common stockholders or to repurchase securities ranking junior to or ratably with the Preferred Stock unless Emmis is current on the Preferred Stock dividend payments; (3) a right to sell the stock back to Emmis at $50 per share, plus any outstanding dividends, if the Company goes private; (4) the right to elect two Emmis directors if dividends are not paid for six consecutive quarters; and (5) the requirement that any issuance of senior-ranking stock or any adverse amendment to the terms of the Preferred Stock be approved by two-thirds of the outstanding Preferred Stock.

Attempts to Take Emmis Private

In 2006, Emmis CEO, Jeff Smulyan, proposed to take Emmis private by purchasing the Company's common stock at $15.25 per share. However, a committee of disinterested directors of the Board of Directors ("the Board") rejected his proposal and Emmis remained a public company. Two years later, in October 2008, Emmis, like other entities in the radio and media industry, was hit hard by the nationwide financial crisis and was forced to cut its workforce, reduce employee benefits, and cut wages and salaries. Emmis also ceased paying dividends to its Preferred Shareholders at that time and has not paid dividends since.[1] The current amount of accrued unpaid dividends is $12.12 per share.

In 2010, two years after the financial crisis, the market price of Emmis's Common Stock had fallen to less than $3.00 per share. Mr. Smulyan, fueled by the belief that the Common Stock was undervalued

1 In August 2009, the holders of Emmis's senior debt demanded that loan covenants be amended to prohibit the Company from paying dividends on the Preferred Stock. This prohibition continues today.

by the market, proposed another go-private transaction. As part of that deal, Emmis asked the Preferred Shareholders to relinquish their right to sell their stock back to Emmis at $50.00 per share plus unpaid dividends (which would have eliminated any potential profit from the go-private transaction) and instead requested that they exchange their shares for subordinated debt instruments. That proposed amendment to the terms of the Preferred Stock failed to win the required two-thirds' approval, however. As a result, Emmis's financier, preferred holder Alden Global Distressed Opportunities Master Fund ("Alden"), pulled out of the deal, and the initiative collapsed. * * *

Emmis's Proposal to Acquire Preferred Stock Using Total Return Swaps

In the summer of 2011, Emmis's senior management was contacted by a few of the Preferred Shareholders who sought liquidity for their shares. According to Defendants, Emmis recognized the benefits to its capital structure of repurchasing its Preferred Stock at the then-prevailing market rate. Repurchasing the Preferred Stock for approximately 25 cents on the dollar would be treated by credit rating agencies as the extinguishment of debt at a substantial discount, making it easier for Emmis to refinance senior debt at lower interest rates, which would in turn have the effect of improving the Company's overall financial health, increasing the value of Emmis's common stock and possibly the remaining Preferred Stock as well.

In September 2011, Emmis's senior management negotiated with Zell Credit Opportunities Master Fund, LLC ("Zell") for financing that would enable Emmis to repurchase the Preferred Stock. At approximately that same time, in September and October 2011, Emmis began approaching its ten largest Preferred Shareholders to determine whether there was interest in selling. In mid-October, after a sufficient number of the approached Preferred Shareholders had expressed interest in selling their shares at the current market value, Emmis finalized a loan commitment of up to $35 million with Zell (the "Zell Financing") to fund those purchases.

Emmis's senior management presented the proposal to repurchase Preferred Stock using the Zell Financing at the Board's October 25, 2011 meeting. * * *

One of the goals of the purchase proposal was not simply to acquire Preferred Stock, but also to preserve the voting rights of the Preferred Stock it did acquire. Under Indiana law, any shares of Preferred Stock that Emmis acquired through outright purchases would have to be retired and could not be voted. Thus, the Preferred Stock repurchase proposal included the possibility of using total return swap ("TRS") transactions[3] and TRS Voting Agreements rather than ordinary

[3] Plaintiffs' expert witness, Edward Adams, explained that total return swaps are financial derivative contracts in which: "Party A agrees to pay the total returns to Party B in exchange for Party B making generally periodic payments to Party A. So if the asset goes up in value from 50 to a hundred dollars, then Party A is going to pay that to B. If it goes down in

purchase agreements, which proposal was presented to the Board as a way to preserve the voting rights of the Preferred Stock. Basically, Preferred Shareholders would be offered a price per share for certain interests in their Preferred Stock; and, although they would lose the economic rights in those shares, they would retain record ownership of the stock. In addition, Emmis would enter into voting agreements with these Preferred Shareholders pursuant to which they would agree to vote their shares as Emmis directed. It was proposed that Emmis would make this offer only to its largest holders of Preferred Stock, and the Board was informed that, if Emmis succeeded in acquiring two-thirds of the vote, the use of the total return swaps "would allow flexibility" to seek amendments to the terms of the Preferred Stock.

The proposal was approved by unanimous vote of the directors, including all of its independent directors as well as the Preferred Shareholders' representative on the Board, David Gale. Gale did express concern regarding what Emmis planned to do if it acquired voting control of two-thirds of the Preferred Stock. However, after being informed that the Board would not take any action on that issue at that meeting, he ultimately voted in favor of the Preferred Stock repurchase proposal, including the use of TRS transactions and accompanying TRS Voting Agreements.

Emmis's Acquisition of Preferred Stock Using Total Return Swaps

With authorization from the Board, Emmis's senior management finalized the Zell Financing and proceeded with the discussions with the ten targeted Preferred Shareholders about acquisition of their shares. On November 10, 2011, Emmis signed the loan agreement with Zell and the next day announced it would acquire Preferred Stock from certain holders pursuant to TRS transactions. Because at that point Emmis had entered into these discussions with only ten of its Preferred Shareholders regarding the acquisition of their shares, the announcement that Emmis made on November 11 was the first notice to the remaining Preferred Shareholders of Emmis's acquisition plans. On November 14, 2011, in a 8-K filing submitted to the Securities Exchange Commission ("SEC"), Emmis disclosed that it had secured the Zell financing and that it had "entered into securities purchase agreements with certain holders of its Preferred Stock," and that, "[t]he transactions will settle pursuant to the terms of total return swaps . . ., the terms of which provide that until final settlement of these arrangements, the seller agree[d] to vote its shares in accordance with the prior written instructions of Emmis." Emmis further disclosed that it "may enter into additional transactions to purchase its Preferred Stock in the future. According to an 8-K form filed on November 15, 2011, Emmis had already acquired 645,504 shares

value, Party B's got to pay that to A. So what happens in a total return swap is Party B doesn't really own the asset. It owns the economics of the asset. Party A continues to own the asset and vote it. Party B has the economics, so if it goes up, Party B benefits. If it goes down, Party B pays."

of Preferred Stock, mainly through TRS transactions, and, by that date, had secured the ability to direct the vote of approximately 23% of the Preferred Stock.

One week later, on November 22, 2011, as part of a broader agreement to settle all litigation related to its pullout from the 2010 go-private transaction, Alden Capital agreed to enter into a TRS transaction with Emmis involving over 1,000,000 shares of Preferred Stock. These shares represented approximately 34% of the outstanding Preferred Stock and increased the percentage of shares over which Emmis had secured voting control to 56.8%. Defendants claim that it was only at this point that Emmis's senior management first believed that the Company might be able to gain control of two-thirds of the outstanding shares of the Preferred Stock.

On that same day, the Board met to discuss the merits of a tender offer and the implications of acquiring voting control over at least two-thirds of the outstanding Preferred Stock. The minutes of that meeting state that no decision was being made at that time "with respect to any possible amendments to the terms of the preferred stock," and that, "such a determination, if any," would be made at a separate meeting. The Board did, however, approve by an 8–1 margin[5] a modified "Dutch auction" tender offer for its Preferred Stock at the November 22 meeting.

The Dutch Auction Tender Offer

On November 30, 2011, Emmis announced that it would conduct a modified Dutch auction tender offer to purchase up to $6 million in Preferred Stock at a price between $12.50 and $15.56 per share. The next day, on December 1, 2011, Emmis submitted its tender offer filing to the SEC. In that filing, Emmis stated that if it succeeded in obtaining two-thirds of the vote, it "may elect to, among other things, amend various provisions applicable to the Preferred Shares." By December 12, 2011, in response to the disclosures made in Emmis's December 1 filing, four of the five Plaintiffs had entered into a formal lockup agreement in an attempt to gain a blocking position by controlling at least one-third of the vote of the Preferred Stock.

On January 5, 2012, Emmis announced that it had purchased through the December tender offer 164,400 shares of Preferred Stock. Because those shares were purchased rather than acquired through TRS transactions, they were retired and returned to the status of authorized but unissued Preferred Stock, thereby reducing the number of shares of outstanding Preferred Stock, which in turn increased the percentage of shares over which Emmis controlled the vote to 60.6%.

On January 20, 2012, with the term of the Zell Financing set to expire within two weeks, Emmis used the last of those funds to purchase and retire an additional 25,700 shares of Preferred Stock at prices of up to $30 per share. Emmis announced the acquisition in its January 30,

[5] Gale, the Preferred Shareholders' representative on the Board was the only dissenter.

2012 Form 8-K, stating that the total of "authorized but unissued" shares had reached 452,680, and that, if it reissued 390,604 of those shares to a third party with a voting agreement allowing Emmis to direct the vote, it would have voting control over two-thirds of the Preferred Stock. In the Form 8-K, Emmis further disclosed that, if it were able to acquire voting control, it "may elect" to use that power to amend the rights of the Preferred Shareholders.

Creation of Employee Retention Plan Trust and Reissuance of Preferred Stock

In January 2012, Emmis entered into negotiations with its lenders, Zell and Canyon Capital Advisors, whereby Emmis proposed to reissue to the lenders approximately 400,000 shares of Preferred Stock which amount was needed to reach the two-thirds threshold. However, in early February 2012, Zell and Canyon concluded that the possible return on an investment in the Preferred Stock was not worth the risk of litigation with the lockup group and declined to invest.

Once negotiations with Zell and Canyon stalled, Emmis's senior management decided to create an employee benefit plan trust ("the Retention Plan Trust") to which it could issue the 400,000 shares of Preferred Stock, which would be voted as directed by the Board.[7] On February 29, 2012, senior management presented this idea to the Board, which approved the plan at its March 8, 2012 meeting. According to Defendants, there were two purposes for creating the Retention Plan Trust; first, to enable Emmis to acquire voting control over two-thirds of the Preferred Stock, and second, to provide a means of retaining and rewarding employees who remained with the company for at least two years.

Before the proxy for approval of the Retention Plan Trust was tendered, Emmis made a separate filing on March 13, 2012, announcing its intention to conduct a vote amending the rights of the remaining Preferred Shareholders by using the shares that it planned to issue to the not-yet-created Trust. The March 13 filing also noted that the shares in the Retention Plan Trust would vote in favor of the proposed amendments. On April 2, 2012, the Trust, with Mr. Smulyan as Trustee, was approved by shareholder vote. Emmis then contributed 400,000 shares of Preferred Stock in return for a voting agreement allowing the Company to direct the vote of those shares, giving Emmis control of over two-thirds of the Preferred Stock.

Board Approval and Disclosure of Proposed Amendments

At the February 29 and March 8 Board meetings when the Retention Plan Trust was discussed and adopted, the Board for the first time also discussed the details of specific Amendments to the Articles of

[7] Indiana law allows corporations to vote their own shares when held "in or for an employee benefit plan." Ind. Code § 23–1–30–2(c). [Eds. Similar language appears in the Model Act § 7.21(c).]

Incorporation affecting the terms of the Preferred Stock (at the February 29 meeting) and approved the Proposed Amendments for consideration by the Company's shareholders (at the March 8 meeting). The Proposed Amendments would, inter alia: (1) eliminate Emmis's obligation to pay Preferred Stock dividends accumulated since October 2008; (2) change the Preferred Stock from "Cumulative" to "Non-Cumulative"; (3) eliminate the right of Preferred Shareholders to elect directors in the event of nonpayment of dividends; (4) remove the restrictions on Emmis's ability to pay dividends or make distributions on or repurchase its Common Stock or other junior stock prior to paying accumulated dividends or distributions on the Preferred Stock; and (5) eliminate the right of the holders of the Preferred Stock to require Emmis to repurchase all of their shares upon certain going-private transactions.

Emmis filed a preliminary proxy statement on March 13, 2012, in which it disclosed the exact terms of the Proposed Amendments and its expectation that the holders of two-thirds of the Preferred Stock would vote in favor of the Amendments, based on the terms of the TRS and Retention Plan Trust Voting Agreements. Id. The preliminary proxy also provided as follows:

> The Emmis board of directors, with the exception of Dave Gale who was appointed as a director by the holders of the Preferred Stock, believes the Proposed Amendments will have a positive effect on the overall capital structure of Emmis, which will have a beneficial impact on holders of the Common Stock. Accordingly, the board of directors, with the exception of Mr. Gale, believes that the Proposed Amendments are in the best interests of Emmis and the holders of the Common Stock and recommends that the holders of the Common Stock vote FOR the Proposed Amendments.

The Instant Litigation

On April 16, 2012, Plaintiffs filed their Complaint as well as the instant motion for injunctive relief, alleging that Defendants' acquisition of Preferred Stock through TRS transactions and the reissuance of Preferred Stock to the Retention Plan Trust violated various federal securities laws as well as the laws governing the conduct of Indiana corporations.

Legal Analysis

* * *

II. Likelihood of Success on the Merits

A. State Law Claims

* * *

2. Indiana Code § 23–1–30–2

a. Stock acquired through TRS transactions

Plaintiffs argue that Defendants cannot vote the shares of Preferred Stock they acquired through total return swaps because they are no longer "outstanding" as defined by Indiana statute. According to Plaintiffs, regardless of the label Defendants put on those transactions, they were sales in all respects but name, and consequently, the TRS shares should have been retired. Defendants rejoin that the total return swaps were not sales. Emmis made no outright purchases of those shares (because the Preferred Shareholder counterparties retain record ownership), and thus, that the TRS shares remain outstanding and retain their voting rights. Defendants maintain that they are authorized to direct the vote of the TRS shares pursuant to the voting agreements executed by the Preferred Shareholder counterparties as part of the total return swap.

It is undisputed that the transactions Defendants call total return swaps are not typical TRS transactions. However, the label given to the transaction is largely immaterial for our purposes. The court's task here is not to determine whether the transactions in fact fit the mold of what is traditionally called a total return swap, but rather to determine whether, regardless of the label given to the transaction, the manner in which Defendants structured the transactions to ensure the shares remain outstanding is permissible under Indiana law.

The Indiana Business Corporation Law ("IBCL") expressly allows Indiana corporations to vote and "deal in" their own shares except as otherwise prohibited in the statute. Ind. Code § 23–1–22–2(6). Indiana Code § 23–1–30–2(a) grants voting rights to shares that are "outstanding." Under Indiana law, issued shares remain outstanding "until they are reacquired, redeemed, converted, or cancelled." Ind. Code § 23–1–25–3. Emmis's Articles provide that, in accordance with Indiana law, shares that are reacquired by the company "will be retired and canceled promptly after reacquisition."

Plaintiffs contend that, although the Preferred Shareholder counterparties retain record ownership, the TRS transactions are nevertheless tantamount to sales because Emmis acquired everything of value, to wit, both the economic rights and the right to direct the vote of the shares pursuant to the accompanying voting agreements.[11] However, although they clearly effected a substantial transfer of interest, these transactions were not complete exchanges of the entire bundle of rights of ownership. Further, they do not reflect the parties' intention to transfer all ownership rights, as evidenced by the fact that the

---

11 In materials submitted to the SEC, Emmis concedes that it represented that the total return swap "arrangement had the same economic and voting effect as a purchase of those shares." However, this characterization is not controlling here as to whether Defendants acted in contravention of the applicable provisions of the IBCL in structuring the transactions in the manner that they did.

counterparties to the transactions retain record ownership of the shares, which is one traditional indicia of ownership. See Meridian Mortg. Co. v. Indiana, 182 Ind. App. 328, 395 N.E.2d 433, 439 (Ind. Ct. App. 1979) (discussing general indicia of ownership as including title, possession, and control). As both parties' experts conceded at the hearing, while unusual, nothing prohibits two consenting parties from disaggregating the bundle of ownership rights and tailoring a transaction in such a manner. Moreover, although we concede that it is difficult to articulate what concrete value remains with mere record ownership, it is not meaningless under Indiana law. The IBCL provides that one definition of "shareholder" is "the person in whose name shares are registered in the records of a corporation." Ind. Code § 23–1–20–24. Similarly, Section 2.10 of Emmis's bylaws state that "[t]he original stock register or transfer book . . . shall be the only evidence as to who are the Shareholders entitled . . . to notice of or to vote at any meeting."

Given these facts, we cannot conclude that Plaintiffs are likely to succeed in establishing that the TRS Stock is not outstanding, at least not within the meaning of the IBCL, since record ownership remains with the Preferred Shareholder counterparty. Nor have Plaintiffs shown a likelihood of success in establishing that Emmis cannot lawfully direct the vote of the TRS Stock via the TRS Voting Agreements. The IBCL expressly authorizes voting agreements between two or more shareholders providing for "the manner in which they will vote their shares." Ind. Code § 23–1–31–2. Moreover, the only limitation on the general rule that each outstanding share is entitled to vote is contained in Indiana Code § 23–1–30–2(b), which prohibits a subsidiary from voting the shares of its parent if the parent owns a majority of the subsidiary's shares. The Official Comments make clear, however, that subsection (b) "does not prohibit . . . the voting of a corporation's own shares in other circumstances where the corporation may have the power to direct the voting, such as shares owned by a limited partnership of which the corporation is the general partner." (emphasis added).

In sum, unlike statutes governing corporations in certain other states, the IBCL expressly permits an Indiana corporation to vote its own shares. The IBCL also affords the board of directors broad discretion to act in the best interest of the corporation unless otherwise prohibited by the statute. Although the manner in which Defendants structured the TRS transactions to retain the voting rights is admittedly unusual, having clearly been creatively devised to serve the company's purposes, we are not persuaded that Plaintiffs are likely to prevail on a claim that the IBCL prohibits their actions.

* * *

b. Stock reissued to Retention Plan Trust

Under Indiana Code § 23–1–30–2(c), a corporation is allowed to "vote any shares, including its own shares, held by it in or for an employee benefit plan or in any other fiduciary capacity." Plaintiffs argue that, despite this clear and unconditional allowance under Indiana law, Defendants should nevertheless be prohibited from voting the 400,000 shares of the Preferred Stock that they reissued to the Retention Plan Trust because the Trust is a "sham," created not for the benefit of Emmis employees, but solely to allow Emmis to strip away the rights of the remaining holders of the Preferred Stock.

The only authority Plaintiffs cite in support of this argument is the Southern District of Ohio's decision in NCR Corporation v. AT&T Co., 761 F. Supp. 475 (S.D. Ohio 1991), in which the court, applying Maryland law, held that an employee stock ownership plan ("ESOP") created by NSR [sic] was invalid and unenforceable because the primary purpose of the ESOP was to thwart a competitor's takeover offer rather than to provide employees with benefits, and thus, was in violation of Maryland's "primary purpose test." Under Maryland law, the "primary purpose test" is applied to determine the validity of stock issuances that have the effect of consolidating or perpetuating management control. See Mountain Manor Realty, Inc. v. Buccheri, 55 Md. App. 185, 461 A.2d 45, 53 (Md. Ct. Spec. App. 1983). Under that test, transactions can be deemed invalid if a court finds "that the purpose of the transaction was primarily one of management's self-perpetuation and that that purpose outweighed any other legitimate business purpose."

It is undisputed that one purpose of Emmis's creating the Retention Plan Trust and reissuing to it the 400,000 shares of Preferred Stock was to sufficiently dilute the number of Preferred Stock shares to enable Defendants to acquire voting control. However, Plaintiffs are unlikely to be successful in establishing that such a purpose or strategy renders the employee benefit plan invalid under Indiana law, thereby preventing Defendants from voting those shares. Plaintiffs have not pointed to, nor are we aware of any test under Indiana law similar to Maryland's primary purpose test. To the contrary, the IBCL expressly repudiates the application of legal decisions from other states that apply stricter scrutiny on directors' decisions than that provided for under Indiana's business judgment rule, which states in relevant part as follows:

> Certain judicial decisions in Delaware and other jurisdictions, which might otherwise be looked to for guidance in interpreting Indiana corporate law, including decisions relating to potential change of control transactions that impose a different or higher degree of scrutiny on actions taken by directors in response to a proposed acquisition of control of the corporation, are inconsistent with the proper application of the business judgment rule under this article.

Ind. Code § 23–1–35–1(f); see also 20 Indiana Practice § 47.11 n.11 (citing NCR as an example of a case that would be inapplicable under Indiana law).

Indiana law clearly provides that a corporation may vote its own shares if they are held in an employee benefit plan. It imposes no further qualifications on the creation of such a plan. In the case at bar, the Board exercised its business judgment in deciding to approve the resolutions establishing the Retention Plan Trust and in allowing Emmis to direct the vote of the stock placed therein, a decision of which a majority of the disinterested directors approved. Although Plaintiffs accuse Defendants of nefarious motives in creating the Retention Plan Trust, the evidence shows that Emmis employees have been told that the shares placed in the Trust were placed there for their benefit and will be available for distribution to employees who remain with the company for at least two years. Given these facts, Plaintiffs have failed to establish that they have a reasonable likelihood of establishing that the Retention Plan Trust is nothing more than an illegal sham, the creation of which violates Indiana law.

* * *

IV. Balance of Harms and the Public Interest

For the reasons detailed above, we have found that Plaintiffs have failed to meet any of the threshold requirements for injunctive relief. We therefore need not address the balance of harms or public interest factors. Nonetheless, we note that, had Plaintiffs met the threshold requirements, the balance of harms is, if anything, a toss-up: Defendants have shown a likelihood that, if an injunction were to issue and the vote be enjoined, both Emmis's stock price as well as its efforts to refinance before the November 2012 deadline could be seriously and adversely affected. As for the public interest, it is served best in our judgment by allowing the decisions made by this Indiana corporation to stand when, given the circumstances presented here, they appear to have acted in compliance with their statutory prerogatives. At this preliminary stage of the litigation, Plaintiffs have failed to show that Defendants' actions contravened either the IBCL or the relevant federal securities disclosure laws.

V. Conclusion

For the foregoing reasons, we hereby DENY Plaintiffs' request for injunctive relief.

IT IS SO ORDERED.

QUESTIONS

1. What ownership rights did the preferred holders that engaged in the swap transaction retain? If there were any, what value would they be likely to have?
2. The initial repurchase offer was a selective offer to ten large preferred shareholders. If the remaining shareholders were not offered exit at similar values, can they complain about unequal treatment?

3. Was this a coercive offer that preferred shareholders could not refuse? See Chancellor Allen's opinion in Katz v. Oak Industries in Chapter 6.

4. Note that Richard Gale, the preferred's representative on the board, approved the TRS swap proposal. Did Mr. Gale have a conflict of interest in his vote? Does it depend upon which preferred holder he represented, or does he represent all of them? Or does he represent the collective body of common and preferred shareholders?

5. Some commentators have suggested that the result in this case might be different under Delaware law. DGCL § 160(c) provides:

   > (c) Shares of its own capital stock belonging to the corporation or to another corporation, if a majority of the shares entitled to vote in the election of directors of such other corporation is held, directly or indirectly, by the corporation, shall neither be entitled to vote nor be counted for quorum purposes. Nothing in this section shall be construed as limiting the right of any corporation to vote stock, including but not limited to its own stock, held by it in a fiduciary capacity.

   Do you agree that the outcome of the case might have differed if Emmis were a Delaware corporation?

6. Can you make an argument that the board of directors was acting in the best interests of the corporation? Of the common stockholders? Of all the stockholders?

NOTE

In an excerpted section of the Emmis opinion, the court also discussed who is a "beneficial owner" of the preferred stock under the Williams Act, which requires public reporting of shares that are "beneficially owned" by persons holding more than 5% of the company's voting power. There, the court declined to address whether the TRS arrangements were part of a plan to avoid these reporting requirements. In CSX Corporation v. The Children's Investment Fund, 562 F.Supp. 2d 511 (S.D. N.Y. 2008), however, the federal court for the Southern District of New York addressed the question in a closely-followed proxy fight over the board of directors of CSX Corporation and the hedge funds The Children's Investment Fund Management (UK) LLP ("CIFM") and 3G Capital Partners Ltd. ("3G"). In anticipation of the proxy fight, CIFM and 3G had entered into total return swaps that, together with shares directly owned by them, covered more than 5% of CSX's voting power. In the case, the court considered whether the use of such swaps by CIFM and 3G constituted "beneficial ownership" of the subject stock under the theory that CIFM and 3G knew that the counterparty banks would actually purchase CSX shares in order to hedge their positions under the swaps and that those hedge counterparties were likely to vote in line with CIFM and 3G.

Both the district court and the Second Circuit were ultimately unable to resolve the matter, but the CSX decision nevertheless educated corporate counsel that hostile bidders could surreptitiously accumulate a target's shares without disclosure under the Williams Act. Moreover, this strategy could in theory thwart the purpose of a poison pill or shareholder rights plan. As discussed elsewhere in the casebook, these plans are triggered if prospective bidders reach specific ownership levels of a target's outstanding securities. Under these plans, ownership is generally defined in the terms used by federal regulations under Section 13(d) of the Williams Act, which defines the concept of "beneficial ownership." In addition to alerting corporate counsel to the risk that swaps could allow parties to evade a poison pill, the CSX case also prompted some firms to revise their poison pills to redefine the definition of "beneficial ownership." Consider, for instance, the following language from the poison pill for the JC Penney Company, Inc.:*

> (f) A Person shall be deemed the "Beneficial Owner" of, and shall be deemed to "beneficially own," any securities:
>
> * * *
>
> (iv) that are the subject of a derivative transaction entered into by such Person or any of such Person's Affiliates or Associates . . . that gives such Person or any of such Person's Affiliates or Associates the economic equivalent of ownership of an amount of such securities due to the fact that the value of the derivative is explicitly determined by reference to the price or value of such securities, or which provides such Person or any of such Person's Affiliates or Associates an opportunity, directly or indirectly, to profit, or to share in any profit, derived from any change in the value of such securities, in any case without regard to whether (a) such derivative conveys any voting rights in such securities to such Person or any of such Person's Affiliates or Associates, (b) the derivative is required to be, or capable of being, settled through delivery of such securities, or (c) such Person or any of such Person's Affiliates or Associates may have entered into other transactions that hedge the economic effect of such derivative. In determining the number of shares of Common Stock "beneficially owned" by virtue of the operation of this Section 1(f)(iv), the subject Person shall be deemed to "beneficially own" (without duplication) the notional or other number of shares of Common Stock specified in the documentation evidencing the derivative position as being subject to be acquired upon the exercise or settlement of the applicable right or as the basis upon which the value or settlement amount of such right, or the opportunity of the holder of such right to profit or share in any profit, is to be calculated in whole or in part, and in any case (or if no such number of shares of Common Stock is specified in such documentation or otherwise), as determined by the Board in good faith to be the number of shares of Common Stock to which the derivative position relates. . .

* See JC Penney Company, Inc., Form 8-K, filed August 21, 2013, available at https://www.sec.gov/Archives/edgar/data/1166126/000116612613000064/certificatedesig.htm.

If you were drafting a preferred stock provision for prospective investors, how might you use similar language to protect them from a maneuver like the one in *Emmis*?

---

5. FIDUCIARY DUTIES AND THE PREFERRED STOCK CONTRACT

In Chapter 6, we saw that a perennial challenge for debt investors concerns the problem of incomplete contracts: No contract can anticipate all future states of the world. As a result, a situation may arise where the interests of debt investors conflict with those of the common stockholders, but the debt contract is silent with respect to how it should be resolved. Moreover, because directors of corporations are elected by common stockholders, debt investors must anticipate that directors will use their authority to exploit any contractual gaps to advance the interests of common stockholders rather than those of debt investors. And while directors' exercise of discretion must comport with their fiduciary duties, cases such as Simons v. Cogan, 549 A.2d 300, 303 (Del. 1988) and North American Catholic Education Programming Foundation Inc v. Gheewalla, 930 A. 2d 92 (Del. 2007) make clear that these fiduciary duties do not run to debt investors, unless a company is insolvent.

Preferred stockholders also face the incomplete contracting problem. Indeed, the *Benchmark Capital* case from earlier in this chapter provides a clear example: Believing they had secured a veto right over adverse changes to their preferred stock, the Series A and Series B Preferred Stock investors ultimately discovered that their negotiated protections did not cover adverse changes made by way of a subsidiary merger. A similar problem faced the preferred stockholders in *Emmis*: Through the creative use of total return swaps, Emmis was able to acquire more than two-thirds of the preferred stock voting power, enabling the company to strip the preferred stock of important rights. In the process, the company shifted value from preferred stockholders to common stockholders.

Yet, in contrast to debt investors, preferred stockholders are formally stockholders. As a result, this fact raises the possibility that in addition to whatever express contract provisions they have secured, the preferred stock bargain might also be protected by the fiduciary duties owed to preferred stockholders. Indeed, as noted in Vice Chancellor Noble's opinion (in footnote 14), Benchmark made precisely this type of argument, although it was not raised in their request for a preliminary injunction (the subject of Vice Chancellor Noble's opinion). We explore in this section what, if any, fiduciary duties are owed to preferred stockholders.

Additionally, a board's fiduciary duties can potentially shape the preferred stock bargain in another way when preferred stockholders secure a representative on a company's board of directors. As we have seen, preferred stockholders will sometimes have the right to nominate one or more directors. This is especially common in venture capital investments and in situations where publicly traded companies have not paid earmarked dividends. (As you may recall, this was the reason why preferred stockholders had a board member in the *Emmis* case.) Yet these director-nominees often face an inescapable dilemma: As directors of the corporation, they clearly owe a fiduciary duty to the corporation and its stockholders, but as employees and/or directors of the preferred stockholder entity, they may also owe a duty of loyalty to the preferred stockholder itself. This should not pose a problem when a board's decision seeks to benefit all investors. But what if the exercise of board discretion would benefit the preferred stockholders at the expense of common stockholders (or vice-versa)? How is a director-nominee supposed to act when the decision involves a zero-sum game between these two investor classes? In this section we will also explore how courts have sought to answer these latter questions of inherent conflict.

A. BOARD DUTIES TO PREFERRED SHAREHOLDERS

Mary G. Dalton v. American Investment Company

490 A.2d 574 (Del. Ch. 1985)

■ BROWN, CHANCELLOR.

This action is brought by certain preferred shareholders of American Investment Company, a Delaware corporation. The suit charges that the individual defendants, in their capacity as the board of directors of American Investment Company (hereafter "AIC"), breached the fiduciary duty owed by them to the plaintiffs during the course of a merger whereby AIC was merged into Leucadia American Corp., a wholly-owned subsidiary of Leucadia, Inc. ("Leucadia"). In that merger, the common shareholders of AIC were eliminated from their equity position in the corporation at a price of $13 per share. However, the preferred shareholders of AIC were not cashed out, but were left as preferred shareholders of the corporation surviving the merger. Plaintiffs contend that AIC's board looked only to the interests of the common shareholders in seeking a merger partner for AIC and, by so doing, unfairly froze the preferred shareholders into the post merger AIC as completely controlled by Leucadia. Thus, the suit is unusual in that the plaintiff shareholders are complaining about being unfairly frozen in as shareholders as opposed to the more normal shareholder lament that they were unfairly cashed out.

The plaintiffs also contend that the benefit allegedly given to them in the merger—an increase in their preferred dividend percentage plus the creation of a sinking fund and a plan for the mandatory redemption of the preferred shares—was wrongfully accomplished since it was done without their approval. They say that this constituted a change which adversely affected their existing preference rights and that as a consequence they were entitled to vote as a class on the merger proposal. They say that the failure of the defendants to permit them to vote as a class rendered shareholder approval of the merger illegal and wrongfully forced them into their present predicament. Under either theory plaintiffs seek a recovery of money damages against the individual defendants as well as against Leucadia indirectly through its subsidiary, AIC.

* * *

I.

* * *

Aside from operating . . . insurance companies, AIC was in the business of consumer finance. In essence, it borrowed money wholesale in order to lend it at retail rates through a chain of offices scattered throughout the country. It is my impression that consumer finance was the primary business of AIC during the 1970's.

[Eds. During the late 1970s AIC found that rising interest rates were squeezing its profits. As a consumer finance company, it borrowed money at wholesale (presumably at low rates) and lent at retail (presumably at significantly higher rates). By April 1980, however, the prime rate (at which banks lend to their best customers) reached 20%, and other interest rates, as well as dividend rates on newly issued preferred stock, were correspondingly high. These high rates on new issues depressed the value of existing preferred stocks carrying lower dividend rates. Why didn't AIC just raise rates on its consumer lending activity? In many jurisdictions, consumer lending was subject to rate ceilings imposed by law, which could explain AIC's squeeze. In 1977 the AIC board retained Kidder, Peabody & Co., Inc. ("Kidder Peabody") to seek a prospective purchaser or merger partner.]

* * *

Kidder, Peabody sent out many letters and pursued numerous merger candidates. Eventually, in 1978, Household Finance Corporation ("HFC") came forth with an offer to acquire all outstanding shares of AIC. The offer of HFC was $12 per share for the common stock and $25 per share for the two series of preferred stock. At the time Kidder, Peabody had valued AIC's common stock within a range of $9 to $11, and the $12 figure offered by HFC approximated the then book value of the common shares. At the $25 redemption and liquidation value, the price offered for the preferred shares represented their book value also. The preferred shares were trading for about $9 per share at the time.

This offer by HFC was approved as fair by Kidder, Peabody and was accepted by AIC's board. It was also approved overwhelmingly by AIC's shareholders, both common and preferred. However, the United States Department of Justice entered the picture and sought to prohibit the acquisition by HFC on antitrust grounds. Ultimately, the acquisition of AIC by HFC was enjoined by the federal courts and HFC's merger proposal was terminated.

[Thereafter AIC's President, Brockmann, took an active role in seeking a new buyer. Because HFC's $12 per share price was approximately the book value of AIC's common stock at the time of its offer, Brockman used book value to suggest a floor for any new offers, in part because AIC's book value per share of common. Stock was rising to $13.50 even as its business deteriorated. HFC's offer of $25 for preferred stock trading at $9 was regarded as a "Christmas present" for the preferred shareholders. Brockman never suggested a $13.50 price for the common stock, but the HFC total bid was approximately $75 million, which was well known by market participants.]

* * *

In February, 1980, Leucadia, a company also in the consumer finance business, submitted a written offer to AIC whereby it proposed to acquire all common shares of AIC for $13 per share. The proposal contained no offer for the preferred shares but rather it proposed to leave them in place. Later, presumably as a result of Brockmann's suggestion that something should be done for the holders of the preferred, Leucadia revised its proposal by offering to make available to AIC's preferred shareholders immediately following the merger a Leucadia debenture worth 40% of the face value of the preferred shares, with interest at 13%, which could be exchanged for the preferred shares. Still later, however, because of declining economic conditions, Leucadia withdrew its offer altogether.

In August, 1980, Leucadia reappeared. This time it offered $13 per share for all outstanding shares of AIC's common stock and offered further to increase the dividend rate on the preferred shares from 5 ½% to 7%. In addition, and again because of Brockmann's expression of concern for the preferred shareholders, Leucadia added a "sweetener" in the form of a sinking fund to redeem the preferred shares over a period of 20 years at the rate of 5% each year. Any such redemptions were to continue to be made by lot as provided by AIC's original preference designations, but subject, however, to the added proviso that any market purchases or other acquisitions of preferred shares made during a given year could be credited against the annual 5% redemption requirement.

Kidder, Peabody opined that this offer was fair to AIC and its shareholders, stressing the fairness of the price to the common (AIC was trading for $11 per share on the day prior to the announcement of the approval of the merger in principle) and the safety that the proposal would provide to the rights of the preferred. The board of AIC accepted the offer and, when put to the vote of the shareholders, it was overwhelmingly approved by AIC's common shareholders and was approved unanimously by the holders of the other series of preferred stock. However, the holders of the Series B preferred, including the plaintiffs, voted some 170,000 of the 280,000 Series B shares against the proposal. Nonetheless, with all shares being accorded an equal vote, the plan of merger was adopted and AIC was merged into Leucadia American Corp., the wholly-owned subsidiary of Leucadia, with the name of the surviving corporation being changed to AIC. The former common shareholders of AIC were cashed out at $13 per share. Leucadia became the owner of all of AIC's common stock while the preferred shareholders were continued on as shareholders of AIC, albeit at the increased dividend rate and with the added redemption and sinking fund provisions.

Other relevant factors may be summarized as follows. On the same day that Leucadia submitted the offer that was ultimately accepted by AIC, another company, Dial Financial Corporation, still another company engaged in the consumer finance business, also submitted a merger proposal to AIC. The offer of Dial Financial Corporation (hereafter "Dial") was $13.50 per share for the common stock and nothing for the preferred other than the creation of a sinking fund for redemption purposes. The AIC board considered both offers but opted to take the Leucadia offer even though it was 50 cents per share lower for the common stock because the board viewed Leucadia's offer to be better from the standpoint of the preferred shareholders and because it avoided potential antitrust problems since Dial was a direct competitor of AIC in certain market areas.

* * *

II.

Addressing first the plaintiffs breach of fiduciary duty claims, it is their contention that the individual defendants, in their capacity as directors, owed a duty of fair dealing to all shareholders of AIC, both the common and the preferred, in negotiating and agreeing to any plan of merger. They say, however, that the defendant directors violated this duty to the extent that it was owed to the preferred shareholders once the HFC proposal had aborted. They charge that the defendants did so following the cancellation of the HFC offer by discreetly seeking to channel the whole of any prospective purchase price toward the payment for the common shares of AIC alone, and to the deliberate exclusion of the preferred shares.

[Plaintiffs argued that Brockmann sought to capture the whole of any $75 million offer for the common stockholders by suggesting book value as a floor on any bid, which would result in common shareholders receiving the entire purchase price to the exclusion of any benefit for the preferred.]

* * *

Plaintiffs . . . argue that even though they were minority preferred shareholders of AIC, they were nonetheless entitled to the protections of the fiduciary duty of fairness imposed upon those who were in a position to guide the fortunes of the corporation. They contend that the recent decision in Weinberger v. UOP, Inc., Del. Supr., 457 A.2d 701 (1984) makes it clear that they were owed a duty of fair dealing by AIC's board in its search for financial assistance for the company through the merger route. They say that our law is well established that where the real and only purpose of a merger is to promote the interests of one class of shareholders to the detriment, or at the expense, of another class of minority shareholders, the duty to deal fairly with all shareholders is violated and the merger transaction itself is rendered improper.

* * *

In response, the defendants take the position that the arguments of the plaintiffs ignore the economic and legal realities of the situation. They point out first that the preference rights applicable to the Series B preferred were negotiated in 1961 as a result of arms-length bargaining surrounding the purchase of the two insurance companies by AIC. They suggest that if the original preferred shareholders failed to negotiate for redemption or other rights in the event of a merger or sale of substantial assets, they had nobody to blame but themselves. Defendants suggest that the Series B shareholders were probably unable to get such rights because they traded them off in order to get what was then a highly favorable 5 ½% dividend rate, guaranteed indefinitely. But, say the defendants, the fact that what had been a good deal in 1961 had turned sour by 1980—when interest rates were hovering near 20%—did not impose a fiduciary duty on AIC's board to get the Series B preferred shareholders out of that deal, or to negotiate a new deal for them.

In short, defendants argue that the rights of preferred shareholders are contract rights and that as against the rights of the common shareholders they are fixed by the contractual terms agreed upon when the class of preferred stock is created. Since the preferred shareholders had no contractual right to be bought out as part of the acquisition of AIC by Leucadia—either at par value or at any other price—defendants argue that the board of AIC had no fiduciary duty to bargain on their behalf in an effort to obtain a cash-out deal for them also.

* * *

III.

Having considered the foregoing arguments in light of the evidence, I am satisfied that the answer to the plaintiffs' charges of breach of fiduciary duty lies somewhere between the legal positions advocated by the parties, and that it turns on the factual determination of whether or not Leucadia's offer was made in response to a solicitation by Brockmann and the other directors defendants. I find on the evidence that it was not, and accordingly I rule in favor of the defendants on this point.

As framed, the issue appears to be a troublesome one on the surface. However, it can be placed in perspective if certain factors are first weeded out. To begin with, I have no doubt that Brockmann and the AIC board were attempting to invite an offer of $13.50 for the common stock while at the same time they were seeking nothing specific for the preferred shares. One could scarcely reach any other conclusion. I am convinced also that they well suspicioned that if a third party offered anything near that amount for the common stock there would be little, if anything, offered for the preferred. I think that the inference to be drawn from the evidence on this point clearly preponderates in favor of the plaintiffs.

* * *

Given that Brockmann's approach of alluding to the book value of the common shares can, in the context of matters, be reasonably interpreted as a solicitation for an offer for the common shares only without a corresponding offer for the preferred, what the plaintiffs proceed to do in their argument is to then assume that the Leucadia offer was made in response to that solicitation and as a direct result of it. Because only if that were so can the plaintiffs establish that the predicament in which they now find themselves was caused by the conduct of the AIC directors, and only then would we reach the legal question of whether or not it was a breach of the fiduciary duty owed by the directors to the preferred shareholders for them to have engaged in such conduct.

I find that we do not have to reach this legal question because the inference of causal connection which the plaintiffs attempt to draw from the sequence of events as they happened is adequately rebutted by the direct evidence offered by Leucadia. When the trimmings of precedent and fiduciary duty are brushed aside, plaintiffs' argument, reduced to its simplest terms, is (1) that between the HFC proposal in 1978 and the Leucadia merger in 1980 the price per share for the common stock was increased from $12 to $13 per share while the preferred shareholders went from $25 per share to no cash consideration whatever, and (2) that during the interval between the two events Brockmann and the AIC board were soliciting offers at book value, or $13.50, for the common shares while seeking nothing for the preferred. From these two premises plaintiffs proceed to the conclusion that the difference between the HFC and Leucadia proposals was necessarily a direct result of the efforts by the AIC board to increase the cash consideration from the common stock with knowledge that such an increase would be at the expense of the preferred shares. Having thus bridged the gap to arrive at this factual conclusion, plaintiffs then plug it into the legal principle which holds that it is improper for those in a fiduciary position to utilize the merger process solely to promote the interests of one class of shareholders to the detriment, and at the expense, of the members of a minority class of shareholders. Thus plaintiffs reach their final position that they have been injured momentarily by the failure of the defendant directors to adhere to their fiduciary duty to deal fairly with all shareholders in a merger context.

The weakness in the plaintiffs' argument, as I see it, is making the factual assumption that because Brockmann's solicitation of an offer from Leucadia and the subsequent Leucadia offer crossed each other, the latter must have been a direct result of the former. It is the "but for" assumption. It is an argument that "but for" Brockmann's solicitation of an offer for the common stock alone with nothing sought for the preferred, Leucadia would likely have followed HFC's lead and proposed a buy-out of both classes of stock at a price of something less than $13 per share for the common and at a price either equating or approaching the liquidation value of the preferred. In addition to being speculative, such a proposition does not comport with the evidence.

The evidence indicates that the Leucadia offer was formulated and put forth by two of Leucadia's principle officers and shareholders, Ian M. Chumming and Joseph S. Steinberg. * * *

Overall, Steinberg's testimony indicates that Leucadia had its own economic justification for not cashing out the preferred shareholders, that Leucadia was advised by its attorneys that it was not legally necessary that the preferred shares be bought out, and that Leucadia reached its decision to offer to purchase the common shares only for its own reasons and not because of anything said by Brockmann or anyone else on behalf of AIC.

Accordingly, I find on the evidence that Leucadia's offer in the form in which it was put forth was not made in direct response to a veiled solicitation by Brockmann. Rather, I find that the Leucadia offer was made by knowledgeable and experienced businessmen who chose to take advantage of an existing situation of which they were well aware for business reasons peculiar to the interests of their company. Thus, I cannot find that the terms of the merger which left the plaintiffs as continuing preferred shareholders of AIC were brought about as a result of any breach of fiduciary duty on the part of the defendant directors of AIC, even assuming without deciding that the conduct of Brockmann and the AIC board in seeking a merger partner in the manner they did would have constituted a breach of fiduciary duty owed to AIC's preferred shareholders.

* * *

For the reasons given, judgment will be entered in favor of the defendants.

QUESTIONS

1. Why would Leucadia not be interested in purchasing the preferred stock at this time?

2. Does the court intimate that the directors owed duties to the preferred to see that it was sold along with the common? If no bid has yet been received, could the board seek a buyer solely for the common?

3. If you represent the AIC board when it is considering a sale of the company, and you have advised it that the holders of the Series B Preferred have no right to redemption, what would you advise the board about its duties to the Series B Preferred?

4. If the board has not received any offers but judges that the entire company is worth $75 million, must it seek to include the preferred in any sale? Must it seek $25 for a stock trading at $9? If it obtains such an offer, would the common stockholders have a claim against the board for not seeking more for the common?

5. Can you draft a provision that would have solved this problem for the Series B Preferred if the provision had been included in the terms of the Series B Preferred when this stock was first issued?

NOTE: SO WHAT FIDUCIARY DUTIES ARE OWED TO PREFERRED STOCKHOLDERS?

Preferred stock is often viewed as an investment hybrid, something in between debt and common stock. Despite this perception, the rights of preferred stockholders are generally seen as contractual, rather than deriving from fiduciary duties.* The standard recital of the courts is that "it is well established that the rights of preferred stockholders are contract rights." Baron v. Allied Artists Pictures Corporation, 337 A.2d 653, 657 (Del. Ch. 1975). Noting that preferred contract rights are protected in a limited way by the implied covenant of good faith and fair dealing, Vice Chancellor Jacobs stated that "[t]o allow a fiduciary claim to coexist in parallel with an implied contractual claim, would undermine the primacy of contract law over fiduciary law in matters involving the essentially contractual rights and obligations of preferred shareholders." Gale v. Bershad, 23 Del. J. Corp. L. 1294, 1306 (Del. Ch. 1998). The flintiness of the law in this area was famously demonstrated in Federal United Corp. v. Havender, discussed *supra* in this chapter, where the Delaware Supreme Court permitted the destruction of accrued arrearages on preferred stock, because the statute permitting exchanges of securities in mergers antedated the issuance of the preferred and was thus part of the shareholders' contract.

Notwithstanding these cases, other cases have made clear that preferred stockholders are owed some degree of fiduciary duties, making it difficult to articulate a clear standard by which to evaluate a company's treatment of preferred stockholders. The greatest confusion arises, predictably, in connection with acquisition and sale transactions. The blurring of the lines between contract and fiduciary duties is quite ancient here. For instance, in 1928 preferred stockholders complained that a merger agreement did not provide them with a fair amount of the purchase price, pleading that it was "grossly unfair and fraudulent with respect to the

* Victor Brudney, *Contract and Fiduciary Duty in Corporate Law*, 38 B. C. L. REV. 595, 649–51 (1997) (noting the exceptions to the doctrine).

preferred stockholders. . ." MacFarlane v. North American Cement Corp., 157 A. 396, 397 (Del. Ch. 1928). The court saw its duty as to determine whether the terms of the merger were "so grossly unfair and inequitable to the preferred stockholders . . . as to be a fraud upon them and entitle them to equitable relief."

While the opinion did not invoke fiduciary duties, they were invoked by Chancellor Allen in 1986, when he explained that while stated preferences were strictly governed by contract, "where however the right asserted is not to a preference as against the common stock but rather a right shared equally with the common, the existence of such right and the scope of the correlative duty may be measured by equitable as well as legal standards," and that a claim to a fair allocation of merger proceeds "fairly implicate fiduciary duties and ought not be evaluated wholly from the point of view of the contractual terms of the preferred stock designations." Jedwab v. MGM Grand Hotels, Inc., 509 A.2d 584, 594 (Del. Ch. 1986). Imposing a duty of "fair sharing" on directors is such an open standard that room for litigation should always exist. At about the same time, in the *Dalton* case, Chancellor Brown addressed the complaint of preferred shareholders left behind in their corporation when the common stock was acquired. In the face of defendants' claim that preferred stockholders were limited to their contract rights and preferred stockholders' claims of a breach of fiduciary duties owed them, Chancellor Brown, in Solomonic fashion, ruled that "the answer . . . lies somewhere between the positions advocated by the parties. . ." As illustrated in the opinion, the court then engaged in a fact-intensive analysis of whether the terms of the acquisition were initiated by the buyer or the seller, ultimately concluding that (even assuming a duty was owed to the preferred stockholders), the preferred stockholders failed to show that their damages were "caused" by the board's breach of this duty. The resulting body of law is something less than clear and invited further litigation.

For instance, Winston v. Mandor, 710 A.2d 835 (Del. Ch. 1997), involved a series of transactions in which a controlling common stockholder caused the corporation to purchase troubled real estate investments owned by the stockholder at an allegedly sweetheart price. This was followed by a transfer of the corporation's original properties to a newly created subsidiary and a spin-off of the shares of the subsidiary as a dividend to the common stockholders, leaving the convertible preferred stockholders with claims against a very different and allegedly inferior pool of assets. The preferred stockholders had no voting rights on the transactions, and thus the court held they had no claim that a stockholder vote was required for the spin-off, as a sale of substantially all assets under DGCL § 271. As for claims of breach of the board's fiduciary duty to the preferred stockholders, the court stated ". . . the corporation's duties and obligations to preferred stockholders include fiduciary responsibilities where their acts extend beyond the bounds of the contractual relationship contemplated by the certificate [of incorporation]. When, however, the corporate actions complained of are expressly contemplated by a certificate, the duties and obligations of the corporation and its preferred stockholders are governed exclusively by their contract. And so it is here." The court noted that the sale of substantially all assets and a dividend to common stockholder were covered by conversion and price adjustment provisions of the certificate of incorporation.

Another departure from the equitable allocation doctrine suggested in *Dalton* was provided by then Vice Chancellor Strine in LC Capital Master Fund, Ltd. v. James, 990 A.2d 435 (Del. Ch. 2010). The facts of the case arose from a merger where the convertible preferred stock was entitled to merger consideration on an "as-converted-to-common-stock" basis. When the merger provided exactly that, the preferred stockholders sued, arguing that the directors owed them a fiduciary duty to consider allocating more of the merger consideration to the preferred in recognition that in liquidation it would have been entitled to more proceeds than were paid in the merger. The court, however, rejected this argument, distinguishing cases such as *Jedwab* on the basis that the charter in *Jedwab* made no specific provision for the preferred in the event of a merger, leaving only the default rule of fair treatment to all classes.

The emphasis these decisions placed on deferring to the preferred stock contract (as opposed to fiduciary duties) to advance the interests of preferred stockholders clearly underscores the need for clear and precise contract drafting for preferred stockholders. But what about cases alleging that a board breached its fiduciary duties to preferred stockholders by exercising discretion in ways that undermined the preferred stockholders' express contractual rights in order to benefit the common stockholders?

In general, these cases have also not fared well for preferred stockholders. For instance, efforts by preferred stockholders to argue that a board's fiduciary duties should constrain a company's ability to engage in heavy-handed bargaining with the preferred stockholders have generally failed. As an example, in Gradient OC Master, Ltd. v. NBC Universal, Inc. 930 A.2d 104 (Del. Ch. 2007), Vice Chancellor Parsons examined an exchange offer being made by a company to its preferred stockholders as part of a recapitalization. In the exchange offer, each tendering preferred stockholder would receive subordinated debt and newly issued preferred stock having seniority over the prior preferred stock; however, as a condition to tendering their shares, each holder of prior preferred stock would be required to consent to the removal of various covenants protecting the prior preferred stock. The exchange offer thus posed the same type of "coercive" exchange offer at issue in Katz v. Oak Indus., 508 A.2d 873, 880 (Del. Ch. 1986), examined in Chapter 6.

In response to claims that the exchange offer violated fiduciary duties owed to the preferred stockholders, Vice Chancellor Parsons denied the claim, focusing instead on whether the exchange offer complied with the preferred stock's formal contract rights:

> Should a majority of the 14¼% Preferred Stock choose to support the Company's decision to recapitalize in this manner, the elimination of the non-tendered shares' covenants is merely an effect of the reality that a majority of the 14¼% peers have disagreed with the non-tendering shareholders and concluded that accepting the Exchange Offer is in their best interest. The

> amendment of the [Certificate of Designations ("CD")] for the 14¼% Preferred Stock by the holders of a majority of that class of stock is authorized by the CD.

For Vice Chancellor Parsons, this limited focus on compliance with preferred stockholders' formal contract rights was appropriate because the Board's duty is to the overall corporation and not to one group of stockholders: "To suggest that the Board must fashion an imitative recapitalization or favor one group of shareholders over the overall benefit to the corporation here would contravene the fundamental principle that a board may freely make decisions that benefit [the firm] as a whole." In other words, a Board's aggressive approach to preferred stock rights is perfectly acceptable so long as the Board does so to maximize the value of the firm (and consequently, the value of its residual claimants).

Indeed, Vice Chancellor Laster has suggested that a Board's fiduciary duties may even require it to *breach* the preferred stock contract if doing so maximizes the value of the corporation and its residual claimants. Specifically, in Frederick Hsu Living Trust v. ODN Holding Corporation, 2017 WL 1437308 (Del. Ch. 2017), Vice Chancellor Laster articulated a Board's fiduciary duty as requiring it "to promote the value of the corporation for the benefit of its stockholders," noting that "the question naturally arises: which stockholders?" For Vice Chancellor Laster the "answer is the stockholders in the aggregate in their capacity as residual claimants, which means the undifferentiated equity as a collective, without regard to any special rights." Under this understanding of a Board's duties, any action by the Board that depleted the value of the residual claim, such as entering into a contract for less than fair value, would violate a Board's fiduciary duty. But so too would the failure of the Board to consider the corporation's alternatives given its *existing* contractual obligations, including those owed to preferred stockholders:

> Even with an iron-clad contractual obligation, there remains room for fiduciary discretion because of the doctrine of efficient breach. Under that doctrine, a party to a contract may decide that its most advantageous course is to breach and pay damages. Just like any other decision maker, a board of directors may choose to breach if the benefits (broadly conceived) exceed the costs (again broadly conceived). . . . A corollary of this principle is that directors who choose to comply with a contract when it would be value-maximizing (broadly conceived) to breach could be subject, in theory, to a claim for breach of duty. For a contract with a third party, the business judgment rule typically will govern and prevent such a claim from getting beyond the pleading stage, but the fiduciary standard of conduct remains operative and the underlying legal theory therefore exists.

Thus, even with something as clear as an immediate preferred stock redemption right, the fiduciary duties owed to a corporation's "stockholders" might require the Board to consider breaching the redemption right if doing so would grow the overall residual claim held across all stockholders.* Do these cases help explain why Benchmark Capital chose not to pursue a fiduciary claim as the basis for its preliminary injunction request? Similarly, what types of corporate conduct would clearly justify a preferred stockholder in bringing a fiduciary duty claim against a board of directors in light of the language used in *ODN*? A fuller discussion of Delaware cases is found in Marilyn B. Cane et al., *Recent Developments Concerning Stockholder Rights Under Delaware Law*, 5 Va. L. & Bus. Rev. 377 (2011).

B. DUTIES OF A PREFERRED-CONTROLLED BOARD

Orban v. Field

1997 WL 153831 (Del. Ch. 1997)

■ ALLEN, CHANCELLOR.

This is a stockholders' suit brought by certain holders of common stock of Office Mart Holdings Corp. ("Office Mart"). The suit arises out of a series of transactions culminating in a June 23, 1992 stock-for-stock merger between Office Mart and a subsidiary of Staples, Inc. The first of the transactions was a November 15, 1991 recapitalization in which, in exchange for forgiveness of principal and interest of outstanding notes, Office Mart creditors accepted a package of securities including common stock warrants and a new Series C Preferred stock. The second step was board action of May 1992 facilitating the exercise of certain warrants held by the holders of preferred stock. The concluding transaction was the merger with Staples. In that merger, various classes of Office Mart preferred stock were entitled to liquidation preferences that together exceed the value of the consideration paid. Thus, the Office Mart common stock received no consideration in the merger. The merger was an arm's-length transaction and it is not contended in this suit that the price paid by Staples was not a fair price or the best price reasonably available.

In summary, the claims made are now two. First, it is asserted that the Office Mart board breached its duty to the common stock by facilitating steps that enabled the holders of preferred stock to exercise warrants that enabled the preferred to overcome a practical power that

---

* The implications of this case were not lost on the drafters of the NVCA model documents. As noted in the NVCA Model Charter, the prevailing version of the model charter includes a provision that requires a company to pay interest at the maximum permitted rate under applicable state law in the event a preferred stock redemption request is not honored. As noted in the comments to the model charter, "Including this type of interest provision to induce compliance with a redemption obligation may be even more important following the Delaware Chancery Court's ruling in The Frederick Hsu Living Trust v. ODN Holding Corporation, Case No. C. A. 12108-VCL (Del. Ch. Apr. 14, 2017), in which the court suggested that where the amount of a redemption obligation is fixed and will not increase over time a board of directors may breach its fiduciary duties by complying with such obligation rather than growing the corporation's business for the benefit of the corporation's common stockholders and gradually redeeming shares over a long-term horizon."

the common held to impede the closing of the merger. This claim in essence asserts that the board, which was controlled by holders of preferred stock, exercised corporate power against the common and in favor of the preferred and, thus, breached a duty of loyalty to the common. * * *

* * *

Extensive discovery has now occurred and an amended complaint, which no longer contains claims concerning undisclosed negotiations, has been filed. Defendants have moved for summary judgment.

For the reasons that follow, I conclude that no fact material to the appropriate legal analysis is in dispute and that defendants are entitled to judgment as a matter of law. With respect to the first claim, I conclude that there is no evidence upon which a fact finder could conclude that the board's actions (as explained below) in facilitating the exercise by holders of preferred stock of their legal rights to exercise warrants represented a disloyal act towards the common stock. Even assuming, as I do, that in facilitating the exercise of the warrants in these circumstances (where the warrants were used to overcome Mr. Orban's resistance to the merger) the board has a burden to establish either the reasonableness of its actions or its fairness, the record is in my judgment, entirely consistent with that conclusion and wholly inconsistent with the opposite conclusion.

* * *

I. Relevant Facts

George Orban, the principal plaintiff in this action, founded Office Mart in 1987; served as its CEO until 1989; and as a director until March 1992. From 1987 to 1992, Office Mart developed and operated a chain of ten "WORKplace" office supply superstores in and around Tampa, Florida. The company was, however, never well capitalized. That fact became rather quickly apparent when the company sought to expand into the California market in 1988, from which it was forced to retreat.

Capital structure: Initially, the company was capitalized largely with equity in the form of voting preferred stock from institutional investors. Mr. Orban, who in this litigation, characterizes himself as a "venture capitalist," invested only approximately $15,000 in exchange for which he received all of the common stock. (Later other employees of the firm came to hold modest amounts of the common as well). The substantial capital came in several tranches from financial institutions. 2,422,750 shares of Series A preferred stock were issued in 1987 to raise $2,950,000 in initial capital. In May 1988, an additional $17,084,080 was raised by the private placement of 6,833,632 shares of Series B preferred stock.

All classes of equity voted together. Mr. Orban was the largest holder of common stock, however, he held only 14.32% of the total voting power. Series A and Series B preferred stockholders held 22.59% and 63.18%, respectively, of the company's total voting rights. Both classes of preferred stock were convertible into common stock and entitled to vote on an as-converted basis, both had anti-dilution rights and possessed liquidation preferences payable in the event of a merger.* The common stock, of course, had no such rights.

Continuing need for long term capital: Relatively early on, by June 1989, Office Mart's board was forced to conclude that it either had to find additional capital to pursue an aggressive growth strategy, or had to sell the company. At that point, Mr. Orban resigned as CEO and Stephen Westerfield agreed to assume the duties of CEO. He had had no prior involvement with Office Mart [although he was an experienced former president of another company]. Mr. Westerfield began taking steps to address these issues. The investment banking firm of Donaldson Lufkin & Jenrette was hired to assist in these efforts, but no potential investors or acquirors were identified and the financial position of the company continued to worsen.

Recognizing that it would be difficult for Office Mart to borrow necessary capital from commercial lenders, the company began to consider means to attract additional capital from the company's current investors. In April 1990, a group of Series B stockholders (including affiliates of Prudential Insurance, and Manufacturers Hanover Bank) provided the company with a $5.2 million line of credit in consideration of the issuance by the company of its 13% secured notes and warrants to acquire 40% of the company's fully diluted equity shares, exercisable at a price of $1.39 per share. The notes matured in three years (due on March 31, 1993) but could be prepaid at par plus accrued interest.

Office Mart began to draw down its credit facility shortly after its establishment. The company had difficulty from the beginning in meeting the interest payments on the debt. In order to ameliorate this situation in January 1991, an agreement was reached with creditors pursuant to which the company's interest obligations were deferred, in consideration of the grant of additional common stock warrants. The warrants covered common stock equal to 1.75% of total equity for each quarter of interest deferred, for a maximum of up to 10.575% of total equity. Despite the credit facility and deferred interest agreement, Office Mart continued to have financial difficulties throughout 1991.

The recapitalization: On September 5, 1991, Mr. Westerfield recommended that a recapitalization plan be adopted in order to eliminate the debt burden on the company's balance sheet. During a telephone meeting on September 27, 1991, Mr. Westerfield expressed his opinion that the recapitalization was necessary for the company to continue as a going concern; the board approved a proposed recapitalization plan at that time. On November 14, 1991, the Board again unanimously voted on the terms of the recapitalization,

* Eds. We discuss anti-dilution rights in Chapter 8.

authorizing the company's officers to effectuate the transaction on the following day. At that meeting, Mr. Westerfield informed the Board that "there was no significant activity" with respect to efforts that had been made to locate potential investors or buyers of the company.

The material elements of the recapitalization plan: First, a new senior, nonconvertible Series C Senior Cumulative Redeemable Preferred Stock was created.[5] In exchange for 5.2 million shares of the Series C preferred stock and 2,136,976 new shares of common stock (equal to more than half of all then outstanding common stock and equal to 10% of the fully diluted equity of the company), the holders of the debt agreed to its cancellation and released the company from the repayment of the $5.2 million principal amount and $607,800 in accrued interest. Finally, the company reduced the exercise price on the warrants issued to the creditors in connection with the original extension of the $5.2 million credit, from $1.39 to $0.75 per share.

Mr. Orban voted in favor of the recapitalization as a member of the Board and, subsequently, in his capacity as a Series A preferred stockholder. Although the common stockholders never were asked to approve the recapitalization plan in a shareholders' vote, it went into effect on November 15, 1991.[6]

As a result of the recapitalization plan, the following changes in the company's capital structure were to be made. As to Mr. Orban, his combined ownership of common and preferred stock was diluted from 13.27% to 2.54%. As to the common stockholders as a group, since the total number of shares of common stock outstanding had been increased from 1,548,411 to 3,683,387 shares, the percentage of voting power held by the holders of the pre-recap common was reduced from 14% to less than 3%. As to the former creditors, the recapitalization was structured to provide them with a potential for 50% voting interest in the company, with the Series A and B preferred stockholders now capable of voting 10.54% and 36.92% of the equity respectively, and with the remainder 3% voted by the common stockholders.

[Shortly after the recapitalization Westerfield began his search for an investor. His efforts resulted in an offer from Office Depot valuing the company at approximately $30 million. The board rejected the offer and instructed management to keep negotiating and to solicit offers from others. No other offers were received within two months, and the board

---

5 In the event of a liquidation or merger of the company, the new Series C preferred stock would entitle its owners to receive an initial preference of $7.5 million and a secondary preference of $1.5 million to be paid only after $12 million had been distributed to the A and B preferred stockholders. After the satisfaction of the secondary preference, the remaining proceeds would first go to the A and B preferred stockholders in order to meet their still unpaid liquidation preferences. The common stockholders would not receive any distributions until all of these preferences had been satisfied in full.

6 This Court has determined that the common stockholders were not legally entitled to vote as a class on the recapitalization plan. *See Orban*, Mem. Op. at 19. The plan was approved by the Board and holders of Class A and B preferred stock which together constituted a majority of the total voting power of the company.

instructed Westerfield to renew negotiations for an improved offer with Office Depot. Shortly after the board meeting, Staples, concerned that Office Depot might acquire the company, expressed interest in acquiring Office Mart. By February 22, Staples had agreed to acquire Office Mart for Staples Stock valued at $35 million, based on the current price of Staples' stock.]

The Staples proposal was for a merger qualifying as a tax free merger and for "pooling of interests" accounting treatment. In order to assure that the transaction qualified for pooling of interest treatment, Staples demanded a contract clause requiring that holders of each class of Office Mart stock approve the transaction with a 90% vote.

[Eds. Prior to its elimination in 2001, pooling of interest accounting allowed a merger to occur without any need for the acquiring firm to recognize goodwill arising from the transaction. Because goodwill was required to be amortized prior to 2001, a transaction that could be structured as a pooling-of-interest transaction minimized future accounting charges. In order to qualify for pooling-of-interest treatment, however, a merger had to meet a number of criteria, inducing Staples to make the demand for common stockholder approval of the merger.]

* * *

Third, the parties had to agree upon a stock allocation date upon which to determine the proportionate distribution of the Staples shares to Office Mart stockholders. Due to the fact that the total consideration was of less value than the total preferred stock preferences, as of the date of the letter agreement, this issue was particularly important to the common stockholders. The common stockholders could only receive merger consideration if the value of the Staples shares exceeded $35,062,470—the total amount of preferences to which the preferred were entitled—on the stock allocation date. The Board elected the date of May 29, the date of the signing of the definitive merger agreement. In hindsight, we know that the stock allocation date was inconsequential for the common stockholders because they would not have received merger proceeds on any of the possible stock allocation dates.

[The Staples agreement was conditioned not only on a 90% vote of all shares eligible to vote, but also on the approval of 90% of the shares of each class. Because Mr. Orban held more than 10% of the common stock, and expressed opposition to a merger in which the common would receive nothing, the board met with him in a series of unsuccessful negotiations to resolve the dispute.]

Dilution of Mr. Orban's common stock interest: Instead of continuing negotiations with Mr. Orban, the Board removed the impediment to the closure of the transaction by facilitating the exercise of warrants to acquire common stock by the Series A and B stockholders.

Several steps were required to effectuate this readjustment of proportionate ownership. First, the company's certificate of incorporation had to be amended to increase the authorized common stock from 25 to 56 million and preferred stock shares from 15 to 16.175 million. Second, to compensate for the issuance of additional shares, the Board adjusted the conversion ratio of the Series A and B and proportionately increase the number of warrants held by the holders of Series C preferred. Third, the Board proportionately reduced the exercise price of the warrants from $.75 to $.28726 in order to maintain the total exercise price of $6.4 million. Finally, the Board authorized the redemption of 2,089,714 shares held by Series C preferred stockholders, on a non-pro rata basis. In doing so, the company extended sufficient consideration to the Series C holders ($3,013,995) to enable them to exercise warrants to permit them, as a group, to hold more than 90% of Office Mart's outstanding common stock. The aggregate effect of these steps was to assure that Mr. Orban was entitled to vote less than 10% of the company's common stock.

The merger: When Office Mart and Staples entered into the definitive merger agreement on May 29, 1992, the agreement received the approval of 90% of each class of outstanding stock. As of May 29, the stock valuation date, the 1,093,750 shares of Staples common stock were worth a total of $31,992,188. When the transaction closed on June 23, that amount was used to allocate the merger proceeds to be distributed to each class of Office Mart stock in accord with the preferences of the preferred stockholders.

Since the merger consideration was insufficient to satisfy all of the contractual preferences of Office Mart's preferred stockholders, Mr. Orban and the other common stockholders received no proceeds. It might be noted, however, that Mr. Orban would have received no proceeds from the merger even if the recapitalization and related transactions had never occurred.

* * *

II. Analysis

Plaintiffs contend that the Board breached its fiduciary duty of loyalty to the common stockholders by facilitating the exercise of legal rights of preferred stockholders in transactions aimed at eliminating the leverage of the common stockholders by diluting their ownership interest below 10%.[23] The basic theory of Mr. Orban's case is that although the common stock was practically under water (i.e., valueless in a liquidation context) as of the spring of 1992, when evaluating the merger consideration in relation to the preferred stock preferences, *the pooling provision requiring a 90% approval vote of each class of stock gave Mr. Orban stock a certain value.* That value was destroyed when the Board took actions to assist the preferred stockholders to exercise their warrants, diluting the plaintiffs' common stock interest below 10%.

---

[23] There is no claim that the Board engaged in fraud or that the merger itself was not in the best interests of the corporation.

In response, defendants contend that the contested actions taken by the Board did not constitute any breach of fiduciary duty because they were legal and necessary to effectuate a merger in the best interest of the company. Further, defendants argue that the business judgment rule should apply to all of the challenged acts of the Board because the directors neither stood on both sides of the transactions nor received distinct personal benefits from such transactions.[24] According to defendants, all of the challenged acts of the Board were approved by a fully informed majority of disinterested directors and then ratified by an informed majority of the stockholders. *Williams v. Geier*, Del. Supr., 671 A.2d 1368 (1996).*

For purposes of this motion for summary judgment, I will assume that the business judgment rule is not applicable to the actions challenged by Mr. Orban's breach of fiduciary duty claim. Unquestionably in this instance the board of directors exercised corporate power—most pointedly in authorizing a non-pro-rata redemption of preferred shares for the purpose of funding the exercise by holders of preferred stock of warrants to buy common stock. That act was directed against the common stock who found themselves with a certain leverage because of the requirements for pooling treatment. A board may certainly deploy corporate power against its own shareholders in some circumstances—the greater good justifying the action—but when it does, it should be required to demonstrate that it acted both in good faith and reasonably. See Phillips v. Insituform, Inc., Del. Ch., C.A. No. 9173, 1987 Del. Ch. LEXIS 474, Allen, C. (Aug. 27, 1987); *Unocal Corp. v. Mesa Petroleum Co.*, Del. Supr., 493 A.2d 946 (1985); *see also Unitrin, Inc. v. American General Corp.*, Del. Supr., 651 A.2d 1361 (1995). The burden is upon defendants, the party moving for summary judgment, to show that their conduct was taken in good faith pursuit of valid ends and was reasonable in the circumstances.

While such a test is inevitably one that must be applied in the rich particularity of context, it is not inconsistent with summary adjudication where no material facts are in dispute or disputed facts may be assumed in favor of non-movant. In my opinion, the record established, satisfies the defendants' burden.

As a preliminary matter, it is important to note that there is no evidence, or even remaining allegation, that the November recapitalization was part of a scheme to deprive the common stockholders of consideration in the subsequent merger. The recapitalization was

24 Defendants stress that the fact that a director represents a large shareholder of the company is insufficient alone to find that a director was interested in the transaction. *See Citron v. Fairchild Camera and Instrument Corp.*, Del. Supr., 569 A.2d 53, 65 (1989). Although this is true even where other shareholders are in potential conflict with the affiliated shareholder, it is inapplicable if there had been special treatment of the affiliated shareholders, as is alleged in this case. *Id.*

* Eds. In addition to Orban, the other three directors were Westerfield, alleged by Orban to have a conflict because of his right to severance payments on a sale or merger, and two officers of corporate owners of Series B preferred stock.

legally effectuated by the Board, validly altering the existing ownership structure of the company. Certainly, when viewed as an isolated event, the recapitalization was fair, authorized appropriately, and if it were to be tested under a fairness test, it would satisfy that standard.

The subsequent conduct of the Board, while requiring a more involved analysis, was, in my opinion, fair as a matter of law as well.

Duty of loyalty: Dilution of Mr. Orban's common stock interest: Once Orban attempted to use a potential power to deprive the transaction of pooling treatment, the Board was inevitably forced to decide whether it would support the common stock's (Mr. Orban's) effort to extract value from the preferred position or whether it would seek to accomplish the negotiated transaction, which it believed to be the transaction at the highest available price.

Certainly in some circumstances a board may elect (subject to the corporation's answering in contract damages) to repudiate a contractual obligation where to do so provides a net benefit to the corporation. To do so may in some situations be socially efficient. *See, e.g.,* Richard Craswell, *Contract Remedies, Renegotiation, and the Theory of Efficient Breach,* 61 S. CAL. L. REV. 629 (1988). But it would be bizarre to take this fact of legal life so far as to assert, as Mr. Orban must, that the Board had a duty to common stock to refrain from recognizing the corporation's legal obligations to its other classes of voting securities.[26]

To resolve this situation, the Board decided not to negotiate with Mr. Orban, but rather to effectuate the transaction as intended, respecting the preferential rights of the preferred stockholders. In my opinion, it cannot be said that the Board breached a duty of loyalty in making this decision. Whereas the preferred stockholders had existing legal preferences, the common stockholders had no legal right to a portion of the merger consideration under Delaware law or the corporate charter. The Staples' transaction appeared reasonably to be the best available transaction. Mr. Orban's threat to impede the realization of that transaction by the corporation was thwarted by legally permissible action that was measured and appropriate in the circumstances.

* * *

Based on the foregoing, defendants' motion for summary judgment is granted.

---

[26] In economic terms, Mr. Orban's position does not represent an allocatively efficient transaction, the presence of which may make efficient breach socially desirable. Rather, it could be preferable to deny the preferred their full liquidation preference (or the fullest amount of it available) only on the assumption that, as a practical matter, Office Mart would not be required to repair the loss with damages.

QUESTIONS

1. What was the nature of Orban's complaint that the board acted in a self-interested way to favor the preferred shareholders? Was it the recapitalization? Was it the repurchase of preferred shares?
2. If the board owes fiduciary duties to all shareholders, did it owe any duty to allocate some part of the merger consideration to the common stockholders, in exchange for their (diluted) veto power, as "tribute," in the words of the district judge in Goldman v. Postal Telegraph, Inc.?
3. Does this decision give a preferred-controlled board the power to ignore the welfare of the common in a merger?
4. If Orban had dissented from the merger and demanded the appraised fair value of his shares, would he have a better case than this complaint about fiduciary duties?

In re Trados Incorporated Shareholder Litigation

73 A.3d 17 (Del. Ch. 2013)

■ LASTER, VICE CHANCELLOR.

TRADOS Inc. ("Trados" or the "Company") obtained venture capital in 2000 to support a growth strategy that could lead to an initial public offering. The VC firms received preferred stock and placed representatives on the Trados board of directors (the "Board"). Afterwards, Trados increased revenue year-over-year but failed to satisfy its VC backers. In 2004, the VC directors began looking to exit. As part of that process, the Board adopted a management incentive plan (the "MIP") that compensated management for achieving a sale even if the transaction yielded nothing for the common stock.

In July 2005, SDL plc acquired Trados for $60 million in cash and stock (the "Merger"). Under Trados's certificate of incorporation, the Merger constituted a liquidation that entitled the preferred stockholders to a liquidation preference of $57.9 million. Without the MIP, the common stockholders would have received $2.1 million. The MIP took the first $7.8 million of the Merger consideration. The preferred stockholders received $52.2 million. The common stockholders received nothing.

* * *

The plaintiff contended that instead of selling to SDL, the Board had a fiduciary duty to continue operating Trados independently in an effort to generate value for the common stock. Despite the directors' failure to follow a fair process and their creation of a trial record replete with contradictions and less-than-credible testimony, the defendants carried their burden of proof on this issue. Under Trados's business plan, the common stock had no economic value before the Merger, making it fair for its holders to receive in the Merger the substantial equivalent of what they had before. The appraised value of the common stock is likewise zero.

I. FACTUAL BACKGROUND

[Eds. Trados began life as a company selling desktop translation software in 1984. It became the dominant product in the desktop software market, but by the late 1990s the founders wanted to expand into the corporate "enterprise" market. By this time its annual sales were $11–$14 million, and it sought venture capital financing. As is usually the case, this financing was done in stages, with the first stage (Series A Participating Preferred) sold to Wachovia Capital Partners in 2000. The stock carried an 8% cumulative dividend. Wachovia designated Scanlan as its representative on the board. At about the same time, Hg Capital invested in the company's Series C and Series D Preferred Stock, and Hg designated Stone as its representative on the board. Both Wachovia and Hg made follow-on investments. Each series of preferred stock had a liquidation preference equal to the purchase price plus accrued dividends.

In the following years Trados made steady gains in revenue. In 2002 Trados acquired Uniscape, a software company, in a stock-for-stock merger. Uniscape's principal venture capital backer, Sequoia Capital, exchanged its Uniscape preferred stock for Trados' Series E Preferred Stock on terms similar to those of the other venture capitalists, and Sequoia designated Gandhi and Prang as its representatives on the Trados board. Later in 2002 Invision AG, a Swiss firm, invested in the company's Series F Preferred Stock, on terms similar to the earlier series. Invision designated Laidig as its representative on the board.

Trados' progress was steady if not exciting. Annual sales reached $24.8 million in 2003. By 2004 progress was slowing. The CEO, Dev Ganesan, lowered revenue projections for the year and maintained current employment levels, despite declining cash reserves. In early 2004 the board asked Kevin McClelland at the investment bank JMP, to meet with Ganesan to begin setting the table for a sale by discussing "opportunities for Trados in the public equity and M & A markets." In April the board terminated Ganesan and named one of the founders, Hummel, as Acting President, but told him to consult with two of the directors before taking any important action. One director was appointed as a search committee for a new CEO, while the board sent Hummel to contact Trados' major commercial relationships, Microsoft, Bowne Global Solutions, and Documentum, Inc., to see if they had any interest in acquiring Trados. When none of these companies showed any interest, the board searched more broadly. When this search turned up one interested party (named SDL), the board retained JMP, an investment bank, to serve as advisor and search for additional potential buyers.

At the same time the board hired Joseph Campbell as a new CEO, with the understanding that there would be an incentive plan to reward the top executives for a successful sale of Trados. The board understood that otherwise managers might not have sufficient incentives to remain with the company through a sale. McClellan presented JMP's valuation calculations, which ranged from $20.4 million to $169.8 million, using various methodologies, and identified a number of potential targets, most of which had no interest in Trados. Only SDL seemed serious. After further meetings with Stone of Trados, Lancaster of SDL offered $10 million cash and $30 million in SDL stock, which the Trados directors rejected. At the July 7, 2004 board meeting the board approved hiring Campbell as CEO, and Scanlan suggested the board adopt a plan to motivate management to pursue a sale. It was at this time that the board adopted the MIP.

As Campbell took over as CEO, he wanted to focus on growing the business rather than keeping a "for sale" sign on it, and he terminated the relationship with JMP. Campbell solved a short-term liquidity problem by borrowing $4 million. By the fourth quarter of 2004, revenues reached a record level and profits of $1.1 million were also a record. By early 2005 Lancaster told director Stone that SDL remained interested in pursuing an acquisition. Scanlan inquired about what price would be acceptable to Trados, and the board asked Campbell to prepare a model showing cash distributions at $50, $60 and $70 million. When the numbers were ready, Invision, the last of the investors, indicated it would not sell below its investment valuation of $60 million, and the board decided that Campbell would seek $60 million from SDL. Shortly thereafter Campbell presented his projections to the board, showing substantial growth in revenues through 2007 by concentrating on the enterprise market, where Trados' market share was lower than in the desktop market.

SDL eventually offered $50 million cash and $10 million in stock for Trados, and the venture capital investors agreed to the price. By this time other mergers in this field made SDL the only likely buyer for Trados. After the board approved the deal, the company's revenues and profits continued to grow. As negotiations with SDL continued, SDL agreed that Campbell would become President of the combined company, and would join SDL's board. Prior to the closing in June of 2005, the board approved a $250,000 bonus for Campbell and a smaller one for Budge, Trados's CFO.]

At the time of the Merger, the total liquidation preference on the preferred stock was $57.9 million, including accumulated dividends. The proceeds remaining after the MIP payments—approximately $52.2 million—went to satisfy the liquidation preference. Each of the preferred stockholders received less than their full liquidation preference but more than their initial investment. * * *

As events turned out, the preferred stockholders actually received somewhat less. Under the Merger agreement, approximately $4 million of the consideration was set aside in escrow to address indemnification claims. Only $968,000 from the escrow was dispersed to the preferred stockholders, leaving them with total proceeds of $49.2 million. The common stockholders received nothing.

At the June 15, 2005 meeting, the Board determined that the Merger was "advisable and in the best interests of the Company and its stockholders" and formally "authorized, adopted and approved" it. The Board also approved and recommended to stockholders an amendment to the Company's certificate of incorporation that reset the liquidation preferences of the preferred stock at the specific amounts they would receive in the Merger.

All that remained were the necessary stockholder approvals, one by the preferred and one by the common. Trados management anticipated getting both votes handily. . . .

On June 17, 2005, Trados's stockholders approved the Merger. Microsoft abstained, advising Campbell that "the economic result from the perspective of our equity interest is not such that we are prepared to actively vote in favor. . . ."

P. The Plaintiff Sues.

Plaintiff Marc Christen owned about 5% of Trados's common stock. On July 21, 2005, he sought appraisal for his 1,753,298 shares.

* * *

On July 3, 2008, based on discovery from the appraisal action, Christen filed a second lawsuit, individually and on behalf of a class of Trados's common stockholders, alleging that the former Trados directors breached their duty of loyalty by approving the Merger. After the actions were consolidated, the defendants moved to dismiss the new claims and obtained a stay of discovery in both actions pending the outcome of the motion. With one exception, Chancellor Chandler denied the motion. * * *

In 2010, the action was reassigned to me [from former Chancellor Chandler]. * * * On March 11, 2011, I certified a class "consist[ing] of all beneficial owners of Trados, Inc.'s common stock whose shares were extinguished by a merger on July 7, 2005, with the exception of defendants. . ." At the close of discovery, the defendants again moved for summary judgment. After the motion was denied, the case proceeded to trial.

II. LEGAL ANALYSIS

* * * The breach of fiduciary duty claim seeks an equitable remedy that requires a finding of wrongdoing. The appraisal proceeding seeks a statutory determination of fair value that does not require a finding of wrongdoing. * * * Consistent with the Delaware Supreme Court's instructions, this decision starts with the plaintiff's claim for breach of fiduciary duty, then turns to the appraisal. It also considers the plaintiff's request for leave to file an application for fee shifting under the bad faith exception to the American Rule.

A. The Breach of Fiduciary Duty Claim

* * *

Under Delaware law, the standard of review depends initially on whether the board members (i) were disinterested and independent (the business judgment rule), (ii) faced potential conflicts of interest because of the decisional dynamics present in particular recurring and recognizable situations (enhanced scrutiny), or (iii) confronted actual conflicts of interest such that the directors making the decision did not comprise a disinterested and independent board majority (entire fairness). The standard of review may change further depending on whether the directors took steps to address the potential or actual conflict, such as by creating an independent committee, conditioning the transaction on approval by disinterested stockholders, or both. * * *

1. The Standard Of Conduct

Delaware corporate law starts from the bedrock principle that "[t]he business and affairs of every corporation . . . shall be managed by or under the direction of a board of directors." 8 Del. C. § 141(a). When exercising their statutory responsibility, the standard of conduct requires that directors seek "to promote the value of the corporation for the benefit of its stockholders."

* * *

A Delaware corporation, by default, has a perpetual existence. Equity capital, by default, is permanent capital. In terms of the standard of conduct, the duty of loyalty therefore mandates that directors maximize the value of the corporation over the long-term for the benefit of the providers of equity capital, as warranted for an entity with perpetual life in which the residual claimants have locked in their investment. When deciding whether to pursue a strategic alternative that would end or fundamentally alter the stockholders' ongoing investment in the corporation, the loyalty-based standard of conduct requires that the alternative yield value exceeding what the corporation otherwise would generate for stockholders over the long-term. Value, of course, does not just mean cash. It could mean an ownership interest in an entity, a package of other securities, or some combination, with or without cash, that will deliver greater value over the anticipated investment horizon.

The duty to act for the ultimate benefit of stockholders does not require that directors fulfill the wishes of a particular subset of the stockholder base. * * * More pertinent to the current case, a particular class or series of stock may hold contractual rights against the corporation and desire outcomes that maximize the value of those rights.

* * *

A board does not owe fiduciary duties to preferred stockholders when considering whether or not to take corporate action that might trigger or circumvent the preferred stockholders' contractual rights. Preferred stockholders are owed fiduciary duties only when they do not invoke their special contractual rights and rely on a right shared equally with the common stock. Under those circumstances, "the existence of such right and the correlative duty may be measured by equitable as well as legal standards." Thus, for example, just as common stockholders can challenge a disproportionate allocation of merger consideration, so too can preferred stockholders who do not possess and are not limited by a contractual entitlement. Under those circumstances, the decision to allocate different consideration is a discretionary, fiduciary determination that must pass muster under the appropriate standard of review, and the degree to which directors own different classes or series of stock may affect the standard of review.

To reiterate, the standard of conduct for directors requires that they strive in good faith and on an informed basis to maximize the value of the corporation for the benefit of its residual claimants, the ultimate beneficiaries of the firm's value, not for the benefit of its contractual claimants. In light of this obligation, "it is the duty of directors to pursue the best interests of the corporation and its common stockholders, if that can be done faithfully with the contractual promises owed to the preferred. Put differently, "generally it will be the duty of the board, where discretionary judgment is to be exercised, to prefer the interests of the common stock—as the good faith judgment of the board sees them to be—to the interests created by the special rights, preferences, etc. . . of preferred stock. This principle is not unique to preferred stock; it applies equally to other holders of contract rights against the corporation. Consequently, as this court observed at the motion to dismiss stage, "in circumstances where the interests of the common stockholders diverge from those of the preferred stockholders, it is possible that a director could breach her duty by improperly favoring the interests of the preferred stockholders over those of the common stockholders."

In this case, the directors made the discretionary decision to sell Trados in a transaction that triggered the preferred stockholders' contractual liquidation preference, a right that the preferred stockholders otherwise could not have exercised. The plaintiff contends that the Board should not have agreed to the Merger and had a duty to continue operating Trados on a stand-alone basis, because that alternative had the potential to maximize the value of the corporation for the ultimate benefit of the common stock. The Trados directors, of course, contend that they complied with their fiduciary duties.

2. The Standards Of Review

To determine whether directors have met their fiduciary obligations, Delaware courts evaluate the challenged decision through the lens of a standard of review. In this case, the Board lacked a majority of disinterested and independent directors, making entire fairness the applicable standard. * * *

Entire fairness, Delaware's most onerous standard, applies when the board labors under actual conflicts of interest. Once entire fairness applies, the defendants must establish "to the court's satisfaction that the transaction was the product of both fair dealing and fair price." "Not even an honest belief that the transaction was entirely fair will be sufficient to establish entire fairness. Rather, the transaction itself must be objectively fair, independent of the board's beliefs."

To obtain review under the entire fairness test, the stockholder plaintiff must prove that there were not enough independent and disinterested individuals among the directors making the challenged decision to comprise a board majority. To determine whether the directors approving the transaction comprised a disinterested and independent board majority, the court conducts a director-by-director analysis.

In this case, the plaintiff proved at trial that six of the seven Trados directors were not disinterested and independent, making entire fairness the operative standard. This finding does not mean that the six directors necessarily breached their fiduciary duties, only that entire fairness is the lens through which the court evaluates their actions.

a. The Management Directors: Campbell and Hummel

Two of the directors—Campbell and Hummel—received personal benefits in the Merger [through the Management Incentive Plan]. The plaintiff proved that the benefits were material to them, rendering Campbell and Hummel interested in the decision to approve the Merger.

In Trados I, this court recognized that "a director is interested in a transaction if 'he or she will receive a personal financial benefit from a transaction that is not equally shared by the stockholders.'" This court further recognized that for purposes of fiduciary review, "the benefit received by the director and not shared with stockholders must be 'of a sufficiently material importance, in the context of the director's economic circumstances, as to have made it improbable that the director could perform her fiduciary duties . . . without being influenced by her overriding personal interest.'

At trial, the plaintiff proved that Campbell personally received $2.34 million from the MIP, portions of which were recharacterized as a bonus and as payment for his non-competition agreement. Campbell bargained for and obtained post-transaction employment as SDL's President and Chief Strategy Officer. He also became a member of SDL's board, where he earned $50,000 per year for his service (later bumped to $60,000 per year).

During discovery, the plaintiff asked Campbell about his personal wealth to explore materiality. Defense counsel objected, and Campbell initially refused to provide any specifics. He then only agreed to estimate that his net worth at the time was $5–10 million. Defense counsel instructed him not to answer any further questions on the subject.

Campbell's post-transaction SDL board membership, standing alone, would not be sufficient to create a disqualifying interest. Taken collectively, however, the benefits Campbell received were material. The payments represented 23% to 47% of his net worth at the time of the Merger and paid him nearly ten times what he would make annually by continuing to manage Trados as a stand-alone entity, triggering golden parachute. * * * It is also fair to infer that the payments were material in light of defense counsel's objections and the defendants' failure to produce any countervailing evidence. * * *

At trial, the plaintiff similarly proved that Hummel personally received material benefits. Hummel's employment with Trados provided his sole source of income between 1984 and 2005; at the time of the Merger, he was earning approximately $190,000 plus an annual bonus. SDL employed Hummel post-transaction at the same level of compensation. Hummel originally was entitled to 12% of the MIP, representing $0.936 million of the Merger proceeds. Just before the Merger, Hummel complained to Campbell about some of the "strings" imposed by the MIP, such as his one year non-competition agreement. After Hummel complained, his MIP percentage increased from 12% to 14% for total proceeds of $1.092 million. Two days later, Budge described Hummel as "obviously a lock" to vote for the Merger.

* * *

Taken collectively, the direct financial benefits Hummel received were material to him. He admitted that the $1 million payday was significant. His post-transaction employment also was a material benefit.

* * *

b. The VC Directors: Gandhi, Scanlan, and Stone

Three of the directors—Gandhi, Scanlan, and Stone—were fiduciaries for VC funds that received disparate consideration in the Merger in the form of a liquidation preference. Each faced the dual fiduciary problem identified in Weinberger v. UOP, Inc., 457 A.2d 701, 710 (Del. 1983), where the Delaware Supreme Court held that there was "no dilution" of the duty of loyalty when a director "holds dual or multiple" fiduciary obligations. If the interests of the beneficiaries to whom the dual fiduciary owes duties are aligned, then there is no conflict. But if the interests of the beneficiaries diverge, the fiduciary faces an inherent conflict of interest. "There is no 'safe harbor' for such divided loyalties in Delaware." The plaintiff proved at trial that Gandhi, Scanlan, and Stone faced a conflict of interest as dual fiduciaries.

In Trados I, Chancellor Chandler recognized that the VC firms' ability to receive their liquidation preference could give the VC directors a divergent interest in the Merger that conflicted with the interests of the common stock. In moving to dismiss, the defendants argued that because the preferred stockholders did not receive their full liquidation preference, and because the Series A and BB were participating preferred, the preferred stockholders would benefit from a higher price and their interests were aligned with the common. Chancellor Chandler rejected their argument:

> Even accepting this proposition as true, however, it is not the case that the interests of the preferred and common stockholders were aligned with respect to the decision of whether to pursue a sale of the [C]ompany or continue to operate the Company without pursuing a transaction at that time.
>
> The [M]erger triggered the $57.9 million liquidation preference of the preferred stockholders, and the preferred stockholders received approximately $52 million dollars as a result of the [M]erger. In contrast, the common stockholders received nothing as a result of the [M]erger, and lost the ability to ever receive anything of value in the future for their ownership interest in Trados. It would not stretch reason to say that this is the worst possible outcome for the common stockholders.

The Chancellor held that it was "reasonable to infer from the factual allegations in the Complaint that the interests of the preferred and common stockholders were not aligned with respect to the decision to pursue a transaction that would trigger the liquidation preference of the preferred and result in no consideration for the common stockholders."

Although Chancellor Chandler clearly understood the point, the fact that preferred and common "may have incentives to pursue different exit strategies is not obvious." Both are equity securities which give their holders incentives to maximize value of the firm. But preferred stock carries special rights that create specific economic incentives that differ from those of common stock. VCs also operate under a business model that causes them to seek outsized returns and to liquidate (typically via a sale) even profitable ventures that fall short of their return hurdles and which otherwise would require investments of time and resources that could be devoted to more promising ventures.

i. Economic Incentives

VCs invest through preferred stock with highly standardized features, although individual details vary. VC preferred stock typically carries a preference upon liquidation, defined to include a sale of the company, that entitles the holders to receive specified value before the common stock receives anything. It usually earns a cumulative dividend which, if unpaid, steadily increases the liquidation preference. It also entitles the preferred holder to convert into common stock at a specified ratio in lieu of receiving the liquidation preference. The preferred stock in this case carried each of these features.

There is nothing inherently pernicious about the standard features of VC preferred stock. The sophisticated contract rights, the use of staged financing, and the gradual acquisition of board control over the course of multiple financing rounds help VCs reduce the risk of entrepreneur opportunism and management agency costs. See [Jesse M. Fried & Mira Ganor, Agency Costs of Venture Capitalist Control in Startups, 81 N.Y.U. L. Rev. 967, 983–84 (2006) (hereinafter Agency Costs); D. Gordon Smith,

The Exit Structure of Venture Capital, 53 UCLA L. Rev. 315, 318–24 (2005) (hereinafter Exit Structure); Manuel A. Utset, Reciprocal Fairness, Strategic Behavior & Venture Survival: A Theory of Venture Capital-Financed Firms, 2002 Wis. L. Rev. 45, 56–68 (hereinafter Venture Survival)]; Nevertheless, "[w]hile each of the . . . contracting techniques helps VC investors minimize agency risk, they also give rise to the possibility that the venture capitalist may use the contract rights opportunistically." Robert P. Bartlett, III, Venture Capital, Agency Costs, and the False Dichotomy of the Corporation, 54 UCLA L. Rev. 37, 56 n.78 (2006) [hereinafter False Dichotomy]; accord Ronald J. Gilson, Engineering a Venture Capital Market: Lessons from the American Experience, 55 Stan. L. Rev. 1067, 1085 (2003) ("Reducing the agency costs of the entrepreneur's discretion by transferring it to the venture capital fund also transfers to the venture capitalist . . . the opportunity to use that discretion opportunistically against the entrepreneur.").

The cash flow rights of typical VC preferred stock cause the economic incentives of its holders to diverge from those of the common stockholders. See Theory of Preferred, supra, at 1832 (noting "the preferred's financial interest is defined by contract rights that conflict intrinsically with the interests of the common"). "[T]o the extent that VCs retain their preferred stock, their cash flow rights are debt-like; to the extent that they convert, their preferred stock offers the same cash flow rights as common." Agency Costs, supra, at 982. "Because of the preferred shareholders' liquidation preferences, they sometimes gain less from increases in firm value than they lose from decreases in firm value. This effect may cause a board dominated by preferred shareholders to choose lower-risk, lower-value investment strategies over higher-risk, higher-value investment strategies." Id. at 994. The different cash flow rights of preferred stockholders are particularly likely to affect the choice between (i) selling or dissolving the company and (ii) maintaining the company as an independent private business. "In particular, preferred dominated boards may favor immediate 'liquidity events' (such as dissolution or sale of the business) even if operating the firm as a stand-alone going concern would generate more value for shareholders." In these situations, "[l]iquidity events promise a certain payout, much [or all] of which the preferred shareholders can capture through their liquidation preferences. Continuing to operate the firm as an independent company may expose the preferred-owning VCs to risk without sufficient opportunity for gain." Agency Costs, supra, at 993–94; accord Theory of Preferred, supra, at 1886 ("Preferred, as a senior claim, will avoid taking value-enhancing risk in a case where common, as the at-the-margin residual interest, would assume the risk.").

The distorting effects "are most likely to arise when, as is often the case, the firm is neither a complete failure nor a stunning success." Agency Costs, supra, at 996; accord Theory of Preferred, supra, at 1833, 1875. When the venture is a stunning success (everybody wins) or a complete failure (everybody loses), the outcomes are "cut and dried." William W. Bratton, Venture Capital on the Downside: Preferred Stock and Corporate Control, 100 Mich. L. Rev. 891, 896 (2002) [hereinafter Downside]. But in intermediate cases, preferred stockholders have incentives to "act opportunistically." Agency Costs, supra, at 993. "The costs of this value-reducing behavior are borne, in the first instance, by common shareholders." Id. at 995; see Exit Structure, supra, at 351. "[B]ecause VCs in . . . sales often exit as preferred shareholders with liquidation preferences that must be paid in full before common shareholders receive any payout, common shareholders may receive little (if any) payout. At the same time, the sale eliminates any 'option value' (upside potential) of the common stock." Carrots & Sticks, supra, at 3.[25]

ii. Personal Incentives

The VC business model reinforces the economic incentives that the preferred stock's cash flow rights create.

> Before venture capitalists invest, they plan for exit. . . The ability to control exit is crucial to the venture capitalist's business model of short-term funding of nascent business opportunities. Exit allows venture capitalists to reallocate funds and the nonfinancial contributions that accompany them. . . It also allows fund investors to evaluate the quality of their venture capitalists. . . Finally, the credible threat of exit by venture capitalists may work to minimize the temptation towards self-dealing by the entrepreneurs who manage the venture-backed companies.

Exit Structure, supra, at 316. * * * The timing and form of exit are critical because VCs seek very high rates of return, usually a ten-fold return of capital over a five year period.

Three forms of exit are common. An IPO is the gold standard and most lucrative; liquidation via sale to a larger company (a trade sale) is a second-best solution; and a write-off is the least attractive. "[V]enture capitalists will sometimes liquidate an otherwise viable firm, if its

---

25 Professors Brian J. Broughman and Jesse M. Fried offer a simple illustration: "Consider, for example, a startup with $50 million in aggregate liquidation preferences. Assume there is a 50% likelihood that, within one year, the firm will be worth $90 million and a 50% likelihood that it will be worth $0. A hypothetical risk-neutral buyer content to earn a $0 return would pay $45 million for all of the equity of the startup. Preferred shareholders would get $45 million; common shareholders would get $0. But if the startup were to remain independent, the common stock would have an expected value of $20 million." Brian J. Broughman & Jesse M. Fried, Carrots & Sticks: How VCs Induce Entrepreneurial Teams to Sell Startups 12 n.47 (Harvard Law & Econ., Discussion Paper No. 742, 2013), available at http://ssrn.com/abstract=2221033 [hereinafter Carrots & Sticks]. The preferred stockholders will prefer their sure $45 million over the risk-adjusted $25 million. The common stockholders will prefer the opportunity to receive a risk-adjusted $20 million over a sure zero. If the preferred have the power to force a sale, then the $20 million is "the 'option value' of the common stock that is lost in the sale of the firm today for $45 million." Id.; see also Agency Costs, supra, at 995–97 (providing more detailed examples). Of course, this is not the only possibility. Under other scenarios, the preferred stockholders' incentives can lead to defensible results. See, e.g., Theory of Preferred, supra, at 1886.

expected returns are not what they (or their investors) expected, or not worth pursuing further, given limited resources and the need to manage other portfolio firms." This may seem irrational, but "it makes perfect economic sense when viewed from the venture capitalist's need to allocate [his] time and resources among various ventures." Venture Survival, supra, at 110 n.218. "Although the individual company may be economically viable, the return on time and capital to the individual venture capitalist is less than the opportunity cost." William A. Sahlman, The Structure and Governance of Venture-Capital Organizations, 27 J. Fin. Econ. 473, 507 (1990). VC firms strive to avoid a so-called "sideways situation," also known as a "zombie company" or "the living dead," in which the entity is profitable and requires ongoing VC monitoring, but where the growth opportunities and prospects for exit are not high enough to generate an attractive internal rate of return. These companies "are routinely liquidated," usually via trade sales, "by venture capitalists hoping to turn to more promising ventures."

iii. The Evidence That The VC Directors Faced A Conflict In This Case

At the pleadings stage, Chancellor Chandler recognized that it was reasonably conceivable that the VC directors faced a conflict of interest. At trial, the plaintiff had the burden to prove on the facts of this case, by a preponderance of evidence, that (i) the interests of the VC firms in receiving their liquidation preference as holders of preferred stock diverged from the interests of the common stock and (ii) the VC directors faced a conflict of interest because of their competing duties. * * *

Campbell testified in his first deposition, taken on September 20, 2006, just over a year after the Merger and before anyone was sued for breach of fiduciary duty, that his mission upon joining Trados "was to help the company understand its future path, which in the mind[s] of the outside board members at that time was some type of either merger or acquisition event." Campbell perceived "degrees of aggressiveness" among the directors based on how long they had invested in Trados. From his "first week" at the Company, he perceived Gandhi as "probably the most aggressive," Scanlan next, then Stone. * * *

Consistent with Campbell's deposition testimony, the evidence at trial established that Gandhi faced a conflict and acted consistent with Sequoia's interest in exiting from Trados and moving on. As Gandhi explained at trial, when Sequoia invests, it hopes for "really fast" growth and "very large outsized returns." Within six months after the Uniscape merger, Gandhi had concluded that Trados would not deliver outsized returns and that Sequoia's "real opportunity" was only "to recover a fraction" of its $13 million investment in Uniscape. By the end of 2002, Gandhi had decided not to put significant time into Trados beyond Board meetings and only to attend by phone unless meetings were held locally. From his perspective, this was simply a matter of prioritizing his time based on how Trados would perform for Sequoia relative to other opportunities with "a lot of upside." He later elaborated: "[M]y most, you know, limited resource is just where I'm putting my time. And it's just better to work on something brand-new that has a chance .... Is [the next Sequoia investment] going to be Google?"

Gandhi saw a sale as a means of liquidating Sequoia's investment and moving on to better things. * * * The evidence at trial established that Scanlan had similar incentives, consistent with Campbell's deposition testimony. * * * Scanlan also recommended and designed the MIP to incentivize top management to favor a sale even at valuations where the common stock would receive zero. * * *

As Campbell testified, Stone was the least aggressive in seeking an exit. The evidence at trial nevertheless established that Stone had the same desire to exit and faced the same conflict of interest as Gandhi and Scanlan, although she was more open to considering a sale in 12–18 months rather than pushing for a near-term outcome. Stone candidly admitted that "[a]ll private equity firms, ourselves included, are always, from the moment we buy [ ] a business, looking for an exit." Indeed, when Hg invested in 2000, its investment thesis included an "explicit agreement with the management team" to pursue "an IPO in 18 to 24 months."

Based on this evidence and other materials on which the plaintiff relied, the plaintiff carried his burden to show that Gandhi, Scanlan, and Stone were not independent with respect to the Merger. They wanted to exit, consistent with the interests of the VC firms they represented.

c. The Outside Directors: Laidig And Prang

Two of the directors—Laidig and Prang—were neither members of management nor dual fiduciaries. The plaintiff did not challenge Laidig's disinterestedness and independence. By contrast, the plaintiff contended that (i) Prang was not independent because of his close business relationship with Gandhi and Sequoia, and (ii) he was not disinterested because he beneficially owned preferred stock through Mentor, his investment vehicle, and received a liquidation preference for his shares.

Because of the web of interrelationships that characterizes the Silicon Valley startup community, scholars have argued that "so-called 'independent directors'" on VC-backed startup boards "are often not truly independent of the VCs." Agency Costs, supra, at 988. "Many of these directors are chosen by the VCs, who tend to have much larger professional networks than the entrepreneurs or other common shareholders." Id. If there is a "conflict of interest" between the VCs and common stockholders, the "independent directors" have incentives to side with the VCs. Id. at 989. * * *

Prang had a long history with Sequoia, dating back to Sequoia's investment in Aspect Development, where Prang was President and COO. After Aspect Development, Sequoia asked Prang to work with them on other companies, and Gandhi recalled "a number where we worked very collaboratively. . ." One was Uniscape. The relationship led to Prang investing about $300,000 in three Sequoia funds, including Sequoia X, which owned Trados preferred stock. At the time of the Merger, Prang was also the CEO of Conformia Software, a company backed by Sequoia where Gandhi served on the board. When Sequoia obtained the right to designate two members of Trados's Board, Sequoia designated Gandhi and Prang. Having considered these facts as a whole and evaluated Prang's demeanor, I find that Prang's current and past relationships with Gandhi and Sequoia resulted in a sense of "owingness" that compromised his independence for purposes of determining the applicable standard of review.

The plaintiff also introduced sufficient evidence at trial to establish that the $220,633 that Prang received in the Merger (through Mentor) was material to him. * * *

3. Entire Fairness

A reviewing court deploys the entire fairness test to determine whether the members of a conflicted board of directors complied with their fiduciary duties. * * * "The concept of fairness has two basic aspects: fair dealing and fair price." Weinberger, 457 A.2d at 711. Fair dealing "embraces questions of when the transaction was timed, how it was initiated, structured, negotiated, disclosed to the directors, and how the approvals of the directors and the stockholders were obtained." Fair price "relates to the economic and financial considerations of the proposed merger, including all relevant factors: assets, market value, earnings, future prospects, and any other elements that affect the intrinsic or inherent value of a company's stock." Although the two aspects may be examined separately, "the test for fairness is not a bifurcated one as between fair dealing and price. All aspects of the issue must be examined as a whole since the question is one of entire fairness." Id. But "perfection is not possible, or expected. . ."

a. Fair Dealing

The evidence pertinent to fair dealing weighed decidedly in favor of the plaintiff. Indeed, there was no contemporaneous evidence suggesting that the directors set out to deal with the common stockholders in a procedurally fair manner. Nor were the defendants able to recharacterize their actions retrospectively to show that they somehow blundered unconsciously into procedural fairness, notwithstanding their vigorous and coordinated efforts at trial to achieve this elusive goal.

i. Transaction Initiation

Fair dealing encompasses an evaluation of how the transaction was initiated. In this case, the VC directors pursued the Merger because Trados did not offer sufficient risk-adjusted upside to warrant either the continuing investment of their time and energy or their funds' ongoing exposure to the possibility of capital loss. An exit addressed these risks by enabling the VCs to devote personal resources to other, more promising investments and by returning their funds' invested capital plus a modest return. The VC directors did not make this decision after evaluating Trados from the perspective of the common stockholders, but rather as holders of preferred stock with contractual cash flow rights that diverged materially from those of the common stock and who sought to generate returns consistent with their VC funds' business model.[32]

* * *

In his first deposition, Campbell testified that upon joining Trados, he understood that his "mission" was to "help the company understand its future path, which in the mind[s] of the outside board members at that time was some type of either merger or acquisition event." * * * The contemporaneous documents overwhelmingly support this account. It also comports with how VCs who found themselves at or beyond their typical hold period naturally would regard a seemingly sideways if not stumbling portfolio company. * * * The contemporaneous documentary evidence and Campbell's far more credible deposition testimony, backed up by Budge[, the CFO], establish that the VC directors wanted to exit. They were not interested in continuing to manage the Company to increase its value for the common. They initiated a sale process and pursued the Merger to take advantage of their special contractual rights.

ii. Transaction Negotiation and Structure

Fair dealing encompasses questions of how the transaction was negotiated and structured. To analyze these aspects of the Merger requires an understanding of the MIP. * * *

The MIP paid a percentage of the total consideration achieved in any sale to senior management, before any amounts went to the preferred or

---

32 From a broader market or even societal perspective, there is nothing inherently wrong with a VC exit under these circumstances. It may well be that facilitating exit results in greater aggregate returns and maximizes overall societal wealth. This court's task, at least as I understand it, is not to apply its own normative balancing of broader policy concerns, but rather to evaluate the fairness of the defendants' actions in terms of an entity-specific arrangement of contract rights and fiduciary duties. The VC contracts in this case did not attempt to incorporate any mechanism for side-stepping fiduciary duties (such as a drag-along right if the VC funds sold their shares), nor did they explicitly seek to realign the directors' fiduciary duties in a manner that might alter the traditional analysis. See 8 Del. C. § 141(a) ("The business and affairs of every corporation organized under this chapter shall be managed by or under the direction of a board of directors, except as may be otherwise provided in this chapter or in its certificate of incorporation. If any such provision is made in the certificate of incorporation, the powers and duties conferred or imposed upon the board of directors by this chapter shall be exercised or performed to such extent and by such person or persons as shall be provided in the certificate of incorporation." (emphasis added)). This decision provides no opportunity for expressing a view as to the effectiveness of any such mechanism or realignment, and it does not intimate one. In the current case, the absence of any attempt at explicit contracting over exit-related conflicts does mean that to deviate from traditional fiduciary analysis would require giving credence to an implicit waiver or constructive fiduciary realignment. Setting aside the inherently ambiguous nature of the exercise—whether the common accepted a typical VC investment structure because they implicitly consented to a VC-dominated exit or because they believed fiduciary duties would protect them and therefore did not bargain over the issue—the structure of the DGCL and longstanding common law authority require that any such arrangement be explicit. See, e.g., 8 Del. C. §§ 102(b)(7), 141(a), 151(a), 202. See generally supra Part II.A.1.

the common. The percentage payout increased as the value of the deal increased as follows:

Deal Value	MIP Percentage
< $30 million	0%
> $30 million but < $40 million	6%
> $40 million but < $50 million	11%
> $50 million but < $90 million	13%
> $90 million but < $120 million	14%
> $120 million	15%

Although the MIP nominally provided for a range of deal consideration, SDL had offered $40 million for Trados in July 2004, when the Company had no CEO and was coming off a terrible first half of the year. No one has contended in this case that any suitor would have paid more than $90 million for Trados. The real issue was whether management would get 11% or 13%.

As a practical matter, at deal prices below the preferred stockholders' liquidation preference, the preferred bore the entire cost of the MIP because the common would not be entitled to any proceeds. Nothing about that is procedurally or substantively unfair. Once the deal price exceeded the liquidation preference, however, the MIP took value away from the common. At the time of the Merger, for example, the total liquidation preference was $57.9 million. The $60 million in consideration exceeded the preference, so without the MIP, the preferred stockholders would have received $57.9 million and the common stockholders $2.1 million. With the MIP, management received $7.8 million, the preferred stockholders received $52.2 million, and the common stockholders received zero. To fund the MIP, the common stockholders effectively paid $2.1 million, and the preferred stockholders effectively paid $5.7 million. As a result, the common stockholders contributed 100% of their ex-MIP proceeds while the preferred stockholders only contributed 10% ($5.7 million / $57.9 million).

There is no evidence in the record that the Board ever considered how to allocate fairly any incremental dollars above the liquidation preference. Until the Merger proceeds cleared the preference, each dollar was allocated between management and the preferred stockholders, with management receiving its assigned percentage and the preferred taking the rest. But once the consideration topped the preference, thereby implicating the rights of the common, the additional dollars were not fairly allocated. All of the additional dollars went to management and the preferred. The common would not receive anything until the deal price exceeded the preference by more than the MIP payout.

The break-even deal value was $66.5 million. At that point, the MIP payout would be $8.6 million, and the residual proceeds would be sufficient to pay the $57.9 million preference. Above $66.5 million, the common would receive consideration, but would still fund the MIP disproportionately. For example, at $70 million, the MIP receives $9.1 million, the preferred receive $57.9 million, and the common receive $3.0 million. Without the MIP, the preferred would receive $57.9 million, and the common would receive $12.1 million. The common effectively fund the MIP with 75% of the consideration they otherwise would receive, retaining only 25%. The preferred stockholders would not lose a dime. The following graph shows the relative contribution of the common and the preferred at different deal values:

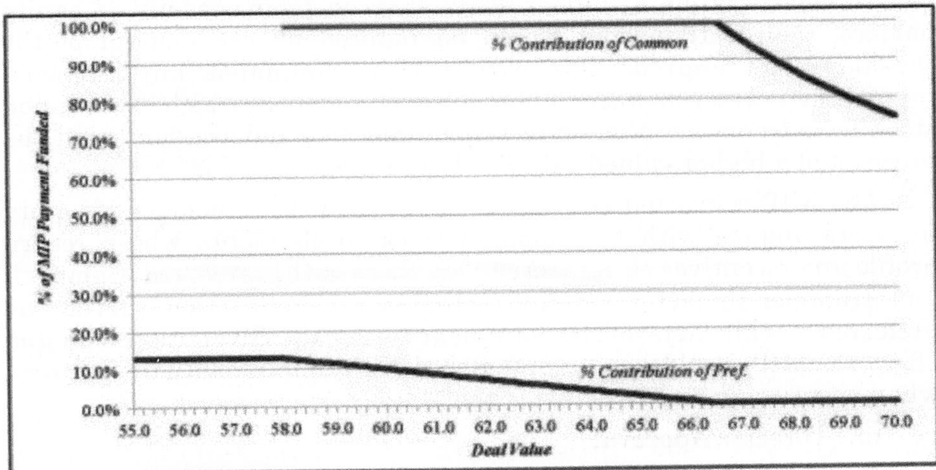

For purposes of fair dealing, the MIP skewed the negotiation and structure of the Merger in a manner adverse to the common stockholders. In February 2005, the Board reached a consensus that Campbell would seek $60 million from SDL. The defendants focused on this number after Campbell provided the waterfall analysis that Scanlan requested reflecting the allocation of deal proceeds at prices of $50, $60, and $70 million. The price target was also influenced significantly by Invision's desire not to take a capital loss by selling below its pre-money entry price of $60 million. At that price, the preferred stockholders would receive back all of their capital and make a nominal profit. There was never any effort to explore prices above $60 million or to consider whether alternatives to the Merger might generate value for the common.

Without the MIP, in a transaction that valued Trados at $60 million, Campbell, Budge, and Hummel would have received nothing for their options, and Hummel would have received approximately $0.5 million for his common stock (excluding any participation by the Series A and BB). In confronting that reality, their personal financial interests would have been aligned with the interests of the common stockholders as a whole, giving them strong reasons to evaluate critically whether the Board should pass on the Merger and continue to operate Trados as a stand-alone entity with the prospect of a higher-valued exit in the future. Perhaps the Board would have reached the same decision, but the process would have been different.

The MIP changed matters dramatically. In a transaction at $60 million, the MIP allocated $7.8 million to senior management, with Campbell, Budge, and Hummel collectively receiving $4.2 million. Instead of $0.5 million, Hummel's share was $1.092 million. The MIP accomplished this result by reallocating to the MIP recipients 100% of the consideration that the common stockholders would receive in a transaction valued at $66.5 million or less. On top of that, the MIP's cutback feature ensured that to the extent any MIP participants might receive consideration at higher deal values in their capacity as equity holders, their MIP payout would be reduced by the amount of the consideration received. The combination eliminated any financial incentive for senior management to push for a price at which the common stock would receive value or to favor remaining independent with the prospect of a higher valued sale at a later date.

The MIP converted the management team from holders of equity interests aligned with the common stock to claimants whose return profile and incentives closely resembled those of the preferred. Campbell and Hummel in fact acted and voted in a manner that served the preferred stockholders' desire for a near-term sale. Given its design and effect, the MIP is evidence that the Board dealt unfairly with the common when negotiating and structuring the Merger.

iii. Director Approval

Fair dealing encompasses questions of how director approval was obtained. Except for Laidig, all of the directors were financially interested in the Merger or faced a conflict of interest because they owed fiduciary duties to entities whose interests diverged from those of the common stockholders. The MIP played a role here as well, because it gave Campbell and Hummel a direct and powerful incentive to vote in favor of the deal.

The element of Board approval also encompasses how the directors reached their decision. A director's failure to understand the nature of his duties can be evidence of unfairness. Directors who cannot perceive a conflict or who deny its existence cannot meaningfully address it. The defendants in this case did not understand that their job was to maximize the value of the corporation for the benefit of the common stockholders, and they refused to recognize the conflicts they faced.

During his deposition, Laidig volunteered that the Trados directors never considered the common stockholders:

> Q: . . . Was it the best thing for the common stockholders to sell the company?

> Laidig: To tell you the truth, between common and preferred was only a topic which really popped up through this court case. I didn't even remember this thing as being a debate or discussion on the board. . .
>
> Q: You don't recall any discussion at the board level as between the interests of the common stockholders[?]
>
> Laidig: No. . . It only once came up, you know, in conjunction with the stock option plan, you know, when we reduced the value. That's what I have a vague memory of.

Laidig's deposition testimony comports with the documentary record, which does not reflect any serious consideration of the common stock or the divergence of interests between the common and the preferred.

* * *

When pressed, the [other] directors could not recall any specific discussion of the common stock, and they could not comprehend the possibility that the economic interests of the preferred stockholders might diverge from those of the common. * * *

Conflict blindness and its lesser cousin, conflict denial, have long afflicted the financially sophisticated. Given the directors' intelligence, educational background, and experience, I believe they fully appreciated the diverging interests of the VCs, senior management, and the common stockholders. Despite this reality, the defendants did not consider forming a special committee to represent the interests of the common stockholders.[39] They also chose not to obtain a fairness opinion to analyze the Merger or evaluate other possibilities from the perspective of the common stockholders. * * * Taken as a whole, the manner in which director approval was obtained provides evidence of unfair dealing.

iv. Stockholder Approval

Finally, fair dealing encompasses questions of how stockholder approval was obtained. The defendants never considered conditioning the Merger on the vote of a majority of disinterested common stockholders. The vote on the Merger was delivered by the preferred, who controlled a majority of the Company's voting power on an as-converted basis, and other "[l]arge [f]riendlies," such as Hummel. Hummel originally was entitled to 12% of the MIP, but when he seemed to be having second thoughts just before the Merger, his MIP percentage was increased from 12% to 14%. Two days later, Budge described Hummel as "obviously a lock" to vote in favor of the Merger. Other common

[39] The decision not to form a special committee had significant implications for this litigation. The Merger was not a transaction where a controller stood on both sides, and the plaintiff did not challenge Laidig's independence or disinterestedness. If a duly empowered and properly advised committee had approved the Merger, it could well have resulted in business judgment deference. Admittedly, under those circumstances, the plaintiff likely would have found reason to criticize Laidig.

stockholders reached different conclusions. One of the largest common stockholders, Microsoft, abstained because it could not stomach "the economic result" of the Merger, i.e. the fact that it would receive nothing. The plaintiff, who owned 5% of the common stock, sought appraisal.

"Stockholders in Delaware corporations have a right to control and vote their shares in their own interest." Bershad v. Curtiss-Wright Corp., 535 A.2d 840, 845 (Del. 1987). "They are limited only by any fiduciary duty owed to other stockholders. It is not objectionable that their motives may be for personal profit, or determined by whim or caprice, so long as they violate no duty owed [to] other shareholders." The fact that the preferred stockholders voted in their own interest is therefore not evidence of unfair dealing. The failure to condition the deal on a vote of the disinterested common stockholders is likewise not evidence of unfairness; it simply deprives the defendants of otherwise helpful affirmative evidence of fairness. The effect of the MIP on Hummel's voting preferences, however, provides some additional evidence of unfairness.

b. Evidence Pertinent To Fair Price

In contrast to the evidence on fair dealing, which decidedly favored the plaintiff, the evidence on fair price was mixed. Consistent with the amount of consideration that the common stockholders received in the Merger, the defendants strived at trial to demonstrate that the common stock had no value. As with their trial testimony on issues relevant to fair dealing, the defendants adopted aggressive positions that were contrary to the contemporaneous documents and their earlier testimony. But as will be seen in the unitary fairness determination, their evidence on price fairness was ultimately persuasive.

[The court ultimately found the DCF valuation conducted by the company's valuation expert to be more persuasive than the valuation conducted by the plaintiff's expert. The former valued the company at $51.9 million in the event it remained an independent entity, which was less than the Merger proceeds of $60 million, indicating that the common stock had no economic value.]

Although the defendant directors did not adopt any protective provisions, failed to consider the common stockholders, and sought to exit without recognizing the conflicts of interest presented by the Merger, they nevertheless proved that the transaction was fair. The Delaware Supreme Court has characterized the proper "test of fairness" as whether "the minority stockholder shall receive the substantial equivalent in value of what he had before." Sterling v. Mayflower Hotel Corp., 93 A.2d 107, 114 (Del. 1952); accord Rosenblatt v. Getty Oil Co., 493 A.2d 929, 940 (Del. 1985). If Trados's common stock had no economic value before the Merger, then the common stockholders received the substantial equivalent in value of what they had before, and the Merger satisfies the test of fairness. * * *

In light of this reality, the directors breached no duty to the common stock by agreeing to a Merger in which the common stock received nothing. The common stock had no economic value before the Merger, and the common stockholders received in the Merger the substantial equivalent in value of what they had before.

Under the circumstances of this case, the fact that the directors did not follow a fair process does not constitute a separate breach of duty. As the Delaware Supreme Court has recognized, an unfair process can infect the price, result in a finding of breach, and warrant a potential remedy. On these facts, such a finding is not warranted. The defendants' failure to deploy a procedural device such as a special committee resulted in their being forced to prove at trial that the Merger was entirely fair. Having done so, they have demonstrated that they did not commit a fiduciary breach.

* * *

QUESTIONS

1. What are duties of the board in resolving conflicting desires of the common and preferred?
2. If you were advising the board on its fiduciary duties, what would you suggest to convince a court that the board had considered the interests of the common?
3. Gandhi testified that he thought like a common shareholder because the VC's preferred was convertible into common if the investment was a success. "We never made money on preferred instruments. Preferred for us, . . . [is] a thinly veiled version of common." Yet the court refers to this as "conflict blindness." What does that mean? Why does the court reject Gandhi's claim?
4. The court held that the allocation of the cost of the Management Incentive Plan was unfair to the common stockholders. How could you revise the plan to avoid this criticism?
5. The court noted that without the MIP management's options were worthless, which might have motivated management to "evaluate critically whether the Board should pass on the Merger and continue to operate Trados as a stand-alone entity with the prospect of a higher-valued exit in the future." Does that skew the manager's motivations to favor risky prospects at the expense of the preferred? Where do their fiduciary duties lie in that case?
6. The court relies on *Weinberger v. UOP* for a showing that interested directors voting in a conflict situation must demonstrate both procedural fairness (which the defendants failed to do) and fair price (where they succeeded). This suggests that fair price trumps any procedural concerns. If this is so, why does the court examine procedural fairness in such meticulous detail?

7. In an excerpted footnote, Vice Chancellor Laster states that *Trados* is consistent with *Orban* given that "I read [Orban] as a case in which the common stock had no economic value such that a transaction in which the common stockholders received nothing was fair to them." Is this an accurate reading of Chancellor Allen's opinion in *Orban*? Is it consistent with Vice Chancellor Laster's statement regarding efficient breach in *ODN* discussed previously?

NOTE: A CONTRACTUAL RESPONSE TO *TRADOS*?

Following *Trados*, a number of commentators raised concerns that the decision would make it difficult for a board to approve the sale of a firm for less than its preferred stock liquidation preferences. To the extent this conclusion is accurate, the decision would undermine the very purpose of the preferred stock liquidation preference as it is used in the venture capital context. In response, the model voting agreement maintained by the National Venture Capital Association was modified to include a new "Sale Rights" provision. Under this provision, preferred stockholders holding a specified percentage of the outstanding shares of preferred stock have the power to force the company to initiate a sale and to follow specific procedures to conclude one, including the hiring of a financial advisor, to be overseen by a designated representative of the preferred stockholders (the "Holder Representative"). As with personal service contracts, however, compelling compliance with this Sale Rights provision raises clear enforceability issues. To address this possibility, the provision also includes the following term:

> __.1.3 Approval of the Terms and Conditions of a Proposed Sale of the Company; Failure to Approve a Sale of the Company.
>
> (a) The Company shall cause its management, together with the Financial Advisor and Deal Counsel, to deliver regular updates to its Board regarding material developments in the Sale Process and summarizing the status of the negotiation of the terms and conditions of the Sale of the Company. The Company shall, upon request of the Holder Representative, either call a meeting of its Board or seek the written consent of the Board approving the Sale of the Company and the entering into of the definitive agreements relating thereto.
>
> (b) In the event that the Board approval described in ([a]) above has not been obtained within the time period requested by the Holder Representative (such time period not to be less than three (3) business days), the Electing Holders shall have the right by written notice (the "Redemption Notice") to require the Company to redeem all of the then outstanding shares of capital stock held by the Electing Holders at a price equal to the amount of proceeds that would have been paid in respect of their shares of capital stock were the Sale of the Company consummated or, in the case of a Sale of the Company that is structured as a sale of all or substantially all of the Company's assets, the amount of proceeds

> that would have been paid in respect of their investment in the Company had all proceeds from the proposed Sale of the Company been distributed in a Deemed Liquidation Event (a "Preferred Redemption"). The Company and each Investor shall be obligated to effect the Preferred Redemption within ten (10) days of the delivery of the Redemption Notice.

Comments to this provision note that "since this section provides for redemption rights additional to any that may be included in the Certificate of Incorporation, selling the company may be the only means by which the Board is able to honor this contractual 'put' obligation." To what extent do you believe this contract provision will allow a company's board to avoid a *Trados*-type claim?

CHAPTER 8

OPTIONS AND CONVERTIBLE SECURITIES

1. INTRODUCTION

Consider the following hypothetical.

It is three years after your law school graduation, and your favorite client, Perpetual Youth ("PY") (our start-up from Chapter 2), is looking to hire a general counsel. Through Leon Ponce's leadership, the company has scaled successfully and closed two rounds of venture capital finance provided by some of the world's most famous venture capitalists. Given the excellent legal services you have provided PY, Leon calls you first to offer you the job.

PONCE: Look, I really need you working full time for Perpetual Youth as we prepare for an IPO down the road. However, we need to minimize our burn-rate, so I can only pay you a fraction of what you make now. But I can also sell you 5,000,000 shares, which is 1% of the fully-diluted stock. You'll be rich when we go public.

YOU: I'm intrigued, but that's a big pay cut. And I'm trying to save for a down payment on a house. How much would the shares cost me?

PONCE: Our last financing was wildly oversubscribed; unicorn club, here we come! Based on the last valuation, you'd need to pay 5.

YOU: thousand?

PONCE: No. Million.

YOU: WHAT??!

PONCE: Sorry, we have a valuation expert who says our common stock is now $1 per share. What if I threw in some free killer chia kombucha pills?

YOU: How about this. Let's have PY offer to sell me 5,000,000 shares of Common Stock at $1.00/share, and let's also make the offer non-revocable for a period of 10 years. That way, if things go really well and the value of the company continues to climb, it will make sense for me to accept the offer and pay $5 million for the shares. And if things go south, I don't have to lose any money, and you don't have to sell me any shares. Plus, given the meager salary, I obviously will have a strong incentive to work hard to increase the value of the stock. What do you think?

PONCE: You drive a hard bargain, but I guess that's why I know you're the right person for the job. Assuming the other directors agree, you have deal!

Your proposal to Ponce should hopefully seem familiar, as it borrows from a concept covered in a standard first-year Contracts course. Rather than accept the company's offer to sell you 5,000,000 shares by paying $5,000,000, your suggestion was for PY to make the offer irrevocable for a period of 10 years giving you the opportunity to take a wait-and-see approach. As you may recall from your Contracts class, an enforceable promise not to revoke an offer is called an *"option contract,"* and it means that PY's offer to sell you 5,000,000 shares at $1.00/share stands ready for your acceptance—at any time—for a period of 10 years. All you would need to do to accept it is to notify PY and pay the $5,000,000. (Recall that under the Common Law, offers are generally revocable at any time until acceptance; hence, the need for an option contract if you want an offer to be irrevocable.)

Your proposal may also sound familiar because it is an extremely common way for companies to compensate employees, particularly start-up firms like PY. Employment offer letters might refer to these commitments as "stock options" or "stock option grants." For instance, when Eric Schmidt joined Google as its Chief Executive Officer, his offer letter included the following language:

> We will recommend to the Board that, at a meeting to be held on the Effective Date, you be granted a stock option to purchase 3,582,927 shares of the Company's Common Stock (which number represents 7% of the Company's fully diluted equity) on the date of grant at an exercise price equal to the then current fair market value as determined by the Board at that meeting (with such fair market value currently anticipated to be $1.20 per share) (the "Option").*

When a company offers its employees "stock options," it is simply making an irrevocable offer to sell shares at a specified price per share (for tax purposes, this price is generally set at the fair market value of the stock on the day of the stock option grant). As suggested in the hypothetical, stock options are attractive to employees because they do not require employees to put any money at risk but still allow for upside gain. The employee can wait to accept the offer and pay the specified exercise price only if the stock increases. For the same reason, options can provide powerful incentives for employees to work hard to increase the firm's value.

However, employee stock option grants are just one type of option in finance. Indeed, as a matter of contract law, possession of an irrevocable offer can be valuable in a variety of contexts. For instance, what if you suspected that a city was contemplating the construction of a new baseball stadium near an abandoned railyard. If you had an irrevocable offer to purchase nearby real estate at current prices, you would have

* See Offer Letter to Eric Schmidt, March 14, 2001, Exhibit 10.11 to Google, Inc. Form S-1/A, filed August 9, 2004, available at https://www.sec.gov/Archives/edgar/data/1288776/000119312504135503/dex1011.htm.

development rights over property that might become quite valuable. And you can wait to purchase the property until you are certain about plans for the new stadium. As this example shows, option contracts can thus be useful for investment and, by extension, speculation. Likewise, what if you had an irrevocable offer from a large insurance company to buy your car at any time for $10,000. If the car declines in value (perhaps because you get in an accident), you can receive $10,000 simply by delivering them the damaged car. In other words, option contracts can also be used as a form of insurance or as a way to hedge the risk of adverse events.

Of course, no one would agree to such lopsided bargains without a proper inducement, which is why acquiring an option is not costless. In fact, you may recall from your Contracts class that forming an enforceable option contract generally requires both a promise not to revoke and consideration. In the employment context, the presence of consideration is pretty obvious: Google granted Eric Schmidt an option to buy 7% of the company's equity for $1.20/share because it wanted to induce him to quit his job at Novell and join Google. To obtain a real estate option or an insurance option, you would likely need to pay a fair sum of money to secure such a commitment, which would also satisfy the requirement for consideration. Importantly, buying an option does not commit you to ever execute on the underlying transaction (buying the land or selling your car); you simply have the legal right to do so for a specified period of time if you wish.

For many students, option theory can seem like an arcane, highly technical corner of corporate finance. However, focusing on the formal concept of an option contract can help demystify the subject and illuminate why it's so relevant for lawyers working in corporate finance. Fundamentally, every option contract requires (a) a promise by one party not to revoke an offer and (b) some type of consideration. In other words, we should expect every option contract to provide another party with a unilateral right to do something (e.g., to buy 3,582,927 shares of Google stock at $1.20/share, to buy a parcel of land at a specified price, or to sell a car for $10,000). And we should also expect that this unliteral right will be worth something. The task of the lawyer is to implement different versions of this "wait-and-see" bargain and, to the extent possible, ensure that it remains intact for as long as it exists. We shall approach the subject, with this task in mind, by examining the following three topics:

1. Identifying options and implementing the unliteral right to exercise;
2. Valuing options; and
3. Protecting the option bargain.

2. IDENTIFYING OPTIONS AND IMPLEMENTING THE UNILATERAL RIGHT TO EXERCISE

A. OVERVIEW

Let's again consider the stock option issued to Eric Schmidt:

Figure 8-1: Schmidt Option Contract

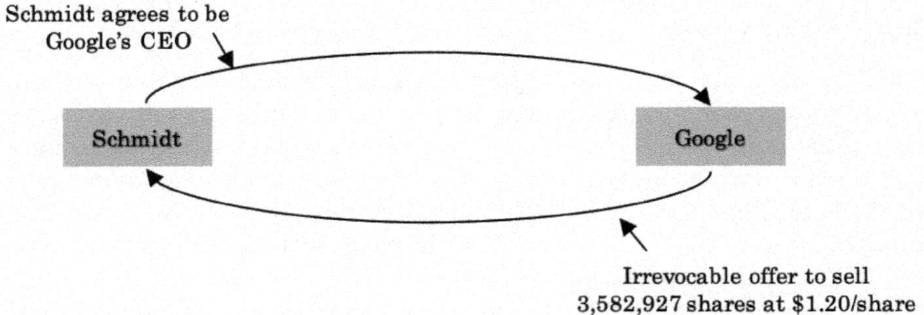

In exchange for Schmidt's agreement to become Google's CEO, Google made an irrevocable offer to sell Schmidt 3,582,927 shares of Google Common Stock at $1.20/share. Elsewhere, Google agreed that the term of this offer would last for 10 years. As with all offers, this empowered Schmidt to accept the offer at any time during the term of the option by notifying Google of his election to do so and by delivering the purchase price of $1.20 per share. Thus, if accepted by Schmidt, the following exchange would take place:

Figure 8-2: Acceptance of Schmidt Option Contract

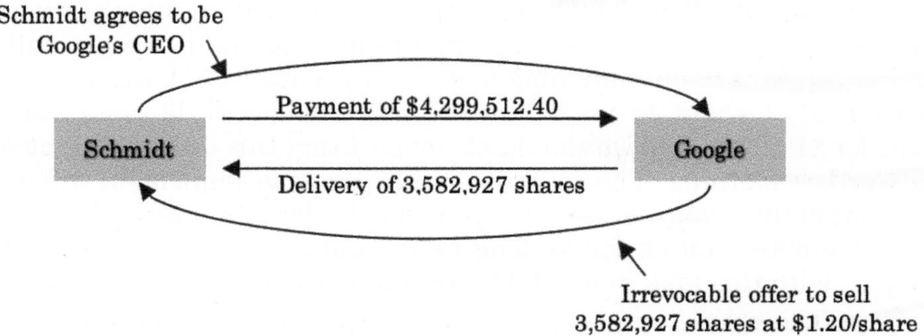

While we could continue to use the language of contracts to analyze this arrangement, option theory uses a different set of terms to describe all options. How would this deal be expressed in the language of option theory? First, because this option gives Schmidt the right to *purchase* something, option theory would regard this as a *call option*. (Below, we will look at the inverse situation where someone has the right to *sell*

something at a specific price, which is called a *put option.*) Second, Schmidt's decision to accept the offer and purchase the shares would be regarded as a decision to *exercise* the option and pay the *exercise price*, which is sometimes called the *strike price*. We would also refer to the 10-year period during which Schmidt is allowed to exercise the option as the *option term* or *option duration*. Over the term of an option, the profitability of exercising an option will naturally change as the price of the underlying stock changes, and an option is said to be *"in-the-money"* if it would be profitable to exercise the option. Conversely, an option that is *"out-of-the-money"* would be unprofitable to exercise. This would occur, for example, if Google's stock price dropped to $1 per share right after Schmidt joined the company. (When the exercise price is exactly equal to the value of the stock—as is typically the case upon the initial grant of an employee stock option—it is an *"at-the-money"* option.) Finally, because Schmidt has the right to exercise the option at any time during its term, we would refer to this option as an *American option*. As such, it differs from a *European option*, which can only be exercised at its expiration (i.e., if this was a European option, Schmidt could only elect to exercise the stock purchase at the end of the 10-year term).

Returning to our legal analysis, to implement this bargain a company will ordinarily issue a formal stock option agreement outlining the shares covered by the option, its duration, the exercise price, the method for notifying the company, and any other terms that the company wishes to make a part of the option. For instance, the option might state that if Schmidt purchases shares pursuant to the option, the company retains the right to repurchase the stock at cost in the event Schmidt were to quit working at Google—until a certain period of time elapses (i.e., a vesting provision).* The option agreement will also include a provision that specifies the method of exercise. Google's 2000 Stock Plan, for instance, included a form "Stock Option Agreement" with the following provision:

> (b) <u>Method of Exercise</u>. This Option shall be exercisable by delivery of an exercise notice in the form attached as Exhibit A (the "Exercise Notice") which shall state the election to exercise the Option, the number of Shares with respect to which the Option is being exercised, and such other representations and agreements as may be required by the Company. The Exercise

* Employee stock option agreements typically include these types of vesting agreements. Among technology companies, vesting provisions generally permit the company to repurchase any shares from an employee who stops working for the company, with the percentage available for repurchase declining the longer the employee remains an employee at the company. Traditionally, the standard vesting schedule has been for the company to have the right to repurchase 100% of the employee's shares until the one-year anniversary of the option's grant date. On this date, the company loses the right to repurchase (i.e., the employee "vests in") 25% of the shares covered by the option. After that, the employee vests (i.e., the company loses the right to repurchase shares) in 1/36 of the total shares covered by the option for every month the employee works at the company. After four full years of employment, the employee would thus be vested in 100% of the shares.

> Notice shall be accompanied by payment of the aggregate Exercise Price as to all Exercised Shares.

It also included the following section specifying the method of payment:

> 5. Method of Payment. Payment of the aggregate Exercise Price shall be by any of the following, or a combination thereof, at the election of the Optionee:
>
> (a) cash;
>
> (b) check;*

The notion that an employee must pay by cash or check might seem trivial, but it turns out to be a vitally important part of the agreement. Let's imagine, for instance, that the option agreement omitted Section 5. As long as Eric Schmidt delivers $4,299,512.40 worth of "stuff" he would appear to have triggered Google's obligation to deliver the 3,582,927 shares. This, in turn, could open up a vast number of possibilities. Consider just a few:

- Suppose Schmidt is an avid investor in baseball cards. He delivers five cards to Google having a market value of $4,299,512.40 as consideration for the 3,582,927 shares.
- Schmidt, having loaned Google money in the past, is owed exactly $4,299,512.40 by Google. He agrees to cancel this debt as consideration for the 3,528,927 shares.
- Schmidt, having tired of eating at Subway Restaurants, delivers a few hundred thousand Subway gift cards he previously purchased as consideration for the 3,528,927 shares. The gift cards entitle the holders to $4,299,512.40 of Subway meals.

Indeed, it would seem Schmidt could convert all sorts of things into 3,582,927 shares of Google stock!

Of course, these fanciful examples are not permitted under Google's actual stock option agreement. But they highlight how simple it is to draft a call option that can be exercised using non-cash consideration. And it turns out that this is precisely how convertible securities are created.

To illustrate, let's return to Lyft's convertible preferred stock, the terms of which are contained in its Certificate of Incorporation which is reproduced in the Appendix. Section 4 of Article IV(B) of Lyft's Charter provides that shares of preferred stock are convertible into shares of

---

* As is typical of employee options, the agreement also permitted employees to pay with a promissory note as well as by a "cashless exercise"; under this latter provision, if the value of the stock exceeds the specified purchase price, the employee can surrender the option and receive the value of stock equal to the difference between the fair value of all shares offered by the company and the total purchase price required to be paid. So, for example, if Schmidt decided to pursue a cashless exercise for 200 shares at a moment when Google stock traded at $2.40, he would pay no cash and receive 100 shares of Google. Do you see why?

common stock. (Recall that Lyft sub-divided its preferred stock into 10 separate series.) Section 4(a) begins with the following language:

> (a) Right to Convert. Each share of Preferred Stock shall be convertible, at the option of the holder thereof, at any time after the date of issuance of such share at the office of this Corporation or any transfer agent for such stock, into such number of fully paid and nonassessable shares of Common Stock as is determined by dividing the Original Issue Price for each such series of Preferred Stock by the Conversion Price applicable to such share, determined as hereafter provided, in effect on the date the certificate is surrendered for conversion.

Following this sentence, the next sentence (omitted here for brevity) then defines the "Conversion Price applicable to such share" as being equal to the Original Issue Price for that series of preferred stock.

Thus, to convert shares of preferred stock into shares of common stock, a holder of preferred stock needs to deliver its shares of preferred stock to the company. That sounds a lot like paying for Lyft common stock using preferred stock instead of cash. However, if the conversion is effectively the purchase of common stock, we need some additional information to understand the mechanics of this right. In particular, what is the price per share of the common stock being purchased with the preferred stock? And what value should we place on each share of preferred stock being tendered? The aforementioned provision in the Certificate of Incorporation gives us an answer to both of these questions: Each share of preferred stock will be valued at its Original Issue Price, and the purchase price of the common stock will be the Conversion Price for the series (which is initially the same as the Original Issue Price but, as we will see, might be adjusted by some later events). Like Eric's Schmidt call option for Google Common Stock, this provision thus gives each holder of preferred stock a call option for Lyft Common Stock.

How do we know that this is the intention of the provision? Let's look at the formula specified in Section 4(a):

$$\frac{\textit{Original Issue Price}}{\textit{Conversion Price}} = \textit{number of shares of Common Stock received}$$

If you have only a dollar in your wallet and want to buy as many apples as you can at \$0.50 per apple, you will obviously be able to buy 2 apples (i.e., \$1.00 payment/purchase price). For the same reason, if a holder of Series A Preferred Stock of Lyft wants to buy shares of Lyft Common Stock, Section 4(a) gives this stockholder the unilateral right to do so by simply tendering a share of Series A Preferred Stock, which will be valued at its Original Issue Price of \$0.762666667 per share. (The Original Issue Price for the Series A Preferred Stock is defined in Article IV(B), Section 2 of Lyft's Charter.) Having delivered \$0.762666667 of consideration, the denominator tells us how much each share of Common Stock costs and, consequently, how many shares will be purchased. Since the Conversion Price is also $0.762666667 per share, the stockholder will receive 1 share of Common Stock. Hence, the initial 1:1 conversion ratio discussed in Chapter 7. In short, convertible securities are effectively embedded call options that can be exercised by tendering the original securities.

Convertible debt securities, such as convertible notes and convertible bonds, work in a very similar manner. In a convertible note transaction, the issuer will sell notes to investors promising to repay principal and interest according to a fixed schedule set forth in the note. But the note will also give an investor the right to convert the note into the issuer's equity securities by surrendering the note to the company. Because surrendering the note cancels the debt obligation, an investor who converts the note is delivering consideration equal to the amount of the debt that has just been cancelled. The number of shares issuable to the investor is then determined by dividing this amount by a conversion price specified in the note, just as in the case of Lyft's convertible preferred stock.*

Nor are call options the only type of option that can be embedded in another financing instrument. As mentioned earlier, the inverse of a call option is a put option, which entitles the holder to sell an asset at a fixed price to the party who sells the put (sometimes called the "writer" of the option). Let's return, for example, to the Perpetual Youth hypothetical at the beginning of this chapter. Assume that PY continues to grow and that it eventually conducts an IPO at $3.00 per share. You exercise your option for $5,000,000, receiving 5,000,000 shares valued at $15 million. Congratulations! While pleased, you also worry that so much of your personal wealth is now tied up in PY stock. Your financial advisor offers you the following proposition: For a sizeable fee, it will agree to purchase up to 5,000,000 shares of PY from you at a price of $1.00 per share.

Figure 8-3: Option Contract for Put Option

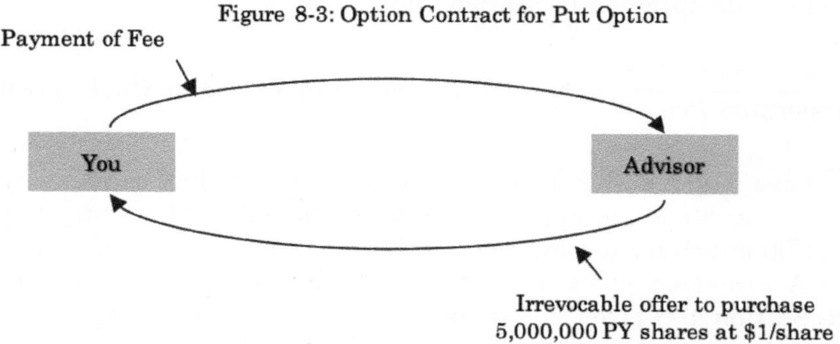

---

* Convertible bonds issued pursuant to an indenture will often stipulate a fixed conversion ratio for every $1,000 of principal that is being converted; in these cases, the effective exercise price of the embedded option is $1,000 divided by the conversion ratio.

Thus, if the price of PY falls below $1.00 per share, you can exercise the option and force the advisor to pay you $5,000,000 for your 5,000,000 shares. This arrangement allows you to hedge your concentrated position in PY stock; you might sleep better at night knowing that even if the price drops down to nothing, you'll still be able to receive $5 million from exercising your put (assuming, of course, your financial advisor is solvent and able to honor its financial obligations).

Figure 8-4: Acceptance of Put Option Contract

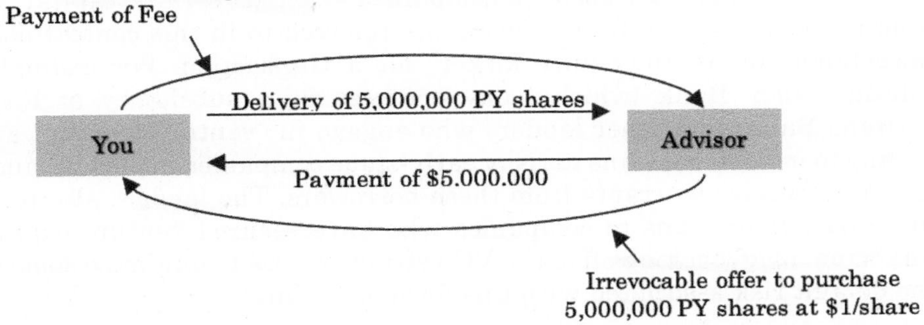

Note that this right to have stock purchased at a fixed price is effectively the same as the preferred stock redemption provisions studied in Chapter 7. Said differently, investor redemption rights represent a put option with an exercise price equal to the redemption price. Moreover, as we saw in Chapter 7, preferred stock can be redeemable *and* convertible. Thus, it is possible for a security to have multiple embedded options. Since the exercise of these two options remains in the discretion of the investor, the investor is free to choose the option (including retaining the original security) that maximizes its ultimate payout.

B. WARRANTS AND LISTED OPTIONS

The options we have discussed so far are just a few of the many instances where they are used. Because formal options are simply irrevocable offers, anyone who has the capacity to contract can form them. Moreover, options are useful for both investment purposes and risk management purposes, and they are pervasive in the world of finance. Consider two other types of formal options commonly observed in practice: Warrants and Listed Options.

Warrants. We briefly introduced warrants in Chapter 4. Technically, a warrant is the same thing as an employee stock option. That is, a company issuing a warrant makes an irrevocable promise to sell the warrant holder shares of the company's equity at a fixed price per share. The primary difference is that warrants are issued to non-employees. For instance, start-up companies routinely issue warrants to consultants as a form of incentive compensation. A start-up company might also issue warrants as a mode of partial payment in other contracts, such as a real estate or equipment lease. Commercial real estate firms that operate in areas permeated by start-up companies understand that across all their tenants, there are likely to be a handful that will be extremely successful. Holding a portfolio of warrants in their tenants can therefore be a way to acquire the right to invest in the successful ventures and to do so at a price per share that reflects the valuation of the company when it entered into the lease. And warrants can conceivably be used for more than just rent payments; if a vendor is amenable to it, a company can issue warrants as a partial form of payment in any contract setting.

Warrants are also used by companies seeking to raise capital. In practice, it is common to hear warrants referred to in this context as a "sweetener" or as an "equity kicker" for a transaction. For example, Silicon Valley Bank (which today operates as a subsidiary of First Citizens Bank) and other lenders who engage in "venture lending" are willing to make term loans to risky early-stage companies in part because they also receive warrants from these borrowers. The lenders also tend to restrict their loans to companies who have secured venture capital financing, piggybacking off of the VC vetting process to minimize some of the default risk associated with this form of lending.

Imagine, for instance, a company that is seeking venture debt after having just completed its Series C Preferred Stock financing at a price of $2.00 per share. As an inducement to entering into a $5 million term loan facility, a venture lender may require 10% of "warrant coverage" in the company's Series C Preferred Stock.* What does this mean? Upon closing the loan, the company would issue the lender a warrant to purchase $500,000 of Series C Preferred Stock (or 250,000 shares) at an exercise price of $2.00 per share. While the lender will make short-term returns through loan fees and interest payments, these warrants provide the potential for long-term returns that can help offset some of the (inevitable) losses from a business model that makes loans to risky start-up companies.

Outside the start-up context, companies likewise use warrants in both public and private offerings of debt and equity. For example, smaller, growing businesses may conduct a public "unit offering" in which they seek to raise capital by selling units consisting of a share of common stock and a warrant to purchase the company's common stock at an exercise price at or near the offering price of the unit. While sold initially as a combined unit, the warrants typically "detach" after a specified number of days from the offering date and thereafter become freely tradeable. (To facilitate secondary trading, the company will generally list both the common stock and the warrants on an exchange.) While the theoretical rationale for these unit offerings remains disputed, one common explanation is that the warrant kicker may induce some investors to participate in offerings by smaller, riskier firms who need growth capital. Furthermore, any future exercises of the warrants will

* The amount of warrant coverage typically ranges between 10–20% of the loan amount.

provide additional financing to the company at the exercise price, thereby securing additional financing without the need to incur incremental costs from a seasoned offering (i.e., a follow-on issue of securities by a public company).*

More generally, warrants can be bundled with any bond or preferred stock offering to grant investors the option of participating in the issuer's residual claim. In this context, the effect of the warrants can be very similar to an investment in convertible bonds or convertible preferred stock. Consider, for instance, Berkshire Hathaway's $5 billion investment in Bank of America in 2011. In the financing, Berkshire Hathaway purchased 50,000 shares of Bank of America's Cumulative Perpetual Preferred Stock for $100,000 per share. Each share had a liquidation preference of $100,000 and paid a 6% cumulative dividend. In connection with the financing, Berkshire Hathaway also received warrants to purchase 700,000,000 shares of Bank of America common stock at an exercise price of approximately $7.14. The aggregate exercise price was therefore $5,000,000,000, and the warrant exercise price could be paid by surrendering the 50,000 shares of preferred stock. And Berkshire Hathaway did exactly that a few years later by surrendering all 50,000 shares of preferred stock to obtain 700,000,000 shares of common stock. At the time, Bank of America's common stock was trading near $25 per share for an aggregate value of $17.5 billion—not a bad return! The ultimate result was the same as if Berkshire Hathaway had originally purchased convertible preferred stock with a conversion price of $7.14 per share.

Listed Options. Investors can also buy and sell on specialized option exchanges options relating to the common stock of most publicly traded firms. Unlike warrants, these listed options are not typically sold by the underlying company; they simply represent an exchange of contract rights between buyer and seller. For instance, we present below the "option chain" showing all outstanding options for The Progressive Corporation (whose common stock has the trading symbol "PGR") in April 2019:

* Note that investors will rationally exercise the warrants only when the underlying stock price is valued at more than the exercise price. A company that relies on warrant exercises rather than a seasoned offering for future financing needs is therefore assuming that the costs of a seasoned offering will exceed the money that the company leaves on the table by selling stock at the warrant exercise price rather than at the current value of the company's common stock.

Figure 8-5: Option Chain for PGR in April 2019

Apr 19 | May 19 | Aug 19 | Nov 19 | Jan 20 | Jan 21 | Near Term | All

Option Chain for Progressive Corporation (The) (PGR)

Calls	Last	Chg	Bid	Ask	Vol	Open Int	Root	Strike	Puts	Last	Chg	Bid	Ask	Vol	Open Int
Apr 18, 2019	17.10		17.30	18.10	0	11.00	PGR	55	Apr 18, 2019				0.30	0	0
Apr 18, 2019	12.80		12.3	13.10	0	10	PGR	60	Apr 18, 2019	0.07			0.25	0	50
Apr 18, 2019			9.8	10.50	0	0	PGR	62.5	Apr 18, 2019	0.05			0.10	0	65
Apr 18, 2019	7.00		7.1	8.00	0	9	PGR	65	Apr 18, 2019	0.05			0.15	42	345
Apr 18, 2019	4.60		5	5.70	0	35	PGR	67.5	Apr 18, 2019	0.27		0.10	0.25	0	62
Apr 18, 2019	2.80	0.2	2.8	3.20	3	59	PGR	70	Apr 18, 2019	0.52	-0.08	0.45	0.55	9	2656
Apr 18, 2019	1.25	0.25	1.25	1.45	37	215	PGR	72.5	Apr 18, 2019	1.26	-0.44	1.10	1.35	14	1725
Apr 18, 2019	0.40	0.1	0.3	0.50	62	3753	PGR	75	Apr 18, 2019	2.90	0.01	2.70	3.00	2	19
Apr 18, 2019	0.10			0.15	13	9283	PGR	77.5	Apr 18, 2019	5.02		4.60	5.30	0	1
Apr 18, 2019	0.05			0.15	0	45	PGR	80	Apr 18, 2019			7.20	7.80	0	0
Apr 18, 2019				0.35	0	0	PGR	82.5	Apr 18, 2019			9.50	10.40	0	0
Apr 18, 2019				0.30	0	0	PGR	85	Apr 18, 2019			12.20	12.70	0	0
Apr 18, 2019				0.30	0	0	PGR	90	Apr 18, 2019			17.20	17.20	0	0

The left half of the listings are call options having an expiration date of April 18, 2019 and strike prices (listed in the center) ranging from $55 per share to $90 per share. At the time, PGR's stock was trading at $72.61, so the top seven calls (shaded in grey) were in-the-money. The right half of the figure contains listings for put options having the same expiration date and strike prices, so the bottom six puts were in-the-money (also shaded in grey).

The availability of listed options can be quite useful for investors looking to hedge investment positions. For instance, an investor who holds shares of PGR and is concerned about a decline in PGR's stock price might purchase one of the seven out-of-the-money put options to guard against this risk. The cost of acquiring this insurance is simply the price of the put. By paying the ask price of $1.35 for the seventh put on the list, for example, the investor gets the right through April 18, 2019 to sell a share of PGR to the writer of the put for $72.50. If the price of PGR stock drops below this strike price, the investor will exercise the put to hedge the investment. Listed options are typically American options, so the holder of a listed call or put can exercise the option at any time until the expiration date. Options are also available for many stock indexes (e.g., the S&P500), but these are often in the form of European options (i.e., they are only exercisable on the expiration date, not before).

Options on U.S. equities and stock indices are currently listed on more than a dozen option exchanges. (The listing of options for PGR reflects the consolidated quotes from all exchanges where PGR options are traded.) The two most active exchanges are the Chicago Board of Options Exchange ("CBOE") and the NYSE American Options Exchange ("NYSE"). As with any contract, the buyer of an option necessarily faces the risk that the seller of the contract will default on their contractual obligation, which would seem especially relevant when trading on exchanges with anonymous counterparties. To minimize this risk, all listed options must be centrally cleared through The Options Clearing Corporation ("OCC"), which serves as the counterparty to all listed option trades. Thus, the OCC is a direct participant in every purchase and sale of a listed option contract. As shown in Figure 8-6, when an option writer or holder sells its option contract to someone else, the OCC serves as an intermediary in the transaction; the option writer sells its contract to the

OCC and the option buyer buys it from the OCC. Formally, the OCC thus carries on its books the options positions of the brokerage firms that are clearing members of OCC, and the clearing members in turn carry on their books the options positions of their customers. The OCC closely regulates the capital requirements of its clearing members, helping to ensure that they honor the options that they write on behalf of their customers.

Figure 8-6: The Options Clearing Corporation

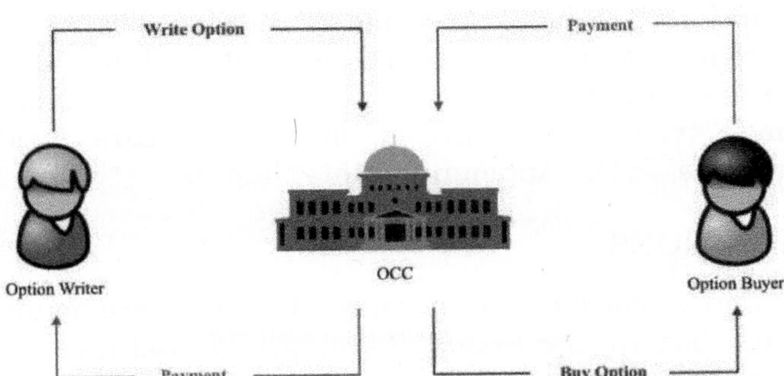

Listed options have standardized terms that are determined by both the exchanges and the OCC. For example, every listed equity option for a given stock will have at least four expiration months that are currently trading, with the expiration date for each month typically occurring on the third Friday of that month. In the case PGR, a trader in early April 2019 could buy and sell options expiring on April 19, 2019, which was the third Friday of that month, as well as options expiring on the third Friday of May 2019 (the following month) and options expiring on the third Fridays of August 2019 and November 2019. While every equity will have options expiring in the current month and the following month, the remaining two months are based on where the stock has been assigned within the "option cycle" set by the OCC. More specifically, for stocks assigned to option cycle 1, the remaining two months are the ensuing January, April, July or October months; for option cycle 2, they are the ensuing February, May, August or November months; and for option cycle 3, they are the ensuing March, June, September or December months. PGR is in option cycle 2, so for a trader looking to buy or sell PGR options in April 2019, the final two months are August 2019 and November 2019.

In addition, some stocks may have long-term equity anticipation securities (LEAPS), which are simply options with an expiration date one or two years in the future. If a stock has LEAPS, then new LEAPS are issued in May, June or July depending on the cycle to which the stock is assigned and typically have a January expiration date. In the case of PGR, for instance, a trader could buy LEAPS in April 2019 that had expiration dates of January 17, 2020 and January 15, 2021.

For heavily traded stocks and indices, some exchanges also permit "weekly" options. For instance, the CBOE introduced weekly options that expire on Fridays in 2005, and in 2016, it listed weekly options that expire on Wednesdays. By 2022, CBOE had introduced weekly options with expirations on every trading day of the week. Thus, for some securities, it is now possible to buy or sell an option on any given trading day which will expire later that same day—a scenario that has given rise to a dramatic uptick in the trading of so-called zero days to expiration (or 0DTE) options. These are not for the faint of heart!

Listed options are just one of many possible derivative securities that investors may trade in the capital markets. While a full canvasing of derivatives is beyond the scope of this chapter, we summarize several other common types of derivatives, including futures contracts and forward contracts, in the Appendix to this chapter.

C. REAL OPTIONS

In addition to formal option contracts, there are many economic arrangements that are the equivalent of options, and it can be useful to think of them in that manner. For instance, an investor may have the choice to continue or to abandon an investment in a project. A classic example is the concept of staged financing in venture capital finance. Typically, a venture capitalist will make a small initial investment in a start-up company and retain contract rights to continue to fund the venture in the future if the company meets future performance milestones. If, however, the company fails to perform as expected, the venture capitalist can decline to make further investments, thus "exercising" its option to abandon the investment. Similarly, when a manufacturing company buys a vacant parcel of land next to a plant, it is creating the option to expand in the future. When an inventor files a patent application, she is likewise creating an exclusive option to exploit the invention in the future. Oil and gas leases are another example of de facto options. The typical lease on undeveloped mineral rights calls for a nominal "delay rental," often $1.00 per acre per year, for as long as the lessee does not produce oil and gas. This, in effect, is an option to the lessee to develop the mineral rights by drilling at the time of its choice (at which time higher royalty payments replace the delay rentals).

These arrangements are often known as "real options" because, like financial options, they convey a right but not an obligation to take some action in the future. Real options can also have significant implications for the valuation of an investment. All options have value, but conventional approaches to valuation, such as DCF analysis, typically ignore the option value created by a real option. Consider, for instance, a project that requires an investment of $150 today and is expected to generate the following possible revenues in one year:

Revenues	Investment	Income	Probability
$200	$150	$50	1/3
$150	$150	$0	1/3
$40	$150	−$110	1/3

Based on these probabilities, the expected net income from the investment is −$20 ($50/3 + $0/3 + −$110/3), making it a poor use of investment funds (you don't even need to know the discount rate). The reason is clear enough: there's a 1/3 probability that the project is a failure and produces a −$110 loss. But what if the investor had the right to delay the $150 investment until the investor had more information about whether this "bad news" scenario was likely to occur? This is analogous to the venture capitalist's option to abandon and would dramatically change the determination of whether the full $150 investment should be made. In this situation, the expected investment income turns positive: $50 × 1/3 + $0 × 1/3 + $0 × 1/3, or $16.67. In short, without the option to abandon, the investor will pass on the investment. With the option to abandon, the investor can skip the $150 payment if information emerges that the project will tank. This, in turn, yields an expected cash flow of $16.67, making this an attractive proposition (assuming that the discount rate, which we have ignored here for simplicity, is not too high).

As you spend more time thinking about real options theory, you will often uncover benefits in unexpected contexts. For example, real options can be useful when valuing the equity of a distressed firm. For a heavily indebted corporation, where shareholders have limited liability, shareholders hold a de facto option to buy the company by paying off the debt. To see why, imagine a leveraged company that has fallen on hard times. It has $100 of bonds outstanding, and its assets are worth just $90. The bonds are not yet due and no default has occurred, but the bondholders effectively "own" the firm assuming nothing changes. But does this mean that the stock price has zero value? Since the bonds are not yet due and there is no default, the possibility exists that things could change for better, boosting the value of the company's assets above $100 and causing the stockholders to repay the debt. In effect, the stockholders would be exercising their option to purchase the firm's assets from the bondholders by paying them $100. From this perspective, stockholders hold a call option on the assets of the firm, which is why the stock price of distressed firms—even those that have filed for bankruptcy—can continue to trade with positive value. Moreover, thinking about common stock as a call option on the assets of a leveraged firm also tells us something about why common stockholders might want the company to undertake risky business strategies: As we shall see below, the value of a call option increases with the volatility of the underlying asset. In other words, a firm that takes on riskier investments will increase the value of the common stock "call option."*

> **Quick Check: Was *Trados* Correctly Decided?**
>
> Recall that in the *Trados* opinion covered in Chapter 7, Vice Chancellor Travis Laster evaluated whether the decision to sell Trados to SDL complied with the board's fiduciary duties under the entire fairness standard of review. The case was brought by holders of Trados common stock who received nothing in the acquisition due to the preferred stock's liquidation preferences. Vice Chancellor Laster concluded that, while the board's decision-making failed the "fair process" prong of the entire fairness review, it nevertheless met the "fair price" prong because the fair value of the common stock was zero. If you were representing the plaintiffs, does the foregoing discussion of real options theory tell you anything about what you should be looking for in a valuation expert?

3. OPTION VALUATION

A key concept to keep in mind when working with options is that they are binary contracts. If an investor holds a call option that allows the investor to purchase a stock at a particular price, the option is worthless if the stock trades below the exercise price and profitable if it trades above the exercise price. Similarly, if an investor holds a put option to sell a stock at a certain price, it is worthless if the stock rises above that price, but worth the difference between the exercise price and the current market price of the stock if the stock price falls below the exercise price.

Options are also bilateral agreements, and they are necessarily a zero-sum game. If you buy a call option and it expires unexercised, you will have lost the value of the price of the option, but the seller of the option will have pocked your purchase price. Conversely, when you exercise the option, the seller will have to deliver the stock, no matter what the price it might cost to acquire it.

These binary outcomes, and their consequences for buyers and sellers of options, determine the ultimate value of any given option. Accordingly, in this section, we begin our discussion of option valuation with an exploration of the cash flows to buyers and sellers of options.

A. UNDERSTANDING OPTION CASH FLOWS

Investors who buy-and-hold a stock are often referred to as being "long" the stock in the sense that the investor expects to earn returns

---

* This observation, of course, is simply another way to explain why the stockholders of a distressed firm will try to engage in asset substitution and some of the other risk-enhancing strategies discussed in Chapter 6.

based on any long-term increases in the price of the stock. In contrast, an investor who is "short" a stock expects to earn returns from *decreases* in the price of the stock. To execute a short position, an investor will (i) borrow shares from his or her broker for a fee, (ii) sell the shares in the market, and (iii) wait for the price to decline. Once it does, the investor can then repurchase shares in the market at that lower price and return them to the broker, closing out the position. As with a long investor, the short investor earns a return equal to the difference between the price at which the stock was sold and the price at which the stock was purchased; the main difference for a short investor is that the "sell" transaction occurs before the "buy" transaction.

Buyers and sellers of options can also be "long" and "short" options, depending on their net economic position when buying or selling.

i. LONG AND SHORT POSITIONS IN CALL OPTIONS

Just as with stock, someone who purchases a call option is said to have a long position in the option. The payoff from a call option on its expiration date is a function of the stock price and the exercise price. Imagine, for instance, an investor who has purchased a European call option for a share of IBM. If the exercise price is $100, and the value of the stock is less than $100, then the option is worthless (and the investor is also out the option's initial purchase price). If the stock price is greater than $100, however, the option is worth the stock price minus the exercise price. We can show this in the following chart:

	Call Option Payoff on Expiration Date	
Contingent States:	If stock price < $100	If stock price > $100
Call Option Value:	0	Stock price – $100

Notice that there is no upper limit to the potential value of a call option at maturity; no matter how high the price of the underlying stock rises, the *intrinsic value* of the option (i.e., the difference between the stock price and the exercise price) rises accordingly. In Figure 8-7 we introduce a payoff diagram to illustrate the intrinsic value of this hypothetical option at expiration as a function of IBM's stock price. The vertical axis is the intrinsic value of the option at maturity, representing the dollars the investor will gain from exercise on that date. The horizontal axis represents the stock's price on the same date. The bold line represents the intrinsic value of the option at various stock prices. Note that once the stock price reaches and exceeds the exercise price, the intrinsic value of the option rises with the value of the stock on a dollar-for-dollar basis.

Figure 8-7: Payout of Call Option at Expiration

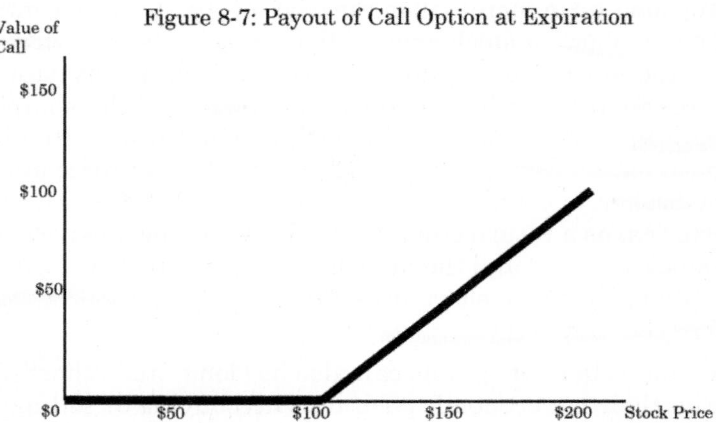

As shown in the figure, the buyer of an option runs the risk that the option will be worthless at the expiration date. This defines the extent of the buyer's risk of loss; it is limited to the price paid for the option. However, the same is not true for the buyer's potential gain. Regardless of how high the value of the underlying asset climbs, the buyer can obtain it for the exercise price. Thus, in Figure 8-7 there is no upper bound on the diagonal line: potential gains to the holder of a call option are infinite.*

For every buyer of a call option (i.e., being long an option), there is someone who has written (sold) the option, and thus has taken a short position. This seller receives the proceeds of the initial price of the call option and bears the risk of having to deliver the stock if its price rises above the option exercise price. Why would anyone take this economic position? The investor who writes a call option may hold IBM stock and might believe that it is a good long-term investment, but that, for some reason, the stock will not do so well in the short run. Indeed, the investor might even believe IBM's stock price will decline over the next six months. The investor could, of course, sell IBM stock now with an intent to repurchase it in the future. But the investor will incur two sets of transaction costs—both selling and buying IBM stock. And in addition to brokerage costs, some investors may also incur tax costs. Alternatively, our gloomy investor could hold the IBM stock and sell a call option on it. The option price will generate a profit for our gloomy investor, so long as the option expires unexercised (i.e., IBM stock declines or does not rise

* Note that Figure 8-7 shows the value of the call option without taking the initial purchase price of the call into consideration. For example, if it costs the investor $5 to buy the option, then the net economic gain if IBM stock rises to $150 is $45 ($50 from exercising the option minus $5 to buy the option). We can also graph the net position value from buying the option, which includes the initial purchase price, by simply shifting the line in Figure 8-7 down by the cost of the option. So, continuing the example, we might shift the line down by $5 to illustrate that the net position from buying the call is −$5 for any closing price below $100 (i.e., the investor loses the cost of purchasing the call). As the price of IBM stock rises above $100, the purchase price is offset until the investor eventually breaks even at $105 and generates actual profits from the investment at stock prices above that amount.

above $100 per share). Said differently, our option writer has partially hedged the risk of a decline in IBM stock. Of course, our option writer is at risk if the stock price rises above $100 during the life of the option; in that case, the option will be exercised and the option writer will need to cover his position by delivering shares of IBM.

While this example has assumed the writer of the call option holds shares of IBM, we know from our prior discussion that this doesn't have to be the case. Another investor who holds the same gloomy expectations about IBM's stock price can also write call options on shares of IBM and collect a fee for every option she sells. These are called "naked" options. (Where the writer of a call option owns the underlying stock that must be delivered upon exercise of the option, this is referred to as a "covered" option.) If the writer of a naked option is correct in her prediction about the stock price of IBM, the option will expire unexercised and the investor's profit arises from the option price charged to the buyer of the option. However, if IBM's stock price increases beyond $100 per share, the option will be exercised, and the writer of the option will need to purchase shares of IBM in the open market at the prevailing market price to cover the position. As a result, the potential losses for a writer of a naked call option are, in theory, limitless. We can see the position of a writer of a naked call option in Figure 8-8.

Figure 8-8: Liability of Call Option Writer at Expiration

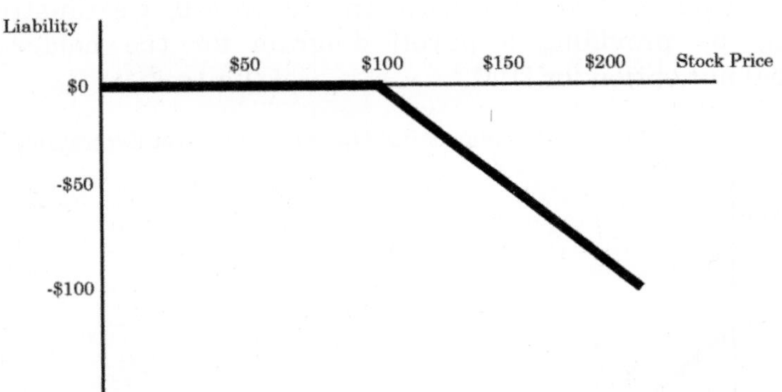

Why would any investor ever wish to take the losing position shown in Figure 8-8? Recall that a call option writer will get paid when she sells these options.* If this initial payment for the option is sufficient to compensate the writer of the call option for this risk, then she might still come out ahead. (The business model is analogous to that of an insurance firm who collects premiums and then pays out only if bad events happen.)

* As noted above, if we want to graph the net position of the call option writer, then we would need to shift the graph up by the initial price of the option which is paid by the buyer of the option.

We discuss below how we might value the fair price for selling a call option.

ii. LONG AND SHORT POSITIONS IN PUT OPTIONS

A put option is the opposite of a call option. It gives the holder the right to sell (put) the underlying asset to the writer of the option at a previously specified exercise price. In our previous example, if the IBM stockholder fears a decline in IBM's stock price, she can also hedge that risk by buying an option giving her the right to sell IBM stock for $100 at the expiration date (once again, assuming a European option). Thus, if IBM stock turns out to be worth $75 at the expiration date, the proceeds upon exercising the put option will be $100. Indeed, if IBM stock turns out to be worthless, the proceeds from exercising the put option remain $100. In both cases the option should be exercised. In contrast, if the price of IBM stock is at $100 or more at the expiration date, the put option should not be exercised. We can see that there is an inverse relationship between the intrinsic value of the put option and the value of the common stock: For every dollar that IBM stock falls below $100 on the expiration date, the intrinsic value of the put option increases by the same amount. The intrinsic value of the put option can therefore be expressed as:

Put Option Intrinsic Value = Exercise Price – Market Price of Stock

Note that, as reflected in this equation, the intrinsic value of a put option can never be less than zero. In Figure 8-9, we illustrate this relationship by providing a payoff diagram for the holder of our hypothetical put option for IBM.*

Figure 8-9: Value of Put Option to Holder at Expiration

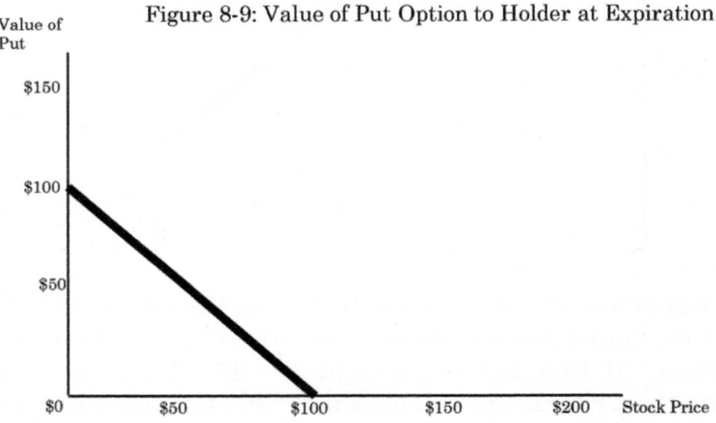

* As before, the net position for the purchaser of a put is graphed by shifting the entire payoff line down by the price paid for the put.

Quick Check Question 8.1

Using long and short positions in other financial instruments (e.g., shares of IBM and call options on these shares), can you synthesize the position of the writer of a put option, to achieve the position shown in Figure 8-9? Keep in mind that some instruments have unlimited upsides and downsides, while the payout on a put option is confined, as shown in Figure 8-9.

What about the cash flows to the seller (writer) of a put option? This investor has the obligation to buy the stock at the stated price ($100, in our example). Following the collection of the purchase price for the put option, the writer of the put option would expect cash flows as reflected in Figure 8-10, which illustrates these cash flows at various stock prices.

Figure 8-10: Liability of Put Option Writer at Expiration

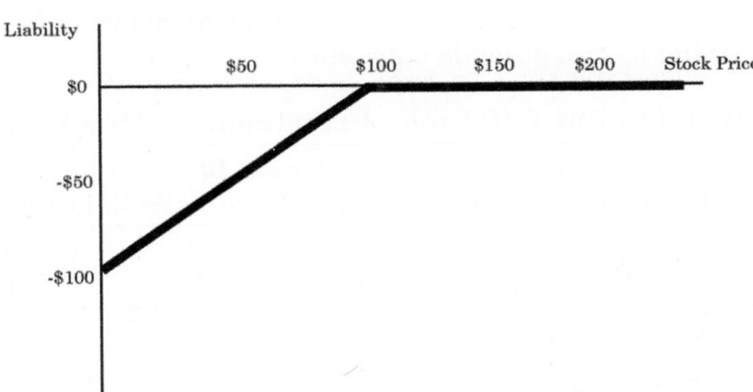

We can summarize the foregoing discussion in terms of "winners" and "losers" from buying and selling options as follows:

Summary: Option Outcomes at Expiration

Value of Underlying Stock	**Winners**	**Losers**
High (relative to exercise price)	Call Holder	Call Writer
	Put Writer	Put Holder
Low (relative to exercise price)	Call Writer	Call Holder
	Put Holder	Put Writer

B. COMBINING OPTIONS, STOCKS AND BONDS; PUT-CALL PARITY

In addition to illustrating how options function, the preceding discussion of option payoff diagrams can help illuminate how call options, put options, and shares of the underlying stock can be combined to replicate the expected cash flows for other investments. As we shall see, this turns out to be a key insight that informs how we estimate the fair value for an option.

To illustrate, assume that our IBM investor holds one share of IBM stock which currently trades at $100 per share. Now, suppose the investor enters into two option transactions, both involving one-year European options. First, she buys a one-year European put option on IBM stock with a $100 exercise price. Under this option, if the price of IBM in one year's time is less than $100, the investor will exercise the option and will receive $100 in cash. Second, the investor sells a one-year European call option with an exercise price of $100. The term of this option is also one year. Let's call this combination of investment positions (i.e., "long" a share of stock, "long" a put option and "short" a call option), the "Put-Call-Stock Investment."

Now let's consider the expected payoffs to the investor given these transactions, ignoring for the moment the fees paid or received for the options. In one year, the stock price will either be above or below $100 per share, giving us two possible outcomes:

Payoffs to Put-Call-Stock Investment at One Year

Outcome A: Stock Price Rises Above $100		***Outcome B:*** Stock Price Falls Below $100	
Action Taken:	Cash to Investor	Action Taken:	Cash to Investor
Put option expires.	0	Call expires	0
Call is exercised against investor, obligating investor to sell IBM stock, to receive exercise price of $100.	$100	Investor exercises put, selling the stock for the exercise price of $100.	$100
TOTAL	$100		$100

In either outcome, the investor will receive $100 in one year's time. In effect, we have replicated the outcome of an investor who, instead of engaging in this sequence of transactions, simply invests a sum of money in a bank account for a year that grows to $100 by the end of this one-year period. In fact, assuming no default by the writer of the put option, we have replicated the position of an investor in a risk-free zero-coupon bond that matures at the exercise price of both options (i.e., $100) in one year.*

We can also see this by going back to our payoff diagram. Again, assuming the investor (a) holds one share of IBM with a market price of $100, (b) writes (i.e., sells) a one-year European call option with an exercise price of $100, and (c) buys a one-year European put option with an exercise price of $100, the cash flows to the investor at different IBM stock prices in one year are illustrated in Figure 8-11:

Figure 8-11: Value of Put-Call-Stock Investment in 1 Year

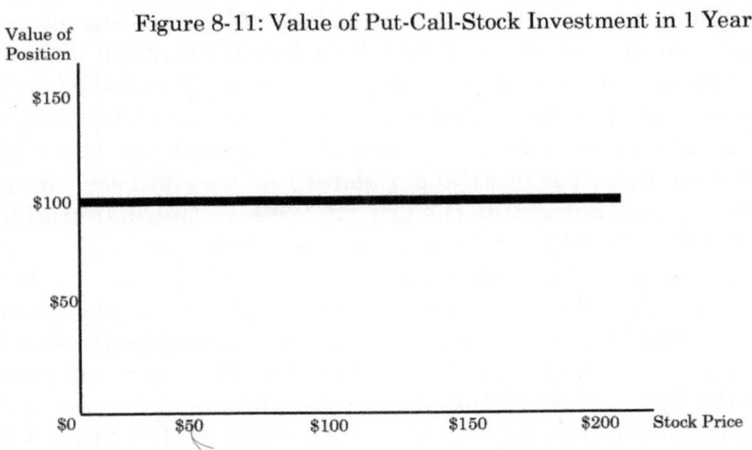

Whether the stock rises or falls, the investor's position in one year is the same as holding a zero-coupon bond paying $100 in one year. For example, if the risk-free rate is 10%, Figure 8-11 reflects exactly the same payout an investor will receive if she simply invests $90.91 in a risk-free 1-year $100 zero-coupon bond and waits one-year for the $100 payment. In either case, the investor expects exactly $100 in one year, regardless of the stock price of IBM.

We can take this logic a bit further. First, if markets are efficient at pricing financial assets, then we should expect the fair market value of the Put-Call-Stock Investment to equal the fair market value of an investment in a risk-free zero-coupon bond that matures in one year at the exercise price of these options. After all, the two investments yield exactly the same payout in one year, so they should be valued the same (i.e., the "law of one price" should apply). We can express this formally as follows:

Value of 1-year $100 Zero-Coupon Bond = *Value of Put-Call-Stock Investment*

---

* A zero-coupon bond pays only a stated principal obligation at maturity. Its current value is represented by the discounted present value of this maturity payment, using the appropriate discount rate. (See Chapter 3.)

Second, we can break-down each side of the equation. On the left-hand side, the value of a 1-year \$100 zero-coupon bond is simply the present value of a bond that pays \$100 in one year, discounted at the risk-free rate. The value of the Put-Call-Stock Investment is a bit more complicated. To make this investment, an investor must purchase two items (a share of IBM and a put option) and sell one item (a call option on IBM). The call option, if exercised, will require the investor to deliver a share of IBM stock in exchange for the exercise price, and it will not be exercised unless the value of IBM exceeds the exercise price. This means that the call option represents a type of liability for the investor insofar that it will require the investor to take a loss if exercised. (This can be seen most clearly in the case of an investor who writes a naked call option on IBM with a strike price of \$100: Any exercise of the call option for \$100 will require the investor to go into the stock market and buy a share of IBM at a price in excess of \$100 per share.) As we shall see, the point of option pricing is to determine the present value of this potential liability given both its probability and potential magnitude. Thus, in competitive markets, the seller of an option takes on a liability having a value equal to the price received for the option (otherwise, why would the seller agree to this risk?). The buyer of an option, conversely, acquires an asset having a value equal to the price paid for the option. With this information, a holder of the Put-Call-Stock Investment therefore holds a position having a market value equal to: Market Value of 1 share of IBM Stock + Market Value of Put Option – Market Value of Call Option.

Substituting this information into the equation above gives us the following relationship:

$$\frac{Exercise\ Price}{(1 + risk\ free\ rate)^T} = Value\ of\ Share + Value\ of\ Put - Value\ of\ Call$$

Where "Exercise Price" is the \$100 exercise price of the put option and the call option, and T is the duration of the two options (here, 1 year). Finally, by re-arranging terms, we can re-write this equation as follows:

$$\frac{Exercise\ Price}{(1 + risk\ free\ rate)^T} + Value\ of\ Call = Value\ of\ Share + Value\ of\ Put$$

Written in this latter form, we now have an important equation showing *put-call parity*. Under the put-call parity theorem, if we know the value of three out of the four components of the equation, we can determine the value of the fourth. In practice, this means that if we know the value of a call option on stock S with duration T and strike price X, we will be able to determine the value of a put option on the same security S with duration T and strike price X. Why? Because the values for two of the components—$X/(1 + risk\ free\ rate)^T$ and *Value of Share*—should always be available given that the risk free rate and the trading price of S are both observable. This means that the put-call parity theorem should allow us to calculate the value of a put option or a call option if we can observe the value of one but not the other.

Sidebar: Using Put-Call Parity to Replicate Other Investments

Using the put-call parity theorem, we can replicate a wide range of financial instruments. We have already demonstrated how we can replicate a 1-year zero-coupon bond paying $100 with a combination of a share of stock and put and call options on that share of stock having a term of one year and a strike price of $100. Using similar logic, we can replicate any of the four components of the put-call parity equation. For instance, what if rather than buying a share of IBM, we wanted to replicate the economics of holding a share of IBM using (a) a zero-coupon bond, (b) a call option and (c) a put option? We begin by re-writing the put-call parity equation to isolate the value of IBM stock on the left-hand side:

$$Value\ of\ Share = \frac{Exercise\ Price}{(1 + risk\ free\ rate)^T} + Value\ of\ Call - Value\ of\ Put$$

This tells us that to create a "synthetic" long position in a share of IBM, we need to buy a call option, sell a put option, and invest the present value of the exercise price of the options in a risk-free one-year zero coupon bond (using the risk-free rate as the discount rate). So long as the term of the options matches the term of the zero-coupon bond and so long as the put and the call options have the same exercise price, we can replicate the economics of holding a share of IBM.

To illustrate, assume that the risk-free rate is 10% and that IBM currently trades at $100. To create a synthetic long position, you sell a one-year put option on the stock and you buy a one-year call option, both having an exercise price of $100. You also invest $90.91 (i.e., $100/1.1) at the risk-free rate for one year. Now let's look at your payouts assuming that IBM either rises to $150 or declines to $50 in exactly one year.

Payouts on Expiration Date of Position

Outcome A: Stock Price Rises to $150		***Outcome B:*** Stock Price Falls to $50	
Payout on Bond	$100	Payout on Bond	$100
Put expires unexercised	0	You let call expire	0

You exercise call option at $100 using payout from bond	($100)	You buy stock @$100 on exercise of put against you using payout from bond	($100)
Value of stock purchased	$150	Value of stock purchased	$50
TOTAL	$150	TOTAL	$50

If you had simply purchased a share of IBM at $100 at the beginning of the period, you would, of course, have a share worth $150 if the stock price rose to $150 and a share worth $50 if it declined to $50. Thus, we have replicated the economics of being long one share of IBM. Again, this works because the call and put options have the same expiration and strike price, and they cover the same share of stock that we are using to replicate the position.

Suppose that a regulatory agency bans all put options on IBM in a clumsy effort to promote higher stock prices. You think IBM faces poor future prospects, however, and that its share price will fall. Using put-call parity, can you replicate a put option on IBM, assuming the same parameters as before?

C. THE BLACK-SCHOLES MODEL

In the prior subsection, we saw how the put-call parity theorem can be used to calculate the value of a put option if we know the value of a call option and vice versa. However, this still requires us to know the value of either a call option or a put option for a particular stock. How does one find the value of either a call option or put option that can then be used in the put-call parity equation?

For exchange-traded options, the answer to this question is straightforward: look at the market price for the option. As we saw previously when discussing listed options, the market value of put and call options for firms like The Progressive Corporation can be seen by examining option chains published in any number of financial websites, including Yahoo Finance.* But what if an option is not traded? For instance, employee stock options issued by both private and publicly-held companies are not listed for trading. How much are these worth? Moreover, even exchange-traded options are presumably valued in the market according to some underlying principles. What theory might explain how rational investors arrive at these market prices?

* The option chain for The Progressive Corporation can be found at https://finance.yahoo.com/quote/PGR/options/.

To answer this inquiry, one might be tempted to return to the valuation techniques of Chapter 3 where we examined ways to calculate the present value of various financial instruments. Unfortunately, this approach is not helpful when valuing options. Finding the opportunity cost of capital is not practical, because the risk of an option changes every time the price of the stock changes. For example, when you buy a call option, you are taking a position in the stock, but using less money. As a result, the option is riskier than the underlying stock. This means that the expected rate of return investors demand should vary constantly, as the stock price changes—and this is not easy to model with a standard discounted cash flow formula.

So instead of discounting future cash flows, option pricing models typically rely on replicating option payoffs (as discussed in the prior subsection). To illustrate, let's consider again the payoffs from a one-year European call option for a share of IBM. Assume that IBM currently trades at $100 and that the exercise price for the call option is also $100. To keep the math simple, let's also assume that the price of IBM in one year's time can be only $80 or $120. Finally, assume that the risk-free rate is 10%. Our task is to find the fair price to pay today for this European call option.

Start by considering the possible payoffs from this option at the end of the year:

Payoff to Option Holder in 1 Year:

	Outcome A (Bad State):	**Outcome B (Good State):**
	Stock price = $80	Stock price = $120
Net Payoff:	$0 (option expires unexercised)	$20 (option exercised for $100)

Next, as we did in the prior subsection, we will replicate these payoffs by making an investment that does not utilize a call option. If we can find such an investment, then the law of one price should dictate that the cost of making this replicating investment should be a fair price to pay for the call option. The replicating investment we shall consider combines a risk-free loan and the purchase of a share of IBM. Specifically, we will buy a share of IBM at $100 (the current market price), funding a portion of the purchase price with borrowed funds at a 10% interest rate. The goal is to borrow just enough money so that in one year's time we will owe $80—the value of IBM in the "bad state" of the world. Why? Let's take a look at the payoffs from this investment strategy. At 10% interest, we would need to borrow $72.73 so that we owe exactly $80 in one year. If a share of IBM costs $100 today, that means we would need to pay $27.27 with our own funds to come up with the $100 purchase price. Here are the payoffs:

Payoff to Leveraged Investment in 1 Year:

	Outcome A (Bad State):	Outcome B (Good State):
	Stock price = $80	Stock price = $120
Net Payoff:	$0 (sell stock; repay loan balance of $80)	$40 (sell stock for $120; repay loan balance of $80)

As expected, we have replicated the payoff of the call option in the "bad state" of the world: In the event IBM stock falls to $80 in one year, we can repay the loan by selling the stock, netting $0 which matches the option's payoff if IBM trades at $80 upon the option's expiration. However, the payoff in the "good" state of the world is too high. The option holder's payoff is just $20 when IBM trades at $120, but this leveraged investment leaves us with a payoff of $40. But what if we just bought ½ of a share of IBM using the same leveraged strategy? One-half of a share would cost $50, and in one year, this one-half share would be either $40 (in the bad state) or $60 (in the good state). As above, our goal is to buy the one-half share for $50 using just enough borrowed funds so that in one year's time we owe the value of our investment in the bad state of the world. We can accomplish this by borrowing $36.36 (i.e., $40/1.1) and covering the rest of the $50 purchase price with $13.64 of personal cash. Now let's look at the payoffs from this investment:

Payoff to Leveraged Investment in 1 Year:

	Outcome A (Bad State):	Outcome B (Good State):
	Stock price (½ share) = $40	Stock price (½ share) = $60
Net Payoff:	$0 (sell stock; repay loan balance of $40)	$20 (sell ½ share for $60; repay loan balance of $40)

Using this alternative strategy, we have now replicated the option payoffs perfectly. And the total out-of-pocket cost to us was $13.64, which represents the amount of our personal savings that we put at risk in making this investment. $13.64 must therefore be the fair value of buying the call option on IBM. Why? Any other price would lead to arbitrage: If the call option was priced at more than $13.64, we could earn risk-free profits by writing a call and buying the replicating portfolio; if the option was priced at less than \$13.64, we could buy the underpriced call option and sell the replicating portfolio.*

To summarize, we can calculate the value of a call option (C) as follows:

$$C = \Delta S - B$$

Where Δ ("delta") is the fraction of a share of IBM we purchase in our replication strategy, S is the current value of IBM stock, and B is the amount we borrow at 10% interest. The number of shares needed to replicate an option (i.e., Δ) is often called the *hedge ratio* or the *option delta.*

While this approach provides a conceptual basis for estimating the value of our IBM call option, it relies on the unrealistic assumption that IBM's stock price will take only one of two values in one year. In the real world, of course, IBM's stock price is likely to move in a much more complicated pattern. Consider, for instance, what happens to our replication analysis if we assume that IBM could move up or down by \$20 after *six* months and that, in the following six months, it could also move up or down by \$20. We would have several potential price paths:

* To sell the replicating portfolio, you would sell short ½ share of IBM and loan \$36.36 at the risk-free rate. For instance, if this hypothetical call option was trading at \$10, one could earn risk free profits of \$3.64 by (i) buying the underpriced option for \$10, (ii) selling ½ share of IBM for \$50, and (iii) loaning \$36.36 at the risk-free rate. In one year, the total cash flows would be as follows:

	Stock price (½ share) = \$40	Stock price (½ share) = \$60
Payment for call:	−\$10.00	−\$10.00
Extension of loan:	−\$36.36	−\$36.36
Cash Received from shorting ½ share	\$50.00	\$50.00
Cost of covering short in 1 year	−\$40.00	−\$60.00
Cash received on repayment of Loan	\$40.00	\$40.00
Profit on exercise of call option	\$0	\$20.00
Net profit:	\$3.64	\$3.64

Figure 8-12: IBM Price Paths

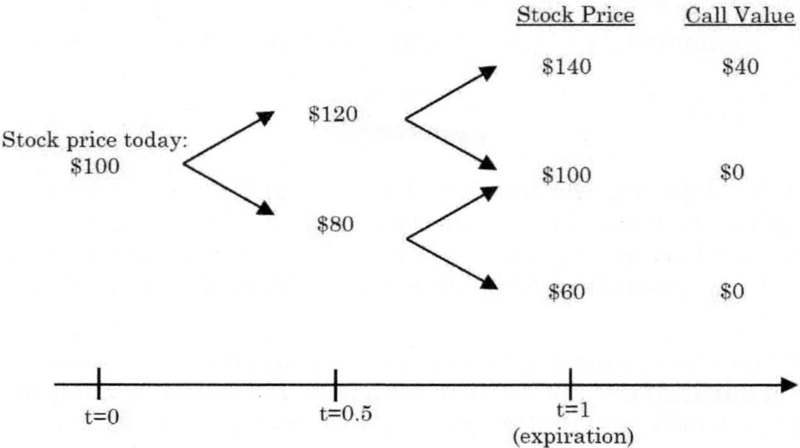

Attempting to replicate the value of the same European call option received at t = 0 is now more complicated. As before, we know what the value of the option will be at the end of all three possible outcomes. Since the price of IBM will be $140, $100, or $60, this means that the payoff from the call option will be $40, $0, or $0, respectively. The likelihood of each outcome, however, depends on where the stock price is at t = 0.5. Midway through the year, there are two possible outcomes ($120 and $80), which will present two separate call option possibilities. That is, if IBM moves to $120 at t=0.5, the holder will have a call option that will be worth either $40 or $0 at expiration. Conversely, if IBM moves to $80 at t=0.5, the holder will have a call option that will be worth $0 with certainty at expiration. So rather than replicating the value of one call option, as we did previously, we now need to replicate the value of the two call options at t = 0.5.

It turns out that buying one share of IBM at $120 using borrowed funds of $95.24 and $24.76 of out-of-pocket cash will replicate the first option. The value of this call is therefore $24.76. (Note that interest will accrue only for six months, or 5%.) And because the other option has a $0 value with certainty, its value is $0. With this information, we can now replicate the value of the option as of t=0 because we know this option will have a value of either $24.76 or $0 at t=0.5. Using the same replication technique, it turns out that purchasing 0.619 shares of IBM with borrowed funds of $47.16 and personal cash of $14.74 will replicate these two possible payoffs. The value of the call option at t=0 is therefore $14.74. Notice that the value of this call option is slightly higher than the $13.64 obtained previously. These calculations are summarized visually in Figure 8-13:*

* The text in the figure walks through how to calculate option delta (Δ) and the replicating loan (B) at *t*=0 and *t*=0.5. For instance, to determine how to replicate the payout at *t*=0.5 for the setting where S=120, we need a Δ and B that will yield a net payout of $40 if the

Figure 8-13: Replicating the Payout for an IBM Call Option

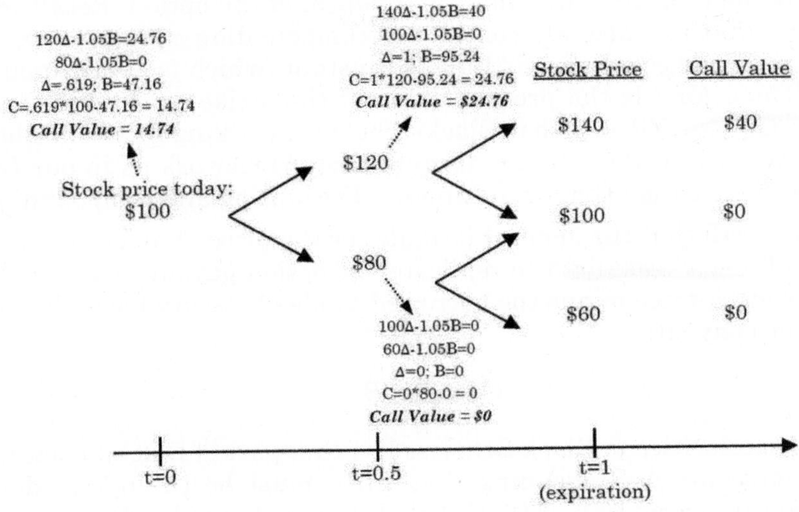

Even this model of IBM's price, however, is far too simplistic. Ideally, we would do this for even shorter increments of time within the one-year duration of the option. For instance, we could do the same exercise but rather than predict prices at six-month intervals, we could predict prices at the end of each month, or better yet, at the end of each day. Indeed, with some fairly complicated calculus, we could do this exercise across infinitesimal slices of time. And it turns out that this latter approach is a fair way to conceive of the *Black-Scholes option pricing model*, which is the most common model for valuing options. The model, which was originally developed by Fisher Black and Myron Scholes, and subsequently refined with Robert Merton, would ultimately earn Scholes and Merton the 1997 Nobel Prize in Economics (Fisher Black having died).

Deriving the model is far beyond the scope of this book (it is related to a heat transfer equation in physics!). But the preceding discussion should allow you to understand the intuition behind the model. Formally, the model is as follows and produces the price for a European call option (we define the variables below):

$$C = S_t \cdot N(d_1) - Ke^{-rt} \cdot N(d_2)$$

The complexity of Black-Scholes is captured in calculating $N(d_1)$ and $N(d_2)$, so we will postpone discussing those concepts for now except to say

final stock price is $140 (to match the payout on the call option if the final stock price is $140) and that will yield a net payout of $0 if the stock price is $100 (to match the payout on the call option if the final stock price is $100). Or in other words, we need to solve Δ and B for both of these equations: 140Δ − 1.05B=40 and 100Δ − 1.05B=0. By re-arranging terms for the latter equation, we know that B=(−100Δ / −1.05). We can therefore solve for Δ by replacing B in the first equation with (−100Δ / −1.05): 140Δ−1.05*(−100Δ / −1.05) = 40, or Δ = 1. With this information, we can then solve for B: 100 – 1.05B = 0, or B = 95.24.

that they yield real numbers. S_t is the current stock price, K is the strike price, r is the risk-free rate, and t is the term of the option. Recall from Chapter 3 that we calculate continuous compounding at interest rate r over time t using e^{rt} where e is Euler's constant (which is approximately 2.718). Thus, Ke^{-rt} is the present value of the strike price, discounted continuously at r. (Recall that Black-Scholes is working in a continuous time framework, rather than a discrete time framework as in our IBM examples, hence the need for continuous discounting and compounding.)

Now recall that the general formula for the price of an option is the fraction of a stock required to replicate the option payout (option delta) times the stock price minus the borrowed funds necessary for replicating the option's payout:

$$C = \Delta S - B$$

Note the similarities to Black-Scholes. The first part of Black-Scholes, S_t $N(d_1)$, represents Δ S, meaning that $N(d_1)$ must be the option delta. Likewise, the second half of Black-Scholes, Ke^{-rt} $N(d_2)$, is effectively the amount of borrowed funds (B) one needs to replicate the option in the continuous time framework of Black-Scholes.

In short, Black-Scholes calculates option prices using an extension of the same replicating portfolio technique we used earlier to value a call option on a share of IBM. The primary difference is that, rather than estimate discrete price changes at various points in time, it replicates the option payoffs continuously through the duration of the option assuming the stock price follows a specific type of random walk.* The model captures this nuance in the calculation of $N(d_1)$ and $N(d_2)$. The function $N(\bullet)$ represents the cumulative distribution function (CDF) for the standard normal distribution, which we describe in the Sidebar. d_1 and d_2 are defined in the Black-Scholes model as follows:

$$d_1 = \frac{\ln\left(\frac{S}{K}\right) + \left(r + \frac{\sigma^2}{2}\right)t}{\sigma\sqrt{t}}$$

$$d_2 = d_1 - \sigma\sqrt{t}$$

The variables are the same as those in the main equation, except for σ, which represents the standard deviation of stock returns (i.e., return volatility). Using the Black-Scholes model, we can therefore estimate the price of a European call option if we know five key parameters:

t: Duration of the option.

---

* More specifically, the stock price is assumed to evolve following geometric Brownian motion. This means that returns on a stock have a lognormal distribution with constant volatility (i.e., stock prices cannot "jump"). This assumption constitutes a well-known limitation of the Black-Scholes model insofar that stock prices are known to exhibit random "jumps" and volatility is not constant over time.

K: strike price of the option.

S: current price of the underlying stock.

σ: standard deviation of the stock's returns (i.e., its volatility).

r: risk-free rate of interest.

(Note that *t, r,* and *σ* must all be in the same units of time; for example, if the *t* and *r* are in years, *σ* must also be annualized).

In the Sidebar, we discuss how to use the Black-Scholes model with Microsoft Excel. We also discuss how the model can be modified slightly to accommodate the potential payment of dividends which can significantly affect the value of call and put options. In addition to constructing a Black-Scholes pricing model, you can also use Excel to easily examine how changes to the different variables will impact the value of an option.

While this discussion of option pricing may initially seem complicated and tangential to a lawyer's job, we should mention that option pricing can often require a lawyer's attention. Within the context of securities regulation, for instance, FASB Statement No. 123R requires a firm to treat the value of employee stock options issued during an accounting period as a compensation expense. Moreover, SEC disclosure rules require SEC-reporting companies to state the fair value of all option awards made to corporate executives in their SEC filings.* Thus, a lawyer drafting an IPO prospectus or a proxy statement must have a basic knowledge of option pricing in order to assess whether a firm is in compliance with its reporting obligations. If something seems off, you might want to suggest that an option pricing calculation be rechecked. More generally, as a matter of corporate governance, having a working knowledge of how options are valued can provide important insights into how stock options affect management incentives. We explore this latter issue in more detail in another Sidebar below.

Sidebar: Cumulative Distribution Function (CDF) for the Standard Normal Distribution

The CDF for the Standard Normal Distribution is used to calculate the probability of observing a particular value within a population or sample. To understand the concept, it is necessary to recall how we calculate the mean and standard deviation for a sample (which we discussed in Chapter 3). Recall that the standard deviation of an observation tells us how far it is from the mean of the data. For instance, imagine we have 100 exam answers and the mean (average) of the scores is 75%. To calculate the standard deviation of the scores, we first take each individual score and subtract 0.75 and square the result to remove any negative numbers. The average of these numbers is the variance, and the square root of this number is the standard

* See Item 402 of Regulation S–K, 17 CFR § 229.402.

deviation. If the standard deviation of the scores is 10%, this gives us helpful information about where a score of, say, 95% sits within the test scores. 95% is two standard deviations above the mean, which indicates it is much higher than the mean, and the student excelled on the exam. A score of 80%, by contrast, is one-half a standard deviation above the mean, meaning that the student did well but likely performed the same as many other students. The standard deviation therefore tells us the "distance" an observation is from the mean of the sample. Indeed, it is so common to think about the "distance" of an observation from the mean that we often standardize observations to reflect this distance. For the sample of tests, for instance, we can assign a "distance-from-the-mean" number for each test by subtracting the mean score from each student's score and then dividing the difference by the standard deviation. A student who scored a 95% would have a standardized "distance score" (called a z-score) equal to 2.0, or (.95 – .75)/.1.

If a sample or population is "normally distributed" we can infer even more information from the student's z-score. As you may know, if the standardized scores are normally distributed, the distribution will be bell-shaped as follows:

Figure 8-14: Standard Normal Distribution

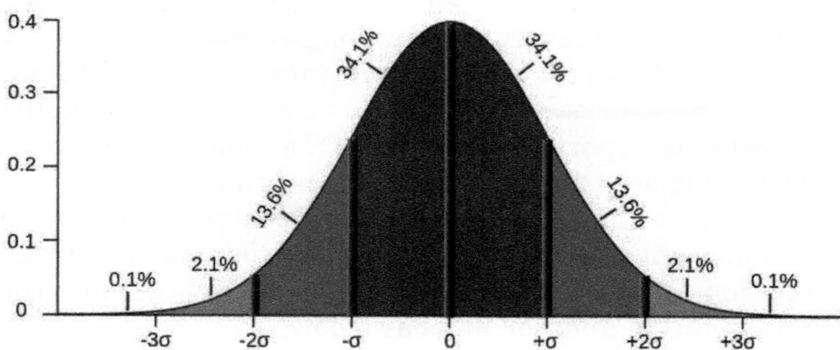

This figure reflects a histogram. In a standard normal distribution, the x-axis represents the z-score assigned to an observation, so it is measured in standard deviations. The y-axis reflects the percent of observations having each score. Thus, it visually presents the distribution of test scores within the overall class; our student with a 2.0 z-score would be represented in the right "tail", which contains very few individuals. As shown in the histogram, an important property of a standard normal distribution is that 68.2% of the observations fall within plus/minus one standard deviation of the mean, and 95.4% of the observations fall within plus/minus two standard deviations of the mean. Only 2.2% (i.e., 0.1% + 2.1%) of observations are below a z-score of –2.0, and only 2.2% of observations are above a z-score of 2.0. Accordingly, if we observe a standardized score of 2.0, it means that it equals or exceeds 97.7% of all observed scores (i.e., 0.1% + 2.1% + 13.6%

+ 34.1% + 34.1% + 13.6%), assuming the distribution of scores is normal.

N(•) is a short-hand notation for representing this idea for a given z-score. For instance, N(2.0) tells us that approximately 97.7% of values lie below a z-score of 2.0. In the Black-Scholes formula, d_1 and d_2 produce numbers that *N(•)* transforms into percentages. In particular, $N(d_1)$ produces option delta (the fraction of a share required to create the replicating portfolio) and $N(d_2)$ produces a percentage that, when multiplied by the present value of the strike price, yields the loan necessary to create the replicating portfolio. As we discuss in the following Sidebar, Microsoft Excel has a built-in function that can quickly calculate *N(•)*.

Sidebar: Using Microsoft Excel to Calculate Option Prices

For many students, the Black-Scholes formula can be intimidating due to the need to calculate the CDF for the Standard Normal Distribution. Fortunately, Microsoft Excel has a built-in function for conducting this calculation, which makes calculating option prices a straightforward procedure (assuming you have the input variables required by the Black-Scholes equation). We provide an example in the Option Valuation Worksheet on the Casebook website. In the worksheet we make a slight modification to the classical Black-Scholes equation to account for the possibility that a stock pays dividends. If a stock pays a dividend, this reduces the value of the stock to future investors because the value of the dividend is removed from the corporation. A holder of a call option on a dividend-paying stock will therefore anticipate that if a stock trades today at $100, the value of the stock upon exercise will be reduced by any dividends paid during the term of the option. Because Black-Scholes works in a continuous time environment, we account for this fact by discounting the price of the stock by the dividend yield (i.e., the annual dividend/today's stock price). In particular, the modified Black-Scholes formula is:

$$C = S_{te}^{-yt}N(d_1) - Ke^{-rt} \cdot N(d_2)$$

Where y is the annual dividend yield. d_1 is also modified slightly to become:

$$d_1 = \frac{\ln\left(\frac{S}{K}\right) + \left(r - y + \frac{\sigma^2}{2}\right)t}{\sigma\sqrt{t}}$$

d_2 remains the same. The worksheet also calculates the value of a corresponding European put option using put-call parity. Once again, however, the value of the stock in the put-call parity formula must be multiplied by e^{-yt} to account for the expected dividends. As shown in the worksheet, entering "exp( )" instructs Excel to exponent Euler's constant by the number in the parentheses (which can also be a cell reference to a number).

In the worksheet, we calculate the value of a European call option with the following attributes:

Current Stock Price (S):	$120
Strike Price (K):	$120
Option life (T) (years):	1
Standard Deviation in Stock Returns (σ) (annual)	15.00%
Dividend yield (dividends/Current value of stock) (annual)	2.50%
Riskless Rate (r) (annual):	2.0%

As shown in the worksheet, implementing the formula is largely a straight-forward matter of plugging these variables into the formula (including d_1 and d_2). The only wrinkle is the calculation of $N(d_1)$ and $N(d_2)$. To make these latter calculations, we make use of the Excel function NORMSDIST( ) which returns the CDF for the Standard Normal Distribution for any number placed in the parentheses.

We recommend that you use the worksheet to explore how increases/ decreases in each of these variables affects the price of the call option. Which variable do you think matters the most?

Sidebar: Stock Options and Incentives for Risk-Taking

In exploring the option pricing worksheet, you may have noticed that increasing a stock's volatility also increases the value of the call option. We can also illustrate this relationship visually. In Figure 8-15A we present 100 simulations that examine how a stock price might evolve over the course of a year assuming the stock follows the same type of random walk used in the Black-Scholes model (i.e., geometric Brownian motion). In the simulation, we assume the stock has an expected annual return of just 5% and an annual volatility of 5%. The stock price at the beginning of the year is $100.

Now assume that the CEO of this firm holds a deeply out-of-the-money call option having a strike price of $125 that is exercisable in one year. As shown in the figure, none of the simulations result in a stock price above $125 at the end of the year (the x-axis has 252 days because there are 252 trading days in the year).

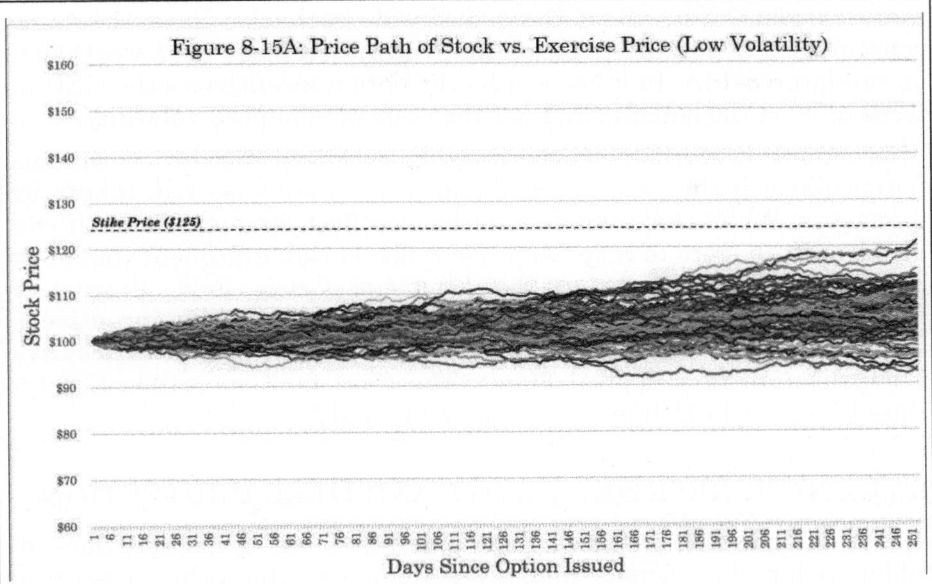

Figure 8-15A: Price Path of Stock vs. Exercise Price (Low Volatility)

Now compare the situation if the stock has the same expected return of 5% but annual volatility is 10%—double the volatility used to produce Figure 8-15A. We present the results from running 100 simulations under these assumptions in Figure 8-15B.

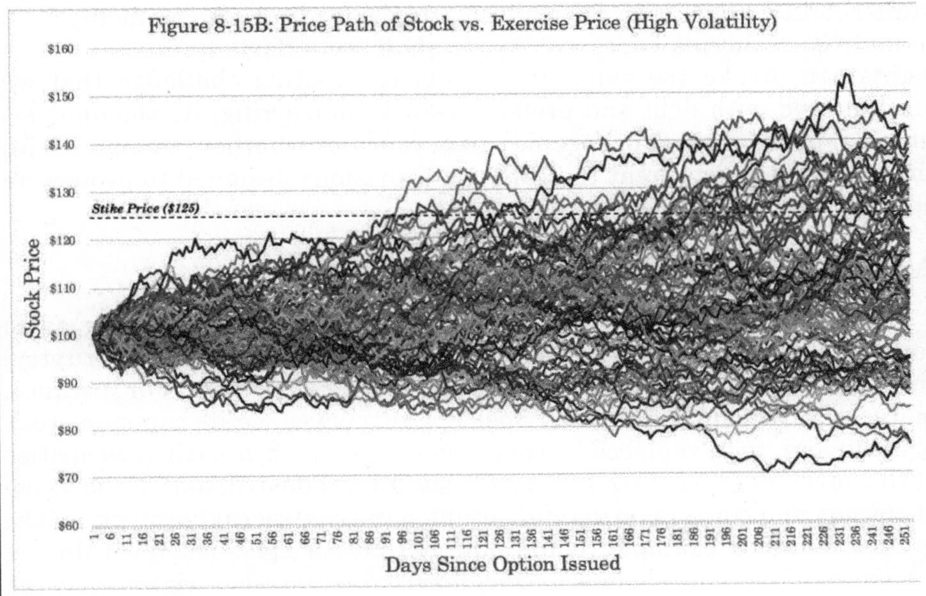

Figure 8-15B: Price Path of Stock vs. Exercise Price (High Volatility)

Notice the dramatic effect on the value of the call option to the CEO. In the first scenario, there was no realistic expectation that the option would move into the money. Now, however, a significant portion of the simulations result in a stock price above $125 by the end of the year. Of course, the downside possibilities from this greater volatility are also more extreme. Yet, all of these downside scenarios have the same consequence to our CEO insofar that the option will expire worthless, as in Figure 8-15A. In other words, the option incentivizes the CEO to focus only on the benefits and not the costs of enhanced volatility.

This simple exercise illustrates the potential for stock options (particularly if they are out-of-the-money) to enhance risk-taking by managers. While this may be a desirable effect for some firms, it can also lead managers to take excessive risks. For an argument that such risks helped contribute to the Financial Crisis (and alternative compensation arrangements that might reduce risk-taking incentives), see Jeffrey N. Gordon, "Corporate Governance and Executive Compensation in Financial Firms: The Case for Convertible Equity-Based Pay," 2012 Colum. Bus. L. Rev 834 (2012).

4. CONVERTIBLE SECURITIES AND DEAL PROTECTION

As the preceding section has illustrated, an option provides its holder with real economic value. Fundamentally, this value arises from the fact that an option gives the holder the power to exercise or not exercise a right or privilege, such as buying or selling an asset at a fixed price. Yet, because options are long-term contracts, an option holder is also vulnerable to actions taken by the contractual counterparty that can reduce or even destroy the option's value. In this section, we examine this vulnerability, along with the contract provisions that are commonly used to address recurring concerns. As we shall see, efforts to protect option rights can invoke the same incomplete contracting challenge that we encountered with debt and preferred stock contracting. As the analysis unfolds, in the context of specific cases, consider whether you agree with the way that courts treat the contract provisions designed to protect an option's value.

A. DESTRUCTION OF THE OPTION

There are a number of voluntary corporate actions (leaving aside corporate disasters such as operating losses, defaults and bankruptcy) that can destroy the value of options and conversion rights. For instance, mergers in which the company does not survive cause its common stock to disappear, to be replaced by some other asset such as cash or securities of the surviving corporation. This causes a total destruction of the value of options and conversion rights, absent some contractual protection. Or, to take another example, while options have a specified term during which they can be exercised, the term of conversion rights may be rendered uncertain by the ability of the issuing corporation to call the underlying securities for redemption. For instance, if a company can unilaterally redeem its outstanding shares of convertible preferred stock, the preferred stock investors would receive the redemption proceeds but would be stripped of their option to convert into common stock. The following cases explore how holders of options can address the possibility that certain corporate actions can destroy an option's value.

Simons v. Cogan

542 A.2d 785 (Del. Ch. 1987),
aff'd 549 A.2d 300 (Del. 1988)

■ ALLEN, CHANCELLOR.

It has now become firmly fixed in our law that among the duties owed by directors of a Delaware corporation to holders of that corporations' debt instruments, there is no duty of the broad and exacting nature characterized as a fiduciary duty. Unlike shareholders, to whom such duties are owed, holders of debt may turn to documents that exhaustively detail the rights and obligations of the issuer, the trustee under the debt indenture, and of the holders of the securities.

Such documents are typically carefully negotiated at arms-length. In a public offering, the underwriter of the debt, and to some extent the indenture trustee, have an interest in negotiating in that fashion; in a private placement, the purchaser has a similar interest. More importantly, the purchaser of such debt is offered, and voluntarily accepts, a security whose myriad terms are highly specified. Broad and abstract requirements of a "fiduciary" character ordinarily can be expected to have little or no constructive role to play in the governance of such a negotiated, commercial relationship.

Accordingly, it is elementary that rights of bondholders are ordinarily fixed by and determinable from the language of documents that create and regulate the security. In a publicly distributed debenture the notes themselves and a trust indenture serve this function, but other documents such as a note agreement or, in the case of secured bonds, security agreements may be involved. Of course, in some circumstances, bondholders may have rights against an issuer that are not expressly created by the indenture or other original documents. Most palpably this is the case where a statute has been violated or when bondholders allege and prove fraud in the inducement of the purchase of the bonds. In addition, the contractual documents creating the debenture and the duties of the issuer may, in narrow circumstances, be held to imply obligations arising from an implied covenant of good faith and fair dealing. See, e.g., Katz v. Oak Industries, Inc., Del. Ch., 508 A.2d 873, (1986) note 7 (1986); Van Gemert v. Boeing Co., 520 F.2d 1373, 1383 (2d Cir.1975) (applying New York law).

This case is a purported class action brought on behalf of the holders of 8-1/8% Convertible Subordinated Debentures of Knoll International, Inc. The complaint seeks various relief against the issuer of these bonds, and, among others, its controlling shareholder. Central to the theories of recovery urged is the contention that the defendants, in the particular circumstances presented, do owe a fiduciary duty to the bondholders[2] and have breached that duty. In addition, as amplified at oral argument, plaintiffs' position is that the facts alleged also state a claim for fraud, and for breach of contract, including a breach of an implied contractual duty of good faith.

Defendants have moved to dismiss the complaint for failure to state a claim upon which relief may be granted. For the reasons set forth below, I conclude that, assuming the well-pleaded factual allegations of the complaint to be true, those facts do not state a legal wrong to the class of bondholders. The pending motion will therefore be granted.

I.

The debentures here involved were issued in 1983 pursuant to a public offering and had an original maturity of twenty years. As issued, they were convertible at the option of the holder into the Company's Class A Common Stock at a rate of one share for each $19.20 principal amount of debentures and were redeemable, at the Company's option, after August 15, 1985, at a stated premium which decreased as the securities matured. The bonds were subordinated and bore interest at 8-1/8%.

The issuer of these convertible debentures, Knoll International, Inc. ("Knoll"), is controlled through a series of subsidiaries by defendant Knoll International Holdings, Inc., which, in turn, is controlled by defendant Marshall S. Cogan. The gist of the complaint is that defendants caused the minority shareholders of Knoll to be eliminated through a two-stage transaction involving a $12 cash tender offer followed by a cash for stock merger at the same price. The merger that culminated this process occurred on January 22, 1987 and left Knoll, the issuer, as the surviving corporation and a wholly-owned subsidiary (indirectly) of Holdings. In connection with that merger, a Supplemental Indenture was executed by the issuer and the indenture trustee providing that, instead of each $19.20 of principal amount of the debentures being convertible into one share of Knoll Class A Common Stock, such principal amount would henceforth be convertible into the consideration received by the public Class A shareholders in the merger, $12 cash. The core complaint is that the substitution of a right to convert to $12 in lieu of a right to convert to Class A Common Stock is unfair and a wrong.[3]

The complaint states that the issuer owes a fiduciary duty to the holders of its convertible debentures and asserts a lengthy list of facts that are said to constitute violations of that duty. For example, it is said that the self-dealing merger transaction was effected at a particularly

---

[2] For purposes of this opinion, I use the term "bonds" and "debentures" interchangeably, overlooking for the moment their technical differences relating to whether or not the note is secured.

[3] Knoll's Class A common was trading at 9¼ on the day before announcement of the $12 cash-out transaction; the 8-1/8% debentures were trading at 86 at that time. Complaint para. 15(g). The debentures, however, allegedly declined in value upon announcement of the supplemental indenture, trading at 73-¼ immediately thereafter.

disadvantageous time from the point of view of the minority stockholders; it was not negotiated by an independent committee; and the offering circular in connection with the tender offer leg of the transaction contained false and misleading information. Twelve dollars per share is said to be an unfairly low price, and inadequate consideration for loss of a Class A share; the right to convert to $12, thus, is seen as an inadequate substitute for the right to convert into a Class A share.

It is concluded (para. 17) that, "the defendants have ignored and breached the fiduciary duty of fair dealing they owe Knoll's debenture holders in structuring and proposing the Merger."

While it is not the principal theory of the complaint, a breach of contract theory can be detected in that pleading. Paragraph 13 asserts that the First Supplemental Indenture—which changed the conversion right from Class A Common Stock to cash—was entered "without the consent of the debenture holders as provided in § 15.02 of the original Indenture." At oral argument a somewhat different breach of contract theory—breach of a contractual obligation of good faith—was alluded to.

Finally, it is also asserted that the complaint states a claim of common law fraud. Various assertions of inadequate disclosure in the tender offer document and in the 1983 prospectus published in connection with the original distribution of the debentures, are urged in support of this theory, although a reading of the complaint makes it utterly clear that, when drafted, those allegations were intended not to make out a claim of fraud but to bolster plaintiffs' principal, roll-it-all-into-a-ball, theory of breach of a fiduciary duty of entire fairness.

The complaint seeks, among other relief, rescission of the merger or the establishment of a new conversion rate and damages.

II.

I turn first to an evaluation of plaintiff's principal contention—that defendants owe to him as a holder of convertible debentures a fiduciary duty of loyalty and fairness. The answer to that central contention begins with a recognition that the courts of this state have consistently recognized that neither an issuer of debentures nor a controlling shareholder owes to holders of the company's debt securities duties of the special sort characterized as fiduciary in character. Those cases establish in this jurisdiction "that (i) a debenture holder has no independent right to maintain a claim for breach of fiduciary duty, and (ii) in the absence of fraud, insolvency or a statutory violation, a debenture holder's rights are defined by the terms of the indenture." In so holding, of course, our cases are directed to claims against an issuer not to those directed against an indenture trustee.

Under this traditional approach, it has no particular significance that the debentures in question are convertible into stock at the option of the holder. As early as 1889 Justice Holmes noted that such a conversion right is:

> . . . simply an option to take stock as it may turn out to be when the time for choice arrives. The bondholder does not become a stockholder by his contract, in equity any more than at law . . .

Parkinson v. West End Street Railway Co., Mass. Supr., 173 Mass. 446, 53 N.E. 891 (1899). This court made the same observation in Harff v. Kerkorian, Del. Ch., 324 A.2d at 219 in concluding that holders of a corporation's convertible debt were not stockholders in equity entitled to act as corporate representatives in derivative litigation. The implication of Harff was, of course, that, as creditors, holders of such debt were not the beneficiaries of fiduciary duties.

In so holding, the courts of this state have announced and applied well-established, conventional legal doctrine:

> Courts traditionally have directed bondholders to protect themselves against . . . self-interested issuer action with explicit contractual provisions. Holders of senior securities, such as bonds, are outside the legal model of the firm for protective purposes: a heavy black-letter line bars the extension of corporate fiduciary protections to them.

Bratton, The Economics and Jurisprudence of Convertible Bonds, 1984 Wisc.L.Rev. 667, 668 (1984). See also American Bar Foundation, Commentaries on Model Debenture Indenture Provisions (1971) at 527 (hereafter "ABF Commentaries").

This traditional view, which continues to be applied in other jurisdictions as well as in Delaware has not gone altogether unchallenged in the modern cases. In Broad v. Rockwell International Corp.,[6] a panel of the Fifth Circuit Court of Appeals held that an issuer of convertible debentures does owe a duty of fidelity to holders of such securities, although at its critical point, the doctrinal analysis of that point fails rather completely. See 614 F.2d at 430–31.[7] In all events, on en banc review, that opinion was vacated and, while the full court assumed for purposes of its decision the existence of such a duty, one cannot fairly read the later opinion except as an endorsement of the traditional conceptualization of the basis for the legal relationship between an issuer of convertible bonds and the holders of such securities. In Van Gemert v. Boeing Co., 520 F.2d 1373 (2d Cir. 1975), the Second Circuit Court of Appeals, applying New York law, found a covenant of good faith and fair

---

[6] 614 F.2d 418 (5th Cir. 1980) ["Broad I"] vacated, 642 F.2d 929 (5th Cir. 1980) (en banc) ["Broad II"] cert. denied 454 U.S. 965, 70 L. Ed. 2d 380, 102 S. Ct. 506 (1981).

[7] Reliance by the panel in Broad I on identical dicta of Justice Douglas in two cases (Pepper v. Litton, 308 U.S. 295, 311, 60 S. Ct. 238, 84 L. Ed. 281 (1939) and Superintendent of Insurance v. Bankers Life & Casualty Co., 404 U.S. 6, 12, 92 S. Ct. 165, 30 L. Ed. 2d 128 (1971)) surely provides too frail a support for the conclusion reached. I need not now dilate upon those cases (although they are cited by plaintiff here) except to say that they were actions brought by a trustee in bankruptcy (not creditors) on behalf of a bankrupt corporation against a controlling shareholder for breach of fiduciary duty. They were properly maintained under perfectly conventional principles of fiduciary duty and legitimately raise no question about the existence of such a duty towards creditors. Pepper acknowledges as much. See 308 U.S. at 307.

dealing implied in a convertible debenture indenture. Judge Oaks alone on that panel indicated a willingness to go further and find an "underlying duty of fair treatment . . . owed by the corporation or majority stockholders or controlling directors and officers" to bondholders. 520 F.2d at 1385. But another panel of that court, in a later phase of that same case has made clear that the rationale for the result reached in Van Gemert was contractual, not fiduciary. See 553 F.2d 812 (2d Cir. 1977).

And in Pittsburgh Terminal Corp. v. Baltimore & O.R. Co., 680 F.2d 933 (3d Cir. 1982), Judge Gibbons of the Third Circuit Court of Appeals noted, without citation of authority or elaboration, that he "would be very much surprised if Maryland or any other state would today hold that no [fiduciary] obligations were owed by an issuer of [convertible] securities and its directors." The two other members of that panel, however, specifically disavowed any such conclusion.

Finally, in a case relied upon by plaintiff here, the United States District Court for the Southern District of New York purported to find in our Supreme Court's reversal in part of this court's opinion in Harff v. Kerkorian authority for the imposition of fiduciary obligations running from the issuer and its directors to holders of convertible securities. See Green v. Hamilton, S.D.N.Y., 1981 U.S. Dist. LEXIS 13439 (1981).

Thus, there exists a body of judicial opinion willing to extend the protection offered by the fiduciary concept to the relationship between an issuer and the holders of its convertible debt securities. These seeds, however, have fallen upon stones. None of the appellate opinions actually represent a holding so extending that concept and, indeed, each of those cases evidence the fact that prevailing judicial opinion remains to the contrary.

* * *

That a convertibility feature of a debt security creates an economic interest in the issuer's stock price that the holder of a straight debt instrument would not have is plain. But, it does not follow at all that from such additional economic interest, fiduciary duties of loyalty, etc. necessarily or properly flow. Such duties and the restriction on self-dealing, etc. that they entail have been imposed upon those to whom property has been entrusted to manage for the benefit of another. Trusts are the prototype, but the concept has long been extended to corporate officers and directors, agents, partners. But it has not been extended to negotiated commercial transactions where the original property owner transfers it with a contractual right to repayment. Thus, for example, no case holds that the relationship between a bank and its borrower involves a fiduciary duty running from the borrower; nor, indeed, in the case of a deposit relationship from the bank to its depositor.

While the convertibility feature of convertible bonds creates an economic interest in an issuer's stock price, so long as the right to convert is not exercised, it remains merely an option, and the holder of it retains all of the benefits of his creditor status. Until the moment of exercise, his investment is not held subject to the risks that the fiduciary duty concept was designed to address, but is held pursuant to a negotiated contract detailing rights and duties and conferring upon the creditor a legal right to repayment. Thus, what Justice Holmes said in 1899 in Parkinson v. West End Street Railway remains true; the holder of a convertible bond is and only is a corporate creditor to whom contractual but not fiduciary duties are owed unless he acts to end his entitlement to the legal protections his contract affords him and to assume the risks of stockholder status through exercise of the power of conversion.

Accordingly, were I free to pass upon the question presented in Harff and Norte & Co. for the first time, I could find nothing in Green or in the other federal opinions cited above to suggest that an alteration in the traditional structure governing the legal relationship between corporations and holders of their convertible debt is warranted. That traditional approach has not been shown to be inadequate in any important way. Underwriters of convertible securities do have an interest in negotiating protections on points regarded as material by ultimate purchasers of those securities. The development of elaborate anti-destruction and anti-dilution provisions in indentures attests to the relative effectiveness of this mechanism of defining rights and obligations of issuers. See ABF Commentaries at 290–301.

The tide has no doubt long run away from a world of hard and fast rules with predictable outcomes and towards a world in which it is common for courts to evaluate specific behavior in the light cast by broadly worded principles.[10] Working amid such flows, however, courts must be wary of the danger to useful structures that they entail. To introduce the powerful abstraction of "fiduciary duty" into the highly negotiated and exhaustively documented commercial relationship between an issuer of convertible securities and the holders of such securities would, or so it now appears to me, risk greater insecurity and uncertainty than could be justified by the occasional increment in fairness that might be hoped for. See generally Bratton, The Economics and Jurisprudence of Convertible Bonds, *supra,* at 730–739. I conclude that plaintiff has failed to state a claim of breach of fiduciary duty upon which relief may be granted.

* * *

For the foregoing reasons, defendants' motion to dismiss the complaint shall be granted.

---

[10] Professor P. S. Atiyah has brilliantly captured the zeitgeist in his inaugural lecture at Oxford University, which has been reprinted by the Iowa Law Review. See Atiyah, From Principles to Pragmatism: Changes in the Function of the Judicial Process and the Law, 65 Iowa L. Rev. 1249 (1980).

QUESTIONS

1. Why doesn't Chancellor Allen treat debt covenants as contracts of adhesion? Underwriters are hired by the issuer to market the debt securities. Why would they provide protection to investors?
2. Does the right to convert each $19.20 of principal amount of debenture into the merger consideration have any value to debenture holders?
3. In footnote 3 Chancellor Allen notes that the debentures were trading at $86 before announcement of the cash-out merger, and allegedly declined in value upon the announcement of the supplemental indenture to $73¼. The expectation of an event that would affect the value of a debt security typically results in bond rating agencies placing the debentures on immediate "credit watch," followed shortly by a downgrade. Markets typically respond more quickly. If the bonds were formerly convertible into common stock at $19.20 per share, what value does the market appear to attribute to the conversion right per share? If you were the defendant, what kind of evidence might you offer that the entire decline was not attributable to the announcement of the supplemental indenture?
4. Chancellor Allen holds that holders of convertible debentures aren't entitled to the benefit of fiduciary duties until they exercise their conversion rights. Is this pure formalism, or can you think of other reasons that might justify such a rule? Are there real differences in the situations of shareholders and holders of convertible debentures? What would happen if directors owed duties to both shareholders and convertible debenture holders?

NOTE ON BROAD V. ROCKWELL INTERNATIONAL CORPORATION

As Chancellor Allen noted, similar issues arose in Broad v. Rockwell International Corporation, 642 F.2d 929 (en banc, 5th Cir.), cert. denied 454 U.S. 965 (1981). Collins Radio Company had issued debentures convertible into its common stock at $72.50 per Collins share, at a time when Collins stock was trading at around $60. But Collins then fell on hard times, and its stock price declined to as low as $9.75, when Rockwell stepped in. At first Rockwell invested in convertible preferred stock of Collins, but then proceeded with a tender offer and cash-out merger at $25 per Collins share, a premium over the market. The indenture governing the convertible debentures provided that upon a merger in which Collins disappeared, the conversion rights would become exercisable for the same consideration received by a Collins shareholder in the merger—in this case $25 cash.

The company's holders of convertible debentures sued, alleging breach of contract. Their primary contract claim asserted that, under the indenture, the holders' right to convert into common stock should survive a merger of Collins into another company, and that every holder of debentures should thereafter have the right to convert its debentures into common stock of the surviving company as long as the debentures remained outstanding. After discussing the long history of courts' emphasis on contractual language in determining bondholders' rights, the court found that the debenture holders had been provided exactly what the contract required—the right to convert each $1,000 debenture into $344.75 in cash (i.e., $1,000/$72.50 × $25.00), and that this "adequately accords to the holders of Debentures their valid rights under the Indenture." The court then proceeded to reject plaintiff's argument that an implied covenant of fair dealing under New York law required more for the debenture holders, stating ". . . this implied covenant of good faith and fair dealing cannot give the holders of Debentures any rights inconsistent with those explicitly set out in the Indenture. '[W]here the instrument contains an express covenant in regard to any subject, no covenants are to be implied with respect to the same subject.' "

What kind of contract language might have provided the plaintiffs in *Simons v. Cogan* or *Broad v. Rockwell* with the right to convert into common shares of the surviving firm at their option? The following is a fairly typical provision that offers some protection for options or conversion rights against the risk of destruction:

> In case at any time the Company shall be a party to any transaction . . . in which the previously outstanding Capital Stock shall be changed into or exchanged for different securities of the Company or common stock or other securities of another corporation . . . then, as a condition of the consummation of the Transaction, lawful and adequate provisions shall be made so that each holder of Conversion Rights, upon the exercise thereof at any time on or after the Consummation Date, shall be entitled to receive, and such Conversion Rights shall thereafter represent the right to receive, in lieu of the Capital Stock issuable upon such exercise prior to the Consummation Date, the highest amount of securities or other property to which such holder would actually have been entitled as a shareholder upon the consummation of the Transaction if such holder had exercised such Conversion Rights immediately prior thereto. . .

Anti-destruction provisions are also critical components for a shareholder rights plan. Recall that poison pill rights plans are often designed to "flip over" into stock of a hostile bidder when triggered, thus representing a form of option on the common shares of a future bidder. Typically, these rights provide for a bargain purchase of the bidders' shares at a 50% discount from the market value of the issuer. The standard structure is for the rights to begin as rights to acquire shares in the issuing firm that "flip over" into rights to acquire stock of the hostile bidder. To be effective, these rights must thus survive the "destruction" of the issuer's stock in the event of its merger. Below is an example of anti-destruction language:

> "(a) In the event the Company shall consolidate with, or merge with and into, any other Person. . . then . . . proper

> provision shall be made so that (i) each holder of a Right (except as otherwise provided herein) shall thereafter have the right to receive, upon the exercise thereof at a price equal to the then current Purchase Price multiplied by the number of shares of Common Stock of the Company for which a Right is then exercisable, such number of validly issued, fully paid, nonassessable and freely tradable shares of Common Stock of the Principal Party, not subject to any liens, encumbrances, preemptive rights, rights of first refusal or other adverse claims, as shall equal the result obtained by (A) multiplying the then current Purchase Price by the number of shares of Common Stock for which a Right is then exercisable and dividing that product by (B) 50% of the then Current Per Share Market Price of the Common Stock of such Principal Party (determined pursuant to Section 11(d) hereof) on the date of consummation of such consolidation, merger, sale or transfer. . .

As a final example, anti-destruction provisions are also highly relevant for employee stock options. These options typically have ten-year terms and are intended to encourage company executives to pursue value maximizing transactions, which could ultimately mean the sale of the company. What happens if the company is sold and the options can no longer be exercised for company stock? There are at least two solutions. One approach is to accelerate vesting of unvested options and allow the employee or director to exercise the options before the merger that destroys the company's stock. This allows the option holder to obtain the same benefits as the other shareholders. Another approach is to convert the options into the right to receive the same consideration that the shareholders will receive at the merger. Here is typical language to implement this latter approach:

> In case at any time the Company shall be a party to any transaction . . . in which the previously outstanding Capital Stock shall be changed into or exchanged for different securities of the Company or common stock or other securities of another corporation . . . then, as a condition of the consummation of the Transaction, lawful and adequate provisions shall be made so that each holder of option, upon the exercise thereof at any time on or after the Consummation Date, shall be entitled to receive, and such option rights shall thereafter represent the right to receive, in lieu of the Capital Stock issuable upon such exercise prior to the Consummation Date, the highest amount of securities or other property to which such holder would actually have been entitled as a shareholder upon the consummation of the Transaction if such holder had exercised such option rights immediately prior thereto . . .

If the consideration is stock, this gets the employee the right to purchase stock in the acquiring firm. If the option's duration remains unchanged, the employee has the opportunity to profit from increases in the acquiring firm's stock price over time. Note, however, that if the consideration is cash, the option holder will only be entitled to cash; consequently, in a cash-out transaction, the option holder will continue to face destruction of the option.*

We conclude this section on anti-destruction provisions with a discussion of the proper remedy for when a company destroys option value in violation of a contractual clause, such as the ones just presented. In particular, must the holder of the options pursue a remedy for breach under contract law, or can the holder use other remedies afforded by corporate law? *Simons v. Cogan* makes clear that a breach of fiduciary duty claim will be unavailable. But what about appraisal rights in the wake of a merger that seeks to cash out a firm's option holders? As the following case illustrates, courts have not been receptive to these claims.

Andaloro v. PFPC Worldwide, Inc.

830 A.2d 1232 (Del. Ch. 2003)

■ STRINE, VICE CHANCELLOR.

This is an appraisal action brought by petitioners John J. Andaloro and Robert J. Perslweig against respondent PFPC Worldwide, Inc. The petitioners seek appraisal of the value of the shares and options they owned in PFPC before it was merged with an acquisition vehicle of PFPC's indirect parent, PNC Financial Services Group, Inc., in a short-form merger under 8 Del. C. § 253 in which PFPC was the surviving entity. Both of the petitioners were PFPC executives before the merger.

The issue now before the court is a discrete one that is purely legal in nature: Can the petitioners seek appraisal under § 262 to receive the "fair value" of the options they were forced to give up in the merger in exchange for certain other consideration? The petitioners argue that the equities demand recognition of such a right. In support of that contention, the petitioners have filed affidavits suggesting that PFPC failed to provide the petitioners with adequate information or otherwise make fair provisions for the petitioners to convert their options into stock before the effective time of the merger, despite the fact that the relevant option agreements provided that the petitioners' options would vest upon the occurrence of a change of control, including a § 253 merger. For example, the petitioners have provided evidence to demonstrate that the PFPC board did not undertake a fair valuation process for the options but simply imposed a take-it-or-leave-it value on the petitioners in an offer that required them to waive a host of legal rights.

Without contesting in this action that the petitioners might have equitable or contractual claims regarding the treatment of their options,

* While not typically applicable to employee stock options, the risk that a cash merger will destroy an option's value (regardless of antidestruction provisions) is one of the reasons why venture capital investors negotiate for veto rights over a sale of a portfolio company.

the respondent PFPC has moved for partial summary judgment advancing a simple proposition: § 262 is a limited statutory remedy that is available only to stockholders. Under the settled authority of Lichtman v. Recognition Equipment, Inc.,[2] the right of appraisal is not available to option holders. "It is limited to stockholders of the merged corporation."

I see no proper basis to deviate from the holding in Lichtman, which tracks the language of § 262 itself. The statute by its own terms . . . applies to "shares of stock,"[4] a definition that excludes options.

Nor do the equities require straining the linguistic reach of the statute's words. In this case, for example, the petitioners have advanced arguments that, if true, might well constitute a breach of the relevant option agreements. In a breach-of-contract action, the petitioners would be free to show that they were deprived of their options (or of their contractual rights of vesting and conversion) in violation of their contractual rights. A fitting remedy for such a breach might well be an award of damages that equals a judicial assessment of the fair value of the options that the petitioners lost.[5] In this sense, the petitioners would have access to what in some equitable corporate cases is referred to as a "quasi-appraisal" award of damages.[6]

But, as a predicate to such an award, the petitioners would be required to make an independent showing that is not contemplated within a § 262 proceeding; namely, a showing that the petitioners suffered a contractual or equitable injury at the hands of the respondent, PFPC. Importantly, that type of case might well involve claims against parties other than the surviving corporation, which is the only proper respondent to a § 262 action. In fact, the petitioners have brought just this type of action against PFPC and other parties in this court and that action has also been assigned to me for resolution.

The reality that the petitioners have to prove a predicate breach of duty (of some kind) before getting to the point where a damages award would be assessable against PFPC demonstrates that the petitioners' desire for appraisal of their options cannot be squared with § 262. Shoehorning their claims into § 262 would distort the statute's intended

---

2 295 A.2d 771 (Del. Ch. 1972). One of the major treatises on Delaware law treats Lichtman as having settled the question of whether options can be appraised under § 262 by providing an authoritative negative answer. See 2 Rodman Ward, Jr. et al., Folk on the Delaware General Corporation Law § 262.2.1, at GCL–IX–182 (4th ed. Supp. 2002–1).

4 8 Del. C. § 262(a) ("The words 'stock' and 'share' mean and include what is ordinarily meant by those words. . ."). See also id. § 262(d)(2) ("Appraisal rights are available for any or all shares of such class or series of stock of [the] constituent corporation. . .").

5 The parties have not discussed whether the petitioners believe that the directors of their former corporation owed them fiduciary duties as option holders in connection with the merger. I therefore concentrate on the obvious rights of the petitioners as option holders—their contract rights.

6 See, e.g., Erickson v. Centennial Beauregard Cellular, L.L.C., 2003 Del. Ch. LEXIS 38, 2003 WL 1878583, at *3 (Del. Ch. Apr. 11, 2003); Tansey v. Trade Show News Networks, Inc., 2001 Del. Ch. LEXIS 142, 2001 WL 1526306, at *7 n.30 (Del. Ch. Nov. 27, 2001); Weinberger v. UOP, Inc., 457 A.2d 701 (Del. 1983).

focus as a limited and efficient remedy focused solely on the fair value of stock.[7]

For these same reasons, I reject the petitioners' alternative argument that under principles of equity, their options should be treated as having already been exercised before the merger and converted into "stock," and that the resulting (hypothetical) "stock" should be included in the appraisal action. It is undisputed that the petitioners did not actually exercise their options before the merger. The petitioners argue, however, that they "would have" exercised the options before the merger had PFPC provided certain requested information, and that PFPC "treated" the options as stock in various ways during the transaction. This argument, however, is precisely the kind of breach-of-duty question that has no place in a statutory appraisal, and that must be raised in a separate plenary action. The petitioners cite no relevant authority for the proposition that equitable breach-of-duty claims may be raised in an appraisal proceeding,[9] and I decline to interpret § 262 to permit consideration of issues unrelated to the appraisal of the fair value of actual stock. To do otherwise would be to dishonor the General Assembly's determination of the proper scope of a § 262 action.

Finally, because the petitioners have the right to and, as noted, have already filed a separate plenary action seeking relief for breach of contract and fiduciary duty in connection with the treatment of their options, other judicial tools exist that can facilitate an efficient resolution of all of their claims. To the extent that the petitioners are able to prove a breach of contract or fiduciary duty, the remedy might well be one in the nature of an appraisal determination. After hearing from the parties to this action and the separate plenary action, the court might also conclude that the actions should be consolidated for many or all purposes.

---

[7] See Lichtman, 295 A.2d at 772 (stating that permitting option holders to seek appraisal would inject collateral issues not contemplated by § 262 into appraisal proceedings).

[9] The petitioners cite various cases in their surreply brief for the proposition that it is necessary in an appraisal proceeding to determine what stock is validly at issue in the appraisal. Without quibbling with that statement, I note that these cases do not support the proposition that equity may require this court to ignore the simple fact that petitioners are seeking appraisal for options, not stock. Indeed, in all of the cases cited by petitioners that involve appraisal proceedings, the petitioners actually held, in some form or another, shares of stock for which appraisal was being sought. See Salomon Bros., Inc. v. Interstate Bakeries Corp., 576 A.2d 650 (Del. Ch. 1989) (holding that stockholder who purchased shares with notice of merger plans was not foreclosed from seeking appraisal); Neal v. Alabama By-Prods. Corp., 1988 Del. Ch. LEXIS 135, 1988 WL 105754 (Del. Ch. Oct. 11, 1988) (holding appraisal demand by beneficial holder of stock invalid because demand was not by or on behalf of record holder as required by § 262); Engel v. Magnavox Co., 1976 Del. Ch. LEXIS 165, 1976 WL 1705, at *5 (Del. Ch. Apr. 22, 1976) (holding that stockholder's submission of blank proxy constituted vote in favor of merger and therefore barred appraisal); Scott v. Arden Farms Co., 26 Del. Ch. 283, 28 A.2d 81 (Del. Ch. 1942) (holding that voting trustee's vote in favor of merger precluded stockholder from seeking appraisal). Other of the cases cited by petitioners deal with proceedings under other statutes in which the consideration of equitable claims is necessarily contemplated by the very nature of the statutory right of action, such as 8 Del. C. § 225, and are therefore irrelevant. See Agranoff v. Miller, 1999 Del. Ch. LEXIS 78, 1999 WL 219650, at *17–18 (Del. Ch. Apr. 12, 1999) (explaining proper scope of § 225), aff'd & remanded, 737 A.2d 530 (Del. 1999) (TABLE).

The option to consolidate eliminates any need to distort the § 262 remedy in the name of equity or efficiency.

For all these reasons, therefore, PFPC's motion for partial summary judgment is granted and the petitioners' claim for appraisal of their options is dismissed. IT IS SO ORDERED.

B. DILUTION OF OPTION RIGHTS

Even when an issuer lacks the authority to destroy an option, it can still take other actions that might greatly reduce the option's value. Consider, for instance, the Black-Scholes option pricing formula. We know from our prior discussion that the value of an option under this formula will depend on the following parameters:

Parameter	Relationship to Call Option Value
t: duration of the option	Positive
K: strike price of option	Negative
S: current price of stock	Positive
σ: standard deviation	Positive
r: risk-free rate	Positive
y: dividend yield	Negative

Corporate actions that affect any of these parameters can therefore change the value of an option. Indeed, the destruction of the option problem in the last section can be viewed as a corporate action that reduces the term of the option (t) to 0. Likewise, a company that decreases its stock price volatility (σ) will decrease the value of its common stock options. While the provisions of an option contract can, in theory, seek to address changes to any of these parameters, our focus here is on corporate actions that affect the value of S (the underlying security). Specifically, we focus on legal strategies that option holders might deploy to protect against diminution in the value of S arising from dilutive stock splits and dividends as well as dilutive stock issuances.

i. STOCK SPLITS AND DIVIDENDS

We begin with stock splits and stock dividends. In a stock split, a company amends its charter to cause each outstanding share of common stock to be sub-divided into a specified number of shares. For instance, if a company's board of directors chooses to conduct a 3-for-1 stock split, for every one share held by an investor, that investor would thereafter hold three shares. A stock dividend has a similar effect but, in contrast to a stock split, will not typically require a charter amendment. Suppose a firm wants to mimic a 3-for-1 stock split using a stock dividend. Assuming there are sufficient authorized but unissued shares of common stock, the board of directors can declare a common stock dividend of two shares payable to every outstanding share of common stock. Thereafter, for every one share held by an investor, that investor will now hold three shares (i.e., the same result as a 3-for-1 stock split).

What's the impact of a stock split or stock dividend on an option holder? To illustrate, let's return to our hypothetical company, NewCo, Inc., from Chapter 5. There, we saw that Francis Founder had started the company by purchasing 40 shares of common stock. Francis then sold 60 shares of common stock to Janet (an angel investor) for $10/share, giving the company a post-financing valuation of $1,000 (i.e., 100 shares x $10/share). Because the focus of Chapter 5 was on common stock, we assumed that Janet had acquired shares of common stock, but now let's imagine that Janet received shares of convertible preferred stock—as is often the case with early-stage financings. Let us further assume that, as is also typical, the conversion price of the preferred stock is the original issue price of $10/share, so that the initial conversion ratio is 1:1 (i.e., $10 original issue price / $10 conversion price). Following Janet's investment, the capitalization table looks like this:

Table 8-1:
Capitalization of NewCo Following Janet's Investment

Stockholder	Common Stock	Preferred Stock	Fully Diluted Shares	% of Fully Diluted Stock
Francis	40	0	40	40%
Janet	0	60	60	60%
Total	**40**	**60**	**100**	**100%**

Now, what happens if NewCo conducts a 3-for-1 stock split of the common stock. Following the split, the capitalization table will change as follows:

Table 8-2:
Capitalization of NewCo Following 3-for-1 Stock Split

Stockholder	Common Stock	Preferred Stock	Fully Diluted Shares	% of Fully Diluted Stock
Francis	120	0	120	66.67%
Janet	0	60	60	33.33%
Total	**120**	**60**	**180**	**100%**

Notice the dramatic effect on Janet's position. Assuming the company is still worth $1,000 and there is no debt outstanding, her election to convert into common stock only entitles her to a claim having a fair value of $333.33, as opposed to the $600 claim she held prior to the stock split. Given the dilutive effect of a stock split, it is very common for options and convertible securities to contain anti-dilution provisions that are designed to address this exact problem.

As an example, consider Section 4(d)(iii) from Article IV(B) of Lyft's Certificate of Incorporation, which is set forth in the Appendix to this book. Section 4(d) is entitled "Conversion Price Adjustments of Preferred Stock" and subsection (iii) states:

> (iii) In the event this Corporation should at any time or from time to time after the Filing Date fix a record date for the effectuation of a split or subdivision of the outstanding shares of Common Stock or the determination of holders of Common Stock entitled to receive a dividend or other distribution payable in additional shares of Common Stock or other securities or rights convertible into, or entitling the holder thereof to receive directly or indirectly, additional shares of Common Stock (hereinafter referred to as "**Common Stock Equivalents**") without payment of any consideration by such holder for the additional shares of Common Stock or the Common Stock Equivalents (including the additional shares of Common Stock issuable upon conversion or exercise thereof), then, as of such record date (or the date of such dividend distribution, split or subdivision if no record date is fixed), the Conversion Prices of each series of Preferred Stock shall be appropriately decreased so that the number of shares of Common Stock issuable on conversion of each share of such series shall be increased in proportion to such increase in the aggregate number of shares of Common Stock outstanding and those issuable with respect to such Common Stock Equivalents.

Notice that the effect of this provision is to lower the conversion price in a way that preserves the initial benefit of the option. Had this provision applied to Janet's preferred stock, it would require a reduction in the $10 conversion price of her shares so that the number of shares of common stock she would receive upon conversion is increased in proportion to the tripling of the outstanding shares of common stock held by Francis. That is, the conversion price of the preferred stock would drop from $10 to $3.33, such that each share of preferred stock would thereafter entitle Janet to receive 3 shares of common stock upon conversion. The capitalization table would therefore look like the following after the stock split:

Table 8-3: Capitalization of NewCo Following 3-for-1 Stock Split with Conversion Price Adjustment				
Stockholder	Common Stock	Preferred Stock	Fully Diluted Shares	% of Fully Diluted Stock
Francis	120	0	120	40%
Janet	0	60	180	60%
Total	**120**	**60**	**300**	**100%**

Janet's equity position, on a fully-diluted basis, now remains the same as before the split. Recall that the conversion price for convertible securities is effectively the exercise price for buying the underlying common stock. And each share of preferred will be valued at its original issue price. So the punchline of this provision is simply to say that if the company does a stock split and Janet later converts a share of preferred stock that is valued at $10 (i.e., its original issue price), she will be treated as if she is buying common stock at a discounted price of $3.33 per share, entitling her to three shares for each share of preferred. This reduced conversion price, in turn, ensures that she is not diluted by the stock split.

What about dividends of cash and tangible property? This represents another risk to the value of the option because a company might declare a large cash dividend (or dividend of other valuable property) to common stockholders before the option holder elects to exercise/convert. In the case of NewCo, for instance, imagine that the board of directors declares a dividend of $10/share for each share of common stock. After the distribution of this $400 to the common stockholders, the total value of the firm will naturally be $400 lower, diminishing the value of converting Janet's shares of preferred stock into common stock. While she initially had a conversion right valued at 60% of $1000, or $600, after the dividend, she will only have a conversion claim worth 60% of $600, or $360.

To avoid this scenario, the preferred stock held by Janet needs to have some form of protection, such as a veto right over dividends of cash or other property, or the right to participate in such dividends as if she had already converted her shares of preferred stock. Companies may expect to have flexibility to declare cash dividends, however, and whether Janet will be successful in demanding such protections often depends on the relative bargaining positions and preferences of the parties. There is also room for some middle-ground provisions that might restrict, but not fully prohibit, dividend payments (we saw some examples of this in Chapter 6 because debt investors are also concerned about large common stock dividends).

For investments in early-stage companies, it is quite common for the preferred stock acquired by angel investors and venture capitalists to contain a participation feature. Consider, for instance, the dividend provisions contained in Section 1 of Article IV(B) of Lyft's charter (you may recall from Chapter 7 that Lyft's preferred stock had an 8% preferential dividend):

> (b) After payment of any dividends pursuant to Article IV.B.1(a) [i.e., the preferred stock dividends], any additional dividends shall be distributed among all holders of Common Stock and all holders of Preferred Stock in proportion to the number of shares of Common Stock which would be held by each such holder if all shares of such series of Preferred Stock were converted to Common Stock at the then-effective conversion rate for each such series of Preferred Stock.

Again, we can see how this works by returning to the NewCo example. If Janet had negotiated for this same provision, and the firm decided to make a $400 cash dividend, then she would be entitled to participate in this dividend on an as-converted basis.* She would take 60% of the $400, or $240, and the rest of the cash dividend would go to Francis. Notice that the $240 received by Janet plus the remaining $360 conversion value (calculated above) equals $600—thereby preserving the benefit of Janet's initial bargain.

An alternative to this type of participation right is for the terms of the preferred stock to include a conversion price adjustment, as we saw in the case of a stock split or stock dividend. The case that follows, however, underscores how difficult it can be to draft these provisions, particularly when the dividend consists of property other than cash, such as an entire corporate subsidiary.

NOTE: THE RESTRUCTURING OF MARRIOTT CORPORATION

The following case arose from an extensive restructuring transaction by the Marriott Corporation. Marriott had invested heavily in hotels during the 1970s and 1980s, financing most of its rapid expansion with large amounts of borrowing. In the late 1980s real estate values declined nationwide, however, and the company's debt burden posed a formidable challenge for the company's growth prospects. In light of this situation, Marriott engaged in a restructuring designed to get its profitable growing businesses—hotel management and services—out from under the load of its existing debt. To accomplish the restructuring, Marriott created a new corporation, Marriott International ("International"), which would hold Marriott's lodging, food services and facilities management, and senior living service businesses. The existing Marriott Corporation would change its name to Marriott Host

* Note that if the preferred stock had a preferential dividend (such as the 8% preferential dividend that applied to Lyft's preferred stock), NewCo could declare this common stock dividend only after first paying the preferential dividend on all shares of preferred stock.

Corporation ("Host"), and would retain Marriott's real estate, airport, toll road and stadium concessions, and some other properties.

The result of the restructuring was to leave the service business—International—with $900 million in long-term debt, $7.4 billion in revenues, and $500 million in cash flows.* Host, on the other hand, would have over $2 billion in debt, $1.7 billion in revenues, and cash flow of $368 million. Interest expense for Host would be $196 million, and Host would also show losses because of large depreciation expenses.

The price of Marriott's common stock jumped 12% on the date of announcement, but the price of Marriott's bonds dropped 30% in 2 days.† Bond rating services downgraded the Marriott bonds from investment grade to junk bonds. The bonds had no covenants to prevent this distribution, and you can bet that these investors were not pleased. Marriott also had convertible preferred stock outstanding.

HB Korenvaes Investments, L.P. v. Marriott Corporation

1993 WL 257422 (Del. Ch. 1993)

■ ALLEN, CHANCELLOR.

In this action holders of Series A Cumulative Convertible Preferred Stock of Marriott Corporation seek to enjoin a planned reorganization of the businesses owned by that corporation. The reorganization involves the creation of a new corporate subsidiary, Marriott International, Inc., ("International"), the transfer to International of the greatest part of Marriott's cash-generating businesses, followed by the distribution of the stock of International to all of the holders of Marriott common stock, as a special dividend.

Plaintiffs assert that the proposed special dividend would leave the residual Marriott endangered by a disproportionate debt burden and would deprive them of certain rights created by the certificate of designation that defines the special rights, etc., of the preferred stock. More particularly, they claim: (1) that the proposed transaction, taken together with a recently declared intention to discontinue the payment of dividends on the preferred stock, constitutes coercive action designed wrongfully to force them to exercise their conversion privilege and thus surrender their preference rights; (2) that the planned payment of cash dividends on International's common stock, while plaintiffs' preferred dividend will have been suspended, violates the preferred stock's dividend preference; (3) that the authorization by the directors of Marriott of the spin-off transaction, without the affirmative vote of the holders of preferred stock, violates the voting rights of the preferred conferred by the certificate of designation; and (4) that the distribution

* Eric W. Orts, *The Complexity and Legitimacy of Corporate Law*, 50 WASH. & LEE L. REV. 1565, 1607–08 (1993).

† *Id.*

of the dividend will violate the provisions of Section 5(e)(iv) of the certificate of designation of the preferred stock. Section 5(e)(iv) is designed to protect the economic interests of the preferred stock in the event of a special dividend. Finally, plaintiffs allege (5) that defendants have made false statements upon which they have relied in buying preferred stock in the market and that defendants are liable for fraud.

The Series A Cumulative Convertible Preferred Stock is Marriott's only outstanding issue of preferred stock. Plaintiffs are four institutional investors who have acquired more than 50% of the preferred stock. They present their case as one involving manipulation, deception and a legalistic interpretation of rights, which, if permitted and generalized will impose a material future cost on the operation of capital markets.

Defendants assert that the reorganization, and more particularly the special dividend, constitutes a valid, good faith attempt to maximize the interests of Marriott's common stockholders. Marriott asserts the right to deal with the preferred stock at arm's length,[1] to afford them their legal rights arising from the certificate of designation, but also to take steps not inconsistent with those rights to maximize the economic position of Marriott's common stock. It claims that this is what the proposed special dividend does. Defendants also deny that they have intentionally misled plaintiffs.

Pending is plaintiffs' motion for a preliminary injunction prohibiting the distribution of the special dividend. It is presently anticipated by defendants that the holders of Marriott's common stock will approve the proposed transaction at the Company's annual meeting now scheduled for July 23, 1993 and that the distribution, if not enjoined, will occur in August or September of this year.

* * *

For the reasons that follow, I conclude that plaintiffs have not shown a reasonable likelihood of success with respect to those aspects of their claims that appear to state a claim upon which relief might be granted. Certain theories plaintiffs advance do not appear to state such a claim and will be dismissed.

I.

Except as otherwise indicated, I take the following background facts to be non-controversial.

(a) The Company

Marriott Corporation, as presently constituted, is in the business (1) of owning and operating hotels, resorts, and retirement homes, (2) of providing institutional food service and facilities management, and (3) of operating restaurants and food, beverage and merchandise concessions

[1] Plaintiffs contention that, with respect to this transaction Marriott owes to the holders of its preferred stock fiduciary duties was rejected and a claim based on the existence of such a duty has been dismissed.

at airports, tollway plazas and other facilities. Its common stock has a present market value of approximately $2.6 billion. In December 1991 Marriott issued $200,000,000 face amount of convertible preferred stock bearing an 8 ¼% cumulative dividend, the stock owned by plaintiffs. Marriott has substantial debt, including Liquid Yield Option Notes ("LYONS") with an accreted value of $228 million;[2] and long-term debt of $2.732 billion. According to its proxy statement, the book value of Marriott's assets is $6.560 billion.

In the fiscal year ending January 1, 1993 Marriott's sales were $8.722 billion; earnings before interest, taxes, depreciation and amortization (EBITDA) was $777 million; earnings before interest and corporate expenses was $496 million; and net income was $85 million. Each common share has received an annual cash dividend of $0.28 per share and the preferred stock dividends have been paid over its short life.

(b) The terms of the preferred stock in brief

The preferred stock is entitled to an 8¼% cumulative dividend and no more. It ranks prior to the common stock with respect to dividends and distribution of assets. It has in total, a face amount of $200,000,000 and that, plus the amount of any unpaid cumulated dividends, "and no more" is the amount of its liquidation preference. The corporation may, at its option, redeem any or all of the preferred stock after January 15, 1996, at prices set forth in the certificate.

The preferred stock is convertible at the option of the holder into common stock at a conversion price set forth in the certificate. Generally that means that every $50.00 face amount share of preferred stock may be converted into 2.87 shares of common stock. The certificate provides a mechanism to adjust the conversion price "in case the Corporation shall, by dividend . . . distribute to all holders of Common Stock . . . assets (including securities). . ."

The value of the right to convert is protected by a notice provision. The certificate provides that "in the event the Corporation shall declare a dividend . . . on its Common Stock payable otherwise than in cash or out of retained earnings," the Corporation shall give written notice to the holders of the preferred stock 15 days in advance of the record date.

There are no express restrictions on the payment of dividends other than the requirement that the quarterly dividend on the preferred must be paid prior to the distribution of dividend payments to common stock.

(c) Announcement of the proposed transaction

On October 5, 1993, Marriott announced a radical rearrangement of the legal structure of the Company's businesses. The restructuring was said to be designed to separate Marriott's "ownership of real estate . . .

---

[2] A leading finance text notes that "a liquid yield option note (LYON) is a callable and retractable, convertible zero coupon bond (and you can't get much more complicated than that)." An example set forth in that text explains the security. See Richard A. Brealey and Stewart C. Myers, Principles of Corporate Finance, 3d ed. (1988) at p. 586.

and other capital intensive businesses from its management and services businesses." The latter constitute Marriott's most profitable and fastest growing business segments. As indicated above, following this transfer Marriott intends to "spin-off" this new subsidiary by distributing all its stock as a dividend to Marriott's common stockholders.

(d) Marriott International

International is anticipated to be highly profitable from its inception and to be well positioned for future growth. It is expected to pay to its common stockholders the same dividend that has been paid to Marriott's common stock. Marriott's proxy statement describes International's proposed business activities as follows:

> Pursuant to existing long-term management, lease and franchise agreements with hotel owners, and [similar] . . . agreements to be entered into with Host Marriott with respect to lodging facilities and senior living properties to be owned by Host Marriott, Marriott international will operate or franchise a total of 242 Marriott full service hotels, 207 Courtyard by Marriott hotels, 179 Residence Inns, 118 Fairfield Inns and 16 senior living communities. Marriott International will also conduct the Company's food and facilities management businesses, as well as the Company's vacation timesharing operations.

According to its pro forma balance sheet for the quarter ending March 26, 1993, after the distribution (and assuming the Exchange Offer described below is effectuated) International will have assets of $3.048 billion, long-term debt of $902 million, and shareholders equity of $375 million.

Had International, with all the assets it will hold, been operated as a separate company in 1992, it would have had sales of $7.787 billion, earnings before interest and corporate expenses of $331 million and net income of $136 million. Marriott's adviser, S.G. Warburg & Company, has estimated that in 1993 International will have sales of $8.210 billion, and EBIT of $368 million.

(e) Host Marriott

Marriott's remaining assets will consist of large real estate holdings and Marriott's airport and tollway concession business. Marriott will be renamed Host Marriott ("Host"). The assets retained by Host have a value of several billion dollars but will be burdened with great debt and produce little cash-flow after debt service.

> Host Marriott will retain [ownership of] most of the Company's [Marriott's] existing real estate properties, including 136 lodging and senior living properties. Host Marriott will also complete the Company's existing real estate development projects and manage the Company's holdings of undeveloped real estate. Host Marriott will seek to maximize the cash flow

> from . . . its real estate holdings . . . Host Marriott . . . will also be the leading operator of airport and toll-road food and merchandise concessions in the U.S., holding contracts at 68 major airports and operating concessions at nearly 100 toll-road units.

Assuming the Exchange Offer is effectuated, after the special dividend Host will have, according to its pro forma balance sheet as of March 26, 1993, assets of $3.796 billion, long-term debt of 2.130 billion and shareholders' equity of $516 million. Host's pro forma income statement for the fiscal year ending January 1, 1993, would reflect sales of $1.209 billion, earnings before corporate expenses and interest of $152 million, interest expense of $196 million, corporate expenses of $46 million, and a net loss of $44 million.

When he announced the spin-off transaction on October 5, 1992, Stephen Bollenbach, Marriott's Chief Financial Officer stated, with respect to the future of Host:

> Net cash flow of Host Marriott will be used primarily to service and retire debt. The Company does not plan to pay dividends on its common stock . . . I am very comfortable with the way Host Marriott has been structured. I believe this approach represents the best way for Marriott shareholders to unlock the value of our long-term assets. Secondly, the transaction gives Host Marriott the staying power needed if the recovery is slower than anticipated in arriving. I am convinced Host Marriott has the financial means to meet all its obligations to employees, suppliers, lenders and other stakeholders."[6]

Mr. Bollenbach reiterated this position two weeks later at a meeting of securities analysts.

* * *

(h) Plaintiffs' acquisition of preferred stock and short sales of common.

Plaintiffs began for the first time to purchase substantial amounts of Marriott's preferred stock following the announcement of the special dividend.

Since the preferred stock is convertible at the option of the holder into 2.87 shares of Marriott common stock and bears a dividend of 8¼%

---

[6] Plaintiff has put forth substantial documentary support for their assertion that at the time this statement was made it was the expectation of the senior Marriott executives that the preferred stock dividend would not be paid following the distribution. This alleged undisclosed fact forms an important part of the predicate for their fraud claim in this lawsuit. Defendants deny that Marriott's responsible officers had at that time made the determination, which was later (March 15, 1993) announced, that preferred dividends would be discontinued. This factual dispute cannot be settled on this motion. For present purposes I assume that in October 1992 Marriott's responsible officers knew that no final decision on preferred dividends had been made, but expected such dividends to be discontinued; thus the lawyerly use of the term "obligation."

on its stated (liquidation) value of $50 per share, the market value of a share of preferred stock includes two possible components of value: the value of the conversion right and the value of the preferences. The presence of a presently exercisable conversion right will assure that the market value of the preferred will not fail below the market value of the security or property into which the preferred might convert, in this case 2.87 shares of common stock (less transaction costs of the conversion). The stated dividend, the dividend preference and the liquidation preference and other features of the preferred will ordinarily assure that the preferred trades at some premium to the value of the conversion right.

In this instance plaintiffs have acquired a majority of the shares of the preferred stock. Plaintiffs, however, did not simply acquire preferred stock. The record shows that each of the plaintiffs, except one, have hedged their risk by entering short sales contracts with respect to Marriott common stock. In this way plaintiffs have isolated their risk to that part of the preferred stock trading value represented by that stock's preference rights. Any change in the market price of the preferred stock caused by movement in the value of the underlying common stock will in their case be offset by change in the extent of their obligations under the short sales contracts.

(i) Marriott common and preferred stock price changes

The prices of both Marriott common stock and Marriott preferred stock have increased substantially since the announcement of the special dividend. On the last trading day before the announcement of the transaction Marriott's common stock closed at $17.125 per share. The day of the announcement the price increased to $19.25 and by June 4, 1993 it had reached $25.75, for a total increase of approximately 50.3%.

The price of Marriott preferred stock closed on the last trading day before the announcement at $62.75, which represented a premium of $13.54 over the value of the 2.8736 common shares into which each preferred share could convert. The day of the announcement the preferred stock increased to $68.875. On June 4, 1993 the price of the preferred stock closed at $77.00 per share, an increase of 22.8% over the pre-announcement market price. The premium that the preferred stock commanded over the common into which it could convert (i.e., the market value of the preferences) however, had by June 4th, shrunk, to $3.00.

Thus while both common stock and preferred stock have experienced substantial increases in the market value of their securities, because of the impact of their hedging strategy, plaintiffs are in a different position than are non-hedged holders of preferred stock. The reduction of the premium at which the preferred stock trades has resulted in losses on their short sales, leading some plaintiffs, as of June 4, 1993, to net unrealized losses on their investments.

For example, plaintiff, The President and Fellows of Harvard College, ("Harvard") as of June 4, 1993 owned 480,300 shares of preferred stock, which were purchased for $33,580,108 and which had a market value on that day of $37,724,801. Thus, this plaintiff has an unrealized profit of $4,144,693 on its investment in the preferred stock. Harvard also entered into short sales of 1,338,300 shares of Marriott common stock, approximately 2.8 times the number of preferred shares it purchased. It received $30,949,383 on these short sales. The cost to cover these short sales, however, has increased to $34,609,056, or $3,659,673 more than was received on the sales, representing an unrealized loss in that amount. Thus, as of June 4, 1993, although the value of the preferred stock owned by this plaintiff has increased in value by over $4 million, the total value of its investment position has increased by only $485,020.[9]

* * *

V. The Section 5(e)(iv) Claim

I turn now to analysis of that which I regard as the centrally important certificate provision, Section 5(e)(iv). That section affords protection against dilution of the conversion component of the market value of the preferred stock by providing an adjustment to the conversion price when the corporation declares a dividend of assets, including securities. The principle that appears embedded in Section 5(e)(iv) is that when the assets of the Firm are depleted through a special distribution to shareholders, the preferred will be protected by the triggering of a conversion price adjustment formula. Under Section 5(e)(iv) the number of shares into which the preferred can convert will be proportionately increased in order to maintain the value of the preferred's conversion feature. The principle seems clear enough; the realization of it will inevitably involve problems.

> (a) Section 5(e)(iv) of the certificate of designation requires Marriott, when effectuating a special dividend, to leave sufficient net assets in the corporation to permit that Section to function as intended to protect the predisposition value of the preferred stock.

The language of the certificate of designation is as follows:

> 5. *Conversion Rights.* The holders of shares of Convertible Preferred Stock shall have the right at their option, to convert such shares into shares of Common Stock on the following terms and conditions:
>
> (a) Shares of Convertible Preferred Stock shall be convertible at any time into fully paid and nonassessable shares of Common

---

[9] At least two other plaintiffs have entered into similar transactions. AKT Associates L.P., had as of June 4, 1993, an unrealized profit on its preferred stock of $2,033,495 and increased cost to cover short sales of $2,036,777 for an unrealized loss of $3,282. HB Korenvaes Investments, L.P. had an unrealized gain of $3,555,648 on its preferred and a loss of $3,793,089 on its short position for an unrealized loss of $237,441. * * *

> Stock at a conversion price of $17.40 per share of Common Stock (the "Conversion Price").
>
> * * *
>
> (e) The conversion Price shall be adjusted from time to time as follows:
>
> (iv) In case the Corporation shall, by dividend or otherwise, distribute to all holders of its Common Stock . . . assets (including securities . . .), the Conversion Price shall be adjusted so that the same shall equal the price determined by multiplying the Conversion Price in effect immediately prior to the close of business on the date fixed for the determination of stockholders entitled to receive such distribution by a fraction of which the numerator shall be the current market price per share (determined as provided in subsection (vi) below) of the Common Stock on the date fixed for such determination less the then fair market value (as determined by the Board of Directors, whose determination shall be conclusive and shall be described in a statement filed with the transfer agent for the Convertible Preferred Stock) of the portion of the evidences of indebtedness or assets so distributed applicable to one share of Common Stock and the denominator shall be such current market price per share of the Common Stock, such adjustment to become effective immediately prior to the opening of business on the day following the date fixed for the determination of stockholders entitled to receive such distribution. (emphasis added).

Thus, stated simply, whenever Marriott distributes assets to its common stockholders this provision protects the value of the preferred conversion right by reducing the conversion price. Protection of this type may be important to the buyer of preferred stock and presumably its inclusion will permit an issuer to arrange the sale of preferred stock on somewhat more advantageous terms than would otherwise be available. What is intuitively apparent is that in a narrow range of extreme cases, a dividend of property may be so large relative to the corporation's net worth, that following the distribution, the firm, while still solvent,[16] will not represent sufficient value to preserve the pre-dividend value of the preferred's conversion right.

Appended to this opinion are three hypothetical cases in which the Section 5(e)(iv) formula is employed. Case 1 involves a dividend of 40% of the issuing corporation's net asset value. Case 2 is a dividend of 90% of net asset value. Case 3 displays the consequences of a dividend of 95% of asset value. Given the assumptions of the examples (i.e. preferred

16 Traditionally preferred stockholders have not been treated as creditors for the amount of the liquidation preference and the preference does not count as a "claim" for fraudulent conveyance purposes.

conversion rights equal 9.1% of total pre-distribution value), only in the last case does the Section 5(e)(iv) formula fail to function.

In light of the mathematical effect demonstrated in the appended examples, a court that must construe Section 5(e)(iv) is required to conclude, in my opinion, that Marriott has voluntarily and effectively bound itself not to declare and distribute special dividends of a proportion that would deprive the preferred stockholders of the protection that that provision was intended to afford. In providing a mechanism to maintain pre-distribution value (putting to one side for the moment, how pre-distribution value is determined) the issuer impliedly but unmistakably and necessarily undertook to refrain from declaring a dividend so large that what is left in the corporation is itself worth less than the pre-distribution value of the preferred stock. No other interpretation of the certificate of designation gives the language of Section 5(e)(iv) its intended effect in all circumstances. Thus, were the facts of Case 3 the facts of this case, I would be required to find that the special dividend violated the rights of the preferred stockholders created by the certificate of designation.

Such a holding would not be inconsistent with those cases that hold that rights of preference are to be strictly construed. This strict construction perspective on the interpretation of certificates of designation has long been the law of this jurisdiction and others. While that principle does define the court's approach to construction and interpretation of the documents that create preferred stock, that principle does not excuse a court from the duty to interpret the legal meaning of the certificate of designation. Thus where the necessary implication of the language used is the existence of a right or a duty, a court construing that language is duty bound to recognize the existence of that right or that duty.

(b) Plaintiffs have failed to introduce evidence from which it could be concluded at this time that it is reasonably probable that they will prevail on a claim that the special dividend violates Section 5(e)(iv).

(i) The value that Section 5(e)(iv) intends to protect is the market value of the conversion feature at the time the board authorizes a special dividend transaction.

The determination that Section 5 of the certificate creates by necessary implication an obligation on the part of the corporation to leave sufficient value in the corporation following a special dividend to permit the protections it creates to function with the intended effect, raises the further question, what value does Section 5 intend to protect. Plainly it is the value of the conversion feature, that is what all of Section 5 is about, but measured at what point in time?

On the last day of trading before the announcement of the special dividend, Marriott's common stock closed at $17.125. The preferred's conversion feature, (its right to convert into 11,494,400 common shares) had a value at that time of $196,842,000. Beginning the first trading day after the announcement of the special dividend, Marriott common stock rose greatly in price. By May 21, 1993, it had increased to approximately $26.00 per share and the value of the preferred's conversion right had increased to $298.5 million.

Plaintiffs' position is that this value, as effected by the prospect of the dividend attacked, is the value that must be left in the corporation.

I cannot accept this interpretation of what good faith adherence to the provisions of the certificate requires of Marriott. Section 5(e)(iv) operates to prevent the confiscation of the value of the preferred conversion right through a special dividend. By necessary implication it limits the board's discretion with respect to the size of special dividends. But that limitation is one that has its effect when it is respected by the board of directors at the time it takes corporate action to declare the dividend. If, when declared, the dividend will leave the corporation with sufficient assets to preserve the conversion value that the preferred possesses at that time, it satisfies the limitation that such a protective provision necessarily implies. That is, Section 5(e)(iv) does not, in my opinion, explicitly or by necessary implication grant the preferred a right to assurance that any increase in the value of their conversion rights following the authorization of a special dividend be maintained.

(ii) Plaintiffs have failed to introduce evidence that establishes a reasonable probability of their proving that the net value remaining in Host after distribution of the special dividend is or is reasonably likely to be insufficient to maintain the pre-distribution value of the preferred's conversion right.

In attempting to demonstrate that the special dividend will confiscate some part of their property, plaintiffs rely on the affidavit of Charles R. Wright, a certified public accountant. Mr. Wright states that following the special dividend the value of Host's equity will not exceed $200 million. This opinion is based upon analyses conducted by Wolfensohn, Inc. in October 1992, concerning the transaction as planned at that time. But the transaction of October 1992 reflected a very different financial structure than that now planned; it contemplated Host bearing substantially more debt than the transaction currently envisioned. * * *

The later projections by Wolfensohn and S.G. Warburg, provide a different picture of Host's financial status than the earlier ones upon which Mr. Wright relies. On May 7, 1993, Wolfensohn provided Marriott's board with current valuations of Host and International. Wolfensohn concluded that, assuming the Exchange Offer closes, Host will have a total equity value of between $371 million and $556 million.

A discounted cash flow valuation of Host produced by Wolfensohn on April 20, 1993 and based on the assumption that the Exchange Offer will be effectuated, produced a range of values from $270 million (assuming a 14% discount rate; and a multiple of 7 times EBITDA) to $884 million (assuming a 12% discount rate and a multiple of 9 times EBITDA) with a middle case of $567 million (assuming a 13% discount rate and a multiple of 8 times EBITDA.)

S.G. Warburg's valuation of Host, dated May 6, 1993, estimated the trading value of Host, assuming the Exchange Offer closes, at $1.38 to $2.84 per share or an aggregate of $179 million to $368 million. Warburg also estimated that the summary business value of Host would be in the range of $551 to $830 million or $4.25 to $6.40 per share.

The lower end of S.G. Warburg's estimate of the likely range of trading values for Host stock falls below the $196.8 million that represents the value of plaintiffs' conversion rights prior to the announcement of the distribution. Unspecified assertions by plaintiffs' expert that "major assumptions used in the discounted cash flow analysis are inappropriate" and that companies used for comparison are not comparable to Host, do not, however, provide a basis upon which to conclude that it is more likely that Host's common stock will have a value in the lower end of this range of values rather than in the higher part. The mere possibility that this will be the case is not enough to support the grant of a preliminary injunction. I assume the shape of a graph of the probabilities of any of these values in the range being "correct" would form a bell shaped curve. That is to say it is more likely that, upon more exhaustive analysis or with a more definitive valuation technique, the intrinsic value of Host would be the mean number of these ranges rather than either expressed limit of them. These higher probability mean estimates are all in excess of $196 million.

Thus, I am unable to conclude that plaintiffs have shown a sufficient probability of demonstrating that the protective functions of Section 5(e)(iv) will be frustrated by the size of the special dividend to justify the issuance of an injunction preventing the effectuation of the planned reorganization of Marriott.

(c) Plaintiffs have not shown that defendants have breached (or are about to breach) the agreed upon formula for implementing Section 5(e)(iv).

In its June 19, 1993 proxy statement, Marriott described the process that it intends to employ with respect to the operation of Section 5(e)(iv) of the certificate. After paraphrasing the certificate language quoted above, the proxy statement states:

> The Board currently intends to determine the "fair market value" of the Distribution, for purposes of this calculation, by ascertaining the relative, intrinsic values of Host Marriott and Marriott International (with reference to all factors which it deems relevant) and by designating the allocable portion of the

Current Market Price attributable to Marriott International as the fair market value of the Distribution.

In this litigation defendants have amplified their proposed method for determining fair market value of the individual distribution. Marriott intends to first determine "with reference to all relevant factors" the "intrinsic values" of International and Host. Then the fraction of the value of a Marriott share represented by International would be determined by dividing International's "intrinsic value" by the sum of the intrinsic values of International and Host. This fraction would then be multiplied by the current trading value of Marriott to determine the fair market value (per share) of International and thus of the distribution. Therefore, the fair market value of the distribution (i.e., International) is treated by the board's proposed valuation method as fraction of the market value of Marriott prior to the distribution of the dividend. The premise of this methodology is the assertion that as long as Host common stock trades at some positive value, the fair market value of International for purposes of applying Section 5(e)(iv) must be less than the current market value of Marriott; the whole (Marriott) cannot be less than the sum of its parts (International plus Host).

Defendants claim that this method of determining fair market value is consistent with the certificate and that it reaches a determination of the fair market value of the distribution that can meaningfully be compared to the current market value of Marriott. Indeed, they assert that any alternative technique which yields a value for International that is higher than the market value of Marriott must (as long as Host trades at a positive value) be faulty.

* * *

In my opinion, Marriott's proposed technique for determining the values to employ in the contractual formula is one valid way to do what the company is contractually bound to do. It follows that this claim presents no grounds to justify the issuance of a preliminary injunction.

* * *

Defendants' intended technique for estimating the "fair market value applicable to one share" would appear to serve the purpose of the section. As explained above, the equation is intended to operate to reduce the conversion price by the same percentage that the total assets of the company are being reduced. Assuming again that Host will have some positive net worth, it is clear that less than 100% of the assets of Marriott are being distributed. Therefore, in such a case the conversion price should be reduced by less than 100%. The method adopted by the company for determining applicable fair market value would, if fairly and competently applied, provide for the adjustment of the conversion price in a manner that effectuates the purposes of the clause. The certificate of course confers broad discretion on Marriott in implementing the formula of Section 5(e)(iv) and makes its choices "conclusive." While that grant may too imply a duty of commercial good faith, the facts adduced do not suggest that the employment of the formula by defendants has been other than in good faith.

Thus, I am unable to conclude that plaintiffs have shown a reasonable probability of success on the merits of their claim that the method of determining the fair market value of the assets to be distributed "applicable to one share of [Marriott] common stock", that defendants have announced they will employ, violates Section 5(e)(iv).

* * *

APPENDIX

The following three hypotheticals demonstrate how section 5(e)(iv) operates to preserve the economic value of the conversion rights of the preferred when the company's assets are distributed as dividends to the common stockholders, and how at extreme levels it could fail.

CASE I

Assume a company, Corporation Y, with $1 billion in assets and no debts. It has 10 million shares of common stock and 1 million shares of cumulative convertible preferred stock having a face amount and liquidation preference of $100 million. The preferred is convertible into common stock at a price of $100 face amount per common share or into 1 million common shares, in total. The certificate of designation contains a provision identical to Section 5(e)(iv).

Assume further that the capital markets operate efficiently and the common stock trades at price reflecting Corporation Y's asset values on a fully diluted basis.

Under these assumptions at time T[1], Current Market Price ("CMP") is determined as follows:

CMP = $1 billion × 1/11 million shares = $90.9091 per share

Preferred Conversion Value = 1 million shares × $90.9091/1 share = $90,909,100

At time T[2] Corporation Y declares a dividend of assets with a fair market value of $400 million or $40 per outstanding common share, leaving the company with $600 million in assets.

The conversion price would be adjusted by the same formula as applies in section 5(e)(iv)

ACP = CP x CMP – FMV/CMP

Where: ACP=Adjusted Conversion Price

CP=Conversion Price;

FMV=Fair Market Value

CMP=Current Market Price common stock

ACP = 100 × $90.9091 – $40/$90.9091 = $56.0000

The preferred would become convertible into 1,785,710 common shares, $100,000,000 × 1 common share/$56.0000 = 1,785,870 common shares with an aggregate value of $90,908,900, $600,000,000 × 1,785,710 converted shares/11,785,710 common shares = $90,908,900

Thus in this case the anti-dilution provision of the certificate would serve to preserve the economic value of the preferred stock despite the diversion of 40% of Corporation Y's net worth out of the company.

CASE II

Now assume alternatively that Corporation Y declares a special dividend to its common stockholders of $900 million of its assets or $90 per outstanding share.

The conversion price adjustment formula would work to adjust the conversion price from $100 to 1.00 per share:

ACP = $100 × $90.9091 – $90/$90.9091 = $1.0000

The preferred would become convertible into 100,000,000 shares, (91% of all common stock) at T[2].

$100,000,000 × 1 common share/$1.0000 = 100,000,000 shares

But the aggregate value of the preferred portion would remain unchanged at $90,909,091:

100,000,000 converted shares/110,000,000 common shares × $100,000,000 = $90,909,091

Thus, on these assumptions, even if 90% of Corporation Y's assets are distributed to the common stockholders, the conversion value of the preferred is maintained at its pre-distribution level by the Section 5(e)(iv) gross-up provision.

CASE III

When the special dividend is so large that insufficient equity remains in Corporation Y to maintain the value of the preferred upon conversion the gross up provisions will fail to work.[1] In such a situation the gross-up equation provides for a negative adjusted conversion price and is therefore meaningless.

For example: If Corporation Y declared a dividend of $950 million of its assets, the gross-up equation would give the following result:

ACP = CP × CMP – FMV/CMP

ACP = $100 × $90.9091 – $95.00/$90.9091 = –($4.499)

Thus, a distribution of $950 million leaves only $50 million in assets in the corporation, making it impossible for the preferred to maintain its

---

1 They may also fail, in the specific case of Section 5(e)(iv) because the measurement period for "current market price" is somewhat historical while the measurement period for "fair market value" of assets distributed is current. Thus, it may happen, given the potentials for fluctuating market prices, for a negative number to be generated simply as an artifact of the formula.

pre-distribution conversion value of $90.909 million. For that reason it also causes Section 5(e)(iv) to fail to work meaningfully.

QUESTIONS

1. What did the plaintiffs expect to achieve by selling Marriott common stock short? What is their net position? How would they earn a return?
2. If the announcement of the special dividend meant that no dividends were likely to be paid on the preferred stock, why did the market value of the preferred stock increase from $62.75 to $77.00 on June 4, 1993?
3. What does the court mean when it says that "the premium that the preferred stock commanded over the common into which it could convert (i.e., the market value of the preferences) however, had by June 4th, shrunk, to $3.00"?
4. The opinion states that on the last trading day before announcement of the special dividend, the right to convert the preferred into 11,494,400 common shares, had a value of $196,842,000. This represents the market value of the common. Is that the correct measure of the conversion right's value? Is it the correct measure under the certificate of designation for the preferred? Is there a difference between the market value of the conversion right of the preferred and its value on the date of a hypothetical conversion?
5. Chancellor Allen holds that Marriott must leave enough assets in Host to preserve the conversion value of the preferred. What is the source of this holding?
6. Some experts (namely S.G. Warburg, plaintiffs' expert), found potential trading values of the common stock between $179,000,000 and $368,000,000, with the lower end below the conversion value of $196,000,000 used by the court as a minimum. Why doesn't the court hold that this breaches the implied covenant?
7. The Plaintiffs complain about how Marriott calculated the formula for valuing the distribution. What is the nature of their complaint? Marriott argues that the fair market value of International must be less than the current market value of Marriott. Is this necessarily true?

---

ii. "CHEAP" STOCK ISSUANCES

We previously discussed in Chapter 5 how a stockholder can experience economic dilution through a "cheap" stock issuance. There, we illustrated the concept using two examples involving NewCo following a $600 investment by Janet. In the first example, NewCo issued 100 shares to Arigo Ventures for free, thereby doubling the number of outstanding shares. Assuming the company originally had a value of $1,000 (i.e., $10/share paid by Janet × 100 total shares), this issuance resulted in an immediate dilution in the value of each share of common stock held by Janet. Before the issuance Janet held 60 shares of common stock worth $600, but after the issuance of 100 shares to Arigo Ventures each share of common stock was worth just $5/share (i.e., $1,000 valuation / 200 shares), meaning that the value of her as-converted-to-common-stock position plunged to just $300. This example is an extreme illustration of a general point: Any time a company issues stock below fair market value, each share of common stock will decline in value.

In the second example, we assumed that NewCo issued Arigo Ventures 100 shares of common stock at $8/share, $2 less than what Janet paid. We stipulated that $8/share was the fair value of each share of stock, but Janet still experienced a decline in the value of her position. While such a situation may reflect an overpayment by Janet or a decline in the value of the firm, we noted that such "cheap stock" issuances nevertheless provide evidence of a decline in the value of the common stock. For holders of options in this common stock, they likewise represent declines in the value of the options.

Just as common stockholders may seek to protect against such dilutive stock issuances, option holders and holders of convertible securities can likewise negotiate for protections from the dilution of option value arising from cheaper stock sales. The principal mechanism for achieving this protection involves a decrease in the exercise price or conversion price, similar to what we saw previously in the context of stock splits. The goal of these adjustments is the same as those we discussed in Chapter 5 with Janet and Arigo Ventures. In particular, one way for Janet to avoid suffering economic dilution from the company's sale of stock at $8/share is for the company to issue her new shares to ensure that her overall position in the firm retains a value of $600.

To see how a conversion price adjustment can accomplish this same result, let us assume that, instead of acquiring 60 shares of common stock in NewCo at $10/share, Janet acquires 60 shares of preferred stock at $10/share and that each share has a conversion price of $10/share. Thus, her conversion ratio is initially 1:1 and the capitalization is the same as that set forth in Table 8-1. That is, upon conversion of her preferred shares, Janet would hold 60% of the company's common stock. Assuming NewCo is valued at $1,000 and has no outstanding debt, the value of her position (post-conversion) would therefore be $600. The purpose of antidiliution protection is to protect the value of Janet's position (post-conversion) as the value of the common stock declines in future issuances.

Now assume that the company's charter contained the following provision:

> In the event the Corporation issues additional shares of common stock without consideration or for a consideration per share less than the applicable Conversion Price for the Preferred Stock in effect immediately prior to such issue, then the Conversion Price of the Preferred Stock shall be reduced, concurrently with such

issue, to the consideration per share received by the Corporation for such issue of the additional shares of Common Stock.

This contract language is generally referred to as *full ratchet* antidilution protection and means that if the company sells stock at a price below the conversion price of the preferred stock, the conversion price is automatically reduced to the price per share of the stock sold by the company. In our example, NewCo's sale of common stock to Arigo Ventures for $8/share would therefore mean that the conversion price of Janet's preferred stock is reduced to $8/share. Because her conversion ratio is determined by dividing the $10 original issue price by the conversion price, she will now be entitled to 1.25 shares of common stock (i.e., $10/$8) for each share of preferred stock. Following the transaction, the company's capitalization table would look like this:

Table 8-4: Capitalization of NewCo Following Stock Sale Triggering Antidilution Adjustment

Stockholder	Common Stock	Preferred Stock	Fully Diluted Shares	% of Fully Diluted Stock
Francis	40	0	40	18.6%
Janet	0	60	75	34.9%
Arigo Ventures	100	0	100	46.5%
Total	**140**	**60**	**215**	**100%**

This would implement the full ratchet provision in the preferred stock, but there is one other issue to consider. Note that Arigo Ventures now holds less than 50% of the company's fully-diluted capitalization. As discussed in Chapter 5, Arigo Ventures would almost certainly object to this outcome because it is investing $800 in a firm that has a pre-money valuation of $800 (i.e., $8/share × 100 pre-financing shares, fully-diluted). Under these conditions, Arigo would expect 50% of the company's fully-diluted capitalization (i.e., $800 investment/($800 investment + $800 pre-financing valuation)).* Accordingly, upon discovery of the preferred stock

* In this example, we adopt the conventional, simple approach to equity pricing in which an investor calculates the price per share by (a) determining the pre-financing value of the company (here, $800) and (b) dividing this number by the fully-diluted capitalization of the company (here, initially 100 shares). Indeed, this is the standard approach even for venture capital investors who purchase *convertible preferred stock* rather than common stock. In effect, this pricing equation assumes that all pre-existing stockholders hold common stock and that the new investors are purchasing common stock. Why would investors assume away the preferred stock preferences when pricing the transaction? The most straightforward answer is that these investors (both pre-existing investors and new investors) are investing in a firm that will become sufficiently valuable that all investors will elect to convert into common stock. In such an event, the preferred stock preferences become irrelevant, and what matters for the investors is the fraction of the outstanding common stock received on conversion (i.e., the value of their conversion option). Hence, investors focus on pricing the transaction to ensure that their as-converted equity stake (as reflected on the fully-diluted capitalization table) is equal to the

anti-dilution protection, Arigo Ventures will no doubt price the transaction by treating the conversion price adjustment as occurring immediately before the transaction—so as to avoid any dilution from it. (We discuss this technique in the Sidebar). The end result is the issuance of 160 shares of common stock to Arigo Ventures at $5/share. This, in turn, means that the full ratchet antidilution protection drops the conversion price of the preferred stock to $5/share, resulting in a 2:1 conversion ratio. In other words, this approach will ensure that Arigo Ventures receives its expected 50% of the fully-diluted capitalization while still honoring the preferred stock antidilution protection. The resulting positions of Francis, Janet and Arigo Ventures are shown in Table 8-5.

Table 8-5: Capitalization of NewCo Following Stock Sale Triggering Antidilution Adjustment Priced by Arigo Ventures

Stockholder	Common Stock	Preferred Stock	Fully Diluted Shares	% of Fully Diluted Stock
Francis	40	0	40	12.5%
Janet	0	60	120	37.5%
Arigo Ventures	160	0	160	50.0%
Total	**200**	**60**	**320**	**100%**

Where does all of this ultimately leave Janet? Recall that the pre-financing value of the company is $800 and Arigo Ventures is investing $800, meaning that the post-financing value of the company must be $1,600. If Janet were to convert her preferred stock, she would hold a 37.5% equity claim, or an equity claim worth exactly $600 (i.e., 37.5% x $1,600). In short, the full ratchet antidilution protection has ensured that she suffers no economic dilution of the value of her option to convert. For this reason, when options and convertible securities have full ratchet anti-dilution protection, they are often said to have "full price protection."

As you may have noticed, one downside of issuing options and convertible securities with full ratchet antidilution protection is the adverse economic consequence for the company's pre-existing common stockholders. In effect, a full ratchet anti-dilution provision guarantees that the preferred stock investors will be entitled to a portion of the fully-diluted capitalization equal to the dollar value of their original investment. Since any new investors will also demand a portion of the

value of their investment relative to the total post-financing value of the company. Despite its popularity, this approach to equity pricing ignores the very real value of the embedded options associated with the company's convertible preferred stock. For a discussion of this issue in the context of venture capital finance, see Robert Bartlett, "Preferred Stock Liquidation Preferences", in *The Palgrave Encyclopedia of Private Equity* (2024).

fully-diluted capitalization equal to the dollar value of their new investment, this means that the pre-existing common stockholders will see a dramatic decline in their ownership stake. In the case of NewCo, for example, Arigo Ventures will expect an equity stake worth $800, and Janet's full ratchet antidilution protection will provide her with an equity stake worth $600. But look at poor Francis! If the entire company is valued at $1,600, this means that Francis must have an equity claim of just $200 (i.e., $1,600 – $800 – $600 = $200). Before the financing, Francis's 40 shares of common stock represented a claim of 40% in a company valued at $800. In short, the value of Francis' equity stake declined from $320 (.4 × $800) to $200.

It is for this reason that full ratchet antidilution protection for cheap stock issuances is far from a guaranteed preferred stock term. Indeed, it is commonly resisted by firms issuing options and convertible securities, and only investors in the strongest negotiating position are likely to obtain this term.* Instead, investors who are concerned about future cheap-stock issuances may seek a more modest form of antidilution protection, known as *weighted-average* antidilution protection, as a potential compromise. With weighted-average antidilution protection, if the company issues stock at a price below the conversion price of the preferred stock, the conversion price is still adjusted downward—but more modestly. Rather than just pegging the conversion price to the price of the newly issued "cheap stock," the conversion price is adjusted using a formula, such as the following:

$$New\ Conversion\ Price = Old\ Conversion\ Price \times \frac{CSO + NSOP}{CSO + NIS}$$

This is the formula for weighted average antidilution protection used in the model Certificate of Incorporation published on the website of the National Venture Capital Association. The terms in the formula are defined as follows:

CSO: Common Stock Outstanding immediately before the cheap stock issuance, assuming the conversion and

* This is not to say that all investors necessarily prefer full ratchet antidilution protection, even if a company were willing to provide it. In the context of venture capital finance, for instance, an early-stage investor must anticipate that whatever preferred stock terms it receives on its shares of preferred stock will also be demanded by subsequent investors on their shares of preferred stock. Imagine, for instance, the first venture capital investor in a company acquires shares of Series A Preferred Stock at $0.50/share with full ratchet antidilution protection. Two years later the company sells Series B Preferred Stock at $5.00/share. Given that the company provided the Series A investor with full ratchet antidilution protection, it would hardly be surprising for this new investor to ask for full ratchet antidilution protection for the Series B Preferred Stock. To the extent this occurs, however, the Series A investor will now face the risk that the company will sell stock at a price below the Series B conversion price of $5.00 but above the Series A conversion price of $0.50, which would trigger the Series B full ratchet antidilution protection and thereby dilute *both* the holders of common stock and the holders of Series A Preferred Stock. For this reason, an early-stage investor who receives full ratchet antidilution protection could come to regret receiving this contract provision.

exercise of all outstanding convertible and exercisable securities.

NSOP: Number of shares of stock that would have been issued had the company sold the new shares at the old conversion price instead of the "cheap stock" price.

NIS: Number of new shares actually sold at the "cheap stock" price.

In the case of NewCo, if Janet's preferred stock was entitled to weighted-average antidilution protection, the adjustment would look like the following when the Company sold 100 shares of common stock to Arigo Ventures at $8/share.

$$New\ Conversion\ Price = \$10 \times \frac{100 + \$800/\$10}{100 + \$800/\$8}$$

Under this formula, the new conversion price would therefore become $9 (i.e., $10 × 180/200), making the new conversion ratio 1.11 (i.e., $10 original issue price / $9 conversion price means that each share of preferred stock can convert into 1.11 shares of common stock).

While visually complicated, the gist of the formula is to reduce the conversion price based on (a) the amount of financing completed at the "cheap" price, and (b) how much this financing affects the company's fully-diluted capitalization. (In this regard, note that the ratchet is triggered *regardless* of how much stock is actually issued at the lower price.) These two features of the weighted-average formula can be seen by the fact that (a) the denominator grows—and thus, the conversion price adjustment grows—with each additional share sold at the "cheap" price, and (b) the adjustment is moderated by the size of CSO, which represents the pre-financing shares outstanding. For instance, as CSO approaches infinity, the ratio approaches 1 and no adjustment is made to the conversion price; conversely, as CSO approaches zero, the ratio converges to a simple full ratchet.*

Finally, as with the full ratchet example, Arigo Ventures will seek to avoid being diluted by the conversion price adjustment by pricing the transaction as if the adjustment occurs immediately prior to its investment. (As mentioned above, we discuss this type of calculation in the Sidebar.) The end result will be the issuance of 110 shares of common stock to Arigo Ventures for its $800 investment at a price per share of $7.27. Using this price in the weighted-average formula above, the

---

* For instance, if CSO were zero in the case of NewCo, the formula would be:

$$New\ Conversion\ Price = \$10 \times \frac{0 + \$800/\$10}{0 + \$800/\$8}$$

Or $10 × 80/100, producing a new conversion price of $8, which is the same result as a full ratchet.

preferred stock conversion price is reduced to $8.57, producing a conversion ratio of 1.17. The post-financing capitalization table would therefore appear as follows:

Table 8-6: Capitalization of NewCo Following Stock Sale Triggering Antidilution Adjustment Priced by Arigo Ventures

Stockholder	Common Stock	Preferred Stock	Fully Diluted Shares	% of Fully Diluted Stock
Francis	40	0	40	18.2%
Janet	0	60	70	31.8%
Arigo Ventures	110	0	110	50.0%
Total	**150**	**60**	**220**	**100%**

Assuming, as before, that the post-financing value of the company is $1,600, the as-converted equity stake of Arigo is $800 (50% x $1,600), Janet's stake is approximately $509 (31.8% x $1,600), and Francis' stake is approximately $291 (18.2% x $1,600). Thus, relative to the full ratchet, Janet experiences a modest amount of economic dilution of her option value (though not as much as if she had no antidilution protection). This, in turn, causes more value to remain in Francis's equity claim than in the full ratchet example.

Finally, we close this discussion of antidilution protection with two drafting issues that commonly arise in this context. First, our examples have all assumed that NewCo sells shares of common stock at the "cheap" price. But what if a company subsequently issues other securities, such as convertible preferred stock or common stock options? In general, an investor will be concerned about any issuance of securities at a "cheap" price that dilutes its ownership stake in the company's residual claim (i.e., an investor will worry about any issuance of securities that are included in the fully-diluted capitalization). As a result, antidilution provisions can typically be triggered by the sale of common stock or securities that can be converted into (or exercised for) common stock. In the case of convertible and exercisable securities, the relevant question to ask is whether the conversion price or exercise price of these securities is less than the conversion price of the stock having antidilution protection. If so, their issuance will generally trigger the antidilution provision as if the underlying shares of common stock were sold at the conversion/exercise price.

Second, the drafter of antidilution protection must be careful to ask whether *every* cheap stock issuance should trigger an antidilution adjustment. This is especially important in the context of a ratchet provision where a single share of stock issued at a cheap price can trigger a conversion price adjustment. In practice, it is typical to exclude the issuance of shares from triggering an antidilution adjustment if the issuance relates to a cheap stock issuance that is for non-financing purposes, such as the issuance of stock and stock options to employees or consultants in the ordinary course of business.

Problem 8.1

In light of the foregoing drafting considerations, review Section 4(d)(i) and Section 4(d)(ii) of Article IV(B) of Lyft's Charter as set forth in the Appendix to this book. These two provisions describe the antidilution protection that applies to Lyft's preferred stock. What type of antidilution protection does Section 4(d)(i) reflect? Which of the two drafting considerations discussed in the main text is addressed in Section 4(d)(i) (E)? Which is addressed in Section 4(d)(ii)?

Sidebar: Pricing an Equity Financing That Triggers Antidilution Protection in Options and Convertible Securities

In Chapter 5, we introduced the concept of antidilution protection in the context of an all common stock capital structure. There, we examined how a common stockholder can protect itself against the economic dilution that arises from a cheap stock issuance by securing a contractual right to be issued new shares if the company sells stock in the future at a price below the price paid by the investor. As you may recall, this contract right was secured by Texas Pacific Group in its common stock investment in Washington Mutual in 2008.

In effect, this type of provision is similar to the concept of using a conversion price adjustment in the wake of a cheap stock issuance. As shown in the examples above, the end result of these conversion price adjustments is for the protected preferred stock to have the right to convert into a greater number of shares of common stock, thereby diminishing the dilution of the preferred stock's conversion value. As with the direct issuance of new shares considered in Chapter 5, new investors will seek to include the increase in the preferred stock's underlying common shares in the company's pre-financing fully-diluted capitalization when setting a price per share for the financing. Otherwise, the conversion price adjustment will dilute the new investor and cause the investor to hold less of an ownership claim than it expects from the economics of the financing.

As was done in Chapter 5, we can accomplish this pricing modification by including any "antidilution" shares as part of the pre-financing fully-diluted capitalization. Using the share pricing equation from Chapter 5, the investor would calculate the price per share as:

$$\frac{\textit{Pre-Financing Valuation}}{\textit{Actual Pre-Financing FDS} + \textit{“Antidilution Shares”}} = \textit{New Issuance Price}$$

While conceptually simple, implementing this approach is complicated by the fact that the conversion price adjustment (and therefore, the number of antidilution shares) depends on the New Issuance Price, which (as shown in the equation) depends on the number of antidilution shares. As discussed in Chapter 5, we can use Excel's iterative calculation to solve this problem by creating a spreadsheet that has two components. In one component, we calculate the *New Issuance Price;* in the other, we calculate the conversion price adjustment and the number of *Antidilution Shares*, taking care that the calculation of New Issuance Price is linked to the cell calculating the Antidilution Shares and vice versa. The spreadsheet entitled “Pricing Model with Preferred Stock Antidilution Protection” on the casebook website provides an example of this calculation using Arigo Ventures' $800 investment in NewCo. In the tab entitled “Ratchet Model,” we assume that the 60 shares of preferred stock held by Janet have full ratchet antidilution protection. Assuming Arigo Ventures uses an $800 pre-financing valuation of the company, the left-side of the spreadsheet calculates the price per share in Cell C12:

	A	B	C	D	E	F
1	**Pricing Model Where Preferred Stock Has Full Ratchet Antidilution Protection**					
2						
3		**Pricing Formula:**			**Conversion Price Adjustment:**	
4						
5		**Numerator:**			Original Conversion Price	10
6		Pre-Money Valuation:	800		New Conversion Price	=C12
7		**Denominator:**			New Preferred Stock Conversion Ratio:	=10/F6
8		Outstanding Common Stock (as converted)	=60+40			
9		"Antidilution Shares"	=F12		Pre-financing Preferred Stock (as-converted):	60
10		*total:*	=SUM(C8:C9)		Post-financing Preferred Stock (as converted):	=F9*F7
11						
12		**Price (Numerator/Denominator):**	=C6/C10		"Antidilution Shares"	=F10-F9

Note that the denominator of the pricing equation (C10) includes both the actual shares outstanding prior to the financing (C8) and the “Antidilution Shares” (C9), which references the cell F12. F12 (the number of Antidilution Shares) is calculated on the right side of the spreadsheet. Since the preferred stock has a full ratchet antidilution protection, the new conversion price (F6) simply cross-references the price per share calculated in C12, which is then used to calculate the new conversion ratio (F7) and the number of Antidilution Shares (F12). Of course, given the contents of C12 and F6, we now have a circular system of references. However, by turning on the “iterative” calculation functionality (see Chapter 5), Excel will converge on the correct price per share, which in this case is $5/share:

	A	B	C	D	E	F
1	**Pricing Model Where Preferred Stock Has Full Ratchet Antidilution Protection**					
2						
3		**Pricing Formula:**			**Conversion Price Adjustment:**	
4						
5		**Numerator:**			Original Conversion Price	$10.00
6		Pre-Money Valuation:	$800		New Conversion Price	$5.00
7		**Denominator:**			New Preferred Stock Conversion Ratio:	2.00
8		Outstanding Common Stock (as converted)	100			
9		"Antidilution Shares"	60		Pre-financing Preferred Stock (as-converted):	60
10		*total:*	160		Post-financing Preferred Stock (as converted):	120
11						
12		**Price (Numerator/Denominator):**	$5.00		"Antidilution Shares"	60

The spreadsheet also provides an example of this calculation when the preferred stock has weighted-average antidilution protection.

While this discussion of antidilution protection has focused on the use of antidilution protection in the context of convertible preferred stock, the risk of a cheap stock issuance is a general one faced by holders of all types of common stock options and convertible securities. As a result, it is common to see antidilution protection incorporated into other types of options and convertibles securities, such as warrants and convertible notes. We shall see examples of the use of antidilution protection in these other contexts in some of the cases we explore in the following section.

C. CONVERTIBLE SECURITIES AND THE INCOMPLETE CONTRACTING PROBLEM

In the earlier chapters on debt and preferred stock financing, we discovered that investors in these securities face a challenging incomplete contracting problem. These instruments can create conflicts of interest between common stockholders and the more senior investors. Accordingly, it is often wise to negotiate for contract provisions that seek to protect against corporate actions that enrich common stockholders at the expense of debt and preferred stock investors. Yet, contracts are necessarily incomplete because investors can't anticipate all future states of the world where a firm's directors and managers (who are presumably loyal to common stockholders) will be able to take opportunistic actions. Further, while various contract doctrines exist to address the challenge of incomplete contracts (e.g., the duty of good faith and fair dealing and exceptions to the parol evidence rule), these doctrines are given a narrow construction in the context of debt and preferred stock contracting. In the following cases, do courts seem to take a similar approach to the incomplete contracting problem that faces holders of options and convertible securities? If not, do they conform to the classical rules of contract law, or is there some other legal principle that seems to apply to these agreements?

Stephenson v. Plastics Corporation of America, Inc.

276 Minn. 400, 150 N.W.2d 668 (1967)

■ SHERAN, JUSTICE.

Action was instituted by plaintiffs against defendants on the theory that defendant Plastics Corporation of America, Inc., (hereafter called Plastics) breached contract obligations springing from stock purchase warrants issued by it, and that defendant United Fabricators and Electronics, Inc., (hereafter called United) participated in the resulting wrong to the plaintiffs by conduct constituting willful and malicious interference with the contract relationship. Defendant Plastics denied the claimed breach of contract and cross-claimed for indemnity as against United in the event plaintiffs should prevail. United denied the alleged breach of contract and the asserted unlawful interference. Each defendant moved for judgment on the pleadings. United's motion was granted; Plastics' was denied.

* * *

The Warrants

The stock subscription warrants are dated December 16, 1960. It will be helpful, at the outset, to place their provisions in these compartments:

(A) The principal object of the agreements.

(B) Corporate changes conceived as affecting the principal object of the agreements.

(C) Mechanisms provided for preserving the principal object of the agreements in the event of such changes.

(D) Provisions for notice of such corporate changes.

A. Principal Object

The principal object of the agreements was to afford the holders or their assigns (such as these plaintiffs) the option for a period of 5 years to obtain 30,000 shares of the "capital" stock of the company at the price of $1 per share. It is specifically provided that the warrants were not to entitle the holders to any voting rights or other rights as a stockholder of the company.

B. Anticipated Corporate Changes

In an apparent effort to prevent a defeat of the basic purpose of the warrants by a change in corporate circumstances, 12 different possible situations are anticipated in paragraph 3 of the agreements:

(1) A distribution upon capital stock payable in capital stock, i.e., a "stock dividend."[2]

---

[2] 3(a). "In case the Company shall declare any dividend or other distribution upon its outstanding capital stock payable in capital stock or shall subdivide its outstanding shares of capital stock into a greater number of shares, then the number of shares of capital stock which may thereafter be purchased upon the exercise of the rights represented hereby shall be

(2) A division ("split") of the outstanding capital stock.[2]

(3) A combining ("reverse split") of outstanding capital stock.[2]

(4) A cash dividend upon stock not payable from net earnings or earned surplus.[3]

(5) Such a dividend upon stock but not payable in cash.[3]

(6) A capital "reorganization."[4]

(7) A reclassification of stock.[4]

(8) A consolidation with another corporation.[4]

(9) A merger with another corporation.[4]

(10) The sale of all or substantially all of the assets of the corporation to another corporation.[4]

(11) An offer to holders of capital stock for pro rata subscription for additional shares of stock or any other rights.[5]

(12) A voluntary or involuntary dissolution.[5]

---

increased in proportion to the increase through such dividend or subdivision and the purchase price per share shall be decreased in such proportion. In case the Company shall at any time combine the outstanding shares of its capital stock into a smaller number of shares, the number of shares of capital stock which may thereafter be purchased upon the exercise of the rights represented hereby shall be decreased in proportion to the decrease through such combination and the purchase price per share shall be increased in such proportion."

3 3(b). "In case the Company shall declare a dividend upon the capital stock payable otherwise than out of earnings or surplus (other than paid-in surplus) or otherwise than in capital stock, the purchase price per share in effect immediately prior to the declaration of such dividend shall be reduced by an amount equal, in the case of a dividend in cash, to the amount thereof payable per share of the capital stock or, in the case of any other dividend, to the fair value thereof per share of the capital stock as determined by the Board of Directors of the Company. For the purposes of the foregoing a dividend other than in cash shall be considered payable out of earnings or surplus (other than paid-in surplus) only to the extent that such earnings or surplus are charged an amount equal to the fair value of such dividend as determined by the Board of Directors of the Company. Such reductions shall take effect as of the date on which a record is taken for the purpose of such dividend, or, if a record is not taken, the date as of which the holders of capital stock of record entitled to such dividend are to be determined."

4 3(c). "If any capital reorganization or reclassification of the capital stock of the Company, or consolidation or merger of the Company with another corporation, or the sale of all or substantially all of its assets to another corporation shall be effected, then, as a condition of such reorganization, reclassification, consolidation, merger or sale, lawful and adequate provision shall be made whereby the holder hereof shall thereafter have the right to purchase and receive upon the basis and upon the terms and conditions specified in this Warrant and in lieu of the shares of the capital stock of the Company immediately theretofore purchasable and receivable upon the exercise of the rights represented hereby, such shares of stock, securities or assets as may be issued or payable with respect to or in exchange for a number of outstanding shares of such capital stock equal to the number of shares of such capital stock immediately theretofore purchasable and receivable upon the exercise of the rights represented hereby had such reorganization, reclassification, consolidation, merger or sale not taken place, and in any such case appropriate provision shall be made with respect to the rights and interests of the holder of this Warrant to the end that the provisions hereof (including without limitation provisions for adjustment of the purchase price per share and of the number of shares purchasable upon the exercise of this Warrant) shall thereafter be applicable, as nearly as may be in relation to any shares of stock, securities or assets thereafter deliverable upon the exercise hereof." (Italics supplied.)

5 Reference to situations 11 and 12 is to be found in the notice provision set out in footnote 11.

C. Contemplated Adjustment

In the event of the occurrence of situations 1 to 3 (stock dividends; splits; reverse splits) the warrants provide for adjustment by decrease or increase in the number of shares purchasable and the price per share to be paid.[6]

In situations 4 and 5 (depleting dividend) the adjustment is to be accomplished by reducing the purchase price per share (i.e., $1 per share) by (a) the amount of the dividend, if paid in cash, and (b) the fair value of distributed assets other than cash.[7]

In situations 6 to 10 (reorganization; stock reclassification; consolidation; merger; sale of all or substantially all assets) it is required by paragraph 3(c) of the agreement that "appropriate provision" be made for the protection of the rights and interests of the warrant holders.[8]

Paragraph 3(c) which deals with situations 6 to 10 concludes with this sentence:

> " * * * Any such shares of stock, securities or assets which the holder hereof may be entitled to purchase pursuant to this paragraph (c) shall be included within the term 'capital stock' as used herein."

This sentence becomes significant when considered in conjunction with paragraph 2 of the agreements which concludes with this sentence:

> " * * * The Company further covenants and agrees that during the period within which the rights represented by this Warrant may be exercised, the Company will at all times have authorized, and reserved, a sufficient number of shares of capital stock to provide for the exercise of the rights represented by this Warrant * * *." (Italics supplied.)

We interpret these provisions, considered together, to impose on Plastics an obligation to have reserved a sufficient number of shares of United stock to provide for the exercise of the rights represented by the warrants if the arrangement planned and executed by the seven directors of the two corporations, described hereinafter, amounted to a reorganization; stock reclassification; consolidation; merger; or a sale of all or substantially all of Plastics' assets to United.

Paragraph 3(c) provided with respect to situations 8 to 10 (consolidation; merger; sale of all or substantially all of assets) that the successor corporation should be required to assume "the obligation to deliver to such [warrant] holder such shares of stock, securities or assets

[6] See footnote 2, supra.

[7] See footnote 3, supra.

[8] See footnote 4, supra.

as, in accordance with the foregoing provisions, such holder may be entitled to purchase."[9]

D. Notice Provisions

In situations 1 to 3 (stock dividends; splits; reverse splits) set out above, the company obligates itself to give notice to the warrant holder stating "the purchase price per share resulting from such adjustment and the increase or decrease, if any, in the number of shares purchasable at such price upon the exercise of this Warrant."[10]

In situations 1 (stock dividend) and 4 to 12 (dividends; reorganization; reclassification; consolidation; merger; sale of all or substantially all of assets; subscription offer; dissolution) a 20-day notice to the warrant holder is required by paragraph 3(e) which notice in situations 4 and 5 (dividends), 11 (subscription offer), and 12 (dissolution) at least, must specify "the date on which the holders of capital stock shall be entitled thereto," and in situations 6 (reorganization), 7 (reclassification), 8 (consolidation), 9 (merger), 10 (sale) and 12 (dissolution) must specify "the date on which the holders of capital stock shall be entitled to exchange their capital stock for securities or other property."[11]

---

[9] 3(c). " * * * The Company shall not effect any such consolidation, merger or sale, unless prior to or simultaneously with the consummation thereof the successor corporation (if other than the Company) resulting from such consolidation or merger or the corporation purchasing such assets shall assume by written instrument executed and mailed or delivered to the holder hereof at the last address of such holder appearing on the books of the Company, the obligation to deliver to such holder such shares of stock, securities or assets as, in accordance with the foregoing provisions, such holder may be entitled to purchase."

[10] 3(d). "Upon any adjustment of the number of shares of capital stock which may be purchased upon the exercise of the rights represented hereby and/or of the purchase price per share, then and in each such case the Company shall give written notice thereof, by first class mail, postage prepaid, addressed to the holder of this Warrant at the address of such holder as shown on the books of the Company, which notice shall state the purchase price per share resulting from such adjustment and the increase or decrease, if any, in the number of shares purchasable at such price upon the exercise of this Warrant, setting forth in reasonable detail the method of calculation and the facts upon which such calculation is based."

[11] 3(e). "In case at any time:

"(1) the Company shall pay any dividend payable in stock upon its capital stock or make any distribution (other than regular cash dividends paid at an established annual rate) to the holders of its capital stock;

"(2) the Company shall offer for subscription pro rata to the holders of its capital stock any additional shares of stock of any class or other rights;

"(3) there shall be any capital reorganization, or reclassification of the capital stock of the Company, or consolidation or merger of the Company with, or sale of all or substantially all of its assets to, another corporation; or

"(4) there shall be a voluntary or involuntary dissolution, liquidation or winding up of the Company; then, in any one or more of such cases, the Company shall give to the holder of this Warrant (aa) at least twenty days' prior written notice of the date on which the books of the Company shall close or a record shall be taken for such dividend, distribution or subscription rights or for determining rights to vote in respect of any such reorganization, reclassification, consolidation, merger, sale, dissolution, liquidation or winding up, and (bb) in the case of any such reorganization, reclassification, consolidation, merger, sale, dissolution, liquidation or winding up, at least twenty days' prior written notice of the date when the same shall take place. Such notice in accordance with the foregoing clause (aa) shall also specify, in the case of any such dividend, distribution or subscription rights, the date on which the holders of capital stock shall be entitled thereto, and such notice in accordance with the foregoing clause (bb) shall also

The Corporate Change

In the latter part of 1964 and at a time when the warrants analyzed above were outstanding, Plastics was controlled and governed by a board of seven directors who agreed among themselves:

(1) A part of the assets of Plastics then devoted to the production of thermoplastic products by one of the divisions of Plastics should be transferred to a newly created corporation; the newly created corporation should, in exchange, transfer all of its stock to Plastics. (The new corporation, United Fabricators and Electronics, Inc., which we refer to as "United," was incorporated March 11, 1965.)

(2) All of the stock of the newly created corporation to be transferred to Plastics should be distributed to Plastics shareholders of record on February 22, 1965, and warrant holders exercising their stock options by March 16, 1965. (This agreement to distribute all of the stock of the newly created corporation to Plastics shareholders of necessity made it impossible for Plastics to reserve a sufficient number of shares of United's stock to provide for the exercise of an option with respect to such stock after March 16, 1965, but before expiration of the 5-year option period.)

(3) Three of the seven directors then in control of Plastics should resign and become the directors of United. The four remaining should continue in control of Plastics.

(4) The United stock to be acquired by the four directors of Plastics as a result of the distribution contemplated by step (2) above should be exchanged for the Plastics stock held by the three departing directors so that the one group would be in control of United and the other in control of Plastics when the transaction was completed.

Agreements were made intending to bind the seven directors and the corporations (Plastics and United) to this plan, and these agreements have been fully executed.

On February 24, 1965, Plastics gave notice to holders of stock purchase warrants, including plaintiffs, reading as follows:

> "You are hereby notified that the Directors of Plastics Corporation of America, Inc. have authorized a distribution on March 31, 1965 to the common shareholders of said corporation of one (1) share of United Fabricators & Electronics, Inc. for each two (2) shares of Plastics Corporation of America, Inc. held of record on February 22, 1965.
>
> "Inasmuch as the holders of Stock Purchase Warrants of Plastics Corporation of America, Inc. are entitled to twenty

---

specify the date on which the holders of capital stock shall be entitled to exchange their capital stock for securities or other property deliverable upon such reorganization, reclassification, consolidation, merger, sale, dissolution, liquidation or winding up, as the case may be. Each such written notice shall be given by first class mail, postage prepaid, addressed to the holder of this Warrant at the address of such holder as shown on the books of the Company."

days' notice of such distribution, the Directors have established March 16, 1965 as the record date for such distribution for the holders of Stock Purchase Warrants who shall hereafter become a shareholder by reason of the exercise of such Warrants."

Plaintiffs did not undertake to exercise their option to purchase Plastics stock until December 1965. We assume for present purposes (but do not decide) that they made an effective exercise of the option embodied in the warrants before the expiration of the 5-year period specified in it.

The theory of plaintiffs' pleading is that they are entitled upon exercise of their option before the expiration of the 5-year period to have the shares of Plastics stock specified in the warrants and in addition that number of the shares of United stock which would have been distributed to plaintiffs had they been stockholders when the distribution of United stock was in fact made; and that if specific performance is impossible, damages should be awarded.

1. In our opinion, the order of the trial court granting judgment for United against plaintiffs on the pleadings can be sustained if, but only if, any one of these legal conclusions follow from the facts summarized:

(a) The warrants created no right in plaintiffs to share in the distribution of United stock in any event.

* * *

2a. If the distribution of United stock was a dividend not charged to net earnings or earned surplus, plaintiffs would have no right as against United because in such event, by the terms of the warrants, plaintiffs' position was to be protected by reducing the purchase price per share of Plastics stock by the fair value of the United stock determined as of the date of distribution. In our opinion, it cannot be held on the present record that the parties to the warrants intended a transaction of this kind to be treated as a dividend.

* * *

There is a difference between the transactions involved in the present case and a "dividend" in the usual sense of that word. In Hoberg v. John Hoberg Co., 170 Wis. 50, 173 N.W. 639, 173 N.W. 952, it was held that a corporation's pro rata distribution to its stockholders of recently acquired stock of another corporation was not a dividend, emphasizing that no attempt was made to meet a dividend obligation by the transfer. In determining whether a transaction constitutes a "dividend," consideration must be given to the context in which the term "dividend" is used; the consequences that turn upon the answer to the question; and the facts of the particular case. We believe that it would be premature to rule as a matter of law upon the limited record now before us that the present transaction was intended to be a "dividend" within the meaning of the warrants.

Ordinarily the object of a dividend is to enable the shareholders to enjoy the fruits of a corporate operation. It is at least indexable that the purpose of the distribution of United's stock to Plastics shareholders was intended primarily (a) to enable the directors who remained with Plastics to acquire the stock of that corporation distributed to the three directors who were taking over the management of United and (b) to give the three departing directors control of the newly created corporation through exchange of their Plastics stock for the distributed shares of United coming into the hands of the four Plastics directors who remained. In fact it is reasonable to infer that this exchange of United's stock for Plastics after the distribution was an essential part of the agreement between the seven directors and that but for this understanding the "spin-off" would never have taken place. So considered, we cannot say that the warrants declare clearly and unambiguously that a transaction of this character was intended to be treated as a "dividend" within the meaning of the language of the warrants.

We do not disagree with United's contention that a "spin-off" can involve or be executed by a means of a dividend of a new company's stock to the old company's shareholders. See, Rockefeller v. United States, 257 U.S. 176, 42 S. Ct. 68, 66 L. Ed. 186; Siegel, When Corporations Divide: A Statutory and Financial Analysis, 79 Harv. L. Rev. 534. We hold only that the question cannot be resolved in the present situation without the aid of extrinsic evidence.

2b. If the transaction does not represent a "dividend" within the meaning of the warrants, then what was it? Plaintiffs contend that it was a capital reorganization (situation 6 above) or a sale of all or substantially all of the assets of the corporation to another corporation (situation 10 above). If so (unless the notice set out above served to accelerate the time within which plaintiffs' option was exercisable with respect to the distribution), the corporation was obligated by the terms of the warrants to reserve a sufficient number of shares of United stock to permit the exercise of the right of the warrant holders to acquire it for the full 5-year term of the warrants. This is so because paragraph 3(c) of the agreement provides that, in the event of any capital reorganization or the sale of all or substantially all of the corporate assets to another corporation, "lawful and adequate provision shall be made whereby the holder hereof shall thereafter have the right to purchase and receive * * * such shares of stock, securities or assets as may be issued or payable with respect to or in exchange for a number of outstanding shares of such capital stock equal to the number of shares or such capital stock immediately theretofore purchasable and receivable upon the exercise of the rights represented hereby had such reorganization, * * * or sale not taken place." The obligation to hold the required number of shares of United in reserve follows from the concluding sentence of paragraph 3(c)[12] requiring that any such shares of stock or assets be included within the term "capital stock" as used in the warrants.

2c. Although not free from ambiguity, we believe it would be possible for the plaintiffs to establish that the transaction here involved was a "capital reorganization" within the meaning of the warrants. The net result was that each Plastics shareholder held an interest represented by stock in exactly the same assets after the transaction as before. Before the transaction this interest was represented by stock in one corporation only; after the transaction the interest was represented by stock held in two corporations. All that was changed was the "organization."

The pertinent Federal and Minnesota income tax provisions declare transactions of this kind to be "reorganizations."[13]

* * *

United points out that the warrant contracts provide that upon reorganization a warrant holder is entitled to receive "*in lieu of* the shares of the capital stock of the Company immediately theretofore purchasable and receivable" certain stock or other assets of the transferee corporation. (Italics supplied.) It asserts that this shows that the parties to the warrant contracts contemplated that upon the reorganization a new corporation would take over and completely supersede the old one.

However, this provision does not compel the interpretation defendant would give it. It may simply mean that the warrant holder is entitled to a certain amount of stock of the old corporation, and in addition thereto (and in lieu merely of more stock of the old corporation),

---

12 The sentence, to which reference has been made, reads: "Any such shares of stock, securities or assets which the holder hereof may be entitled to purchase pursuant to this paragraph (c) shall be included within the term 'capital stock' as used herein."

13 Section 368(a) of the 1954 Internal Revenue Code, 68A Stat. 120, 26 USCA, § 368(a), provides in part:

> "(a) Reorganization.—
>
> "(1) In General.—For purposes of parts I and II and this part, the term 'reorganization' means—
>
> * * *
>
> "(D) a transfer by a corporation of all or a part of its assets to another corporation if immediately after the transfer the transferor, or one or more of its shareholders (including persons who were shareholders immediately before the transfer), or any combination thereof, is in control of the corporation to which the assets are transferred; but only if, in pursuance of the plan, stock or securities of the corporation to which the assets are transferred are distributed in a transaction which qualifies under section 354, 355, or 356."

Section 355 covers, inter alia, a corporation's distributions to its shareholders of stock of a corporation which it controlled immediately before the distribution.

Minn. St. 290.136, subd. 9(a)(1)(D), is identical to the Federal provision.

United asserts that the present transaction was taxed as an ordinary dividend rather than as a reorganization, but this fact does not establish that it was a dividend as the term is used in the warrant.

a certain amount of stock of the new corporation. Especially is this interpretation justifiable in light of the fact that the words in question also control where there has been a sale of "all or substantially all" of Plastics' assets. In the event of a sale of only substantially all of Plastics' assets, the agreement probably contemplates the warrant holder receiving both Plastics stock and stock of the vendee.

Defendant points out that the stock warrants' reference to Plastics' duty to require the "successor corporation" to assume the duty to honor the stock warrants covers only situations of consolidation, merger, or sale of all or substantially all of Plastics' assets and urges that this must mean that "capital reorganization" comprehends only situations involving a structural change within Plastics. But a change in Plastics' structure resulting in the birth of a new corporation is not necessarily excluded from the term "capital reorganization" by this language. The same may be said of the fact that the warrants referred to the giving of 20-day notice of the date that the books would close and a record would be taken "for determining rights to vote in respect of any such reorganization." Defendant insists this means that only "reorganizations" upon which shareholders vote in accordance with § 301.55 are included. Again, the argument is persuasive, but not so clear that plaintiffs should not be allowed to present evidence on the matter.

2d. In the alternative, plaintiffs urge that the evidence may establish that the transaction was a sale of "all or substantially all" of Plastics' assets. The complaint does not allege any particular proportion of Plastics' assets as having been transferred, merely stating that "the assets of its United Fabricators and Electronics Division, and certain other assets" were transferred.[15] Thus, at this stage of the proceedings, no proper evidence has been adduced on such matters as the proportion of Plastics' assets which were transferred; the nature of those assets (as compared to that of the assets retained); the relationship of the assets transferred and of those retained to Plastics' past and present objects and purposes; or the degree to which the transfer was unusual and out of the ordinary course of Plastics' business.

* * *

Conclusion

The difficulty we have had with this case comes from the fact that the provisions of the warrants do not seem to deal specifically with a situation such as that described in the pleadings where, in an apparent effort to resolve a conflict in business judgment as between the directors, the assets of the original corporation are divided with one group given

[15] Defendant asserts that the claim that transfer was of substantially all of Plastics' assets "is clearly refuted by facts contained in the pleadings which make it clear that the spin-off involved something less than one-half of PCA's net worth," citing a portion of the complaint and certain documents made part of Plastics' pleadings. Plastics' pleadings are not to be considered as admitted on this motion on the pleadings; moreover, the portions cited do not clearly support defendant's assertion.

operating control of one phase of the corporate activity and the other assuming control of the balance. It is reasonable, in view of the elaborate effort to anticipate all possible changes that might affect the rights of warrant holders, to attribute to Plastics a general intent that the option rights of persons in the position of these plaintiffs should not be diminished by an arrangement which seems to have been particularly responsive to the needs of those in control of the corporation. But the language of the warrants is not so clear and unequivocal as to give a solution to the present problem without affording the parties an opportunity to present such evidence as may be available to clarify the ambiguities which have been discussed.

* * *

Reversed and remanded.

QUESTIONS

1. Why isn't this a dividend not payable in cash, covered by Paragraph 3(b) of the agreement?
2. Does this opinion suggest that no spin-off transaction, in which shareholders receive shares in a former subsidiary, would ever be covered by the adjustment for dividends other than in cash?
3. If the court had treated this transaction as a dividend not payable in cash, what provision would have been made to protect the warrant holders?
4. What exactly is a "capital reorganization"? Is this a defined term in the agreements quoted? See if you can find a clear definition on the Internet.

Wood v. Coastal States Gas Corporation

401 A.2d 932 (Del. 1979)

■ DUFFY, J.

This appeal is from an order of the Court of Chancery dismissing the complaints in a consolidated class action filed by the owners of two series of preferred stock[1] in Coastal States Gas Corporation (Coastal), a Delaware corporation. The suit is against Coastal, two of its subsidiaries and its chief executive officer. While this litigation is part of a complex controversy in a mosaic of many persons and disputes, it is entirely between the owners of Coastal's preferred stock and the owners of its common stock.

---

[1] One series is designated, "$1.83 Cumulative Convertible Preferred Stock, Series B," and the other, "$1.19 Cumulative Convertible Preferred Stock, Series A." The certificate of rights and preferences for each series is identical and thus what is said herein of one is applicable to both. We will refer to the stock in the singular as "Series A," or "Series B," or the "preferred stock."

I

The facts out of which the dispute arises involve the sale and delivery of natural gas to many cities and corporate users in the State of Texas and, although our involvement is limited, we must recite some of them to put the appeal into context. For that purpose, the relevant facts are these:

A significant part of Coastal's business is the gathering, transporting and marketing of natural gas, all of which is conducted by a subsidiary, Coastal States Gas Producing Co. (Producing), also a defendant in this action. Producing, in turn, has a subsidiary, Lo-Vac. Gathering Co. (Lo-Vac.), another defendant, which supplies the gas to intrastate customers in Texas, including the Cities of Austin, Brownsville, Corpus Christi and San Antonio.

As a result of several factors associated with the "energy crisis" in the early 1970s, the wellhead price of natural gas increased significantly (from about 20 cents per 1000 cubic feet to about $2.00 for the same quantity) and Lo-Vac. was unable to honor its obligations to deliver gas to its customers at contract prices. In 1973, Lo-Vac. sought and obtained interim permission from the Railroad Commission of Texas (the agency vested with jurisdiction over intrastate utilities in Texas) to increase its rates; that authorization permitted Lo-Vac. to pass to its customers certain of its own cost increases. After the higher rates went into effect, a large number of Lo-Vac. industrial and municipal customers filed suits against Lo-Vac., Producing, Coastal and Oscar Wyatt (Coastal's chief executive officer, the owner of the single largest block of its common stock and a defendant in this suit) for breach of contract.

In December 1977, the Commission entered a final order denying Lo-Vac.'s original petition for rate relief and, in effect, rescinding the interim order which had authorized the increase. The Commission then directed Lo-Vac. to comply with the contract rates and ordered Coastal, Producing and Lo-Vac. to refund the rate increment which had been charged to customers under the 1973 interim order. It is estimated that the refundable amount exceeds $1.6 billion—which is about three times Coastal's net worth.

Given this state of affairs, with its obvious and enormous implications for a large section of Texas, settlement negotiations were undertaken and, eventually, a complex plan evolved. It is unnecessary for us to detail the plan, but the following summary states its substance:

(1) The substantial litigation and disputes between the natural gas sales customers of Lo-Vac. and Coastal, Producing, Lo-Vac. and Wyatt, which developed as a result of the "Lo-Vac. problem," will be settled;

(2) Producing will be renamed "Valery Energy Corporation," restructured into a corporate enterprise and spun off from Coastal; it will consist principally of Producing's present gas

utility pipe-line and extraction plant operations, including Lo-Vac., and a Texas retail gas distribution division of Coastal;

(3) There will be transfers to a trust for the benefit of the customers who adopt the settlement plan ("Settling Customers") of: (a) approximately 1,196,218 shares (or about 5.3%) of the voting securities of Coastal; (b) a one-year interest-bearing promissory note of Valery in the principal amount of $8,000,000; (c)) 13.4% of the outstanding shares of the common stock of Valery; and (d) 1,150,000 shares ($115,000,000 aggregate liquidation value) of Valery Preferred Stock, $8.50 Cumulative Series A;

(4) Coastal will issue to Valery approximately 805,130 shares (with approximately $80,513,000 aggregate liquidation value) of Coastal's $8.50 Cumulative Preferred Stock, Series D, $.33 1/3 par value (which is a new class of stock);

(5) A long-term program will be established providing for the expenditure of $180,000,000 to $230,000,000 (subject to certain increases or decreases, with a maximum commitment estimated at $495,000,000), by Coastal to find and develop gas reserves to be made available to the Lo-Vac. System and to be offered for sale by Coastal to Valery at discounted prices and, in turn, resold to Lo-Vac. (or, in some instances, to third parties) at higher prices, with the net proceeds (in excess of the cost of gas) received by Valery on such resale to be paid to the trust for the benefit of certain Settling Customers;

(6) There will be a new gas sales rate structure for Lo-Vac. designed to stabilize it as a viable public utility.

In addition, there will be a distribution by Coastal, in the form of an extraordinary dividend chargeable to earned surplus, to its common stockholders (except Wyatt) of the balance (86.6%) of the Valery common stock not transferred to the trust referred to in (3)(c)) above.[2] Shareholders will receive one share of Valery for each share of Coastal common held at the time of the spin-off. It is this distribution which is at the center of this litigation between the preferred and common stockholders of Coastal. And Coastal's dividend history of annual payments to the preferred but none (with one exception) to the common suggests a reason for this. Coastal has paid regular quarterly dividends of $.2975 per share on the $1.19 Series A and $.4575 per share on the $1.83 Series B since each was issued. Only one dividend of $.075 per share has been paid on the common in the last twenty years.

---

2 The Valero shares trade on a "when issued" basis at $6.50 to $7.00 per share (against an assumed market value of $6.50 per share).

Coastal's Board of Directors unanimously approved the settlement[3] and, in August 1978, the Commission gave its approval. The Coastal management then submitted the plan for approval at a special meeting of its stockholders called for November 10.

* * *

Holders of the Series A and Series B preferred stock, (plaintiffs), filed an action in the Court of Chancery to enjoin the special shareholders meeting. They alleged that the settlement plan breaches the "Certificate of the Designations, Preferences and Relative, Participating Optional or other Special Rights" (Certificate) of the Series A and Series B preferred stock. In essence, plaintiffs say that the plan violates their Certificate rights because the preferred will not receive any of the Valery shares, that is, the 86.6% to be distributed entirely to the Coastal common.

After a trial on the merits, the Vice Chancellor entered judgment for defendants and ordered plaintiffs to pay the costs of giving notice to the members of the class of the pendency of the action. The Court determined that the settlement plan and, more specifically, the spin-off of Producing and the distribution of Valery stock to the common stockholders of Coastal, is not a "recapitalization" within the meaning of the Certificate. (If it is, all parties concede that the preferred is entitled to participate in the distribution of the Valery shares.) The Vice Chancellor reasoned that a key phrase, "in lieu of," in the Certificate implies that the existing shares of Coastal common must be exchanged for something else before there is a "recapitalization" which creates rights in the preferred. And he found support for that conclusion in another Certificate provision which permits Coastal to pay a dividend to holders of common stock, in other than its own common, without affecting the rights of the preferred.

The Court also ruled that the holders of the preferred stock were not entitled to vote as a class on the settlement plan, because the requirements of the Certificate for such a vote had not been met.

Finally, the Court considered plaintiffs' claims that the settlement plan is unfair to the preferred, unjustly enriched the common and did not have a proper business purpose, and concluded that the rights of the preferred are found, under the circumstances of this case, solely in the Certificate, not in concepts of fairness or fiduciary duty.

On appeal, plaintiffs challenge each of these rulings, as well as the order requiring them to pay the costs of giving notice to the class.

---

[3] Fletcher Yarbrough, who had been nominated by the Securities and Exchange Commission to serve as a director on the Coastal Board, testified at trial that the

> ". . . complex of problems relating to Lo-Vaca, both before the Railroad Commission and in the litigation, simply had to be settled, that there was a truly unacceptably high risk that this problem could destroy the corporation and the value of the shares of the corporation. . ."

II

Before discussing the merits of the controversy, we emphasize that this lawsuit is not a general attack upon the settlement plan. On the contrary, plaintiffs say that they approve the plan and hope to see it executed. As we have observed, the case involves a dispute between the preferred vis-a-vis the common over participation rights in the Valery stock to be distributed as part of the spin-off. As we understand it, that is the extent of plaintiffs' attack upon the plan.

The preferred has a conversion right to exchange for the common on a one-to-one basis. Briefly stated, the preferred argues that a distribution of Valery stock to the common only, and without provision for permitting the preferred to share therein now or at the time of conversion, violates its Certificate rights. We now examine those rights in some detail.

* * *

B.

For most purposes, the rights of the preferred shareholders as against the common shareholders are fixed by the contractual terms agreed upon when the class of preferred stock is created. And, as to the conversion privilege, it has been said that the rights of a preferred shareholder are "least affected by rules of law and most dependent on the share contract." Buxbaum, "Preferred Stock—Law and Draftsmanship," 42 Cal.L.Rev. 243, 279 (1954).

Our duty, then, is to construe the contract governing the preferred shares. In so doing, we employ the methods used to interpret contracts generally; that is, we consider the entire instrument and attempt to reconcile all of its provisions "in order to determine the meaning intended to be given to any portion of it." More to the point, we must construe the several qualifications of the conversion privilege which are stated in Sections (c)(4)–(7) of the Certificate.

C.

The basic conversion privilege is stated in Section (a) of the Certificate: at the option of the holder, each share of preferred is convertible into one share of common. * * * But, assuming silence on the subject in the conversion contract (as here), the preferred has no right to any particular market price ratio between the shares. However, the preferred is ordinarily given (as here) anti-dilution or anti-destruction rights in the conversion contract.

Section (c)(4) in the Coastal Certificate is such an "anti-dilution" clause. It provides for a proportionate change in the conversion ratio in the event of a stock split or a stock combination (that is, a reverse split). In each of those events, the number of outstanding shares of Coastal common would change so, in order to preserve the parity relationship, a proportionate adjustment to the conversion ratio is essential.[4] In brief, (c)(4) prohibits the common from diluting the conversion right by requiring a proportionate adjustment if the number of outstanding shares is increased (and a similar adjustment if there is a decrease resulting from a reverse split).

Section (c)(6) is directed to the same antidilution purpose. While (c)(4) applies to subdivisions and combinations (which enlarge or decrease the number of outstanding shares), (c)(6) is directed to a stock dividend, that is, the issuance of Coastal shares to its stockholders as a dividend. That, too, is a circumstance which, by definition, would dilute the prior parity relationship and, to prevent that, the conversion ratio is "proportionately increased" by (c)(6).

Since Coastal is neither splitting nor reverse-splitting its shares, nor distributing them as a dividend, (c)(4) and (6) do not directly apply to this case.

D.

This brings us to (c)(5) which plaintiffs contend is the heart of the matter. The short of it is that unless the plaintiffs can find something in this paragraph which, directly or by implication, prohibits Coastal from distributing the Valery stock to the holders of its common, without giving its preferred a right to participate therein (now or at the time of conversion), then, under our settled law, restated only eighteen months ago in Judah and running back at least to 1929 in Gaskill v. Gladys Belle Oil Co., Del. Ch., 16 Del. Ch. 289, 146 A. 337, 339, the preferred has no such right. The Vice Chancellor found none. Nor do we.

Given the significance of (c)(5) in the dispute, we quote it again, this time omitting the references to consolidations, mergers, sales, and so on, which are not directly germane here. Thus:

> "In the event that the Corporation shall be recapitalized, [consolidated with or merged into any other corporation or shall sell or convey to any other corporation all or substantially all of its property as an entirety], provision shall be made as part of the terms of such recapitalization, . . . so that any holder of . . . Preferred Stock may thereafter receive in lieu of the Common Stock otherwise issuable to him upon conversion of his . . . Preferred Stock, but at the conversion ratio stated in this Article . . . which would otherwise be applicable at the time of conversion, the same kind and amount of securities or assets as may be distributable upon such recapitalization, . . . with respect to the Common Stock of the Corporation."

After noting that the "recapitalization" has no generally accepted meaning in law or accounting, the Vice Chancellor focused on the phrase,

---

[4] For example: if the Coastal common were split three for one, the number of outstanding shares would be tripled and, upon conversion thereafter, a preferred stockholder would be entitled to receive three shares of common for each share of preferred surrendered.

"in lieu of," as it appears in (c)(5) and concluded that, before the Section becomes applicable, the "Common Shares of Coastal must cease to exist and something [must] be given in lieu of them." Since the Coastal shares will continue in being after the spin-off, he concluded that the plan is not a recapitalization within the meaning of the Certificate.

Plaintiffs contend that Section (c)(5) is the key to analysis of the Certificate. They say that the settlement plan constitutes a "recapitalization" of Coastal, which triggers the adjustment called for in that section.

Relying on the significant changes which the plan will effect in Coastal's capital structure, plaintiffs argue that there will be a recapitalization in fact and law.

Section (c)(5) contains what is typically considered to be "anti-destruction" language. Transactions listed therein—a merger or consolidation, for example—are the kind of events that will not merely dilute the conversion privilege by altering the number of shares of common but, rather, may destroy the conversion privilege by eliminating the stock into which a preferred share is convertible. We focus, however, on the preferred's claim of right if Coastal "shall be recapitalized."

At trial, both sides offered the testimony of experts as to what "recapitalization" means. Professor Sametz noted that there is not a precise or specific definition, but the term implies a "fundamental realignment of relationships amongst a company's securities" or a "reshuffling of the capital structure."

The parties have also cited cases[7] from other jurisdictions, but we are not persuaded that such cases considered language reasonably comparable to that at issue here; so they are of little help. And the same is true of general financial terminology. The point is that we must decide the controversy under the facts in this case and, for present purposes, that means the Certificate language.

We agree with plaintiffs that the changes which the plan will bring to Coastal's financial structure are enormous. And it may be concluded that, collectively, these amount to a "reshuffling of the capital structure" under the general definition to which Professor Sametz testified. But that is not the test. The critical question concerns what is said in the contract.

Section (c)(5) provides that in the event of "recapitalization" one of the provisions shall be that a holder of preferred may "thereafter" receive—something. When he may receive it is clear: he may receive it "upon conversion" after the recapitalization has taken place. After that event, he may receive, not what he would have received before recapitalization; that was the common stock which was "otherwise

7 See, for example, Stephenson v. Plastics Corporation of America, Minn. Supr., 276 Minn. 400, 150 N.W.2d 668 (1967); United Gas Improvement Co. v. Commissioner of Internal Revenue, 3 Cir., 142 F.2d 216, 218 (1944); Commissioner of Internal Revenue v. Neustadt's Trust, 2 Cir., 131 F.2d 528 (1942).

issuable to him upon conversion." Certainly this clause is meaningless if the common share remains issuable to him after recapitalization. And so is the remainder of the paragraph which requires that the same conversion ratio be retained by distributing to the preferred, upon conversion, the "same kind and amount of securities or assets as may be distributable upon said recapitalization . . . with respect to the Common." The "same kind and amount" would be distributable to the common only if the common had been exchanged for something else. This was the situation the draftsman contemplated by the provision that the preferred "may receive" the "same kind and amount" of property "in lieu of the Common Stock."

Since the settlement plan does not include an exchange of the common and, given the added circumstances that the dividend or liquidated preference of the preferred is not threatened and that earned surplus is ample to support the distribution of the Valery shares to the common, the settlement plan does not include a recapitalization within the meaning of Section (c)(5).

E.

We turn now to (c)(7) which, we think, is related to what is said in (c)(5) and our construction of it; (c)(7) states:

> "No adjustment of the conversion ratio shall be made by reason of any declaration or payment to the holders of the Common Stock of the Corporation of a dividend or distribution payable in any property or securities other than Common Stock, any redemption of the Common Stock, any issuance of any securities convertible into Common Stock, or for any other reason, except as expressly provided herein."

This section, plainly and clearly, lists transactions which do not call for an adjustment to the conversion ratio. Thus an adjustment is not made for:

(1) a dividend payable to holders of the common in property other than Coastal common,

(2) a redemption of the common,

(3) an issuance of securities convertible into common,

(4) "any other reason."

Section (c)(7) concludes with the phrase, "except as expressly provided herein," which creates an ambiguity that must be resolved.

Plaintiffs contend that the phrase relates to all of Section (c), including (c)(5), and thus if a property dividend (the Valery stock) is regarded as a "recapitalization," the latter section controls. It is somewhat difficult to follow that argument but, as we understand it, plaintiffs contend that (c)(7) does not apply here.

In our opinion, the phrase, "except as expressly provided herein," refers to those paragraphs of Section (c) which "expressly . . . [provide]" for a change in the conversion ratio. In so doing, the phrase does modify the preceding phrase, "any other reason" (which is all-encompassing). But the transactions referred to are those in (c)(4) and (c)(6), and thus they are the exceptions "expressly provided" for. There are no exceptions provided for in (c)(7) and, therefore, the phrase would be meaningless if it were construed as applying to (c)(7).

Section (c)(7) states flatly that an adjustment shall not be made in the conversion ratio in the event any of the three specified events occurs: a dividend in property other than Coastal common, a redemption of the common or the issue of securities convertible into common. And the three specifics are enlarged by the general reference to "any other reason." Given what we believe to be mandatory language ("[no] adjustment . . . shall be made") prohibiting a change in the conversion ratio, we conclude that such a change may be made only if it is "expressly provided" in Section (c), and, as we have said, that means by the anti-dilution provisions of (c)(4) and (c)(6), I. e., by a stock split, reverse split or a stock dividend. It is only in those paragraphs that provisions are found for an adjustment in the conversion ratio.[8] Section (c)(5), on the other hand, is not directed merely to an adjustment in the exchange ratio; it is directed toward maintaining parity between the common and the preferred after a specified event has occurred: thus a conversion after recapitalization, merger or consolidation shall be "at the conversion ratio stated in this Article." The "conversion ratio" referred to here is the parity referred to throughout the Article (i.e., the Certificate).[9]

But even if one were to find some inconsistency or contradiction between (c)(5) and (c)(7), then, under familiar and well-settled rules of construction, the specific language of (c)(7) (as applied to the Valery stock) controls over any general language in (c)(5) regarding recapitalization.

F.

We have reviewed Sections (c)(4) through (c)(7) independently but failed to find therein any merit to the contentions which plaintiffs argue. And considering the paragraphs together, * * * So viewed, the basic scheme is that parity between the common and preferred is maintained through any changes in the number of outstanding shares which are unaccompanied by other balance sheet changes: thus a stock split, reverse split or stock dividend changes only the number of shares outstanding without any change in corporate assets. Sections (c)(4) and

8 The adjustment called for is an increase or decrease, as the case may be, of the number of shares of common to be received for each share of preferred which is converted.

9 Assuming Section (c)(5) could possibly be interpreted to contemplate an adjustment of the conversion ratio, none would be appropriate under our view of these facts since we have concluded that the settlement plan here does not include a recapitalization within the meaning of Section (c)(5).

(c)(6) provide for continuing parity by making the appropriate adjustment to the conversion ratio (that is, what will be given for one share of preferred) in such instance. But it appears that a reduction in assets by distribution to the common may be made without adjustment to that exchange basis. Thus a cash dividend is permissible under (c)(7),[10] or other corporate assets (stock in a listed company, for example) may be distributed under that paragraph. And if the distribution of assets is in the form of a redemption of the common, that, too, is permissible. In short, dividends and other distribution of corporate assets are permissible without change in the exchange basis. Speaking generally, such distributions are the ordinary and permissible way in which the holders of common stock share in the earnings of the enterprise. In saying this, we emphasize once more that there is not a charge here that the liquidation preference or the dividend of the preferred is in any way threatened. Nor is fraud involved.

* * *

In summary, we conclude that a distribution of the Valery stock to the holders of coastal common is permissible under Section (c)(7) and may be made without adjustment to the conversion ratio; such distribution is not a recapitalization under Section (c)(5).

* * *

Affirmed.

QUESTIONS

1. In footnote 7 the court distinguishes the *Stephenson* case based on differences in the contractual language of the preferred stock. Can you determine what language differences might be critical to the court's decision?
2. Why does Section (c)(5) cover sales of all or substantially all of Coastal's property (for which Coastal would presumably receive equivalent value), but not a dividend of stock of a subsidiary, for which Coastal receives nothing? What is the effect of Section (c)(7)?
3. If you were drafting to protect the preferred stockholders under these facts, what kind of protective language would you suggest? Would paragraph 3(b) in the warrants of Plastics Corporation of America (footnote 3 in the *Stephenson* case, *supra*) have solved the problem?
4. These provisions, as interpreted by the court, provide a large hole in the protection of the preferred's conversion rights. Why would holders of preferred accept such provisions? Does the language governing the preferred's conversion rights represent a drafting error?

---

[10] Mr. Katzin testified that Coastal has a substantial earned surplus to which the Valery distribution is to be charged.

NOTE ON LOHNES V. LEVEL 3 COMMUNICATIONS, INC.

The question of how to interpret the scope of contractual antidilution protection also arose in Lohnes v. Level 3 Communications, Inc., 272 F.3d 49 (1st Cir. 2001). Lohnes, as trustee of a real estate trust, had leased office space to a corporation later acquired by Level 3 and had obtained warrants to purchase common stock in the original lessee. After the acquisition, the warrants were adjusted to be exercisable in Level 3's stock. When Level 3 engaged in a two for one stock split, Lohnes insisted on an adjustment of the warrants to cover twice as many shares, and Level 3 declined. Lacking language that directly addressed stock splits, Lohnes argued that his rights were governed by the terms "capital reorganization" and "reclassification of stock." "Capital reorganization" was not a defined term in the warrant, and the court looked to Wood v. Coastal States Gas Corp., *supra*, and other cases to conclude that "capital reorganization" is a " 'general term describing corporate amalgamations or readjustments occurring, for example, when one corporation acquires another in a merger or acquisition, a single corporation divides into two or more entities, or a corporation makes a substantial change in its capital structure.' Black's Law Dictionary 1298 (6th ed. 1990). The first two prongs of this definition are clearly inapposite here. That leaves only the question of whether a stock split entails a 'substantial change in [a corporation's] capital structure.' We think not."

Turning to the phrase "reclassification of stock," the court concluded that the "sine qua non of a reclassification of stock is the modification of existing shares into something fundamentally different," a test not met by a stock split.

Cofman v. Acton Corporation

958 F.2d 494 (1st Cir. 1992)

■ ALDRICH, SENIOR CIRCUIT JUDGE.

Twelve partnerships, hereinafter Partnerships, having equal claims against defendant Acton Corporation, engaged in settlement negotiations of a prior suit. Acton offered $60,000; ($5,000 apiece); Partnerships countered with $180,000, and Acton responded with $120,000. Partnerships were agreeable to $120,000 if there were an added "sweetener," and suggested stock warrants, but Acton did not wish this complication. Instead, Section 2.2 was added to each of the twelve settlement contracts; hereinafter the agreement:

> The Partnership shall be entitled to receive, upon written demand made within the three years following the execution of the Settlement Agreement (the "Exercise Date"), the following one time payment: the sum of "X" times a multiple of 7,500 where "X" equals the "price" of one share of Acton Corporation's common stock on the Exercise Date less $7.00. The "price" on

> the Exercise Date shall be equal to the average closing price of one share of the common stock of Acton Corporation on the American Stock Exchange for any period, selected by the Partnership, consisting of thirty (30) consecutive trading days prior to the Exercise Date. Acton CATV shall make such payment as necessary within 30 days after receipt of the written demand. The Partnership's rights hereunder shall expire three years after the date of this Agreement and shall not be assignable.

The manifestly implicit concept, quite apart from the parol evidence, is that if Acton did better, presumably reflected in its stock, it could afford to pay more for the settlement. At the same time, the chances that this would bear much fruit, if any, were not considered large, as Acton was not doing well, and its stock was fluctuating between $1.50 and $3.12. These circumstances are to be considered with the contract language regardless of the parol evidence rule.

About a year after the making of the agreement, Acton's stock not having increased in price, it concluded that there were psychological market advantages in artificially shrinking the number of outstanding shares, and thereby increasing the per share price. It accordingly executed a so-called reverse stock split, as the result of which each stockholder owned one-fifth the original number of shares, with the new shares having five times the par value and, at the outset, approximately five times the immediately preceding price on the Stock Exchange, viz., substantially more than the $7.00 figure in the agreement.

Surprisingly, Acton did not consult Partnerships before engaging in this maneuver; it merely sent a letter explaining that it was of no consequence.

> This is to advise you that the stockholders of Acton Corporation have authorized a one-for-five reverse stock split of Acton Corporation's common shares effective June 25, 1987. This means that one share of stock will represent five shares of Acton Corporation's common stock prior to that date. The reverse stock split will affect Section 2.2 of the above-referenced Agreement such that the price $7.00 as referenced in such Section shall become $35.00.

Partnerships immediately rejected this conclusion. At the same time their present contention that Acton's letter, sent the very day of the change, was a recognition of its substantive effect on the agreement, and an "attempted amendment," is a flight of fancy.

The fight was on. Under Partnerships' interpretation of the agreement the twelve Partnerships together are owed $1,218,600 for their abandoned $60,000, based on a per share price of $20.54, although, had the number of shares not been reduced by the reverse split the per share price would have been some $4.11, sparking nothing. After a bench trial the court, in an opinion reported at 768 F. Supp. 392 (D. Mass. 1991), found for defendants. Partnerships appeal. We affirm.

Partnerships' position is simple and straightforward. This is precisely the way the agreement reads; it is unambiguous, and integrated,[3] and even were parol evidence admissible, which they deny, there was no prior discussion suggesting exceptions. The court, taking up this last fact, stated that the agreement "did not address an eventuality such as a reverse stock split," and the very fact that the parties had not considered it supplied the answer. "An expression may be complete . . . and yet ambiguous. Indeed, human limitations make it inevitable that every expression will be less than complete in a thoroughly comprehensive sense. Ambiguity will remain about some matters that might have been addressed and were not."[4] 768 F. Supp. at 395. Finding that the parties had not thought about dilution—a finding that binds Partnerships here—the court found the omission was an ambiguity in the agreement, and resolved it by concluding that the reasonable provision would have been that stock splits would have no effect.

We might turn one of Partnerships' arguments back on them in support of this result. The agreement provided that Partnerships had three years in which to pick a thirty day high price. During the negotiations Partnerships inquired what would happen if, during that period, Acton went private, as a result of which business success would not be reflected on the Exchange. Interestingly enough, while Partnerships are normally hostile to pre-agreement evidence, they narrate this. Acton "refused to give them any protection if Acton went private . . . the Partnerships were 'at risk' on that issue." (Emphasis in original.) During trial—not subsequently repeated—the court suggested that this indicated Partnerships also took the risk if Acton made a stock split increasing the number of shares. Partnerships assert this implication. If there is any inference, we would draw just the opposite. Inclusio unius, exclusio alterius. But certainly this did not mean that Partnerships were accepting any and all defeating actions that Acton might take.

The court ultimately so concluded. "It defies common sense" that Partnerships would have agreed that Acton could effectively escape the specified consequences of a rising market price by increasing the number of shares. And if Partnerships would not suffer from any increasing, it would follow, since a contract must be construed consistently, Acton should not suffer from any decreasing.

---

3 Integration. This Agreement contains the entire agreement between the parties hereto with respect to the transactions and matters contemplated herein and . . . supersedes all prior agreements, if any, between the parties hereto. . .

4 More simply put, "Paragraph 6 is not self-interpreting—no form of words is—and the evidence could be received and used to elucidate its meaning in context." See Antonellis v. Northgate Construction Corp., 362 Mass. 847, 851, 291 N.E.2d 626 (1973). (Emphasis supplied).

No doubt recognizing this symbiosis, when the district court inquired, as later did we, whether Acton could have avoided all liability under the agreement simply by increasing the number of shares, counsel answered affirmatively. The court characterized his proffered concession as "gallant." We can only say that if this particular counsel would have been too gallant to make a claim, surely some less chivalrous could have been found. How could so meaningless an undertaking have been considered a sweetener? It is a fundamental principle that a contract is to be construed as meaningful and not illusory. As the court said in Clark, 270 Mass. at 153,

> The construction of a written instrument to be adopted is the one which appears to be in accord with justice and common sense and the probable intention of the parties. It is to be interpreted as a business transaction entered into by practical men to accomplish an honest and straightforward end.

It is true that contracts cannot be rewritten simply to "rescue a firm from a sinkhole of its own design." Adding a whole new provision is normally permissible only when additional terms are "essential to a determination." Assuming that rule applicable, which we need not decide, Partnerships contends there was no necessity here; they may have been affirmatively content at the time of contracting to there being no antidilution provision. There are two answers to this. The first is that the court has found the parties gave no thought to dilution, and this finding cannot be said to be plainly wrong. Second, this is precisely a case where to read the contract as meaning that Partnerships should not suffer by dilution—and hence Acton by reverse dilution—is a necessity, or "essential to a determination." There is every reason to presume Partnerships did not intend to acquire nothing,[5] and saving from unenforceability ranks as a necessity.

Whether we reach that result by implying a provision to meet a circumstance not envisaged by the parties, or by construing the word "share" as including following the res, is immaterial. "[A] legal instrument is to be construed with reference to all of its language and to its general structure and purpose and in the light of the circumstances under which it was executed. These factors may qualify and control the literal signification of particular terms and phrases as effectually as if express qualifying words were found in the instrument." In any event, the rules of construction do not call for Partnership's wooden interpretation.

Affirmed.

---

[5] We do not pause over Partnership's sought analogy to convertible debentures, where the rule is that anti-dilution must be expressly stated. Broad v. Rockwell International Corp., 642 F.2d 929, 940–45 (5th Cir.) (en banc), cert. denied, 454 U.S. 965, 70 L. Ed. 2d 380, 102 S. Ct. 506 (1981); Parkinson v. West End Street Ry., 173 Mass. 446, 53 N.E. 891 (1899). These are formal, and complicated commercial structures, prepared with care for the general public. Purchasers have the bonds in any event. Here we have a simple agreement between individuals, not even assignable.

QUESTIONS

1. We've now seen several cases involving both bonds and preferred stock where courts adopt a narrow perspective of the parol evidence rule, confining their analysis to the 4-corners of the investment agreement. Why doesn't the *Acton* court follow the reasoning of those cases? What's different here?
2. If you were drafting on behalf of Acton, what kind of adjustment clause would you want to include in these agreements?
3. Does giving no thought to a subject in drafting always lead to its automatic insertion? Should it? See Ayres and Gertner, "Filling Gaps in Incomplete Contracts: An Economic Theory of Default Rules," 99 Yale L. J. 87 (1989), who argue that such contracts ought to be construed against the more knowledgeable and experienced party, thus providing incentives for such parties to disclose their real intentions. How would that argument apply here?

NOTE: TO IMPLY OR NOT IMPLY AN ADJUSTMENT FOR A STOCK SPLIT?

The question of whether a court should imply an automatic share adjustment provision for common stock options in the event of a stock split has continued to divide courts. For instance, Reiss v. Financial Performance Corp., 764 N.E.2d 958 (N.Y. 2001) involved warrants granted to a director that contained no adjustment provision, and the company subsequently conducted a reverse stock split. Nonetheless, the company took the position that the number of shares underlying the warrants and the exercise price should be proportionately adjusted based on the reverse stock split. The trial court agreed; however, the only evidence to support the trial court's conclusion involved company disclosures made after the reverse split, which took the position that the warrant had been adjusted. The Appellate Division affirmed, but on contextual grounds, that an adjustment clause was an essential term of the warrants that the court could supply, regardless of the parties' intent. 715 N.Y.S.2d 29 (App. Div. 2000). In justifying its approach, the Appellate Division declined to "disregard common sense and slavishly bow to the written word where to do so would plainly ignore the true intentions of the parties in making the contract." 279 A.D.2d 13 at 20. Criticizing this approach (and implicitly that of the court in the previous case), Miriam Albert argues that the Restatement of Contracts 2d § 204 (1981) does not permit supplying an omitted term as a matter of interpretation, but only where it is necessary to effectuate the contract. Miriam Albert, Common Sense for Common Stock Options: Inconsistent Interpretation of Anti-Dilution Provisions in Options and Warrants, 34 Rutgers L. J. 321 (2003).

In contrast, in Sanders v. Wang, 1999 Del. Ch. LEXIS 203, 25 Del. J. Corp. L. 1036 (Del. Ch. 1999), the Delaware Chancery Court came to a different conclusion in evaluating the number of shares that could be awarded to employees under a Key Employee Stock Option Plan (KESOP) adopted by Computer Associates International, Inc. The terms of the KESOP provided for stock grants to participants of up to 6 million shares if the company's stock reached a price of $180 for at least 60 trading days. The plan contained no adjustment clause for changing the total number of shares awardable under the plan in the event of a forward stock split. However, the company's compensation committee was permitted under the plan to adjust the target stock price of $180 to account for any stock splits that occurred following the adoption of the plan.

After three forward stock splits, the compensation committee of the board determined that the stock had reached the required price, after adjusting for the splits. It then proceeded to issue employees 20.25 million shares under the plan, which was equivalent to 6 million shares after adjusting for the three stock splits. In a derivative action brought by shareholders to challenge the grants, the court held for the plaintiffs, that there was no authority under the KESOP for an adjustment in the number of shares to account for the splits, despite the explicit language that allowed the compensation committee to adjust the performance target price to reflect any stock splits.

CL Investments, L.P. v. Advanced Radio Telecom Corp.

2000 WL 1868096 (Del. Ch. 2000)

■ JACOBS, VICE CHANCELLOR.

This action is brought to enforce the terms of a stock purchase warrant that entitles the plaintiff, who is the warrant-holder, to purchase a specific number of shares of the issuer upon exercising the warrant. Importantly, the warrant also requires two different kinds of adjustments of the type and number of shares the warrant-holder is entitled to purchase. The first type of adjustment occurs if the issuer of the warrant merges with another corporation. In that event the exercising warrant-holder becomes entitled to purchase the same securities it would have received in the merger if it were a shareholder. The second type of adjustment occurs if the company engages in specified transactions that dilute its shares. In that event, an adjustment is made to offset the effect of the dilution.

Both types of adjustments are implicated in this case. After the warrant was issued, the issuer merged with another corporation and as a result, the stock of the issuer was canceled and exchanged for stock of the acquiring corporation. It is undisputed that the merger triggered the first type of adjustment, thereby entitling the plaintiff warrant-holder to purchase stock of the acquiring corporation when the warrant is exercised.

What is disputed is the number of shares that the plaintiff, upon exercising the warrant, would be entitled to purchase. That dispute arises because after the merger, the acquiror entered into various dilutive transactions in its own stock. The plaintiff claims that those transactions triggered its right to the second type of adjustment, under the "anti-dilution" provision of the warrant. The defendant acquiror contends that in these circumstances the anti-dilution adjustment provision is not applicable. That dispute led to the filing of this action to enforce the warrant's anti-dilution provision. The defendants have moved to dismiss the complaint for failure to state a claim, and the plaintiff has cross-moved for partial judgment on the pleadings. This Opinion decides both motions.

I. FACTUAL BACKGROUND

* * *

B. The Merger

On October 28, 1996,[5] seven months after the Warrant was issued, Telecom entered into a Merger Agreement and Plan of Reorganization (the "Merger Agreement") with the co-defendant, Advanced Radio Telecom Corp. ("ART"). Under the Merger Agreement, ART acquired Telecom in a transaction in which (i) a wholly owned shell subsidiary of ART (the "merger-subsidiary") was merged into Telecom, (ii) Telecom became the surviving corporation,[6] (iii) all of Telecom's shares were exchanged for ART shares, and (iv) the Telecom shares were canceled.

C. Subsequent Dilutive Transactions

ART acknowledges that as a result of the Merger, the plaintiff, upon exercising the Warrant, would be entitled to purchase ART common stock instead of Telecom stock.[7] After the Merger took place, however, ART issued to third parties, in various transactions, ART common stock, securities convertible into ART common stock, and warrants and options to purchase ART common stock. These transactions diluted the ART stock to which the plaintiff would be entitled upon exercising the Warrant. The plaintiff claims that unless it receives an adjustment under the Warrant's anti-dilution provision (Section 7), those dilutive ART stock transactions will have improperly diminished the value of its Warrant. The defendants took the position, however, that the Warrant, by its own terms, does not entitle the plaintiff to any Section 7 adjustment to offset the dilutive effect of these transactions.

In its amended complaint, (the "Complaint"), the plaintiff alleges two Causes of Action that embody three separate claims: (1) breach of contract (i.e., the Warrant) for refusing to acknowledge the plaintiff's

---

5 The plaintiff purchased the Warrant as part of bridge financing to help defendants ART and combine their businesses and then offer common stock to the public. At that time, ART was named Advanced Radio Technologies Corporation.

6 ART and Telecom are collectively "the defendants."

7 All of Telecom's stock is now owned by ART.

entitlement to the Section 7 adjustments, (2) breach of the Warrant for refusing to produce an Accountants' Certificate, and (3) unjust enrichment.

II. THE APPLICABLE STANDARDS AND THE PARTIES' CONTENTIONS

A. The Procedural Standards

The defendants have moved to dismiss the Complaint under Court of Chancery Rule 12(b)(6) for failure to state a claim upon which relief can be granted. The plaintiff, in response, has cross-moved under Rule 12(c) for partial judgment on the pleadings on its claim that the defendants have breached the Warrant.

* * *

B. The Contentions

The plaintiff contends that it is entitled to judgment on the pleadings on its claim the defendants breached the Warrant. The alleged contractual breaches consist of the defendants' (i) failure to acknowledge the plaintiff's right to an anti-dilution adjustment under Section 7, and (ii) refusal to deliver an Accountants' Certificate. The bases for the claim are that as a result of the Merger the plaintiff became entitled to purchase ART common stock upon exercising the Warrant, and that ART's dilutive stock transactions after the Merger entitle the plaintiff to a dilution-offsetting adjustment under Section 7 of the Warrant.

* * *

The defendants respond that all of the plaintiff's claims must be dismissed as a matter of law, for three reasons. First, to the extent the breach of contract claim is based upon Section 7 of the Warrant, that claim is legally deficient because under the terms of the Warrant itself, the ART stock transactions in question could not, and did not, implicate Section 7. Second, to the extent the breach of contract claim rests on ART's alleged failure to deliver an Accountants' Certificate, that claim is invalid on its face and is also time-barred. * * *

III. ANALYSIS

* * *

B. The Breach of Contract Claim

1. The Issues

* * *

The parties agree that the dispute is governed by Sections 6 and 7 of the Warrant. Section 6 provides:

> In case the Company after the Original Issue Date shall (a) effect a reorganization, (b) consolidate with or merge into any other person, or (c) transfer all or substantially all of its properties or assets to any other person under any plan or

> arrangement contemplating the dissolution of the Company, then, in each such case, the holder of this Warrant, upon the exercise hereof as provided in Section 3 at any time after the consummation of such reorganization, consolidation or merger or the effective date of such dissolution, as the case may be, shall be entitled to receive (and the Company shall be entitled to deliver), in lieu of the Common Stock (or Other Securities) issuable upon such exercise prior to such consummation or such effective date, the stock and other securities and property (including cash) to which such holder would have been entitled upon such consummation or in connection with such dissolution as the case may be, if such holder had so exercised this Warrant immediately prior thereto, *all subject to further adjustment thereafter as provided in Sections 5 and 7 hereof.*

And Section 7 provides:

> Where *the Company* shall issue or sell shares of its Common Stock after the Original Issue Date without consideration or for a consideration per share less than the Purchase Price in effect pursuant to the terms of this Warrant at the time of the issuance or sale of such additional shares . . . then the Purchase Price in effect hereunder shall simultaneously with such issuance or sale be reduced to a price determined by [a formula specified in the Warrant].

Section 7 is (to repeat) an "anti-dilution" provision designed to offset any dilution of the issuer's stock caused by stock issuances made for consideration less than the stipulated "Purchase Price." Section 7 accomplishes that by lowering the purchase price per share that an exercising warrant-holder would pay, which would thereby increase the number of shares to be purchased. But, because in this case the dilutive transactions involved stock issued by ART, Section 7 would not apply to those transactions unless ART is "the Company" referred to in the above quoted first line of Section 7. That is the key question upon which the pending motions turn.

"The Company" is a defined term in the Warrant. The definition, found in the Warrant's preamble, states:

> As used herein the following terms, unless the context otherwise requires, have the following respective meanings:
>
> (a) The term "Company" includes any corporation which shall *succeed to or assume* the obligations of the Company [Telecom] hereunder.

As earlier stated, the applicability of Section 7 turns on whether ART is "the Company" within the meaning of that Section. As that term is defined, there are only two ways that ART could be deemed "the Company." The first is if ART "succeed[ed] to or assumed" the obligations of Telecom under the Warrant in the Merger. The second is if the "context" of the term "the Company" in Section 7 "otherwise requires" that ART be deemed "the Company." The plaintiff contends that under either prong of the definition ART must be deemed "the Company." The defendants argue that the pled facts alleged in the Complaint implicate neither prong. Because both prongs of the definition are in issue, each must be separately analyzed.

2. Did ART Succeed to or Assume Telecom's Warrant Obligations?

The defendants argue that ART neither succeeded to nor assumed any obligations of Telecom, including its obligations under the Warrant, because nothing in the Merger Agreement provides for an assumption of those obligations. Indeed, the defendants urge, under Section 3(f) of the Merger Agreement Telecom is the surviving corporation. Nor, defendants say, did ART assume Telecom's liabilities by operation of law, because the Merger Agreement states that "the corporate existence, franchises and rights of Telecom . . . shall continue unaffected and unimpaired by the Merger."

In response, the plaintiff urges that ART "succeed[ed] to or assumed" Telecom's obligations under the Warrant by agreeing to a merger involving the exchange of Telecom's stock for ART stock and the cancellation of all Telecom stock. As support, the plaintiff points to Section 4(c) of the Merger Agreement, which provides that: "At the Effective Time . . . each 2.75 issued shares of Telecom Common Stock . . . shall be converted into the right to receive one share of ART Common Stock." The plaintiff also relies upon the language of Section 6(b), that: "after the Effective Time each certificate which represented outstanding shares of Telecom Common Stock . . . prior to the Effective Time shall be deemed for all corporate purposes to evidence the ownership of the shares of ART Common Stock . . . provided in Section 4." By virtue of the exchange of Telecom stock for ART stock and the cancellation of Telecom stock, the plaintiff concludes that ART must necessarily (albeit implicitly) have assumed Telecom's obligations in the Merger.

Having considered the arguments raised by both sides, I determine that in the Merger, ART did not succeed to or assume Telecom's Warrant obligations. Section 3(f) of the Merger Agreement explicitly provides that Telecom will continue as a functioning entity after the Merger. Nowhere does the Merger Agreement expressly provide for any assumption by ART of the liabilities and obligations of Telecom. Nor, given the structure of the Merger, did ART assume the obligations of Telecom by operation of law. As a purely structural matter, had Telecom merged into the merger-subsidiary so that the latter became the surviving corporation, then Telecom would no longer exist. In that case, ART would necessarily have "succeed[ed] to or assumed" the obligations of Telecom by virtue of 8 Del. C. § 259. Here, however, Telecom was the surviving corporation in the Merger, and therefore ART did not by operation of law "succeed to or assume" Telecom's Warrant obligations under § 259.

Because ART did not "succeed to or assume" the obligations of Telecom under the Warrant, the only way that ART could be deemed "the Company" under Section 7 of the Warrant is if the "context otherwise requires." I turn to that issue.

3. Does "the Context Otherwise Require" That ART Be Deemed "the Company For Purposes of Section 7 of the Warrant?

a. *The Contentions*

The plaintiff urges that this Court must find as a matter of law that ART is "the Company" under the Warrant, as provided in the second prong of the definition of "the Company." The Court must so conclude (the plaintiff argues) for three reasons.

First, plaintiff contends, the context of "the Company" as used in Section 7 requires that "the Company" be read to mean ART. The argument runs as follows: By application of Section 6 of the Warrant and as a result of the Merger, the plaintiff, upon exercising the Warrant, can purchase only ART stock. But Section 6 does more than merely substitute ART stock for Telecom stock as the security the Warrant-holder is entitled to purchase. Section 6 also expressly makes that stock subject to "further adjustment . . . as provided in . . . Section 7." Because ART common stock is the only stock the plaintiff may now purchase upon exercising the Warrant, and because the Warrant defines Common Stock as "the common stock of the Company and its successors," the term "Common Stock" as used in Section 7, must mean ART common stock. Otherwise, the provision of Section 6 that (i) entitles the exercising Warrant-holder to purchase the stock or other securities received in a merger, and then (ii) makes that stock subject to adjustment under Section 7, would become meaningless and effectively be read out of the Warrant contract.

Second, the plaintiff argues that to read that Warrant in any different way would be inequitable. Because of the Merger, Telecom can no longer discharge its original obligation under the Warrant to deliver Telecom shares—adjusted for any dilutive transactions—to exercising warrant-holders. Now those warrant-holders can receive only ART shares. Unless ART is "the Company" under Section 7 of the Warrant, those ART shares could be diluted with impunity—a result that would be legally prohibited if the shares being purchased were the Telecom shares for which the ART shares were substituted. Under the defendants' interpretation, the plaintiff Warrant-holder, will be deprived of the anti-dilution protections that it bargained for.

* * *

Third, the plaintiff urges that its reading of "the Company" is the only interpretation that is faithful to "the rules of construction of contracts [which] require us to adopt an interpretation which gives meaning to every provision of a contract or, in the negative, no provision of a contract should be left without force and effect." Section 6 entitles the plaintiff to receive ART stock, and also expressly makes that stock "subject to further adjustment thereafter as provided in Sections 5 and 7 hereof." Only if "the Company" in Section 7 means ART, can a Section 7 adjustment occur. Any different construction would render the "further adjustment" provision in Section 6 meaningless. For these three reasons, the plaintiff concludes, it is entitled to judgment on the pleadings on its breach of contract claim.

The defendants respond by arguing, also as a matter of law, that ART is not "the Company." Therefore, the plaintiff's contractual claim of entitlement to an adjustment under Section 7 is not legally cognizable and must be dismissed, for two reasons.

The defendants first argue that it cannot be implied either from the Merger or from the context of Section 6 of the Warrant, that ART succeeded to or assumed the Warrant obligations of Telecom, which still exists as a wholly-owned subsidiary of ART. To find that ART implicitly assumed Telecom's obligations as a matter of "context" would contravene the established principle that a parent-subsidiary relationship, without more, cannot render a parent corporation liable for the obligations of its subsidiary even where the subsidiary is wholly owned. Nothing in the Merger Agreement alters this basic principle. On the contrary, defendants say, that Agreement provides that "the corporate existence, franchises and rights of Telecom, with its purposes, powers and objects, shall continue unaffected and unimpaired by the Merger."

Second, the defendants contend that the context in which the term "Company" appears does not "otherwise require" that "the Company" be read to mean ART. Rather, the definition of that term means that "the Company" is (i) Telecom, and that (ii) unless the context otherwise requires, "the Company" also means an entity that succeeds to or assumes Telecom's obligations under the Warrant. To put it differently, the defendants contend that the definitional language "unless the context otherwise requires," operates to limit, not expand, the universe of entities that could be "the Company." Accordingly, defendants conclude, nothing in the "context" of the Warrant justifies reading the term "the Company" broadly to include any other entity except one that expressly succeeds to or assumes liabilities of Telecom under the Warrant. Because ART did not succeed to or assume Telecom's Warrant liabilities, it cannot be "the Company."

b. *Discussion*

Having considered the parties' colliding views, I conclude as a matter of contract construction that ART must be deemed "the Company," as that term is used in Section 7 of the Warrant. Both legally and equitably, the "context" requires that result. The defendants rely essentially upon the technical structure they chose for the Merger as their reason for not recognizing a Section 7 adjustment that Sections 6 and 7 on their face expressly require.

Assume (counterfactually) that the Merger had resulted in ART's merger-subsidiary swallowing up Telecom and becoming the surviving corporation. In that case, the subsidiary would have, "succeeded to or assumed" the obligations of Telecom by operation of law under 8 Del. C. § 259, and a Section 7 adjustment would be required. Here, however, the merger-subsidiary was merged into Telecom, leaving Telecom as the surviving corporation. Under that structure, no obligations of Telecom were assumed by operation of law. But that does not end the analysis, because the definition of "the Company" also permits the Court to consider the "context." The definition of "the Company" is not narrowly confined to entities that succeed to or assume Telecom's liabilities under the Warrant. Indeed, that reading impermissibly conflates both prongs of the definition into only one prong. Nor does Section 6 (which makes the ART stock "subject to further adjustment under . . . Section 7") distinguish between mergers where the original issuer of the Warrant is—or is not—the surviving corporation. If Section 6 made such a distinction, then one would have expected the defendants to argue that the plaintiff is not entitled to receive ART stock when the Warrant is exercised. Yet the defendants concede that the plaintiff would be entitled to purchase ART stock.

In this case the relevant "context" is this: the plaintiff bargained for certain anti-dilution protections, and for other protections in the event of a merger that converted the stock the Warrant-holder was originally entitled to purchase into securities of the acquiring company. Both protections are mandated by the same Section—Section 6—which directs that adjustments be made to the stock received by reason of a merger under Sections 5 and 7. Unless the "context" from which both of these protections arise is respected, the defendants will be permitted to use the structure of the Merger self-servingly as both a shield and a sword—a sword to force the plaintiff warrant-holder to accept ART stock upon exercising the Warrant, and a shield to prevent that warrant-holder from enforcing anti-dilution provisions that are part and parcel of the same package of contractual protections. That simply cannot be.

The defendants respond that despite the linkage (in Section 6) between the Section 6 and Section 7 adjustments, and despite the plaintiff's entitlement under Section 6 to purchase ART stock when it exercises the Warrant, the plaintiff is not entitled to the anti-dilution adjustments under Section 7. The reason, defendants say, is that Telecom continues, post-Merger, as a viable entity capable of satisfying its obligations under the Warrant. But that argument is hopelessly flawed. To make it, the defendants must first de-couple Sections 6 and 7, and then assert that a Section 7 adjustment need not necessarily or inevitably follow or accompany a Section 6 adjustment.[25] The flaw is that

[25] The defendants cite as an example, a Section 6 merger for cash. It is true that in that case, there would be no Section 7 adjustment. But the example is irrelevant, because cash need not be "adjusted" to prevent stock dilution, since the warrant-holder would not be receiving any stock that is capable of dilution.

unless "the Company" means ART in this context, Section 7 will essentially be read out of the Warrant contract. Unless the stock of "the Company" received by virtue of a Section 6 (merger) adjustment is the same as the stock of "the Company" that is adjusted (for dilution) under Section 7, then no post-merger dilution of the stock underlying the Warrant would ever trigger a Section 7 adjustment. That result would violate the explicit command of Section 6, which makes the stock received in the Merger "subject to adjustment under Section 7." Only by interpreting "the Company" in Section 7 as the same "Company" whose stock will be received by the warrant-holder under Section 6, can the Court avoid a construction that would render Section 7 superfluous and disregard a critical provision in Section 6. The defendants' interpretation would contravene New York's rule of construction, which prohibits a reading that would render a provision of a contract superfluous as "unsupportable under standard principles of contract interpretation."

In short, the context requires that ART be deemed "the Company" under Section 7. First, the anti-dilution adjustment formula in Section 7 works only if the stock triggering the anti-dilution adjustment is the same as the stock that is the subject matter of the Warrant. Second, at present the subject matter of the Warrant is, by virtue of the Merger, and Section 6, ART stock. Third, transactions involving ART stock are the only transactions that are capable of diluting the value of the Warrant. If ART is not "the Company" after its stock has been substituted for that of Telecom, then what entity can be? It cannot be Telecom. Logically and by process of elimination, the "context requires" that "the Company" be ART.

* * *

IV. CONCLUSION

For the foregoing reasons, (1) with respect to the plaintiff's claims for breach of contract (including its claim of right to receive an Accountants' Certificate), the plaintiff's motion for judgment on the pleadings is granted and the defendants' motion to dismiss is denied; and (2) with respect to the plaintiff's claim for unjust enrichment, the defendants' motion to dismiss is granted.

QUESTIONS

1. How does the court determine that ART, which was not one of the merging corporations, "*succeed[s] to or assume[s]* the obligations of the Company [Telecom]" under the merger agreement?
2. Section 7 provides antidilution protection where "the Company" issues or sells its shares at a price below the "Purchase Price" (a defined term). How could this apply to ART after the merger of its subsidiary with Telecom given that Telecom remains in existence following the merger?

3. Recall that Delaware courts have adopted a *de facto* "strict construction" approach in interpreting the terms of preferred stock. As noted by the court in the *Benchmark* case examined in Chapter 7, "Any rights, preferences and limitations of preferred stock that distinguish that stock from common stock must be expressly and clearly stated, as provided by statute." Given the ambiguous contract language in the Telecom warrant regarding Section 7, why doesn't the court adopt a similar perspective in determining the rights held by the warrant holders?

Appendix

Forward and Futures Contracts

Listed options are one type of derivative security that can be used for hedging and trading purposes. Two other common derivative products are *forwards* and *futures*, which we briefly summarize here.

A *Forward Contract* is simply a contract for delivery of a good that is executory on both sides. For example, assume that Farmer Jones is nervous that today's price of wheat ($7.00 per bushel) may decline before the harvest in September. Because Farmer Brown is undiversified, being wholly invested (long) in wheat, he may prefer to sell now. At the same time, assume that a cereal manufacturer, such as Kellogg's, is concerned that the price of wheat may rise, leading to a production cost increase, while competitors who focus on rice and oat cereals won't face this problem. Both parties may benefit from a forward contract, in which Farmer Brown agrees to deliver his wheat to Kellogg's on September 15 at $7.00 per bushel. Each has managed to reduce the risk that wheat prices will move against them in the future. Forward contracts are not marked to market and are generally private, non-exchange agreements between two parties. Thus, a party to a forward contract must worry about default risk by the counterparty to the contract.

Futures Contracts, unlike forward contracts, are standardized agreements traded on regulated exchanges. Farmer Jones, looking to secure a price for his upcoming wheat harvest, might engage with the Chicago Board of Trade (CBOT), a major global commodity exchange. Through a brokerage firm, he enters into a futures contract to sell his wheat at $7.00 per bushel in September. The CBOT provides the platform where Farmer Jones's contract is listed and traded, detailing the commodity's quality, quantity, and specified delivery month. As September approaches and Farmer Jones is ready to fulfill his contract, he communicates with his broker, who in turn liaises with the CBOT-associated clearing house. This clearing house, such as the one operated by the Chicago Mercantile Exchange (CME) Group, is central to the process. It ensures financial integrity by acting as the counterparty to every trade. When Farmer Jones signifies his intent to deliver wheat, the clearing house identifies a corresponding buyer with a matching September wheat futures contract. This buyer could be a manufacturer like Kellogg's, intending to use the wheat, or a speculative investor. If the buyer does not require the physical wheat, they will typically resell the contract on the market, potentially to a business that needs it.

The Dodd-Frank Wall Street Reform and Consumer Protection Act of 2010, enacted in response to the 2007–2008 financial crisis, requires standardized derivatives, including futures contracts, to be traded transparently and cleared through a central counterparty. This structure ensures that every futures contract has a counterbalancing buyer and seller, with the exchange facilitating and the clearing house guaranteeing the transactions.

In contrast to Forward Contracts, an integral part of futures trading is the "marking to market" process. For Farmer Jones's wheat contract, this means its value is adjusted daily to reflect the current market price of wheat for September delivery. If market prices rise, the value of his position decreases because he is obligated to sell at a lower price than the current market rate. Conversely, if market prices fall, the value of his position increases as he can sell at a higher price than the market rate. The clearing house calculates these daily valuation changes. An increase in the value of his position may result in excess funds in his account, which he can withdraw or retain for potential future margin calls. On the other hand, a decrease in value might lead to a "margin call," requiring Farmer Jones to deposit additional funds into his brokerage account to cover the loss. This daily settlement process minimizes the risk of default, keeping the contract's value aligned with market fluctuations. While Farmer Jones has locked in a selling price for his wheat, he remains subject to the market's daily ebb and flow until he either fulfills or closes out his contract.

* * *

In addition to options, futures and forwards, traders may also enter into a wide variety of other derivatives. Broadly defined, a derivative is any security whose value depends upon the value of something else—so the possibilities for creating derivatives is limited only to the imagination of an investment banker. One example is the credit default swap, in which a buyer pays a sum in order to receive a payment from the counterparty if a debtor defaults on a specific debt instrument. (You might recall credit default swaps from the Quadrant Structured Products v. Vertin case we studied earlier in Chapter 4.) Issuance of credit default swaps caused the collapse of American International Group (AIG) and its subsequent bailout by the U.S. government in 2008. Dodd Frank now requires most swaps to be traded and cleared on a registered clearing organization, to improve transparency of trading and mitigate counterparty risk. These organizations must provide security of payment for swap settlements.

CHAPTER 9

DIVIDENDS AND DISTRIBUTIONS

1. INTRODUCTION

Imagine that a few more years have passed and that your skilled work as general counsel for Perpetual Youth (PY) has helped the firm thrive. PY's IPO was a huge success. The company used the additional funds to develop a comprehensive line of kale-coated collagen supplements that have taken the market by storm. PY is now in the enviable position of having millions of spare dollars, which the CFO has temporarily parked in safe short-term government bonds.

One day, PY's CEO and CFO stroll into your office with pensive looks on their faces. "We're having a bit of an argument," they tell you in unison, "and we could use your counsel." The conversation goes something like this:

CEO: "Our kale-coated collagen campaign has put us in a great position, but we can't just rest on our laurels. I think I've identified a fantastic new opportunity involving IV amino acid drip bags. We've got about $180 million in spare cash, and this should be just enough to develop this product and establish a new growth horizon for PY."

CFO: "Look, we've invented some great products so far, but developing the IV amino drip would be like playing hopscotch in a minefield. Injectable supplements are a completely different business, and they bring a host of new risks. I've also started to hear from our public stockholders that they might like to see a cash dividend one of these days. We haven't paid them anything! We've got 30 million shares outstanding, and we should really use that $180 million in spare cash to pay a special $6 per share dividend. The investors will love it, and our stock price will jump."

CEO: "No way. If we just give the money back to investors, then everyone will recognize that we've run out of good ideas. We've got to keep pushing new initiatives to develop innovative products."

Both [turning to you]: "What do you think we should do?"

Conversations like this will inevitably arise for successful firms. As we've been discussing all along, investors expect a return. Debt investors make money through interest payments. Preferred stock might get an earmarked cumulative dividend that keeps accumulating until paid. What about common stockholders? Do they expect dividends as well? If not, is there some other way that a firm can (or should) distribute the benefits of business success to these residual investors? And what are the legal restrictions that might prevent a company from issuing a dividend—even when the entire leadership team is convinced that such a move makes sense? This chapter considers all these topics and brings our exploration of the corporate finance business cycle to a close.

Note that we will sometimes use the word "distributions" rather than "dividends" to emphasize that there are a variety of ways that shareholders can obtain a return from their investment in a company. Cash dividends generally come to mind first when we think of distributions, but they are not the only way to offer a return. For example, a company may choose to return cash to shareholders by repurchasing shares; this allows a self-selection process among those shareholders willing to bear the tax consequences of realizing capital gains. Or a firm may give shareholders a non-cash benefit through a spin-off transaction, in which a corporation declares a dividend of the shares of a subsidiary company. We will see all these, along with some other distributions like stock splits and tracking stocks, in this final chapter.

But let's start with a fundamental question: Is it a good idea to pay a cash dividend? Will the decision to declare a dividend increase the value of the corporation? This inquiry is sometimes known as the *dividend policy* question.

2. DIVIDEND POLICY: THEORY AND PRACTICE

Ask a group of financial economists a simple question—like whether increasing a dividend will increase the value of a firm and its common stock—and you're likely to get more than one answer. Indeed, if you ask this question to a large enough gathering, you might get three very different answers. One group may say "absolutely: an increase in dividend payout will *increase* firm value." A second group may respond "do what you want: an increase in dividend payout will have *no impact* on firm value." And a third group might say "no way, an increase in dividend payout will *decrease* firm value."

How can we reconcile these different views? Let's consider each perspective in turn.

A. WHY INCREASING DIVIDENDS MIGHT INCREASE VALUE (THE HISTORICAL PERSPECTIVE)

When developing a valuation model for stocks, it is often tempting to discount net earnings (or some variant, such as EBITDA) to present value. And while this may provide a rough estimate of value, investors don't own firm earnings. Indeed, a firm can retain profits for decades without paying any of the earnings out to shareholders. Actual cash dividends are only paid at the discretion of the directors, subject to a few legal requirements (as we shall see in more detail shortly). Historically, this simple fact caused analysts to suggest that dividends are the only thing that should matter for stock valuation. Consider two representative perspectives:

> [I]nvestors buy the firm's dividends, not its earnings. The intuitive rationale is quite straightforward: dividends constitute the only cash flows produced by the firm for its shareholders and therefore represent the one observable return they receive on their investment. They put up a sum of money to purchase a share of stock—i.e., they forego present consumption—in order to lay claim to a series of subsequent payments that will permit future consumption at a higher level. This trade-off, as perceived by the multitude of individuals who populate the capital markets, is in fact the essence of the community's collective investment decision. Such individuals cannot spend a firm's retained earnings on goods and services; they can spend only the dividends—the *cash* payments—they receive. Retained earnings are not necessarily irrelevant, but they are relevant only insofar as they generate higher *future* dividends. Unless some incremental cash flow eventually occurs, a corporation's retentions have absolutely no value to its stockholders.

Wilbur G. Lewellen, The Cost of Capital 88–89 (J. Fred Weston & Allan Meltzer eds., 1969).

> **Historical Primacy of Dividends**. For the vast majority of common stocks the dividend record and prospects have always been the most important factor controlling investment quality and value. The success of the typical concern has been measured by its ability to pay liberal and steadily increasing dividends on its capital. In the majority of cases the price of common stocks has been influenced more markedly by the dividend rate than by the reported earnings. The 'outside,' or noncontrolling, stockholders of any company can reap benefits from their investment in only two ways—through dividends and through an increase in the market value of their shares. Since the market value in most cases has depended primarily upon the dividend rate, the latter could be held responsible for nearly all the gains ultimately realized by investors.

Benjamin Graham, David L. Dodd & Sidney Cottle, SECURITY ANALYSIS: PRINCIPLES AND TECHNIQUE (4th ed. 1962) 480.

The assertion that "cash in king" seems to make some sense for stock valuation. And this theory can also explain why a share of stock of a firm like Alphabet (the parent of Google, Inc.), which has never paid dividends (as of this publication), can be worth hundreds of dollars. At some point, analysts expect that the firm will decide to make large dividend payments, and these future cash flows can be discounted back to present value to support the current share price.

During the 1960s, however, while Graham Dodd and Cottle were writing their views about dividend policy, a revolution was brewing. Led by two familiar figures from Chapter 4, this insurrection posited that dividend policy might not matter for common stock value.

B. WHY DIVIDENDS MIGHT NOT MATTER

Franco Modigliani and Merton Miller (now both Nobel laureates) revolutionized thinking about dividends as much as they did about capital structure (see Chapter 4). They argued that dividends were irrelevant to the value of the firm and offered mathematical proofs of their assertion. Miller & Modigliani, "Dividend Policy, Growth and the Valuation of Shares," 34 Journal of Business 411 (1961).

As before, Modigliani and Miller's work is mostly theoretical in nature. And they again use several simplifying assumptions in their model:

- All traders have perfect and costless access to information about the company and its stock price.
- There are no transaction costs, such as brokerage fees or transaction taxes.
- There are no tax differentials between distributed and undistributed profits and between dividends and capital gains. (It's easiest to think of this as a world of zero taxes, but it could also occur with equal tax rates on dividends and capital gains.)
- Investors are rational wealth-seekers indifferent about how they hold their wealth—whether in cash or shares, assuming compensation for risk.

Modigliani and Miller broadened the discussion by showing that a share should be valued on the basis of its entire stream of future benefits to shareholders—which includes both the discounted present value of dividends *and* the discounted present value of the proceeds from selling the investment. They then presented two essential insights:

- Firm values depend on investment policies, not dividend policies. That is, investment policies that obtain returns in excess of the firm's cost of capital will create more value for investors, whether in the form of higher current dividends or higher terminal values for the shareholder's investment when sold. If the firm's investments simply earn the firm's cost of capital, investors will be satisfied because they are earning their expected return. But they will also be indifferent between allowing the firm to grow its earnings annually by reinvesting retained earnings or receiving dividends that the shareholders can invest in other assets with the same expected return. In the latter case, the firm can only grow by selling new capital, but new investors will demand the same return on their capital (i.e., the company's cost of capital), so the value of their claims will exactly equal the capitalized value of the new earnings from expansion.

- Shareholders can "home-make" dividends by selling shares.

Let's take a closer look at how Modigliani and Miller's irrelevance hypothesis works. Suppose a firm decides that it wants to pay a dividend of one-third of its total value to shareholders. But it also has a new project, offering a return equal to the firm's cost of capital, that it would like to finance. Finally, let's imagine that the cost of the new project is precisely equal to the proposed dividend and that there is only enough current cash to support one of the two initiatives. Now, if the firm declares the dividend, the moment that the shares trade "ex dividend" (when subsequent stock purchasers no longer have the right to receive the dividend because it will be sent to the former stock owners), the market value of the shares should drop by precisely one-third to reflect the fact that this cash is effectively gone from the firm.

At this point, to finance the project the firm needs to sell new shares equal to the amount of the dividend. Because the firm is now worth one-third less than before, it must raise an amount equal to one-half of its remaining value. In short, the new investors must replace the funds paid out in the dividend. If the new project will earn the cost of the firm's capital, the firm must sell new shares equal to one-half of the currently outstanding shares. This leaves the new investors with one-third of the total shares outstanding after the financing is completed. Each share is now worth the value of a share ex dividend, which is one-third less than before the dividend. Essentially, the original shareholders have swapped cash for share value. This is illustrated by Figure 9-1:

Figure 9-1. Dividend Funded by Additional Equity

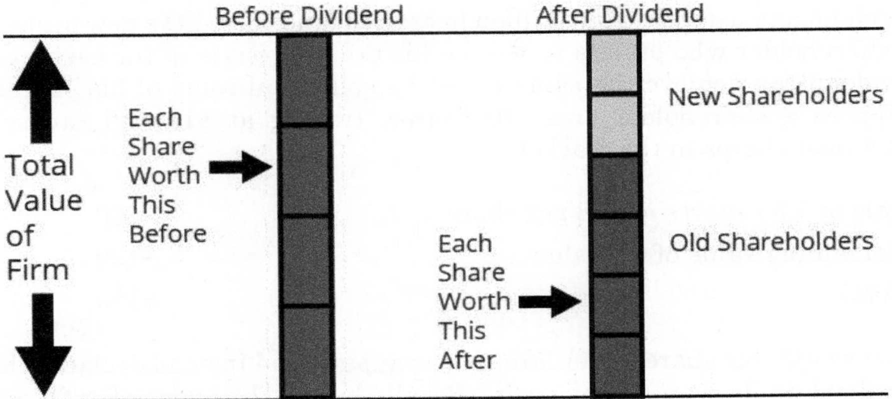

We can illustrate this numerically by returning to the PY hypothetical at the beginning of the chapter. Suppose PY has 30 million shares outstanding that are valued at $18 each, for a total market value of $540 million. And let's assume that the firm earns $54 million annually, which is capitalized at a 10% rate. Now suppose PY declares a $180 million total cash dividend (or $6 per share). After the dividend is paid, the firm has one third fewer assets, and we will assume that the firm's earning power has been reduced pro rata, so it now earns $36 million. The situation of the shareholders can be described as follows (in millions):

Total firm value	=	$360
Shareholders cash	=	$180
Shareholder wealth:	=	$540

Note that each share is now worth $12 ($360 million divided by 30 million shares). If the firm has a new $180 million project that is expected to generate $18 million in annual earnings it must calculate how many shares it needs to sell at $12 each in order to raise the necessary funding:

$$\frac{\$180{,}000{,}000}{\$12} = 15 \text{ million shares}$$

Thus, the new shareholders will hold one third of total outstanding shares (calculated as 15 million / 45 million) after completion of the financing. This leaves the old shareholders with shares worth $360 million and $180 million in cash. Presumably they can reinvest that cash in another firm with a similar level of risk and a similar cost of capital if they wish. So, economically, the old shareholders are exactly where they were before. And paying the dividend will have no effect on firm value if new funds are raised to replace the money used for the dividend.

Now let's see what happens if the firm decided not to pay the dividend and uses the $180 million in cash to fund the CEO's new project. A shareholder who prefers to receive his pro rata share of the cash as a dividend can achieve the same result by selling off some of his shares. Suppose a shareholder owns 10 shares, trading at $18 and can sell fractional shares in the market.

Sale of 3.33 shares at $18 per share		$60
Remaining value of 6.67 shares	=	$120
Total		$180

How would this shareholder fare if the company had instead declared the dividend as discussed previously? Recall that in the event of a $6 per share dividend, each share would decline in value to $12 per share once the dividend was declared. However, because each share would be entitled to $6 per share in dividends, our shareholder would own an economic entitlement equal to exactly $180 (i.e., $12 per share × 10 + $6 per share × 10).

Another way to think about this is that shareholders can raise cash from outside investors by selling them shares in the marketplace, or they can raise cash by receiving a dividend and having the firm sell new shares to outside investors. Figure 9-2 illustrates these choices:

Figure 9-2. Shareholder Options for Obtaining Cash

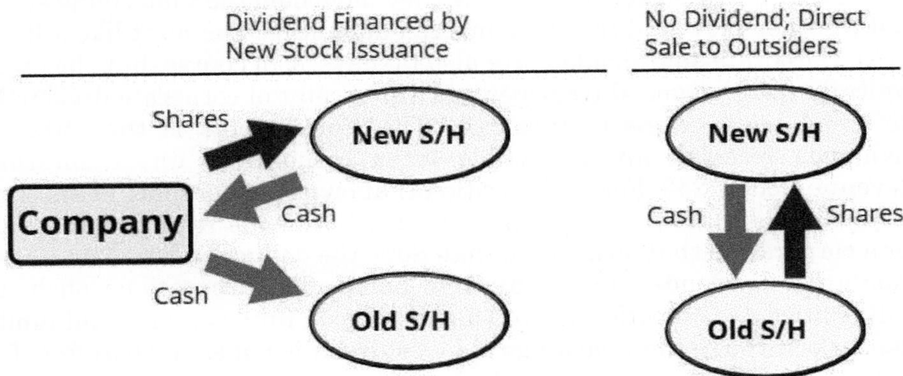

Therefore, under the conditions Modigliani and Miller have posited, investors should not really care whether corporations pay dividends or not. This is sometimes referred to as the Indifference Proposition. It is also important to observe that there is no link between dividend policy and investment policy: a firm may raise capital in capital markets as easily as it may retain earnings for reinvestment.

While Modigliani and Miller established these relationships with formal proofs, we (and they) know that this theory involves simplifying assumptions. We know that some, but not all firms, do elect to pay dividends. And we know that disagreements about dividend policy can sometimes lead to lawsuits (as we will soon see in more detail). So just like in Chapter 4, we again advise you not to tell your clients that dividends really don't matter. The indifference proposition can't offer the final word about how firms really make dividend decisions. Instead, we need to ask how relaxing the assumptions underlying the indifference proposition might prompt a more empirical analysis of the dividend policy question in a way that is connected to actual corporate decisions.

C. WHY DIVIDENDS MIGHT DECREASE FIRM VALUE

As we start to relax some of Modigliani and Miller's assumptions, we now arrive at a third perspective on dividends: they might actually *decrease* the value of a firm and its stock. There are several reasons why this might be true.

i. SHAREHOLDER PREFERENCES AND CLIENTELE EFFECTS

Investors may have very different preferences about dividends, perhaps stemming from the fact that that some shareholders pay taxes while others do not. Consider a firm with three types of shareholders: an individual investor, another corporation, and a university endowment. Individual shareholders typically have to pay income taxes on dividends, though their marginal rates may differ based on their tax bracket and some other factors (such as how long they have held the underlying stock and whether they hold the stock in a tax-advantaged account like a Roth IRA). Corporate shareholders are also taxpayers, of course, but they will typically receive special treatment for the receipt of corporate dividends (to avoid triple levels of taxation). The general rule is that 50% of dividends received are deductible for a corporation under Internal Revenue Code § 243. For a corporation that owns 20% or more of another corporation's shares, the deduction for the dividends rises to 65%. And for a corporation that owns more than 80%, the deduction becomes 100%. Similarly, dividends are tax-free for non-profit corporations such as universities and charities, as well as for pension funds and mutual funds that pass through their earnings to investors. It is not easy, therefore, for a board of directors to reach a clear understanding about the shareholder-level tax bill that will accompany a dividend payment.

What about asking individual shareholders whether they would like to receive cash now or whether they are content to just let the earnings build up inside the firm? Under a "life cycle theory of investing," we might expect younger investors to be happy with zero dividend policies that support saving for long-term goals, such as providing higher education for children and funding their own retirement.* Older investors will, when they retire, prefer investments that yield current income to support them in retirement. This might suggest that firms should consider the average age of their investor base when making a dividend decision.

But wait—Modigliani and Miller have something to say about this as well. Recall that a shareholder who wants cash when the company decides not to declare a dividend can "home-make" a dividend by selling off some shares. Moreover, a shareholder who prefers to remain fully invested in the company, when the company does pay a dividend, can just use the cash that they receive to buy more shares. Does this take us back to a dividend indifference world where the firm can do what it wants, and

* For a literature review, see Franco Modigliani, *Life Cycle, Individual Thrift, and the Wealth of Nations*, 76 AMERICAN ECONOMIC REVIEW 297 (1986). This description omits part of Modigliani's description. Younger adults, such as college and law students, often borrow funds, not only to pay tuition but also to provide living expenses, as they invest in their human capital. Once they complete this phase and move into the employment market, they may borrow to buy capital assets—homes, autos and appliances. Modigliani's theory is that individuals borrow and save in an effort to level out their standard of living throughout their lives, which maximizes total lifetime utility.

shareholders can self-adjust according to their preferences? Not necessarily. There are two problems with this strategy, as we shall discuss in the following subsections—transaction costs and tax costs.

ii. TRANSACTION COSTS OF SELLING OR BUYING SHARES

In Modigliani and Miller's model it's possible for a firm to sell more shares to fund new investments if it wants to use current cash for a dividend. While this is true, it is obvious that selling stock is not costless. Stock issuances involve underwriting commissions and other professional fees, and many firms will ultimately find it cheaper to retain earnings rather than sell shares for such purposes. There might also be a second type of cost if the sale of new shares is greeted with a decline in the market price of stock. Some investors may infer, for instance, that managers believe their stock is overpriced and wish to take advantage of investor ignorance. Under these circumstances, managers seeking outside financing may prefer to issue new debt, which, while it incurs transaction costs, is unlikely to cause the stock price to fall because of a negative signal that managers believe stock prices have reached a peak. (This all takes us back to Chapter 4, of course, where we discussed optimal capital structure planning.)

Similarly, shareholders can incur transaction costs if they wish to reinvest dividends in their company. There are brokerage fees to start with, though these have dropped significantly in recent years. Some companies also have dividend reinvestment programs that allow investors to avoid brokerage fees. But there may be psychological or decision costs for individual shareholders as well: should they reinvest in the same firm, or would they do better elsewhere? If a firm pays no dividends, there's no need to think about investment alternatives as directly.

What is the upshot of these various transaction costs? Note that firms incur the costs if they need to raise money to fund a dividend, while (some) investors incur the costs if they want to reinvest cash receipts in additional shares. If the first category of transaction costs is larger than the second, this might support a theory that issuing dividends will decrease the value of the firm. It seems difficult to evaluate this empirically, however, and the opposite might certainly be true for some firms. For this reason, the main argument against issuing dividends comes down to a tax minimization strategy.

iii. TAXES

You've probably spotted another obvious real-world error in the previous example of using a dividend payment to buy more shares. Our shareholder's cash dividend is subject to a personal income tax, so after paying taxes she has less money to reinvest in company stock. Recall the PY example above, where shareholders receive $180 million in dividends, and suppose now that all shareholders want to remain invested in the firm's stock. If the average dividend tax rate is 20%, they will pay $36 million in taxes, leaving only $144 million to reinvest in shares. This will buy just 12 million shares at $12 each. Thus, they wind up with shares with a market value of $144 million, and the rest of the money goes to the IRS. Notice that the investors bear this tax loss regardless of whether they simply keep the cash dividend or reinvest it.

But now assume that the company pays no dividends and reinvests the $180 million in new productive ventures earning its cost of capital, so the firm retains its value. If all shareholders wish to replicate the dividend above, then they will sell a third of their shares to raise cash. What is the tax impact here? This, of course, depends on the size of the shareholder's gain from the sale. If the shareholder paid $18 for their shares, then there is no gain and no tax on the transaction. The worst case would arise if the shareholders paid nothing for the shares; they would have a zero-cost basis and a gain of $180 million. If the shares have been held for one year or more, they are taxed at the long-term capital gains rate. Historically, this has often been less than the tax rate on dividends. And even if it is the same rate, 20% in this example, the total shareholder tax burden remains $36 million. But that's the worst-case scenario; most shareholders will have some cost basis to offset the gains. Furthermore, each shareholder can decide for themselves whether to incur the tax bill or just wait and keep the shares. Thus, for many investors, home-made dividends have looked a lot more attractive than cash dividends.

This is the core of the argument for financial economists who believe that a dividend increase will lead to lower firm value. If dividends are taxed at a higher rate than capital gains (as was historically the case), a firm can minimize the tax bill of distributing cash to shareholders by engaging in stock buybacks instead of dividends. (Don't forget that state income taxes are an added burden for taxpayers.) And even if the tax rates are the same (as has been the case more recently*), the ability of shareholders to offset some of their taxes with a cost basis supports the same strategy.

Moreover, there may be other tax reasons to avoid paying dividends. U.S. companies have historically held vast profits overseas. Prior to the introduction of the Tax Cuts and Jobs Act (TCJA) in 2017, U.S. corporate tax rates were often among the highest in the world. Under the pre-TCJA regime, if large corporations operated through foreign subsidiaries, their profits were often taxed at the lower rates of the nations where they were earned. While a U.S. corporation would receive a credit against its U.S. tax liability if it returned the funds to the U.S. to make them available

* "Qualified dividends" have been taxed at capital gain rates since 2003. Recently, for instance, qualified dividends are taxed at 20% for high-bracket taxpayers. To be qualified, the taxpayer must have held the stock for more than 60 days during the 121-day period that begins 60 days before the ex-dividend date. Prior to 2003, dividends were taxed at the individual's ordinary income tax rate, with the exception of the first $500, until 1985, when they were fully taxed. Source: http://www.dividend.com/taxes/a-brief-history-of-dividend-tax-rates/.

for distribution to shareholders, it would have to pay the difference between the foreign taxes paid and the U.S.'s higher rate, historically around 35%. As a result, multinational corporations often sought to limit their U.S. tax liability by deferring the repatriation of income earned abroad to their U.S.-based parent company in the form of dividends. The TCJA significantly altered this dynamic by reducing the incentive to keep cash outside the United States. However, it remains important to consider how tax rules might affect a firm's willingness to pay dividends, particularly those that would require the repatriation of overseas earnings.

For many, then, effective tax planning dictates that a corporation should never pay cash dividends. The firm should focus on investing cash in positive net present value projects that earn more than the cost of capital. Indeed, it should even use retained earnings to take on projects that simply return the cost of capital. If the firm lacks such projects but has a large cash balance, then it might consider an acquisition, a short-term investment in the securities of other corporations, or perhaps a stock buyback plan (more on this soon).

D. WHY DIVIDENDS MIGHT INCREASE FIRM VALUE (REVISITED)

Despite the plausible appeal of divided abstention policies that seek to minimize taxes, we see firms paying out cash dividends all the time. Many firms even try to increase their dividends on a regular basis. Why? To answer this question, we need to revisit the initial argument that dividends might increase firm value by considering some other assumptions of the Modigliani and Miller's indifference proposition.

i. IMPERFECT CAPITAL MARKETS AND THE SIGNALING VALUE OF DIVIDENDS

Modigliani and Miller assumed perfect capital markets in which all traders have equal and costless access to all relevant information about shares. But traders act as if markets are not perfect, or course, when they engage in research to locate valuable information not yet observed by other traders—and thus not yet reflected in stock prices. Indeed, that leads to the Efficient Capital Markets Paradox: that it is the disbelief of traders in market efficiency that keeps markets efficient.* Of course corporate frauds, insider trading, and other events demonstrate that capital markets cannot be perfectly efficient—efficiency is only a relative concept. Similarly, traders recognize that corporate managers frequently have superior information about firm prospects. For example, when companies sell stock, traders often infer that managers believe stock prices have peaked. As a result, new issues can depress current stock

* Sanford Grossman & Joseph Stiglitz, *On the Impossibility of Informationally Efficient Markets*, 70 AMERICAN ECONOMIC REVIEW 393 (1980).

prices for the issuer. Another way of saying this is that traders infer that managers believe their company's stock is currently overvalued. This is a negative "signal" that traders will operate on.

What kind of signal does a new corporate dividend send? Often it is read as a sign that management expects earnings or cash flows to increase, so it can "afford" to pay a higher dividend while maintaining its target payout rate. So perhaps a dividend increase predicts management's expectations about future earnings increases. On the other hand, recall that management should invest in all new positive net present value projects. Under this view, a dividend increase could be read as an announcement that the company's markets have matured, and fewer exceptional investment opportunities are expected in the future. Which story is more consistent with empirical observations in the market? Typically, a dividend decrease announcement appears to be read as a signal that management expects earnings to decline, and that the company will not be able to "afford" to continue the dividend at its current level. In response, stock prices often decline on the announcement of a dividend reduction. Similarly, an announced dividend increase is often taken, rightly or wrongly, as a signal of good things to come.

To be sure, this is not always the case. For instance, during the economic downturn in 2007 and 2008, some suffering financial institutions announced a dividend cut. The market response: stock prices increased. Why? Many analysts felt like this was a signal that managers at these firms recognized the extent of their troubles and that they were prepared to take the steps necessary to counteract any difficulties. This was an unusual context, however, and many people continue to think that a dividend increase, during normal times, carries a positive signal.

ii. AGENCY COST EXPLANATIONS OF DIVIDENDS

Thus far we have explored various factors that might influence directors' choices about paying dividends, including the choice between dividends and repurchases, the changing influence of taxes, investor expectations, investment opportunities, and the signaling effect of dividends. Implicit in some of these discussions has been the possibility that managers might refrain from making distributions to invest in negative net present value projects—a form of agency cost. There are various possible reasons for this—poor judgment or attempts to build a larger empire in order to justify higher compensation. The literature on acquisitions, for example, shows that acquiring firms can often destroy some shareholder value—explained by one author as management "hubris."

In other cases, managers may refrain from making distributions because they are overly risk-averse. After all, a firm's failure will have disastrous effects on their own careers and personal wealth. They may therefore avoid high-risk projects that offer substantial positive net present value, in favor of lower-risk, lower-return projects that offer more safety. In addition, for firms with existing debt, foregoing dividends and financing new projects from retained earnings increases the proportion of equity in the firm's balance sheet. This has the effect of lowering the riskiness of existing firm debt and providing creditors with an additional unbargained-for benefit.

However, all of these agency cost explanations might help explain why firms *avoid* distributions. Are there also agency cost explanations that might explain why managers *make* distributions? Frank Easterbook offers a "bonding" theory for the regular payment of dividends.* Recognizing the power of Modigliani and Miller's thesis that investment policy rather than dividend policy determines firm value, he offers the hypothesis that dividends, accompanied by regular trips to the capital market for new financing, offer a way for managers to commit to being faithful agents. As we have discussed previously, shareholders face collective action problems in monitoring. Easterbrook argues that a policy of regular dividends plus outside financing assures that the debt-equity ratio remains stable or increases the percentage of debt in the capital structure. In this regard, a strong distribution policy has the same effect as taking on debt insofar that it makes managers more efficient in their use of corporate resources. Moreover, by forcing the firm to return to the capital markets for external financing, managers will undergo careful scrutiny of the firm, its management, and the quality of proposed new investments. For instance, both creditors and investment bankers serving as underwriters will perform their own "due diligence" to assure that the firm promises future success. Securing outside capital will also require a firm to prepare audited financial statements. And in many industries the primary buyers of new securities offerings will be large financial institutions who have the capacity to perform their own due diligence and analysis. They may be prepared to undertake a large enough investment to justify expending more money and effort on due diligence than the average shareholder would consider.

Thus, a commitment to pay regular dividends is a commitment that, as the firm encounters new investment opportunities, it will regularly submit itself to inspection. This, in turn, might assure existing investors that agency costs will be constrained by management's anticipation of such continuing scrutiny. Share repurchases often tend to be sporadic, and thus might not offer the same scrutiny expectations of regular distributions.

E. WHAT DO FIRMS ACTUALLY DO?

As we have seen, the theoretical arguments about dividend policy point in different directions. There are plausible reasons to avoid paying dividends, and there are other effects that might commend such a strategy. What do firms actually do? Here we offer a description of

* Frank H. Easterbrook, *Two Agency-Cost Explanations of Dividends*, 74 AMERICAN ECONOMIC REVIEW 650 (1984).

dividend practices, without any theory. In part this is because some practices do not seem to conform to any rational theory that economists have been able to propound, leaving us with the conclusion that dividends remain something of a mystery. For purposes of this discussion we also include other forms of payout—including share repurchases.

The earliest modern study of dividend practices was published in 1956 by John Lintner—well before computers allowed massive empirical studies.* As a result, his study included only 28 companies. Lintner found what today's behavioralist economists would describe as an anchoring bias—discussions of dividends were always referenced to the current dividend policy and whether the dividend should be increased or decreased. Managers also apparently believed that investors valued predictability of dividends, so that an unexpected decrease from an "overly generous" dividend the previous year would harm the company's stock price. This led to conservative year-to-year adjustments. As a result, dividend policy was not guided by decisions about the need for new investment or the lack of investment opportunities. Most companies had a fixed idea of what "fair share" of firm earnings should be paid to shareholders—a "payout ratio"—but this was only a broad guideline, and adjustments were not made annually to rigorously maintain that ratio; they only occurred incrementally over time. At the time Lintner studied these practices, target ratios varied from 20% to 80%, with most companies aiming for a payout of 40% to 60% of earnings. Anticipated capital needs of the business could influence current payout decisions. During this era share repurchases were apparently negligible, and Lintner did not discuss them as part of corporate distribution policy.

Where Lintner's early effort shed some light on dividend decisions, modern economists have had the advantage of large corporate accounting datasets and more comprehensive analysis. Eugene Fama and Kenneth R. French reported in 2001 on a study of all New York Stock Exchange, American Stock Exchange and NASDAQ firms.† They concluded that "[t]he percent of firms paying dividends declines sharply after 1978. In 1973, 52.8% of publicly traded non-financial non-utility firms pay dividends. The proportion of payers rises to a peak of 66.5% in 1978. It then falls rather relentlessly. In 1999, only 20.8% of firms pay dividends." They attribute this in part to a growing awareness of the tax disadvantage of dividends, which were then taxed to individual shareholders at their marginal ordinary income tax rates. At the same time, they noted the growth of share repurchases, where, as discussed above, only the sum in excess of a taxpayer's cost basis is taxed (and often at more favorable capital gains rates). In 2003, part of the dividend tax disadvantage disappeared when rates on dividends were reduced to the

* John Lintner, *Distribution of Incomes of Corporations Among Dividends, Retained Earnings, and Taxes*, 46 AMERICAN ECONOMIC REVIEW 97 (1956).

† Eugene Fama and Kenneth R. French, *Disappearing Dividends: Changing Firm Characteristics or Lower Propensity to Pay?*, 60 JOURNAL OF FINANCIAL ECONOMICS 3 (2001).

capital gains rate. But the entire amount of a dividend payment is taxed, of course, while only the gain on a sale of shares is taxed.

Yet dividends seemed to reverse course right about the time that Fama and French published their article. From 2001 to 2007, U.S. firms paid out cash through both dividends and repurchases, both in absolute amounts and relative to earnings, that exceeded levels at any time in modern history according to a paper by Eric Floyd et al.* While repurchases exceeded dividends, both forms of payouts increased steadily after 2002 for both industrial firms and banks. Could this mean that managers agreed with Easterbrook's analysis that dividends offered a credible commitment to submit to outside monitoring? Part of the explanation appears related to the growth of LBOs about this time. During an era of historically low interest rates beginning in 2002 and continuing until a speculative bubble drove them up in 2005–2008, and then back down to extremely low levels, there were numerous leveraged buyouts by private equity funds and other financial investors. These were heavily financed with debt, but often the investors repaid themselves by increasing dividends to levels that allowed repayment of some if not all the debt. Still, given the overall magnitude of payouts during this period, leveraged buyouts and their aftermath probably explain only a small amount of the phenomenon.

Floyd et al. were surprised to observe the "stickiness" of dividends during the financial crisis, perhaps echoing Lintner's earlier observations. Dividends for both industrial and financial corporations persisted from 2007–2009, with only 1% of payers discontinuing dividends, and aggregate dividends declining by only 2%. More surprising, perhaps, they found that large banks that participated in the government bail-out were reluctant to cut their dividends, with most delaying cuts until after the first round of bail-out funding in October 2008.

The authors also note that dividends grew and persisted during this period, despite the view of economists that repurchases are a more tax-efficient and thus superior payout vehicle. They return to the possibility that a consistent dividend policy may reduce agency costs and satisfy the needs of some investor clientele groups for a steady dividend policy. They also found that a relatively small number of large highly profitable firms account for the bulk of payouts (dividends + repurchases) in their sample. Finally, they examined the evidence of whether the tax reforms of 2003 that reduced dividend rates to the same level as capital gains rates had any effect on payout practices. One might have expected a shift toward a relatively greater share of payouts in the form of dividends, but the evidence is to the contrary—a greater proportion of payouts through repurchases.

* Eric Floyd, Nan Li, and Douglas J. Skinner, *Payout Policy Through the Financial Crisis: The Growth of Repurchases and the Resilience of Dividends*, 118 JOURNAL OF FINANCIAL ECONOMICS 299 (2015).

In summary, the only thing that can be safely said is that dividend practices differ widely among firms. Some managers seem to eschew payouts, while others persist in declaring large dividends. Accordingly, we cannot offer a definitive conclusion about whether paying a dividend will increase firm value. Instead, we now turn our attention to the legal considerations that a firm will face when it does chart a distribution strategy.

3. BOARD DISCRETION AND DUTIES IN DECLARING DIVIDENDS

We begin our legal discussion with some basics. Statutes generally reserve dividend decisions for the board of directors. See DGCL § 170(a) ("The directors of every corporation . . . may declare and pay dividends upon the shares of its capital stock. . .") and Model Act § 6.40(a) ("A board of directors may authorize and the corporation may make distributions to its shareholders. . ."). Every jurisdiction treats a declared dividend as an indebtedness of the corporation. But when does it accrue, and who owns it? These questions become critical when ownership is transferred, and in large public corporations millions of shares may trade each day.

Caleb & Co. v. E. I. Dupont de Nemours & Company

615 F.Supp. 96 (S.D.N.Y. 1985)

■ SWEET, D.J.

This securities action, arising from the tender offer by E. I. DuPont de Nemours and Co. ("DuPont") for Conoco ("Conoco"), returns as the result of an amended complaint and a renewed motion to dismiss pursuant to Fed.R.Civ.P. 12(b)(6). The motion is granted in part and denied in part, as set forth below.

* * *

Facts

[On July 15, 1981, DuPont issued its prospectus to all Conoco shareholders, including Caleb, offering them a choice of $95 cash or 1.7 DuPont shares for every Conoco share tendered in accordance with the offer. Two weeks later, because DuPont's tender offer was hotly contested by two other bidders, Joseph E. Seagram & Sons, Inc. and Mobil Oil Corporation, DuPont increased the number of shares it would accept for cash, and on August 4, DuPont increased its cash offer to $98.00 per share, prompting Mobil to increase its offer to $120.00 per share.]

[I]t is alleged that the Board of Directors of Conoco declared a dividend on July 31, 1981, payable to shareholders of record as of August 14, 1981. * * *

The Complaint

On the facts alleged, Caleb asserts four causes of action. * * *

The fourth cause of action alleges that DuPont and First Jersey violated contractual and fiduciary obligations owed to Caleb by prematurely transferring the shares to DuPont thereby permitting DuPont wrongfully to receive the dividend payable to shareholders of record on August 14, 1981.

DuPont and First Jersey have moved to dismiss each of the four counts of the amended complaint, and the counts will be addressed sequentially.

* * *

Count Four: Entitlement to the Dividend

The amended complaint alleges that First Jersey improperly permitted DuPont to acquire the tendered shares, prior to payment, before the August 14 record date for the \$0.65 quarterly Conoco dividend, thereby permitting DuPont improperly to receive the dividend. It is undisputed that Conoco declared a \$0.65 per share dividend on July 31, 1981, payable on September 14 to stockholders of record on August 14. DuPont accepted and purchased the shares on August 5, although it did not pay for them until after August 14. The issues that must be resolved are first whether DuPont's acceptance without payment on August 5 made it the record owner on August 14, and second, which holder has the right to a cash dividend when the dividend is declared before a sale of stock, but the shares are sold before the record date but after the declaration.

A. DuPont's August 5 Acceptance

DuPont's acceptance of tendered shares on August 5 vested in DuPont the right to be considered the record owner on August 14, even though payment for the shares postdated August 14. The principle was explained and held to be uniformly applicable by Professor Williston, who stated:

> The uniform statutes, in force in all of the states in one form or another, definitely provide . . . that legal title to stock passes to the buyer upon delivery of the certificate in proper form. But the passing of legal title may, or may not, be coterminous with the passing of the risks, and the rights of ownership, in the shares. Moreover, all of the rights, or obligations, of ownership may not pass at the same time. Thus, the purchaser of shares, absent any agreement to the contrary, is generally entitled to dividends, rights and all the privileges of a shareholder, except voting power, from the time he makes the purchase contract, whether or not he has made payment, has taken legal title or has been registered on the corporation records as a shareholder.

8 Williston on Contracts § 953 at 320–21 (1964) (footnotes omitted) (emphasis added).

In Lafountain & Woolson Co. v. Brown, 91 Vt. 340, 101 A. 36, 37 (1917), the court explained that "the principle of equitable assignments applies. The purchaser of shares of corporate stock is held to acquire an equitable interest in the stock before the transfer is completed, if the agreement of purchase and sale is binding between the parties." Id. The contract between the tendering shareholders and DuPont became binding on August 5, and DuPont thereby could benefit from the principle of equitable assignments in order to be considered the owner of record.

B. Declaration Date v. Record Owner

An examination of the Delaware authorities, recognized by both parties to be binding here, establishes that an owner as of the record date but not the declaration date is the beneficiary of the dividend. A sale between the declaration and record dates causes the dividend to inure to the benefit of the purchaser.

The tension between the declaration date and the record date results from the desire of corporations to clarify their own liability for dividend payments. Before the record date problem arose, the courts with very few exceptions held that dividends belonged to the owner of the stock on the date the dividend was declared. However, the practice of most corporations today is to declare the dividend to be payable to shareholders on a date of record between the declaration date and the date set for payment. The original purpose of such a practice was undoubtedly to protect the corporation, so that when it paid a dividend to the person registered on the books on the record date no liability would fall on the corporation if such person were not the actual owner on that date. However, many courts have held that the record date is the effective date of the dividend and that the actual owner on the date of record is entitled to the dividend even though he may not be the owner registered on the books of the corporation. Some courts have not accepted this view and retain the rule that title vests on the date of the declaration. The numerical majority follows the reasoning of the Connecticut Supreme Court in Richter & Co. v. Light, whereas the minority in number is led by New Jersey.

> "It would seem clear that the majority of states, both in number and importance, favors the Connecticut rule, and that the trend is increasingly in that direction."

Note, Dividends—To Whom Payable When Record Date Is Given, 7 Ohio St. U.L.J. 431, 437–39 (1941) (footnotes omitted).

When there is both a declaration date and a record date, the declaration of the dividend creates a debtor-creditor relationship between the corporation and the owner of the stock on the date of declaration:

> It seems to be true that upon the declaration of a lawful dividend by a Board of Directors that the relation of debtor and creditor is set up between the corporation and the stockholder. In most cases the right set up in the stockholder is an irrevocable right

> and the declaration of the lawful dividend creates an obligation of the corporation and there exists a right to action on the part of the stockholder to enforce its payment. The right of action is in the nature of a contract and grows out of the declaration of a lawful dividend. The actual wording of the Resolution, the physical minutes, constitute mere matter of Record.

Selly v. Fleming Coal Co., 37 Del. 34, 180 A. 326, 328 (1935).

> The theory [is] that when a dividend is declared, it is, in effect, set aside by the corporation, as money in hand, for the benefit of the stockholder entitled, though it is not then payable. Wheeler v. Northwestern Sleigh Co., C.C., 39 F. 347; Cogswell v. Second Nat'l Bank, 78 Conn. 75, 60 A. 1059; 38 Harv. Law. Rev. 247. This creates a debtor and creditor relation, and if such dividend is not paid when due it may be recovered in an appropriate action by the stockholders.

Wilmington Trust Co. v. Wilmington Trust Co., 25 Del. Ch. 193, 15 A.2d 665, 667 (1940). However, the ultimate beneficiary of the dividend will still be controlled by owner of the stock on the record date. As the court explained in Wilmington Trust, supra, the debtor-creditor relationship between the corporation and stock owner arising at the time of declaration of the dividend was not ultimately controlling.

> The general rule is that the estate of the life beneficiary of the income is entitled to all regular cash dividends that have been declared during her lifetime, for the benefit of the stockholders of record on dates prior to her death, though such dividends are not actually payable or receivable by the trustees until dates subsequent thereto.

The Delaware Code also establishes the supremacy of the record date over the declaration date for the establishment of shareholder rights:

> (a) In order that the corporation may determine the stockholders entitled to notice of or to vote at any meeting of stockholders or any adjournment thereof, or to express consent to corporate action in writing without a meeting, or entitled to receive payment of any dividend or other distribution or allotment of any rights, or entitled to exercise any rights in respect of any change, conversion or exchange of stock or for the purpose of any other lawful action, the board of directors may fix, in advance, a record date, which shall not be more than 60 nor less than 10 days before the date of such meeting, nor more than 60 days prior to any other action.

See Fletcher, Cyclopedia of the Law of Private Corporations § 5379 (citing Del. Code Title 8, § 213 as statutory alteration of rule of declaration date entitlement); 12 Del. Code Ann. Title 12 § 6104(e) (establishing priority of corporate specified record date over declaration date).

* * *

Even though neither Wilmington Trust, supra, nor the Delaware Code section cited above, directly resolve the confrontation here, I conclude that their clear implication is that the owner as of the record date is the proper recipient of the dividend. Caleb's final cause of action is therefore dismissed.

QUESTIONS

1. Why would the transfer agent for Conoco's stock, First Jersey, transfer title to the shares before the receipt of the purchase price?
2. Why bother separating the declaration date from the record date? Can't a board just pay (or owe) dividends to current shareholders as soon as it announces the payout decision?
3. Based on our earlier discussion, what effect would you expect the declaration of a dividend to have on a stock's price between the declaration date and the date of record? After the date of record? Is it possible to make an accurate prediction?

How do the fiduciary duties of a board interact with dividend decisions? Is the board of directors completely free, as a matter of fiduciary law, to declare, increase, or reduce a dividend as it sees fit? Consider the next case:

Berwald v. Mission Development Company

185 A.2d 480 (Del. 1962)

■ SOUTHERLAND, CHIEF JUSTICE.

Plaintiffs, owners of 248 shares of the stock of Mission Development Corporation, brought suit to compel the liquidation of Mission and the distribution of its assets to its stockholders. Mission answered and filed a motion for summary judgment, based on affidavits and depositions. Plaintiffs tendered no contradictory proof. The Vice Chancellor granted the motion and the plaintiffs appeal.

The facts are as follows:

Defendant, Mission Development, is a holding company. Its sole significant asset is a block of nearly seven million shares of Tidewater Oil Company. Tidewater is a large integrated oil company, qualified to do business in all the States of the Union. It is controlled, through Mission Development and Getty Oil Company, by J. Paul Getty.

Mission Development was formed in 1948 for the purpose of acquiring a block of 1,416,693 shares of Tidewater common stock. . . * * *

The shares of both Mission Development and Tidewater are listed on the New York Stock Exchange.

From 1948 to 1951 Mission acquired an additional 1,050,420 shares of Tidewater. Thereafter, and by 1960, Mission's holdings of Tidewater, through a 100% stock dividend and annual stock dividends of five per cent, increased to 6,943,957 shares.

In 1954 Tidewater discontinued the payment of cash dividends, thus effecting a discontinuance of Mission's income. Mission, as above noted, received thereafter until 1960 an annual 5% stock dividend, but Mission's proportionate ownership of Tidewater was not thereby increased, and its management accordingly deemed it unwise to distribute the shares as a dividend, since to do so would have decreased its proportionate ownership of Tidewater.

As hereafter shown, Tidewater's discontinuance of cash dividends was prompted by the adoption in 1954 of a policy of corporate expansion and modernization. The use of its available cash for this purpose left it without funds for dividends.

* * *

All of the foregoing facts were reported to Mission stockholders by letter of J. Paul Getty, President of the corporation, dated April 11, 1955.

We pause to note that some of the plaintiff's stock in Mission Development was bought in 1956 and 1959.

* * *

From September 1960 to and including August 1961 Getty Oil Company acquired 510,200 shares of Mission. Some of these were purchased off the market.

In November 1960 this suit was filed.

As above indicated, plaintiffs seek to compel a complete or partial liquidation of the defendant and the distribution of its assets, either through the medium of a winding-up receivership, or by means of a court order compelling the management to distribute, or to offer to distribute, at least part of the Tidewater shares in exchange for Mission shares.

The extreme relief of receivership to wind up a solvent going business is rarely granted. To obtain it there must be a showing of imminent danger of great loss resulting from fraud or mismanagement. Like caution is dictated in considering an application to compel a corporation to make a partial distribution.

Since no showing is made of fraud or mismanagement inflicting injury upon the corporation, what is the basis of plaintiff's case?

Plaintiff's argument proceeds as follows:

There is an inherent conflict of interest between the controlling stockholder of Mission, Mr. J. Paul Getty, and the minority stockholders. This arises out of the dividend policy of Tidewater. Because of high income taxes, Mr. Getty, it is said, is not interested in receiving dividends; he is interested in acquiring more shares of Tidewater. To achieve this end, it is charged, he has caused Tidewater to discontinue all dividends and to announce, in 1960, that no dividends could be expected for five years. The necessary effect of this policy, plaintiffs say, was to depress the market value of Mission shares, and enable Mr. Getty to buy more Mission shares at an artificially low price, at the expense of Mission's minority stockholders. This, plaintiffs charge, is just what he has done, as is proved by Getty Oil's purchases of stock in 1960 and 1961. Thus he and Mission have inflicted a serious wrong upon the minority stockholders.

It is quite true that in some cases the interests of a controlling stockholder and of the minority stockholders in respect of the receipt of dividends may conflict, because of the existence of very high income taxes.* And in some cases this may work hardship on the minority. But we find no such situation here.

It is plain that the whole argument based on a charge of conflict of interest rests upon the claim that Tidewater's dividend policy, and its public announcement of it, were designed to serve the selfish interest of Mr. Getty and not to further its own corporate interests. If the opposite is true—if Tidewater's policy was adopted in furtherance of its own corporate interest—then Mission's stockholders have not been subjected to an actionable wrong and have no complaint. The fact of Mr. Getty's purchase of Mission Development stock then becomes irrelevant.

What does the record show with respect to Tidewater's dividend policy?

In the ten years prior to 1953 Tidewater's expenditure for capital improvements did not exceed $41,100,000 in any one year. Shortly prior to 1954 Tidewater began to expand and modernize its facilities. In February 1955 it closed and subsequently sold its obsolete refinery at Bayonne, New Jersey, and built a new and modern refinery in New Castle County, Delaware at a cost in excess of $200,000,000. Also, it commenced and still continues the expansion and modernization of its refinery facilities at Avon, California, and the increase of its crude oil and natural gas resources. As of November 3, 1960, the budget for new capital projects to be begun in 1961 was $111,000,000.

It is unnecessary to elaborate the point. It is entirely clear from the facts set forth in the affidavits that Tidewater's cash has since 1960 been largely devoted to capital improvements and that, in the opinion of management, funds were not available for dividends. These facts are uncontradicted, and they constitute a refutation of the basic argument of plaintiffs that dividends were discontinued to enable J. Paul Getty to buy Mission stock at a depressed price.

---

* Eds. During this era the maximum marginal Federal Income Tax rate for individuals was 91%.

Some point is sought to be made of the unusual action of the Tidewater management in announcing that dividends could not be expected for five years. As defendant's counsel says, this was done out of common fairness to its stockholders and to prospective purchasers of its stock.

It is earnestly argued that plaintiffs should be allowed to go to trial and adduce testimony on the issue of the selfish motives of the controlling stockholder. Plaintiffs say that they could show by expert testimony that the market price of Mission common was artificially depressed.

It is first to be noted that the record of market prices put in by the plaintiffs themselves fails to show any drop in prices coincident with or closely following the announcement of the cessation of dividends. Plaintiffs reply that this fact is meaningless because at that time the market was steadily going up, and say that expert testimony will establish this. The answer to this argument is that if plaintiffs had such proof they should have come forward with it. "In such a situation, a duty is cast upon the plaintiff to disclose evidence which will demonstrate the existence of a genuine issue of fact * * * if summary judgment * * * is to be denied."

There are other facts in this case that support the conclusion above indicated. The sole corporate purpose of Mission is and has been to hold Tidewater stock. Any investor in its shares could readily ascertain this fact. Because of this he knows, or should know, that he is buying for growth and not for income.

* * *

However the various arguments are put they come to this: Plaintiffs are in effect seeking to wind up the corporation, either wholly or partially, because it is doing exactly what it was lawfully organized to do.

We think the plaintiffs have failed to make a case.

The judgment below is affirmed.

QUESTIONS

1. One of the requests for relief of the plaintiffs was for Mission to distribute part of the Tidewater shares in exchange for Mission shares. Both Mission and Tidewater were listed on the New York Stock Exchange. How would this relief have benefitted the plaintiffs?
2. If you represented the defendants, what argument could you make from finance in response to plaintiff's claim that the Tidewater dividends were eliminated to depress the market value of Mission shares, and thus to allow Getty to buy more Mission shares at a depressed price?
3. The court concedes that the interests of minority and majority shareholders may conflict because of high tax rates, and that in some

cases this may work a hardship on the minority. Would you expect this to be a problem in a large publicly traded corporation? Why or why not?

4. Mission's stock price did not fall in reaction to the announcement of the dividend cut. The plaintiff attributes this to a generally rising stock market. Can you think of a more refined way to examine the effect of the announcement?

NOTE

Many readers will recall Dodge v. Ford Motor Co., 204 Mich. 459, 170 N.W. 668 (1919), where Henry Ford, as controlling shareholder, caused the company to reduce dividend payments drastically in the face of efforts by the Dodge brothers, 10% shareholders, to start their own automobile company. Henry Ford testified that he thought profits were "too large," and that he wanted to reduce car prices and increase sales to employ more workers. While the court rejected Ford's "charitable" justifications for the company's decisions, it declined to interfere with investments in an expanded plant, saying:

> "We are not, however, persuaded that we should interfere with the proposed expansion of the business of the Ford Motor Company. In view of the fact that the selling price of products may be increased at any time, the ultimate results of the larger business cannot be certainly estimated. The judges are not business experts. It is recognized that plans must often be made for a long future, for expected competition, for a continuing as well as an immediately profitable venture. The experience of the Ford Motor Company is evidence of capable management of its affairs. . ."

The court did, however, order Ford to reinstate large special dividends that had recently been discontinued—claiming that the firm needed to be run for the benefit of shareholders and not as a semi-charitable organization. Is such judicial intrusion into board dividend decision-making justifiable?

A more recent challenge to board discretion regarding dividends can be seen in Gabelli & Co. Profit Sharing Plan v. Liggett Group, Inc., 479 A.2d 276 (Del. 1984). Gabelli, a stockholder in Liggett, sued because the Liggett board declined to pay its regular quarterly dividend on its common stock after it had agreed to be acquired by Grand Metropolitan Limited. Grand Met completed a tender offer that obtained 87% of Liggett's common stock, and then prepared for a cash-out merger at the same price. The Chancery Court granted summary judgment for the defendant directors and was affirmed on appeal. The Supreme Court found no fraud or gross abuse of discretion, which it stated must be shown before the courts would interfere with a dividend decision. The court found two justifications for the failure to declare this dividend:

> On the record before us, the non-payment of a final dividend by the Liggett Board in the final stages of the cash-out merger, is reasonably "explicable" . . . for at least 2 reasons: (1) It would have been unfair to the holders of 87% of the stock who accepted the tender offer upon the recommendation of the Board, to reward by a

"farewell" or "bonus" dividend the holders of the remaining 13% who, for some unannounced reason, declined to accept the tender offer and held out for the merger cash-out with the risk-free assurance of receiving the same price per share; and (2) It would have been unreasonable to supplement the $69 per share, which had been approved by the Board as a fair price for Liggett and all of its assets, by a last minute dividend declared in the final stages of the merger cash-out process.

Some readers may also recall Sinclair Oil Corp. v. Levien, 280 A.2d 717 (Del. 1971), where a minority shareholder in a subsidiary of Sinclair's complained that the corporation was paying out excessive dividends, rather than causing the subsidiary to invest in new opportunities. He complained that Sinclair was causing the subsidiary to pay these dividends because of Sinclair's need for funds to make investments at the parent company level. Once again, the top marginal individual tax rate ranged from 77–91% during this period, and Sinclair, as owner of more than 80% of the subsidiary's stock, received a deduction for 100% of the dividends received (facts not discussed in the opinion). Recall that the court dismissed the dividend claim since all shareholders were treated alike—it was not important that the impact of receipt of dividends on them was quite different. Is this a good rule? Would your answer change if Sinclair was paying out large dividends because it feared nationalization of the subsidiary by the Venezuelan government?

What if there are only a handful of shareholders? Dividend disputes in close corporations can vary somewhat from this deferential rule. Many cases take the same approach as the cases above. Gottfried v. Gottfried, 73 N.Y.S.2d 692 (Sup. 1947) involved the typical falling out between brothers, with one brother's employment terminated while the other held control. The controlling family members continued to draw salaries and, in one case, received a share of the profits of a major subsidiary as compensation. They also received loans from the corporation. Other funds were spent on expansion, and the court could not conclude that the failure to pay dividends, or to pay modest dividends, was in bad faith. It therefore denied relief. In other cases, courts have ruled that they lacked power to order the payment of a dividend, but they have offered a remedy for oppressive conduct by a majority in the form of dissolution or the appointment of a receiver. White v. Perkins, 213 Va. 129, 189 S.E.2d 315 (1972).

And some courts have been willing to go further by ordering the payment of dividends. See Miller v. Magline, Inc., 76 Mich. App. 284, 256 N.W.2d 761 (1977). In this dispute, two of the three officers and directors left full-time employment with the company, and thereafter received neither salaries nor dividends, while the remaining officer-director took larger and larger compensation as the corporation prospered over the next six years. Earned surplus grew to over $2.5 million. The court ordered dividend payments for the most recent five years. Citing Dodge v. Ford Motor Co., 204 Mich. 459, 170 N.W. 668 (1919), the court noted that the controlling officer-director was taking a share of profits as compensation, while denying the other shareholders any part of the profits, and characterized it as "inequitable in not giving consideration properly to the needs and requirements of all of the stockholders of the corporation." The court rejected the defendant's arguments that a dividend was inappropriate because the company had a working capital shortage, had outmoded equipment that needed replacement, and was in a cyclical business. The controlling officer-director had not cut back his own compensation because of these concerns.

Another highly publicized dispute over non-payment of dividends did not reach the courts but generated a takeover attempt of the company. Chrysler Corporation had come perilously close to bankruptcy in the late 1970s, due to a series of unsuccessful models. Under the new leadership of Lee Iacocca, Chrysler restructured its debt and obtained government guarantees for this new debt. Iacocca led a successful revival of Chrysler in the 1980s, so that by the 1990s the company was once again solvent. Iacocca was succeeded as Chrysler CEO in 1992 by Robert Eaton, who was hired from General Motors. Financier Kirk Kerkorian began accumulating Chrysler stock in 1990 and increased its holdings to nearly 10% by 1994. As profits increased, Chrysler had increased its dividends only modestly, retaining most of its earnings. Chrysler's management explained that it needed to retain cash because it was in a cyclical business, where large profits could be followed by equally large losses, but the need to introduce new models continued. One suspects that this buildup of cash had at least some connection to its previous financial crisis; Chrysler management may have been uncertain about its ability to go to the capital markets for funding during hard times. By the end of 1994, Chrysler projected that its cash reserves would be $7.5 billion, and $11.5 billion by the end of 1996. At the same time, Chrysler's stock fell from $63.50 in January 1994 to $45 by mid-November of that year.

Kerkorian (now allied with the retired Iacocca) urged Chrysler to increase its dividends and engage in large stock repurchases to return cash to shareholders. At the same time, he urged the board to eliminate Chrysler's poison pill so he could acquire more than 15% of its stock and force a change in management. In December of 1994, Chrysler raised its dividend and announced a $1 billion stock buy-back program, which was completed in 1995. In 1995 Kerkorian, still unsatisfied, launched a $20 billion hostile takeover attempt, but this faltered as he struggled to finance the transaction. During this period Chrysler's stock rose as high as $52.50 on the first announcement of the initial offer, and fell to $44 after the second bid and the announcement of a possible proxy fight. Eventually, Chrysler raised its dividend several times and doubled the size of its stock buy-back program to $2 billion. Ultimately, it entered into a settlement with Kerkorian in which he agreed to keep his holdings below 13.7% and Chrysler agreed to an additional share repurchase program and placement of a Kerkorian representative on the board.

In more recent years, similar strategic battles have occurred between activist shareholders, who sometimes seek greater distributions, and the managers at profitable technology companies, like Apple or Dell. In many cases, the firms have accumulated large cash hoards but seem unwilling to dip into the money to fund shareholder distributions. Resolution of these debates can differ from situation to situation.

4. LEGAL RESTRICTIONS ON DIVIDENDS AND OTHER DISTRIBUTIONS TO SHAREHOLDERS

In Chapter 6 we discussed the role of indenture covenants and loan agreements in protecting creditors from shareholder attempts to strip the assets from the debtor corporation. We saw a variety of approaches: restricting dividends to some defined portion of earnings or retained earnings, requiring maintenance of some minimum net worth or tangible net worth, and requiring maintenance of certain ratios that impose an indirect limit on dividends, such as current ratios or debt-equity ratios. These restrictions protect not only the lenders obtaining the covenants, but other creditors as well. Unsecured contract and tort creditors, for instance, can free ride on the limits imposed on the debtor by covenants in bond indentures and loan agreements.

Beyond any contractually negotiated limits on distributions, a firm might also need to worry about some other legal restrictions. In earlier chapters we alluded to legal capital requirements and fraudulent transfer concerns. We now examine these legal limits on corporate distributions more closely. The rules here are not always intuitive or straightforward, and these legal restrictions can sometimes serve as a trap for unwary directors who seek to pay out dividends.

A. LEGAL CAPITAL REQUIREMENTS

Early "legal capital" rules were designed to assure the initial contribution of value to a corporation in exchange for its shares. These rules were also meant to ensure that some portion of this capital remained in the corporation as a "fund" to lessen the risk of insolvency. Imagine, for instance, that we started a corporation with no equity capital and obtained all of our operating funds by borrowing $100, which we used to buy equipment for exactly $100. Even a modest drop in the value of our equipment would render the company formally insolvent (i.e., the liquidation value of our assets would be less than our liabilities). In contrast, if we started the company by purchasing $10 of stock and borrowed $90 to buy $100 of equipment, the value of our equipment would have to drop below $90 before the company was formally insolvent.

Yet, creating and identifying a fund of capital to protect creditors is one thing; preserving it is another. Historically, the primary means to ensure that this fund of capital remained in the corporation was to restrict payments of any dividends to a corporation's profits. While the current Model Act no longer takes this approach, it persists in some states, and thus is worthy of mention. To understand how these restrictions operate, it is helpful to set forth some important nomenclature from § 2 of the Model Act (1950):

"Par value" means the amount specified in a company's charter as the minimum value that a corporation can receive for a share of capital stock. (It is also permissible to authorize stock with no par value, in which

case a corporation's directors generally specify the minimum amount the corporation may receive for its stock.)

"*Stated capital*" means par value times the number of shares outstanding, or the amount of consideration for no-par shares assigned to stated capital. (The default rule is the whole amount goes to stated capital under Model Act § 19 (1950).)

"*Net assets*" means assets minus liabilities.

"*Surplus*" means the excess of the net assets over stated capital. Surplus can be broken down into two kinds:

"*Earned Surplus*," which is the accumulated net profits not paid to shareholders, minus accumulated losses.

"*Capital Surplus*" is the rest of the surplus (sometimes called paid-in surplus).

Model Act § 19 (1950) provided that the excess paid for shares over par value (or the amount paid for no-par shares over the amount allocated to stated capital) is "capital surplus." These Model Act rules remained in effect until 1980. However, even today, Delaware continues to use these concepts of stated capital and capital surplus. DGCL § 154

The 1950 Model Act suggested that capital was meant to be preserved. In theory, this would help maintain the stability of a corporation and provide creditors with an equity cushion to protect their investment. Dividends could only be paid from current or past profits. Specifically, Model Act § 40 (1950), provided that dividends could be paid "only out of the unreserved and unrestricted earned surplus of the corporation. . ." Section 40, 1st paragraph, contained another limitation: dividends could be paid "except when the corporation is insolvent or when the payment thereof would render the corporation insolvent. . ."

DGCL § 170 continues to take a similar approach:

> "(a) The directors of every corporation . . . may declare and pay dividends upon the shares of its capital stock . . . either (1) out of its surplus, as defined in and computed in accordance with §§ 154 and 244 of this title, or (2) in case there shall be no surplus, out of its net profits for the fiscal year in which the dividend is declared and/or the preceding fiscal year. * * * "

Note that, while Model Act § 40 (1950) restricted dividends to earned surplus, Delaware law does not treat amounts paid for shares in excess of par value as part of permanent capital. Distributions (a return of capital) can therefore be made from these funds (capital surplus). (As with the Model Act (1950), however, a shareholder distribution in a Delaware corporation cannot result in the insolvency of the firm.)* This suggests an obvious loophole for the firm seeking to minimize legal capital restrictions: couple these rules with the use of low par stock—

* This issue was analyzed in the *Thoughtworks* case discussed in Chapter 7.

authorized under all U.S. statutes—and formal legal capital rules will preserve very little capital (aside from insolvency limitations).

Related evasions were also possible. Under the older Model Act, capital could be reduced by reducing par value through a shareholder vote that amended the articles of incorporation. Model Act § 53 (1950) permitted amendments of the articles that would reduce par value of both issued and unissued shares. This might free up funds, which could be paid out to shareholders as capital surplus. Similar results are possible in Delaware.

A second way to sidestep legal capital requirements arose through "nimble dividends." Model Act § 45(a) (alternative) (2d ed. 1967) provided as follows:

> "(a) Dividends may be declared and paid in cash or in property only out of the unreserved and unrestricted earned surplus of the corporation, *or out of the unreserved and unrestricted net earnings of the current fiscal year and the next preceding fiscal year taken as a single period, except as otherwise provided in this section.*" (Emphasis added.)

This meant that even if a corporation had negative earned surplus it could pay dividends if it had two good years. DGCL § 170(a)(2), quoted above, contains a similar provision. Indeed, this is slightly more flexible than the old Model Act provision because the corporation can pay so called nimble dividends even if the negative earned surplus exceeds capital surplus (funds paid in excess of par value for shares or resulting from reduction of par value).

Accordingly, the legal capital rules represented a maze that was navigable by corporations determined to pay dividends to their shareholders. The only real restriction for well-advised firms seemed to be insolvency.*

---

* Former Model Act § 40(a) (1950), dealing with dividends being paid only from surplus, allowed payment "except when the corporation is insolvent or when the declaration or payment thereof would render the corporation insolvent . . ." Former Model Act § 41(a) (1950), dealing with distributions from capital surplus (in partial liquidation) provided:

"(a) No such distribution shall be made at a time when the corporation is insolvent or when such distribution would render the corporation insolvent."

DGCL § 170(a) provides in part:

"(a) * * * If the capital of the corporation, computed in accordance with §§ 154 and 244 of this title, shall have been diminished by depreciation in the value of its property, or by losses, or otherwise, to an amount less than the aggregate amount of the capital represented by the issued and outstanding stock of all classes having a preference upon the distribution of assets, the directors of such corporation shall not declare and pay out of such net profits any dividends upon any shares of any classes of its capital stock until the deficiency in the amount of capital represented by the issued and outstanding stock of all classes having a preference upon the distribution of assets shall have been repaired. Nothing in this subsection shall invalidate or otherwise affect a note, debenture or other obligation of the corporation paid by it as a dividend on shares of its stock, or any payment made thereon, if at the time such note, debenture or obligation was delivered by the corporation, the corporation had either surplus or net profits as provided in clause (1) or (2) of this subsection from which the dividend could lawfully have been paid." (Emphasis added.)

These statutes applied the same approach to share repurchases, which also return money to shareholders. Model Act § 5 (1950) authorized share repurchases, "but it shall not purchase,

What happens if a board makes a mistake and pays a dividend that violates the legal capital rules? As we will see shortly, Section 7 of the Uniform Fraudulent Transfer Act provides that creditors of a transferring debtor may avoid the transfer, seek to enjoin further transfers, or seek a receiver to take charge of the transferred assets. Yet corporate laws go further. For example, Model Act § 8.33(a) provides for personal liability of directors!

> § 8.33 Directors' Liability for Unlawful Distributions
>
> (a) A director who votes for or assents to a distribution in excess of what may be authorized and made pursuant to section 6.40(a) or 14.09(a) [distributions in liquidation] is personally liable to the corporation for the amount of the distribution that exceeds what could have been distributed without violating section 6.40(a) or 14.09(a) if the party asserting liability establishes that when taking the action the director did not comply with section 8.30.

DGCL § 174 follows suit:

§ 174 Liability of Directors for Unlawful Payment of Dividend or Unlawful Stock Purchase or Redemption; Exoneration From Liability; Contribution Among Directors; Subrogation

> (a) In case of any willful or negligent violation of the provisions of sections 160 [share repurchases] or 173 [dividends] of this title, the directors under whose administration the same may happen shall be jointly and severally liable, at any time within six years after paying such unlawful dividend or after such lawful stock purchase or redemption, to the corporation, and to its creditors in the event of dissolution or insolvency, to the full amount of the dividend unlawfully paid, or to the full amount unlawfully paid for the purchase or redemption of the corporation's stock, with interest from the time such liability accrued.

You can bet that the prospect of personal liability for excessive distributions means that a board of directors who stumbles into this trap will be extremely upset.

---

either directly or indirectly, its own shares except out of its earned surplus or, with the affirmative vote of the holders of at least two-thirds of all shares entitled to vote thereon, out of its capital surplus."

DGCL § 160(a)1. suggests the same result:

"(a) Every corporation may purchase, redeem, receive, take or otherwise acquire, own and hold, sell, lend, exchange, transfer or otherwise dispose of, pledge, use and otherwise deal in and with its own shares; provided, however, that no corporation shall—

"1. Purchase or redeem its own shares of capital stock for cash or other property when the capital of the corporation is impaired or when such purchase or redemption would cause any impairment of the capital of the corporation. . .".

Klang v. Smith's Food & Drug Centers, Inc.

702 A.2d 150 (Del. 1997)

■ VEASEY, CHIEF JUSTICE.

This appeal calls into question the actions of a corporate board in carrying out a merger and self-tender offer. Plaintiff in this purported class action alleges that a corporation's repurchase of shares violated the statutory prohibition against the impairment of capital. Plaintiff also claims that the directors violated their fiduciary duty of candor by failing to disclose material facts prior to seeking stockholder approval of the transactions in question.

No corporation may repurchase or redeem its own shares except out of "surplus," as statutorily defined, or except as expressly authorized by provisions of the statute not relevant here. Balance sheets are not, however, conclusive indicators of surplus or a lack thereof. Corporations may revalue assets to show surplus, but perfection in that process is not required. Directors have reasonable latitude to depart from the balance sheet to calculate surplus, so long as they evaluate assets and liabilities in good faith, on the basis of acceptable data, by methods that they reasonably believe reflect present values, and arrive at a determination of the surplus that is not so far off the mark as to constitute actual or constructive fraud.

We hold that, on this record the Court of Chancery was correct in finding that there was no impairment of capital and there were no disclosure violations. Accordingly, we affirm.

Facts

Smith's Food & Drug Centers, Inc. ("SFD") is a Delaware corporation that owns and operates a chain of supermarkets in the Southwestern United States. Slightly more than three years ago, Jeffrey P. Smith, SFD's Chief Executive Officer, began to entertain suitors with an interest in acquiring SFD. At the time, and until the transactions at issue, Mr. Smith and his family held common and preferred stock constituting 62.1% voting control of SFD. Plaintiff and the class he purports to represent are holders of common stock in SFD.

On January 29, 1996, SFD entered into an agreement with The Yucaipa Companies ("Yucaipa"), a California partnership also active in the supermarket industry. Under the agreement, the following would take place:

(1) Smitty's Supermarkets, Inc. ("Smitty's"), a wholly-owned subsidiary of Yucaipa that operated a supermarket chain in Arizona, was to merge into Cactus Acquisition, Inc. ("Cactus"), a subsidiary of SFD, in exchange for which SFD would deliver to Yucaipa slightly over 3 million newly-issued shares of SFD common stock;

(2) SFD was to undertake a recapitalization, in the course of which SFD would assume a sizable amount of new debt, retire old debt, and offer to repurchase up to fifty percent of its outstanding shares (other than those issued to Yucaipa) for $36 per share; and

(3) SFD was to repurchase 3 million shares of preferred stock from Jeffrey Smith and his family.

SFD hired the investment firm of Houlihan Lokey Howard & Zukin ("Houlihan") to examine the transactions and render a solvency opinion. Houlihan eventually issued a report to the SFD Board replete with assurances that the transactions would not endanger SFD's solvency, and would not impair SFD's capital in violation of 8 Del. C. § 160. On May 17, 1996, in reliance on the Houlihan opinion, SFD's Board determined that there existed sufficient surplus to consummate the transactions, and enacted a resolution proclaiming as much. On May 23, 1996, SFD's stockholders voted to approve the transactions, which closed on that day. The self-tender offer was over-subscribed, so SFD repurchased fully fifty percent of its shares at the offering price of $36 per share.

Disposition in the Court of Chancery

This appeal came to us after an odd sequence of events in the Court of Chancery. On May 22, 1996, the day before the transactions closed, plaintiff Larry F. Klang filed a purported class action in the Court of Chancery against Jeffrey Smith and his family, various members of the SFD Board, Yucaipa, Yucaipa's managing general partner Ronald W. Burkle, Smitty's and Cactus. On May 30, 1996, plaintiff filed an amended complaint as well as a motion to have the transactions voided or rescinded, advancing a variety of claims, only two of which are before us on appeal. First, he contended that the stock repurchases violated 8 Del. C. § 160[1] by impairing SFD's capital. Second, he alleged that SFD's directors violated their fiduciary duties by failing to disclose material facts relating to the transactions prior to obtaining stockholder approval.

* * *

---

[1] Section 160(a) provides in part:

(a) Every corporation may purchase, redeem, receive, take or otherwise acquire, own and hold, sell, lend exchange, transfer or otherwise dispose of, pledge, use and otherwise deal in and with its own shares; provided, however, that no corporation shall:

(1) Purchase or redeem its own shares of capital stock for cash or other property when the capital of the corporation is impaired or when such purchase or redemption would cause any impairment of the capital of the corporation, except that a corporation may purchase or redeem out of capital any of its own shares which are entitled upon any distribution of its assets, whether by dividend or in liquidation, to a preference over another class or series of its stock, or, if no shares entitled to such a preference are outstanding, any of its own shares, if such shares will be retired upon their acquisition and the capital of the corporation reduced in accordance with §§ 243 and 244 of this title.

Plaintiff's Capital-Impairment Claim

A corporation may not repurchase its shares if, in so doing, it would cause an impairment of capital, unless expressly authorized by Section 160. A repurchase impairs capital if the funds used in the repurchase exceed the amount of the corporation's "surplus," defined by 8 Del. C. § 154 to mean the excess of net assets over the par value of the corporation's issued stock.

Plaintiff asked the Court of Chancery to rescind the transactions in question as violative of Section 160. As we understand it, plaintiff's position breaks down into two analytically distinct arguments. First, he contends that SFD's balance sheets constitute conclusive evidence of capital impairment. He argues that the negative net worth that appeared on SFD's books following the repurchase compels us to find a violation of Section 160. Second, he suggests that even allowing the Board to "go behind the balance sheet" to calculate surplus does not save the transactions from violating Section 160. In connection with this claim, he attacks the SFD Board's off-balance-sheet method of calculating surplus on the theory that it does not adequately take into account all of SFD's assets and liabilities. Moreover, he argues that the May 17, 1996 resolution of the SFD Board conclusively refutes the Board's claim that revaluing the corporation's assets gives rise to the required surplus. We hold that each of these claims is without merit.

SFD's balance sheets do not establish a violation of 8 Del. C. § 160

In an April 25, 1996 proxy statement, the SFD Board released a pro forma balance sheet showing that the merger and self-tender offer would result in a deficit to surplus on SFD's books of more than $100 million. A balance sheet the SFD Board issued shortly after the transactions confirmed this result. Plaintiff asks us to adopt an interpretation of 8 Del. C. § 160 whereby balance-sheet net worth is controlling for purposes of determining compliance with the statute. Defendants do not dispute that SFD's books showed a negative net worth in the wake of its transactions with Yucaipa, but argue that corporations should have the presumptive right to revalue assets and liabilities to comply with Section 160.

Plaintiff advances an erroneous interpretation of Section 160. We understand that the books of a corporation do not necessarily reflect the current values of its assets and liabilities. Among other factors, unrealized appreciation or depreciation can render book numbers inaccurate. It is unrealistic to hold that a corporation is bound by its balance sheets for purposes of determining compliance with Section 160. Accordingly, we adhere to the principles of Morris v. Standard Gas & Electric Co.[7] allowing corporations to revalue properly its assets and liabilities to show a surplus and thus conform to the statute.

It is helpful to recall the purpose behind Section 160. The General Assembly enacted the statute to prevent boards from draining

---

[7] Morris v. Standard Gas & Electric Co., 31 Del. Ch. 20, 63 A.2d 577 (1949).

corporations of assets to the detriment of creditors and the long-term health of the corporation. That a corporation has not yet realized or reflected on its balance sheet the appreciation of assets is irrelevant to this concern. Regardless of what a balance sheet that has not been updated may show, an actual, though unrealized, appreciation reflects real economic value that the corporation may borrow against or that creditors may claim or levy upon. Allowing corporations to revalue assets and liabilities to reflect current realities complies with the statute and serves well the policies behind this statute.

The SFD Board appropriately revalued corporate assets to comply with 8 Del. C. § 160.

Plaintiff contends that SFD's repurchase of shares violated Section 160 even without regard to the corporation's balance sheets. Plaintiff claims that the SFD Board was not entitled to rely on the solvency opinion of Houlihan, which showed that the transactions would not impair SFD's capital given a revaluation of corporate assets. The argument is that the methods that underlay the solvency opinion were inappropriate as a matter of law because they failed to take into account all of SFD's assets and liabilities. In addition, plaintiff suggests that the SFD Board's resolution of May 17, 1996 itself shows that the transactions impaired SFD's capital, and that therefore we must find a violation of 8 Del. C. § 160. We disagree, and hold that the SFD Board revalued the corporate assets under appropriate methods. Therefore the self-tender offer complied with Section 160, notwithstanding errors that took place in the drafting of the resolution.

On May 17, 1996, Houlihan released its solvency opinion to the SFD Board, expressing its judgment that the merger and self-tender offer would not impair SFD's capital. Houlihan reached this conclusion by comparing SFD's "Total Invested Capital" of $1.8 billion—a figure Houlihan arrived at by valuing SFD's assets under the "market multiple" approach—with SFD's long-term debt of $1.46 billion. This comparison yielded an approximation of SFD's "concluded equity value" equal to $346 million, a figure clearly in excess of the outstanding par value of SFD's stock. Thus, Houlihan concluded, the transactions would not violate 8 Del. C. § 160.

Plaintiff contends that Houlihan's analysis relied on inappropriate methods to mask a violation of Section 160. Noting that 8 Del. C. § 154 defines "net assets" as "the amount by which total assets exceeds total liabilities," plaintiff argues that Houlihan's analysis is erroneous as a matter of law because of its failure to calculate "total assets" and "total liabilities" as separate variables. In a related argument, plaintiff claims that the analysis failed to take into account all of SFD's liabilities, i.e., that Houlihan neglected to consider current liabilities in its comparison of SFD's "Total Invested Capital" and long-term debt. Plaintiff contends that the SFD Board's resolution proves that adding current liabilities into the mix shows a violation of Section 160. The resolution declared the value of SFD's assets to be $1.8 billion, and stated that its "total liabilities" would not exceed $1.46 billion after the transactions with Yucaipa. As noted, the $1.46 billion figure described only the value of SFD's long-term debt. Adding in SFD's $372 million in current liabilities, plaintiff argues, shows that the transactions impaired SFD's capital.

We believe that plaintiff reads too much into Section 154. The statute simply defines "net assets" in the course of defining "surplus." It does not mandate a "facts and figures balancing of assets and liabilities" to determine by what amount, if any, total assets exceeds total liabilities. The statute is merely definitional. It does not require any particular method of calculating surplus, but simply prescribes factors that any such calculation must include. Although courts may not determine compliance with Section 160 except by methods that fully take into account the assets and liabilities of the corporation, Houlihan's methods were not erroneous as a matter of law simply because they used Total Invested Capital and long-term debt as analytical categories rather than "total assets" and "total liabilities."

We are satisfied that the Houlihan opinion adequately took into account all of SFD's assets and liabilities. Plaintiff points out that the $1.46 billion figure that approximated SFD's long-term debt failed to include $372 million in current liabilities, and argues that including the latter in the calculations dissipates the surplus. In fact, plaintiff has misunderstood Houlihan's methods. The record shows that Houlihan's calculation of SFD's Total Invested Capital is already net of current liabilities. Thus, subtracting long-term debt from Total Invested Capital does, in fact, yield an accurate measure of a corporation's net assets.

The record contains, in the form of the Houlihan opinion, substantial evidence that the transactions complied with Section 160. Plaintiff has provided no reason to distrust Houlihan's analysis. In cases alleging impairment of capital under Section 160, the trial court may defer to the board's measurement of surplus unless a plaintiff can show that the directors "failed to fulfill their duty to evaluate the assets on the basis of acceptable data and by standards which they are entitled to believe reasonably reflect present values." In the absence of bad faith or fraud on the part of the board, courts will not "substitute [our] concepts of wisdom for that of the directors." Here, plaintiff does not argue that the SFD Board acted in bad faith. Nor has he met his burden of showing that the methods and data that underlay the board's analysis are unreliable or that its determination of surplus is so far off the mark as to constitute actual or constructive fraud.[12] Therefore, we defer to the board's

[12] We interpret 8 Del. C. § 172 to entitle boards to rely on experts such as Houlihan to determine compliance with 8 Del. C. § 160. Plaintiff has not alleged that the SFD Board failed to exercise reasonable care in selecting Houlihan, nor that rendering a solvency opinion is outside Houlihan's realm of competence. Compare 8 Del. C. § 141(e) (providing that directors may rely in good faith on records, reports, experts, etc.).

determination of surplus, and hold that SFD's self-tender offer did not violate 8 Del. C. § 160.

* * *

The judgment of the Court of Chancery is affirmed.

QUESTIONS

1. While the opinion isn't exactly clear on this subject, what do you think Houlihan Lokey Howard & Zukin did to determine the value of assets through a "market multiple" approach?
2. Should SFD's balance sheet constitute exclusive evidence of capital impairment? How could it show a negative net worth while Houlihan Lokey is giving an opinion that capital isn't impaired?
3. Plaintiffs argued that the definition of "net assets" in § 154, "the amount by which total assets exceed total liabilities," requires a calculation of total assets and total liabilities as separate variables, and that Houlihan Lokey failed to do this. Why do Plaintiffs make this argument, and how does the court respond?
4. The court says "net assets" is "merely definitional." What does that mean?

The revolution in legal capital rules: Model Act § 6.40.

In 1979 the Model Act abandoned the legal capital approach. See the Report of the Committee on Corporate Laws, 34 Bus. Law. 1867 (1979):

> "It has long been recognized by practitioners and legal scholars that the pervasive statutory structure in which "par value" and "stated capital" are basic to state corporation statutes does not today serve the original purpose of protecting creditors and senior security holders from payments to junior security holders, and may, to the extent security holders are led to believe that it provides some protection, tend to be misleading."
>
> "In light of this recognized fact, the Committee on Corporate Laws has, as part of a fundamental revision of the financing provisions of the Model Act, deleted the mandatory concepts of stated capital and par value. In the Model Act as in effect prior to the amendments, dividends and stock repurchases could not lawfully be made by a corporation if, after giving effect thereto, the corporation would be insolvent in the equity sense, i.e., unable to pay its obligations as they become due in the ordinary course of business. The committee concluded that this is the fundamentally important test and should be retained without change. * * *

"Upon elimination of par value and stated capital, the committee considered at length the question of what, if any, new or different standards should control dividends and share repurchases in addition to the equity-insolvency test. The Committee concluded that the Model Act should also contain a balance sheet test. In a departure from existing statutory provisions, the balance sheet test is explicitly authorized to be determined on the basis of either financial statements prepared under accounting practices and principles that are reasonable in the circumstances, or, in the alternative, a fair valuation or other method that is reasonable in the circumstances."

Set out below is Model Act § 6.40, which is the current version of that reform:

§ 6.40. Distributions to shareholders

"(a) A board of directors may authorize and the corporation may make distributions to its shareholders subject to restriction by the articles of incorporation and the limitation in subsection (c).

"(b) If the board of directors does not fix the record date for determining shareholders entitled to a distribution (other than one involving a purchase, redemption, or other reacquisition of the corporation's shares), it is the date the board of directors authorizes the distribution.

"(c) No distribution may be made if, after giving it effect:

"(1) The corporation would not be able to pay its debts as they become due in the usual course of business; or

"(2) The corporation's total assets would be less than the sum of its total liabilities plus (unless the articles of incorporation permit otherwise) the amount that would be needed, if the corporation were to be dissolved at the time of the distribution, to satisfy the preferential rights upon dissolution of shareholders whose preferential rights are superior to those receiving the distribution.

"(d) The board of directors may base a determination that a distribution is not prohibited under subsection (c) either on financial statements prepared on the basis of accounting practices and principles that are reasonable in the circumstances or on a fair valuation or other method that is reasonable in the circumstances.*

"(e) Except as provided in subsection (g), the effect of a distribution under subsection (c) is measured:

* Eds. The official commentary to Model Act § 6.40(d)states that:

"The board of directors should in all circumstances be entitled to rely upon reasonably current financial statements prepared on the basis of generally accepted accounting principles in determining whether or not the balance sheet test of section 6.40(c)(2) has been met, unless the board is then aware that it would be unreasonable to rely on the financial statements because of newly-discovered or subsequently-arising facts or circumstances."

"(1) in the case of distribution by purchase, redemption, or other acquisition of the corporation's shares, as of the earlier of (i) the date money or other property is transferred or debt incurred by the corporation; or (ii) The date the shareholder ceases to be a shareholder with respect to the acquired shares;

"(2) in the case of any other distribution of indebtedness, as of the date the indebtedness is distributed; and

"(3) in all other cases, as of (i) the date the distribution is authorized if payment occurs within 120 days after the date of authorization; or (ii) the date the payment is made if it occurs more than 120 days after the date of authorization.

"(f) A corporation's indebtedness to a shareholder incurred by reason of a distribution made in accordance with this section is at parity with the corporation's indebtedness to its general, unsecured creditors except to the extent subordinated by agreement.

"(g) Indebtedness of a corporation, including indebtedness issued as a distribution, is not considered a liability for purposes of determinations under subsection (c) if its terms provide that payment of principal and interest are to be made only if and to the extent that payment of a distribution to shareholders could then be made under this section. If the indebtedness is issued as a distribution, each payment of principal or interest is treated as a distribution, the effect of which is measured on the date the payment is actually made."

B. FRAUDULENT TRANSFERS

We have thus seen how legal capital rules have evolved (mostly) into a requirement that firms do not make distributions while insolvent. If so, then this restriction will dovetail with (duplicate?) longstanding rules against fraudulent transfers by insolvent debtors. Since the Statute of 13 Elizabeth c. 5 (1570), there have been general prohibitions against conveyances by debtors that were either designed to or had the effect of removing debtor assets from the reach of creditors.

The modern version of these laws is the Uniform Fraudulent Transfer Act. Consider some key provisions:

§ 4. Transfers Fraudulent as to Present and Future Creditors

(a) A transfer made or obligation incurred by a debtor is fraudulent as to a creditor, whether the creditor's claim arose before or after the transfer was made or the obligation was incurred, if the debtor made the transfer or incurred the obligation:

(1) with actual intent to hinder, delay, or defraud any creditor of the debtor; or

(2) without receiving a reasonably equivalent value in exchange for the transfer or obligation, and the debtor:

(i) was engaged or was about to engage in a business or a transaction for which the remaining assets of the debtor were unreasonably small in relation to the business or transaction; or

(ii) intended to incur, or believed or reasonably should have believed that he or she would incur, debts beyond his or her ability to pay as they became due.

(b) In determining actual intent under subsection (a)(1), consideration may be given, among other factors, to whether:

(1) the transfer or obligation was to an insider;

(2) the debtor retained possession or control of the property transferred after the transfer;

* * *

(7) the debtor removed or concealed assets;

(8) the value of the consideration received by the debtor was reasonably equivalent to the value of the asset transferred or the amount of the obligation incurred;

(9) the debtor was insolvent or became insolvent shortly after the transfer was made or the obligation was incurred;

(10) the transfer occurred shortly before or shortly after a substantial debt was incurred; and

(11) the debtor transferred the essential assets of the business to a lienor who transferred the assets to an insider of the debtor.

§ 5. Transfers Fraudulent as to Present Creditors

(a) A transfer made or obligation incurred by a debtor is fraudulent as to a creditor whose claim arose before the transfer was made or the obligation was incurred if the debtor made the transfer or incurred the obligation without receiving a reasonably equivalent value in exchange for the transfer or obligation and the debtor was insolvent at that time or the debtor became insolvent as a result of the transfer or obligation.

(b) A transfer made by a debtor is fraudulent as to a creditor whose claim arose before the transfer was made if the transfer was made to an insider for an antecedent debt, the debtor was insolvent at that time, and the insider had reasonable cause to believe that the debtor was insolvent.

§ 7. Remedies of Creditors

(a) In an action for relief against a transfer or obligation under this article, a creditor . . . may obtain:

(1) avoidance of the transfer or obligation to the extent necessary to satisfy the creditor's claim;

* * *

(3) subject to applicable principles of equity and in accordance with applicable rules of civil procedure:

(i) an injunction against further disposition by the debtor or a transferee, or both, of the asset transferred or of other property;

(ii) appointment of a receiver to take charge of the asset transferred or of other property of the transferee; or

(iii) any other relief the circumstances may require.

(b) If a creditor has obtained a judgment on a claim against the debtor, the creditor, if the court so orders, may levy execution on the asset transferred or its proceeds.

§ 8. Defenses, Liability, and Protection of Transferee

(a) A transfer or obligation is not voidable under Section 4(a)(1) against a person who took in good faith and for a reasonably equivalent value or against any subsequent transferee or obligee.

(b) Except as otherwise provided in this section, to the extent a transfer is voidable in an action by a creditor under section 7(a)(1), the creditor may recover judgment for the value of the asset transferred, or the amount necessary to satisfy the creditor's claim, whichever is less. The judgment may be entered against:

(1) the first transferee of the asset or the person for whose benefit the transfer was made; or

(2) any subsequent transferee other than a good faith transferee or obligee who took for value or from any subsequent transferee or obligee.

(c) If the judgment under subsection (b) section is based upon the value of the asset transferred, the judgment must be for an amount equal to the value of the asset at the time of the transfer, subject to adjustment as the equities may require.

(d) Notwithstanding voidability of a transfer or an obligation under this article, a good faith transferee or obligee is entitled, to the extent of the value given the debtor for the transfer or obligation, to:

(1) a lien on or a right to retain any interest in the asset transferred;

(2) Enforcement of any obligation incurred; or

(3) A reduction in the amount of the liability on the judgment.

The most obvious example of a fraudulent transfer involves a corporation that is about to file for bankruptcy. If the firm pays a huge dividend to shareholders on the eve of the filing, this payment will probably be treated as a fraudulent transfer. (And, as we have seen, it is also likely to violate legal capital rules). Another example might occur if the bankrupt firm "sells" its last valuable asset (e.g., a key parcel of land) to another entity for a tiny price (especially if the buyer is a related party). The obvious goal of fraudulent transfer laws is to prevent a borrower from shuffling assets away to another legal entity right before collection efforts by the creditor are initiated.

Might a leveraged buyout transaction, or LBO, also give rise to a fraudulent transfer? At first blush leveraged buyouts don't seem to belong in a chapter on distributions—recall from earlier chapters that a third party buys the corporate shares from the existing shareholders in a leveraged buyout. The buyer raises the funds for the purchase largely through borrowings that are ultimately secured by the subject corporation's assets. Prime candidates for LBOs are companies with steady and predictable cash flows that enable the company to service its debt, and companies with relatively large proportions of fungible and marketable assets that can be liquidated quickly in the event of default. These are the most attractive kinds of assets for lenders, because a security interest in them has real value.

The prototypical LBO, spawning cases such as the two that follow, involves the LBO sponsor (typically a private equity fund) creating an Acquisition Subsidiary, which is wholly owned by the sponsor. The sponsor will invest some equity into this subsidiary—whatever amount is demanded by the prospective lenders. The Acquisition Subsidiary then secures loan agreements from lenders and agrees to pledge all of its property to secure the loans. The Acquisition Subsidiary and the "Target" corporation then merge, with the surviving corporation succeeding to all of the obligations of the constituent corporations—including the Acquisition Subsidiary's loans, security agreements and mortgages. The cash proceeds are paid to the Target shareholders, who then exit the scene.

When the smoke clears, this transaction leaves the pre-existing unsecured creditors of the Target with very large amounts of secured debt having a priority over their claims. And the former Target shareholders have been paid large amounts of cash. Could this be fraudulent transfer? We exclude for purposes of this discussion the possibility that the debtor incurs the debts with actual intent to hinder, delay or defraud its creditors under subsection (1) of the Uniform Fraudulent Transfer Act—all participants hope the debtor prospers, and is able to repay all of its obligations on schedule.

But note that subsection (2) might be invoked when debt is incurred without receiving reasonably equivalent value in exchange for the debt incurred or the property transferred. LBO lenders seem to have given reasonably equivalent value for the loan obligations and pledges: they have lent cash. And the Target shareholders seem to have also given value for the cash they receive: they have surrendered their shares. Does this mean that fraudulent transfer laws are inapplicable? Or should we consider collapsing the two steps if it turns out that the post-LBO firm is unable to honor its debt obligations?

United States of America v. Tabor Court Realty Corp.

803 F.2d 1288 (3d Cir. 1986)

■ ALDISERT, CHIEF JUDGE.

We have consolidated appeals from litigation involving one of America's largest anthracite coal producers. . . Ultimately, we have to decide whether the court erred in entering judgment in favor of the United States in reducing to judgment certain federal corporate tax assessments made against the coal producers, in determining the priority of the government liens, and in permitting foreclosure on the liens. To reach these questions, however, we must examine a very intricate leveraged buy-out and decide whether mortgages given in the transaction were fraudulent conveyances within the meaning of the constructive and intentional fraud sections of the Pennsylvania Uniform Fraudulent Conveyances Act (UFCA), and if so, whether a later assignment of the mortgages was void as against creditors.

* * * We are told that this case represents the first significant application of the UFCA to leveraged buy-out financing.

We will address seven issues presented by the appellants and an amicus curiae, the National Commercial Finance Association, and by the United States and a trustee in bankruptcy as cross appellants:

- whether the court erred in applying the UFCA to a leveraged buy-out;
- whether the court erred in denying the mortgage assignee, McClellan Realty, a "lien superior to all other creditors";
- whether the court erred in "collapsing" two separate loans for the leveraged buy-out into one transaction;
- whether the court erred in holding that the mortgages placed by the borrowers on November 26, 1973 were invalid under the UFCA;
- whether the court erred in holding that the mortgages placed by the guarantors were invalid for lack of fair consideration;
- in the government's cross-appeal, whether the court erred in determining that the mortgage assignee, McClellan Realty, was entitled to an equitable lien for municipal taxes paid; and
- in the government's and trustee in bankruptcy's cross-appeal, whether the court erred in placing the mortgage

assignee, McClellan Realty, on the creditor list rather than removing it entirely.

We will summarize a very complex factual situation and then discuss these issues seriatim.

I.

These appeals arise from an action by the United States to reduce to judgment delinquent federal income taxes, interest, and penalties assessed and accrued against Raymond Colliery Co., Inc. and its subsidiaries (the Raymond Group) for the fiscal years of June 30, 1966 through June 30, 1973 and to reduce to judgment similarly assessed taxes owed by Great American Coal Co., Inc. and its subsidiaries for the fiscal year ending June 30, 1975.

* * *

Raymond Colliery, incorporated in 1962, was owned by two families, the Gillens and the Clevelands. It owned over 30,000 acres of land in Lackawanna and Luzerne counties in Pennsylvania and was one of the largest anthracite coal producers in the country. In 1966, Glen Alden Corporation sold its subsidiary, Blue Coal Corporation, to Raymond for $6 million. Raymond paid $500,000 in cash and the remainder of the purchase price with a note secured by a mortgage on Blue Coal's land. Lurking in the background of the financial problems present here are two important components of the current industrial scene: first, the depressed economy attending anthracite mining in Lackawanna and Luzerne Counties, the heartland of this industry; and second, the Pennsylvania Department of Environmental Resources' 1967 order directing Blue Coal to reduce the amount of pollutants it discharged into public waterways in the course of its deep mining operations, necessitating a fundamental change from deep mining to strip or surface mining.

Very serious problems surfaced in 1971 when Raymond's chief stockholders—the Gillens and Clevelands—started to have disagreements over the poor performance of the coal producing companies. The stockholders decided to solve the problem by seeking a buyer for the group. On February 2, 1972, the shareholders granted James Durkin, Raymond's president, an option to purchase Raymond for $8.5 million. The stockholders later renewed Durkin's option at a reduced price of $7.2 million.

Durkin had trouble in raising the necessary financing to exercise his option. He sought help from the Central States Pension Fund of the International Brotherhood of Teamsters and also from the Mellon Bank of Pittsburgh. Mellon concluded that Blue Coal was a bad financial risk. Moreover, both Mellon and Central States held extensive discussions with Durkin's counsel concerning the legality of encumbering Raymond's assets for the purpose of obtaining the loan, a loan which was not to be used to repay creditors but rather to buy out Raymond's stockholders.

After other unsuccessful attempts to obtain financing for the purchase, Durkin incorporated a holding company, Great American, and assigned to it his option to purchase Raymond's stock. Although the litigation in the district court was far-reaching, most of the central issues have their genesis in 1973 when the Raymond Group was sold to Durkin in a leveraged buy-out through the vehicle of Great American.

A leveraged buy-out is not a legal term of art. It is a shorthand expression describing a business practice wherein a company is sold to a small number of investors, typically including members of the company's management, under financial arrangements in which there is a minimum amount of equity and a maximum amount of debt. The financing typically provides for a substantial return of investment capital by means of mortgages or high risk bonds, popularly known as "junk bonds." The predicate transaction here fits the popular notion of a leveraged buy-out. Shareholders of the Raymond Group sold the corporation to a small group of investors headed by Raymond's president; these investors borrowed substantially all of the purchase price at an extremely high rate of interest secured by mortgages on the assets of the selling company and its subsidiaries and those of additional entities that guaranteed repayment.

To effectuate the buy-out, Great American obtained a loan commitment from Institutional Investors Trust on July 24, 1973, in the amount of $8,530,000. The 1973 interrelationship among the many creditors of the Raymond Group, and the sale to Great American—a seemingly empty corporation which was able to perform the buy-out only on the strength of the massive loan from IIT—forms the backdrop for the relevancy of the Pennsylvania Uniform Fraudulent Conveyance Act, one of the critical legal questions presented for our decision.

Durkin obtained the financing through [a loan from IIT, in which the assets of the Raymond Group companies were pledged to secure repayment.] * * * We must decide whether the borrowers' mortgages were invalid under the UFCA and whether there was consideration for the guarantors' mortgages.

* * *

When the financial dust settled after the closing on November 26, 1973, this was the situation at Raymond: Great American paid $6.7 million to purchase Raymond's stock, the shareholders receiving $6.2 million in cash and a $500,000 note; at least $4.8 million of this amount was obtained by mortgaging Raymond's assets.

Notwithstanding the cozy accommodations for the selling stockholders, the financial environment of the Raymond Group at the time of the sale was somewhat precarious. At the time of the closing, Raymond had multi-million dollar liabilities for federal income taxes, trade accounts, pension fund contributions, strip mining and back-filling obligations, and municipal real estate taxes. The district court calculated that the Raymond Group's existing debts amounted to at least $20 million on November 26, 19[7]3.

Under Durkin's control after the buy-out, Raymond's condition further deteriorated. Following the closing the Raymond Group lacked the funds to pay its routine operating expenses, including those for materials, supplies, telephone, and other utilities. It was also unable to pay its delinquent and current real estate taxes. Within two months of the closing, the deep mining operations of Blue Coal were shut down; within six months of the closing, the Raymond Group ceased all strip mining operations. Consequently, the Raymond Group could not fulfill its existing coal contracts and became liable for damages for breach of contract. The plaintiffs in the breach of contract actions exercised their right of set-off against accounts they owed the Raymond Group. Within seven months of the closing, the Commonwealth of Pennsylvania and the Anthracite Health & Welfare Fund sued the Raymond Group for its failures to fulfill back-filling requirements in the strip mining operations and to pay contributions to the Health & Welfare Fund. This litigation resulted in injunctions against the Raymond Group companies which prevented them from moving or selling their equipment until their obligations were satisfied.... Finally, on September 15, 1976, IIT notified the borrowing and guarantor Raymond companies that their mortgage notes were in default. On September 29, 1976, IIT confessed judgments against the borrowing companies for the balance due on the loan and began to solicit a buyer for the Raymond Group mortgages.* * *

[The IIT mortgages were ultimately sold to Pagnotti Enterprises, another large anthracite producer, who subsequently sold the mortgages to McClellan Realty.]

* * *

II.

The instant action was commenced by the United States on December 12, 1980 to reduce to judgment certain corporate federal tax assessments made against the Raymond Group and Great American. The government sought to assert the priority of its tax liens and to foreclose against the property that Raymond had owned at the time of the assessments as well as against properties currently owned by Raymond. The United States argued that the IIT mortgages executed in November 1973 should be set aside under the Uniform Fraudulent Conveyance Act and further that the purported assignment of these mortgages to Pagnotti should be voided because at the inception Pagnotti had purchased the mortgages with knowledge that they had been fraudulently conveyed.

As heretofore stated, after a bench trial, the district court issued three separate published opinions. In Gleneagles I the court concluded, inter alia, that the mortgages given by the Raymond Group to IIT on November 26, 1973 were fraudulent conveyances within the meaning of the constructive and intentional fraud sections of the Pennsylvania Uniform Fraudulent Conveyances Act. In Gleneagles II the court further held that the mortgages to McClellan Realty were void as against the other Raymond Group creditors. * * *

The Raymond Group . . . has appealed. * * * For the purpose of this appeal, we shall refer to the Raymond Group as "appellants", or "McClellan".

* * *

III.

McClellan initially challenges the district court's application of the Pennsylvania Uniform Fraudulent Conveyances Act to the leveraged buy-out loan made by IIT to the mortgagors, and to the acquisition of the mortgages from IIT by McClellan. The district court determined that IIT lacked good faith in the transaction because it knew, or should have known, that the money it lent the mortgagors was used, in part, to finance the purchase of stock from the mortgagors' shareholders, and that as a consequence of the loan, IIT and its assignees obtained a secured position in the mortgagors' property to the detriment of creditors. Because this issue involves the interpretation and application of legal precepts, review is plenary.

In applying section [3](a) of the UFCA, the district court stated:

> The initial question ... is whether the transferee, IIT, transferred its loan proceeds in good faith ... IIT knew or strongly suspected that the imposition of the loan obligations secured by the mortgages and guarantee mortgages would probably render insolvent both the Raymond Group and each individual member thereof. In addition, IIT was fully aware that no individual member of the Raymond Group would receive fair consideration within the meaning of the Act in exchange for the loan obligations to IIT. Thus, we conclude that IIT does not meet the standard of good faith under Section [3](a) of the Act.

McClellan argues that "the only reasonable and proper application of the good faith criteria as it applies to the lender in structuring a loan is one which looks to the lender's motives as opposed to his knowledge." McClellan argues that good faith is satisfied when "the lender acted in an arms-length transaction without ulterior motive or collusion with the debtor to the detriment of creditors."

Section [4] of the UFCA is a "constructive fraud" provision. It establishes that a conveyance made by a person "who is or will be thereby rendered insolvent, is fraudulent as to creditors, without regard to his actual intent, if the conveyance is made . . . without a fair consideration." Section [3] defines fair consideration as an exchange of a "fair equivalent . . . in good faith." Because section [4] excludes an examination of intent, it follows that "good faith" must be something other than intent; because section [4] also focuses on insolvency, knowledge of insolvency is a rational interpretation of the statutory language of lack of "good faith." McClellan would have us adopt "without ulterior motive or collusion with the debtor to the detriment of creditors" as the good faith standard. We are uneasy with such a standard because these words come very close to describing intent.

Surprisingly, few courts have considered this issue. In Epstein v. Goldstein, 107 F.2d 755, 757 (2d Cir. 1939), the court held that because a transferee had no knowledge of the transferor's insolvency, it could not justify a finding of bad faith, implying that a showing of such knowledge would support a finding of bad faith. In Sparkman and McClean Co. v. Derber, 4 Wash. App. 341, 481 P.2d 585 (1971), the court considered a mortgage given to an attorney by a corporation on the verge of bankruptcy to secure payment for his services. The trial court found that the transaction had violated section 3 of the UFCA . . . because it had been made in bad faith. On appeal the Washington Court of Appeals stated that "prior cases . . . have not precisely differentiated the good faith requirement . . . of fair consideration [in UFCA section 3] from the actual intent to defraud requirement of [UFCA section 7]." The court then set forth a number of factors to be considered in determining good faith: 1) honest belief in the propriety of the activities in question; 2) no intent to take unconscionable advantage of others; and 3) no intent to, or knowledge of the fact that the activities in question will, hinder, delay, or defraud others. Where "any one of these factors is absent, lack of good faith is established and the conveyance fails."

We have decided that the district court reached the right conclusion here for the right reasons. It determined that IIT did not act in good faith because it was aware, first, that the exchange would render Raymond insolvent, and second, that no member of the Raymond Group would receive fair consideration. We believe that this determination is consistent with the statute and case law.

McClellan and amicus curiae also argue that as a general rule the UFCA should not be applied to leveraged buy-outs. They contend that the UFCA, which was passed in 1924, was never meant to apply to a complicated transaction such as a leveraged buy-out. The Act's broad language, however, extends to any "conveyance" which is defined as "every payment of money . . . and also the creation of any lien or incumbrance." [UFCA § 1]. This broad sweep does not justify exclusion of a particular transaction such as a leveraged buy-out simply because it is innovative or complicated. If the UFCA is not to be applied to leveraged buy-outs, it should be for the state legislatures, not the courts, to decide.

In addition, although appellants' and amicus curiae's arguments against general application of the Act to leveraged buy-outs are not without some force, the application of fraudulent conveyance law to certain leveraged buy-outs is not clearly bad public policy.[2] In any event, the circumstances of this case justify application. Even the policy arguments offered against the application of fraudulent conveyance law to leveraged buy-outs assume facts that are not present in this case. For example, in their analysis of fraudulent conveyance law, Professors Baird and Jackson assert that their analysis should be applied to leveraged buy-outs only where aspects of the transaction are not hidden from creditors and the transaction does not possess other suspicious attributes. See Baird and Jackson, Fraudulent Conveyance Law and Its Proper Domain, 38 Vand. L. Rev. 829, 843 (1985). In fact, Baird and Jackson conclude their article by noting that their analysis is limited to transactions in which "the transferee parted with value when he entered into the transaction and that transaction was entered in the ordinary course." Id. at 855 (footnote omitted). In the instant case, however, the severe economic circumstances in which the Raymond Group found itself, the obligation, without benefit, incurred by the Raymond Group, and the small number of shareholders benefited by the transaction suggest that the transaction was not entered in the ordinary course, that fair consideration was not exchanged, and that the transaction was anything but unsuspicious. The policy arguments set forth in opposition to the application of fraudulent conveyance law to leveraged buy-outs do not justify the exemption of transactions such as this.[3]

IV.

* * *

E.

McClellan next contends that the district court erred in not crediting McClellan for that portion of the IIT loan that was not passed through to Raymond's shareholders: although "the District Court acknowledged

---

[2] A major premise of the policy arguments opposing application of fraudulent conveyance law to leveraged buy-outs is that such transactions often benefit creditors and that the application of fraudulent conveyance law to buy-outs will deter them in the future. See Douglas Baird and Thomas Jackson, *Fraudulent Conveyance Law and Its Proper Domain*, 38 VAND. L. REV. 829, 855 (1985). An equally important premise is that creditors can protect themselves from undesirable leveraged buy-outs by altering the terms of their credit contracts. Id. at 835. This second premise ignores, however, cases such as this one in which the major creditors (in this instance the United States and certain Pennsylvania municipalities) are involuntary and do not become creditors by virtue of a contract. The second premise also ignores the possibility that the creditors attacking the leveraged buy-out (such as many of the creditors in this case) became creditors before leveraged buy-outs became a common financing technique and thus may not have anticipated such leveraged transactions so as to have been able to adequately protect themselves by contract. These possibilities suggest that Baird and Jackson's broad proscription against application of fraudulent conveyance law to leveraged buy-outs may not be unambiguously correct.

[3] It should also be noted that another basic premise of the Baird and Jackson analysis is that as a general matter fraudulent conveyance law should be applied only to those transactions to which a rational creditor would surely object. Baird and Jackson, at 834. Although a rational creditor might under certain circumstances consent to a risky but potentially beneficial leveraged buy-out of a nearly insolvent debtor, no reasonable creditor would consent to the intentionally fraudulent conveyance the district court correctly found this transaction to be. Thus, the application of fraudulent conveyance law to the instant transaction appears consistent even with Baird and Jackson's analysis.

that $2,915,000, or approximately 42 percent, of the IIT loan proceeds originally went for the benefit of . . . creditors, IIT and McClellan received no credit therefor in regard to the partial validity of their liens." McClellan argues the district court determined that "the wrong committed upon the creditors . . . [was] the diversion of some 58 percent of the loan proceeds from the IIT loan to [Raymond's] shareholders." It concludes that to invalidate the entire mortgage would be to provide Raymond's creditors with a "double recovery." We understand the dissent to agree with McClellan's analysis when noting that " 'creditors have causes of action in fraudulent conveyance law only to the extent they have been damaged.' "

McClellan and, by implication, the dissent mischaracterize the district court's findings and conclusions regarding the fraudulent nature of the IIT loans. The district court did not determine that the loan transaction was only partially—or, to use McClellan's formulation, 58%—fraudulent. Nor did the district court conclude that Raymond's creditors had been wronged by only a portion of the transaction. Instead, the district court stated that:

> McClellan Realty's argument rests on the incorrect assumption that some portions of the IIT mortgages are valid as against the Creditors. In Gleneagles I, 565 F. Supp. at 580, 586, this Court found that IIT and Durkin engaged in an intentionally fraudulent transaction on November 26, 1973. The IIT mortgages are therefore invalid in their entirety as to creditors.

In essence, the district court ruled that the aggregate transaction was fraudulent, notwithstanding the fact that a portion of the loan proceeds was allegedly used to pay existing creditors.

This determination is bolstered by the fact that most of the $2,915,000 allegedly paid to the benefit of Raymond's creditors went to only one creditor—Chemical Bank. In Gleneagles I, the district court found that $2,186,247 of the IIT loan proceeds were paid to Chemical Bank in satisfaction of the mortgage that Raymond had taken to purchase Blue Coal (a Raymond subsidiary). The purpose of this payment is of critical significance:

> The Gillens and the Clevelands [Raymond's selling shareholders] required satisfaction of the Chemical Bank mortgage as a condition of the sale of their Raymond Colliery stock at least in part because Royal Cleveland had personally guaranteed repayment of that loan.

McClellan does not challenge this finding on appeal. Thus, of the $2.9 million allegedly paid to benefit Raymond's creditors, $2.2 million were actually intended to benefit Raymond's shareholders and to satisfy a condition for the sale. The remaining amounts allegedly paid to benefit Raymond's creditors were applied to the closing costs of the transaction.

On this record, the district court's characterization of the transaction as a whole as fraudulent cannot reasonably be disputed. The court's consequent determination that the "IIT mortgages are . . . invalid in their entirety as to creditors" is supported by precedent. See Newman v. First National Bank, 76 F.2d 347, 350–51 (3d Cir. 1935).

* * *

VI.

McClellan next faults the district court's determination that the Raymond Group was rendered insolvent by "the IIT transaction and the instantaneous payment to the selling stockholders of a substantial portion of the IIT loan in exchange for their stock." McClellan disputes the method of computation used by the district court. The question of insolvency is a mixed question of law and fact. * * *

A.

Section [2] of the UFCA defines insolvency as "when the present, fair, salable value of [a person's] assets is less than the amount that will be required to pay his probable liability on his existing debts as they become absolute and matured." As heretofore stated, the district court calculated the Raymond Group's existing debts as "at least $20,000,000 on November 26, 1973." The court then compared Raymond's debt to the "present, fair, salable value" of its assets and found the Group insolvent. In doing so, the court relied on Larrimer v. Feeney, where the Pennsylvania Supreme Court stated:

> A reasonable construction of the . . . statutory definition of insolvency indicates that it not only encompasses insolvency in the bankruptcy sense i.e. a deficit net worth, but also includes a condition wherein a debtor has insufficient presently salable assets to pay existing debts as they mature. If a debtor has a deficit net worth, then the present salable value of his assets must be less than the amount required to pay the liability on his debts as they mature. A debtor may have substantial paper net worth including assets which have a small salable value, but which if held to a subsequent date could have a much higher salable value. Nevertheless, if the present salable value of [his] assets [is] less than the amount required to pay existing debts as they mature the debtor is insolvent.

Guided by this teaching, the court found that: (1) the Raymond Group's coal production, which had been unprofitable since 1969, "could not produce a sufficient cash flow to pay the company's obligations in a timely manner"; (2) the sale of the Raymond Group's surplus lands, which had provided a substantial cash flow, was "abruptly cut off" by the terms of the IIT agreement; and (3) sale of its equipment could not generate adequate cash to meet Raymond's existing debts as they matured.

* * *

We conclude that McClellan has not demonstrated that this finding was clearly erroneous. We are satisfied that the district court followed the guidance of Pennsylvania courts in analyzing the Raymond Group's insolvency. Its application of the law was not clearly in error, nor were its factual determinations clearly erroneous.

QUESTIONS

1. The court states at the start of Part III of its opinion that IIT "obtained a secured position in the mortgagors' property to the detriment of [general unsecured] creditors." Isn't this always the case in secured lending? What more does it take to make the security interest a fraudulent conveyance?
2. If the Raymond Group had essentially no funds before the loan, did the pass-through of the funds create or exacerbate its insolvency?
3. The district court found that Raymond was indebted by at least $20 million at the time of the IIT loan and mortgage, and found that the present fair, salable value of its assets meant it was insolvent. Further, the court found that its coal production was insufficient to produce a cash flow to meet Raymond's debts in a timely manner. Why would Durkin seek to acquire control of an insolvent corporation, that he had just caused, through the IIT mortgage, to become more heavily indebted?
4. If you are an attorney representing prospective LBO lenders after this decision, what can you do to protect your client from subsequent charges of fraudulent transfers?

As we've seen, fraudulent transfer laws and legal capital requirements both govern distributions by insolvent firms. Might legal capital restrictions provide another angle of attack for highly leveraged buyouts? Recall that directors are personally liable for distributions made in contravention of these rules.

Matter of Munford, Inc., d.b.a. Majik Market, Debtor

97 F.3d 456 (11th Cir.1996)

■ HATCHETT, CHIEF JUDGE.

In this corporate leveraged-buy-out merger case, we affirm the district court's ruling that Georgia's stock distribution and repurchase statutes apply.

FACTS

In May 1988, the Panfida Group offered to purchase Munford, Inc., a public company on the New York Stock Exchange, through a leverage buy out (LBO) structured as a reverse triangle merger for $18 per share. Under the terms of the proposed merger agreement, the Panfida Group agreed to create Alabama Acquisition Corporation (AAC) and a subsidiary, Alabama Merger Corporation (AMC), and through AAC or AMC deposit the funds necessary to purchase Munford, Inc.'s outstanding stock with Citizens & Southern Trust Company. As evidence of its commitment to purchase Munford, Inc., the Panfida Group bought 291,100 of Munford, Inc.'s stock. In June 1988, the Panfida Group also told Munford, Inc.'s board of directors that it, upon the sale of Munford, Inc., intended to put additional capital into Munford, Inc. but would only invest as much as Citibank required to finance the proposed merger.

After consulting its lawyers and financial experts at Shearson Lehman Brothers (Shearson), the board of directors accepted the Panfida Group's offer pending shareholder approval of the purchase agreement. Prior to the directors seeking shareholder approval, the Panfida Group learned that Munford, Inc. had potential environmental liability. Consequently, the Panfida Group reduced the purchase price from $18.50 a share to $17 a share. On October 18, 1988, the shareholders approved the merger plan. On November 29, 1988, the sale of Munford, Inc. to the Panfida Group closed. Pursuant to the purchase agreement, the LBO transaction converted each share of common stock into the right to receive the merger price of $17 per share and extinguished the shareholders' ownership in Munford, Inc. On January 2, 1990, thirteen months after the merger, Munford, Inc. filed for Chapter 11 proceedings in bankruptcy court.

PROCEDURAL HISTORY

On June 17, 1991, Munford, Inc. brought an adversary proceeding in bankruptcy court in the Northern District of Georgia on behalf of itself and unsecured creditors pursuant to 11 U.S.C. §§ 544(b) and 1107(a) (1988), seeking to avoid transfers of property, disallow claims and recover damages against former shareholders, officers, directors, and Shearson. In Count III of its complaint, Munford, Inc. asserted that the directors violated legal restrictions under Georgia's distribution and share repurchase statutes in approving the LBO merger. Specifically, Munford, Inc. asserts that the LBO transaction constituted a distribution of corporate assets that rendered Munford, Inc. insolvent. The directors moved for summary judgment contending that the Georgia distribution and repurchase statutes did not apply to LBO mergers. On August 10, 1994, the district court, adopting the bankruptcy court's report and recommendation in part, denied the directors' motion for summary judgment on Munford, Inc.'s stock repurchase and distribution claim, ruling that Georgia's stock distributions and repurchase restrictions applied to LBO transactions. The district court also found that a genuine issue of material fact existed as to whether the LBO merger rendered Munford, Inc. insolvent in violation of Georgia law. On August 26, 1994, the district court amended its order and entered final judgment pursuant to Federal Rules of Civil Procedure 54(b) to permit this appeal. Fed.R.Civ.P. 54(b).

CONTENTIONS

The directors contend that the district court erred in concluding that the LBO merger constituted a distribution of assets within the meaning of Georgia's distribution and repurchase statutes. They contend that these statutes do not apply to an arm's-length sale of a company to a third party through an LBO merger. In the alternative, the directors contend that they should not face personal liability for alleged violations of Georgia's distribution and repurchase statutes because they approved the LBO merger in good faith with the advice of legal counsel.

Munford, Inc. contends that the district court properly denied the directors' motion for summary judgment on this claim.

ISSUE

The sole issue on appeal is whether the district court erred in ruling that Georgia's stock distribution and repurchase statutes apply to a leverage acquisition of a corporation.

DISCUSSION

* * *

Georgia's capital surplus distribution statute provides, in pertinent part:

> (a) The board of directors of a corporation may from time to time distribute to shareholders out of capital surplus of the corporation a portion of its assets in cash or property subject to the following [provision]:
>
> > (1) No such distribution shall be made at a time when the corporation is insolvent or when such distribution would render the corporation insolvent[.]

Similarly, Georgia's stock repurchasing statute prohibits directors of a corporation from repurchasing the corporation's shares when such purchase would render the corporation insolvent. Under both statutes, directors who vote for or assent to a corporate distribution or stock repurchase in violation of these statutes are jointly and severally liable for the amount distributed or paid to the extent the payments violated the restrictions.

The directors appeal the district court's denial of summary judgment contending that Georgia's distribution and share repurchase statutes do not apply to LBO mergers. The directors argue that Georgia's distribution and repurchase statutes only apply in circumstances where the directors take assets of the corporation and either distribute them to shareholders or use them to repurchase shares. In both cases, the directors assert, control of the company does not change hands and the directors determine the source of the assets used. The directors note that in this case the Panfida Group owned Munford, Inc. at the completion of the LBO merger and thereafter ran the company. The directors therefore argue that only Georgia's merger statutes apply to this transaction.

The district court denied the directors' motion for summary judgment adopting the reasoning of the bankruptcy court. The bankruptcy court, in analyzing the LBO merger, considered the substance of the transaction and equated the LBO merger to a stock distribution or repurchase, disregarding the fact that Munford, Inc. had new owners and stockholders as a result of the merger at the time the shareholders received the LBO payments. The bankruptcy court specifically found that: (1) the directors "approved or assented to the underlying merger agreement which structured and required payment to the shareholders"; (2) the merger agreement contemplated the Panfida Group's pledging of "virtually all of Munford[, Inc.]'s assets as collateral" for the loan that funded the LBO payments made to the shareholders; and (3) the directors knew or should have known "the source, purpose, or use of" Munford, Inc.'s assets prior to or at the time the directors approved the merger plan. Based on these findings, the bankruptcy court concluded that a reasonable jury could conclude that the merger rendered Munford, Inc. insolvent in violation of Georgia's distribution and stock repurchase statutes.

In reaching its conclusion, the bankruptcy court rejected a Fourth Circuit case that refused to apply Virginia's corporate distribution statute to recapture payments made to shareholders pursuant to an LBO merger. See C-T of Virginia, Inc. v. Barrett, 958 F.2d 606 (4th Cir.1992).

In C-T of Virginia, the Fourth Circuit held that the LBO merger did not constitute a distribution within the meaning of Virginia's share repurchase and distribution statutes reasoning that Virginia's distribution statute

> [was] not intended to obstruct an arm's-length acquisition of an enterprise by new owners who have their own plans for commercial success. The reason for this distinction is simple: a corporate acquisition, structured as a merger, is simply a different animal from a distribution.

C-T of Virginia, 958 F.2d at 611. The court in C-T of Virginia further reasoned that because such distribution statutes derive from the regulation of corporate dividends courts should limit their restriction to situations in which shareholders after receiving the transfer from the corporation retain their status as owners of the corporation.

The bankruptcy court, in this case, rejected this line of reasoning, reasoning that the legislature enacted the distribution and share repurchase statutes of the Georgia Code to protect creditors "by prohibiting transfers at a time when a corporation is insolvent or would be rendered insolvent." Such intent, the bankruptcy court noted, "furthers the longstanding principle that creditors are to be paid before shareholders." We agree with the district court and the reasoning of the bankruptcy court and decline to join the Fourth Circuit in holding that "[a] corporate acquisition, structured as a merger, is simply a different animal from a distribution." C-T of Virginia, Inc., 958 F.2d at 611.

We note that the LBO transaction in this case did not merge two separate operating companies into one combined entity. Instead, the LBO transaction represented a "paper merger" of Munford, Inc. and AMC, a shell corporation with very little assets of its own. To hold that Georgia's distribution and repurchase statutes did not apply to LBO mergers such as this, while nothing in these statutes precludes such a result, would frustrate the restrictions imposed upon directors who authorize a corporation to distribute its assets or to repurchase shares from stockholders when such transactions would render the corporation insolvent. We therefore affirm the district court's ruling that Georgia's restrictions on distribution and stock repurchase apply to LBO.

In the alternative, the directors argue that their approval of the LBO merger should not subject them to liability under the distribution and repurchase statutes because they approved the merger in good faith and with the advice of legal counsel. Because we are not aware of any Georgia courts that recognize good faith or reasonable reliance on legal counsel's advice as an affirmative defense to liability under Georgia's distribution and repurchase statutes, we reject this argument.

CONCLUSION

For the reasons stated above, we affirm the district court's denial of the directors' motion for summary judgment on Munford, Inc.'s stock distribution and repurchase claim.

Affirmed.

QUESTIONS

1. Georgia adopted the Model Act effective in 1989. Would Model Act § 6.40(d) have changed the outcome in this case?
2. The Court of Appeals characterized the LBO transaction as merely a "paper merger" that did not escape the regulation of the distribution statutes. O.C.G.A. § 14–2–103, as it became effective in 1989, after the Munford transaction, provides "Each provision of this chapter shall have independent legal significance." The notes to this section state an intent to adopt the rule of construction of Delaware, under such cases as Hariton v. Arco Electronics, 188 A.2d 123 (Del. Supr. 1963). Would the presence of this statute make a difference in future cases?
3. In C-T of Virginia, Inc. v. Barrett, 958 F.2d 606 (4th Cir.1992), cited in Munford, the Court of Appeals noted that at the time of the cash payment, the recipients were "former shareholders" rather than

shareholders of the corporation, because their shares had been canceled in the merger. Is this a persuasive distinction?

4. If directors have decided to sell the company, and a proposed LBO offers the highest price for the company, how can directors satisfy their duty to obtain the highest price for shareholders without running a risk of liability under distribution provisions?

5. Assuming that the directors resign at the effective time of the merger, what causes the subsequent insolvency, the decision to borrow against the corporation's assets or the manner in which the corporation is financed and operated subsequent to the merger?

6. Should an infusion of new working capital by the buyers make a difference in directors' liability if the company still becomes insolvent? Should it matter if lenders agree only to fund the LBO if the buyer agrees to contribute what the lender believes is adequate working capital?

5. STOCK REPURCHASES

Stock repurchases have increased in recent decades, due, in part, to the tax advantages of buybacks that we explored earlier in this chapter. The economic effect on shareholders (assuming a pro-rata buyback) is very similar to that of a cash dividend: money flows out of the firm and into the pocket of equity investors. But from a legal standpoint, stock repurchases can raise some distinct, and important, issues.

From the perspective of a creditor, stock repurchases perform precisely the same function as dividends, by causing the corporation to pay funds to its shareholders. For that reason, the Model Act doesn't define "dividend," but rather defines "distribution" as a "transfer of money or other property (except its own shares) . . . to or for the benefit of its shareholders in respect of any of its shares." Model Act § 1.40(6). This is an economically realistic way to look at share repurchases because, absent taxes and transaction costs, shareholders in the aggregate will be indifferent between receiving a cash dividend and having a portion of their shares repurchased.

Dividends must always be paid pro rata. 11 Fletcher Cyclopedia Corporations § 5352 (2003 Rev. Vol.). By contrast, a corporation can repurchase its shares from some, but not all, of its shareholders. It is this possibility for discriminatory treatment of shareholders that creates most of the conflicts and law in this area, as we will see shortly.*

---

* Note that the pro rata requirement applies only to shareholders holding the same class of stock; where a corporation has more than one class of stock (e.g., where it a corporation has preferred stock and common stock), the corporation is entitled to declare a dividend on one class of stock without declaring a dividend on another class.

A. THE ECONOMICS OF STOCK REPURCHASES

Let's begin with a brief numerical review: why, again, are buybacks economically similar to cash dividends? Assume a corporation has a market value of $10,000 with 100 shares outstanding, each trading at $100. Let's also assume that there are 10 total shareholders who each hold 10 shares. Finally, suppose that the firm has $1000 in surplus cash from last year's earnings. If the corporation declares a dividend of $10 per share, the value of the stock ex dividend will drop to $90, and each shareholder will have $10 cash per share, resulting in a total position of $1000 ($900 worth of stock and $100 worth of cash from the dividend). Alternatively, the corporation could distribute the $1000 by repurchasing 100 shares @ $10 each. The remaining 900 shares will be worth $9000, and the stock price will continue to be $10 per share.

What is the effect of this buyback on a shareholder's economic position? If each of the 10 shareholders participates in the buyback, then they will receive $100 from the sale of 10 shares to the firm and hold 90 shares worth $10 each. Their total position remains $1000. What if a shareholder doesn't want to sell? No problem: they will still hold 100 shares worth $10 each, for a net position of $1000. And of course, if a shareholder sells all her shares, then she will receive the entire $1000 in cash. Because the buyback is taking place at fair value, every investor can participate as they see fit without the fear of economic repercussions. (This is not true, as we shall see in more detail shortly, if the buyback occurs at a higher or lower price.)

Note that, all else being equal, the repurchase decision will have an effect on earnings per share (EPS)—because the total earnings will be divided by a smaller number of shares. Sometimes the financial press focuses on increased EPS from buybacks, as if it offers a real benefit for the remaining shareholders—and should therefore increase the value of the firm. Obviously, as we discussed in Chapter 4, in efficient markets with no transaction costs or taxes this cannot be so.

As mentioned earlier, taxes can make a large difference in the desirability of repurchases over dividends if dividends are taxed at a higher rate than the capital gains realized on repurchase. Continuing with the example above, suppose the shareholders have individual tax rates of 40% on dividend payouts and capital gains rates of 20%.* Even at first glance, the total amount of after-tax cash paid to investors will differ greatly:

Dividend:	*$1000 less $400 taxes = $600.*
Repurchase:	*$1000 less $200 taxes = $800.*

* This disparity existed until 2003, when taxes on Qualified Dividends were reduced to capital gains rates. The use of 20% and 40% in these examples is for simplification purposes.

However, this calculation is unrealistic in that it assumes the entire \$1000 represents a capital gain—that is, the shareholders paid nothing for their shares, and thus had no tax basis. The repurchase alternative is even more beneficial if shareholders have a substantial basis in the shares. For example, if the shareholders' basis is \$5 per share, then the tax on the capital gain of \$500 will be \$100 (i.e., (\$1,000 – (\$5 × 100 shares)) × 20%):

Repurchase if basis is \$500: \$1000 less \$100 taxes = \$900.

As of publication, the tax rate on qualified dividends is identical to the maximum capital gains rate, so high bracket stockholders will be indifferent from a tax perspective if their capital gains are the entire amount received. But if they have any basis whatsoever, the capital gains recognized will be less than the taxable dividend received, and the taxpayers should still prefer repurchases.

Sometimes managers explain or justify share repurchases by stating that they believe their company's shares are a "good investment." In efficient markets, how can this be so?* One way to explain this "good investment" rationale is that management believes the company has no positive net present value investments at present, so the board has simply decided to return cash to the shareholders. Yet if this is the case, why not use a dividend? Indeed, some companies that pay dividends also repurchase shares, and the obvious question is why they don't simply raise the dividend rate.

One possible answer seems to be that boosting a dividend is regarded as a more permanent commitment; a subsequent dividend reduction could be viewed as a negative signal. A more cynical answer might be that managers prefer distribution strategies that prop up or maintain the price of the firm's stock in order to support personal stock option benefits and perceptions of effective leadership. (Note how in the example above, the cash dividend alternative decreases the stock price to \$9 per share, while the buyback strategy maintains a price of \$10 per share. If you hold one million warrants with a strike price of \$9.50 and no antidilution protection, the choice here might matter a lot!) Of course, the managers might always respond to this criticism, with some justification, that they are only seeking to get the cash to investors in the most tax efficient manner.

Once a company has determined to do a share repurchase, there are three major ways to repurchase stock in a public corporation. First, a corporation can repurchase its shares in the market through trading transactions, just like any other investor (subject to disclosure rules set out in the next subsection). Second, a company can make a "self-tender offer," in which it publicly offers to buy back a certain amount of its stock,

* For a skeptical view of managerial arguments along these lines, see Vice Chancellor Strine's opinion in Chesapeake Corp. v. Shore, 771 A.2d 293 (Del. Ch. 2000).

generally at a premium over market prices (subject to a different set of disclosure rules). Typically, the right to sell shares back to the firm in a self-tender is implemented on a pro rata basis if the offer is oversubscribed. Finally, a company might engage in a "targeted repurchase," which usually involves a firm buying out a large shareholder, who is threatening a hostile takeover, at a premium price in exchange for their promise to just go away. This carries the pejorative name of "greenmail." But greenmail is not a very effective anti-takeover strategy because subsequent raiders might simply buy up new blocks of shares and put *their* hands out for an additional payout. Moreover, greenmail has been effectively outlawed by punitive tax treatment to the raider on the capital gains.

B. REGULATION OF SHARE REPURCHASES

i. LEGAL AUTHORITY FOR SHARE REPURCHASES

Should corporations even be allowed to buy their own shares? The leading English case of Trevor v. Whitworth, 12 App. Cas. 400 (1887) held that a corporation lacked the power to purchase its own shares; if it bought them to resell them, it would be "trafficking in shares" rather than engaging in the business for which it was organized. If it bought them to reduce equity capital, it would be reducing capital without the court approval required by the English Companies Act.

Yet today this outcome is an anomaly. All American statutes expressly grant corporations the power to repurchase their own shares, subject to the legal capital restrictions discussed earlier in this chapter. See, e.g., DGCL § 160 and Model Act § 6.31.

ii. MARKET REPURCHASES

Market repurchases always run the risk of being made when a company is in possession of material inside information, and thus violating Rule 10b–5. Because stock repurchases can increase the market price of a stock, a company repurchasing its own stock could also risk running afoul of Section 9(a)(2) of the Exchange Act, which prohibits stock purchases that have the purpose of raising or depressing the price of a stock. Rule 10b–18 and Rule 10b5–1 provide a solution to these twin challenges. First, Rule 10b–18 provides a company with a safe harbor from liability under Section 9 if a company repurchase its common stock in accordance with the *manner of purchase condition* (the company must use a single broker or dealer each day it repurchases its stock), the *timing condition* (the company may not engage in repurchases during certain times of the trading day), the *price condition* (the company is limited in the price it pays for its stock), and the *volume condition* (the company is limited in the amount of common stock it may repurchase on any single day). Second Rule 10b5–1 provides a safe harbor for Rule 10b–5. In general, it provides that if the company adopts a repurchase plan at a time when it is not in possession of material, non-public information, purchases subsequently made in accordance with the plan are deemed not to be made "on the basis of" that information. To obtain this benefit, the issuer must create a written repurchase plan and comply with some other technical conditions. Rule 10b5–1(c)(1)(B) provides that the plan must either (1) specify the amount of securities to be purchased, the purchase price and the date of purchase—a requirement that would limit the repurchase essentially to a one-time action; (2) include a formula or algorithm or computer program for determining the amount, price and date for the securities to be bought; or (3) empower the agent executing the plan to exercise discretion about how, when, and whether to effect purchases—provided that the agent is not in possession of material nonpublic information. Of course, this does not address state law concerns about asymmetric information in repurchases, although it may well be persuasive.

Market repurchases can also be manipulative. Companies may be tempted to engage in repurchases in an effort to influence the price of their shares. In one sense, this appears to conflict with CAPM, which teaches that all stocks are fungible, and that they are priced fairly in relation to each other because they are only tools in building a portfolio. But purchases and sales can have signaling effects; substantial sales by insiders (which must be disclosed within two days under Exchange Act section 16) generally lead to a price decline—apparently because uninformed traders believe these insiders have superior information about the company's prospects. Myron Scholes, "The Market for Securities: Substitution versus Price Pressure and the Effects of Information on Share Prices," 45 J. Bus. 179 (1972). In 2023, the SEC bolstered buyback disclosure requirements by requiring companies to (1) disclose daily repurchase data in 10-Q and 10-K filings; (2) indicate whether any company executives or directors participated in the trading of the company's equity securities; and (3) provide narrative disclosure about the repurchase program, including objectives and rationale.

Our learning about how stock prices behave also depends upon stocks trading in what the Supreme Court has called "open and developed" securities markets. Basic Inc. v. Levinson, 424 U.S. 224, 241 (1988). Thin markets, where trading is infrequent and the stock is not widely followed by analysts and traders, are generally understood to be especially susceptible to manipulation. Are there times when even the market for a widely traded stock might act as if it were thin? The SEC has thought so, and acted accordingly. While the following case predates widespread knowledge and acceptance of efficient market learning, it illustrates the type of behavior with which the SEC was concerned when it adopted Rule 10b–18.

Securities and Exchange Commission v. Georgia-Pacific Corporation

U.S. District Court for the Southern District of New York, 66 Civil Action No. 1215, April 27, 1966. Excerpts from Complaint. Federal Securities Law Reporter (CCH) (1964–66 Decisions) ¶ 91,680

COUNT ONE

Section 10(b) of the Securities Exchange Act and Rule 10b–5 thereunder

11. Since on or about May 26, 1961 [Georgia-Pacific ("GP")] has merged with other corporations or has acquired substantially all of the stock or assets of other corporations in return for stock in GP pursuant to agreements which provided that the total number of shares of GP stock to be issued in return for the interests in such other corporations would be dependent on the price of GP common stock on the NYSE at certain times or during certain periods of time (hereafter referred to as valuation periods).

12. During and immediately prior to certain of such valuation periods the defendants GP, CHEATHAM and PAMPLIN (individually and as trustees of the Georgia-Pacific Stock Bonus Trust), and MRS. BROOKS, intentionally caused GP common stock to be bid for and purchased for the Stock Bonus Plan and for the GP treasury on the NYSE in a manner which would and did, directly and indirectly, cause the price of GP common stock on the NYSE to rise in order that GP's obligations to issue additional shares of its common stock in return for the interests in other corporations would be avoided or reduced.

13. In making such purchases for the Stock Bonus Plan the defendants CHEATHAM, PAMPLIN, and MRS. BROOKS did not attempt to have them executed in a manner which would have tended to result in purchases at the lowest prices possible and thus did not act exclusively in the interest of the Stock Bonus Plan participants.

* * *

THE ST. CROIX PAPER COMPANY

16. From January 17, 1963 to about February 27, 1963 GP made an offer to exchange a maximum of 587,714 shares of GP common stock for the common stock of St. Croix Paper Company (St. Croix), a Maine corporation, which then had approximately 2,700 shareholders. The offer provided that up to 470,172 shares of GP common stock would initially be issued to the St. Croix shareholders at the rate of 8/10 of a GP share for each St. Croix share. The offer further provided that GP was obligated to issue additional GP shares, up to the limit of 2/10 of a GP share for each St. Croix share exchanged, to make up any difference should the last sale price on the NYSE of GP common stock not average $50 per share for a period of 30 consecutive trading days next preceding any date to be later selected by GP within the next 2½ years. The offer also

provided that GP was obligated to issue the additional 2/10 of a GP share for each St. Croix share exchanged if within 2½ years GP did not select such a date.

17. On March 7, 1963 GP acquired 94.6% of the St. Croix stock under this offer, and on April 10, 1963 GP acquired an additional 4.16% of the St. Croix stock under the same terms.

18. On nine occasions between February 15 and April 9, 1963 the three trustees of the Stock Bonus Plan passed resolutions authorizing purchases of a total of 23,100 shares of GP common stock to be made at the discretion of either CHEATHAM or PAMPLIN. Pursuant to these authorizations, 22,900 shares of GP common stock (or 50.66% of the GP common stock purchased for the Stock Bonus Plan in 1963) were purchased for the Stock Bonus Plan on the NYSE on 25 of the 36 trading days from February 21 through April 15, 1963. Such purchases were effected at the discretion of MRS. BROOKS under the general direction of CHEATHAM.

19. During this period, CHEATHAM, PAMPLIN, and MRS. BROOKS did not attempt to have such purchases executed in a manner which would have tended to result in purchases at the lowest prices possible. Instead, such purchases were caused to be executed predominantly through the use of several orders at the market* on the same day (on one occasion as many as 11 separate orders on the same day), sometimes through two or more brokerage firms on the same day and at the same times during one day and on most occasions without placing any price limit on such orders. In addition, such purchases were caused to be concentrated near the close of the market on many days during this period.

20. Purchases of 9.6% of the GP stock made for the Stock Bonus Plan from March 28 through April 15, 1963 were executed at prices higher than those on the preceding transactions (on "plus ticks") or at the same price as the preceding transactions, the last change in price having been upward (on "zero plus ticks"). Consequently, the prices at which such purchases were executed led advances and retarded declines in the price of GP common stock on the NYSE. Between March 28 and April 15, 1963 such purchases accompanied an advance in the market price of GP common stock from 49 to 52¾. When the price of GP common stock appeared to be averaging above the price required to eliminate GP's obligation to issue additional shares under the St. Croix offer, such purchasing was discontinued, although funds still remained in the Stock Bonus Plan. In addition, on April 2, April 9, and April 10 such purchases (on plus and zero-plus ticks) were the last purchases of the day. In summary, such purchases were intentionally effected in a manner which would and did, directly and indirectly, cause the last sale price of GP common stock on the NYSE to rise in order that GP's obligation to issue

* Eds. A purchase "at the market" is an order to a broker to purchase at the best price currently available in the market.

additional shares of its common stock under the St. Croix offer would be avoided or reduced.

Georgia Pacific entered into a consent decree with the SEC which, in the words of SEC Litigation Release No. 3511 (May 23, 1966), provided as follows:

> In addition, the judgment enjoins Georgia-Pacific and the individual defendants (so long as they are associated with Georgia-Pacific) from bidding for or purchasing any Georgia-Pacific security (1) during serious negotiations looking toward the acquisition of another company in exchange for Georgia-Pacific securities, (2) during or within 10 business days immediately prior to any period of time during which the market price of any security of Georgia-Pacific is to be used to determine the amount of Georgia-Pacific securities to be issued in connection with an acquisition, (3) during a distribution of Georgia-Pacific securities, and (4) at any other time except in accordance with specified limitations intended to minimize the impact of such purchases on the market price of Georgia-Pacific stock and to cause such purchases to follow rather than lead changes in the market price of Georgia-Pacific stock.

As we've seen, the ultimate resolution of the SEC's concerns in this area is Rule 10b–18, 17 C.F.R. § 240.10b–18. Does it adequately address the problem identified above? Does it make sense in terms of what we know about efficient capital markets and CAPM?

iii. GOING-PRIVATE TRANSACTIONS

Most stock repurchase programs by publicly-traded companies involve the issuer repurchasing only a small fraction of its total outstanding stock. However, it is also possible for a company to repurchase enough stock to cease being a publicly-traded entity entirely. How is this possible? While a full discussion of the rules is beyond the scope of this book, the short answer is that if a company's "holders of record" of its common stock are fewer than 300 persons, the company can immediately terminate its registration of its common stock under the Exchange Act. See Exchange Act Rule 12g–4. (For companies that have more than 300 holders of record of its common stock, there are also additional rules that might achieve this end; a full class on securities regulation will generally cover them). Once a company terminates its Exchange Act registration and delists its securities from any stock exchange, a company will therefore have no obligation to file Exchange Act reports. Thus, a company that conducts an issuer self-tender that reduces its shareholder count below 300 can choose to deregister and "go private."

Transactions to cash out public shareholders, and to return companies to non-public status, first achieved prominence in the early 1970s. A bull market in the late 1960s was followed by a market drop in 1969 and 1970. Many companies that had conducted public offerings during the 1960s discovered that being a public company was not producing the benefits expected, in terms of a highly valued stock, liquidity, and providing a medium for stock options to retain employees. As a result, controlling shareholders at some firms began to propose going-private transactions. While some of these transactions took the form of an issuer self-tender offer, others were structured as a "takeout merger," similar to an LBO. In particular, a controlling stockholder might form a shell corporation (a "merger sub") that is capitalized with the stockholder's stock of the controlled company and additional funds that are used to buy out the company's public shareholders in a merger of the company with the merger sub. After the transaction, the previously public company would then be owned entirely by the controlling stockholder. While these cash-outs were generally conducted at market premiums, in some instances they nevertheless occurred below initial public offering prices. Many commentators railed against these transactions.

We will not repeat the Delaware jurisprudence on going-private transactions here, except to note the concern of the Delaware Supreme Court that the terms of these transactions are often set unilaterally by a controlling shareholder who also dominates the board of directors. This has led the Delaware courts to impose a duty of "entire fairness" on the controlling shareholder, which includes both fair dealing (candor and full disclosure) and fair price. Weinberger v. UOP, Inc., 457 A.2d 701 (Del. 1983). The burden can be shifted to the plaintiff, however, or even transformed into the more lenient business judgement standard of review, if the controlling shareholder structures the deal carefully. Usually this means conditioning the transaction on the approval of an independent board committee and a positive, informed vote of the minority shareholders (often called a "MOM" vote because a "Majority of the Minority" must vote yes). See Kahn v. M & F Worldwide Corp., 88 A.3d 635 (Del. 2014).

Another structural possibility arises if the corporation (or the controlling shareholder) makes a tender offer for public shares that results in the acquisition of at least 90% of the target's stock. This can be followed by a statutory short form merger under DGCL § 253 to take the firm completely private. See In re Siliconix Incorporated Shareholder Litigation, 2001 WL 716787 (Del. Ch. 2001) and Glassman v. Unocal Corp., 777 A.2d 242 (Del. 2001).

In addition to these state law considerations, an issuer considering a going-private transaction must also comply with its federal disclosure obligations under the Exchange Act. In particular, in 1977 the SEC proposed a rule for going-private transactions. Exchange Act Release No.

14185 (Nov. 17, 1977). The initial version of the proposed rule was strict: it would be a fraudulent, deceptive or manipulative act or practice to purchase securities in a going-private transaction if it was "unfair to unaffiliated securityholders." After much debate a final version of the rule was adopted in 1979 without such a substantive fairness requirement.

As adopted, Rule 13e–3, 17 C.F.R. § 240.13e–3, is a disclosure rule. It requires issuers subject to the Exchange Act who are about to engage in a going-private transaction to file Schedule 13E-3. These disclosures give shareholders all the conventional financial information about an issuer, along with a discussion about the fairness of the transaction (Item 8) and the disclosure of any reports, opinions or appraisals received by the issuer or its affiliates relating to the fairness of the transaction. It should also be noted that the Delaware courts have taken disclosure requirements (as part of a board's fiduciary duties) beyond federal standards of materiality to encompass any other information shareholders might like to know.

In recent years there has been an explosion in shareholder litigation relating to mergers, especially for going-private transactions. You might recall that the Dell transaction, discussed earlier in the context of appraisal valuation (Chapter 3) and capital structure adjustments (Chapter 4), involved a going-private merger. Here is another notable dispute:

Howing Co. v. Nationwide Corporation

826 F.2d 1470 (6th Cir.1987),
cert. denied 486 U.S. 1059 (1988)

■ MERRITT, CIRCUIT JUDGE.

Under § 13(e) of the Securities Exchange Act of 1934, a Williams Act provision enacted in 1968, a company that has issued publicly traded stock is prohibited from buying it back unless the issuer complies with rules promulgated by the SEC. This appeal raises issues concerning the existence of a private right of action under § 13e–3, the nature of the disclosure duty imposed by Rule 13e–3, and the interrelationship of this provision with other antifraud rules.

Pursuant to its authority under § 13e–3, the SEC has issued Rule 13e–3 and Schedule 13e-3, a long and detailed set of disclosure requirements governing such "going private" transactions. Schedule 13e-3 accompanying the Rule requires that numerous items of information about the transaction be filed with the Commission, including three items pertinent to this case, i.e., Items 7, 8 and 9. Item 7 covers the "reasons" for the transaction; Item 8 requires a statement concerning the fairness of the transaction; and Item 9 requires disclosure of appraisals and other information concerning the value of the stock. The Rule also provides that this same information be disclosed to the selling shareholders.

The basic questions presented in this case are: (1) whether the plaintiffs have a private right of action under § 13e–3 to police non-compliance with Rule 13e–3; (2) and if so, whether the disclosure requirements of Rule 13e–3 have been met; and (3) if those requirements have not been met, whether defendant's conduct in violating Rule 13e–3 also gives rise to liability under the antifraud provisions of Rules 10b–5 and 14a–9.

Parties and Summary of Disposition Below

Defendant Nationwide Corporation is one of the largest life insurance holding companies in the United States. Originally incorporated in 1947 as Service Insurance Agency, the company has enjoyed steady growth since its affiliation with the Nationwide group of insurance companies in September 1955. As a result of this affiliation, the company adopted its present name and issued a special class of common stock (Class B common) which was held entirely by two Nationwide companies: Nationwide Mutual Insurance Company and Nationwide Mutual Fire Insurance Company. The Class A common stock continued in the hands of individual shareholders.

* * *

Nationwide Mutual and Nationwide Mutual Fire began to eliminate public ownership of Nationwide Corporation in December 1978 when these companies made a tender offer to buy the Class A shares for $20.00 per share net in cash. By January 1979, Nationwide Mutual and Nationwide Mutual Fire had purchased 4,074,695 Class A shares through this offer. After the tender offer, Nationwide Mutual and Nationwide Mutual Fire continued to purchase shares in the open market at prices ranging between $22.50 and $24.62 per share. These transactions ultimately gave Nationwide Mutual and Nationwide Mutual Fire ownership of 85.6% of the Class A common stock formerly held by the public.

In November 1982, the Board of Directors of Nationwide Corporation approved a transaction in which Nationwide Mutual and Nationwide Mutual Fire would acquire the remaining Class A shares at $42.50 per share. As a result, Nationwide Corporation would become a wholly-owned subsidiary of the two mutuals, and would have no public ownership. * * *

The present class action began with an action by Belle Efros, a Nationwide shareholder, seeking a preliminary injunction with respect to a vote on the proposed merger. Following the denial of the Efros motion for a preliminary injunction, the merger was approved by 94.7% of the voted public shares. * * * The final amended complaint in this action raised claims under the Securities Exchange Act of 1934 §§ 10(b), 13(e), and 14(a) and rules promulgated thereunder as well as state law claims based on a breach of fiduciary duty.

The defendants moved for summary judgment and plaintiffs filed a cross-motion for partial summary judgment. The District Court granted defendants' motion, denied plaintiffs' cross-motion, and dismissed the amended complaint.

* * *

The District Court concluded overall that the proxy statement satisfied the requirements of Rule 13e–3. The District Court stated:

> Most important, there was sufficient information disclosed in the proxy statement to enable the stockholders to make an informed decision on what to do. It is the conclusion of the Court, therefore, that there is no genuine issue of material fact concerning the adequacy of the proxy statement when measured against the standards set forth in Rule 13e–3, and that any omissions pointed out by plaintiffs were not material as defined by the Court in TSC Industries, Inc. v. Northway, Inc., 426 U.S. at 449, 96 S. Ct. at 2132.

* * *

Rule 13e–3 Compliance

Going private transactions raise unique problems because of their inherently coercive nature: minority shareholders are forced to exchange their shares for cash or other consideration. The coercive effect of these transactions is reinforced by the fact that the majority shareholders control the timing and terms of the transaction.

* * *

Rule 13e–3 does not require that the issuer's Schedule 13e-3 filing with the Commission be reproduced in its entirety in the communication with shareholders. Most items from that Schedule may be summarized. However, Items 7, 8 and 9 must be disclosed verbatim. The rationale behind complete disclosure of these items is that they go to the essence of the transaction. Item 7 requires full disclosure of the purposes, alternatives, reasons, and effects of the transaction; Item 8 requires a statement as to the fairness of the transaction and the factors upon which such belief is based; and Item 9 requires disclosure of reports, opinions, appraisals and certain negotiations.

* * *

B. *Item 8 Disclosure*

The instructions accompanying Schedule 13e-3 are quite definite in the level of specificity required in certain disclosures.[5] The Instruction to

---

[5] The Instructions to Item 8(b) of the Schedule identify the following factors to be discussed in the disclosure:

Item 8 states that "conclusory statements, such as 'The Rule 13e–3 transaction is fair to unaffiliated security holders in relation to net book value, going concern value and future prospects of the issuer' *will not be considered sufficient disclosure in response to Item 8(a).*" (emphasis added.)

The Commission has expressed special concern with disclosures under Item 8(b) of Schedule 13e-3, the Item concerning the factors underlying a belief as to the fairness of the transaction. The Commission has issued the following guidance to prospective issuers:

> The Division is concerned that in many instances the Item 8(b) disclosure being made to security holders is vague and non-specific and is therefore of limited utility to security holders. . . Each such factor which is material to the transaction should be discussed and, in particular, if any of the sources of value indicate a value higher than the value of the consideration offered to unaffiliated security holders, the discussion should specifically address such difference and should include a statement of the bases for the belief as to fairness in light of the difference.

Exchange Act Release No. 34–17719, at 17,245–42.

The most serious problem in defendants' proxy statement concerns Item 8(b) compliance. Our review of the proxy statement indicates that defendants have made precisely the kind of conclusory statements prohibited by the Rule. In describing the fairness of the transaction as required by Item 8(b), defendants have done nothing more than provide a laundry list of factors considered by their investment banker.[6]

This kind of non-specific disclosure runs counter not only to the SEC's position taken in the Commission release discussed above but also to the Instruction to Item 8(b) of Schedule 13e-3. The Instruction states that the issuer shall "discuss in reasonable detail the material factors upon which the belief stated in Item 8(a) is based and, to the extent practicable, the weight assigned to each factor." (emphasis added). Thus, the proxy statement is incomplete in that we are not provided with any indication of the weights given the various factors as required by Rule 13e–3, incorporating Schedule 13e-3. Moreover, we therefore have no indication as to whether any of the "sources of value indicate a value

---

Instructions. (1) The factors which are important in determining the fairness of a transaction to unaffiliated security holders and the weight, if any, which should be given to them in a particular context will vary. Normally such factors will include, among others, those referred to in paragraphs (c), (d) and (e) of this Item and whether the consideration offered to unaffiliated security holders constitutes fair value in relation to: (i) Current market prices, (ii) Historical market prices, (iii) Net book value, (iv) Going concern value, (v) Liquidation value, (vi) The purchase price paid in previous purchases disclosed in Item 1(f) of Schedule 13e-3, (vii) Any report, opinion, or appraisal described in Item 9 and (viii) Firm offers of which the issuer or affiliate is aware made by any unaffiliated person, other than the person filing this statement, during the preceding eighteen months . . .

6 See Appendix A for the relevant language from the proxy statement.

higher than the value of the consideration offered to unaffiliated security holders." Exchange Act Release No. 34–17719, at 17,245–42.

Instead of providing this itemized disclosure called for by Rule 13e–3, defendants rely heavily on the First Boston opinion letter to discharge their disclosure obligations.[7] Indeed, the proxy materials state specifically, "Although the Evaluation Committee did not give specific weight to each of the various factors considered in evaluating the fairness of the proposed merger, particular emphasis was placed upon the receipt of the opinion of First Boston."

While the Commission has stated that an issuer in a going private transaction can rely on an investment banker's opinion to meet its disclosure obligations, such opinion itself must fully analyze the factors enumerated in Item 8(b) as well as be "expressly adopted" by the issuer. Exchange Act Release No. 34–17719, at 17,245–42. The issuer in this case did not conduct its own investigation but chose to rely on the expertise of First Boston. The problem with defendants adopting the First Boston opinion letter as their disclosure to shareholders is that this one-page letter is itself woefully inadequate when measured against the specific disclosure requirements of the Rule. An issuer cannot insulate itself from 13e-3 liability by relying on an investment banker's opinion letter which itself does not comply with the specific disclosure requirements of the Rule. Therefore, defendants' conclusory statements are not cured by conclusory statements made by First Boston in its opinion letter.

Somewhere in the proxy materials the Nationwide shareholders should have received a reasonably detailed analysis of the various financial valuation methods discussed by the Rule and the weights attached thereto. Even if certain valuation methods were not particularly relevant, this should itself have been noted and explained. See Exchange Act Release No. 34–17719, at 17,245–42. Without this disclosure, Nationwide shareholders did not possess the information necessary to make an informed decision concerning the going private transaction.

* * *

The Antifraud Claims

In addition to liability under subsection (b)(2) of Rule 13e–3, plaintiffs also contend that the defendants breached the antifraud provisions of Rules 10b–5, 13e–3(b)(1), and 14a–9. In essence, plaintiffs contend that a failure to disclose information required by Rule 13e–3 ipso facto constitutes an "omission" actionable under the antifraud provisions. They argue that Rules 10b–5 and 14a–9 incorporate Rule 13e–3 by reference in the going private context.

The three antifraud provisions at issue here spring from distinct statutes which have unique texts and histories. All three, however,

7 See Appendix B for the language from the First Boston opinion letter which appears in the proxy statement as Exhibit II.

parallel the common law of fraud and deceit. Absent special circumstances, an action for deceit would lie at common law for both falsehoods and half-truths, but not for a complete failure to disclose. See III L. Loss, Securities Regulation at 1433–35. As was noted by this circuit almost fifty years ago with regard to a similarly worded antifraud provision in the Securities Act of 1933:

> The statute did not require appellant to state every fact about stock offered that a prospective purchaser might like to know or that might, if known, tend to influence his decision, but it did require appellant not "to obtain money or property by means of any untrue statement of a material fact or any omission to state a material fact necessary in order to make the statements made, in the light of the circumstances under which they were made, not misleading.

Otis & Co. v. SEC, 106 F.2d 579, 582 (6th Cir.1939) (emphasis in original) (construing § 17(a)(2) of the Securities Act of 1933).

The second clauses of Rules 10b–5 and 13e–3(b)(1), and similar language in Rule 14a–9, adopt the common law rule and prohibit silence only where the omitted information is necessary to prevent inaccuracy in existing disclosure. As a result, these provisions have been considered by commentators and the courts alike to be concerned with half-truth rather than omissions per se.

The essence of plaintiff's claim is that a failure to provide items of disclosure required by Rule 13e–3(e) always constitutes a material omission under the antifraud rules. This is tantamount to incorporating the disclosure provisions of the securities laws into the antifraud provisions. No longer would omissions be actionable only where a half-truth resulted. Instead, any failure to comply with SEC disclosure obligations would be actionable by private litigants under the antifraud provisions.

Although the antifraud rules are the "catch-all" provisions of the securities laws, the Supreme Court has emphasized in the Rule 10b–5 context that they apply only where some fraud has been committed. See Chiarella v. United States, 445 U.S. 222, 234–35, 63 L. Ed. 2d 348, 100 S. Ct. 1108 (1980). Congress did not enact sections 10(b), 13(e), or 14(a) to give private litigants the same enforcement powers granted to the Commissioner of the SEC. Allowing private suits based on any non-disclosure, without regard to the "half-truth" limitation, would contravene the congressional intent behind these statutes. Therefore, we hold that omission of disclosure required by Rule 13e–3(e) will constitute a violation of the antifraud provisions of sections 10(b), 13(e), and 14(a) only where the information is necessary to prevent half-truth. The violations of Rule 13e–3, Item 8, itemized above, do not constitute "fraud" under sections 10(b) and 14(a) but should be considered as violations only of the specific rule in question.[11]

* * *

Accordingly, the judgment of the District Court is reversed and remanded for proceedings consistent with this opinion.

APPENDIX A

The proxy statement provides in pertinent part:

The members of the Evaluation Committee believe that, from a financial point of view, the terms of the proposed merger are fair to the public shareholders of the Corporation. The committee members considered important, as an indication of the fairness of the proposed merger, the receipt of the written opinion of First Boston. The committee members also considered important a number of other factors discussed with the representatives of First Boston. These factors are the current market price of the Class A Common shares as compared with stock prices of other comparable entities; past and current earnings of the Corporation; past and current price/earnings ratios of the Corporation and other companies having similar operations; past and current price/equity ratios of the Corporation (as computed in accordance with generally accepted accounting principles); and the premium over market price offered to the public shareholders in other similar transactions as well as in other recent acquisitions in the life insurance industry generally. In its discussions with the representatives of First Boston, upon whose opinion the Evaluation Committee has concluded that it is appropriate to rely, these representatives stated that in addition to the above noted factors they had also considered the current overall level of the stock market; historical market prices of the Class A Common shares as compared with market prices for the stock of other comparable entities; going concern value of the Corporation; net book value of the Corporation; liquidation value of the Corporation; various financial ratios; present revenues, expenses, earnings and dividends of the Corporation and trends with respect thereto; the purchase price paid to holders of Class A Common shares by Nationwide Mutual in connection with the December 1978 tender offer for the Class A Common shares; present value of projected future cash flows of the Corporation; replacement value of the Corporation; off balance sheet items of the Corporation; significant trends in the insurance business; competitive environment of the insurance industry; regulatory environment of the insurance industry; and the impact of inflation on the Corporation.

APPENDIX B

The First Boston opinion letter reads in its entirety as follows:

---

11 Under certain circumstances, violations of Rule 13e–3 may be indicative of a "scheme or artifice to defraud" which would violate the antifraud provisions. Such is not the case here, however, where non-disclosure is claimed to be a violation standing alone.

November 1, 1982

Board of Directors
Nationwide Corporation
One Nationwide Plaza
Columbus, Ohio 43216

Gentlemen:

You have asked us to advise you as to the fairness to the shareholders of Nationwide Corporation, other than Nationwide Mutual Insurance Company and Nationwide Mutual Fire Insurance Company, of the financial terms of a proposed merger whereby the owners of 685,545 publicly held Class A common shares would receive cash for their shares and Nationwide Mutual Insurance Company and Nationwide Mutual Fire Insurance Company would become the only shareholder of Nationwide Corporation. The terms of the merger transaction are that Nationwide Corporation shareholders will be entitled to receive $42.50 for each share of Nationwide Corporation Class A common shares.

In connection with our review, Nationwide Corporation furnished to us certain business and financial data concerning Nationwide Corporation. This information was furnished specifically for the purpose of our advising you as to the fairness of the financial terms of the proposed merger, and our Corporation's representation that the information is complete and accurate in all material respects. We have not independently verified the information. We have also reviewed certain publicly available information that we considered relevant and have had discussions with certain members of Nationwide Corporation's management.

In arriving at our opinion we have also considered, among other matters we deemed relevant, the historical financial record, operating statistics, current financial position and general prospects of Nationwide Corporation and the stock market performance of the Class A common shares of Nationwide Corporation. In addition, we have considered the terms and conditions of the proposed transaction as compared with the terms and conditions of comparable transactions.

Based on our analysis of the foregoing and of such other factors as we have considered necessary for the purpose of this opinion and in reliance upon the accuracy and completeness of the information furnished to us by Nationwide Corporation, it is our opinion that the financial terms of the proposed transaction are fair to the minority shareholders of Nationwide Corporation.

VERY TRULY YOURS,

THE FIRST BOSTON
CORPORATION

QUESTIONS

1. The court found that the proxy statement did not comply sufficiently with Item 8(b) of Schedule 13e-3. If you were advising corporate officials after this decision, what kinds of disclosures would you want to explore?

2. Why didn't the First Boston letter satisfy the obligations of the Board on fairness disclosures? Why can't you rely on the recommendation of experts concerning the fairness of the price offered? Suppose the Board really has no idea about what price is fair except the information they obtain from its investment bankers, who provide a letter like that provided by First Boston. What else can the Board say about fairness? Is there a reason why First Boston has provided such a short letter on a complex topic? Would a lawyer be well advised to provide a short opinion letter on a complex legal question?

3. Why doesn't a failure to comply with Item 8(b) necessarily constitute fraud under Rule 10b–5 and related statutes? Do you agree with the Sixth Circuit's conclusion? Note that in the context of omitting information in a company's annual report on Form 10-K or quarterly report on Form 10-Q, the Second Circuit has stated that "This Court and our sister circuits have long recognized that a duty to disclose under Section 10(b) can derive from statutes or regulations that obligate a party to speak. And this conclusion stands to reason—for omitting an item required to be disclosed on a 10-Q can render that financial statement misleading. Like registration statements and prospectuses, Form 10-Qs are mandatory filings that "speak . . . to the entire market." Stratte-McClure v. Morgan Stanley, 776 F.3d 94 (2d Cir. 2015) (citations omitted). Shouldn't similar reasoning apply to omissions in a Schedule 13e-3?

---

iv. REPURCHASES DURING HOSTILE TENDER OFFERS

During a hostile tender offer, a target company may decide to repurchase its own shares in the market. These transactions are governed by the disclosure requirements of Securities Exchange Act Rule 13e–1, 17 CFR § 240.13e–1, set out below.

Rule 13e–1. Purchase of Securities by the Issuer During a Third-Party Tender Offer.

An issuer that has received notice that it is the subject of a tender offer made under Section 14(d)(1) of the Act (15 U.S.C. 78n), that has commenced under § 240.14d–2 must not purchase any of its equity securities during the tender offer unless the issuer first:

(a) Files a statement with the Commission containing the following information:

(1) The title and number of securities to be purchased;

(2) The names of the persons or classes of persons from whom the issuer will purchase the securities;

(3) The name of any exchange, inter-dealer quotation system or any other market on or through which the securities will be purchased;

(4) The purpose of the purchase;

(5) Whether the issuer will retire the securities, hold the securities in its treasury, or dispose of the securities. If the issuer intends to dispose of the securities, describe how it intends to do so;

(6) The source and amount of funds or other consideration to be used to make the purchase. If the issuer borrows any funds or other consideration to make the purchase or enters any agreement for the purpose of acquiring, holding, or trading the securities, describe the transaction and agreement and identify the parties; and

(7) [Provides an exhibit that sets forth various fees to be paid by the company].

(b) Pays the fee required by Rule 0–11 when it files the initial statement and any amendment with respect to which an additional fee is due.

(c) Submits to the Commission the exhibit required by paragraph (a)(7) of this section . . . .

(d) This section does not apply to periodic repurchases in connection with an employee benefit plan or other similar plan of the issuer so long as the purchases are made in the ordinary course and not in response to the tender offer.

An alternative means for a target to battle a hostile tender offer is through its own tender offer for its shares, at a higher price than the bidder offers. "Self-tenders" are regulated by the disclosure requirements of Securities Exchange Act Rule 13e–4, 17 CFR § 240.13e–4, not included here because of its length. Delaware also has its own rules for the fiduciary duties of boards of directors in this context, as illustrated in the following case.

AC Acquisitions Corp. v. Anderson, Clayton & Co.

519 A.2d 103 (Del.Ch.1986)

■ ALLEN, CHANCELLOR.

This case involves a contest for control of Anderson, Clayton & Co., a Delaware corporation ("Anderson, Clayton" or the "Company"). Plaintiffs, Bear, Stearns & Co., Inc., Gruss Petroleum Corp. and Gruss

Partners ("BS/G") are shareholders of Anderson, Clayton who, through a newly formed corporation—AC Acquisitions Corp.—are currently making a tender offer for any and all shares of Anderson, Clayton at $56 per share cash. That offer, which may close no earlier than midnight tonight, is subject to several important conditions as detailed below. BS/G has announced an intention, if it succeeds through its tender offer in acquiring 51% of the Company's stock, to do a follow-up merger at $56 per share cash.

BS/G publicly announced its tender offer on August 21, 1986, having failed to bring defendants to the bargaining table despite attempts over several months. On the following day, Anderson, Clayton announced the commencement of a self-tender offer for approximately 65% of its outstanding stock at $60 per share cash. The Company also announced that, in connection with the closing of the self-tender offer, the Company would sell stock to a newly-formed Employee Stock Ownership Plan ("ESOP") amounting to 25% of all issued and outstanding stock following such sale. This alternative transaction (the "Company Transaction") itself is a continuation in another form of a recapitalization of the Company that had been approved by the Company's Board in February 1986.

* * * Pending before the Court at this time is plaintiffs' motion for an order preliminarily enjoining the Company from (1) buying any shares of the Company's stock pursuant to its pending self-tender offer, (2) selling any of the Company's stock to the newly-established ESOP and (3) taking any steps to finance the self-tender offer or (4) attempting to apply or enforce a "fair price" provision contained in Article 11 of the Company's restated certificate of incorporation to any BS/G second-step merger at $56 per share.

In summary, plaintiffs contend that this relief is justified because the Company Transaction is an economically coercive transaction that deprives shareholders of the option presented by the BS/G offer, which provides demonstrably greater current value than is offered in the Company Transaction; and that in structuring the Company Transaction and in its timing the Board has breached its fiduciary duties of care and loyalty to the shareholders because the Company Transaction is designed and effective to deprive shareholders of effective choice, to entrench the existing Board and protect it from the discipline of the market for corporate control.

* * *

[Anderson, Clayton was faced with the prospect that four aging stockholders, owning 30% of its shares, would need to sell some of their stock for estate planning purposes. Accordingly, the AC board retained First Boston & Co. to explore alternatives. A management buyout foundered, and First Boston was asked to explore the sale of the company. Plaintiffs alleged that First Boston's efforts in this respect were weak, since neither it nor another obvious candidate were contacted. Instead of a sale or liquidation of the company, First Boston recommended a recapitalization, involving a merger and a shareholder vote, that would result in a partial liquidation, involving payment of substantial amounts of cash to shareholders and the issuance of large amounts of debt by the recapitalized company. First Boston estimated the value of this transaction at between $43 and $47 per share. When the recapitalization transaction was approved by the AC board and recommended to the shareholders, BS/G offered $54 per share all cash. The AC board never entered into meaningful negotiations with BS/G. Instead, it revised the transaction in the form of a share repurchase at $60 per share, coupled with the sale of a substantial portion of stock to the company's ESOP. The results were essentially the same as the previous recapitalization but would not require a shareholder vote. First Boston was able to raise its estimate of the value of the Company Transaction to a range of $52.34 to $57.34, depending on the value of the remaining common stock (the "stub shares.")]

III.

* * *

Ordinarily when a court is required to review the propriety of a corporate transaction challenged as constituting a breach of duty or is asked to enjoin a proposed transaction on that ground, it will, in effect, decline to evaluate the merits or wisdom of the transaction once it is shown that the decision to accomplish the transaction was made by directors with no financial interest in the transaction adverse to the corporation and that in reaching the decision the directors followed an appropriately deliberative process. This deference—the business judgment rule—is, of course, simply a recognition of the allocation of responsibility made by section 141(a) of the General Corporation Law and of the limited institutional competence of courts to assess business decisions.

* * *

Because the effect of the proper invocation of the business judgment rule is so powerful and the standard of entire fairness so exacting, the determination of the appropriate standard of judicial review frequently is determinative of the outcome of derivative litigation. Perhaps for that reason, the Delaware Supreme Court recognized in Unocal Corp. v. Mesa Petroleum Co., Del. Supr., 493 A.2d 946 (1985) that where a board takes action designed to defeat a threatened change in control of the company, a more flexible, intermediate form of judicial review is appropriate. In such a setting the "omnipresent specter that a board may be acting primarily in its own interests," 493 A.2d at 954 (emphasis added), justifies the utilization of a standard that has two elements. First, there must be shown some basis for the Board to have concluded that a proper corporate purpose was served by implementation of the defensive measure and, second, that measure must be found reasonable in relation to the threat posed by the change in control that instigates the action. See Unocal, 493 A.2d at 955; . . .

* * *

It is this standard of review applicable to corporate steps designed to defeat a threat to corporate control that I believe is applicable to the pending case. While this proposed stock repurchase derives from an earlier proposed recapitalization that itself may be said to have been defensive only in a general, preemptive way, there are elements of the present Company Transaction that are crucial to this case and that do not derive from the abandoned recapitalization. These elements are unmistakably reactive to the threat to corporate control posed by the BS/G $56 cash offer. Specifically, the timing of the self-tender offer and the decision to tender for 65.5% of the outstanding stock at $60 per share (rather than, as just one example, distributing the available $480,000,000 through an offer for 69% of the Company's 12,207,644 shares at $57) are elements of the transaction that go to the heart of plaintiff's complaint about coercion and that were obviously fixed in reaction to the timing and price of the BS/G offer.

I turn then to the two legs of the Unocal test.

A.

The first inquiry concerns the likelihood that defendants will be able to demonstrate a "reasonable ground for believing that a danger to corporate policy or effectiveness" exists by reason of the BS/G offer. Unocal, 493 A.2d at 955. Stated in these precise terms, the Company Transaction may seem not to satisfy this aspect of the Unocal test. There is no evidence that the BS/G offer—which is non-coercive and at a concededly fair price—threatens injury to shareholders or to the enterprise. However, I take this aspect of the test to be simply a particularization of the more general requirement that a corporate purpose, not one personal to the directors, must be served by the stock repurchase. As so understood, it seems clear that a self-tender in these circumstances meets this element of the appropriate test.

Unlike most of our cases treating defensive techniques, the Board does not seek to justify the Company Transaction as necessary to fend off an offer that is inherently unfair. Rather, Defendants account for their creation of the Company Transaction as the creation of an option to shareholders to permit them to have the benefits of a large, tax-advantaged cash distribution together with a continuing participation in a newly-structured, highly-leveraged Anderson, Clayton. The Board recognizes that the BS/G offer—being for all shares and offering cash consideration that the Board's expert advisor could not call unfair—is one that a rational shareholder might prefer. However, the Board asserts—and it seems to me to be unquestionably correct in this that a rational shareholder might prefer the Company Transaction. One's choice, if given an opportunity to effectively choose, might be dictated by any number of factors most of which (such as liquidity preference, degree of aversion to risk, alternative investment opportunities and even desire or disinterest in seeing the continuation of a distinctive Anderson, Clayton identity) are distinctive functions of each individual decision-maker. Recognizing this, the Board contends that "the decision in this fundamentally economic contest lies properly with the shareholders" and that the Board "has preserved the ability of the stockholders to choose between these two options."

The creation of such an alternative, with no other justification, serves a valid corporate purpose (certainly so where, as here, that option is made available to all shareholders on the same terms). That valid corporate purpose satisfies the first leg of the Unocal test.

B.

The fatal defect with the Company Transaction, however, becomes apparent when one attempts to apply the second leg of the Unocal test and asks whether the defensive step is "reasonable in relation to the threat posed." The BS/G offer poses a "threat" of any kind (other than a threat to the incumbency of the Board) only in a special sense and on the assumption that a majority of the Company's shareholders might prefer an alternative to the BS/G offer. On this assumption, it is reasonable to create an option that would permit shareholders to keep an equity interest in the firm, but, in my opinion, it is not reasonable in relation to such a "threat" to structure such an option so as to preclude as a practical matter shareholders from accepting the BS/G offer. As explained below, I am satisfied that the Company Transaction, if it proceeds in its current time frame, will have that effect.

If all that defendants have done is to create an option for shareholders, then it can hardly be thought to have breached a duty. Should that option be, on its merits, so attractive to shareholders as to command their majority approval, that fact alone, while disappointing to BS/G, can hardly be thought to render the Board's action wrongful. But plaintiffs join issue on defendants' most fundamental assertion that the Board has acted to create an option and to "preserve the ability of the stockholders to choose." Plaintiffs contend to the contrary that the Company Transaction was deliberately structured so that no rational shareholder can risk tendering into the BS/G offer. Plaintiffs say this for two related reasons: (1) Stockholders tendering into the BS/G offer have no assurance that BS/G will take down their stock at $56 a share since that offer is subject to conditions including a minimum number of shares tendered and abandonment of the Company Transaction; and (2) Tendering shareholders would thereby preclude themselves from participating in the "fat" front-end of the Company Transaction and risk having the value of all their shares fall very dramatically. In such circumstances, plaintiffs say, to characterize the Board's action as an attempt to preserve the ability of shareholders to choose is a charade.

They claim the Company Transaction is coercive in fact and in the circumstances presented, improperly so in law.

May the Company Transaction be said to be coercive in the sense that no rational profit-maximizing shareholder can reasonably be expected to reject it? If it is concluded that the Company Transaction is coercive in this sense, one must ask why it is so and if, in these particular circumstances, this coercive aspect precludes a determination that the action is reasonable in light of the "threat" posed by the BS/G offer.

I conclude as a factual matter for purposes of this motion that no rational shareholder could afford not to tender into the Company's self-tender offer at least if that transaction is viewed in isolation. The record is uncontradicted that the value of the Company's stock following the effectuation of the Company Transaction will be materially less than $60 per share. The various experts differ only on how much less. Shearson, Lehman opines that the Company's stock will likely trade in a range of $22–$31 per share after consummation of the Company Transaction. First Boston is more hopeful, informally projecting a range of $37–52. What is clear under either view, however, is that a current shareholder who elects not to tender into the self-tender is very likely, upon consummation of the Company Transaction, to experience a substantial loss in market value of his holdings. The only way, within the confines of the Company Transaction, that a shareholder can protect himself from such an immediate financial loss, is to tender into the self-tender so that he receives his pro rata share of the cash distribution that will, in part, cause the expected fall in the market price of the Company's stock.[11]

I conclude that an Anderson, Clayton stockholder, acting with economic rationality, has no effective choice as between the contending offers as presently constituted. Even if a shareholder would prefer to sell all of his or her holdings at $56 per share in the BS/G offer, he or she may not risk tendering into that proposal and thereby risk being frozen out of the front end of the Company Transaction, should the BS/G offer not close.[12]

Thus, I conclude that if the Board's purpose was both to create an option to BS/G's any-and-all cash tender offer and to "preserve the ability of the shareholders to choose between those options" it has, as a practical matter, failed in the latter part of its mission.

---

[11] As a matter of fairly rudimentary economics, it can readily be seen that a self-tender, being for less than all shares, can always be made at a price higher than the highest rational price that can be offered for all of the enterprises stock. See Michael Bradley and Michael Rosenzweig, *Defensive Stock Repurchases*, 99 HARV. L. REV. 1378 (May 1986).

[12] BS/G could, by making its tender offer subject to no conditions, cure the coercive aspect of the Company Transaction, but it has no legal duty to extend an unconditional offer whereas the Board does have a legal duty to its shareholders to exercise its judgment to promote the stockholders' interests. Thus, in assessing the legal consequences in these circumstances of the conclusion that the Company Transaction has a coercive impact, I do not consider it relevant that plaintiffs, were they willing to do so, could counter that coercive effect by assuming additional risk.

The creation of an option of the kind represented by the Company Transaction need not have the collateral effect of foreclosing possible acceptance of the BS/G option by those shareholders who might prefer that alternative. The problem and its solution is one of timing. It would, in my opinion, be manifestly reasonable in relation to the limited "threat" posed by the BS/G any-and-all cash offer, for the Company to announce an alternative form of transaction (perhaps even a "front-end loaded" transaction of the kind the self-tender doubtlessly is)[13] to be available promptly should a majority not tender into the BS/G offer. An alternative timed in such a way would be a defensive step, in that it would make the change in control threatened by the BS/G offer less likely; it would afford to shareholders an alternative that, due to the non-coercive nature of the BS/G offer, would be readily available to shareholders if a majority of the shareholders in fact prefers it; and it would leave unimpaired the ability of shareholders effectively to elect the BS/G option if a majority of shareholders in fact prefers that option. A board need not be passive, Unocal, 493 A.2d at 954, even in the face of an any-and-all cash offer at a fair price with an announced follow up merger offering the same consideration. But in that special case, a defensive step that includes a coercive self-tender timed to effectively preclude a rational shareholder from accepting the any-and-all offer cannot, in my opinion, be deemed to be reasonable in relation to any minimal threat posed to stockholders by such offer.

What then is the legal consequence of a conclusion that the Company Transaction is a defensive step that is not reasonable in relation to the threat posed? The first consequence is that the Board's action does not qualify for the protections afforded by the business judgment rule. In the light of that fact, the obvious entrenchment effect of the Company Transaction and the conclusion that that transaction cannot be justified as reasonable in the circumstances, I conclude that it is likely to be found to constitute a breach of a duty of loyalty, albeit a possibly unintended one. (I need not and do not express any opinion on the question of subjective intent.) Where director action is not protected by the business judgment rule, mere good faith will not preclude a finding of a breach of the duty of loyalty. Rather, in most such instances (which happen to be self-dealing transactions), the transaction can only be sustained if it is objectively or intrinsically fair; an honest belief that the transaction was entirely fair will not alone be sufficient.

[The court determined it would issue a preliminary injunction but ordered further hearings on its form.]

---

[13] That is the $60 cash consideration offered is of greater current value than the stock with which a non-tendering shareholder will be left following consummation of the Company Transaction.

QUESTIONS

1. If AC was offering $60 per share in its tender offer and BS/G offered $56 per share, how could AC's offer possibly be inferior to the BS/G offer?
2. If the BS/G deal is indeed better, then why can't the shareholders simply decide to take that deal and reject the AC offer?
3. What will cause a court to abandon the deference of the business judgment rule in reviewing a transaction and impose a "more flexible, intermediate form of judicial review" under Unocal Corp. v. Mesa Petroleum Co.? Why does it believe that such a shift is justified here?
4. How could the board have made the Company Transaction non-coercive? Would this have provided shareholders a meaningful choice?

---

v. TARGETED REPURCHASES

Perhaps the most controversial repurchases of the 1980s involved the buyback of stock from someone who threatened a takeover attempt. As we mentioned earlier in this chapter, stock repurchase offers were sometimes used to persuade a potential hostile bidder to just go away—and the bidder might indeed accept the offer if the price was right. These repurchases are called "greenmail." The incidence of greenmail declined rapidly by the 1990s, however, because an extra 50% penalty tax on gains from greenmail was imposed by Internal Revenue Code § 5881 in 1987.

Yet targeted repurchases can still occur. The transaction described in the following case, for instance, was not covered by the greenmail provisions of IRC § 5881, which are only triggered if a stockholder makes or threatens to make a takeover offer before being bought out.

Grobow v. Perot

539 A.2d 180 (Del. 1988)

■ HORSEY, JUSTICE.

In these consolidated shareholder derivative suits, plaintiffs-shareholders appeal the Court of Chancery's dismissal of their suits for failure of plaintiffs to make presuit demand under Court of Chancery Rule 23.1. The Court of Chancery held that plaintiffs' complaints as amended failed to allege particularized facts which, if taken as true, would excuse demand under the demand futility test of Aronson v. Lewis, Del. Supr., 473 A.2d 805 (1984). The Court interpreted Aronson's "reasonable doubt" standard for establishing demand futility as requiring plaintiffs to plead particularized facts sufficient to sustain "a judicial finding" either of director interest or lack of director independence, or whether the directors exercised proper business judgment in approving the challenged transaction, placing the transaction beyond the protection of the business judgment rule. We find the Vice Chancellor to have erred in formulating an excessive criterion for satisfying Aronson's reasonable doubt test. Moreover, the Vice Chancellor erred in his statement that fairness is a "pivotal" question under an Aronson analysis. Unless the presumption of the business judgment rule is overcome by the pleadings, questions of fairness play no part in the analysis. However, applying the correct standard, we conclude that the complaints (singly or collectively) fail to state facts which, if taken as true, would create a reasonable doubt either of director disinterest or independence, or that the transaction was other than the product of the Board's valid exercise of business judgment. Therefore, we affirm the decision below, finding the Court's error to have been harmless.

I

* * *

A.

In 1984, General Motors Corporation ("GM") acquired 100 percent of Electronic Data Systems' ("EDS") stock. Under the terms of the merger, H. Ross Perot, founder, chairman and largest stockholder of EDS, exchanged his EDS stock for GM Class E stock and contingent notes. Perot became GM's largest shareholder, holding 0.8 percent of GM voting stock. Perot was also elected to GM's Board of Directors (the "Board") while remaining chairman of EDS.

The merger proved mutually beneficial to both corporations and was largely a success. However, management differences developed between Perot and the other officers and directors of GM's Board over the way GM was running EDS, and Perot became increasingly vocal in his criticism of GM management. By mid-1986, Perot announced to GM that he could no longer be a "company man." Perot demanded that GM allow him to run EDS as he saw fit or that GM buy him out. Perot then began publicly criticizing GM management with such statements as: "Until you nuke the old GM system, you'll never tap the full potential of your people"; and "GM cannot become a world-class and cost-competitive company simply by throwing technology and money at its problems." Thereafter, GM and American Telephone and Telegraph entered into exploratory negotiations for AT & T's purchase of EDS from GM allegedly as a means of GM's eliminating Perot. However, their negotiations did not proceed beyond the preliminary stage.

By late fall of 1986, Perot, anxious, for tax reasons, for a definitive decision before year-end, offered to sell his entire interest in GM. GM responded with a purchase proposal. Perot replied, suggesting additional terms, which Perot characterized as "a giant premium." When a definitive agreement was reached, the Board designated a three-member Special Review Committee ("SRC"), chaired by one of the Board's outside directors to review its terms. The SRC met on November 30, 1986 to consider the repurchase proposal and unanimously recommended that

GM's Board approve its terms. The following day, December 1, 1986, the GM Board of Directors met and approved the repurchase agreement.

Under the terms of the repurchase, GM acquired all of Perot's GM Class E stock and contingent notes and those of his close EDS associates for nearly $745,000,000. GM also received certain commitments, termed "covenants," from Perot. In addition to resigning immediately from GM's Board and as Chairman of EDS, Perot further agreed: (1) to stop criticizing GM management, in default of which Perot agreed to pay GM damages in a liquidated sum of up to $7.5 million;[3] (2) not to purchase GM stock or engage in a proxy contest against the Board for five years; and (3) not to compete with EDS for three years or recruit EDS executives for eighteen months.

At all relevant times, a majority of the GM Board of Directors consisted of outside directors. The exact number and composition of the GM Board at the time is not clear. However, from the limited record, it appears that the Board was comprised of twenty-six directors (excluding Perot), of whom eighteen were outside directors.

The GM repurchase came at a time when GM was experiencing financial difficulty and was engaged in cost cutting. Public reaction to the announcement ranged from mixed to adverse. The repurchase was sharply criticized by industry analysts and by members within GM's management ranks as well. The criticism focused on two features of the repurchase: (1) the size of the premium over the then market price of GM class E stock;[4] and (2) the hush mail provision.

B.

Plaintiffs filed separate derivative actions (later consolidated) against GM, EDS, GM's directors, H. Ross Perot, and three of Perot's EDS associates. The suits collectively allege: (i) that the GM director defendants breached their fiduciary duties to GM and EDS by paying a grossly excessive price for the repurchase of Perot's and the EDS associates' Class E stock of GM; (ii) that the repurchase included a unique hush mail feature to buy not only Perot's resignation, but his silence, and that such a condition lacked any valid business purpose and was a waste of GM assets; and (iii) that the repurchase was entrenchment motivated and was carried out principally to save GM's

---

3 This commitment by Perot would later be characterized as the "hush mail" feature of the agreement. The colloquial term is not defined in the pleadings but is assumed by this Court to combine the terms "green mail" and "hush money" to connote a variation on an unlawful and secret payment to assure silence. Here, the commitment is cast in the form of an explicit liquidated damage clause for future breach of contract. See infra section III B.

4 Plaintiffs allege that the total repurchase price per share ($31.375) was double the market price of the GM class E stock on the last day of trading before consummation of the repurchase ($61.90) [Sic. The trial court opinion makes clear that the "total sell-out price" was $61.90 per share, or double the stock's market value. 526 A.2d 914, 919, n. 6 (Del. Ch. 1987)]. However, the extent of premium over market cannot be mathematically calculated with any precision without disregarding the value of the contingent notes. The total repurchase price per share includes not only the price paid for the class E stock, but also the price paid for the contingent notes and the value of the special interest federal tax compensation. See infra note 7.

Board from further public embarrassment by Perot. The complaints charge the individual defendants with acting out of self-interest and with breaching their duties of loyalty and due care to GM and EDS.

* * *

III

* * *

As previously noted, the business judgment rule is but a presumption that directors making a business decision, not involving self-interest, act on an informed basis, in good faith and in the honest belief that their actions are in the corporation's best interest. Thus, good faith and the absence of self-dealing are threshold requirements for invoking the rule. Assuming the presumptions of director good faith and lack of self-dealing are not rebutted by well-pleaded facts, a shareholder derivative complainant must then allege further facts with particularity which, "taken as true, support a reasonable doubt that the challenged transaction was [in fact] the product of a valid exercise of business judgment." The complaints as amended do not even purport to plead a claim of fraud, bad faith, or self-dealing in the usual sense of personal profit or betterment. Therefore, we must presume that the GM directors reached their repurchase decision in good faith.

* * *

A. Disinterest and Independence

* * *

Having failed to plead financial interest with any particularity, plaintiffs' complaints must raise a reasonable doubt of director disinterest based on entrenchment. Plaintiffs attempt to do so mainly through reliance on Unocal Corp. v. Mesa Petroleum Co., Del. Supr., 493 A.2d 946 (1985); Unocal, however, is distinguishable. The enhanced duty of care that the Unocal directors were found to be under was triggered by a struggle for corporate control and the inherent presumption of director self-interest associated with such a contest. Here there was no outside threat to corporate policy of GM sufficient to raise a Unocal issue of whether the directors' response was reasonable to the threat posed.

Plaintiffs also do not plead any facts tending to show that the GM directors' positions were actually threatened by Perot, who owned only 0.8 percent of GM's voting stock, nor do plaintiffs allege that the repurchase was motivated and reasonably related to the directors' retention of their positions on the Board. Plaintiffs merely argue that Perot's public criticism of GM management could cause the directors embarrassment sufficient to lead to their removal from office. Such allegations are tenuous at best and are too speculative to raise a reasonable doubt of director disinterest. Speculation on motives for undertaking corporate action are wholly insufficient to establish a case of demand excusal. Therefore, we agree with the Vice Chancellor that plaintiffs' entrenchment theory is based largely on supposition rather than fact.

Plaintiffs' remaining allegations bearing on the issue of entrenchment are: the rushed nature of the transaction during a period of GM financial difficulty; the giant premium paid;[7] and the criticism (after the fact) of the repurchase by industry analysts and top GM management. Plaintiffs argue that these allegations are sufficient to raise a reasonable doubt of director disinterest. We cannot agree. Not one of the asserted grounds would support a reasonable belief of entrenchment based on director self-interest. The relevance of these averments goes largely to the issue of due care, next discussed. Such allegations are patently insufficient to raise a reasonable doubt as to the ability of the GM Board to act with disinterest. Thus, we find plaintiffs' entrenchment claim to be essentially conclusory and lacking in factual support sufficient to establish excusal based on director interest.

* * *

B. Director Due Care

Having concluded that plaintiffs have failed to plead a claim of financial interest or entrenchment sufficient to excuse presuit demand, we examine the complaints as amended to determine whether they raise a reasonable doubt that the directors exercised proper business judgment in the transaction. By proper business judgment we mean both substantive due care (purchase terms), and procedural due care (an informed decision).

With regard to the nature of the transactions and the terms of repurchase, especially price, plaintiffs allege that the premium paid Perot constituted a prima facie waste of GM's assets. Plaintiffs argue that the transaction, on its face, was "so egregious as to be afforded no presumption of business judgment protection." * * *

The law of Delaware is well established that, in the absence of evidence of fraud or unfairness, a corporation's repurchase of its capital stock at a premium over market from a dissident shareholder is entitled to the protection of the business judgment rule. We have already determined that plaintiffs have not stated a claim of financial interest or entrenchment as the compelling motive for the repurchase, and it is equally clear that the complaints as amended do not allege a claim of fraud. They allege, at most, a claim of waste based on the assertion that

7 The formula plaintiffs use to establish the existence of a "giant premium" is ambiguous, making the allegation conclusory. The total repurchase price includes not only the price paid for the class E stock, but also the price paid for the contingent notes and the value of the tax compensation. Ambiguity is caused when these items are factored in, especially the contingent note discounts. For example, in their complaints, plaintiffs appear to discount the contingent notes by \$16.20, reflecting present value (\$62.50–\$46.30). The GM directors, however, discount the notes by \$6.00. This disparity appears to be due to plaintiffs' use of a base figure of \$46.30, which is \$16.20 less than that used by the defendants. The plaintiffs fail to explain this disparity with particularity, thus failing to satisfy their burden under Aronson.

GM's Board paid such a premium for the Perot holdings as to shock the conscience of the ordinary person.

Thus, the issue becomes whether the complaints state a claim of waste of assets, i.e., whether "what the corporation has received is so inadequate in value that no person of ordinary, sound business judgment would deem it worth that which the corporation has paid." By way of reinforcing their claim of waste, plaintiffs seize upon the hush-mail feature of the repurchase as being the motivating reason for the "giant premium" approved by the GM Board. Plaintiffs then argue that buying the silence of a dissident within management constitutes an invalid business purpose. Ergo, plaintiffs argue that a claim of waste of corporate assets evidencing lack of director due care has been well pleaded.

The Vice Chancellor was not persuaded by this reasoning to reach such a conclusion and neither are we. Plaintiffs' assertions by way of argument go well beyond their factual allegations, and it is the latter which are controlling. Plaintiffs' complaints as amended fail to plead with particularity any facts supporting a conclusion that the primary or motivating purpose of the Board's payment of a "giant premium" for the Perot holdings was to buy Perot's silence rather than simply to buy him out and remove him from GM's management team. To the contrary, plaintiffs themselves state in their complaints as amended several legitimate business purposes for the GM Board's decision to sever its relationship with Perot: (1) the Board's determination that it would be in GM's best interest to retain control over its wholly-owned subsidiary, EDS; and (2) the decision to rid itself of the principal cause of the growing internal policy dispute over EDS' management and direction.

* * *

In addition to regaining control over the management affairs of EDS, GM also secured, through the complex repurchase agreement, significant covenants from Perot, of which the hush-mail provision was but one of many features and multiple considerations of the repurchase. Quite aside from whatever consideration could be attributed to buying Perot's silence, GM's Board received for the $742.8 million paid: all the class E stock and contingent notes of Perot and his fellow EDS directors; Perot's covenant not to compete or hire EDS employees; his promise not to purchase GM stock or engage in proxy contests; Perot's agreement to stay out of and away from GM's and EDS' affairs, plus the liquidated damages provision should Perot breach his no-criticism covenant.

Plaintiffs' effort to quantify the size of the premium paid by GM is flawed, as we have already noted, by their inability to place a dollar value on the various promises made by Perot, particularly his covenant not to compete with EDS or to attempt to hire away EDS employees. (See supra notes 2, 4, and 7.) Thus, viewing the transaction in its entirety, we must agree with the Court of Chancery that plaintiffs have failed to plead with particularity facts sufficient to create a reasonable doubt that the substantive terms of the repurchase fall within the protection of the business judgment rule.

* * *

[The court also rejected plaintiff's claim that the directors did not make an informed decision.]

IV. Conclusion

Apart from whether the Board of Directors may be subject to criticism for the premium paid Perot and his associates for the repurchase of their entire interest in GM, on the present record the repurchase of dissident Perot's interests can only be viewed legally as representing an exercise of business judgment by the General Motors Board with which a court may not interfere. Only through a considerable stretch of the imagination could one reasonably believe this Board of Directors to be "interested" in a self-dealing sense in Perot's ouster from GM's management. We view a board of directors with a majority of outside directors, such as this Board, as being in the nature of overseers of management. So viewed, the Board's exercise of judgment in resolving an internal rift in management of serious proportions and at the highest executive level should be accorded the protection of the business judgment rule absent well-pleaded averments implicating financial self-interest, entrenchment, or lack of due care. These complaints fall far short of stating a claim for demand excusal.

* * * The Trial Court, therefore, correctly dismissed the suits under Del. Ch. Ct. R. 23.1 for failure of plaintiffs to make presuit demand upon the GM Board.

Affirmed.

QUESTIONS

1. Why does the Court reject the plaintiff's claim? Can you imagine any allegations of bad faith that would excuse demand?
2. If the way to assign a value to the premium paid for the class E stock is to separately value the other consideration, what methodology would you use to assign a value to the Contingent Notes? Each contingent note, on maturity, entitles the holder to the difference between (i) $62.50 and (ii) the then-current market price per share of Class E stock, for each Class E share received in the merger, plus "Special Interest" to offset certain federal tax consequences.
3. How would you value a covenant not to compete?
4. Can you put a value on what GM paid Perot to stop criticizing GM management? What about Perot's promise to "stand still" and not purchase GM stock or engage in a proxy fight for 5 years?

5. Should a company ever be able to buyout a single shareholder at a premium to market prices? Why or why not?

---

6. OTHER TYPES OF DISTRIBUTIONS

A. STOCK DIVIDENDS AND STOCK SPLITS

The rationale for cash dividends and share buybacks are easy enough to understand: A company has more cash than it has good investment opportunities, resulting in the company's decision to distribute cash to shareholders. But sometimes companies declare stock dividends, which simply distribute more stock units *pro rata* among existing shareholders. Every share, for example, might receive one or two new shares as a dividend. Necessarily, the market value of each share must decline in proportion to the percentage of new shares issued. Nothing on the company's balance sheet has changed except the number of shares outstanding—shareholders' equity remains the same. And each shareholder has the same proportion of equity as before. Corporate statutes generally don't concern themselves much with stock dividends—they aren't "distributions" under the Model Act, and thus aren't subject to the restrictions on distributions.

The obvious question about a stock dividend is "why bother?" If you're just slicing the same sized pie into more pieces, isn't this a waste of time? There's another, related situation that raises the same question: stock splits. A split involves subdividing the existing shares. A two-for-one stock split, for example, involves issuing one new share for each outstanding share. The economic effect is exactly the same as that of a stock dividend—the market price of the stock should decline by one-half as the total number of shares doubles. The 1984 version of the Model Act eliminated any references to stock splits, and simply provides stock dividends as the sole means of issuing new shares pro rata to shareholders. Model Act § 6.23. Stock splits can still be accomplished, however, through amendments of the articles of incorporation, and the Model Act § 10.05(4) permits stock splits by board action alone, even though this requires an amendment of the articles of incorporation. In some jurisdictions, however, a firm may need to go through the normal processes—including soliciting shareholder approval—to amend the articles of incorporation and thereby execute the split. See, e.g., Blades v. Wisehart, 2010 WL 4638603 (Del. Ch. 2010). This usually makes a stock dividend easier to execute than a stock split. But again, the practical question remains: "why bother?"

One theory is that a stock dividend or stock split may be a subtle way to announce a permanent increase in dividend payments. If the cash dividend per share remains unchanged, a 10% stock dividend is effectively a 10% increase in cash dividends. But it would be just as easy—and more obvious—to raise the cash dividend by 10%, wouldn't it? One important study looked at the cumulative abnormal returns to stocks at the time of stock splits. They found substantial positive returns (33%) in the 30 months leading up to a stock split, and none after the date of the split. Gains continued after the announcement, which generally would be a month or two before the actual split date. Eugene F. Fama, Michael Jensen and Richard Roll, The Adjustment of Stock Prices to New Information, 10 International Economic Review 1 (1969). This suggests that the decision to split the stock was a product of the price rise, and that once announced it caused a further rise. One explanation given for this is that splits signal future dividend increases, even though the dividend increases weren't announced at the time of the stock split.*

Another explanation for splits is premised on the idea that there is a "popular price range" for trading stocks. When a stock's price rises too far above this level, perhaps into three or four figures, some companies become concerned that many investors may be reluctant to buy a "round lot" of 100 shares, the most common trading unit. Keeping stocks in the popular price range may assure greater "retail" ownership of the stock by individual investors. Keeping more investors interested in a stock produces greater liquidity, and thus greater value, as the story goes. There is some support for this.† But the counter-story is that this really doesn't matter: more and more stocks are held by institutional investors, who usually buy far more than 100 shares at a time. Would managers care whether their shares are held by individuals or institutions? They might. Individual investors tend to be more passive as voting stockholders than some institutions, which have become relatively active participants in corporate governance in recent years. But today, most retail brokers allow investors to purchase stocks using fractional share investments. Fractional share investing—which typically allows investors to purchase as little of a dollar worth of a particular stock—eliminates price as a binding constraint for retail traders.

As an illustration of this last point, consider the Class A common shares of Warren Buffet's Berkshire Hathaway, Inc. In recent years, it has traded in the six figures—that's right, you might need to pay $500,000, or so, for one share of stock. (And that's *after* a 50–1 stock split in 2010.) For most of its recent history, average daily trading volume can be less than 300 shares. Why does Warren Buffet not care about

---

* Additional research bolsters this hypothesis. In particular, Helen Mason and Roger Shalor, *Stock Splits: An Institutional Investor Preference*, 33 FINANCE REVIEW 33 (1998), find that institutional investors are attracted to stocks that are about to split. Josef Lakonishok and Baruch Lev, *Stock Splits and Stock Dividends: Why, Who and When*, 42 JOURNAL OF FINANCE 913 (1987), find that stock dividend announcements are followed by large cash dividend increases.

† See Christopher G. Lamoureux and Percy Poon, *The Market Reaction to Stock Splits*, 42 JOURNAL OF FINANCE 1347 (1987) (finding that the number of shareholders increases after a split) and Lakonishok and Lev, *supra* (finding that stocks that split have been priced above control firms).

conventional wisdom? Or does he? Berkshire Hathaway also has a class B common that trades at one-1500th of the price of the A shares. This latter class of stock has an average daily trading volume closer to four million shares. Buffet famously resisted splitting the Class A shares for years, grousing that such a move would do nothing except rack up additional transaction fees required to execute the change. But eventually he relented. Whatever Buffet's reason for preferring a high stock price for Class A shares, it hardly seems to matter to retail investors in this new era of fractional share trading. As of this writing, most of the reported trading volume in the Class A shares of Berkshire Hathaway reflects retail fractional share trades.*

Some have suggested other reasons, apart from the transaction costs necessary to conduct a split, that might cause stock splits and stock dividends to raise investor costs. For example, brokerage fees tend to be a higher percentage of value for lower-priced stocks. Some trading costs are relatively fixed and don't go down with the price of the stock. Similarly, in over-the-counter stocks, the bid-ask spread may rise as a percentage of the value of the stock. Thus, if a dealer offers to buy a stock for $49.50 and to sell the same stock for $50.00, the spread is $0.50. But if the dealer offers to buy a stock for $9.50 and sell it for $10.00, the $0.50 spread is a much greater percentage of value.† So just like our earlier discussion on cash dividends, the jury is still out on whether stock splits will create incremental value. Nevertheless, they continue to be a common occurrence in today's markets.

As mentioned above, a stock dividend only requires directors' approval. By contrast, an amendment of the charter is required for stock splits. In Model Act states, however, there is an interesting exception to the normal rule that shareholders need to vote on such an amendment:

§ 10.05 Amendment by Board of Directors

Unless the articles of incorporation provide otherwise, a corporation's board of directors may adopt amendments to the corporation's articles of incorporation without shareholder approval:

* * *

(4) if the corporation has only one class of shares outstanding:

(a) to change each issued and unissued share of the class into a greater or lesser number of whole shares of that class; or

(b) to increase the number of authorized shares of the class to the extent necessary to permit the issuance of shares as a share dividend; . . .

---

* See Robert Bartlett, Justin McCrary, and Maureen O'Hara, *Tiny Trades, Big Questions: Fractional Share Trades*, JOURNAL OF FINANCIAL ECONOMICS (forthcoming).

† T. Copeland, *Liquidity Changes Following Stock Splits*, 34 JOURNAL OF FINANCE 115 (1979).

Likewise, Model Act § 6.23(a) permits the board to issue shares as a dividend:

§ 6.23 Share Dividends

(a) Unless the articles of incorporation provide otherwise, shares may be issued pro rata and without consideration to the corporation's shareholders or to the shareholders of one or more classes or series. An issuance of shares under this subsection is a share dividend.

Because there are no legal capital rules, the board has authority to do this without restriction, unless the articles of incorporation prohibit it. And because there are no legal capital rules in the Model Act, no surplus has to be allocated to par value (stated capital). Thus, large numbers of shares can be issued as a dividend, equivalent to a stock split under the Model Act, without a shareholder vote (if there are enough authorized but unissued shares, or the board increases the authorized shares under Model Act § 10.05(4)).

In contrast, Delaware law still takes legal capital seriously, which has implications for a company that conducts a stock dividend. DGCL § 173 provides that dividends may be paid in cash, property or shares of the corporation's stock. If they are paid in authorized but unissued stock, the board shall designate as capital an amount at least equal to the par value of the shares being dividended (presumably from surplus):

§ 173. Declaration and Payment of Dividends

No corporation shall pay dividends except in accordance with the provisions of this chapter. Dividends may be paid in cash, in property, or in shares of the corporation's capital stock. If the dividend is to be paid in shares of the corporation's theretofore unissued capital stock the board of directors shall, by resolution, direct that there be designated as capital in respect of such shares an amount which is not less than the aggregate par value of par value shares being declared as a dividend and, in the case of shares without par value shares being declared as a dividend, such amount as shall be determined by the board of directors. No such designation of capital shall be necessary if shares are being distributed by a corporation pursuant to a split-up or division of its stock rather than as a payment of a dividend declared payable in stock of the corporation.

A stock split, which changes the number of shares, also requires a shareholder vote to amend the certificate of incorporation under DGCL § 242(a):

§ 242 Amendment of Certificate of Incorporation After Receipt of Payment for Stock; Non-Stock Corporation

(a) After a corporation has received payment for any of its capital stock . . . it may amend its certificate of incorporation, from time to time, in any and as many respects as may be desired, so long as its certificate of incorporation as amended would contain only such provisions at it would be lawful and proper to insert in an original certificate of incorporation filed at the time of the filing of the amendment; and if a change in stock or the rights of stockholders, or an exchange, reclassification, subdivision, combination or cancellation of stock or rights of stockholders is to be made, such provisions as may be necessary to effect such change, exchange, reclassification, subdivision, combination or cancellation. In particular, and without limitation upon such general power of amendment, a corporation may amend its certificate of incorporation, from time to time, so as:

* * *

(3) To increase or decrease its authorized capital stock or to reclassify the same, by changing the number, par value, designations, preferences, or relative, participating, optional, or other special rights of the shares. . .

The principal legal concern with stock dividends is deception—fear that shareholders will either believe that a stock dividend somehow represents a distribution of profits or believe that a stock split is a sign of good things to come. Consider the following excerpt from the NYSE Listed Company Manual § 703.02, which provides general guidance about stock splits, and attempts to provide a distinction between stock splits and stock dividends:

703.02 (part 1) Stock Split/Stock Rights/Stock Dividend Listing Process

(A) Introduction

Stock Splits—There are many factors which a company must consider in evaluating the merits of splitting its stock. Studies by the Exchange indicate that a properly timed stock split can contribute to an increase in and broadening of the shareholder base and can also be an important means of improving market liquidity. Generally speaking, a properly timed stock split, when effected under appropriate circumstances, serves as an excellent means of generating greater investor interest. Postsplit price is also an important consideration, especially when a company is competing in the financial marketplace for investor attention with other high quality securities.

Exchange statistics indicate a preferential price range within which a significant percentage of Exchange round-lot volume is generated. This preference tends to be strongly reinforced when demand for a particular security is supported by a strong corporate image, widely recognized product lines, a strong financial picture and a good dividend history.

Furthermore, a stock split can present an opportunity for long-term holders to consider the possibility of selling a portion of their position. This could have the effect of creating additional round-lot holders and thereby act as an aid in obtaining additional liquidity, thus assisting in broadening the floating supply of the stock.

A stock split also acts as a means of converting odd-lot holders into round-lot holders. It is the round-lot holder that plays a very important role in a stock's marketability and liquidity on the Exchange.

Today, liquidity is probably the most important element in the investment decision, other than the financial condition or suitability of the security under consideration. Optimum liquidity is measured by the relative ease and promptness with which a security may be traded with a minimum price change from the previous transaction. Accordingly, a further objective of a stock split is to lower the market price sufficiently in order to broaden marketability.

Consideration of a stock split is therefore justified when a company's shares are selling at a relatively high price, and when such action is accompanied by healthy operating results and a strong financial condition. When these factors are further supported by anticipated growth as evidenced by a steady increase in earnings, dividends, book value and revenue, a strong foundation is in place for a stock split decision.

While not having any fixed formula for determination of the appropriate ratio for a stock split, the Exchange is of the view that a stock split in a ratio of less than two shares for one (i.e., one additional share for each share outstanding), is not likely to achieve, to a satisfactory degree, the constructive purposes of a stock split. Experience has shown that frequently, when a stock split in a lesser proportion has been effected, the company has felt it necessary to follow it up with a further small stock split within a relatively short period in order to obtain the desired result. Adjustments of that nature, following each other too closely, may have effects upon the market not consistent with the best interests of the company, of its shareholders, or those of the general investing public.

As it appears to the Exchange, a stock split should be effected on a basis designed to produce, in one step, and to the full extent deemed beneficial, the adjustments of price and distribution indicated by current and anticipated conditions. If those conditions do not indicate clearly that a stock split of at least two-for-one proportion is warranted, it is questionable whether they warrant any stock split at all.

Furthermore, recurring stock splits in a ratio less than two-for-one may give rise to the question of whether such stock splits are not, in effect, periodic stock dividends to which the accounting requirement and other phases of the Exchange's stock dividend policy apply.

The Exchange also takes the position that a stock split is not in the public interest in the case of a company which, because of the nature of its business, its capitalization, or other factors, has a record of widely fluctuating earnings with alternating years of substantial profits and heavy losses.

* * *

Stock Dividends—

Many listed companies find it preferable at times to pay dividends in stock rather than cash, particularly in those cases in which a substantial part of earnings is retained by the company for use in its business. In order to guard against possible misconception by the shareowners of the effect of stock dividends on their equity in the company, and of their relation to current earnings, the Exchange has adopted certain standards of disclosure and accounting treatment.

Distinction between a Stock Dividend, a Partial Stock Split, and a Stock Split in Exchange Policy:

Stock Dividend—A distribution of less than 25% of the outstanding shares (as calculated prior to the distribution).

Partial Stock Split—A distribution of 25% or more but less than 100% of the outstanding shares (as calculated prior to the distribution).

Stock Split—A distribution of 100% or more of the outstanding shares (as calculated prior to the distribution).

* * *

Avoidance of the Word "Dividend"—

A stock split is frequently effected by means of a distribution to shareholders upon the same authority, and in the same manner as a stock dividend. However, in order to preserve the distinction between a stock split and a stock dividend, the use of the word "dividend" should be avoided in any reference to a stock split when such a distribution does not result in the capitalization of retained earnings of the fair market value of the shares distributed. Such usage may otherwise tend to obscure the real nature of the distribution. Where legal considerations require the use of the word "dividend", the distribution should be described, for example, as a "stock split effected in the form of a stock dividend."

Notice to Shareholders with Stock Dividend Distribution—

A notice should be sent to shareholders with the distribution advising them of the amount capitalized in the aggregate and per share, the relation of such aggregate amount to current earnings and retained earnings, the account or accounts to which such aggregate has been charged and credited, the reason for issuance of the stock dividend, and that sale of the dividend shares would reduce their proportionate equity in the company.

In 1968 the SEC proposed Rule10b–12, which would have codified the NYSE's approach, but the rule was never adopted.

B. REVERSE STOCK SPLITS

Reverse stock splits are barely mentioned in standard finance texts. In a reverse stock split, the number of issued and outstanding shares is reduced, as in a one-for-three reverse split, where one new share is issued for every three shares outstanding. There are a number of situations that disfavor low-priced shares, and these problems can be overcome through reverse stock splits. For example, if a share's average trading price drops below $1.00 on NYSE or if the average minimum bid on NASDAQ is below $1.00, this can provide grounds for delisting the stock from the trading exchange.

So-called "penny stocks" get harsher treatment from Congress and the SEC as well. Exchange Act § 3(51)(A) authorizes the SEC to define a "penny stock." The SEC has adopted Exchange Act Rule 3a51–1, which defines a penny stock as any stock trading below $5.00. Section 15(g) of the Exchange Act requires brokers to provide customers with warnings about the risks of penny stocks, and descriptions of dealer markets not required for other securities. Section 21E(b) excludes penny stocks from the benefits of the safe harbor created for forward-looking statements.

Some commentators mention transaction costs as a factor—that brokerage fees fall as a percentage of the trading price as stock prices rise. On the other hand, reducing the number of shares outstanding may reduce liquidity and the proportion of stock held by individual investors. Finally, companies can reduce the cost of serving shareholders by eliminating holders of small amounts through a reverse stock split. Why would a reverse stock split eliminate shareholders? Because a sufficiently large reverse stock split will result in some shareholders holding less than 1 whole share, and corporate statutes generally allow companies to cash out any fractional shares. Should the purging of shareholders in this manner raise any legal concerns?

Applebaum v. Avaya

812 A.2d 880 (Del. 2002)

■ VEASEY, CHIEF JUSTICE.

In this appeal, we affirm the judgment of the Court of Chancery holding that a corporation could validly initiate a reverse stock split and selectively dispose of the fractional interests held by stockholders who no longer hold whole shares. The Vice Chancellor interpreted Section 155 of the Delaware General Corporation Law to permit the corporation, as part of a reverse/forward stock split, to treat its stockholders unequally by cashing out the stockholders who own only fractional interests while opting not to dispose of fractional interests of stockholders who will end up holding whole shares of stock as well as fractional interests. In the latter instance the fractional shares would be reconverted to whole shares in an accompanying forward stock split.

We hold that neither the language of Section 155 nor the principles guiding our interpretation of statutes dictate a prohibition against the disparate treatment of stockholders, for this purpose. We also hold that the corporation may dispose of those fractional interests pursuant to Section 155(1) by aggregating the fractional interests and selling them on behalf of the cashed-out stockholders where this method of disposition has a rational business purpose of saving needless transaction costs.

A further issue we address is whether, as an alternative method of compensation, the corporation may satisfy the "fair price" requirement of Section 155(2) by paying the stockholders an amount based on the average trading price of the corporation's stock. Here, the Vice Chancellor properly held that the trading price of actively-traded stock of a corporation, the stock of which is widely-held, will provide an adequate measure of fair value for the stockholders' fractional interests for purposes of a reverse stock split under Section 155.

Facts

Avaya, Inc. is a Delaware corporation that designs and manages communications networks for business organizations and large non-profit agencies. The enterprise is a descendant of the industry standard-bearer, AT&T. Avaya was established as an independent company in October of 2000 when it was spun off from Lucent Technologies. Lucent itself is a spin-off of AT&T. Because its capital structure is the product of two spin-off transactions, the outstanding stock of Avaya is one of the most widely-held on the New York Stock Exchange. Over 3.3 million common stockholders own fewer than 90 shares of Avaya stock each.

Although a large number of stockholders hold a small stake in the corporation, Avaya incurs heavy expenses to maintain their accounts. Avaya spends almost $4 million per year to print and mail proxy statements and annual reports to each stockholder as well as to pay transfer agents and other miscellaneous fees. Stockholders who own their stock in street names cost Avaya an additional $3.4 million in similar administrative fees.

Since the cost of maintaining a stockholder's account is the same regardless of the number of shares held, Avaya could reduce its administrative burden, and thereby save money for its stockholders, by decreasing its stockholder base. In February of 2002, at the corporation's annual meeting, the Avaya board of directors presented the stockholders with a transaction designed to accomplish this result. The Avaya board asked the stockholders to grant the directors authorization to engage in one of three alternative transactions:

(1) a reverse 1-for-30 stock split followed immediately by a forward 30-for-1 stock split of the Common stock

(2) a reverse 1-for-40 stock split followed immediately by a forward 40-for-1 stock split of the Common stock

(3) a reverse 1-for-50 stock split followed immediately by a forward 50-for-1 stock split of the Common stock.

We refer in this opinion to all three of these alternative transactions as the "Proposed Transaction" or the "Reverse/Forward Split." Regardless of the particular ratio the board chooses, at some future date the Reverse Split will occur at 6:00 p. m., followed by a Forward Split one minute later. Once selected, the effective date of the Split will be posted on Avaya's website.

The transaction will cash out stockholders who own stock below the minimum number ultimately selected by the directors for the Reverse/Forward Split pursuant to those three alternative options. Stockholders who do not hold the minimum number of shares necessary to survive the initial Reverse Split will be cashed out and receive payment for their resulting fractional interests (the "cashed-out stockholders" or "targeted stockholders"). Stockholders who own a sufficient amount of stock to survive the Reverse Split will not have their fractional interests cashed out. Once the Forward Split occurs, their fractional holdings will be converted back into whole shares of stock.

Avaya will compensate the cashed-out stockholders through one of two possible methods. Avaya may combine the fractional interests and sell them as whole shares on the open market. In the alternative, the corporation will pay the stockholders the value of their fractional interests based on the trading price of the stock averaged over a ten-day period preceding the Reverse Split. * * *

To illustrate the Proposed Transaction through a hypothetical, assume Stockholder A owns fifteen shares of stock and Stockholder B owns forty-five shares of stock. If Avaya chooses to initiate a Reverse 1-for-30 Stock Split, Stockholder A will possess a fractional interest equivalent to one-half a share of stock. Stockholder B will hold one whole share of Avaya stock and a fractional interest equivalent to one-half a share. Using the provisions of Section 155(1) or (2) of the Delaware General Corporation Law,[2] Avaya would cash out Stockholder A since he

---

[2] 8 *Del. C.* § 155 provides: Fractions of shares. A corporation may, but shall not be required to, issue fractions of a share. If it does not issue fractions of a share, it shall (1) arrange for the disposition of fractional interests by those entitled thereto, (2) pay in cash the fair value of fractions of a share as of the time when those entitled to receive such fractions are determined or (3) issue scrip or warrants in registered form (either represented by a certificate or uncertificated) or in bearer form (represented by a certificate) which shall entitle the holder to receive a full share upon the surrender of such scrip or warrants aggregating a full share. A

no longer possesses a whole share of stock. Stockholder A would no longer be an Avaya stockholder. Stockholder B will remain a stockholder because Avaya will not cash out the fractional interest held by her. Stockholder B's fractional interest remains attached to a whole share of stock. When Avaya executes the accompanying Forward 30-for-1 Stock Split, Stockholder B's interest in one and one-half shares will be converted into forty-five shares of stock, the same amount that she held prior to the Transaction.

At the annual meeting, Avaya stockholders voted to authorize the board to proceed with any one of the three alternative transactions. Applebaum, a holder of twenty-seven shares of Avaya stock, filed an action in the Court of Chancery to enjoin the Reverse/Forward Split. Under any one of the three alternatives Applebaum would be cashed out because he holds less than thirty shares.

Proceedings in the Court of Chancery

Applebaum asked the Court of Chancery to enjoin the Proposed Transaction, alleging that Avaya's treatment of fractional interests will not comport with the requirements set forward in Title 8, Section 155 of the Delaware Code. Applebaum argued that Section 155 does not permit Avaya to issue fractional shares to some stockholders but not to others in the same transaction. Even if Avaya could issue fractional shares selectively, Applebaum contended that the methods by which Avaya plans to cash-out the smaller stockholders do not comply with subsections (1) and (2) of Section 155.

After considering cross-motions for summary judgment, the Court of Chancery denied Applebaum's request for an injunction and held that the Reverse/Forward Split would comply with Section 155 and dispose of the cashed-out stockholders' interests in a fair and efficient manner. Applebaum appeals the final judgment entered for the defendants. We affirm.

Issues on Appeal

Applebaum claims the Court of Chancery erred by: (1) holding that Title 8, Section 155 permits Avaya to issue fractional shares to the surviving stockholders but not issue fractional shares to the cashed-out stockholders; (2) holding that Avaya can combine the fractional interests and sell them on the open market; (3) holding that Avaya can instruct nominees to participate in the Split even if a particular nominee holds a sufficient amount of stock on behalf of all of its beneficial holders to

---

certificate for a fractional share or an uncertificated fractional share shall, but scrip or warrants shall not unless otherwise provided therein, entitle the holder to exercise voting rights, to receive dividends thereon and to participate in any of the assets of the corporation in the event of liquidation. The board of directors may cause scrip or warrants to be issued subject to the conditions that they shall become void if not exchanged for certificates representing the full shares or uncertificated full shares before a specified date, or subject to the conditions that the shares for which scrip or warrants are exchangeable may be sold by the corporation and the proceeds thereof distributed to the holders of scrip or warrants, or subject to any other conditions which the board of directors may impose.

survive the Split; (4) granting summary judgment and holding that the payment of cash for fractional interests based on a ten-day average of the trading price of Avaya stock constitutes "fair value" under Section 155; and (5) holding that the meaning of "fair value" in Sections 155(2) is different from Section 262 and thus failing to value the fractional shares as proportionate interests in a going concern.

Section 155 Does Not Prevent Avaya From Disposing of Fractional Interests Selectively

Applebaum questions the board's authority to treat stockholders differently by disposing of the fractional interests of some stockholders but not others. Applebaum contends that Avaya will issue fractional shares in violation of Section 155. According to this view of the transaction, during the one minute interval between the two stock splits the corporation will not issue fractional shares to stockholders who possess holdings below the minimum amount. Those stockholders will be cashed out. Stockholders who hold stock above the minimum amount, by contrast, will be issued fractional shares that will be reconverted in the Forward Split into the same number of whole shares owned by those stockholders before the Reverse Split.

Applebaum argues that Section 155 prevents Avaya from achieving this disparate result by providing that:

> A corporation may, but shall not be required to, issue fractions of a share. If it does not issue fractions of a share, it shall (1) arrange for the disposition of fractional interests by those entitled thereto, (2) pay in cash the fair value of fractions of a share as of the time when those entitled to receive such fractions are determined. . .

Applebaum reads Section 155 to mean that Avaya can employ the cash-out methods provided in Section 155 only if the corporation "does not issue fractions of a share."

This Court reviews de novo the Court of Chancery's decision to grant Avaya's motion for summary judgment. We need not reach the merits of Applebaum's interpretation of Section 155 because he has based his argument on the flawed assumption that Avaya will issue fractional shares. Since the Reverse/Forward Split is an integrated transaction, Avaya need not issue any fractional shares. The initial Reverse Split creates a combination of whole *shares* and fractional *interests*. Avaya will use either Section 155(1) or (2) to cash out the fractional interests of stockholders who no longer possess a whole share of stock. Fractional *interests* that are attached to whole *shares* will not be disposed of. Nor will they be represented by fractions of a share. Fractional shares are unnecessary because the surviving fractional interests will be reconverted into whole shares in the Forward Split.

Applebaum correctly notes that Avaya stockholders are not treated equally in the Proposed Transaction. The disparate treatment, however, does not arise by issuing fractional shares selectively. It occurs through the selective disposition of some fractional interests but not others. The provisions of Section 155 do not forbid this disparate treatment. While principles of equity permit this Court to intervene when technical compliance with a statute produces an unfair result, equity and equality are not synonymous concepts in the Delaware General Corporation Law. Moreover, this Court should not create a safeguard against stockholder inequality that does not appear in the statute.[10] Here there is no showing that Applebaum was treated inequitably. From all that appears on this record, the proposed transaction was designed in good faith to accomplish a rational business purpose-saving transaction costs.[11]

Our jurisprudence does not prevent Avaya from properly using Section 155 in a creative fashion that is designed to meet its needs as an on-going enterprise.[12] The subsections listed in Section 155 merely require the corporation to compensate its stockholders when it chooses not to recognize their fractional interests in the form of fractional shares.[13] Based upon this record, we conclude that Avaya is free to recognize the fractional interests of some stockholders but not others so long as the corporation follows the procedures set forth in Section 155.

Avaya May Proceed with Any of Its Alternative Plans to Dispose of the Fractional Interests

The balance of Applebaum's appeal challenges the alternative methods by which Avaya proposes to dispose of the fractional interests. The Court of Chancery concluded that Avaya could proceed under Section 155(1) by aggregating the fractional interests and selling them on behalf of the cashed-out stockholders. The Court also held that Avaya could employ Section 155(2), which requires payment of the "fair value" of the fractional interests, by paying the cashed-out stockholders an amount based on the average trading price of Avaya stock. We agree with the decision of the Court of Chancery and address separately the issues based on each subsection of the statute.

---

[10] *See, e. g.,* Williams v. Geier, 671 A.2d 1368, 1385 n. 36 (Del. 1996) (noting "Directors and investors must be able to rely on the stability and absence of judicial interference with the State's statutory prescriptions"); *Nixon*, 626 A.2d at 1379–81 (absent legislation there should be no "special, judicially-created rules for minority investors"); American Hardware Corp. v. Savage Arms. Corp., 37 Del. Ch. 59, 136 A.2d 690, 693 (Del. 1957) (rejecting argument based on an interpretation that would "import serious confusion and uncertainty into corporate procedure").

[11] *See* Sinclair v. Levien, 280 A.2d 717, 720 (Del. 1971) (board action presumed valid if it "can be attributed to any rational business purpose"); *see also* Williams [v. Geier], 671 A.2d at 1377–78 (board action in recommending charter amendment for stockholder action covered by business judgment rule in the absence of rebuttal demonstrating violation of fiduciary duty).

[12] *See* Grimes v. Alteon Inc., 804 A.2d 256, 266 (Del. 2002) (noting that corporations "should have the freedom to enter into new and different forms of transactions") (citations omitted).

[13] *See* WARD, WELCH & TUREZYN, FOLK ON THE DELAWARE GENERAL CORPORATION LAW § 155.1 (4th ed. 2002) (stating "a corporation may refuse to issue share fractions . . . [but] If the corporation chooses to ignore share fractions, it must elect one of the three alternatives authorized by Section 155 . . .").

Section 155(1) Permits Avaya to Sell the Factional Interest on Behalf of the Stockholders

The stockholders have authorized Avaya to compensate the cashed-out stockholders by combining their fractional interests into whole shares and then selling them on the stockholders' behalf. Section 155(1) permits Avaya to "arrange for the disposition of fractional interests by those entitled thereto."

Applebaum claims that Avaya cannot use Section 155(1) because the corporation will sell whole shares rather than "fractional interests." According to this rendition of the transaction, the fractional interests held by the targeted stockholders must be reconverted into whole shares in the Forward Split. Otherwise, their fractional interests will be diluted. Avaya must reconvert the interests back to their initial value as whole shares in order to sell the combined fractional interests. Thus, Avaya would be selling whole shares rather than fractional interests.

Applebaum's argument incorrectly assumes that Avaya must issue fractions of a share in the Proposed Transaction. After the Reverse Split takes place, the stockholders holding shares below the minimum amount will be cashed out. The fractional interests will not be represented as shares and are therefore not involved in the Forward Split. Avaya will then aggregate the fractional interests and repackage them as whole shares which the corporation will sell on the open market. The statute does not mandate any set procedure by which the fractional interests must be disposed of so long as those interests are sold in a manner that secures the proportionate value of the cashed-out holdings.

Applebaum also contends that Avaya cannot sell the fractional interests on behalf of the cashed-out stockholders. If Avaya sells the interests for the stockholders, Applebaum argues that the corporation will not comply with Section 155(1) because the interests are not disposed of by "those entitled thereto." As the Vice Chancellor noted, Applebaum presents a strained reading of Section 155(1). The Court of Chancery correctly reasoned that "In the eyes of equity, such sales would be 'by' " the stockholders.

Applebaum's interpretation also ignores the corporation's responsibility under Section 155(1) to "arrange" for the disposition of fractional interests. Since fractional shares cannot be listed on the major stock exchanges, the corporation must arrange for their aggregation in order to sell them. Aggregation is normally performed by

> affording to the stockholder an election to sell the fractional share or to purchase an additional fraction sufficient to make up a whole share. The elections are forwarded to a trust company or other agent of the corporation who matches up the purchases and sales and issues certificates for the whole shares or checks for payment of the fractional shares. . ."

The general practice requires the corporation to act as an intermediary to package the fractional interests into marketable shares. If the corporation were not permitted to do so, the fractional interests of the cashed-out stockholders would be dissipated through the transaction costs of finding other fractional holders with whom to combine and sell fractional interests in the market.

* * *

The Ten-Day Trading Average by which Avaya Proposes to Compensate the Cashed-Out Stockholders Constitutes "Fair Value" under Section 155(2)

As an alternative to selling the fractional interests on behalf of the stockholders, Avaya may opt to pay the stockholders cash in an amount based on the trading price of Avaya stock averaged over a ten-day period preceding the Proposed Transaction. To do so, Avaya relies on Section 155(2), which provides that a corporation may "pay in cash the fair value of fractions of a share as of the time when those entitled to receive such fractions are determined."

The corporation owes its cashed-out stockholders payment representing the "fair value" of their fractional interests. The cashed-out stockholders will receive fair value if Avaya compensates them with payment based on the price of Avaya stock averaged over a ten-day period preceding the Proposed Transaction. While market price is not employed in all valuation contexts,[28] our jurisprudence recognizes that in many circumstances a property interest is best valued by the amount a buyer will pay for it.[29] The Vice Chancellor correctly concluded that a well-informed, liquid trading market will provide a measure of fair value superior to any estimate the court could impose.

Applebaum relies on two instances where the Court of Chancery intimated that a Section 155(2) valuation may be similar to a going concern valuation employed in an appraisal proceeding. In *Chalfin v. Hart Holdings Co.*,[31] the Court of Chancery rejected a market price offered by a majority stockholder because the stock was not traded in an active market. In *Metropolitan Life Ins. Co. v. Aramark Corp.*,[32] the Court of Chancery declined to apply a private company discount presented by a

---

[28] *See e. g.*, 8 *Del. C.* § 262(h) ("In determining . . . fair value," in an appraisal proceeding, "the Court shall take into account all relevant factors."); *Smith v. Van Gorkom*, 488 A.2d 858, 876 (Del. 1985) (holding that a decision by the board of directors to approve a merger did not fall within the proper exercise of business judgment because the directors failed to consider the intrinsic worth of the corporation where the stock traded at a depressed market value).

[29] *Cf.* 8 *Del. C.* § 262(b)(1) (denying appraisal rights for stock listed on a national securities exchange, interdealer quotation system by the National Association of Securities Dealers, Inc. or held of record by more than 2,000 holders); *Revlon, Inc. v. MacAndrews & Forbes Holdings*, 506 A.2d 173, 182 (Del. 1986) (noting that an auction for the sale of a corporation is an appropriate method by which to secure the best price for the stockholders); *Baron v. Pressed Metals of America, Inc.*, 35 Del. Ch. 581, 123 A.2d 848, 854 (Del. 1956) (noting that the "best price" a corporation could hope to obtain for the sale of a corporate asset "was what someone would be willing to pay" for it).

[31] *Chalfin v. Hart Holdings Co.*, 1990 Del. Ch. LEXIS 188, 1990 WL 181958 (Del. Ch.).

[32] *Metropolitan Life Ins. Co. v. Aramark Corp.*, 1998 Del. Ch. LEXIS 70 (Del. Ch.).

controlling stockholder seeking to squeeze out the minority stockholders. Neither case applies here.

The court cannot defer to market price as a measure of fair value if the stock has not been traded actively in a liquid market. In *Chalfin*, for example, the Court of Chancery held that the controlling stockholder could not offer as "fair value" in a reverse stock split the same amount alleged to be the past trading value because the stock had not been publicly traded for "some time." The "market price" offered by the controlling stockholder was based on stale information. An active trading market did not exist to monitor the corporation's performance. Thus, a more thorough valuation would have been necessary.

Avaya stock, by contrast, is actively traded on the NYSE. The concerns noted in *Chalfin* are not pertinent to the Proposed Transaction because the market continues to digest information currently known about the company. The value of Avaya's stock is tested daily through the purchase and sale of the stock on the open market.

In a related argument, Applebaum contends that the trading price cannot represent fair value because the stock price is volatile, trading at a range of prices from $13.70 per share to $1.12 per share over the past year. The volatility in trading does not necessarily mean that the market price is not an accurate indicator of fair value. Avaya stock is widely-held and actively traded in the market. The ten-day average has been recognized as a fair compromise that will hedge against the risk of fluctuation. Corporations often cash out fractional interests in an amount based on the average price over a given trading period.

Applebaum also misunderstands the appropriate context for which a going-concern valuation may be necessary under Section 155(2). In both *Chalfin* and *Aramark*, the Court of Chancery recognized that a transaction employing Section 155 may warrant a searching inquiry of fair value if a controlling stockholder initiates the transaction. When a controlling stockholder presents a transaction that will free it from future dealings with the minority stockholders, opportunism becomes a concern. Any shortfall imposed on the minority stockholders will result in a transfer of value to the controlling stockholder. The discount in value could be imposed deliberately or could be the result of an information asymmetry where the controlling stockholder possesses material facts that are not known in the market.[41] Thus, a Section 155(2) inquiry may resemble a Section 262 valuation if the controlling stockholder will

---

[41] *See, e.g., Glassman v. Unocal Exploration Corp.*, 777 A.2d 242, 248 (De. 2001) (a fair value determination must be based on "all relevant factors" in a short-form merger because the transaction presented by the controlling stockholder may be "timed to take advantage of a depressed market, or a low point in the company's cyclical earnings, or to precede an anticipated positive development . . ."). *See also* Robert B. Thompson, *Exit, Liquidity, and Majority Rule: Appraisal's Role in Corporate Law*, 84 Geo. L.J. 1, 36 (1995) (arguing that an appraisal valuation may be necessary in a squeeze-out context if "the minority does not have a choice and is being forced out, perhaps because of an anticipated increase in value that will only become visible after the transaction, [in which case] exclusion [of the minority stockholders] can easily become a basis for oppression of the minority").

benefit from presenting a suspect measure of valuation, such as an outdated trading price, or a wrongfully imposed private company discount.

Although the Reverse/Forward Split will cash out smaller stockholders, the transaction will not allow the corporation to realize a gain at their expense. Unlike the more typical "freeze-out" context, the cashed-out Avaya stockholders may continue to share in the value of the enterprise. Avaya stockholders can avoid the effects of the proposed transaction either by purchasing a sufficient amount of stock to survive the initial Reverse Split or by simply using the payment provided under Section 155(2) to repurchase the same amount of Avaya stock that they held before the transaction.

The Reverse/Forward Split merely forces the stockholders to choose affirmatively to remain in the corporation. Avaya will succeed in saving administrative costs only if the board has assumed correctly that the stockholders who received a small interest in the corporation through the Lucent spin off would prefer to receive payment, free of transaction costs, rather than continue with the corporation. The Transaction is not structured to prevent the cashed-out stockholders from maintaining their stakes in the company. A payment based on market price is appropriate because it will permit the stockholders to reinvest in Avaya, should they wish to do so.

The Meaning of "Fair Value" under Section 155(2) is not Identical to the Concept of "Fair Value" in Section 262

The Court of Chancery correctly interpreted "fair value" in Section 155 to have a meaning independent of the definition of "fair value" in Section 262 of the Delaware General Corporation Law.[44] Relying on the maxim that the same words used in different sections must be construed to have the same meaning, Applebaum argues that "fair value" under Section 155(2) requires the court to perform a valuation similar to an appraisal proceeding. Borrowing from appraisal concepts that require that shares of stock be valued as proportionate interests in a going concern, Applebaum contends that the average trading price would be inadequate because the market price possesses an inherent discount that accounts for the holder's minority stake in the company.

The Delaware General Assembly could not have intended Section 155(2) to have the same meaning as the fair value concept employed in Section 262.[47] The reference to fair value in Section 155 first appeared in

---

[44] 8 *Del. C.* § 262(a) (providing that "Any stockholder of a corporation of this State who holds shares of stock on the date of the making of a demand pursuant to subsection (d) . . . who continuously holds such shares through the effective date of the merger or consolidation . . . who has neither voted in favor of the merger or consolidation nor consented thereto . . . shall be entitled to an appraisal by the Court of Chancery of the fair value of the stockholder's shares of stock. . .).

[47] Hariton v. Arco Electronics, Inc., 41 Del. Ch. 74, 188 A.2d 123, 124 (Del. 1963) ("[t]he general theory of the Delaware Corporation Law that action taken pursuant to the authority of the various sections of that law constitute acts of independent legal significance and their validity is not dependent on other sections of the Act.") (quoting Langfelder v. Universal Laboratories, 68 F. Supp. 209, 211 (D. Del. 1946)).

1967. The General Assembly did not place the term fair value in Section 262 until 1976. Furthermore, the case law developing the concept of fair value under the appraisal statute did not acquire its present form until this Court discarded the Delaware block method and underscored the necessity of valuing a corporation as a going concern. This Court has not suggested similar valuation guidelines for the right to receive "fair value" under Section 155(2). Finally, Section 262(b)(2)(c) expressly excludes fractional interests from the appraisal remedy when the stock is traded on a national exchange. When applied in the context of a merger or consolidation, Applebaum's interpretation of "fair value" under Section 155(2) would accord the stockholder of a constituent corporation an appraisal of fractional interests to which the stockholder is not entitled under the "market out" exception provided in Section 262.[51]

As this Court noted in *Alabama By-Products v. Cede & Co.*, the right to an appraisal is a narrow statutory right that seeks to redress the loss of the stockholder's ability under the common law to stop a merger. The Reverse/Forward Split permitted under Section 155 does not present the same problem and is ill-suited for the same solution provided for in Section 262.

The valuation of a stockholder's interest as a "going concern" is necessary only when the board's proposal will alter the nature of the corporation through a merger. When a corporation merges with another corporation, the dissenting stockholder is entitled to the value of the company as a going concern because the nature of the corporation's future "concern" will be vastly different. In a merger requiring an appraisal, the dissenting stockholder's share must be measured as a proportionate interest in a going concern because the proponents of the merger will realize the full intrinsic worth of the company rather than simply the market price of the stock. Thus, when a minority stockholder is confronted with a freeze-out merger, the Section 262 appraisal process will prevent the proponents of the merger from "reaping a windfall" by placing the full value of the company as a going concern into the merged entity while compensating the dissenting stockholder with discounted consideration.[54]

Avaya will not capture its full going-concern value in the Reverse/Forward Split. As the Vice Chancellor noted, if the cashed-out stockholders were awarded the value of the company as a going concern, they, rather than the corporation, would receive a windfall. The cashed-out stockholders could capture the full proportionate value of the

[51] Section 262(b)(1) denies appraisal rights to stockholders of a merging corporation if their stock is listed on a national securities exchange, interdealer quotation system, or held of record by more than 2,000 holders. 8 *Del. C.* § 262(b)(1). Similarly, under Section 262(b)(2)(c), those same stockholders are not afforded an appraisal right for cash they receive "in lieu of fractional shares" of the stock. 8 *Del. C.* § 262(b)(2)(c).

[54] *See Cavalier Oil*, 564 A.2d at 1145 ("To fail to accord to a minority shareholder the full proportionate value of his shares imposes a penalty for lack of control, and unfairly enriches the majority shareholder who may reap a windfall from the appraisal process by cashing out a dissenting shareholder, a clearly undesirable result.").

fractional interest, return to the market and buy the reissued stock at the market price, and realize the going concern value a second time should Avaya ever merge or otherwise become subject to a change of control transaction.

QUESTIONS

1. Avaya could have achieved the same result through a merger with a newly created corporation under DGCL § 251, in which Avaya shareholders would receive one share of the new corporation for each 30, 40 or 50 shares, and those holding fewer shares were cashed out or given appraisal rights under DGCL § 262. Why do you suppose Avaya didn't choose this method?
2. How does the court determine that the meaning of "fair value" in section 155 is different from its meaning in the appraisal section of the Delaware Act, § 262? Does this make economic sense?
3. Applebaum argued that section 155 permitted cashing out fractional shareholders only if Avaya didn't issue fractional shares, and that holders of one whole share received fractional shares while holders of fewer shares did not, which wasn't authorized by section 155. How does the court respond to this objection?
4. One of the basic principles of corporation law is equality of treatment of similarly situated shareholders. Here Applebaum objects that his fractional shares will be treated differently from fractional shares held by those with more than 30, 40 or 50 shares. How does the court deal with this equality argument?

C. SPIN-OFFS AND SPLIT-OFFS

Spin-off transactions involve another form of dividend—this time of the stock of a subsidiary. Corporations may dividend out the stock of an existing subsidiary, or may take an operating division, put its assets into a newly created subsidiary, and then dividend out the shares of the newly created subsidiary.

There are a variety of reasons for spin-off transactions. The excesses of the conglomerate movement of the 1960s and 1970s left many companies with operations that did not fit well with the rest of the businesses owned, in terms of creating operating synergies. Remember, diversification can be home-made, so investors won't value diversification within a firm without a good reason. In many cases these "misfits" were ignored by top management and received little in the way of new capital to pursue good opportunities, even when the expected rates of return were higher than those on projects in more favored divisions. In some cases, top management had little knowledge or understanding of these divisions.

Many of these divisions were sold off during the 1980s. In some cases, divisional management would seek outside financing and engage in a leveraged buyout of the division. In others, competitors might be the buyers. Finally, a corporation without such offers might simply spin the subsidiary's shares off to its own shareholders. The finance literature suggests that spinning off divisions is generally a value-enhancing strategy for shareholders.* One example is Sara Lee's spin-off of Coach, the handbag maker. Since its spin-off in 2000 Coach's stock has increased more than 1500%. Not bad!

One other use of the spin-off is less benign. Beginning in the early 1970s mass tort claims began to be brought against makers of asbestos, makers of products containing asbestos, and makers of products that used asbestos in their manufacturing process. The largest maker of asbestos was Johns Manville Corporation, which was also one of the first to file for Chapter 11 reorganization in 1982. It was soon followed into bankruptcy by other asbestos manufacturers. By the mid-1980s the writing was on the wall: any association with asbestos was likely to bankrupt a company. Some dealt with this issue through corporate reorganizations. The companies would reorganize into a structure in which the shareholders first received shares in a holding company that owned all of the stock of the potential bankrupt. The parent corporation would then proceed to purchase the non-asbestos businesses from the potential bankrupt, placing them in newly created subsidiaries. The parent corporation could then dividend out the shares of the new subsidiaries to the parent's shareholders, thus separating the asbestos assets from the other assets. Litigation centered around whether these transactions were fraudulent conveyances, which depended on the potential insolvency of the defendant and the intent of its management in creating this series of transactions. For one variation on this technique, in which the parent then sold the defendant entity and retained the viable enterprises, see Raytech Corp. v. White, 54 F.3d 187 (3d Cir. 1995).

One advantage of the spin-off is that unlike many other distributions, it is tax free under I.R.C. § 355, if certain conditions are met. The parent must distribute all of the shares of the subsidiary, or at least enough to constitute control under section 368(c), which requires a minimum of 80% of the voting power and value of the stock.

A split-off is a similar transaction, under which the parent corporation distributes the subsidiary's shares in exchange for its own shares. For this exchange transaction to be tax free, the parent corporation must distribute stock of the controlled subsidiary that represents at least 80% of the voting power and value of the subsidiary.

---

* See James A. Miles and James D. Rosenfeld, *The Effect of Voluntary Spin-off Announcements on Shareholder Wealth*, 38 JOURNAL OF FINANCE 1597 (1983) and James D. Rosenfeld, *Additional Evidence on the Relation Between Divestiture Announcements and Shareholder Wealth*, 39 JOURNAL OF FINANCE 1437 (1984).

D. TRACKING STOCKS

Tracking stock is a variation on a spin-off. It generally involves the creation of a new subsidiary, into which a corporation pours the assets of an operating division, although an existing subsidiary could also be used. The parent remains owner of 100% of the subsidiary's stock but issues a tracking stock to its shareholders.

Tracking stock is a class of common stock of the parent corporation, with special rights. The subsidiary's assets and businesses are typically segregated, and separate financial statements are prepared and published.* The parent board can declare dividends as it wishes on each class of stock. Dividends on the tracking stock, however, are limited to the amount that is legally available if the subsidiary were a separate corporation—and the tracking shares were actually shares in the subsidiary. Voting rights of the tracking shares vary, and some tracking stocks will not vote at all. Similarly, liquidation rights can vary, although tracking shares have no separate claim on the subsidiary's assets. Thus, in bankruptcy, the holders of the tracking stock have no priority over the parent's common stockholders to the assets of the subsidiary.

General Motors was one of the first corporations to issue tracking stock in 1984, when it acquired Electronic Data Systems from Ross Perot and the public stockholders of EDS. It issued a new Class "E" common stock tied to the earnings of the EDS operations. It used the same technique when it acquired Hughes Aircraft in 1985 and issued "H" common. Other companies have also issued targeted stock. For an account of these transactions, see Julia D'Souza and John Jacob, Why Firms Issue Targeted Stock, 56 Journal of Financial Economics 459 (2000).

Distributing tracking stock is claimed to have some advantages over spin-offs. By remaining one large diversified corporation, all businesses owned by the entity might benefit from a lower cost of capital that is sometimes available to larger corporations. Similarly, overhead costs are

---

* This can create potential tax issues, including whether the tracking stock is really stock of the parent or the subsidiary. If the IRS treats it as stock of the parent, the following tax consequences will exist:

1. A distribution of tracking stock to stockholders of the parent will qualify as a nontaxable stock dividend under IRC § 305(a).
2. Such a distribution will be tax-free to the parent under IRC § 311.

If, on the other hand, the IRS treats it as stock of the subsidiary, here are the major tax consequences:

1. If the tracking stock transaction doesn't qualify as a § 355 spin-off, tracking stock distributed to the parent's stockholders would be taxable as dividends under § 301.
2. If the tracking stock transaction doesn't qualify as a § 355 spin-off, the difference between the fair market value and the basis of the tracking stock would be recognized as gain to the parent under § 311 of the Code.

See Hass, *supra*, 94 MICH. L. REV. at 2111, citing Hard R. Handler & Dickson G. Brown, Tracking Stock, *6 Tax Strategies for Corporate Acquisitions, Dispositions, Spin-Offs, Joint Ventures and Other Strategic Alliances, Financings, Reorganizations and Restructurings 1993*, at 369 (PLI TAX LAW AND ESTATE PLANNING COURSE NO. J–346, 1993).

spread over one, not two entities. And the larger entity might also be better protected from unsolicited takeover bids, although a corporation created before a spin-off can be well protected in advance.

But tracking stock can create some difficult conflicts between the parent and subsidiary boards and shareholders. The parent's directors will elect the board of the subsidiary, and the parent board will owe fiduciary duties to two discrete groups—holders of its own common stock and holders of its tracking stock. These difficulties are discussed in Jeffrey J. Hass, "Directorial Fiduciary Duties in a Tracking Stock Equity Structure: The Need for a Duty of Fairness," 94 Mich. L. Rev. 2089 (1996).

The EDS transaction illustrated one of the difficulties with tracking stock. If General Motors acquired EDS, at least in part, to provide services to General Motors, how should it set a price for those services that is fair to both GM and the E shareholders? While some commentators suggest that using targeted stock may increase value because it enhances the transparency of financial reporting—since the corporation must now separate its financial results by division quite clearly—most tracking stocks have not had long-term success. Firms issuing these shares will often retire them.

APPENDIX

AMENDED AND RESTATED CERTIFICATE OF INCORPORATION OF LYFT, INC.

Article I.

The name of this corporation is **Lyft, Inc.** (the "**Corporation**").

Article II.

The address of the registered office of this Corporation in the State of Delaware is 3500 South Dupont Highway, City of Dover, County of Kent, Delaware 19901. The name of its registered agent at such address is Incorporating Services, Ltd.

Article III.

The nature of the business of this Corporation and the objects or purposes to be transacted, promoted or carried on by it are to engage in any lawful act or activity for which corporations may be organized under the General Corporation Law of the State of Delaware (the "**DGCL**").

Article IV.

A. Classes of Stock. As of the date on which this Amended and Restated Certificate of Incorporation is accepted for filing by the Secretary of State of the State of Delaware (the "**Filing Date**"), the authorized capital stock of the Corporation shall be as follows:

This Corporation is authorized to issue two classes of stock to be designated, respectively, "**Common Stock**" and "**Preferred Stock**." This Corporation is authorized to issue 340,000,000 shares of Common Stock, par value of $0.00001 per share. This Corporation is authorized to issue 227,328,900 shares of Preferred Stock, par value of $0.00001 per share, 6,063,921 of which shall be designated "**Series Seed Preferred Stock**," 8,129,364 of which shall be designated "**Series A Preferred Stock**," 7,067,771 of which shall be designated "**Series B Preferred Stock**," 14,479,445 of which shall be designated "**Series C Preferred Stock**," 24,674,534 of which shall be designated "**Series D Preferred Stock**," 47,099,094 of which shall be designated "**Series E Preferred Stock**," 37,263,568 of which shall be designated "**Series F Preferred Stock**," 18,662,127 of which shall be designated "**Series G Preferred Stock**," 42,771,492 of which shall be designated "**Series H Preferred Stock**" and 21,117,584 of which shall be designated "**Series I Preferred Stock**."

B. Rights, Preferences and Restrictions of Preferred Stock. The rights, preferences, privileges, and restrictions granted to and imposed on the each series of Preferred Stock are as set forth below in this Article IV.B.

1. Dividend Provisions.

(a) The holders of shares of Preferred Stock shall be entitled to receive dividends, on a *pari passu* basis, out of any assets legally available therefor, prior and in preference to any declaration or payment of any dividend (payable other than in Common Stock or other securities and rights convertible into or entitling the holder thereof to receive, directly or indirectly, additional shares of Common Stock of this Corporation) on the Common Stock of this Corporation, at the rate of (i) $0.01801333 per share per annum for the Series Seed Preferred Stock, (ii) $0.06101333 per share per annum for the Series A Preferred Stock, (iii) $0.16820000 per share per annum for the Series B Preferred Stock, (iv) $0.339792 per share per annum for the Series C Preferred Stock, (v) $0.810552 per share per annum for the Series D Preferred Stock, (vi) $1.5556 per share per annum for the Series E Preferred Stock, (vii) $2.143112 per share per annum for the Series F Preferred Stock, (viii) $2.572 per share per annum for the Series G Preferred Stock, (ix) $3.179688 per share per annum for the Series H Preferred Stock and (x) $3.788312 per share per annum for the Series I Preferred Stock (each as adjusted for any stock splits, stock dividends, combinations, recapitalizations or the like (collectively, "**Recapitalizations**")), and as otherwise set forth elsewhere herein, payable when, as, and if declared by the Board of Directors of this Corporation (the "**Board of Directors**"). Such dividends shall not be cumulative. Any partial payment shall be made *pro rata* among the holders of Preferred Stock in proportion to the payment each such holder would receive if the full amount of such dividends were paid.

(b) After payment of any dividends pursuant to Article IV.B.1(a), any additional dividends shall be distributed among all holders of Common Stock and all holders of Preferred Stock in proportion to the number of shares of Common Stock which would be held by each such holder if all shares of such series of Preferred Stock were converted to Common Stock at the then-effective conversion rate for each such series of Preferred Stock.

(c) To the extent one or more sections of any other state corporations code setting forth minimum requirements for this Corporation's retained earnings and/or net assets are applicable to this Corporation's repurchase of shares of Common Stock, such code sections shall not apply, to the greatest extent permitted by applicable law, in whole or in part with respect to repurchases by this Corporation of its Common Stock from employees, officers, directors, advisors, consultants or other persons performing services for this Corporation or any subsidiary pursuant to agreements under which this Corporation has the right to repurchase such shares at cost upon the occurrence of certain events, such as the termination of employment. In the case of any such repurchases, distributions by this Corporation may be made without regard to the "preferential dividends arrears amount" or any "preferential rights amount," as such terms may be defined in such other state's corporations code.

2. Liquidation Preference.

(a) In the event of a Liquidation Event (as defined below), either voluntary or involuntary, the holders of Preferred Stock shall be entitled to receive, prior and in preference to any distribution of any of the assets of this Corporation to the holders of Common Stock by reason of their ownership thereof, on a *pari passu* basis, an amount per share equal to (i) in the case of the Series Seed Preferred Stock, the sum of $0.225166667 (the "**Original Series Seed Issue Price**") for each outstanding share of Series Seed Preferred Stock and an amount equal to all declared but unpaid dividends on such share, (ii) in the case of the Series A Preferred Stock, the sum of $0.762666667 (the "**Original Series A Issue Price**") for each outstanding share of Series A Preferred Stock and an amount equal to all declared but unpaid dividends on such share, (iii) in the case of the Series B Preferred Stock, the sum of $2.1025 (the "**Original Series B Issue Price**") for each outstanding share of Series B Preferred Stock and an amount equal to all declared but unpaid dividends on such share, (iv) in the case of the Series C Preferred Stock, the sum of $4.2474 (the "**Original Series C Issue Price**") for each outstanding share of Series C Preferred Stock and an amount equal to all declared but unpaid dividends on such share, (v) in the case of the Series D Preferred Stock, the sum of $10.1319 (the "**Original Series D Issue Price**") for each outstanding share of Series D Preferred Stock and an amount equal to all declared but unpaid dividends on such share, (vi) in the case of the Series E Preferred Stock, the sum of $19.4456 (the "**Original Series E Issue Price**") for each outstanding share of Series E Preferred Stock and an amount equal to all declared but unpaid dividends on such share, (vii) in the case of the Series F Preferred Stock, the sum of $26.7889 (the "**Original Series F Issue Price**") for each outstanding share of Series F Preferred Stock and an amount equal to all declared but unpaid dividends on such share, (viii) in the case of the Series G Preferred Stock, the sum of $32.1500 (the "**Original Series G Issue Price**") for each outstanding share of Series G Preferred Stock and an amount equal to all declared but unpaid dividends on such share, (ix) in the case of the Series H Preferred Stock, the sum of $39.7461 (the "**Original Series H Issue Price**") for each outstanding share of Series H Preferred Stock and an amount equal to all declared but unpaid dividends on such share and (x) in the case of the Series I Preferred Stock, the sum of $47.3539 (the "**Original Series I Issue Price**" and along with each of the Original Series Seed Issue Price, the Original Series A Issue Price, the Original Series B Issue Price, the Original Series C Issue Price, the Original Series D Issue Price, the Original Series E Issue Price, the Original Series F Issue Price, the Original Series G Issue Price and the Original Series H Issue Price may be referred to herein as an "**Original Issue Price**") for each outstanding share of Series I Preferred Stock and an amount equal to all declared but unpaid dividends on such share (each as adjusted for Recapitalizations and as otherwise set forth elsewhere herein). If, upon the occurrence of such event, the assets and funds thus distributed among the holders of the Preferred Stock shall be insufficient to permit the payment to such holders of the full aforesaid preferential amounts, then the entire assets and funds of this Corporation legally available for distribution to stockholders shall be distributed *pro rata* among the holders of the Preferred Stock in proportion to the full preferential amount each such holder is otherwise entitled to receive under this Article IV.B.2(a).

(b) Upon completion of the distributions required by Article IV.B.2(a) all of the remaining assets of this Corporation available for distribution to stockholders shall be distributed among the holders of Common Stock *pro rata* based on the number of shares of Common Stock held by each.

(c) Notwithstanding the above, for purposes of determining the amount each holder of shares of Preferred Stock is entitled to receive with respect to a Liquidation Event, each such holder of shares of Preferred Stock shall be deemed to have converted (regardless of whether such holder actually converted) such holder's shares of Preferred Stock into shares of Common Stock immediately prior to such Liquidation Event if, as a result of an actual conversion, such holder would receive, in the aggregate, an amount greater than the amount that would be distributed to such holder if such holder did not convert such Preferred Stock into shares of Common Stock. If any such holder shall be deemed to have converted shares of Preferred Stock into Common Stock pursuant to this paragraph, then such holder shall not be entitled to receive any distribution that would otherwise be made to holders of Preferred Stock that have not converted (or have not been deemed to have converted) into shares of Common Stock.

(d) Deemed Liquidation Events.

(i) A "**Liquidation Event**" shall mean (unless the holders of (x) a majority of the Preferred Stock, voting together as a single class on an as-converted basis, (y) a majority of the Series C Preferred Stock and the Series D Preferred Stock, voting together as a single class on an as-converted basis, (z) a majority of the Series E Preferred Stock, voting as a separate series, (aa) a majority of the Series F Preferred Stock, voting as a separate series, (bb) a majority of the Series G Preferred Stock, voting as a separate series, (cc) the "**Series H Requisite Approval**" (which shall mean a majority of the Series H Preferred Stock, *provided, however,* that for so long as any person that is a holder of Series H Preferred Stock as of the Filing Date, together with its affiliates, holds at least 12,579,855 shares of Series H Preferred Stock, "Series H Requisite Approval" shall mean at least seventy-one percent

(71%) of the Series H Preferred Stock), in each case, voting as a separate series, and (dd) a majority of the Series I Preferred Stock, voting as a separate series, shall determine otherwise):

(A) any liquidation, dissolution, or winding up of the Corporation, whether voluntary or involuntary;

(B) the acquisition of this Corporation by another entity by means of any reorganization, merger or consolidation (but excluding any reorganization, merger or consolidation effected exclusively for the purpose of changing the domicile of this Corporation), or any transaction or series of related transactions in which this Corporation's stockholders of record as constituted immediately prior to such transaction or series of related transactions will, immediately after such transaction or series of related transactions (by virtue of securities issued in such transaction or series of related transactions) fail to hold at least 50% of the voting power of the resulting or surviving corporation (but excluding any sale of Preferred Stock to investors for the principal purpose of raising capital);

(C) a sale, lease, transfer or other disposition (whether by merger or otherwise), in a single transaction or any series of related transactions, by this Corporation of all or substantially all of the assets of this Corporation to any person or entity other than a wholly owned subsidiary of this Corporation; or

(D) the grant of an exclusive license to all or substantially all of this Corporation's intellectual property in a single transaction or series of related transactions to any person or entity other than a wholly owned subsidiary of this Corporation.

For purposes hereof, "**person**" shall mean any individual, firm, corporation, partnership, association, limited liability company, trust or any other entity and any person shall be deemed an "**affiliate**" of another person who, directly or indirectly, controls, is controlled by or is under common control with such person, including, without limitation, any general partner, managing member, officer or director of such person or any venture capital fund now or hereafter existing that is controlled by one or more general partners or managing members of, or shares the same management company with, such person.

(ii) In any of such events, if the consideration received by this Corporation is other than cash, its value will be deemed its fair market value as determined in good faith by the Board of Directors (including at least one of the Preferred Directors (as defined below)). Any securities shall be valued as follows:

(A) For securities not subject to investment letter or other similar restrictions on free marketability (other than restrictions arising solely by virtue of a stockholder's status as an affiliate or former affiliate):

(1) If traded on a national securities exchange, the value shall be deemed to be the average of the closing prices of the securities on such exchange over the 30-day period (or portion thereof) ending three days prior to the closing;

(2) If actively traded over-the-counter, the value shall be deemed to be the average of the closing bid or sale prices (whichever is applicable) over the 30-day period (or portion thereof) ending three days prior to the closing; and

(3) If there is no active public market, the value shall be the fair market value thereof, as determined by the Board of Directors (including at least one of the Preferred Directors).

(B) For securities subject to investment letter or other restrictions on free marketability (other than restrictions arising solely by virtue of a stockholder's status as an affiliate or former affiliate), the value shall be deemed to be the value determined as described above in Article IV.B.2(d)(ii)(A) marked down by an appropriate discount to reflect the approximate fair market value thereof, as determined by the Board of Directors (including at least one of the Preferred Directors).

(iii) In the event the requirements of Article IV.B.2 are not complied with, this Corporation shall forthwith either:

(A) Cause such closing to be postponed until such time as the requirements of Article IV.B.2 have been complied with; or

(B) Cancel such transaction, in which event the rights, preferences and privileges of the holders of the Preferred Stock shall revert to and be the same as such rights, preferences and privileges existing immediately prior to the date of the first notice referred to in Article IV.B.2(d)(iv) hereof.

(iv) This Corporation shall give each holder of record of Preferred Stock written notice of such impending transaction not later than 20 days prior to the date for determining the right to vote with respect to such transaction, or 20 days prior to the closing of such transaction, whichever is earlier, and shall also notify such holders in writing of the final approval of such transaction. The first of such notices shall describe the material terms and conditions of the impending transaction, and this Corporation shall thereafter give such holders prompt notice of any material changes to such terms and conditions. The transaction shall in no event take place sooner than 20 days after this Corporation has given the first notice provided for herein or sooner than 10 days after this Corporation has given notice of any material changes provided for herein; provided that such periods may be shortened or waived prospectively or retrospectively upon the written consent of the holders of Preferred Stock that are entitled to such notice rights or similar notice rights and that represent a majority of the voting power of the then-outstanding shares of such Preferred Stock, voting together as a single class on an as-converted basis.

3. Redemption. Neither this Corporation nor the holders of Preferred Stock shall have the unilateral right to call or redeem or cause to have called or redeemed any shares of the Preferred Stock.

4. Conversion. The holders of Preferred Stock shall have conversion rights as follows (the "**Conversion Rights**"):

(a) Right to Convert. Each share of Preferred Stock shall be convertible, at the option of the holder thereof, at any time after the date of issuance of such share at the office of this Corporation or any transfer agent for such stock, into such number of fully paid and nonassessable shares of Common Stock as is determined by dividing the Original Issue Price for each such series of Preferred Stock by the Conversion Price applicable to such share, determined as hereafter provided, in effect on the date the certificate is surrendered for conversion. As of the Filing Date, the Conversion Price per share for shares of Series Seed Preferred Stock shall be the Original Series Seed Issue Price, the Conversion Price per share for shares of Series A Preferred Stock shall be the Original Series A Issue Price, the Conversion Price per share for shares of Series B Preferred Stock shall be the Original Series B Issue Price, the Conversion Price per share for shares of Series C Preferred Stock shall be the Original Series C Issue Price, the Conversion Price per share for shares of Series D Preferred Stock shall be the Original Series D Issue Price, the Conversion Price per share for shares of Series E Preferred Stock shall be the Original Series E Issue Price, the Conversion Price per share for shares of Series F Preferred Stock shall be the Original Series F Issue Price, the Conversion Price per share for shares of Series G Preferred Stock shall be the Original Series G Issue Price, the Conversion Price per share for shares of Series H Preferred Stock shall be the Original Series H Issue Price and the Conversion Price per share for shares of Series I Preferred Stock shall be the Original Series I Issue Price; *provided, that* the Conversion Price for each series of Preferred Stock shall be subject to adjustment as set forth in Article IV.B.4(d).

(b) Automatic Conversion. Each share of Preferred Stock shall automatically be converted into shares of Common Stock at the Conversion Price then in effect for such series of Preferred Stock as adjusted pursuant to Article IV.B.4(d)(ii)(C), if applicable, immediately upon the earlier of (i) except as provided in Article IV.B.4(c), immediately prior to the closing of this Corporation's sale of its Common Stock in a firm commitment underwritten public offering pursuant to an effective registration statement under the Securities Act of 1933, as amended (the "**Act**"), resulting in gross proceeds to the Corporation (before deducting underwriter discounts and commissions) of at least $150,000,000 (provided, that any adjustment of the Conversion Price for shares of Series F Preferred Stock, Series G Preferred Stock, Series H Preferred Stock and/or Series I Preferred Stock pursuant to Article IV.B.4(d)(ii)(C) in respect of the issuance of shares of Common Stock in such public offering shall be made immediately prior to conversion of such shares of Preferred Stock into shares of Common Stock pursuant to this Article IV.B.4(b), notwithstanding that such conversion takes place prior to the actual issuance of such shares of Common Stock) and (ii) the date, or the occurrence of an event, specified by written consent of the holders of a majority of the then-outstanding shares of Preferred Stock, voting together as a single class and on an as-converted basis; *provided, however*, (x) the Series C Preferred Stock shall not be converted pursuant to this subsection (ii) without the approval of the holders of a majority of the then-outstanding shares of Series C Preferred Stock, voting as a separate series, (y) the Series D Preferred Stock shall not be converted pursuant to this subsection (ii) without the approval of the holders of a majority of the then-outstanding shares of Series D Preferred Stock, voting as a separate series, (z) the Series E Preferred Stock shall not be converted pursuant to this subsection (ii) without the approval of the holders of a majority of the then-outstanding shares of Series E Preferred Stock, voting as a separate series, (aa) the Series F Preferred Stock shall not be converted pursuant to this subsection (ii) without the approval of the holders of a majority of the then-outstanding shares of Series F Preferred Stock, voting as a separate series, (bb) the Series G Preferred Stock shall not be converted pursuant to this subsection (ii) without the approval of the holders of a majority of the then-outstanding shares of Series G Preferred Stock, voting as a separate series, (cc) the Series H Preferred Stock shall not be converted pursuant to this subsection (ii) without the Series H Requisite Approval, voting as a separate series, and (dd) the Series I Preferred Stock shall not be converted pursuant to this subsection (ii) without the approval of the holders of a majority of the then-outstanding shares of Series I Preferred Stock, voting as a separate series.

(c) Mechanics of Conversion. Before any holder of Preferred Stock shall be entitled to convert the same into shares of Common Stock, he, she or it shall surrender the certificate or certificates therefor, duly endorsed, at the office of this Corporation or of any transfer agent for the Preferred Stock (or shall notify the Corporation or its transfer agent that such certificates have been lost, stolen or destroyed and shall execute an agreement satisfactory to the Corporation to indemnify the Corporation from any loss incurred by it in connection with such certificate or certificates), and shall give written notice to this Corporation at its principal corporate office, of the election to convert the same and shall state therein the name or names in which the certificate or certificates for shares of Common Stock are to be issued. This Corporation shall, as soon as practicable thereafter, issue and deliver at such office to such holder of Preferred Stock, or to the nominee or nominees of such holder, a certificate or certificates for the number of shares of Common Stock to which such holder shall be entitled. Such conversion shall be deemed to have been made immediately prior to the close of business on the date of such surrender of the shares of Preferred

Stock to be converted, and the person or persons entitled to receive the shares of Common Stock issuable upon such conversion shall be treated for all purposes as the record holder or holders of such shares of Common Stock as of such date. If the conversion is in connection with an underwritten offering of securities registered pursuant to the Act, the conversion may, at the option of any holder tendering Preferred Stock for conversion, be conditioned upon the closing with the underwriters of the sale of securities pursuant to such offering, in which event the persons entitled to receive the Common Stock upon conversion of the Preferred Stock shall not be deemed to have converted such Preferred Stock until immediately prior to the closing of such sale of securities.

(d) Conversion Price Adjustments of Preferred Stock. The Conversion Price for any series of Preferred Stock shall be subject to adjustment from time to time as follows:

(i) (A) If this Corporation shall issue, at any time or from time to time after the Filing Date, any Additional Stock (as defined below) without consideration or for a consideration per share less than the Conversion Price for any such series of Preferred Stock, as such price is in effect immediately prior to the issuance of such Additional Stock, the Conversion Price for such series of Preferred Stock, as such price is in effect immediately prior to each such issuance shall (except as otherwise provided in this Article IV.B.4(d)(i)) be adjusted concurrently with such issuance to a price computed using the following formula:

$$CP_N = CP_O \times \frac{CS_O + \frac{M_N}{CP_O}}{CS_O + AS_N}$$

Where CP_N is the adjusted Conversion Price for such series of Preferred Stock;

CP_O is the Conversion Price for such series of Preferred Stock, as such price is in effect immediately prior to such issuance;

CS_O is the number of shares of Common Stock Outstanding (as defined below) immediately prior to such issuance;

M_N is the aggregate consideration received by the Corporation for such issuance; and

AS_N is the number of shares of such Additional Stock.

For purposes of this Article IV.B.4(d)(i), the term "**Common Stock Outstanding**" shall mean and include the following: (1) then-outstanding shares of Common Stock; (2) shares of Common Stock issuable upon conversion of outstanding shares of Preferred Stock; (3) shares of Common Stock issuable upon exercise of then-outstanding stock options or settlement of then-outstanding restricted stock unit awards; (4) shares of Common Stock issuable upon exercise (and, in the case of warrants to purchase Preferred Stock, conversion) of then-outstanding warrants; and (5) the maximum number of shares of Common Stock issuable upon conversion of any other then-outstanding security convertible directly or indirectly into Common Stock. Shares described in the immediately preceding clauses (1) through (5) shall be included whether vested or unvested, and whether exercisable or not yet exercisable.

(B) Except to the limited extent provided for in Article IV.B.4(d)(i)(E)(3) and Article IV.B.4(d)(i)(E)(4), no adjustment of such Conversion Price pursuant to this Article IV.B.4(d)(i) shall have the effect of increasing the Conversion Price above the applicable Conversion Price in effect immediately prior to such adjustment.

(C) In the case of the issuance of Additional Stock for cash, the consideration shall be deemed to be the amount of cash paid therefor before deducting any reasonable discounts, commissions or other expenses allowed, paid or incurred by this Corporation for any underwriting or otherwise in connection with the issuance and sale thereof.

(D) In the case of the issuance of the Additional Stock for a consideration in whole or in part other than cash, the consideration other than cash shall be deemed to be the fair value thereof as determined by the Board of Directors (including at least one of the Preferred Directors) irrespective of any accounting treatment.

(E) In the case of the issuance of options to purchase or rights to acquire Common Stock, securities by their terms convertible into or exchangeable for Common Stock or options to purchase or rights to acquire such convertible or exchangeable securities, the following provisions shall apply for purposes of determining the number of shares of Additional Stock issued and the consideration paid therefor:

(1) The aggregate maximum number of shares of Common Stock deliverable upon exercise (assuming the satisfaction of any conditions to exercisability, including, without limitation, the passage of time) of such options to purchase or rights to acquire Common Stock shall be deemed to have been issued at the time such options or rights were issued and for a consideration equal to the consideration (determined in the manner provided in Article IV.B.4(d)(i)(C) and Article IV.B.4(d)(i)(D)), if any, received by this Corporation upon the issuance of such options or rights plus the minimum exercise price provided in such options or rights for the Common Stock covered thereby.

(2) The aggregate maximum number of shares of Common Stock deliverable upon conversion of, or in exchange

(assuming the satisfaction of any conditions to convertibility or exchangeability, including, without limitation, the passage of time) for any such convertible or exchangeable securities or upon the exercise of options to purchase or rights to acquire such convertible or exchangeable securities and subsequent conversion or exchange thereof shall be deemed to have been issued at the time such securities were issued or such options or rights were issued and for a consideration equal to the consideration, if any, received by this Corporation for any such securities and related options or rights (excluding any cash received on account of accrued interest or accrued dividends), plus the minimum additional consideration, if any, to be received by this Corporation upon the conversion or exchange of such securities or the exercise of any related options or rights (the consideration in each case to be determined in the manner provided in Article IV.B.4(d)(i)(C) and Article IV.B.4(d)(i)(D)).

(3) In the event of any change in the number of shares of Common Stock deliverable or in the consideration payable to this Corporation upon exercise of such options or rights or upon conversion of or in exchange for such convertible or exchangeable securities, including, but not limited to, a change resulting from the antidilution provisions thereof, the Conversion Price of each series of Preferred Stock, to the extent in any way affected by or computed using such options, rights or securities, shall be recomputed to reflect such change, but no further adjustment shall be made for the actual issuance of Common Stock or any payment of such consideration upon the exercise of any such options or rights or the conversion or exchange of such securities.

(4) Upon the expiration of any such options or rights, the termination of any such rights to convert or exchange or the expiration of any options or rights related to such convertible or exchangeable securities, the Conversion Price of each series of Preferred Stock, to the extent in any way affected by or computed using such options, rights or securities or options or rights related to such securities, shall be recomputed to reflect the issuance of only the number of shares of Common Stock (and convertible or exchangeable securities that remain in effect) actually issued upon the exercise of such options or rights, upon the conversion or exchange of such securities or upon the exercise of the options or rights related to such securities.

(5) The number of shares of Common Stock deemed issued and the consideration deemed paid therefor pursuant to Article IV.B.4(d)(i)(E)(1) and Article IV.B.4(d)(i)(E)(2) shall be appropriately adjusted to reflect any change, termination or expiration of the type described in either Article IV.B.4(d)(i)(E)(3) or Article IV.B.4(d)(i)(E)(4).

(ii) "**Additional Stock**" shall mean any shares of Common Stock issued (or deemed to have been issued pursuant to Article IV.B.4(d)(i)(E)) by this Corporation on or after the Filing Date other than:

(A) shares of Common Stock issued pursuant to a transaction described in Article IV.B.4(d)(iii) hereof;

(B) shares of Common Stock issued or deemed issued to employees, consultants, officers or directors (if in transactions with primarily non-financing purposes) of this Corporation directly or pursuant to a stock option plan, restricted stock purchase plan or other equity incentive plan approved by the Board of Directors;

(C) shares of Common Stock issued (I) in a bona fide, firmly underwritten public offering under the Act in connection with which all outstanding shares of Preferred Stock will be automatically converted to Common Stock, or (II) upon exercise of warrants or rights granted to underwriters in connection with such a public offering; *provided, however, that,* solely with respect to: (i) the Conversion Price of the Series F Preferred Stock, any shares of Common Stock described in this Article IV.B.4(d)(ii)(C)(I) above issued without consideration or for consideration per share less than the Conversion Price for the Series F Preferred Stock, as such price is in effect immediately prior to the issuance of such Additional Stock, shall be deemed "Additional Stock," (ii) the Conversion Price of the Series G Preferred Stock, any shares of Common Stock described in Article IV.B.4(d)(ii)(C)(I) above issued without consideration or for consideration per share less than the Conversion Price for the Series G Preferred Stock, as such price is in effect immediately prior to the issuance of such Additional Stock, shall be deemed "Additional Stock," (iii) the Conversion Price of the Series H Preferred Stock, any shares of Common Stock described in Article IV.B.4(d)(ii)(C)(I) above issued without consideration or for consideration per share less than the Conversion Price for the Series H Preferred Stock, as such price is in effect immediately prior to the issuance of such Additional Stock, shall be deemed "Additional Stock" and (iv) the Conversion Price of the Series I Preferred Stock, any shares of Common Stock described in Article IV.B.4(d)(ii)(C)(I) above issued without consideration or for consideration per share less than the Conversion Price for the Series I Preferred Stock, as such price is in effect immediately prior to the issuance of such Additional Stock, shall be deemed "Additional Stock";

(D) shares of Common Stock issued pursuant to the conversion of Preferred Stock;

(E) shares of Common Stock issued pursuant to the exercise of convertible or exercisable securities (other than Preferred Stock) outstanding on the Filing Date;

(F) shares of Common Stock issued or deemed issued in connection with a bona fide business acquisition of or by this Corporation, whether by merger, consolidation, sale of assets, sale or exchange of stock or otherwise, each as approved by the Board of Directors (including at least one of the Preferred Directors);

(G) shares of Common Stock issued or deemed issued pursuant to Article IV.B.4(d)(i)(E) as a result of a decrease in the Conversion Price of any Series of Preferred Stock resulting from the operation of Article IV.B.4(d)(i)(E);

(H) shares of Common Stock issued or deemed issued to persons or entities with which this Corporation has business relationships, including, but not limited to, strategic partnerships or joint ventures, equipment lease financings, bank credit agreements, company advisors and other providers of goods and services that are for other than primarily equity financing purposes, as approved by the Board of Directors (including at least one of the Preferred Directors); or

(I) shares of Common Stock issued or deemed issued in connection with any transaction where such securities so issued are excepted from the definition "Additional Stock" by the affirmative vote of (i) a majority of the then-outstanding shares of Series D Preferred Stock and Series C Preferred Stock, voting together as a single class, not as separate series and on an as converted basis, (ii) a majority of the then-outstanding shares of Series E Preferred Stock, voting as a separate series, (iii) a majority of the then-outstanding shares of Series F Preferred Stock, voting as a separate series, (iv) a majority of the then-outstanding shares of Series G Preferred Stock, voting as a separate series, (v) the Series H Requisite Approval, voting as a separate series, (vi) a majority of the then-outstanding shares of Series I Preferred Stock, voting as a separate series, and (vii) a majority of the then-outstanding shares of Preferred Stock, voting together as a single class, not as separate series and on an as converted basis.

(iii) In the event this Corporation should at any time or from time to time after the Filing Date fix a record date for the effectuation of a split or subdivision of the outstanding shares of Common Stock or the determination of holders of Common Stock entitled to receive a dividend or other distribution payable in additional shares of Common Stock or other securities or rights convertible into, or entitling the holder thereof to receive directly or indirectly, additional shares of Common Stock (hereinafter referred to as "**Common Stock Equivalents**") without payment of any consideration by such holder for the additional shares of Common Stock or the Common Stock Equivalents (including the additional shares of Common Stock issuable upon conversion or exercise thereof), then, as of such record date (or the date of such dividend distribution, split or subdivision if no record date is fixed), the Conversion Prices of each series of Preferred Stock shall be appropriately decreased so that the number of shares of Common Stock issuable on conversion of each share of such series shall be increased in proportion to such increase in the aggregate number of shares of Common Stock outstanding and those issuable with respect to such Common Stock Equivalents.

(iv) If the number of shares of Common Stock outstanding at any time after the Filing Date is decreased by a combination of the outstanding shares of Common Stock, then, following the record date of such combination, the Conversion Prices for each series of Preferred Stock shall be appropriately increased so that the number of shares of Common Stock issuable on conversion of each share of such series shall be decreased in proportion to such decrease in outstanding shares.

(e) Other Distributions. In the event this Corporation shall declare a distribution payable in securities of other persons, evidences of indebtedness issued by this Corporation or other persons, assets (excluding cash dividends) or options or rights not referred to in Article IV.B.4(d)(iii), then, in each such case for the purpose of this Article IV.B.4(e), the holders of each series of Preferred Stock shall be entitled to a proportionate share of any such distribution as though they were the holders of the number of shares of Common Stock of this Corporation into which their shares of such series of Preferred Stock are convertible as of the record date fixed for the determination of the holders of Common Stock of this Corporation entitled to receive such distribution.

(f) Recapitalizations. If at any time or from time to time there shall be a recapitalization of the Common Stock (other than a subdivision, combination or merger or sale of assets transaction provided for elsewhere in Article IV.B.2 or this Article IV.B.4) provision shall be made so that the holders of each series of the Preferred Stock shall thereafter be entitled to receive upon conversion of such series of Preferred Stock the number of shares of stock or other securities or property of this Corporation or otherwise, to which a holder of the number of shares of Common Stock deliverable upon conversion of the Preferred Stock held by such holder would have been entitled on such recapitalization. In any such case, appropriate adjustment shall be made in the application of the provisions of this Article IV.B.4 with respect to the rights of the holders of each series of Preferred Stock after the recapitalization to the end that the provisions of this Article IV.B.4 (including adjustment of the Conversion Price then in effect and the number of shares purchasable upon conversion of each such series of Preferred Stock) shall be applicable after that event as nearly equivalent as may be practicable.

(g) No Fractional Shares and Certificate as to Adjustments,

(i) No fractional shares shall be issued upon the conversion of any share or shares of Preferred Stock. In lieu of any fractional shares to which the holder would otherwise be entitled, this Corporation shall pay cash equal to such fraction multiplied by the then fair market value of a share of Common Stock as determined in good faith by the Board of Directors. The number of shares of Common Stock to be issued upon such conversion shall be determined on the basis of the total number of shares of Preferred Stock the holder is at the time converting into Common Stock and the number of shares of Common Stock issuable upon such aggregate conversion.

(ii) Upon the occurrence of each adjustment or readjustment of the Conversion Price of any series of Preferred Stock pursuant to this Article IV.B.4, this Corporation, at its expense, shall promptly compute such adjustment or readjustment in accordance with the terms hereof and prepare and furnish to each holder of such series of Preferred Stock a certificate setting forth such adjustment or readjustment and showing in detail the facts upon which such adjustment or readjustment is based. This Corporation shall, upon the written request at any time of any holder of Preferred Stock, furnish or cause to be furnished to such holder a like certificate setting forth (A) such adjustment and readjustment, (B) the Conversion Price for such series of Preferred Stock at the time in effect, and (C) the number of shares of Common Stock and the amount, if any, of other property that at the time would be received upon the conversion of a share of such series of Preferred Stock.

(h) Notices of Record Date. In the event of any taking by this Corporation of a record of the holders of any class of securities for the purpose of determining the holders thereof who are entitled to receive any dividend (other than a cash dividend) or other distribution, any right to subscribe for, purchase or otherwise acquire any shares of stock of any class or any other securities or property, or to receive any other right, this Corporation shall mail to each holder of Preferred Stock, at least 20 days prior to the date specified therein, a notice specifying the date on which any such record is to be taken for the purpose of such dividend, distribution or right, and the amount and character of such dividend, distribution or right.

(i) Reservation of Stock Issuable Upon Conversion. This Corporation shall at all times reserve and keep available out of its authorized but unissued shares of Common Stock, solely for the purpose of effecting the conversion of the shares of Preferred Stock, such number of its shares of Common Stock as shall from time to time be sufficient to effect the conversion of all outstanding shares of Preferred Stock; and if at any time the number of authorized but unissued shares of Common Stock shall not be sufficient to effect the conversion of all then-outstanding shares of Preferred Stock, in addition to such other remedies as shall be available to the holder of such Preferred Stock, this Corporation will take such corporate action as may, in the opinion of its counsel, be necessary to increase its authorized but unissued shares of Common Stock to such number of shares as shall be sufficient for such purposes, including, without limitation, engaging in best efforts to obtain the requisite stockholder approval of any necessary amendment to this Certificate of Incorporation.

(j) Notices. Any notice required by the provisions of this Article IV.B.4 to be given to the holders of shares of Preferred Stock shall be deemed given if deposited in the United States mail, postage prepaid, and addressed to each holder of record at his address appearing on the books of this Corporation, or sent by electronic communication in compliance with the provisions of the DGCL, and shall be deemed given upon such electronic transmission.

(k) Waiver of Adjustment to Conversion Prices. Notwithstanding anything herein to the contrary, any downward adjustment of the Conversion Price of any series of Preferred Stock may be waived, either prospectively or retroactively and either generally or in a particular instance solely by the vote of a majority of the then-outstanding shares of such series of Preferred Stock (and with respect to the Series H Preferred Stock, the Series H Requisite Approval). Any such waivers shall be binding upon all current and future holders of shares of the affected series of Preferred Stock.

5. Voting Rights.

(a) General. On any matter presented to the stockholders of the Corporation for their action or consideration at any meeting of stockholders of the Corporation (or by written consent of stockholders in lieu of a meeting), the holder of each share of Preferred Stock shall have the right to one vote for each share of Common Stock into which such share of Preferred Stock could then be converted. With respect to such vote, and except as otherwise expressly provided herein or as required by applicable law, such holder shall have full voting rights and powers equal to the voting rights and powers of the holders of Common Stock, and shall be entitled, notwithstanding any provision hereof, to notice of any stockholders' meeting in accordance with the Bylaws of this Corporation, and shall be entitled to vote, together with holders of Common Stock as a single class, with respect to any matter upon which holders of Common Stock have the right to vote. Fractional votes shall not, however, be permitted and any fractional voting rights available on an as-converted basis (after aggregating all shares into which shares of Preferred Stock held by each holder could be converted) shall be rounded to the nearest whole number (with one-half being rounded upward).

(b) Election of Directors.

(i) The holders of shares of Series H Preferred Stock shall be entitled, voting separately as a single class, to elect one director of this Corporation (the "**Series H Director**") at each meeting or pursuant to written consent of this Corporation's stockholders for the election of directors, to remove from office such director, to fill any vacancy caused by the resignation or death of such director and to fill any vacancy caused by the removal of such director.

(ii) The holders of shares of Series F Preferred Stock shall be entitled, voting separately as a single class, to elect one director of this Corporation (the "**Series F Director**") at each meeting or pursuant to written consent of this Corporation's stockholders for the election of directors, to remove from office such director, to fill any vacancy caused by the resignation or death of such director and to fill any vacancy caused by the removal of such director.

(iii) The holders of shares of Series E Preferred Stock shall be entitled, voting separately as a single class, to elect two directors of this Corporation (the "**Series E Directors**") at each meeting or pursuant to written consent of this Corporation's stockholders for the election of directors, to remove from office such director, to fill any vacancy caused by the resignation or death of such director and to fill any vacancy caused by the removal of such director.

(iv) The holders of shares of Series C Preferred Stock shall be entitled, voting separately as a single class, to elect one director of this Corporation (the "**Series C Director**") at each meeting or pursuant to written consent of this Corporation's stockholders for the election of directors, to remove from office such director, to fill any vacancy caused by the resignation or death of such director and to fill any vacancy caused by the removal of such director.

(v) The holders of shares of Series B Preferred Stock shall be entitled, voting separately as a single class, to elect one director of this Corporation (the "**Series B Director**," and together with the Series C Director, the Series E Directors, the Series F Director and the Series H Director, the "**Preferred Directors**") at each meeting or pursuant to written consent of this Corporation's stockholders for the election of directors, to remove from office such director, to fill any vacancy caused by the resignation or death of such director and to fill any vacancy caused by the removal of such director.

(vi) The holders of shares of Common Stock shall be entitled, voting separately as a single class, to elect four directors of this Corporation at each meeting or pursuant to written consent of this Corporation's stockholders for the election of directors, and to remove from office such directors, to fill any vacancy caused by the resignation or death of such directors and to fill any vacancy caused by the removal of any such directors.

(vii) The holders of shares of Common Stock and Preferred Stock shall be entitled, each voting as a separate class on an as-converted basis, to elect any remaining directors of this Corporation at each meeting or pursuant to written consent of this Corporation's stockholders for the election of directors, and to remove from office such directors to fill any vacancy caused by the resignation or death of such director and to fill any vacancy caused by the removal of any such director.

(viii) No person entitled to vote at an election for directors may cumulate votes to which such person is entitled, unless, at the time of such election, Section 2115 of the California General Corporation Law ("**CGCL**") purports to apply to the Corporation. During such time or times that Section 2115(b) of the CGCL purports to apply to the Corporation, every stockholder entitled to vote at an election for directors may cumulate such stockholder's votes and give one candidate a number of votes equal to the number of directors to be elected multiplied by the number of votes to which such stockholder's shares are otherwise entitled, or distribute the stockholder's votes on the same principle among as many candidates as such stockholder desires. No stockholder, however, shall be entitled to so cumulate such stockholder's votes unless (i) the names of such candidate or candidates have been placed in nomination prior to the voting and (ii) the stockholder has given notice at the meeting, prior to the voting, of such stockholder's intention to cumulate such stockholder's votes. If any stockholder has given proper notice to cumulate votes, all stockholders may cumulate their votes for any candidates who have been properly placed in nomination. Under cumulative voting, the candidates receiving the highest number of votes, up to the number of directors to be elected, are elected.

(ix) During such time or times that Section 2115(b) of the CGCL purports to apply to the Corporation, one or more directors may be removed from office at any time without cause by the affirmative vote of the holders of a majority of the outstanding shares entitled to vote for that director as provided above; *provided, however*, that unless the entire Board is removed, no individual director may be removed when the votes cast against such director's removal, or not consenting in writing to such removal, would be sufficient to elect that director if voted cumulatively at an election at which the same total number of votes were cast (or, if such action is taken by written consent, all shares entitled to vote were voted) and the entire number of directors authorized at the time of such director's most recent election were then being elected.

6. Protective Provisions.

(a) So long as at least 12,000,000 shares of Preferred Stock (as adjusted from time to time for Recapitalizations) are outstanding, this Corporation shall not, directly or indirectly, by amendment, merger, consolidation or otherwise, without first obtaining the approval (by vote or written consent, as provided by law) of the holders of a majority of the then-outstanding shares of Preferred Stock voting together as a single class on an as-converted basis:

(i) alter or change, whether by merger, consolidation or otherwise, the rights, preferences or privileges of the shares of Preferred Stock;

(ii) increase or decrease the total number of authorized shares of Preferred Stock or Common Stock;

(iii) authorize, designate or issue, or obligate itself to issue, whether by merger, consolidation or otherwise, any other equity security, including any other security convertible into or exercisable for any equity security, having a preference over, or being on a parity with, any series of Preferred Stock with respect to dividends, liquidation, voting or redemption;

(iv) effect any reclassification or recapitalization of outstanding capital stock into shares having preferences superior to or on parity with the Preferred Stock;

(v) effect a Liquidation Event;

(vi) change the authorized number of directors of this Corporation;

(vii) pay dividends or make other distributions on the capital stock of this Corporation (other than a dividend payable solely in shares of Common Stock);

(viii) incur or guaranty any indebtedness in excess of $20,000,000 in one transaction or a series of related transactions, unless approved by the Board of Directors;

(ix) increase the number of shares of Common Stock reserved for issuance under the Corporation's equity incentive plan or create any new equity incentive or benefit plan;

(x) engage in any transaction with one or more of the Corporation's directors or officers, or with any other corporation, partnership, association, or other organization in which one or more of the Corporation's directors or officers are directors or officers and have a material financial interest, unless approved by the Board of Directors (including a majority of disinterested directors);

(xi) permit any subsidiary of the Corporation to issue any equity securities other than to the Corporation or a wholly-owned subsidiary of the Corporation;

(xii) redeem, purchase or otherwise acquire (or pay into or set aside for a sinking fund for such purpose) any share or shares of Preferred Stock or Common Stock; *provided, however*, that this restriction shall not apply to the repurchase of shares of Common Stock from employees, officers, directors, consultants or other persons performing services for this Corporation or any subsidiary (A) pursuant to agreements under which this Corporation has the option to repurchase such shares, at no greater than cost, upon the occurrence of certain events, such as the termination of employment or service or (B) in connection with the settlement or exercise of awards issued pursuant to equity incentive plans of the Company; or

(xiii) amend the Corporation's Certificate of Incorporation or Bylaws.

(b) So long as at least 3,000,000 shares of Series I Preferred Stock (as adjusted for Recapitalizations) are outstanding, this Corporation shall not, directly or indirectly, by amendment of the Corporation's Certificate of Incorporation or Bylaws, merger, consolidation or otherwise, without first obtaining the approval (by vote or written consent, as provided by law) of the holders of a majority of the then-outstanding shares of Series I Preferred Stock voting as a separate class:

(i) increase or decrease the total number of authorized shares of Series I Preferred Stock;

(ii) alter or change the powers, preferences or special rights of the Series I Preferred Stock so as to affect them adversely;

(iii) amend Article IV.B.4(b)(ii)(dd), Article IV.B.4(d)(ii)(C)(iv), or Article IV.B.4(k) of this Corporation's Certificate of Incorporation;

(iv) authorize or issue any security with rights upon a Liquidation Event that are senior to the rights of the Series I Preferred Stock; or

(v) authorize or issue any security with rights upon a Liquidation Event that either (x) are both *pari passu* with the rights of the Series I Preferred Stock and that provide for a liquidation preference that is greater than one times the original issue price of such new security or (y) provide for distribution of additional proceeds to holders of such new security after payment of the original issue price of such new security plus declared but unpaid dividends of such new security but prior to conversion (or deemed conversion pursuant to Article IV.B.2(c) regardless of whether any such conversion actually occurred) of such new security into Common Stock.

(c) So long as at least 3,000,000 shares of Series H Preferred Stock (as adjusted for Recapitalizations) are outstanding, this Corporation shall not, directly or indirectly, by amendment of the Corporation's Certificate of Incorporation or Bylaws, merger, consolidation or otherwise, without first obtaining the Series H Requisite Approval (by vote or written consent, as provided by law), voting as a separate class:

(i) increase or decrease the total number of authorized shares of Series H Preferred Stock;

(ii) alter or change the powers, preferences or special rights of the Series H Preferred Stock so as to affect them adversely;

(iii) amend Article IV.B.4(b)(ii)(cc), Article IV.B.4(d)(ii)(C)(iii), Article IV.B.5(b)(i) or Article IV.B.4(k) of this Corporation's Certificate of Incorporation;

(iv) authorize or issue any security with rights upon a Liquidation Event that are senior to the rights of the Series H Preferred Stock; or

(v) authorize or issue any security with rights upon a Liquidation Event that either (x) are both *pari passu* with the rights of the Series H Preferred Stock and that provide for a liquidation preference that is greater than one times the original issue price of such new security or (y) provide for distribution of additional proceeds to holders of such new security after payment of the original issue price of such new security plus declared but unpaid dividends of such new security but prior to conversion (or deemed conversion pursuant to Article IV.B.2(c) regardless of whether any such conversion actually occurred) of such new security into Common Stock.

(d) So long as at least 3,000,000 shares of Series G Preferred Stock (as adjusted for Recapitalizations) are outstanding, this Corporation shall not, directly or indirectly, by amendment of the Corporation's Certificate of Incorporation or Bylaws, merger, consolidation or otherwise, without first obtaining the approval (by vote or written consent, as provided by law) of the holders of a majority of the then-outstanding shares of Series G Preferred Stock voting as a separate class:

(i) increase or decrease the total number of authorized shares of Series G Preferred Stock;

(ii) alter or change the powers, preferences or special rights of the Series G Preferred Stock so as to affect them adversely;

(iii) amend Article IV.B.4(b)(ii)(bb), Article IV.B.4(d)(ii)(C)(ii), or Article IV.B.4(k) of this Corporation's Certificate of Incorporation;

(iv) authorize or issue any security with rights upon a Liquidation Event that are senior to the rights of the Series G Preferred Stock; or

(v) authorize or issue any security with rights upon a Liquidation Event that either (x) are both *pari passu* with the rights of the Series G Preferred Stock and that provide for a liquidation preference that is greater than one times the original issue price of such new security or (y) provide for distribution of additional proceeds to holders of such new security after payment of the original issue price of such new security plus declared but unpaid dividends of such new security but prior to conversion (or deemed conversion pursuant to Article IV.B.2(c) regardless of whether any such conversion actually occurred) of such new security into Common Stock.

(e) So long as at least 3,000,000 shares of Series F Preferred Stock (as adjusted for Recapitalizations) are outstanding, this Corporation shall not, directly or indirectly, by amendment of the Corporation's Certificate of Incorporation or Bylaws, merger, consolidation or otherwise, without first obtaining the approval (by vote or written consent, as provided by law) of the holders of a majority of the then-outstanding shares of Series F Preferred Stock voting as a separate class:

(i) increase or decrease the total number of authorized shares of Series F Preferred Stock;

(ii) alter or change the powers, preferences or special rights of the Series F Preferred Stock so as to affect them adversely;

(iii) amend Article IV.B.4(b)(ii)(aa), Article IV.B.4(d)(ii)(C)(i), Article IV.B.5(b)(ii), or Article IV.B.4(k) of this Corporation's Certificate of Incorporation;

(iv) authorize or issue any security with rights upon a Liquidation Event that are senior to the rights of the Series F Preferred Stock; or

(v) authorize or issue any security with rights upon a Liquidation Event that either (x) are both *pari passu* with the rights of the Series F Preferred Stock and that provide for a liquidation preference that is greater than one times the original issue price of such new security or (y) provide for distribution of additional proceeds to holders of such new security after payment of the original issue price of such new security plus declared but unpaid dividends of such new security but prior to conversion (or deemed conversion pursuant to Article IV.B.2(c) regardless of whether any such conversion actually occurred) of such new security into Common Stock.

(f) So long as at least 3,000,000 shares of Series E Preferred Stock (as adjusted for Recapitalizations) are outstanding, this Corporation shall not, directly or indirectly, by amendment of the Corporation's Certificate of Incorporation or Bylaws, merger, consolidation or otherwise, without first obtaining the approval (by vote or written consent, as provided by law) of the holders of a majority of the then-outstanding shares of Series E Preferred Stock voting as a separate class:

(i) increase or decrease the total number of authorized shares of Series E Preferred Stock;

(ii) alter or change the powers, preferences or special rights of the Series E Preferred Stock so as to affect them adversely;

(iii) amend Article IV.B.4(b)(ii)(z) of this Corporation's Certificate of Incorporation;

(iv) authorize or issue any security with rights upon a Liquidation Event that are senior to the rights of the Series E Preferred Stock; or

(v) authorize or issue any security with rights upon a Liquidation Event that either (x) are both *pari passu* with the rights of the Series E Preferred Stock and that provide for a liquidation preference that is greater than one times the original issue price of such new security or (y) provide for distribution of additional proceeds to holders of such new security after payment of the original issue price of such new security plus declared but unpaid dividends of such new security but prior to conversion (or deemed conversion pursuant to Article IV.B.2(c) regardless of whether any such conversion actually occurred) of such new security into Common Stock.

(g) So long as at least 3,000,000 shares of Series D Preferred Stock (as adjusted for Recapitalizations) are outstanding, this Corporation shall not, directly or indirectly, by amendment of the Corporation's Certificate of Incorporation or Bylaws, merger, consolidation or otherwise, without first obtaining the approval (by vote or written consent, as provided by law) of the holders of a majority of the then-outstanding shares of Series D Preferred Stock voting as a separate class:

(i) increase or decrease the total number of authorized shares of Series D Preferred Stock;

(ii) alter or change the powers, preferences or special rights of the Series D Preferred Stock so as to affect them adversely;

(iii) alter or change any required approvals of the Series D Preferred Stock in which the holders of such shares of Series D Preferred Stock may vote as a separate class or series;

(iv) amend Article IV.B.4(b)(ii)(y) of this Corporation's Certificate of Incorporation;

(v) authorize or issue any security with rights upon a Liquidation Event that are senior to the rights of the Series D Preferred Stock; or

(vi) authorize or issue any security with rights upon a Liquidation Event that either (x) are both *pari passu* with the rights of the Series D Preferred Stock and that provide for a liquidation preference that is greater than one times the original issue price of such new security or (y) provide for distribution of additional proceeds to holders of such new security after payment of the original issue price of such new security plus declared but unpaid dividends of such new security but prior to conversion (or deemed conversion pursuant to Article IV.B.2(c) regardless of whether any such conversion actually occurred) of such new security into Common Stock.

(h) So long as at least 3,000,000 shares of Series C Preferred Stock (as adjusted for Recapitalizations) are outstanding, this Corporation shall not, directly or indirectly, by amendment, merger, consolidation or otherwise, without first obtaining the approval (by vote or written consent, as provided by law) of the holders of a majority of the then-outstanding shares of Series C Preferred Stock voting as a separate class:

(i) increase or decrease the total number of authorized shares of Series C Preferred Stock;

(ii) amend the Corporation's Certificate of Incorporation or Bylaws so as to adversely impact the powers, designations, preferences and restrictions of the Series C Preferred Stock in a manner different from the Series I Preferred Stock, the Series H Preferred Stock, Series G Preferred Stock, Series F Preferred Stock, the Series E Preferred Stock, the Series D Preferred Stock, the Series B Preferred Stock, the Series A Preferred Stock or the Series Seed Preferred Stock; or

(iii) amend Article IV.B.4(b)(ii)(x) of this Corporation's Certificate of Incorporation.

(i) So long as at least 3,000,000 shares of Series B Preferred Stock (as adjusted for Recapitalizations) are outstanding, this Corporation shall not, directly or indirectly, by amendment, merger, consolidation or otherwise, without first obtaining the approval (by vote or written consent, as provided by law) of the holders of a majority of the then-outstanding shares of Series B Preferred Stock voting as a separate class:

(i) increase or decrease the total number of authorized shares of Series B Preferred Stock; or

(ii) amend the Corporation's Certificate of Incorporation or Bylaws so as to adversely impact the powers, designations, preferences and restrictions of the Series B Preferred Stock in a manner different from the Series I Preferred Stock, the Series H Preferred Stock, Series G Preferred Stock, Series F Preferred Stock, the Series E Preferred Stock, the Series D Preferred Stock, the Series C Preferred Stock, the Series A Preferred Stock or the Series Seed Preferred Stock.

(j) So long as at least 3,000,000 shares of Series A Preferred Stock (as adjusted for Recapitalizations) are outstanding, this Corporation shall not, directly or indirectly, by amendment, merger, consolidation or otherwise, without first obtaining the approval (by vote or written consent, as provided by law) of the holders of a majority of the then-outstanding shares of Series A Preferred Stock voting as a separate class:

(i) increase or decrease the total number of authorized shares of Series A Preferred Stock; or

(ii) amend the Corporation's Certificate of Incorporation or Bylaws so as to adversely impact the powers, designations, preferences and restrictions of the Series A Preferred Stock in a manner different from the Series I Preferred Stock, the Series H Preferred Stock, Series G Preferred Stock, Series F Preferred Stock, the Series E Preferred Stock, the Series D Preferred Stock, the Series C Preferred Stock, the Series B Preferred Stock or the Series Seed Preferred Stock.

(k) So long as at least 3,000,000 shares of Series Seed Preferred Stock (as adjusted for Recapitalizations) are outstanding, this Corporation shall not, directly or indirectly, by amendment, merger, consolidation or otherwise, without first obtaining the approval (by vote or written consent, as provided by law) of the holders of a majority of the then-outstanding shares of Series Seed Preferred Stock voting as a separate class:

(i) increase or decrease the total number of authorized shares of Series Seed Preferred Stock; or

(ii) amend the Corporation's Certificate of Incorporation or Bylaws so as to adversely impact the powers, designations, preferences and restrictions of the Series Seed Preferred Stock in a manner different from the Series I Preferred Stock, the Series H Preferred Stock, Series G Preferred Stock, Series F Preferred Stock, the Series E Preferred Stock, the Series D Preferred Stock, the Series C Preferred Stock, the Series B Preferred Stock or the Series A Preferred Stock.

7. Status of Redeemed or Converted Stock. In the event any shares of Preferred Stock shall be redeemed or converted pursuant to Article IV.B.3 or Article IV.B.4, the shares so redeemed or converted shall be cancelled and shall not be issuable by this Corporation.

C. Common Stock. The rights, preferences, privileges and restrictions granted to and imposed on the Common Stock are as set forth below in this Article IV.C.

1. Dividend Rights. Subject to the prior rights of holders of all classes of stock at the time outstanding having prior rights as to dividends, the holders of the Common Stock shall be entitled to receive, when and as declared by the Board of Directors, out of any assets of this Corporation legally available therefor, such dividends as may be declared from time to time by the Board of Directors.

2. Liquidation Rights. Upon a Liquidation Event, the assets of this Corporation shall be distributed as provided in Article IV.B.2.

3. Redemption. Except as may otherwise be provided in a written agreement between this Corporation and a holder of Common Stock or the Bylaws of this Corporation, neither this Corporation nor the holders of Common Stock shall have the unilateral right to call or redeem or cause to have called or redeemed any shares of Common Stock.

4. Voting Rights. The holder of each share of Common Stock shall have the right to one vote for each such share, and shall be entitled to notice of any stockholders' meeting in accordance with the Bylaws of this Corporation, and shall be entitled to vote upon such matters and in such manner as may be provided by law. Subject to the other terms of this Restated Certificate, the number of authorized shares of Common Stock may be increased or decreased (but not below the number of shares then outstanding) by the affirmative vote of the holders of shares of stock of this Corporation representing a majority of the votes represented by all outstanding shares of stock of this Corporation entitled to vote, irrespective of the provisions of Section 242(b)(2) of the DGCL.

Article V.

For the management of the business and for the conduct of the affairs of this Corporation, and in further definition, limitation, and regulation of the powers of this Corporation and of its directors and of its stockholders or any class thereof, as the case may be, it is further provided:

A. The management of the business and the conduct of the affairs of this Corporation shall be vested in its Board of Directors. The number of directors which shall constitute the whole Board of Directors shall be fixed by, or in the manner provided in, the Bylaws. The phrase "whole Board" and the phrase "total number of directors" shall be deemed to have the same meaning, to wit, the total number of directors that this Corporation would have if there were no vacancies. Elections of directors need not be by written ballot unless the Bylaws of this Corporation shall so provide.

B. Except as otherwise provided in this Restated Certificate, the power to adopt, amend, or repeal the Bylaws of this Corporation may be exercised by the Board of Directors of this Corporation.

Article VI.

To the fullest extent permitted by applicable law, this Corporation is authorized to provide indemnification of (and advancement of expenses to) directors, officers, employees and agents of this Corporation (and any other persons to which the DGCL permits this Corporation to provide indemnification) through Bylaw provisions, agreements with such persons, vote of stockholders or disinterested directors or otherwise, in excess of the indemnification and advancement otherwise permitted by Section 145 of the DGCL, subject only to limits created by applicable law (statutory or non-statutory), with respect to actions for breach of duty to this Corporation, its stockholders, and others.

Any amendment, repeal or modification of the foregoing provisions of this Article VI shall not adversely affect any right or protection of a director, officer, employee, agent or other person existing at the time of, or increase the liability of any such person with respect to any acts or omissions of such person occurring prior to, such amendment, repeal or modification.

Article VII.

A director of the Corporation shall not be liable to this Corporation or its stockholders for monetary damages for breach of fiduciary duty as a director, except to the extent such exemption from liability or limitation thereof is not permitted under the DGCL as the same exists or may hereafter be amended. Any amendment, modification or repeal of the foregoing sentence shall not adversely affect any right or protection of a director of the Corporation hereunder in respect of any act or omission occurring prior to the time of such amendment, modification or repeal.

Any amendment, repeal or modification of the foregoing provisions of this Article VII by the stockholders of this Corporation shall not adversely affect any right or protection of a director of this Corporation existing at the time of, or increase the liability of any director of this Corporation with respect to any acts or omissions of such director occurring prior to, such amendment, repeal or modification.

Article VIII.

This Corporation renounces, to the fullest extent permitted by law, any interest or expectancy of this Corporation in, or in being offered an opportunity to participate in, any Excluded Opportunity. An "**Excluded Opportunity**" is any matter, transaction or interest that is presented to, or acquired, created or developed by, or which otherwise comes into the possession of, (i) any director of this Corporation who is not an employee of this Corporation or any of its subsidiaries, or (ii) any holder of Preferred Stock or any partner, member, director, stockholder, employee or agent of any such holder, if such holder is not an employee of this Corporation or of any of its subsidiaries (collectively, "**Covered Persons**"), unless such matter, transaction or interest is presented to, or acquired, created or developed by, or otherwise comes into the possession of, a Covered Person expressly and solely in such Covered Person's capacity as a director of this Corporation.

Article IX.

Unless the Corporation consents in writing to an alternative forum, the sole and exclusive forum for (i) any derivative action or proceeding brought on behalf of the Corporation, (ii) any action asserting a claim of breach of a fiduciary duty owed by any director, officer, or other employee of the Corporation to the Corporation or the Corporation's stockholders, (iii) any action asserting a claim arising under any provision of the DGCL, the certificate of incorporation, or the Bylaws of the Corporation, or (iv) any action asserting a claim governed by the internal-affairs doctrine shall be a state or federal court located within the State of Delaware in all cases subject to the court's having personal jurisdiction over the indispensable parties named as defendants.

Unless the Corporation consents in writing to the selection of an alternative forum, the federal district courts of the United States of America shall be the exclusive forum for the resolution of any complaint stating any claim against the Corporation, or any director, officer, employee, control person, underwriter or agent of the Corporation arising under the Act.

Any person or entity purchasing or otherwise acquiring any interest in any security of the Corporation shall be deemed to have notice of and consented to the provisions of this Amended and Restated Certificate of Incorporation.

If any provision or provisions of this Article IX shall be held to be invalid, illegal or unenforceable as applied to any person or entity or circumstance for any reason whatsoever, then, to the fullest extent permitted by law, the validity, legality and enforceability of such provisions in any other circumstance and of the remaining provisions of this Article IX (including, without limitation, each portion of any sentence of this Article IX containing any such provision held to be invalid, illegal or unenforceable that is not itself held to be invalid, illegal or unenforceable) and the application of such provision to other persons or entities and circumstances shall not in any way be affected or impaired thereby.

INDEX

References are to Pages